LITTLE,
BROWN
SPARK

LARGE
PRINT

NOISE

A Flaw in Human Judgment

DANIEL KAHNEMAN
OLIVIER SIBONY
CASS R. SUNSTEIN

Fountaindale Public Library District
300 W. Briarcliff Rd.
Bolingbrook, IL 60440

LITTLE, BROWN **SPARK**
LARGE PRINT EDITION

Hachette Book Group supports the right to free expression and the value of copyright. The purpose of copyright is to encourage writers and artists to produce the creative works that enrich our culture.

The scanning, uploading, and distribution of this book without permission is a theft of the author's intellectual property. If you would like permission to use material from the book (other than for review purposes), please contact permissions@hbgusa.com. Thank you for your support of the author's rights.

Little, Brown Spark
Hachette Book Group
1290 Avenue of the Americas, New York, NY 10104
littlebrownspark.com

First Edition: May 2021

Little, Brown Spark is an imprint of Little, Brown and Company, a division of Hachette Book Group, Inc. The Little, Brown Spark name and logo are trademarks of Hachette Book Group, Inc.

The publisher is not responsible for websites (or their content) that are not owned by the publisher.

ISBN 978-0-316-45140-6 (hardcover) / 978-0-316-26665-9 (int'l edition) / 978-0-316-32227-0 (large print)

LCCN 2020951207

Printing 1, 2021

LSC-C

Printed in the United States of America

For Noga, Ori and Gili — DK
For Fantin and Lélia — OS
For Samantha — CRS

Contents

CONTENTS

CONTENTS

NOISE

INTRODUCTION

Two Kinds of Error

I magine that four teams of friends have gone to a shooting arcade. Each team consists of five people; they share one rifle, and each person fires one shot. Figure 1 shows their results.

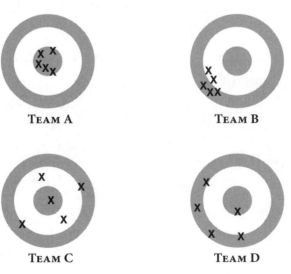

TEAM A

TEAM B

TEAM C

TEAM D

FIGURE 1: *Four teams*

In an ideal world, every shot would hit the bull's-eye.

That is nearly the case for Team A. The team's shots are tightly clustered around the bull's-eye, close to a perfect pattern.

We call Team B *biased* because its shots are systematically off target. As the figure illustrates, the consistency of the bias supports a prediction. If one of the team's members were to take another shot, we would bet on its landing in the same area as the first five. The consistency of the bias also invites a causal explanation: perhaps the gunsight on the team's rifle was bent.

We call Team C *noisy* because its shots are widely scattered. There is no obvious bias, because the impacts are roughly centered on the bull's-eye. If one of the team's members took another shot, we would know very little about where it is likely to hit. Furthermore, no interesting hypothesis comes to mind to explain the results of Team C. We know that its members are poor shots. We do not know why they are so noisy.

Team D is both biased and noisy. Like Team B, its shots are systematically off target; like Team C, its shots are widely scattered.

But this is not a book about target shooting. Our topic is human error. Bias and noise—systematic deviation and random scatter—are different components of error. The targets illustrate the difference.

The shooting range is a metaphor for what can go wrong in human judgment, especially in the diverse decisions that people make on behalf of organizations. In these situations, we will find the two types of error illustrated in figure 1. Some judgments are biased; they are systematically off target. Other judgments are noisy, as people who are expected to agree end up at very different points around the target. Many organizations, unfortunately, are afflicted by both bias and noise.

Figure 2 illustrates an important difference between bias and noise. It shows what you would see

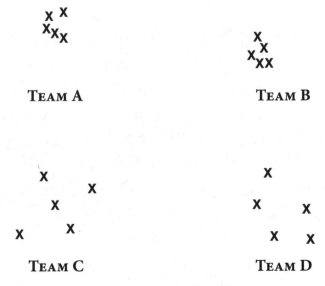

FIGURE 2: *Looking at the back of the target*

at the shooting range if you were shown only the backs of the targets at which the teams were shooting, without any indication of the bull's-eye they were aiming at.

From the back of the target, you cannot tell whether Team A or Team B is closer to the bull's-eye. But you can tell at a glance that Teams C and D are noisy and that Teams A and B are not. Indeed, you know just as much about scatter as you did in figure 1. A general property of noise is that you can recognize and measure it while knowing nothing about the target or bias.

The general property of noise just mentioned is essential for our purposes in this book, because many of our conclusions are drawn from judgments whose true answer is unknown or even unknowable. When physicians offer different diagnoses for the same patient, we can study their disagreement without knowing what ails the patient. When film executives estimate the market for a movie, we can study the variability of their answers without knowing how much the film eventually made or even if it was produced at all. We don't need to know who is right to measure how much the judgments of the same case vary. All we have to do to measure noise is look at the back of the target.

To understand error in judgment, we must understand both bias and noise. Sometimes, as we will see, noise is the more important problem. But in public conversations about human error and in organizations all over the world, noise is rarely recognized. Bias is the star of the show. Noise is a bit player, usually off-stage. The topic of bias has been discussed in thousands of scientific articles and dozens of popular books, few of which even mention the issue of noise. This book is our attempt to redress the balance.

In real-world decisions, the amount of noise is often scandalously high. Here are a few examples of the alarming amount of noise in situations in which accuracy matters:

- *Medicine is noisy.* Faced with the same patient, different doctors make different judgments about whether patients have skin cancer, breast cancer, heart disease, tuberculosis, pneumonia, depression, and a host of other conditions. Noise is especially high in psychiatry, where subjective judgment is obviously important. However, considerable noise is also found in areas where it might not be expected, such as in the reading of X-rays.

- *Child custody decisions are noisy.* Case managers in child protection agencies must assess whether children are at risk of abuse and, if so, whether to place them in foster care. The system is noisy, given that some managers are much more likely than others to send a child to foster care. Years later, more of the unlucky children who have been assigned to foster care by these heavy-handed managers have poor life outcomes: higher delinquency rates, higher teen birth rates, and lower earnings.

- *Forecasts are noisy.* Professional forecasters offer highly variable predictions about likely sales of a new product, likely growth in the unemployment rate, the likelihood of bankruptcy for troubled companies, and just about everything else. Not only do they disagree with each other, but they also disagree with themselves. For example, when the same software developers were asked on two separate days to estimate the completion time for the same task, the hours they projected differed by 71%, on average.

- *Asylum decisions are noisy.* Whether an asylum seeker will be admitted into the United States depends on something like a lottery. A study of cases that were randomly allotted to different judges found that one judge admitted 5% of applicants, while another admitted 88%. The title of the study says it all: "Refugee Roulette." (We are going to see a lot of roulette.)

- *Personnel decisions are noisy.* Interviewers of job candidates make widely different assessments of the same people. Performance ratings of the same employees are also highly variable and depend more on the person doing the assessment than on the performance being assessed.

- *Bail decisions are noisy.* Whether an accused person will be granted bail or instead sent to jail pending trial depends partly on the identity of the judge who ends up hearing the case. Some judges are far more lenient than others. Judges also differ markedly in their assessment of which defendants present the highest risk of flight or reoffending.

- *Forensic science is noisy.* We have been trained to think of fingerprint identification as infallible. But fingerprint examiners sometimes differ in deciding whether a print found at a crime scene matches that of a suspect. Not only do experts disagree, but the same experts sometimes make inconsistent decisions when presented with the same print on different occasions. Similar variability has been documented in other forensic science disciplines, even DNA analysis.

- *Decisions to grant patents are noisy.* The authors of a leading study on patent applications emphasize the noise involved: "Whether the patent office grants or rejects a patent is significantly related to the happenstance of which examiner is assigned the application." This variability is obviously troublesome from the standpoint of equity.

All these noisy situations are the tip of a large iceberg. Wherever you look at human judgments, you are likely to find noise. To improve the quality of our judgments, we need to overcome noise as well as bias.

This book comes in six parts. In part 1, we explore the difference between noise and bias, and we show that both public and private organizations can be noisy, sometimes shockingly so. To appreciate the problem, we begin with judgments in two areas. The first involves criminal sentencing (and hence the public sector). The second involves insurance (and hence the private sector). At first glance, the two areas could not be more different. But with respect to noise, they have much in common. To establish that point, we introduce the idea of a noise audit, designed to measure how much disagreement there is among professionals considering the same cases within an organization.

In part 2, we investigate the nature of human judgment and explore how to measure accuracy and error. Judgments are susceptible to both bias and noise. We describe a striking equivalence in the roles of the two types of error. Occasion noise is the variability in judgments of the same case by the same person or group on different occasions. A surprising amount of occasion noise arises in group discussion because of seemingly irrelevant factors, such as who speaks first.

Part 3 takes a deeper look at one type of judgment that has been researched extensively: predictive judgment. We explore the key advantage of rules, formulas, and algorithms over humans when it comes to making predictions: contrary to popular belief, it is not so much the superior insight of rules but their noiselessness. We discuss the ultimate limit on the quality of predictive judgment—objective ignorance of the future—and how it conspires with noise to limit the quality of prediction. Finally, we address a question that you will almost certainly have asked yourself by then: if noise is so ubiquitous, then why had you not noticed it before?

Part 4 turns to human psychology. We explain the central causes of noise. These include interpersonal differences arising from a variety of factors, including personality and cognitive style; idiosyncratic variations in the weighting of different considerations; and the different uses that people make of the very same scales. We explore why people are oblivious to noise and are frequently unsurprised by events and judgments they could not possibly have predicted.

Part 5 explores the practical question of how you can improve your judgments and prevent error. (Readers who are primarily interested in practical applications of noise reduction might skip the discussion of the challenges of prediction and of the psychology of judgment in parts 3 and 4 and move directly to this part.) We investigate efforts to tackle noise in medicine, business, education, government, and elsewhere. We introduce several noise-reduction techniques that we collect under the label of *decision hygiene.* We present five case studies of domains in which there is much documented noise and in which people have made sustained efforts to reduce it, with instructively varying degrees of success. The case studies include unreliable medical diagnoses, performance ratings, forensic science, hiring decisions, and forecasting in general. We conclude by offering a system we call the *mediating assessments protocol:* a general-purpose approach to the evaluation of options that incorporates several key practices of decision hygiene and aims to produce less noisy and more reliable judgments.

What is the right level of noise? Part 6 turns to this question. Perhaps counterintuitively, the right level is not zero. In some areas, it just isn't feasible to eliminate noise. In other areas, it is too expensive to do so. In still other areas, efforts to reduce noise would compromise important competing values. For example, efforts to eliminate noise could undermine morale and give people a sense that they are being treated like cogs in a machine. When algorithms are part of the answer, they raise an assortment of objections; we address some of them here. Still, the current level of noise is unacceptable. We urge both private and public organizations to conduct noise audits and to undertake, with unprecedented seriousness, stronger efforts to reduce noise. Should they do so, organizations could reduce widespread unfairness — and reduce costs in many areas.

With that aspiration in mind, we end each chapter with a few brief propositions in the form of quotations. You can use these statements as they are or adapt them for any issues that matter to you, whether they involve health, safety, education, money, employment, entertainment, or something else. Understanding the problem of noise, and trying to solve it, is a work in progress and a collective endeavor. All of us have opportunities to contribute to this work. This book is written in the hope that we can seize those opportunities.

PART I

Finding Noise

It is not acceptable for similar people, convicted of the same offense, to end up with dramatically different sentences — say, five years in jail for one and probation for another. And yet in many places, something like that happens. To be sure, the criminal justice system is pervaded by bias as well. But our focus in chapter 1 is on noise — and in particular, on what happened when a famous judge drew attention to it, found it scandalous, and launched a crusade that in a sense changed the world (but not enough). Our tale involves the United States, but we are confident that similar stories can be (and will be) told about many other nations. In some of those nations, the problem of noise is likely to be even worse than it is in the United States. We use the example of sentencing in part to show that noise can produce great unfairness.

Criminal sentencing has especially high drama, but we are also concerned with the private sector, where the stakes can be large, too. To illustrate the point, we turn in chapter 2 to a large insurance company. There, underwriters have the task of setting insurance premiums for potential clients, and claims adjusters must judge the value of claims. You might predict that these tasks would be simple and mechanical and that different professionals would come up with roughly the same amounts. We conducted a carefully designed experiment — a noise audit — to test that prediction. The results surprised us, but more importantly they astonished and dismayed the company's leadership. As we learned, the sheer volume of noise is costing the company a great deal of money. We use this example to show that noise can produce large economic losses.

Both of these examples involve studies of a large number of people making a large number of judgments. But many important judgments are *singular* rather than repeated: how to handle an apparently unique business opportunity, whether to launch a whole new product, how to deal with a pandemic, whether to hire someone who just doesn't meet the standard profile. Can noise be found in decisions about unique situations like these? It is tempting to think that it is absent there. After all, noise is unwanted variability, and how can you have variability with singular decisions? In chapter 3, we try to answer this question. The judgment that you make, even in a seemingly unique situation, is one in a cloud of possibilities. You will find a lot of noise there as well.

The theme that emerges from these three chapters can be summarized in one sentence, which will be a key theme of this book: *wherever there is judgment, there is noise—and more of it than you think.* Let's start to find out how much.

CHAPTER 1

Crime and Noisy Punishment

Suppose that someone has been convicted of a crime—shoplifting, possession of heroin, assault, or armed robbery. What is the sentence likely to be?

The answer should not depend on the particular judge to whom the case happens to be assigned, on whether it is hot or cold outside, or on whether a local sports team won the day before. It would be outrageous if three similar people, convicted of the same crime, received radically different penalties: probation for one, two years in jail for another, and ten years in jail for another. And yet that outrage can be found in many nations—not only in the distant past but also today.

All over the world, judges have long had a great deal of discretion in deciding on appropriate sentences. In many nations, experts have celebrated this discretion and have seen it as both just and humane. They have insisted that criminal sentences should be based on a host of factors involving not only the crime but also the defendant's character and circumstances. Individualized tailoring was the order of the day. If judges were constrained by rules, criminals would be treated in a dehumanized way; they would not be seen as unique individuals entitled to draw attention to the details of their situation. The very idea of due process of law seemed, to many, to call for open-ended judicial discretion.

In the 1970s, the universal enthusiasm for judicial discretion started to collapse for one simple reason: startling evidence of noise. In 1973, a famous judge, Marvin Frankel, drew public attention to the problem. Before he became a judge, Frankel was a defender of freedom of speech and a passionate human rights advocate who helped found the Lawyers' Committee for Human Rights (an organization now known as Human Rights First).

Frankel could be fierce. And with respect to noise in the criminal justice system, he was outraged. Here is how he describes his motivation:

> *If a federal bank robbery defendant was convicted, he or she could receive a maximum of 25 years.*

That meant anything from 0 to 25 years. And where the number was set, I soon realized, depended less on the case or the individual defendant than on the individual judge, i.e., on the views, predilections, and biases of the judge. So the same defendant in the same case could get widely different sentences depending on which judge got the case.

Frankel did not provide any kind of statistical analysis to support his argument. But he did offer a series of powerful anecdotes, showing unjustified disparities in the treatment of similar people. Two men, neither of whom had a criminal record, were convicted for cashing counterfeit checks in the amounts of $58.40 and $35.20, respectively. The first man was sentenced to fifteen *years,* the second to 30 *days.* For embezzlement actions that were similar to one another, one man was sentenced to 117 *days* in prison, while another was sentenced to 20 *years.* Pointing to numerous cases of this kind, Frankel deplored what he called the "almost wholly unchecked and sweeping powers" of federal judges, resulting in "arbitrary cruelties perpetrated daily," which he deemed unacceptable in a "government of laws, not of men."

Frankel called on Congress to end this "discrimination," as he described those arbitrary cruelties. By that term, he mainly meant noise, in the form of inexplicable variations in sentencing. But he was also concerned about bias, in the form of racial and socioeconomic disparities. To combat both noise and bias, he urged that differences in treatment of criminal defendants should not be allowed unless the differences could be "justified by relevant tests capable of formulation and application with sufficient objectivity to ensure that the results will be more than the idiosyncratic ukases of particular officials, justices, or others." (The term *idiosyncratic ukases* is a bit esoteric; by it, Frankel meant personal edicts.) Much more than that, Frankel argued for a reduction in noise through a "detailed profile or checklist of factors that would include, wherever possible, some form of numerical or other objective grading."

Writing in the early 1970s, he did not go quite so far as to defend what he called "displacement of people by machines." But startlingly, he came close. He believed that "the rule of law calls for a body of impersonal rules, applicable across the board, binding on judges as well as everyone else." He explicitly argued for the use of "computers as an aid toward orderly thought in sentencing." He also recommended the creation of a commission on sentencing.

Frankel's book became one of the most influential in the entire history of criminal law — not only in the

United States but also throughout the world. His work did suffer from a degree of informality. It was devastating but impressionistic. To test for the reality of noise, several people immediately followed up by exploring the level of noise in criminal sentencing.

An early large-scale study of this kind, chaired by Judge Frankel himself, took place in 1974. Fifty judges from various districts were asked to set sentences for defendants in hypothetical cases summarized in identical pre-sentence reports. The basic finding was that "absence of consensus was the norm" and that the variations across punishments were "astounding." A heroin dealer could be incarcerated for one to ten years, depending on the judge. Punishments for a bank robber ranged from five to eighteen years in prison. The study found that in an extortion case, sentences varied from a whopping twenty years imprisonment and a $65,000 fine to a mere three years imprisonment and no fine. Most startling of all, in sixteen of twenty cases, there was no unanimity on whether any incarceration was appropriate.

This study was followed by a series of others, all of which found similarly shocking levels of noise. In 1977, for example, William Austin and Thomas Williams conducted a survey of forty-seven judges, asking them to respond to the same five cases, each involving low-level offenses. All the descriptions of the cases included summaries of the information used by judges in actual sentencing, such as the charge, the testimony, the previous criminal record (if any), social background, and evidence relating to character. The key finding was "substantial disparity." In a case involving burglary, for example, the recommended sentences ranged from five years in prison to a mere thirty days (alongside a fine of $100). In a case involving possession of marijuana, some judges recommended prison terms; others recommended probation.

A much larger study, conducted in 1981, involved 208 federal judges who were exposed to the same sixteen hypothetical cases. Its central findings were stunning:

> *In only 3 of the 16 cases was there a unanimous agreement to impose a prison term. Even where most judges agreed that a prison term was appropriate, there was a substantial variation in the lengths of prison terms recommended. In one fraud case in which the mean prison term was 8.5 years, the longest term was life in prison. In another case the mean prison term was 1.1 years, yet the longest prison term recommended was 15 years.*

As revealing as they are, these studies, which involve tightly controlled experiments, almost certainly understate the magnitude of noise in the real world of criminal justice. Real-life judges are exposed to far more information than what the study participants received in the carefully specified vignettes of these experiments. Some of this additional information is relevant, of course, but there is also ample evidence that irrelevant information, in the form of small and seemingly random factors, can produce major differences in outcomes. For example, judges have been found more likely to grant parole at the beginning of the day or after a food break than immediately before such a break. If judges are hungry, they are tougher.

A study of thousands of juvenile court decisions found that when the local football team loses a game on the weekend, the judges make harsher decisions on the Monday (and, to a lesser extent, for the rest of the week). Black defendants disproportionately bear the brunt of that increased harshness. A different study looked at 1.5 million judicial decisions over three decades and similarly found that judges are more severe on days that follow a loss by the local city's football team than they are on days that follow a win.

A study of six million decisions made by judges in France over twelve years found that defendants are given more leniency on their birthday. (The defendant's birthday, that is; we suspect that judges might be more lenient on their own birthdays as well, but as far as we know, that hypothesis has not been tested.) Even something as irrelevant as outside temperature can influence judges. A review of 207,000 immigration court decisions over four years found a significant effect of daily temperature variations: when it is hot outside, people are less likely to get asylum. If you are suffering political persecution in your home country and want asylum elsewhere, you should hope and maybe even pray that your hearing falls on a cool day.

Reducing Noise in Sentencing

In the 1970s, Frankel's arguments, and the empirical findings supporting them, came to the attention of Edward M. Kennedy, brother of the slain president John F. Kennedy, and one of the most influential members of the US Senate. Kennedy was shocked and appalled. As early as 1975, he introduced sentencing reform legislation; it didn't go anywhere. But Kennedy was relentless. Pointing to the evidence, he continued to press for the enactment of that legislation, year after year. In 1984, he succeeded. Responding to the evidence of unjustified variability, Congress enacted the Sentencing Reform Act of 1984.

The new law was intended to reduce noise in the system by reducing "the unfettered discretion the law confers on those judges and parole authorities responsible for imposing and implementing the sentences." In particular, members of Congress referred to "unjustifiably wide" sentencing disparity, specifically citing findings that in the New York area, punishments for identical actual cases could range from three years to twenty years of imprisonment. Just as Judge Frankel had recommended, the law created the US Sentencing Commission, whose principal job was clear: to issue sentencing guidelines that were meant to be mandatory and that would establish a restricted range for criminal sentences.

In the following year, the commission established those guidelines, which were generally based on average sentences for similar crimes in an analysis of ten thousand actual cases. Supreme Court Justice Stephen Breyer, who was heavily involved in the process, defended the use of past practice by pointing to the intractable disagreement within the commission: "Why didn't the Commission sit down and really go and rationalize this thing and not just take history? The short answer to that is: we couldn't. We couldn't because there are such good arguments all over the place pointing in opposite directions.... Try listing all the crimes that there are in rank order of punishable merit.... Then collect results from your friends and see if they all match. I will tell you they won't."

Under the guidelines, judges have to consider two factors to establish sentences: the crime and the defendant's criminal history. Crimes are assigned one of forty-three "offense levels," depending on their seriousness. The defendant's criminal history refers principally to the number and severity of a defendant's previous convictions. Once the crime and the criminal history are put together, the guidelines offer a relatively narrow range of sentencing, with the top of the range authorized to exceed the bottom by the greater of six months or 25%. Judges are permitted to depart from the range altogether by reference to what they see as aggravating or mitigating circumstances, but departures must be justified to an appellate court.

Even though the guidelines are mandatory, they are not entirely rigid. They do not go nearly as far as Judge Frankel wanted. They offer judges significant room to maneuver. Nonetheless, several studies, using a variety of methods and focused on a range of historical periods, reach the same conclusion: the guidelines cut the noise. More technically, they "reduced the net variation in sentence attributable to the happenstance of the identity of the sentencing judge."

The most elaborate study came from the commission itself. It compared sentences in bank robbery, cocaine distribution, heroin distribution, and bank embezzlement cases in 1985 (before the guidelines went into effect) with the sentences imposed between January 19, 1989, and September 30, 1990. Offenders were matched with respect to the factors deemed relevant to sentencing under the guidelines. For every offense, variations across judges were much smaller in the later period, after the Sentencing Reform Act had been implemented.

According to another study, the expected difference in sentence length between judges was 17%, or 4.9 months, in 1986 and 1987. That number fell to 11%, or 3.9 months, between 1988 and 1993. An independent study covering different periods found similar success in reducing interjudge disparities, which were defined as the differences in average sentences among judges with similar caseloads.

Despite these findings, the guidelines ran into a firestorm of criticism. Some people, including many judges, thought that some sentences were too severe — a point about bias, not noise. For our purposes, a much more interesting objection, which came from numerous judges, was that guidelines were deeply unfair because they prohibited judges from taking adequate account of the particulars of the case. The price of reducing noise was to make decisions unacceptably mechanical. Yale law professor Kate Stith and federal judge José Cabranes wrote that "the need is not for blindness, but for insight, for equity," which "can only occur in a judgment that takes account of the complexities of the individual case."

This objection led to vigorous challenges to the guidelines, some of them based on law, others based on policy. Those challenges failed until, for technical reasons entirely unrelated to the debate summarized here, the Supreme Court struck the guidelines down in 2005. As a result of the court's ruling, the guidelines became merely advisory. Notably, most federal judges were much happier after the Supreme Court decision. Seventy-five percent preferred the advisory regime, whereas just 3% thought the mandatory regime was better.

What have been the effects of changing the guidelines from mandatory to advisory? Harvard law professor Crystal Yang investigated this question, not with an experiment or a survey but with a massive data set of actual sentences, involving nearly four hundred thousand criminal defendants. Her central finding is that by multiple measures, interjudge disparities increased significantly after 2005. When the guidelines were mandatory, defendants who had been sentenced by a relatively harsh judge were sentenced to 2.8 months longer than if they had been sentenced by an average judge. When the guidelines became merely advisory, the disparity was doubled. Sounding much like Judge Frankel from forty years before, Yang writes that her "findings raise large equity concerns because the identity of the assigned sentencing judge contributes significantly to the disparate treatment of similar offenders convicted of similar crimes."

After the guidelines became advisory, judges became more likely to base their sentencing decisions on their personal values. Mandatory guidelines reduce bias as well as noise. After the Supreme Court's decision, there was a significant increase in the disparity between the sentences of African American defendants and white people convicted of the same crimes. At the same time, female judges became more likely than male judges were to exercise their increased discretion in favor of leniency. The same is true of judges appointed by Democratic presidents.

Three years after Frankel's death in 2002, striking down the mandatory guidelines produced a return to something more like his nightmare: law without order.

———

The story of Judge Frankel's fight for sentencing guidelines offers a glimpse of several of the key points we will cover in this book. First, judgment is difficult because the world is a complicated, uncertain place. This complexity is obvious in the judiciary and holds in most other situations requiring professional judgment. Broadly, these situations include judgments made by doctors, nurses, lawyers, engineers, teachers, architects, Hollywood executives, members of hiring committees, book publishers, corporate executives of all kinds, and managers of sports teams. Disagreement is unavoidable wherever judgment is involved.

Second, the extent of these disagreements is much greater than we expect. While few people object to the principle of judicial discretion, almost everyone disapproves of the magnitude of the disparities it produces. *System noise,* that is, unwanted variability in judgments that should ideally be identical, can create rampant injustice, high economic costs, and errors of many kinds.

Third, noise can be reduced. The approach advocated by Frankel and implemented by the US Sentencing Commission — rules and guidelines — is one of several approaches that successfully reduce noise. Other approaches are better suited to other types of judgment. Some methods adopted to reduce noise can simultaneously reduce bias as well.

Fourth, efforts at noise reduction often raise objections and run into serious difficulties. These issues must be addressed, too, or the fight against noise will fail.

Speaking of Noise in Sentencing

"Experiments show large disparities among judges in the sentences they recommend for identical cases. This variability cannot be fair. A defendant's sentence should not depend on which judge the case happens to be assigned to."

"Criminal sentences should not depend on the judge's mood during the hearing, or on the outside temperature."

"Guidelines are one way to address this issue. But many people don't like them, because they limit judicial discretion, which might be necessary to ensure fairness and accuracy. After all, each case is unique, isn't it?"

CHAPTER 2

A Noisy System

Our initial encounter with noise, and what first triggered our interest in the topic, was not nearly so dramatic as a brush with the criminal justice system. Actually, the encounter was a kind of accident, involving an insurance company that had engaged the consulting firm with which two of us were affiliated.

Of course, the topic of insurance is not everyone's cup of tea. But our findings show the magnitude of the problem of noise in a for-profit organization that stands to lose a lot from noisy decisions. Our experience with the insurance company helps explain why the problem is so often unseen and what might be done about it.

The insurance company's executives were

weighing the potential value of an effort to increase consistency — to reduce noise — in the judgments of people who made significant financial decisions on the firm's behalf. Everyone agreed that consistency is desirable. Everyone also agreed that these judgments could never be entirely consistent, because they are informal and partly subjective. Some noise is inevitable.

Disagreement emerged when it came to its magnitude. The executives doubted that noise could be a substantial problem for their company. Much to their credit, however, they agreed to settle the question by a kind of simple experiment that we will call a *noise audit*. The result surprised them. It also turned out to be a perfect illustration of the problem of noise.

A Lottery That Creates Noise

Many professionals in any large company are authorized to make judgments that bind the company. For example, this insurance company employs numerous underwriters who quote premiums for financial risks, such as insuring a bank against losses due to fraud or rogue trading. It also employs many claims adjusters who forecast the cost of future claims and also negotiate with claimants if disputes arise.

Every large branch of the company has several

qualified underwriters. When a quote is requested, anyone who happens to be available may be assigned to prepare it. In effect, the particular underwriter who will determine a quote is selected by a lottery.

The exact value of the quote has significant consequences for the company. A high premium is advantageous if the quote is accepted, but such a premium risks losing the business to a competitor. A low premium is more likely to be accepted, but it is less advantageous to the company. For any risk, there is a Goldilocks price that is just right — neither too high nor too low — and there is a good chance that the average judgment of a large group of professionals is not too far from this Goldilocks number. Prices that are higher or lower than this number are costly — this is how the variability of noisy judgments hurts the bottom line.

The job of claims adjusters also affects the finances of the company. For example, suppose that a claim is submitted on behalf of a worker (the claimant) who permanently lost the use of his right hand in an industrial accident. An adjuster is assigned to the claim — just as the underwriter was assigned, because she happens to be available. The adjuster gathers the facts of the case and provides an estimate of its ultimate cost to the company. The same adjuster then takes charge of negotiating with the claimant's representative to ensure that the claimant receives the benefits promised in the policy while also protecting the company from making excessive payments.

The early estimate matters because it sets an implicit goal for the adjuster in future negotiations with the claimant. The insurance company is also legally obligated to reserve the predicted cost of each claim (i.e., to have enough cash to be able to pay it). Here again, there is a Goldilocks value from the perspective of the company. A settlement is not guaranteed, as there is an attorney for the claimant on the other side, who may choose to go to court if the offer is miserly. On the other hand, an overly generous reserve may allow the adjuster too much latitude to agree to frivolous demands. The adjuster's judgment is consequential for the company—and even more consequential for the claimant.

We use the word *lottery* to emphasize the role of chance in the selection of one underwriter or adjuster. In the normal operation of the company, a single professional is assigned to a case, and no one can ever know what would have happened if another colleague had been selected instead.

Lotteries have their place, and they need not be unjust. Acceptable lotteries are used to allocate "goods," like courses in some universities, or "bads," like the draft in the military. They serve a purpose.

But the judgment lotteries we talk about allocate nothing. They just produce uncertainty. Imagine an insurance company whose underwriters are noiseless and set the optimal premium, but a chance device then intervenes to modify the quote that the client actually sees. Evidently, there would be no justification for such a lottery. Neither is there any justification for a system in which the outcome depends on the identity of the person randomly chosen to make a professional judgment.

Noise Audits Reveal System Noise

The lottery that picks a particular judge to establish a criminal sentence or a single shooter to represent a team creates variability, but this variability remains unseen. A noise audit — like the one conducted on federal judges with respect to sentencing — is a way to reveal noise. In such an audit, the same case is evaluated by many individuals, and the variability of their responses is made visible.

The judgments of underwriters and claims adjusters lend themselves especially well to this exercise because their decisions are based on written information. To prepare for the noise audit, executives of the company constructed detailed descriptions of five representative cases for each group (underwriters and adjusters). Employees were asked to evaluate two or three cases each, working independently. They were not told that the purpose of the study was to examine the variability of their judgments.

Before reading on, you may want to think of your own answer to the following questions: In a well-run insurance company, if you randomly selected two qualified underwriters or claims adjusters, how different would you expect their estimates for the same case to be? Specifically, what would be the difference between the two estimates, as a percentage of their average?

We asked numerous executives in the company for their answers, and in subsequent years, we have obtained estimates from a wide variety of people in different professions. Surprisingly, one answer is clearly more popular than all others. Most executives of the insurance company guessed 10% or less. When we asked 828 CEOs and senior executives from a variety of industries how much variation they expected to find in similar expert judgments, 10% was also the median answer and the most frequent one (the second most popular was 15%). A 10% difference would mean, for instance, that one of the two underwriters set a premium of $9,500 while the other quoted $10,500. Not a negligible difference, but one that an organization can be expected to tolerate.

Our noise audit found much greater differences. By our measure, the median difference in underwriting was 55%, about five times as large as was expected by most people, including the company's executives. This result means, for instance, that when one underwriter sets a premium at $9,500, the other does not set it at $10,500 — but instead quotes $16,700. For claims adjusters, the median ratio was 43%. We stress that these results are medians: in half the pairs of cases, the difference between the two judgments was even larger.

The executives to whom we reported the results of the noise audit were quick to realize that the sheer volume of noise presented an expensive problem. One senior executive estimated that the company's annual cost of noise in underwriting — counting both the loss of business from excessive quotes and the losses incurred on underpriced contracts — was in the hundreds of millions of dollars.

No one could say precisely how much error (or how much bias) there was, because no one could know for sure the Goldilocks value for each case. But no one needed to see the bull's-eye to measure the scatter on the back of the target and to realize that the variability was a problem. The data showed that the price a customer is asked to pay depends to an uncomfortable extent on the lottery that picks the employee who will deal with that transaction. To say the least, customers would not be pleased to hear that they were signed up for such a lottery without their consent. More generally, people who deal with organizations expect a system that reliably delivers consistent judgments. They do not expect system noise.

Unwanted Variability Versus Wanted Diversity

A defining feature of system noise is that it is *unwanted,* and we should stress right here that variability in judgments is not always unwanted.

Consider matters of preference or taste. If ten film critics watch the same movie, if ten wine tasters rate the same wine, or if ten people read the same novel, we do not expect them to have the same opinion. Diversity of tastes is welcome and entirely expected. No one would want to live in a world in which everyone has exactly the same likes and dislikes. (Well, almost no one.) But diversity of tastes can help account for errors if a personal taste is mistaken for a professional judgment. If a film producer decides to go forward with an unusual project (about, say, the rise and fall of the rotary phone) because she personally likes the script, she might have made a major mistake if no one else likes it.

Variability in judgments is also expected and welcome in a competitive situation in which the best
judgments will be rewarded. When several companies
(or several teams in the same organization) compete
to generate innovative solutions to the same customer
problem, we don't want them to focus on the same
approach. The same is true when multiple teams of
researchers attack a scientific problem, such as the
development of a vaccine: we very much want them to
look at it from different angles. Even forecasters sometimes behave like competitive players. The analyst
who correctly calls a recession that no one else has
anticipated is sure to gain fame, whereas the one who
never strays from the consensus remains obscure. In
such settings, variability in ideas and judgments is
again welcome, because variation is only the first step.
In a second phase, the results of these judgments will
be pitted against one another, and the best will tri-
umph. In a market as in nature, selection cannot work
without variation.

Matters of taste and competitive settings all pose
interesting problems of judgment. But our focus is on
judgments in which variability is undesirable. System
noise is a problem of systems, which are organizations,
not markets. When traders make different assessments of the value of a stock, some of them will make
money, and others will not. Disagreements make

markets. But if one of those traders is randomly chosen to make that assessment on behalf of her firm, and if we find out that her colleagues in the same firm would produce very different assessments, then the firm faces system noise, and that is a problem.

An elegant illustration of the issue arose when we presented our findings to the senior managers of an asset management firm, prompting them to run their own exploratory noise audit. They asked forty-two experienced investors in the firm to estimate the fair value of a stock (the price at which the investors would be indifferent to buying or selling). The investors based their analysis on a one-page description of the business; the data included simplified profit and loss, balance sheet, and cash flow statements for the past three years and projections for the next two. Median noise, measured in the same way as in the insurance company, was 41%. Such large differences among investors in the same firm, using the same valuation methods, cannot be good news.

Wherever the person making a judgment is randomly selected from a pool of equally qualified individuals, as is the case in this asset management firm, in the criminal justice system, and in the insurance company discussed earlier, noise is a problem. System noise plagues many organizations: an assignment process that is effectively random often decides which doctor sees you in a hospital, which judge hears your case in a courtroom, which patent examiner reviews your application, which customer service representative hears your complaint, and so on. Unwanted variability in these judgments can cause serious problems, including a loss of money and rampant unfairness.

A frequent misconception about unwanted variability in judgments is that it doesn't matter, because random errors supposedly cancel one another out. Certainly, positive and negative errors in a judgment about the same case will tend to cancel one another out, and we will discuss in detail how this property can be used to reduce noise. But noisy systems do not make multiple judgments of the same case. They make noisy judgments of different cases. If one insurance policy is overpriced and another is underpriced, pricing may on average look right, but the insurance company has made two costly errors. If two felons who both should be sentenced to five years in prison receive sentences of three years and seven years, justice has not, on average, been done. In noisy systems, errors do not cancel out. They add up.

The Illusion of Agreement

A large literature going back several decades has documented noise in professional judgment. Because we were aware of this literature, the results of the insurance company's noise audit did not surprise us. What did surprise us, however, was the reaction of the executives to whom we reported our findings: no one at the company had expected anything like the amount of noise we had observed. No one questioned the validity of the audit, and no one claimed that the observed amount of noise was acceptable. Yet the problem of noise—and its large cost—seemed like a new one for the organization. Noise was like a leak in the basement. It was tolerated not because it was thought acceptable but because it had remained unnoticed.

How could that be? How could professionals in the same role and in the same office differ so much from one another without becoming aware of it? How could executives fail to make this observation, which they understood to be a significant threat to the performance and reputation of their company? We came to see that the problem of system noise often goes unrecognized in organizations and that the common inattention to noise is as interesting as its prevalence. The noise audits suggested that respected professionals— and the organizations that employ them—maintained an *illusion of agreement* while in fact disagreeing in their daily professional judgments.

To begin to understand how the illusion of agreement arises, put yourself in the shoes of an underwriter on a normal working day. You have more than five years of experience, you know that you are well regarded among your colleagues, and you respect and like them. You know you are good at your job. After thoroughly analyzing the complex risks faced by a financial firm, you conclude that a premium of $200,000 is appropriate. The problem is complex but not much different from those you solve every day of the week.

Now imagine being told that your colleagues at the office have been given the same information and assessed the same risk. Could you believe that at least half of them have set a premium that is either higher than $255,000 or lower than $145,000? The thought is hard to accept. Indeed, we suspect that underwriters who heard about the noise audit and accepted its validity never truly believed that its conclusions applied to them personally.

Most of us, most of the time, live with the unquestioned belief that the world looks as it does because that's the way it is. There is one small step from this belief to another: "Other people view the world much the way I do." These beliefs, which have been called *naive realism,* are essential to the sense of a reality we share with other people. We rarely question these beliefs. We hold a single interpretation of the world around us at any one time, and we normally invest little effort in generating plausible alternatives to it. One interpretation is enough, and we experience it as true. We do not go through life imagining alternative ways of seeing what we see.

In the case of professional judgments, the belief that others see the world much as we do is reinforced every day in multiple ways. First, we share with our colleagues a common language and set of rules about the considerations that should matter in our decisions. We also have the reassuring experience of agreeing with others on the absurdity of judgments that violate these rules. We view the occasional disagreements with colleagues as lapses of judgment on their part. We have little opportunity to notice that our agreed-on rules are vague, sufficient to eliminate some possibilities but not to specify a shared positive response to a particular case. We can live comfortably with colleagues without ever noticing that they actually do not see the world as we do.

One underwriter we interviewed described her experience in becoming a veteran in her department: "When I was new, I would discuss seventy-five percent of cases with my supervisor. . . . After a few years, I didn't need to—I am now regarded as an expert. . . . Over time, I became more and more confident in my judgment." Like many of us, this person had developed confidence in her judgment mainly by exercising it.

The psychology of this process is well understood. Confidence is nurtured by the subjective experience of judgments that are made with increasing fluency and ease, in part because they resemble judgments made in similar cases in the past. Over time, as this underwriter learned to agree with her past self, her confidence in her judgments increased. She gave no indication that—after the initial apprenticeship phase—she had learned to agree with others, had checked to what extent she did agree with them, or had even tried to prevent her practices from drifting away from those of her colleagues.

For the insurance company, the illusion of agreement was shattered only by the noise audit. How had the leaders of the company remained unaware of their noise problem? There are several possible answers here, but one that seems to play a large role in many settings is simply the discomfort of disagreement. Most organizations prefer consensus and harmony over dissent and conflict. The procedures in place often seem expressly designed to minimize the frequency of exposure to actual disagreements and, when such disagreements happen, to explain them away.

Nathan Kuncel, a professor of psychology at the University of Minnesota and a leading researcher on the prediction of performance, shared with us a story that illustrates this problem. Kuncel was helping a school's admissions office review its decision process. First a person read an application file, rated it, and then handed it off with ratings to a second reader, who then also rated it. Kuncel suggested — for reasons that will become obvious throughout this book — that it would be preferable to mask the first reader's ratings so as not to influence the second reader. The school's reply: "We used to do that, but it resulted in so many disagreements that we switched to the current system." This school is not the only organization that considers conflict avoidance at least as important as making the right decision.

Consider another mechanism that many companies resort to: postmortems of unfortunate judgments. As a learning mechanism, postmortems are useful. But if a mistake has truly been made — in the sense that a judgment strayed far from professional norms — discussing it will not be challenging. Experts will easily conclude that the judgment was way off the consensus. (They might also write it off as a rare exception.) Bad judgment is much easier to identify than good judgment. The calling out of egregious mistakes and the marginalization of bad colleagues will not help professionals become aware of how much they disagree when making broadly acceptable judgments. On the contrary, the easy consensus about bad judgments may even reinforce the illusion of agreement. The true lesson, about the ubiquity of system noise, will never be learned.

We hope you are starting to share our view that system noise is a serious problem. Its existence is not a surprise; noise is a consequence of the informal nature of judgment. However, as we will see throughout this book, the amount of noise observed when an organization takes a serious look almost always comes as a shock. Our conclusion is simple: wherever there is judgment, there is noise, and more of it than you think.

Speaking of System Noise in the Insurance Company

"We depend on the quality of professional judgments, by underwriters, claims adjusters, and others. We assign each case to one expert, but we operate under the wrong assumption that another expert would produce a similar judgment."

"System noise is five times larger than we thought — or than we can tolerate. Without a noise audit, we would never have realized that. The noise audit shattered the illusion of agreement."

"System noise is a serious problem: it costs us hundreds of millions."

"Wherever there is judgment, there is noise — and more of it than we think."

CHAPTER 3

Singular Decisions

The case studies we have discussed thus far involve judgments that are made repeatedly. What is the right sentence for someone convicted of theft? What is the right premium for a particular risk? While each case is in some sense unique, judgments like these are *recurrent decisions*. Doctors diagnosing patients, judges hearing parole cases, admissions officers reviewing applications, accountants preparing tax forms—these are all examples of recurrent decisions.

Noise in recurrent decisions is demonstrated by a noise audit, such as those we introduced in the previous chapter. Unwanted variability is easy to define and measure when interchangeable professionals make decisions in similar cases. It seems much harder, or perhaps even impossible, to apply the idea of noise to a category of judgments that we call *singular decisions*.

Consider, for instance, the crisis the world faced in 2014. In West Africa, numerous people were dying from Ebola. Because the world is interconnected, projections suggested that infections would rapidly spread all over the world and hit Europe and North America particularly hard. In the United States, there were insistent calls to shut down air travel from affected regions and to take aggressive steps to close the borders. The political pressure to move in that direction was intense, and prominent and well-informed people favored those steps.

President Barack Obama was faced with one of the most difficult decisions of his presidency — one that he had not encountered before and never encountered again. He chose not to close any borders. Instead he sent three thousand people — health workers and soldiers — to West Africa. He led a diverse, international coalition of nations that did not always work well together, using their resources and expertise to tackle the problem at its source.

Singular Versus Recurrent

Decisions that are made only once, like the president's Ebola response, are singular because they are not made recurrently by the same individual or team, they lack a prepackaged response, and they are marked by genuinely unique features. In dealing with Ebola, President Obama and his team had no real precedents on which to draw. Important political decisions are often good examples of singular decisions, as are the most fateful choices of military commanders.

In the private realm, decisions you make when choosing a job, buying a house, or proposing marriage have the same characteristics. Even if this is not your first job, house, or marriage, and despite the fact that countless people have faced these decisions before, the decision feels unique to you. In business, heads of companies are often called on to make what seem like unique decisions to them: whether to launch a potentially game-changing innovation, how much to close down during a pandemic, whether to open an office in a foreign country, or whether to capitulate to a government that seeks to regulate them.

Arguably, there is a continuum, not a category difference, between singular and recurrent decisions. Underwriters may deal with some cases that strike them as very much out of the ordinary. Conversely, if you are buying a house for the fourth time in your life, you have probably started to think of home buying as a recurrent decision. But extreme examples clearly suggest that the difference is meaningful.

Going to war is one thing; going through annual budget reviews is another.

Noise in Singular Decisions

Singular decisions have traditionally been treated as quite separate from the recurrent judgments that interchangeable employees routinely make in large organizations. While social scientists have dealt with recurrent decisions, high-stakes singular decisions have been the province of historians and management gurus. The approaches to the two types of decisions have been quite different. Analyses of recurrent decisions have often taken a statistical bent, with social scientists assessing many similar decisions to discern patterns, identify regularities, and measure accuracy. In contrast, discussions of singular decisions typically adopt a causal view; they are conducted in hindsight and are focused on identifying the causes of what happened. Historical analyses, like case studies of management successes and failures, aim to understand how an essentially unique judgment was made.

The nature of singular decisions raises an important question for the study of noise. We have defined noise as undesirable variability in judgments of the same problem. Since singular problems are never exactly repeated, this definition does not apply to them. After all, history is only run once. You will never be able to compare Obama's decision to send health workers and soldiers to West Africa in 2014 with the decisions other American presidents made about how to handle that particular problem at that particular time (though you can speculate). You may agree to compare your decision to marry that special someone with the decisions of other people like you, but that comparison will not be as relevant to you as the one we made between the quotes of underwriters on the same case. You and your spouse are unique. There is no direct way to observe the presence of noise in singular decisions.

Yet singular decisions are not free from the factors that produce noise in recurrent decisions. At the shooting range, the shooters on Team C (the noisy team) may be adjusting the gunsight on their rifle in different directions, or their hands may just be unsteady. If we observed only the first shooter on the team, we would have no idea how noisy the team is, but the sources of noise would still be there. Similarly, when you make a singular decision, you have to imagine that another decision maker, even one just as competent as you and sharing the same goals and values, would not reach the same conclusion from the same facts. And as the decision maker, you should recognize that you might have made a different decision if some irrelevant aspects of the situation or of the decision-making process had been different.

In other words, we cannot measure noise in a singular decision, but if we think counterfactually, we know for sure that noise is there. Just as the shooter's unsteady hand implies that a single shot *could* have landed somewhere else, noise in the decision makers and in the decision-making process implies that the singular decision *could* have been different.

Consider all the factors that affect a singular decision. If the experts in charge of analyzing the Ebola threat and preparing response plans had been different people, with different backgrounds and life experiences, would their proposals to President Obama have been the same? If the same facts had been presented in a slightly different manner, would the conversation have unfolded the same way? If the key players had been in a different mood or had been meeting during a snowstorm, would the final decision have been identical? Seen in this light, the singular decision does not seem so determined. Depending on many factors that we are not even aware of, the decision could plausibly have been different.

For another exercise in counterfactual thinking, consider how different countries and regions responded to the COVID-19 crisis. Even when the virus hit them roughly at the same time and in a similar manner, there were wide differences in responses. This variation provides clear evidence of noise in different countries' decision making. But what if the epidemic had struck a single country? In that case, we wouldn't have observed any variability. But our inability to observe variability would not make the decision less noisy.

Controlling Noise in Singular Decisions

This theoretical discussion matters. If singular decisions are just as noisy as recurrent ones, then the strategies that reduce noise in recurrent decisions should also improve the quality of singular decisions.

This is a more counterintuitive prescription than it seems. When you have a one-of-a-kind decision to make, your instinct is probably to treat it as, well, one of a kind. Some even claim that the rules of probabilistic thinking are entirely irrelevant to singular decisions made under uncertainty and that such decisions call for a radically different approach.

Our observations here suggest the opposite advice. From the perspective of noise reduction, *a singular decision is a recurrent decision that happens only once.* Whether you make a decision only once or a hundred times, your goal should be to make it in a way that reduces both bias and noise. And practices that reduce error should be just as effective in your one-of-a-kind decisions as in your repeated ones.

Speaking of Singular Decisions

"The way you approach this unusual opportunity exposes you to noise."

"Remember: a singular decision is a recurrent decision that is made only once."

"The personal experiences that made you who you are are not truly relevant to this decision."

PART II

Your Mind Is a Measuring Instrument

Measurement, in everyday life as in science, is the act of using an instrument to assign a value on a scale to an object or event. You measure the length of a carpet in inches, using a tape measure. You measure the temperature in degrees Fahrenheit or Celsius by consulting a thermometer.

The act of making a judgment is similar. When judges determine the appropriate prison term for a crime, they assign a value on a scale. So do underwriters when they set a dollar value to insure a risk, or doctors when they make a diagnosis. (The scale need not be numerical: "guilty beyond a reasonable doubt," "advanced melanoma," and "surgery is recommended" are judgments, too.)

Judgment can therefore be described as *measurement in which the instrument is a human mind.* Implicit in the notion of measurement is the goal of accuracy — to approach truth and minimize error. The goal of judgment is not to impress, not to take a stand, not to persuade. It is important to note that the concept of judgment as we use it here is borrowed from the technical psychological literature, and that it is a much narrower concept than the same word has in everyday language. *Judgment* is not a synonym for *thinking,* and *making accurate judgments* is not a synonym for *having good judgment.*

As we define it, a judgment is a conclusion that can be summarized in a word or phrase. If an intelligence analyst writes a long report leading to the conclusion that a regime is unstable, only the conclusion is a judgment. *Judgment,* like *measurement,* refers both to the mental activity of making a judgment and to its product. And we will sometimes use *judge* as a technical term to describe people who make judgments, even when they have nothing to do with the judiciary.

Although accuracy is the goal, perfection in achieving this goal is never achieved even in scientific measurement, much less in judgment. There is always some error, some of which is bias and some of which is noise.

To experience how noise and bias contribute to error, we invite you to play a game that will take you less than one minute. If you have a smartphone with a stopwatch, it probably has a lap function, which enables you to measure consecutive time intervals without stopping the stopwatch or even looking at the display. Your goal is to produce five consecutive laps of exactly ten seconds without looking at the phone. You may want to observe a ten-second interval a few times before you begin. Go.

Now look at the lap durations recorded on your phone. (The phone itself was not free from noise, but there was very little of it.) You will see that the laps are not all exactly ten seconds and that they vary over a substantial range. You tried to reproduce the same timing exactly, but you were unable to do so. The variability you could not control is an instance of noise.

This finding is hardly surprising, because noise is universal in physiology and psychology. Variability across individuals is a biological given; no two peas in a pod are truly identical. Within the same person, there is variability, too. Your heartbeat is not exactly regular. You cannot repeat the same gesture with perfect precision. And when you have your hearing examined by an audiologist, there will be some sounds so soft you never hear them, and others so loud you always do. But there will also be some sounds that you will sometimes hear and sometimes miss.

Now look at the five numbers on your phone. Do you see a pattern? For instance, are all five laps shorter than ten seconds, a pattern suggesting that your internal clock is running fast? In this simple task, the bias is the difference, positive or negative, between the mean of your laps and ten seconds. Noise constitutes the variability of your results, analogous to the scatter of shots we saw earlier. In statistics, the most common measure of variability is *standard deviation,* and we will use it to measure noise in judgments.

We can think of most judgments, specifically *predictive* judgments, as similar to the measurements you just made. When we make a prediction, we attempt to come close to a true value. An economic forecaster aims to be as close as possible to the true value of the growth in next year's gross domestic product; a doctor aims to make the correct diagnosis. (Note that the term *prediction,* in the technical sense used in this book, does not imply predicting the future: for our purposes, the diagnosis of an existing medical condition is a prediction.)

We will rely extensively on the analogy between judgment and measurement because it helps explain the role of noise in error. People who make predictive judgments are just like the shooter who aims at the bull's-eye or the physicist who strives to measure the true weight of a particle. Noise in their judgments implies error. Simply put, when a judgment aims at a true value, two different judgments cannot both be right. Like measuring instruments, some people generally show more error than others in a particular task—perhaps because of deficiencies in skill or training. But, like measuring instruments, the people who make judgments are never perfect. We need to understand and measure their errors.

Of course, most professional judgments are far more complex than the measurement of a time interval. In chapter 4, we define different types of professional judgments and explore what they aim at. In chapter 5, we discuss how to measure error and how to quantify the contribution of system noise to it. Chapter 6 dives deeper into system noise and identifies its components, which are different types of noise. In chapter 7, we explore one of these components: occasion noise. Finally, in chapter 8, we show how groups often amplify noise in judgments.

A simple conclusion emerges from these chapters: like a measuring instrument, the human mind is imperfect—it is both biased and noisy. Why, and by how much? Let's find out.

CHAPTER 4

Matters of Judgment

This book is about professional judgments, broadly understood, and it assumes that whoever makes such a judgment is competent and aiming to get it right. However, the very concept of judgment involves a reluctant acknowledgment that you can never be certain that a judgment is right.

Consider the phrases "matter of judgment" or "it's a judgment call." We do not consider the proposition that the sun will rise tomorrow or that the formula of sodium chloride is NaCl to be matters of judgment, because reasonable people are expected to agree perfectly on them. A matter of judgment is one with some uncertainty about the answer and where we allow for the possibility that reasonable and competent people might disagree.

But there is a limit to how much disagreement is

admissible. Indeed, the word *judgment* is used mainly where people believe they should agree. Matters of judgment differ from matters of opinion or taste, in which unresolved differences are entirely acceptable. The insurance executives who were shocked by the result of the noise audit would have no problem if claims adjusters were sharply divided over the relative merits of the Beatles and the Rolling Stones, or of salmon and tuna.

Matters of judgment, including professional judgments, occupy a space between questions of fact or computation on the one hand and matters of taste or opinion on the other. They are defined by the *expectation of bounded disagreement.*

Exactly how much disagreement is acceptable in a judgment is itself a judgment call and depends on the difficulty of the problem. Agreement is especially easy when a judgment is absurd. Judges who differ widely in the sentences they set in a run-of-the-mill fraud case will concur that a fine of one dollar and a life sentence are both unreasonable. Judges at wine competitions differ greatly on which wines should get medals, but are often unanimous in their contempt for the rejects.

The Experience of Judgment: An Example

Before we further discuss the experience of judgment, we now ask you to make one yourself. You will absorb more from the rest of this chapter if you do this exercise and carry it out to completion.

Imagine that you are a member of a team charged with evaluating candidates for the position of chief executive in a moderately successful regional financial firm that faces increasing competition. You are asked to assess the probability that the following candidate will be successful after two years on the job. Successful is defined simply as the candidate's having kept the CEO job at the end of the two years. Express the probability on a scale from 0 (impossible) to 100 (certain).

Michael Gambardi is thirty-seven years old. He has held several positions since he graduated from Harvard Business School twelve years ago. Early on, he was a founder and an investor in two start-ups that failed without attracting much financial support. He then joined a large insurance company and quickly rose to the position of regional chief operating officer for Europe. In that post, he initiated and managed an important improvement in the timely resolution of claims. He was described by colleagues and subordinates as effective but also as domineering and abrasive, and there was significant turnover of executives during his tenure. Colleagues and subordinates also attest to his integrity and willingness to take responsibility for failures. For the last two years, he has served as CEO of a medium-sized financial company that was initially at risk of failing. He stabilized the company, where he is considered successful though difficult to work with. He has indicated an interest in moving on. Human resources specialists who interviewed him a few years ago gave him superior grades for creativity and energy but also described him as arrogant and sometimes tyrannical.

Recall that Michael is a candidate for a CEO position in a regional financial firm that is moderately successful and that faces increasing competition. What is the probability that Michael, if hired, will still be in his job after two years? Please decide on a specific number in the range of 0 to 100 before reading on. Read the description again if you need to.

If you engaged in the task seriously, you probably found it difficult. There is a mass of information, much of it seemingly inconsistent. You had to struggle to form the coherent impression that you needed to produce a judgment. In constructing that impression, you focused on some details that appeared important and you very likely ignored others. If asked to explain your choice of a number, you would mention a few salient facts but not enough of them for a full accounting of your judgment.

The thought process you went through illustrates several features of the mental operation we call judgment:

- Of all the cues provided by the description (which are only a subset of what you might need to know), you attended to some more than others without being fully aware of the choices you made. Did you notice that Gambardi is an Italian name? Do you remember the school he attended? This exercise was designed to overload you so that you could not easily recover all the details of the case. Most likely, your recollection of what we presented would be different from that of other readers. Selective attention and selective recall are a source of variability across people.

- Then, you informally integrated these cues into an overall impression of Gambardi's prospects.

69

The key word here is *informally*. You did not construct a plan for answering the question. Without being fully aware of what you were doing, your mind worked to construct a coherent impression of Michael's strengths and weaknesses and of the challenges he faces. The informality allowed you to work quickly. It also produces variability: a formal process such as adding a column of numbers guarantees identical results, but some noise is inevitable in an informal operation.

- Finally, you converted this overall impression into a number on a probability scale of success. Matching a number between 0 and 100 to an impression is a remarkable process, to which we will return in chapter 14. Again, you do not know exactly why you responded as you did. Why did you choose, say, 65 rather than 61 or 69? Most likely, at some point, a number came to your mind. You checked whether that number felt right, and if it did not, another number came to mind. This part of the process is also a source of variability across people.

Since each of these three steps in a complex judgment process entails some variability, we should not be surprised to find a lot of noise in answers about Michael Gambardi. If you ask a few friends to read the case, you will probably find that your estimates of his probability of success are scattered widely. When we showed the case to 115 MBA students, their estimates of Gambardi's probability of success ranged from 10 to 95. That is a great deal of noise.

Incidentally, you may have noticed that the stopwatch exercise and the Gambardi problem illustrate two types of noise. The variability of judgments over successive trials with the stopwatch is noise within a single judge (yourself), whereas the variability of judgments of the Gambardi case is noise between different judges. In measurement terms, the first problem illustrates *within-person* reliability, and the second illustrates *between-person* reliability.

What Judgment Aims to Achieve: The Internal Signal

Your answer to the Gambardi question is a predictive judgment, as we have defined the term. However, it differs in important ways from other judgments that we call predictive, including tomorrow's peak temperature in Bangkok, the result of tonight's football game, or the outcome of the next presidential election. If you disagree with a friend about these problems, you will, at some point, find out who is right. But if you disagree about Gambardi, time will *not* tell who was right, for a simple reason: Gambardi does not exist.

Even if the question referred to a real person and we knew the outcome, a single probability judgment (other than 0 or 100%) cannot be confirmed or disconfirmed. The outcome does not reveal what the ex ante probability was. If an event that was assigned a probability of 90% fails to happen, the judgment of probability was not necessarily a bad one. After all, outcomes that are just 10% likely to happen end up happening 10% of the time. The Gambardi exercise is an example of a *nonverifiable* predictive judgment, for two separate reasons: Gambardi is fictitious and the answer is probabilistic.

Many professional judgments are nonverifiable. Barring egregious errors, underwriters will never know, for instance, whether a particular policy was overpriced or underpriced. Other forecasts may be nonverifiable because they are conditional. "If we go to war, we will be crushed" is an important prediction, but it is likely to remain untested (we hope). Or forecasts may be too long term for the professionals who make them to be brought to account—like, for instance, an estimate of mean temperatures by the end of the twenty-first century.

Did the nonverifiable nature of the Gambardi task change how you approached it? Did you, for instance, ask yourself whether Gambardi was real or fictitious? Did you wonder whether the outcome would be revealed later in the text? Did you reflect on the fact that, even if that were the case, the revelation would not give you the answer to the question you were facing? Probably not, because these considerations did not seem relevant when you answered the question.

Verifiability does not change the experience of judgment. To some degree, you might perhaps think harder about a problem whose answer will be revealed soon, because the fear of being exposed concentrates the mind. Conversely, you might refuse to give much thought to a problem so hypothetical as to be absurd ("If Gambardi had three legs and could fly, would he be a better CEO?"). But, by and large, you address a plausible, hypothetical problem in much the same way that you tackle a real one. This similarity is important to psychological research, much of which uses made-up problems.

Since there is no outcome—and you probably did not even ask yourself whether there would ever be one—you were not trying to minimize error relative to that outcome. You tried to get the judgment right, to land on a number in which you had enough confidence to make it your answer. Of course, you were not perfectly confident in that answer, in the way you would be perfectly confident that four times six is twenty-four. You were aware of some uncertainty (and, as we will see, there is probably more of it than you recognized). But at some point, you decided that you were no longer making progress and settled for an answer.

What made you feel you got the judgment right, or at least right enough to be your answer? We suggest this feeling is an *internal signal of judgment completion,* unrelated to any outside information. Your answer felt right if it seemed to fit comfortably enough with the evidence. An answer of 0 or 100 would not give you that sense of fit: the confidence it implies is inconsistent with the messy, ambiguous, conflicting evidence provided. But the number on which you settled, whatever it is, gave you the sense of coherence you needed. The aim of judgment, as you experienced it, was the achievement of a coherent solution.

The essential feature of this internal signal is that the sense of coherence is part of the experience of judgment. It is not contingent on a real outcome. As a result, the internal signal is just as available for non-verifiable judgments as it is for real, verifiable ones. This explains why making a judgment about a fictitious character like Gambardi feels very much the same as does making a judgment about the real world.

How Judgment Is Evaluated: The Outcome and the Process

Verifiability does not change the experience of judgment as it takes place. It does, however, change its evaluation after the fact.

Verifiable judgments can be scored by an objective observer on a simple measure of error: the difference between the judgment and the outcome. If a weather forecaster said today's high temperature would be seventy degrees Fahrenheit and it is sixty-five degrees, the forecaster made an error of plus five degrees. Evidently, this approach does not work for nonverifiable judgments like the Gambardi problem, which have no true outcome. How, then, are we to decide what constitutes good judgment?

The answer is that there is a second way to evaluate judgments. This approach applies both to verifiable and nonverifiable ones. It consists in evaluating the *process* of judgment. When we speak of good or bad judgments, we may be speaking either about the output (e.g., the number you produced in the Gambardi case) or about the process—what you did to arrive at that number.

One approach to the evaluation of the process of judgment is to observe how that process performs when it is applied to a large number of cases. For instance, consider a political forecaster who has assigned probabilities of winning to a large number of candidates in local elections. He described one hundred of these candidates as being 70% likely to win. If seventy of them are eventually elected, we have a good indication of the forecaster's skill in using the probability scale. The judgments are verifiable as an ensemble, although no single probability judgment can be declared right or wrong. Similarly, bias for or against a particular group can best be established by examining statistical results for a substantial number of cases.

Another question that can be asked about the process of judgment is whether it conforms to the principles of logic or probability theory. A large body of research on cognitive biases of judgment has been in this vein.

Focusing on the process of judgment, rather than its outcome, makes it possible to evaluate the quality of judgments that are not verifiable, such as judgments about fictitious problems or long-term forecasts. We may not be able to compare them to a known outcome, but we can still tell whether they have been made incorrectly. And when we turn to the question of *improving* judgments rather than just evaluating them, we will focus on process, too. All the procedures we recommend in this book to reduce bias and noise aim to adopt the judgment process that would minimize error over an ensemble of similar cases.

We have contrasted two ways of evaluating a judgment: by comparing it to an *outcome* and by assessing the quality of the *process* that led to it. Note that when the judgment is verifiable, the two ways of evaluating it may reach different conclusions in a single case. A skilled and careful forecaster using the best possible tools and techniques will often miss the correct number in making a quarterly inflation forecast. Meanwhile, in a single quarter, a dart-throwing chimpanzee will sometimes be right.

Scholars of decision-making offer clear advice to resolve this tension: focus on the process, not on the outcome of a single case. We recognize, however, that this is not standard practice in real life. Professionals are usually evaluated on how closely their judgments match verifiable outcomes, and if you ask them what they aim for in their judgments, a close match is what they will answer.

In summary, what people usually claim to strive for in verifiable judgments is a prediction that matches the outcome. What they are effectively trying to achieve, regardless of verifiability, is the internal signal of completion provided by the coherence between the facts of the case and the judgment. And what they should be trying to achieve, normatively speaking, is the judgment process that would produce the best judgment over an ensemble of similar cases.

Evaluative Judgments

So far in this chapter, we have focused on predictive judgment tasks, and most of the judgments we will discuss are of that type. But chapter 1, which discusses Judge Frankel and noise in sentencing by federal judges, examines another type of judgment. Sentencing a felon is not a prediction. It is an *evaluative judgment* that seeks to match the sentence to the severity of the crime. Judges at a wine fair and restaurant critics make evaluative judgments. Professors who grade essays, judges at ice-skating competitions, and committees that award grants to research projects make evaluative judgments.

A different kind of evaluative judgment is made in decisions that involve multiple options and trade-offs between them. Consider managers who choose among candidates for hiring, management teams that must decide on strategic options, or even presidents choosing how to respond to an epidemic in Africa. To be sure, all these decisions rely on predictive judgments that provide input—for instance, how a candidate will perform in her first year, how the stock market will respond to a given strategic move, or how quickly the epidemic will spread if left unchecked. But the final decisions entail trade-offs between the pros and cons of various options, and these trade-offs are resolved by evaluative judgments.

Like predictive judgments, evaluative judgments entail an expectation of bounded disagreement. No self-respecting federal judge is likely to say, "This is the punishment I like best, and I don't care a bit if my colleagues think otherwise." And decision makers who choose from several strategic options expect colleagues and observers who have the same information and share the same goals to agree with them, or at least not to disagree too much. Evaluative judgments partly depend on the values and preferences of those making them, but they are not mere matters of taste or opinion.

For that reason, the boundary between predictive and evaluative judgments is fuzzy and people who make judgments are often unaware of it. Judges who set sentences or professors who grade essays think hard about their task and strive to find the "right" answer. They develop confidence in their judgments and in the justifications they have for them. Professionals feel much the same, act much the same, and speak much the same to justify themselves when their judgments are predictive ("How well will this new product sell?") and when they are evaluative ("How well did my assistant perform this year?").

What's Wrong with Noise

The observation of noise in predictive judgments always indicates that something is wrong. If two doctors disagree on a diagnosis or two forecasters disagree about the next quarter's sales, at least one of them must be in error. The error may happen because one of them is less skilled, and therefore more likely to be wrong, or because of some other source of noise. Regardless of the cause, failing to make the correct judgment can have serious consequences for those who rely on the diagnoses and forecasts of these individuals.

Noise in evaluative judgments is problematic for a different reason. In any system in which judges are assumed to be interchangeable and assigned quasi-randomly, large disagreements about the same case violate expectations of fairness and consistency. If there are large differences in sentences given to the same defendant, we are in the domain of the "arbitrary cruelties" that Judge Frankel denounced. Even judges who believe in the value of individualized sentencing and who disagree on a robber's sentence will agree that a level of disagreement that turns a judgment into a lottery is problematic. The same is true (if less dramatically so) when vastly different grades are given to the same essay, different safety ratings to the same restaurant, or different scores to the same ice-skater — or when one person, suffering from depression, gets social security disability benefits, while another person with the same condition gets nothing.

Even when unfairness is only a minor concern, system noise poses another problem. People who are affected by evaluative judgments expect the values these judgments reflect to be those of the system, not of the individual judges. Something must have gone badly wrong if one customer, complaining of a defective laptop, gets fully reimbursed, and another gets a mere apology; or if one employee who has been with a firm for five years asks for a promotion and gets exactly that, while another employee, whose performance is otherwise identical, is politely turned down. System noise is inconsistency, and inconsistency damages the credibility of the system.

Undesirable but Measurable

All we need to measure noise is multiple judgments of the same problem. We do not need to know a true value. As the shooting-range story in the introduction illustrates, when we look at the back of the target, the bull's-eye is invisible, but we can see the scatter of the shots. As soon as we know that all the shooters were aiming at the same bull's-eye, we can measure noise. This is what a noise audit does. If we ask all our forecasters to estimate next quarter's sales, the scatter in their forecasts is noise.

This difference between bias and noise is essential for the practical purpose of improving judgments. It may seem paradoxical to claim that we can improve judgments when we cannot verify whether they are right. But we can — if we start by measuring noise. Regardless of whether the goal of judgment is just accuracy or a more complex trade-off between values, noise is undesirable and often measurable. And once noise is measured, as we will discuss in part 5, it is often possible to reduce it.

Speaking of Professional Judgment

"This is a matter of judgment. You can't expect people to agree perfectly."

"Yes, this is a matter of judgment, but some judgments are so far out that they are wrong."

"Your choice between the candidates was just an expression of taste, not a serious judgment."

"A decision requires both predictive and evaluative judgments."

CHAPTER 5

Measuring Error

It is obvious that a consistent bias can produce costly errors. If a scale adds a constant amount to your weight, if an enthusiastic manager routinely predicts that projects will take half the time they end up taking, or if a timid executive is unduly pessimistic about future sales year after year, the result will be numerous serious mistakes.

We have now seen that noise can produce costly errors as well. If a manager most often predicts that projects will take half the time they ultimately take, and occasionally predicts they will take twice their actual time, it is unhelpful to say that the manager is "on average" right. The different errors add up; they do not cancel out.

An important question, therefore, is how, and how

much, bias and noise contribute to error. This chapter aims to answer that question. Its basic message is straightforward: in professional judgments of all kinds, whenever accuracy is the goal, *bias and noise play the same role in the calculation of overall error.* In some cases, the larger contributor will be bias; in other cases it will be noise (and these cases are more common than one might expect). But in every case, a reduction of noise has the same impact on overall error as does a reduction of bias by the same amount. For that reason, the measurement and reduction of noise should have the same high priority as the measurement and reduction of bias.

This conclusion rests on a particular approach to the measurement of error, which has a long history and is generally accepted in science and in statistics. In this chapter, we provide an introductory overview of that history and a sketch of the underlying reasoning.

Should GoodSell Reduce Noise?

Begin by imagining a large retail company named GoodSell, which employs many sales forecasters. Their job is to predict GoodSell's market share in various regions. Perhaps after reading a book on the topic of noise, Amy Simkin, head of the forecasting department at GoodSell, has conducted a noise audit. All forecasters produced independent estimates of the market share in the same region.

Figure 3 shows the (implausibly smooth) results of the noise audit. Amy can see that the forecasts were distributed in the familiar bell-shaped curve, also known as the normal or Gaussian distribution. The most frequent forecast, represented by the peak of the bell curve, is 44%. Amy can also see that the forecasting system of the company is quite noisy: the forecasts, which would be identical if all were accurate, vary over a considerable range.

We can attach a number to the amount of noise in GoodSell's forecasting system. Just as we did when you used your stopwatch to measure laps, we can compute the *standard deviation* of the forecasts. As its name indicates, the standard deviation represents a

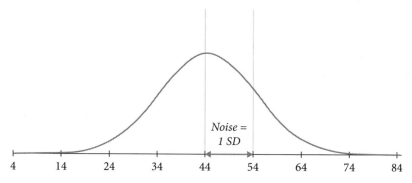

FIGURE 3: *Distribution of GoodSell's market share forecasts for one region*

typical distance from the mean. In this example, it is 10 percentage points. As is true for every normal distribution, about two-thirds of the forecasts are contained within one standard deviation on either side of the mean — in this example, between a 34% and a 54% market share. Amy now has an estimate of the amount of system noise in the forecasts of market share. (A better noise audit would use several forecasting problems for a more robust estimate, but one is enough for our purpose here.)

As was the case with the executives of the real insurance company of chapter 2, Amy is shocked by the results and wants to take action. The unacceptable amount of noise indicates that the forecasters are not disciplined in implementing the procedures they are expected to follow. Amy asks for authority to hire a noise consultant to achieve more uniformity and discipline in her forecasters' work. Unfortunately, she does not get approval. Her boss's reply seems sensible enough: how, he asks, could we reduce errors when we don't know if our forecasts are right or wrong? Surely, he says, if there is a large average error in the forecasts (i.e., a large bias), addressing it should be the priority. Before undertaking anything to improve its forecasts, he concludes, GoodSell must wait and find out if they are correct.

One year after the original noise audit, the

outcome that the forecasters were trying to predict is known. Market share in the target region turned out to be 34%. Now we also know each forecaster's error, which is simply the difference between the forecast and the outcome. The error is 0 for a forecast of 34%, it is 10% for the mean forecast of 44%, and it is –10% for a lowball forecast of 24%.

Figure 4 shows the distribution of errors. It is the same as the distribution of forecasts in figure 3, but the true value (34%) has been subtracted from each forecast. The shape of the distribution has not changed, and the standard deviation (our measure of noise) is still 10%.

The difference between figures 3 and 4 is analogous to the difference between a pattern of shots seen from the back and the front of the target in figures 1

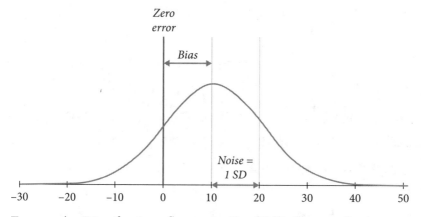

FIGURE 4: *Distribution of errors in GoodSell's forecasts for one region*

and 2 (see the introduction). Knowing the position of the target was not necessary to observe noise in shooting; similarly, knowing the true outcome adds nothing at all to what was already known about noise in forecasting.

Amy Simkin and her boss now know something they did not know earlier: the amount of bias in the forecasts. Bias is simply the average of errors, which in this case is also 10%. Bias and noise, therefore, happen to be numerically identical in this set of data. (To be clear, this equality of noise and bias is by no means a general rule, but a case in which bias and noise are equal makes it easier to understand their roles.) We can see that most forecasters had made an optimistic error—that is, they overestimated the market share that would be achieved: most of them erred on the right-hand side of the zero-error vertical bar. (In fact, using the properties of the normal distribution, we know that is the case for 84% of the forecasts.)

As Amy's boss notes with barely concealed satisfaction, he was right. There was a lot of bias in the forecasts! And indeed, it is now evident that reducing bias would be a good thing. But, Amy still wonders, would it have been a good idea a year ago—and would it be a good idea now—to reduce noise, too? How would the value of such an improvement compare with the value of reducing bias?

Mean Squares

To answer Amy's question, we need a "scoring rule" for errors, a way to weight and combine individual errors into a single measure of overall error. Fortunately, such a tool exists. It is the *method of least squares,* invented in 1795 by Carl Friedrich Gauss, a famous mathematical prodigy born in 1777, who began a career of major discoveries in his teens.

Gauss proposed a rule for scoring the contribution of individual errors to overall error. His measure of overall error — called *mean squared error* (MSE) — is the average of the squares of the individual errors of measurement.

Gauss's detailed arguments for his approach to the measurement of overall error are far beyond the scope of this book, and his solution is not immediately obvious. Why use the squares of errors? The idea seems arbitrary, even bizarre. Yet, as you will see, it builds on an intuition that you almost certainly share.

To see why, let us turn to what appears to be a completely different problem but turns out to be the same one. Imagine that you are given a ruler and asked to measure the length of a line to the nearest millimeter. You are allowed to make five measurements. They are represented by the downward-pointing triangles on the line in figure 5.

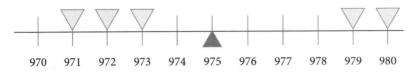

FIGURE 5: *Five measurements of the same length*

As you can see, the five measurements are all between 971 and 980 millimeters. What is your best estimate of the true length of the line? There are two obvious contenders. One possibility is the median number, the measurement that sits between the two shorter measurements and the two longer ones. It is 973 millimeters. The other possibility is the arithmetic mean, known in common parlance as the average, which in this example is 975 millimeters and shown here as an upward-pointing arrow. Your intuition probably favors the mean, and your intuition is correct. The mean contains more information; it is affected by the size of the numbers, while the median is affected only by their order.

There is a tight link between this problem of estimation, about which you have a clear intuition, and the problem of overall error measurement that concerns us here. They are, in fact, two sides of the same coin. That is because the best estimate is one that minimizes the overall error of the available measurements. Accordingly, if your intuition about the mean being the best estimate is correct, the formula you use to measure overall error should be one that yields the arithmetic mean as the value for which error is minimized.

MSE has that property—and it is the only definition of overall error that has it. In figure 6, we have computed the value of MSE in the set of five measurements for ten possible integer values of the line's true length. For instance, if the true value was 971, the errors in the five measurements would be 0, 1, 2, 8, and 9. The squares of these errors add up to 150, and their mean is 30. This is a large number, reflecting the fact that some measurements are far from the true value. You can see that MSE decreases as we get closer

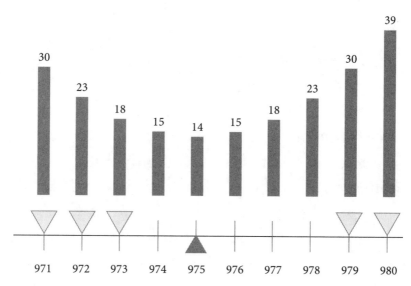

FIGURE 6: *Mean squared error (MSE) for ten possible values of the true length*

to 975 — the mean — and increases again beyond that point. The mean is our best estimate because it is the value that minimizes overall error.

You can also see that the overall error increases rapidly when your estimate diverges from the mean. When your estimate increases by just 3 millimeters, from 976 to 979, for instance, MSE doubles. This is a key feature of MSE: squaring gives large errors a far greater weight than it gives small ones.

You now see why Gauss's formula to measure overall error is called mean squared error and why his approach to estimation is called the least squares method. The squaring of errors is its central idea, and no other formula would be compatible with your intuition that the mean is the best estimate.

The advantages of Gauss's approach were quickly recognized by other mathematicians. Among his many feats, Gauss used MSE (and other mathematical innovations) to solve a puzzle that had defeated the best astronomers of Europe: the rediscovery of Ceres, an asteroid that had been traced only briefly before it disappeared into the glare of the sun in 1801. The astronomers had been trying to estimate Ceres's trajectory, but the way they accounted for the measurement error of their telescopes was wrong, and the planet did not reappear anywhere near the location their results suggested. Gauss redid their calculations, using the least squares method. When the astronomers trained their telescopes to the spot that he had indicated, they found Ceres!

Scientists in diverse disciplines were quick to adopt the least squares method. Over two centuries later, it remains the standard way to evaluate errors wherever achieving accuracy is the goal. The weighting of errors by their square is central to statistics. In the vast majority of applications across all scientific disciplines, MSE rules. As we are about to see, the approach has surprising implications.

The Error Equations

The role of bias and noise in error is easily summarized in two expressions that we will call *the error equations*. The first of these equations decomposes the error in a single measurement into the two components with which you are now familiar: bias — the average error — and a residual "noisy error." The noisy error is positive when the error is larger than the bias, negative when it is smaller. The average of noisy errors is zero. Nothing new in the first error equation.

Error in a single measurement = Bias + Noisy Error

The second error equation is a decomposition of

MSE, the measure of overall error we have now introduced. Using some simple algebra, MSE can be shown to be equal to the sum of the squares of bias and noise. (Recall that noise is the standard deviation of measurements, which is identical to the standard deviation of noisy errors.) Therefore:

Overall Error (MSE) = Bias² + Noise²

The form of this equation — a sum of two squares — may remind you of a high-school favorite, the Pythagorean theorem. As you might remember, in a right triangle, the sum of the squares of the two shorter sides equals the square of the longest one. This suggests a simple visualization of the error equation, in which MSE, Bias², and Noise² are the areas of three squares on the sides of a right triangle. Figure 7 shows how MSE (the area of the darker square) equals the

FIGURE 7: *Two decompositions of MSE*

sum of the areas of the other two squares. In the left panel, there is more noise than bias; in the right panel, more bias than noise. But MSE is the same, and the error equation holds in both cases.

As the mathematical expression and its visual representation both suggest, bias and noise play identical roles in the error equation. They are independent of each other and equally weighted in the determination of overall error. (Note that we will use a similar decomposition into a sum of squares when we analyze the components of noise in later chapters.)

The error equation provides an answer to the practical question that Amy raised: how will reductions in either noise or bias by the same amount affect overall error? The answer is straightforward: bias and noise are interchangeable in the error equation, and the decrease in overall error will be the same, regardless of which of the two is reduced. In figure 4, in which bias and noise happen to be equal (both are 10%), their contributions to overall error are equal.

The error equation also provides unequivocal support for Amy Simkin's initial impulse to try to reduce noise. Whenever you observe noise, you should work to reduce it! The equation shows that Amy's boss was wrong when he suggested that GoodSell wait to measure the bias in its forecasts and only then decide what to do. In terms of overall error, noise and bias are independent: the benefit of reducing noise is the same, regardless of the amount of bias.

This notion is highly counterintuitive but crucial. To illustrate it, figure 8 shows the effect of reducing bias and noise by the same amount. To help you appreciate what has been accomplished in both panels, the original distribution of errors (from figure 4) is represented by a broken line.

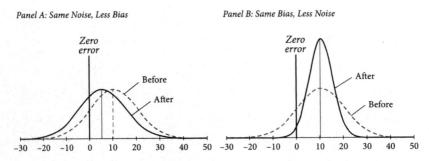

FIGURE 8: *Distribution of errors with bias reduced by half vs. noise reduced by half*

In panel A, we assume that Amy's boss decided to do things his way: he found out what the bias was, then somehow managed to reduce it by half (perhaps by providing feedback to the overoptimistic forecasters). Nothing was done about noise. The improvement is visible: the whole distribution of forecasts has shifted closer to the true value.

In panel B, we show what would have happened if Amy had won the argument. Bias is unchanged, but noise is reduced by half. The paradox here is that noise reduction seems to have made things worse. The forecasts are now more concentrated (less noisy) but not more accurate (not less biased). Whereas 84% of forecasts were on one side of the true value, almost all (98%) now err in the direction of overshooting the true value. Noise reduction seems to have made the forecasts more precisely wrong—hardly the sort of improvement for which Amy hoped!

Despite appearances, however, overall error has been reduced just as much in panel B as in panel A. The illusion of deterioration in panel B arises from an erroneous intuition about bias. The relevant measure of bias is not the imbalance of positive and negative errors. It is average error, which is the distance between the peak of the bell curve and the true value. In panel B, this average error has not changed from the original situation—it is still high, at 10%, but not worse. True, the presence of bias is now more striking, because it accounts for a larger proportion of overall error (80% rather than 50%). But that is because noise has been reduced. Conversely, in panel A, bias has been reduced, but noise has not. The net result is that MSE is the same in both panels: reducing noise or reducing bias by the same amount has the same effect on MSE.

As this example illustrates, MSE conflicts with

common intuitions about the scoring of predictive judgments. To minimize MSE, you must concentrate on avoiding large errors. If you measure length, for example, the effect of reducing an error from 11cm to 10cm is 21 times as large as the effect of going from an error of 1cm to a perfect hit. Unfortunately, people's intuitions in this regard are almost the mirror image of what they should be: people are very keen to get perfect hits and highly sensitive to small errors, but they hardly care at all about the difference between two large errors. Even if you sincerely believe that your goal is to make accurate judgments, your emotional reaction to results may be incompatible with the achievement of accuracy as science defines it.

Of course, the best solution here would be to reduce both noise and bias. Since bias and noise are independent, there is no reason to choose between Amy Simkin and her boss. In that regard, if GoodSell decides to reduce noise, the fact that noise reduction makes bias more visible — indeed, impossible to miss — may turn out to be a blessing. Achieving noise reduction will ensure that bias reduction is next on the company's agenda.

Admittedly, reducing noise would be less of a priority if bias were much larger than noise. But the GoodSell example offers another lesson worth highlighting. In this simplified model, we have assumed that noise and bias are equal. Given the form of the error equation, their contributions to total error are equal, too: bias accounts for 50% of overall error, and so does noise. Yet, as we have noted, 84% of the forecasters err in the same direction. It takes a bias this large (six out of seven people making mistakes in the same direction!) to have as much effect as noise has. We should not be surprised, therefore, to find situations in which there is more noise than bias.

We illustrated the application of the error equation to a single case, one particular region of GoodSell's territory. Of course, it is always desirable to carry out a noise audit on multiple cases at once. Nothing changes. The error equation is applied to the separate cases; and an overall equation is obtained by taking the averages of MSE, bias squared and noise squared over the cases. It would have been better for Amy Simkin to obtain multiple forecasts for several regions, either from the same or from different forecasters. Averaging results would give her a more accurate picture of bias and noise in the forecasting system of GoodSell.

The Cost of Noise

The error equation is the intellectual foundation of this book. It provides the rationale for the goal of reducing system noise in predictive judgments, a goal that is in principle as important as the reduction of statistical bias. (We should emphasize that statistical bias is not a synonym for social discrimination; it is simply the average error in a set of judgments.)

The error equation and the conclusions we have drawn from it depend on the use of MSE as the measure of overall error. The rule is appropriate for purely predictive judgments, including forecasts and estimates, all of which aim to approach a true value with maximum accuracy (the least bias) and precision (the least noise).

The error equation does not apply to evaluative judgments, however, because the concept of error, which depends on the existence of a true value, is far more difficult to apply. Furthermore, even if errors could be specified, their costs would rarely be symmetrical and would be unlikely to be precisely proportional to their square.

For a company that makes elevators, for example, the consequences of errors in estimating the maximum load of an elevator are obviously asymmetrical: underestimation is costly, but overestimation could be catastrophic. Squared error is similarly irrelevant to the decision of when to leave home to catch a train. For that decision, the consequences of being either one minute late or five minutes late are the same. And when the insurance company of chapter 2 prices policies or estimates the value of claims, errors in both directions are costly, but there is no reason to assume that their costs are equivalent.

These examples highlight the need to specify the roles of predictive and evaluative judgments in decisions. A widely accepted maxim of good decision making is that you should not mix your values and your facts. Good decision making must be based on objective and accurate predictive judgments that are completely unaffected by hopes and fears, or by preferences and values. For the elevator company, the first step would be a neutral calculation of the maximum technical load of the elevator under different engineering solutions. Safety becomes a dominant consideration only in the second step, when an evaluative judgment determines the choice of an acceptable safety margin to set the maximum capacity. (To be sure, that choice will also greatly depend on factual judgments involving, for example, the costs and benefits of that safety margin.) Similarly, the first step in deciding when to leave for the station should be an objective determination of the probabilities of different travel times. The respective costs of missing your train and of wasting time at the station become relevant only in your choice of the risk you are willing to accept.

The same logic applies to much more consequential decisions. A military commander must weigh many considerations when deciding whether to launch an offensive, but much of the intelligence on which the leader relies is a matter of predictive judgment. A government responding to a health crisis, such as a pandemic, must weigh the pros and cons of various options, but no evaluation is possible without accurate predictions about the likely consequences of each option (including the decision to do nothing).

In all these examples, the final decisions require evaluative judgments. The decision makers must consider multiple options and apply their values to make the optimal choice. But the decisions depend on underlying predictions, which should be value-neutral. Their goal is accuracy — hitting as close as possible to the bull's-eye — and MSE is the appropriate measure of error. Predictive judgments will be improved by procedures that reduce noise, as long as they do not increase bias to a larger extent.

Speaking of the Error Equation

"Oddly, reducing bias and noise by the same amount has the same effect on accuracy."

"Reducing noise in predictive judgment is always useful, regardless of what you know about bias."

"When judgments are split 84 to 16 between those that are above and below the true value, there is a large bias — that's when bias and noise are equal."
"Predictive judgments are involved in every decision, and accuracy should be their only goal. Keep your values and your facts separate."

CHAPTER 6

The Analysis of Noise

The previous chapter discussed variability in the measurement or judgment of a single case. When we focus on a single case, all variability of judgment is error, and the two constituents of error are bias and noise. Of course, the judgment systems we are examining, including those involving courts and insurance companies, are designed to deal with different cases and to discriminate among them. Federal judges and claims adjusters would be of little use if they returned the same judgment for all the cases that come their way. Much of the variability in judgments of different cases is intentional.

However, variability in judgments of the same case is still undesirable — it is system noise. As we will show, a noise audit in which the same people make judgments about several cases permits a more detailed analysis of system noise.

A Noise Audit of Sentencing

To illustrate the analysis of noise with multiple cases, we turn to an exceptionally detailed noise audit of sentencing by federal judges. The analysis was published in 1981 as part of the movement toward sentencing reform that we described in chapter 1. The study narrowly focused on sentencing decisions, but the lessons it offers are general and bear on other professional judgments. The goal of the noise audit was to go beyond the vivid but anecdotal evidence of noise assembled by Judge Frankel and others and to "determine the extent of sentencing disparity" more systematically.

The study's authors developed sixteen hypothetical cases in which the defendant had been found guilty and was to be sentenced. The vignettes depicted either robberies or cases of fraud and differed on six other dimensions, including whether the defendant was a principal or an accomplice in the crime, whether he had a criminal record, whether (for the robbery cases) a weapon had been used, and so on.

The researchers organized carefully structured interviews with a national sample of 208 active federal judges. In the course of ninety minutes, the judges were presented with all sixteen cases and asked to set a sentence.

To appreciate what can be learned from this study, you will find an exercise in visualization helpful. Picture a large table with sixteen columns for the crimes, labeled from A to P, and 208 rows for the judges, labeled 1 to 208. Each cell, from A1 to P208, shows the prison term set for a particular case by a particular judge. Figure 9 illustrates what this 3,328-cell table would look like. To study noise, we will want to focus on the sixteen columns, each of which is a separate noise audit.

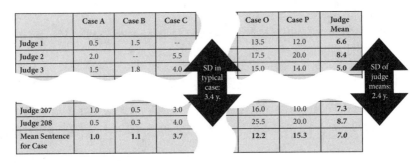

	Case A	Case B	Case C		Case O	Case P	Judge Mean
Judge 1	0.5	1.5	--		13.5	12.0	6.6
Judge 2	2.0	--	5.5		17.5	20.0	8.4
Judge 3	1.5	1.8	4.0		15.0	14.0	5.0
Judge 207	1.0	0.5	3.0		16.0	10.0	7.3
Judge 208	0.5	0.3	4.0		25.5	20.0	8.7
Mean Sentence for Case	1.0	1.1	3.7		12.2	15.3	7.0

SD in typical case: 3.4 y.

SD of judge means: 2.4 y.

FIGURE 9: *A representation of the sentencing study*

Mean Sentences

There is no objective way to determine what the "true value" of a sentence is for a particular case. In what follows, we treat the average of the 208 sentences for each case (mean sentence) as if it were the "just" sentence for that case. As we noted in chapter 1, the US Sentencing Commission made the same assumption when it used the average practice in past cases as the foundation for establishing sentencing guidelines. This label assumes zero bias in the mean judgment of each case.

We are fully aware that, in reality, this assumption is wrong: the average judgment of some cases is quite likely to be biased relative to the average judgment of other, highly similar cases, for example because of racial discrimination. The variance of biases across cases — some positive, some negative — is an important source of error and unfairness. Confusingly, this variance is what is often referred to as "bias." Our analysis in this chapter — and in this book — is focused on noise, which is a distinct source of error. Judge Frankel emphasized the injustice of noise, but also drew attention to bias (including racial discrimination). Similarly, our focus on noise should not be taken to diminish the importance of measuring and combating shared biases.

For convenience, the mean sentence for each case is indicated in the bottom row of the table. The cases are arranged in increasing order of severity: the mean sentence in Case A is 1 year; in Case P it is 15.3 years. The average prison term for all sixteen cases is 7 years.

Now imagine a perfect world in which all judges are flawless measuring instruments of justice, and sentencing is noise-free. What would figure 9 look like in such a world? Evidently, all the cells in the Case A column would be identical, because all judges would give the defendant in case A the same sentence of exactly one year. The same would be true in all the other columns. The numbers in each row, of course, would still vary, because the cases are different. But each row would be identical to the one above it and below it. The differences between the cases would be the only source of variability in the table.

Unfortunately, the world of federal justice is not perfect. The judges are not identical, and variability within columns is large, indicating noise in the judgments of each case. There is more variability in sentences than there should be, and the study's aim is to analyze it.

The Sentencing Lottery

Start from the picture of the perfect world we described above, in which all cases receive the same punishment from every judge. Each column is a series of 208 identical numbers. Now, add noise by going down each column and changing some numbers here and there—sometimes by adding prison time to the mean sentence, sometimes by subtracting from it. Because the changes you make are not all the same, they create variability within the column. This variability is noise.

The essential result of this study is the large amount of noise observed *within the judgments of each case.* The measure of noise within each case is the standard deviation of the prison terms assigned to that case. For the average case, the mean sentence was 7.0 years, and the standard deviation around that mean was 3.4 years.

While you may well be familiar with the term *standard deviation*, you may find a concrete description useful. Imagine that you randomly pick two judges and compute the difference between their judgments of a case. Now repeat, for all pairs of judges and all cases, and average the results. This measure, the *mean absolute difference,* should give you a sense of the lottery that faces the defendant in a federal courtroom. Assuming that the judgments are normally distributed, it is 1.128 times the standard deviation, which implies that the average difference between two randomly chosen sentences of the same case will be 3.8 years. In chapter 3, we spoke of the lottery that faces the client who needs specialized underwriting from an insurance company. The criminal defendant's lottery is, to say the least, more consequential.

A mean absolute difference of 3.8 years between judges when the average sentence is 7.0 years is a disturbing and, in our view, unacceptable result. Yet there are good reasons to suspect that there is even more noise in the actual administration of justice. First, the participants in the noise audit dealt with artificial cases, which were unusually easy to compare and were presented in immediate succession. Real life does not provide nearly as much support for the maintenance of consistency. Second, judges in a courtroom have much more information than they had here. New information, unless it is decisive, provides more opportunities for judges to differ from one another. For these reasons, we suspect that the amount of noise defendants face in actual courtrooms is even larger than what we see here.

Some Judges Are Severe: Level Noise

In the next step of the analysis, the authors broke down noise into separate components. The first interpretation of noise that probably came to your mind— as it did to Judge Frankel's mind—is that noise is due to variation among judges in their disposition to set severe sentences. As any defense lawyer will tell you, judges have reputations, some for being harsh "hanging judges," who are more severe than the average judge, and others for being "bleeding-heart judges," who are more lenient than the average judge. We refer to these deviations as *level errors*. (Again: error is defined here as a deviation from the average; an error may in fact correct an injustice, if the average judge is wrong.)

Variability in level errors will be found in any judgment task. Examples are evaluations of performance where some supervisors are more generous than others, predictions of market share where some forecasters are more optimistic than others, or recommendations for back surgery where some orthopedists are more aggressive than others.

Each row in figure 9 shows the sentences set by one judge. The mean sentence set by each judge, shown in the rightmost column of the table, is a measure of the judge's level of severity. As it turns out, judges vary widely on this dimension. The standard deviation of the values in the rightmost column was 2.4 years. This variability has nothing to do with justice. Instead, as you might suspect, differences in average sentencing reflect variation among judges in other characteristics—their backgrounds, life experiences, political opinions, biases, and so on. The researchers examined the judges' attitudes to sentencing in general—for example, whether they think the main goal of sentencing is incapacitation (removing the criminal from society), rehabilitation, or deterrence. They found that judges who think that the main goal is rehabilitation tend to assign shorter prison sentences and more supervised time than do judges who pointed to deterrence or incapacitation. Separately, judges located in the American South assigned significantly longer sentences than did their counterparts in other parts of the country. Not surprisingly, conservative ideology was also related to severity of sentences.

The general conclusion is that the average level of sentencing functions like a personality trait. You could use this study to arrange judges on a scale that ranges from very harsh to very lenient, just as a personality test might measure their degree of extraversion or agreeableness. Like other traits, we would expect severity of sentencing to be correlated with genetic factors, with life experiences, and with other aspects of personality. None of these has anything to do with the case or the defendant. We use the term *level noise* for the variability of the judges' average judgments, which is identical to the variability of level errors.

Judges Differ: Pattern Noise

As the black arrows show in figure 9, level noise is 2.4 years and system noise is 3.4 years. This difference indicates that there is more to system noise than differences in average severity across individual judges.

112

We will call this other component of noise *pattern noise.*

To understand pattern noise, consider again figure 9, and focus on one randomly chosen cell—say, cell C3. The mean sentence in Case C is shown at the bottom of the column; as you can see, it is 3.7 years. Now, look at the rightmost column to find the mean sentence given by Judge 3 across all cases. It is 5.0 years, just 2.0 years less than the grand mean. If the variation in judges' severity were the only source of noise in column 3, you would predict that the sentence in cell C3 is 3.7 – 2.0 = 1.7 years. But the actual entry in cell C3 is 4 years, indicating that Judge 3 was especially harsh in sentencing that case.

The same simple, additive logic would let you predict every sentence in every column of the table, but in fact you would find deviations from the simple model in most cells. Looking across a row, you will find that judges are not equally severe in their sentencing of all cases: they are harsher than their personal average in some and more lenient in others. We call these residual deviations *pattern errors.* If you wrote down these pattern errors in each cell of the table, you would find that they add up to zero for every judge (row) and that they also add up to zero for every case (column). However, the pattern errors do not cancel out in their contribution to noise, because the values in all cells are squared for the computation of noise.

There is an easier way to confirm that the simple additive model of sentencing does not hold. You can see in the table that the mean sentences at the bottom of each column increase steadily from left to right, but the same is not true within the rows. Judge 208, for example, set a much higher sentence to the defendant in Case O than to the defendant in Case P. If individual judges ranked the cases by the prison time they thought appropriate, their rankings would not be the same.

We use the term *pattern noise* for the variability we just identified, because that variability reflects a complex pattern in the attitudes of judges to particular cases. One judge, for instance, may be harsher than average in general but relatively more lenient toward white-collar criminals. Another may be inclined to punish lightly but more severely when the offender is a recidivist. A third may be close to the average severity but sympathetic when the offender is merely an accomplice and tough when the victim is an older person. (We use the term *pattern noise* in the interest of readability. The proper statistical term for pattern noise is *judge × case interaction*—pronounced "judge-by-case." We apologize to people with statistical training for imposing the burden of translation on them.)

In the context of criminal justice, some of the idiosyncratic reactions to cases may reflect the judge's personal philosophy of sentencing. Other responses may result from associations of which the judge is barely aware, such as a defendant who reminds him of a particularly hateful criminal or who perhaps looks like his daughter. Whatever their origin, these patterns are not mere chance: we would expect them to recur if the judge saw the same case again. But because pattern noise is, in practice, difficult to predict, it adds uncertainty to the already-unpredictable lottery of sentencing. As the study's authors noted, "Patterned differences between judges in the influence of offense/offender characteristics" are "an additional form of sentence disparity."

You may have noticed that the decomposition of system noise into level noise and pattern noise follows the same logic as the error equation in the previous chapter, which decomposed error into bias and noise. This time, the equation can be written as follows:

System Noise^2 = Level Noise^2 + Pattern Noise^2

This expression can be represented visually in the same manner as the original Error Equation (Figure 10). We have represented the two sides of the triangle as equal. That is because, in the study of sentencing,

115

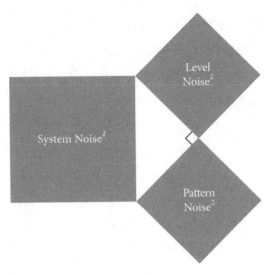

FIGURE 10: *Decomposing system noise*

pattern noise and level noise contribute approximately equally to system noise.

Pattern noise is pervasive. Suppose that doctors are deciding whether to admit people for hospitalization, that companies are deciding whom to hire, that lawyers are deciding which cases to bring, or that Hollywood executives are deciding which television shows to produce. In all these cases, there will be pattern noise, with different judges producing different rankings of the cases.

The Components of Noise

Our treatment of pattern noise glossed over a significant complexity: the possible contribution of random error.

Recall the stopwatch exercise. When you tried to measure ten seconds repeatedly, your results varied from one lap to the next; you showed within-person variability. By the same token, the judges would not have set precisely the same sentences to the sixteen cases if they had been asked to judge them again on another occasion. Indeed, as we will see, they would not have set the same sentences if the original study had been conducted on another day of the same week. If a judge is in a good mood because something nice happened to her daughter, or because a favorite sports team won yesterday, or because it is a beautiful day, her judgment might be more lenient than it would otherwise be. This within-person variability is conceptually distinct from the stable between-person differences that we have just discussed—but it is difficult to tell these sources of variability apart. Our name for the variability that is due to transient effects is *occasion noise*.

We effectively ignored occasion noise in this study and chose to interpret the judges' idiosyncratic patterns of sentencing in the noise audit as indicating stable attitudes. This assumption is certainly optimistic, but there are independent reasons to believe that occasion noise did not play a large role in this study. The highly experienced judges who participated in it surely brought with them some set ideas about the significance of various features of offenses and of defendants.

In the next chapter, we discuss occasion noise in greater detail and show how it can be separated from the stable component of pattern noise.

To summarize, we discussed several types of noise. *System noise* is undesirable variability in the judgments of the same case by multiple individuals. We have identified its two major components, which can be separated when the same individuals evaluate multiple cases:

- ❏ *Level noise* is variability in the average level of judgments by different judges.
- ❏ *Pattern noise* is variability in judges' responses to particular cases.

In the present study, the amounts of level noise and pattern noise were approximately equal. However, the component that we identified as pattern noise certainly contains some *occasion noise*, which can be treated as random error.

We have used a noise audit in the judicial system as an illustration, but the same analysis can be applied to any noise audit — in business, medicine, government, or elsewhere. Level noise and pattern noise (which includes occasion noise) both contribute to system noise, and we will encounter them repeatedly as we proceed.

Speaking of Analyzing Noise

"Level noise is when judges show different levels of severity. Pattern noise is when they disagree with one another on which defendants deserve more severe or more lenient treatment. And part of pattern noise is occasion noise — when judges disagree with themselves."

"In a perfect world, defendants would face justice; in our world, they face a noisy system."

CHAPTER 7

Occasion Noise

Aprofessional basketball player is preparing for a free throw. He stands at the foul line. He concentrates—and shoots. This is a precise sequence of moves he has practiced countless times. Will he make the shot?

We don't know, and neither does he. In the National Basketball Association, players typically make about three-quarters of their attempts. Some players, obviously, are better than others, but no player scores 100% of the time. The all-time best make a little over 90% of their free throws. (At the time of this writing, they are Stephen "Steph" Curry, Steve Nash, and Mark Price.) The all-time worst are around 50%. (The great Shaquille O'Neal, for example, made only about 53% of his shots.) Although the hoop is always exactly ten feet high and fifteen feet away, and the ball always weighs twenty-two ounces, the ability to repeat the precise sequence of gestures required to score does not come easily. Variability is expected, not just between players but within players. The free throw is a form of lottery, with a much higher chance of success if the shooter is Curry than if he is O'Neal, but it is a lottery nonetheless.

Where does this variability come from? We know that countless factors can influence the player at the foul line: the fatigue of a long game, the mental pressure of a tight score, the cheers of the home court, or the boos of the opposing team's fans. If someone like Curry or Nash misses, we will invoke one of these explanations. But in truth, we are unlikely to know the exact role these factors play. The variability in a shooter's performance is a form of noise.

The Second Lottery

Variability in free throws or in other physical processes comes as no surprise. We are used to variability in our bodies: our heart rate, our blood pressure, our reflexes, the tone of our voice, and the trembling of our hands are different at different times. And however hard we try to produce the same signature, it is still slightly different on every check.

It is less easy to observe the variability of our minds. Of course, we have all had the experience of changing our minds, even without new information. The film that made us laugh out loud last night now seems mediocre and forgettable. The person we judged severely yesterday now seems to deserve our indulgence. An argument that we had not liked or understood sinks in and now appears essential. But as these examples suggest, we usually associate such changes with relatively minor and largely subjective matters.

In reality, our opinions do change without apparent reason. This point holds even for matters of careful, considered judgment by professional experts. For instance, it is common to obtain significantly different diagnoses from the same physicians when they are presented twice with the same case (see chapter 22). When wine experts at a major US wine competition tasted the same wines twice, they scored only 18% of the wines identically (usually, the very worst ones). A forensic expert can reach different conclusions when examining the same fingerprints twice, just a few weeks apart (see chapter 20). Experienced software consultants can offer markedly different estimates of the completion time for the same task on two occasions. Simply put, just like a basketball player who never throws the ball twice in exactly the same way, we do not always produce identical judgments when faced with the same facts on two occasions.

We have described the process that picks an underwriter, a judge, or a doctor as a lottery that creates system noise. Occasion noise is the product of a second lottery. This lottery picks the moment when the professional makes a judgment, the professional's mood, the sequence of cases that are fresh in mind, and countless other features of the occasion. This second lottery usually remains much more abstract than the first. We can see how the first lottery could have selected a different underwriter, for instance, but the alternatives to the actual responses of the selected underwriter are abstract counterfactuals. We know only that the judgment that did occur was picked from a cloud of possibilities. Occasion noise is the variability among these unseen possibilities.

Measuring Occasion Noise

Measuring occasion noise is not easy — for much the same reason that its existence, once established, often surprises us. When people form a carefully considered professional opinion, they associate it with the reasons that justify their point of view. If pressed to explain their judgment, they will usually defend it with arguments that they find convincing. And if they are presented with the same problem a second time and recognize it, they will reproduce the earlier answer both to minimize effort and maintain consistency. Consider this example from the teaching profession: if a teacher gives an excellent grade to a student essay and then rereads the same essay a week later after seeing the original grade, he will be unlikely to give it a very different grade.

For this reason, direct measurements of occasion noise are hard to obtain whenever cases are easily memorable. If, for example, you show an underwriter or a criminal judge a case that they previously decided, they will probably recognize the case and just repeat their previous judgment. One review of research on variability in professional judgment (technically known as *test-retest reliability,* or *reliability* for short) included many studies in which the experts made the same judgment twice in the same session. Not surprisingly, they tended to agree with themselves.

The experiments we mentioned above bypassed this issue by using stimuli that the experts would not recognize. The wine judges took part in a blind tasting. The fingerprint examiners were shown pairs of prints they had already seen, and the software experts were asked about tasks they had already worked on — but some weeks or months later and without being told that these were cases they had already examined.

There is another, less direct way to confirm the existence of occasion noise: by using big data and econometric methods. When a large sample of past professional decisions is available, analysts can sometimes check whether these decisions were influenced by occasion-specific, irrelevant factors, such as time of day or outside temperature. Statistically significant effects of such irrelevant factors on judgments are evidence of occasion noise. Realistically speaking, there is no hope of discovering all the extraneous sources of occasion noise, but those that can be found illustrate the great variety of these sources. If we are to control occasion noise, we must try to understand the mechanisms that produce it.

One Is a Crowd

Think of this question: what percentage of the world's airports are in the United States? As you thought about it, an answer probably came to your mind. But it did not occur to you in the same way that you would remember your age or your phone number. You are aware that the number you just produced is an estimate. It is not a random number — 1% or 99% would clearly be wrong answers. But the number you came up with is just one in a range of possibilities that you would not rule out. If someone added or subtracted 1 percentage point from your answer, you would probably not find the resulting guess much less plausible than yours. (The correct answer, in case you wonder, is 32%.)

Two researchers, Edward Vul and Harold Pashler, had the idea of asking people to answer this question (and many similar ones) not once but twice. The subjects were not told the first time that they would have to guess again. Vul and Pashler's hypothesis was that the average of the two answers would be more accurate than either of the answers on its own.

The data proved them right. In general, the first guess was closer to the truth than the second, but the best estimate came from averaging the two guesses.

Vul and Pashler drew inspiration from the well-known phenomenon known as the *wisdom-of-crowds effect:* averaging the independent judgments of different people generally improves accuracy. In 1907, Francis Galton, a cousin of Darwin and a famous polymath, asked 787 villagers at a country fair to estimate the weight of a prize ox. None of the villagers guessed the actual weight of the ox, which was 1,198 pounds, but the mean of their guesses was 1,200, just 2 pounds off, and the median (1,207) was also very close. The villagers were a "wise crowd" in the sense that although their individual estimates were quite noisy, they were unbiased. Galton's demonstration surprised him: he had little respect for the judgment of ordinary people, and despite himself, he urged that his results were "more creditable to the trustworthiness of a democratic judgment than might have been expected."

Similar results have been found in hundreds of situations. Of course, if questions are so difficult that only experts can come close to the answer, crowds will not necessarily be very accurate. But when, for instance, people are asked to guess the number of jelly beans in a transparent jar, to predict the temperature in their city one week out, or to estimate the distance between two cities in a state, the average answer of a large number of people is likely to be close to the truth. The reason is basic statistics: averaging several independent judgments (or measurements) yields a new judgment, which is less noisy, albeit not less biased, than the individual judgments.

Vul and Pashler wanted to find out if the same effect extends to occasion noise: can you get closer to the truth by combining two guesses from the same person, just as you do when you combine the guesses of different people? As they discovered, the answer is yes. Vul and Pashler gave this finding an evocative name: *the crowd within.*

Averaging two guesses by the same person does not improve judgments as much as does seeking out an independent second opinion. As Vul and Pashler put it, "You can gain about 1/10th as much from asking yourself the same question twice as you can from getting a second opinion from someone else." This is not a large improvement. But you can make the effect much larger by waiting to make a second guess. When Vul and Pashler let three weeks pass before asking their subjects the same question again, the benefit rose to one-third the value of a second opinion. Not bad for a technique that does not require any additional information or outside help. And this result certainly provides a rationale for the age-old advice to decision makers: "Sleep on it, and think again in the morning."

Working independently of Vul and Pashler but at about the same time, two German researchers, Stefan Herzog and Ralph Hertwig, came up with a different implementation of the same principle. Instead of merely asking their subjects to produce a second estimate, they encouraged people to generate an estimate that—while still plausible—was as different as possible from the first one. This request required the subjects to think actively of information they had not considered the first time. The instructions to participants read as follows:

First, assume that your first estimate is off the mark. Second, think about a few reasons why that could be. Which assumptions and considerations could have been wrong? Third, what do these new considerations imply? Was the first estimate rather too high or too low? Fourth, based on this new perspective, make a second, alternative estimate.

Like Vul and Pashler, Herzog and Hertwig then averaged the two estimates thus produced. Their technique, which they named *dialectical bootstrapping,* produced larger improvements in accuracy than did a simple request for a second estimate immediately following the first. Because the participants forced themselves to consider the question in a new light, they sampled another, more different version of themselves — two "members" of the "crowd within" who were further apart. As a result, their average produced a more accurate estimate of the truth. The gain in accuracy with two immediately consecutive "dialectical" estimates was about half the value of a second opinion.

The upshot for decision makers, as summarized by Herzog and Hertwig, is a simple choice between procedures: if you can get independent opinions from others, do it — this real wisdom of crowds is highly likely to improve your judgment. If you cannot, make the same judgment yourself a second time to create an "inner crowd." You can do this either after some time has passed—giving yourself distance from your first opinion—or by actively trying to argue against yourself to find another perspective on the problem. Finally, regardless of the type of crowd, unless you have very strong reasons to put more weight on one of the estimates, your best bet is to average them.

Beyond practical advice, this line of research confirms an essential insight about judgment. As Vul and Pashler put it, "Responses made by a subject are sampled from an internal probability distribution, rather than deterministically selected on the basis of all the knowledge a subject has." This observation echoes the experience you had when answering the question about airports in the United States: Your first answer did not capture all your knowledge or even the best of it. The answer was just one point in the cloud of possible answers that your mind could have generated. The variability we observe in judgments of the same problem by the same person is not a fluke observed in a few highly specialized problems: occasion noise affects all our judgments, all the time.

Sources of Occasion Noise

There is at least one source of occasion noise that we have all noticed: mood. We've all experienced how our own judgments can depend on how we feel—and we are certainly aware that the judgments of others vary with their moods, too.

The effect of moods on judgment has been the subject of a vast amount of psychological research. It is remarkably easy to make people temporarily happy or sad and to measure the variability of their judgments and decisions after these moods have been induced. Researchers use a variety of techniques to do this. For example, participants are sometimes asked to write a paragraph recalling either a happy memory or a sad one. Sometimes they simply view a video segment taken either from a funny movie or from a tearjerker.

Several psychologists have spent decades investigating the effects of mood manipulation. Perhaps the most prolific is Australian psychologist Joseph Forgas. He has published around a hundred scientific papers on the subject of mood.

Some of Forgas's research confirms what you already think: People who are in a good mood are generally more positive. They find it easier to recall happy memories than sad ones, they are more approving of people, they are more generous and helpful, and so on. Negative mood has the opposite effects. As Forgas writes, "The same smile that is seen as friendly by a person in a good mood may be judged as awkward when the observer is in a negative mood; discussing the weather could be seen as poised when the person is in a good mood but boring when that person is in a bad mood."

In other words, mood has a measurable influence on what you think: what you notice in your environment, what you retrieve from your memory, how you make sense of these signals. But mood has another, more surprising effect: it also changes *how* you think. And here, the effects are not those you might imagine. Being in a good mood is a mixed blessing, and bad moods have a silver lining. The costs and benefits of different moods are situation-specific.

In a negotiation situation, for instance, good mood helps. People in a good mood are more cooperative and elicit reciprocation. They tend to end up with better results than do unhappy negotiators. Of course, successful negotiations make people happy, too, but in these experiments, the mood is not caused by what is going on in the negotiation; it is induced before people negotiate. Also, negotiators who shift from a good mood to an angry one during the negotiation often achieve good results — something to remember when you're facing a stubborn counterpart!

On the other hand, a good mood makes us more likely to accept our first impressions as true without challenging them. In one of Forgas's studies, participants read a short philosophical essay, to which a picture of the author was appended. Some readers saw a stereotypical philosophy professor — male, middle-aged, and wearing glasses. Others saw a young woman. As you can guess, this is a test of the readers' vulnerability to stereotypes: do people rate the essay more favorably when it is attributed to a middle-aged man than they do when they believe that a young woman wrote it? They do, of course. But importantly, the difference is larger in the good-mood condition. People who are in a good mood are more likely to let their biases affect their thinking.

Other studies tested the effect of mood on gullibility. Gordon Pennycook and colleagues have conducted many studies of people's reactions to meaningless, pseudo-profound statements generated by assembling randomly selected nouns and verbs from the sayings of popular gurus into grammatically correct sentences, such as "Wholeness quiets infinite phenomena" or "Hidden meaning transforms unparalleled abstract beauty." The propensity to agree with such statements is a trait known as *bullshit receptivity*. (*Bullshit* has become something of a technical term since Harry Frankfurt, a philosopher at Princeton University, published an insightful book, *On Bullshit*, in which he distinguished bullshit from other types of misrepresentation.)

Sure enough, some people are more receptive than

others to bullshit. They can be impressed by "seemingly impressive assertions that are presented as true and meaningful but are actually vacuous." But here again, this gullibility is not merely a function of permanent, unchanging dispositions. Inducing good moods makes people more receptive to bullshit and more gullible in general; they are less apt to detect deception or identify misleading information. Conversely, eyewitnesses who are exposed to misleading information are better able to disregard it—and to avoid false testimony—when they are in a bad mood.

Even moral judgments are strongly influenced by mood. In one study, researchers exposed subjects to the footbridge problem, a classic problem in moral philosophy. In this thought experiment, five people are about to be killed by a runaway trolley. Subjects are to imagine themselves standing on a footbridge, underneath which the trolley will soon pass. They must decide whether to push a large man off the footbridge and onto the tracks so that his body will stop the trolley. If they do so, they are told, the large man will die, but the five people will be saved.

The footbridge problem illustrates the conflict between approaches to moral reasoning. Utilitarian calculation, associated with English philosopher Jeremy Bentham, suggests that the loss of one life is preferable to the loss of five. Deontological ethics, associated with Immanuel Kant, prohibits killing someone, even in the service of saving several others. The footbridge problem clearly contains a salient element of personal emotion: physically pushing a man off a bridge into the path of an oncoming trolley is a particularly repugnant act. Making the utilitarian choice to push the man off the bridge requires people to overcome their aversion to a physically violent act against a stranger. Only a minority of people (in this study, fewer than one in ten) usually say they would do so.

However, when the subjects were placed in a positive mood — induced by watching a five-minute video segment — they became three times more likely to say that they would push the man off the bridge. Whether we regard "Thou shalt not kill" as an absolute principle or are willing to kill one stranger to save five should reflect our deepest values. Yet our choice seems to depend on what video clip we have just watched.

We have described these studies of mood in some detail because we need to emphasize an important truth: *you are not the same person at all times.* As your mood varies (something you are, of course, aware of), some features of your cognitive machinery vary with it (something you are *not* fully aware of). If you are shown a complex judgment problem, your mood in the moment may influence your approach to the problem and the conclusions you reach, even when you believe that your mood has no such influence and even when you can confidently justify the answer you found. In short, you are noisy.

Many other incidental factors induce occasion noise in judgments. Among the extraneous factors that should not influence professional judgments, but do, are two prime suspects: stress and fatigue. A study of nearly seven hundred thousand primary care visits, for instance, showed that physicians are significantly more likely to prescribe opioids at the end of a long day. Surely, there is no reason why a patient with a 4 pm appointment should be in greater pain than one who shows up at 9 am. Nor should the fact that the doctor is running behind schedule influence prescription decisions. And indeed, prescriptions of other pain treatments, such as nonsteroidal anti-inflammatory drugs and referrals to physical therapy, do not display similar patterns. When physicians are under time pressure, they are apparently more inclined to choose a quick-fix solution, despite its serious downsides. Other studies showed that, toward the end of the day, physicians are more likely to prescribe antibiotics and less likely to prescribe flu shots.

Even the weather has a measurable influence on professional judgments. Since these judgments are often made in air-conditioned rooms, the effect of weather is probably "mediated" by mood (that is, the weather does not directly affect decisions but modifies the decision maker's mood, which in turn does change how they decide). Bad weather is associated with improved memory; judicial sentences tend to be more severe when it is hot outside; and stock market performance is affected by sunshine. In some cases, the effect of the weather is less obvious. Uri Simonsohn showed that college admissions officers pay more attention to the academic attributes of candidates on cloudier days and are more sensitive to nonacademic attributes on sunnier days. The title of the article in which he reported these findings is memorable enough: "Clouds Make Nerds Look Good."

Another source of random variability in judgment is the order in which cases are examined. When a person is considering a case, the decisions that immediately preceded it serve as an implicit frame of reference. Professionals who make a series of decisions in sequence, including judges, loan officers, and baseball umpires, lean toward restoring a form of balance: after a streak, or a series of decisions that go in the same direction, they are more likely to decide in the opposite direction than would be strictly justified. As a result, errors (and unfairness) are inevitable. Asylum judges in the United States, for instance, are 19% less likely to grant asylum to an applicant when the previous two cases were approved. A person might be approved for a loan if the previous two applications were denied, but the same person might have been rejected if the previous two applications had been granted. This behavior reflects a cognitive bias known as the *gambler's fallacy:* we tend to underestimate the likelihood that streaks will occur by chance.

Sizing Occasion Noise

How large is occasion noise relative to total system noise? Although no single number applies to all situations, a general rule emerges. In terms of their size, the effects we have described in this chapter are smaller than stable differences between individuals in their levels and patterns of judgments.

As noted, for instance, the chance that an asylum applicant will be admitted in the United States drops by 19% if the hearing follows two successful ones by the same judge. This variability is certainly troubling. But it pales in comparison with the variability between judges: in one Miami courthouse, Jaya Ramji-Nogales and her co-authors found that one judge would grant asylum to 88% of applicants and another to only 5%. (This is real data, not a noise audit, so the applicants were different, but they were quasi-randomly assigned, and the authors checked that differences in country of origin did not explain the discrepancies.) Given such disparities, reducing one of these numbers by 19% does not seem like such a big deal.

Similarly, fingerprint examiners and physicians sometimes disagree with themselves, but they do so less often than they disagree with others. In every case we reviewed in which the share of occasion noise in total system noise could be measured, occasion noise was a smaller contributor than were differences among individuals.

Or to put it differently, you are not always the same person, and you are less consistent over time than you think. But somewhat reassuringly, you are more similar to yourself yesterday than you are to another person today.

Occasion Noise, Inner Causes

Mood, fatigue, weather, sequence effects: many factors may trigger unwanted variations in the judgment of the same case by the same person. We might hope to construct a setting in which all the extraneous factors bearing on decisions are known and controlled. In theory at least, such a setting should reduce occasion noise. But even this setting would probably not be sufficient to eliminate occasion noise entirely.

Michael Kahana and his University of Pennsylvania colleagues study memory performance. (Memory is not a judgment task by our definition, but it is a cognitive task for which conditions can be rigorously controlled and variations in performance easily measured.) In one study, they asked seventy-nine subjects to participate in an exceptionally thorough analysis of their memory performance. The subjects sat through twenty-three sessions on separate days, during each of which they had to recall words from twenty-four different lists of twenty-four words each. The percentage of words recalled defines memory performance.

Kahana and his colleagues were not interested in the differences between subjects but rather in the predictors of variability in the performance of each subject. Would performance be driven by how alert the subjects felt? By how much sleep they got the previous night? By the time of day? Would their performance increase with practice from one session to the next? Would it deteriorate within each session as they got tired or bored? Would some lists of words prove easier to memorize than others?

The answer to all these questions was yes, but not by very much. A model that incorporated all these predictors explained only 11% of the variation in the performance of a given subject. As the researchers put it, "We were struck by how much variability remained after removing the effects of our predictor variables." Even in this tightly controlled setting, exactly what factors drive occasion noise was a mystery.

Of all the variables the researchers studied, the most powerful predictor of a subject's performance on a particular list was not an external factor. Performance on one list of words was best predicted by how well a subject had performed on the list that immediately preceded it. A successful list was likely to be followed by another relatively successful one, and a mediocre one by another mediocre one. Performance did not vary randomly from list to list: within each session, it ebbed and flowed over time, with no obvious external cause.

These findings suggest that memory performance is driven in large part by, in Kahana and coauthors' words, "the efficiency of endogenous neural processes that govern memory function." In other words, the moment-to-moment variability in the efficacy of the brain is not just driven by external influences, like the weather or a distracting intervention. It is a characteristic of the way our brain itself functions.

It is very likely that intrinsic variability in the functioning of the brain also affects the quality of our judgments in ways that we cannot possibly hope to control. This variability in brain function should give pause to anyone who thinks occasion noise can be eliminated. The analogy with the basketball player at the free-throw line was not as simplistic as it may have initially appeared: just as the player's muscles never execute exactly the same gesture, our neurons never operate in exactly the same way. If our mind is a measuring instrument, it will never be a perfect one.

We can, however, strive to control those undue influences that can be controlled. Doing so is especially important when judgments are made in groups, as we will see in chapter 8.

Speaking of Occasion Noise

"Judgment is like a free throw: however hard we try to repeat it precisely, it is never exactly identical."

"Your judgment depends on what mood you are in, what cases you have just discussed, and even what the weather is. You are not the same person at all times."

"Although you may not be the same person you were last week, you are less different from the 'you' of last week than you are from someone else today. Occasion noise is not the largest source of system noise."

CHAPTER 8

How Groups Amplify Noise

Noise in individual judgment is bad enough. But group decision making adds another layer to the problem. Groups can go in all sorts of directions, depending in part on factors that should be irrelevant. Who speaks first, who speaks last, who speaks with confidence, who is wearing black, who is seated next to whom, who smiles or frowns or gestures at the right moment — all these factors, and many more, affect outcomes. Every day, similar groups make very different decisions, whether the question involves hiring, promotion, office closings, communications strategies, environmental regulations, national security, university admissions, or new product launches.

It might seem odd to emphasize this point, since we noted in the previous chapter that aggregating the judgments of multiple individuals reduces noise. But because of group dynamics, groups can add noise, too. There are "wise crowds," whose mean judgment is close to the correct answer, but there are also crowds that follow tyrants, that fuel market bubbles, that believe in magic, or that are under the sway of a shared illusion. Minor differences can lead one group toward a firm yes and an essentially identical group toward an emphatic no. And because of the dynamics among group members—our emphasis here—the level of noise can be high. That proposition holds whether we are speaking of noise across similar groups or of a single group whose firm judgment on an important matter should be seen as merely one in a cloud of possibilities.

Noise in the Music

For evidence, we begin in what might seem to be an unlikely place: a large-scale study of music downloads by Matthew Salganik and his coauthors. As the study was designed, the experimenters created a control group of thousands of people (visitors to a moderately popular website). Members of the control group could hear and download one or more of seventy-two songs by new bands. The songs were vividly named: "Trapped in an Orange Peel," "Gnaw," "Eye Patch,"

"Baseball Warlock v1," and "Pink Aggression." (Some of the titles sound directly related to our concerns here: "Best Mistakes," "I Am Error," "The Belief Above the Answer," "Life's Mystery," "Wish Me Luck," and "Out of the Woods.")

In the control group, the participants were told nothing about what anyone else had said or done. They were left to make their own independent judgments about which songs they liked and wished to download. But Salganik and his colleagues also created eight other groups, to which thousands of other website visitors were randomly assigned. For members of those groups, everything was the same, with just one exception: people could see how many people in their particular group had previously downloaded every individual song. For example, if "Best Mistakes" was immensely popular in one group, its members would see that, and so too if no one was downloading it.

Because the various groups did not differ along any important dimension, the study was essentially running history eight times. You might well predict that in the end, the good songs would always rise to the top and the bad ones would always sink to the bottom. If so, the various groups would end up with identical or at least similar rankings. Across groups, there would be no noise. And indeed, that was the precise question that Salganik and his coauthors meant to explore. They were testing for a particular driver of noise: *social influence.*

The key finding was that group rankings were wildly disparate: across different groups, there was a great deal of noise. In one group, "Best Mistakes" could be a spectacular success, while "I Am Error" could flop. In another group, "I Am Error" could do exceedingly well, and "Best Mistakes" could be a disaster. If a song benefited from early popularity, it could do really well. If it did not get that benefit, the outcome could be very different.

To be sure, the very worst songs (as established by the control group) never ended up at the very top, and the very best songs never ended up at the very bottom. But otherwise, almost anything could happen. As the authors emphasize, "The level of success in the social influence condition was more unpredictable than in the independent condition." In short, social influences create significant noise across groups. And if you think about it, you can see that individual groups were noisy, too, in the sense that their judgment in favor of one song, or against it, could easily have been different, depending on whether it attracted early popularity.

As Salganik and his coauthors later demonstrated, group outcomes can be manipulated fairly easily, because popularity is self-reinforcing. In a somewhat fiendish follow-up experiment, they inverted the rankings in the control group (in other words, they lied about how popular songs were), which meant that people saw the least popular songs as the most popular, and vice versa. The researchers then tested what the website's visitors would do. The result was that most of the unpopular songs became quite popular, and most of the popular songs did very poorly. Within very large groups, popularity and unpopularity bred more of the same, even when the researchers misled people about which songs were popular. The single exception is that the very most popular song in the control group did rise in popularity over time, which means that the inverted ranking could not keep the best song down. For the most part, however, the inverted ranking helped determine the ultimate ranking.

It should be easy to see how these studies bear on group judgments in general. Suppose that a small group consisting of, say, ten people is deciding whether to adopt some bold new initiative. If one or two advocates speak first, they might well shift the entire room in their preferred direction. The same is true if skeptics speak first. At least this is so if people are influenced by one another—and they usually are. For this reason, otherwise similar groups might end up making very different judgments simply because of who spoke first and initiated the equivalent of early downloads. The popularity of "Best Mistakes" and "I Am Error" have close analogues in professional judgments of all kinds. And if groups do not hear the analogue to the popularity rankings of such songs—loud enthusiasm, say, for that bold initiative—the initiative might not go anywhere, simply because those who supported it did not voice their opinion.

Beyond Music Downloads

If you are skeptical, you might be thinking that the case of music downloads is unique or at least distinctive and that it tells us little about judgments by other groups. But similar observations have been made in many other areas as well. Consider, for example, the popularity of proposals for referenda in the United Kingdom. In deciding whether to support a referendum, people must of course judge whether it is a good idea, all things considered. The patterns are similar to those observed by Salganik and his coauthors: an initial burst of popularity is self-reinforcing, and if a proposal attracts little support on the first day, it is essentially doomed. In politics, as in music, a great deal depends on social influences and, in particular, on whether people see that other people are attracted or repelled.

Building directly on the music downloads experiment, sociologist Michael Macy of Cornell University and his collaborators asked whether the visible views of other people could suddenly make identifiable political positions popular among Democrats and unpopular among Republicans — or vice versa. The short answer is yes. If Democrats in an online group saw that a particular point of view was obtaining initial popularity among Democrats, they would endorse that point of view, ultimately leading most Democrats, in the relevant group, to favor it. But if Democrats in a different online group saw that the very same point of view was obtaining initial popularity among Republicans, they would reject that point of view, ultimately leading most Democrats, in the relevant group, to reject it. Republicans behaved similarly. In short, political positions can be just like songs, in the sense that their ultimate fate can depend on initial popularity. As the researchers put it, "chance variation in a small number of early movers" can have major effects in tipping large populations — and in getting both Republicans and Democrats to embrace a cluster of views that actually have nothing to do with each other.

Or consider a question that bears directly on group decisions in general: how people judge comments on websites. Lev Muchnik, a professor at the Hebrew University of Jerusalem, and his colleagues carried out an experiment on a website that displays diverse stories and allows people to post comments, which can in turn be voted up or down. The researchers automatically and artificially gave certain comments on stories an immediate up vote — the first vote that a comment would receive. You might well think that after hundreds or thousands of visitors and ratings, a single initial vote on a comment could not possibly matter. That is a sensible thought, but it is wrong. After seeing an initial up vote (and recall that it was entirely artificial), the next viewer became 32% more likely to give an up vote.

Remarkably, this effect persisted over time. After five months, a single positive initial vote artificially increased the mean rating of comments by 25%. The effect of a single positive early vote is a recipe for noise. Whatever the reason for that vote, it can produce a large-scale shift in overall popularity.

This study offers a clue about how groups shift and why they are noisy (again in the sense that similar groups can make very different judgments, and single groups can make judgments that are merely one in a cloud of possibilities). Members are often in a position to offer the functional equivalent of an early up vote (or down vote) by indicating agreement, neutrality, or dissent. If a group member has given immediate approval, other members have reason to do so as well.

There is no question that when groups move in the direction of some products, people, movements, and ideas, it may not be because of their intrinsic merits but instead because of the functional equivalent of early up votes. Of course Muchnik's own study involved very large groups. But the same thing can happen in small ones, in fact even more dramatically, because an initial up vote — in favor of some plan, product, or verdict — often has a large effect on others.

There is a related point. We have pointed to the wisdom of crowds: if you take a large group of people and ask them a question, there is a good chance that the average answer will be close to the target. Aggregating judgments can be an excellent way of reducing noise, and therefore error. But what happens if people are listening to one another? You might well think that their doing so is likely to help. After all, people can learn from one another and thus figure out what is right. Under favorable circumstances, in which people share what they know, deliberating groups can indeed do well. But independence is a prerequisite for the wisdom of crowds. If people are not making their own judgments and are relying instead on what other people think, crowds might not be so wise after all.

Research has revealed exactly that problem. In simple estimation tasks — the number of crimes in a city, population increases over specified periods, the length of a border between nations—crowds were indeed wise as long as they registered their views independently. But if they learned the estimates of other people—for example, the average estimate of a group of twelve—the crowd did worse. As the authors put it, social influences are a problem because they reduce "group diversity without diminishing the collective error." The irony is that while multiple independent opinions, properly aggregated, can be strikingly accurate, even a little social influence can produce a kind of herding that undermines the wisdom of crowds.

Cascades

Some of the studies we are describing involve *informational cascades*. Such cascades are pervasive. They help explain why similar groups in business, government, and elsewhere can go in multiple directions and why small changes can produce such different outcomes and hence noise. We are able to see history only as it was actually run, but for many groups and group decisions, there are clouds of possibilities, only one of which is realized.

To see how informational cascades work, imagine that ten people are in a large office, deciding whom to hire for an important position. There are three main candidates: Thomas, Sam, and Julie. Assume that the group members are announcing their views in sequence. Each person attends, reasonably enough, to the judgments of others. Arthur is the first to speak. He suggests that the best choice is Thomas. Barbara now knows Arthur's judgment; she should certainly go along with his view if she is also enthusiastic about Thomas. But suppose she isn't sure about who is the best candidate. If she trusts Arthur, she might simply agree: Thomas is the best. Because she trusts Arthur well enough, she supports his judgment.

Now turn to a third person, Charles. Both Arthur and Barbara have said that they want to hire Thomas, but Charles's own view, based on what he knows to be limited information, is that Thomas is not the right person for the job and that Julie is the best candidate. Even though Charles has that view, he might well ignore what he knows and simply follow Arthur and Barbara. If so, the reason is not that Charles is a coward. Instead it is because he is a respectful listener. He may simply think that both Arthur and Barbara have evidence for their enthusiasm.

Unless David thinks that his own information is really better than that of those who preceded him, he should and will follow their lead. If he does that, David is in a cascade. True, he will resist if he has very strong grounds to think that Arthur, Barbara, and Charles are wrong. But if he lacks those grounds, he will likely go along with them.

Importantly, Charles or David may have information or insights about Thomas (or the other candidates) — information or insights of which Arthur and Barbara are unaware. If it had been shared, this private information might have changed Arthur's or Barbara's views. If Charles and David had spoken first, they would not only have expressed their views about the candidates but also contributed information that might have swayed the other participants. But since they speak last, their private information might well remain private.

Now suppose that Erica, Frank, and George are expected to express their views. If Arthur, Barbara, Charles, and David have previously said that Thomas is best, each of them might well say the same thing even if they have good reason to think that another choice would be better. Sure, they might oppose the growing consensus if it is clearly wrong. But what if the decision isn't clear? The trick in this example is that Arthur's initial judgment has started a process by which several people are led to participate in a cascade, leading the group to opt unanimously for Thomas — even if some of those who support him actually have no view and even if others think he is not the best choice at all.

This example, of course, is highly artificial. But within groups of all kinds, something like it happens all the time. People learn from others, and if early speakers seem to like something or want to do something, others might assent. At least this is so if they do not have reason to distrust them and if they lack a good reason to think that they are wrong.

For our purposes, the most important point is that informational cascades make noise across groups possible and even likely. In the example we have given, Arthur spoke first and favored Thomas. But suppose that Barbara had spoken first and favored Sam. Or suppose that Arthur had felt slightly differently and preferred Julie. On plausible assumptions, the group would have turned to Sam or Julie, not because they are better but because that is how the cascade would have worked itself out. That is the central finding of the music download experiment (and its cousins).

Note that it is not necessarily irrational for people to participate in informational cascades. If people are unsure about whom to hire, they might be smart to follow others. As the number of people who share the same view gets larger, relying on them becomes smarter still. Nonetheless, there are two problems. First, people tend to neglect the possibility that most of the people in the crowd are in a cascade, too—and are not making independent judgments of their own.

When we see three, ten, or twenty people embracing some conclusion, we might well underestimate the extent to which they are all following their predecessors. We might think that their shared agreement reflects collective wisdom, even if it reflects the initial views of just a few people. Second, informational cascades can lead groups of people in truly terrible directions. After all, Arthur might have been wrong about Thomas.

Information is not, of course, the only reason that group members are influenced by one another. Social pressures also matter. At a company or in government, people might silence themselves so as not to appear uncongenial, truculent, obtuse, or stupid. They want to be team players. That is why they follow the views and actions of others. People think that they know what is right or probably right, but they nonetheless go along with the apparent consensus of the group, or the views of early speakers, to stay in the group's good graces.

With minor variations, the hiring tale just told can proceed in the same way, not because people are learning from one another about the merits of Thomas but because they do not want to look disagreeable or silly. Arthur's early judgment in favor of Thomas might start a kind of bandwagon effect, ultimately imposing strong social pressure on Erica, Frank, or George, simply because everyone else has favored Thomas. And as with informational cascades, so with social pressure cascades: people might well exaggerate the conviction of those who have spoken before them. If people are endorsing Thomas, they might be doing so not because they really prefer Thomas but because an early speaker, or a powerful one, endorsed him. And yet group members end up adding their voice to the consensus and thus increasing the level of social pressure. This is a familiar phenomenon in companies and government offices, and it can lead to confidence about, and unanimous support for, a judgment that is quite wrong.

Across groups, social influences also produce noise. If someone starts a meeting by favoring a major change in the company's direction, that person might initiate a discussion that leads a group unanimously to support the change. Their agreement might be a product of social pressures, not of conviction. If someone else had started the meeting by indicating a different view, or if the initial speaker had decided to be silent, the discussion might have headed in an altogether different direction—and for the same reason. Very similar groups can end up in divergent places because of social pressures.

Group Polarization

In the United States and in many other countries, criminal cases (and many civil cases) are generally tried by a jury. One would hope that, through their deliberations, juries make wiser decisions than do the individuals who constitute these deliberative bodies. However, the study of juries uncovers a distinct kind of social influence that is also a source of noise: *group polarization*. The basic idea is that when people speak with one another, they often end up at a more extreme point in line with their original inclinations. If, for example, most people in a seven-person group tend to think that opening a new office in Paris would be a pretty good idea, the group is likely to conclude, after discussion, that opening that office would be a terrific idea. Internal discussions often create greater confidence, greater unity, and greater extremism, frequently in the form of increased enthusiasm. As it happens, group polarization does not only occur in juries; teams that make professional judgments often become polarized, too.

In a series of experiments, we studied the decisions of juries that award punitive damages in product liability cases. Each jury's decision is a monetary amount, which is intended to punish the company for its wrongdoing and be a deterrent to others. (We will return to these studies and describe them in greater detail in chapter 15.) For our purposes here, consider an experiment that compares real-world deliberating juries and "statistical juries." First, we presented the 899 participants in our study with case vignettes and asked them to make their own independent judgments about them, using a seven-degree scale to express their outrage and punitive intent and a dollar scale for monetary awards (if any). Then, with the aid of the computer, we used these individual responses to create millions of statistical juries, that is, virtual six-person groups (assembled randomly). In each statistical jury, we took the median of the six individual judgments as the verdict.

We found, in short, that the judgments of these statistical juries were much more consistent. Noise was substantially reduced. The low noise was a mechanical effect of statistical aggregation: the noise present in the independent, individual judgments is always reduced by averaging them.

Real-world juries are not, however, statistical juries; they meet and discuss their views of the case. You could reasonably wonder whether deliberating juries would, in fact, tend to arrive at the judgment of their median members. To find out, we followed up the first experiment with another, this one involving more than three thousand jury-eligible citizens and more than five hundred six-person juries.

The results were straightforward. Looking at the same case, deliberating juries were far noisier than statistical juries—a clear reflection of social influence noise. Deliberation had the effect of increasing noise.

There was another intriguing finding. When the

median member of a six-person group was only moderately outraged and favored a lenient punishment, the verdict of the deliberating jury typically ended up more lenient still. When, on the contrary, the median member of a six-person group was quite outraged and expressed a severe punitive intent, the deliberating jury typically ended up more outraged and more severe still. And when this outrage was expressed as a monetary award, there was a systematic tendency to come up with monetary awards that were higher than that of the jury's median member. Indeed, 27% of juries chose an award as high as, or even higher than, that of their most severe member. Not only were deliberating juries noisier than statistical juries, but they also accentuated the opinions of the individuals composing them.

Recall the basic finding of group polarization: after people talk with one another, they typically end up at a more extreme point in line with their original inclinations. Our experiment illustrates this effect. Deliberating juries experienced a shift toward greater leniency (when the median member was lenient) and a shift toward greater severity (when the median member was severe). Similarly, juries that were inclined to impose monetary punishments ended up imposing more severe punishments than what their median members had favored.

The explanations for group polarization are, in turn, similar to the explanations for cascade effects. Information plays a major role. If most people favor a severe punishment, then the group will hear many arguments in favor of severe punishment — and fewer arguments the other way. If group members are listening to one another, they will shift in the direction of the dominant tendency, rendering the group more unified, more confident, and more extreme. And if people care about their reputation within the group, they will shift in the direction of the dominant tendency, which will also produce polarization.

Group polarization can, of course, produce errors. And it often does. But our main focus here is on variability. As we have seen, an aggregation of judgments will reduce noise, and for those purposes, the more judgments, the better. This is why statistical juries are less noisy than individual jurors. At the same time, we found that deliberating juries are noisier than statistical juries. When similarly situated groups end up differing, group polarization is often the reason. And the resulting noise can be very loud.

In business, in government, and everywhere else, cascades and polarization can lead to wide disparities between groups looking at the same problem. The potential dependence of outcomes on the judgments of a few individuals — those who speak first or who have the largest influence — should be especially worrisome now that we have explored how noisy individual judgments can be. We have seen that level noise and pattern noise make differences between the opinions of group members larger than they should be (and larger than we would expect). We have also seen that occasion noise — fatigue, mood, comparison points — may affect the judgment of the first person who speaks. Group dynamics can amplify this noise. As a result, deliberating groups tend to be noisier than statistical groups that merely average individual judgments.

Since many of the most important decisions in business and government are made after some sort of deliberative process, it is especially important to be alert to this risk. Organizations and their leaders should take steps to control noise in the judgments of their individual members. They should also manage deliberating groups in a way that is likely to reduce noise, not amplify it. The noise-reduction strategies we will propose aim to achieve that goal.

Speaking of Group Decisions

"Everything seems to depend on early popularity. We'd better work hard to make sure that our new release has a terrific first week."

"As I always suspected, ideas about politics and economics are a lot like movie stars. If people think that other people like them, such ideas can go far."

"I've always been worried that when my team gets together, we end up confident and unified—and firmly committed to the course of action that we choose. I guess there's something in our internal processes that isn't going all that well!"

PART III

Noise in Predictive Judgments

Many judgments are predictions, and since verifiable predictions can be evaluated, we can learn a lot about noise and bias by studying them. In this part of the book, we focus on predictive judgments.

Chapter 9 compares the accuracy of predictions made by professionals, by machines, and by simple rules. You will not be surprised by our conclusion that the professionals come third in this competition. In chapter 10, we explore the reasons for this outcome and show that noise is a major factor in the inferiority of human judgment.

To reach these conclusions, we must evaluate the

quality of predictions, and to do that, we need a measure of predictive accuracy, a way to answer this question: How closely do the predictions *co-vary* with the outcomes? If the HR department routinely rates the potential of new hires, for example, we can wait a few years to find out how employees perform and see how closely ratings of potential co-vary with evaluations of performance. Predictions are accurate to the extent that the employees whose potential was rated high when they were hired also earn high evaluations for their work.

A measure that captures this intuition is the *percent concordant (PC),* which answers a more specific question: Suppose you take a pair of employees at random. What is the probability that the one who scored higher on an evaluation of potential also performs better on the job? If the accuracy of the early ratings were perfect, the PC would be 100%: the ranking of two employees by potential would be a perfect prediction of their eventual ranking by performance. If the predictions were entirely useless, concordance would occur by chance only, and the "higher-potential" employee would be just as likely as not to perform better: PC would be 50%. We will discuss this example, which has been studied extensively, in chapter 9. For a simpler example, PC for foot length and height in adult men is 71%. If you look at two people, first at their head and then at their feet, there is a 71% chance that the taller of the two also has the larger feet.

PC is an immediately intuitive measure of covariation, which is a large advantage, but it is not the standard measure that social scientists use. The standard measure is the *correlation coefficient* (r), which varies between 0 and 1 when two variables are positively related. In the preceding example, the correlation between height and foot size is about .60.

There are many ways to think about the correlation coefficient. Here is one that is intuitive enough: the correlation between two variables is their percentage of shared determinants. Imagine, for instance, that some trait is entirely genetically determined. We would expect to find a .50 correlation on that trait between siblings, who have 50% of their genes in common, and a .25 correlation between first cousins, who have 25% of their genes in common. We can also read the .60 correlation between height and foot size as suggesting that 60% of the causal factors that determine height also determine shoe size.

The two measures of covariation we have described are directly related to each other. Table 1 presents the PC for various values of the correlation coefficient. In the rest of this book, we always present the two measures together when we discuss the performance of humans and models.

Table 1: *Correlation coefficient and percentage concordant (PC)*

Correlation coefficient	Percentage concordant (PC)
.00	50%
.10	53%
.20	56%
.30	60%
.40	63%
.60	71%
.80	79%
1.00	100%

In chapter 11, we discuss an important limit on predictive accuracy: the fact that most judgments are made in a state of what we call *objective ignorance,* because many things on which the future depends can simply not be known. Strikingly, we manage, most of the time, to remain oblivious to this limitation and make predictions with confidence (or, indeed, overconfidence). Finally, in chapter 12, we show that objective ignorance affects not just our ability to predict events but even our capacity to understand them—an important part of the answer to the puzzle of why noise tends to be invisible.

CHAPTER 9

Judgments and Models

M any people are interested in forecasting people's future performance on the job — their
own and that of others. The forecasting of performance is therefore a useful example of predictive professional judgment. Consider, for instance, two
executives in a large company. Monica and Nathalie
were assessed by a specialized consulting firm when
they were hired and received ratings on a 1-to-10 scale
for leadership, communication, interpersonal skills,
job-related technical skills, and motivation for the
next position (table 2). Your task is to predict their
performance evaluations two years after they were
hired, also using a 1-to-10 scale.

Table 2: *Two candidates for an executive position*

	Leader-ship	*Communi-cation*	*Interpersonal skills*	*Technical skills*	*Motiva-tion*	*Your prediction*
Monica	4	6	4	8	8	
Nathalie	8	10	6	7	6	

Most people, when faced with this type of problem, simply eyeball each line and produce a quick judgment, sometimes after mentally computing the average of the scores. If you just did that, you probably concluded that Nathalie was the stronger candidate and that the difference between her and Monica was 1 or 2 points.

Judgment or Formula?

The informal approach you took to this problem is known as *clinical judgment.* You consider the information, perhaps engage in a quick computation, consult your intuition, and come up with a judgment. In fact, clinical judgment is the process that we have described simply as judgment in this book.

Now suppose that you performed the prediction task as a participant in an experiment. Monica and Nathalie were drawn from a database of several hundred managers who were hired some years ago, and who received ratings on five separate dimensions. You used these ratings to predict the managers' success on the job. Evaluations of their performance in their new roles are now available. How closely would these evaluations align with your clinical judgments of their potential?

This example is loosely based on an actual study of performance prediction. If you had been a participant in that study, you would probably not be pleased with its results. Doctoral-level psychologists, employed by an international consulting firm to make such predictions, achieved a correlation of .15 with performance evaluations (PC = 55%). In other words, when they rated one candidate as stronger than another—as you did with Monica and Nathalie—the probability that their favored candidate would end up with a higher performance rating was 55%, barely better than chance. To say the least, that is not an impressive result.

Perhaps you think that accuracy was poor because the ratings you were shown were useless for prediction. So we must ask, how much useful predictive information do the candidates' ratings actually contain? How can they be combined into a predictive score that will have the highest possible correlation with performance?

A standard statistical method answers these questions. In the present study, it yields an optimal correlation of .32 (PC = 60%), far from impressive but substantially higher than what clinical predictions achieved.

This technique, called *multiple regression,* produces a predictive score that is a weighted average of the predictors. It finds the optimal set of weights, chosen to maximize the correlation between the composite prediction and the target variable. The optimal weights minimize the MSE (mean squared error) of the predictions—a prime example of the dominant role of the least squares principle in statistics. As you might expect, the predictor that is most closely correlated with the target variable gets a large weight, and useless predictors get a weight of zero. Weights could also be negative: the candidate's number of unpaid traffic tickets would probably get a negative weight as a predictor of managerial success.

The use of multiple regression is an example of *mechanical prediction.* There are many kinds of mechanical prediction, ranging from simple rules ("hire anyone who completed high school") to sophisticated artificial intelligence models. But linear regression models are the most common (they have been called "the workhorse of judgment and decision-making research"). To minimize jargon, we will refer to linear models as *simple models.*

The study that we illustrated with Monica and Nathalie was one of many comparisons of clinical and mechanical predictions, which all share a simple structure:

❑ A set of *predictor variables* (in our example, the ratings of candidates) are used to predict a *target outcome* (the job evaluations of the same people);
❑ Human judges make *clinical predictions;*
❑ A rule (such as multiple regression) uses the same predictors to produce *mechanical predictions* of the same outcomes;
❑ The overall accuracy of clinical and mechanical predictions is compared.

Meehl: The Optimal Model Beats You

When people are introduced to clinical and mechanical prediction, they want to know how the two compare. How good is human judgment, relative to a formula?

The question had been asked before, but it attracted much attention only in 1954, when Paul Meehl, a professor of psychology at the University of Minnesota, published a book titled *Clinical Versus Statistical Prediction: A Theoretical Analysis and a Review of the Evidence*. Meehl reviewed twenty studies in which a clinical judgment was pitted against a mechanical prediction for such outcomes as academic success and psychiatric prognosis. He reached the strong conclusion that simple mechanical rules were generally superior to human judgment. Meehl discovered that clinicians and other professionals are distressingly weak in what they often see as their unique strength: the ability to integrate information.

To appreciate how surprising this finding is, and how it relates to noise, you have to understand how a simple mechanical prediction model works. Its defining characteristic is that the same rule is applied to all the cases. Each predictor has a weight, and that weight does not vary from one case to the next. You might think that this severe constraint puts models at a great disadvantage relative to human judges. In our example, perhaps you thought that Monica's combination of motivation and technical skills would be an important asset and would offset her limitations in other areas. And perhaps you also thought that Nathalie's weaknesses in these two areas would not be a serious issue, given her other strengths. Implicitly, you imagined different routes to success for the two women. These plausible clinical speculations effectively assign different weights to the same predictors in the two cases — a subtlety that is out of the reach of a simple model.

Another constraint of the simple model is that an

increase of 1 unit in a predictor always produces the same effect (and half the effect of an increase of 2 units). Clinical intuition often violates this rule. If, for instance, you were impressed by Nathalie's perfect 10 on communication skills and decided this score was worth a boost in your prediction, you did something that a simple model will not do. In a weighted-average formula, the difference between a score of 10 and a score of 9 must be the same as the difference between a 7 and a 6. Clinical judgment does not obey that rule. Instead, it reflects the common intuition that the same difference can be inconsequential in one context and critical in another. You may want to check, but we suspect that no simple model could account exactly for your judgments about Monica and Nathalie.

The study we used for these cases was a clear example of Meehl's pattern. As we noted, clinical predictions achieved a .15 correlation (PC = 55%) with job performance, but mechanical prediction achieved a correlation of .32 (PC = 60%). Think about the confidence that you experienced in the relative merits of the cases of Monica and Nathalie. Meehl's results strongly suggest that any satisfaction you felt with the quality of your judgment was an illusion: the *illusion of validity*.

The illusion of validity is found wherever

predictive judgments are made, because of a common failure to distinguish between two stages of the prediction task: evaluating cases on the evidence available and predicting actual outcomes. You can often be quite confident in your assessment of which of two candidates *looks* better, but guessing which of them will actually *be* better is an altogether different kettle of fish. It is safe to assert, for instance, that Nathalie looks like a stronger candidate than Monica, but it is not at all safe to assert that Nathalie will be a more successful executive than Monica. The reason is straightforward: you know most of what you need to know to assess the two cases, but gazing into the future is deeply uncertain.

Unfortunately, the difference gets blurred in our thinking. If you find yourself confused by the distinction between cases and predictions, you are in excellent company: Everybody finds that distinction confusing. If you are as confident in your predictions as you are in your evaluation of cases, however, you are a victim of the illusion of validity.

Clinicians are not immune to the illusion of validity. You can surely imagine the response of clinical psychologists to Meehl's finding that trivial formulas, consistently applied, outdo clinical judgment. The reaction combined shock, disbelief, and contempt for the shallow research that pretended to study the marvels of clinical intuition. The reaction is easy to understand: Meehl's pattern contradicts the subjective experience of judgment, and most of us will trust our experience over a scholar's claim.

Meehl himself was ambivalent about his findings. Because his name is associated with the superiority of statistics over clinical judgment, we might imagine him as a relentless critic of human insight, or as the godfather of quants, as we would say today. But that would be a caricature. Meehl, in addition to his academic career, was a practicing psychoanalyst. A picture of Freud hung in his office. He was a polymath who taught classes not just in psychology but also in philosophy and law and who wrote about metaphysics, religion, political science, and even parapsychology. (He insisted that "there is something to telepathy.") None of these characteristics fits the stereotype of a hard-nosed numbers guy. Meehl had no ill will toward clinicians—far from it. But as he put it, the evidence for the advantage of the mechanical approach to combining inputs was "massive and consistent."

"Massive and consistent" is a fair description. A 2000 review of 136 studies confirmed unambiguously that mechanical aggregation outperforms clinical judgment. The research surveyed in the article covered a wide variety of topics, including diagnosis of jaundice, fitness for military service, and marital satisfaction. Mechanical prediction was more accurate in 63 of the studies, a statistical tie was declared for another 65, and clinical prediction won the contest in 8 cases. These results understate the advantages of mechanical prediction, which is also faster and cheaper than clinical judgment. Moreover, human judges actually had an unfair advantage in many of these studies, because they had access to "private" information that was not supplied to the computer model. The findings support a blunt conclusion: *simple models beat humans.*

Goldberg: The Model of You Beats You

Meehl's finding raises important questions. Why, exactly, is the formula superior? What does the formula do better? In fact, a better question would be to ask what humans do worse. The answer is that people are inferior to statistical models in many ways. One of their critical weaknesses is that they are noisy.

To support this conclusion, we turn to a different stream of research on simple models, which began in the small city of Eugene, Oregon. Paul Hoffman was a wealthy and visionary psychologist who was impatient with academia. He founded a research institute where he collected under one roof a few extraordinarily effective researchers, who turned Eugene into a world-famous center for the study of human judgment.

One of these researchers was Lewis Goldberg, who is best known for his leading role in the development of the Big Five model of personality. In the late 1960s, following earlier work by Hoffman, Goldberg studied statistical models that describe the judgments of an individual.

It is just as easy to build such a model of a judge as it is to build a model of reality. The same predictors are used. In our initial example, the predictors are the five ratings of a manager's performance. And the same tool, multiple regression, is used. The only difference is the target variable. Instead of predicting a set of real outcomes, the formula is applied to predict a set of judgments — for instance, *your* judgments of Monica, Nathalie, and other managers.

The idea of modeling your judgments as a weighted average may seem altogether bizarre, because this is not how you form your opinions. When you thought clinically about Monica and Nathalie, you didn't apply the same rule to both cases. Indeed, you did not apply any rule at all. The model of the judge is not a realistic description of how a judge actually judges.

However, even if you do not actually compute a linear formula, you might still make your judgments *as if* you did. Expert billiard players act as if they have solved the complex equations that describe the mechanics of a particular shot, even if they are doing nothing of the kind. Similarly, you could be generating predictions as if you used a simple formula—even if what you actually do is vastly more complex. An as-if model that predicts what people will do with reasonable accuracy is useful, even when it is obviously wrong as a description of the process. This is the case for simple models of judgment. A comprehensive review of studies of judgment found that, in 237 studies, the average correlation between the model of the judge and the judge's clinical judgments was .80 (PC = 79%). While far from perfect, this correlation is high enough to support an as-if theory.

The question that drove Goldberg's research was how well a simple model of the judge would predict real outcomes. Since the model is a crude approximation of the judge, we could sensibly assume that it cannot perform as well. How much accuracy is lost when the model replaces the judge?

The answer may surprise you. Predictions did not lose accuracy when the model generated predictions. They improved. In most cases, the model out-predicted the professional on which it was based. The ersatz was better than the original product.

This conclusion has been confirmed by studies in many fields. An early replication of Goldberg's work involved the forecasting of graduate school success. The researchers asked ninety-eight participants to predict the GPAs of ninety students from ten cues. On the basis of these predictions, the researchers built a linear model of each participant's judgments and compared how accurately the participants and the models of the participants predicted GPA. For every one of the ninety-eight participants, the model did better than the participant did! Decades later, a review of fifty years of research concluded that models of judges consistently outperformed the judges they modeled.

We do not know if the participants in these studies received personal feedback on their performance. But you can surely imagine your own dismay if someone told you that a crude model of your judgments—almost a caricature—was actually more accurate than you were. For most of us, the activity of judgment is complex, rich, and interesting precisely because it does not fit simple rules. We feel best about ourselves and about our ability to make judgments when we invent and apply complex rules or have an insight that makes an individual case different from others—in short, when we make judgments that are not reducible to a plain operation of weighted averaging. The model-of-the-judge studies reinforce Meehl's conclusion that the subtlety is largely wasted.

Complexity and richness do not generally lead to more accurate predictions.

Why is that so? To understand Goldberg's finding, we need to understand what accounts for the differences between you and the model of you. What causes the discrepancies between your actual judgments and the output of a simple model that predicts them?

A statistical model of your judgments cannot possibly add anything to the information they contain. All the model can do is subtract and simplify. In particular, the simple model of your judgments will not represent any complex rules that you consistently follow. If you think that the difference between 10 and 9 on a rating of communications skill is more significant than the difference between 7 and 6, or that a well-rounded candidate who scores a solid 7 on all dimensions is preferable to one who achieves the same average with clear strengths and marked weaknesses, the model of you will not reproduce your complex rules—even if you apply them with flawless consistency.

Failing to reproduce your subtle rules will result in a loss of accuracy when your subtlety is valid. Suppose, for instance, that you must predict success at a difficult task from two inputs, skill and motivation. A weighted average is not a good formula, because no amount of motivation is sufficient to overcome a severe skill deficit, and vice versa. If you use a more complex combination of the two inputs, your predictive accuracy will be enhanced and will be higher than that achieved by a model that fails to capture this subtlety. On the other hand, complex rules will often give you only the illusion of validity and in fact harm the quality of your judgments. Some subtleties are valid, but many are not.

In addition, a simple model of you will not represent the pattern noise in your judgments. It cannot replicate the positive and negative errors that arise from arbitrary reactions you may have to a particular case. Neither will the model capture the influences of the momentary context and of your mental state when you make a particular judgment. Most likely, these noisy errors of judgment are not systematically correlated with anything, which means that for most purposes, they can be considered random.

The effect of removing noise from your judgments will always be an improvement of your predictive accuracy. For example, suppose that the correlation between your forecasts and an outcome is .50 (PC = 67%), but 50% of the variance of your judgments consists of noise. If your judgments could be made noise-free—as a model of you would be—their correlation with the same outcome would jump to .71 (PC = 75%). Reducing noise mechanically increases the validity of predictive judgment.

In short, replacing you with a model of you does two things: it eliminates your subtlety, and it eliminates your pattern noise. The robust finding that the model of the judge is more valid than the judge conveys an important message: the gains from subtle rules in human judgment—when they exist—are generally not sufficient to compensate for the detrimental effects of noise. You may believe that you are subtler, more insightful, and more nuanced than the linear caricature of your thinking. But in fact, you are mostly noisier.

Why do complex rules of prediction harm accuracy, despite the strong feeling we have that they draw on valid insights? For one thing, many of the complex rules that people invent are not likely to be generally true. But there is another problem: even when the complex rules are valid in principle, they inevitably apply under conditions that are rarely observed. For example, suppose you have concluded that exceptionally original candidates are worth hiring, even when their scores on other dimensions are mediocre. The problem is that exceptionally original candidates are, by definition, exceptionally rare. Since an evaluation of originality is likely to be unreliable, many high scores on that metric are flukes, and truly original talent often remains undetected. The performance evaluations that could confirm that "originals" end up as superstars are also imperfect. Errors of measurement at both ends inevitably attenuate the validity of predictions—and rare events are particularly likely to be missed. The advantages of true subtlety are quickly drowned in measurement error.

A study by Martin Yu and Nathan Kuncel reported a more radical version of Goldberg's demonstration. This study (which was the basis for the example of Monica and Nathalie) used data from an international consulting firm that employed experts to assess 847 candidates for executive positions, in three separate samples. The experts scored the results on seven distinct assessment dimensions and used their clinical judgment to assign an overall predictive score to each, with rather unimpressive results.

Yu and Kuncel decided to compare judges not to the best simple model of themselves but to a *random* linear model. They generated ten thousand sets of random weights for the seven predictors, and applied the ten thousand random formulas to predict job performance.

Their striking finding was that *any* linear model, when applied consistently to all cases, was likely to outdo human judges in predicting an outcome from the same information. In one of the three samples, 77% of the ten thousand randomly weighted linear models did better than the human experts. In the other two samples, 100% of the random models outperformed the humans. Or, to put it bluntly, it proved almost impossible in that study to generate a simple model that did worse than the experts did.

The conclusion from this research is stronger than the one we took away from Goldberg's work on the model of the judge—and indeed it is an extreme example. In this setting, human judges performed very poorly in absolute terms, which helps explain why even unimpressive linear models outdid them. Of course, we should not conclude that any model beats any human. Still, the fact that mechanical adherence to a simple rule (Yu and Kuncel call it "mindless consistency") could significantly improve judgment in a difficult problem illustrates the massive effect of noise on the validity of clinical predictions.

This quick tour has shown how noise impairs clinical judgment. In predictive judgments, human experts are easily outperformed by simple formulas—models of reality, models of a judge, or even randomly generated models. This finding argues in favor of using noise-free methods: rules and algorithms, which are the topic of the next chapter.

Speaking of Judgments and Models

"People believe they capture complexity and add subtlety when they make judgments. But the complexity and the subtlety are mostly wasted—usually they do not add to the accuracy of simple models."

"More than sixty years after the publication of Paul Meehl's book, the idea that mechanical prediction is superior to people is still shocking."

"There is so much noise in judgment that a noise-free model of a judge achieves more accurate predictions than the actual judge does."

CHAPTER 10

Noiseless Rules

In recent years, artificial intelligence (AI), particularly machine-learning techniques, has enabled machines to perform many tasks formerly regarded as quintessentially human. Machine-learning algorithms can recognize faces, translate languages, and read radiology images. They can solve computational problems, such as generating driving directions for thousands of drivers at once, with astonishing speed and accuracy. And they perform difficult prediction tasks: machine-learning algorithms forecast the decisions of the US Supreme Court, determine which defendants are more likely to jump bail, and assess which calls to child protective services most urgently require a case worker's visit.

Although nowadays these are the applications we have in mind when we hear the word *algorithm*, the

term has a broader meaning. In one dictionary's definition, an algorithm is a "process or set of rules to be
followed in calculations or other problem-solving
operations, especially by a computer." By this definition, simple models and other forms of mechanical
judgment we described in the previous chapter are
algorithms, too.

In fact, many types of mechanical approaches, from
almost laughably simple rules to the most sophisticated and impenetrable machine algorithms, can outperform human judgment. And one key reason for this
outperformance—albeit not the only one—is that all
mechanical approaches are noise-free.

To examine different types of rule-based approaches
and to learn how and under what conditions each
approach can be valuable, we start our journey with
the models of chapter 9: simple models based on multiple regression (i.e., linear regression models). From
this starting point, we will travel in the two opposite
directions on the spectrum of sophistication—first to
seek extreme simplicity, then to add greater sophistication (figure 11).

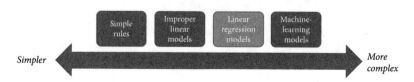

FIGURE 11: *Four types of rules and algorithms*

More Simplicity: Robust and Beautiful

Robyn Dawes was another member of the Eugene, Oregon, team of stars that studied judgment in the 1960s and 1970s. In 1974, Dawes achieved a breakthrough in the simplification of prediction tasks. His idea was surprising, almost heretical: instead of using multiple regression to determine the precise weight of each predictor, he proposed giving all the predictors equal weights.

Dawes labeled the equal-weight formula an *improper linear model*. His surprising discovery was that these equal-weight models are about as accurate as "proper" regression models, and far superior to clinical judgments.

Even the proponents of improper models admit that this claim is implausible and "contrary to statistical intuition." Indeed, Dawes and his assistant, Bernard Corrigan, initially struggled to publish their paper in scientific journals; editors simply did not believe them. If you think about the example of Monica and Nathalie in the previous chapter, you probably believe that some predictors matter more than others. Most people, for instance, would give leadership a higher weight than technical skills. How can a straight unweighted average predict someone's performance better than a carefully weighted average, or better than the judgment of an expert?

Today, many years after Dawes's breakthrough, the statistical phenomenon that so surprised his contemporaries is well understood. As explained earlier in this book, multiple regression computes "optimal" weights that minimize squared errors. But multiple regression minimizes error *in the original data.* The formula therefore adjusts itself to predict every random fluke in the data. If, for instance, the sample includes a few managers who have high technical skills and who also performed exceptionally well for unrelated reasons, the model will exaggerate the weight of technical skill.

The challenge is that when the formula is applied *out of sample*—that is, when it is used to predict outcomes in a different data set—the weights will no longer be optimal. Flukes in the original sample are no longer present, precisely because they were flukes; in the new sample, managers with high technical skills are not all superstars. And the new sample has different flukes, which the formula cannot predict. The correct measure of a model's predictive accuracy is its performance in a new sample, called its *cross-validated correlation.* In effect, a regression model is *too* successful in the original sample, and a cross-validated correlation is almost always lower than it was in the original data. Dawes and Corrigan compared equal-weight models to multiple regression models (cross-validated) in several situations. One of their examples involved predictions of the first-year GPA of ninety graduate students in psychology at the University of Illinois, using ten variables related to academic success: aptitude test scores, college grades, various peer ratings (e.g., extroversion), and various self-ratings (e.g., conscientiousness). The standard multiple regression model achieved a correlation of .69, which shrank to .57 (PC = 69%) in cross-validation. The correlation of the equal-weight model with first-year GPA was about the same: .60 (PC = 70%). Similar results have been obtained in many other studies.

The loss of accuracy in cross-validation is worst when the original sample is small, because flukes loom larger in small samples. The problem Dawes pointed out is that the samples used in social science research are generally so small that the advantage of so-called optimal weighting disappears. As statistician Howard Wainer memorably put it in the subtitle of a scholarly article on the estimation of proper weights, "It Don't Make No Nevermind." Or, in Dawes's words, "we do not need models more precise than our measurements." Equal-weight models do well because they are not susceptible to accidents of sampling.

The immediate implication of Dawes's work deserves to be widely known: you can make valid statistical predictions without prior data about the outcome that you are trying to predict. All you need is a collection of predictors that you can trust to be correlated with the outcome.

Suppose you must make predictions of the performance of executives who have been rated on a number of dimensions, as in the example in chapter 9. You trust that these scores measure important qualities, but you have no data about how well each score predicts performance. Nor do you have the luxury of waiting a few years to track the performance of a large sample of managers. You could nevertheless take the seven scores, do the statistical work required to weight them equally, and use the result as your prediction. How good would this equal-weight model be? Its correlation with the outcome would be .25 (PC = 58%), far superior to clinical predictions (r = .15, PC = 55%), and surely quite similar to a cross-validated regression model. And it does not require any data you don't have or any complicated calculations.

To use Dawes's phrase, which has become a meme among students of judgment, there is a "robust beauty" in equal weights. The final sentence of the seminal article that introduced the idea offered another pithy summary: "The whole trick is to decide what variables to look at and then to know how to add."

Even More Simplicity: Simple Rules

Another style of simplification is through *frugal models,* or *simple rules.* Frugal models are models of reality that look like ridiculously simplified, back-of-the-envelope calculations. But in some settings, they can produce surprisingly good predictions.

These models build on a feature of multiple regression that most people find surprising. Suppose you are using two predictors that are strongly predictive of the outcome — their correlations with the outcome are .60 (PC = 71%) and .55 (PC = 69%). Suppose also that the two predictors are correlated to each other, with a correlation of .50. How good would you guess your prediction is going to be when the two predictors are optimally combined? The answer is quite disappointing. The correlation is .67 (PC = 73%), higher than before, but not much higher.

The example illustrates a general rule: the combination of two or more correlated predictors is barely more predictive than the best of them on its own. Because, in real life, predictors are almost always correlated to one another, this statistical fact supports the use of frugal approaches to prediction, which use a small number of predictors. Simple rules that can be applied with little or no computation have produced impressively accurate predictions in some settings, compared with models that use many more predictors.

A team of researchers published in 2020 a large-scale effort to apply a frugal approach to a variety of prediction problems, including the choice that bail judges face when they decide whether to release or retain defendants pending trial. That decision is an implicit prediction of the defendant's behavior. If wrongly denied bail, that person will be detained needlessly, at a significant cost to the individual and to society. If bail is granted to the wrong defendant, the person may flee before trial or even commit another crime.

The model that the researchers built uses just two inputs known to be highly predictive of a defendant's likelihood to jump bail: the defendant's age (older people are lower flight risks) and the number of past court dates missed (people who have failed to appear before tend to recidivate). The model translates these two inputs into a number of points, which can be used as a risk score. The calculation of risk for a defendant does not require a computer—in fact, not even a calculator.

When tested against a real data set, this frugal model performed as well as statistical models that used a much larger number of variables. The frugal model did better than virtually all human bail judges did in predicting flight risk.

The same frugal approach, using up to five features weighted by small whole numbers (between –3 and +3), was applied to tasks as varied as determining the severity of a tumor from mammographic data, diagnosing heart disease, and predicting credit risk. In all these tasks, the frugal rule did as well as more complex regression models did (though generally not as well as machine learning did).

In another demonstration of the power of simple rules, a separate team of researchers studied a similar but distinct judicial problem: recidivism prediction. Using only two inputs, they were able to match the validity of an existing tool that uses 137 variables to assess a defendant's risk level. Not surprisingly, these two predictors (age and the number of previous convictions) are closely related to the two factors used in the bail model, and their association with criminal behavior is well documented.

The appeal of frugal rules is that they are transparent and easy to apply. Moreover, these advantages are obtained at relatively little cost in accuracy relative to more complex models.

More Complexity: Toward Machine Learning

For the second part of our journey, let us now travel in the opposite direction on the spectrum of sophistication. What if we could use many more predictors, gather much more data about each of them, spot relationship patterns that no human could detect, and model these patterns to achieve better prediction? This, in essence, is the promise of AI.

Very large data sets are essential for sophisticated analyses, and the increasing availability of such data sets is one of the main causes of the rapid progress of AI in recent years. For example, large data sets make it possible to deal mechanically with *broken-leg exceptions.* This somewhat cryptic phrase goes back to an example that Meehl imagined: Consider a model that was designed to predict the probability that people will go to the movies tonight. Regardless of your confidence in the model, if you happen to know that a particular person just broke a leg, you probably know better than the model what their evening will look like.

When using simple models, the broken-leg principle holds an important lesson for decision makers: it tells them when to override the model and when not to. If you have decisive information that the model could not take into consideration, there is a true broken leg, and you should override the model's recommendation. On the other hand, you will sometimes disagree with a model's recommendation even if you lack such private information. In those cases, your temptation to override the model reflects a personal pattern you are applying to the same predictors. Since this personal pattern is highly likely to be invalid, you should refrain from overriding the model; your intervention is likely to make the prediction less accurate.

One of the reasons for the success of machine-learning models in prediction tasks is that they are capable of discovering such broken legs—many more than humans can think of. Given a vast amount of data about a vast number of cases, a model tracking the behavior of moviegoers could actually learn, for example, that people who have visited the hospital on their regular movie day are unlikely to see a film that evening. Improving predictions of rare events in this way reduces the need for human supervision.

What AI does involves no magic and no understanding; it is mere pattern finding. While we must admire the power of machine learning, we should remember that it will probably take some time for an AI to understand *why* a person who has broken a leg will miss movie night.

An Example: Better Bail Decisions

At about the same time that the previously mentioned team of researchers applied simple rules to the problem of bail decisions, another team, led by Sendhil Mullainathan, trained sophisticated AI models to perform the same task. The AI team had access to a bigger set of data—758,027 bail decisions. For each case, the team had access to information also available to the judge: the defendant's current offense, rap sheet, and prior failures to appear. Except for age, no other demographic information was used to train the algorithm. The researchers also knew, for each case, whether the defendant was released and, if so, whether the individual failed to appear in court or was rearrested. (Of the defendants, 74% were released, and of these, 15% failed to appear in court and 26% were rearrested.) With this data, the researchers trained a machine-learning algorithm and evaluated its performance. Since the model was built through machine learning, it was not restricted to linear combinations. If it detected a more complex regularity in the data, it could use this pattern to improve its predictions.

The model was designed to produce a prediction of flight risk quantified as a numerical score, rather than a bail/no-bail decision. This approach recognizes that the maximum acceptable risk threshold, that is, the level of risk above which a defendant should be denied bail, requires an evaluative judgment that a model cannot make. However, the researchers calculated that, no matter where the risk threshold is set, using their model's predictive score would result in improvements over the performance of human judges. If the risk threshold is set so that the number of people who are denied bail remains the same as when the judges decide, Mullainathan's team calculated, crime rates could be reduced by up to 24%, because the people behind bars would be the ones most likely to recidivate. Conversely, if the risk threshold is set to reduce the number of people denied bail as much as possible without increasing crime, the researchers calculated that the number of people detained could be reduced by up to 42%. In other words, the machine-learning model performs much better than human judges do at predicting which defendants are high risks.

The model built by machine learning was also far more successful than linear models that used the same information. The reason is intriguing: "The machine-learning algorithm finds significant signal in combinations of variables that might otherwise be missed." The algorithm's ability to find patterns easily missed by other methods is especially pronounced for the defendants whom the algorithm classifies as highest risk. In other words, some patterns in the data, though rare, strongly predict high risk. This finding—that the algorithm picks up rare but decisive patterns— brings us back to the concept of broken legs.

The researchers also used the algorithm to build a model of each judge, analogous to the model of the judge we described in chapter 9 (but not restricted to simple linear combinations). Applying these models to the entire set of data enabled the team to simulate the decisions judges would have made if they had seen the same cases, and to compare the decisions. The results indicated considerable system noise in bail decisions. Some of it is level noise: when judges are sorted by leniency, the most lenient quintile (that is, the 20% of judges who have the highest release rates) released 83% of the defendants, whereas the least lenient quintile of judges released only 61%. Judges also have very different patterns of judgments about which defendants are higher flight risks. A defendant who is seen as a low flight risk by one judge can be considered a high flight risk by another judge, who is not stricter in general. These results offer clear evidence of pattern noise. A more detailed analysis revealed that differences between cases accounted for 67% of the variance, and system noise for 33%. System noise included some level noise, i.e., differences in average severity, but most of it (79%) was pattern noise.

Finally, and fortunately, the greater accuracy of the machine-learning program does not come at the expense of other identifiable goals that the judges might have pursued — notably, racial fairness. In theory, although the algorithm uses no racial data, the program might inadvertently aggravate racial disparities. These disparities could arise if the model used predictors that are highly correlated with race (such as zip code) or if the source of the data on which the algorithm is trained is biased. If, for instance, the number of past arrests is used as a predictor, and if past arrests are affected by racial discrimination, then the resulting algorithm will discriminate as well.

While this sort of discrimination is certainly a risk in principle, the decisions of this algorithm are in important respects less racially biased than those of the judges, not more. For instance, if the risk threshold is set to achieve the same crime rate as the judges' decisions did, then the algorithm jails 41% fewer people of color. Similar results are found in other scenarios: the gains in accuracy need not exacerbate racial disparities—and as the research team also showed, the algorithm can easily be instructed to reduce them.

Another study in a different domain illustrates how algorithms can simultaneously increase accuracy and reduce discrimination. Bo Cowgill, a professor at Columbia Business School, studied the recruitment of software engineers at a large tech company. Instead of using (human) résumé screeners to select who would get an interview, Cowgill developed a machine-learning algorithm to screen the résumés of candidates and trained it on more than three hundred thousand submissions that the company had received and evaluated. Candidates selected by the algorithm were 14% more likely than those selected by humans to receive a job offer after interviews. When the candidates received offers, the algorithm group was 18% more likely than the human-selected group to accept them. The algorithm also picked a more diverse group of candidates, in terms of race, gender, and other metrics; it was much more likely to select "nontraditional" candidates, such as those who did not graduate from an elite school, those who lacked prior work experience, and those who did not have a referral. Human beings tended to favor résumés that checked all the boxes of the "typical" profile for a software engineer, but the algorithm gave each relevant predictor its proper weight.

To be clear, these examples do not prove that algorithms are always fair, unbiased, or nondiscriminatory. A familiar example is an algorithm that is supposed to predict the success of job candidates, but is actually trained on a sample of past promotion decisions. Of course, such an algorithm will replicate all the human biases in past promotion decisions.

It is possible, and perhaps too easy, to build an algorithm that perpetuates racial or gender disparities, and there have been many reported cases of algorithms that did just that. The visibility of these cases explains the growing concern about bias in algorithmic decision making. Before drawing general conclusions about algorithms, however, we should remember that some algorithms are not only more accurate than human judges but also fairer.

Why Don't We Use Rules More Often?

To summarize this short tour of mechanical decision making, we review two reasons for the superiority of rules of all kinds over human judgment. First, as described in chapter 9, all mechanical prediction techniques, not just the most recent and more sophisticated ones, represent significant improvements on human judgment. The combination of personal patterns and occasion noise weighs so heavily on the quality of human judgment that simplicity and noiselessness are sizable advantages. Simple rules that are merely sensible typically do better than human judgment.

Second, the data is sometimes rich enough for sophisticated AI techniques to detect valid patterns and go well beyond the predictive power of a simple model. When AI succeeds in this way, the advantage of these models over human judgment is not just the absence of noise but also the ability to exploit much more information.

Given these advantages and the massive amount of

evidence supporting them, it is worth asking why algorithms are not used much more extensively for the types of professional judgments we discuss in this book. For all the spirited talk about algorithms and machine learning, and despite important exceptions in particular fields, their use remains limited. Many experts ignore the clinical-versus-mechanical debate, preferring to trust their judgment. They have faith in their intuitions and doubt that machines could do better. They regard the idea of algorithmic decision making as dehumanizing and as an abdication of their responsibility.

The use of algorithms in medical diagnosis, for instance, is not yet routine, notwithstanding impressive advances. Few organizations use algorithms in their hiring and promotion decisions. Hollywood studio executives green-light movies on the basis of their judgment and experience, not according to a formula. Book publishers do the same thing. And if the tale of the statistics-obsessed Oakland Athletics baseball team, as told in Michael Lewis's bestseller *Moneyball,* has made such an impression, it is precisely because algorithmic rigor had long been the exception, not the rule, in the decision-making process of sports teams. Even today, coaches, managers, and people who work with them often trust their gut and insist that statistical analysis cannot possibly replace good judgment.

In a 1996 article, Meehl and a coauthor listed (and rebutted) no fewer than seventeen types of objections that psychiatrists, physicians, judges, and other professionals had to mechanical judgment. The authors concluded that the resistance of clinicians can be explained by a combination of sociopsychological factors, including their "fear of technological unemployment," "poor education," and a "general dislike of computers."

Since then, researchers have identified additional factors that contribute to this resistance. We do not aim to offer a full review of that research here. Our goal in this book is to offer suggestions for the improvement of human judgment, not to argue for the "displacement of people by machines," as Judge Frankel would have put it.

But some findings about what drives human resistance to mechanical prediction are relevant to our discussion of human judgment. One key insight has emerged from recent research: people are not systematically suspicious of algorithms. When given a choice between taking advice from a human and an algorithm, for instance, they often prefer the algorithm. Resistance to algorithms, or *algorithm aversion,* does not always manifest itself in a blanket refusal to adopt new decision support tools. More often, people are willing to give an algorithm a chance but stop trusting it as soon as they see that it makes mistakes.

On one level, this reaction seems sensible: why bother with an algorithm you can't trust? As humans, we are keenly aware that we make mistakes, but that is a privilege we are not prepared to share. We expect machines to be perfect. If this expectation is violated, we discard them.

Because of this intuitive expectation, however, people are likely to distrust algorithms and keep using their judgment, even when this choice produces demonstrably inferior results. This attitude is deeply rooted and unlikely to change until near-perfect predictive accuracy can be achieved.

Fortunately, much of what makes rules and algorithms better can be replicated in human judgment. We cannot hope to use information as efficiently as an AI model does, but we can strive to emulate the simplicity and noiselessness of simple models. To the extent that we can adopt methods that reduce system noise, we should see improvements in the quality of predictive judgments. How to improve our judgments is the main theme of part 5.

Speaking of Rules and Algorithms

"When there is a lot of data, machine-learning algorithms will do better than humans and better than simple models. But even the simplest rules and algorithms have big advantages over human judges:

they are free of noise, and they do not attempt to apply complex, usually invalid insights about the predictors."

"Since we lack data about the outcome we must predict, why don't we use an equal-weight model? It will do almost as well as a proper model, and will surely do better than case-by-case human judgment."

"You disagree with the model's forecast. I get it. But is there a broken leg here, or do you just dislike the prediction?"

"The algorithm makes mistakes, of course. But if human judges make even more mistakes, whom should we trust?"

CHAPTER 11

Objective Ignorance

W e have often had the experience of sharing with audiences of executives the material of the last two chapters, with its sobering findings about the limited achievements of human judgment. The message we aim to convey has been around for more than half a century, and we suspect that few decision makers have avoided exposure to it. But they are certainly able to resist it.

Some of the executives in our audiences tell us proudly that they trust their gut more than any amount of analysis. Many others are less blunt but share the same view. Research in managerial decision making has shown that executives, especially the more senior and experienced ones, resort extensively to something variously called *intuition, gut feel,* or, simply, *judgment* (used in a different sense from the one we use in this book).

In short, decision makers like to listen to their gut, and most seem happy with what they hear. Which raises a question: what, exactly, do these people, who are blessed with the combination of authority and great self-confidence, hear from their gut?

One review of intuition in managerial decision making defines it as "a judgment for a given course of action that comes to mind with an aura or conviction of rightness or plausibility, but without clearly articulated reasons or justifications—essentially 'knowing' but without knowing why." We propose that this sense of knowing without knowing why is actually the *internal signal* of judgment completion that we mentioned in chapter 4.

The internal signal is a self-administered reward, one people work hard (or sometimes not so hard) to achieve when they reach closure on a judgment. It is a satisfying emotional experience, a pleasing sense of coherence, in which the evidence considered and the judgment reached feel right. All the pieces of the jigsaw puzzle seem to fit. (We will see later that this sense of coherence is often bolstered by hiding or ignoring pieces of evidence that don't fit.)

What makes the internal signal important—and misleading—is that it is construed not as a feeling but as a belief. This emotional experience ("the evidence feels right") masquerades as rational confidence in the validity of one's judgment ("I know, even if I don't know why").

Confidence is no guarantee of accuracy, however, and many confident predictions turn out to be wrong. While both bias and noise contribute to prediction errors, the largest source of such errors is not the limit on how good predictive judgments *are*. It is the limit on how good they *could be*. This limit, which we call *objective ignorance*, is the focus of this chapter.

Objective Ignorance

Here is a question you can ask yourself if you find yourself making repeated predictive judgments. The question could apply to any task—picking stocks, for instance, or predicting the performance of professional athletes. But for simplicity, we'll choose the same example we used in chapter 9: the selection of job candidates. Imagine you have evaluated a hundred candidates over the years. You now have a chance to assess how good your decisions were, by comparing the evaluations you had made with the candidates' objectively assessed performance since then. If you pick a pair of candidates at random, how often would your ex ante judgment and the ex post evaluations agree? In other words, when comparing any two candidates, what is the probability that the one you thought had more potential did in fact turn out to be the higher performer?

We often informally poll groups of executives on this question. The most frequent answers are in the 75–85% range, and we suspect that these responses are constrained by modesty and by a wish not to appear boastful. Private, one-on-one conversations suggest that the true sense of confidence is often even higher.

Since you are now familiar with the percent concordant statistic, you can easily see the problem this evaluation raises. A PC of 80% roughly corresponds to a correlation of .80. This level of predictive power is rarely achieved in the real world. In the field of personnel selection, a recent review found that the performance of human judges does not come close to this number. On average, they achieve a predictive correlation of .28 (PC = 59%).

If you consider the challenge of personnel selection, the disappointing results are not that surprising. A person who starts a new job today will encounter many challenges and opportunities, and chance will intervene to change the direction of her life in many ways. She may encounter a supervisor who believes in her, creates opportunities, promotes her work, and builds her self-confidence and motivation. She may also be less lucky and, through no fault of her own, start her career with a demoralizing failure. In her personal life, too, there may be events that affect her job performance. None of these events and circumstances can be predicted today—not by you, not by anyone else, and not by the best predictive model in the world. This intractable uncertainty includes everything that cannot be known at this time about the outcome that you are trying to predict.

Furthermore, much about the candidates is in principle knowable but is not known when you make your judgment. For our purposes, it does not matter whether these gaps in knowledge come from the lack of sufficiently predictive tests, from your decision that the cost of acquiring more information was not justified, or from your own negligence in fact-finding. One way or the other, you are in a state of less-than-perfect information.

Both intractable uncertainty (what cannot possibly be known) and imperfect information (what could be known but isn't) make perfect prediction impossible. These unknowns are not problems of bias or noise in your judgment; they are objective characteristics of the task. This objective ignorance of important unknowns severely limits achievable accuracy. We take a terminological liberty here, replacing the commonly used *uncertainty* with *ignorance.* This term helps limit the risk of confusion between uncertainty, which is about the world and the future, and noise, which is variability in judgments that should be identical.

There is more information (and less objective ignorance) in some situations than in others. Most professional judgments are pretty good. With respect to many illnesses, doctors' predictions are excellent, and for many legal disputes, lawyers can tell you, with great accuracy, how judges are likely to rule.

In general, however, you can safely expect that people who engage in predictive tasks will underestimate their objective ignorance. Overconfidence is one of the best-documented cognitive biases. In particular, judgments of one's ability to make precise predictions, even from limited information, are notoriously overconfident. What we said of noise in predictive judgments can also be said of objective ignorance: wherever there is prediction, there is ignorance, and more of it than you think.

Overconfident Pundits

A good friend of ours, the psychologist Philip Tetlock, is armed with a fierce commitment to truth and a mischievous sense of humor. In 2005, he published a book titled *Expert Political Judgment.* Despite that neutral-sounding title, the book amounted to a devastating attack on the ability of experts to make accurate predictions about political events.

Tetlock studied the predictions of almost three hundred experts: prominent journalists, respected academics, and high-level advisers to national leaders. He asked whether their political, economic, and social forecasts came true. The research spanned two decades; to find out whether long-term predictions are right, you need patience.

Tetlock's key finding was that in their predictions about major political events, the supposed experts are stunningly unimpressive. The book became famous for its arresting punch line: "The average expert was roughly as accurate as a dart-throwing chimpanzee." A more precise statement of the book's message was that experts who make a living "commenting or offering advice on political and economic trends" were not "better than journalists or attentive readers of the *New York Times* in 'reading' emerging situations." For sure, the experts told great stories. They could analyze a situation, paint a compelling picture of how it would evolve, and refute, with great confidence, the objections of those who disagreed with them in television studios. But did they actually know what would happen? Hardly.

Tetlock reached this conclusion by cutting through the storytelling. For each issue, he asked the experts to assign probabilities to three possible outcomes: status quo, more of something, or less of it. A dart-throwing chimp would "choose" each of these outcomes with the same probability—one-third—regardless of reality. Tetlock's experts barely exceeded this very low standard. On average, they assigned slightly higher probabilities to events that occurred than to those that did not, but the most salient feature of their performance was their excessive confidence in their predictions. Pundits blessed with clear theories about how the world works were the most confident and the least accurate.

Tetlock's findings suggest that detailed long-term predictions about specific events are simply impossible. The world is a messy place, where minor events can have large consequences. For example, consider the fact that at the instant of conception, there was an even chance that every significant figure in history (and also the insignificant ones) would be born with a different gender. Unforeseeable events are bound to occur, and the consequences of these unforeseeable events are also unforeseeable. As a result, objective ignorance accumulates steadily the further you look into the future. The limit on expert political judgment is set not by the cognitive limitation of forecasters but by their intractable objective ignorance of the future.

Our conclusion, then, is that pundits should not be blamed for the failures of their distant predictions. They do, however, deserve some criticism for attempting an impossible task and for believing they can succeed in it.

Some years after his shocking discovery of the futility of much long-term forecasting, Tetlock teamed up with his spouse, Barbara Mellers, to study how well people do when asked to forecast world events in the relatively short term — usually less than a year. The team discovered that short-term forecasting is difficult but not impossible, and that some people, whom Tetlock and Mellers called *superforecasters,* are consistently better at it than most others, including professionals in the intelligence community. In the terms we use here, their new findings are compatible with the notion that objective ignorance increases as we look further into the future. We return to superforecasters in chapter 21.

Poor Judges and Barely Better Models

Tetlock's early research demonstrated people's general inability to do well in long-term political forecasting. Finding even one person with a clear crystal ball would have changed the conclusions completely. A task can be deemed impossible only after many credible actors have tried their hand and failed. As we have shown that mechanical aggregation of information is often superior to human judgment, the predictive accuracy of rules and algorithms provides a better test of how intrinsically predictable, or unpredictable, outcomes are.

The previous chapters may have given you the impression that algorithms are crushingly superior to predictive judgments. That impression, however, would be misleading. Models are consistently better than people, but not much better. There is essentially no evidence of situations in which people do very poorly and models do very well with the same information.

In chapter 9, we mentioned a review of 136 studies that demonstrated the superiority of mechanical aggregation over clinical judgment. While the evidence of that superiority is indeed "massive and consistent," the performance gap is not large. Ninety-three of the studies in the review focused on binary decisions and measured the "hit rate" of clinicians and formulas. In the median study, clinicians were right 68% of the time, formulas 73% of the time. A smaller subset of 35 studies used the correlation coefficient as a measure of accuracy. In these studies, clinicians achieved a median correlation with the outcome of

.32 (PC = 60%), while formulas achieved .56 (PC = 69%). On both metrics, formulas are consistently better than clinicians, but the limited validity of the mechanical predictions remains striking. The performance of models does not change the picture of a fairly low ceiling of predictability.

What about artificial intelligence? As we noted, AI often performs better than simpler models do. In most applications, however, its performance remains far from perfect. Consider, for instance, the bail-prediction algorithm we discussed in chapter 10. We noted that, keeping constant the number of people who are denied bail, the algorithm could reduce crime rates by up to 24%. This is an impressive improvement on the predictions of human bail judges, but if the algorithm could predict with perfect accuracy which defendants will reoffend, it could reduce the crime rate much more. The supernatural predictions of future crimes in *Minority Report* are science fiction for a reason: there is a large amount of objective ignorance in the prediction of human behavior.

Another study, led by Sendhil Mullainathan and Ziad Obermeyer, modeled the diagnosis of heart attacks. When patients present signs of a possible heart attack, emergency room physicians must decide whether to prescribe additional tests. In principle, patients should be tested only when the risk of a heart attack is high enough: because testing is not just costly but also invasive and risky, it is undesirable for low-risk patients. Thus a physician's decision to prescribe tests requires an assessment of heart attack risk. The researchers built an AI model to make this assessment. The model uses more than twenty-four hundred variables and is based on a large sample of cases (4.4 million Medicare visits by 1.6 million patients). With this amount of data, the model probably approaches the limits of objective ignorance.

Not surprisingly, the AI model's accuracy is distinctly superior to that of physicians. To evaluate the performance of the model, consider the patients whom the model placed in the highest decile of risk. When these patients were tested, 30% of them turned out to have had a heart attack, whereas 9.3% of the patients in the middle of the risk distribution had experienced one. This level of discrimination is impressive, but it is also far from perfect. We can reasonably conclude that the performance of the physicians is limited at least as much by the constraints of objective ignorance as by the imperfections of their judgments.

The Denial of Ignorance

By insisting on the impossibility of perfect prediction, we might seem to be stating the obvious. Admittedly, asserting that the future is unpredictable is hardly a conceptual breakthrough. However, the obviousness of this fact is matched only by the regularity with which it is ignored, as the consistent findings about predictive overconfidence demonstrate.

The prevalence of overconfidence sheds new light on our informal poll of gut-trusting decision makers. We have noted that people often mistake their subjective sense of confidence for an indication of predictive validity. After you reviewed the evidence in chapter 9 about Nathalie and Monica, for instance, the internal signal you felt when you reached a coherent judgment gave you confidence that Nathalie was the stronger candidate. If you were confident in that prediction, however, you fell for the illusion of validity: the accuracy you can achieve with the information you were given is quite low.

People who believe themselves capable of an impossibly high level of predictive accuracy are not just overconfident. They don't merely deny the risk of noise and bias in their judgments. Nor do they simply deem themselves superior to other mortals. They also believe in the predictability of events that are in fact unpredictable, implicitly denying the reality of uncertainty. In the terms we have used here, this attitude amounts to a *denial of ignorance*.

The denial of ignorance adds an answer to the

puzzle that baffled Meehl and his followers: why his message has remained largely unheeded, and why decision makers continue to rely on their intuition. When they listen to their gut, decision makers hear the internal signal and feel the emotional reward it brings. This internal signal that a good judgment has been reached is the voice of confidence, of "knowing without knowing why." But an objective assessment of the evidence's true predictive power will rarely justify that level of confidence.

Giving up the emotional reward of intuitive certainty is not easy. Tellingly, leaders say they are especially likely to resort to intuitive decision making in situations that they perceive as highly uncertain. When the facts deny them the sense of understanding and confidence they crave, they turn to their intuition to provide it. The denial of ignorance is all the more tempting when ignorance is vast.

The denial of ignorance also explains another puzzle. When faced with the evidence we have presented here, many leaders draw a seemingly paradoxical conclusion. Their gut-based decisions may not be perfect, they argue, but if the more systematic alternatives are also far from perfect, they are not worth adopting. Recall, for instance, that the average correlation between the ratings of human judges and employee performance is .28 (PC = 59%). According to the same study, and consistent with the evidence we reviewed, mechanical prediction might do better, but not by much: its predictive accuracy is .44 (PC = 65%). An executive might ask: why bother?

The answer is that in something as important as decisions about whom to hire, this increase in validity has a great deal of value. The same executives routinely make significant changes in their ways of working to capture gains that are not nearly as large. Rationally, they understand that success can never be guaranteed and that a higher chance of success is what they are striving for in their decisions. They also understand probability. None of them would buy a lottery ticket that had a 59% chance of winning if they could buy, for the same price, one with a 65% chance.

The challenge is that the "price" in this situation is not the same. Intuitive judgment comes with its reward, the internal signal. People are prepared to trust an algorithm that achieves a very high level of accuracy because it gives them a sense of certainty that matches or exceeds that provided by the internal signal. But giving up the emotional reward of the internal signal is a high price to pay when the alternative is some sort of mechanical process that does not even claim high validity.

This observation has an important implication for the improvement of judgment. Despite all the evidence in favor of mechanical and algorithmic prediction methods, and despite the rational calculus that clearly shows the value of incremental improvements in predictive accuracy, many decision makers will reject decision-making approaches that deprive them of the ability to exercise their intuition. As long as algorithms are not nearly perfect—and, in many domains, objective ignorance dictates that they will never be—human judgment will not be replaced. That is why it must be improved.

Speaking of Objective Ignorance

"Wherever there is prediction, there is ignorance, and probably more of it than we think. Have we checked whether the experts we trust are more accurate than dart-throwing chimpanzees?"

"When you trust your gut because of an internal signal, not because of anything you really know, you are in denial of your objective ignorance."

"Models do better than people, but not by much. Mostly, we find mediocre human judgments and slightly better models. Still, better is good, and models are better."

"We may never be comfortable using a model to make these decisions—we just need the internal signal to have enough confidence. So let's make sure we have the best possible decision process."

CHAPTER 12

The Valley of the Normal

We now turn to a broader question: how do we achieve comfort in a world in which many problems are easy but many others are dominated by objective ignorance? After all, where objective ignorance is severe, we should, after a while, become aware of the futility of crystal balls in human affairs. But that is not our usual experience of the world. Instead, as the previous chapter suggested, we maintain an unchastened willingness to make bold predictions about the future from little useful information. In this chapter, we address the prevalent and misguided sense that events that could not have been predicted can nevertheless be understood.

What does this belief really mean? We raise that question in two contexts: the conduct of social science and the experience of the events of daily life.

Predicting Life Trajectories

In 2020, a group of 112 researchers, led by Sara McLanahan and Matthew Salganik, both professors of sociology at Princeton University, published an unusual article in the *Proceedings of the National Academy of Sciences.* The researchers aimed to figure out how much social scientists actually understand about what will happen in the life trajectories of socially fragile families. Knowing what they know, how well can social scientists predict events in a family's life? Specifically, what level of accuracy can experts achieve when predicting life events, using the information that sociologists normally collect and apply in their research? In our terms, the aim of the study was to measure the level of objective ignorance that remains in these life events after sociologists have done their work.

The authors drew material from the Fragile Families and Child Wellbeing Study, a large-scale longitudinal investigation of children who were followed from birth to fifteen years of age. The huge database contains several thousand items of information about the families of almost five thousand children, most of them born to unmarried parents in large US cities. The data covers topics such as the education and employment of the child's grandparents, details about the health of all family members, indices of economic and social status, answers to multiple questionnaires, and tests of cognitive aptitude and personality. This is an extraordinary wealth of information, and social scientists have made good use of it: more than 750 scientific articles have been written based on data from the Fragile Families study. Many of these papers used the background data about children and their families to explain life outcomes such as high school grades and criminal record.

The study led by the Princeton team focused on the predictability of six outcomes observed when the child was fifteen years old, including the occurrence of a recent eviction, the child's GPA, and a general measure of the household's material circumstances. The organizers used what they called the "common task method." They invited teams of researchers to compete in generating accurate predictions of the six chosen outcomes, using the mass of data available about each family in the Fragile Families study. This type of challenge is novel in the social sciences but common in computer science, where teams are often invited to compete in tasks such as machine translation of a standard set of texts or detection of an animal in a large set of photographs. The achievement of the winning team in these competitions defines the state of the art at a point in time, which is always exceeded in the next competition. In a social science prediction task, where rapid improvement is not expected, it is reasonable to use the most accurate prediction achieved in the competition as a measure of the predictability of the outcome from these data — in other words, the residual level of objective ignorance.

The challenge evoked considerable interest among researchers. The final report presented results from 160 highly qualified teams drawn from a much larger international pool of applicants. Most of the selected competitors described themselves as data scientists and used machine learning.

In the first stage of the competition, the participating teams had access to all the data for half of the total sample; the data included the six outcomes. They used this "training data" to train a predictive algorithm. Their algorithms were then applied to a hold-out sample of families that had not been used to train the algorithm. The researchers measured accuracy using MSE: the prediction error for each case was the square of the difference between the real outcome and the algorithm's prediction.

How good were the winning models? The sophisticated machine-learning algorithms trained on a large data set did, of course, outperform the predictions of simple linear models (and would, by extension, out-predict human judges). But the improvement the AI models delivered over a very simple model was slight, and their predictive accuracy remained disappointingly low. When predicting evictions, the best model achieved a correlation of .22 (PC = 57%). Similar results were found for other single-event outcomes, such as whether the primary caregiver had been laid off or had been in job training and how the child would score on a self-reported measure of "grit," a personality trait that combines perseverance and passion for a particular goal. For these, the correlations fell between .17 and .24 (PC = 55 – 58%).

Two of the six target outcomes were aggregates, which were much more predictable. The predictive correlations were .44 (PC = 65%) with the child's GPA, and .48 (PC = 66%) with a summary measure of material hardship during the preceding twelve months. This measure was based on eleven questions, including "Were you ever hungry?" and "Was your telephone service canceled?" Aggregate measures are widely known to be both more predictive and more predictable than are measures of single outcomes. The main conclusion of the challenge is that a large mass of predictive information does not suffice for the prediction of single events in people's lives—and even the prediction of aggregates is quite limited.

The results observed in this research are typical,

and many correlations that social scientists report fall in this range. An extensive review of research in social psychology, covering 25,000 studies and involving 8 million subjects over one hundred years, concluded that "social psychological effects typically yield a value of r [correlation coefficient] equal to .21." Much higher correlations, like the .60 we mentioned earlier between adult height and foot size, are common for physical measurements but are very rare in the social sciences. A review of 708 studies in the behavioral and cognitive sciences found that only 3% of reported correlations were .50 or more.

Such low correlation coefficients may come as a surprise if you are used to reading about findings that are presented as "statistically significant" or even "highly significant." Statistical terms are often misleading to the lay reader, and "significant" may be the worst example of this. When a finding is described as "significant," we should not conclude that the effect it describes is a strong one. It simply means that the finding is unlikely to be the product of chance alone. With a sufficiently large sample, a correlation can be at once very "significant" and too small to be worth discussing.

The limited predictability of single outcomes in the challenge study carries a troubling message about the difference between understanding and prediction.

The Fragile Families study is considered a treasure trove of social science, and as we have seen, its data has been used in a vast body of research. The scholars who produced that research surely felt that their work advanced the understanding of the lives of fragile families. Unfortunately, this sense of progress was not matched by an ability to make granular predictions about individual events in individual lives. The introductory abstract of the multiauthored report on the Fragile Families challenge contained a stark admonition: "Researchers must reconcile the idea that they understand life trajectories with the fact that none of the predictions were very accurate."

Understanding and Prediction

The logic behind this pessimistic conclusion requires some elaboration. When the authors of the Fragile Families challenge equate understanding with prediction (or the absence of one with the absence of the other), they use the term *understanding* in a specific sense. There are other meanings of the word: if you say you understand a mathematical concept or you understand what love is, you are probably not suggesting an ability to make any specific predictions.

However, in the discourse of social science, and in

most everyday conversations, a claim to understand something is a claim to understand what *causes* that thing. The sociologists who collected and studied the thousands of variables in the Fragile Families study were looking for the causes of the outcomes they observed. Physicians who understand what ails a patient are claiming that the pathology they have diagnosed is the cause of the symptoms they have observed. To understand is to describe a causal chain. The ability to make a prediction is a measure of whether such a causal chain has indeed been identified. And correlation, the measure of predictive accuracy, is a measure of how much causation we can explain.

This last statement may surprise you if you have been exposed to elementary statistics and remember the often-repeated warning that "correlation does not imply causation." Consider, for instance, the correlation between shoe size and mathematical ability in children: obviously, one variable does not cause the other. The correlation arises from the fact that both shoe size and math knowledge increase with a child's age. The correlation is real and supports a prediction: if you know that a child has large feet, you should predict a higher math level than you would if you know that the child has small feet. But you should not infer a causal link from this correlation.

We must, however, remember that while correlation does not imply causation, causation *does* imply correlation. Where there is a causal link, we should find a correlation. If you find no correlation between age and shoe size among adults, then you can safely conclude that after the end of adolescence, age does not make feet grow larger and that you have to look elsewhere for the causes of differences in shoe size.

In short, wherever there is causality, there is correlation. It follows that where there is causality, we should be able to predict — and correlation, the accuracy of this prediction, is a measure of how much causality we understand. Hence the conclusion of the Princeton researchers is this: the extent to which sociologists can predict events like evictions, as measured by a correlation of .22, is an indication of how much — or how little — they understand about the life trajectories of these families. Objective ignorance sets a ceiling not only on our predictions but also on our understanding.

What, then, do most professionals mean when they confidently claim to understand their field? How can they make pronouncements about what causes the phenomena they are observing and offer confident predictions about them? In short, why do professionals — and why do we all — seem to underestimate our objective ignorance of the world?

Causal Thinking

If, as you read the first part of this chapter, you asked yourself what drives evictions and other life outcomes among fragile families, you engaged in the same sort of thinking as that of the researchers whose efforts we described. You applied *statistical thinking:* you were concerned with ensembles, such as the population of fragile families, and with the statistics that describe them, including averages, variances, correlations, and so on. You were not focused on individual cases.

A different mode of thinking, which comes more naturally to our minds, will be called here *causal thinking.* Causal thinking creates stories in which specific events, people, and objects affect one another. To experience causal thinking, picture yourself as a social worker who follows the cases of many underprivileged families. You have just heard that one of these families, the Joneses, has been evicted. Your reaction to this event is informed by what you know about the Joneses. As it happens, Jessica Jones, the family's breadwinner, was laid off a few months ago. She could not find another job, and since then, she has been unable to pay the rent in full. She made partial payments, pleaded with the building manager several times, and even asked you to intervene (you did, but he remained unmoved). Given this context, the

Joneses' eviction is sad but not surprising. It feels, in fact, like the logical end of a chain of events, the inevitable denouement of a foreordained tragedy.

When we give in to this feeling of inevitability, we lose sight of how easily things could have been different—how, at each fork in the road, fate could have taken a different path. Jessica could have kept her job. She could have quickly found another one. A relative could have come to her aid. You, the social worker, could have been a more effective advocate. The building manager could have been more understanding and allowed the family a few weeks of respite, making it possible for Jessica to find a job and catch up with the rent.

These alternate narratives are as unsurprising as the main one—if the end is known. Whatever the outcome (eviction or not), once it has happened, causal thinking makes it feel entirely explainable, indeed predictable.

Understanding in the Valley of the Normal

There is a psychological explanation for this observation. Some events are surprising: a deadly pandemic, an attack on the Twin Towers, a star hedge fund that turns out to be a Ponzi scheme. In our personal lives as well, there are occasional shocks: falling in love with a stranger, the sudden death of a young sibling, an unexpected inheritance. Other events are actively expected, like a second-grader's return from school at the appointed time.

But most human experience falls between these two extremes. We are sometimes in a state in which we actively expect a specific event, and we are sometimes surprised. But most things take place in the broad valley of the normal, where events are neither entirely expected nor especially surprising. At this moment, for example, you have no specific expectation of what is coming in the next paragraph. You would be surprised to find we suddenly switched to Turkish, but there is a wide range of things we could say without shocking you.

In the valley of the normal, events unfold just like the Joneses' eviction: they appear normal in hindsight, although they were not expected, and although we could not have predicted them. This is because the process of understanding reality is backward-looking. An occurrence that was not actively anticipated (the eviction of the Jones family) triggers a search of memory for a candidate cause (the tough job market, the inflexible manager). The search stops when a good narrative is found. Given the opposite outcome, the search would have produced equally compelling causes (Jessica Jones's tenacity, the understanding manager).

As these examples illustrate, many events in a normal story are literally self-explanatory. You may have noted that the building manager in the two versions of the eviction story was not really the same person: the first one was unsympathetic, the second was kind. But your only clue to the manager's character was the behavior that his character exhibits. Given what we now know about him, his behavior appears coherent. It is the occurrence of the event that tells you its cause.

When you explain an unexpected but unsurprising outcome in this way, the destination that is eventually reached always makes sense. This is what we mean by *understanding* a story, and this is what makes reality appear predictable — in hindsight. Because the event explains itself as it occurs, we are under the illusion that it could have been anticipated.

More broadly, our sense of understanding the world depends on our extraordinary ability to construct narratives that explain the events we observe. The search for causes is almost always successful because causes can be drawn from an unlimited reservoir of facts and beliefs about the world. As anyone who listens to the evening news knows, for example, few large movements of the stock market remain unexplained. The same news flow can "explain" either a fall of the indices (nervous investors are worried about the news!) or a rise (sanguine investors remain optimistic!).

When the search for an obvious cause fails, our first resort is to produce an explanation by filling a blank in our model of the world. This is how we infer a fact we had not known before (for instance, that the manager was an unusually kind person). Only when our model of the world cannot be tweaked to generate the outcome do we tag this outcome as surprising and start to search for a more elaborate account of it. Genuine surprise occurs only when routine hindsight fails.

This continuous causal interpretation of reality is how we "understand" the world. Our sense of understanding life as it unfolds consists of the steady flow of hindsight in the valley of the normal. This sense is fundamentally causal: new events, once known, eliminate alternatives, and the narrative leaves little room for uncertainty. As we know from classic research on hindsight, even when subjective uncertainty does exist for a while, memories of it are largely erased when the uncertainty is resolved.

Inside and Outside

We have contrasted two ways of thinking about events: statistical and causal. The causal mode saves us much effortful thinking by categorizing events in real time as normal or abnormal. Abnormal events quickly mobilize costly effort in a search for relevant information, both in the environment and in memory. Active expectation—attentively waiting for something to happen—also demands effort. In contrast, the flow of events in the valley of the normal requires little mental work. Your neighbor may smile as your paths cross or may appear preoccupied and just nod—neither of these events will attract much attention if both have been reasonably frequent in the past. If the smile is unusually wide or the nod unusually perfunctory, you may well find yourself searching your memory for a possible cause. Causal thinking avoids unnecessary effort while retaining the vigilance needed to detect abnormal events.

In contrast, statistical thinking is effortful. It requires the attention resources that only System 2, the mode of thinking associated with slow, deliberate thought, can bring to bear. Beyond an elementary level, statistical thinking also demands specialized training. This type of thinking begins with ensembles and considers individual cases as instances of broader categories. The eviction of the Joneses is not seen as resulting from a chain of specific events but is viewed as a statistically likely (or unlikely) outcome, given prior observations of cases that share predictive characteristics with the Joneses.

The distinction between these two views is a recurring theme of this book. Relying on causal thinking about a single case is a source of predictable errors. Taking the statistical view, which we will also call the *outside view*, is a way to avoid these errors.

At this point, all we need to emphasize is that the causal mode comes much more naturally to us. Even explanations that should properly be treated as statistical are easily turned into causal narratives. Consider assertions such as "they failed because they lacked experience" or "they succeeded because they had a brilliant leader." It would be easy for you to think of counterexamples, in which inexperienced teams succeeded and brilliant leaders failed. The correlations of experience and brilliance with success are at best moderate and probably low. Yet a causal attribution is readily made. Where causality is plausible, our mind easily turns a correlation, however low, into a causal and explanatory force. Brilliant leadership is accepted as a satisfactory explanation of success, and inexperience as an explanation of failure.

The reliance on flawed explanations is perhaps inevitable, if the alternative is to give up on understanding our world. However, causal thinking and the illusion of understanding the past contribute to overconfident predictions of the future. As we will see, the preference for causal thinking also contributes to the neglect of noise as a source of error, because noise is a fundamentally statistical notion.

Causal thinking helps us make sense of a world that is far less predictable than we think. It also explains why we view the world as far more predictable than it really is. In the valley of the normal, there are no surprises and no inconsistencies. The future seems as predictable as the past. And noise is neither heard nor seen.

Speaking of the Limits of Understanding

"Correlations of about .20 (PC = 56%) are quite common in human affairs."

"Correlation does not imply causation, but causation does imply correlation."

"Most normal events are neither expected nor surprising, and they require no explanation."

"In the valley of the normal, events are neither expected nor surprising — they just explain themselves."

"We think we understand what is going on here, but could we have predicted it?"

PART IV

How Noise Happens

W hat is the origin of noise—and of bias? What mental mechanisms give rise to the variability of our judgments and to the shared errors that affect them? In short, what do we know about the psychology of noise? These are the questions to which we now turn.

First, we describe how some of the operations of fast, *System 1* thinking are responsible for many judgment errors. In chapter 13, we present three important judgment heuristics on which System 1 extensively relies. We show how these heuristics cause predictable, directional errors (statistical bias) as well as noise.

Chapter 14 focuses on matching—a particular operation of System 1—and discusses the errors it can produce.

In chapter 15, we turn to an indispensable accessory in all judgments: the scale on which the judgments are made. We show that the choice of an appropriate scale is a prerequisite for good judgment and that ill-defined or inadequate scales are an important source of noise.

Chapter 16 explores the psychological source of what may be the most intriguing type of noise: the patterns of responses that different people have to different cases. Like individual personalities, these patterns are not random and are mostly stable over time, but their effects are not easily predictable.

Finally, in chapter 17, we summarize what we have learned about noise and its components. This exploration leads us to propose an answer to the puzzle we raised earlier: why is noise, despite its ubiquity, rarely considered an important problem?

CHAPTER 13

Heuristics, Biases, and Noise

This book extends half a century of research on intuitive human judgment, the so-called heuristics and biases program. The first four decades of this research program were reviewed in *Thinking, Fast and Slow,* which explored the psychological mechanisms that explain both the marvels and the flaws of intuitive thinking. The central idea of the program was that people who are asked a difficult question use simplifying operations, called *heuristics.* In general, heuristics, which are produced by fast, intuitive thinking, also known as *System 1 thinking,* are quite useful and yield adequate answers. But sometimes they lead to biases, which we have described as systematic, predictable errors of judgment.

The heuristics and biases program focused on what

people have in common, not on how they differ. It showed that the processes that cause judgment errors are widely shared. Partly because of this history, people who are familiar with the notion of psychological bias often assume that it always produces *statistical bias,* a term we use in this book to mean measurements or judgments that mostly deviate from the truth in the same direction. Indeed, psychological biases create statistical bias when they are broadly shared. However, psychological biases create system noise when judges are biased in different ways, or to a different extent. Whether they cause statistical bias or noise, of course, psychological biases always create error.

Diagnosing Biases

Judgment biases are often identified by reference to a true value. There is bias in predictive judgments if errors are mostly in one direction rather than the other. For instance, when people forecast how long it will take them to complete a project, the mean of their estimates is usually much lower than the time they will actually need. This familiar psychological bias is known as the *planning fallacy.*

Often, though, there is no true value to which judgments can be compared. Given how much we stressed that statistical bias can be detected only when the true value is known, you may wonder how psychological biases can be studied when the truth is unknown. The answer is that researchers confirm a psychological bias either by observing that a factor that should not affect judgment does have a statistical effect on it, or that a factor that should affect judgment does not.

To illustrate this method, let us return to the shooting range analogy. Imagine that Teams A and B have taken their shots, and we are looking at the back of the target (figure 12). In this example, you don't know where the bull's-eye is (the true value is unknown). Therefore, you don't know how biased the two teams are relative to the center of the target. However, you are told that, in panel 1, the two teams were aiming at the same bull's-eye, and that, in panel 2, Team A was aiming at one bull's-eye and Team B at a different one.

In spite of the absence of a target, both panels

Panel 1
Aiming at *the same* bull's-eye,
but hitting different spots

Panel 2
Aiming at *different* bull's-eyes,
but hitting the same area

FIGURE 12: *A look at the back of the target in an experiment to test for bias*

provide evidence of systematic bias. In panel 1, the shots of the two teams differ, although they should be identical. This pattern resembles what you would see in an experiment in which two groups of investors read business plans that are substantively identical but printed in a different font and on a different paper. If these irrelevant details make a difference in the investors' judgment, there is psychological bias. We don't know if the investors who were impressed by the sleek font and glossy paper are too positive or if those who read the rougher version are too negative. But we know their judgments are different, although they should not be.

Panel 2 illustrates the opposite phenomenon. Since the teams were aiming at different targets, the clusters of shots should be distinct, but they are centered on the same spot. For example, imagine that two groups of people are asked the same question you were asked in chapter 4 about Michael Gambardi, but with a twist. One group is asked, as you were, to estimate the probability that Gambardi will still be in his job in two years; the other is asked to estimate the probability that he will still be in his job in three years. The two groups should reach different conclusions, because there are obviously more ways to lose your job in three years than in two. However, the evidence suggests that the probability estimates of the two groups will differ little, if at all. The answers should be clearly different, but they are not, suggesting that a factor that should influence judgments is ignored. (This psychological bias is called *scope insensitivity*.)

Systematic errors of judgment have been demonstrated in many fields, and the term *bias* is now used in many domains, including business, politics, policy-making, and law. As the word is commonly used, its meaning is broad. In addition to the cognitive definition we use here (referring to a psychological mechanism and to the error that this mechanism typically produces), the word is frequently used to suggest that someone is biased against a certain group (e.g., gender biases or racial biases). It can also mean that someone favors a particular conclusion, as when we read that someone is biased by a conflict of interest or by a political opinion. We include these types of bias in our discussion of the psychology of judgment errors because all psychological biases cause both statistical bias and noise.

There is one usage to which we strongly object. In this usage, costly failures are attributed to unspecified "bias," and acknowledgments of error are accompanied by promises to "work hard to eliminate biases in our decision making." These statements mean nothing more than "mistakes were made" and "we will try hard to do better." To be sure, some failures truly are caused by predictable errors associated with specific psychological biases, and we believe in the feasibility of interventions to reduce bias (and noise) in judgments and decisions. But blaming every undesirable outcome on biases is a worthless explanation. We recommend reserving the word *bias* for specific and identifiable errors and the mechanisms that produce them.

Substitution

To experience the heuristic process, please try your hand at answering the following question, which illustrates several essential themes of the heuristics and biases approach. As usual, you will get more from the example if you produce your own answers.

> *Bill is thirty-three years old. He is intelligent but unimaginative, compulsive, and generally lifeless. In school, he was strong in mathematics but weak in social studies and humanities.*
>
> *The following is a list of eight possibilities for Bill's current situation.*
>
> *Please go over the list and select the two that you consider* most probable.

- ❑ *Bill is a physician who plays poker as a hobby.*
- ❑ *Bill is an architect.*
- ❑ *Bill is an accountant.*

❑ *Bill plays jazz as a hobby.*
❑ *Bill surfs as a hobby.*
❑ *Bill is a reporter.*
❑ *Bill is an accountant who plays jazz as a hobby.*
❑ *Bill climbs mountains as a hobby.*
Now, go back over the list and select the two categories where Bill most resembles *a typical person in that category. You may pick the same or different categories as before.*

We are almost certain that you picked the same categories as highest in probability and in resemblance. The reason for our confidence is that multiple experiments have shown that people give identical answers to the two questions. But similarity and probability are actually quite different. For example, ask yourself, which of the following statements makes more sense?

❑ *Bill fits my idea of a person who plays jazz as a hobby.*
❑ *Bill fits my idea of an accountant who plays jazz as a hobby.*

Neither of these statements is a good fit, but one of them is clearly less awful than the other. Bill has more in common with an accountant who plays jazz as a hobby than with a person who plays jazz as a hobby.

Now consider this: which of the following is more probable?

❑ *Bill plays jazz as a hobby.*
❑ *Bill is an accountant who plays jazz as a hobby.*

You may be tempted to pick the second answer, but logic won't allow it. The probability that Bill plays jazz as a hobby *must be* higher than the probability of his being a jazz-playing accountant. Remember your Venn diagrams! If Bill is a jazz player and an accountant, he is certainly a jazz player. Adding detail to a description can only make it less probable, although it can make it more representative, and thus a better "fit," as in the present case.

The theory of judgment heuristics proposes that people will sometimes use the answer to an easier question in responding to the harder one. So, which question is more easily answered: "How similar is Bill to a typical amateur jazz player?" or "How probable is it that Bill is an amateur jazz player?" By acclamation, the similarity question is easier, which makes it likely that it was the one that people answer when asked to assess probability.

You have now experienced the essential idea of the heuristics and biases program: a heuristic for answering a difficult question is to find the answer to an easier one. The substitution of one question for the other causes predictable errors, called psychological biases.

This sort of bias is manifest in the Bill example. Errors are bound to occur when a judgment of similarity is substituted for a judgment of probability, because probability is constrained by a special logic. In particular, Venn diagrams apply only to probability, not to similarity. Hence the predictable logical error that many people make.

For another example of a neglected statistical property, recall how you thought about the Gambardi question in chapter 4. If you are like most people, your assessment of Michael Gambardi's chances of success was based entirely on what the case told you about him. You then attempted to match his description to the image of a successful CEO.

Did it occur to you to consider the probability that a randomly chosen CEO will still hold the same job two years later? Probably not. You can think of this *base-rate information* as a measure of the difficulty of surviving as a CEO. If this approach seems odd, consider how you would estimate the probability that a particular student would pass a test. Surely, the proportion of students who fail the test is relevant, as it gives you an indication of how difficult the test is. In the same manner, the base rate of CEO survival is relevant to the Gambardi problem. Both questions are examples of taking what we have called the outside view: when you take this view, you think of the student, or of Gambardi, as a member of a class of similar cases. You think statistically about the class, instead of thinking causally about the focal case.

Taking the outside view can make a large difference and prevent significant errors. A few minutes of research would reveal that estimates of CEO turnover in US companies hover around 15% annually. This statistic suggests that the average incoming CEO has a roughly 72% probability of still being around after two years. Of course, this number is only a starting point, and the specifics of Gambardi's case will affect your final estimate. But if you focused solely on what you were told about Gambardi, you neglected a key piece of information. (Full disclosure: We wrote the Gambardi case to illustrate noisy judgment; it took us weeks before we realized that it was also a prime example of the bias we describe here, which is called *base-rate neglect*. Thinking of base rates is no more automatic for the authors of this book than for anyone else.)

Substitution of one question for another is not restricted to similarity and probability. Another example is the replacement of a judgment of frequency by an impression of the ease with which instances come to mind. For example, the perception of the risk of airplane crashes or hurricanes rises briefly after well-publicized instances of such events. In theory, a judgment of risk should be based on a long-term average. In reality, recent incidents are given more weight because they come more easily to mind. Substituting a judgment of how easily examples come to mind for an assessment of frequency is known as the *availability heuristic.*

The substitution of an easy judgment for a hard one is not limited to these examples. In fact, it is very common. Answering an easier question can be thought of as a general-purpose procedure for answering a question that could stump you. Consider how we tend to answer each of the following questions by using its easier substitute:

Do I believe in climate change?
  Do I trust the people who say it exists?

Do I think this surgeon is competent?
  Does this individual speak with confidence and
    authority?

Will the project be completed on schedule?
  Is it on schedule now?

Is nuclear energy necessary?
  Do I recoil at the word **nuclear**?

Am I satisfied with my life as a whole?
  What is my mood right now?

Regardless of the question, substituting one question for another will lead to an answer that does not give different aspects of the evidence their appropriate weights, and incorrect weighting of the evidence inevitably results in error. For example, a full answer to a question about life satisfaction clearly requires consulting more than your current mood, but evidence suggests that mood is in fact overly weighted.

In the same manner, substituting similarity for probability leads to neglect of base rates, which are quite properly irrelevant when judging similarity. And factors such as irrelevant variations in the aesthetics of the document that presents a business plan should be given little or no weight in assessing the value of a company. Any impact they have on the judgment is likely to reflect a misweighting of the evidence and will produce error.

Conclusion Biases

At a key moment in the development of the screenplay for *Return of the Jedi,* the third Star Wars film, George Lucas, the mastermind behind the series, had a heated debate with his great collaborator Lawrence Kasdan. Kasdan strongly advised Lucas, "I think you should kill Luke and have Leia take over." Lucas promptly rejected the idea. Kasdan suggested that if Luke lived, another major character should die. Lucas again disagreed, adding, "You don't go around killing people." Kasdan responded with a heartfelt claim about the nature of cinema. He explained to Lucas that "the movie has more emotional weight if someone you love is lost along the way; the journey has more impact."

Lucas's response was quick and unequivocal: "I don't like that and I don't believe that."

The thought process here looks quite different from the one you experienced when you thought about Bill, the jazz-playing accountant. Read Lucas's answer again: "Not liking" precedes "Not believing." Lucas had an automatic response to Kasdan's suggestion. That response helped motivate his judgment (even if it turned out to be right).

This example illustrates a different type of bias, which we call *conclusion bias,* or *prejudgment.* Like Lucas, we often start the process of judgment with an inclination to reach a particular conclusion. When we do that, we let our fast, intuitive System 1 thinking suggest a conclusion. Either we jump to that conclusion and simply bypass the process of gathering and integrating information, or we mobilize System 2 thinking — engaging in deliberate thought — to come up with arguments that support our prejudgment. In that case, the evidence will be selective and distorted: because of *confirmation bias* and *desirability bias*, we will tend to collect and interpret evidence selectively to favor a judgment that, respectively, we already believe or wish to be true.

People often come up with plausible rationalizations for their judgments and will actually think that they are the cause of their beliefs. A good test of the role of prejudgment is to imagine that the arguments seemingly supporting our belief are suddenly proven invalid. Kasdan, for instance, might well have pointed out to Lucas that "You don't go around killing people" is hardly a compelling argument. The author of *Romeo and Juliet* would not have agreed with Lucas, and if the writers of *The Sopranos* and *Game of Thrones* had decided against killings, both shows would probably have been canceled in their first season. But we can bet that a strong counterargument wouldn't have changed Lucas's mind. Instead, he would have come up with other arguments to support his judgment. (For example, "Star Wars is different.")

Prejudgments are evident wherever we look. Like Lucas's reaction, they often have an emotional component. The psychologist Paul Slovic terms this the *affect heuristic:* people determine what they think by consulting their feelings. We like most things about politicians we favor, and we dislike even the looks and the voices of politicians we dislike. That is one reason that smart companies work so hard to attach a positive affect to their brand. Professors often notice that in a year when they get high marks for teaching, students also give the course material a high rating. In a year when students don't like the professor so much, they give a low rating to the identical assigned readings. The same mechanism is at work even when emotion is not involved: regardless of the true reasons for your belief, you will be inclined to accept any argument that appears to support it, even when the reasoning is wrong.

A subtler example of a conclusion bias is the *anchoring effect*, which is the effect that an arbitrary number has on people who must make a quantitative judgment. In a typical demonstration, you might be presented with a number of items whose price is not easy to guess, such as an unfamiliar bottle of wine. You are asked to jot down the last two digits of your Social Security number and indicate whether you would pay that amount for the bottle. Finally, you are asked to state the maximum amount you would be willing to pay for it. The results show that anchoring on your Social Security number will affect your final buying price. In one study, people whose Social Security numbers generated a high anchor (more than eighty dollars) stated that they were willing to pay about three times more than those with a low anchor (less than twenty dollars).

Clearly, your Social Security number should not have a large effect on your judgment about how much a bottle of wine is worth, but it does. Anchoring is an extremely robust effect and is often deliberately used in negotiations. Whether you're haggling in a bazaar or sitting down for a complex business transaction, you probably have an advantage in going first, because the recipient of the anchor is involuntarily drawn to think of ways your offer could be reasonable. People always attempt to make sense of what they hear; when they encounter an implausible number, they automatically bring to mind considerations that would reduce its implausibility.

Excessive Coherence

Here is another experiment that will help you experience a third type of bias. You will read a description of a candidate for an executive position. The description consists of four adjectives, each written on a card. The deck of cards has just been shuffled. The first two cards have these two descriptors:

Intelligent, Persistent.

It would be reasonable to suspend judgment until the information is complete, but this is not what has happened: you already have an evaluation of the candidate, and it is positive. This judgment simply happened. You had no control over the process, and suspending judgment was not an option.

Next, you draw the last two cards. Here is the full description now:

Intelligent, Persistent, Cunning, Unprincipled.

Your evaluation is no longer favorable, but it did not change enough. For comparison, consider the following description, which another shuffling of the deck could have produced:

Unprincipled, Cunning, Persistent, Intelligent.

This second description consists of the same adjectives, and yet — because of the order in which they are introduced — it is clearly much less appealing than the first. The word *Cunning* was only mildly negative when it followed *Intelligent* and *Persistent,* because we still believed (without reason) that the executive's intentions were good. Yet when it follows *Unprincipled,* the word *Cunning* is awful. In this context, persistence and intelligence are not positives anymore: they make a bad person even more dangerous.

This experiment illustrates *excessive coherence:* we

form coherent impressions quickly and are slow to change them. In this example, we immediately developed a positive attitude toward the candidate, in light of little evidence. Confirmation bias—the same tendency that leads us, when we have a prejudgment, to disregard conflicting evidence altogether—made us assign less importance than we should to subsequent data. (Another term to describe this phenomenon is the *halo effect,* because the candidate was evaluated in the positive "halo" of the first impression. We will see in chapter 24 that the halo effect is a serious problem in hiring decisions.)

Here is another example. In the United States, public officials have required chain restaurants to include calorie labels to ensure that consumers see the calories associated with, for example, cheeseburgers, hamburgers, and salads. After seeing those labels, do consumers change their choices? The evidence is disputed and mixed. But in a revealing study, consumers were found to be more likely to be affected by calorie labels if they were placed to the left of the food item rather than the right. When calories are on the left, consumers receive that information first and evidently think "a lot of calories!" or "not so many calories!" before they see the item. Their initial positive or negative reaction greatly affects their choices. By contrast, when people see the food item first, they apparently think "delicious!" or "not so great!" before they see the calorie label. Here again, their initial reaction greatly affects their choices. This hypothesis is supported by the authors' finding that for Hebrew speakers, who read right to left, the calorie label has a significantly larger impact if it is on the right rather than the left.

In general, we jump to conclusions, then stick to them. We think we base our opinions on evidence, but the evidence we consider and our interpretation of it are likely to be distorted, at least to some extent, to fit our initial snap judgment. As a result, we maintain the coherence of the overall story that has emerged in our mind. This process is fine, of course, if the conclusions are correct. When the initial evaluation is erroneous, however, the tendency to stick to it in the face of contradictory evidence is likely to amplify errors. And this effect is difficult to control, because information that we have heard or seen is impossible to ignore and often difficult to forget. In court, judges sometimes instruct jurors to disregard an inadmissible piece of evidence they have heard, but this is not a realistic instruction (although it may be helpful in jury deliberation, where arguments explicitly based on this evidence can be rejected).

Psychological Biases Cause Noise

We have briefly presented three types of biases that operate in different ways: substitution biases, which lead to a misweighting of the evidence; conclusion biases, which lead us either to bypass the evidence or to consider it in a distorted way; and excessive coherence, which magnifies the effect of initial impressions and reduces the impact of contradictory information. All three types of biases can, of course, produce statistical bias. They can also produce noise.

Let's start with substitution. Most people judge the probability that Bill is an accountant by the similarity of his profile to a stereotype: the result, in this experiment, is a shared bias. If every respondent makes the same mistake, there is no noise. But substitution does not always produce such unanimity. When the question "Is there climate change?" is replaced with "Do I trust the people who say it is real?," it is easy to see that the answer will vary from one person to the next, depending on that person's social circles, preferred sources of information, political affiliation, and so on. The same psychological bias creates variable judgments and between-person noise.

Substitution can also be a source of occasion noise. If a question on life satisfaction is answered by consulting one's immediate mood, the answer will inevitably vary for the same person from one moment to the next. A happy morning can be followed by a distressing afternoon, and changing moods over time can lead to very different reports of life satisfaction depending on when the interviewer happens to call. In chapter 7, we reviewed examples of occasion noise that can be traced to psychological biases.

Prejudgments also produce both bias and noise. Return to an example we mentioned in the introduction: the shocking disparities in the percentage of asylum seekers that judges admit. When one judge admits 5% of applicants and another in the same courthouse admits 88%, we can be quite certain that they are biased in different directions. From a broader perspective, individual differences in biases can cause massive system noise. Of course, the system can also be biased to the extent that most or all judges are biased similarly.

Finally, excessive coherence can produce either bias or noise, depending on whether the sequence of information and the meaning assigned to it are identical for all (or most) judges. Consider, for instance, a physically attractive candidate whose good looks create an early positive impression in most recruiters. If physical appearance is irrelevant to the position for which the candidate is considered, this positive halo will result in a shared error: a bias.

On the other hand, many complex decisions require compiling information that arrives in an essentially random order. Consider the claims adjusters of chapter 2. The order in which data about a claim becomes available varies haphazardly from one adjuster to the next and from one case to the next, causing random variation in initial impressions. Excessive coherence means that these random variations will produce random distortions in the final judgments. The effect will be system noise.

———

In short, psychological biases, as a mechanism, are universal, and they often produce shared errors. But when there are large individual differences in biases (different prejudgments) or when the effect of biases depends on context (different triggers), there will be noise.

Both bias and noise create error, which suggests that anything that reduces psychological biases will improve judgment. We will return to the topic of debiasing, or removing bias, in part 5. But for now, we continue our exploration of the process of judgment.

Speaking of Heuristics, Biases, and Noise

"We know we have psychological biases, but we should resist the urge to blame every error on unspecified 'biases.'"

"When we substitute an easier question for the one we should be answering, errors are bound to occur.

For instance, we will ignore the base rate when we judge probability by similarity."

"Prejudgments and other conclusion biases lead people to distort evidence in favor of their initial position."

"We form impressions quickly and hold on to them even when contradictory information comes in. This tendency is called excessive coherence."

"Psychological biases cause statistical bias if many people share the same biases. In many cases, however, people differ in their biases. In those cases, psychological biases create system noise."

CHAPTER 14

The Matching Operation

Look at the sky. How likely is it to rain in two hours?

You probably had no difficulty answering this question. The judgment you made — for example, that it is "very likely" to rain soon — was produced effortlessly. Somehow, your evaluation of the sky's darkness was converted into a probability judgment.

What you just performed is an elementary example of *matching*. We have described judgment as an operation that assigns a value on a scale to a subjective impression (or to an aspect of an impression). Matching is an essential part of that operation. When you answer the question "On a scale of 1 to 10, how good is your mood?" or "Please give one to five stars to your shopping experience this morning," you are matching: your task is to find a value on the judgment scale that matches your mood or experience.

Matching and Coherence

You met Bill in the previous chapter, and here he is again: "Bill is thirty-three years old. He is intelligent but unimaginative, compulsive and generally lifeless. In school, he was strong in mathematics but weak in social studies and humanities." We asked you to estimate the probability that Bill had various occupations and hobbies, and we saw that you answered this question by substituting a judgment of similarity for one of probability. You did not really ask how likely Bill was to be an accountant, but how similar he was to the stereotype of that profession. We now turn to a question we left unanswered: how you made that judgment.

It is not difficult to assess the degree to which Bill's description matches the stereotypes of professions and hobbies. Bill is clearly less similar to a typical jazz player than to an accountant, and he is even less similar to a surfer. The example illustrates the extraordinary versatility of matching, which is particularly obvious in judgments about people. There is hardly a limit to the questions you could have answered about Bill. For example, how would you feel about being stranded on a desert island with him? You probably had an immediate intuitive answer to this question on the basis of the scant information provided. Yet, we have news for you: Bill, as we know him, happens to be a hardened explorer with extraordinary survival skills. If this surprises you (and it probably does), you just experienced a failure to achieve coherence.

The surprise is intense because the new information is incompatible with the image of Bill that you had constructed earlier. Now imagine that Bill's prowess and survival skills had been included in the original description. You would have ended up with a different overall image of the man, perhaps as a person who comes alive only in the great outdoors. The overall impression of Bill would have been less coherent, and therefore more difficult to match to categories of professions or hobbies, but you would have experienced far less dissonance than you just did.

Conflicting cues make it more difficult to achieve a sense of coherence and to find a judgment that is a satisfactory match. The presence of conflicting cues characterizes complex judgments, in which we expect to find a lot of noise. The Gambardi problem, where some of the indications were positive and others negative, was such a judgment. We return to complex judgments in chapter 16. In the remainder of this chapter we focus on relatively simple judgments—especially those made on *intensity scales*.

Matching Intensities

Some of the scales on which we express judgments are qualitative: professions, hobbies, and medical diagnoses are examples. They are identified by the fact that the values of the scale are not ordered: red is neither more nor less than blue.

Many judgments, however, are made on quantitative intensity scales. Physical measurements of size, weight, brightness, temperature, or loudness; measures of cost or value; judgments of probability or frequency—all these are quantitative. So are judgments on more abstract scales, like confidence, strength, attractiveness, anger, fear, immorality, or the severity of punishments.

The distinctive feature shared by these quantitative dimensions is that the question "Which is more?" can be answered about any pair of values on the same dimension. You can tell that a flogging is a more severe punishment than a slap on the wrist or that you like *Hamlet* more than you liked *Waiting for Godot,* just as you can tell that the sun is brighter than the moon, that an elephant weighs more than a hamster, and that the average temperature in Miami is higher than in Toronto.

People have a remarkable intuitive ability to match intensities across unrelated dimensions, by mapping one intensity scale onto another. You can match the intensity of your affection for different singers to the height of buildings in your city. (If you think that Bob Dylan is especially great, for example, you might match your level of enthusiasm for him to the tallest building in your city.) You could match the current level of political discord in your country to a summer temperature in a city you know well. (If there is remarkable political harmony, you might match it to a breezy seventy-degree summer day in New York.) And if you were asked to express your appreciation of a restaurant by comparing it to the length of a novel instead of the usual 1-to-5-star rating scale, this request would strike you as quite bizarre but not at all infeasible. (Your favorite restaurant might be like *War and Peace*.) In each case, it is — oddly — quite clear what you mean.

In ordinary conversation, the range of values for a scale is a function of the context. The comment "She has been saving a lot of money" has a different meaning when you are toasting the retirement of a successful investment banker than it has when you are congratulating a teenager who has been babysitting. And the meaning of words like *large* and *small* depends entirely on a frame of reference. We can, for example, make sense of a statement like "The large mouse ran up the trunk of the small elephant."

The Bias of Matching Predictions

The following puzzle illustrates both the power of matching and a systematic judgment error that is associated with it.

Julie is a graduating student at a university. Read the following piece of information about her, then guess her GPA (on the standard scale of 0.0 to 4.0):

Julie read fluently when she was four years old.

What is her GPA?

If you are familiar with the grade point average system in the United States, a number came to your mind quite quickly, and it was probably close to 3.7 or 3.8. How a guess about Julie's GPA instantly came to your mind illustrates the matching process we just described.

First, you evaluated how precocious a reader Julie was. The evaluation was easy because Julie read unusually early, and that precociousness placed Julie in a category on some scale. If you had to describe the scale you used, you would probably say its highest category is something like "extraordinarily precocious," and you would note that Julie does not quite belong in that category (some children read before they are two). Julie probably belongs in the next one, the band of "unusually but not extraordinarily precocious" children.

In the second step, you matched a judgment of GPA to your evaluation of Julie. Although you were unaware of doing so, you must have been looking for a value of GPA that would also fit the label "unusual but not extraordinary." A *matching prediction* came to your mind, seemingly out of nowhere, when you heard Julie's story.

Deliberately carrying out the calculations required to perform these tasks of evaluation and matching would take quite a while, but in fast, System 1 thinking, the judgment is achieved quickly and effortlessly. The story we tell here about guessing Julie's GPA involves a complex, multistage sequence of mental events that cannot be directly observed. The specificity of the mental mechanism of matching is unusual in psychology — but the evidence for it is unusually conclusive. We can be certain from many similar experiments that the following two questions, when posed to different groups of people, will elicit exactly the same numbers:

❑ *What percentage of Julie's class read at an earlier age than she did?*
❑ *What percentage of Julie's class has a higher GPA than she does?*

The first question is manageable on its own: it simply asks you to evaluate the evidence you were given about Julie. The second question, which requires a distant prediction, is certainly harder — but it is intuitively tempting to answer it by answering the first.

The two questions we ask about Julie are analogous to two questions that we described as universally confusing in an earlier discussion of the illusion of validity. The first question about Julie requires you to evaluate the "intensity" of the information you have about her case. The second question asks about the intensity of a prediction. And we suspect that they are still difficult to tell apart.

The intuitive prediction of Julie's GPA is a case of the psychological mechanism that we described in chapter 13: the substitution of an easy question for a difficult one. Your System 1 simplifies a difficult prediction question by answering a much easier one: how impressive was Julie's achievement as a four-year-old reader? An extra step of matching is required to move directly from reading age, measured in years, to GPA, measured in points.

The substitution happens, of course, only if the available information is relevant. If all you knew about Julie was that she was a fast runner or a mediocre dancer, you would have no information at all. But any fact that can be interpreted as a plausible indication of intelligence is likely to be an acceptable substitute.

Substituting one question for another inevitably causes errors when the true answers to the two questions are different. Substituting reading age for GPA, though seemingly plausible, is manifestly absurd. To see why, think of events that could have happened since Julie was four years old. She could have been in a terrible accident. Her parents could have had a traumatic divorce. She could have encountered an inspiring teacher who influenced her greatly. She could have become pregnant. Any of these events and many more could have affected her work in college.

The matching prediction can be justified only if reading precocity and college GPA are perfectly correlated, which is clearly not the case. On the other hand, completely ignoring the information about Julie's reading age would also be a mistake, because her reading age does provide some relevant information. The optimal prediction must lie between these two extremes of perfect knowledge and zero knowledge.

What do you know about a case when you know nothing specific about it—only the category to which it belongs? The answer to that question is what we have called the outside view of the case. If we were asked to predict Julie's GPA but given no information about her, we would surely predict the average—perhaps 3.2. This is the outside-view prediction. The best estimate of Julie's GPA must therefore be higher than 3.2 and lower than 3.8. The precise location of the estimate depends on the predictive value of the information: the more you trust reading age as a predictor of GPA, the higher the estimate. In Julie's case, the information is certainly quite weak, and the most reasonable prediction will accordingly be closer to the average GPA. There is a technical but fairly easy way to correct the error of matching predictions; we detail it in appendix C.

Although they lead to statistically absurd predictions, predictions that match the evidence are hard to resist. Sales managers often assume that the salesperson who was more successful than the rest of the sales team last year will continue to overperform. Senior executives sometimes meet an exceptionally talented candidate and imagine how the new hire will rise to the top of the organization. Producers routinely anticipate that the next movie of a director whose previous movie was a hit will be just as successful.

These examples of matching predictions are more likely than not to end in disappointment. On the other hand, matching predictions that are made when things are at their worst are more likely than not to be overly negative. Intuitive predictions that match the evidence are too extreme, both when they are optimistic and when they are pessimistic. (The technical term for such prediction errors is that they are *nonregressive,* because they fail to take into account a statistical phenomenon called *regression to the mean.*)

It should be noted, however, that substitution and matching do not always govern predictions. In the language of two systems, the intuitive System 1 proposes quick associative solutions to problems as they arise, but these intuitions must be endorsed by the more reflective System 2 before they become beliefs. Matching predictions are sometimes rejected in favor of more complex responses. For example, people are more reluctant to match predictions to unfavorable than to favorable evidence. We suspect that you would hesitate to make a matching prediction of inferior college performance if Julie had been a late reader. The asymmetry between favorable and unfavorable predictions disappears when more information is available.

We offer the outside view as a corrective for intuitive predictions of all kinds. In an earlier discussion of Michael Gambardi's future prospects, for example, we recommended anchoring your judgment about Michael's probability of success on the relevant base rate (the two-year success rate for incoming CEOs). In the case of quantitative predictions such as Julie's GPA, taking the outside view means anchoring your prediction on the average outcome. The outside view can be neglected only in very easy problems, when the information available supports a prediction that can be made with complete confidence. When serious judgment is necessary, the outside view must be part of the solution.

Noise in Matching: Limitations of Absolute Judgment

Our limited ability to distinguish categories on intensity scales constrains the accuracy of the matching operation. Words such as *large* or *rich* assign the same label to a range of values on the dimension of size or wealth. This is a potentially important source of noise.

The retiring investment banker surely deserves the label *rich,* but how rich is she? We have many adjectives to choose from: *well-off, affluent, comfortable, wealthy, super-rich,* and others. If you were given detailed descriptions of the wealth of some individuals and had to attach an adjective to each, how many distinct categories could you form — without resorting to detailed comparisons across cases?

The number of categories that we can distinguish on an intensity scale is given in the title of an all-time classic article in psychology, published in 1956: "The Magical Number Seven, Plus or Minus Two." Beyond this limit, people tend to start to make errors — for instance, to assign A to a higher category than B when they would in fact rate B higher than A in a head-to-head comparison.

Imagine a set of lines of four different lengths of between 2 and 4 inches, each line the same amount longer than the next one. You are shown one line at a time and have to call out a number between 1 and 4, where 1 goes with the shortest line and 4 with the longest. The task is easy. Now suppose you are shown lines of five different lengths and have to repeat the task calling out numbers 1 through 5. Still easy. When will you start making errors? Around the magical number of seven lines. Surprisingly, this number depends very little on the range of line lengths: if the lines were spaced between 2 and 6 inches, rather than between 2 and 4, you would still start making mistakes beyond seven lines. Much the same result is obtained when you are presented with tones that vary in loudness, or with lights of different brightness. There is a genuine limit on people's ability to assign distinct labels to stimuli on a dimension, and that limit is around seven labels.

This limit of our discriminating power matters, because our ability to match values across intensity dimensions cannot be better than our ability to assign values on these dimensions. The matching operation is a versatile tool of fast, System 1 thinking and the core of many intuitive judgments, but it is crude.

The magical number is not an absolute constraint. People can be trained to make finer distinctions by hierarchical categorization. For example, we can certainly discriminate several categories of wealth among multimillionaires, and judges can discriminate degrees of severity in multiple categories of crimes, themselves ordered in severity. For this refinement process to work, however, the categories must exist in advance and their boundaries must be clear. When assigning labels to a set of lines, you cannot decide to separate the longer lines from the shorter ones and treat them as two separate categories. Categorization is not under voluntary control when you are in the fast-thinking mode.

There is a way to overcome the limited resolution of adjective scales: instead of using labels, use comparisons. Our ability to compare cases is much better than our ability to place them on a scale.

Consider what you would do if instructed to use a twenty-point scale of quality to evaluate a large set of restaurants, or singers. A five-star scale would be easily manageable, but you could not possibly maintain perfect reliability with a twenty-point scale. (Joe's Pizza is worth three stars, but is it an eleven or a twelve?) The solution to this problem is simple, if time-consuming. You would first rate the restaurants, or singers, using the five-point rating scale to sort them into five categories. You would then rank the cases within each category, which you will usually be able to do with only a few ties: you probably know whether you prefer Joe's Pizza to Fred's Burgers, or Taylor Swift to Bob Dylan, even if you assigned them to the same category. To keep things simple, you could now distinguish four levels within each of the five categories. You can probably discriminate levels of contempt even among the singers you most dislike.

The psychology of this exercise is straightforward. Explicit comparisons between objects of judgment support much finer discriminations than do ratings of objects evaluated one at a time. Judgments of line length tell a similar story: your ability to compare the length of lines that are shown in immediate succession is much better than your ability to label lengths, and you will be even more accurate when comparing lines that are in view at the same time.

The advantage of comparative judgments applies to many domains. If you have a rough idea of people's wealth, you will do better comparing individuals in the same range than you would by labeling their wealth individually. If you grade essays, you will be more precise when you rank them from best to worst than you are when you read and grade essays one by one. Comparative or relative judgments are more sensitive than categorical or absolute ones. As these examples suggest, they are also more effortful and time-consuming.

Rating objects individually on scales that are explicitly comparative retains some of the benefits of comparative judgment. In some contexts, notably in education, recommendations of candidates for acceptance or promotion often require the recommender to locate the candidate in the "top 5%" or "top 20%" of some designated population, such as "students that you have taught" or "programmers with the same level of experience." These ratings rarely deserve to be taken at face value because there is no way to keep the recommenders accountable for using the scale properly. Accountability is possible in some contexts: when managers rate employees or when analysts assess investments, a person who assigns 90% of cases to the "top 20%" category can be identified and corrected. The use of comparative judgments is one of the remedies for noise that we will discuss in part 5.

Many tasks of judgment require matching individual cases to a category on a scale (for instance, a seven-point agreement scale) or using an ordered set of adjectives (for example, "unlikely" or "extremely unlikely" in rating the probabilities of events). This type of matching is noisy because it is crude. Individuals may differ in the interpretation of labels even when they agree on the substance of the judgment. A procedure that compels explicitly comparative judgments is likely to reduce noise. In the next chapter, we further explore how using the wrong scales can add to noise.

Speaking of Matching

"Both of us say this movie is very good, but you seem to have enjoyed it a lot less than I did. We're using the same words, but are we using the same scale?"

"We thought Season 2 of this series would be just as spectacular as Season 1. We made a matching prediction, and it was wrong."

"It is hard to remain consistent when grading these essays. Should you try ranking them instead?"

CHAPTER 15

Scales

I magine yourself a juror in a civil trial. You have heard the evidence summarized below, and you will be required to make some judgments about it.

Joan Glover v. General Assistance

Joan Glover, a six-year-old child, ingested a large number of pills of Allerfree, a nonprescription allergy medicine, and required an extensive hospital stay. Because the overdose weakened her respiratory system, she will be more susceptible to breathing-related diseases such as asthma and emphysema for the rest of her life. The Allerfree bottle used an inadequately designed childproof safety cap.

The manufacturer of Allerfree is General Assistance, a large company (with annual *profits of $100 million to $200 million) that produces a variety of nonprescription medicines. A federal regulation requires childproof safety caps on all medicine bottles. General Assistance has systematically ignored the intent of this regulation by using a childproof safety cap that had a much higher failure rate than that of others in the industry. An internal company document says that "this stupid, unnecessary federal regulation is a waste of our money" and states that the risk of being punished is low. The document adds that, in any case, "the punishments for violating the regulation are extremely mild; basically we'd be asked to improve the safety caps in the future." Although it was warned about its safety cap by an official of the US Food and Drug Administration, the company decided to take no corrective action.*

Next we ask you to make three judgments. Please slow down enough to choose your answers.

Outrage:

Which of the following best expresses your opinion of the defendant's actions? (Please circle your answer.)

Completely acceptable		*Objectionable*		*Shocking*		*Absolutely outrageous*
0	1	2	3	4	5	6

Punitive intent:

In addition to paying compensatory damages, how much should the defendant be punished? (Please circle the number that best expresses your opinion of the appropriate level of punishment.)

No punishment		Mild punishment		Severe punishment		Extremely severe punishment
0	1	2	3	4	5	6

Damages: In addition to paying compensatory damages, what amount of *punitive* damages (if any) should the defendant be required to pay as punishment and to deter the defendant and others from similar actions in the future? (Please write your answer in the blank below.)

$ ....

The story of Joan Glover is a slightly abbreviated version of a case used in a study that two of us (Kahneman and Sunstein, along with our friend and collaborator David Schkade) reported in 1998. We describe this study in some detail in this chapter, and we wanted you to experience one of the tasks the study includes, because we now see it as an instructive example of a noise audit, which reprises many of the themes of this book.

This chapter focuses on the role of the *response scale* as a pervasive source of noise. People may differ in their judgments, not because they disagree on the substance but because they use the scale in different ways. If you were rating the performance of an employee, you might say that on a scale of 0 to 6, the performance was a 4—which, in your view, is pretty good. Someone else might say that on the same scale, the employee's performance was a 3—which, in his view, is also pretty good. Ambiguity in the wording of scales is a general problem. Much research has been conducted on the difficulties of communication that arise from vague expressions such as "beyond a reasonable doubt," "clear and convincing evidence," "outstanding performance," and "unlikely to happen." Judgments that are expressed in such phrases are inevitably noisy because they are interpreted differently by both speakers and listeners.

In the study for which the Joan Glover case was written, we observed the effects of an ambiguous scale in a situation in which it has serious consequences. The topic of the study was noise in jury-awarded punitive damages. As you could infer from the third question about Joan Glover's case, the law in the United States (and in some other countries) allows juries in civil cases to impose punitive damages on a defendant whose actions were particularly egregious. Punitive damages are supplemental to compensatory awards, which are designed to make injured people whole. When, as in the Glover example, a product has caused injuries and plaintiffs have successfully sued the company, they will be awarded money to pay their medical bills and any lost wages. But they could also receive a punitive award, intended to send the defendant and similar companies a warning. The behavior of General Assistance in this case was obviously reprehensible; it falls in the range of actions for which a jury could reasonably impose punitive damages.

A major concern about the institution of punitive damages has been their unpredictability. The same wrongdoing may be punished by damages that range from very modest to massive. Using the terminology of this book, we would say the system is noisy. Requests for punitive damages are often denied, and even when they are granted, the awards frequently do not add much to compensatory damage. There are striking exceptions, however, and the very large amounts that juries sometimes award appear surprising and arbitrary. An often-mentioned example is a punitive award of $4 million imposed on a car dealership for nondisclosure of the fact that the plaintiff's new BMW had been repainted.

In our study of punitive damages, 899 participants were asked to evaluate Joan Glover's case and nine other similar cases — all of them involving plaintiffs who had suffered some harm and sued the company that was allegedly responsible. Unlike you, the participants answered only one of the three questions (outrage, punitive intent, or dollar amount) for all ten cases. The participants were further divided into smaller groups, each assigned to one version of each case. The different versions varied the harm suffered by the plaintiff and the revenue of the defendant company. There were a total of twenty-eight scenarios. Our goals were to test a theory about the psychology of punitive damages and to investigate the role of the monetary scale (here dollars) as a main source of noise in this legal institution.

The Outrage Hypothesis

How to determine a just punishment has been debated by philosophers and legal scholars for centuries. Our hypothesis, however, was that the question that philosophers find difficult is quite easy for ordinary people, who simplify the task by substituting an easy question for the hard one. The easy question, which is answered immediately when you are asked how much General Assistance should be punished is, "How angry am I?" The intensity of the intended punishment will then be matched to the intensity of the outrage.

To test this outrage hypothesis, we asked different groups of participants to answer either the punitive intent question or the outrage question. We then compared the average ratings obtained on the two questions for the twenty-eight scenarios used in the study. As expected from the substitution idea, the correlation between the mean ratings of outrage and of punitive intent was a close-to-perfect 0.98 (PC = 94%). This correlation supports the outrage hypothesis: the emotion of outrage is the primary determinant of punitive intent.

Outrage is the main driver of punitive intent but not the only one. Did you notice anything in Joan's story that attracted more attention when you rated punitive intent than when you rated outrage? If you did, we suspect it was the harm she suffered. You can tell whether a behavior is outrageous without knowing its consequences; in this instance, the behavior of General Assistance was surely outrageous. In contrast, intuitions about punitive intent have a retributive aspect, which is crudely expressed in the eye-for-an-eye principle. The urge for retribution explains why attempted murder and murder are treated differently by the law and by juries; a would-be murderer who is lucky enough to miss his target will be punished less severely.

To find out whether harm does indeed make a difference in punitive intent but not in outrage, we showed different groups of respondents "severe-harm" and "mild-harm" versions of the Joan Glover case and of several others. The severe-harm version is the one you saw. In the mild-harm version, Joan "had to spend several days in a hospital and is now deeply traumatized by pills of any kind. When her parents try to get her to take even beneficial medications such as vitamins, aspirin, or cold remedies, she cries uncontrollably and says that she is afraid." This version describes a traumatic experience for the child, but a much lower level of harm than the long-term medical damage described in the first version you read. As expected, the average ratings of outrage were almost identical for the severe-harm version (4.24) and the mild-harm version (4.19). Only the defendant's behavior matters to outrage; its consequences do not. In contrast, the ratings of punitive intent averaged 4.93 for severe harm and 4.65 for mild harm, a small but statistically reliable difference. The median monetary awards were two million dollars for the severe-harm version and one million for the milder version. Similar results were obtained for several other cases.

These findings highlight a key feature of the process of judgment: the subtle effect of the judgment task on the weighting of different aspects of the evidence. The participants who rated punitive intent and outrage were not aware that they were taking a stand on the philosophical issue of whether justice should be retributive. They were not even aware of assigning weights to the various features of the case. Nevertheless, they assigned a near-zero weight to harm when rating outrage and a significant weight to the same factor when determining punishment. Recall that the participants saw only one version of the story; their assignment of a higher punishment to the worse harm was not an explicit comparison. It was the outcome of an automatic operation of matching in the two conditions. The responses of participants relied more on fast than on slow thinking.

Noisy Scales

The second goal of the study was to find out why punitive damages are noisy. Our hypothesis was that jurors generally agree on how severely they wish the defendant to be punished but differ widely in how they translate their punitive intent onto the scale of dollars.

The design of the study allows us to compare the amount of noise in judgments of the same cases on three scales: outrage, punitive intent, and damage awards in dollars. To measure noise, we apply the method that was used to analyze the results of the noise audit of federal judges in chapter 6. We assume, as we did in that analysis, that the average of individual judgments of a case can be treated as an unbiased, just value. (This is an assumption for purposes of analysis; we emphasize that it might be wrong.) In an ideal world, all jurors who use a particular scale would agree in their judgments of every case. Any deviation from the average judgment counts as an error, and these errors are the source of system noise.

As we also noted in chapter 6, system noise can be broken down into level noise and pattern noise. Here, level noise is the variability among jurors in how severe they are in general. Pattern noise is the variability in how a given juror responds to particular cases, relative to this juror's own average. We can therefore break down the overall variance of judgments into three elements:

Variance of Judgments =
    Variance of Just Punishments + (Level Noise)^2 +
    (Pattern Noise)^2

This analysis, decomposing the variance of judgments into three terms, was conducted separately for the three judgments of outrage, punitive intent, and dollar award.

Figure 13 shows the results. The least noisy scale is punitive intent, where system noise accounts for 51% of the variance—there is about as much noise as there is justice. The outrage scale is distinctly noisier: 71% noise. And the dollar scale is by far the worst: fully 94% of the variance in judgments is noise!

The differences are striking because the three scales are, in terms of their content, almost identical. We saw earlier that the just values of outrage and punitive intent were almost perfectly correlated, as implied by the outrage hypothesis. The ratings of punitive intent and the dollar awards answer precisely the same question — how severely General Assistance should be punished — in different units. How can we explain the large differences seen in figure 13?

We can probably agree that outrage is not a very precise scale. True, there is such a thing as "completely acceptable" behavior, but if there is a limit to how angry you can get at General Assistance or at the other

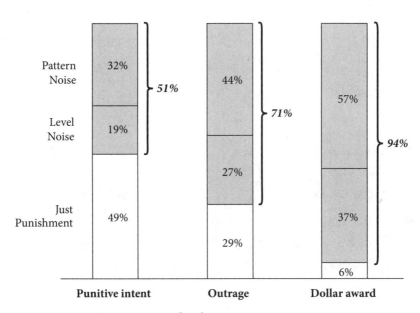

FIGURE 13: *Components of judgment variance*

defendants, that limit is rather vague. What does it mean for a behavior to be "absolutely outrageous"? The lack of clarity on the upper end of the scale makes some noise inevitable.

Punitive intent is more specific. "Severe punishment" is more precise than "absolutely outrageous," because an "extremely severe punishment" is bounded by the maximum prescribed by the law. You may wish to "throw the book" at the culprit, but you may not, for instance, recommend putting the CEO of General Assistance and its entire executive team to death. (We hope.) The punitive-intent scale is less ambiguous because its upper bound is more clearly specified. As we might expect, it is also less noisy.

Outrage and punitive intent were both measured on similar rating scales, defined more or less clearly by verbal labels. The dollar scale belongs to a different family, which is far more problematic.

Dollars and Anchors

The title of our academic paper expresses its central message: "Shared Outrage and Erratic Awards: The Psychology of Punitive Damages." There was a fair amount of agreement among our experimental jurors in their ratings of punitive intent; the ratings were mostly explained by outrage. However, the dollar measure most closely simulated the courtroom situation, and it was unacceptably noisy.

The reason is not mysterious. If you actually generated a specific dollar amount of damages in the Joan Glover case, you surely experienced the feeling that your choice of a number was essentially arbitrary. The feeling of arbitrariness conveys important information: it tells you that other people will make widely different arbitrary decisions and that the judgments will be very noisy. This turns out to be a characteristic of the family of scales to which dollar awards belong.

The legendary Harvard psychologist S. S. Stevens discovered the surprising fact that people share strong intuitions about the *ratios* of intensity of many subjective experiences and attitudes. They can adjust a light so that it appears "twice as bright" as another, and they agree that the emotional significance of a ten-month prison sentence is not nearly ten times as bad as that of a sentence of one month. Stevens called scales that draw on such intuitions *ratio scales*.

You can tell that our intuitions about money are expressed in ratios from the ease with which we understand such expressions as "Sara got a 60% raise!" or "Our rich neighbor lost half his wealth overnight." The dollar scale of punitive damages is a ratio scale for the measurement of the intention to punish. Like other ratio scales, it has a meaningful zero (zero dollars) and is unbounded at the top.

Stevens discovered that a ratio scale (like the dollar scale) can be tied down by a single intermediate anchor (the jargon term is *modulus*). In his laboratory, he would expose observers to a light of a certain brightness, with the instruction to "call the brightness of that light 10 (or 50, or 200) and assign numbers to other brightnesses accordingly." As expected, the numbers that observers assigned to lights of different brightness were proportional to the arbitrary anchor they were instructed to adopt. An observer who was anchored on the number 200 would make judgments that were 20 times higher than if the anchor had been 10; the standard deviation of the observer's judgments would also be proportional to the anchor.

In chapter 13, we described an amusing example of anchoring, in which people's willingness to pay for an object was strongly influenced by asking them first if they would pay (in dollars) the last two digits of their Social Security number. A more striking result was that the initial anchor also affected their willingness to pay for a whole list of other objects. Participants who were induced to agree to pay a large amount for a cordless trackball agreed to pay a correspondingly larger amount for a cordless keyboard. It appears that people are much more sensitive to the *relative* value of comparable goods than to their absolute value. The authors of the study named the persistent effect of a single anchor "coherent arbitrariness."

To appreciate the effect of an arbitrary anchor in the Joan Glover case, suppose that the text at the beginning of this chapter included the following information:

> *In a similar case involving another pharmaceutical company, a little girl who was the victim suffered moderate psychological trauma (as in the mild-harm version you read earlier). The punitive damages were set at $1.5 million.*

Notice that the problem of setting a punishment for General Assistance has suddenly become much easier. Indeed, an amount may have come to your mind already. There is a multiplier (or ratio) of the dollar awards that corresponds to the contrast between the severe harm that was done to Joan and the mild harm suffered by the other little girl. Furthermore, the single anchor you read ($1.5 million) is sufficient to tie down the entire dollar scale of punishment. It is now easy for you to set damages for cases both more severe and milder than the two considered so far.

If anchors are required to make judgments on a

ratio scale, what happens when people are not given an anchor? Stevens reported the answer. In the absence of guidance from the experimenter, people are forced to make an arbitrary choice when they use the scale for the first time. From that point, they make their judgments consistently, using their first answer as an anchor.

You may recognize the task you faced in setting damages for the Joan Glover case as an instance of scaling without an anchor. Like the anchorless observers in Stevens's lab, you made an arbitrary decision about the correct punishment for General Assistance. The participants in our study of punitive damages faced the same problem: they were also compelled to make an initial arbitrary decision about the first case they saw. Unlike you, however, they did not just make one arbitrary decision: they went on to set punitive damages for nine other cases. These nine judgments were not arbitrary because they could be made consistent with the initial anchoring judgment, and therefore with one another.

The findings of Stevens's laboratory suggest that the anchor that individuals produce should have a large effect on the absolute values of their subsequent dollar judgments but no effect whatsoever on the relative positions of the ten cases. A large initial judgment causes all the other judgments to be proportionately large without affecting their relative size. This reasoning leads to a surprising conclusion: although they appear hopelessly noisy, dollar judgments actually reflect the judges' punitive intentions. To discover these intentions, we need only replace the absolute dollar values with relative scores.

To test this idea, we repeated the analysis of noise after replacing each dollar award by its rank among an individual's ten judgments. The highest dollar award was scored 1, the next highest was scored 2, and so forth. This transformation of dollar awards to ranks eliminates all juror-level errors, because the 1 to 10 distribution of ranks is the same for everyone, except for occasional ties. (In case you wondered, there were multiple versions of the questionnaire because each individual judged ten of the twenty-eight scenarios. We conducted the analysis separately for each group of participants who had responded to the same ten scenarios, and we report an average.)

The results were striking: the proportion of noise in the judgments dropped from 94% to 49% (figure 14). Transforming the dollar awards into rankings revealed that jurors were actually in substantial agreement about the appropriate punishment in different cases. Indeed, the rankings of dollar awards were, if anything, slightly *less* noisy than the original ratings of punitive intent.

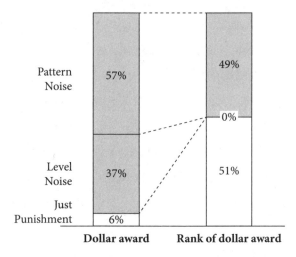

FIGURE 14: *Noise in value vs. noise in ranking*

An Unfortunate Conclusion

The results are consistent with the theory we have outlined: dollar awards for all cases were anchored on the arbitrary number that each juror picked for the first case they saw. The relative ranking of cases reflects attitudes with fair accuracy and is thus not very noisy, but the absolute values of the dollar awards are essentially meaningless because they depend on the arbitrary number chosen in the first case.

Ironically, the case that jurors assess in real trials is the first and only one they see. American legal practice requires civil juries to set a dollar award for one case, without the benefit of any guiding anchor. The law explicitly prohibits any communication to the jury of the size of punitive awards in other cases. The assumption implicit in the law is that jurors' sense of justice will lead them directly from a consideration of an offense to the correct punishment. This assumption is psychological nonsense—it assumes an ability that humans do not have. The institutions of justice should acknowledge the limitations of the people who administer it.

The example of punitive damages is extreme; professional judgments are rarely expressed on scales that are so hopelessly ambiguous. Nonetheless, ambiguous scales are common, which means that the punitive-damages study holds two general lessons, applicable in business, education, sports, government, and elsewhere. First, the choice of a scale can make a large difference in the amount of noise in judgments, because ambiguous scales are noisy. Second, replacing absolute judgments with relative ones, when feasible, is likely to reduce noise.

Speaking of Scales

"There is a lot of noise in our judgments. Could this be because we understand the scale differently?"

"Can we agree on an anchor case that will serve as a reference point on the scale?"

"To reduce noise, maybe we should replace our judgments with a ranking?"

CHAPTER 16

Patterns

Remember Julie, the precocious child whose college GPA you tried to guess in chapter 14? Here is a fuller description.

Julie was an only child. Her father was a successful lawyer, her mother an architect. When Julie was about three years old, her father contracted an autoimmune disease that forced him to work at home. He spent a lot of time with Julie and patiently taught her to read. She was reading fluently when she was four years old. Her dad also tried to teach her arithmetic, but she found that topic difficult. Julie was a good pupil in elementary school, but she was emotionally needy and rather unpopular. She spent much time alone and became a passionate bird-watcher after being inspired by watching birds with her favorite uncle.

Her parents divorced when she was eleven, and Julie took the divorce hard. Her grades plummeted, and she had frequent outbursts at school. In high school, she did very well in some subjects, including biology and creative writing. She surprised everyone by excelling in physics. But she neglected most of her other subjects, and she graduated from high school a B student.

Not admitted to the prestigious schools to which she applied, Julie eventually attended a good state school, where she majored in environmental studies. During her first two years in college, she continued a pattern of frequent emotional entanglements and smoked pot fairly regularly. In her fourth semester, however, she developed a strong wish to go to medical school and began to take her work much more seriously.

What is your best guess about Julie's graduating GPA?

Problems: Hard and Easy

Obviously, this problem (let's call it Julie 2.0) has become much more difficult. All you knew about

Julie 1.0 was that she could read when she was four. With only one cue, the power of matching did the work, and an intuitive estimate of her GPA came quickly to mind.

Matching would still be available if you had several cues that pointed in the same general direction. For instance, when you read a description of Bill, the jazz-playing accountant, all the information you had ("unimaginative," "strong in mathematics," "weak in social studies") painted a coherent, stereotypical picture. Similarly, if most of the events in the life of Julie 2.0 were consistent with a story of precociousness and superior achievement (with perhaps a few data points suggesting merely "average" performance), you would not find the task so difficult. When the evidence available paints a coherent picture, our fast, System 1 thinking has no difficulty making sense of it. Simple judgment problems like these are easily resolved, and most people agree on their solution.

Not so with Julie 2.0. What makes this problem difficult is the presence of multiple, conflicting cues. There are indications of ability and motivation but also of character weaknesses and mediocre achievement. The story seems to be all over the place. It does not easily make sense, because the elements cannot be fit in a coherent interpretation. Of course, the incoherence does not make the story unrealistic or even implausible. Life is often more complex than the stories we like to tell about it.

Multiple, conflicting cues create the ambiguity that defines difficult judgment problems. Ambiguity also explains why complex problems are noisier than simple ones. The rule is simple: if there is more than one way to see anything, people will vary in how they see it. People can pick different pieces of evidence to form the core of their narrative, so there are many possible conclusions. If you found it difficult to construct a story that makes sense of Julie 2.0, you can be quite certain that other readers will construct different stories that justify judgments other than yours. This is the variability that produces pattern noise.

When do you feel confident in a judgment? Two conditions must be satisfied: the story you believe must be comprehensively coherent, and there must be no attractive alternatives. Comprehensive coherence is achieved when all the details of the chosen interpretation fit with the story and reinforce each other. Of course, you can also achieve coherence, albeit less elegantly, by ignoring or explaining away whatever does not fit. It is the same with alternative interpretations. The true expert who has "solved" a judgment problem knows not only why her explanatory story is correct; she is equally fluent in explaining why other stories are wrong. Here again, a person can gain confidence of equal strength but poorer quality by failing to consider alternatives or by actively suppressing them.

The main implication of this view of confidence is that subjective confidence in one's judgment by no means guarantees accuracy. Moreover, the suppression of alternative interpretations — a well-documented process in perception — could induce what we have called the *illusion of agreement* (see chapter 2). If people cannot imagine possible alternatives to their conclusions, they will naturally assume that other observers must reach the same conclusion, too. Of course, few of us have the good fortune of being highly confident about all our judgments, and all of us have had the experience of uncertainty, perhaps as recently as your reading about Julie 2.0. We are not all highly confident all the time, but most of the time we are more confident than we should be.

Pattern Noise: Stable or Transient

We have defined a pattern error as an error in an individual's judgment of a case that cannot be explained by the sum of the separate effects of the case and the judge. An extreme example may be the normally lenient judge who is unusually severe in sentencing a particular kind of defendant (say, people who have committed traffic offenses). Or, say, the normally cautious investor who drops his usual caution when shown the plan of an exciting start-up. Of course, most pattern errors are not extreme: we observe a moderate pattern error in the lenient judge who is less lenient than usual when dealing with recidivists, or even more lenient than usual when sentencing young women.

Pattern errors arise from a combination of transient and permanent factors. The transient factors include those we have described as sources of occasion noise, such as a judge's good mood at the relevant moment or some unfortunate recent occurrence that is currently on the judge's mind. Other factors are more permanent — for example, an employer's unusual enthusiasm for people who attended certain universities or a doctor's unusual propensity to recommend hospitalization for people with pneumonia. We can write a simple equation that describes an error in a single judgment:

Pattern Error = Stable Pattern Error + Transient (Occasion) Error

Because stable pattern error and transient (occasion) error are independent and uncorrelated, we can extend the equation above to analyze their variances:

(Pattern Noise)^2 = (Stable Pattern Noise)^2 + (Occasion Noise)^2

As we did for other components of error and noise, we can represent this equation graphically as a sum of squares on the sides of a right triangle (Figure 15):

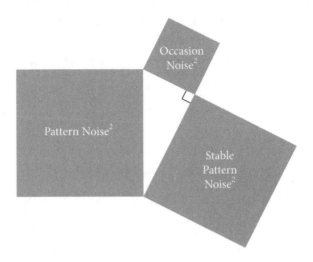

FIGURE 15: *Decomposing pattern noise*

For a simple case of stable pattern noise, consider recruiters who predict the future performance of executives on the basis of a set of ratings. In chapter 9 we spoke of a "model of the judge." The model of an individual recruiter assigns a weight to each rating, which corresponds to its importance in that recruiter's judgments. The weights vary among recruiters: leadership may count more for one recruiter, communication skills for another. Such differences produce variability in the recruiters' ranking of candidates—an instance of what we call stable pattern noise.

Personal reactions to individual cases can also produce patterns that are stable but highly specific. Consider what led you to pay more attention to some aspects of Julie's story than to others. Some details of the case may resonate with your life experience. Perhaps something about Julie reminds you of a close relative who kept almost succeeding but ultimately failing, because of what you believe are deep character flaws that were evident since that relative's teenage years. Conversely, Julie's story may evoke memories of a close friend who, after a troubled adolescence, did make it to medical school and is now a successful specialist. The associations that Julie evokes in different people are idiosyncratic and unpredictable, but they are likely to be stable: if you had read Julie's story last week, you would have been reminded of the same people and would have seen her story in the same distinctively personal light.

Individual differences in the quality of judgments are another source of pattern noise. Imagine a single forecaster with crystal-ball powers that no one knows about (including herself). Her accuracy would make her deviate in many cases from the average forecast. In the absence of outcome data, these deviations would be regarded as pattern errors. When judgments are unverifiable, superior accuracy will look like pattern noise.

Pattern noise also arises from systematic differences in the ability to make valid judgments about different dimensions of a case. Consider the process of selection for professional sports teams. Coaches may focus on skills in various aspects of the game, physicians on susceptibility to injuries, and psychologists on motivation and resilience. When these different specialists evaluate the same players, we can expect a considerable amount of pattern noise. Similarly, professionals in the same generalist role may be more skilled at some aspects of the judgment task than at others. In such cases, pattern noise is better described as variability in what people know than as error.

When professionals make decisions on their own, variability in skills is simply noise. However, when management has the opportunity to construct teams that will reach judgments together, diversity of skills becomes a potential asset, because different professionals will cover different aspects of the judgment and complement one another. We discuss this opportunity — and what is required to capture it — in chapter 21.

In earlier chapters, we spoke of the two lotteries that face the client of an insurance company or the defendant who is assigned the judge who will try him. We can now see that the first lottery, which picks a professional from a group of colleagues, selects much more than the average level of that professional's judgments (the level error). The lottery also selects a kaleidoscopic assemblage of values, preferences, beliefs, memories, experiences, and associations that are unique to this particular professional. Whenever you make a judgment, you carry your own baggage, too. You come with the habits of mind you formed on the job and the wisdom you gained from your mentors. You bring along the successes that built your confidence and the mistakes that you are careful not to repeat. And somewhere in your brain are the formal rules you remember, those you forgot, and those you learned that it is okay to ignore. No one is exactly like you in all these respects; your stable pattern errors are unique to you.

The second lottery is the one that picks the moment when you make your judgment, the mood you are in, and other extraneous circumstances that should not affect your judgment but do. This lottery creates occasion noise. Imagine, for instance, that shortly before you read Julie's case, you read a newspaper article about drug use on college campuses. The piece featured the story of a gifted student who was determined to go to law school and worked hard—but was unable to make up for the deficit he had accumulated while using drugs in his early years of college. Because it is fresh in your mind, this story will lead you to pay more attention to Julie's pot-smoking habit in your assessment of her overall chances. However, you probably would not remember the article if you encountered the question about Julie in a couple of weeks (and you would obviously not have known about it if you had read the case yesterday). The effect of reading the newspaper article is transient; it is occasion noise.

As this example illustrates, there is no sharp discontinuity between stable pattern noise and the unstable variant that we call occasion noise. The main difference is whether a person's unique sensitivity to some aspects of the case is itself permanent or transient. When the triggers of pattern noise are rooted in our personal experiences and values, we can expect the pattern to be stable, a reflection of our uniqueness.

The Personality Analogy

The idea of uniqueness in the responses of particular people to certain features or combinations of features is not immediately intuitive. To understand it, we might consider another complex combination of features that we all know well: the personalities of people around us. In fact, the event of a judge making a judgment about a case should be seen as a special case of a broader topic that is the domain of personality research: how a person acts in a situation. There is something to be learned about judgment from the decades of intensive study of the broader topic.

Psychologists have long sought to understand and measure individual differences in personality. People differ from one another in many ways; an early attempt to scan the dictionary for terms that may describe a person identified eighteen thousand words. Today, the dominant model of personality, the Big Five model, combines traits into five groupings (extraversion, agreeableness, conscientiousness, openness to experience, neuroticism), with each of the Big Five covering a range of distinguishable traits. A personality trait is understood as a predictor of actual behaviors. If someone is described as conscientious, we expect to observe some corresponding behaviors (arriving on time, keeping commitments, and so on). And if Andrew scores higher than Brad on a measure of aggressiveness, we should observe that, in most situations, Andrew behaves more aggressively than Brad does. In fact, however, the validity of broad traits for predicting specific behaviors is quite limited; a correlation of .30 (PC = 60%) would be considered high.

Common sense suggests that while behavior may be driven by personality, it is also strongly affected by *situations*. In some situations no one is aggressive, and in other situations everyone is. When consoling a bereaved friend, neither Andrew nor Brad will act aggressively; at a football game, however, both will display some aggression. In short—and unsurprisingly—behaviors are a function of personalities *and* of situations.

What makes people unique and endlessly interesting is that this joining of personality and situation is not a mechanical, additive function. For example, the situations that trigger more or less aggression are not the same for all people. Even if Andrew and Brad are equally aggressive on average, they do not necessarily display equal aggressiveness in every context. Perhaps Andrew is aggressive toward his peers but docile with superiors, whereas Brad's level of aggressiveness is not sensitive to hierarchical level. Perhaps Brad is particularly prone to aggression when criticized and unusually restrained when physically threatened.

These signature patterns of response to situations are likely to be fairly stable over time. They constitute much of what we consider someone's *personality*, although they do not lend themselves to a description by a broad trait. Andrew and Brad may share the same score on a test of aggression, but they are unique in their pattern of response to aggression triggers and contexts. Two people who share a trait level—if, for example, they are equally obstinate or equally generous — should be described by two distributions of behaviors that have the same average but not necessarily the same pattern of responses to different situations.

You can now see the parallel between this discussion of personality and the model of judgment we have presented. Level differences between judges correspond to the differences among scores on personality traits, which represent an average of behaviors in multiple situations. Cases are analogous to situations. A person's judgment of a particular problem is only moderately predictable from that person's average level, just as specific behaviors are only moderately predictable from personality traits. The ranking of individuals by their judgment varies substantially from one case to another because people differ in their reaction to the features and combinations of features that they find in each case. The signature of an individual who makes judgments and decisions is a unique pattern of sensitivity to features and a correspondingly unique pattern in the judgment of cases.

The uniqueness of personality is normally a cause for celebration, but this book is concerned with professional judgments, where variation is problematic and noise is error. The point of the analogy is that pattern noise in judgment is not random — even if we have little hope of explaining it and even if the individuals who make distinctive judgments could not explain them.

Speaking of Pattern Noise

"You seem confident in your conclusion, but this is not an easy problem: there are cues pointing in different directions. Have you overlooked alternative interpretations of the evidence?"

"You and I have interviewed the same candidate, and usually we are equally demanding interviewers. Yet we have completely different judgments. Where does this pattern noise come from?"

"The uniqueness of people's personalities is what makes them capable of innovation and creativity, and simply interesting and exciting to be around. When it comes to judgment, however, that uniqueness is not an asset."

CHAPTER 17

The Sources of Noise

W e hope that by now, you agree that wherever there is judgment, there is noise. We also hope that for you, there is no longer more of it than you think. This mantra about noise motivated us when we started our project, but our thinking about the topic has evolved over the years of working on it. We now review the main lessons we have learned about the components of noise, about their respective importance in the general picture of noise, and about the place of noise in the study of judgment.

The Components of Noise

Figure 16 offers a combined graphical representation of the three equations we introduced in chapters 5, 6,

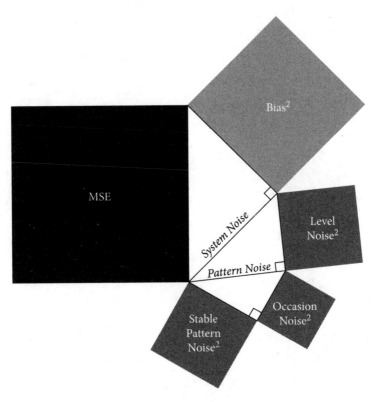

FIGURE 16: *Error, bias, and the components of noise*

and 16. The figure illustrates three successive breakdowns of error:

- error into bias and system noise,

- system noise into level noise and pattern noise,

- pattern noise into stable pattern noise and occasion noise.

You can now see how MSE breaks down into the squares of bias and of the three components of noise we have discussed.

When we began our research, we were focusing on the relative weights of bias and noise in total error. We soon concluded that noise is often a larger component of error than bias is, and certainly well worth exploring in more detail.

Our early thinking on the constituents of noise was guided by the structure of complex noise audits, in which multiple people make individual judgments about multiple cases. The study of federal judges was an example, and the study of punitive damages another. Data from these studies provided solid estimates of level noise. On the other hand, because every participant judges every case but does so only once, there is no way of telling whether the residual error, which we have called pattern error, is transient or stable. In the conservative spirit of statistical analysis, the residual error is commonly labeled an error term and is treated as random. In other words, the default interpretation of pattern noise is that it consists entirely of occasion noise.

This conventional interpretation of pattern noise as random error constrained our thinking for a long time. It seemed natural to focus on level noise—the consistent differences between harsh and lenient judges or between optimistic and pessimistic forecasters. We were also intrigued by evidence of the influence on judgments of the irrelevant and transient circumstances that create occasion noise.

The evidence gradually led us to realize that the noisy judgments that different people make are largely determined by something that is neither a general bias of the individual nor transient and random: the persistent personal reactions of particular individuals to a multitude of features, which determine their reactions to specific cases. We eventually concluded that our default assumption about the transient nature of pattern noise should be abandoned.

Though we want to be careful not to overgeneralize from what remains a limited selection of examples, the studies we have assembled, taken together, suggest that stable pattern noise is actually more significant than the other components of system noise. Because we rarely have a full picture of the components of error in the same study, it requires some triangulation to formulate this tentative conclusion. In short, here is what we know—and what we don't.

Sizing the Components

First, we have several estimates of the relative weights of level noise and pattern noise. Overall, it appears that pattern noise contributes more than level noise. In the insurance company of chapter 2, for instance, differences between underwriters in the average of the premiums they set accounted for only 20% of total system noise; the remaining 80% was pattern noise. Among the federal judges of chapter 6, level noise (differences in average severity) represented slightly less than half of total system noise; pattern noise was the larger component. In the punitive damages experiment, the total amount of system noise varied widely depending on the scale used (punitive intent, outrage, or damages in dollars), but the share of pattern noise in that total was roughly constant: it accounted for 63%, 62%, and 61% of total system noise for the three scales used in the study. Other studies we will review in part 5, notably on personnel decisions, are consistent with this tentative conclusion.

The fact that in these studies level noise is generally not the larger component of system noise is already an important message, because level noise is the only form of noise that organizations can (sometimes) monitor without conducting noise audits. When cases are assigned more or less randomly to individual professionals, the differences in the average level of their decisions provide evidence of level noise. For example, studies of patent offices observed large differences in the average propensity of examiners to grant patents, with subsequent effects on the incidence of litigation about these patents. Similarly, case officers in child protection services vary in their propensity to place children in foster care, with long-term consequences for the children's welfare. These observations are based solely on an estimation of level noise. If there is more pattern noise than level noise, then these already-shocking findings understate the magnitude of the noise problem by at least a factor of two. (There are exceptions to this tentative rule. The scandalous variability in the decisions of asylum judges is almost certainly due more to level noise than to pattern noise, which we suspect is large as well.)

The next step is to analyze pattern noise by separating its two components. There are good reasons to assume that stable pattern noise, rather than occasion noise, is the dominant component. The audit of the sentences of federal judges illustrates our reasoning. Start with the extreme possibility that all pattern noise is transient. On that assumption, sentencing would be unstable and inconsistent over time, to an extent that we find implausible: we would have to expect that the average difference between judgments of *the same case by the same judge* on different occasions is about 2.8 years. The variability of average sentencing among judges is already shocking. The same variability in the sentences of an individual judge over occasions would be grotesque. It seems more reasonable to conclude that judges differ in their reactions to different defendants and different crimes and that these differences are highly personal but stable.

To quantify more precisely how much of pattern noise is stable and how much is occasion noise, we need studies in which the same judges make two independent assessments of each case. As we have noted, obtaining two independent judgments is generally impossible in studies of judgment, because it is difficult to guarantee that the second judgment of a case is truly independent of the first. Especially when the judgment is complex, there is a high probability that the individual will recognize the problem and repeat the original judgment.

A group of researchers at Princeton, led by Alexander Todorov, has designed clever experimental techniques to overcome this problem. They recruited participants from Amazon Mechanical Turk, a site where individuals provide short-term services, such as answering questionnaires, and are paid for their time. In one experiment, participants viewed pictures of faces (generated by a computer program, but perfectly indistinguishable from the faces of real people) and rated them on various attributes, such as likability and trustworthiness. The experiment was repeated, with the same faces and the same respondents, one week later.

It is fair to expect less consensus in this experiment than in professional judgments such as those of sentencing judges. Everyone might agree that some people are extremely attractive and that others are extremely unattractive, but across a significant range, we expect reactions to faces to be largely idiosyncratic. Indeed, there was little agreement among observers: on the ratings of trustworthiness, for instance, differences among pictures accounted for only 18% of the variance of judgments. The remaining 82% of the variance was noise.

It is also fair to expect less stability in these judgments, because the quality of judgments made by participants who are paid to answer questions online is often substantially lower than in professional settings. Nevertheless, the largest component of noise was stable pattern noise. The second largest component of noise was level noise — that is, differences among observers in their average ratings of trustworthiness. Occasion noise, though still substantial, was the smallest component.

The researchers reached the same conclusions when they asked participants to make other judgments — about preferences among cars or foods, for example, or on questions that are closer to what we call professional judgments. For instance, in a replication of the study of punitive damages discussed in chapter 15, participants rated their punitive intent in ten cases of personal injury, on two separate occasions separated by a week. Here again, stable pattern noise was the largest component. In all these studies, individuals generally did not agree with one another, but they remained quite stable in their judgments. This "consistency without consensus," in the researchers' words, provides clear evidence of stable pattern noise.

The strongest evidence for the role of stable patterns comes from the large study of bail judges we mentioned in chapter 10. In one part of this exceptional study, the authors created a statistical model that simulated how each judge used the available cues to decide whether to grant bail. They built custom-made models of 173 judges. Then they applied the simulated judges to make decisions about 141,833 cases, yielding 173 decisions for each case—a total of more than 24 million decisions. At our request, the authors generously carried a special analysis in which they separated the variance judgments into three components: the "true" variance of the average decisions for each of the cases, the level noise created by differences among judges in their propensity to grant bail, and the remaining pattern noise.

This analysis is relevant to our argument because pattern noise, as measured in this study, is entirely stable. The random variability of occasion noise is not represented, because this is an analysis of *models* that predict a judge's decision. Only the verifiably stable individual rules of prediction are included.

The conclusion was unequivocal: this stable pattern noise was almost four times larger than level noise (stable pattern noise accounted for 26%, and level noise 7%, of total variance). The stable, idiosyncratic individual patterns of judgment that could be identified were much larger than the differences in across-the-board severity.

All this evidence is consistent with the research on occasion noise that we reviewed in chapter 7: while the existence of occasion noise is surprising and even disturbing, there is no indication that within-person variability is larger than between-person differences. The most important component of system noise is the one we had initially neglected: stable pattern noise, the variability among judges in their judgments of particular cases.

Given the relative scarcity of relevant research, our conclusions are tentative, but they do reflect a change in how we think about noise — and about how to tackle it. In principle at least, level noise — or simple, across-the-board differences between judges — should be a relatively easy problem to measure and address. If there are abnormally "tough" graders, "cautious" child custody officers, or "risk-averse" loan officers, the organizations that employ them could aim to equalize the average level of their judgments. Universities, for instance, address this problem when they require professors to abide by a predetermined distribution of grades within each class.

Unfortunately, as we now realize, focusing on level noise misses a large part of what individual differences are about. Noise is mostly a product not of level differences but of interactions: how different judges deal with particular defendants, how different teachers deal with particular students, how different social workers deal with particular families, how different leaders deal with particular visions of the future. Noise is mostly a by-product of our uniqueness, of our "judgment personality." Reducing level noise is still a worthwhile objective, but attaining only this objective would leave most of the problem of system noise without a solution.

Explaining Error

We found a lot to say about noise, but the topic is almost entirely absent from public awareness and from discussions of judgment and error. Despite the evidence of its presence and the multiple mechanisms that produce it, noise is rarely mentioned as a major factor in judgment. How is this possible? Why do we never invoke noise to explain bad judgments, whereas we routinely blame biases? Why is it so unusual to give much thought to noise as a source of error, despite its ubiquity?

The key to this puzzle is that although the average of errors (the bias) and the variability of errors (the noise) play equivalent roles in the error equation, we think about them in profoundly different ways. And our ordinary way of making sense of the world around us makes it all but impossible to recognize the role of noise.

Earlier in this book, we noted that we easily make sense of events in hindsight, although we could not have predicted them before they happened. In the valley of the normal, events are unsurprising and easily explained.

The same can be said of judgments. Like other events, judgments and decisions mostly happen in the valley of the normal; they usually do not surprise us. For one thing, judgments that produce satisfactory outcomes are normal, and seldom questioned. When the shooter who is picked for the free kick scores the goal, when the heart surgery is successful, or when a start-up prospers, we assume that the reasons the decision makers had for their choices must have been the right ones. After all, they have been proven right. Like any other unsurprising story, a success story explains itself once the outcome is known.

We do, however, feel a need to explain abnormal outcomes: the bad ones and, occasionally, the surprisingly good ones—such as the shocking business gamble that pays off. Explanations that appeal to error or to special flair are far more popular than they deserve to be, because important gambles of the past easily become acts of genius or folly when their outcome is known. A well-documented psychological bias called the *fundamental attribution error* is a strong tendency to assign blame or credit to agents for actions and outcomes that are better explained by luck or by objective circumstances. Another bias, hindsight, distorts judgments so that outcomes that could not have been anticipated appear easily foreseeable in retrospect.

Explanations for errors of judgment are not hard to come by; finding reasons for judgments is, if anything, easier than finding causes for events. We can always invoke the motives of the people making the judgments. If that is not sufficient, we can blame their incompetence. And another explanation for poor judgments has become common in recent decades: psychological bias.

A substantial body of research in psychology and behavioral economics has documented a long list of psychological biases: the planning fallacy, overconfidence, loss aversion, the endowment effect, the status quo bias, excessive discounting of the future ("present bias"), and many others — including, of course, biases for or against various categories of people. Much is known about the conditions under which each of these biases is likely to influence judgments and decisions, and a fair amount is known that would allow an observer of decision making to recognize biased thinking in real time.

A psychological bias is a legitimate causal explanation of a judgment error if the bias could have been predicted in advance or detected in real time. A psychological bias that is identified only after the fact can still provide a useful, if tentative, explanation if it also offers a prediction about the future. For example, the surprising rejection of a strong woman candidate for a position may suggest a more general hypothesis of gender bias that future appointments by the same committee will confirm or refute. Consider, in contrast, a causal explanation that applies only to one event: "In that case they failed, so they must have been overconfident." The statement is completely vacuous, but it provides an illusion of understanding that can be quite satisfying. Business school professor Phil Rosenzweig has convincingly argued that empty explanations in terms of biases are common in discussions of business outcomes. Their popularity attests to the prevalent need for causal stories that make sense of experience.

Noise Is Statistical

As we noted in chapter 12, our normal way of thinking is causal. We naturally attend to the particular, following and creating causally coherent stories about individual cases, in which failures are often attributed to errors, and errors to biases. The ease with which bad judgments can be explained leaves no space for noise in our accounts of errors.

The invisibility of noise is a direct consequence of causal thinking. Noise is inherently statistical: it becomes visible only when we think statistically about an ensemble of similar judgments. Indeed, it then becomes hard to miss: it is the variability in the backward-looking statistics about sentencing decisions and underwriting premiums. It is the range of possibilities when you and others consider how to predict a future outcome. It is the scatter of the hits on the target. Causally, noise is nowhere; statistically, it is everywhere.

Unfortunately, taking the statistical view is not easy. We effortlessly invoke causes for the events we observe, but thinking statistically about them must be learned and remains effortful. Causes are natural; statistics are difficult.

The result is a marked imbalance in how we view bias and noise as sources of error. If you have been exposed to any introductory psychology, you probably remember the illustrations in which a salient and richly detailed figure stands out from an indistinct background. Our attention is firmly fixed on the figure even when it is small against the background. The figure/ground demonstrations are an apt metaphor for our intuitions about bias and noise: bias is a compelling figure, while noise is the background to which we pay no attention. That is how we remain largely unaware of a large flaw in our judgment.

Speaking of the Sources of Noise

"We easily see differences in the average level of judgments, but how large is the pattern noise we do not see?"

"You say this judgment was caused by biases, but would you say the same thing if the outcome had been different? And can you tell if there was noise?"

"We are rightly focused on reducing biases. Let's also worry about reducing noise."

PART V

Improving Judgments

How can an organization improve the judgments its professionals make? In particular, how can an organization reduce judgment noise? If you were in charge of answering these questions, how would you go about it?

A necessary first step is to get the organization to recognize that noise in professional judgments is an issue that deserves attention. To get to that point, we recommend a noise audit (see appendix A for a detailed description). In a noise audit, multiple individuals judge the same problems. Noise is the variability of these judgments. There will be cases in which this variability can be attributed to incompetence: some judges know what they are talking about, others do not. When there is such a skill gap (either in general, or on certain types of cases), the priority should of course be to improve the deficient skills. But, as we have seen, there can be a large amount of noise even in the judgments of competent and well-trained professionals.

If the amount of system noise is worth addressing, replacing judgment with rules or algorithms is an option that you should consider, as it will eliminate noise entirely. But rules have their own problems (as we will see in part 6), and even the most enthusiastic proponents of AI agree that algorithms are not, and will not soon be, a universal substitute for human judgment. The task of improving judgment is as urgent as ever, and it is the topic of this part of the book.

A sensible way to improve judgments is, of course, to select the best possible human judges. At the shooting range, some shooters have an especially good aim. The same is true of any professional judgment task: the most highly skilled will be both less noisy and less biased. How to find the best judges is sometimes obvious; if you want to solve a chess problem, ask a grandmaster, not the authors of this book. But in most problems, the characteristics of superior judges are harder to discern. These characteristics are the subject of chapter 18.

Next, we discuss approaches to the reduction of

judgment errors. Psychological biases are implicated in both statistical bias and noise. As we see in chapter 19, there have been many attempts to counteract psychological biases, with some clear failures and some clear successes. We briefly review debiasing strategies and suggest a promising approach that, to our knowledge, has not been systematically explored: asking a designated *decision observer* to search for diagnostic signs that could indicate, in real time, that a group's work is being affected by one or several familiar biases. Appendix B provides an example of a bias checklist that a decision observer could use.

We then proceed to our main focus in this part of the book: the fight against noise. We introduce the theme of *decision hygiene,* the approach we recommend to reduce noise in human judgments. We present case studies in five different domains. In each domain, we examine the prevalence of noise and some of the horror stories it generates. We also review the success—or the lack of success—of efforts to reduce noise. In each domain, of course, multiple approaches have been used, but for ease of exposition, each chapter emphasizes a single decision hygiene strategy.

We start in chapter 20 with the case of forensic science, which illustrates the importance of *sequencing information.* The search for coherence leads people to form early impressions based on the limited evidence available and then to confirm their emerging prejudgment. This makes it important not to be exposed to irrelevant information early in the judgment process.

In chapter 21, we turn to the case of forecasting, which illustrates the value of one of the most important noise-reduction strategies: *aggregating multiple independent judgments.* The "wisdom of crowds" principle is based on the averaging of multiple independent judgments, which is guaranteed to reduce noise. Beyond straight averaging, there are other methods for aggregating judgments, also illustrated by the example of forecasting.

Chapter 22 offers a review of noise in medicine and efforts to reduce it. It points to the importance and general applicability of a noise-reduction strategy we already introduced with the example of criminal sentencing: *judgment guidelines.* Guidelines can be a powerful noise-reduction mechanism because they directly reduce between-judge variability in final judgments.

In chapter 23, we turn to a familiar challenge in business life: performance evaluations. Efforts to reduce noise there demonstrate the critical importance of using a *shared scale grounded in an outside view.* This is an important decision hygiene strategy for a simple reason: judgment entails the translation of an impression onto a scale, and if different judges use different scales, there will be noise.

Chapter 24 explores the related but distinct topic of personnel selection, which has been extensively researched over the past hundred years. It illustrates the value of an essential decision hygiene strategy: *structuring complex judgments.* By *structuring,* we mean decomposing a judgment into its component parts, managing the process of data collection to ensure the inputs are independent of one another, and delaying the holistic discussion and the final judgment until all these inputs have been collected.

We build on the lessons learned from the field of personnel selection to propose, in chapter 25, a general approach to option evaluation called the *mediating assessments protocol,* or MAP for short. MAP starts from the premise that "options are like candidates" and describes schematically how structured decision making, along with the other decision hygiene strategies mentioned above, can be introduced in a typical decision process for both recurring and singular decisions.

A general point before we embark: it would be valuable to be able to specify, and even to quantify, the likely benefits of each decision hygiene strategy in various contexts. It would also be valuable to know which of the strategies is most beneficial and how to compare them. When the information flow is controlled, to what extent is noise reduced? If the goal is to reduce noise, in practice, how many judgments should be aggregated? Structuring judgments can be valuable, but exactly how valuable is it in different contexts?

Because the topic of noise has attracted little attention, these remain open questions, which research could eventually address. For practical purposes, the benefits of one or another strategy will depend on the particular setting in which it is being used. Consider the adoption of guidelines: they will sometimes produce massive benefits (as we will see in some medical diagnoses). In other settings, however, the benefits of adopting guidelines might be modest — perhaps because there is not a lot of noise to begin with or perhaps because even the best possible guidelines do not reduce error much. In any given context, a decision maker should aspire to achieve a more precise understanding of the likely gains from each decision hygiene strategy — and of the corresponding costs, which we discuss in part 6.

CHAPTER 18

Better Judges for Better Judgments

Thus far, we have mostly spoken of human judges without distinguishing among them. Yet it is obvious that in any task that requires judgment, some people will perform better than others will. Even a wisdom-of-crowds aggregate of judgments is likely to be better if the crowd is composed of more able people. An important question, then, is how to identify these better judges.

Three things matter. Judgments are both less noisy and less biased when those who make them are well trained, are more intelligent, and have the right cognitive style. In other words: good judgments depend on what you know, how well you think, and *how* you think. Good judges tend to be experienced and smart, but they also tend to be actively open-minded and willing to learn from new information.

Experts and Respect-Experts

It is almost tautological to say that the skill of judges affects the quality of their judgments. For instance, radiologists who are skilled are more likely to diagnose pneumonia correctly, and in forecasting world events there are "superforecasters" who reliably outpredict their less-than-super peers. If you assemble a group of lawyers who are true specialists in some area of law, they are likely to make similar, and good, predictions about the outcome of common legal disputes in court. Highly skilled people are less noisy, and they also show less bias.

These people are true experts at the tasks in question. Their superiority over others is verifiable, thanks to the availability of outcome data. In principle at least, we can choose a doctor, forecaster, or lawyer according to how often they have been right in the past. (For obvious reasons, this approach may be difficult in practice; we don't recommend that you attempt to subject your family practitioner to a proficiency exam.)

As we have also noted, many judgments are not verifiable. Within certain boundaries, we cannot easily know or uncontroversially define the true value at which judgments are aiming. Underwriting and criminal sentencing fall in this category, as do wine tasting, essay grading, book and movie reviewing, and innumerable other judgments. Yet some professionals in these domains come to be called experts. The confidence we have in these experts' judgment is entirely based on the respect they enjoy from their peers. We call them *respect-experts*.

The term *respect-expert* is not meant to be disrespectful. The fact that some experts are not subject to an evaluation of the accuracy of their judgments is not a criticism; it is a fact of life in many domains. Many professors, scholars, and management consultants are respect-experts. Their credibility depends on the respect of their students, peers, or clients. In all these fields, and many more, the judgments of one professional can be compared only with those of her peers.

In the absence of true values to determine who is right or wrong, we often value the opinion of respect-experts even when they disagree with one another. Picture, for instance, a panel on which several political analysts have sharply different perspectives on what caused a diplomatic crisis and how it will unfold. (This disagreement is not unusual; it would not be a very interesting panel if they all agreed.) All the analysts believe that there is a correct view and that their own view is the one closest to it. As you listen, you may find several of the analysts equally impressive and their arguments equally convincing. You cannot know then which of them is correct (and you may not even know later, if their analyses are not formulated as clearly verifiable predictions). You know that at least some of the analysts are wrong, because they are in disagreement. Yet you respect their expertise.

Or consider a different set of experts, not making predictions at all. Three moral philosophers, all of them well trained, are gathered in a room. One of them follows Immanuel Kant; another, Jeremy Bentham; and a third, Aristotle. With respect to what morality requires, they disagree intensely. The issue might involve whether and when it is legitimate to lie, or the rights of animals, or the goal of criminal punishment. You listen closely. You might admire the clarity and precision of their thinking. You tend to agree with one philosopher, but you respect them all.

Why do you do that? More generally, how do people who are themselves respected for the quality of their judgment decide to trust someone as an expert when there is no data to establish expertise objectively? What makes a respect-expert?

Part of the answer is the existence of shared norms, or professional doctrine. Experts often obtain professional qualifications from professional communities and receive training and supervision in their organizations. Doctors who complete their residency and young lawyers who learn from a senior partner do not just learn the technical tools of their trade; they are trained to use certain methods and follow certain norms.

Shared norms give professionals a sense of which inputs should be taken into account and how to make and justify their final judgments. In the insurance company, for instance, claims adjusters had no difficulty agreeing on and describing the relevant considerations that should be included in a checklist to assess a claim.

This agreement, of course, did not stop the claims adjusters from varying widely in their claims assessments, because doctrine does not fully specify how to proceed. It is not a recipe that can be mechanically followed. Instead, doctrine leaves room for interpretation. Experts still produce judgments, not computations. That is why noise inevitably occurs. Even identically trained professionals who agree on the doctrine they are applying will drift away from one another in their application of it.

Beyond a knowledge of shared norms, experience is necessary, too. You can be a young prodigy if your specialty is chess, concert piano, or throwing the javelin, because results validate your level of performance. But underwriters, fingerprint examiners, or judges usually need some years of experience for credibility. There are no young prodigies in underwriting.

Another characteristic of respect-experts is their ability to make and explain their judgments with confidence. We tend to put more trust in people who trust themselves than we do in those who show their doubts. The confidence heuristic points to the fact that in a group, confident people have more weight than others, even if they have no reason to be confident. Respect-experts excel at constructing coherent stories. Their experience enables them to recognize patterns, to reason by analogy with previous cases, and to form and confirm hypotheses quickly. They easily fit the facts they see into a coherent story that inspires confidence.

Intelligence

Training, experience, and confidence enable respect-experts to command trust. But these attributes do not guarantee the quality of their judgments. How can we know which experts are likely to make good judgments?

There is good reason to believe that general intelligence is likely to be associated with better judgment. Intelligence is correlated with good performance in virtually all domains. All other things being equal, it is associated not only with higher academic achievement but also with higher job performance.

Many debates and misunderstandings arise in discussions of measures of intelligence or of general mental ability (GMA, the term now used in preference to intelligence quotient, or IQ). There are lingering misconceptions about the innate nature of intelligence; in fact, tests measure developed abilities, which are partly a function of heritable traits and partly influenced by the environment, including educational opportunities. Many people also have concerns about the adverse impact of GMA-based selection on identifiable social groups and the legitimacy of using GMA tests for selection purposes.

We need to separate these concerns about the use of tests from the reality of their predictive value. Since the US Army started using tests of mental ability more than a century ago, thousands of studies have measured the link between cognitive test scores and subsequent performance. The message that emerges from this mass of research is unambiguous. As one review put it, "GMA predicts both occupational level attained and performance within one's chosen occupation and does so better than any other ability, trait, or disposition and better than job experience." Of course, other cognitive abilities matter too (more on this later). So do many personality traits—including conscientiousness and *grit,* defined as perseverance and passion in the pursuit of long-term goals. And yes, there are various forms of intelligence that GMA tests do not measure, such as practical intelligence and creativity. Psychologists and neuroscientists distinguish between crystallized intelligence, the ability to solve problems by relying on a store of knowledge about the world (including arithmetical operations), and fluid intelligence, the ability to solve novel problems.

Yet for all its crudeness and limitations, GMA, as measured by standardized tests containing questions on verbal, quantitative, and spatial problems, remains by far the best single predictor of important outcomes. As the previously mentioned review adds, the predictive power of GMA is "larger than most found in psychological research." The strength of the association between general mental ability and job success increases, quite logically, with the complexity of the job in question: intelligence matters more for rocket scientists than it does for those with simpler tasks. For jobs of high complexity, the correlations that can be observed between standardized test scores and job performance are in the .50 range (PC = 67%). As we have noted, a correlation of .50 indicates a very strong predictive value by social-science standards.

Especially in discussions of skilled professional judgments, an important and frequent objection to the relevance of intelligence measures is that all those who make such judgments are likely to be high-GMA individuals. Doctors, judges, or senior underwriters are much more educated than the general population and highly likely to score much higher on any measure of cognitive ability. You might reasonably believe that high GMA makes little difference among them—that it is merely the entry ticket into the pool of high achievers, not the source of achievement differences within that pool.

This belief, although widespread, is incorrect. No doubt the range of GMAs found in a given occupation is wider at the bottom of the range of occupations than at the top: there are high-GMA individuals in lower-level occupations but almost no people with below-average GMA among lawyers, chemists, or engineers. From that perspective, therefore, high mental ability is apparently a necessary condition for gaining access to high-status professions.

However, this measure fails to capture differences in achievement *within* these groups. Even among the top 1% of people as measured by cognitive ability (evaluated at age thirteen), exceptional outcomes are strongly correlated with GMA. Compared with those who are in the bottom quartile of this top 1%, those who are in the top quartile are two to three times more likely to earn a doctoral-level degree, publish a book, or be granted a patent. In other words, not only does the difference in GMA matter between the 99th percentile and the 80th or 50th, but it still matters — a lot! — between the 99.88th percentile and the 99.13th.

In another striking illustration of the link between ability and outcomes, a 2013 study focused on the CEOs of Fortune 500 companies and the 424 American billionaires (the top 0.0001% of Americans by wealth). It found, predictably, that these hyper-elite groups are composed of people drawn from the most intellectually able. But the study also found that *within* these groups, higher education and ability levels are related to higher compensation (for CEOs) and net worth (for billionaires). Incidentally, famous college dropouts who become billionaires, such as Steve Jobs, Bill Gates, and Mark Zuckerberg, are the trees that hide the forest: whereas about one-third of American adults have earned a college degree, 88% of billionaires did so.

The conclusion is clear. GMA contributes significantly to the quality of performance in occupations that require judgment, even within a pool of high-ability individuals. The notion that there is a threshold beyond which GMA ceases to make a difference is not supported by the evidence. This conclusion in turn strongly suggests that if professional judgments are unverifiable but assumed to reach for an invisible bull's-eye, then the judgments of high-ability people are more likely to be close. If you must pick people to make judgments, picking those with the highest mental ability makes a lot of sense.

But this line of reasoning has an important limitation. Since you cannot give standardized tests to everyone, you will have to guess who the higher-GMA people are. And high GMA improves performance on many fronts, including the ability to convince others that you're right. People of high mental ability are more likely than others to make better judgments and to be true experts, but they are also more likely to impress their peers, earn others' trust, and become respect-experts in the absence of any reality feedback. Medieval astrologers must have been among the highest-GMA people of their time.

It can be sensible to place your trust in people who look and sound intelligent and who can articulate a compelling rationale for their judgments, but this strategy is insufficient and may even backfire. Are there, then, other ways to identify real experts? Do people with the best judgment have other recognizable traits?

Cognitive Style

Regardless of mental ability, people differ in their *cognitive style*, or their approach to judgment tasks. Many instruments have been developed to capture cognitive styles. Most of these measures correlate with GMA (and with one another), but they measure different things.

One such measure is the *cognitive reflection test* (CRT), made famous by the now-ubiquitous question about the ball and the bat: "A bat and a ball cost $1.10 in total. The bat costs $1.00 more than the ball. How much does the ball cost?" Other questions that have been proposed to measure cognitive reflection include this one: "If you're running a race and you pass the person in second place, what place are you in?" CRT questions attempt to measure how likely people are to override the first (and wrong) answer that comes to mind ("ten cents" for the ball-and-bat question, and "first" for the race example). Lower CRT scores are associated with many real-world judgments and beliefs, including belief in ghosts, astrology, and extrasensory perception. The scores predict whether people will fall for blatantly inaccurate "fake news." They are even associated with how much people will use their smartphones.

The CRT is seen by many as one instrument to measure a broader concept: the propensity to use reflective versus impulsive thought processes. Simply put, some people like to engage in careful thought, whereas others, faced with the same problem, tend to trust their first impulses. In our terminology, the CRT can be seen as a measure of people's propensity to rely on slow, System 2 thinking rather than on fast, System 1 thinking.

Other self-assessments have been developed to measure this propensity (and all these tests are, of course, intercorrelated). The need-for-cognition scale, for instance, asks people how much they like to think hard about problems. To score high on the scale, you would have to agree that "I tend to set goals that can be accomplished only by expending considerable mental effort" and disagree with "Thinking is not my idea of fun." People with a high need for cognition tend to be less susceptible to known cognitive biases. Some more bizarre associations have been reported, too: if you avoid movie reviews with a spoiler alert, you probably have a high need for cognition; those who are low on the need-for-cognition scale prefer spoiled stories.

Because that scale is a self-assessment and because the socially desirable answer is fairly obvious, the scale raises fair questions. Someone who is trying to impress is hardly likely to endorse the statement "Thinking is not my idea of fun." For that reason, other tests try to measure skills instead of using self-descriptions.

One example is the Adult Decision Making Competence scale, which measures how prone people are to make typical errors in judgment like overconfidence or inconsistency in risk perceptions. Another is the Halpern Critical Thinking Assessment, which focuses on critical thinking skills, including both a disposition toward rational thinking and a set of learnable skills. Taking this assessment, you would be asked questions like this: "Imagine that a friend asks you for advice about which of two weight-loss programs to choose. Whereas one program reports that clients lose an average of twenty-five pounds, the other program reports that they lose an average of thirty pounds. What questions would you like to have answered before choosing one of the programs?" If you answered, for instance, that you would want to know how many people lost this much weight and whether they maintained that weight loss for a year or more, you would score points for applying critical thinking. People who score well on the Adult Decision Making Competence scale or on the Halpern assessment seem to make better judgments in life: they experience fewer adverse life events driven by bad choices, such as needing to pay late fees for a movie rental and experiencing an unwanted pregnancy.

It seems sensible to assume that all these measures of cognitive style and skill—and many others—generally predict judgment. Their relevance seems, however, to vary with the task. When Uriel Haran,

Ilana Ritov, and Barbara Mellers looked for the cognitive styles that might predict forecasting ability, they found that the need for cognition did not predict who would work harder to seek additional information. They also did not find that the need for cognition was reliably associated with higher performance.

The only measure of cognitive style or personality that they found to predict forecasting performance was another scale, developed by psychology professor Jonathan Baron to measure "actively open-minded thinking." To be actively open-minded is to actively search for information that contradicts your preexisting hypotheses. Such information includes the dissenting opinions of others and the careful weighing of new evidence against old beliefs. Actively open-minded people agree with statements like this: "Allowing oneself to be convinced by an opposing argument is a sign of good character." They disagree with the proposition that "changing your mind is a sign of weakness" or that "intuition is the best guide in making decisions."

In other words, while the cognitive reflection and need for cognition scores measure the propensity to engage in slow and careful thinking, actively open-minded thinking goes beyond that. It is the humility of those who are constantly aware that their judgment is a work in progress and who yearn to be corrected.

We will see in chapter 21 that this thinking style characterizes the very best forecasters, who constantly change their minds and revise their beliefs in response to new information. Interestingly, there is some evidence that actively open-minded thinking is a teachable skill.

We do not aim here to draw hard-and-fast conclusions about how to pick individuals who will make good judgments in a given domain. But two general principles emerge from this brief review. First, it is wise to recognize the difference between domains in which expertise can be confirmed by comparison with true values (such as weather forecasting) and domains that are the province of respect-experts. A political analyst may sound articulate and convincing, and a chess grandmaster may sound timid and unable to explain the reasoning behind some of his moves. Yet we probably should treat the professional judgment of the former with more skepticism than that of the latter.

Second, some judges are going to be better than their equally qualified and experienced peers. If they are better, they are less likely to be biased or noisy. Among many things that explain these differences, intelligence and cognitive style matter. Although no single measure or scale unambiguously predicts judgment quality, you may want to look for the sort of people who actively search for new information that could contradict their prior beliefs, who are methodical in integrating that information into their current perspective, and who are willing, even eager, to change their minds as a result.

The personality of people with excellent judgment may not fit the generally accepted stereotype of a decisive leader. People often tend to trust and like leaders who are firm and clear and who seem to know, immediately and deep in their bones, what is right. Such leaders inspire confidence. But the evidence suggests that if the goal is to reduce error, it is better for leaders (and others) to remain open to counterarguments and to know that they might be wrong. If they end up being decisive, it is at the end of a process, not at the start.

Speaking of Better Judges

"You are an expert. But are your judgments verifiable, or are you a respect-expert?"

"We have to choose between two opinions, and we know nothing about these individuals' expertise and track record. Let's follow the advice of the more intelligent one."

"Intelligence is only part of the story, however. *How* people think is also important. Perhaps we should pick the most thoughtful, open-minded person, rather than the smartest one."

CHAPTER 19

Debiasing and Decision Hygiene

Many researchers and organizations have pursued the goal of debiasing judgments. This chapter examines their central findings. We will distinguish between different types of debiasing interventions and discuss one such intervention that deserves further investigation. We will then turn to the reduction of noise and introduce the idea of decision hygiene.

Ex Post and Ex Ante Debiasing

A good way to characterize the two main approaches to debiasing is to return to the measurement analogy. Suppose that you know that your bathroom scale adds, on average, half a pound to your weight. Your scale is biased. But this does not make it useless. You can address its bias in one of two possible ways. You can correct every reading from your unkindly scale by subtracting half a pound. To be sure, that might get a bit tiresome (and you might forget to do it). An alternative might be to adjust the dial and improve the instrument's accuracy, once and for all.

These two approaches to debiasing measurements have direct analogues in interventions to debias judgments. They work either ex post, by correcting judgments after they have been made, or ex ante, by intervening before a judgment or decision.

Ex post, or corrective, debiasing is often carried out intuitively. Suppose that you are supervising a team in charge of a project and that the team estimates that it can complete its project in three months. You might want to add a buffer to the members' judgment and plan for four months, or more, thus correcting a bias (the planning fallacy) you assume is present.

This kind of bias correction is sometimes undertaken more systematically. In the United Kingdom, HM Treasury has published *The Green Book*, a guide on how to evaluate programs and projects. The book urges planners to address optimistic biases by applying percentage adjustments to estimates of the cost and duration of a project. These adjustments should ideally be based on an organization's historic levels of optimism bias. If no such historical data is available, *The Green Book* recommends applying generic adjustment percentages for each type of project.

Ex ante or preventive debiasing interventions fall in turn into two broad categories. Some of the most promising are designed to modify the environment in which the judgment or decision takes place. Such modifications, or *nudges,* as they are known, aim to reduce the effect of biases or even to enlist biases to produce a better decision. A simple example is automatic enrollment in pension plans. Designed to overcome inertia, procrastination, and optimistic bias, automatic enrollment ensures that employees will be saving for retirement unless they deliberately opt out. Automatic enrollment has proved to be extremely effective in increasing participation rates. The program is sometimes accompanied by Save More Tomorrow plans, by which employees can agree to earmark a certain percentage of their future wage increases for savings. Automatic enrollment can be used in many places — for example, automatic enrollment in green energy, in free school meal plans for poor children, or in various other benefits programs.

Other nudges work on different aspects of choice architecture. They might make the right decision the easy decision—for example, by reducing administrative burdens for getting access to care for mental health problems. Or they might make certain characteristics of a product or an activity salient—for example, by making once-hidden fees explicit and clear. Grocery stores and websites can easily be designed to nudge people in a way that overcomes their biases. If healthy foods are put in prominent places, more people are likely to buy them.

A different type of ex ante debiasing involves training decision makers to recognize their biases and to overcome them. Some of these interventions have been called *boosting;* they aim to improve people's capacities—for example, by teaching them statistical literacy.

Educating people to overcome their biases is an honorable enterprise, but it is more challenging than it seems. Of course, education is useful. For instance, people who have taken years of advanced statistics classes are less likely to make errors in statistical reasoning. But teaching people to avoid biases is hard. Decades of research have shown that professionals who have learned to avoid biases in their area of expertise often struggle to apply what they have learned to different fields. Weather forecasters, for instance, have learned to avoid overconfidence in their forecasts. When they announce a 70% chance of rain, it rains, by and large, 70% of the time. Yet they can be just as overconfident as other people when asked general-knowledge questions. The challenge of learning to overcome a bias is to recognize that a new problem is similar to one we have seen elsewhere and that a bias that we have seen in one place is likely to materialize in other places.

Researchers and educators have had some success using nontraditional teaching methods to facilitate this recognition. In one study, Carey Morewedge of Boston University and his colleagues used instructional videos and "serious games." Participants learned to recognize errors caused by confirmation bias, anchoring, and other psychological biases. After each game, they received feedback on the errors they had made and learned how to avoid making them again. The games (and, to a lesser extent, the videos) reduced the number of errors that participants made on a test immediately afterward and again eight weeks later, when they were asked similar questions. In a separate study, Anne-Laure Sellier and her colleagues found that MBA students who had played an instructional video game in which they learned to overcome confirmation bias applied this learning when solving a business case in another class. They did so even though they were not told that there was any connection between the two exercises.

A Limitation of Debiasing

Whether they correct biases ex post or prevent their effects through nudging or boosting, most debiasing approaches have one thing in common: they target a specific bias, which they assume is present. This often-reasonable assumption is sometimes wrong.

Consider again the example of project planning. You can reasonably assume that overconfidence affects project teams in general, but you cannot be sure that it is the only bias (or even the main one) affecting a particular project team. Maybe the team leader has had a bad experience with a similar project and so has learned to be especially conservative when making estimates. The team thus exhibits the opposite error from the one you thought you should correct. Or perhaps the team developed its forecast by analogy with another similar project and was anchored on the time it took to complete that project. Or maybe the project team, anticipating that you would add a buffer to its estimate, has preempted your adjustment by making its recommendation even more bullish than its true belief.

Or consider an investment decision. Overconfidence about the investment's prospects may certainly be at work, but another powerful bias, loss aversion, has the opposite effect, making decision makers loath to risk losing their initial outlay. Or consider a company allocating resources across multiple projects. Decision makers may be both bullish about the effect of new initiatives (overconfidence again) and too timid in diverting resources from existing units (a problem caused by *status quo bias,* which, as the name indicates, is our preference for leaving things as they are).

As these examples illustrate, it is difficult to know exactly which psychological biases are affecting a judgment. In any situation of some complexity, multiple psychological biases may be at work, conspiring to add error in the same direction or offsetting one another, with unpredictable consequences.

The upshot is that ex post or ex ante debiasing—which, respectively, correct or prevent specific psychological biases—are useful in some situations. These approaches work where the general direction of error is known and manifests itself as a clear statistical bias. Types of decisions that are expected to be strongly biased are likely to benefit from debiasing interventions. For instance, the planning fallacy is a sufficiently robust finding to warrant debiasing interventions against overconfident planning.

The problem is that in many situations, the likely direction of error is not known in advance. Such situations include all those in which the effect of psychological biases is variable among judges and essentially unpredictable — resulting in system noise. To reduce error under circumstances like these, we need to cast a broader net to try to detect more than one psychological bias at a time.

The Decision Observer

We suggest undertaking this search for biases neither before nor after the decision is made, but in real time. Of course, people are rarely aware of their own biases when they are being misled by them. This lack of awareness is itself a known bias, the *bias blind spot*. People often recognize biases more easily in others than they do in themselves. We suggest that observers can be trained to spot, in real time, the diagnostic signs that one or several familiar biases are affecting someone else's decisions or recommendations.

To illustrate how the process might work, imagine a group that attempts to make a complex and consequential judgment. The judgment could be of any type: a government deciding on possible responses to a pandemic or other crisis, a case conference in which physicians are exploring the best treatment for a patient with complex symptoms, a corporate board deciding on a major strategic move. Now imagine a *decision observer,* someone who watches this group and uses a checklist to diagnose whether any biases may be pushing the group away from the best possible judgment.

A decision observer is not an easy role to play, and no doubt, in some organizations it is not realistic. Detecting biases is useless if the ultimate decision makers are not committed to fighting them. Indeed, the decision makers must be the ones who initiate the process of decision observation and who support the role of the decision observer. We certainly do not recommend that you make yourself a self-appointed decision observer. You will neither win friends nor influence people.

Informal experiments suggest, however, that real progress can be made with this approach. At least, the approach is helpful under the right conditions, especially when the leaders of an organization or team are truly committed to the effort, and when the decision observers are well chosen — and not susceptible to serious biases of their own.

Decision observers in these cases fall in three categories. In some organizations, the role can be played by a supervisor. Instead of monitoring only the substance of the proposals that are submitted by a project team, the supervisor might also pay close attention to the *process* by which they are developed and to the team's dynamics. This makes the observer alert to biases that may have affected the proposal's development. Other organizations might assign a member of each working team to be the team's "bias buster"; this guardian of the decision process reminds teammates in real time of the biases that may mislead them. The downside of this approach is that the decision observer is placed in the position of a devil's advocate inside the team and may quickly run out of political capital. Finally, other organizations might rely on an outside facilitator, who has the advantage of a neutral perspective (and the attending disadvantages in terms of inside knowledge and costs).

To be effective, decision observers need some training and tools. One such tool is a checklist of the biases they are attempting to detect. The case for relying on a checklist is clear: checklists have a long history of improving decisions in high-stakes contexts and are particularly well suited to preventing the repetition of past errors.

Here is an example. In the United States, federal agencies must compile a formal regulatory impact analysis before they issue expensive regulations designed to clean the air or water, reduce deaths in the workplace, increase food safety, respond to public health crises, reduce greenhouse gas emissions, or increase homeland security. A dense, technical document with an unlovely name (OMB Circular A-4)

and spanning nearly fifty pages sets out the requirements of the analysis. The requirements are clearly
designed to counteract bias. Agencies must explain
why the regulation is needed, consider both more and
less stringent alternatives, consider both costs and
benefits, present the information in an unbiased manner, and discount the future appropriately. But in
many agencies, government officials have not com-
plied with the requirements of that dense, technical
document. (They might not even have read it.) In
response, federal officials produced a simple checklist,
consisting of just one and one-half pages, to reduce
the risk that agencies will ignore, or fail to attend to,
any of the major requirements.

To illustrate what a bias checklist might look like,
we have included one as appendix B. This generic
checklist is merely an example; any decision observer
will certainly want to develop one that is customized
to the needs of the organization, both to enhance its
relevance and facilitate its adoption. Importantly, a
checklist is not an exhaustive list of all the biases that
can affect a decision; it aims to focus on the most frequent and most consequential ones.

Decision observation with appropriate bias checklists can help limit the effect of biases. Although we
have seen some encouraging results in informal,
small-scale efforts, we are not aware of any systematic

exploration of the effects of this approach or of the pros and cons of the various possible ways to deploy it. We hope to inspire more experimentation, both by practitioners and by researchers, of the practice of real-time debiasing by decision observers.

Noise Reduction: Decision Hygiene

Bias is error we can often see and even explain. It is directional: that is why a nudge can limit the detrimental effects of a bias, or why an effort to boost judgment can combat specific biases. It is also often visible: that is why an observer can hope to diagnose biases in real time as a decision is being made.

Noise, on the other hand, is unpredictable error that we cannot easily see or explain. That is why we so often neglect it—even when it causes grave damage. For this reason, strategies for noise reduction are to debiasing what preventive hygiene measures are to medical treatment: the goal is to prevent an unspecified range of potential errors before they occur.

We call this approach to noise reduction *decision hygiene*. When you wash your hands, you may not know precisely which germ you are avoiding—you just know that handwashing is good prevention for a variety of germs (especially but not only during a pandemic). Similarly, following the principles of decision hygiene means that you adopt techniques that reduce noise without ever knowing which underlying errors you are helping to avoid.

The analogy with handwashing is intentional. Hygiene measures can be tedious. Their benefits are not directly visible; you might never know what problem they prevented from occurring. Conversely, when problems do arise, they may not be traceable to a specific breakdown in hygiene observance. For these reasons, handwashing compliance is difficult to enforce, even among health-care professionals, who are well aware of its importance.

Just like handwashing and other forms of prevention, decision hygiene is invaluable but thankless. Correcting a well-identified bias may at least give you a tangible sense of achieving something. But the procedures that reduce noise will not. They will, statistically, prevent many errors. Yet you will never know *which* errors. Noise is an invisible enemy, and preventing the assault of an invisible enemy can yield only an invisible victory.

Given how much damage noise can cause, that invisible victory is nonetheless worth the battle. The following chapters introduce several decision hygiene strategies used in multiple domains, including forensic science, forecasting, medicine, and human resources. In chapter 25, we will review these strategies and show how they can be combined in an integrated approach to noise reduction.

Speaking of Debiasing and Decision Hygiene

"Do you know what specific bias you're fighting and in what direction it affects the outcome? If not, there are probably several biases at work, and it is hard to predict which one will dominate."

"Before we start discussing this decision, let's designate a decision observer."

"We have kept good decision hygiene in this decision process; chances are the decision is as good as it can be."

CHAPTER 20

Sequencing Information in Forensic Science

I n March 2004, a series of bombs placed in commuter trains killed 192 people and injured more than 2,000 in Madrid. A fingerprint found on a plastic bag at the crime scene was transmitted via Interpol to law enforcement agencies worldwide. Days later, the US Federal Bureau of Investigation (FBI) crime lab conclusively identified the fingerprint as belonging to Brandon Mayfield, an American citizen living in Oregon.

Mayfield looked like a plausible suspect. A former officer in the US Army, he had married an Egyptian woman and converted to Islam. As a lawyer, he had represented men charged with (and later convicted of) attempting to travel to Afghanistan to join the Taliban. He was on the FBI's watch list.

Mayfield was placed under surveillance, his house bugged and searched, his phones wiretapped. When this scrutiny failed to yield any material information, the FBI arrested him. But he was never formally charged. Mayfield had not left the country in a decade. While he was in custody, the Spanish investigators, who had already informed the FBI that they considered Mayfield a negative match for the fingerprint on the plastic bag, matched that print to another suspect.

Mayfield was released after two weeks. Eventually, the US government apologized to him, paid him a $2 million settlement, and ordered an extensive investigation into the causes of the mistake. Its key finding: "The error was a human error and not a methodology or technology failure."

Fortunately, such human errors are rare. They are nonetheless instructive. How could the best fingerprint experts in the United States mistakenly identify a fingerprint as belonging to a man who had never come close to the crime scene? To find out, we first need to understand how fingerprint examination works and how it relates to other examples of professional judgment. We will learn that forensic fingerprinting, which we tend to think of as an exact science, is in fact subject to the psychological biases of examiners. These biases can create more noise, and thus more error, than we would imagine. And we will see how the forensic science community is taking steps to tackle this problem by implementing a decision hygiene strategy that can apply to all environments: a tight control over the flow of information used to make judgments.

Fingerprints

Fingermarks are the impressions left by the friction ridges of our fingers on the surfaces we touch. Although there are examples of fingerprints being used as apparent identification marks in ancient times, modern fingerprinting dates back to the late nineteenth century, when Henry Faulds, a Scottish physician, published the first scientific paper suggesting the use of fingerprints as an identification technique.

In subsequent decades, fingerprints gained traction as identification marks in criminal records, gradually replacing the anthropometric measurement techniques developed by Alphonse Bertillon, a French police officer. Bertillon himself codified, in 1912, a formal system for the comparison of fingerprints. Sir Francis Galton, whom we previously encountered as the discoverer of the wisdom of crowds, had developed a similar system in England. (Still, it is no wonder that these founding fathers are rarely celebrated.

Galton believed that fingerprints would be a useful tool for classifying individuals according to their race, and Bertillon, probably because of anti-Semitic prejudice, contributed decisive—and flawed—expert testimony during the 1894 and 1899 trials of Alfred Dreyfus.)

Police officers soon discovered that fingerprints could do more than serve as identification marks for repeat offenders. In 1892, Juan Vucetich, a police officer in Argentina, was the first to compare a latent fingerprint left at a crime scene with a suspect's thumb. Since then, the practice of collecting *latent prints* (those left by their owner at the scene of a crime) and comparing them with *exemplar prints* (those collected in controlled conditions from known individuals) has been the most decisive application of fingerprinting and has provided the most widely used form of forensic evidence.

If you have ever come across an electronic fingerprint reader (like those used by immigration services in many countries), you probably think of fingerprint comparison as a straightforward, mechanical, and easily automated task. But comparing a latent print collected from a crime scene with an exemplar print is a much more delicate exercise than matching two clean prints. When you press your fingers firmly on a reader purposely built to record a fingerprint impression, you produce a neat, standardized image. By contrast, latent prints are often partial, unclear, smudged, or otherwise distorted; they do not provide the same quantity and quality of information as does a print collected in a controlled and dedicated environment. Latent prints often overlap with other prints, either by the same person or by someone else, and include dirt and other artifacts present on the surface. Deciding whether they match a suspect's exemplar prints requires expert judgment. It is the job of human fingerprint examiners.

When provided with a latent print, examiners routinely follow a process called ACE-V, which stands for analysis, comparison, evaluation, and verification. First, they must analyze the latent print to determine whether it is of sufficient value for comparison. If it is, they compare it to an exemplar print. The comparison leads to an evaluation, which can produce an *identification* (the prints originated from the same person), an *exclusion* (the prints do not originate from the same person), or an inconclusive decision. An identification decision triggers the fourth step: verification by another examiner.

For decades, the reliability of this procedure remained unquestioned. Although eyewitness testimonies have been shown to be dangerously unreliable and even confessions can be false, fingerprints were accepted—at least until the advent of DNA analysis—as the most credible form of evidence. Until 2002, fingerprint evidence had never been successfully challenged in an American courtroom. The FBI website at the time, for example, was adamant: "Fingerprints offer an *infallible* means of personal identification." In the very rare cases when errors did happen, they were blamed on incompetence or fraud.

Fingerprint evidence remained unchallenged for so long in part because of the difficulty in proving it wrong. The true value of a set of fingerprints, that is, the ground truth of who actually committed the crime, is often unknown. For Mayfield and a handful of similar cases, the mistake was especially egregious. But in general, if a suspect disputes the examiner's conclusions, the fingerprint evidence will, of course, be considered more reliable.

We have noted that not knowing the true value is neither unusual nor an impediment to measuring noise. How much noise is there in fingerprint analysis? Or more precisely, given that fingerprint examiners, unlike sentencing judges or underwriters, do not produce a number but make a categorical judgment, how often do they disagree, and why? This question is what Itiel Dror, a cognitive neuroscience researcher at University College London, was the first to set out to study. He conducted what amounts to a series of noise audits in a field that had assumed it did not have a noise problem.

Occasion Noise in Fingerprint Analysis

It may seem odd for a cognitive scientist — a psychologist — to challenge fingerprint examiners. After all, as you may have seen on TV shows like *CSI: Crime Scene Investigation* and subsequent series of the CSI franchise, these are latex-glove-wearing, microscope-wielding hard-science types. But Dror realized that examining fingerprints was clearly a matter of judgment. And as a cognitive neuroscientist, he reasoned that wherever there is judgment, there must be noise.

To test this hypothesis, Dror focused first on occasion noise: the variability between the judgments of *the same* experts looking at *the same* evidence twice. As Dror puts it, "If experts are not reliable in the sense that they are not consistent with themselves, then the basis of their judgments and professionalism is in question."

Fingerprints provide a perfect test bed for an audit of occasion noise because unlike the cases that a physician or a judge encounters, pairs of prints are not easily memorable. Of course, a suitable interval of time must be allowed to pass to ensure that examiners do not remember the prints. (In Dror's studies, some brave, open-minded experts agreed that, *at any time in the next five years,* they would take part in studies, without their knowledge.) Additionally, the experiment must happen in the course of the experts' routine casework, so that they are not aware that their skills are being tested. If, under these circumstances, the examiners' judgments change from one test to the next, we are in the presence of occasion noise.

The Forensic Confirmation Bias

In two of his original studies, Dror added an important twist. When seeing the prints for the second time, some of the examiners were exposed to additional biasing information about the case. For instance, fingerprint examiners who had earlier found the prints to be a match were told, this time, that "the suspect has an alibi" or that "firearms evidence suggests it's not him." Others, who had first concluded that a suspect was innocent or that the prints were inconclusive, were told the second time that "the detective believes the suspect is guilty," "eyewitnesses identified him," or "he confessed to the crime." Dror called this experiment a test of the experts' "biasability," because the contextual information supplied activated a psychological bias (a confirmation bias) in a given direction.

Indeed, the examiners turned out to be susceptible to bias. When the same examiners considered the same prints they had seen earlier, but this time with biasing information, their judgments changed. In the first study, four out of five experts altered their previous identification decision when presented with strong contextual information that suggested an exclusion. In the second study, six experts reviewed four pairs of prints; biasing information led to changes in four of the twenty-four decisions. To be sure, most of their decisions did not change, but for these kinds of decisions, a shift of one in six can be counted as large. These findings have since been replicated by other researchers.

Predictably, the examiners were more likely to change their minds when the decision was a difficult one to start with, when the biasing information was strong, and when the change was from a conclusive to an inconclusive decision. It is, nonetheless, troubling that "expert fingerprint examiners made decisions on the basis of the context, rather than on the basis of the actual information contained in the print."

The effect of biasing information is not restricted to the examiner's conclusion (identification, inconclusive, or exclusion). Biasing information actually changes *what* the examiner perceives, in addition to *how* that perception is interpreted. In a separate study,

Dror and colleagues showed that examiners who have been placed in a biased context literally do not see the same things as those who have not been exposed to biasing information. When the latent print is accompanied by a target exemplar print, the examiners observe significantly fewer details (called *minutiae*) than they do when they see the latent print alone. A later, independent study confirmed this conclusion and added that "how [it] occurs is not obvious."

Dror coined a term for the impact of biasing information: the *forensic confirmation bias*. This bias has since been documented with other forensic techniques, including blood pattern analysis, arson investigation, the analysis of skeletal remains, and forensic pathology. Even DNA analysis—widely regarded as the new gold standard in forensic science—can be susceptible to confirmation bias, at least when experts must assess complex DNA mixtures.

The susceptibility of forensic experts to confirmation bias is not just a theoretical concern because, in reality, no systematic precautions are in place to make sure that forensic experts are not exposed to biasing information. Examiners often receive such information in the transmittal letters that accompany the evidence submitted to them. Examiners are also often in direct communication with police, prosecutors, and other examiners.

Confirmation bias raises another problem. An important safeguard against errors, built into the ACE-V procedure, is the independent verification by another expert before an identification can be confirmed. But most often, only identifications are independently verified. The result is a strong risk of confirmation bias, as the verifying examiner knows that the initial conclusion was an identification. The verification step therefore does not provide the benefit normally expected from the aggregation of independent judgments, because verifications are not, in fact, independent.

A cascade of confirmation biases seems to have been at work in the Mayfield case, in which not two but three FBI experts concurred on the erroneous identification. As the later investigation of the error noted, the first examiner appears to have been impressed by "the power of the correlation" from the automated system searching the databases of fingerprints for a possible match. Although he was, apparently, not exposed to Mayfield's biographical details, the results provided by the computerized system performing the initial search, "coupled with the inherent pressure of working an extremely high-profile case," were enough to produce the initial confirmation bias. Once the first examiner made an erroneous identification, the report continues, "the subsequent examinations were tainted." As the first examiner was a highly respected supervisor, "it became increasingly difficult for others in the agency to disagree." The initial error was replicated and amplified, resulting in a near-certainty that Mayfield was guilty. Tellingly, even a highly respected independent expert, appointed by the court to examine the evidence on behalf of Mayfield's defense, concurred with the FBI in confirming the identification.

The same phenomenon can be at work in other forensic disciplines and across them. Latent print identification is reputed to be among the most objective of the forensic disciplines. If fingerprint examiners can be biased, so can experts in other fields. Moreover, if a firearms expert knows that the fingerprints are a match, this knowledge may bias that expert's judgment, too. And if a forensic odontologist knows that DNA analysis has identified a suspect, that expert is probably less likely to suggest that the bite marks do not match the suspect. These examples raise the specter of bias cascades: just as in the group decisions we described in chapter 8, an initial error prompted by confirmation bias becomes the biasing information that influences a second expert, whose judgment biases a third one, and so on.

Having established that biasing information creates variability, Dror and his colleagues uncovered more evidence of occasion noise. Even when fingerprint experts are not exposed to biasing information, they sometimes change their minds about a set of prints they have seen before. As we would expect, changes are less frequent when no biasing information is supplied, but they happen nonetheless. A 2012 study commissioned by the FBI replicated this finding on a larger scale by asking seventy-two examiners to look again at twenty-five pairs of prints they had evaluated about seven months earlier. With a large sample of highly qualified examiners, the study confirmed that fingerprint experts are sometimes susceptible to occasion noise. About one decision in ten was altered. Most of the changes were to or from the inconclusive category, and none resulted in false identifications. The study's most troubling implication is that some fingerprint identifications that led to convictions could potentially have been judged inconclusive at another time. When the same examiners are looking at the same prints, even when the context is not designed to bias them but is instead meant to be as constant as possible, there is inconsistency in their decisions.

Some Noise, but How Much Error?

The practical question raised by these findings is the possibility of judicial errors. We cannot ignore questions about the reliability of experts who testify in court: validity requires reliability because, quite simply, it is hard to agree with reality if you cannot agree with yourself.

How many errors, exactly, are caused by faulty forensic science? A review of 350 exonerations obtained by the Innocence Project, a nonprofit that works to overturn wrongful convictions, concluded that the misapplication of forensic science was a contributing cause in 45% of cases. This statistic sounds bad, but the question that matters to judges and jurors is different: To know how much trust they should accord the examiner taking the stand to testify, they need to know how likely forensic scientists, including fingerprint examiners, are to make consequential errors.

The most robust set of answers to this question can be found in a report by the President's Council of Advisors on Science and Technology (PCAST), an advisory group of the nation's leading scientists and engineers, which in 2016 produced an in-depth review of forensic science in criminal courts. The report summarizes the available evidence on the validity of fingerprint analysis and especially on the likelihood of erroneous identifications (false positives) such as the one involving Mayfield.

This evidence is surprisingly sparse, and as PCAST

notes, it is "distressing" that work to produce it did not begin until recently. The most credible data come from the only published large-scale study of fingerprint identification accuracy, which was conducted by FBI scientists themselves in 2011. The study involved 169 examiners, each comparing approximately one hundred pairs of latent and exemplar fingerprints. Its central finding was that very few erroneous identifications occurred: the false-positive rate was about one in six hundred.

An error rate of one in six hundred is low but, as the report noted, is "*much higher* than the general public (and, by extension, most jurors) would likely believe based on longstanding claims about the accuracy of fingerprint analysis." Furthermore, this study contained no biasing contextual information, and the participating examiners knew they were taking part in a test—which may have caused the study to underestimate the errors that occur in real casework. A subsequent study conducted in Florida arrived at much higher numbers of false positives. The varied findings in the literature suggest that we need more research on the accuracy of fingerprint examiner decisions and how these decisions are reached.

One reassuring finding that does seem consistent across all studies, however, is that the examiners appear to err on the side of caution. Their accuracy is not perfect, but they are aware of the consequences of their judgments, and they take into account the asymmetrical cost of possible errors. Because of the very high credibility of fingerprinting, an erroneous identification can have tragic effects. Other types of error are less consequential. For instance, FBI experts observe, "in most casework, an exclusion has the same operational implications as an inconclusive." In other words, the fact that a fingerprint is found on the murder weapon is sufficient to convict, but the absence of that print is not sufficient to exonerate a suspect.

Consistent with our observation of examiner caution, the evidence suggests that experts think twice — or much more than twice — before making an identification decision. In the FBI study of identification accuracy, less than one-third of "mated" pairs (where the latent and the exemplar are from the same person) were judged (accurately) as identifications. Examiners also make far fewer false-positive identifications than false-negative exclusions. They are susceptible to bias, but not equally in both directions. As Dror notes, "It is easier to bias forensic experts towards the non-committal conclusion of 'inconclusive' than to the definitive 'identification' conclusion."

Examiners are trained to consider erroneous identification as the deadly sin to be avoided at all costs. To their credit, they act in accordance with this principle. We can only hope that their level of care keeps erroneous identifications, like those in the Mayfield case and a handful of other high-profile cases, extremely rare.

Listening to Noise

To observe that there is noise in forensic science should not be seen as a criticism of forensic scientists. It is merely a consequence of the observation we have made repeatedly: Wherever there is judgment, there is noise, and more of it than you think. A task like the analysis of fingerprints seems objective, so much so that many of us would not spontaneously regard it as a form of judgment. Yet it leaves room for inconsistency, disagreement, and, occasionally, error. However low the error rate of fingerprint identification may be, it is not zero, and as PCAST noted, juries should be made aware of that.

The first step to reduce noise must be, of course, to acknowledge its possibility. This admission does not come naturally to members of the fingerprint community, many of whom were initially highly skeptical of Dror's noise audit. The notion that an examiner can be unwittingly influenced by information about the case irked many experts. In a reply to Dror's study, the chair of the Fingerprint Society wrote that "any fingerprint examiner who...is swayed either way in that decision making process...is so immature he/she should seek employment in Disneyland." A director of a major forensic laboratory noted that having access to case information—precisely the sort of information that could bias the examiner—"provides some personal satisfaction which allows [examiners] to enjoy their job *without actually altering their judgment.*" Even the FBI, in its internal investigation of the Mayfield case, noted that "latent print examiners routinely conduct verifications in which they know the previous examiners' results *and yet those results do not influence the examiner's conclusions.*" These remarks essentially amount to a denial of the existence of confirmation bias.

Even when they are aware of the risk of bias, forensic scientists are not immune to the bias blind spot: the tendency to acknowledge the presence of bias in others, but not in oneself. In a survey of four hundred professional forensic scientists in twenty-one countries, 71% agreed that "cognitive bias is a cause for concern in the forensic sciences as a whole," but only 26% thought that their "own judgments are influenced by cognitive bias." In other words, about half of these forensic professionals believe that their colleagues' judgments are noisy but that their own are not. Noise can be an invisible problem, even to people whose job is to see the invisible.

Sequencing Information

Thanks to the persistence of Dror and his colleagues, attitudes are slowly changing and a growing number of forensic laboratories have begun taking new measures to reduce error in their analyses. For example, the PCAST report commended the FBI laboratory for redesigning its procedures to minimize the risk of confirmation bias.

The necessary methodological steps are relatively simple. They illustrate a decision hygiene strategy that has applicability in many domains: *sequencing information to limit the formation of premature intuitions.* In any judgment, some information is relevant, and some is not. More information is not always better, especially if it has the potential to bias judgments by leading the judge to form a premature intuition.

In that spirit, the new procedures deployed in forensic laboratories aim to protect the independence of the examiners' judgments by giving the examiners only the information they need, when they need it. In other words, the laboratory keeps them as much in the dark about the case as possible and reveals information only gradually. To do that, the approach Dror and colleagues codified is called *linear sequential unmasking.*

Dror has another recommendation that illustrates

the same decision hygiene strategy: examiners should document their judgments at each step. They should document their analysis of a latent fingerprint *before* they look at exemplar fingerprints to decide whether they are a match. This sequence of steps helps experts avoid the risk that they see only what they are looking for. And they should record their judgment on the evidence before they have access to contextual information that risks biasing them. If they change their mind after they are exposed to contextual information, these changes, and the rationale for them, should be documented. This requirement limits the risk that an early intuition biases the entire process.

The same logic inspires a third recommendation, which is an important part of decision hygiene. When a different examiner is called on to verify the identification made by the first person, the second person should not be aware of the first judgment.

The presence of noise in forensic science is, of course, of concern because of its potential life-or-death consequences. But it is also revealing. That we remained for so long entirely unaware of the possibility of error in fingerprint identification shows how our confidence in expert human judgment can sometimes be exaggerated and how a noise audit can reveal an unexpected amount of noise. The ability to mitigate these shortcomings through relatively simple process changes should be encouraging to all those who care about improving the quality of decisions.

The main decision hygiene strategy this case illustrates — sequencing information — has broad applicability as a safeguard against occasion noise. As we have noted, occasion noise is driven by countless triggers, including mood and even outside temperature. You cannot hope to control all these triggers, but you can attempt to shield judgments from the most obvious ones. You already know, for instance, that judgments can be altered by anger, fear, or other emotions, and perhaps you have noted that it is a good practice, if you can, to revisit your judgment at different points in time, when the triggers of occasion noise are likely to be different.

Less obvious is the possibility that your judgment can be altered by another trigger of occasion noise: information — even when it is accurate information. As in the example of the fingerprint examiners, as soon as you know what others think, confirmation bias can lead you to form an overall impression too early and to ignore contradictory information. The titles of two Hitchcock movies sum it up: a good decision maker should aim to keep a "shadow of a doubt," not to be "the man who knew too much."

Speaking of Sequencing Information

"Wherever there is judgment, there is noise — and that includes reading fingerprints."

"We have more information about this case, but let's not tell the experts everything we know before they make their judgment, so as not to bias them. In fact, let's tell them only what they absolutely need to know."

"The second opinion is not independent if the person giving it knows what the first opinion was. And the third one, even less so: there can be a bias cascade."

"To fight noise, they first have to admit that it exists."

CHAPTER 21

Selection and Aggregation in Forecasting

Many judgments involve forecasting. What is the unemployment rate likely to be in the next quarter? How many electric cars will be sold next year? What will be the effects of climate change in 2050? How long will it take to complete a new building? What will be the annual earnings of a particular company? How will a new employee perform? What will be the cost of a new air pollution regulation? Who will win an election? The answers to such questions have major consequences. Fundamental choices of private and public institutions often depend on them.

Analysts of forecasting—of when it goes wrong and why—make a sharp distinction between bias and noise (also called inconsistency or unreliability). Everyone agrees that in some contexts, forecasters are biased. For example, official agencies show unrealistic optimism in their budget forecasts. On average, they project unrealistically high economic growth and unrealistically low deficits. For practical purposes, it matters little whether their unrealistic optimism is a product of a cognitive bias or political considerations.

In addition, forecasters tend to be overconfident: if asked to formulate their forecasts as confidence intervals rather than as point estimates, they tend to pick narrower intervals than they should. For instance, an ongoing quarterly survey asks the chief financial officers of US companies to estimate the annual return of the S&P 500 index for the next year. The CFOs provide two numbers: a minimum, below which they think there is a one-in-ten chance the actual return will be, and a maximum, which they believe the actual return has a one-in-ten chance of exceeding. Thus the two numbers are the bounds of an 80% confidence interval. Yet the realized returns fall in that interval only 36% of the time. The CFOs are far too confident in the precision of their forecasts.

Forecasters are also noisy. A reference text, J. Scott Armstrong's *Principles of Forecasting,* points out that even among experts, "unreliability is a source of error in judgmental forecasting." In fact noise is a major source of error. Occasion noise is common; forecasters do not always agree with themselves. Between-person noise is also pervasive; forecasters disagree with one another, even if they are specialists. If you ask law professors to predict Supreme Court rulings, you will find a great deal of noise. If you ask specialists to project the annual benefits of air pollution regulation, you will find massive variability, with ranges of, for example, $3 billion to $9 billion. If you ask a group of economists to make forecasts about unemployment and growth, you will also find great variability. We have already seen many examples of noisy forecasts, and research on forecasting uncovers many more.

Improving Forecasts

The research also offers suggestions for reducing noise and bias. We will not review them exhaustively here, but we will focus on two noise-reduction strategies that have broad applicability. One is an application of the principle we mentioned in chapter 18: selecting better judges produces better judgments. The other is one of the most universally applicable decision hygiene strategies: aggregating multiple independent estimates.

The easiest way to aggregate several forecasts is to average them. Averaging is mathematically guaranteed to reduce noise: specifically, it divides it by the square root of the number of judgments averaged.

This means that if you average one hundred judgments, you will reduce noise by 90%, and if you average four hundred judgments, you will reduce it by 95% — essentially eliminating it. This statistical law is the engine of the wisdom-of-crowds approach, discussed in chapter 7.

Because averaging does nothing to reduce bias, its effect on total error (MSE) depends on the proportions of bias and noise in it. That is why the wisdom of crowds works best when judgments are independent, and therefore less likely to contain shared biases. Empirically, ample evidence suggests that averaging multiple forecasts greatly increases accuracy, for instance in the "consensus" forecast of economic forecasters of stock analysts. With respect to sales forecasting, weather forecasting, and economic forecasting, the unweighted average of a group of forecasters outperforms most and sometimes all individual forecasts. Averaging forecasts obtained by different methods has the same effect: in an analysis of thirty empirical comparisons in diverse domains, combined forecasts reduced errors by an average of 12.5%.

Straight averaging is not the only way to aggregate forecasts. A *select-crowd* strategy, which selects the best judges according to the accuracy of their recent judgments and averages the judgments of a small number of judges (e.g., five), can be as effective as straight averaging. It is also easier for decision makers who respect expertise to understand and adopt a strategy that relies not only on aggregation but also on selection.

One method to produce aggregate forecasts is to use *prediction markets,* in which individuals bet on likely outcomes and are thus incentivized to make the right forecasts. Much of the time, prediction markets have been found to do very well, in the sense that if the prediction market price suggests that events are, say, 70% likely to happen, they happen about 70% of the time. Many companies in various industries have used prediction markets to aggregate diverse views.

Another formal process for aggregating diverse views is known as the Delphi method. In its classic form, this method involves multiple rounds during which the participants submit estimates (or votes) to a moderator and remain anonymous to one another. At each new round, the participants provide reasons for their estimates and respond to the reasons given by others, still anonymously. The process encourages estimates to converge (and sometimes forces them to do so by requiring new judgments to fall within a specific range of the distribution of previous-round judgments). The method benefits both from aggregation and social learning.

The Delphi method has worked well in many

situations, but it can be challenging to implement. A simpler version, *mini-Delphi,* can be deployed within a single meeting. Also called *estimate-talk-estimate,* it requires participants first to produce separate (and silent) estimates, then to explain and justify them, and finally to make a new estimate in response to the estimates and explanations of others. The consensus judgment is the average of the individual estimates obtained in that second round.

The Good Judgment Project

Some of the most innovative work on the quality of forecasting, going well beyond what we have explored thus far, started in 2011, when three prominent behavioral scientists founded the Good Judgment Project. Philip Tetlock (whom we encountered in chapter 11 when we discussed his assessment of long-term forecasts of political events); his spouse, Barbara Mellers; and Don Moore teamed up to improve our understanding of forecasting and, in particular, why some people are good at it.

The Good Judgment Project started with the recruitment of tens of thousands of volunteers—not specialists or experts but ordinary people from many walks of life. They were asked to answer hundreds of questions, such as these:

- ❏ *Will North Korea detonate a nuclear device before the end of the year?*
- ❏ *Will Russia officially annex additional Ukrainian territory in the next three months?*
- ❏ *Will India or Brazil become a permanent member of the UN Security Council in the next two years?*
- ❏ *In the next year, will any country withdraw from the eurozone?*

As these examples show, the project has focused on large questions about world events. Importantly, efforts to answer such questions raise many of the same problems that more mundane forecasts do. If a lawyer is asking whether a client will win in court, or if a television studio is asked whether a proposed show will be a big hit, forecasting skills are involved. Tetlock and his colleagues wanted to learn whether some people are especially good forecasters. They also wanted to learn whether the ability to forecast could be taught or at least improved.

To understand the central findings, we need to explain some key aspects of the method adopted by Tetlock and his team to evaluate forecasters. First, they used a large number of forecasts, not just one or a few, where luck might be responsible for success or failure. If you predict that your favorite sports team will win its next game, and it does, you are not necessarily a good forecaster. Maybe you *always* predict that your favorite team will win: if that's your strategy, and if they win only half the time, your forecasting ability is not especially impressive. To reduce the role of luck, the researchers examined how participants did, on average, across numerous forecasts.

Second, the researchers asked participants to make their forecasts in terms of probabilities that an event would happen, rather than a binary "it will happen" or "it will not happen." To many people, forecasting means the latter—taking a stand one way or the other. However, given our objective ignorance of future events, it is much better to formulate probabilistic forecasts. If someone said in 2016, "Hillary Clinton is 70% likely to be elected president," he is not necessarily a bad forecaster. Things that are correctly said to be 70% likely will not happen 30% of the time. To know whether forecasters are good, we should ask whether their probability estimates map onto reality. Suppose that a particular forecaster named Margaret says that 500 different events are 60% likely. If 300 of them actually happen, then we can conclude that Margaret's confidence is well *calibrated*. Good calibration is one requirement for good forecasting.

Third, as an added refinement, Tetlock and

colleagues did not just ask their forecasters to make *one* probability estimate about whether an event would happen in, say, twelve months. They gave the participants the opportunity to revise their forecasts continuously in light of new information. Suppose that you had estimated, back in 2016, that the United Kingdom had only a 30% chance of leaving the European Union before the end of 2019. As new polls came out, suggesting that the "Leave" vote was gaining ground, you probably would have revised your forecast upward. When the result of the referendum was known, it was still uncertain whether the United Kingdom would leave the union within that time frame, but it certainly looked a lot more probable. (Brexit technically happened in 2020.)

With each new piece of information, Tetlock and his colleagues allowed the forecasters to update their forecasts. For scoring purposes, each one of these updates is treated as a new forecast. That way, participants in the Good Judgment Project are incentivized to monitor the news and update their forecasts continuously. This approach mirrors what is expected of forecasters in business and government, who should also be updating their forecasts frequently on the basis of new information, despite the risk of being criticized for changing their minds. (A well-known response to this criticism, sometimes attributed to John Maynard

Keynes, is, "When the facts change, I change my mind. What do *you* do?")

Fourth, to score the performance of the forecasters, the Good Judgment Project used a system developed by Glenn W. Brier in 1950. *Brier scores,* as they are known, measure the distance between what people forecast and what actually happens.

Brier scores are a clever way to get around a pervasive problem associated with probabilistic forecasts: the incentive for forecasters to hedge their bets by never taking a bold stance. Think again of Margaret, whom we described as a well-calibrated forecaster because she rated 500 events as 60% likely, and 300 of those events did happen. This result may not be as impressive as it seems. If Margaret is a weather forecaster who *always* predicts a 60% chance of rain and there are 300 rainy days out of 500, Margaret's forecasts are well calibrated but also practically useless. Margaret, in essence, is telling you that, just in case, you might want to carry an umbrella every day. Compare her with Nicholas, who predicts a 100% chance of rain on the 300 days when it will rain, and a 0% chance of rain on the 200 dry days. Nicholas has the same perfect calibration as Margaret: when either forecaster predicts that X% of the days will be rainy, rain falls precisely X% of the time. But Nicholas's forecasts are much more valuable: instead of hedging his bets, he is willing to tell you whether you should take an umbrella. Technically, Nicholas is said to have a high *resolution* in addition to good calibration.

Brier scores reward both good calibration and good resolution. To produce a good score, you have not only to be right on average (i.e., well calibrated) but also to be willing to take a stand and differentiate among forecasts (i.e., have high resolution). Brier scores are based on the logic of mean squared errors, and lower scores are better: a score of 0 would be perfect.

So, now that we know how they were scored, how well did the Good Judgment Project volunteers do? One of the major findings was that the overwhelming majority of the volunteers did poorly, but about 2% stood out. As mentioned earlier, Tetlock calls these well-performing people superforecasters. They were hardly unerring, but their predictions were much better than chance. Remarkably, one government official said that the group did significantly "better than the average for intelligence community analysts who could read intercepts and other secret data." This comparison is worth pausing over. Intelligence community analysts are trained to make accurate forecasts; they are not amateurs. In addition, they have access to classified information. And yet they do not do as well as the superforecasters do.

Perpetual Beta

What makes superforecasters so good? Consistent with our argument in chapter 18, we could reasonably speculate that they are unusually intelligent. That speculation is not wrong. On GMA tests, the super-forecasters do better than the average volunteer in the Good Judgment Project (and the average volunteer is significantly above the national average). But the difference isn't all that large, and many volunteers who do extremely well on intelligence tests do not qualify as superforecasters. Apart from general intelligence, we could reasonably expect that superforecasters are unusually good with numbers. And they are. But their real advantage is not their talent at math; it is their ease in thinking analytically and probabilistically.

Consider superforecasters' willingness and ability to structure and disaggregate problems. Rather than form a holistic judgment about a big geopolitical question (whether a nation will leave the European Union, whether a war will break out in a particular place, whether a public official will be assassinated), they break it up into its component parts. They ask, "What would it take for the answer to be yes? What would it take for the answer to be no?" Instead of offering a gut feeling or some kind of global hunch, they ask and try to answer an assortment of subsidiary questions.

Superforecasters also excel at taking the outside view, and they care a lot about base rates. As explained for the Gambardi problem in chapter 13, before you focus on the specifics of Gambardi's profile, it helps to know the probability that the average CEO will be fired or quit in the next two years. Superforecasters systematically look for base rates. Asked whether the next year will bring an armed clash between China and Vietnam over a border dispute, superforecasters do not focus only or immediately on whether China and Vietnam are getting along right now. They might have an intuition about this, in light of the news and analysis they have read. But they know that their intuition about one event is generally not a good guide. Instead they start by looking for a base rate: they ask how often past border disputes have escalated into armed clashes. If such clashes are rare, superforecasters will begin by incorporating that fact and only then turn to the details of the China–Vietnam situation.

In short, what distinguishes the superforecasters isn't their sheer intelligence; it's *how* they apply it. The skills they bring to bear reflect the sort of cognitive style we described in chapter 18 as likely to result in better judgments, particularly a high level of "active open-mindedness." Recall the test for actively open-minded thinking: it includes such statements as "People should take into consideration evidence that goes against their beliefs" and "It is more useful to pay attention to people who disagree with you than to pay attention to those who agree." Clearly, people who score high on this test are not shy about updating their judgments (without overreacting) when new information becomes available.

To characterize the thinking style of superforecasters, Tetlock uses the phrase "perpetual beta," a term used by computer programmers for a program that is not meant to be released in a final version but that is endlessly used, analyzed, and improved. Tetlock finds that "the strongest predictor of rising into the ranks of superforecasters is perpetual beta, the degree to which one is committed to belief updating and self-improvement." As he puts it, "What makes them so good is less what they are than what they do — the hard work of research, the careful thought and self-criticism, the gathering and synthesizing of other perspectives, the granular judgments and relentless updating." They like a particular cycle of thinking: "try, fail, analyze, adjust, try again."

Noise and Bias in Forecasting

At this point, you might be tempted to think that people can be trained to be superforecasters or at least to perform more like them. And indeed, Tetlock and his collaborators have worked to do exactly that. Their efforts should be considered the second stage of understanding why superforecasters perform so well and how to make them perform better.

In an important study, Tetlock and his team randomly assigned regular (nonsuper) forecasters to three groups, in which they tested the effect of different interventions on the quality of subsequent judgments. These interventions exemplify three of the strategies we have described to improve judgments:

1. *Training:* Several forecasters completed a tutorial designed to improve their abilities by teaching them probabilistic reasoning. In the tutorial, the forecasters learned about various biases (including base-rate neglect, overconfidence, and confirmation bias); the importance of averaging multiple predictions from diverse sources; and considering reference classes.

2. *Teaming (a form of aggregation):* Some forecasters were asked to work in teams in which they could see and debate one another's predictions. Teaming could increase accuracy by encouraging forecasters to deal with opposing arguments and to be actively open-minded.

3. *Selection:* All forecasters were scored for accuracy, and at the end of a full year, the top 2% were designated as superforecasters and given the

opportunity to work together in elite teams the following year.

As it turns out, all three interventions worked, in the sense that they improved people's Brier scores. Training made a difference, teaming made a larger one, and selection had an even larger effect.

This important finding confirms the value of aggregating judgments and selecting good judges. But it is not the full story. Armed with data about the effects of each intervention, Ville Satopää, who collaborated with Tetlock and Mellers, developed a sophisticated statistical technique to tease out how, exactly, each intervention improved forecasts. In principle, he reasoned, there are three major reasons why some forecasters can perform better or worse than others:

1. They can be more skilled at finding and analyzing data in the environment that are relevant to the prediction they have to make. This explanation points to the importance of information.

2. Some forecasters may have a general tendency to err on a particular side of the true value of a forecast. If, out of hundreds of forecasts, you systematically overestimate or underestimate the probability that certain changes from the status quo will occur,

you can be said to suffer from a form of bias, in favor of either change or stability.

3. Some forecasters may be less susceptible to noise (or random errors). In forecasting, as in any judgment, noise can have many triggers. Forecasters may overreact to a particular piece of news (this is an example of what we have called pattern noise), they may be subject to occasion noise, or they may be noisy in their use of the probability scale. All these errors (and many more) are unpredictable in their size and direction.

Satopää, Tetlock, Mellers, and their colleague Marat Salikhov called their model the BIN (bias, information, and noise) model for forecasting. They set out to measure how much each of the three components was responsible for the performance improvement in each of the three interventions.

Their answer was simple: all three interventions worked primarily by reducing noise. As the researchers put it, "Whenever an intervention boosted accuracy, it worked mainly by suppressing random errors in judgment. Curiously, the original intent of the training intervention was to reduce bias."

Since the training was designed to reduce biases, a less-than-super forecaster would have predicted that bias reduction would be the major effect of the training. Yet the training worked by reducing noise. The surprise is easily explained. Tetlock's training is designed to fight *psychological* biases. As you now know, the effect of psychological biases is not always a statistical bias. When they affect different individuals on different judgments in different ways, psychological biases produce noise. This is clearly the case here, as the events being forecast are quite varied. The same biases can lead a forecaster to overreact or underreact, depending on the topic. We should not expect them to produce a *statistical* bias, defined as the general tendency of a forecaster to believe that events will happen or not happen. As a result, training forecasters to fight their psychological biases works—by reducing noise.

Teaming had a comparably large effect on noise reduction, but it also significantly improved the ability of the teams to extract information. This result is consistent with the logic of aggregation: several brains that work together are better at finding information than one is. If Alice and Brian are working together, and Alice has spotted signals that Brian has missed, their joint forecast will be better. When working in groups, the superforecasters seem capable of avoiding the dangers of group polarization and information cascades. Instead, they pool their data and insights and, in their actively open-minded way, make the most of the combined information. Satopää and his colleagues explain this advantage: "Teaming—unlike training...allows forecasters to harness the information."

Selection had the largest total effect. Some of the improvement comes from a better use of information. Superforecasters are better than others at finding relevant information—possibly because they are smarter, more motivated, and more experienced at making these kinds of forecasts than is the average participant. But the main effect of selection is, again, to reduce noise. Superforecasters are less noisy than regular players or even trained teams. This finding, too, was a surprise to Satopää and the other researchers: " 'Superforecasters' may owe their success more to superior discipline in tamping down measurement error, than to incisive readings of the news" that others cannot replicate.

Where Selection and Aggregation Work

The success of the superforecasting project highlights the value of two decision hygiene strategies: *selection* (the superforecasters are, well, super) and *aggregation* (when they work in teams, forecasters perform better). The two strategies are broadly applicable in many judgments. Whenever possible, you should aim to combine the strategies, by constructing teams of judges (e.g., forecasters, investment professionals, recruiting officers) who are selected for being both good at what they do *and* complementary to one another.

So far, we have considered the improved precision that is achieved by averaging multiple independent judgments, as in the wisdom-of-crowds experiments. Aggregating the estimates of higher-validity judges will further improve accuracy. Yet another gain in accuracy can be obtained by combining judgments that are both independent and complementary. Imagine that four people are witnesses to a crime: it is essential, of course, to make sure that they do not influence one another. If, in addition, they have seen the crime from four different angles, the quality of the information they provide will be much better.

The task of assembling a team of professionals to make judgments together resembles the task of assembling a battery of tests to predict the future performance of candidates at school or on the job. The standard tool for that task is multiple regression (introduced in chapter 9). It works by selecting variables in succession. The test that best predicts the outcome is selected first. However, the next test to be included is not necessarily the second most valid. Instead, it is the one that *adds* the most predictive power to the first test, by providing predictions that are both valid and not redundant with the first. For example, suppose you have two tests of mental aptitude, which correlate .50 and .45 with future performance, and a test of personality that correlates only .30 with performance but is uncorrelated with aptitude tests. The optimal solution is to pick the more valid aptitude test first, then the personality test, which brings more new information.

Similarly, if you are assembling a team of judges, you should of course pick the best judge first. But your next choice may be a moderately valid individual who brings some new skill to the table rather than a more valid judge who is highly similar to the first one. A team selected in this manner will be superior because the validity of pooled judgments increases faster when the judgments are uncorrelated with one another than when they are redundant. Pattern noise will be relatively high in such a team because individual judgments of each case will differ. Paradoxically, the average of that noisy group will be more accurate than the average of a unanimous one.

An important caveat is in order. Regardless of diversity, aggregation can only reduce noise if judgments are truly independent. As our discussion of noise in groups has highlighted, group deliberation often adds more error in bias than it removes in noise. Organizations that want to harness the power of diversity must welcome the disagreements that will arise when team members reach their judgments independently. Eliciting and aggregating judgments that are both independent and diverse will often be the easiest, cheapest, and most broadly applicable decision hygiene strategy.

Speaking of Selection and Aggregation

"Let's take the average of four independent judgments — this is guaranteed to reduce noise by half."

"We should strive to be in perpetual beta, like the superforecasters."

"Before we discuss this situation, what is the relevant base rate?"

"We have a good team, but how can we ensure more diversity of opinions?"

CHAPTER 22

Guidelines in Medicine

S ome years ago, a good friend of ours (let's call him Paul) was diagnosed with high blood pressure by his primary care doctor (we will call him Dr. Jones). The doctor advised Paul to try medication. Dr. Jones prescribed a diuretic, but it had no effect; Paul's blood pressure remained high. A few weeks later, Dr. Jones responded with a second medication, a calcium channel blocker. Its effect was also modest.

These results baffled Dr. Jones. After three months of weekly office visits, Paul's high blood pressure readings had dropped slightly, but they were still too high. It wasn't clear what the next steps would be. Paul was anxious and Dr. Jones was troubled, not least because Paul was a relatively young man in good health. Dr. Jones contemplated trying a third medication.

At that point, Paul happened to move to a new city, where he consulted a new primary care doctor (we will call him Dr. Smith). Paul told Dr. Smith the story of his continuing struggles with high blood pressure. Dr. Smith immediately responded, "Buy a home blood pressure kit, and see what the readings are. I don't think you have high blood pressure at all. You probably just have white coat syndrome—your blood pressure goes up in doctors' offices!"

Paul did as he was told, and sure enough, his blood pressure was normal at home. It has been normal ever since (and a month after Dr. Smith told him about white coat syndrome, it became normal in doctors' offices as well).

A central task of doctors is to make diagnoses—to decide whether a patient has some kind of illness and, if so, to identify it. Diagnosis often requires some kind of judgment. For many conditions, the diagnosis is routine and largely mechanical, and rules and procedures are in place to minimize noise. It's usually easy for a doctor to determine whether someone has a dislocated shoulder or a broken toe. Something similar can be said about problems that are more technical. Quantifying tendon degeneration produces little noise. When pathologists evaluate core needle biopsies of breast lesions, their evaluations are relatively straightforward, with little noise.

Importantly, some diagnoses do not involve judgment at all. Health care often progresses by removing the element of judgment—by shifting from judgment to calculation. For strep throat, a doctor will begin with a rapid antigen test on a swab sample from a patient's throat. In a short period, the test can detect strep bacteria. (Without the rapid antigen result, and to some extent even with it, there is noise in diagnosis of strep throat.) If you have a fasting blood sugar level of 126 milligrams per deciliter or higher or an HbA1c (an average measure of blood sugar over the prior three months) of at least 6.5, you are considered to have diabetes. During the early stages of the COVID-19 pandemic, some doctors initially made diagnoses as a result of judgments reached after considering symptoms; as the pandemic progressed, testing became much more common, and the tests made judgment unnecessary.

Many people know that when doctors do exercise judgment, they can be noisy, and they might err; a standard practice is to advise patients to get a second opinion. In some hospitals, a second opinion is even mandatory. Whenever the second opinion diverges from the first, we have noise—though of course it may not be clear which doctor has it right. Some patients (including Paul) have been astonished to see how much the second opinion diverges from the first. But the surprise is not the existence of noise in the medical profession. It is its sheer magnitude.

Our goals in this chapter are to elaborate that claim and to describe some of the approaches to noise reduction used by the medical profession. We will focus on one decision hygiene strategy: the development of diagnostic guidelines. We are keenly aware that an entire book could easily be written about noise in medicine and the various steps that doctors, nurses, and hospitals have been taking by way of remedy. Notably, noise in medicine is hardly limited to noise in diagnostic judgments, which is our focus here. Treatments can also be noisy, and an extensive literature addresses this topic as well. If a patient has a heart problem, doctors' judgments about the best treatment are shockingly variable, whether the question involves the right medication, the right kind of surgery, or whether to get surgery at all. The Dartmouth Atlas Project has dedicated itself, for more than twenty years, to documenting "glaring variations in how medical resources are distributed and used in the United States." Similar conclusions hold in numerous nations. For our purposes, however, a brief exploration of noise in diagnostic judgments will be sufficient.

A Tour of the Horizon

There is an immense literature on noise in medicine. While much of the literature is empirical, testing for the presence of noise, much of it is also prescriptive.

Those involved in health care are continuing to search for noise-reduction strategies, which take many forms and are a gold mine of ideas worth considering in many fields.

When there is noise, one physician may be clearly right and the other may be clearly wrong (and may suffer from some kind of bias). As might be expected, skill matters a lot. A study of pneumonia diagnoses by radiologists, for instance, found significant noise. Much of it came from differences in skill. More specifically, "variation in skill can explain 44% of the variation in diagnostic decisions," suggesting that "policies that improve skill perform better than uniform decision guidelines." Here as elsewhere, training and selection are evidently crucial to the reduction of error, and to the elimination of both noise and bias.

In some specialties, such as radiology and pathology, doctors are well aware of the presence of noise. Radiologists, for example, call diagnostic variation their "Achilles' heel." It is not clear whether noise in the fields of radiology and pathology receives particular attention because there is truly more noise in these fields than in others or simply because noise is more easily documented there. We suspect that ease of documentation may be more important. Clean, simple tests of noise (and sometimes error) are easier to conduct in radiology. For example, you can return to scans or slides to reevaluate a previous assessment.

In medicine, between-person noise, or *interrater reliability,* is usually measured by the *kappa statistic.* The higher the kappa, the less noise. A kappa value of 1 reflects perfect agreement; a value of 0 reflects exactly as much agreement as you would expect between monkeys throwing darts onto a list of possible diagnoses. In some domains of medical diagnosis, reliability as measured by this coefficient has been found to be "slight" or "poor," which means that noise is very high. It is often found to be "fair," which is of course better but which also indicates significant noise. On the important question of which drug-drug interactions are clinically significant, generalist physicians, reviewing one hundred randomly selected drug-drug interactions, showed "poor agreement." To outsiders and to many doctors, diagnosis of the various stages of kidney disease might seem relatively straightforward. But nephrologists show only "slight to moderate agreement" in their judgments about the meaning of standard tests used in the evaluation of patients with kidney disease.

On the question of whether a breast lesion was cancerous, one study found only "fair" agreement among pathologists. In diagnosing breast proliferative lesions, agreement was again only "fair." Agreement was also "fair" when physicians assessed MRI scans for the degree of spinal stenosis. It is worth pausing over these findings. We have said that in some domains, the level of noise in medicine is very low. But in some areas that are fairly technical, doctors are far from noise-free. Whether a patient will be diagnosed with a serious disease, such as cancer, might depend on a kind of lottery, determined by the particular doctor that she will see.

Consider just a few other findings from the literature, drawn from areas in which the volume of noise seems especially noteworthy. We describe these findings not to give authoritative statements about the current state of medical practice, which continues to evolve and improve (in some cases rapidly), but to convey a general sense of the pervasiveness of noise, both in the relatively recent past and in the present.

1. Heart disease is the leading cause of death in both men and women in the United States. Coronary angiograms, a primary method used to test for heart disease, assess the degree of blockage in the heart's arteries in both acute and nonacute settings. In nonacute settings, when a patient presents with recurrent chest pain, treatment — such as stent placement — is often pursued if more than 70% of one or more arteries is found to be blocked. However, a degree of variability in interpreting angiograms has been documented, potentially leading to unnecessary procedures. An early study found that 31% of the time,

physicians evaluating angiograms disagreed on whether a major vessel was more than 70% blocked. Despite widespread awareness by cardiologists of potential variability in reading angiograms, and despite continuing efforts and corrective steps, the problem has yet to be solved.

2. Endometriosis is a disorder in which endometrial tissue, normally lining the inside of the uterus, grows outside the uterus. The disorder can be painful and lead to fertility problems. It is often diagnosed through laparoscopy, in which a small camera is surgically inserted into the body. Digital videos of laparoscopies in three patients, two of whom had endometriosis of varying degrees of severity and one of whom did not, were shown to 108 gynecological surgeons. The surgeons were asked to judge the number and location of endometriotic lesions. They disagreed dramatically, with weak correlations on both number and location.

3. Tuberculosis (TB) is one of the most widespread and deadly diseases worldwide — in 2016 alone, it infected more than 10 million people and killed almost 2 million. A widely used method for detecting TB is a chest X-ray, which allows examination of the lungs for the empty space caused by the TB bacteria. Variability in diagnosis of TB has been

well documented for almost seventy-five years. Despite improvements over the decades, studies have continued to find significant variability in diagnosis of TB, with "moderate" or just "fair" interrater agreement. There is also variability in TB diagnoses between radiologists in different countries.

4. When pathologists analyzed skin lesions for the presence of melanoma — the most dangerous form of skin cancer — there was only "moderate" agreement. The eight pathologists reviewing each case were unanimous or showed only one disagreement just 62% of the time. Another study at an oncology center found that the diagnostic accuracy of melanomas was only 64%, meaning that doctors misdiagnosed melanomas in one of every three lesions. A third study found that dermatologists at New York University failed to diagnose melanoma from skin biopsies 36% of the time. The authors of the study conclude that "the clinical failure to diagnose melanoma correctly has grievous implications for survival of patients with that potentially fatal disease."

5. There is variability in radiologists' judgments with respect to breast cancer from screening mammograms. A large study found that the range of false negatives among different radiologists varied from 0% (the radiologist was correct every time) to

greater than 50% (the radiologist incorrectly identified the mammogram as normal more than half of the time). Similarly, false-positive rates ranged from less than 1% to 64% (meaning that nearly two-thirds of the time, the radiologist said the mammogram showed cancer when cancer was not present). False negatives and false positives, from different radiologists, ensure that there is noise.

These cases of interpersonal noise dominate the existing research, but there are also findings of occasion noise. Radiologists sometimes offer a different view when assessing the same image again and thus disagree with themselves (albeit less often than they disagree with others). When assessing the degree of blockage in angiograms, twenty-two physicians disagreed with themselves between 63 and 92% of the time. In areas that involve vague criteria and complex judgments, intrarater reliability, as it is called, can be poor.

These studies offer no clear explanation of this occasion noise. But another study, not involving diagnosis, identifies a simple source of occasion noise in medicine—a finding worth bearing in mind for both patients and doctors. In short, doctors are significantly more likely to order cancer screenings early in the morning than late in the afternoon. In a large sample, the order rates of breast and colon screening tests were highest at 8 a.m., at 63.7%. They decreased throughout the morning to 48.7% at 11 a.m. They increased to 56.2% at noon—and then decreased to 47.8% at 5 p.m. It follows that patients with appointment times later in the day were less likely to receive guideline-recommended cancer screening.

How can we explain such findings? A possible answer is that physicians almost inevitably run behind in clinic after seeing patients with complex medical problems that require more than the usual twenty-minute slot. We already mentioned the role of stress and fatigue as triggers of occasion noise (see chapter 7), and these elements seem to be at work here. To keep up with their schedules, some doctors skip discussions about preventive health measures. Another illustration of the role of fatigue among clinicians is the lower rate of appropriate handwashing during the end of hospital shifts. (Handwashing turns out to be noisy, too.)

Less Noisy Doctors: The Value of Guidelines

It would be a major contribution not only to medicine but also to human knowledge to provide a comprehensive account of the existence and magnitude of noise in the context of different medical problems.

We are unaware of any such account; we hope that it will be produced in the fullness of time. But even now, existing findings provide some clues.

At one extreme, diagnosis for some problems and illnesses is essentially mechanical and allows no room for judgment. In other cases, the diagnosis is not mechanical but straightforward; anyone with medical training is highly likely to reach the same conclusion. In still other cases, a degree of specialization — among, say, lung cancer specialists — will be sufficient to ensure that noise exists but is minimal. At the other extreme, some cases present a great deal of room for judgment, and the relevant criteria for diagnosis are so open-ended that noise will be substantial and difficult to reduce. As we will see, this is the case in much of psychiatry.

What might work to reduce noise in medicine? As we mentioned, training can increase skill, and skill certainly helps. So does the aggregation of multiple expert judgments (second opinions and so forth). Algorithms offer an especially promising avenue, and doctors are now using deep-learning algorithms and artificial intelligence to reduce noise. For example, such algorithms have been used to detect lymph node metastases in women with breast cancer. The best of these have been found to be superior to the best pathologist, and, of course, algorithms are not noisy.

Deep-learning algorithms have also been used, with considerable success, for the detection of eye problems associated with diabetes. And AI now performs at least as well as radiologists do in detecting cancer from mammograms; further advances in AI will probably demonstrate its superiority.

The medical profession is likely to rely on algorithms more and more in the future; they promise to reduce both bias and noise and to save lives and money in the process. But our emphasis here will be on human-judgment guidelines, because the domain of medicine helpfully illustrates how they produce good or even excellent results in some applications and more mixed results in others.

Perhaps the most famous example of a guideline for diagnosis is the Apgar score, developed in 1952 by the obstetric anesthesiologist Virginia Apgar. Assessing whether a newborn baby is in distress used to be a matter of clinical judgment for physicians and midwives. Apgar's score gave them a standard guideline instead. The evaluator measures the baby's color, heart rate, reflexes, muscle tone, and respiratory effort, sometimes summarized as a "backronym" for Apgar's name: *appearance* (skin color), *pulse* (heart rate), *grimace* (reflexes), *activity* (muscle tone), and *respiration* (breathing rate and effort). In the Apgar test, each of these five measures is given a score of 0, 1, or

2. The highest possible total score is 10, which is rare. A score of 7 or above is considered indicative of good health (table 3).

Table 3: *Apgar Scoring Guidelines*

Category	Number of points assigned
Appearance (skin color)	0: Entire body is blue or pale 1: Good color in body but blue hands or feet 2: Completely pink or normal color
Pulse (heart rate)	0: No heart rate 1: <100 beats per minute 2: >100 beats per minute
Grimace (reflexes)	0: No response to airways being stimulated 1: Grimace during stimulation 2: Grimace and cough or sneeze during stimulation
Activity (muscle tone)	0: Limp 1: Some flexing (bending) of arms and legs 2: Active motion
Respiration (breathing rate and effort)	0: Not breathing 1: Weak cry (whimpering, grunting) 2: Good, strong cry

Note that heart rate is the only strictly numerical component of the score and that all the other items involve an element of judgment. But because the judgment is decomposed into individual elements, each of which is straightforward to assess, practitioners with even a modest degree of training are unlikely to disagree a great deal — and hence Apgar scoring produces little noise.

The Apgar score exemplifies how guidelines work and why they reduce noise. Unlike rules or algorithms, guidelines do not eliminate the need for judgment: the decision is not a straightforward computation. Disagreement remains possible on each of the components and hence on the final conclusion. Yet guidelines succeed in reducing noise because they decompose a complex decision into a number of easier subjudgments on predefined dimensions.

The benefits of this approach are clear when we view the problem in terms of the simple prediction models discussed in chapter 9. A clinician making a judgment about a newborn's health is working from several predictive cues. Occasion noise might be at work: on one day but not another, or in one mood but not another, a clinician could pay attention to relatively unimportant predictors or ignore important ones. The Apgar score focuses the health professional on the five that are empirically known to matter. Then, the score provides a clear description of how to evaluate each cue, which greatly simplifies each cue-level judgment and hence reduces its noise. Finally, the Apgar score specifies how to weight the predictors mechanically to produce the overall judgment required, whereas human clinicians would otherwise differ on the weights they assign to the cues. A focus on the relevant predictors, simplification of the predictive model, and mechanical aggregation—all of these reduce noise.

Analogous approaches have been used in many medical domains. One example is the Centor score to guide diagnosis of strep throat. A patient is given one point for each of the following symptoms or signs (whose terms, like the Apgar score, constitute a backronym for the last name of Robert Centor, who with his colleagues first summarized this guideline): absence of a *cough*, presence of *exudates* (white patches on the back of throat), tender or swollen lymph *nodes* in the neck, and a *temperature* greater than 100.4 degrees. Depending on the number of points a patient is assigned, a throat swab to diagnose strep pharyngitis may be recommended. Assessment and scoring are relatively straightforward using this scale, which has effectively reduced the number of people undergoing unnecessary testing and treatment for strep throat.

Similarly, guidelines have been developed for breast cancer diagnosis with the Breast Imaging Reporting and Data System (BI-RADS), which reduces noise in the interpretations of mammograms. One study found that BI-RADS increased interrater agreement on the assessments of mammograms, demonstrating that guidelines can be effective in reducing noise in an area where variability has been significant. In pathology, there have been many successful efforts to use guidelines for the same purpose.

The Depressing Case of Psychiatry

In terms of noise, psychiatry is an extreme case. When diagnosing the same patient using the same diagnostic criteria, psychiatrists frequently disagree with one another. For that reason, noise reduction has been a major priority for the psychiatric community since at least the 1940s. And as we will see, despite being constantly refined, guidelines have provided only modest help in reducing noise.

A 1964 study involving 91 patients and ten experienced psychiatrists found that the likelihood of an agreement between two opinions was just 57%. Another early study, involving 426 state hospital patients diagnosed independently by two psychiatrists, found agreement merely 50% of the time in their diagnosis of the kind of mental illness that was present. Yet another early study, involving 153 outpatients, found 54% agreement. In these studies, the source of the noise was not specified. Interestingly, however, some psychiatrists were found to be inclined to assign patients to specific diagnostic categories. For example, some psychiatrists were especially likely to diagnose patients with depression, and others with anxiety.

As we shall soon see, levels of noise continue to be high in psychiatry. Why is this? Specialists lack a single, clear answer (which means that the explanations for noise are themselves noisy). The large set of diagnostic categories is undoubtedly one factor. But in a preliminary effort to answer that question, researchers asked one psychiatrist to interview a patient first, and then had a second psychiatrist conduct another interview after a short resting period. The two psychiatrists met afterward and, if they disagreed, discussed why they did so.

One frequent reason was "inconstancy of the physician": different schools of thought, different training, different clinical experiences, different interview styles. While a "clinician with developmental training might explain the hallucinatory experience as part of posttraumatic experience of past abuse," a different clinician "with a biomedical orientation might explain the same hallucinations as part of a schizophrenic process." Such differences are examples of pattern noise.

Beyond physician differences, however, the main reason for noise was "inadequacy of the nomenclature."

Such observations and widespread professional dissatisfaction with psychiatric nomenclature helped motivate the 1980 revision (the third edition) of the *Diagnostic and Statistical Manual of Mental Disorders* (DSM-III). The manual included, for the first time, explicit and detailed criteria for diagnosing mental disorders, a first step in the direction of introducing diagnostic guidelines.

DSM-III led to a dramatic increase in the research on whether diagnoses were noisy. It also proved helpful in reducing noise. But the manual was far from a complete success. Even after a significant 2000 revision of the fourth edition, DSM-IV (originally published in 1994), research showed that the level of noise remained high. On the one hand, Ahmed Aboraya and his colleagues conclude that "the use of diagnostic criteria for psychiatric disorders has been shown to increase the reliability of psychiatric diagnoses." On the other hand, there continues to be a serious risk that "admissions of a single patient will reveal multiple diagnoses for the same patient."

Another version of the manual, DSM-5, was released in 2013. The American Psychiatric Association had hoped that DSM-5 would reduce noise because the new edition relied on more objective, clearly scaled criteria. But psychiatrists continue to show significant noise. For example, Samuel Lieblich and his colleagues find that "psychiatrists have a hard time agreeing on who does and does not have major depressive disorder." Field trials for DSM-5 found "minimal agreement," which "means that highly trained specialist psychiatrists under study conditions were only able to agree that a patient has depression between 4 and 15% of the time." According to some field trials, DSM-5 actually made things worse, showing increased noise "in all major domains, with some diagnoses, such as mixed anxiety-depressive disorder...so unreliable as to appear useless in clinical practice."

The major reason for the limited success of guidelines seems to be that, in psychiatry, "the diagnostic criteria of some disorders are still vague and difficult to operationalize." Some guidelines reduce noise by decomposing judgment into criteria on which disagreement is reduced, but to the extent that such criteria are relatively open-ended, noise remains likely. With this point in mind, prominent proposals call for more standardized diagnostic guidelines. These include (1) clarifying diagnostic criteria, moving away from vague standards; (2) producing "reference definitions" of symptoms and their level of severity, on the theory that when "clinicians agree on the presence or absence of symptoms, they are more likely to agree on the diagnosis"; and (3) using structured interviews of patients in addition to open conversation. One proposed interview guide includes twenty-four screening questions that allow for more reliable diagnosis of, for example, anxiety, depression, and eating disorders.

These steps sound promising, but it is an open question to what extent they would succeed in reducing noise. In the words of one observer, "the reliance on the patient's subjective symptoms, the clinician's interpretation of the symptoms, and the absence of objective measure (such as a blood test) implant the seeds of diagnostic unreliability of psychiatric disorders." In this sense, psychiatry may prove especially resistant to attempts at noise reduction.

On that particular question, it is too soon to make a confident prediction. But one thing is clear. In medicine in general, guidelines have been highly successful in reducing both bias and noise. They have helped doctors, nurses, and patients and greatly improved public health in the process. The medical profession needs more of them.

Speaking of Guidelines in Medicine

"Among doctors, the level of noise is far higher than we might have suspected. In diagnosing cancer and heart disease — even in reading X-rays — specialists sometimes disagree. That means that the treatment a patient gets might be a product of a lottery."

"Doctors like to think that they make the same decision whether it's Monday or Friday or early in the morning or late in the afternoon. But it turns out that what doctors say and do might well depend on how tired they are."

"Medical guidelines can make doctors less likely to blunder at a patient's expense. Such guidelines can also help the medical profession as a whole, because they reduce variability."

CHAPTER 23

Defining the Scale in Performance Ratings

Let's start with an exercise. Take three people you know; they might be friends or colleagues. Rate them on a scale of 1 to 5, where 1 is the lowest and 5 is the highest, in terms of three characteristics: kindness, intelligence, and diligence. Now ask someone who knows them well—your spouse, best friend, or closest colleague—to do the same thing with respect to the same three people.

There is a good chance that on some of the ratings, you and the other rater came up with different numbers. If you (and your counterpart) are willing, please discuss the reasons for the differences. You might find that the answer lies in how you used the scale—what we have called level noise. Perhaps you thought a 5 requires something truly extraordinary, whereas the other rater thought that it merely requires something unusually good. Or perhaps you differed because of your differing views of the people being rated: your understanding of whether they are kind, and how exactly to define that virtue, might be different from that of the other rater.

Now imagine that for the three people you rated, a promotion or bonus is at stake. Suppose that you and the other rater are engaged in performance ratings at a company that values kindness (or collegiality), intelligence, and diligence. Would there be a difference between your ratings? Would it be as large as in the earlier exercise? Even larger? However those questions are answered, differences in policies and scaling are likely to produce noise. And in fact, that is what is pervasively observed in performance ratings across organizational settings.

A Judgment Task

In almost all large organizations, performance is formally evaluated on a regular basis. Those who are rated do not enjoy the experience. As one newspaper headline put it, "Study Finds That Basically Every Single Person Hates Performance Reviews." Every single person also knows (we think) that performance reviews are subject to both bias and noise. But most people do not know just how noisy they are.

In an ideal world, evaluating people's performance

would not be a judgment task; objective facts would be sufficient to determine how well people are doing. But most modern organizations have little in common with Adam Smith's pin factory, in which every worker had a measurable output. What would that output be for a chief financial officer or for a head of research? Today's knowledge workers balance multiple, sometimes contradictory objectives. Focusing on only one of them might produce erroneous evaluations and have harmful incentive effects. The number of patients a doctor sees every day is an important driver of hospital productivity, for example, but you would not want physicians to focus single-mindedly on that indicator, much less to be evaluated and rewarded only on that basis. Even quantifiable performance metrics — say, sales for a salesperson or number of lines of code written for a programmer — must be evaluated in context: not all customers are equally difficult to serve, and not all software development projects are identical. In light of these challenges, many people cannot be evaluated entirely on the basis of objective performance metrics. Hence the ubiquity of judgment-based performance reviews.

One-Quarter Signal, Three-Quarters Noise

Thousands of research articles have been published on the practice of performance appraisals. Most researchers find that such appraisals are exceedingly noisy. This sobering conclusion comes mostly from studies based on 360-degree performance reviews, in which multiple raters provide input on the same person being rated, usually on multiple dimensions of performance. When this analysis is conducted, the result is not pretty. Studies often find that true variance, that is, variance attributable to the person's performance, accounts for no more than 20 to 30% of the total variance. The rest, 70 to 80% of the variance in the ratings, is system noise.

Where does this noise come from? Thanks to multiple studies of variance in job performance ratings, we know that all the components of system noise are present.

These components are quite easy to picture in the context of a performance rating. Consider two raters, Lynn and Mary. If Lynn is lenient and Mary tough, in the sense that Lynn gives higher ratings than Mary does, on average, to all people being evaluated, then we have level noise. As noted in our discussion of judges, this noise may mean either that Lynn and Mary form truly different impressions or that the two raters merely use the rating scale differently to express the same impression.

Now, if Lynn is evaluating you and happens to have a distinctly poor opinion of you and your contributions, her general leniency may be offset by her idiosyncratic (and negative) reaction to you. This is what we have called a stable pattern: a specific rater's reaction to a specific person being rated. Because the pattern is unique to Lynn (and to her judgment of you), it is a source of pattern noise.

Finally, Mary may have discovered that someone dented her car in the company parking lot just before she filled in a rating form, or Lynn may just have received her own, surprisingly generous, bonus, which put her in an unusually good mood as she evaluated your performance. Such events may, of course, produce occasion noise.

Different studies come to different conclusions on the breakdown of system noise into these three components (level, pattern, and occasion), and we can certainly imagine reasons why it should vary from one organization to the next. But all forms of noise are undesirable. The basic message that emerges from this research is a simple one: most ratings of performance have much less to do with the performance of the person being rated than we would wish. As one review summarizes it, "the relationship between job performance and ratings of job performance is likely to be weak or at best uncertain."

In addition, there are many reasons why ratings in organizations might not reflect the rater's perception of an employee's true performance. For example, raters might not in fact attempt to evaluate performance accurately but might rate people "strategically." Among other motives, the evaluators might intentionally inflate a rating to avoid a difficult feedback conversation, to favor a person who is seeking a long-awaited promotion, or even, paradoxically, to get rid of an underperforming team member who needs a good evaluation to be allowed to transfer to another division.

These strategic calculations certainly affect ratings, but they are not the only source of noise. We know this thanks to a sort of natural experiment: some 360-degree feedback systems are used solely for developmental purposes. With these systems, the respondents are told that the feedback will not be used for evaluation purposes. To the extent that the raters actually believe what they are told, this approach discourages them from inflating — or deflating — ratings. As it turns out, the developmental review does make a difference in the quality of the feedback, but system noise remains high and still accounts for much more variance than does the performance of the person being rated. Even when the feedback is purely developmental, ratings remain noisy.

A Problem Long Recognized but Not Solved

If performance rating systems are so badly broken, the people who measure performance should take notice and improve them. Indeed, over the past several decades, organizations have experimented with countless reforms to those systems. The reforms have employed some of the noise-reduction strategies we have outlined. In our view, much more could be done.

Almost all organizations use the noise-reduction strategy of *aggregation*. Aggregate ratings are often associated with 360-degree rating systems, which became the standard in large corporations in the 1990s. (The journal *Human Resources Management* had a special issue on 360-degree feedback in 1993.)

While averaging ratings from several raters should help to reduce system noise, it is worth noting that 360-degree feedback systems were not invented as a remedy for that problem. Their primary purpose is to measure much more than what a boss sees. When your peers and subordinates, and not just your boss, are asked to contribute to your performance evaluation, the nature of what is valued is changed. The theory is that this shift is for the better, because today's jobs entail more than pleasing your boss. The rise in popularity of 360-degree feedback coincided with the generalization of fluid, project-based organizations.

Some evidence suggests that 360-degree feedback is a useful tool in that it predicts objectively measurable performance. Unfortunately, the use of this feedback system has created its own problems. As computerization made it effortless to add more questions to feedback systems, and as the proliferation of multiple corporate objectives and constraints added dimensions to job descriptions, many feedback questionnaires became absurdly complex. Overengineered questionnaires abound (one example involves forty-six ratings on eleven dimensions for each rater and person being rated). It would take a superhuman rater to recall and process accurate, relevant facts about numerous people being evaluated on so many dimensions. In some ways, this overly complicated approach is not only useless but also pernicious. As we have seen, the halo effect implies that supposedly separate dimensions will in fact not be treated separately. A strong positive or negative rating on one of the first questions will tend to pull answers to subsequent questions in the same direction.

Even more importantly, the development of 360-degree systems has exponentially increased the amount of time devoted to providing feedback. It is not uncommon for middle managers to be asked to complete dozens of questionnaires on their colleagues at all levels — and sometimes on their counterparts in other organizations, because many companies now request feedback from customers, vendors, and other business partners. However well intentioned, this explosion in the demands placed on time-constrained raters cannot be expected to improve the quality of the information they supply. In this case, the reduction of noise may not be worth the cost—a problem that we will discuss in part 6.

Finally, 360-degree systems are not immune to a near-universal disease of all performance measurement systems: creeping ratings inflation. One large industrial company once observed that 98% of its managers had been rated as "fully meeting expectations." When almost everyone receives the highest possible rating, it is fair to question the value of these ratings.

In Praise of Relative Judgments

A theoretically effective solution to the problem of ratings inflation is to introduce some standardization in ratings. One popular practice that aims to do this is *forced ranking*. In a forced ranking system, raters are not only prevented from giving everyone the highest possible rating but also forced to abide by a predetermined distribution. Forced ranking was advocated by Jack Welch when he was CEO of General Electric, as a way to stop inflation in ratings and to ensure "candor" in performance reviews. Many companies adopted it, only to abandon it later, citing undesirable side effects on morale and teamwork.

Whatever their flaws, rankings are less noisy than ratings. We saw in the example of punitive damages that there is much less noise in relative judgments than in absolute ones, and this relationship has been shown to apply in performance ratings, too.

To appreciate why, consider figure 17, which shows two examples of scales for evaluating employees. Panel A, in which an employee is rated on an absolute scale, requires what we have called a matching operation: finding the score that most closely matches your impression of the employee's "work quality." Panel B, by contrast, requires each individual to be compared

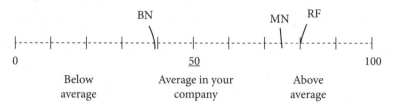

Panel A

Work quality of Employee A: _____

	1	2	3	4	5
	Very poor	Poor	Fair	Good	Excellent

Panel B

Please rate your subordinates on *safety*. *Safety* refers to how well the employees follow the proper rules and regulations; behave in a safe manner on the job; and demonstrate awareness and understanding of safe work practices.

FIGURE 17: *Examples of absolute and relative rating scales*

with a group of others on a specific dimension—safety. The supervisor is asked to state the rank (or percentile) of an employee in a specified population, using a percentile scale. We can see that a supervisor has placed three employees on this common scale.

The approach in panel B has two advantages. First, rating all employees on one dimension at a time (in this example, safety) exemplifies a noise-reduction strategy we will discuss in more detail in the next chapter: *structuring* a complex judgment into several dimensions. Structuring is an attempt to limit the halo effect, which usually keeps the ratings of one individual on different dimensions within a small range. (Structuring, of course, works only if the ranking is done on each dimension separately, as in this example: ranking employees on an ill-defined, aggregate judgment of "work quality" would not reduce the halo effect.)

Second, as we discussed in chapter 15, a ranking reduces both pattern noise and level noise. You are less likely to be inconsistent (and to create pattern noise) when you compare the performance of two members of your team than when you separately give each one a grade. More importantly, rankings mechanically eliminate level noise. If Lynn and Mary are evaluating the same group of twenty employees, and Lynn is more lenient than Mary, their average ratings will be different, but their average rankings will not. A lenient ranker and a tough ranker use the same ranks.

Indeed, noise reduction is the main stated objective of forced ranking, which ensures that all raters have the same mean and the same distribution of evaluations. Rankings are "forced" when a distribution of ratings is mandated. For instance, a rule might state that no more than 20% of the people being rated can be put in the top category and that no less than 15% can be put in the bottom one.

Rank but Do Not Force

In principle, therefore, forced ranking should bring about much-needed improvements. Yet it often backfires. We do not intend here to review all its possible unwanted effects (which are often related to poor implementation rather than principle). But two issues with forced ranking systems offer some general lessons.

The first is the confusion between absolute and relative performance. It is certainly impossible for 98% of the managers of any company to be in the top 20%, 50%, or even 80% of their peer group. But it is not impossible that they all "meet expectations," if these expectations have been defined ex ante *and in absolute terms*.

Many executives object to the notion that nearly all employees can meet expectations. If so, they argue, the expectations must be too low, perhaps because of a culture of complacency. Admittedly this interpretation may be valid, but it is also possible that most employees really do meet *high* expectations. Indeed, this is exactly what we would expect to find in a high-performance organization. You would not sneer at the leniency of the National Aeronautics and Space Administration's performance management procedures if you heard that all the astronauts on a successful space mission have fully met expectations.

The upshot is that a system that depends on relative evaluations is appropriate only if an organization cares about relative performance. For example, relative ratings might make sense when, regardless of people's absolute performance, only a fixed percentage of them can be promoted — think of colonels being evaluated for promotion to general. But forcing a relative ranking on what purports to measure an *absolute* level of performance, as many companies do, is illogical. And mandating that a set percentage of employees be rated as failing to meet (absolute) expectations is not just cruel; it is absurd. It would be foolish to say that 10% of an elite unit of the army must be graded "unsatisfactory."

The second problem is that the forced distribution

of the ratings is assumed to reflect the distribution of the underlying true performances — typically, something close to a normal distribution. Yet even if the distribution of performances in the population being rated is known, the same distribution may not be reproduced in a smaller group, such as those assessed by a single evaluator. If you randomly pick ten people from a population of several thousand, there is no guarantee that exactly two of them will belong to the top 20% of the general population. ("No guarantee" is an understatement: the probability that this will be the case is just 30%.) In practice, the problem is even worse, because the composition of teams is not random. Some units may be staffed almost entirely with high performers, and others with subpar employees.

Inevitably, forced ranking in such a setting is a source of error and unfairness. Suppose that one rater's team is composed of five people whose performances are indistinguishable. Forcing a differentiated distribution of ratings on this undifferentiated reality does not reduce error. It increases it.

Critics of forced ranking have often focused their attacks on the principle of ranking, which they decry as brutal, inhumane, and ultimately counterproductive. Whether or not you accept these arguments, the fatal flaw of forced ranking is not the "ranking," but the "forced." Whenever judgments are forced onto an inappropriate scale, either because a relative scale is used to measure an absolute performance or because judges are forced to distinguish the indistinguishable, the choice of the scale mechanically adds noise.

What's Next?

In light of all the efforts that organizations have made to improve performance measurement, it is an understatement to say that the results have been disappointing. As a result of those efforts, the cost of performance evaluations skyrocketed. In 2015, Deloitte calculated that it was spending 2 million hours each year evaluating its sixty-five thousand people. Performance reviews continue to be one of the most dreaded rituals of organizations, hated almost as much by those who have to perform them as by those who receive them. One study found that a staggering 90% of managers, employees, and HR heads believe that their performance management processes fail to deliver the results they expected. Research has confirmed what most managers have experienced. Although performance feedback, when associated with a development plan for the employee, can bring about improvements, performance ratings as they are most often practiced demotivate as often as they motivate. As one review article summarized, "No matter what has been tried over decades to improve [performance management] processes, they continue to generate inaccurate information and do virtually nothing to drive performance."

In despair, a small but growing number of companies are now considering the radical option of eliminating evaluation systems altogether. Proponents of this "performance management revolution," including many technology companies, some professional services organizations, and a handful of companies in traditional sectors, aim to focus on developmental, future-oriented feedback rather than on evaluative, backward-looking assessment. A few have even made their evaluations numberless, which means that they abandon traditional performance ratings.

For companies that are not giving up on performance ratings (and they are the overwhelming majority), what can be done to improve them? One noise-reduction strategy has to do, again, with picking the right scale. The aim is to ensure a *common frame of reference*. Research suggests that a combination of improved rating formats and training of the raters can help achieve more consistency between raters in their use of the scale.

At a minimum, performance rating scales must be anchored on descriptors that are sufficiently specific to be interpreted consistently. Many organizations use *behaviorally anchored rating scales* in which each degree on the scale corresponds to a description of specific behaviors. The left panel of figure 18 provides an example.

Evidence suggests, however, that behaviorally anchored rating scales are not sufficient to eliminate noise. A further step, *frame-of-reference training,* has been shown to help ensure consistency between raters. In this step, raters are trained to recognize different dimensions of performance. They practice rating performance using videotaped vignettes and then learn how their ratings compare with "true" ratings provided by experts. The performance vignettes act as reference cases; each vignette defines an anchor point on the performance scale, which becomes a *case scale,* such as the one shown on the right panel of figure 18.

With a case scale, each rating of a new individual is a comparison with the anchor cases. It becomes a

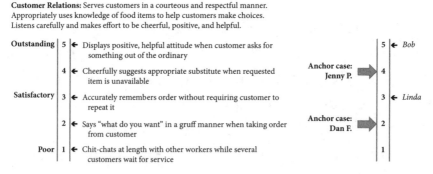

FIGURE 18: *Example of a behaviorally anchored rating scale (left) and case scale (right)*

relative judgment. Because comparative judgments are less susceptible to noise than ratings are, case scales are more reliable than scales that use numbers, adjectives, or behavioral descriptions.

Frame-of-reference training has been known for decades and provides demonstrably less noisy and more accurate ratings. Yet it has gained little ground. It is easy to guess why. Frame-of-reference training, case scales, and other tools that pursue the same goals are complex and time-consuming. To be valuable, they usually need to be customized for the company and even for the unit conducting the evaluations, and they must be frequently updated as job requirements evolve. These tools require a company to add to its already-large investment in its performance management systems. Current fashion goes in the opposite direction. (In part 6, we shall have more to say about the costs of reducing noise.)

In addition, any organization that tames the noise attributable to raters also reduces their ability to influence ratings in pursuit of their own goals. Requiring managers to undergo additional rater training, to invest more effort in the rating process, and to give up some of the control they have over outcomes is certain to generate considerable resistance. Tellingly, the majority of studies of frame-of-reference rater training have so far been conducted on students, not on actual managers.

The large subject of performance evaluation raises many questions, both practical and philosophical. Some people ask, for instance, to what extent the notion of individual performance is meaningful in today's organizations, where outcomes often depend on how people interact with one another. If we believe the notion is indeed meaningful, we must wonder how levels of individual performance are distributed among people in a given organization — for instance, whether performance follows a normal distribution or whether there exists "star talent" making a hugely disproportionate contribution. And if your goal is to bring out the best in people, you can reasonably ask whether measuring individual performance and using that measurement to motivate people through fear and greed is the best approach (or even an effective one).

If you are designing or revising a performance management system, you will need to answer these questions and many more. Our aspiration here is not to examine these questions but to make a more modest suggestion: if you do measure performance, your performance ratings have probably been pervaded by system noise and, for that reason, they might be essentially useless and quite possibly counterproductive. Reducing this noise is a challenge that cannot be solved by simple technological fixes. It requires clear thinking about the judgments that raters are expected to make. Most likely, you will find that you can improve judgments by clarifying the rating scale and training people to use it consistently. This noise-reduction strategy is applicable in many other fields.

Speaking of Defining the Scale

"We spend a lot of time on our performance ratings, and yet the results are one-quarter performance and three-quarters system noise."

"We tried 360-degree feedback and forced ranking to address this problem, but we may have made things worse."

"If there is so much level noise, it is because different raters have completely different ideas of what 'good' or 'great' means. They will only agree if we give them concrete cases as anchors on the rating scale."

CHAPTER 24

Structure in Hiring

If you have ever held a job of any kind, the words *recruiting interview* might evoke some vivid and stressful memories. Job interviews, in which a candidate meets with a future supervisor or an HR professional, are a rite of passage required to enter many organizations.

In most cases, interviews follow a well-rehearsed routine. After exchanging some pleasantries, interviewers ask candidates to describe their experience or elaborate on specific aspects of it. Questions are asked about achievements and challenges, motivations for the job, or improvement ideas for the company. Often the interviewers ask candidates to describe their personality and explain why they would be a good fit for the position or the company's culture. Hobbies and interests are sometimes discussed. Toward the end, the candidate usually gets to ask a few questions, which are duly evaluated for relevance and insightfulness.

If you are now in a position to hire employees, your selection methods probably include some version of this ritual. As one organizational psychologist noted, "It is rare, even unthinkable, for someone to be hired without some type of interview." And almost all professionals rely to some degree on their intuitive judgments when making hiring decisions in these interviews.

The ubiquity of the employment interview reflects a deep-seated belief in the value of judgment when it comes to choosing the people we will work with. And as a judgment task, personnel selection has a great advantage: because it is so ubiquitous and so important, organizational psychologists have studied it in great detail. The inaugural issue of the *Journal of Applied Psychology*, published in 1917, identified hiring as the "supreme problem... because human capacities are after all the chief national resources." A century later, we know a lot about the effectiveness of various selection techniques (including standard interviews). No complex judgment task has been the focus of so much field research. This makes it a perfect test case, offering lessons that can be extrapolated to many judgments involving a choice among several options.

The Dangers of Interviews

If you are unfamiliar with research on the employment interview, what follows may surprise you. In essence, if your goal is to determine which candidates will succeed in a job and which will fail, standard interviews (also called unstructured interviews to distinguish them from structured interviews, to which we will turn shortly) are not very informative. To put it more starkly, they are often useless.

To reach this conclusion, innumerable studies estimated the correlation between the rating an evaluator gives a candidate after an interview and the candidate's eventual success on the job. If the correlation between the interview rating and success is high, then interviews — or any other recruiting techniques for which correlation is computed in the same manner — can be assumed to be a good predictor of how candidates will perform.

A caveat is needed here. The definition of success is a nontrivial problem. Typically, performance is evaluated on the basis of supervisor ratings. Sometimes, the metric is length of employment. Such measures raise questions, of course, especially given the questionable validity of performance ratings, which we noted in the previous chapter. However, for the purpose of evaluating the quality of an employer's judgments when selecting employees, it seems reasonable to use the judgments that the same employer makes when evaluating the employees thus hired. Any analysis of the quality of hiring decisions must make this assumption.

So what do these analyses conclude? In chapter 11, we mentioned a correlation between typical interview ratings and job performance ratings of .28. Other studies report correlations that range between .20 and .33. As we have seen, this is a very good correlation by social science standards—but not a very good one on which to base your decisions. Using the percent concordant (PC) we introduced in part 3, we can calculate a probability: given the preceding levels of correlation, if all you know about two candidates is that one appeared better than the other in the interview, the chances that this candidate will indeed perform better are about 56 to 61%. Somewhat better than flipping a coin, for sure, but hardly a fail-safe way to make important decisions.

Admittedly, interviews serve other purposes besides making a judgment about a candidate. Notably, they provide an opportunity to sell the company to promising candidates and to start building rapport with future colleagues. Yet from the perspective of an organization that invests time and effort in talent selection, the main purpose of interviews is clearly one of selection. And at that task, they are not exactly a terrific success.

Noise in Interviewing

We can easily see why traditional interviews produce error in their prediction of job performance. Some of this error has to do with what we have termed objective ignorance (see chapter 11). Job performance depends on many things, including how quickly the person you hire adjusts to her new position or how various life events affect her work. Much of this is unpredictable at the time of hiring. This uncertainty limits the predictive validity of interviews and, indeed, any other personnel selection technique.

Interviews are also a minefield of psychological biases. In recent years, people have become well aware that interviewers tend, often unintentionally, to favor candidates who are culturally similar to them or with whom they have something in common, including gender, race, and educational background. Many companies now recognize the risks posed by biases and try to address them through specific training of recruiting professionals and other employees. Other biases have also been known for decades. For instance, physical appearance plays a large part in the evaluation of candidates, even for positions where it should matter little or not at all. Such biases are shared by all or most recruiters and, when applied to a given candidate, will thus tend to produce a shared error—a negative or positive bias in the candidate's evaluation.

You will not be surprised to hear that there is noise as well: Different interviewers respond differently to the same candidate and reach different conclusions. Measures of the correlation between the ratings that two interviewers produce after interviewing the same candidate range between .37 and .44 (PC = 62–65%). One reason is that the candidate may not behave in exactly the same way with different interviewers. But even in panel interviews, where several interviewers are exposed to the same interviewee behavior, the correlation between their ratings is far from perfect. One meta-analysis estimates a correlation of .74 (PC = 76%). This means that you and another interviewer, after seeing the *same* two candidates in the *same* panel interview, will still disagree about which of two candidates is better about one-quarter of the time.

This variability is largely the product of pattern noise, the difference in interviewers' idiosyncratic reactions to a given interviewee. Most organizations fully expect this variability and, for that reason, require several interviewers to meet the same candidate, with the results aggregated in some way. (Typically, the aggregate opinion is formed through a discussion in which some sort of consensus must be reached—a procedure that creates its own problems, as we have already noted.)

A more surprising finding is the presence of much occasion noise in interviews. There is strong evidence, for instance, that hiring recommendations are linked to impressions formed in the informal rapport-building phase of an interview, those first two or three minutes where you just chat amicably to put the candidate at ease. First impressions turn out to matter—a lot.

Perhaps you think that judging on first impressions is unproblematic. At least some of what we learn from first impressions is meaningful. All of us know that we do learn something in the first seconds of interaction with a new acquaintance. It stands to reason that this may be particularly true of skilled interviewers. But the first seconds of an interview reflect exactly the sort of superficial qualities you associate with first impressions: early perceptions are based mostly on a candidate's extraversion and verbal skills. Even the quality of a handshake is a significant predictor of hiring recommendations! We may all like a firm handshake, but few recruiters would consciously choose to make it a key hiring criterion.

The Psychology of Interviewers

Why do first impressions end up driving the outcome of a much longer interview? One reason is that in a traditional interview, interviewers are at liberty to steer the interview in the direction they see fit. They are likely to ask questions that confirm an initial impression. If a candidate seems shy and reserved, for instance, the interviewer may want to ask tough questions about the candidate's past experiences of working in teams but perhaps will neglect to ask the same questions of someone who seems cheerful and gregarious. The evidence collected about these two candidates will not be the same. One study that tracked the behavior of interviewers who had formed a positive or negative initial impression from résumés and test scores found that initial impressions have a deep effect on the way the interview proceeds. Interviewers with positive first impressions, for instance, ask fewer questions and tend to "sell" the company to the candidate.

The power of first impressions is not the only problematic aspect of interviews. Another is that as interviewers, we want the candidate sitting in front of us to *make sense* (a manifestation of our excessive tendency, discussed in chapter 13, to seek and find coherence). In one striking experiment, researchers assigned students to play the role of interviewer or interviewee and told both that the interview should consist only of closed-ended, yes-or-no questions. They then asked some of the interviewees to answer questions *randomly*. (The first letter of the questions as formulated determined if they should answer yes or no.) As the researchers wryly note, "Some of the interviewees were initially concerned that the random interview would break down and be revealed to be nonsense. No such problems occurred, and the interviews proceeded." You read that right: *not a single interviewer* realized that the candidates were giving random answers. Worse, when asked to estimate whether they were "able to infer a lot about this person given the amount of time we spent together," interviewers in this "random" condition were as likely to agree as those who had met candidates responding truthfully. Such is our ability to create coherence. As we can often find an imaginary pattern in random data or imagine a shape in the contours of a cloud, we are capable of finding logic in perfectly meaningless answers.

For a less extreme illustration, consider the following case. One of the present authors had to interview a candidate who was, in his former position, chief financial officer at a midsize company. He noticed that the candidate had left this position after a few months and asked him why. The candidate explained that the reason was a "strategic disagreement with the CEO." A colleague also interviewed the candidate, asked the same question, and got the same answer. In the debrief that followed, however, the two interviewers had radically different views. One, having so far formed a positive evaluation of the candidate, saw the candidate's decision to leave the company as an indication of integrity and courage. The other, who had formed a negative first impression, construed the same fact as a sign of inflexibility, perhaps even of immaturity. The story illustrates that however much we would like to believe that our judgment about a candidate is based on facts, our interpretation of facts is colored by prior attitudes.

The limitations of traditional interviews cast serious doubt on our ability to draw any meaningful conclusions from them. Yet impressions formed in an interview are vivid, and the interviewer is usually confident about them. When combining the conclusions reached in an interview with other cues about the candidate, we tend to give too much weight to the interview and too little to other data that may be more predictive, such as test scores.

A story may help bring this observation to life. Professors who interview for a faculty position are often asked to teach in front of a panel of their peers to ensure that their teaching skills are up to the institution's standards. It is, of course, a higher-stakes situation than an ordinary class. One of us once witnessed a candidate making a bad impression in this exercise, clearly because of the stress of the situation: the candidate's résumé mentioned outstanding teaching evaluations and several awards for teaching excellence. Yet the vivid impression produced by his failure in one highly artificial situation weighed more heavily in the final decision than did the abstract data about his excellent past teaching performance.

A final point: when interviews are not the only source of information about candidates — for instance, when there are also tests, references, or other inputs — these various inputs must be combined into an overall judgment. The question this raises is one you now recognize: should the inputs be combined using judgment (a clinical aggregation) or a formula (a mechanical aggregation)? As we saw in chapter 9, the mechanical approach is superior both in general and in the specific case of work performance prediction. Unfortunately, surveys suggest that the overwhelming majority of HR professionals favor clinical aggregation. This practice adds yet another source of noise to an already-noisy process.

Improving Personnel Selection Through Structure

If traditional interviews and judgment-based hiring decisions have limited predictive validity, what can we do about them? Fortunately, research has also produced some advice on how to improve personnel selection, and some companies are paying attention.

One example of a company that has upgraded its personnel selection practices and reported on the results is Google. Laszlo Bock, its former senior vice president of People Operations, tells the tale in his book *Work Rules!* Despite being focused on hiring talent of the highest caliber and devoting considerable resources to finding the right people, Google was struggling. An audit of the predictive validity of its recruiting interviews found "zero relationship (...), a complete random mess." The changes Google implemented to address this situation reflect principles that have emerged from decades of research. They also illustrate decision hygiene strategies.

One of these strategies should be familiar by now: aggregation. Its use in this context is not a surprise. Almost all companies aggregate the judgments of multiple interviewers on the same candidate. Not to be outdone, Google sometimes had candidates suffer through twenty-five interviews! One of the conclusions of Bock's review was to reduce that number to four, as he found that additional interviews added almost no predictive validity to what was achieved by the first four. To ensure this level of validity, however, Google stringently enforces a rule that not all companies observe: the company makes sure that the interviewers rate the candidate separately, *before* they communicate with one another. Once more:

aggregation works—but only if the judgments are independent.

Google also adopted a decision hygiene strategy we haven't yet described in detail: *structuring complex judgments.* The term *structure* can mean many things. As we use the term here, a structured complex judgment is defined by three principles: decomposition, independence, and delayed holistic judgment.

The first principle, *decomposition*, breaks down the decision into components, or *mediating assessments.* This step serves the same purpose as the identification of the subjudgments in a guideline: it focuses the judges on the important cues. Decomposition acts as a road map to specify what data is needed. And it filters out irrelevant information.

In Google's case, there are four mediating assessments in the decomposition: general cognitive ability, leadership, cultural fit (called "googleyness"), and role-related knowledge. (Some of these assessments are then broken down into smaller components.) Note that a candidate's good looks, smooth talk, exciting hobbies, and any other aspects, positive or negative, that a recruiter might notice in an unstructured interview are not on the list.

Creating this sort of structure for a recruiting task may seem like mere common sense. Indeed, if you are hiring an entry-level accountant or an administrative assistant, standard job descriptions exist and specify the competencies needed. As professional recruiters know, however, defining the key assessments gets difficult for unusual or senior positions, and this step of definition is frequently overlooked. One prominent headhunter points out that defining the required competencies in a sufficiently specific manner is a challenging, often overlooked task. He highlights the importance for decision makers of "investing in the problem definition": spending the necessary time up front, before you meet any candidates, to agree on a clear and detailed job description. The challenge here is that many interviewers use bloated job descriptions produced by consensus and compromise. The descriptions are vague wish lists of all the characteristics an ideal candidate would possess, and they offer no way to calibrate the characteristics or make trade-offs among them.

The second principle of structured judgment, *independence*, requires that information on each assessment be collected independently. Just listing the components of the job description is not enough: most recruiters conducting traditional interviews also know the four or five things they look for in a candidate. The problem is that, in the conduct of the interview, they do not evaluate these elements separately. Each assessment influences the others, which makes each assessment very noisy.

To overcome this problem, Google orchestrated ways to make assessments in a fact-based manner and independently of one another. Perhaps its most visible move was to introduce *structured behavioral interviews*. The interviewers' task in such interviews is not to decide whether they like a candidate overall; it is to collect data about each assessment in the evaluation structure and to assign a score to the candidate on each assessment. To do so, interviewers are required to ask predefined questions about the candidate's behaviors in past situations. They must also record the answers and score them against a predetermined rating scale, using a unified rubric. The rubric gives examples of what average, good, or great answers look like for each question. This shared scale (an example of the behaviorally anchored rating scales we introduced in the preceding chapter) helps reduce noise in judgments.

If this approach sounds different from a traditional, chatty interview, it is. In fact, it can feel more like an exam or interrogation than a business encounter, and there is some evidence that both interviewees and interviewers dislike structured interviews (or at least prefer unstructured ones). There is continuing debate about exactly what an interview must include to qualify as structured. Still, one of the most consistent findings to emerge from the literature on interviewing is that structured interviews are far more predictive of future performance than are traditional, unstructured ones. Correlations with job performance range between .44 and .57. Using our PC metric, your chances of picking the better candidate with a structured interview are between 65 and 69%, a marked improvement over the 56 to 61% chance an unstructured interview would give you.

Google uses other data as inputs on some of the dimensions it cares about. To test job-related knowledge, it relies in part on *work sample tests*, such as asking a candidate for a programming job to write some code. Research has shown that work sample tests are among the best predictors of on-the-job performance. Google also uses "backdoor references," supplied not by someone the candidate has nominated but by Google employees with whom the candidate has crossed paths.

The third principle of structured judgment, *delayed holistic judgment,* can be summarized in a simple prescription: do not exclude intuition, but delay it. At Google, the final hiring recommendation is made collegially by a hiring committee, which reviews a complete file of all the ratings the candidates have obtained on each assessment in each interview and other relevant information in support of these assessments. On the basis of that information, the committee then decides whether to extend an offer.

Despite the famously data-driven culture of this company, and despite all the evidence that a mechanical combination of data outperforms a clinical one, the final hiring decision is *not* mechanical. It remains a judgment, in which the committee takes all the evidence into account and weighs it holistically, engaging in a discussion of the question "Will this person be successful at Google?" The decision is not merely computed.

In the next chapter, we will explain why we believe that this approach to making the final decision is a sensible one. But note that while they are not mechanical, Google's final hiring decisions are anchored on the average score assigned by the four interviewers. They are also informed by the underlying evidence. In other words, Google allows judgment and intuition in its decision-making process only after all the evidence has been collected and analyzed. Thus, the tendency of each interviewer (and hiring committee member) to form quick, intuitive impressions and rush to judgment is kept in check.

The three principles—once more, decomposition, independent assessment on each dimension, and delayed holistic judgment—do not necessarily provide a template for all organizations trying to improve their selection processes. But the principles are broadly consistent with the recommendations that organizational psychologists have formulated over the years. In fact, the principles bear some resemblance to the selection method that one of us (Kahneman) implemented in the Israeli army as early as 1956 and described in *Thinking, Fast and Slow.* That process, like the one Google put in place, formalized an evaluation structure (the list of personality and competence dimensions that had to be evaluated). It required interviewers to elicit objective evidence relevant to each dimension in turn and to score that dimension before moving on to the next. And it allowed recruiters to use judgment and intuition to reach a final decision — but only after the structured evaluation had taken place.

———

There is overwhelming evidence of the superiority of structured judgment processes (including structured interviews) in hiring. Practical advice is available to guide executives who want to adopt them. As the example of Google illustrates and as other researchers have noted, structured judgment methods are also less costly — because few things are as costly as face time.

Nevertheless, most executives remain convinced of the irreplaceable value of informal, interview-based methods. Remarkably, so do many candidates who believe that only a face-to-face interview will enable them to show a prospective employer their true mettle. Researchers have called this "the persistence of an illusion." One thing is clear: recruiters and candidates severely underestimate the noise in hiring judgments.

Speaking of Structure in Hiring

"In traditional, informal interviews, we often have an irresistible, intuitive feeling of understanding the candidate and knowing whether the person fits the bill. We must learn to distrust that feeling."

"Traditional interviews are dangerous not only because of biases but also because of noise."

"We must add structure to our interviews and, more broadly, to our selection processes. Let's start by defining much more clearly and specifically what we are looking for in candidates, and let's make sure we evaluate the candidates independently on each of these dimensions."

CHAPTER 25

The Mediating Assessments Protocol

S ome time ago, two of us (Kahneman and Sibony), together with our friend Dan Lovallo, described a method of decision making in organizations. We called the method, which was designed with noise mitigation as a primary objective, the *mediating assessments protocol*. It incorporates most of the decision hygiene strategies that we have introduced in the preceding chapters. The protocol can be applied broadly and whenever the evaluation of a plan or an option requires considering and weighting multiple dimensions. It can be used, and adapted in various ways, by organizations of all kinds, including diverse companies, hospitals, universities, and government agencies.

We illustrate the protocol here with a stylized

example that is a composite of several real cases: a fictitious corporation we'll call Mapco. We will follow the steps Mapco takes as it studies the opportunity to make a major, transformative acquisition, and we will highlight how these differ from the usual steps a company takes in such a situation. As you will see, the differences are significant, but subtle — an inattentive observer might not even notice them.

The First Meeting: Agreeing on the Approach

The idea of acquiring Roadco, a competitor, had been percolating at Mapco, and had matured sufficiently so that the company's leaders were contemplating a board meeting to discuss it. Joan Morrison, the CEO of Mapco, convened a meeting of the board's strategy committee for a preliminary discussion of the possible acquisition and of what should be done to improve the board's deliberations about it. Early in the meeting, Joan surprised the committee with a proposal:

"I would like to propose that we try a new procedure for the board meeting where we will decide on the Roadco acquisition. The new procedure has an unappealing name, the mediating assessments protocol, but the idea is really quite simple. It is inspired by the similarity between the evaluation of a strategic option and the evaluation of a job candidate.

"You are certainly familiar with the research that shows that structured interviews produce better results than unstructured ones, and more broadly with the idea that structuring a hiring decision improves it. You know that our HR department has adopted these principles for its hiring decisions. A vast amount of research shows that structure in interviews leads to much higher accuracy—unstructured interviews as we used to practice them don't even come close.

"I see a clear similarity between the evaluation of candidates and the evaluation of options in big decisions: *options are like candidates.* And this similarity leads me to the idea that we should adapt the method that works for evaluating candidates to our task, which is to evaluate strategic options."

The committee members were initially puzzled by the analogy. The recruiting process, they argued, is a well-oiled machine that makes numerous, similar decisions and is not under severe time pressure. A strategic decision, on the other hand, requires a great deal of ad hoc work and must be made quickly. Some committee members made clear to Joan that they would be hostile to any proposal that delayed the decision. They were also worried about adding to the due-diligence requirements from Mapco's research staff.

Joan responded directly to these objections. She assured her colleagues that the structured process would not delay the decision. "This is all about setting the agenda for the board meeting in which we will discuss the deal," she explained. "We should decide in advance on a list of assessments of different aspects of the deal, just as an interviewer starts with a job description that serves as a checklist of traits or attributes a candidate must possess. We will make sure the board discusses these assessments separately, one by one, just as interviewers in structured interviews evaluate the candidate on the separate dimensions in sequence. Then, and only then, will we turn to a discussion of whether to accept or reject the deal. This procedure will be a much more effective way to take advantage of the collective wisdom of the board.

"If we agree on this approach, of course, it has implications for how the information should be presented and for how the deal team should work to prepare the meeting. That's why I wanted to get your thoughts now."

One committee member, still skeptical, asked Joan what benefits the structure brought to the quality of decision making in hiring and why she believed these benefits would transfer to a strategic decision. Joan walked him through the logic. Using the mediating assessments protocol, she explained, maximizes the value of information by keeping the dimensions of the evaluation independent of each other. "The board discussions we usually have look a lot like unstructured interviews," she observed. "We are constantly aware of the final goal of reaching a decision, and we process all the information in light of that goal. We start out looking for closure, and we achieve it as soon as we can. Just like a recruiter in an unstructured interview, we are at risk of using all the debate to confirm our first impressions.

"Using a structured approach will force us to postpone the goal of reaching a decision until we have made all the assessments. We will take on the separate assessments as intermediate goals. This way, we will consider all the information available and make sure that our conclusion on one aspect of the deal does not change our reading on another, unrelated aspect."

The committee members agreed to try out the approach. But, they asked, what were the mediating assessments? Was there a predefined checklist that Joan had in mind? "No," she replied. "That might be the case if we applied the protocol to a routine decision, but in this case, we need to define the mediating assessments ourselves. This is critically important: deciding on the major aspects of the acquisition that should be assessed is up to us." The strategy committee agreed to meet again the next day to do that.

The Second Meeting: Defining the Mediating Assessments

"The first thing we are going to do," Joan explained, "is draw up a comprehensive list of independent assessments about the deal. These will be assessed by Jeff Schneider's research team. Our task today is to construct the list of assessments. It should be comprehensive in the sense that any relevant fact you can think of should find its place and should influence at least one of the assessments. And what I mean by 'independent' is that a relevant fact should preferably influence only one of the assessments, to minimize redundancy."

The group got to work and generated a long list of facts and data that seemed relevant. It then organized them into a list of assessments. The challenge, the participants soon discovered, was to make the list short, comprehensive, and composed of nonoverlapping assessments. But the task was manageable. Indeed, the group's final list of seven assessments was superficially similar to the table of contents the board would expect in a regular report presenting an acquisition proposal. In addition to the expected financial modeling, the list included, for instance, an evaluation of the quality of the target's management team and an assessment of the likelihood that the anticipated synergies would be captured.

Some of the strategy committee members were disappointed that the meeting did not produce novel insights about Roadco. But, Joan explained, that was not the goal. The immediate objective was to brief the deal team in charge of studying the acquisition. Each assessment, she said, would be the subject of a different chapter in the deal team's report and would be discussed separately by the board.

The deal team's mission, as Joan saw it, was not to tell the board what it thought of the deal as a whole — at least, not yet. It was to provide an objective, independent evaluation on each of the mediating assessments. Ultimately, Joan explained, each chapter in the deal team's report should end with a rating that answers a simple question: "Leaving aside the weight we should give this topic in the final decision, how strongly does the evidence on this assessment argue for or against the deal?"

The Deal Team

The leader of the team in charge of evaluating the deal, Jeff Schneider, got his team together that afternoon to organize the work. The changes from the team's usual way of working were not many, but he stressed their importance.

First, he explained, the team's analysts should try

to make their analyses as objective as possible. The evaluations should be based on facts—nothing new about that—but they should also use an *outside view* whenever possible. Since the team members were unsure of what he meant by "outside view," Jeff gave them two examples, using two of the mediating assessments Joan had identified. To evaluate the probability that the deal would receive regulatory approval, he said, they would need to start by finding out the *base rate,* the percentage of comparable transactions that are approved. This task would, in turn, require them to define a relevant *reference class,* a group of deals considered comparable enough.

Jeff then explained how to evaluate the technological skills of the target's product development department—another important assessment Joan had listed. "It is not enough to describe the company's recent achievements in a fact-based way and to call them 'good' or 'great.' What I expect is something like, 'This product development department is in the second quintile of its peer group, as measured by its recent track record of product launches.'" Overall, he explained, the goal was to make evaluations as comparative as possible, because relative judgments are better than absolute ones.

Jeff had another request. In keeping with Joan's instructions, he said, assessments should be as independent of one another as possible, to reduce the risk that one assessment would influence the others. Accordingly, he assigned different analysts to the different assessments, and he instructed them to work independently.

Some of the analysts expressed surprise. "Isn't teamwork better?" they asked him. "What's the point of assembling a team if you don't want us to communicate?"

Jeff realized he needed to explain the need for independence. "You probably know about the halo effect in recruiting," he said. "That is what happens when the general impression of a candidate influences your assessment of the candidate's skills on a specific dimension. That's what we are trying to avoid." Since some of the analysts seemed to think that this effect was not a serious problem, Jeff used another analogy: "If you have four witnesses to a crime, would you let them talk to each other before testifying? Obviously not! You don't want one witness to influence the others." The analysts did not find the comparison particularly flattering, but it got the message across, Jeff thought.

As it happened, Jeff did not have enough analysts to achieve the goal of perfectly independent assessments. Jane, an experienced member of the team, was charged with two assessments. Jeff chose the two to be as different from each other as possible, and he instructed Jane to complete the first assessment and prepare the report on it before turning to the other. Another concern was the evaluation of the quality of the management team; Jeff was worried that his analysts would struggle to dissociate their assessment of the team's intrinsic quality from judgments about the company's recent results (which the team would, of course, study in detail). To address this issue, Jeff asked an outside HR expert to weigh in on the quality of the management team. This way, he thought, he would obtain a more independent input.

Jeff had another instruction that the team found somewhat unusual. Each chapter should focus on one assessment and, as requested by Joan, lead to a conclusion in the form of a rating. However, Jeff added, the analysts should include in each chapter all the relevant factual information about the assessment. "Don't hide anything," he instructed them. "The general tone of the chapter will be consistent with the proposed rating, of course, but if there is information that seems inconsistent or even contradictory with the main rating, don't sweep anything under the rug. Your job is not to sell your recommendation. It is to represent the truth. If it is complicated, so be it — it often is."

In the same spirit, Jeff encouraged the analysts to

be transparent about their level of confidence in each assessment. "The board knows that you do not have perfect information; it will help them if you tell them when you're really in the dark. And if you run into something that really gives you pause—a potential deal breaker—you should, of course, report it immediately."

The deal team proceeded as instructed. Fortunately, it found no major deal breakers. It assembled a report for Joan and the board, covering all the assessments identified.

The Decision Meeting

As she read the team's report to prepare for the decision meeting, Joan immediately noticed something important: while most of the assessments supported doing the deal, they did not paint a simple, rosy, all-systems-go picture. Some of the ratings were strong; others were not. These differences, she knew, were a predictable result of keeping the assessments independent of one another. When excessive coherence is kept in check, reality is not as coherent as most board presentations make it seem. "Good," Joan thought. "These discrepancies between assessments will raise questions and trigger discussions. That's just what we need to have a good debate in the board. The diverse results will not make the decision easier, for sure—but they will make it better."

Joan convened a meeting of the board to review the report and come to a decision. She explained the approach that the deal team followed, and she invited the board members to apply the same principle. "Jeff and his team have worked hard to keep the assessments independent of each other," she said, "and our task now is to review them independently, too. This means we will consider each assessment separately, before we start discussing the final decision. We are going to treat each assessment as a distinct agenda item."

The board members knew that following this structured approach would be difficult. Joan was asking them not to form a holistic view of the deal before all assessments were discussed, but many of them were industry insiders. They *had* a view on Roadco. Not discussing it felt a bit artificial. Nevertheless, because they understood what Joan was trying to achieve, they agreed to play by her rules and refrain temporarily from discussing their overall views.

To their surprise, the board members found that this practice was highly valuable. During the meeting, some of them even changed their mind about the deal (although no one would ever know, since they had kept their views to themselves). The way Joan ran the meeting played a large part: she used the *estimate-talk-estimate* method, which combines the advantages of deliberation and those of averaging independent opinions.

Here is how she proceeded. On each assessment, Jeff, on behalf of the deal team, briefly summarized the key facts (which the board members had read in detail beforehand). Then Joan asked the board members to use a voting app on their phones to give their own rating on the assessment — either the same as the deal team's proposed rating or a different one. The distribution of ratings was projected immediately on the screen, without identifying the raters. "This is not a vote," Joan explained. "We are just taking the temperature of the room on each topic." By getting an immediate read on each board member's independent opinion before starting a discussion, Joan reduced the danger of social influence and information cascades.

On some assessments, there was immediate consensus, but on others, the process revealed opposing views. Naturally, Joan managed the discussion to spend more time on the latter. She made sure that board members on each side of the divide spoke up, encouraging them to express their viewpoints with facts and arguments but also with nuance and humility. Once, when a board member who felt strongly about the deal got carried away, she reminded him that "we are all reasonable people and we disagree, so this must be a subject on which reasonable people can disagree."

When the discussion of an assessment drew to a close, Joan asked the board members to vote again on a rating. Most of the time, there was more convergence than in the initial round. The same sequence— a first estimate, a discussion, and a second estimate—was repeated for each assessment.

Finally, it was time to reach a conclusion about the deal. To facilitate the discussion, Jeff showed the list of assessments on the whiteboard, with, for each assessment, the average of the ratings that the board had assigned to it. The board members were looking at the profile of the deal. How should they decide?

One board member had a simple suggestion: use a straight average of the ratings. (Perhaps he knew about the superiority of mechanical aggregation over holistic, clinical judgment, as discussed in chapter 9.) Another member, however, immediately objected that, in her view, some of the assessments should be given a much higher weight than others. A third person disagreed, suggesting a different hierarchy of the assessments.

Joan interrupted the discussion. "This is not just about computing a simple combination of the assessment ratings," she said. "We have delayed intuition, but now is the time to use it. What we need now is your judgment."

Joan did not explain her logic, but she had learned this lesson the hard way. She knew that, particularly with important decisions, people reject schemes that tie their hands and do not let them use their judgment. She had seen how decision makers game the system when they know that a formula will be used. They change the ratings to arrive at the desired conclusion — which defeats the purpose of the entire exercise. Furthermore, although this was not the case here, she remained alert to the possibility that decisive considerations could emerge that were not anticipated in the definition of assessments (the broken-leg factors discussed in chapter 10). If such unanticipated deal breakers (or, conversely, deal clinchers) appeared, a purely mechanical decision process based on the average of the assessments might lead to a serious mistake.

Joan also knew that letting the board members use their intuition at this stage was very different from having them use it earlier in the process. Now that the assessments were available and known to all, the final decision was safely anchored on these fact-based, thoroughly discussed ratings. A board member would need to come up with strong reasons to be against the deal while staring at a list of mediating assessments that mostly supported it. Following this logic, the board discussed the deal and voted on it, in much the same way all boards do.

The Mediating Assessments Protocol in Recurring Decisions

We have described the mediating assessments protocol in the context of a one-off, singular decision. But the procedure applies to recurring decisions, too. Imagine that Mapco is not making a single acquisition but is a venture capital fund that makes repeated investments in start-ups. The protocol would be just as applicable and the story would be much the same, with just two twists that, if anything, make it simpler.

First, the initial step — defining the list of mediating assessments — needs to be done only once. The fund has investment criteria, which it applies to all its prospective investments: these are the assessments. There is no need to reinvent them each time.

Second, if the fund makes many decisions of the same type, it can use its experience to calibrate its judgments. Consider, for instance, an assessment that every fund will want to make: evaluating the quality of the management team. We suggested that such evaluations should be made relative to a reference class. Perhaps you sympathized with the analysts of Mapco: gathering data about comparable companies, in addition to evaluating a specific target, is challenging.

Comparative judgments become much easier in the context of a recurring decision. If you have evaluated the management teams of dozens, even hundreds of companies, you can use this shared experience as a reference class. A practical way to do this is to create a case scale defined by anchor cases. You might say, for instance, that the target management team is "as good as the management team of ABC Company when we acquired it" but not quite "as good as the management team of DEF Company." The anchor cases must, of course, be known to all the participants (and periodically updated). Defining them requires an up-front investment of time. But the value of this approach is that relative judgments (comparing this team to the ones at ABC and DEF) are much more reliable than are absolute ratings on a scale defined by numbers or adjectives.

What the Protocol Changes

For ease of reference, we summarize the main changes that the mediating assessments protocol entails in table 4.

Table 4: *Main steps of the mediating assessments protocol*

1. At the beginning of the process, structure the decision into mediating assessments. *(For recurring judgments, this is done only once.)*

2. Ensure that whenever possible, mediating assessments use an outside view. *(For recurring judgments: use relative judgments, with a case scale if possible.)*

3. In the analytical phase, keep the assessments as independent of one another as possible.

4. In the decision meeting, review each assessment separately.

5. On each assessment, ensure that participants make their judgments individually; then use the estimate-talk-estimate method.

6. To make the final decision, delay intuition, but don't ban it.

You may have recognized here an implementation of several of the decision hygiene techniques we presented in the preceding chapters: sequencing information, structuring the decision into independent assessments, using a common frame of reference grounded in the outside view, and aggregating the independent judgments of multiple individuals. By implementing these techniques, the mediating assessments protocol aims to change the decision *process* to introduce as much decision hygiene as possible.

No doubt this emphasis on process, as opposed to the content of decisions, may raise some eyebrows. The reactions of the research team members and the board members, as we have described them, are not unusual. Content is specific; process is generic. Using intuition and judgment is fun; following process is not. Conventional wisdom holds that good decisions — especially the very best ones — emerge from the insight and creativity of great leaders. (We especially like to believe this when we are the leader in question.) And to many, the word *process* evokes bureaucracy, red tape, and delays.

Our experience with companies and government agencies that have implemented all or some of the components of the protocol suggests that these concerns are misguided. To be sure, adding complexity to the decision-making processes of an organization that is already bureaucratic will not make things better. But decision hygiene need not be slow and certainly doesn't need to be bureaucratic. On the contrary, it promotes challenge and debate, not the stifling consensus that characterizes bureaucracies.

The case for decision hygiene is clear. Leaders in business and in the public sector are usually entirely unaware of noise in their largest and most important decisions. As a result, they take no specific measures to reduce it. In that respect, they are just like the recruiters who continue to rely on unstructured interviews as their sole personnel selection tool: oblivious to the noise in their own judgment, more confident in its validity than they should be, and unaware of procedures that could improve it.

Handwashing does not prevent all diseases. Likewise, decision hygiene will not prevent all mistakes. It will not make every decision brilliant. But like handwashing, it addresses an invisible yet pervasive and damaging problem. Wherever there is judgment, there is noise, and we propose decision hygiene as a tool to reduce it.

Speaking of the Mediating Assessments Protocol

"We have a structured process to make hiring decisions. Why don't we have one for strategic decisions? After all, options are like candidates."

"This is a difficult decision. What are the mediating assessments it should be based on?"

"Our intuitive, holistic judgment about this plan is very important—but let's not discuss it yet. Our intuition will serve us much better once it is informed by the separate assessments we have asked for."

PART VI

Optimal Noise

In 1973, Judge Marvin Frankel was right to call for a sustained effort to reduce noise in criminal sentencing. His informal, intuitive noise audit, followed by more formal and systematic efforts, uncovered unjustified disparities in the treatment of similar people. Those disparities were outrageous. They were also startling.

Much of this book can be understood as an effort to generalize Frankel's arguments and to offer an understanding of their psychological foundations. To some people, noise in the criminal justice system seems uniquely intolerable, even scandalous. But in countless other contexts, it is not exactly tolerable, as supposedly interchangeable people in the private and public sectors make different judgments on the job. In insurance, recruitment and evaluation of employees, medicine, forensic science, education, business, and government, interpersonal noise is a major source of error. We have also seen that each of us is subject to occasion noise, in the sense that supposedly irrelevant factors can lead us to make different judgments in the morning and in the afternoon, or on Monday and Thursday.

But as the intensely negative judicial reaction to the sentencing guidelines suggests, noise-reduction efforts often run into serious and even passionate objections. Many people have argued that the guidelines are rigid, dehumanizing, and unfair in their own way. Almost everyone has had the experience of making a reasonable request to a company, an employer, or a government, only to be met with the response "We really would love to help you, but our hands are tied. We have clear rules here." The rules in question may seem stupid and even cruel, but they may have been adopted for a good reason: to reduce noise (and perhaps bias as well).

Even so, some efforts to reduce noise raise serious concerns, perhaps above all if they make it difficult or impossible for people to get a fair hearing. The use of algorithms and machine learning has put that objection in a new light. No one is marching under a banner that says "Algorithms now!"

An influential critique comes from Kate Stith of Yale Law School and José Cabranes, a federal judge. They offered a vigorous attack on the sentencing guidelines and, in a sense, on one of our central arguments here. Their argument was limited to the area of criminal sentencing, but it can be offered as an objection to many noise-reduction strategies in education, business, sports, and everywhere else. Stith and Cabranes maintain that the sentencing guidelines are animated "by a fear of the exercise of discretion — by a fear of judging — and by a technocratic faith in experts and central planning." They argue that "fear of judging" operates to forbid consideration of "the particulars of each case at hand." In their view, "no mechanical solution can satisfy the demands of justice."

These objections are worth examining. In settings that involve judgments of all kinds, people often view the "demands of justice" as forbidding any sort of mechanical solution — and hence allowing or even mandating processes and approaches that turn out to guarantee noise. Many people call for attention to "the particulars of each case at hand." In hospitals, schools, and firms large and small, this call has deep intuitive appeal. We have seen that decision hygiene includes diverse strategies for reducing noise, and most of them do not involve mechanical solutions;

when people decompose a problem into its component parts, their judgments need not be mechanical. Even so, many people would not welcome the use of decision hygiene strategies.

We have defined noise as unwanted variability, and if something is unwanted, it should probably be eliminated. But the analysis is more complicated and more interesting than that. Noise may be unwanted, other things being equal. But other things might not be equal, and the costs of eliminating noise might exceed the benefits. And even when an analysis of costs and benefits suggests that noise is costly, eliminating it might produce a range of awful or even unacceptable consequences for both public and private institutions.

There are seven major objections to efforts to reduce or eliminate noise.

First, reducing noise can be expensive; it might not be worth the trouble. The steps that are necessary to reduce noise might be highly burdensome. In some cases, they might not even be feasible.

Second, some strategies introduced to reduce noise might introduce errors of their own. Occasionally, they might produce systematic bias. If all forecasters in a government office adopted the same unrealistically optimistic assumptions, their forecasts would not be noisy, but they would be wrong. If all doctors at a hospital prescribed aspirin for every illness, they would not be noisy, but they would make plenty of mistakes.

We explore these objections in chapter 26. In chapter 27, we turn to five more objections, which are also common and which are likely to be heard in many places in coming years, especially with increasing reliance on rules, algorithms, and machine learning.

Third, if we want people to feel that they have been treated with respect and dignity, we might have to tolerate some noise. Noise can be a by-product of an imperfect process that people end up embracing because the process gives everyone (employees, customers, applicants, students, those accused of crime) an individualized hearing, an opportunity to influence the exercise of discretion, and a sense that they have had a chance to be seen and heard.

Fourth, noise might be essential to accommodate new values and hence to allow moral and political evolution. If we eliminate noise, we might reduce our ability to respond when moral and political commitments move in new and unexpected directions. A noise-free system might freeze existing values.

Fifth, some strategies designed to reduce noise might encourage opportunistic behavior, allowing people to game the system or evade prohibitions. A little noise, or perhaps a lot of it, might be necessary to prevent wrongdoing.

Sixth, a noisy process might be a good deterrent. If people know that they could be subject to either a small penalty or a large one, they might steer clear of wrongdoing, at least if they are risk-averse. A system might tolerate noise as a way of producing extra deterrence.

Finally, people do not want to be treated as if they are mere things, or cogs in some kind of machine. Some noise-reduction strategies might squelch people's creativity and prove demoralizing.

Although we will address these objections as sympathetically as we can, we by no means endorse them, at least not if they are taken as reasons to reject the general goal of reducing noise. To presage a point that will recur throughout: whether an objection is convincing depends on the particular noise-reduction strategy to which it is meant to apply. You might, for example, object to rigid guidelines while also agreeing that aggregation of independent judgments is a good idea. You might object to the use of the mediating assessments protocol while strongly favoring the use of a shared scale grounded in the outside view. With these points in mind, our general conclusion is that even when the objections are given their due, noise reduction remains a worthy and even an urgent goal. In chapter 28, we defend this conclusion by exploring a dilemma that people face every day, even if they are not always aware of it.

CHAPTER 26

The Costs of Noise Reduction

Whenever people are asked to eliminate noise, they might object that the necessary steps are just too expensive. In extreme circumstances, noise reduction is simply not possible. We have heard this objection in business, education, government, and elsewhere. There is a legitimate concern here, but it is easily overstated, and it is often just an excuse.

To put the objection in its most appealing light, consider the case of a high school teacher who grades twenty-five essays by tenth-graders during each week of the school year. If the teacher spends no more than fifteen minutes on each essay, the grading might be noisy and therefore inaccurate and unfair. The teacher might consider a little decision hygiene, perhaps reducing the noise by asking a colleague to grade the essays as well, so that two people are reading every paper. Perhaps the teacher could accomplish the same goal by spending more time reading each essay, structuring the relatively complex process of assessment, or by reading the essays more than once and in different orders. A detailed grading guideline used as a checklist might help. Or perhaps the educator could make sure to read each essay at the same time of day, so as to reduce occasion noise.

But if the teacher's own judgments are pretty accurate and not terribly noisy, it might be sensible not to do any of these things. It might not be worth the bother. The teacher might think that using a checklist or asking a colleague to read the same papers would be a form of overkill. To know whether it is, a disciplined analysis might be necessary: how much more accuracy would the teacher gain, how important is more accuracy, and how much time and money would be required by the effort to reduce noise? We could easily imagine a limit on how much to invest in noise reduction. We could just as easily see that this limit should be different when the essays are written by ninth-graders or as senior theses, where university admission may be on the line and the stakes are higher.

The basic analysis might be extended to more complex situations faced by private and public organizations of all kinds, leading them to reject some noise-reduction strategies. For some diseases, hospitals and doctors might struggle to identify simple guidelines to eliminate variability. In the case of divergent medical diagnoses, efforts to reduce noise have particular appeal; they might save lives. But the feasibility and costs of those efforts need to be taken into account. A test might eliminate noise in diagnoses, but if the test is invasive, dangerous, and costly, and if variability in diagnoses is modest and has only mild consequences, then it might not be worthwhile for all doctors to require all patients to take the test.

Rarely does the evaluation of employees involve life and death. But noise can result in unfairness for employees and high costs for the firm. We have seen that efforts to reduce noise should be feasible. Are they worthwhile? Cases involving clearly mistaken evaluations might get noticed and seem embarrassing, shameful, or worse. Nonetheless, an institution might think that elaborate corrective steps are not worth the effort. Sometimes that conclusion is shortsighted, self-serving, and wrong, even catastrophically so. Some form of decision hygiene might well be worthwhile. But the belief that it is too expensive to reduce noise is not always wrong.

In short, we have to compare the benefits of noise reduction with the costs. That is fair, and it is one reason noise audits are so important. In many situations, the audits reveal that noise is producing outrageous levels of unfairness, very high costs, or both. If so, the cost of noise reduction is hardly a good reason not to make the effort.

Less Noise, More Mistakes?

A different objection is that some noise-reduction efforts might themselves produce unacceptably high levels of error. The objection might be convincing if the instruments used to reduce noise are too blunt. In fact, some efforts at noise reduction might even increase bias. If a social media platform such as Facebook or Twitter introduced firm guidelines that call for removing all posts containing certain vulgar words, its decisions will be less noisy, but it will be taking down numerous posts that should be allowed to stay up. These false positives are a directional error — a bias.

Life is full of institutional reforms that are designed to reduce the discretion of people and practices that generate noise. Many such reforms are well motivated, but some cures are worse than the disease. In *The Rhetoric of Reaction,* economist Albert Hirschman points to three common objections to reform efforts. First, such efforts might be perverse, in the sense that they will aggravate the very problem they are intended to solve. Second, they might be futile; they might not change things at all. Third, they put other important values in jeopardy (such as when an effort to protect labor unions and the right to unionize is said to hurt economic growth). Perversity, futility, and jeopardy might be offered as objections to noise reduction, and of the three, claims of perversity and jeopardy tend to be the most powerful. Sometimes these objections are just rhetoric — an effort to derail a reform that will actually do a great deal of good. But some noise-reduction strategies could jeopardize important values, and for others the risk of perversity might not be readily dismissed.

The judges who objected to the sentencing guidelines were pointing to that risk. They were well aware of Judge Frankel's work, and they did not deny that discretion produces noise. But they thought that reducing discretion would produce more mistakes, not fewer. Quoting Václav Havel, they insisted, "We have to abandon the arrogant belief that the world is merely a puzzle to be solved, a machine with instructions for use waiting to be discovered, a body of information to be fed into a computer in the hope that, sooner or later, it will spit out a universal solution." One reason for rejecting the idea of universal solutions is an insistent belief that human situations are highly varied and that good judges address the variations—which might mean tolerating noise, or at least rejecting some noise-reduction strategies.

In the early days of computer chess, a large airline offered a chess program for international passengers, who were invited to play against a computer. The program had several levels. At the lowest level, the program used a simple rule: place your opponent's king in check whenever you can. The program was not noisy. It played the same way every time; it would always follow its simple rule. But the rule ensured a great deal of error. The program was terrible at chess. Even inexperienced chess players could defeat it (which was undoubtedly the point; winning air travelers are happy air travelers).

Or consider the criminal sentencing policy adopted in some US states and called "three strikes and you're out." The idea is that if you commit three felonies, your sentence is life imprisonment—period. The policy reduces the variability that comes from random assignment of the sentencing judge. Some of its proponents were especially concerned about level noise and the possibility that some judges were too lenient with hardened criminals. Eliminating noise is the central point of the three-strikes legislation.

But even if the three-strikes policy succeeds in its noise-reduction goal, we can reasonably object that the price of this success is too high. Some people who have committed three felonies should not be put away for life. Perhaps their crimes were not violent. Or their awful life circumstances might have helped lead them to crime. Maybe they show a capacity for rehabilitation. Many people think that a life sentence, inattentive to the particular circumstances, is not only too harsh but also intolerably rigid. For that reason, the price of that noise-reduction strategy is too high.

Consider the case of *Woodson v. North Carolina,* in which the US Supreme Court held that a mandatory death sentence was unconstitutional not because it was too brutal but *because it was a rule.* The whole point of the mandatory death sentence was to ensure against noise — to say that under specified circumstances, murderers would have to be put to death. Invoking the need for individualized treatment, the court said that "the belief no longer prevails that every offense in a like legal category calls for an identical punishment without regard to the past life and habits of a particular offender." According to the Supreme Court, a serious constitutional shortcoming of the mandatory death sentence is that it "treats all persons convicted of a designated offense not as uniquely individual human beings, but as members of a faceless, undifferentiated mass to be subjected to the blind infliction of the penalty of death."

The death penalty involves especially high stakes, of course, but the court's analysis can be applied to many other situations, most of them not involving law at all. Teachers evaluating students, doctors evaluating patients, employers evaluating employees, underwriters setting insurance premiums, coaches evaluating athletes—all these people might make mistakes if they apply overly rigid, noise-reducing rules. If employers use simple rules for evaluating, promoting, or suspending employees, those rules might eliminate noise while neglecting important aspects of the employees' performance. A noise-free scoring system that fails to take significant variables into account might be worse than reliance on (noisy) individual judgments.

Chapter 27 considers the general idea of treating people as "uniquely individual," rather than as "members of a faceless, undifferentiated mass." For now, we are focusing on a more prosaic point. Some noise-reduction strategies ensure too many mistakes. They might be a lot like that foolish chess program.

Still, the objection seems far more convincing than it actually is. If one noise-reduction strategy is error-prone, we should not rest content with high levels of noise. We should instead try to devise a better noise-reduction strategy—for example, aggregating judgments rather than adopting silly rules or developing wise guidelines or rules rather than foolish ones. In the interest of noise reduction, a university could say, for example, that people with the highest test scores will be admitted, and that's it. If that rule seems too crude, the school could create a formula that takes account of test scores, grades, age, athletic achievements, family background, and more. Complex rules might be more accurate — more attuned to the full range of relevant factors. Similarly, doctors have complex rules for diagnosing some illnesses. The guidelines and rules used by professionals are not always simple or crude, and many of them help reduce noise without creating intolerably high costs (or bias). And if guidelines or rules will not work, perhaps we could introduce other forms of decision hygiene, suited to the particular situation, that will; recall aggregating judgments or using a structured process such as the mediating assessments protocol.

Noiseless, Biased Algorithms

The potentially high costs of noise reduction often come up in the context of algorithms, where there are growing objections to "algorithmic bias." As we have seen, algorithms eliminate noise and often seem appealing for that reason. Indeed, much of this book might be taken as an argument for greater reliance on algorithms, simply because they are noiseless. But as we have also seen, noise reduction can come at an intolerable cost if greater reliance on algorithms increases discrimination on the basis of race and gender, or against members of disadvantaged groups.

There are widespread fears that algorithms will in fact have that discriminatory consequence, which is undoubtedly a serious risk. In *Weapons of Math Destruction,* mathematician Cathy O'Neil urges that reliance on big data and decision by algorithm can embed prejudice, increase inequality, and threaten democracy itself. According to another skeptical account, "potentially biased mathematical models are remaking our lives — and neither the companies responsible for developing them nor the government is interested in addressing the problem." According to ProPublica, an independent investigative journalism organization, COMPAS, an algorithm widely used in recidivism risk assessments, is strongly biased against members of racial minorities.

No one should doubt that it is possible — even easy — to create an algorithm that is noise-free but also racist, sexist, or otherwise biased. An algorithm that explicitly uses the color of a defendant's skin to determine whether that person should be granted bail would discriminate (and its use would be unlawful in many nations). An algorithm that takes account of whether job applicants might become pregnant would discriminate against women. In these and other cases, algorithms could eliminate unwanted variability in judgment but also embed unacceptable bias.

In principle, we should be able to design an algorithm that does *not* take account of race or gender. Indeed, an algorithm could be designed that disregards race or gender entirely. The more challenging problem, now receiving a great deal of attention, is that an algorithm could discriminate and, in that sense, turn out to be biased, even when it does not overtly use race and gender as predictors.

As we have suggested, an algorithm might be biased for two main reasons. First, by design or not, it could use predictors that are highly correlated with race or gender. For example, height and weight are correlated with gender, and the place where people grew up or where they live might well be correlated with race.

Second, discrimination could also come from the source data. If an algorithm is trained on a data set that is biased, it will be biased, too. Consider "predictive policing" algorithms, which attempt to predict crime, often in order to improve the allocation of police resources. If the existing data about crime reflects the overpolicing of certain neighborhoods or the comparative overreporting of certain types of offenses, then the resulting algorithms will perpetuate or exacerbate discrimination. Whenever there is bias in the training data, it is quite possible to design, intentionally or unintentionally, an algorithm that encodes discrimination. It follows that even if an algorithm does not expressly consider race or gender, it could turn out to be as biased as human beings are. Indeed, in this regard, algorithms could be worse: since they eliminate noise, they could be more *reliably* biased than human judges.

For many people, a key practical consideration is whether an algorithm has a disparate impact on identifiable groups. Exactly how to test for disparate impact, and how to decide what constitutes discrimination, bias, or fairness for an algorithm, are surprisingly complex topics, well beyond the scope of this book.

The fact that this question can be raised at all, however, is a distinct advantage of algorithms over human judgments. For starters, we recommend careful assessment of algorithms to ensure that they do not consider inadmissible inputs and to test whether they discriminate in an objectionable way. It is much harder to subject individual human beings, whose judgments are often opaque, to the same kind of scrutiny; people sometimes discriminate unconsciously and in ways that outside observers, including the legal system, cannot easily see. So in some ways, an algorithm can be more transparent than human beings are.

Undoubtedly, we need to draw attention to the costs of noiseless but biased algorithms, just as we need to consider the costs of noiseless but biased rules. The key question is whether we can design algorithms that do better than real-world human judges on a combination of criteria that matter: accuracy and noise reduction, and nondiscrimination and fairness. A great deal of evidence suggests that algorithms can outperform human beings on whatever combination of criteria we select. (Note that we said *can* and not *will*.) For instance, as described in chapter 10, an algorithm can be more accurate than human judges with respect to bail decisions while producing less racial discrimination than human beings do. Similarly, a résumé-selection algorithm can select a better *and more diverse* pool of talent than human résumé screeners do.

These examples and many others lead to an inescapable conclusion: although a predictive algorithm in an uncertain world is unlikely to be perfect, it can be far less imperfect than noisy and often-biased human judgment. This superiority holds in terms of both validity (good algorithms almost always predict better) and discrimination (good algorithms can be less biased than human judges). If algorithms make fewer mistakes than human experts do and yet we have an intuitive preference for people, then our intuitive preferences should be carefully examined.

Our broader conclusions are simple and extend well beyond the topic of algorithms. It is true that noise-reduction strategies can be costly. But much of the time their costs are merely an excuse—and not a sufficient reason to tolerate the unfairness and costs of noise. Of course, efforts to reduce noise might produce errors of their own, perhaps in the form of bias. In that case we have a serious problem, but the solution is not to abandon noise-reduction efforts; it is to come up with better ones.

Speaking of the Costs of Noise Reduction

"If we tried to eliminate noise in education, we would have to spend a lot of money. When they grade students, teachers are noisy. We can't have five teachers grading the same paper."

"If, instead of relying on human judgment, a social network decides that no one may use certain words, whatever the context, it will eliminate noise, but also create a lot of errors. The cure might be worse than the disease."

"True, there are rules and algorithms that are biased. But people have biases, too. What we should ask is, can we design algorithms that are both noise-free and less biased?"

"It might be costly to remove noise — but the cost is often worth incurring. Noise can be horribly unfair. And if one effort to reduce noise is too crude — if we end up with guidelines or rules that are unacceptably rigid or that inadvertently produce bias — we shouldn't just give up. We have to try again."

CHAPTER 27

Dignity

Suppose you have been denied a mortgage, not because any person has studied your situation but because a bank has a firm rule that people with your credit rating simply cannot get a mortgage. Or suppose you have terrific qualifications and an interviewer at a firm was greatly impressed with you, but your application for employment is rejected because you were convicted of a drug offense fifteen years ago— and the firm has a flat prohibition on hiring anyone who has been convicted of a crime. Or maybe you are accused of a crime and denied bail not after an individualized hearing before an actual human being but because an algorithm has decided that people with your characteristics have a flight risk that exceeds the threshold that would allow for bail.

In such cases, many people would object. They

want to be treated as individuals. They want a real human being to look at their particular circumstances. They may or may not be aware that individualized treatment would produce noise. But if that is the price of such treatment, they insist that it is a price worth paying. They might complain whenever people are treated, in the Supreme Court's words, "not as uniquely individual human beings, but as members of a faceless, undifferentiated mass to be subjected to the blind infliction" of some penalty (see chapter 26).

Many people insist on an individualized hearing, free from what they see as the tyranny of rules, to give people a sense that they are being treated as individuals and hence with a kind of respect. The idea of due process, taken as part of ordinary life, might seem to require an opportunity for a face-to-face interaction in which a human being, authorized to exercise discretion, considers a wide range of factors.

In many cultures, this argument for case-by-case judgment has deep moral foundations. It can be found in politics, law, theology, and even literature. Shakespeare's *Merchant of Venice* is easily read as an objection to noise-free rules and a plea for a role of mercy in law and in human judgment generally. Hence Portia's closing argument:

> *The quality of mercy is not strained;*
> *It droppeth as the gentle rain from heaven*

Upon the place beneath. It is twice blest;
It blesseth him that gives and him that takes:
(...)
It is enthroned in the hearts of kings,
It is an attribute to God himself;
And earthly power doth then show likest God's
When mercy seasons justice.

Because it is not bound by rules, mercy is noisy. Nonetheless, Portia's plea can be made in many situations and in countless organizations. It often resonates. An employee might be seeking a promotion. A would-be homeowner might be applying for a loan. A student might be applying to university. Those who are making decisions about such cases might reject some noise-reduction strategies, above all firm rules. If they do not, it might be because they think, with Portia, that the quality of mercy is not strained. They might know that their own approach is noisy, but if it ensures that people feel that they have been treated with respect and that someone has listened to them, they might embrace it anyway.

Some noise-reduction strategies do not run into this objection. If three people, rather than merely one, are making a decision, people are still given an individualized hearing. Guidelines may leave decision makers with significant discretion. But some efforts to reduce noise, including rigid rules, do eliminate that discretion and might lead people to object that the resulting process offends their sense of dignity.

Are they right? Certainly, people often care about whether they receive an individualized hearing. There is an unquestionable human value in the opportunity to be heard. But if individualized hearings produce more deaths, more unfairness, and much higher costs, they should not be celebrated. We have emphasized that in situations like hiring, admissions, and medicine, some noise-reduction strategies might turn out to be crude; they might forbid forms of individualized treatment that, while noisy, would produce fewer errors on balance. But if a noise-reduction strategy is crude, then, as we have urged, the best response is to try to come up with a better strategy—one attuned to a wide range of relevant variables. And if that better strategy eliminates noise and produces fewer errors, it would have obvious advantages over individualized treatment, even if it reduces or eliminates the opportunity to be heard.

We are not saying that the interest in individualized treatment does not matter. But there is a high price to pay if such treatment leads to all sorts of terrible consequences, including palpable unfairness.

Changing Values

Imagine that a public institution succeeds in eliminating noise. Let's say that a university defines *misconduct* so that every faculty member and every student knows what it does and does not include. Or suppose that a large firm specifies exactly what *corruption* means, so that anyone in the firm would know what is permitted and what is forbidden. Or imagine that a private institution reduces noise significantly, perhaps by saying that it will not hire anyone who has not majored in certain subjects. What happens if an organization's values change? Some noise-reduction strategies would seem unable to make space for them, and their inflexibility might be a problem, one that is closely connected with the interest in individualized treatment and dignity.

A famously puzzling decision in American constitutional law helps make the point. Decided in 1974, the case involved a school system's firm rule requiring pregnant teachers to take unpaid leave five months before the expected date of childbirth. Jo Carol LaFleur, a teacher, argued that she was perfectly fit to teach, that the rule was discriminatory, and that five months was excessive.

The US Supreme Court agreed. But it did not speak of sex discrimination, and it did not say that five months was necessarily excessive. Instead it objected that LaFleur had not been given an opportunity to show that there was no physical need for her, in particular, to stop working. In the court's own words,

> *there is no individualized determination by the teacher's doctor — or the school board's — as to*

any particular teacher's ability to continue at her job. The rules contain an irrebuttable presumption of physical incompetency, and that presumption applies even when the medical evidence as to an individual woman's physical status might be wholly to the contrary.

A mandatory period of five months off does seem absurd. But the court did not emphasize that point. Instead it complained of the "irrebuttable presumption" and the absence of an "individualized determination." In so saying, the court was apparently arguing, with Portia, that the quality of mercy is not strained and that a particular person should be required to look at LaFleur's particular circumstances.

But without some decision hygiene, that is a recipe for noise. Who decides LaFleur's case? Will the decision be the same for her as for many other, similarly situated women? In any case, many rules amount to irrebuttable presumptions. Is a specified speed limit unacceptable? A minimum age for voting or drinking? A flat prohibition on drunk driving? With such examples in mind, critics objected that an argument against "irrebuttable presumptions" would prove too much — not least because their purpose and effect are to reduce noise.

Influential commentators at the time defended the court's decision by emphasizing that moral values change over time and hence the need to avoid rigid rules. They argued that with respect to women's role in society, social norms were in a state of great flux. They contended that individualized determinations were especially suitable in that context because they would allow for incorporation of those changing norms. A rule-bound system might eliminate noise, which is good, but it might also freeze existing norms and values, which is not so good.

In sum, some people might insist that an advantage of a noisy system is that it will allow people to accommodate new and emerging values. As values change, and if judges are allowed to exercise discretion, they might begin to give, for example, lower sentences to those convicted of drug offenses or higher sentences to those convicted of rape. We have emphasized that if some judges are lenient and others are not, then there will be a degree of unfairness; similarly situated people will be treated differently. But unfairness might be tolerated if it allows room for novel or emerging social values.

The problem is hardly limited to the criminal justice system or even to law. With respect to any number of policies, companies might decide to allow some flexibility in their judgments and decisions, even if doing so produces noise, because flexibility ensures that as new beliefs and values arise, they can change policies over time. We offer a personal example: when one of us joined a large consulting firm some years ago, the not-so-recent welcome pack he received specified the travel expenses for which he was allowed to claim reimbursement ("one phone call home on safe arrival; a pressing charge for a suit; tips for bellboys"). The rules were noise-free but clearly outdated (and sexist). They were soon replaced with standards that can evolve with the times. For example, expenses must now be "proper and reasonable."

The first answer to this defense of noise is simple: Some noise-reduction strategies do not run into this objection at all. If people use a shared scale grounded in an outside view, they can respond to changing values over time. In any event, noise-reduction efforts need not and should not be permanent. If such efforts take the form of firm rules, those who make them should be willing to make changes over time. They might revisit them annually. They might decide that because of new values, new rules are essential. In the criminal justice system, the rule makers might reduce sentences for certain crimes and increase them for others. They might decriminalize some activity altogether—and criminalize an activity that had previously been considered perfectly acceptable.

But let's step back. Noisy systems can make room for emerging moral values, and that can be a good thing. But in many spheres, it is preposterous to defend high levels of noise with this argument. Some of the most important noise-reduction strategies, such as aggregating judgments, do allow for emerging values. And if different customers, complaining of a malfunctioning laptop, are treated differently by a computer company, the inconsistency is unlikely to be because of emerging values. If different people get different medical diagnoses, it is rarely because of new moral values. We can do a great deal to reduce noise or even eliminate it while still designing processes to allow values to evolve.

Gaming the System, Evading the Rules

In a noisy system, judges of all kinds can adapt as the situation requires—and respond to unexpected developments. By eliminating the power of adaptation, some noise-reduction strategies can have the unintended consequence of giving people an incentive to game the system. A potential argument for tolerating noise is that it may turn out to be a by-product of approaches that private and public institutions adopt to prevent that kind of gaming.

The tax code is a familiar example. On the one hand, the tax system should not be noisy. It should be clear and predictable; identical taxpayers ought not to be treated differently. But if we eliminated noise in the tax system, clever taxpayers would inevitably find a way to evade the rules. Among tax specialists, there is a lively debate about whether it is best to have clear rules, eliminating noise, or instead to have a degree of vagueness, allowing for unpredictability but also reducing the risk that clear rules will produce opportunistic or self-interested behavior.

Some companies and universities forbid people to engage in "wrongdoing," without specifying what that means. The inevitable result is noise, which is not good and may even be very bad. But if there is a specific list of what counts as wrongdoing, then terrible behavior that is not explicitly covered by the list will end up being tolerated.

Because rules have clear edges, people can evade them by engaging in conduct that is technically exempted but that creates the same or analogous harms. (Every parent of a teenager knows this!) When we cannot easily design rules that ban all conduct that ought to be prohibited, we have a distinctive reason to tolerate noise, or so the objection goes.

In some circumstances, clear, defined rules eliminating noise do give rise to the risk of evasion. And this risk might be a reason to adopt some other strategy for reducing noise, such as aggregation, and perhaps to tolerate an approach that allows for some noise. But the words *might be* are crucial. We need to ask how much evasion there would be—and how much noise there would be. If there is only a little evasion and a lot of noise, then we are better off with approaches that reduce noise. We will return to this question in chapter 28.

Deterrence and Risk Aversion

Suppose that the goal is to deter misconduct—by employees, by students, by ordinary citizens. A little unpredictability, or even a lot of it, might not be the worst thing. An employer might think, "If the punishment of certain kinds of wrongdoing is a fine, a suspension, or a dismissal, then my employees will not engage in those kinds of wrongdoing." Those who run a criminal justice system might think, "We don't much mind if would-be criminals have to guess about the likely punishment. If the prospect of a punishment lottery discourages people from crossing the line, maybe the resulting noise can be tolerated."

In the abstract, these arguments cannot be dismissed, but they are not terribly convincing. At first glance, what matters is the expected value of the punishment, and a 50% chance of a $5,000 fine is equivalent to the certainty of a $2,500 fine. Of course, some people might focus on the worst-case scenario. Risk-averse people might be more deterred by the 50% chance of a $5,000 fine — but risk-seeking people will be less deterred by it. To know whether a noisy system imposes more deterrence, we need to know whether potential wrongdoers are risk-averse or risk-seeking. And if we want to increase deterrence, wouldn't it be better to increase the penalty and eliminate the noise? Doing that would eliminate unfairness as well.

Creativity, Morale, and Fresh Ideas

Might some noise-reduction efforts squelch motivation and engagement? Might they affect creativity and prevent people from making big breakthroughs? Many organizations think so. In some cases, they might be right. To know whether they are, we need to specify the noise-reduction strategy to which they are objecting.

Recall the intensely negative reaction of many judges to the sentencing guidelines. As one judge put it, "We must learn once again to trust the exercise of judgment in the courtroom." In general, people in positions of authority do not like to have their discretion taken away. They may feel diminished as well as constrained — even humiliated. When steps are taken to reduce their discretion, many people will rebel.

They value the opportunity to exercise judgment; they might even cherish it. If their discretion is removed so that they will do what everyone else does, they might feel like cogs in a machine.

In short, a noisy system might be good for morale not because it is noisy but because it allows people to decide as they see fit. If employees are allowed to respond to customer complaints in their own way, evaluate their subordinates as they think best, or establish premiums as they deem appropriate, then they might enjoy their jobs more. If the company takes steps to eliminate noise, employees might think that their own agency has been compromised. Now they are following rules rather than exercising their own creativity. Their jobs look more mechanical, even robotic. Who wants to work in a place that squelches your own capacity to make independent decisions?

Organizations might respond to these feelings not only because they honor them but also because they want to give people space to come up with new ideas. If a rule is in place, it might reduce ingenuity and invention.

These points apply to many people in organizations but, of course, not all of them. Different tasks must be evaluated differently; noisy diagnoses of strep throat or hypertension might not be a good place to exercise creativity. But we might be willing to tolerate noise if it makes for a happier and more inspired work-force. Demoralization is itself a cost and leads to other costs, such as poor performance. To be sure, we should be able to reduce noise while remaining receptive to fresh ideas. Some noise-reduction strategies, such as structuring complex judgments, do exactly that. If we want to reduce noise while maintaining good morale, we might select decision hygiene strategies that have that consequence. And those who are in charge might make it clear that even when firm rules are in place, a process exists to challenge and rethink them — but not to break them by exercising case-by-case discretion.

In a series of energetic books, Philip Howard, a distinguished lawyer and thinker, makes similar points in favor of allowing more flexible judgments. Howard wants policies to take the form not of prescriptive rules, which eliminate noise, but of general principles: "be reasonable," "act prudently," "do not impose excessive risks."

In Howard's view, the modern world of government regulation has gone mad, simply because it is so rigid. Teachers, farmers, developers, nurses, doctors — all of these experts, and many more, are burdened by rules that tell them what to do and exactly how to do it. Howard thinks that it would be much better to allow people to use their own creativity to figure out how to achieve the relevant goals, whether the goals are better educational outcomes, reduced accidents, cleaner water, or healthier patients.

Howard makes some appealing arguments, but it is important to ask about the consequences of the approaches he favors, including potential increases in noise and bias. Most people do not love rigidity in the abstract, but it might be the best way of reducing noise and eliminating bias and error. If only general principles are in place, noise in their interpretation and enforcement will follow. That noise might well be intolerable, even scandalous. At the very least, the costs of noise have to be given careful consideration—and they usually are not. Once we see that noise produces widespread unfairness and high costs of its own, we will often conclude that it is unacceptable and that we should identify noise-reduction strategies that do not compromise important values.

Speaking of Dignity

"People value and even need face-to-face interactions. They want a real human being to listen to their concerns and complaints and to have the power to make things better. Sure, those interactions will inevitably produce noise. But human dignity is priceless."

"Moral values are constantly evolving. If we lock everything down, we won't make space for changing values. Some efforts to reduce noise are just too rigid; they would prevent moral change."

"If you want to deter misconduct, you should tolerate some noise. If students are left wondering about the penalty for plagiarism, great—they will avoid plagiarizing. A little uncertainty in the form of noise can magnify deterrence."

"If we eliminate noise, we might end up with clear rules, which wrongdoers will find ways to avoid. Noise can be a price worth paying if it is a way of preventing strategic or opportunistic behavior."

"Creative people need space. People aren't robots. Whatever your job, you deserve some room to maneuver. If you're hemmed in, you might not be noisy, but you won't have much fun and you won't be able to bring your original ideas to bear."

"In the end, most of the efforts to defend noise aren't convincing. We can respect people's dignity, make plenty of space for moral evolution, and allow for human creativity without tolerating the unfairness and cost of noise."

CHAPTER 28

Rules or Standards?

If the goal is to reduce noise or decide how and whether to do so (and to what degree), it is useful to distinguish between two ways of regulating behavior: rules and standards. Organizations of all kinds often choose one or the other or some combination of the two.

In business, a company might say that employees have to be at work between specified hours, that no one may take vacations of more than two weeks, and that if anyone leaks to the press, the person will be fired. Alternatively, it might say that employees must be at work "for a reasonable working day," that vacations will be decided "on a case-by-case basis, consistent with the needs of the firm," and that leaks "will be punished appropriately."

In law, a rule might say that no one may exceed a numerical speed limit, that workers may not be exposed to carcinogens, or that all prescription drugs must come with specific warnings. By contrast, a standard might say that people must drive "prudently," that employers must provide safe workplaces "to the extent feasible," or that in deciding whether to offer warnings for prescription drugs, companies must act "reasonably."

These examples illustrate the central distinction between rules and standards. Rules are meant to eliminate discretion by those who apply them; standards are meant to grant such discretion. Whenever rules are in place, noise ought to be severely reduced. Those who interpret rules must answer a question of fact: How fast did the driver go? Was a worker exposed to a carcinogen? Did the drug have the required warnings?

Under rules, the enterprise of fact-finding may itself involve judgment and so produce noise or be affected by bias. We have encountered many examples. But people who design rules aim to reduce those risks, and when a rule consists of a number ("no one may vote until they reach the age of eighteen" or "the speed limit is sixty-five miles per hour"), noise should be reduced. Rules have an important feature: *they reduce the role of judgment.* On that count, at least, judges (understood to include all those who apply rules) have less work to do. They follow the rules. For better or worse, they have far less room to maneuver.

Standards are altogether different. When standards are in place, judges have to do a lot of work to specify the meaning of open-ended terms. They might have to make numerous judgments to decide what counts as (for example) "reasonable" and "feasible." In addition to finding facts, they must give content to relatively vague phrases. Those who devise standards effectively export decision-making authority to others. They delegate power.

The kinds of guidelines discussed in chapter 22 might be rules or standards. If they are rules, they dramatically constrain judgment. Even if they are standards, they might be far from open-ended. Apgar scores are guidelines and not rules. They do not forbid some exercise of discretion. When guidelines are tightened so as to eliminate that discretion, they turn into rules. Algorithms work as rules, not standards.

Divisions and Ignorance

It should be clear at the outset that whenever firms, organizations, societies, or groups are sharply divided, it might be far easier to generate standards than rules. Company leaders might agree that managers should not act abusively, without knowing precisely what the proscription means. Managers might oppose sexual harassment in the workplace without deciding whether flirtatious behavior is acceptable. A university might prohibit students from engaging in plagiarism, without specifying the exact meaning of that term. People might agree that a constitution should protect freedom of speech, without deciding whether it should protect commercial advertising, threats, or obscenity. People might agree that environmental regulators should issue prudent rules to reduce greenhouse gas emissions, without defining what constitutes prudence.

Setting standards without specifying details can lead to noise, which might be controlled through some of the strategies we have discussed, such as aggregating judgments and using the mediating assessments protocol. Leaders might want to come up with rules but, as a practical matter, might not be able to agree on them. Constitutions themselves include many standards (protecting, for example, freedom of religion). The same is true of the Universal Declaration of Human Rights ("All human beings are born free and equal in dignity and rights").

The great difficulty of getting diverse people to agree on noise-reducing rules is one reason why standards, and not rules, are put in place. The leaders of a company might be unable to agree on specific words to govern how employees must deal with customers. Standards might be the best that such leaders can do. There are analogies in the public sector. Lawmakers might reach a compromise on a standard (and tolerate the resulting noise) if that is the price of enacting law at all. In medicine, doctors might agree on standards for diagnosing illnesses; attempts to devise rules, on the other hand, might cause intractable disagreement.

But social and political divisions are not the only reason that people resort to standards instead of rules. Sometimes, the real problem is that people lack the information that would enable them to produce sensible rules. A university might be unable to produce rules to govern its decisions about whether to promote a faculty member. An employer might struggle to foresee all the circumstances that would lead it to retain or discipline employees. A national legislature might not know about the appropriate level of air pollutants—particulate matter, ozone, nitrogen dioxide, lead. The best it can do is issue some kind of standard and rely on trusted experts to specify its meaning, even if the consequence is noise.

Rules can be biased in many ways. A rule might forbid women from becoming police officers. It might say that Irish need not apply. Even if they create a large bias, rules will sharply reduce noise (if everyone follows them). If a rule says that everyone over the age of twenty-one is permitted to buy alcoholic beverages and that no one under that age can do so, there will probably be little noise, at least as long as people follow the rule. By contrast, standards invite noise.

Bosses, Controlling Subordinates

The distinction between rules and standards has great importance for all public and private institutions, including businesses of all kinds. The choice between the two arises whenever a principal is trying to control an agent. As described in chapter 2, insurance underwriters work hard to charge the Goldilocks premium (one neither too high nor too low) to benefit their company. Would their bosses give these underwriters standards or rules to guide them? Any leader in a company might direct employees very specifically or more generally ("use your common sense" or "exercise your best judgment"). A doctor might use one or the other approach when offering instructions to a patient. "Take a pill every morning and every night" is a rule; "take a pill whenever you feel you need it" is a standard.

We have noted that a social media company such as Facebook will inevitably be concerned with noise and how to reduce it. The company might tell its employees to take down content when a post violates a clear rule (forbidding, say, nudity). Or it might tell its employees to enforce a standard (such as forbidding bullying or patently offensive materials). Facebook's Community Standards, first made public in 2018, are a fascinating mix of rules and standards, with plenty of both. After they were released, numerous complaints were made by Facebook's users, who argued that the company's standards produced excessive noise (and therefore created both errors and unfairness). A recurring concern was that because many thousands of Facebook's reviewers had to make judgments, the decisions could be highly variable. In deciding whether to take down posts that they reviewed, the reviewers made different decisions about what was allowed and what was forbidden. To see why such variability was inevitable, consider these words from Facebook's Community Standards in 2020:

> *We define hate speech as a direct attack on people based on what we call protected characteristics — race, ethnicity, national origin, religious affiliation, sexual orientation, caste, sex, gender, gender identity, and serious disease or disability. We also provide some protections for immigration status. We define attack as violent or dehumanizing*

speech, statements of inferiority, or calls for exclusion or segregation.

In implementing a definition of this kind, reviewers will inevitably be noisy. What, exactly, counts as "violent or dehumanizing speech"? Facebook was aware of such questions, and in response to them, it moved in the direction of blunt rules, precisely to reduce noise. Those rules were cataloged in a nonpublic document called the Implementation Standards, consisting of about twelve thousand words, which *The New Yorker* obtained. In the public Community Standards, the text governing graphic content started with a standard "We remove content that glorifies violence." (What's that, exactly?) By contrast, the Implementation Standards listed graphic images and explicitly told the content moderators what to do about these images. Examples included "charred or burning human beings" and "the detachment of non-generating body parts." To summarize a complicated story, the Community Standards look more like standards whereas the Implementation Standards look more like rules.

In the same vein, an airline might ask its pilots to abide by either rules or standards. The question might be whether to go back to the gate after ninety minutes on the tarmac or when, exactly, to turn on the seatbelt sign. The airline might like rules because they limit pilots' discretion, thus reducing error. But it might also believe that under some circumstances, pilots ought to use their best judgment. In these situations, standards might be much better than rules, even if they produce some noise.

In all these cases and many more, those who decide between rules and standards must focus on the problem of noise, the problem of bias, or both. Businesses, both large and small, have to make that decision all the time. Sometimes they do so intuitively and without much of a framework.

Standards come in many shapes and sizes. They can have essentially no content: "do what is appropriate, under the circumstances." They can be written so as to approach rules — as, for example, when what is appropriate is specifically defined, to limit judges' discretion. Rules and standards can also be mixed and matched. For example, a personnel office might adopt a rule ("all applicants must have a college degree") to precede the application of the standard ("subject to that constraint, choose people who will do a terrific job").

We have said that rules should reduce or possibly even eliminate noise and that standards will often produce a great deal of it (unless some noise-reduction strategy is adopted). In private and public organizations, noise is often a product of a failure to issue rules.

When the noise is loud enough—when everyone can see that similarly situated people are not being treated similarly—there is often a movement in the direction of rules. As in the case of criminal sentencing, the movement might turn into an outcry. Some sort of noise audit typically precedes that outcry.

The Return of the Repressed

Consider an important question: who counts as disabled, such that they should qualify for economic benefits reserved for those who are unable to work? If the question is phrased that way, judges will make ad hoc decisions that will be noisy and therefore unfair. In the United States, such noisy, unfair decisions were once the norm, and the results were scandalous. Two seemingly identical people in wheelchairs or with severe depression or chronic pain would be treated differently. In response, public officials shifted to something far more like a rule—a *disability matrix*. The matrix calls for relatively mechanical judgments on the basis of education, geographical location, and remaining physical capacities. The goal is to make the decisions less noisy.

The leading discussion of the problem, written by law professor Jerry Mashaw, gives a name to the effort to eliminate noisy judgments: *bureaucratic justice*. The term is worth remembering. Mashaw celebrates the creation of the matrix as fundamentally just, precisely because it promises to eliminate noise. In some situations, however, the promise of bureaucratic justice might not be realized. Whenever an institution shifts to rule-bound decisions, there is a risk that noise will reemerge.

Suppose that rules produce terrible results in particular cases. If so, judges might simply ignore the rules, thinking that they are far too harsh. For that reason, they might exercise discretion through a mild form of civil disobedience, which can be hard to police or even see. In private companies, employees ignore firm rules that seem stupid. Similarly, administrative agencies charged with protecting public safety and health can simply refuse to enforce statutes when they are too rigid and rule-like. In criminal law, *jury nullification* refers to situations in which juries simply refuse to follow the law, on the ground that it is senselessly rigid and harsh.

Whenever a public or private institution tries to control noise through firm rules, it must always be alert to the possibility that the rules will simply drive discretion underground. With the three-strikes policy, the frequent response of prosecutors — to avoid making a felony charge against people who had been convicted twice — was extremely difficult to control and even see.

When such things happen, there will be noise, but no one will hear it. We need to monitor our rules to make sure they are operating as intended. If they are not, the existence of noise might be a clue, and the rules should be revised.

A Framework

In business and in government, the choice between rules and standards is often made intuitively, but it can be made more disciplined. As a first approximation, the choice depends on just two factors: (1) the costs of decisions and (2) the costs of errors.

With standards, the costs of decisions can be very high for judges of all kinds, simply because they have to work to give them content. Exercising judgment can be burdensome. If doctors are told to make their best judgment, they might have to spend time thinking about each case (and the judgments might well be noisy). If doctors are given clear guidelines to decide whether patients have strep throat, their decisions might be fast and relatively straightforward. If the speed limit is sixty-five miles per hour, police officers do not have to think hard about how fast people are allowed to go, but if the standard is that people may not drive "unreasonably fast," officers have to do a lot more thinking (and the enforcement will almost certainly be noisy). With rules, the costs of decisions are typically much lower.

Still, it's complicated. Rules may be straightforward to apply once they are in place, but before a rule is put in place, *someone has to decide what it is.* Producing a rule can be hard. Sometimes it is prohibitively costly. Legal systems and private companies therefore often use words such as *reasonable, prudent,* and *feasible.* This is also why terms like these play an equally important role in fields such as medicine and engineering.

The costs of errors refer to the number and the magnitude of mistakes. A pervasive question is whether agents are knowledgeable and reliable, and whether they practice decision hygiene. If they are, and if they do, then a standard might work just fine—and there might be little noise. Principals need to impose rules when they have reason to distrust their agents. If agents are incompetent or biased and if they cannot feasibly implement decision hygiene, then they should be constrained by rules. Sensible organizations well understand that the amount of discretion they grant is closely connected with the level of trust they have in their agents.

Of course there is a continuum from perfect trust to complete distrust. A standard might lead to numerous errors by less-than-trustworthy agents, but if those errors are minor, they might be tolerable. A rule might lead to only a few mistakes, but if they are catastrophic, we might want a standard. We should be able to see that there is no *general* reason to think that the costs of errors are larger with either rules or standards. If a rule is perfect, of course, it will produce no errors. But rules are rarely perfect.

Suppose that the law says that you can buy liquor only if you are 21 or older. The law aims to protect young people from the various risks associated with alcohol consumption. Understood in this way, the law will produce plenty of mistakes. Some people who are 20 or 19 or 18 or even 17 can do just fine with liquor. Some people who are 22 or 42 or 62 cannot. A standard would produce fewer errors—if we could find a suitable form of words and if people could apply these words accurately. Of course, that is very hard to do, which is why we almost always see simple rules, based on age, for liquor sales.

This example suggests a much larger point. Whenever numerous decisions must be made, there might well be a lot of noise, and there is a strong argument for clear rules. If dermatologists are seeing a large number of patients with itchy rashes and moles, they might make fewer errors if their judgments are constrained by sensible rules. Without such rules, and with open-ended standards, the costs of decisions tend to become impossibly large. For repeated decisions, there are real advantages to moving in the direction of mechanical rules rather than ad hoc judgments. The burdens of exercising discretion turn out to be great, and the costs of noise, or the unfairness it creates, might well be intolerable.

Smart organizations are keenly aware of the disadvantages of both ways of regulating behavior. They enlist rules, or standards that are close to rules, as a way of reducing noise (and bias). And to minimize the costs of errors, they are willing to devote considerable time and attention, in advance, to ensuring that the rules are accurate (enough).

Outlawing Noise?

In many situations, noise should be a scandal. People live with it, but they should not have to do that. A simple response is to shift from open-ended discretion or a vague standard to a rule or something close to it. We now have a sense of when the simple response is the right response. But even when a rule is not feasible or not a good idea, we have identified an assortment of strategies to reduce noise.

All this raises a large question: should the legal system outlaw noise? It would be too simple to answer yes, but the law should be doing much more than it now does to control noise. Here is one way to think about the problem. The German sociologist Max Weber complained of "Kadi justice," which he understood as informal, ad hoc judgments undisciplined by general rules. In Weber's view, Kadi justice was intolerably case by case; it was a violation of the rule of law. As Weber put it, the judge "precisely did not adjudicate according to formal rules and 'without regard to persons.' Just the reverse largely obtained; he judged persons according to their concrete qualities and in terms of the concrete situation, or according to equity and the appropriateness of the concrete result."

This approach, Weber argued, "knows no rational rules of decision." We can easily see Weber as complaining about intolerable noise that Kadi justice ensured. Weber celebrated the rise of bureaucratic judgments, disciplined in advance. (Recall the idea of bureaucratic justice.) He saw specialized, professional, and rule-bound approaches as the final stage in the evolution of law. But long after Weber wrote, it is clear that Kadi justice, or something like it, remains pervasive. The question is what to do about it.

We would not go so far as to say that noise reduction should be part of the Universal Declaration of Human Rights, but in some cases, noise can be counted as a rights violation, and in general, legal systems all over the world should be making much greater efforts to control noise. Consider criminal sentencing; civil fines for wrongdoing; and the grant or denial of asylum, educational opportunities, visas, building permits, and occupational licenses. Or suppose that a large government agency is hiring hundreds or even thousands of people and that its decisions have no rhyme or reason; there is a cacophony of noise. Or suppose that a child custody agency treats young children very differently, depending on whether one or another employee is assigned to the case. How is it acceptable that a child's life and future depend on that lottery?

In many cases, variability in such decisions is clearly driven by biases, including identifiable cognitive biases and certain forms of discrimination. When that is so, people tend to find the situation intolerable, and the law may be invoked as a corrective, requiring new and different practices. Organizations all over the world see bias as a villain. They are right. They do not see noise that way. They should.

In many areas, the current level of noise is far too high. It is imposing high costs and producing terrible unfairness. What we have cataloged here is the tip of the iceberg. The law should do much more to reduce those costs. It should combat that unfairness.

Speaking of Rules and Standards

"Rules simplify life, and reduce noise. But standards allow people to adjust to the particulars of the situations."

"Rules or standards? First, ask which produces more mistakes. Then, ask which is easier or more burdensome to produce or work with."

"We often use standards when we should embrace rules—simply because we don't pay attention to noise."

"Noise reduction shouldn't be part of the Universal Declaration of Human Rights—at least not yet. Still, noise can be horribly unfair. All over the world, legal systems should consider taking strong steps to reduce it."

Taking Noise Seriously

Noise is the unwanted variability of judgments, and there is too much of it. Our central goals here have been to explain why that is so and to see what might be done about it. We have covered a great deal of material in this book, and by way of conclusion, we offer here a brisk review of the main points, as well as a broader perspective.

Judgments

As we use the term, *judgment* should not be confused with "thinking." It is a much narrower concept: judgment is a form of measurement in which the instrument is a human mind. Like other measurements, a judgment assigns a score to an object. The score need not be a number. "Mary Johnson's tumor is probably benign" is a judgment, as are statements like "The national economy is very unstable," "Fred Williams would be the best person to hire as our new manager," and "The premium to insure this risk should be $12,000." Judgments informally integrate diverse pieces of information into an overall assessment. They are not computations, and they do not follow exact rules. A teacher uses judgment to grade an essay, but not to score a multiple-choice test.

Many people earn a living by making professional judgments, and everyone is affected by such judgments in important ways. Professional *judges,* as we call them here, include football coaches and cardiologists, lawyers and engineers, Hollywood executives and insurance underwriters, and many more. Professional judgments have been the focus of this book, both because they have been extensively studied and because their quality has such a large impact on all of us. We believe that what we have learned applies to judgments that people make in other parts of their lives, too.

Some judgments are *predictive,* and some predictive judgments are verifiable; we will eventually know whether they were accurate. This is generally the case for short-term forecasts of outcomes such as the effects of a medication, the course of a pandemic, or the results of an election. But many judgments, including long-term forecasts and answers to fictitious questions, are unverifiable. The quality of such judgments can be assessed only by the quality of the thought process that produces them. Furthermore, many judgments are not predictive but *evaluative:* the sentence set by a judge or the rank of a painting in a prize competition cannot easily be compared to an objective true value.

Strikingly, however, people who make judgments behave as if a true value exists, regardless of whether it does. They think and act as if there were an invisible bull's-eye at which to aim, one that they and others should not miss by much. The phrase *judgment call* implies both the possibility of disagreement and the expectation that it will be limited. Matters of judgment are characterized by an expectation of *bounded disagreement.* They occupy a space between matters of computation, where disagreement is not allowed, and matters of taste, where there is little expectation of agreement except in extreme cases.

Errors: Bias and Noise

We say that *bias* exists when most errors in a set of judgments are in the same direction. Bias is the *average error,* as, for example, when a team of shooters consistently hits below and to the left of the target; when executives are too optimistic about sales, year after year; or when a company keeps reinvesting money in failing projects that it should write off.

Eliminating bias from a set of judgments will not eliminate all error. The errors that remain when bias is removed are not shared. They are the unwanted divergence of judgments, the unreliability of the measuring instrument we apply to reality. They are *noise*. Noise is variability in judgments that should be identical. We use the term *system noise* for the noise observed in organizations that employ interchangeable professionals to make decisions, such as physicians in an emergency room, judges imposing criminal penalties, and underwriters in an insurance company. Much of this book has been concerned with system noise.

Measuring Bias and Noise

The *mean of squared errors (MSE)* has been the standard of accuracy in scientific measurement for two hundred years. The main features of MSE are that it yields the sample mean as an unbiased estimate of the population mean, treats positive and negative errors equally, and disproportionately penalizes large errors. MSE does not reflect the real costs of judgment errors, which are often asymmetric. However, professional decisions always require accurate predictions. For a city facing a hurricane, the costs of under- and overestimating the threat are clearly not the same, but you would not want these costs to influence the meteorologists' forecast of the storm's speed and trajectory. MSE is the appropriate standard for making such predictive judgments, where objective accuracy is the goal.

As measured by MSE, bias and noise are independent and additive sources of error. Obviously, bias is always bad and reducing it always improves accuracy. Less intuitive is the fact that noise is equally bad and that reducing noise is always an improvement. The best amount of scatter is zero, even when the judgments are clearly biased. The goal, of course, is to minimize both bias and noise.

Bias in a set of verifiable judgments is defined by the difference between the average judgment of a case and the corresponding true value. This comparison is impossible for unverifiable judgments. For example, the true value of a premium that an underwriter sets for a particular risk will never be known. Nor can we easily know the true value of the just sentence for a particular crime. Lacking that knowledge, a frequent and convenient (though not always correct) assumption is that judgments are unbiased and that the average of many judges is the best estimate of the true value.

Noise in a system can be assessed by a *noise audit,* an experiment in which several professionals make independent judgments of the same cases (real or fictitious). We can measure noise without knowing a true value, just as we can see, from the back of the target, the scatter of a set of shots. Noise audits can measure the variability of judgments in many systems, including a radiology department and the system of criminal justice. They may sometimes call attention to deficiencies in skill or training. And they will quantify system noise — for instance, when underwriters in the same team differ in their assessments of risks.

Of bias and noise, which is the larger problem? It depends on the situation. The answer might well turn out to be noise. Bias and noise make equal contributions to overall error (MSE) when the mean of errors (the bias) is equal to the standard deviations of errors (the noise). When the distribution of judgments is normal (the standard bell-shaped curve), the effects of bias and noise are equal when 84% of judgments are above (or below) the true value. This is a substantial bias, which will often be detectable in a professional context. When the bias is smaller than one standard deviation, noise is the bigger source of overall error.

Noise Is a Problem

Variability as such is unproblematic in some judgments, even welcome. Diversity of opinions is essential for generating ideas and options. Contrarian thinking is essential to innovation. A plurality of opinions among movie critics is a feature, not a bug. Disagreements among traders make markets. Strategy differences among competing start-ups enable markets to select the fittest. In what we call matters of judgment, however, system noise is always a problem. If two doctors give you different diagnoses, at least one of them is wrong.

The surprises that motivated this book are the sheer magnitude of system noise and the amount of damage that it does. Both of these far exceed common expectations. We have given examples from many fields, including business, medicine, criminal justice, fingerprint analysis, forecasting, personnel ratings, and politics. Hence our conclusion: wherever there is judgment, there is noise, and more of it than you think.

The large role of noise in error contradicts a commonly held belief that random errors do not matter, because they "cancel out." This belief is wrong. If multiple shots are scattered around the target, it is unhelpful to say that, on average, they hit the bull's-eye. If one candidate for a job gets a higher rating than she deserves and another gets a lower one, the wrong person may be hired. If one insurance policy is overpriced and another is underpriced, both errors are costly to the insurance company; one makes it lose business, the other makes it lose money.

In short, we can be sure that there is error if judgments vary for no good reason. Noise is detrimental even when judgments are not verifiable and error cannot be measured. It is unfair for similarly situated people to be treated differently, and a system in which professional judgments are seen as inconsistent loses credibility.

Types of Noise

System noise can be broken down into *level noise* and *pattern noise*. Some judges are generally more severe than others, and others are more lenient; some forecasters are generally bullish and others bearish about market prospects; some doctors prescribe more antibiotics than others do. *Level noise* is the variability of the average judgments made by different individuals. The ambiguity of judgment scales is one of the sources of level noise. Words such as *likely* or numbers (e.g., "4 on a scale of 0 to 6") mean different things to different people. Level noise is an important source of error in judgment systems and an important target for interventions aimed at noise reduction.

System noise includes another, generally larger component. Regardless of the average level of their judgments, two judges may differ in their views of which crimes deserve the harsher sentences. Their sentencing decisions will produce a different *ranking* of cases. We call this variability *pattern noise* (the technical term is *statistical interaction*).

The main source of pattern noise is stable: it is the difference in the personal, idiosyncratic responses of judges to the same case. Some of these differences reflect principles or values that the individuals follow, whether consciously or not. For example, one judge might be especially severe with shoplifters and unusually lenient with traffic offenders; another might show the opposite pattern. Some of the underlying principles or values may be quite complex, and the judge may be unaware of them. For example, a judge could be relatively lenient toward older shoplifters without realizing it. Finally, a highly personal reaction to a particular case could also be stable. A defendant who resembles the judge's daughter might well have evoked the same feeling of sympathy, and hence leniency, on another day.

This *stable pattern noise* reflects the uniqueness of judges: their response to cases is as individual as their personality. The subtle differences among people are often enjoyable and interesting, but the differences become problematic when professionals operate within a system that assumes consistency. In the studies we have examined, the stable pattern noise that such individual differences produce is generally the single largest source of system noise.

Still, judges' distinctive attitudes to particular cases are not perfectly stable. Pattern noise also has a transient component, called *occasion noise*. We detect this kind of noise if a radiologist assigns different diagnoses to the same image on different days or if a fingerprint examiner identifies two prints as a match on one occasion but not on another. As these examples illustrate, occasion noise is most easily measured when the judge does not recognize the case as one seen before. Another way to demonstrate occasion noise is to show the effect of an irrelevant feature of the context on judgments, such as when judges are more lenient after their favorite football team won, or when doctors prescribe more opioids in the afternoon.

The Psychology of Judgment and Noise

The judges' cognitive flaws are not the only cause of errors in predictive judgments. *Objective ignorance* often plays a larger role. Some facts are actually unknowable—how many grandchildren a baby born yesterday will have seventy years from now, or the number of a winning lottery ticket in a drawing to be held next year. Others are perhaps knowable but are not known to the judge. People's exaggerated confidence in their predictive judgment underestimates their objective ignorance as well as their biases.

There is a limit to the accuracy of our predictions, and this limit is often quite low. Nevertheless, we are generally comfortable with our judgments. What gives us this satisfying confidence is an *internal signal,* a self-generated reward for fitting the facts and the judgment into a coherent story. Our subjective confidence in our judgments is not necessarily related to their objective accuracy.

Most people are surprised to hear that the accuracy of their predictive judgments is not only low but also inferior to that of formulas. Even simple linear models built on limited data, or simple rules that can be sketched on the back of an envelope, consistently outperform human judges. The critical advantage of rules and models is that they are noise-free. As we subjectively experience it, judgment is a subtle and complex process; we have no indication that the subtlety may be mostly noise. It is difficult for us to imagine that mindless adherence to simple rules will often achieve higher accuracy than we can—but this is by now a well-established fact.

Psychological biases are, of course, a source of

systematic error, or statistical bias. Less obviously, they are also a source of noise. When biases are not shared by all judges, when they are present to different degrees, and when their effects depend on extraneous circumstances, psychological biases produce noise. For instance, if half the managers who make hiring decisions are biased against women and half are biased in their favor, there will be no overall bias, but system noise will cause many hiring errors. Another example is the disproportionate effect of first impressions. This is a psychological bias, but that bias will produce occasion noise when the order in which the evidence is presented varies randomly.

We have described the process of judgment as the informal integration of a set of cues to produce a judgment on a scale. The elimination of system noise would therefore require judges to maintain uniformity in their use of cues, in the weights they assign to cues, and in their use of the scale. Even leaving aside the random effects of occasion noise, these conditions are rarely met.

Agreement is often fairly high in judgments on single dimensions. Different recruiters will often agree on their evaluations of which of two candidates is more charismatic or more diligent. The shared intuitive process of *matching* across intensity dimensions — such as when people match a high GPA to a precocious reading age—will generally produce similar judgments. The same is true of judgments based on a small number of cues that point in the same general direction.

Large individual differences emerge when a judgment requires the *weighting of multiple, conflicting cues.* Looking at the same candidate, some recruiters will give more weight to evidence of brilliance or charisma; others will be more influenced by concerns about diligence or calm under pressure. When cues are inconsistent and do not fit a coherent story, different people will inevitably give more weight to certain cues and ignore others. Pattern noise will result.

The Obscurity of Noise

Noise is not a prominent problem. It is rarely discussed, and it is certainly less salient than bias. You probably had not given it much thought. Given its importance, the obscurity of noise is an interesting phenomenon in and of itself.

Cognitive biases and other emotional or motivated distortions of thinking are often used as explanations for poor judgments. Analysts invoke overconfidence, anchoring, loss aversion, availability bias, and other biases to explain decisions that turned out badly. Such bias-based explanations are satisfying, because the human mind craves causal explanations. Whenever something goes wrong, we look for a cause — and often find it. In many cases, the cause will appear to be a bias.

Bias has a kind of explanatory charisma, which noise lacks. If we try to explain, in hindsight, why a particular decision was wrong, we will easily find bias and never find noise. Only a *statistical view* of the world enables us to see noise, but that view does not come naturally — we prefer causal stories. The absence of statistical thinking from our intuitions is one reason that noise receives so much less attention than bias does.

Another reason is that professionals seldom see a need to confront noise in their own judgments and in those of their colleagues. After a period of training, professionals often make judgments on their own. Fingerprint experts, experienced underwriters, and veteran patent officers rarely take time to imagine how colleagues might disagree with them — and they spend even less time imagining how they might disagree with themselves.

Most of the time, professionals have confidence in their own judgment. They expect that colleagues would agree with them, and they never find out whether they actually do. In most fields, a judgment may never be evaluated against a true value and will at most be subjected to vetting by another professional who is considered a *respect-expert.* Only occasionally will professionals be faced with a surprising disagreement, and when that happens, they will generally find reasons to view it as an isolated case. The routines of organizations also tend to ignore or suppress evidence of divergence among experts in their midst. This is understandable; from an organizational perspective, noise is an embarrassment.

How to Reduce Noise (and Bias, Too)

There is reason to believe that some people make better judgments than others do. Task-specific skill, intelligence, and a certain cognitive style — best described as being *actively open-minded* — characterize the best judges. Unsurprisingly, good judges will make few egregious mistakes. Given the multiple sources of individual differences, however, we should not expect even the best judges to be in perfect agreement on complex judgment problems. The infinite variety of backgrounds, personalities, and experiences that make each of us unique is also what makes noise inevitable.

One strategy for error reduction is debiasing. Typically, people attempt to remove bias from their judgments either by correcting judgments after the fact or by taming biases before they affect judgments. We propose a third option, which is particularly applicable to decisions made in a group setting: detect biases in real time, by designating a *decision observer* to identify signs of bias (see appendix B).

Our main suggestion for reducing noise in judgment is *decision hygiene.* We chose this term because noise reduction, like health hygiene, is prevention against an unidentified enemy. Handwashing, for example, prevents unknown pathogens from entering our bodies. In the same way, decision hygiene will prevent errors without knowing what they are. Decision hygiene is as unglamorous as its name and certainly less exciting than a victorious fight against predictable biases. There may be no glory in preventing an unidentified harm, but it is very much worth doing.

A noise-reduction effort in an organization should always begin with a noise audit (see appendix A). An important function of the audit is to obtain a commitment of the organization to take noise seriously. An essential benefit is the assessment of separate types of noise.

We described the successes and limitations of noise reduction efforts in various domains. We now recapitulate six principles that define decision hygiene, describe how they address the psychological mechanisms that cause noise, and show how they relate to the specific decision hygiene techniques we have discussed

The goal of judgment is accuracy, not individual expression. This statement is our candidate for the first principle of decision hygiene in judgment. It reflects the narrow, specific way we have defined judgment in this book. We have shown that stable pattern noise is a large component of system noise and that it is a direct consequence of individual differences, of judgment personalities that lead different people to form different views of the same problem. This observation leads to a conclusion that will be as unpopular as it is inescapable: judgment is not the place to express your individuality.

To be clear, personal values, individuality, and creativity are needed, even essential, in many phases of thinking and decision making, including the choice of goals, the formulation of novel ways to approach a problem, and the generation of options. But when it comes to making a judgment about these options, expressions of individuality are a source of noise. When the goal is accuracy and you expect others to agree with you, you should also consider what other competent judges would think if they were in your place.

A radical application of this principle is the

replacement of judgment with rules or algorithms. Algorithmic evaluation is guaranteed to eliminate noise—indeed, it is the only approach that can eliminate noise completely. Algorithms are already in use in many important domains, and their role is increasing. But it is unlikely that algorithms will replace human judgment in the final stage of important decisions—and we consider this good news. However, judgment can be improved, by both the appropriate use of algorithms and the adoption of approaches that make decisions less dependent on the idiosyncrasies of one professional. We have seen, for instance, how decision guidelines can help constrain the discretion of judges or promote homogeneity in the diagnoses of physicians and thus reduce noise and improve decisions.

Think statistically, and take the outside view of the case. We say that a judge takes the outside view of a case when she considers it as a member of a reference class of similar cases rather than as a unique problem. This approach diverges from the default mode of thinking, which focuses firmly on the case at hand and embeds it in a causal story. When people apply their unique experiences to form a unique view of the case, the result is pattern noise. The outside view is a remedy for this problem: professionals who share the same reference class will be less noisy. In addition, the outside view often yields valuable insights.

The outside-view principle favors the anchoring of predictions in the statistics of similar cases. It also leads to the recommendation that predictions should be moderate (the technical term is *regressive;* see appendix C). Attention to the wide range of past outcomes and to their limited predictability should help decision makers calibrate their confidence in their judgments. People cannot be faulted for failing to predict the unpredictable, but they can be blamed for a lack of predictive humility.

Structure judgments into several independent tasks. This divide-and-conquer principle is made necessary by the psychological mechanism we have described as *excessive coherence,* which causes people to distort or ignore information that does not fit a preexisting or emerging story. Overall accuracy suffers when impressions of distinct aspects of a case contaminate each other. For an analogy, think of what happens to the evidentiary value of a set of witnesses when they are allowed to communicate.

People can reduce excessive coherence by breaking down the judgment problem into a series of smaller tasks. This technique is analogous to the practice of structured interviews, in which interviewers evaluate one trait at a time and score it before moving to the next one. The principle of structuring inspires diagnostic guidelines, such as the Apgar score. It is also at the heart of the approach we have called the *mediating assessments protocol.* This protocol breaks down a complex judgment into multiple fact-based assessments and aims to ensure that each one is evaluated independently of the others. Whenever possible, independence is protected by assigning assessments to different teams and minimizing communication among them.

Resist premature intuitions. We have described the internal signal of judgment completion that gives decision makers confidence in their judgment. The unwillingness of decision makers to give up this rewarding signal is a key reason for the resistance to the use of guidelines and algorithms and other rules that tie their hands. Decision makers clearly need to be comfortable with their eventual choice and to attain the rewarding sense of intuitive confidence. But they should not grant themselves this reward prematurely. An intuitive choice that is informed by a balanced and careful consideration of the evidence is far superior to a snap judgment. Intuition need not be banned, but it should be informed, disciplined, and delayed.

This principle inspires our recommendation to *sequence the information:* professionals who make judgments should not be given information that they don't need and that could bias them, even if that information is accurate. In forensic science, for example, it is good practice to keep examiners unaware of other information about a suspect. Control of discussion agendas, a key element of the mediating assessments protocol, also belongs here. An efficient agenda will ensure that different aspects of the problem are considered separately and that the formation of a holistic judgment is delayed until the profile of assessments is complete.

Obtain independent judgments from multiple judges, then consider aggregating those judgments. The requirement of independence is routinely violated in the procedures of organizations, notably in meetings in which participants' opinions are shaped by those of others. Because of cascade effects and group polarization, group discussions often increase noise. The simple procedure of collecting participants' judgments *before* the discussion both reveals the extent of noise and facilitates a constructive resolution of differences.

Averaging independent judgments is guaranteed to reduce system noise (but not bias). A single judgment is a sample of one, drawn from the population of all possible judgments; and increasing sample size improves the precision of estimates. The advantage of averaging is further enhanced when judges have diverse skills and complementary judgment patterns.

The average of a noisy group may end up being more accurate than a unanimous judgment.

Favor relative judgments and relative scales. Relative judgments are less noisy than absolute ones, because our ability to categorize objects on a scale is limited, while our ability to make pairwise comparisons is much better. Judgment scales that call for comparisons will be less noisy than scales that require absolute judgments. For example, a *case scale* requires judges to locate a case on a scale that is defined by instances familiar to everyone.

———

The decision hygiene principles we have just listed are applicable not only to recurrent judgments but also to one-off major decisions, or what we call *singular decisions*. The existence of noise in singular decisions may seem counterintuitive: by definition, there is no variability to measure if you decide only once. Yet noise is there, causing errors. The noise in a team of shooters is invisible if we see only the first shooter in action, but the scatter would become apparent if we saw the other shooters. Similarly, the best way to think about singular judgments is to treat them as *recurrent judgments that are made only once.* That is why decision hygiene should improve them, too.

Enforcing decision hygiene can be thankless. Noise

is an invisible enemy, and a victory against an invisible enemy can only be an invisible victory. But like physical health hygiene, decision hygiene is vital. After a successful operation, you like to believe that it is the surgeon's skill that saved your life—and it did, of course—but if the surgeon and all the personnel in the operating room had not washed their hands, you might be dead. There may not be much glory to be gained in hygiene, but there are results.

How Much Noise?

Of course, the battle against noise is not the only consideration for decision makers and organizations. Noise may be too costly to reduce: a high school could eliminate noise in grading by having five teachers read each and every paper, but that burden is hardly justified. Some noise may be inevitable in practice, a necessary side effect of a system of due process that gives each case individualized consideration, that does not treat people like cogs in a machine, and that grants decision makers a sense of agency. Some noise may even be desirable, if the variation it creates enables a system to adapt over time—as when noise reflects changing values and goals and triggers a debate that leads to change in practice or in the law.

Perhaps most importantly, noise-reduction

strategies may have unacceptable downsides. Many concerns about algorithms are overblown, but some are legitimate. Algorithms may produce stupid mistakes that a human would never make, and therefore lose credibility even if they also succeed in preventing many errors that humans do make. They may be biased by poor design or by training on inadequate data. Their facelessness may inspire distrust. Decision hygiene practices also have their downsides: if poorly managed, they risk bureaucratizing decisions and demoralizing professionals who feel their autonomy is being undermined.

All these risks and limitations deserve full consideration. However, whether an objection to noise reduction makes sense depends on the particular noise-reduction strategy that is under discussion. An objection to aggregating judgments—perhaps on the ground that it is too costly—may not apply to the use of guidelines. To be sure, whenever the costs of noise reduction exceed its benefits, it should not be pursued. Once the cost-benefit calculation is made, it may reveal an optimal level of noise that is not zero. The problem is that in the absence of noise audits, people are unaware of how much noise there is in their judgments. When that is the case, invoking the difficulty of reducing noise is nothing but an excuse not to measure it.

Bias leads to errors and unfairness. Noise does too — and yet, we do a lot less about it. Judgment error may seem more tolerable when it is random than when we attribute it to a cause; but it is no less damaging. If we want better decisions about things that matter, we should take noise reduction seriously.

A Less Noisy World

I magine what organizations would look like if they were redesigned to reduce noise. Hospitals, hiring committees, economic forecasters, government agencies, insurance companies, public health authorities, criminal justice systems, law firms, and universities would be keenly alert to the problem of noise and strive to reduce it. Noise audits would be routine; they might be undertaken every year.

Leaders of organizations would use algorithms either to replace human judgment or to supplement it in far more areas than they do today. People would break down complex judgments into simpler mediating assessments. They would know about decision hygiene and follow its prescriptions. Independent judgments would be elicited and aggregated.

Meetings would look very different; discussions would be more structured. An outside view would be more systematically integrated into the decision process. Overt disagreements would be both more frequent and more constructively resolved.

The result would a be less noisy world. It would save a great deal of money, improve public safety and health, increase fairness, and prevent many avoidable errors. Our aim in writing this book has been to draw attention to this opportunity. We hope that you will be among those who seize it.

APPENDIX A

How to Conduct a Noise Audit

This appendix provides a practical guide for conducting a noise audit. You should read it from the perspective of a consultant who has been engaged by an organization to examine the quality of the professional judgments its employees produce by conducting a noise audit in one of its units.

As implied by its name, the focus of the audit is the prevalence of noise. However, a well-conducted audit will provide valuable information about biases, blind spots, and specific deficiencies in the training of employees and in the supervision of their work. A successful audit should stimulate changes in the operations of the unit, including in the doctrine that guides professionals' judgments, the training they receive, the tools they use to support their judgments, and the routine supervision of their work. If the effort is considered successful, it may be extended to other units of the organization.

A noise audit requires a substantial amount of work and much attention to detail because its credibility will surely be questioned if its findings reveal significant flaws. Every detail of the cases and the procedure should therefore be considered with hostile scrutiny in mind. The process we describe aims to reduce opposition by enlisting the professionals who are the most significant potential critics of the audit to be its authors.

Alongside the consultant (who may be external or internal), the relevant cast of characters includes the following:

- *Project team.* The project team will be responsible for all phases of the study. If the consultants are internal, they will form the core of the project team. If the consultants are external, an internal project team will work closely with them. This will ensure that people in the company view the audit as *their* project and consider the consultants as playing a supporting role. In addition to the consultants who administer the collection of data, analyze the results, and prepare a final report, the project team should include subject matter experts who can construct the cases that the judges will assess. All the members of the project team should have high professional credibility.

- *Clients.* A noise audit will only be useful if it leads to significant changes, which requires early involvement of the leadership of the organization, which is the "client" of the project. You can expect clients to be initially skeptical about the prevalence of noise. This initial skepticism is actually an advantage if it is accompanied by an open-minded attitude, curiosity about the results of the audit, and a commitment to remedy the situation if the consultant's pessimistic expectations are confirmed.

- *Judges.* The clients will designate one or more units to be audited. The selected unit should consist of a substantial number of "judges," the professionals who make similar judgments and decisions on behalf of the company. The judges should be effectively interchangeable; i.e., if one person was unavailable to handle a case, another would be assigned to it and expected to arrive at a similar judgment. The examples that introduced this book were sentencing decisions of federal judges and the setting of risk premiums and claims reserves in an insurance company. For a noise audit, it is best to select a judgment task that (1) can be completed on the basis of written information, and (2) is expressed numerically (e.g., in dollars, probabilities, or ratings).

- *Project manager.* A high-level manager in the administrative staff should be designated as project manager. Specific professional expertise is not required for that task. However, a high position in the organization is of practical significance in overcoming administrative hurdles and is also a demonstration of the importance that the company attaches to the project. The task of the project manager is to provide administrative support to facilitate all phases of the project, including the preparation of the final report and the communication of its conclusions to the leadership of the company.

Construction of Case Materials

The subject matter experts who are part of the project team should have recognized expertise in the task of the unit (e.g., setting premiums for risks or evaluating the potential of possible investments). They will be in charge of developing the cases that will be used in the audit. Designing a credible simulation of the judgments professionals make on the job is a delicate task—especially given the scrutiny that the study will undergo if it reveals serious problems. The team must consider this question: if the results of our simulation indicate a high level of noise, will people in the company accept that there is noise in the actual judgments of the unit? The noise audit is only worth carrying out if the answer is a clear yes.

There is more than one way to achieve a positive response. The noise audit of sentencing described in chapter 1 summarized each case by a brief schematic list of relevant attributes and obtained assessments of sixteen cases in ninety minutes. The noise audit in the insurance company described in chapter 2 used detailed and realistic summaries of complex cases. Findings of high noise in both instances provided acceptable evidence because of the argument that if much disagreement was found in simplified cases, noise could only be worse in real cases.

A questionnaire should be prepared for each case, to provide a deeper understanding of the reasoning that led each judge to a judgment of that case. The questionnaire should be administered only after the completion of all cases. It should include:

- Open questions about the key factors that led the participant to her response.

- A list of the facts of the case, allowing the participant to rate their importance.

- Questions that call for an "outside view" of the category to which the case belongs. For instance, if the cases call for dollar valuations, participants should provide an estimate of how much below or above average the case is compared to all valuations for cases of the same category.

Prelaunch Meeting with Executives

When the case materials to be used in the audit are assembled, a meeting should be scheduled in which the project team will present the audit to the leadership of the company. The discussion in that meeting should consider possible outcomes of the study, including a finding of unacceptable system noise. The purpose of the meeting is to hear objections to the planned study and to obtain from the leadership a commitment to accept its results, whatever they are: there is no point moving on to the next stage without such a commitment. If serious objections are raised, the project team may be required to improve the case materials and try again.

Once the executives accept the design of the noise audit, the project team should ask them to state their expectations about the results of the study. They should discuss questions such as:

- "What level of disagreement do you expect between a randomly selected pair of answers to each case?"
- "What is the maximum level of disagreement that would be acceptable from a business perspective?"
- "What is the estimated cost of getting an evaluation wrong in either direction (too high or low) by a specified amount (e.g., 15%)?"

The answers to these questions should be documented to ensure that they are remembered and believed when the actual results of the audit come in.

Administration of the Study

The managers of the audited unit should be, from the beginning, informed in general terms that their unit has been selected for special study. However, it is important that the term *noise audit* not be used to describe the project. The words *noise* and *noisy* should be avoided, especially as descriptions of people. A neutral term such as *decision-making study* should be used instead.

The managers of the unit will be immediately in charge of the data collection and responsible for briefing the participants about the task, with the participation of the project manager and members of the project team. The intent of the exercise should be described to the participants in general terms, as in *"The organization is interested in how [decision makers] reach their conclusions."*

It is essential to reassure the professionals who participate in the study that individual answers will not be known to anyone in the organization, including the project team. If necessary, an outside firm may be hired to anonymize the data. It is also important to stress that there will be no specific consequences for the unit, which was merely selected as representative of units that perform judgment tasks on behalf of the organization. To ensure the credibility of the results, all qualified professionals in the unit should participate in the study. The allocation of half a working day to the exercise will help convince the participants of its importance.

All participants should complete the exercise at the same time, but they should be kept physically separate and asked not to communicate while the study is in progress. The project team will be available to answer questions during the study.

Analyses and Conclusions

The project team will be in charge of the statistical analyses of the multiple cases evaluated by each participant, including the measurement of the overall amount of noise and its constituents, level noise and pattern noise. If the case materials allow it, it will also identify statistical biases in the responses. The project team will have the equally important task of trying to understand the sources of variability in judgments by examining responses to the questionnaire in which participants explained their reasoning and identified the facts that most influenced their decisions. Focusing mainly on extreme responses at both ends of the distribution, the team will search for patterns in the data. It will look for indications of possible deficiencies in the training of employees, the procedures of the organization, and the information that it provides to its employees.

The consultant and the internal project team will work together to develop tools and procedures that apply principles of decision hygiene and debiasing to improve the judgments and decisions made in the unit. This step of the process is likely to extend over several months. In parallel, the consultant and the professional team will also prepare a report on the project, which they will present to the leadership of the organization.

At this point, the organization will have carried out a sample noise audit in one of its units. If the effort is considered successful, the executive team may decide on a broader effort to evaluate and improve the quality of the judgments and decisions that are produced in the organization.

APPENDIX B

A Checklist for a Decision Observer

This appendix presents a generic example of a checklist to be used by a decision observer (see chapter 19). The checklist presented here roughly follows the chronological sequence of the discussion that leads to an important decision.

The suggested questions that follow each item in the checklist bring additional clarifications. Decision observers should ask themselves these questions while observing the decision process.

This checklist is not intended to be used as it stands. Rather, we hope that it will serve as an inspiration and a starting point for decision observers who will design a custom bias observation checklist of their own.

Bias Observation Checklist

1. Approach to Judgment
1a. Substitution
____ "Did the group's choice of evidence and the focus of their discussion indicate substitution of an easier question for the difficult one they were assigned?"

____ "Did the group neglect an important factor (or appear to give weight to an irrelevant one)?"

1b. Inside view
____ "Did the group adopt the outside view for part of its deliberations and seriously attempt to apply comparative rather than absolute judgment?"

1c. Diversity of views
____ "Is there any reason to suspect that members of the group share biases, which could lead their errors to be correlated? Conversely, can you think of a relevant point of view or expertise that is not represented in this group?

2. Prejudgments and Premature Closure
2a. Initial prejudgments
____ "Do (any of) the decision makers stand to gain more from one conclusion than another?"

____ "Was anyone already committed to a conclusion? Is there any reason to suspect prejudice?"

____ "Did dissenters express their views?"

____ "Is there a risk of escalating commitment to a losing course of action?"

2b. Premature closure; excessive coherence

____ "Was there accidental bias in the choice of considerations that were discussed early?"

____ "Were alternatives fully considered, and was evidence that would support them actively sought?"

____ "Were uncomfortable data or opinions suppressed or neglected?"

3. INFORMATION PROCESSING

3a. Availability and salience

____ "Are the participants exaggerating the relevance of an event because of its recency, its dramatic quality, or its personal relevance, even if it is not diagnostic?"

3b. Inattention to quality of information

____ "Did the judgment rely heavily on anecdotes, stories, or analogies? Did the data confirm them?"

3c. Anchoring

____ "Did numbers of uncertain accuracy or relevance play an important role in the final judgment?"

3d. Nonregressive prediction

____ "Did the participants make nonregressive extrapolations, estimates, or forecasts?"

4. DECISION
4a. Planning fallacy

____ "When forecasts were used, did people question their sources and validity? Was the outside view used to challenge the forecasts?"

____ "Were confidence intervals used for uncertain numbers? Are they wide enough?"

4b. Loss aversion

____ "Is the risk appetite of the decision makers aligned with that of the organization? Is the decision team overly cautious?"

4c. Present bias

____ "Do the calculations (including the discount rate used) reflect the organization's balance of short- and long-term priorities?"

APPENDIX C

Correcting Predictions

Matching predictions are errors caused by our reliance on the intuitive matching process (see chapter 14). We make matching predictions when we rely on the information we have to make a forecast and behave as if this information were perfectly (or very highly) predictive of the outcome.

Recall the example of Julie, who could "read fluently when she was four years old." The question was, what is her GPA? If you predicted 3.8 for Julie's college GPA, you intuitively judged that the four-year-old Julie was in the top 10% of her age group by reading age (although not in the top 3–5%). You then, implicitly, assumed that Julie would also rank somewhere around the 90th percentile of her class in terms of GPA. This corresponds to a GPA of 3.7 or 3.8 — hence the popularity of these answers.

What makes this reasoning statistically incorrect is that it grossly overstates the diagnostic value of the information available about Julie. A precocious four-year-old does not always become an academic over-achiever (and, fortunately, a child who initially struggles with reading will not languish at the bottom of the class forever).

More often than not, in fact, outstanding perfor-mance will become less outstanding. Conversely, very poor performance will improve. It is easy to imagine social, psychological, or even political reasons for this observation, but reasons are not required. The phe-nomenon is purely statistical. Extreme observations in one direction or the other will tend to become less extreme, simply because past performance is not per-fectly correlated with future performance. This ten-dency is called *regression to the mean* (hence the technical term *nonregressive* for matching predictions, which fail to take it into account).

To put it quantitatively, the judgment you made about Julie would be correct if reading age were a per-fect predictor of GPA, that is, if there were a correla-tion of 1 between the two factors. That is obviously not the case.

There is a statistical way to make a judgment that is likely to be more accurate. It is nonintuitive and difficult to find, even for people with some statistical training. Here is the procedure. Figure 19 illustrates it with Julie's example.

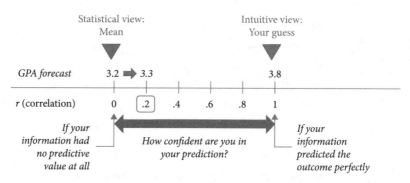

FIGURE 19: *Adjusting an intuitive prediction for regression to the mean*

1. Make your intuitive guess.

Your intuition about Julie, or about any case about which you have information, is not worthless. Your fast, system 1 thinking easily places the information you have onto the scale of your prediction and produces a GPA score for Julie. This guess is the prediction you would make if the information you have were perfectly predictive. Write it down.

2. Look for the mean.

Now, step back and forget what you know about Julie for a moment. What would you say about Julie's GPA *if you knew absolutely nothing about her?* The answer, of course, is straightforward: in the absence of any information, your best guess of Julie's GPA would have to be the mean GPA in her graduating class—probably somewhere around 3.2.

Looking at Julie this way is an application of the broader principle we have discussed above, the *outside view*. When we take the outside view, we think of the case we are considering as an instance of a class, and we think about that class in statistical terms. Recall, for instance, how taking the outside view about the Gambardi problem leads us to ask what the base rate of success is for a new CEO (see chapter 4).

3. Estimate the diagnostic value of the information you have.

This is the difficult step, where you need to ask yourself, "What is the predictive value of the information I have?" The reason this question matters should be clear by now. If all you knew about Julie was her shoe size, you would correctly give this information zero weight and stick to the mean GPA prediction. If, on the other hand, you had the list of grades Julie has obtained in every subject, this information would be perfectly predictive of her GPA (which is their average). There are many shades of gray between these two extremes. If you had data about Julie's exceptional intellectual achievements in high school, this information would be much more diagnostic than her reading age, but less than her college grades.

Your task here is to quantify the diagnostic value of the data you have, expressed as a correlation with the outcome you are predicting. Except in rare cases, this number will have to be a back-of-the-envelope estimate.

To make a sensible estimate, remember some of the examples we listed in chapter 12. In the social sciences, correlations of more than .50 are very rare. Many correlations that we recognize as meaningful are in the .20 range. In Julie's case, a correlation of .20 is probably an upper bound.

4. *Adjust from the outside view in the direction of your intuitive guess, to an extent that reflects the diagnostic value of the information you have.*

The final step is a simple arithmetic combination of the three numbers you have now produced: you must adjust from the mean, in the direction of your intuitive guess, in proportion to the correlation you have estimated.

This step simply extends the observation we have just made: if the correlation were 0, you would stick to the mean; if it were 1, you would disregard the mean and happily make a matching prediction. In Julie's case, then, the best prediction you can make of GPA is one that lies no more than 20% of the way from the mean of the class in the direction of the intuitive estimate that her reading age suggested to you. This computation leads you to a prediction of about 3.3.

We have used Julie's example, but this method can be applied just as easily to many of the judgment problems we have discussed in this book. Consider, for instance, a vice president of sales who is hiring a new salesperson and has just had an interview with an absolutely outstanding candidate. Based on this strong impression, the executive estimates that the candidate should book sales of $1 million in the first year on the job — twice the mean amount achieved by new hires during their first year on the job. How could the vice president make this estimate regressive? The calculation depends on the diagnostic value of the interview. How well does a recruiting interview predict on-the-job success in this case? Based on the evidence we have reviewed, a correlation of .40 is a very generous estimate. Accordingly, a regressive estimate of the new hire's first-year sales would be, at most, $500K + ($1 million – $500K) × .40 = $700K.

This process, again, is not at all intuitive. Notably, as the examples illustrate, corrected predictions will always be more conservative than intuitive ones: they will never be as extreme as intuitive predictions, but instead closer, often *much* closer, to the mean. If you correct your predictions, you will never bet that the tennis champion who has won ten Grand Slam titles will win another ten. Neither will you foresee that a highly successful start-up worth $1 billion will become a behemoth worth several hundred times that. Corrected predictions do not take bets on outliers.

This means that, in hindsight, corrected predictions will inevitably result in some highly visible failures. However, prediction is not done in hindsight. You should remember that outliers are, by definition, extremely rare. The opposite error is much more frequent: when we predict that outliers will remain outliers, they generally don't, because of regression to the mean. That is why, whenever the aim is to maximize accuracy (i.e., minimize MSE), corrected predictions are superior to intuitive, matching predictions.

Acknowledgments

We have many people to thank. Linnea Gandhi has served as our chief of staff, offering substantive guidance and help, keeping us organized, making us smile and laugh, and basically running the show. Aside from all that, she offered numerous valuable suggestions on the manuscript. We couldn't have done it without her. Dan Lovallo played a major part by coauthoring one of the articles that seeded this book. John Brockman, our agent, was enthusiastic, hopeful, sharp, and wise at every stage. We are grateful to him. Tracy Behar, our principal editor and guide, made the book better in ways large and small. Arabella Pike and Ian Straus also provided superb editorial suggestions.

Special thanks too to Oren Bar-Gill, Maya Bar-Hillel, Max Bazerman, Tom Blaser, David Budescu,

ACKNOWLEDGMENTS

Jeremy Clifton, Anselm Dannecker, Vera Delaney, Itiel Dror, Angela Duckworth, Annie Duke, Dan Gilbert, Adam Grant, Anupam Jena, Louis Kaplow, Gary Klein, Jon Kleinberg, Nathan Kuncel, Kelly Leonard, Daniel Levin, Sara McLanahan, Barbara Mellers, Josh Miller, Sendhil Mullainathan, Scott Page, Eric Posner, Lucia Reisch, Matthew Salganik, Eldar Shafir, Tali Sharot, Philip Tetlock, Richard Thaler, Barbara Tversky, Peter Ubel, Crystal Wang, Duncan Watts, and Caroline Webb, who read and commented on draft chapters, and in some cases a draft of the full text. We are grateful for their generosity and help.

We were lucky to benefit from the advice of many great researchers. Julian Parris offered invaluable help on many statistical issues. Our chapters on the achievements of machine learning would not have been possible without Sendhil Mullainathan, Jon Kleinberg, Jens Ludwig, Gregory Stoddard, and Hye Chang. And our discussion of the consistency of judgment owes a lot to Alex Todorov and his Princeton colleagues Joel Martinez, Brandon Labbree, and Stefan Uddenberg, as well as Scott Highhouse and Alison Broadfoot. These amazing teams of researchers not only graciously shared their insights but were kind enough to run special analyses for us. Of course, any misunderstandings or errors are our responsibility. In addition, we thank Laszlo Bock, Bo Cowgill, Jason Dana, Dan Goldstein, Harold Goldstein, Brian Hoffman, Alan Krueger, Michael Mauboussin, Emily Putnam-Horstein, Charles Scherbaum, Anne-Laure Sellier, and Yuichi Shoda for sharing their expertise.

We are also thankful to a veritable army of researchers over the years, including Shreya Bhardwaj, Josie Fisher, Rohit Goyal, Nicole Grabel, Andrew Heinrich, Meghann Johnson, Sophie Mehta, Eli Nachmany, William Ryan, Evelyn Shu, Matt Summers, and Noam Ziv-Crispel. Many of the discussions here involve substantive areas in which we lack expertise, and because of their excellent work, the book has less bias, and less noise, than it otherwise would have.

Finally, collaborating as a three-author, two-continent team is challenging at the best of times, and the year 2020 was not the best of times. We would not have finished this book without the technological magic of Dropbox and Zoom. We are thankful to the people behind these great products.

Notes

Introduction

4. *The targets illustrate:* Using bows and arrows rather than guns, Swiss mathematician Daniel Bernoulli offered the same analogy in 1778 in an essay on problems of estimation. Bernoulli, "The Most Probable Choice Between Several Discrepant Observations and the Formation Therefrom of the Most Likely Induction," *Biometrika* 48, no. 1–2 (June 1961): 3–18, https://doi.org/10.1093/biomet/48.1-2.3.

6. *Child custody decisions:* Joseph J. Doyle Jr., "Child Protection and Child Outcomes: Measuring the Effects of Foster Care," *American Economic Review* 95, no. 5 (December 2007): 1583–1610.

6. *the same software developers:* Stein Grimstad and Magne Jørgensen, "Inconsistency of Expert Judgment-Based Estimates of Software Development Effort," *Journal of Systems and Software* 80, no. 11 (2007): 1770–1777.

6. *Asylum decisions:* Andrew I. Schoenholtz, Jaya Ramji-Nogales, and Philip G. Schrag, "Refugee Roulette: Disparities in Asylum Adjudication," *Stanford Law Review* 60, no. 2 (2007).

7. *Decisions to grant patents:* Mark A. Lemley and Bhaven Sampat, "Examiner Characteristics and Patent Office Outcomes," *Review of Economics*

and Statistics 94, no. 3 (2012): 817–827. See also Iain Cockburn, Samuel Kortum, and Scott Stern, "Are All Patent Examiners Equal? The Impact of Examiner Characteristics," working paper 8980, June 2002, www.nber .org/papers/w8980; and Michael D. Frakes and Melissa F. Wasserman, "Is the Time Allocated to Review Patent Applications Inducing Examiners to Grant Invalid Patents? Evidence from Microlevel Application Data," *Review of Economics and Statistics* 99, no. 3 (July 2017): 550–563.

CHAPTER 1

14. *described his motivation:* Marvin Frankel, *Criminal Sentences: Law Without Order,* 25 Inst. for Sci. Info. Current Contents / Soc. & Behavioral Scis.: This Week's Citation Classic 14, 2A-6 (June 23, 1986), available at http://www.garfield.library.upenn.edu/classics1986/A1986C697400001 .pdf.

14. *"almost wholly unchecked":* Marvin Frankel, *Criminal Sentences: Law Without Order* (New York: Hill and Wang, 1973), 5.

14. *"arbitrary cruelties perpetrated daily":* Frankel, *Criminal Sentences,* 103.

15. *"government of laws, not of men":* Frankel, 5.

15. *"idiosyncratic ukases":* Frankel, 11.

15. *"some form of numerical or other objective grading":* Frankel, 114.

15. *"computers as an aid":* Frankel, 115.

15. *a commission on sentencing:* Frankel, 119.

15. *"absence of consensus was the norm":* Anthony Partridge and William B. Eldridge, *The Second Circuit Sentence Study: A Report to the Judges of the Second Circuit August 1974* (Washington, DC: Federal Judicial Center, August 1974), 9.

16. *"astounding":* US Senate, "Comprehensive Crime Control Act of 1983: Report of the Committee on the Judiciary, United States Senate, on S. 1762, Together with Additional and Minority Views" (Washington, DC: US Government Printing Office, 1983). Report No. 98-225.

16. *A heroin dealer:* Anthony Partridge and Eldridge, *Second Circuit Sentence Study,* A-11.

16. *a bank robber:* Partridge and Eldridge, *Second Circuit Sentence Study,* A-9.

16. *an extortion case:* Partridge and Eldridge, A-5–A-7

16. *a survey of forty-seven judges:* William Austin and Thomas A. Williams III, "A Survey of Judges' Responses to Simulated Legal Cases: Research Note on Sentencing Disparity," *Journal of Criminal Law & Criminology* 68 (1977): 306.

16. *A much larger study:* John Bartolomeo et al., "Sentence Decisionmaking: The Logic of Sentence Decisions and the Extent and Sources of Sentence Disparity," *Journal of Criminal Law and Criminology* 72, no. 2 (1981). (See chapter 6 for a full discussion.) See also Senate Report, 44.

17. *If judges are hungry:* Shai Danziger, Jonathan Levav, and Liora Avnaim-Pesso, "Extraneous Factors in Judicial Decisions," *Proceedings of the National Academy of Sciences of the United States of America* 108, no. 17 (2011): 6889-92.

17. *juvenile court decisions:* Ozkan Eren and Naci Mocan, "Emotional Judges and Unlucky Juveniles," *American Economic Journal: Applied Economics* 10, no. 3 (2018): 171–205.

17. *more severe on days that follow a loss:* Daniel L. Chen and Markus Loecher, "Mood and the Malleability of Moral Reasoning: The Impact of Irrelevant Factors on Judicial Decisions," *SSRN Electronic Journal* (September 21, 2019): 1–70, http://users.nber.org/dlchen/papers/Mood_and_the_Malleability_of_Moral_Reasoning.pdf.

17. *more leniency on their birthday:* Daniel L. Chen and Arnaud Philippe, "Clash of Norms: Judicial Leniency on Defendant Birthdays," (2020) available at SSRN: https://ssrn.com/abstract=3203624.

17. *something as irrelevant as outside temperature:* Anthony Heyes and Soodeh Saberian, "Temperature and Decisions: Evidence from 207,000 Court Cases," *American Economic Journal: Applied Economics* 11, no. 2 (2018): 238–265.

18. *"the unfettered discretion":* Senate Report, 38.

18. *"unjustifiably wide" sentencing disparity:* Senate Report, 38.

18. *the use of past practice:* Justice Breyer is quoted in Jeffrey Rosen, "Breyer Restraint," *New Republic*, July 11, 1994, at 19, 25.

19. *departures must be justified:* United States Sentencing Commission, Guidelines Manual (2018), www.ussc.gov/sites/default/files/pdf/guidelines-manual/2018/GLMFull.pdf.

19. *"reduced the net variation"*: James M. Anderson, Jeffrey R. Kling, and Kate Stith, "Measuring Interjudge Sentencing Disparity: Before and After the Federal Sentencing Guidelines," *Journal of Law and Economics* 42, no. S1 (April 1999): 271–308.

19. *the commission itself*: US Sentencing Commission, *The Federal Sentencing Guidelines: A Report on the Operation of the Guidelines System and Short-Term Impacts on Disparity in Sentencing, Use of Incarceration, and Prosecutorial Discretion and Plea Bargaining*, vols. 1 & 2 (Washington, DC: US Sentencing Commission, 1991).

19. *According to another study:* Anderson, Kling, and Stith, "Interjudge Sentencing Disparity."

19. *An independent study:* Paul J. Hofer, Kevin R. Blackwell, and R. Barry Ruback, "The Effect of the Federal Sentencing Guidelines on Inter-Judge Sentencing Disparity," *Journal of Criminal Law and Criminology* 90 (1999): 239, 241.

20. *"the need is not for blindness…":* Kate Stith and José Cabranes, *Fear of Judging: Sentencing Guidelines in the Federal Courts* (Chicago: University of Chicago Press, 1998), 79.

20. *the Supreme Court struck the guidelines down:* 543 U.S. 220 (2005).

20. *Seventy-five percent preferred the advisory regime:* US Sentencing Commission, "Results of Survey of United States District Judges, January 2010 through March 2010" (June 2010) (question 19, table 19), www.ussc.gov /sites/default/files/pdf/research-and-publications/research-projects-and -surveys/surveys/20100608_Judge_Survey.pdf.

20. *"findings raise…":* Crystal Yang, "Have Interjudge Sentencing Disparities Increased in an Advisory Guidelines Regime? Evidence from Booker," *New York University Law Review* 89 (2014): 1268–1342; pp. 1278, 1334.

CHAPTER 2

26. *To prepare for the noise audit:* Executives of the company constructed detailed descriptions of representative cases, similar to the risks and claims that employees dealt with every day. Six cases were prepared for claims adjusters in the Property and Casualty Division, and four for underwriters specializing in financial risk. The employees were given half a day off

from their regular workload to evaluate two or three cases each. They were instructed to work independently and were not told that the purpose of the study was to examine the variability of their judgments. Altogether, we obtained eight-six judgments from forty-eight underwriters and one hundred thirteen judgments from sixty-eight claims adjusters.

31. *naive realism:* Dale W. Griffin and Lee Ross, "Subjective Construal, Social Inference, and Human Misunderstanding," *Advances in Experimental Social Psychology* 24 (1991): 319–359; Robert J. Robinson, Dacher Keltner, Andrew Ward, and Lee Ross, "Actual Versus Assumed Differences in Construal: 'Naive Realism' in Intergroup Perception and Conflict," *Journal of Personality and Social Psychology* 68, no. 3 (1995): 404; and Lee Ross and Andrew Ward, "Naive Realism in Everyday Life: Implications for Social Conflict and Misunderstanding," *Values and Knowledge* (1997).

PART 2

41. *the most common measure of variability:* The standard deviation of a set of numbers is derived from another statistical quantity, called the *variance.* To compute the variance, we first obtain the distribution of deviations from the mean and then take the square of each of these deviations. Variance is the mean of these squared deviations, and the standard deviation is the square root of the variance.

CHAPTER 4

44. *Judges at wine competitions:* R. T. Hodgson, "An Examination of Judge Reliability at a Major U.S. Wine Competition," *Journal of Wine Economics* 3, no. 2 (2008): 105–113.

52. *trade-offs are resolved by evaluative judgments:* Some students of decision making define decisions as choices between options and view quantitative judgments as a special case of decision, in which there is a continuum of possible choices. In that view, judgments are a special case of decision. Our approach here is different: we view decisions that call for a choice between options as stemming from an underlying evaluative judgment about each option. That is, we regard decisions as a special case of judgment.

CHAPTER 5

59. *invented in 1795:* The method of least squares was first published by Adrien-Marie Legendre in 1805. Gauss claimed that he had first used it ten years earlier, and he later linked it to the development of a theory of error and to the normal error curve that bears his name. The priority dispute has been much discussed, and historians are inclined to believe Gauss's claim (Stephen M. Stigler, "Gauss and the Invention of Least Squares," *Annals of Statistics* 9 [1981]: 465–474; and Stephen M. Stigler, *The History of Statistics: The Measurement of Uncertainty Before 1900* [Cambridge, MA: Belknap Press of Harvard University Press, 1986]).

62. *Using some simple algebra:* We have defined *noise* as the standard deviation of errors; therefore noise squared is the variance of errors. The definition of *variance* is "the mean of the squares minus the square of the mean." Since the mean error is bias, "the square of the mean" is bias squared. Therefore: $\text{Noise}^2 = \text{MSE} - \text{Bias}^2$.

65. *intuitions in this regard:* Berkeley J. Dietvorst and Soaham Bharti, "People Reject Algorithms in Uncertain Decision Domains Because They Have Diminishing Sensitivity to Forecasting Error," *Psychological Science* 31, no. 10 (2020): 1302–1314.

CHAPTER 6

69. *an exceptionally detailed study:* Kevin Clancy, John Bartolomeo, David Richardson, and Charles Wellford, "Sentence Decisionmaking: The Logic of Sentence Decisions and the Extent and Sources of Sentence Disparity," *Journal of Criminal Law and Criminology* 72, no. 2 (1981): 524–554; and INSLAW, Inc. et al., "Federal Sentencing: Towards a More Explicit Policy of Criminal Sanctions III-4," (1981).

70. *asked to set a sentence:* the sentence could include any combination of prison time, supervised time, and fines. For simplicity, we focus here mostly on the main component of the sentences — the prison time — and leave aside the other two components.

71. *This variance is what is often...:* In a multiple-case, multiple-judge setting, the extended version of the error equation we introduced in chapter 5 includes a term that reflects this variance. Specifically, if we define a

grand bias as the average error over all cases, and if this error is not identical across cases, there will be a variance of case biases. The equation becomes: MSE = Grand Bias² + Variance of Case Biases + System Noise².

71. *The average prison term:* The numbers mentioned in this chapter are derived from the original study as follows.

First, the authors report the main effect of the *offense and offender* as accounting for 45% of the total variance (John Bartolomeo et al., "Sentence Decisionmaking: The Logic of Sentence Decisions and the Extent and Sources of Sentence Disparity," *Journal of Criminal Law and Criminology* 72, no. 2 [1981], table 6). However, we are concerned here more broadly with the effect of each case, including all the features presented to the judges—such as whether the defendant had a criminal record or whether a weapon was used in the commission of the crime. By our definition, all these features are part of *true case variance,* not noise. Accordingly, we reintegrated interactions between features of each case in the case variance (these account for 11% of total variance; see Bartolomeo et al., table 10). As a result, we redefine the shares of case variance as 56%, judge main effect (level noise) as 21%, and interactions in total variance as 23%. System noise is therefore 44% of total variance.

The variance of just sentences can be computed from Bartolomeo et al., 89, in the table listing mean sentences for each case: the variance is 15. If this is 56 % of total variance, then total variance is 26.79 and the variance of system noise is 11.79. The square root of that variance is the standard deviation for a representative case, or 3.4 years.

Judge main effect, or level noise, is 21% of total variance. The square root of that variance is the standard deviation that is attributable to judge level noise, or 2.4 years.

72. *3.4 years:* This value is the square root of the average of the variances of sentences for the sixteen cases. We calculated it as explained in the preceding note.

75. *simple, additive logic:* The additivity hypothesis effectively assumes that the harshness of a judge adds a constant amount of prison time. This hypothesis is unlikely to be correct: the harshness of the judge is more likely to add an amount that is proportional to the average sentence. This

issue was ignored in the original report, which provides no way of assessing its importance.

76. *"Patterned differences between judges":* Bartolomeo et al., "Sentence Decisionmaking," 23.

76. *approximately equally:* The following equation holds: (System Noise)^2 = (Level Noise)^2 + (Pattern Noise)^2. The table shows that system noise is 3.4 years and level noise is 2.4 years. It follows that pattern noise is also about 2.4 years. The calculation is shown as an illustration—the actual values are slightly different because of rounding errors.

CHAPTER 7

79. *The all-time best:* See http://www.iweblists.com/sports/basketball/Free ThrowPercent_c.html, consulted Dec. 27, 2020.

79. *Shaquille O'Neal:* See https://www.basketball-reference.com/players/o/one alsh01.html, consulted Dec. 27, 2020.

80. *wine experts:* R. T. Hodgson, "An Examination of Judge Reliability at a Major U.S. Wine Competition," *Journal of Wine Economics* 3, no. 2 (2008): 105–113.

80. *software consultants:* Stein Grimstad and Magne Jørgensen, "Inconsistency of Expert Judgment-Based Estimates of Software Development Effort," *Journal of Systems and Software* 80, no. 11 (2007): 1770–1777.

82. *agree with themselves:* Robert H. Ashton, "A Review and Analysis of Research on the Test–Retest Reliability of Professional Judgment," *Journal of Behavioral Decision Making* 294, no. 3 (2000): 277–294. Incidentally, the author then noted that not a single one of the forty-one studies he reviewed was designed to evaluate occasion noise: "In all cases, the measurement of reliability was a by-product of some other research objectives" (Ashton, 279). This comment suggests that the interest in studying occasion noise is relatively recent.

83. *correct answer:* Central Intelligence Agency, *The World Factbook* (Washington, DC: Central Intelligence Agency, 2020). The figure cited includes all airports or airfields recognizable from the air. The runway or runways may be paved or unpaved and may include closed or abandoned installations.

83. *Edward Vul and Harold Pashler:* Edward Vul and Harold Pashler, "Crowd Within: Probabilistic Representations Within Individuals,"

83. *closer to the truth:* James Surowiecki, *The Wisdom of Crowds: Why the Many Are Smarter Than the Few and How Collective Wisdom Shapes Business, Economies, Societies, and Nations* (New York: Doubleday, 2004).

84. *less noisy:* The standard deviation of the averaged judgments (our measure of noise) decreases in proportion to the square root of the number of judgments.

84. *"You can gain":* Vul and Pashler, "Crowd Within," 646.

84. *Stefan Herzog and Ralph Hertwig:* Stefan M. Herzog and Ralph Hertwig, "Think Twice and Then: Combining or Choosing in Dialectical Bootstrapping?," *Journal of Experimental Psychology: Learning, Memory, and Cognition* 40, no. 1 (2014): 218–232.

85. *"Responses made":* Vul and Pashler, "Measuring the Crowd Within," 647.

86. *Joseph Forgas:* Joseph P. Forgas, "Affective Influences on Interpersonal Behavior," *Psychological Inquiry* 13, no. 1 (2002): 1–28.

86. *"The same smile…":* Forgas, "Affective Influences," 10.

87. *negotiators who shift:* A. Filipowicz, S. Barsade, and S. Melwani, "Understanding Emotional Transitions: The Interpersonal Consequences of Changing Emotions in Negotiations," *Journal of Personality and Social Psychology* 101, no. 3 (2011): 541–556.

87. *participants read a short philosophical essay:* Joseph P. Forgas, "She Just Doesn't Look like a Philosopher…? Affective Influences on the Halo Effect in Impression Formation," *European Journal of Social Psychology* 41, no. 7 (2011): 812–817.

87. *pseudo-profound statements:* Gordon Pennycook, James Allan Cheyne, Nathaniel Barr, Derek J. Koehler, and Jonathan A. Fugelsang, "On the Reception and Detection of Pseudo-Profound Bullshit," *Judgment and Decision Making* 10, no. 6 (2015): 549–563.

87–88. On Bullshit: Harry Frankfurt, *On Bullshit* (Princeton, NJ: Princeton University Press, 2005).

88. *"seemingly impressive assertions":* Pennycook et al., "Pseudo-Profound Bullshit," 549.

88. *more gullible:* Joseph P. Forgas, "Happy Believers and Sad Skeptics?

Affective Influences on Gullibility," *Current Directions in Psychological Science* 28, no. 3 (2019): 306–313.

88. *eyewitnesses:* Joseph P. Forgas, "Mood Effects on Eyewitness Memory: Affective Influences on Susceptibility to Misinformation," *Journal of Experimental Social Psychology* 41, no. 6 (2005): 574–588.

88. *footbridge problem:* Piercarlo Valdesolo and David Desteno, "Manipulations of Emotional Context Shape Moral Judgment," *Psychological Science* 17, no. 6 (2006): 476–477.

89. *opioids at the end of a long day:* Hannah T. Neprash and Michael L. Barnett, "Association of Primary Care Clinic Appointment Time with Opioid Prescribing," *JAMA Network Open* 2, no. 8 (2019); Lindsey M. Philpot, Bushra A. Khokhar, Daniel L. Roellinger, Priya Ramar, and Jon O. Ebbert, "Time of Day Is Associated with Opioid Prescribing for Low Back Pain in Primary Care," *Journal of General Internal Medicine* 33 (2018): 1828.

89. *antibiotics:* Jeffrey A. Linder, Jason N. Doctor, Mark W. Friedberg, Harry Reyes Nieva, Caroline Birks, Daniella Meeker, and Craig R. Fox, "Time of Day and the Decision to Prescribe Antibiotics," *JAMA Internal Medicine* 174, no. 12 (2014): 2029–2031.

89. *flu shots:* Rebecca H. Kim, Susan C. Day, Dylan S. Small, Christopher K. Snider, Charles A. L. Rareshide, and Mitesh S. Patel, "Variations in Influenza Vaccination by Clinic Appointment Time and an Active Choice Intervention in the Electronic Health Record to Increase Influenza Vaccination," *JAMA Network Open* 1, no. 5 (2018): 1–10.

90. *Bad weather:* For comment on improved memory, see Joseph P. Forgas, Liz Goldenberg, and Christian Unkelbach, "Can Bad Weather Improve Your Memory? An Unobtrusive Field Study of Natural Mood Effects on Real-Life Memory," *Journal of Experimental Social Psychology* 45, no. 1 (2008): 254–257. For comment on sunshine, see David Hirshleifer and Tyler Shumway, "Good Day Sunshine: Stock Returns and the Weather," *Journal of Finance* 58, no. 3 (2003): 1009–1032.

90. *"Clouds Make Nerds Look Good":* Uri Simonsohn, "Clouds Make Nerds Look Good: Field Evidence of the Impact of Incidental Factors on Decision Making," *Journal of Behavioral Decision Making* 20, no. 2 (2007): 143–152.

90. gambler's fallacy: Daniel Chen et al., "Decision Making Under the Gambler's Fallacy: Evidence from Asylum Judges, Loan Officers, and Baseball Umpires," *Quarterly Journal of Economics* 131, no. 3 (2016): 1181–1242.

91. *grant asylum:* Jaya Ramji-Nogales, Andrew I. Schoenholtz, and Philip Schrag, "Refugee Roulette: Disparities in Asylum Adjudication," *Stanford Law Review* 60, no. 2 (2007).

91. *memory performance:* Michael J. Kahana et al., "The Variability Puzzle in Human Memory," *Journal of Experimental Psychology: Learning, Memory, and Cognition* 44, no. 12 (2018): 1857–1863.

Chapter 8

95. *study of music downloads:* Matthew J. Salganik, Peter Sheridan Dodds, and Duncan J. Watts, "Experimental Study of Inequality and Unpredictability in an Artificial Cultural Market," *Science* 311 (2006): 854–856. See also Matthew Salganik and Duncan Watts, "Leading the Herd Astray: An Experimental Study of Self-Fulfilling Prophecies in an Artificial Cultural Market," *Social Psychology Quarterly* 71 (2008): 338–355; and Matthew Salganik and Duncan Watts, "Web-Based Experiments for the Study of Collective Social Dynamics in Cultural Markets," *Topics in Cognitive Science* 1 (2009): 439–468.

96. *popularity is self-reinforcing:* Salganik and Watts, "Leading the Herd Astray."

97. *in many other areas:* Michael Macy et al., "Opinion Cascades and the Unpredictability of Partisan Polarization," *Science Advances* (2019): 1–8. See also Helen Margetts et al., *Political Turbulence* (Princeton: Princeton University Press, 2015).

97. *sociologist Michael Macy:* Michael Macy et al., "Opinion Cascades."

98. *comments on websites:* Lev Muchnik et al., "Social Influence Bias: A Randomized Experiment," *Science* 341, no. 6146 (2013): 647–651.

99. *Research has revealed:* Jan Lorenz et al., "How Social Influence Can Undermine the Wisdom of Crowd Effect," *Proceedings of the National Academy of Sciences* 108, no. 22 (2011): 9020–9025.

104. *an experiment that compares:* Daniel Kahneman, David Schkade, and

Cass Sunstein, "Shared Outrage and Erratic Awards: The Psychology of Punitive Damages," *Journal of Risk and Uncertainty* 16 (1998): 49–86.

104. *five hundred mock juries:* David Schkade, Cass R. Sunstein, and Daniel Kahneman, "Deliberating about Dollars: The Severity Shift," *Columbia Law Review* 100 (2000): 1139–1175.

Part 3

108. *percent concordant:* percent concordant (PC) is closely related to Kendall's *W,* also known as the coefficient of concordance.

108. *height and foot size:* Kanwal Kamboj et al., "A Study on the Correlation Between Foot Length and Height of an Individual and to Derive Regression Formulae to Estimate the Height from Foot Length of an Individual," *International Journal of Research in Medical Sciences* 6, no. 2 (2018): 528.

108. *Table 1 presents the PC:* PC is calculated on the assumption that the joint distribution is bivariate-normal. The values shown in the table are approximations based on that assumption. We thank Julian Parris for producing this table.

Chapter 9

112. *actual study of performance prediction:* Martin C. Yu and Nathan R. Kuncel, "Pushing the Limits for Judgmental Consistency: Comparing Random Weighting Schemes with Expert Judgments," *Personnel Assessment and Decisions* 6, no. 2 (2020): 1–10. The .15 correlation achieved by experts is the unweighted average of the three samples studied, including 847 cases in total. The real study differs from this simplified description in several respects.

113. *a weighted average:* A prerequisite for constructing a weighted average is that all predictors must be measured in comparable units. This requirement was satisfied in our introductory example, where all ratings were made on a 0-to-10 scale, but this is not always the case. For example, the predictors of performance might be an interviewer's assessment on a 0-to-10 scale, the number of years of relevant experience, and a score on a test of proficiency. The multiple regression program transforms all

predictors into *standard scores* before combining them. A standard score measures the distance of an observation from the mean of a population, with the standard deviation as a unit. For example, if the mean of the proficiency test is 55 and the standard deviation is 8, a standard score of +1.5 corresponds to a test result of 67. Notably, standardization of each individual's data eliminates any trace of error in the mean or in the variance of individuals' judgments.

113. *gets a large weight:* An important feature of multiple regression is that the optimal weight for each predictor depends on the other predictors. If a predictor is highly correlated with another one, it should not get an equally large weight—this would be a form of "double counting."

113. *"the workhorse…":* Robin M. Hogarth and Natalia Karelaia, "Heuristic and Linear Models of Judgment: Matching Rules and Environments," *Psychological Review* 114, no. 3 (2007): 734.

113. *a simple structure:* A research framework that has been extensively used in this context is the *lens model of judgment,* on which this discussion is based. See Kenneth R. Hammond, "Probabilistic Functioning and the Clinical Method," *Psychological Review* 62, no. 4 (1955): 255–262; Natalia Karelaia and Robin M. Hogarth, "Determinants of Linear Judgment: A Meta-Analysis of Lens Model Studies," *Psychological Bulletin* 134, no. 3 (2008): 404–426.

114. Paul E. Meehl, *Clinical Versus Statistical Prediction: A Theoretical Analysis and a Review of the Evidence* (Minneapolis: University of Minnesota Press, 1954).

116. *A picture of Freud:* Paul E. Meehl, *Clinical Versus Statistical Prediction: A Theoretical Analysis and a Review of the Evidence* (Northvale, NJ: Aronson, 1996), preface.

116. *a polymath:* "Paul E. Meehl," in Ed Lindzey (ed.), *A History of Psychology in Autobiography,* 1989.

116. *"massive and consistent":* "Paul E. Meehl," in *A History of Psychology in Autobiography,* ed. Ed Lindzey (Washington, DC: American Psychological Association, 1989), 362.

116. *A 2000 review:* William M. Grove et al., "Clinical Versus Mechanical Prediction: A Meta-Analysis," *Psychological Assessment* 12, no. 1 (2000): 19–30.

116. *access to "private" information:* William M. Grove and Paul E. Meehl, "Comparative Efficiency of Informal (Subjective, Impressionistic) and Formal (Mechanical, Algorithmic) Prediction Procedures: The Clinical-Statistical Controversy," *Psychology, Public Policy, and Law* 2, no. 2 (1996): 293–323.

117. *In the late 1960s:* Lewis Goldberg, "Man Versus Model of Man: A Rationale, plus Some Evidence, for a Method of Improving on Clinical Inferences," *Psychological Bulletin* 73, no. 6 (1970): 422–432.

118. *nothing of the kind:* Milton Friedman and Leonard J. Savage, "The Utility Analysis of Choices Involving Risk," *Journal of Political Economy* 56, no. 4 (1948): 279–304.

118. *this correlation:* Karelaia and Hogarth, "Determinants of Linear Judgment," 411, table 1.

118. *An early replication:* Nancy Wiggins and Eileen S. Kohen, "Man Versus Model of Man Revisited: The Forecasting of Graduate School Success," *Journal of Personality and Social Psychology* 19, no. 1 (1971): 100–106.

118. *a review of fifty years:* Karelaia and Hogarth, "Determinants of Linear Judgment."

120. *improvement of your predictive accuracy:* The correction of a correlation coefficient for the imperfect reliability of the predictor is known as *correction for attenuation.* The formula is Corrected $r_{xy} = r_{xy}/\sqrt{r_{xx}}$, where r_{xx} is the reliability coefficient (the proportion of true variance in the observed variance of the predictor).

121. *A study by Martin Yu and Nathan Kuncel:* Yu and Kuncel, "Judgmental Consistency."

121. *random formulas:* We discuss equal-weight and random-weight models in greater detail in the next chapter. The weights are constrained to a range of small numbers, and they are constrained to have the right sign.

CHAPTER 10

124. *far superior to clinical judgments:* Robyn M. Dawes and Bernard Corrigan, "Linear Models in Decision Making," *Psychological Bulletin* 81, no. 2 (1974): 95–106. Dawes and Corrigan also proposed using random weights. The study of managerial performance prediction, described in chapter 9, is an application of this idea.

124. *"contrary to statistical intuition"*: Jason Dana, "What Makes Improper Linear Models Tick?," in *Rationality and Social Responsibility: Essays in Honor of Robyn M. Dawes,* ed. Joachim I. Krueger, 71–89 (New York: Psychology Press, 2008), 73.

126. *Similar results:* Jason Dana and Robyn M. Dawes, "The Superiority of Simple Alternatives to Regression for Social Sciences Prediction," *Journal of Educational and Behavior Statistics* 29 (2004): 317–331; Dana, "What Makes Improper Linear Models Tick?"

126. *"It Don't Make"*: Howard Wainer, "Estimating Coefficients in Linear Models: It Don't Make No Nevermind," *Psychological Bulletin* 83, no. 2 (1976): 213–217.

126. *"we do not need"*: Dana, "What Makes Improper Linear Models Tick?," 72.

126. *correlation with the outcome:* Martin C. Yu and Nathan R. Kuncel, "Pushing the Limits for Judgmental Consistency: Comparing Random Weighting Schemes with Expert Judgments," *Personnel Assessment and Decisions* 6, no. 2 (2020): 1–10. As in the previous chapter, the reported correlation is the unweighted average of the three samples studied. The comparison holds in each of the three samples: the validity of clinical expert judgment was .17, .16, and .13, and the validity of equal-weight models was .19, .33, and .22, respectively.

126. *"robust beauty"*: Robyn M. Dawes, "The Robust Beauty of Improper Linear Models in Decision Making," *American Psychologist* 34, no. 7 (1979): 571–582.

127. *"The whole trick"*: Dawes and Corrigan, "Linear Models in Decision Making," 105.

127. *A team of researchers:* Jongbin Jung, Conner Concannon, Ravi Shroff, Sharad Goel, and Daniel G. Goldstein, "Simple Rules to Guide Expert Classifications," *Journal of the Royal Statistical Society, Statistics in Society,* no. 183 (2020): 771–800.

128. *a separate team:* Julia Dressel and Hany Farid, "The Accuracy, Fairness, and Limits of Predicting Recidivism," *Science Advances* 4, no. 1 (2018): 1–6.

128. *only two inputs:* these two examples are linear models based on an

extremely small set of variables (and, in the case of the bail model, on an approximation of the linear weights obtained by a rounding method that transforms the model into a back-of-the-envelope calculation). Another type of "improper model" is a *single-variable rule,* which considers only one predictor and ignores all others. *See* Peter M. Todd and Gerd Gigerenzer, "Précis of Simple Heuristics That Make Us Smart," *Behavioral and Brain Sciences* 23, no. 5 (2000): 727–741.

128. *well documented:* P. Gendreau, T. Little, and C. Goggin, "A Meta-Analysis of the Predictors of Adult Offender Recidivism: What Works!," *Criminology* 34 (1996).

129. *Very large data sets*: Size in this context should be understood as the ratio of the number of observations to predictors. Dawes, "Robust Beauty," suggested that it must be as high as 15 or 20 to 1 before the optimal weights do better on cross-validation than do unit weights. Dana and Dawes, "Superiority of Simple Alternatives," using many more case studies, raised the bar to a ratio of 100 to 1.

130. *another team:* J. Kleinberg, H. Lakkaraju, J. Leskovec, J. Ludwig, and S. Mullainathan, "Human Decisions and Machine Predictions," *Quarterly Journal of Economics* 133 (2018): 237–293.

130. *trained a machine-learning algorithm:* The algorithm was trained on a subset of training data and then evaluated on its ability to predict outcomes on a different, randomly chosen subset.

131. *"The machine-learning algorithm finds"*: Kleinberg et al., "Human Decisions," 16.

131. *System noise included:* Gregory Stoddard, Jens Ludwig, and Sendhil Mullainathan, e-mail exchanges with the authors, June–July 2020.

132. *the recruitment of software engineers:* B. Cowgill, "Bias and Productivity in Humans and Algorithms: Theory and Evidence from Résumé Screening," paper presented at Smith Entrepreneurship Research Conference, College Park, MD, April 21, 2018.

134. *a 1996 article:* William M. Grove and Paul E. Meehl, "Comparative Efficiency of Informal (Subjective, Impressionistic) and Formal (Mechanical, Algorithmic) Prediction Procedures: The Clinical-Statistical Controversy," *Psychology, Public Policy, and Law* 2, no. 2 (1996): 293–323.

135. *prefer the algorithm:* Jennifer M. Logg, Julia A. Minson, and Don A. Moore, "Algorithm Appreciation: People Prefer Algorithmic to Human Judgment," *Organizational Behavior and Human Decision Processes* 151 (April 2018): 90–103.

135. *as soon as they see that it makes mistakes:* B. J. Dietvorst, J. P. Simmons, and C. Massey, "Algorithm Aversion: People Erroneously Avoid Algorithms After Seeing Them Err," *Journal of Experimental Psychology General* 144 (2015): 114–126. See also A. Prahl and L. Van Swol, "Understanding Algorithm Aversion: When Is Advice from Automation Discounted?," *Journal of Forecasting* 36 (2017): 691–702.

135. *If this expectation is violated:* M. T. Dzindolet, L. G. Pierce, H. P. Beck, and L. A. Dawe, "The Perceived Utility of Human and Automated Aids in a Visual Detection Task," *Human Factors: The Journal of the Human Factors and Ergonomics Society* 44, no. 1 (2002): 79–94; K. A. Hoff and M. Bashir, "Trust in Automation: Integrating Empirical Evidence on Factors That Influence Trust," *Human Factors: The Journal of the Human Factors and Ergonomics Society* 57, no. 3 (2015): 407–434; and P. Madhavan and D. A. Wiegmann, "Similarities and Differences Between Human–Human and Human–Automation Trust: An Integrative Review," *Theoretical Issues in Ergonomics Science* 8, no. 4 (2007): 277–301.

CHAPTER 11

137. *Research in managerial decision making:* E. Dane and M. G. Pratt, "Exploring Intuition and Its Role in Managerial Decision Making," *Academy of Management Review* 32, no. 1 (2007): 33–54; Cinla Akinci and Eugene Sadler-Smith, "Intuition in Management Research: A Historical Review," *International Journal of Management Reviews* 14 (2012): 104–122; and Gerard P. Hodgkinson et al., "Intuition in Organizations: Implications for Strategic Management," *Long Range Planning* 42 (2009): 277–297.

137. *One review:* Hodgkinson et al., "Intuition in Organizations," 279.

139. *a recent review:* Nathan Kuncel et al., "Mechanical Versus Clinical Data Combination in Selection and Admissions Decisions: A Meta-Analysis," *Journal of Applied Psychology* 98, no. 6 (2013): 1060–1072. See also chapter 24 for further discussion of personnel decisions.

140. *Overconfidence:* Don A. Moore, *Perfectly Confident: How to Calibrate Your Decisions Wisely* (New York: HarperCollins, 2020).

141. *"commenting or offering advice":* Philip E. Tetlock, *Expert Political Judgment: How Good Is It? How Can We Know?* (Princeton, NJ: Princeton University Press, 2005), 239 and 233.

143. *a review of 136 studies:* William M. Grove et al., "Clinical Versus Mechanical Prediction: A Meta-Analysis," *Psychological Assessment* 12, no. 1 (2000): 19–30.

143. *heart attacks:* Sendhil Mullainathan and Ziad Obermeyer, "Who Is Tested for Heart Attack and Who Should Be: Predicting Patient Risk and Physician Error," 2019. NBER Working Paper 26168, National Bureau of Economic Research.

145. *in situations that they perceive as highly uncertain:* Weston Agor, "The Logic of Intuition: How Top Executives Make Important Decisions," *Organizational Dynamics* 14, no. 3 (1986): 5–18; Lisa A. Burke and Monica K. Miller, "Taking the Mystery Out of Intuitive Decision Making," *Academy of Management Perspectives* 13, no. 4 (1999): 91–99.

146. *prepared to trust an algorithm:* Poornima Madhavan and Douglas A. Wiegmann, "Effects of Information Source, Pedigree, and Reliability on Operator Interaction with Decision Support Systems," *Human Factors: The Journal of the Human Factors and Ergonomics Society* 49, no. 5 (2007).

CHAPTER 12

148. *an unusual article:* Matthew J. Salganik et al., "Measuring the Predictability of Life Outcomes with a Scientific Mass Collaboration," *Proceedings of the National Academy of Sciences* 117, no. 15 (2020): 8398–8403.

150. *total sample:* this included 4,242 families, as some of the families in the Fragile Families study were excluded from this analysis for privacy reasons.

150. *correlation of .22:* To score accuracy, the competition's organizers used the same metric we introduced in part 1: mean squared error, or MSE. For ease of comparability, they also benchmarked the MSE of each model against a "useless" prediction strategy: a one-size-fits-all prediction that each individual case is not different from the mean of the training set. For convenience,

we have converted their results to correlation coefficients. MSE and correlation are related by the expression r^2 = (Var (Y) – MSE) / Var (Y), where Var (Y) is the variance of the outcome variable and (Var (Y) – MSE) is the variance of the predicted outcomes.

151. *An extensive review of research in social psychology:* F. D. Richard et al., "One Hundred Years of Social Psychology Quantitatively Described," *Review of General Psychology* 7, no. 4 (2003): 331–363.

151. *A review of 708 studies:* Gilles E. Gignac and Eva T. Szodorai, "Effect Size Guidelines for Individual Differences Researchers," *Personality and Individual Differences* 102 (2016): 74–78.

152. *"Researchers must reconcile":* One caveat is in order. By design, this study uses an existing descriptive data set, which is very large, but not specifically tailored to predict specific outcomes. This is an important difference with the experts in Tetlock's study, who were free to use any information they saw fit. It may be possible, for instance, to identify predictors of eviction that are not in the database but that could conceivably be collected. Hence, the study does not prove how *intrinsically* unpredictable evictions and other outcomes are but how unpredictable they are *based on this data set,* which is used by numerous social scientists.

152. *a causal chain:* Jake M. Hofman et al., "Prediction and Explanation in Social Systems," *Science* 355 (2017): 486–488; Duncan J. Watts et al., "Explanation, Prediction, and Causality: Three Sides of the Same Coin?," October 2018, 1–14, available through Center for Open Science, https://osf.io/bgwjc.

154. *comes more naturally to our minds:* A closely related distinction contrasts *extensional* from *non-extensional,* or *intentional,* thinking. Amos Tversky and Daniel Kahneman, "Extensional Versus Intuitive Reasoning: The Conjunction Fallacy in Probability Judgment," *Psychological Review* 4 (1983): 293–315.

155. *backward-looking:* Daniel Kahneman and Dale T. Miller, "Norm Theory: Comparing Reality to Its Alternatives," *Psychological Review* 93, no. 2 (1986): 136–153.

156. *classic research on hindsight:* Baruch Fischhoff, "An Early History of Hindsight Research," *Social Cognition* 25, no. 1 (2007): 10–13, doi:10.1521

/soco.2007.25.1.10; Baruch Fischhoff, "Hindsight Is Not Equal to Fore-sight: The Effect of Outcome Knowledge on Judgment Under Uncertainty," *Journal of Experimental Psychology: Human Perception and Performance* 1, no. 3 (1975): 288.

157. *System 2:* Daniel Kahneman, *Thinking, Fast and Slow.* New York: Farrar, Straus and Giroux, 2011.

CHAPTER 13

161. *The first four decades:* Daniel Kahneman, *Thinking, Fast and Slow* (New York: Farrar, Straus and Giroux, 2011).

163. *the evidence suggests:* A caveat is in order. Psychologists who study judgment biases are not content with five participants in each group, as shown in figure 10, for a very good reason: because judgments are noisy, the results for each experimental group will rarely cluster as closely as figure 11 suggests. People vary in their susceptibility to each bias and do not *completely* neglect relevant variables. For example, with a very large number of participants, you could almost certainly confirm that scope insensitivity is imperfect: the average probability assigned to Gambardi's leaving the position is very slightly higher for three years than it is for two. Still, the description of scope insensitivity is appropriate because the difference is a tiny fraction of what it should be.

165. *multiple experiments:* Daniel Kahneman et al., eds., *Judgment Under Uncertainty: Heuristics and Biases* (New York: Cambridge University Press, 1982), chap. 6; Daniel Kahneman and Amos Tversky, "On the Psychology of Prediction," *Psychological Review* 80, no. 4 (1973): 237–251.

167. *estimates of CEO turnover:* See, for example, Steven N. Kaplan and Bernadette A. Minton, "How Has CEO Turnover Changed?," *International Review of Finance* 12, no. 1 (2012): 57–87. See also Dirk Jenter and Katharina Lewellen, "Performance-Induced CEO Turnover," Harvard Law School Forum on Corporate Governance, September 2, 2020, https://corpgov.law.harvard.edu/2020/09/02/performance-induced-ceo-turnover.

168. *At a key moment:* J. W. Rinzler, *The Making of Star Wars: Return of the Jedi: The Definitive Story* (New York: Del Rey, 2013), 64.

168. *development of the screenplay:* Cass Sunstein, *The World According to Star Wars* (New York: HarperCollins, 2016).

169. *selective and distorted:* We are highlighting here the simple case in which a prejudgment exists when the judgment begins. In fact, even in the absence of such a prejudgment, a bias toward a particular conclusion can develop as evidence accumulates, because of the tendency toward simplicity and coherence. As a tentative conclusion emerges, the confirmation bias tilts the collection and interpretation of new evidence in its favor.

170. *even when the reasoning:* This observation has been called the *belief bias.* See J. St. B. T. Evans, Julie L. Barson, and Paul Pollard, "On the Conflict between Logic and Belief in Syllogistic Reasoning," *Memory & Cognition* 11, no. 3 (1983): 295–306.

170. *In a typical demonstration:* Dan Ariely, George Loewenstein, and Drazen Prelec, "'Coherent Arbitrariness': Stable Demand Curves Without Stable Preferences," *Quarterly Journal of Economics* 118, no. 1 (2003): 73–105.

171. *in negotiations:* Adam D. Galinsky and T. Mussweiler, "First Offers as Anchors: The Role of Perspective-Taking and Negotiator Focus," *Journal of Personality and Social Psychology* 81, no. 4 (2001): 657–669.

172. *excessive coherence:* Solomon E. Asch, "Forming Impressions of Personality," *Journal of Abnormal and Social Psychology* 41, no. 3 (1946): 258–290, first used a series of adjectives in different orders to illustrate this phenomenon.

172. *in a revealing study:* Steven K. Dallas et al., "Don't Count Calorie Labeling Out: Calorie Counts on the Left Side of Menu Items Lead to Lower Calorie Food Choices," *Journal of Consumer Psychology* 29, no. 1 (2019): 60–69.

CHAPTER 14

178. *one intensity scale onto another:* S. S. Stevens, "On the Operation Known as Judgment," *American Scientist* 54, no. 4 (December 1966): 385–401. Our use of the term *matching* is more expansive than Stevens's which was restricted to ratio scales, to which we return in chapter 15.

179. *systematic judgment error:* The example was first introduced in Daniel

Kahneman, *Thinking, Fast and Slow* (New York: Farrar, Straus and Giroux, 2011).

180. *exactly the same numbers:* Daniel Kahneman and Amos Tversky, "On the Psychology of Prediction," *Psychological Review* 80 (1973): 237–251.

183. *"The Magical Number Seven":* G. A. Miller, "The Magical Number Seven, Plus or Minus Two: Some Limits on Our Capacity for Processing Information," *Psychological Review* (1956): 63–97.

185. *scales that compel comparisons:* R. D. Goffin and J. M. Olson, "Is It All Relative? Comparative Judgments and the Possible Improvement of Self-Ratings and Ratings of Others," *Perspectives on Psychological Science* 6 (2011): 48–60.

CHAPTER 15

189. *reported in 1998:* Daniel Kahneman, David Schkade, and Cass Sunstein, "Shared Outrage and Erratic Awards: The Psychology of Punitive Damages," *Journal of Risk and Uncertainty* 16 (1998): 49–86, https://link.springer.com/article/10.1023/A:1007710408413; and Cass Sunstein, Daniel Kahneman, and David Schkade, "Assessing Punitive Damages (with Notes on Cognition and Valuation in Law)," *Yale Law Journal* 107, no. 7 (May 1998): 2071–2153. The costs of the research were covered by Exxon in a one-off arrangement, but the company did not pay the researchers and had neither control of the data nor advance knowledge of the results before publication in academic journals.

189. *"reasonable doubt":* A. Keane and P. McKeown, *The Modern Law of Evidence* (New York: Oxford University Press, 2014).

189. *"unlikely to happen":* Andrew Mauboussin and Michael J. Mauboussin, "If You Say Something Is 'Likely,' How Likely Do People Think It Is?," *Harvard Business Review,* July 3, 2018.

190. *new BMW: BMW v. Gore,* 517 U.S. 559 (1996), https://supreme.justia.com/cases/federal/us/517/559.

191. *the emotion of outrage:* For discussions of the role of emotion in moral judgments, see J. Haidt, "The Emotional Dog and Its Rational Tail: A Social Intuitionist Approach to Moral Judgment," *Psychological Review* 108, no. 4 (2001): 814–834; Joshua Greene, *Moral Tribes: Emotion, Reason, and the Gap Between Us and Them* (New York: Penguin Press, 2014).

193. *Figure 13 shows the results:* Given the large amount of noise in these

ratings, you may be puzzled by the very high correlation (.98) between outrage and punitive intent judgments, which provided the support for the outrage hypothesis. The puzzle vanishes when you recall that the correlation was computed between *averages* of judgments. For an average of 100 judgments, noise (the standard deviation of judgments) is reduced by a factor of 10. Noise ceases to be a factor when many judgments are aggregated. See chapter 21.

195. ratios *of intensity:* S. S. Stevens, *Psychophysics: Introduction to Its Perceptual, Neural and Social Prospects* (New York: John Wiley & Sons, 1975).

196. *"coherent arbitrariness":* Dan Ariely, George Loewenstein, and Drazen Prelec, " 'Coherent Arbitrariness': Stable Demand Curves Without Stable Preferences," *Quarterly Journal of Economics* 118, no. 1 (2003): 73–106.

197. *Transforming the dollar awards into rankings:* A transformation into rankings entails a loss of information, as the distances between judgments are not preserved. Suppose that there are only three cases and one juror recommends damages of $10 million, $2 million, and $1 million. Clearly, the juror intends to convey a greater difference in punitive intent between the first two cases than between the second and the third. Once converted to ranks, however, the difference will be the same—a difference of one rank only. This problem could be solved by converting the judgments into standard scores.

CHAPTER 16

202. *process in perception:* R. Blake and N. K. Logothetis, "Visual competition," *Nature Reviews Neuroscience* 3 (2002) 13–21; M. A. Gernsbacher and M. E. Faust, "The Mechanism of Suppression: A Component of General Comprehension Skill," *Journal of Experimental Psychology: Learning, Memory, and Cognition* 17 (March 1991): 245–262; and M. C. Stites and K. D. Federmeier, "Subsequent to Suppression: Downstream Comprehension Consequences of Noun/Verb Ambiguity in Natural Reading," *Journal of Experimental Psychology: Learning, Memory, and Cognition* 41 (September 2015): 1497–1515.

203. *more confident than we should be:* D. A. Moore and D. Schatz, "The three faces of overconfidence," *Social and Personality Psychology Compass* 11, no. 8 (2017), article e12331.

204. *A study of corporate reputation:* S. Highhouse, A. Broadfoot, J. E. Yugo, and S. A. Devendorf, "Examining Corporate Reputation Judgments with Generalizability Theory," *Journal of Applied Psychology* 94 (2009): 782–789. We thank Scott Highhouse and Alison Broadfoot for providing their original data, and Julian Parris for some supplemental analyses.

205. *construct teams:* P. J. Lamberson and Scott Page, "Optimal forecasting groups," *Management Science* 58, no. 4 (2012): 805–10. We thank Scott Page for drawing our attention to this source of pattern noise.

207. *an early attempt to scan:* The work of Allport and Odbert (1936) on English personality-relevant vocabulary is cited in Oliver P. John and Sanjay Srivastava, "The Big-Five Trait Taxonomy: History, Measurement, and Theoretical Perspectives," in *Handbook of Personality: Theory and Research,* 2nd ed., ed. L. Pervin and Oliver P. John (New York: Guilford, 1999).

207. *considered high:* Ian W. Eisenberg, Patrick G. Bissett, A. Zeynep Enkavi et al., "Uncovering the structure of self-regulation through data-driven ontology discovery," *Nature Communications* 10 (2019): 2319.

208. *when physically threatened:* Walter Mischel, "Toward an integrative science of the person," *Annual Review of Psychology* 55 (2004): 1–22.

CHAPTER 17

211. *how MSE breaks down:* Whereas there is no general rule about the breakdown of bias and noise, the proportions in this figure are roughly representative of some of the examples, real or fictitious, that we have reviewed. Specifically, in this figure, bias and noise are equal (as they were in Good-Sell's sales forecasts). The square of level noise accounts for 37% of the square of system noise (as it did in the punitive damages study). The square of occasion noise, as shown, is about 35% of the square of pattern noise.

213. *patent offices:* See references in introduction. Mark A. Lemley and Bhaven Sampat, "Examiner Characteristics and Patent Office Outcomes," *Review of Economics and Statistics* 94, no. 3 (2012): 817–827. See also Iain Cockburn, Samuel Kortum, and Scott Stern, "Are All Patent Examiners Equal? The Impact of Examiner Characteristics," working paper 8980, June 2002, www.nber.org/papers/w8980; and Michael D. Frakes and Melissa F. Wasserman, "Is the Time Allocated to Review Patent

Applications Inducing Examiners to Grant Invalid Patents? Evidence from Microlevel Application Data," *Review of Economics and Statistics* 99, no. 3 (July 2017): 550–563.

213. *child protection services:* Joseph J. Doyle Jr., "Child Protection and Child Outcomes: Measuring the Effects of Foster Care," *American Economic Review* 95, no. 5 (December 2007): 1583–1610.

213. *asylum judges*: Andrew I. Schoenholtz, Jaya Ramji-Nogales, and Philip G. Schrag, "Refugee Roulette: Disparities in Asylum Adjudication," *Stanford Law Review* 60, no. 2 (2007).

214. *about 2.8 years:* This value is estimated from calculations presented in chapter 6, where the interaction variance is 23% of total variance. On the assumption that sentences are normally distributed, the mean absolute difference between two randomly selected observations is 1.128 SD.

214. *A group of researchers at Princeton:* J. E. Martinez, B. Labbree, S. Uddenberg, and A. Todorov, "Meaningful 'noise': Comparative judgments contain stable idiosyncratic contributions" (unpublished ms.).

215. *study of bail judges:* J. Kleinberg, H. Lakkaraju, J. Leskovec, J. Ludwig, and S. Mullainathan, "Human Decisions and Machine Predictions," *Quarterly Journal of Economics* 133 (2018): 237–293.

215. *applied the simulated judges:* The model produced for each judge both an ordering of the 141,833 cases and a threshold beyond which bail would be granted. Level noise reflects the variability of the thresholds, while pattern noise reflects variability in the ordering of cases.

216. *stable pattern noise:* Gregory Stoddard, Jens Ludwig, and Sendhil Mullainathan, e-mail exchanges with authors, June–July 2020.

219. *Phil Rosenzweig has convincingly argued:* Phil Rosenzweig. *Left Brain, Right Stuff: How Leaders Make Winning Decisions* (New York: PublicAffairs, 2014).

CHAPTER 18

225. *crowd is composed of more able people:* Albert E. Mannes et al., "The Wisdom of Select Crowds," *Journal of Personality and Social Psychology* 107, no. 2 (2014): 276–299; Jason Dana et al., "The Composition of Optimally Wise Crowds," *Decision Analysis* 12, no. 3 (2015): 130–143.

228. *confidence heuristic:* Briony D. Pulford, Andrew M. Colmna, Eike K. Buabang, and Eva M. Krockow, "The Persuasive Power of Knowledge: Testing the Confidence Heuristic," *Journal of Experimental Psychology: General* 147, no. 10 (2018): 1431–1444.

229. *it is associated not only:* Nathan R. Kuncel and Sarah A. Hezlett, "Fact and Fiction in Cognitive Ability Testing for Admissions and Hiring Decisions," *Current Directions in Psychological Science* 19, no. 6 (2010): 339–345.

229. *lingering misconceptions:* Kuncel and Hezlett, "Fact and Fiction."

229. *As one review put it:* Frank L. Schmidt and John Hunter, "General Mental Ability in the World of Work: Occupational Attainment and Job Performance," *Journal of Personality and Social Psychology* 86, no. 1 (2004): 162.

229. *conscientiousness and* grit: Angela L. Duckworth, David Weir, Eli Tsukayama, and David Kwok, "Who Does Well in Life? Conscientious Adults Excel in Both Objective and Subjective Success," *Frontiers in Psychology* 3 (September 2012). For grit, see Angela L. Duckworth, Christopher Peterson, Michael D. Matthews, and Dennis Kelly, "Grit: Perseverance and Passion for Long-Term Goals," *Journal of Personality and Social Psychology* 92, no. 6 (2007): 1087–1101.

229. *fluid intelligence:* Richard E. Nisbett et al., "Intelligence: New Findings and Theoretical Developments," *American Psychologist* 67, no. 2 (2012): 130–159.

229. *"larger than most":* Schmidt and Hunter, "Occupational Attainment," 162.

230. *in the .50 range:* Kuncel and Hezlett, "Fact and Fiction."

230. *by social-science standards:* These correlations are derived from meta-analyses that correct the observed correlations for measurement error in the criterion and range restriction. There is some debate among researchers about whether these corrections overstate the predictive value of GMA. However, since these methodological debates apply to other predictors, too, experts generally agree that GMA (along with work sample tests; see chapter 24) is the best available predictor of job success. See Kuncel and Hezlett, "Fact and Fiction."

230. *almost no people with below-average GMA:* Schmidt and Hunter, "Occupational Attainment," 162.

230. *Even among the top 1%:* David Lubinski, "Exceptional Cognitive Ability: The Phenotype," *Behavior Genetics* 39, no. 4 (2009): 350–358.

231. *a 2013 study focused on the CEOs of Fortune 500 companies:* Jonathan Wai, "Investigating America's Elite: Cognitive Ability, Education, and Sex Differences," *Intelligence* 41, no. 4 (2013): 203–211.

232. *Other questions that have been proposed:* Keela S. Thomson and Daniel M. Oppenheimer, "Investigating an Alternate Form of the Cognitive Reflection Test," *Judgment and Decision Making* 11, no. 1 (2016): 99–113.

232. *Lower CRT scores are associated:* Gordon Pennycook et al., "Everyday Consequences of Analytic Thinking," *Current Directions in Psychological Science* 24, no. 6 (2015): 425–432.

232. *fall for blatantly inaccurate "fake news":* Gordon Pennycook and David G. Rand, "Lazy, Not Biased: Susceptibility to Partisan Fake News Is Better Explained by Lack of Reasoning than by Motivated Reasoning," *Cognition* 188 (June 2018): 39–50.

232. *how much people will use their smartphones:* Nathaniel Barr et al., "The Brain in Your Pocket: Evidence That Smartphones Are Used to Supplant Thinking," *Computers in Human Behavior* 48 (2015): 473–480.

232. *the propensity to use reflective:* Niraj Patel, S. Glenn Baker, and Laura D. Scherer, "Evaluating the Cognitive Reflection Test as a Measure of Intuition/Reflection, Numeracy, and Insight Problem Solving, and the Implications for Understanding Real-World Judgments and Beliefs," *Journal of Experimental Psychology: General* 148, no. 12 (2019): 2129–2153.

232. *need-for-cognition scale:* John T. Cacioppo and Richard E. Petty, "The Need for Cognition," *Journal of Personality and Social Psychology* 42, no. 1 (1982): 116–131.

233. *less susceptible to known cognitive biases:* Stephen M. Smith and Irwin P. Levin, "Need for Cognition and Choice Framing Effects," *Journal of Behavioral Decision Making* 9, no. 4 (1996): 283–290.

233. *spoiler alert:* Judith E. Rosenbaum and Benjamin K. Johnson, "Who's Afraid of Spoilers? Need for Cognition, Need for Affect, and Narrative

Selection and Enjoyment," *Psychology of Popular Media Culture* 5, no. 3 (2016): 273–289.

233. *Adult Decision Making Competence scale:* Wandi Bruine De Bruin et al., "Individual Differences in Adult Decision-Making Competence," *Journal of Personality and Social Psychology* 92, no. 5 (2007): 938–956.

233. *Halpern Critical Thinking:* Heather A. Butler, "Halpern Critical Thinking Assessment Predicts Real-World Outcomes of Critical Thinking," *Applied Cognitive Psychology* 26, no. 5 (2012): 721–729.

234. *might predict forecasting ability:* Uriel Haran, Ilana Ritov, and Barbara Mellers, "The Role of Actively Open-Minded Thinking in Information Acquisition, Accuracy, and Calibration," *Judgment and Decision Making* 8, no. 3 (2013): 188–201.

234. *"actively open-minded thinking":* Haran, Ritov, and Mellers, "Role of Actively Open-Minded Thinking."

234. *a teachable skill:* J. Baron, "Why Teach Thinking? An Essay," *Applied Psychology: An International Review* 42 (1993): 191–214; J. Baron, *The Teaching of Thinking: Thinking and Deciding,* 2nd ed. (New York: Cambridge University Press, 1994), 127–148.

CHAPTER 19

236. *their central findings:* For an excellent review, see Jack B. Soll et al., "A User's Guide to Debiasing," in *The Wiley Blackwell Handbook of Judgment and Decision Making,* ed. Gideon Keren and George Wu, vol. 2 (New York: John Wiley & Sons, 2015), 684.

237. The Green Book: HM Treasury, *The Green Book: Central Government Guidance on Appraisal and Evaluation* (London: UK Crown, 2018), https://assets.publishing.service.gov.uk/government/uploads/system/uploads/attachment_data/file/685903/The_Green_Book.pdf.

237. nudges: Richard H. Thaler and Cass R. Sunstein, *Nudge: Improving Decisions about Health, Wealth, and Happiness* (New Haven, CT: Yale University Press, 2008).

238. boosting: Ralph Hertwig and Till Grüne-Yanoff, "Nudging and Boosting: Steering or Empowering Good Decisions," *Perspectives on Psychological Science* 12, no. 6 (2017).

238. *education is useful:* Geoffrey T. Fong et al., "The Effects of Statistical Training on Thinking About Everyday Problems," *Cognitive Psychology* 18, no. 3 (1986): 253–292.

238. *just as overconfident:* Willem A. Wagenaar and Gideon B. Keren, "Does the Expert Know? The Reliability of Predictions and Confidence Ratings of Experts," *Intelligent Decision Support in Process Environments* (1986): 87–103.

239. *reduced the number of errors:* Carey K. Morewedge et al., "Debiasing Decisions: Improved Decision Making with a Single Training Intervention," *Policy Insights from the Behavioral and Brain Sciences* 2, no. 1 (2015): 129–140.

239. *applied this learning:* Anne-Laure Sellier et al., "Debiasing Training Transfers to Improve Decision Making in the Field," *Psychological Science* 30, no. 9 (2019): 1371–1379.

240. *bias blind spot:* Emily Pronin et al., "The Bias Blind Spot: Perceptions of Bias in Self Versus Others," *Personality and Social Psychology Bulletin* 28, no. 3 (2002): 369–381.

241. *biases that may have affected:* Daniel Kahneman, Dan Lovallo, and Olivier Sibony, "Before You Make That Big Decision...," *Harvard Business Review* 89, no. 6 (June 2011): 50–60.

242. *checklists have a long history:* Atul Gawande, *Checklist Manifesto: How to Get Things Right* (New York: Metropolitan Books, 2010).

242. *a simple checklist:* Office of Information and Regulatory Affairs, "Agency Checklist: Regulatory Impact Analysis," no date, www.white house.gov/sites/whitehouse.gov/files/omb/inforeg/inforeg/regpol/RIA _Checklist.pdf.

242. *we have included:* This checklist is partly adapted from Daniel Kahneman et al., "Before You Make That Big Decision," *Harvard Business Review.*

242. *facilitate its adoption:* See Gawande, *Checklist Manifesto.*

CHAPTER 20

246. *"a human error":* R. Stacey, "A Report on the Erroneous Fingerprint Individualisation in the Madrid Train Bombing Case," *Journal of Forensic Identification* 54 (2004): 707–718.

248. *The FBI website:* Michael Specter, "Do Fingerprints Lie?," *The New Yorker,* May 27, 2002. Emphasis added.

249. *As Dror puts it:* I. E. Dror and R. Rosenthal, "Meta-analytically Quantifying the Reliability and Biasability of Forensic Experts," *Journal of Forensic Science* 53 (2008): 900–903.

250. *In the first study:* I. E. Dror, D. Charlton, and A. E. Péron, "Contextual Information Renders Experts Vulnerable to Making Erroneous Identifications," *Forensic Science International* 156 (2006): 74–78.

250. *In the second study:* I. E. Dror amd D. Charlton, "Why Experts Make Errors," *Journal of Forensic Identification* 56 (2006): 600–616.

250. *"expert fingerprint examiners":* I. E. Dror and S. A. Cole, "The Vision in 'Blind' Justice: Expert Perception, Judgment, and Visual Cognition in Forensic Pattern Recognition," *Psychonomic Bulletin and Review* 17 (2010): 161–167, 165. See also I. E. Dror, "A Hierarchy of Expert Performance (HEP)," *Journal of Applied Research in Memory and Cognition* (2016): 1–6.

250. *In a separate study:* I. E. Dror et al., "Cognitive Issues in Fingerprint Analysis: Inter- and Intra-Expert Consistency and the Effect of a 'Target' Comparison," *Forensic Science International* 208 (2011): 10–17.

250. *A later, independent study:* B. T. Ulery, R. A. Hicklin, M. A. Roberts, and J. A. Buscaglia, "Changes in Latent Fingerprint Examiners' Markup Between Analysis and Comparison," *Forensic Science International* 247 (2015): 54–61.

251. *Even DNA analysis:* I. E. Dror and G. Hampikian, "Subjectivity and Bias in Forensic DNA Mixture Interpretation," *Science and Justice* 51 (2011): 204–208.

251. *Examiners often receive:* M. J. Saks, D. M. Risinger, R. Rosenthal, and W. C. Thompson, "Context Effects in Forensic Science: A Review and Application of the Science of Science to Crime Laboratory Practice in the United States," *Science Justice Journal of Forensic Science Society* 43 (2003): 77–90.

251. *the verifying examiner knows:* President's Council of Advisors on Science and Technology (PCAST), *Report to the President: Forensic Science in Criminal Courts: Ensuring Scientific Validity of Feature-Comparison Methods* (Washington, DC: Executive Office of the President, PCAST, 2016).

251. *the later investigation of the error:* Stacey, "Erroneous Fingerprint."

252. *a highly respected independent expert:* Dror and Cole, "Vision in 'Blind' Justice."

252. *bias cascades:* I. E. Dror, "Biases in Forensic Experts," *Science* 360 (2018): 243.

252. *sometimes change their minds:* Dror and Charlton, "Why Experts Make Errors."

252. *A 2012 study:* B. T. Ulery, R. A. Hicklin, J. A. Buscaglia, and M. A. Roberts, "Repeatability and Reproducibility of Decisions by Latent Fingerprint Examiners," *PLoS One* 7 (2012).

253. *the Innocence Project:* Innocence Project, "Overturning Wrongful Convictions Involving Misapplied Forensics," *Misapplication of Forensic Science* (2018): 1–7, www.innocenceproject.org/causes/misapplication-forensic -science. See also S. M. Kassin, I. E. Dror, J. Kukucka, and L. Butt, "The Forensic Confirmation Bias: Problems, Perspectives, and Proposed Solutions," *Journal of Applied Research in Memory and Cognition* 2 (2013): 42–52.

253. *an in-depth review:* PCAST, *Report to the President.*

253. *large-scale study of fingerprint:* B. T. Ulery, R. A. Hicklin, J. Buscaglia, and M. A. Roberts, "Accuracy and Reliability of Forensic Latent Fingerprint Decisions," *Proceedings of the National Academy of Sciences* 108 (2011): 7733–7738.

254. *"much higher":* (PCAST), *Report to the President*, p. 95. Emphasis in original.

254. *subsequent study conducted in Florida:* Igor Pacheco, Brian Cerchiai, and Stephanie Stoiloff, "Miami-Dade Research Study for the Reliability of the ACE-V Process: Accuracy & Precision in Latent Fingerprint Examinations," final report, Miami-Dade Police Department Forensic Services Bureau, 2014, www.ncjrs.gov/pdffiles1/nij/grants/248534.pdf.

254. *"in most casework":* B. T. Ulery, R. A. Hicklin, M. A. Roberts, and J. A. Buscaglia, "Factors Associated with Latent Fingerprint Exclusion Determinations," *Forensic Science International* 275 (2017): 65–75.

254. *far fewer false-positive identifications:* R. N. Haber and I. Haber, "Experimental Results of Fingerprint Comparison Validity and Reliability: A Review and Critical Analysis," *Science & Justice* 54 (2014): 375–389.

254–5. *"It is easier to bias":* Dror, "Hierarchy of Expert Performance," 3.

255. *"seek employment in Disneyland":* M. Leadbetter, letter to the editor, *Fingerprint World* 33 (2007): 231.

255. "without actually altering their judgment": L. Butt, "The Forensic Confirmation Bias: Problems, Perspectives and Proposed Solutions— Commentary by a Forensic Examiner," *Journal of Applied Research in Memory and Cognition* 2 (2013): 59–60. Emphasis added.

255. *Even the FBI:* Stacey, "Erroneous Fingerprint," 713. Emphasis added.

256. *In a survey of four hundred:* J. Kukucka, S. M. Kassin, P. A. Zapf, and I. E. Dror, "Cognitive Bias and Blindness: A Global Survey of Forensic Science Examiners," *Journal of Applied Research in Memory and Cognition* 6 (2017).

257. linear sequential unmasking: I. E. Dror et al., letter to the editor: "Context Management Toolbox: A Linear Sequential Unmasking (LSU) Approach for Minimizing Cognitive Bias in Forensic Decision Making," *Journal of Forensic Science* 60 (2015): 1111–1112.

Chapter 21

259. *official agencies:* Jeffrey A. Frankel, "Over-optimism in Forecasts by Official Budget Agencies and Its Implications," working paper 17239, National Bureau of Economic Research, December 2011, www.nber.org /papers/w17239.

259. *tend to be overconfident:* H. R. Arkes, "Overconfidence in Judgmental Forecasting," in *Principles of Forecasting: A Handbook for Researchers and Practitioners,* ed. Jon Scott Armstrong, vol. 30, International Series in Operations Research & Management Science (Boston: Springer, 2001).

260. *an ongoing quarterly survey:* Itzhak Ben-David, John Graham, and Campell Harvey, "Managerial Miscalibration," *The Quarterly Journal of Economics* 128, no. 4 (November 2013): 1547–1584.

260. *"unreliability is a source":* T. R. Stewart, "Improving Reliability of Judgmental Forecasts," in *Principles of Forecasting: A Handbook for Researchers and Practitioners,* ed. Jon Scott Armstrong, vol. 30, International Series in Operations Research & Management Science (Boston: Springer, 2001) (hereafter cited as *Principles of Forecasting*), 82.

260. *to predict Supreme Court rulings:* Theodore W. Ruger, Pauline T. Kim, Andrew D. Martin, and Kevin M. Quinn, "The Supreme Court Forecasting Project: Legal and Political Science Approaches to Predicting Supreme Court Decision-Making," *Columbia Law Review* 104 (2004): 1150–1209.

260. *air pollution regulation:* Cass Sunstein, "Maximin," *Yale Journal of Regulation* (draft; May 3, 2020), https://papers.ssrn.com/sol3/papers.cfm?abstract_id=3476250.

260. *many examples:* For numerous examples, see Armstrong, *Principles of Forecasting.*

261. *averaging multiple forecasts:* Jon Scott Armstrong, "Combining Forecasts," in *Principles of Forecasting,* 417–439.

261. *outperforms most:* T. R. Stewart, "Improving Reliability of Judgmental Forecasts," in *Principles of Forecasting,* 95.

261. *an average of 12.5%:* Armstrong, "Combining Forecasts."

261. select-crowd: Albert E. Mannes et al., "The Wisdom of Select Crowds," *Journal of Personality and Social Psychology* 107, no. 2 (2014): 276–299.

261. *prediction markets have been found to do very well:* Justin Wolfers and Eric Zitzewitz, "Prediction Markets," *Journal of Economic Perspectives* 18 (2004): 107–126.

262. *used prediction markets:* Cass R. Sunstein and Reid Hastie, *Wiser: Getting Beyond Groupthink to Make Groups Smarter* (Boston: Harvard Business Review Press, 2014).

262. *Delphi method*: Gene Rowe and George Wright, "The Delphi Technique as a Forecasting Tool: Issues and Analysis," *International Journal of Forecasting* 15 (1999): 353–375. See also Dan Bang and Chris D. Frith, "Making Better Decisions in Groups," *Royal Society Open Science* 4, no. 8 (2017).

262. *challenging to implement:* R. Hastie, "Review Essay: Experimental Evidence on Group Accuracy," in B. Grofman and G. Guillermo, eds., *Information Pooling and Group Decision Making* (Greenwich, CT: JAI Press, 1986), 129–157.

262. mini-Delphi: Andrew H. Van De Ven and André L. Delbecq, "The Effectiveness of Nominal, Delphi, and Interacting Group Decision Making Processes," *Academy of Management Journal* 17, no. 4 (2017).

265. *"better than the average"*: *Superforecasting,* 95.

267. *"the strongest predictor":* Superforecasting, 231.

267. *"try, fail, analyze":* Superforecasting, 273.

268. *a sophisticated statistical technique:* Ville A. Satopää, Marat Salikhov, Philip E. Tetlock, and Barb Mellers, "Bias, Information, Noise: The BIN Model of Forecasting," February 19, 2020, 23, https://dx.doi.org/10.2139/ssrn.3540864.

269. *"Whenever an intervention":* Satopää et al., "Bias, Information, Noise," 23.

270. *"Teaming—unlike training":* Satopää et al., 22.

270. *"'Superforecasters' may owe":* Satopää et al., 24.

271. *both independent and complementary:* Clintin P. Davis-Stober, David V. Budescu, Stephen B. Broomell, and Jason Dana. "The composition of optimally wise crowds." *Decision Analysis* 12, no. 3 (2015): 130–143.

CHAPTER 22

274. *Quantifying tendon degeneration produces:* Laura Horton et al., "Development and Assessment of Inter- and Intra-Rater Reliability of a Novel Ultrasound Tool for Scoring Tendon and Sheath Disease: A Pilot Study," *Ultrasound* 24, no. 3 (2016): 134, www.ncbi.nlm.nih.gov/pmc/articles/PMC5105362.

274. *When pathologists evaluate core:* Laura C. Collins et al., "Diagnostic Agreement in the Evaluation of Image-guided Breast Core Needle Biopsies," *American Journal of Surgical Pathology* 28 (2004): 126, https://journals.lww.com/ajsp/Abstract/2004/01000/Diagnostic_Agreement_in_the_Evaluation_of.15.aspx.

274. *Without the rapid antigen result:* Julie L. Fierro et al., "Variability in the Diagnosis and Treatment of Group A Streptococcal Pharyngitis by Primary Care Pediatricians," *Infection Control and Hospital Epidemiology* 35, no. S3 (2014): S79, www.jstor.org/stable/10.1086/677820.

274. *you are considered to have diabetes:* Diabetes Tests, Centers for Disease Control and Prevention, https://www.cdc.gov/diabetes/basics/getting-tested.html (last accessed January 15, 2020).

274. *In some hospitals, a second:* Joseph D. Kronz et al., "Mandatory Second Opinion Surgical Pathology at a Large Referral Hospital," *Cancer* 86 (1999): 2426, https://onlinelibrary.wiley.com/doi/full/10.1002/(SICI)1097-0142(19991201)86:11%3C2426::AID-CNCR34%3E3.0.CO;2-3.

275. *The Dartmouth Atlas Project has dedicated:* Most of the material can be found online; a book-length outline is Dartmouth Medical School, *The Quality of Medical Care in the United States: A Report on the Medicare Program; the Dartmouth Atlas of Health Care 1999* (American Hospital Publishers, 1999).

275. *Similar conclusions hold in:* See, for example, OECD, *Geographic Variations in Health Care: What Do We Know and What Can Be Done to Improve Health System Performance?* (Paris: OECD Publishing, 2014), 137–169; Michael P. Hurley et al., "Geographic Variation in Surgical Outcomes and Cost Between the United States and Japan," *American Journal of Managed Care* 22 (2016): 600, www.ajmc.com/journals /issue/2016/2016-vol22-n9/geographic-variation-in-surgical-outcomes -and-cost-between-the-united-states-and-japan; and John Appleby, Veena Raleigh, Francesca Frosini, Gwyn Bevan, Haiyan Gao, and Tom Lyscom, *Variations in Health Care: The Good, the Bad and the Inexplicable* (London: The King's Fund, 2011), www.kingsfund.org.uk/sites/default/files /Variations-in-health-care-good-bad-inexplicable-report-The-Kings-Fund -April-2011.pdf.

275. *A study of pneumonia diagnoses:* David C. Chan Jr. et al., "Selection with Variation in Diagnostic Skill: Evidence from Radiologists," National Bureau of Economic Research, NBER Working Paper No. 26467, November 2019, www.nber.org/papers/w26467.

275. *Here as elsewhere, training:* P. J. Robinson, "Radiology's Achilles' Heel: Error and Variation in the Interpretation of the Röntgen Image," *British Journal of Radiology* 70 (1997): 1085, www.ncbi.nlm.nih.gov/pubmed /9536897. A relevant study is Yusuke Tsugawa et al., "Physician Age and Outcomes in Elderly Patients in Hospital in the US: Observational Study," *BMJ* 357 (2017), www.bmj.com/content/357/bmj.j1797, which finds that doctors' outcomes get worse the further they are out from training. It follows that there is a trade-off between developing experience, which comes from years of practice, and having familiarity with the most recent evidence and guidelines. The study finds that the best outcomes come from doctors who are in the first few years out of residency, when they have that evidence in mind.

276. *Radiologists, for example, call:* Robinson, "Radiology's Achilles' Heel."

276. the kappa statistic: Like the correlation coefficient, kappa can be negative, although that is rare in practice. Here is one characterization of the meaning of different kappa statistics: "slight (κ = 0.00 to 0.20), fair (κ = 0.21 to 0.40), moderate (κ = 0.41 to 0.60), substantial (κ = 0.61 to 0.80), and almost perfect (κ > 0.80)" (Ron Wald, Chaim M. Bell, Rosane Nisenbaum, Samuel Perrone, Orfeas Liangos, Andreas Laupacis, and Bertrand L. Jaber, "Interobserver Reliability of Urine Sediment Interpretation," *Clinical Journal of the American Society of Nephrology* 4, no. 3 [March 2009]: 567–571, https://cjasn.asnjournals.org/content/4/3/567).

276. *drug-drug interactions:* Howard R. Strasberg et al., "Inter-Rater Agreement Among Physicians on the Clinical Significance of Drug-Drug Interactions," *AMIA Annual Symposium Proceedings* (2013): 1325, www.ncbi.nlm.nih.gov/pmc/articles/PMC3900147.

276. *But nephrologists show only:* Wald et al., "Interobserver Reliability of Urine Sediment Interpretation," https://cjasn.asnjournals.org/content/4/3/567.

276. *whether a breast lesion:* Juan P. Palazzo et al., "Hyperplastic Ductal and Lobular Lesions and Carcinomas in Situ of the Breast: Reproducibility of Current Diagnostic Criteria Among Community- and Academic-Based Pathologists," *Breast Journal* 4 (2003): 230, www.ncbi.nlm.nih.gov/pubmed/21223441.

276. *breast proliferative lesions:* Rohit K. Jain et al., "Atypical Ductal Hyperplasia: Interobserver and Intraobserver Variability," *Modern Pathology* 24 (2011): 917, www.nature.com/articles/modpathol201166.

276. *degree of spinal stenosis:* Alex C. Speciale et al., "Observer Variability in Assessing Lumbar Spinal Stenosis Severity on Magnetic Resonance Imaging and Its Relation to Cross-Sectional Spinal Canal Area," *Spine* 27 (2002): 1082, www.ncbi.nlm.nih.gov/pubmed/12004176.

277. *Heart disease is the leading cause:* Centers for Disease Control and Prevention, "Heart Disease Facts," accessed June 16, 2020, www.cdc.gov/heartdisease/facts.htm.

277. *An early study found that 31%:* Timothy A. DeRouen et al., "Variability in the Analysis of Coronary Arteriograms," *Circulation* 55 (1977): 324, www.ncbi.nlm.nih.gov/pubmed/832349.

277. *They disagreed dramatically:* Olaf Buchweltz et al., "Interobserver Variability in the Diagnosis of Minimal and Mild Endometriosis," *European Journal of Obstetrics & Gynecology and Reproductive Biology* 122 (2005): 213, www.ejog.org/article/S0301-2115(05)00059-X/pdf.

278. *significant variability in diagnosis of TB:* Jean-Pierre Zellweger et al., "Intraobserver and Overall Agreement in the Radiological Assessment of Tuberculosis," *International Journal of Tuberculosis & Lung Disease* 10 (2006): 1123, www.ncbi.nlm.nih.gov/pubmed/17044205. For "fair" interrater agreement, see Yanina Balabanova et al., "Variability in Interpretation of Chest Radiographs Among Russian Clinicians and Implications for Screening Programmes: Observational Study," *BMJ* 331 (2005): 379, www.bmj.com/content /331/7513/379.short.

278. *between radiologists in different countries:* Shinsaku Sakurada et al., "Inter-Rater Agreement in the Assessment of Abnormal Chest X-Ray Findings for Tuberculosis Between Two Asian Countries," *BMC Infectious Diseases* 12, article 31 (2012), https://bmcinfectdis.biomedcentral.com/articles/10 .1186/1471-2334-12-31.

278. *The eight pathologists reviewing:* Evan R. Farmer et al., "Discordance in the Histopathologic Diagnosis of Melanoma and Melanocytic Nevi Between Expert Pathologists," *Human Pathology* 27 (1996): 528, www .ncbi.nlm.nih.gov/pubmed/8666360.

278. *Another study at an oncology center:* Alfred W. Kopf, M. Mintzis, and R. S. Bart, "Diagnostic Accuracy in Malignant Melanoma," *Archives of Dermatology* 111 (1975): 1291, www.ncbi.nlm.nih.gov/pubmed/1190800.

278. *The authors of the study conclude that:* Maria Miller and A. Bernard Ackerman, "How Accurate Are Dermatologists in the Diagnosis of Melanoma? Degree of Accuracy and Implications," *Archives of Dermatology* 128 (1992): 559, https://jamanetwork.com/journals/jamadermatology/fullarticle /554024.

278. *Similarly, false-positive rates ranged:* Craig A. Beam et al., "Variability in the Interpretation of Screening Mammograms by US Radiologists," *Archives of Internal Medicine* 156 (1996): 209, www.ncbi.nlm.nih.gov /pubmed/8546556.

278–279. *Radiologists sometimes offer:* P. J. Robinson et al., "Variation Between Experienced Observers in the Interpretation of Accident and

Emergency Radiographs," *British Journal of Radiology* 72 (1999): 323, www
.birpublications.org/doi/pdf/10.1259/bjr.72.856.10474490.

279. *the degree of blockage in angiograms:* Katherine M. Detre et al., "Observer
Agreement in Evaluating Coronary Angiograms," *Circulation* 52 (1975):
979, www.ncbi.nlm.nih.gov/pubmed/1102142.

279. *In areas that involve vague criteria:* Horton et al., "Inter- and Intra-Rater
Reliability"; and Megan Banky et al., "Inter- and Intra-Rater Variability of
Testing Velocity When Assessing Lower Limb Spasticity," *Journal of
Rehabilitation Medicine* 51 (2019), www.medicaljournals.se/jrm/content
/abstract/10.2340/16501977-2496.

279. *But another study, not involving:* Esther Y. Hsiang et al., "Association of
Primary Care Clinic Appointment Time with Clinician Ordering and
Patient Completion of Breast and Colorectal Cancer Screening," *JAMA
Network Open* 51 (2019), https://jamanetwork.com/journals/jamanet
workopen/fullarticle/2733171.

279. *Another illustration of the role:* Hengchen Dai et al., "The Impact of
Time at Work and Time Off from Work on Rule Compliance: The Case
of Hand Hygiene in Health Care," *Journal of Applied Psychology* 100
(2015): 846, www.ncbi.nlm.nih.gov/pubmed/25365728.

279. *a major contribution:* Ali S. Raja, "The HEART Score Has Substantial
Interrater Reliability," *NEJM J Watch,* December 5, 2018, www.jwatch.org
/na47998/2018/12/05/heart-score-has-substantial-interrater-reliability
(reviewing Colin A. Gershon et al., "Inter-rater Reliability of the HEART
Score," *Academic Emergency Medicine* 26 [2019]: 552).

280. *As we mentioned, training:* Jean-Pierre Zellweger et al., "Intra-observer
and Overall Agreement in the Radiological Assessment of Tuberculosis,"
International Journal of Tuberculosis & Lung Disease 10 (2006): 1123,
www.ncbi.nlm.nih.gov/pubmed/17044205; Ibrahim Abubakar et al.,
"Diagnostic Accuracy of Digital Chest Radiography for Pulmonary
Tuberculosis in a UK Urban Population," *European Respiratory Journal* 35
(2010): 689, https://erj.ersjournals.com/content/35/3/689.short.

280. *So does the aggregation of multiple:* Michael L. Barnett et al., "Comparative Accuracy of Diagnosis by Collective Intelligence of Multiple Physicians
vs Individual Physicians," *JAMA Network Open* 2 (2019): e19009, https://

jamanetwork.com/journals/jamanetworkopen/fullarticle/2726709; Kimberly H. Allison et al., "Understanding Diagnostic Variability in Breast Pathology: Lessons Learned from an Expert Consensus Review Panel," *Histopathology* 65 (2014): 240, https://onlinelibrary.wiley.com/doi/abs/10.1111/his.12387.

280. *The best of these have been found:* Babak Ehteshami Bejnordi et al., "Diagnostic Assessment of Deep Learning Algorithms for Detection of Lymph Node Metastases in Women with Breast Cancer," *JAMA* 318 (2017): 2199, https://jamanetwork.com/journals/jama/fullarticle/2665774.

280. *Deep-learning algorithms have:* Varun Gulshan et al., "Development and Validation of a Deep Learning Algorithm for Detection of Diabetic Retinopathy in Retinal Fundus Photographs," *JAMA* 316 (2016): 2402, https://jamanetwork.com/journals/jama/fullarticle/2588763.

280. *AI now performs at least:* Mary Beth Massat, "A Promising Future for AI in Breast Cancer Screening," *Applied Radiology* 47 (2018): 22, www.appliedradiology.com/articles/a-promising-future-for-ai-in-breast-cancer-screening; Alejandro Rodriguez-Ruiz et al., "Stand-Alone Artificial Intelligence for Breast Cancer Detection in Mammography: Comparison with 101 Radiologists," *Journal of the National Cancer Institute* 111 (2019): 916, https://academic.oup.com/jnci/advance-article-abstract/doi/10.1093/jnci/djy222/5307077.

281 Table 3: Apgar Score, Medline Plus, https://medlineplus.gov/ency/article/003402.htm (last accessed February 4, 2020).

282. *Apgar scoring produces little noise:* L. R. Foster et al., "The Interrater Reliability of Apgar Scores at 1 and 5 Minutes," *Journal of Investigative Medicine* 54, no. 1 (2006): 293, https://jim.bmj.com/content/54/1/S308.4.

283. *Assessment and scoring are relatively:* Warren J. McIsaac et al., "Empirical Validation of Guidelines for the Management of Pharyngitis in Children and Adults," *JAMA* 291 (2004): 1587, www.ncbi.nlm.nih.gov/pubmed/15069046.

283. *One study found that BI-RADS:* Emilie A. Ooms et al., "Mammography: Interobserver Variability in Breast Density Assessment," *Breast* 16 (2007): 568, www.sciencedirect.com/science/article/abs/pii/S0960977607000793.

283. *In pathology, there have been:* Frances P. O'Malley et al., "Interobserver

Reproducibility in the Diagnosis of Flat Epithelial Atypia of the Breast," *Modern Pathology* 19 (2006): 172, www.nature.com/articles/3800514.

283. *For that reason, noise reduction:* See Ahmed Aboraya et al., "The Reliability of Psychiatric Diagnosis Revisited," *Psychiatry (Edgmont)* 3 (2006): 41, www.ncbi.nlm.nih.gov/pmc/articles/PMC2990547. For an overview, see N. Kreitman, "The Reliability of Psychiatric Diagnosis," *Journal of Mental Science* 107 (1961): 876–886, www.cambridge.org/core/journals /journal-of-mental-science/article/reliability-of-psychiatric-diagnosis /92832FFA170F4FF41189428C6A3E6394.

283. *A 1964 study involving 91 patients:* Aboraya et al., "Reliability of Psychiatric Diagnosis Revisited," 43.

284. *But in a preliminary effort to:* C. H. Ward et al., "The Psychiatric Nomenclature: Reasons for Diagnostic Disagreement," *Archives of General Psychiatry* 7 (1962): 198.

284. *While a "clinician with developmental training":* Aboraya et al., "Reliability of Psychiatric Diagnosis Revisited."

284. *DSM-III led to a dramatic:* Samuel M. Lieblich, David J. Castle, Christos Pantelis, Malcolm Hopwood, Allan Hunter Young, and Ian P. Everall, "High Heterogeneity and Low Reliability in the Diagnosis of Major Depression Will Impair the Development of New Drugs," *British Journal of Psychiatry Open* 1 (2015): e5–e7, www.ncbi.nlm.nih.gov/pmc/articles/PMC5000492 /pdf/bjporcpsych_1_2_e5.pdf.

284. *But the manual was far:* Lieblich et al., "High Heterogeneity."

284. *Even after a significant 2000 revision:* See Elie Cheniaux et al., "The Diagnoses of Schizophrenia, Schizoaffective Disorder, Bipolar Disorder and Unipolar Depression: Interrater Reliability and Congruence Between DSM-IV and ICD-10," *Psychopathology* 42 (2009): 296–298, especially 293; and Michael Chmielewski et al., "Method Matters: Understanding Diagnostic Reliability in DSM-IV and DSM-5," *Journal of Abnormal Psychology* 124 (2015): 764, 768–769.

284. *"increase the reliability of psychiatric diagnoses":* Aboraya et al., "Reliability of Psychiatric Diagnosis Revisited," 47.

284. *a serious risk:* Aboraya et al., 47.

285. *Another version of the manual:* See Chmielewski et al., "Method Matters."

285. *The American Psychiatric Association:* See, for example, Helena Chmura Kraemer et al., "DSM-5: How Reliable Is Reliable Enough?," *American Journal of Psychiatry* 169 (2012): 13–15.

285. *psychiatrists continue to show:* Lieblich et al., "High Heterogeneity."

285. *"psychiatrists have a hard time":* Lieblich et al., "High Heterogeneity," e-5.

285. *Field trials for DSM-5 found:* Lieblich et al., e-5.

285. *According to some field trials:* Lieblich et al., e-6.

285. *The major reason for the limited:* Aboraya et al., "Reliability of Psychiatric Diagnosis Revisited," 47.

285. *These include (1) clarifying:* Aboraya et al.

285. *In the words of one observer:* Aboraya et al.

286. *The medical profession needs more:* Some valuable cautionary notes can be found in Christopher Worsham and Anupam B. Jena, "The Art of Evidence-Based Medicine," *Harvard Business Review,* January 30, 2019, https://hbr.org /2019/01/the-art-of-evidence-based-medicine.

CHAPTER 23

288. *one newspaper headline:* Jena McGregor, "Study Finds That Basically Every Single Person Hates Performance Reviews," *Washington Post,* January 27, 2014.

288. *ubiquity of judgment-based:* The digital transformation that many organizations are undergoing may create new possibilities here. In theory, companies can now collect great amounts of granular, real-time information about the performance of every worker. This data may make entirely algorithmic performance evaluations possible for some positions. We focus here, however, on the positions for which judgment cannot be entirely eliminated from the measurement of performance. See E. D. Pulakos, R. Mueller-Hanson, and S. Arad, "The Evolution of Performance Management: Searching for Value," *Annual Review of Organizational Psychology and Organizational Behavior* 6 (2018): 249–271.

289. *Most researchers find:* S. E. Scullen, M. K. Mount, and M. Goff, "Understanding the Latent Structure of Job Performance Ratings," *Journal of Applied Psychology* 85 (2000): 956–970.

289. *The rest, 70 to 80% variance:* A small component—10% of total

variance in some studies—is what researchers call the *rater perspective,* or the *level* effect, in the sense of level in the organization, not of the *level noise* as we define it here. The rater perspective reflects that, in rating the same person, a boss differs systematically from a peer, and a peer from a subordinate. Under a charitable interpretation of results from 360-degree rating systems, one could argue that this is not noise. If people at different levels of the organization systematically see different facets of the same person's performance, their judgment on that person should differ systematically, and their ratings should reflect it.

289. *multiple studies:* Scullen, Mount, and Goff, "Latent Structure"; C. Viswesvaran, D. S. Ones, and F. L. Schmidt, "Comparative Analysis of the Reliability of Job Performance Ratings," *Journal of Applied Psychology* 81 (1996): 557–574. G. J. Greguras and C. Robie, "A New Look at Within-Source Interrater Reliability of 360-Degree Feedback Ratings," *Journal of Applied Psychology* 83 (1998): 960–968; G. J. Greguras, C. Robie, D. J. Schleicher, and M. A. Goff, "A Field Study of the Effects of Rating Purpose on the Quality of Multisource Ratings," *Personnel Psychology* 56 (2003): 1–21; C. Viswesvaran, F. L. Schmidt, and D. S. Ones, "Is There a General Factor in Ratings of Job Performance? A Meta-Analytic Framework for Disentangling Substantive and Error Influences," *Journal of Applied Psychology* 90 (2005): 108–131; and B. Hoffman, C. E. Lance, B. Bynum, and W. A. Gentry, "Rater Source Effects Are Alive and Well After All," *Personnel Psychology* 63 (2010): 119–151.

290. *"the relationship between job performance":* K. R. Murphy, "Explaining the Weak Relationship Between Job Performance and Ratings of Job Performance," *Industrial and Organizational Psychology* 1 (2008): 148–160, especially 151.

290. *an employee's true performance:* In the discussion of sources of noise, we ignored the possibility of case noise arising from systematic biases in the rating of certain employees or categories of employees. None of the studies we could locate on the variability of performance ratings compared them with an externally assessed "true" performance.

290. *rate people "strategically":* E. D. Pulakos and R. S. O'Leary, "Why Is Performance Management Broken?," *Industrial and Organizational Psychology* 4

(2011): 146–164; M. M. Harris, "Rater Motivation in the Performance Appraisal Context: A Theoretical Framework," *Journal of Management* 20 (1994): 737–756; and K. R. Murphy and J. N. Cleveland, *Understanding Performance Appraisal: Social, Organizational, and Goal-Based Perspectives* (Thousand Oaks, CA: Sage, 1995).

290. *purely developmental:* Greguras et al., "Field Study."

291. *predicts objectively measurable:* P. W. Atkins and R. E. Wood, "Self- Versus Others' Ratings as Predictors of Assessment Center Ratings: Validation Evidence for 360-Degree Feedback Programs," *Personnel Psychology* (2002).

291. *Overengineered questionnaires:* Atkins and Wood, "Self- Versus Others' Ratings."

292. *98%:* Olson and Davis, cited in Peter G. Dominick, "Forced Ranking: Pros, Cons and Practices," in *Performance Management: Putting Research into Action,* ed. James W. Smither and Manuel London (San Francisco: Jossey-Bass, 2009), 411–443.

292. *forced ranking:* Dominick, "Forced Ranking."

292. *to apply in performance ratings:* Barry R. Nathan and Ralph A. Alexander, "A Comparison of Criteria for Test Validation: A Meta-Analytic Investigation," *Personnel Psychology* 41, no. 3 (1988): 517–535.

293. *Figure 17:* Adapted from Richard D. Goffin and James M. Olson, "Is It All Relative? Comparative Judgments and the Possible Improvement of Self-Ratings and Ratings of Others," *Perspectives on Psychological Science* 6, no. 1 (2011): 48–60.

296. *Deloitte:* M. Buckingham and A. Goodall, "Reinventing Performance Management," *Harvard Business Review,* April 1, 2015, 1–16, doi:ISSN: 0017-8012.

296. *One study:* Corporate Leadership Council, cited in S. Adler et al., "Getting Rid of Performance Ratings: Genius or Folly? A Debate," *Industrial and Organizational Psychology* 9 (2016): 219–252.

296. *"No matter":* Pulakos, Mueller-Hanson, and Arad, "Evolution of Performance Management," 250.

297. *"performance management revolution":* A. Tavis and P. Cappelli, "The Performance Management Revolution," *Harvard Business Review,* October 2016, 1–17.

297. *Evidence suggests:* Frank J. Landy and James L. Farr, "Performance Rating," *Psychological Bulletin* 87, no. 1 (1980): 72–107.

297. *They practice rating performance:* D. J. Woehr and A. I. Huffcutt, "Rater Training for Performance Appraisal: A Quantitative Review," *Journal of Occupational and Organizational Psychology* 67 (1994): 189–205; S. G. Roch, D. J. Woehr, V. Mishra, and U. Kieszczynska, "Rater Training Revisited: An Updated Meta-Analytic Review of Frame-of-Reference Training," *Journal of Occupational and Organizational Psychology* 85 (2012): 370–395; and M. H. Tsai, S. Wee, and B. Koh, "Restructured Frame-of-Reference Training Improves Rating Accuracy," *Journal of Organizational Behavior* (2019): 1–18, doi:10.1002/job.2368.

298. *Figure 18:* Left panel is adapted from Richard Goffin and James M. Olson, "Is It All Relative? Comparative Judgments and the Possible Improvement of Self-Ratings and Ratings of Others," *Perspectives on Psychological Science* 6, no. 1 (2011): 48–60.

298. *the majority of studies:* Roch et al., "Rater Training Revisited."

299. *"star talent":* Ernest O'Boyle and Herman Aguinis, "The Best and the Rest: Revisiting the Norm of Normality of Individual Performance," *Personnel Psychology* 65, no. 1 (2012): 79–119; and Herman Aguinis and Ernest O'Boyle, "Star Performers in Twenty-First Century Organizations," *Personnel Psychology* 67, no. 2 (2014): 313–350.

CHAPTER 24

300. *"It is rare":* A. I. Huffcutt and S. S. Culbertson, "Interviews," in S. Zedeck, ed., *APA Handbook of Industrial and Organizational Psychology* (Washington, DC: American Psychological Association, 2010), 185–203.

301. *rely to some degree on their intuitive judgments:* N. R. Kuncel, D. M. Klieger, and D. S. Ones, "In Hiring, Algorithms Beat Instinct," *Harvard Business Review* 92, no. 5 (2014): 32.

301. *"supreme problem":* R. E. Ployhart, N. Schmitt, and N. T. Tippins, "Solving the Supreme Problem: 100 Years of Selection and Recruitment at the *Journal of Applied Psychology*," *Journal of Applied Psychology* 102 (2017): 291–304.

302. *Other studies report:* M. McDaniel, D. Whetzel, F. L. Schmidt, and S.

Maurer, "Meta Analysis of the Validity of Employment Interviews," *Journal of Applied Psychology* 79 (1994): 599–616; A. Huffcutt and W. Arthur, "Hunter and Hunter (1984) Revisited: Interview Validity for Entry-Level Jobs," *Journal of Applied Psychology* 79 (1994): 2; F. L. Schmidt and J. E. Hunter, "The Validity and Utility of Selection Methods in Personnel Psychology: Practical and Theoretical Implications of 85 Years of Research Findings," *Psychology Bulletin* 124 (1998): 262–274; and F. L. Schmidt and R. D. Zimmerman, "A Counterintuitive Hypothesis About Employment Interview Validity and Some Supporting Evidence," *Journal of Applied Psychology* 89 (2004): 553–561. Note that validities are higher when certain subsets of studies are considered, especially if research uses performance ratings specifically created for this purpose, rather than existing administrative ratings.

302. *objective ignorance:* S. Highhouse, "Stubborn Reliance on Intuition and Subjectivity in Employee Selection," *Industrial and Organizational Psychology* 1 (2008): 333–342; D. A. Moore, "How to Improve the Accuracy and Reduce the Cost of Personnel Selection," *California Management Review* 60 (2017): 8–17.

303. *culturally similar to them:* L. A. Rivera, "Hiring as Cultural Matching: The Case of Elite Professional Service Firms," *American Sociology Review* 77 (2012): 999–1022.

303. *Measures of the correlation:* Schmidt and Zimmerman, "Counterintuitive Hypothesis"; Timothy A. Judge, Chad A. Higgins, and Daniel M. Cable, "The Employment Interview: A Review of Recent Research and Recommendations for Future Research," *Human Resource Management Review* 10 (2000): 383–406; and A. I. Huffcutt, S. S. Culbertson, and W. S. Weyhrauch, "Employment Interview Reliability: New Meta-Analytic Estimates by Structure and Format," *International Journal of Selection and Assessment* 21 (2013): 264–276.

304. *matter—a lot:* M. R. Barrick et al., "Candidate Characteristics Driving Initial Impressions During Rapport Building: Implications for Employment Interview Validity," *Journal of Occupational and Organizational Psychology* 85 (2012): 330–352; M. R. Barrick, B. W. Swider, and G. L. Stewart, "Initial Evaluations in the Interview: Relationships with

Subsequent Interviewer Evaluations and Employment Offers," *Journal of Applied Psychology* 95 (2010): 1163.

304. *quality of a handshake:* G. L. Stewart, S. L. Dustin, M. R. Barrick, and T. C. Darnold, "Exploring the Handshake in Employment Interviews," *Journal of Applied Psychology* 93 (2008): 1139–1146.

304. *positive first impressions:* T. W. Dougherty, D. B. Turban, and J. C. Callender, "Confirming First Impressions in the Employment Interview: A Field Study of Interviewer Behavior," *Journal of Applied Psychology* 79 (1994): 659–665.

305. *In one striking experiment:* J. Dana, R. Dawes, and N. Peterson, "Belief in the Unstructured Interview: The Persistence of an Illusion," *Judgment and Decision Making* 8 (2013): 512–520.

306. *HR professionals favor:* Nathan R. Kuncel et al., "Mechanical versus Clinical Data Combination in Selection and Admissions Decisions: A Meta-Analysis," *Journal of Applied Psychology* 98, no. 6 (2013): 1060–1072.

307. *"zero relationship":* Laszlo Bock, interview with Adam Bryant, *The New York Times,* June 19, 2013. See also Laszlo Bock, *Work Rules!: Insights from Inside Google That Will Transform How You Live and Lead* (New York: Hachette, 2015).

308. *One prominent headhunter:* C. Fernández-Aráoz, "Hiring Without Firing," *Harvard Business Review,* July 1, 1999.

308. *structured behavioral interviews:* For an accessible guide to structured interviews, see Michael A. Campion, David K. Palmer, and James E. Campion, "Structuring Employment Interviews to Improve Reliability, Validity and Users' Reactions," *Current Directions in Psychological Science* 7, no. 3 (1998): 77–82.

309. *must include to qualify:* J. Levashina, C. J. Hartwell, F. P. Morgeson, and M. A. Campion, "The Structured Employment Interview: Narrative and Quantitative Review of the Research Literature," *Personnel Psychology* 67 (2014): 241–293.

309. *structured interviews are far more predictive:* McDaniel et al., "Meta Analysis"; Huffcutt and Arthur, "Hunter and Hunter (1984) Revisited"; Schmidt and Hunter, "Validity and Utility"; and Schmidt and Zimmerman, "Counterintuitive Hypothesis."

309. *work sample tests:* Schmidt and Hunter, "Validity and Utility."

310. Israeli Army: Kahneman, *Thinking, Fast and Slow,* 229.

311. *Practical advice:* Kuncel, Klieger, and Ones, "Algorithms Beat Instinct." See also Campion, Palmer, and Campion, "Structuring Employment Interviews."

311. *"the persistence of an illusion":* Dana, Dawes, and Peterson, "Belief in the Unstructured Interview."

CHAPTER 25

312. *mediating assessments protocol:* Daniel Kahneman, Dan Lovallo, and Olivier Sibony, "A Structured Approach to Strategic Decisions: Reducing Errors in Judgment Requires a Disciplined Process," *MIT Sloan Management Review* 60 (2019): 67–73.

319. estimate-talk-estimate: Andrew H. Van De Ven and André Delbecq, "The Effectiveness of Nominal, Delphi, and Interacting Group Decision Making Processes," *Academy of Management Journal* 17, no. 4 (1974): 605–621. See also chapter 21.

PART 6

326. *In their view:* Kate Stith and José A. Cabranes, *Fear of Judging: Sentencing Guidelines in the Federal Courts* (Chicago: University of Chicago Press, 1998), 177.

CHAPTER 26

331. *First, such efforts might:* Albert O. Hirschman, *The Rhetoric of Reaction: Perversity, Futility, Jeopardy* (Cambridge, MA: Belknap Press, 1991).

332. *Quoting Václav Havel, they:* Stith and Cabranes, *Fear of Judging.*

332. *"three strikes and you're out":* See, for example, Three Strikes Basics, Stanford Law School, https://law.stanford.edu/stanford-justice-advocacy -project/three-strikes-basics/.

333. *"Woodson v. North Carolina":* 428 U.S. 280 (1976).

355. *can embed prejudice:* Cathy O'Neil, *Weapons of Math Destruction: How Big Data Increases Inequality and Threatens Democracy* (New York: Crown, 2016).

355. *"potentially biased":* Will Knight, "Biased Algorithms Are Everywhere, and No One Seems to Care," *MIT Technology Review,* July 12, 2017.

355. *ProPublica:* Jeff Larson, Surya Mattu, Lauren Kirchner, and Julia Angwin, "How We Analyzed the COMPAS Recidivism Algorithm," *ProPublica,* May 23, 2016, www.propublica.org/article/how-we-analyzed-the-compas -recidivism-algorithm. The claim of bias in this example is disputed, and different definitions of bias may lead to opposite conclusions. For views on this case and more broadly on the definition and measurement of algorithmic bias, see later note, *"Exactly how to test."*

355. *"predictive policing":* Aaron Shapiro, "Reform Predictive Policing," *Nature* 541, no. 7638 (2017): 458–460.

336. *Indeed, in this regard, algorithms:* Although this concern is resurfacing in the context of AI-based models, it is not specific to AI. As early as 1972, Paul Slovic noted that modeling intuition would preserve and reinforce, and perhaps even magnify, existing cognitive biases. Paul Slovic, "Psychological Study of Human Judgment: Implications for Investment Decision Making," *Journal of Finance* 27 (1972): 779.

336. *Exactly how to test:* For an introduction to this debate in the context of the controversy over the COMPAS recidivism-prediction algorithm, see Larson et al., "COMPAS Recidivism Algorithm"; William Dieterich et al., "COMPAS Risk Scales: Demonstrating Accuracy Equity and Predictive Parity," Northpointe, Inc., July 8, 2016, http://go.volarisgroup.com /rs/430-MBX-989/images/ProPublica_Commentary_Final_070616.pdf; Julia Dressel and Hany Farid, "The Accuracy, Fairness, and Limits of Predicting Recidivism," *Science Advances* 4, no. 1 (2018): 1–6; Sam Corbett-Davies et al., "A Computer Program Used for Bail and Sentencing Decisions Was Labeled Biased Against Blacks. It's Actually Not That Clear," *Washington Post,* October 17, 2016, www.washingtonpost.com /news/monkey-cage/wp/2016/10/17/can-an-algorithm-be-racist-our -analysis-is-more-cautious-than-propublicas; Alexandra Chouldechova, "Fair Prediction with Disparate Impact: A Study of Bias in Recidivism Prediction Instruments," *Big Data* 153 (2017): 5; and Jon Kleinberg, Sendhil Mullainathan, and Manish Raghavan, "Inherent Trade-Offs in the Fair Determination of Risk Scores," Leibniz International Proceedings in Informatics, January 2017.

CHAPTER 27

340. *They might know that their:* Tom R. Tyler, *Why People Obey the Law,* 2nd ed. (New Haven, CT: Yale University Press, 2020).

342. *A famously puzzling decision in American: Cleveland Bd. of Educ. v. LaFleur,* 414 U.S. 632 (1974).

343. *Influential commentators at the time:* Laurence H. Tribe, "Structural Due Process," *Harvard Civil Rights–Civil Liberties Law Review* 10, no. 2 (spring 1975): 269.

346. *Recall the intensely negative:* Stith and Cabranes, *Fear of Judging,* 177.

347. *In a series of energetic:* See, for example, Philip K. Howard, *The Death of Common Sense: How Law Is Suffocating America* (New York: Random House, 1995); and Philip K. Howard, *Try Common Sense: Replacing the Failed Ideologies of Right and Left* (New York: W. W. Norton & Company, 2019).

CHAPTER 28

354. *Facebook's Community Standards in 2020* 12. Hate Speech, Facebook: Community Standards, www.facebook.com/communitystandards/hate _speech.

354. *The New Yorker:* Andrew Marantz, "Why Facebook Can't Fix Itself," *The New Yorker,* October 12, 2020.

356. *noisy judgments:* bureaucratic justice: Jerry L. Mashaw, *Bureaucratic Justice* (New Haven, CT: Yale University Press, 1983).

359. *Just the reverse largely obtained:* David M. Trubek, "Max Weber on Law and the Rise of Capitalism," *Wisconsin Law Review* 720 (1972): 733, n. 22 (quoting Max Weber, *The Religion of China* [1951], 149).

About the Authors

Daniel Kahneman is an emeritus professor of psychology and public affairs at Princeton University and the winner of the 2002 Nobel Prize in Economic Sciences and the 2013 Presidential Medal of Freedom. Kahneman is a member of the American Academy of Arts and Sciences and the National Academy of Sciences. He is a fellow of the American Psychological Association, the American Psychological Society, the Society of Experimental Psychologists, and the Econometric Society. He has been the recipient of numerous awards, among them the Distinguished Scientific Contribution Award of the American Psychological Association, the Warren Medal of the Society of Experimental Psychologists, the Hilgard Award for Career Contributions to General Psychology, and the Award for Lifetime Contributions to Psychology from the American Psychological Association. He is the author of *New York Times* bestseller *Thinking, Fast and Slow.* He lives in New York City.

———

Olivier Sibony is a professor of strategy at HEC Paris and an associate fellow at Saïd Business School, Oxford University. Previously, he spent twenty-five years in the Paris and New York offices of McKinsey & Company, where he was a senior partner. Sibony's research on improving the quality of strategic decision making has been featured in many publications, including *Harvard Business Review* and *MIT Sloan Management Review.* He is a graduate of HEC Paris and holds a PhD from Université Paris Sciences et Lettres. He is the author of *You're About to Make a Terrible Mistake!* He lives in Paris. Twitter: @siboliv

———

Cass R. Sunstein is the Robert Walmsley University Professor at Harvard, where he is founder and director of the Program on Behavioral Economics and Public Policy. From 2009 to 2012, he was administrator of the White House Office of Information and Regulatory Affairs. From 2013 to 2014, he served on President Obama's Review Group on Intelligence and

Communications Technologies. Winner of the 2018 Holberg Prize from the government of Norway, Sunstein is the author of many articles and books, including two *New York Times* bestsellers: *The World According to Star Wars* and *Nudge* (with Richard H. Thaler). His other books include *How Change Happens* and *Too Much Information*. Twitter: @casssunstein

INTRODUCTION TO
COMPUTER
ENGINEERING
HARDWARE
AND
SOFTWARE
DESIGN

INTRODUCTION TO
COMPUTER
ENGINEERING
HARDWARE
AND
SOFTWARE
DESIGN
THIRD EDITION

TAYLOR L. BOOTH
University of Connecticut

JOHN WILEY & SONS
New York
Chichester
Brisbane
Toronto
Singapore

Library of Congress Cataloging in Publication Data:

Booth, Taylor L.
   Introduction to computer engineering.

   Rev. ed. of: Digital networks and computer systems.
2nd ed. c1978.
   Includes bibliographical references and index.
   1. Computer engineering.   I. Booth, Taylor L.
Digital networks and computer systems.   II. Title.
TK7885.B583   1984   001.64   84-2252
ISBN 0-471-87321-7

Printed in the United States of America

10 9 8 7 6 5 4 3 2 1

To Aline, Shari, Michael, and Laurine

PREFACE

In 1968, when the first edition of this book was written, digital logic design was dominated by discrete, component technology. Logic circuitry was constructed from individual circuit elements, and printed circuit cards were just coming into widespread use. A single flip-flop or a logic gate could easily cost $25 to $30, and the PDP-8 was considered a major technical breakthrough in minicomputer design. The term digital network was used to describe a complex logic network, and any design involving registers, memory, and a control unit was considered to be a computer system. Thus the title selected for the first edition of this text, "Digital Networks and Computer Systems," was appropriate for that time period. With the present rapid change in technology many of the older terms have taken on new meanings. Digital networks now refer to complex digital systems interconnected by a variety of communication channels, and computer systems may now consist of a number of individual computers. To avoid confusion, this third edition has been given a new title which is a better reflection of the purpose and goals of the text.

A major shift has occurred in the methods used to design digital systems and computers. Integrated circuit technology has sharply reduced the price of both digital computers and basic logic modules. Thus many tasks traditionally performed by analogue circuits and systems are now carried out by digital techniques. The programmable hand calculator and personal computer have become commonplace engineering tools. Many engineers and scientists now find it necessary to understand not only the basic operation of digital systems but how these systems can be designed to carry out a range of information-processing tasks that are associated with their work. These changes have created a need for an introductory undergraduate course that provides an overview of the interrelationship of digital system design, computer organization, and assembly-language programming techniques.

When the first edition of this text was published in 1971, no book existed that presented a comprehensive overview of both hardware and software concepts in an integrated manner. Its success demonstrated the fact that this perceived need did, in fact, exist. The second edition, published in 1978, was able to respond to the changes that were then occurring in the integrated circuit area by reducing the emphasis on the design of individual logic networks from basic logic elements and by increasing the emphasis on the design using logic modules that could be realized as LSI or MSI devices.

Up-to-date computer engineering and computer science curriculums now include one or more basic courses that provide students with an understanding of the hardware and software problems that must be solved when designing complex digital systems and computers. In other areas of engineering and in the physical and life sciences, similar courses have been developed to provide the understanding needed to effectively employ digital devices and computers as basic laboratory tools. Students who complete an introductory course based on this book are provided with the hardware and software concepts needed to effectively employ digital concepts to a wide variety of problems. Special care has been taken to stress general understanding of basic concepts rather than presenting a detailed discussion of the operation of a specific family of logic modules or of one particular microprocessor. Thus the knowledge gained will not be outdated as technology advances. The foundation laid by this approach makes it possible for a student to go on to more advanced courses that specialize in specific areas of digital design or software engineering.

This book is organized to provide an integrated overview of the various classes of digital information-processing systems and devices and the interrelationship between the hardware and software techniques that can be used to solve a particular problem. The unifying theme throughout the book is the concept that the steps involved in solving a problem must first be represented by an algorithm. It is then the designer's task to choose the best techniques to realize the given algorithm. Often it is obvious that either a hardware or a software solution should be used. However, there is an ever-increasing gray area between these two approaches in which many different possibilities must be considered before the best solution can be identified. By giving the student a view of the interdependencies of logic design, digital system design, and machine-level programming, it is possible to provide an appreciation of how all of these different areas of computer technology interact.

At the University of Connecticut, this book is used in the first professional-level computer science and engineering course. It is a required course in both the computer science and engineering and the electrical engineering curricula. Since the only prerequisite to this course is an introductory computing course, students from engineering, mathematics, statistics, the physical sciences, the life sciences, and business also take the course to widen their background or to prepare for advanced work in the computer area. Because of scheduling considerations, most computer science and engineering and electrical engineering students take the course during the first semester of their sophomore year. The other students may take it at any time during the third to sixth semester depending on their area of interest. However, many freshmen and even high school students have completed this course without difficulty, since there is no specific mathematical background required other than an understanding of high school level mathematics.

At other schools this book is suitable for an introductory digital systems course that covers the material in Subject Area 6, Logic Design, and Subject Area 7, Digital System Design, of the IEEE Computer Society Model Program report or course CS-4, Introduction to Computer Organization, of the ACM Curriculum 77 report. The text is also of interest in electrical engineering programs as a first course in digital system design because it provides a broader overview of the computer area than a course limited to microprocessors.

The sequence in which the material is presented provides an orderly and logical transition from the basic ideas of representing digital information and performing basic logical operations through the ideas of complex information processing systems and programming. Chapter 1 gives a brief overview of the various topics discussed in the book and their interrelationships. Chapters 2 to 4 present a discussion of the techniques that can be used to represent and to operate on information in digital form, and Chapter 5 shows how these ideas can be extended to represent the higher level mathematical operations found in normal information processing activities. Chapters 6 and 7 provide an introduction to the basic methods used to design combinational logic networks. The main concepts of switching theory are used to show how a logic expression can be reduced to a combinational logic network. Although a brief discussion of the standard minimization processes is presented, the main emphasis is to show that modern LSI and MSI technology has reduced the need to spend a large amount of design time searching for minimal combinational logic circuit realizations. This material also illustrates many of the standard logic circuits encountered in digital system design.

Chapters 8 to 10 introduce the idea of digital devices with memory. After introducing flip-flops and registers as the basic information storage elements, it is then shown that the use of register transfer notation is a natural method to represent the complex information processing tasks performed at the network level. A hardware programming language, based on register transfer concepts, is then developed to describe the operation of complex digital devices.

Chapters 11 and 12 introduce the general ideas behind the operation of stored program digital computers. In particular, a special simulated educational computer, called SEDCOM II, is introduced to illustrate these ideas. This computer is based on the DEC PDP-11 family of computers, and any program that will run on SEDCOM II will also execute on a PDP-11. The machine language of SEDCOM II is a subset of the PDP-11 machine language. However, a much simpler architecture is used so that the basic system level organization of a typical computer system can be understood without becoming lost in unnecessary details.

Chapters 13 and 14 then present an overview of the techniques used to program a computer in assembly language. The emphasis in this discussion is to illustrate the similarity between the design concepts used to represent a hardware algorithm and a software algorithm.

At the University of Connecticut we cover the first 13 chapters in detail and briefly discuss the material in Chapter 14 as time permits at the end of the semester. Dr. Bernard Lovell of our faculty and Dennis Jurgensen, one of our former undergraduate students, have developed a program to simulate SEDCOM II on the IBM 3081. Scott Lovell has helped to correct a number of the bugs in the initial program and has added other enhancements. Students are required to write and run a number of assembly language programs on the simulated computer. They also use logic system breadboards in the laboratory to obtain additional insight into the operation of both combinational and sequential logic networks.

To aid the student and to help the independent reader, several simple exercises are included at the end of each section to illustrate the material of that section. The answers to many of these exercises are included in Appendix 2. Several home problems are included at the end of each chapter. These problems are comprehensive in nature; they extend the material contained in the chapter and stimulate the student to think about one or more new concepts that will be discussed in detail in one of the following chapters. The references at the ends of the chapters guide those who are interested in the further exploration of a given area. A Teacher's Manual is available from the publisher on request for those instructors who adopt the text for classroom use.

I am indebted to the many faculty members who used the first two editions of this book and who sent me helpful suggestions about ways to improve the presentation of particular topics or about new material to be included. Another very important and continuing source of suggestions have been my colleagues on the faculty of the Computer Science and Engineering Division. I am grateful to them for their many useful comments over the past 12 years as they have taught from various editions of this book. Finally, I thank my wife, Aline, for her patience and encouragement throughout the whole revision process.

Storrs, Connecticut   Taylor L. Booth
1983

CONTENTS

(READ)

INTRODUCTION TO
COMPUTER
ENGINEERING
HARDWARE
AND
SOFTWARE
DESIGN

1

INTRODUCTION TO DIGITAL SYSTEMS

1. INTRODUCTION

Because of the increasing complexity of civilization, man has been forced to continually develop better and more efficient techniques to process and utilize information. Initial attempts at developing information processing aids centered around improving methods of carrying out mechanical manipulations of numbers. During the seventeenth century many of the leading mathematicians and scientists developed calculating devices to aid them in their research. As industrial technology developed during the eighteenth and nineteenth centuries, these basic ideas were refined and extended to develop complex mechanical devices that could be used to control machines and aid businessmen in performing repetitive calculations and bookkeeping tasks.

In the early 1800s Charles Babbage proposed and attempted to construct a device that he referred to as an analytical engine. Conceptually this device was similar to our modern digital computers. Although he was able to build a simple model of his machine, he was never able to complete the construction of a machine that would handle practical problems. One of the reasons for his failure was that the design called for so many moving mechanical parts that the inherent friction between the various parts prevented satisfactory operation of the complete machine. Even though Babbage failed to build a practical device, many of the concepts that he developed laid the foundation for the design concepts of modern computers.

Computers, as we know them today, have become practical only because we have been able to replace mechanical devices with electronic devices. In the late 1930s and early 1940s a series of relay computers were built through the joint effort of Harvard University, Bell Telephone Laboratories, and IBM. Although these computers operated satisfactorily, they were quickly superseded by electronic computers.

In 1946 J. P. Eckert and Dr. J. W. Mauchly developed the first electronic computer, the ENIAC, at the Moore School of Engineering at the University of Pennsylvania. This computer contained 18,000 vacuum tubes. Vacuum tubes were so

1

unreliable at that time that the predicted mean time to failure was shorter than the mean time to repair the device. Nevertheless the computer did work and was used by the U.S. Army for a number of years.

As the capability of computers and digital systems became better understood, many major technical advances were made. With the introduction of the transistor in the early 1950s, it became possible to design and construct highly reliable computers. Discrete transistor circuits have given way to integrated circuit technology. It is now possible to place thousands of electronic components on a silicon chip that is at most a few centimeters square. One visible result of this development is the hand calculator, which can be used to carry out complex numerical calculations.

Integrated circuits have had a major impact on both the design and applications of digital networks and computer systems. Their low cost has greatly expanded the areas of application as well as reduced the price of complete computer systems. We have also reached the point where a large number of manufacturers are producing computers of various sizes and capabilities with prices that range from a few thousands to many millions of dollars.

The majority of people who come in contact with computers can be classified as occasional computer users. Their main interest is to use the computer to carry out the routine data processing task or calculations needed as part of their work. By using procedure-oriented languages such as FORTRAN, Pascal, or PL/1, these people are able to carry out data processing tasks without worrying about the internal organization or structure of the computer.

The high information processing rate of modern computers, however, make it possible to apply computers to a variety of information processing tasks that were not even conceived of before the development of modern computers. Consequently just as engineers or scientists must understand the limitations of the physical laws of nature they must also develop an understanding and appreciation of the laws dealing with the utilization, processing, and transmission of information.

This book has been designed for the person who has reached the point where a computer is viewed as more than a calculating device to solve routine problems. Consequently we first investigate the mathematical techniques that are used to describe and analyze digital networks and systems. Next, the methods that may be used to design combinational and sequential logic networks, which are found in every digital system and computer, are presented. Once the operation of these basic building blocks is understood, we then consider how they can be used to form complex data processing devices and general purpose digital computers. Finally, we consider the various types of programming systems that can be used to program a computer and how they are related to the efficiency of the overall information processing system.

2.   ALGORITHMIC PROCESSES

Two of the major problems in designing a complex digital information processing system concern:

1. The identification of the fundamental information processing tasks that must be accomplished.

2. The specification of the component parts of the system needed to carry out these tasks.

From an abstract viewpoint, the complete computational process carried out by any digital information processor or computer can be formally represented by the mathematical relationship

$$F(x) = y$$

where x represents the data presented to the processor, $F(x)$ represents the computation performed on the data, and y represents the results of this computation. The computation represented by $F(x)$ can take many forms.

In the simplest case, the processor might be a simple logic network that takes the current value of n input variables, $[x_1, x_2, \ldots, x_n]$, and immediately produces an output $f(x_1, x_2, \ldots, x_n)$. On the other hand, the processor might be a large-scale computer system that measures the status of a chemical production process and produces output signals to control the rate at which certain chemical reactions are allowed to take place.

For each of these information processing tasks or any other tasks that we might wish to perform, there is only one restriction that we must place on the computation represented by $F(x)$. We must be sure that there is an explicit and unambiguous set of instructions that tells us how to perform the computation. This set of rules is called an algorithm for the computation of $F(x)$.

Algorithm

We say that an *algorithm* for the computation $F(x) = y$ exists if there is an ordered sequence of discrete steps that can be performed mechanically by a device such that given x the device either:

1. forms $y = F(x)$ by executing these steps in the prescribed order, or
2. indicates that no y exists that satisfies the conditions of the computation.

The device must require only a finite number of steps to reach one or the other of these decisions.

From this definition we see that if we are to implement an algorithm on a digital device we must reduce the steps of the algorithm to a sequence of elementary operations that can be performed by the device. In some cases the device will consist of a simple digital network constructed to perform the complete computation in one step while in other cases the algorithm for the computation will be so complex that it requires a large number of steps and can only be implemented on a large-scale digital computer. We now investigate the general properties of algorithms as they relate to the design and utilization of digital information processing devices. This will, in turn, allow us to gain an insight into the interrelationship between the organization of digital networks and computers and the computational processes that can be carried out by these devices. Our first task is to define what we mean by an "elementary operation."

We automatically carry out an algorithm every time we perform a particular mathematical or logical operation. However, we seldom give any thought to the form that this algorithm takes. This is because our previous experience has taught us to associate fixed reactions and interpretations to different mathematical symbols. However, if we wish to describe how we carried out a given calculation to someone who does not have our background, we must explain, in great detail, how the computation is performed.

For example, assume that we wish to compute the sum of the three two-digit numbers

$$A = a_2a_1 \qquad B = b_2b_1 \qquad D = d_2d_1$$

Normally we would probably carry out the addition in our heads, write down the answer

$$Y = A + B + D = y_3y_2y_1$$

and consider our problem solved. Most computers cannot simultaneously add three numbers together. They must, instead, perform the calculation in two steps as:

Step 1. $R_1 = A + B$

Step 2. $Y = R_1 + D$

Thus, if we assume that we can use the elementary operation of adding two numbers together, our calculation can be completed by using a two-step algorithm. However, consider what would happen if the computing device that we had could add only two digits at a time. Should this be the case we would have to replace both step 1 and step 2 with a sequence of steps that would describe how the two numbers are to be added together digit by digit.

The elementary operation in this case would be digit addition which can be formally defined by

$$
\begin{array}{r}
u_i \\
v_i \\
\hline
c_i \; s_i
\end{array}
$$

where s_i is the *unit sum* of the two digits and c_i is the *carry*.

For example, let $u_i = 9$ and $v_i = 5$. Then

$$
\begin{array}{r}
9 \\
5 \\
\hline
1 \; 4
\end{array}
$$

and we see that $c_i = 1$ and $s_i = 4$.

When we reach this level of refinement we must expand our algorithm to show how two multidigit numbers can be added using the operation of adding two single-digit numbers. To do this suppose that we have a computing device, which we can call a *decimal adder*, that will automatically add two single-digit numbers. The device, which is shown in Figure 1-1a, is assumed to have the ability to compute the two functions

$$\text{Unit Sum} \qquad F_1(u_i, v_i)$$
$$\text{Unit Carry} \qquad F_2(u_i, v_i)$$

Suppose we must use this device to compute

$$Y = A + B + D = a_2a_1 + b_2b_1 + d_2d_1$$

Our first step, as before, is to break the calculation into the two steps

$$R = A + B = r_3r_2r_1$$
$$Y = R + D = r_3r_2r_1 + d_2d_1 = y_3y_2y_1$$

Next we must form each partial sum using the functions $F_1(u_i, v_i)$ and $F_2(u_i, v_i)$. The steps needed to compute R are shown in Figure 1-1b. Using this approach we can develop the following algorithm to compute Y.

	Algorithm to compute $Y = A + B + D$ First Part Compute $R = A + B$	Example of Calculation Performed Using Algorithm $Y = 25 + 34 + 98$
Step 1	$r_1 = F_1(a_1, b_1)$	$r_1 = 9 = F_1(5, 4)$
Step 2	$c_1 = F_2(a_1, b_1)$	$c_1 = 0 = F_2(5, 4)$
Step 3	$p_2 = F_1(a_2, b_2)$	$p_2 = 5 = F_1(2, 3)$
Step 4	$r_2 = F_1(p_2, c_1)$	$r_2 = 5 = F_1(5, 0)$
Step 5	$m_2 = F_2(a_2, b_2)$	$m_2 = 0 = F_2(2, 3)$
Step 6	$n_2 = F_2(p_2, c_1)$	$n_2 = 0 = F_2(5, 0)$
Step 7	$c_2 = F_1(m_2, n_2)$	$c_2 = 0 = F_1(0, 0)$

	Second Part $Y = R + D$	
Step 8	$y_1 = F_1(r_1, d_1)$	$y_1 = 7 = F_1(9, 8)$
Step 9	$c_1' = F_2(r_1, d_1)$	$c_1' = 1 = F_2(9, 8)$
Step 10	$p_2' = F_1(r_2, d_2)$	$p_2' = 4 = F_1(5, 9)$
Step 11	$y_2 = F_1(p_2', c_1')$	$y_2 = 5 = F_1(4, 1)$
Step 12	$m_2' = F_2(r_2, d_2)$	$m_2' = 1 = F_2(5, 9)$
Step 13	$n_2' = F_2(p_2', c_1')$	$n_2' = 0 = F_2(4, 1)$
Step 14	$c_2 = F_1(m_2', n_2')$	$c_2 = 1 = F_1(1, 0)$
Step 15	$y_3 = F_1(c_2', c_2)$	$y_3 = 1 = F_2(1, 0)$

	Result $Y = y_3y_2y_1$	Result $Y = y_3y_2y_1 = 157$

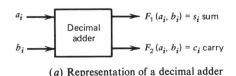

(*a*) Representation of a decimal adder

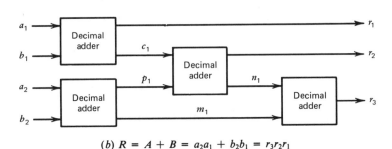

(*b*) $R = A + B = a_2a_1 + b_2b_1 = r_3r_2r_1$

Figure 1-1   Formal summation of two decimal numbers.

This algorithm actually represents the following very simple addition process.

Stage 1	0↖ 0↖		Carry
Compute $R = A + B$	0 ⋮ 2 ⋮ 5		A
	0 ⋮ 3 ⋮ 4		B
	0 ⋮ 5 ⋮ 9		R

Stage 2	1↖ 1↖		Carry
Compute $Y = R + D$	0 ⋮ 5 ⋮ 9		R
	0 ⋮ 9 ⋮ 8		D
	1 5 ⋮ 7		Y

Thus we see that the set of basic operations that we can use affects the complexity of an algorithm. The example also illustrates how we can solve the problem. When we are working with a system there will usually be a sequence of operations that are used enough times to justify attaching a functional name to them. Thus we could define a function

$$F_s(U, V) = U + V$$

that stands for the steps needed to form the sums in the above algorithm. The algorithm then goes back to

Step 1. $R = F_s(A, B)$

Step 2. $Y = F_s(R, D)$

This idea of taking a sequence of simple operations and defining a new operation to represent this sequence is used repeatedly throughout this book. In this way we can concentrate on the important concepts being presented without worrying about the fine details of how each step of the process is actually implemented.

Flowchart Representation of Algorithms

One of the most convenient ways to represent an algorithm is by means of a *flowchart* or *flow diagram*. A flowchart is a graphical representation of a particular algorithm that indicates the logical sequence of operations that are to be performed by the device that executes the algorithm. The flowchart is basically a collection of specially shaped boxes and directed lines. The contents of each box indicate which operations are to be performed while the lines that interconnect the boxes indicate the sequence in which the instructions are to be performed.

A very elaborate flowchart symbology has been evolved by computer programmers. However, for our needs in this book we will limit our flowchart symbols to those illustrated in Figure 1-2. Reference 3 at the end of this chapter presents an extensive discussion of flowcharting techniques.

Each instruction box and decision box will contain one or more expressions describing how the basic operations are used to carry out the calculations. It is assumed that the reader has been introduced to computer programming in sufficient detail to be aware of how flowcharts are used. The following example will serve to review these ideas.

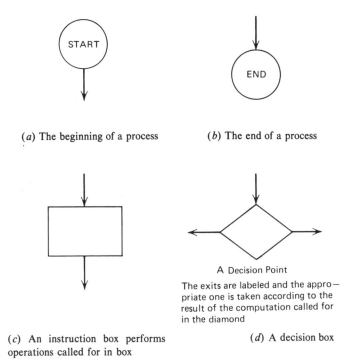

(*a*) The beginning of a process

(*b*) The end of a process

A Decision Point
The exits are labeled and the appro—priate one is taken according to the result of the computation called for in the diamond

(*c*) An instruction box performs operations called for in box

(*d*) A decision box

Figure 1-2   Basic flowchart notation.

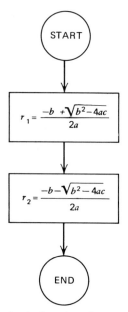

Figure 1-3   A simple flowchart for computing r_1 and r_2.

Assume that we wish to calculate the roots of the equation $ax^2 + bx + c$. If $a \neq 0$ then these roots are given by

$$r_1 = \frac{-b + \sqrt{b^2 - 4ac}}{2a} \qquad r_2 = \frac{-b - \sqrt{b^2 - 4ac}}{2a}$$

The simplest possible flowchart for finding r_1 and r_2 is given in Figure 1-3. However, if we examine this flowchart, we see that it is not much different from our initial statement of the problem. In particular, it assumes that we have two basic operations corresponding to

$$f_1(a, b, c) = \frac{-b + \sqrt{b^2 - 4ac}}{2a}$$

and

$$f_2(a, b, c) = \frac{-b - \sqrt{b^2 - 4ac}}{2a}$$

that can be evaluated to find r_1 and r_2. Since these two functions are somewhat specialized, it becomes desirable to break the calculation down into smaller parts. Before we can do this, we must consider some of the problems that must be overcome.

First, we note that if $a = 0$ we have

$$r_1 = r_2 = -\frac{c}{b}$$

provided we always assume that b is not also 0. Similarly we note that if $b^2 - 4ac \geq 0$ then the roots are real, while if $b^2 - 4ac < 0$ we have the imaginary roots

$$r_1 = \frac{-b + j\sqrt{4ac - b^2}}{2a} \qquad r_2 = \frac{-b - j\sqrt{4ac - b^2}}{2a}$$

where $j = \sqrt{-1}$. Using these observations let us now formulate a much more comprehensive flowchart description of our computation of r_1 and r_2. This flowchart is given in Figure 1-4.

This flowchart is much more complex than the one in Figure 1-3, but we still find boxes that call for complex computations such as $Y = b^2 - 4ac$. If this were the flowchart for a program that is to be written in a programming language such as

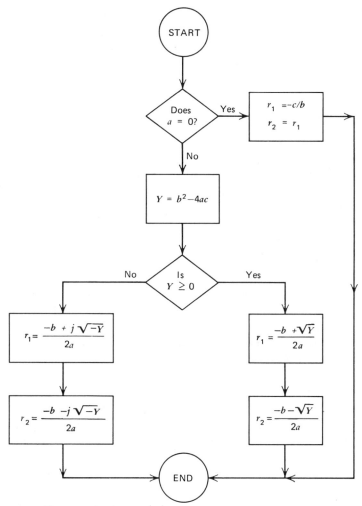

Figure 1-4 A second flowchart for computing r_1 and r_2.

FORTRAN, it would be an acceptable computational step because we could leave the translation of this mathematical statement into a form that the computer can use up to the computer's compiler program. Here again it is also possible to construct a digital network that would accept the variables a, b, and c as inputs and produce Y as an output. However, a network of this type is still too specialized to be of much use.

As a final step in our flowchart example let us take the box that contains $Y = b^2 - 4ac$ and replace it by a set of more basic operations. This is done in Figure 1-5. In this flowchart we have used the operations of multiplication and subtraction as our basic mathematical operations. Similarly we could replace each of the larger boxes of Figure 1-4 with a much more detailed flowchart involving basic operations similar to those illustrated in Figure 1-5.

The discussion of this section has presented a survey of the problems involved in studying the way in which the calculations required in a given information processing task can be described in a formal manner. We paid no attention to the physical problem of how these calculations can actually be performed by a realizable digital device. This problem will now be considered.

3. DIGITAL NETWORKS

For every operation called for as part of an algorithm there must be a digital network or system that will perform the operations. As with algorithms, some of these networks perform very simple operations while there are other, much more complex, digital systems that perform extremely complex tasks. In this section we briefly consider the general forms that these networks and systems can take. A much more extensive discussion of these devices is presented in later chapters.

Combinational Logic

The simplest class of networks are combinational logic networks such as are illustrated in Figure 1-6. Logic networks accept input variables that can take on only one of two values. For convenience these values are arbitrarily designated as 0 and 1. Such a signal is said to carry one *bit* of information.

If the inputs to the logic network are indicated by the variables x_1, x_2, ..., x_l, the current output of the network can be expressed as

$$y = f(x_1, x_2, \ldots, x_l)$$

where y takes on the value 0 or 1 depending on the particular values assigned to the current input variables. Networks of this type can be used alone or can be combined with other circuit elements to form much more complex logic networks.

Registers

In addition to being able to operate on digital signals in a logical manner, a digital network must, in many instances, have the ability to store information about the past behavior or the past inputs to the network. To accomplish this required information

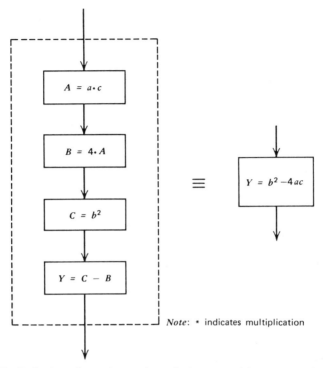

Figure 1-5 Reduction of complex mathematical statement to component operations.

storage, a wide variety of information storage devices has been developed. At present we will refer to the basic storage element as a *cell* and assume that it can store a signal with a value of either a 0 or a 1. The output of each cell has a value corresponding to the quantity stored in the cell. The content of the cell remains constant until an input signal is received instructing the cell to change its content. Figure 1-7a illustrates the symbolic representation that we use for a cell.

Single information storage cells have rather limited storage capabilities since they can store only a single bit of information. If more information must be stored, a collection of cells can be joined together, as shown in Figure 1-7b, to form a *register*. A register with n cells is said to be an *n-bit register*.

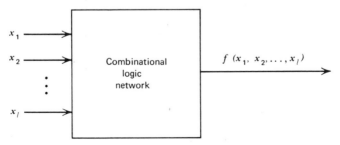

Figure 1-6 General combinational logic network.

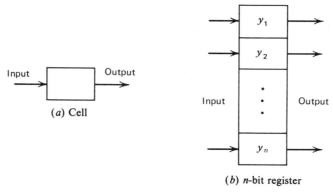

(a) Cell

(b) n-bit register

Figure 1-7   Cells and registers.

Registers by themselves are of relatively little value. They must be combined with combinational logic networks if the stored information is to be used as part of a computation.

Digital Networks

The behavior of any digital network containing a register is dependent on the way in which the inputs to the register are formed. Figure 1-8 shows a completely general model that can be used to represent a digital network that has the ability to store

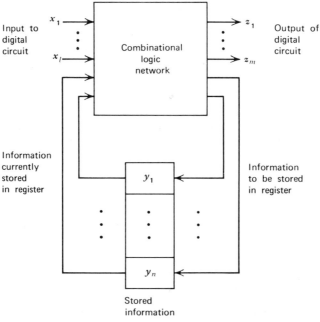

Figure 1-8   General model of a digital circuit.

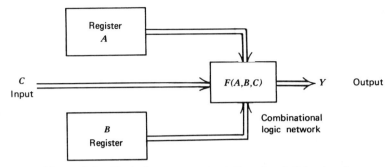

Figure 1-9 Block diagram representation of a digital network.

information. The size of the register in this circuit depends on the amount of information that must be stored, while the overall operation of the network depends on
the form that the combinational logic network takes.

A digital computer is made up of hundreds of these digital networks. Their design
is a straightforward process involving three basic steps.

1. Description of the operation that the network is to perform.
2. Development of a mathematical representation of the logical operations to be
   performed by the combinational logic network.
3. Realization of the network in terms of a particular set of components.

As long as we are interested in the design of a particular network to carry out a
given operation, we must deal with models of the type illustrated in Figure 1-8. However, if we assume that the network is already developed and we wish to investigate
how it is used in a complete system, we can replace the detailed representation of
the network by a block diagram representation such as that illustrated in Figure 1-
9. The content of each register is indicated by a capital letter as are the input and
output signals. The operation performed on this information is represented by a function such as $F(A, B, C)$. In this way we are aware of the overall behavior of the
network without being lost in a mass of details concerning the way that the circuit
is constructed.

This approach is becoming a common design technique using integrated circuit
technology. Many of the common information processing tasks have been standardized, and special *medium-scale integrated* circuits (MSI) or *large-scale integrated*
circuits (LSI) have been developed by electronic manufacturers to carry out these
tasks. Thus a digital system designer can buy these circuits as standard electronic
components without having to worry about how they are constructed.

Digital Systems

Complete information processing systems can be constructed using a small number
of basic digital networks. For example, it is possible to build a digital system that
will observe the output of a radio receiver and sound an alarm whenever a particular
coded message is received.

Another type of digital system is illustrated in Figure 1-10. This system is made

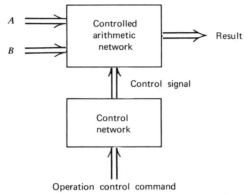

Figure 1-10   A controlled arithmetic processor.

up of two parts, a control network and an arithmetic unit. An external signal is used to select the arithmetic operation that must be performed on the input signals A and B. This operation control command is applied to the control network, which then generates the sequence of commands necessary to make the controlled arithmetic network perform the desired operation. Here again we use a block diagram that shows only the operations that we are interested in and omits the particular details of how the networks, which may be integrated circuits, are actually constructed.

Digital Computers

Although computers are constructed from many different electronic and mechanical elements, the basic organization of a computer can be roughly broken down into the five major parts illustrated in Figure 1-11.

The input to a computer can take many forms depending on the type of infor-mation that must be delivered to the computer. In most large data processing appli-

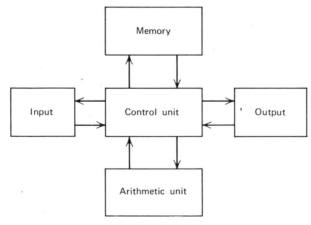

Figure 1-11   A simple block diagram showing the major parts of a computer.

cations, the major input devices are punched cards, magnetic tapes, or magnetic disks. These devices can transfer a large amount of information into the computer in a relatively short period of time.

For other applications it is necessary to provide the capability of human-computer communications. This can be accomplished through the use of such devices as typewriters, display scopes, and graphic position sensors. With devices of this type an operator can guide the operation of a computer by instructing it to perform various operations as intermediate results are made known.

A third type of input situation occurs when the computer is used as part of a complete system such as an automatic flight control system or a chemical processing plant. Applications of this type require the computer to collect input data from a variety of sensor elements. These data might consist of physical quantities such as voltages, temperatures, pressures, or velocity, or the data might be information about the system such as current supply levels, relative anticipated demands for a given system product, or current market prices.

The arithmetic unit of a computer is the center in the computer where the actual operations on the data take place. This unit must be able to hold and manipulate data under the direction of the control unit. The heart of this unit is one or more special registers called *accumulators,* which provide for the temporary storage of information while it is being processed. In addition to these accumulators, this unit also contains the necessary logic circuits to carry out the basic arithmetic and logic operations that the computer has been designed to perform.

A typical computer has four classes of basic operations that can be performed.

1. Arithmetic operations such as addition, subtraction, and multiplication.
2. Logical operations such as greater than, less than, or comparisons.
3. Data manipulation such as shifting the position of data in an accumulator, and transferring data into or out of an accumulator.
4. Decisions on from where to take the next instruction in a program based on the form of the data currently stored in a particular accumulator.

One of the first problems that must be solved when a new computer is being designed is that of selecting the specific set of basic operations, called *instructions,* that can be executed by the computer. These instructions must be selected so that all of the information processing tasks that the computer might be asked to perform can be expressed in terms of an algorithm that makes use of these instructions. The sequence of instructions needed to realize a given algorithm is called a *program.*

Each instruction of the program is encoded into digital form and is stored in the main memory unit. This encoded program is called a *machine-language program.* In addition, the data needed to perform the calculations described by the program are also stored in the memory unit. Such data are directly accessible to the computer.

In addition to main memory, most computers have some form of bulk storage such as magnetic tapes or disks that allow vast amounts of data and information to be stored. These data are usually not directly available to a computer during a calculation. If some of the information stored on one of these devices is needed, it is necessary to transfer this information into main memory.

The actual execution of a given machine-language program is under the direct supervision of the control unit. The control unit reads the current instruction to be executed from memory, interprets the instruction, and then coordinates the operation of all the parts of the computer so that each step needed to carry out the instruction happens in a logical sequence and at the right time. As soon as the computer finishes the operation called for by the current instruction, the control unit goes on to the next instruction in the machine-language program.

The final major section of a computer is the output device. Data can be transferred from the computer in many forms. For a computer mainly devoted to data processing or numerical computations, the output is usually printed. Computers used as an integral part of a much more complex system can have a variety of other forms of outputs.

Control computers usually produce signals that activate some physical process. For example, in a steel mill a computer might control both the amount of raw material and the sequence of operations used in each step of the steel-making process.

The output of a computer might be some form of graphic display so that the user can obtain a dynamic interpretation of the interaction between the various variables of his problem. Outputs of this type are very useful in computer-aided design problems where the operator can vary one parameter of a problem and see how this parameter influences the rest of the problem.

Computer size has been rapidly decreasing in recent years. Integrated circuit technology has reached the point where it is possible to realize a complete computer using only a few integrated circuit modules. Computers of this type are called *microcomputers*. The heart of a microcomputer is a *microprocessor,* which is an integrated circuit that realizes the operations carried out by the arithmetic unit and the control unit. Additional integrated circuits are needed for memory and input/ouput. With this new technology, computer systems that once might have required a large room can be constructed in a few cabinets. Although the size of a computer has been markedly reduced, the theory of operation of a microcomputer is essentially the same as that of any other computer system.

In this section we have briefly considered the general types of hardware that can be used to carry out various classes of logical operations. As the complexity of the operations that we wished to accomplish increased we saw that it became increasingly desirable to carry out the operation as a controlled sequence of logical steps. This approach led us to the concept of a digital computer where the computations carried out by the computer are determined by a program stored in the computer's memory. The problems associated with developing these programs are considered in the next section.

4.   COMPUTER PROGRAMMING

One of the basic assumptions in our discussions of algorithms was that a mechanical device was available to automatically carry out each step of the algorithm. From the last section we know that each digital computer has a set of basic operations that it can perform under the direction of a control element. We also know that the order in which these operations are performed is determined by a machine-language program. Thus, if we wish to use a digital computer to carry out a given calculation, we must first develop an algorithm, using only the allowable computer instructions, that describes how to perform the desired calculation. We must then encode the algorithm into a machine-language program that can be executed by the computer. This section briefly considers the problems associated with generating these programs.

Machine-Language Programming

Every basic instruction associated with a computer is coded as an n-digit sequence of 0's and 1's. For example, the instruction "add A to B" might be encoded as 001010110101. As indicated previously, the set of all the possible encoded instructions is called the machine language of the computer. Any program that is to be executed by a computer must ultimately be expressed in this machine language.

In the earliest computers the machine-language instructions necessary to implement a given algorithm were coded by a programmer directly in the machine language for that computer. For example, the machine-language program to compute

$$Y = A + B - (C + D)$$

might be represented in machine language as

Instruction	Machine-Language Code	Meaning
1	001011010100	Form $S = C + D$
2	011001010101	Form $R = B - S$
3	001010101110	Form $Y = A + R$
4	010000000000	Halt calculation

Obviously a language of this type is very unsatisfactory for general use. There are two major reasons for this conclusion. First, the basic operations that can be performed by the computer are very elementary compared with the operations usually employed in the solution of practical problems. The inclusion of any operation into the set of basic operations of a computer is based on a compromise between the cost of wiring the operation into the computer and the advantages of having this particular operation directly available for use by the computer programmer. This selection process is based primarily on the frequency of use of the operation and the operational advantage gained by wiring it as an elementary operation, rather than performing it as a sequence of elementary operations. Consequently, the more complex the operation the less likely it is to be included as a basic machine operation. The second problem of writing a program in machine language is that it is just too notationally inconvenient for human use.

Higher Level Programming Languages

Although an experienced programmer is usually familiar with the machine language of the computer with which he works, he would much rather use names or other meaningful symbols to help program a given problem. In addition, he would like to have the computer carry out many of the simple bookkeeping jobs that are necessary in programming. This has been the motivating force behind the creation of all the higher level programming languages, such as FORTRAN and PL/1.

A computer is a symbol-manipulating device. Therefore, it is possible to design a special machine-language program that will take symbolic statements written in a high level language, such as FORTRAN, and convert these statements into a machine-language program that can be executed by the computer.

The initial program written by the programmer in the higher level language is called the *source program*, while the resulting machine-language program is called the *object program*. The special machine-language program that converts the source program to the object program is called a *translator*. There are many different types of translator programs and higher level languages.

Assembler Languages

The simplest improvement that can be made is to use short names, called *mnemonics*, to identify each basic computer instruction and the data terms manipulated by these instructions. For example, the instruction

$$001011010100$$

might be represented in mnemonic form as

$$\text{ADD C, D}$$

and correspond to the addition of the two data terms C and D. A translator program can be developed to convert a source program, written in mnemonic form, into the corresponding machine-language object program.

A program, written in mnemonic form, to carry out the computation

$$Y = A + B - (C + D)$$

might have the following form

Instruction	Mnemonic Representation	Meaning
1	S, ADD C, D	Form $S = C + D$
2	R, SUB B, S	Form $R = B - S$
3	Y, ADD A, R	Form $Y = A + R$
4	HLT	Halt calculation

A translator program can be developed to convert these mnemonic terms into their corresponding machine-language representation and carry out other simple programming tasks. Such a translator is called an *assembler* and the corresponding language is called an assembler language. If the above mnemonic source program were processed by an assembler, the resulting object program might have the following form.

$$001011010100$$
$$011001010101$$
$$001010101110$$
$$010000000000$$

The problem with an assembler language is that the basic operations that are represented by this language are essentially the same as those represented by the machine language. Assembler-language programs are very useful to the experienced programmer for developing special programs. However, they are not suitable for the computer user whose main interest is in using a computer to carry out a given task associated with a particular problem. Thus, in order to meet the need for a user-oriented language the concept of higher level programming languages has been developed.

Higher Level Languages

The average computer user does not have the interest, or the time, to master the details of the assembler language or machine language associated with a given computer. A *higher level language* is any language that has been designed so that the statements that make up a program written in that language closely resemble the form of the mathematical statements that are used to describe the problem under investigation. Since these statements cannot be used directly by the computer to carry out the necessary computations, a translation program, called a *compiler,* is used to analyze each source language statement and convert it into the machine-language program used by the computer to carry out the desired computation.

A large number of user-oriented languages have been developed. Among the best known are FORTRAN, which is primarily for engineering and scientific applications; COBOL for business applications; LISP and SNOBOL for the processing of lists of information. PL/1 and Pascal are two new languages that incorporate many of the important features of the above languages.

To solve a problem of adding two numbers, a user-oriented language would use a statement such as the following:

$$Y = A + B - (C + D)$$

The compiler program would then translate this statement into a sequence of machine-language instructions of the form given in the previous examples.

5. SUMMARY

The first digital logic networks and digital computers were very cumbersome and costly relative to the information processing tasks they performed. However, with the advent of modern integrated circuit technology the prices of digital networks and computers have been reduced to the point where it is practical to use digital devices in a wide variety of information processing tasks. This has meant that anyone who wishes to effectively use these devices must fully appreciate their characteristics and limitations.

In this book we will take a comprehensive look at the various aspects of digital circuit and system design. Our approach is designed to provide the insight necessary to understand the relationships that exist between the design considerations and structure of digital devices and the way that these devices can be used. To accomplish this goal we first investigate how information can be represented in digital form. We then investigate the principles involved in logic network design and consider how these networks can be used to carry out specific information processing tasks. This background will then allow us to consider the organization of digital computers and the techniques that can be used to program these computers to carry out specific information processing tasks. Examples and home problems are then used to show how these concepts can be applied to actual digital system design problems.

Since each chapter contains several new and important concepts, the following chapter organization is used to help the reader identify and understand these concepts. At the end of each major section a set of short exercises is inserted to illustrate the important ideas of that section. The answers to many of these exercises are included in the back of the book. In addition, a set of more extensive home problems is included at the end of each chapter. These problems are of a more advanced nature and are designed to further illustrate material contained in the chapter and to relate the current material to that previously considered. The references at the end of each chapter are selected to supplement and indicate the extensions of the material contained in the chapter and home problems.

Reference Notation

Computers and digital systems have had a tremendous impact on engineering and science. Tutorial papers relevant to the various areas of computer science and engineering can be found in *Computer,* the survey and tutorial magazine of the Institute of Electrical and Electronic Engineers (IEEE) Computer Society, *Computer Surveys,* the survey and tutorial journal of the Association for Computing Machinery (ACM), or in general publications such as *Byte* magazine or *Datamation.*

A history of the early development of electronic computers can be found in Reference 5, while Reference 1 gives a general overview of the impact digital computers have had on the industrialized world. The idea of an algorithmic process and the programming process used to realize an algorithm as a computer program is discussed in References 3 and 4. Reference 2 presents an insight into how a number of computer systems evolved as computer technology developed.

REFERENCES

1. Arden, B. W. (ed.) (1980), *What Can Be Automated?* The MIT Press, Cambridge, Mass.
2. Bell, C. G., Mudge, J. C., and McNamara, J. E. (1978), *Computer Engineering—A DEC View of Hardware Systems Design.* Digital Press, Bedford, Mass.
3. Booth, T. L., and Chien, Y. T. (1974), *Computing: Fundamentals and Applications.* Wiley, New York.
4. Graham, N. (1982), *Introduction to Computer Science. A Structured Approach* (second edition). West Publishing Co., St. Paul, Minn.
5. Rosen, S. (1969), "Electronic Computers: A Historical Survey." *Computing Surveys,* Vol. I, No. 1, pp. 7–36, March.

2

REPRESENTATION OF INFORMATION
IN DIGITAL FORM

1. INTRODUCTION

Before we can design a digital system we must decide how to represent the information that will be processed by the system. Sometimes the information will already be in digital form while in other cases we must decide upon which representation to use before we start the design process. This chapter presents a general overview of the various methods used to represent digital information and introduces many of the basic data types used in later chapters. A standard symbology is also introduced.

Scalars

The simplest form of digital information is a single binary variable represented as

$$x_i$$

Single binary variables are called *scalars* and they form the building blocks from which we can construct other digital representations. A binary scalar can take on one of two values, which, for most discussions, will be indicated as 0 or 1. Such a variable represents one *bit* of information.

Tuples

If we group r binary variables together we form an *r-tuple* which is represented as

$$[x_1, x_2, x_3, \ldots, x_r]$$

Since each of the r variables that make up the r-tuple can take on only two values, the r-tuple can assume only

$$2*2*2* \ldots *2 = 2^r$$

different values. For example, if $r = 2$, the four possible values associated with the 2-tuple $[x_1, x_2]$ are

$$[0, 0], [0, 1], [1, 0], [1, 1]$$

The meaning we decide to associate with these possible values will depend upon the particular information being represented by the 2-tuple.

Vectors

There are many situations in which we are interested in the information represented by an r-tuple but not in the details about how the information is represented as a pattern of 0's and 1's. For those cases we refer to the r-tuple as a *vector*. When this occurs we represent the r-tuple by a single vector variable of the form

$$XIN = [x_1, x_2, \ldots, x_r]$$

The variable XIN is thus a vector variable that corresponds to the possible values that can be assigned to the r-tuple of binary variables.

Although information can take a wide variety of forms, it is possible to classify information as either

1. Logical information,
2. Character information, or
3. Numerical information.

In the next sections we introduce techniques that can be used to represent each class of information as well as the standard conventions used to encode information from each class. Throughout this discussion it is unnecessary to refer to any physical device when making our definitions. Thus, the representation techniques developed in this chapter can be applied any time we deal with data in digital form.

2.   INFORMATION REPRESENTATION AND NOTATIONAL CONVENTIONS

A number of notational conventions and terms are used throughout this book to discuss information. Before investigating the techniques used to represent particular types of information, it is useful to discuss these conventions and their relationship to computers and other digital devices.

The following conventions are used to represent scalars and vectors.

1. Identifiers formed from lowercase letters, such as a, x, or mbr, represent scalar binary variables.
2. Identifiers formed from uppercase letters, such as A, X, or MBR, represent vectors.

Since a vector is an r-tuple of scalars, the scalar components of a vector are represented by indexed scalar variables with the same symbolic form used to represent the vector. For example

$$MBR = [mbr_1, mbr_2, \ldots, mbr_k] = [MBR]$$

represents a k-component vector MBR. The notation $[MBR]$ is used to indicate that we wish to consider the individual components of the vector and the values assigned to these components. When we use the notation MBR without the [,], it means that we are interested only in the information represented by the vector and not the internal coding used to represent each specific value. The number of components in a vector is called the *dimension* of the vector.

There are many applications where a vector is formed from two or more subvectors. For example, assume that

$$T = [t_1, \ldots, t_j] \qquad U = [u_1, \ldots, u_k]$$

are two vectors. The $j + k$ component vector V is defined as

$$V = [T, U]$$

where

$$v_i = t_i \qquad i = 1, 2, \ldots, j$$
$$v_{j+m} = u_m \qquad m = 1, 2, \ldots, k$$

In this case we say that the vectors T and U are *subvectors* of V. If we wish to define T and U in terms of V, we use the notation

$$T = V[1, j] \qquad U = V[j + 1, j + k]$$

to indicate that T is the subvector corresponding to the first j components of V and that U is the subvector corresponding to the $(j + 1)$st to $(j + k)$th components of V.

When we partition a vector V into two or more subvectors, the components associated with each subvector are said to form a *field* of the vector V. Thus if

$$V = [T, U]$$

we say that the vector V has two fields T and U corresponding to the subvectors T and U.

In some special cases it is desirable to consider a vector with a single component. Such a vector is represented as a 1-tuple of the form

$$V = [v]$$

where the vector V and the scalar v represent the same information.

Information Representation

In digital circuits and systems it is necessary to differentiate between digital information that is being transmitted between different parts of the system and digital information that is being stored in some manner for later use. Information is transmitted by signals and is stored in registers that are made up of cells. The following conventions are used to describe these signals and storage units.

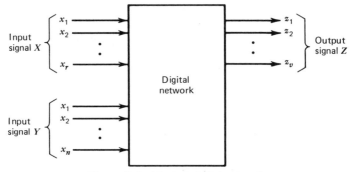

Figure 2-1 Typical digital network.

Signals

A typical digital network is illustrated in Figure 2-1. This network has two input signals, denoted by the vectors X and Y, and one output signal, denoted by the vector Z. Each of these signals is represented by the values assigned to the binary variables that make up the vector. The meaning we associate with such signals depends upon the particular task that we are trying to carry out in the digital network and the encoding that we have selected to assign meaning to each vector. This problem is considered in greater detail in Section 3.

The Basic Storage Unit

The smallest information storage unit is called a *cell*, and it can hold one bit of information. The information contained in a cell is represented by a binary variable, say y_i, and it is assumed that a signal corresponding to y_i is available as an output of the cell. Both of these conditions are represented in Figure 2-2.

As discussed in later chapters, cells are realized in a number of different ways. At this point we use the following conventions to represent the information found in a cell.

1. The binary variable stored in the cell has a value of either 0 or 1.
2. The output of the cell remains constant until some form of input signal is received instructing the cell to change its contents.

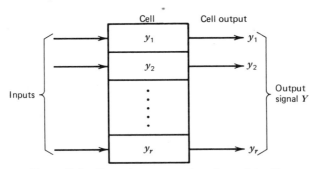

Figure 2-2 General representation of a register Y.

State of a Cell

The value of the binary variable stored in a cell is called the *state* of the cell. Thus a cell can be either in state 0, when it is storing a 0, or in state 1, when it is storing a 1. If we wish to store more information we must use a register.

Registers

An ordered collection of cells forms a *register*. If r cells are used to form a register, then it is called an *r-bit register*. The information stored in an r-bit register can be considered as an r-bit vector. For example, the r-bit register Y shown in Figure 2-2 holds the r-bit vector

$$Y = [y_1, y_2, \ldots, y_r]$$

The variables

$$y_1, y_2, \ldots, y_r$$

which represent the contents of each cell of the register, are called *state variables*. The

$$2^r$$

distinct values that can be associated with the vector Y are called the *states of the register*. For example, if $r = 2$, the four distinct states of a two-cell register are

$$[0, 0] \quad [0, 1] \quad [1, 0] \quad [1, 1]$$

Registers are represented or named using capital letters. It is common practice to use a *mnemonic* for the name of a register that indicates the specific information represented in the register. For example, we can talk about the Memory Buffer Register as the *MBR* register or the Accumulator register as the A register. Again we use the convention that $[A]$ represents the specific cells that make up the register. Thus

$$A = [a_1, a_2, \ldots, a_r] = [A]$$

We also use the convention that the output of a register is a signal that is represented by the same symbolic notation used to name the register. Thus the output of the Y register shown in Figure 2-2 is the vector Y.

The following conventions are used when discussing the contents of registers.

1. The cells may be numbered either left-to-right or right-to-left.

$$A = [a_1, a_2, \ldots, a_r]$$

or

$$A = [a_r, a_{r-1}, \ldots, a_1]$$

2. The cells may be numbered 0 to $r - 1$ or 1 to r.

$$A = [a_{r-1}, a_{r-2}, \ldots, a_0] \text{ or } A = [a_0, a_1, \ldots, a_{r-1}]$$

or

$$A = [a_r, a_{r-1}, \ldots, a_1] \text{ or } A = [a_1, a_2, \ldots, a_r]$$

3. A contiguous collection of cells in a register can be considered a *subregister*. The k-bit subregister starting at the ith cell is indicated as

$$A[i, i + k] = [a_i, a_{i+1}, \ldots, a_{i+k}]$$

4. A single cell may be considered as a 1-bit register. In this case

$$A = [a]$$

indicates that A is a 1-bit register that holds a vector that has the same value as the scalar a.

Some of the notational conventions just introduced may seem confusing. However, as we use them in the following discussions, you will see the reason for this selection.

Nibbles, Bytes, and Words

The number of cells, r, that make up a register or a subregister can be selected in an arbitrary manner. Over the years, a number of factors have led to groupings that have received special names.

It has become standard practice to use a grouping of 8 bits to represent a single character. Such an 8-bit grouping is commonly called a *byte*.

If we restrict our interest to single decimal digits, we can represent such a digit using at most 4 bits, which is half a byte. Some people like to refer to a group of 4 bits as a *nibble*, although this terminology is not as common as the term byte.

Most computer systems have standard-length registers that are used when carrying out a computation. These registers are said to store one *word* of information. Since the manipulation of symbolic data plays a major role in many computer applications, most computers have a word size that is a multiple of 8 bits.

At one time the word size associated with a computer was used to indicate the classification of the computer. For example, microprocessors had 8-bit words, minicomputers had 16-bit or 24-bit words, and regular computers had word sizes of 32 bits, 64 bits, or 128 bits. Modern integrated circuit technology has blurred this distinction. The word size selected for a given computer application is now determined by the application envisioned. Table 2-1 lists some typical computer systems and their associated word size.

Table 2-1   Word Size Associated with Typical Computer Systems

	Typical System	Word Size
Microprocessors	8080, Z80, 6800	8 bits
	8086, Z8000	16 bits
Minicomputer	PDP-11	16 bits
	VAX 11/780	32 bits
Regular Computer	IBM 3033	32 bits
Systems	CDC-6600	60 bits

EXERCISES

$2^4 = 16$

1. List the states of a 4-bit register. $[0,0,0,0]$, $[0001]$ $[0010]$ $[0011]$ $[0100]$
   $[0101]$, $[0110]$ $[0111]$ $[1000]$ $[1001]$ $[1010]$ $[1011]$ $[1100]$ $[1101]$ $[1110]$ $[1111]$
2. A memory unit is made up of 48,000 16-bit words. Estimate the number of pages
   of this text that could be stored in this memory space. 96,000 CHAR
   80 CHAR/LINE, 50 LINES, 2 CHAR/16 bit = 24 pages
3. It is common practice to use the symbol K to mean $1024 = 2^{10}$. A typical microcomputer may be advertised as having a 64K-byte memory. How many bytes
   actually make up such a memory? 65,536

3. REPRESENTING NONNUMERIC INFORMATION

If the rather abstract representation of digital information presented in the previous
section is to be useful, we must have some way to attach meaning to the digital
information contained in a signal or stored in a register. This section presents a number of techniques that can be used to encode logical and character information. The
somewhat more complex problem of representing numerical information is treated
in the next section.

Encoding Logical Information

Many of the analytical techniques used in digital system design have evolved from
the study of mathematical logic that deals with the truth or falsity of declarative
statements. For example, the declarative statement

The ball landed in the box.

may be either TRUE (the ball landed in the box) or FALSE (the ball did not land
in the box). To represent such statements in a mathematical manner, we introduce
the idea of identifying each statement with a scalar variable.

Assume that x is the scalar variable selected to represent the above statement.
Under this interpretation we associate the following meaning to the two possible values, called *truth values,* that x may take on.

$x = 1$ The statement is TRUE. The ball landed in the
box.

$x = 0$ The statement is FALSE. The ball did not land in
the box.

We have introduced the coding that $x = 1$ corresponds to TRUE and that $x = 0$
corresponds to FALSE. This is not the only way that such information can be
encoded.

In a higher level programming language such as FORTRAN or Pascal we might
be faced with the same need to encode a declarative statement. To do this we would

select an identifier, say X, to represent the statement. If the statement was TRUE we would write the following statements

FORTRAN   Pascal

$X = .$ TRUE. $X := $ TRUE

while if the statement was FALSE we would write

FORTRAN   Pascal

$X = .$ FALSE. $X := $ FALSE

As long as we are concerned only with writing a program in one of these languages we do not need to consider how the value associated with X is represented inside the computer that will execute these statements.

Most computers are designed so that they perform computations using information encoded into words or bytes. Thus, a convention must be selected to encode the two truth values TRUE and FALSE. In some higher level languages each truth value is represented as one byte inside a computer. A typical encoding of the truth values in this situation would be

[0, 0, 0, 0, 0, 0, 0, 0]   represents the truth value FALSE

[1, 1, 1, 1, 1, 1, 1, 1]   represents the truth value TRUE

One byte can take on 256 different values. Thus we see that this is a very inefficient encoding since we are using only 2 of the possible 256 values to represent useful information and leaving the remaining 254 values undefined. This is not a problem if we are writing a program with a small number of logical variables.

Sometimes we must develop a program with a large number of logical variables. For example, assume that we are trying to design a "game program" in which a contestant must try to throw eight balls into a box. The outcome of one play of the game could be represented by the vector

$$X = [x_1, x_2, x_3, x_4, x_5, x_6, x_7, x_8]$$

where the following encoding is used

$x_i = 1$ The ith ball is in the box.

$x_i = 0$ The ith ball is not in the box.

With this encoding we see that

$$X = [1, 0, 0, 0, 1, 1, 0, 0]$$

represents the situation that balls 1, 5, and 6 are in the box and all of the others are not.

When we use this type of encoding we find that we can encode a greater number of different logical situations into a single byte. Depending upon the computer system we are using and the types of calculations that we wish to perform, this may or may not present a problem. We must wait until later discussions before we can fully investigate how we might use logical information encoded in this manner.

Encoding Symbolic Information

Symbolic information can take a variety of forms. For example, we might wish to code the alphabet into a digital form or it might be necessary to indicate the operational status of a machine performing a complex manufacturing operation in terms of a digital signal. The problem of encoding information of this type into digital form can be treated in the following general manner.

Assume that we are given a set S of k distinct quantities. Then we can set up a one-to-one relationship that associates a distinct value of the r-tuple $[x_1, x_2, \ldots, x_r]$ with each element of the set provided that

$$k \leq 2^r$$

This correspondence is not unique. In fact there are

$$(2^r)(2^r - 1)(2^r - 2) \cdots (2^r - k + 1) = \frac{(2^r)!}{(2^r - k)!}$$

distinct ways in which this correspondence can be established.

As an example, let us assume that the set S consists of the three commands given in Table 2-2. Information of this type must often be encoded into digital form for use in digital information processing systems. Two possible ways in which this information can be encoded are illustrated in this table. The first method uses a 2-bit signal since $r = 2$ is the smallest value that can be selected. The second encoding uses 3 bits, which is more than absolutely required. The advantage of using this type of encoding is that we can associate a particular symbol with a particular bit of the encoded signal. Thus if $y_1 = 1$ we know that this indicates the addition operation, while $y_2 = 1$ indicates subtraction and $y_3 = 1$ indicates multiplication.

Character Encoding

Since computers are information processing devices, it is quite common to use them to carry out computational tasks on nonnumeric information such as typed text in a word processing system. A standard method must be used to encode the individual characters that make up this information.

Table 2-2 Encoded Symbolic Information

Symbolic Information	Encoding Using $[x_1, x_2]$	Encoding Using $[y_1, y_2, y_3]$
+	[0, 0]	[1, 0, 0]
−	[0, 1]	[0, 1, 0]
*	[1, 0]	[0, 0, 1]

On a typical computer terminal we may have

26	Lowercase letters
26	Uppercase letters
10	Digits
33	Special symbols (such as $+$, $-$, $=$, !, $\langle\rangle$)
33	Special control characters (such as line feed, delete, carriage return, backspace)
128	Total

If we wish to encode each of these 128 symbols in a unique manner, we must use at least 7 bits. There are (128)! different ways that such an encoding could take place. If each designer were allowed to select an individual encoding for these symbols, this would lead to complete chaos when two pieces of equipment had to communicate with each other. Two standard binary codes are in common use to represent the alphabetic, numeric, control, and special symbols found in digital systems.

The most common code used in digital systems and computers is the ASCII (American Standard Code for Information Interchange) code. As defined, this is a 7-bit code. In many applications one or more additional bits may be added to the code for error detection or correction purposes. However, the basic code is 7 bits and the additional bits should not be considered as part of the basic definition of the code. The complete ASCII code is given in Appendix A.

A second common code, used extensively by IBM (International Business Machine Corp.), is the EBCDIC (Extended Binary Coded Decimal Interchange Code). This code, which has the capabilities of representing more than 128 characters, is an 8-bit code. A partial listing of the EBCDIC code is also given in Appendix A.

An inspection of the character encoding in the two codes shows that no simple correspondence exists between the code used to represent the character in ASCII and that used to represent it in EBCDIC.

Encoding Character Sequences

By common agreement the byte is considered to be the standard size of an encoded character. Since a byte corresponds to 8 bits, each EBCDIC character fits into a byte in an obvious manner. When we use the ASCII code we must standardize on the way that it is encoded into the 8 bits that make up the byte. The accepted standard is to place the code for each character in the 7 rightmost bits of the byte. The leftmost bit is then either set to 0 or it is used, as discussed in a home problem, as a parity bit to aid in the detection of possible errors.

To illustrate how symbolic information might be encoded, consider the following sequence of symbols:

$$A(X) = 52*Y + 25;$$

In this sequence we have 13 characters. The end of the sequence is indicated by the symbol ";", which we refer to as an "endmarker." Suppose that we wish to store this sequence in a computer's memory, which stores information as 16-bit words. Each

Table 2-3 Typical ASCII and EBCDIC Codes

Symbol	Code ASCII	Code EBCDIC	Symbol	Code ASCII	Code EBCDIC
A	1000001	11000001	(	0101000	01001101
X	1011000	11100111	)	0101001	01011101
Y	1011001	11101000	=	0111101	01111110
2	0110010	11110010	+	0101011	01001110
5	0110101	11110101	*	0101010	01011100
			;	0111011	01011110

memory location or word corresponds to a register that can hold two bytes. Thus we will need 7 memory locations to hold an encoded representation of the given information. The way that the given 13-character sequence can be "packed" into 7 memory locations is shown in Figure 2-3. An ASCII encoding is shown in Figure 2-3a and an EBCDIC encoding is shown in Figure 2-3b. The ASCII and the EBCDIC codes used to represent each of the distinct characters is listed in Table 2-3.

EXERCISES

1. A computer has a 3-bit instruction register that must indicate which one of the five following instructions is currently being executed by the computer. Give a possible coding of this instruction set.

Instructions

ADD, MULTIPLY, SUBTRACT, DIVIDE, CLEAR

2. Show how the following character sequence can be encoded using both the ASCII and the EBCDIC codes given in Appendix A.

FOR I = 1, 5 DO;

4. NUMBER SYSTEMS

The problem of representing numerical information in digital form is of central importance in the design and use of digital devices and computers. This section provides a brief description of the various number systems that are used in this book, the relationship between these systems, and the methods of encoding numerical values into digital form. This discussion concentrates mainly on the representation of positive numbers. The ideas are extended in later discussions to negative numbers, floating point numbers, and the different operations that can be performed upon numerical information.

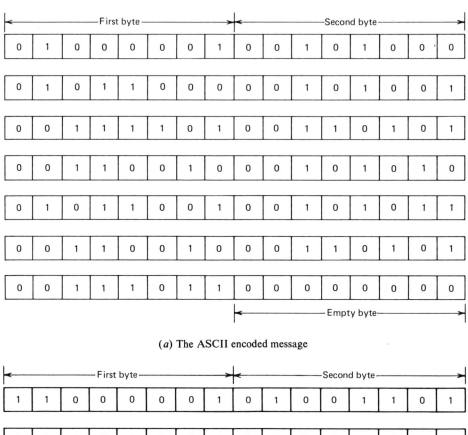

(a) The ASCII encoded message

(b) The EBCDIC encoded message

Figure 2-3   Two typical ways that a symbolic sequence can be stored in a set of registers.

Radix or Base of a Number System

Decimal numbers are so common to our culture that when we see a symbol such as 632.45 we immediately feel that we understand its numerical meaning. This reaction is so common that we forget that each digit of a decimal number has a place value. Thus 632.45 is really a shorthand way of expressing the number

$$N_{10} = 6(10)^2 + 3(10)^1 + 2(10)^0 + 4(10)^{-1} + 5(10)^{-2} = 632.45_{10}$$

A decimal number is said to be expressed in terms of the base 10 since each digit is multiplied by an appropriate power of 10. The number forming the base of a number system is called the *radix* of the system. When it is important to indicate the radix of a number system, we can include it as a subscript. Thus N_{10} indicates that the number N is expressed in the base 10 number system.

The use of 10 as a radix for our number system probably occurred as a natural consequence of the fact that people have 10 fingers. However, as discussed in Reference 2, there is no reason why another number could not be used as the base for a number system. In general any number N can be represented in the base r number system as

$$N_r = a_{n-1}(r)^{n-1} + \cdots + a_1(r) + a_0(r)^0 + a_{-1}(r)^{-1} + \cdots + a_{-m}(r)^{-m}$$

If r is selected as the radix, then the digits a_i of the number take on integer values between 0 and $r - 1$. Since it is too cumbersome to write a number in the above form, we use the shorthand notation

$$N_r = (a_{n-1}a_{n-2} \cdots a_1 a_0 . a_{-1} \cdots a_{-m})_r$$

to indicate that the number is expressed in terms of the base r.

The number N_r is divided into two parts by the *radix point* that appears between a_0 and a_{-1}. The terms to the right of the radix point represent the *fractional* part of the number while the terms to the left represent the *integer* portion of the number. In our later discussions we often need to treat the integer part of a number differently from the fractional part.

Some of the common radices used in the digital area are given in Table 2-4.

Table 2-4 Summary of Common Number Systems

Radix	Name of Number System	Basic Digits Used in System[a]
2	Binary	0, 1
3	Ternary	0, 1, 2
8	Octal	0, 1, 2, 3, 4, 5, 6, 7
10	Decimal	0, 1, 2, 3, 4, 5, 6, 7, 8, 9
16	Hexadecimal	0, 1, 2, 3, 4, 5, 6, 7, 8, 9, A, B, C, D, E, F

[a]The hexadecimal system requires 16 distinct symbols to represent digits. The convention of using the first six letters of the alphabet plus the 10 decimal digits has become common usage.

Suppose that one is given the marks shown below and we wish to indicate the number of marks present.

$$\text{卌} \quad \text{卌} \quad \text{卌} \quad \text{卌} \quad \text{卌} \quad \text{||||}$$

This number, written in the various number systems, would be

$$N_2 = 11101_2 \quad N_{10} = 29_{10}$$
$$N_3 = 1002_3 \quad N_{16} = 1D_{16}$$
$$N_8 = 35_8$$

Range of a Number

When dealing with the base r number system, we find that the values of m and n determine the range of values that can be represented by N_r. The integer portion of N_r will have an equivalent decimal value that falls between 0 and $r^n - 1$. Every integer in this interval can be represented exactly by a base r number with n or fewer digits. Thus if we make n large enough, any particular integer can be represented exactly in any given base r number system.

For example a 16-bit binary number has a range of $\{0, \ldots, 65,535_{10}\}$. Similarly a 6-digit octal number has a range of $\{0, \ldots, 262,143_{10}\}$.

We have a more difficult problem when dealing with the fractional part of a number. A fraction represents a number that falls in the open interval $(0, 1)$. Since this interval represents a continuum of values, there are an uncountable infinite number of points in this interval. However, since m is a finite value, we can represent only $r^m - 1$ fractions in this interval. Thus, as shown in Figure 2-4, there are gaps between each of the fractional points that can be represented. The size of this gap Δ (expressed in base 10 notation) is

$$\Delta_{10} = \left(\frac{1}{r}\right)^m$$

and is called the *resolution interval.* Note that the resolution interval will have a different value for each base.

If we wish to represent a fraction that does not correspond to one of the allowed values, we must approximate the fraction by the closest allowed value. There are two standard ways of doing this: truncation and rounding.

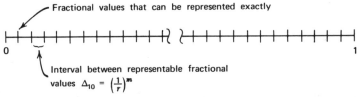

Fractional values that can be represented exactly

0 — 1

Interval between representable fractional values $\Delta_{10} = \left(\frac{1}{r}\right)^m$

Figure 2-4 Graphical illustration of the finite number of fractional values that can be represented by an m-digit fraction.

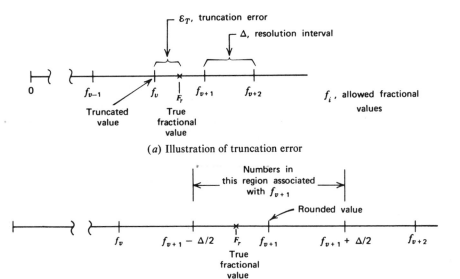

(a) Illustration of truncation error

(b) Illustration of rounding error

Figure 2-5 Errors introduced by uses of finite length fractions.

Truncation

Assume that we have a fraction of the form

$$F_r = .a_{-1}a_{-2}a_{-3} \cdots a_{-m}a_{-(m+1)} \cdots a_{-(m+u)}$$

and we must represent this fraction by using only m digits. This fraction is said to be *truncated* if we simply drop all the digits to the right of a_{-m}. For example, in a base 10 system, $F_{10} = .18763$ would be truncated to .187 if $m = 3$. The maximum error introduced by truncation will always be less than the resolution interval. Thus the decimal value of the truncation error ε_T in a base r system is bounded by

$$\varepsilon_{T10} < \left(\frac{1}{r}\right)^m \qquad \frac{\log \varepsilon_T}{\log r}$$

Figure 2-5a illustrates the form that the truncation error takes.

Rounding

Another way to approximate a fraction is to select the allowed fraction closest to the desired value as the one to represent that variable. This process is called *rounding*. Assume that F_r falls between the fractional values f_v and f_{v+1}. Then

$$f_v \text{ approximates } F_r$$

if

$$(F_r - f_v) \le \frac{\Delta}{2}$$

$$f_{v+1} \text{ approximates } F_r$$

if

$$(F_r - f_v) > \frac{\Delta}{2}$$

The decimal value of the magnitude of the error ε_R in a base r system is bounded by

$$\varepsilon_{R10} \le \frac{1}{2}\left(\frac{1}{r}\right)^m$$

To illustrate rounding, assume a base-10 system with $m = 3$ and $F_{10} = .18763$. Then

$$\frac{\Delta}{2} = \frac{1}{2}\left(\frac{1}{10}\right)^3 = .0005$$

We note that

$$f_v = .187$$
$$f_{v+1} = .188$$

therefore

$$(F_r - f_v) = .00063 > .0005$$

Thus F_r is approximated by the rounded value of .188. Figure 2-5b illustrates the rounding process.

Now that we have a general idea of the different number systems that can be used, our next task is to consider how we can convert numbers from one system to another.

An Application of Binary, Octal, and Hexadecimal Numbers

Binary numbers fit naturally into discussions of digital systems since we describe signals and contents of registers by r-tuples $[x_1, x_2, \ldots, x_r]$ of binary-valued variables. Thus, it is often convenient to think of the contents of a register or the value of a signal as a binary integer even if the actual information represented by the r-tuple has some other meaning.

For example, if the contents of a register are represented by [1, 0, 1, 1, 0, 1, 0, 1, 0], it is just as easy to represent this same information as the binary number $N_2 = 101101010$.

One problem with binary numbers is that they tend to be long and cumbersome to remember. We often find it convenient to use an octal or a hexadecimal number to represent binary information since there is a very easy technique that can be used to convert from one system to the other.

Table 2-5a gives the relationship between the octal digits and their corresponding binary representation, and Table 2-5b gives the same correspondence between hexadecimal digits and their binary representation.

Table 2-5

(a) Octal-Binary Equivalence		(b) Hexadecimal-Binary Equivalence	
Octal Digit	Equivalent Binary Representation	Hexadecimal Digit	Equivalent Binary Representation
0	000	0	0000
1	001	1	0001
2	010	2	0010
3	011	3	0011
4	100	4	0100
5	101	5	0101
6	110	6	0110
7	111	7	0111
		8	1000
		9	1001
		A (10)	1010
		B (11)	1011
		C (12)	1100
		D (13)	1101
		E (14)	1110
		F (15)	1111

It is easy to convert a number from a binary to an octal representation. Starting at the radix point we separately divide the integer portion and the fractional portion of the binary number into groups of three digits and then represent each group of binary digits as a single octal number. The following example illustrates this process.

$$1010111101.11010 \qquad \text{binary number}$$

$$\begin{array}{cccccc} ** & & & & & * \\ 001 & 010 & 111 & 101 & . & 110 & 100 \\ 1 & 2 & 7 & 5 & . & 6 & 4 \end{array} \qquad \begin{array}{l} \text{groups of 3 digits} \\ \text{octal digit equivalent} \end{array}$$

$$1010111101.11010_2 = 1275.64_8$$

*Note the zeros added to fill out groups of three binary digits.

To go in the opposite direction we just reverse the process. For each octal digit we write the corresponding 3-digit binary number and then combine all the resulting binary digits into a single binary number. This process is illustrated by the following example.

$$\begin{array}{cccccc} 1 & 5 & 4 & . & 6 & 3 \\ 001 & 101 & 100 & . & 110 & 011 \end{array} \qquad \begin{array}{l} \text{octal number} \\ \text{3-digit binary representation} \end{array}$$

$$154.63_8 = 1101100.110011_2$$

With a little practice the conversion between binary and octal numbers can be carried out by inspection. The reason behind this conversion process can easily be seen by considering the following steps that we are actually carrying out when we follow this conversion process.

$$N_2 = 101010.101_2 = 1(2)^5 + 0(2)^4 + 1(2)^3 + 0(2)^2 + 1(2) + 0(2)^0$$
$$+ 1(2)^{-1} + 0(2)^{-2} + 1(2)^{-3}$$
$$= [1(2)^2 + 0(2) + 1(2)^0](2)^3 + [0(2)^2 + 1(2) + 0(2)^0]$$
$$+ [1(2)^2 + 0(2) + 1(2)^0](2)^{-3}$$
$$= 5(8)^1 + 2(8)^0 + 5(8)^{-1} = 52.5_8$$

The conversion of a number from binary to hexadecimal form and vice versa is carried out in exactly the same manner except that we form groups of four binary digits rather than groups of three. The following examples illustrate this conversion process. First consider the binary to hexadecimal conversion process.

$$
\begin{array}{llll}
101011 \;.\; 101 & \text{binary number} \\
0010 \;\; 1011 \;.\; 1010 & \text{groups of 4 digits} \\
2 \quad \text{B} \;.\; \text{A} & \text{hexadecimal digit equivalent} \\
101011.101_2 = 2\text{B.A}_{16}
\end{array}
$$

Next consider the hexadecimal to binary conversion process.

$$
\begin{array}{llll}
5 \quad \text{A} \;.\; 6 & \text{hexadecimal number} \\
0101 \quad 1010 \;.\; 0110 & \text{4-digit binary representation} \\
1011010 \;.\; 011 & \text{binary equivalent} \\
5\text{A.6}_{16} = 1011010.011_2
\end{array}
$$

The reason the conversion process between binary, octal, and hexadecimal numbers is so easy is that the radix of each number system is a power of 2. The problem of converting between one of these systems and the decimal system requires a little additional work but it is also easily accomplished.

Binary, Octal, and Hexadecimal to Decimal Conversion

The conversion of a binary, octal, or hexadecimal number to a decimal number is not difficult. For a binary number we simply write the expression for the binary number in powers of 2 notation and then expand and collect these terms to obtain the corresponding decimal number. For example,

$$11010.101_2 = 1(2)^4 + 1(2)^3 + 0(2)^2 + 1(2)^1 + 0(2)^0 + 1(2)^{-1} + 0(2)^{-2}$$
$$+ 1(2)^{-3}$$
$$= 16 + 8 + 2 + .5 + .125 = 26.625_{10}$$

We use a similar process for octal to decimal conversion except that we use the radix 8 instead of 2. To illustrate, consider the following example.

$$613.24_8 = 6(8)^2 + 1(8) + 3(8)^0 + 2(8)^{-1} + 4(8)^{-2}$$
$$= 384 + 8 + 3 + .25 + .0625$$
$$= 395.3125_{10}$$

Similarly the conversion from a hexadecimal to a decimal number can be accomplished as illustrated in the following example. Note that it is necessary to convert the digits A through F to their corresponding decimal values of 10 through 15.

$$5A.E_{16} = 5(16) + A(16)^0 + E(16)^{-1}$$
$$= 5(16) + 10(16)^0 + 14(16)^{-1}$$
$$= 80 + 10 + .875 = 90.875_{10}$$

Decimal to Binary, Octal, or Hexadecimal Conversion

The conversion of a decimal number to a binary, octal, or hexadecimal form can also be handled in a straightforward manner. First, we note that any decimal number can be written

$$N_{10} = \langle\text{integer part}\rangle_{10} . \langle\text{fractional part}\rangle_{10}$$

In the conversion process we first convert the $\langle\text{integer part}\rangle_{10}$ to $\langle\text{integer part}\rangle_r$ and then we convert $\langle\text{fractional part}\rangle_{10}$ to $\langle\text{fractional part}\rangle_r$. These conversions are carried out separately because two different techniques must be employed. After the integer and fractional parts are determined, we can write

$$N_r = \langle\text{integer part}\rangle_r . \langle\text{fractional part}\rangle_r$$

We will consider the complete details of the conversion from decimal to binary numbers. The extension of the conversion technique to the other number systems will then be illustrated by an example.

Suppose the decimal number is given by

$$N_{10} = d_{n-1}d_{n-2} \cdots d_0 . d_{-1}d_{-2} \cdots d_{-m} = I_{10} . F_{10}$$

and we wish to convert it to the binary number

$$N_2 = b_{u-1}b_{u-2} \cdots b_0 . b_{-1}b_{-2} \cdots b_{-v} = I_2 . F_2$$

First, we convert the integer part of the decimal number $I_{10} = d_{n-1}d_{n-2} \cdots d_0$ to the corresponding integer part of the binary number $I_2 = b_{u-1}b_{u-2} \cdots b_0$. This is accomplished by observing that

$$I_{10} = b_{u-1}(2)^{u-1} + b_{u-2}(2)^{u-2} + \cdots + b_1 2 + b_0$$

If we divide I_{10} by 2 we find that we obtain an integer quotient Q_1 and a remainder b_0. That is

$$I_{10} = 2Q_1 + b_0$$

where

$$Q_1 = b_{u-1}(2)^{u-2} + b_{u-2}(2)^{u-3} + \cdots + b_1(2)^0$$

Next we see that if we divide Q_1 by 2 we obtain an integer quotient Q_2 and a remainder b_1. That is

$$Q_1 = 2Q_2 + b_1$$

where

$$Q_2 = b_{u-1}(2)^{u-3} + b_{u-2}(2)^{u-4} + \cdots + b_2(2)^0$$

From this we see that we can continue this process until a value of n is reached such that $Q_n = 0$. The remainder terms generated by this process are then read off as the terms of the binary integer that is equivalent to the original decimal integer.

To illustrate this process let $I_{10} = 25$. Then

$$
\begin{array}{lll}
I_{10} = 2(12) + 1 & Q_1 = 12, & b_0 = 1 \\
Q_1 = 2(6) + 0 & Q_2 = 6, & b_1 = 0 \\
Q_2 = 2(3) + 0 & Q_3 = 3, & b_2 = 0 \\
Q_3 = 2(1) + 1 & Q_4 = 1, & b_3 = 1 \\
Q_4 = 2(0) + 1 & Q_5 = 0, & b_4 = 1
\end{array}
$$

From this result we have

$$I_{10} = 25 \text{ is equivalent to } I_2 = 11001$$

This process can easily be carried out in the following form:

$$
\begin{array}{ll}
\multicolumn{2}{c}{\text{Quotients}} \\
2\,\underline{|\,25} & \\
2\,\underline{|\,12} & \text{Remainders} \\
2\,\underline{|\,6} & b_0 = 1 \\
2\,\underline{|\,3} & b_1 = 0 \\
2\,\underline{|\,1} & b_2 = 0 \\
0 & b_3 = 1 \\
 & b_4 = 1
\end{array}
$$

Thus

$$I_2 = b_4 b_3 b_2 b_1 b_0 = 11001$$

The second step is to convert the fractional part of the decimal number

$$F_{10} = d_{-1} d_{-2} \cdots d_{-m}$$

to the corresponding fractional part of the binary number,

$$F_2 = b_{-1} b_{-2} \cdots b_{-v}$$

There is one difficulty associated with the conversion of fractions that must be pointed out. We often find that a decimal fraction with a finite number of digits will produce a corresponding binary fraction that contains an infinite number of terms. This occurs because the resolution interval is different for binary and decimal numbers. In this situation we must then arbitrarily select a value for the maximum number, v, of digits that we will retain in our binary fraction.

The conversion process is accomplished by observing that

$$F_{10} = b_{-1} 2^{-1} + b_{-2} 2^{-2} + \cdots + b_{-v} 2^{-v} + \cdots$$

Thus if we multiply F_{10} by 2 we have

$$2F_{10} = b_{-1} + b_{-2}2^{-1} + \cdots + b_{-v}2^{-v+1} + \cdots = b_{-1} + C_1$$

where $C_1 < 1$ and b_{-1} is either 1 or 0. Next we multiply C_1 by 2 to obtain

$$2C_1 = b_{-2} + b_{-3}2^{-1} + \cdots + b_{-v}2^{-v+2} + \cdots = b_{-2} + C_2$$

where $C_2 < 1$ and b_{-2} is either 0 or 1. Continuing in this way we finally obtain

$$2C_{v-1} = b_{-v} + C_v$$

where $2^{-v}C_v \leq \varepsilon$ and ε is the largest error that we are willing to tolerate in our conversion process. If $C_v = 0$ for some value of v, then the conversion is exact. Otherwise the resulting binary fraction is an approximation, to within ε, of the original decimal fraction. The two following examples illustrate both situations.

Exact Conversion	Approximate Conversion

Exact Conversion

$$F_{10} = .125$$
$$2(.125) = 0 + .250$$
$$2(.25) = 0 + .5$$
$$2(.5) = 1 + .0$$
$$F_2 = .001$$

Approximate Conversion

$$\varepsilon_{10} = .001$$
$$F_{10} = .3$$
$$2(.3) = 0 + .6$$
$$2(.6) = 1 + .2$$
$$2(.2) = 0 + .4$$
$$2(.4) = 0 + .8$$
$$2(.8) = 1 + .6$$
$$2(.6) = 1 + .2$$
$$2(.2) = 0 + .4$$
$$2(.4) = 0 + .8$$
$$2(.8) = 1 + .6 \quad 2^{-9}(.6) > .001$$
$$2(.6) = 1 + .2 \quad 2^{-10}(.2) < .001$$
$$F_2 \cong .0100110011$$

In many situations it is necessary to specify a value of v that will be used independent of the number being converted. For this case we have

$$(\text{conversion error}) \leq 2^{-v}$$

Now that we have an understanding of the conversion process, the following examples illustrate how we can find the octal or hexadecimal equivalent of a decimal number. The first two examples deal with octal conversion.

Exact Conversion

$$F_{10} = 25.125$$

Integer Part	Fractional Part
8 |25	$(8)(.125) = 1 + .0$
8 |_3_ 1	
0 3	

$$F_8 = 31.1_8$$

Approximate Conversion

$$\varepsilon_{10} = .001$$
$$F_{10} = 25.3$$

Integer Part	Fractional Part
8 |25	$8(.3) = 2 + .4$
8 |_3_ 1	$8(.4) = 3 + .2$
0 3	$8(.2) = 1 + .6$
	$8(.6) = 4 + .8$

$$F_8 \cong 31.2314_8$$

The next two examples deal with the hexadecimal conversion process.

Exact Conversion   **Approximate Conversion**

$\varepsilon_{10} = .001$

$F_{10} = 25.125$ $F_{10} = 25.3$

Integer Part	Fractional Part	Integer Part	Fractional Part
16 ⌊25	$(16)(.125) = 2 + 0$	16 ⌊25	$(16)(.3) = 4 + .8$
16 ⌊1 9		16 ⌊1 9	$(16)(.8) = 12 + .8$
0 1		0 1	$(16)(.8) = 12 + .8$

$F_{16} = 19.2_{16}$ $F_{16} \cong 19.4CC_{16}$

EXERCISES

1. Encode the following numbers into binary form:
    (a) 14.62_8 1100.110010_2
    (b) 123.61_{10} (1101111) $1111011.1001110000l_2$
    (c) $A1B.F12_{16}$ $101000011011.111100010010_2$

2. Convert the following decimal numbers to their equivalent octal and hexadecimal representation:
    (a) 14.65_{10} 16.51463_8 $E.A66_{16}$
    (b) 1568.721_{10} $(0403) = 3040.5611_8$ $(026) = 620.B89$

3. Find the decimal equivalent of the following numbers:
    (a) 110101.110_2 (d) 777.77_8 a) 53.75 d.) 511.984
    (b) 111111.111_2 (e) 777.77_{16} b) 127.875 e.) 1911.4648
    (c) 656.46_8 (f) $FFF.FF_{16}$ x c.) 430.5938 f.) 4095.9961

4. Find the octal and hexadecimal representation for the following binary numbers:
    (a) 010111110101.1101 2765.6648_8 $5F5.D_{16}$
    (b) 110000011.0001 603.04_8 183.1_{16}

5. Find the binary representation for the following numbers:
    (a) 398.788_{10} (d) 777.77_8 a) $(0111000011) = 110001110.11001$
    (b) 111111.111_{10} (e) 777.77_{16} b.) (1110000000100110111)
    (c) 656.46_8 (f) $ABC.DF_{16}$ $1101100100000001111.D00111$
                          c.) 110101110.100110 d.) 1111111111.111111
                          e.) 1110110111.0110111 f.) 1010101110100.1101111

6. How many digits are required in a base r fraction if the truncation error ε_T is to be kept less than 10^{-3}? Let $r = 2, 3, 4, 5, 8, 10, 16$. $\log \varepsilon_T / \log \frac{1}{r} = m$
    $m = 10, 7, 5, 5, 4, 3, 3$

5. ENCODING OF NUMERICAL INFORMATION

The last section introduced the general properties of the binary, octal, decimal, and hexadecimal number systems. We now consider how these ideas are applied to encode numerical information into digital form.

The simplest encoding technique is to take a given number and convert it to its equivalent binary value. This binary number is then taken as the encoded digital value of that number. However, there are certain restrictions and conventions that must be kept in mind.

Binary Point Placement

If a register contains r cells, then we can only deal with binary numbers that have a maximum of r binary digits. This means that any positive decimal integer between 0 and $2^r - 1$ can be represented in an r-bit register. For example, if a 3-bit register contains [0, 1, 0], then we say that the binary number 010 corresponding to 2_{10} is stored in this register.

When dealing with general binary numbers, we do not try to encode the location of the binary point. Instead we assume that the person designing the system in which the number appears also keeps track of where the binary point should be placed and makes appropriate allowance for this whenever the encoded numeric information is used. Thus the binary numbers .101, 1.01, 10.1 and 101. are all encoded in a 3-bit register as [1, 0, 1].

Negative Numbers

If negative, as well as positive, numbers must be encoded, we must use one bit of the register to indicate the sign of the number. Thus, if we have an r-bit register, the first bit can be used as a *sign bit* and the other r-1 bits can be used to encode the value of the magnitude of the number. A 1 in the first bit indicates a negative number and a 0 in this position indicates a positive number. Such a representation is called a *signed-magnitude* representation. Table 2-6 shows the relationship between the signed-magnitude binary numbers and the decimal numbers for $r = 3$.

Generalizing on the example presented in Table 2-6 we see that an r-cell register can represent any binary number between $\pm(2^{r-1} - 1)$. In addition, we note that we have a $+0$ and a -0.

Table 2-6 Signed-Magnitude Binary Numbers and Decimal Equivalent

Binary	Decimal
000	$+0$
001	$+1$
010	$+2$
011	$+3$
100	-0
101	-1
110	-2
111	-3

There are also other methods of representing negative numbers. However, we will postpone our discussion of these methods until Chapter 5, where we discuss binary arithmetic.

Encoding Decimal Numbers

In the above section we saw that the content of a register could be treated as a binary number. However, we live in a decimal world and it is often desirable to retain the decimal character of a number even after it is encoded into digital form. To do this, various coding schemes have been developed. In this section we briefly consider typical codes that have been developed for this purpose.

To encode a decimal digit into a binary form it is necessary to use a minimum of four binary bits. Thus, if we wish to encode a decimal number with u decimal digits and still retain the identity of each digit, we must use a register that has at least $4u$-bits. These bits would be ordered as follows:

first decimal   second decimal uth decimal

digit   digit   digit

$$[x_{1,1},\ x_{1,2},\ x_{1,3},\ x_{1,4},\ \ x_{2,1},\ x_{2,2}\ ,\ x_{2,3},\ x_{2,4},\ \ldots\ ,x_{u,1},x_{u,2},x_{u,3},x_{u,4}]$$

From our previous discussion we know that there are

$$\frac{2^4!}{(2^4 - 10)!} \cong 2.9 \times 10^{10}$$

possible ways that the 10 decimal digits can be encoded as a digital 4-tuple.

The choice of a code is important and influences the design of any digital system that must operate on the numbers represented in the code. Some of the important parameters that must be considered are: ease of performing arithmetic operations, economy of storage space, economy of logic circuitry, error detection and correction, and simplicity of use. These considerations are discussed in Reference 1 listed at the end of this chapter. For this discussion we will limit ourselves to two representative coding schemes.

Weighted Codes

In a weighted code each bit of the 4-tuple $[x_1, x_2, x_3, x_4]$ is assigned a decimal value w_1, w_2, w_3, w_4 called a *weight*. The decimal number represented by a particular 4-tuple is then given by

$$N_{10} = \sum_{i=1}^{4} w_i x_i$$

One of the commonest weighted codes is the *Binary Coded Decimal* (BCD) or 8 4 2 1 code. The decimal digits in this code are represented by their 4-digit binary equivalent. This code is given in Table 2-7.

Table 2-7 BCD Code Representation of
Decimal Digits

Decimal Digit	Weight	BCD Representation 8	4	2	1
0		0	0	0	0
1		0	0	0	1
2		0	0	1	0
3		0	0	1	1
4		0	1	0	0
5		0	1	0	1
6		0	1	1	0
7		0	1	1	1
8		1	0	0	0
9		1	0	0	1

Using this table we can find the BCD representation of any decimal number. For example, the BCD representation of $N_{10} = 7954$ is

$$
\begin{array}{cccc}
7 & 9 & 5 & 4 \\
0111 & 1001 & 0101 & 0100 = 0111100101010100
\end{array}
$$

There are more than 80 possible weighted codes, 17 of which have all positive weights. Two other typical weighted codes are given in Table 2-8.

Unweighted Codes

Sometimes it is desirable, for particular design reasons, to use an unweighted encoding of the decimal numbers. One of the best known unweighted codes is the *excess* 3 code. In this code the decimal digit d is represented by the 4-bit binary number

Table 2-8 Two Typical Weighted Codes

Decimal Digit	Weight	Code 1 2	4	2	1	Code 2 7	4	−2	−1
0		0	0	0	0	0	0	0	0
1		0	0	0	1	0	1	1	1
2		0	0	1	0	0	1	1	0
3		0	0	1	1	0	1	0	1
4		0	1	0	0	0	1	0	0
5		1	0	1	1	1	0	1	0
6		1	1	0	0	1	0	0	1
7		1	1	0	1	1	0	0	0
8		1	1	1	0	1	1	1	1
9		1	1	1	1	1	1	1	0

Table 2-9 Three Unweighted Codes

(a)		(b)		(c)	
					BCD With Even
Excess 3 Code					Parity
Decimal	Coded	Decimal	Coded	Decimal	Code
Digit	Representation	Digit	Representation	Digit	8421P
0	0011	0	0001	0	00000
1	0100	1	0010	1	00011
2	0101	2	0011	2	00101
3	0110	3	0100	3	00110
4	0111	4	0101	4	01001
5	1000	5	0110	5	01010
6	1001	6	1000	6	01100
7	1010	7	1001	7	01111
8	1011	8	1010	8	10001
9	1100	9	1100	9	10010

corresponding to $d + 3$. This code has the property that every code group has at least a single 1. Table 2-9a illustrates this code.

A second example of an unweighted code is given in Table 2-9b. This code has been designed so that no code group has less than one 1 or more than two 1's. This feature is useful since there is a minimal fluctuation in the 0 and 1 values as the encoded variable changes value.

There are many codes that use more than 4 bits to represent a binary number. One of the simplest is the 5-bit even parity code. A fifth bit is introduced that is set so that the total number of 1's in the representation is even.

For example, a BCD encoding with even parity is shown in Table 2-9c. The leftmost 4 bits represent a standard BCD encoding, and the rightmost bit is the parity bit. Thus the BCD representation

$$0101 \quad \text{becomes} \quad 01010$$

since there are already an even number of 1's while

$$0111 \quad \text{becomes} \quad 01111$$

since the initial encoding has an odd number of 1's.

Reflected Numbers and the Gray Code

One of the main problems in a number system using positional notation is that, when going from one number to the next, more than one digit position may change at the same time. For example, when 0111_2 advances to 1000_2, four digits must change simultaneously. This can cause trouble in systems where we are trying to read information, such as the angle or the position of a platform, into a digital system. To

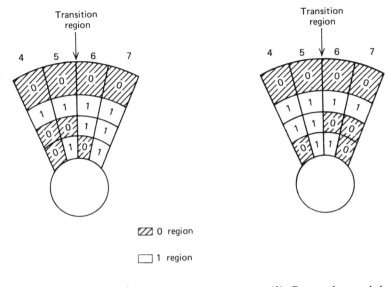

(a) BCD encoded shaft segment

(b) Gray code encoded shaft segment

Figure 2-6 Two methods of encoding shaft position.

illustrate this idea, let us assume that we must read the position of a shaft using a BCD mechanical encoder as shown in Figure 2-6a. As we pass from the 5 to the 6 region we note that the code goes from 0101 to 0110. However, the sensor that we use to measure the coded signal may have problems in the transition region, and it is entirely possible that we might read out some erroneous combination such as 0111 or 0100 while we are going from region 5 to region 6. The coding arrangement shown in Figure 2-6b gets around this problem by allowing only one digit change as we go from region to region. Thus, as we go from region 5 to region 6 the code goes from 0111 to 0101 without any possible erroneous outputs.

The above example illustrates the main feature of a reflected number system. In a reflected number system the coding is set up so that only one digit can change as we go from N to $N + 1$. The way that this is accomplished can be understood if we compare the reflected decimal and binary number systems given in Table 2-10b to the conventional decimal and binary number systems given in Table 2-10a. Examining these tables we note that in the conventional number systems each column systematically advances through the ordered sequence of symbols to the last symbol and then abruptly returns to the symbol at the head of the list. On the other hand, the reflected number system advances each column systematically through the list of ordered symbols until the end of the list is reached. At that point the column then retreats backward through the sequence of symbols rather than snapping back to the head of the list. The binary reflected number system is often called a *gray code*.

The problem of converting a gray coded number to a regular binary number and vice versa can be handled by the following algorithm. Assume that the regular binary

Table 2-10   Conventional and Reflected Decimal and Binary Number Systems

(a) Conventional Number Systems		(b) Reflected Number Systems		
Decimal	Binary	Decimal Value	Reflected Decimal	Reflected Binary
0	0	0	0	0
1	1	1	1	1
2	10	2	2	11
3	11	3	3	10
4	100	4	4	110
5	101	5	5	111
6	110	6	6	101
7	111	7	7	100
8	1000	8	8	1100
9	1001	9	9	1101
10	1010	10	19	1111
11	1011	11	18	1110
12	1100	12	17	1010
13	1101	13	16	1011
14	1110	14	15	1001
15	1111	15	14	1000
16	10000	16	13	11000

number is represented as $A_n A_{n-1} \cdots A_1$ and the gray coded number is represented as $a_n a_{n-1} \cdots a_1$. Then

1. To find a_k, add the digits A_k and A_{k+1} modulo 2 (i.e., disregard the carry). Notice that a_n always equals A_n.
2. To find A_k add a_k through a_n, divide by 2, and the remainder is A_k.

The following examples illustrate this conversion process. First consider the binary-to-gray code conversion. Let

$$A_5 A_4 A_3 A_2 A_1 = 10110$$

be a binary number. Then

$$a_5 = A_5 = 1$$
$$a_4 = A_5 + A_4 = 1 + 0 = 1$$
$$a_3 = A_4 + A_3 = 0 + 1 = 1$$
$$a_2 = A_3 + A_2 = 1 + 1 = 0 + \text{carry } 1 = 0$$
$$a_1 = A_2 + A_1 = 1 + 0 = 1$$

Thus the resulting gray coded number is

$$a_5 a_4 a_3 a_2 a_1 = 11101$$

Next consider the gray code-to-binary conversion. Let

$$a_5a_4a_3a_2a_1 = 11010$$

be a gray coded number. Then

$$A_5 = \frac{a_5}{2} = \frac{1}{2} = 0 + \text{remainder of } 1$$

$$A_4 = \frac{a_5 + a_4}{2} = \frac{2}{2} = 1 + \text{remainder of } 0$$

$$A_3 = \frac{a_5 + a_4 + a_3}{2} = \frac{2}{2} = 1 + \text{remainder of } 0$$

$$A_2 = \frac{a_5 + a_4 + a_3 + a_2}{2} = \frac{3}{2} = 1 + \text{remainder of } 1$$

$$A_1 = \frac{a_5 + a_4 + a_3 + a_2 + a_1}{2} = \frac{3}{2} = 1 + \text{remainder of } 1$$

This gives the resulting binary encoded number

$$A_5A_4A_3A_2A_1 = 10011$$

Digital-to-Analog Conversion

Since the physical world normally deals with continuous signals, there are many situations in which information contained in a digital signal must be transformed into an analog or continuous signal before it can be used. The transformation of a digital signal into an analog signal is called a *digital-to-analog* conversion or simply a D/A conversion. A device that performs this operation is called a *digital-to-analog-converter* or DAC.

There are a number of ways in which this conversion can take place. For the current discussion we assume that it can be accomplished by using a general network of the form shown in Figure 2-7. The digital information contained in the register X is processed by the DAC, which generates an analog signal that has a numerical value equal to the digital number stored in X.

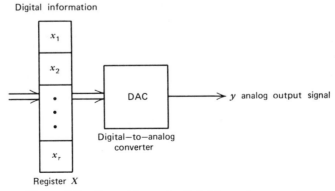

Figure 2-7 General form of a digital-to-analog converter.

The digital information to be processed is placed in the X register. For this discussion we will assume that the register represents the binary number

$$\overbrace{b_s}^{\text{sign bit}} \quad \overbrace{b_{u-1}b_{u-2} \cdots b_1 b_0}^{u \text{ bits}}.\overbrace{b_{-1}b_{-2} \cdots b_{-v}}^{v \text{ bits}}$$

where

b_s indicates the sign of the number

$\quad b_s = 0$ indicates a positive number

$\quad b_s = 1$ indicates a negative number

$b_{u-1} \cdots b_1 b_0$ represents the integer portion of the number

$b_{-1}b_{-2} \cdots b_{-v}$ represents the fractional portion of the number

The value of u and v must be selected so that

$$u + v + 1 = r$$

If $v = 0$, then there will be no fractional part of the number, and if $u = 0$, there will be no integer part of the number.

Under these assumptions the digital signal will take on a value in the range

$$\pm([2^u - 1] + [1 - 2^{-v}])$$

The output analog signal will thus assume values in the same range. Since there are only a finite number of distinct values that can be stored in the register X, the output signal will also take on only a set of discrete values. Each value will be separated by an amount equal to 2^{-v}. For example, let $u = 2$, $v = 2$, and $r = 5$. The distinct digital signals and their corresponding analog values are given in Table 2-11.

Table 2-11   An Example of a D/A Conversion

Digital Number	Analog Output	Digital Number	Analog Output
000.00	0.00	100.00	−0.00
000.01	0.25	100.01	−0.25
000.10	0.50	100.10	−0.50
000.11	0.75	100.11	−0.75
001.00	1.00	101.00	−1.00
001.01	1.25	101.01	−1.25
001.10	1.50	101.10	−1.50
001.11	1.75	101.11	−1.75
010.00	2.00	110.00	−2.00
010.01	2.25	110.01	−2.25
010.10	2.50	110.10	−2.50
010.11	2.75	110.11	−2.75
011.00	3.00	111.00	−3.00
011.01	3.25	111.01	−3.25
011.10	3.50	111.10	−3.50
011.11	3.75	111.11	−3.75

Table 2-12   Typical Values Placed in *X* Register

Time	X	Time	X
0	00001	8	10001
1	00010	9	10010
2	00011	10	10011
3	00100	11	10100
4	00011	12	10011
5	00010	13	10010
6	00001	14	10001
7	00000	15	10000

As long as the signal in the *X* register remains unchanged, the output remains at a constant value. In many applications, the digital signal will take on a sequence of values. For example, assume that the *X* register receives a new value every second. If the sequence of values given in Table 2-12 appears in the *X* register, then the output signal will have the form shown in Figure 2-8.

Examining this figure, we see that the waveform of the output approximates a sine wave. However, the approximation is quite jagged because the output must change in steps of .25 units, since only 2 bits are used in the fractional part of the number.

The difference between two successive values of the output of a digital-to-analog converter is called the *resolution* of the converter. The *range* of the converter is the distance between the most positive and the most negative value that the converter can generate. The converter in the example of Table 2-11 has a resolution of .25 and a range of 3.75 to −3.75. Many commercial digital-to-analog converters have *X*

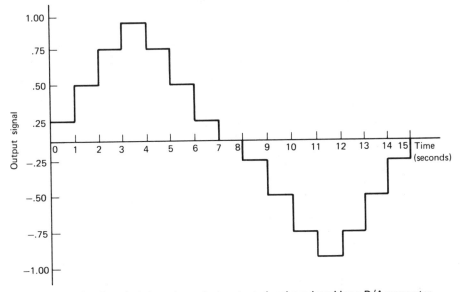

Figure 2-8   A typical time-dependent output signal produced by a D/A converter.

registers with 8 to 12 bits. In some cases, the sign bit is not used and the output is assumed to be a positive number.

Analog-to-Digital Conversion

There are many situations in which the information to be processed by a digital system is initially in continuous or analog form. Thus it is necessary to transform the analog information into digital form. This can be accomplished by using an *analog-to-digital converter* or simply an ADC or *A/D converter*.

There are a number of ways that an A/D conversion can be accomplished. For this discussion we assume that a converter can be represented as shown in Figure 2-9.

The input analog signal $s(t)$ is applied to the A/D converter, which generates a digital signal that is stored in the register X. The relationship between the input signal and the value stored in X is illustrated in Figure 2-10. In this example it is assumed that $s(t)$ will fall in the range $\pm.9$ and that the register X has 4 bits. The digital signal is also assumed to be represented in sign-magnitude form.

Quantization Error

If we examine the input/output relationship illustrated by Figure 2-10, we see that in most cases there will be a conversion error. This error comes about because we cannot exactly represent all values in the continuum $\pm.9$ by the finite number of values that can be represented by the information stored in a 4-bit register. In this example the largest error occurs when the input signal has a value halfway between two adjacent values of X. This is the point at which the value in the X register changes and the error corresponds to $\frac{1}{2}(.125) = .0625$ units.

For the general case assume that the digital signal represents the binary number

$$b_s b_{u-1} \cdots b_1 b_0 \cdot b_{-1} b_{-2} \cdots b_{-v}$$

Then the maximum error will be $\frac{1}{2}(2^{-v}) = 2-(v+1)$.

The error introduced by the digital approximation of a continuous signal is called *quantization error*. The only way to reduce this type of error is to increase the num-

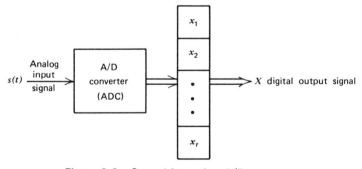

Figure 2-9   General form of an A/D converter.

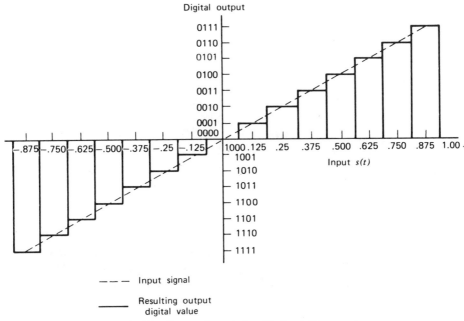

Figure 2-10   Conversion relationship for A/D converter.

ber of bits used in the representation of the digital signal. The choice of the number of bits is determined by the accuracy needed to represent $s(t)$.

Sampling

In most applications where we use A/D converters we are interested in reading the value of the signal every T seconds. Thus the output will be a series of values. This process is called *sampling* the input signal.

For example, assume that the input signal given by

$$s(t) = \sin \omega t$$

where

$$\omega = 12 \text{ radians per second}$$

is to be sampled 11 times in the time interval 0 to 20 seconds. In this case, $T = 2$ and the samples are taken for

$$t = nT \qquad n = 0, 1, \ldots, 10$$

Table 2-13 gives the value of $s(t)$ at these sample points and the corresponding digital value in the output register X. It is assumed that X is a 5-bit register that has a 3-bit fraction part, a 1-bit integer part, and a sign bit.

A graphical interpretation of the information in Table 2-13 is given in Figure 2-11. Note that the value of the input signal will change between the sampling points while the value of the digital signal in the output X register remains constant during

Table 2-13   Sampled Values of sin 12*t*

n	*nT*	sin 15*nT*	*X(nT)*
0	0	0.000	00000
1	2	0.50	00100
2	4	0.866	00111
3	6	1.000	01000
4	8	0.866	00111
5	10	0.50	00100
6	12	0.000	00000
7	14	−0.500	10100
8	16	−0.866	10111
9	18	−1.000	11000
10	20	−0.866	10111

the time between samples. A much more comprehensive discussion of the sampling process and how it influences the accuracy of the information being used in a given information processing task can be found in Reference 3 listed at the end of this chapter.

EXERCISES

1. Find the BCD representation of 145.64_{10}.

2. Find the gray code representation of the following binary numbers:
   (a) 10110101_2
   (b) 11111111_2

3. Encode the following decimal numbers using the 2 4 2 1 and the 7 4 −2 −1 weighted codes.
   (a)   78934
   (b)   345.665

4. Encode the decimal numbers of exercise 3 using the excess 3 code and the BCD code with even parity.

5. What is the range and resolution of a DAC if $u = 4$ and $v = 8$?

6. The following values were placed in a 6-bit X register of a DAC.

   $$100100$$
   $$110101$$
   $$010111$$
   $$001010$$
   $$101111$$

   For each value, what will be the value of the output signal for $v = 0, 1, 3, 5$?

7. An analog signal with a range of ±5 units must be converted to a digital signal

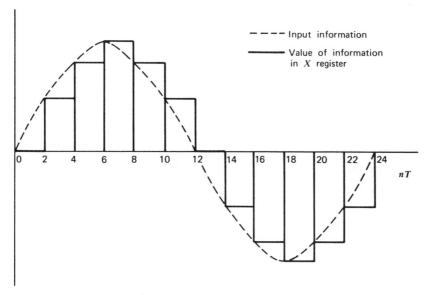

Figure 2-11 Graphical interpretation of the sampling process.

with a quantization error of less than $\pm.01$. How many bits are needed in the output register of the A/D converter?

8. Assume that the signal $s(t)$ given below is to be converted to digital form using an A/D converter that has a 6-bit output register. Let the sampling interval be 1 second. Compute the first 10 output values of the output signal.

$$s(t) = .5 \cos \omega t \qquad \omega = 10 \text{ radians/sec}$$

6. SUMMARY

All information found in a digital system must be represented in binary form. This chapter has presented a summary of the common methods that may be used to represent both numerical and nonnumerical information. Throughout the rest of this book it is assumed that any information under investigation has already been reduced to a suitable digital representation.

In the next chapter we investigate how the different types of digital signals introduced in this chapter can be processed to form new information. Once we have developed an understanding of what operations we might wish to perform on digital information, we can then investigate the techniques that are used to actually perform these operations.

Reference Notation

The paper by Gardner [2] provides a very interesting and informative discussion of why various number systems have been used as civilization evolved. Many modern texts do not provide a comprehensive discussion of the different number systems and coding methods that have been considered as computer systems were developed. The book by Chu [1] provides a comprehensive coverage of this material as it applies to computer design, and Knuth [4] presents a detailed discussion of the theoretical foundation of much of the material presented in this text. The tutorial sequence by Jaeger [3] provides a comprehensive discussion of the A/D and D/A processes found in a wide range of digital systems.

REFERENCES

1. Chu, Y. (1962), *Digital Computer Design Fundamentals*. McGraw-Hill, New York.
2. Gardner, M. (1968), "Counting Systems and Their Relationship Between Numbers and the Real World." *Scientific American,* Vol. 219, No. 3, pp. 218–230, September.
3. Jaeger, R. C. (1982), "Tutorial: Analog Data Acquisition Technology." "Part I—Digital-to-Analog Converters." "Part II—Analog-to-Digital Converters." "Part III—Sample-and-Hold, Instrumentation Amplifiers, and Analog Multiplexers." *IEEE Micro,* Vol. 2, No. 2, 3, 4, May, August, November.
4. Knuth, D. E. (1969), *The Art of Computer Programming,* Vol. 1. Addison-Wesley, Reading, Mass.

HOME PROBLEMS

1. The ternary number system uses 0, 1, 2 as the basic digits to represent a number.
   (a)   Define the basic operations of addition, subtraction, multiplication, and division for the ternary number system.
   (b)   Let

$$A = 110221 \quad \text{and} \quad B = 100212$$

be two ternary numbers. Show how to compute

$$A + B \quad A - B \quad A*B \quad A/B$$

2. (a)   Develop an algorithm that can be used to convert a ternary number directly to an octal number.
   (b)   Develop an algorithm that can be used to convert an octal number directly to a ternary number.

3. The output voltage, v_p, of a pressure transducer has a range of 0 to 2.5 volts. This voltage is to be converted to a binary number, using an analog-to-digital converter, before it is transmitted to a central computer for processing. If the maximum allowable error in indicating v_p must be kept below .1 volt, how many bits must the binary number have in order to represent v_p to the desired degree of precision?

4. Prove that the largest truncation error in a base r system is bounded by

$$\varepsilon_{T_{10}} = (1/r)^m$$

HINT: $1 + a + a^2 + a^3 + \cdots = 1/(1 - a)$ if $|a| < 1$.

5. Although 4 bits are adequate to code a decimal digit, several codes with more than 4 bits are often used in digital systems to simplify logic circuitry or to make it easy to carry out special operations. Derive the code tables for the following codes.
    (a)   The 5 4 3 2 1 0 code. The leftmost bit determines whether the digit is 5 or greater and a single 1 is placed in one of the other 5 bits to determine the complete value of the digit. This is a weighted code.
    (b)   The 5 1 1 1 1 code. The leftmost bit determines whether the digit is 5 or greater and the number and position of the 1's in the other 4 bits determine the rest of the value of the digit. This is a weighted code. How many different ways can this code be defined?

6. When digital data are transmitted between two points in a system, random errors due to noise may occur. Since the presence of an error can lead to the malfunction of the system, digital information is often encoded in a way that allows the system to detect when a single error has occurred.
    One such code is the odd parity check code. If the original digital signal has n bits, then the transmitted signal has $n + 1$ bits. The extra bit is set to 1 if there are an even number of 1's in the first n bits. Otherwise this bit is set equal to zero.
    (a)   Find the parity check code for the 2, 4, 2, 1 code of Table 2-8.
    (b)   An error in transmission of the signal is detected by counting the number of 1's in the received signal. It is known that an odd number of 1's is always transmitted. If the received signal has an even number of 1's, then this indicates that a transmission error has occurred. Is it possible to locate which bit is in error? Explain your answer using an example.

7. Develop an algorithm that can be used to directly calculate the decimal value of a reflected binary number. For example, if the algorithm is given the value 1000, it would produce 15 as the resulting decimal value.

8. For the ASCII code given in Appendix A develop
    (a)   An algorithm that will convert an uppercase letter to a lowercase letter.
    (b)   An algorithm that will detect if the coded character is a number.
    (c)   An algorithm that will detect if the coded character is NOT a letter or a number.

3

BASIC LOGIC OPERATIONS AND SCALAR FUNCTIONS

1.   INTRODUCTION

By itself a digital signal X represented by the r-tuple $[x_1, x_2, \ldots, x_r]$ has limited usefulness. However, when we operate on this signal to form a signal Y, represented by the k-tuple $[y_1, y_2, \ldots, y_k]$, we perform one of the initial steps in the information processing process. Such an information processing task can be assumed to be performed by a logic network as shown in Figure 3-1. If, in addition, we assume that this network does not contain any memory, then the current value of the output, $[y_1, y_2, \ldots, y_k]$, depends only on the current value of the input, $[x_1, x_2, \ldots, x_r]$. Logic networks with this property are called *combinational logic networks*.

The relationship between the input and the individual scalar signals y_i that make up the output vector Y is determined by a set of scalar functions $f_j(x_1, x_2, \ldots, x_r)$. In this chapter we examine the basic properties of these functions and show how any scalar function can be represented in terms of a set of fundamental logic operations. Using these results, we then consider some of the different ways in which these operations and functions are realized using standard integrated circuit logic networks. These representation techniques are used throughout the rest of this book as we investigate the properties of a wide variety of digital systems.

2.   REPRESENTATION OF BASIC LOGIC OPERATIONS AND SCALAR FUNCTIONS

As illustrated in Figure 3-1, scalar functions play a key role in representing the properties of combinational logic networks. During most logic design efforts we first define the set of functions that represent a given network and then realize these functions using a set of standard logic elements. This section presents the mathematical modeling techniques used to describe these functions.

58

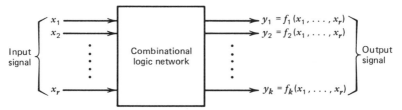

Figure 3-1 General representation of a combinational logic network.

Binary-valued Scalar Functions

Assume that we are given the vector X represented by the ordered r-tuple $[x_1, x_2, \ldots, x_r]$ of r binary variables. There are 2^r distinct values that such an r-tuple can assume. We define a *binary-valued scalar function*

$$f(x_1, x_2, \ldots, x_r) = f(X)$$

of the binary variables $[x_1, x_2, \ldots, x_r]$ to be a unique correspondence that associates a value of either 0 or 1 to each of the 2^r possible values that the r-tuple $[x_1, x_2, \ldots, x_r]$ can take on. For example, assume that $r = 3$. Then $f(0, 1, 1) = 0$ might be the correspondence that we select for the specific value $[0, 1, 1]$.

A number of ways can be used to represent a particular scalar function. The correspondence can be given by listing, in tabular form, all of the possible values of the arguments and the value of the function associated with each such value. The function can also be expressed as a mathematical expression involving the r variables and a set of basic logical operations. We now explore both types of representations.

Truth Tables

One way to describe a scalar function $f(x_1, x_2, \ldots, x_r)$ is to list $[x_1, x_2, \ldots, x_r]$ and the corresponding value of $f(x_1, x_2, \ldots, x_r)$ for each of the 2^r distinct values of the r-tuple $[x_1, x_2, \ldots, x_r]$. Such a listing is called a *truth table* representation of the scalar function $f(x_1, x_2, \ldots, x_r)$. Table 3-1 illustrates how a truth table can be used to represent a typical function when $r = 3$.

Expanding this example to the general case we see that a truth table associated with r variables has 2^r rows. The value of the function associated with each row can be either 0 or 1. Combining these observations we see that there are $(2)^{2^r}$ possible scalar functions of r-variables. Obviously, as r becomes large it is impractical to list all of the possible functions. Fortunately, it is possible to represent any function as a mathematical expression involving a small set of logical operations.

Logical Operations

Some scalar functions occur so often that we give them special names. Such functions are called *logical operators* and the task performed by the function is called a *logical operation.*

Table 3-1   Truth Table (Tabular Representation) of a
Particular Scalar Function

	x_1	x_2	x_3	$f(x_1, x_2, x_3)$	
All possible 3-tuples listed in order of increasing binary value	0	0	0	0	Corresponding value of function
	0	0	1	1	
	0	1	0	1	
	0	1	1	0	
	1	0	0	1	
	1	0	1	0	
	1	1	1	0	
	1	1	1	1	

A logical operator involving only one variable or operand is called a *unary operation,* while a logical operator involving two operands is called a *binary operation.* We could continue is this manner and talk about general *k*-nary operations that would involve *k* operands. However, as we will soon see, any scalar function can be represented using only unary and binary operators.

When we write down an operator and its associated operands, we use *infix notation,* which has the following form:

unary operation   ⟨operator⟩⟨operand⟩
binary operation   ⟨operand⟩⟨operator⟩⟨operand⟩

We now define one unary operation and six binary operations that can be used to construct a formal mathematical description of any binary scalar function of *r* variables.

Unary Operations

The four possible scalar functions of one variable are listed in Table 3-2. Two of these functions,

$$f_1(x) = 0 \quad \text{and} \quad f_4(x) = 1$$

correspond to the functions that take on a constant value independent of the value of the variable *x*. The function

$$f_2(x) = x$$

is simply the *identity function.*

Table 3-2   Unary Function

$[x]$	$f_1(x) = 0$	$f_2(x) = x$	$f_3(x) = \bar{x}$	$f_4(x) = 1$
0	0	0	1	1
1	0	1	0	1

The function $f_3(x)$ is much more interesting. Examining this operation we see that $f_3(x)$ has a value that is opposite to the value of x. For example, assume that x represents the statement

"The door is open."

When this statement is TRUE, x has a value of 1 and when the statement is FALSE, x has a value of 0.

If we apply the function $f_3(x)$ to the statement x, we create the new statement

"The door is *NOT* open"

since when $x = 1$ then $f_3(x) = 0$, and when $x = 0$, $f_3(x) = 1$.

Because of this, we say that the function $f_3(x)$ represents the unary logical operation NOT. This operation can be formally defined as follows where the names in parenthesis indicate other commonly used names for this operation.

NOT (negation, complement) *Operation*

$$f(x) = \overline{x}$$

x	$f(x)$
0	1
1	0

Alternate notation $f(x) = \neg x$, $f(x) = x'$

As we will soon see the NOT operation is a very important logical operation.

Binary Operations

If we let $r = 2$, then there are 16 possible functions of the form

$$f(x_1, x_2) = x_1 \langle \text{operator} \rangle x_2$$

that can be defined. Six of these functions are used so often that we give them special names and include them in our set of basic binary operators. These operations, together with the NOT operation, make up the set of basic logic operations that we can use to define arbitrary scalar functions of r variables.

The following listing formally describes the six binary operations of interest. This listing defines each operation in terms of a truth table description, gives the notational representation that we use to indicate the operation, and gives the name (or names) commonly associated with the operation.

AND Operation (Logical Product)

$$f(x_1, x_2) = x_1 \wedge x_2 = x_1 x_2$$

(Both notations are used extensively in following discussions.)

This operation gives a value of 1 if and only if both x_1 and x_2 equal 1.
Alternate notation $x_1 \cdot x_2$.
The notation $x_1 \cdot x_2$ is reserved in this book to indicate the arithmetic multiplication of numbers.

x_1	x_2	$x_1 \wedge x_2$
0	0	0
0	1	0
1	0	0
1	1	1

OR Operation (Logical Sum, Inclusive OR)

$f(x_1, x_2) = x_1 \vee x_2$
This operation gives a value of 1 if *either* x_1
or x_2 or *both* are equal to 1.
Alternate notation $x_1 + x_2$.
The notation $x_1 + x_2$ is reserved in this book
to indicate the arithmetic sum of two
numbers.

x_1	x_2	$x_1 \vee x_2$
0	0	0
0	1	1
1	0	1
1	1	1

EXCLUSIVE OR Operation

$f(x_1, x_2) = x_1 \oplus x_2$
This operation gives a value of 1 if either x_1
or x_2 but not both equal 1

x_1	x_2	$x_1 \oplus x_2$
0	0	0
0	1	1
1	0	1
1	1	0

COINCIDENCE

$f(x_1, x_2) = x_1 \odot x_2$
The output is 1 if and only if both x_1
and x_2 have the same value

x_1	x_2	$x_1 \odot x_2$
0	0	1
0	1	0
1	0	0
1	1	1

NAND Operation (Sheffer Stroke)

$f(x_1, x_2) = x_1 \uparrow x_2$
This operation equals 1 unless x_1
and x_2 equal 1.
Alternate notation $x_1 | x_2$ $\overline{x_1 x_2}$.

x_1	x_2	$x_1 \uparrow x_2$
0	0	1
0	1	1
1	0	1
1	1	0

NOR Operation (Pierce Arrow)

$f(x_1, x_2) = x_1 \downarrow x_2$
This operation equals 1 if and only
if both x_1 and x_2 equal 0.
Alternate notation $\overline{(x_1 \vee x_2)}$.

x_1	x_2	$x_1 \downarrow x_2$
0	0	1
0	1	0
1	0	0
1	1	0

These basic operations can now be used to define the more complex functions of r
variables.

Composition of Functions

So far we have been taking the operands of the operations to be arbitrary variables.
However, a function is itself a binary variable so any operand in an operation can be
replaced by an arbitrary function. For example, if $f(x_1, x_2, \ldots, x_r)$, $g(y_1, y_2, \ldots,$

y_k), and $h(z_1, z_2)$ are three functions, then $h[f(x_1, x_2, \ldots, x_r), g(y_1, y_2, \ldots, y_k)]$ is also a function. The resulting function is said to be the *composition* of the two functions f and g by the function h.

To illustrate this idea let

$$f(x_1, x_2) = x_1 \oplus x_2$$
$$g(x_2, x_3) = x_2 \downarrow x_3$$
$$h(z_1, z_2) = z_1 \vee z_3$$

Then

$$h[f(x_1, x_2), g(x_2, x_3)] = h(x_1, x_2, x_3) = (x_1 \oplus x_2) \vee (x_2 \downarrow x_3)$$

From this example we see that it is very easy to generate rather complex functions. In fact, any function of r variables can be represented by an expression involving only the operations of AND, OR, and NOT. However, before we can prove this assertion we must further examine some of the basic properties of composite functions.

Evaluation of Composite Functions

The value of a composite function, $f(x_1, x_2, \ldots, x_r)$ for particular values of $[x_1, x_2, \ldots, x_r]$ can be obtained by substituting these values in the expression describing the function and then carrying out the indicated operations.

As in any mathematical system, the order in which operations are performed is important. If we include parentheses around all pairs of terms in an expression that are to be operated on by a given operator, we have no problem in determining the order in which the operators are to be applied. For example, the expression

$$f(x_1, x_2, x_3) = (x_1 \uparrow x_2) \oplus (x_2 \downarrow x_3)$$

is evaluated by first evaluating $y_1 = x_1 \uparrow x_2$ and $y_2 = x_2 \downarrow x_3$. These results are then used to finally evaluate

$$f(x_1, x_2, x_3) = y_1 \oplus y_2$$

Thus if $[x_1, x_2, x_3] = [1, 1, 0]$, then

$$y_1 = 1 \uparrow 1 = 0 \qquad y_2 = 1 \downarrow 0 = 0$$

and

$$f(x_1, x_2, x_3) = 0 \oplus 0 = 0$$

As long as we are dealing with expressions that involve the EXCLUSIVE OR, NAND, or NOR operations, it is best to use parentheses to indicate the two operands that the particular operator operates on. However, in digital logic design most expressions that we work with involve only the operations of AND, OR, and NOT. If we were to include parentheses around all the pairs of terms in an expression that are to be operated on by an operator, we would have a very cumbersome expression. To overcome this problem a set of rules has been established to indicate the *prece-*

dence or order in which these logical operations are to be applied. These rules are as follows.

1. Evaluation of logical expressions without parentheses is accomplished by first applying all instances of the NOT operation to variables in a left-to-right order, then applying all instances of the AND operation in a left-to-right order, and then applying all instances of the OR operation in a left-to-right order.
2. If parentheses are present, this evaluation procedure is applied within the parentheses, and the resulting value entered as an evaluated variable in further evaluation.
3. The NOT operator applied over an expression has the effect of enclosing the expression in parentheses.

$$\text{For example, } \overline{x_1 x_2} \lor x_3 \text{ is equivalent to } \overline{(x_1 x_2)} \lor x_3$$

4. When in doubt, always use parentheses to establish the proper order of evaluation.

To illustrate how these rules are applied, let us assume that we wish to evaluate

$$f(x_1, x_2, x_3, x_4) = \overline{(\overline{x_1 x_4} \lor \overline{x_1} x_3)} x_2 \lor x_1 x_2 x_4 \lor \overline{x_1} x_2 x_3$$

for $x_1 = 0$, $x_2 = 1$, $x_3 = 0$, and $x_4 = 1$.
First we evaluate $\overline{x_1 x_4}$, which gives $\overline{x_1 x_4} = 1$. Then the term $\overline{(1 \lor \overline{x_1} x_3)}$ gives 0. Finally we evaluate the whole expression by performing the NOT operation first, then the AND operations, and finally the OR operation. The resulting value is

$$f(x_1, x_2, x_3, x_4) = 0$$

These rules give rise to the following widely used conventions. When dealing with a sequence of AND operations such as

$$x_1 \land (x_2 \land x_3) \qquad \text{or} \qquad x_1(x_2 x_3)$$

we can omit the parentheses to give

$$x_1 \land x_2 \land x_3 \qquad \text{or} \qquad x_1 x_2 x_3$$

Similarly

$$(x_1 x_2 x_3) \lor ((x_1 \overline{x_2} x_3) \lor (\overline{x_1} \overline{x_2} \overline{x_3}))$$

can be written as

$$x_1 x_2 x_3 \lor x_1 \overline{x_2} x_3 \lor \overline{x_1} \overline{x_2} \overline{x_3}$$

The algebraic properties of these operations are discussed in greater detail in Chapter 4.

The truth table associated with any composite function can be computed by direct enumeration. For example, assume that we wish to create the truth table for the following function

$$f(x_1, x_2, x_3) = (x_1 \overline{x_2} \oplus x_3) \odot (x_1 \lor x_3)$$

To create the truth table we could use a brute force approach and compute each value directly. However, when we are trying to do this task by hand, it is often easier to break the evaluation into stages. The following truth table illustrates one way that we might do this for the above function.

x_1	x_2	x_3	$x_1\bar{x}_2$	$(x_1\bar{x}_2 \oplus x_3)$	$(x_1 \vee x_3)$	$f(x_1, x_2, x_3)$
0	0	0	0	0	0	1
0	0	1	0	1	1	1
0	1	0	0	0	0	1
0	1	1	0	1	1	1
1	0	0	1	1	1	1
1	0	1	1	0	1	0
1	1	0	0	0	1	0
1	1	1	0	1	1	1

Logical Equivalence of Functions

Two functions $f(x_1, \ldots, x_r)$ and $g(x_1, \ldots, x_r)$ defined for the same arguments are *logically equivalent* if and only if

$$f(x_1, \ldots, x_r) = g(x_1, \ldots, x_r)$$

for all possible combinations of the r-tuple $[x_1, \ldots, x_r]$. This is one of the situations where the idea of a truth table representation of a function is very handy. All that we have to do to show that two functions are equivalent is to form the truth table for both functions and see if they compare. If they compare then the two functions are logically equivalent. Otherwise, they are not. The following example illustrates this idea.

Let

$$f(x_1, x_2, x_3) = (x_1 \oplus x_2)(x_2 \vee x_3)$$

$$g(x_1, x_2, x_3) = \bar{x}_1 x_2 \bar{x}_3 \vee \bar{x}_1 x_2 x_3 \vee x_1 \bar{x}_2 x_3$$

The following truth table compares these two functions.

x_1	x_2	x_3	$x_1 \oplus x_2$	$x_2 \vee x_3$	$f(x_1, x_2, x_3)$	$\bar{x}_1 x_2 \bar{x}$	$\bar{x}_1 x_2 x_3$	$x_1 \bar{x}_2 x_3$	$g(x_1, x_2, x_3)$
0	0	0	0	0	0	0	0	0	0
0	0	1	0	1	0	0	0	0	0
0	1	0	1	1	1	1	0	0	1
0	1	1	1	1	1	0	1	0	1
1	0	0	1	0	0	0	0	0	0
1	0	1	1	1	1	0	0	1	1
1	1	0	0	1	0	0	0	0	0
1	1	1	0	1	0	0	0	0	0

Thus we see that $f(x_1, x_2, x_3)$ and $g(x_1, x_2, x_3)$ are logically equivalent.
Similarly we show that $f(x_1, \ldots, x_r)$ is not logically equivalent to $g(x_1, \ldots, x_r)$

by finding one possible value of the r-tuple $[x_1, \ldots, x_r]$ for which the two functions are not equal.

For example

$$(x_1 \odot x_2) \lor x_3$$

is not equivalent to

$$(x_1 \oplus x_2) \land x_3$$

since if $[x_1, x_2, x_3] = [0, 0, 0]$ then

$$(0 \odot 0) \lor 0 = 1$$

but

$$(0 \oplus 0) \land 0 = 0$$

which proves that the two functions are not equivalent.

EXERCISES

1. Show that
    (a) $x_1 \downarrow x_2 = \overline{(x_1 \lor x_2)} = \bar{x}_1 \bar{x}_2$
    (b) $x_1 \uparrow x_2 = \overline{(x_1 \land x_2)} = \bar{x}_1 \lor \bar{x}_2$
    (c) $x_1 \land x_2 = ((\overline{x_1 x_2})(\overline{x_1 x_2}))$
    (d) $(x_1 \lor x_2) \lor x_3 = x_1 \lor (x_2 \lor x_3)$
    (e) $(x_1 \land x_2) \land x_3 = x_1 \land (x_2 \land x_3)$

2. Show that $f(x_1, x_2, x_3, x_4) = g(x_1, x_2, x_3, x_4)$ if

    $$f(x_1, x_2, x_3, x_4) = (x_1 \lor x_3 \lor \overline{x}_2)(x_1 \lor x_3 \lor \overline{x}_4)$$
    $$g(x_1, x_2, x_3, x_4) = x_1 \lor x_3 \lor \overline{x}_2\overline{x}_4$$

3. Let $g(x_1, x_2) = \overline{(\overline{x_1 x_2} \lor \overline{x_1})}$

    $$f(x_2, x_3) = (x_2 \lor x_3) \uparrow (x_2 x_3)$$
    $$h(y_1, y_2) = y_1 y_2 \lor \bar{y}_1 \bar{y}_2$$

    Find the truth table for

    $$m(x_1, x_2, x_3) = h[g(x_1, x_2), f(x_2, x_3)]$$

3. CANONICAL FORMS OF SCALAR FUNCTIONS

In the last section we introduced a number of basic logic operations and showed how they could be used to form scalar functions. We also saw that once such a function was defined it was a straightforward matter to translate the function into a truth table. To complete our discussion we now show that any truth table can be represented by a scalar function that involves only the operations of AND, OR, and NOT.

Minterms and Maxterms

Before considering the general problem, we define two special classes of functions. Let us assume that we are dealing with a function of the r-tuple

$$[x_1, x_2, \ldots, x_r]$$

A *product term* is a function that is defined to be the logical AND (logical product) of a set of terms that are either variables x_i or their negation $\bar{x}_i$. No variable can appear more than once in a product term. For example, if $r = 5$ three typical product terms would be

$$x_1\bar{x}_2x_3x_4\bar{x}_5, \qquad \bar{x}_1\bar{x}_2x_4x_5, \qquad x_3x_4$$

A product term in which all variables appear once and only once is called a *minterm*. Some typical minterms for $r = 5$ are

$$x_1x_2x_3x_4x_5, \qquad x_1\bar{x}_2x_3x_4x_5, \qquad x_1x_2x_3\bar{x}_4\bar{x}_5$$

The reason that these terms are called minterms is that they have a value of 1 for only one of the 2^r possible values of the r-tuple $[x_1, \ldots, x_r]$ and zero for all other values. The following truth table illustrates the form of three typical minterms.

Row Number	x_1	x_2	x_3	$m_7 = x_1x_2x_3$	$m_5 = x_1\bar{x}_2x_3$	$m_1 = \bar{x}_1\bar{x}_2x_3$
0	0	0	0	0	0	0
1	0	0	1	0	0	1
2	0	1	0	0	0	0
3	0	1	1	0	0	0
4	1	0	0	0	0	0
5	1	0	1	0	1	0
6	1	1	0	0	0	0
7	1	1	1	1	0	0

In the above table we have assigned decimal row numbers to each row of the table corresponding to the binary number represented by the input combination associated with the row. These decimal numbers can be used to indicate particular minterms. If we wish to obtain a minterm that has a value of 1 in row d, all that we need do is convert d to its equivalent binary number and then express this number in logical form. This minterm is indicated as m_d. To accomplish this we let each 1 value indicate the unnegated form of the variable and each 0 its negated form. For example let $r = 3$. Then

$$m_7 = x_1x_2x_3 \quad \text{because} \quad 7_{10} = 1\ 1\ 1_2$$
$$m_5 = x_1\bar{x}_2x_3 \quad \text{because} \quad 5_{10} = 1\ 0\ 1_2$$
$$m_1 = \bar{x}_1\bar{x}_2x_3 \quad \text{because} \quad 1_{10} = 0\ 0\ 1_2$$

Note that $m_7 = 1$ if and only if $x_1 = 1$ and $x_2 = 1$ and $x_3 = 1$. Similarly $m_5 = 1$ if and only if $x_1 = 1$ and $x_2 = 0$ and $x_3 = 1$. (How about m_1?)

A *sum term* is a function that is defined to be the logical OR (logical sum) of a set of terms that are either variables x_i or their negation $\overline{x}_i$. No variable can appear more than once in a sum term. For example, if $r = 5$, three typical sum terms would be

$$x_1 \lor \overline{x}_2 \lor x_3 \qquad x_1 \lor x_2 \lor x_3 \lor x_4 \qquad x_1 \lor x_5$$

A sum term in which all variables appear once and only once is called a *maxterm*. Some typical maxterms for $r = 5$ are

$$(x_1 \lor x_2 \lor x_3 \lor x_4 \lor x_5) \qquad (\overline{x}_1 \lor x_2 \lor x_3 \lor \overline{x}_4 \lor \overline{x}_5)$$

The reason that these terms are called maxterms is that they have a value of 0 for only one of the 2^r possible values of the r-tuple $[x_1, \ldots, x_r]$ and 1 for all other values. The truth table below illustrates the form of three typical maxterms.

To indicate a maxterm we can also make use of row numbers. In this case the row number is used to indicate the row in which the 0 value of the term is to appear. Thus we must convert the binary number corresponding to that row into a sum term that has a value of zero when evaluated using these values for the variables.

Row Number	x_1	x_2	x_3	$M_7 = (\overline{x}_1 \lor \overline{x}_2 \lor \overline{x}_3)$	$M_5 = (\overline{x}_1 \lor x_2 \lor \overline{x}_3)$	$M_1 = (x_1 \lor x_2 \lor \overline{x}_3)$
0	0	0	0	1	1	1
1	0	0	1	1	1	0
2	0	1	0	1	1	1
3	0	1	1	1	1	1
4	1	0	0	1	1	1
5	1	0	1	1	0	1
6	1	1	0	1	1	1
7	1	1	1	0	1	1

To accomplish this we let each 0 value indicate the unnegated form of the variable and each 1 value indicate the negated form of the variable. The maxterm corresponding to row d is indicated* as M_d. For example, let $r = 3$. Then

$$M_7 = (\overline{x}_1 \lor \overline{x}_2 \lor \overline{x}_3) \quad \text{because} \quad 7_{10} = 1\ 1\ 1_2$$
$$M_5 = (\overline{x}_1 \lor x_2 \lor \overline{x}_3) \quad \text{because} \quad 5_{10} = 1\ 0\ 1_2$$
$$M_1 = (x_1 \lor x_2 \lor \overline{x}_3) \quad \text{because} \quad 1_{10} = 0\ 0\ 1_2$$

Note that $M_7 = 0$ if and only if $x_1 = 1$, $x_2 = 1$, $x_3 = 1$.

---

*Normally lowercase letters are used to represent scalar values. However, long usage has established the special convention that maxterms are represented by uppercase Ms. This convention is used in this book and should not cause any difficulty.

Canonical Representation of Logic Expressions

Now that we have defined the concept of a minterm and a maxterm, we can use these functions as a set of basic building blocks to represent any arbitrary function that is described by a truth table. The following example illustrates how we can do this.

Assume that a function $f(x_1, x_2, x_3)$ is given by the following truth table and we wish to obtain an expression that describes this function. Examining this truth table

Row Number	x_1	x_2	x_3	$f(x_1, x_2, x_3)$
0	0	0	0	0
1	0	0	1	1
2	0	1	0	0
3	0	1	1	1
4	1	0	0	0
5	1	0	1	1
6	1	1	0	0
7	1	1	1	1

we see that the function takes on a value of 1 in row 1 *or* row 3 *or* row 5 *or* row 7. Therefore, we can represent this function as

$$f(x_1, x_2, x_3) = m_1 \vee m_3 \vee m_5 \vee m_7 = \bar{x}_1\bar{x}_2x_3 \vee \bar{x}_1x_2x_3 \vee x_1\bar{x}_2x_3 \vee x_1x_2x_3$$

This function is said to be represented in the *canonical sum-of-product form* or *disjunctive normal form*. Any binary function can be represented by a unique canonical sum-of-product expression.

A second way to represent a function in a canonical form is to use *maxterms*. Suppose we wish to represent $f(x_1, x_2, x_3)$ in this manner. We note that this function is 0 for row 0 *and* row 2 *and* row 4 *and* row 6. Therefore we can represent this function as

$$f(x_1, x_2, x_3) = M_0 \wedge M_2 \wedge M_4 \wedge M_6$$

This function is said to be represented in the *canonical product-of-sum form* or *conjunctive normal form*. Any binary function can also be represented by a unique canonical product-of-sum expression.

The above discussion has shown that any function of r variables can be represented in terms of the AND, OR, and NOT operations. Therefore, we can conclude that we do not need to introduce any other special operations to represent any function in terms of a logical expression.

EXERCISES

1. For $r = 4$ find the following minterms and maxterms:

$$m_0, m_1, m_2, m_4, m_{11}, m_{13}, m_{15}$$
$$M_0, M_1, M_2, M_4, M_{11}, M_{13}, M_{15}$$

2. Find the canonical sum-of-product and product-of-sum representation for the following truth table.

x_1	x_2	x_3	x_4	$f(x_1, x_2, x_3, x_4)$
0	0	0	0	1
0	0	0	1	1
0	0	1	0	0
0	0	1	1	0
0	1	0	0	1
0	1	0	1	0
0	1	1	0	1
0	1	1	1	1
1	0	0	0	0
1	0	0	1	0
1	0	1	0	0
1	0	1	1	1
1	1	0	0	0
1	1	0	1	1
1	1	1	0	1
1	1	1	1	0

3. Show the canonical forms for the binary operations
   (a) $x_1 \uparrow x_2$
   (b) $x_1 \downarrow x_2$
   (c) $x_1 \oplus x_2$

4.   LOGIC CIRCUIT REPRESENTATION

Up until this point we have considered the general problem of modeling digital signals and the various types of operations that can be performed on these signals. This discussion has concentrated on the various ways that the information could be represented in digital form without concern for the physical form that these signals might take in a digital system. In this section we consider two questions:

1. What are some of the typical physical forms used to represent digital information?
2. What symbolic representations are used to indicate the basic logic operations?

The next section will consider some of the typical integrated circuit logic elements that are commercially available and can be used to realize scalar functions of the type we have been considering.

Logic Circuit Symbols

When we talk about a network, we need a set of symbols that can be used to describe the logic circuit elements that perform the basic operations used to realize a logic network. At one time several different sets of logic circuit symbols were used in the

Table 3-3 Standard Logic Circuit Symbols

Operation	Symbol
NOT (Inversion)	
AND	
OR	
NAND	
NOR	
EXCLUSIVE OR	
COINCIDENCE	or

literature. A set of standard symbols has now been established to represent the basic logic operations (military service standard MIL-STD-8063, American National Standard ANSI Y32.14-1973). The symbols used in this book are given in Table 3-3 and correspond to this standard.

The standard multiple input logic elements are often called *gates*. Thus one might speak of an AND gate, an OR gate, or a NAND gate when talking about a particular hardware element used in a circuit. The NOT logic element is usually called an *inverter*.

The basic elements can easily be expanded to account for any number of inputs. For example, assume that we have the logic expression

$$f(x, y, z) = xy \lor \overline{x}\overline{z} \lor x\overline{y}z$$

This expression can be realized by the network shown in Figure 3-2a if it is assumed that we have the quantities x, $\overline{x}$, y, $\overline{y}$, z and $\overline{z}$ available as inputs. A network of this

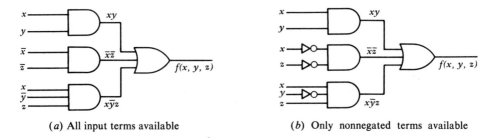

(*a*) All input terms available   (*b*) Only nonnegated terms available

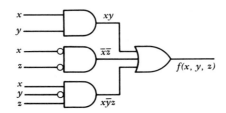

(*c*) Shorthand notation indicating inverters on input

Figure 3-2   Various representations of $f(x, y, z) = xy \lor \bar{x}\bar{z} \lor x\bar{y}z$

type is called a *two level logic* circuit, since only two stages of logic are used. If $\bar{x}$, $\bar{y}$, and $\bar{z}$ are not available, then these quantities must be generated by using inverters as shown in Figure 3-2*b*.

Sometimes when we wish to indicate that the negation of an input term is needed, we use the notation shown in Figure 3-2*c*. If the input line associated with a given term ends in a circle, then that term is negated before the operation indicated by the element symbol is performed. In most instances, an actual inverter, as shown in Figure 3-2*b*, would have to be included in the logic circuit to account for the indicated negation if the negated value of the term is not available as an input. Any line without a circle is assumed to transmit the variable associated with that line directly to the element.

A slightly different situation occurs when the circle is associated with the output of an element. The operation indicated by the element is performed, and then the resulting output is negated. For example, the logic network of Figure 3-3*a* realizes

$$g(x, y, z) = \overline{(x \lor y \lor z)}$$

To illustrate how both of these conventions are used, consider the circuit diagram shown in Figure 3-3*b*. By examining this diagram, we can immediately write down the equation for the network as

$$h(x, y, z) = xy \lor \overline{(x\bar{z})}$$

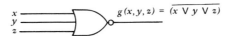

$$g(x, y, z) = \overline{(x \lor y \lor z)}$$

(a) Illustration of output negation convention

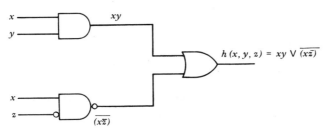

$$h(x, y, z) = xy \lor \overline{(x\bar{z})}$$

$$(x\bar{z})$$

(b) A combinational logic network

Figure 3-3   Logic circuit description.

We see that we can derive the equation for this network by starting on the left and by forming the partial results as we pass each logic element. These results are then combined to produce the final answer.

Realization of Canonical Functions

Any scalar function can be represented in canonical sum-of-product or product-of-sum form. Thus any function can be realized by a two level logic circuit. For example, consider the following function represented in both minterm and maxterm form.

Minterm Form

$$f(x_1, x_2, x_3) = m_1 \lor m_3 \lor m_5 \lor m_7$$

Maxterm Form

$$f(x_1, x_2, x_3) = M_0 \land M_2 \land M_4 \land M_6$$

The logic network representations of these two expressions are shown in Figure 3-4. As we will see in later chapters when we discuss read-only memories and programmed logic arrays, this form of logic network representation of a function can be very useful.

EXERCISES

1. Using the standard logic circuit symbols, draw a logic circuit representation for the following logic expression.

$$f(w, x, y, z) = (w\bar{x} \lor \bar{y}z)(x \lor \bar{y}z)$$

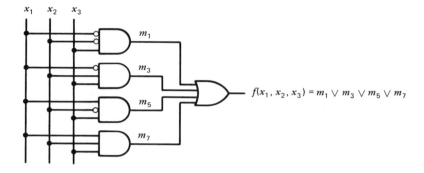

(*a*) Realization of canonical sum-of-product logic expression

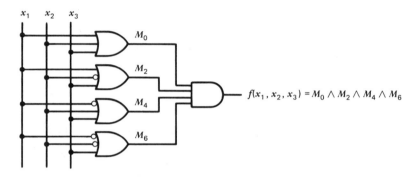

(*b*) Realization of canonical product-of-sum logic expression

Figure 3-4   Realization of canonical form of logic expressions.

    (a)   Assuming negated inputs available.
    (b)   Assuming negated inputs not available.

2.   Draw a logic circuit representation for
    (a) $f(x_1, x_2, x_3) = m_0 \lor m_5 \lor m_6 \lor m_7$
    (b) $f(x_1, x_2, x_3, x_4) = M_0 \land M_5 \land M_7 \land M_{12}$

3.   Find the logic function represented by the following logic diagram.

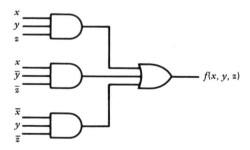

5. ELECTRONIC LOGIC DEVICES

In a digital system the scalar variables can be represented in a wide variety of physical forms. Sometimes the form selected is dictated by the way in which the variable is generated, while in other cases it is up to the logic designer to select the best representation. In this section we discuss some of the basic properties of the electronic circuits used to realize the logic operation that we have been discussing and indicate how these properties influence the physical representation we select to represent binary information.

The following discussion is of a very general nature and does not require a knowledge of electronics. This approach is possible because of a very important technological advance that occurred in the late 1960s. Instead of building individual logic elements from discrete electronic components, it became possible to place a large number of logic elements on a semiconductor chip a few millimeters square. The resulting devices were called *integrated circuits*. With this development, the price of digital logic dropped from the range of dollars per logic operation to cents per logic operation, while the amount of space needed to construct a digital system was drastically reduced. The biggest advantage, as far as we are concerned, is that the logic elements can be treated as the elementary building blocks from which we can make complex systems. We no longer have to be involved with the details of how the individual logic elements are constructed or manufactured.

The Basic Model

Any physical device or phenomenon that exhibits the property of having at least two distinct and reproducible physical states can be used to represent binary information. A detailed analysis of all possible physical devices that are found in digital networks and computers requires more space than we have available in this book. Instead we take a modular viewpoint in discussing the various logical devices. Each device is considered to be a "black box" with a set of input and output terminals. We then discuss the observable external behavior of the device, rather than the physical processes that take place inside the device. This approach is fully consistent with the current design practice of using logic modules in the construction of digital networks. The references listed at the end of this chapter present an extensive analysis of the internal design and behavior of the devices discussed.

A typical logic device can be represented as shown in Figure 3-5. The input signals to the device are voltages and the output is a voltage that can be described as a particular function of the input voltages. In studying this device we must investigate the way it behaves when the input signals remain at a constant value *(steady state*

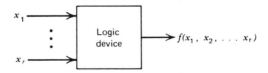

Figure 3-5 General representation of a logic device.

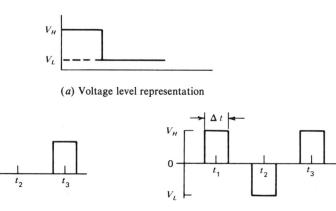

(*a*) Voltage level representation

(*b*) Simple pulses

(*c*) Non-return to zero pulses

Figure 3-6   Typical voltage waveforms.

behavior) and what happens when one or more of the input signals change value (*transient behavior*).

Representation of Logical Variables

Two modes of operation are found in logic networks. In some cases the different variables are represented by voltage levels that remain constant until the value of the variable changes to a new value. A signal of this type is represented in Figure 3-6*a*. When dealing with voltage levels time is not a central parameter. However, many digital networks operate on pulse signals such as are illustrated in Figure 3-6*b* and *c*. When a variable x_1 is used to describe signals of this type, it is implicitly assumed that the signal is defined for a time interval Δt seconds long centered at the time instants $t_1, t_2, \ldots$, etc.

In all these cases we distinguish two distinct values of voltage, V_H corresponding to the higher of the two voltages and V_L corresponding to the lower of the two voltages. There are two ways in which we can assign binary values to these voltages. The first method is called a *positive logic* assignment and it assigns a logical value of 1 to V_H and a value of 0 to V_L. The second method, which is called a *negative logic* assignment, is to let V_H represent the logical value of 0 and V_L represent the logical value of 1.

The choice of either a positive logic or negative logic convention is up to the system designer. The following example, however, illustrates the effect of choosing one or the other assignment.

Let us assume that we have a logic network such as illustrated in Figure 3-7 where

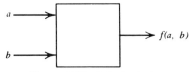

Figure 3-7   A logic device.

Table 3-4   Voltage Levels

a	b	f(a, b)
0	0	0
0	−5	0
−5	0	0
−5	−5	−5

Table 3-5   Truth Table Representation of Device

(a) Positive Logic			(b) Negative Logic		
a	b	f(a, b)	a	b	f(a, b)
1	1	1	0	0	0
1	0	1	0	1	0
0	1	1	1	0	0
0	0	0	1	1	1

$V_H = 0$ and $V_L = -5$ volts, respectively. The relationship between the input and output voltages for this device is given by Table 3-4. If we use a positive logic assignment, we obtain the truth table representation of this device given by Table 3-5a, while we obtain the truth table representation given by Table 3-5b if we use a negative logic assignment. Examining these two tables we see that our device is an OR logic element if we use positive logic and an AND logic element if we use negative logic.

All devices behave in a nonideal manner. Thus we must indicate the range of operating parameters that can be expected when using a particular logic element. The above discussion of logic levels was based on the fact that we could distinguish two distinct voltage levels V_H and V_L. In reality, these voltage levels are nominal values and we must, in practice, indicate a range of voltages we will accept as V_H and V_L. Figure 3-8 illustrates this idea. Inside of the bands representing V_L or V_H the voltage is recognized as representing a specific binary value. However, in the region between these two bands the logical value of the signal is undefined. This transition region is usually very small in most electronic devices.

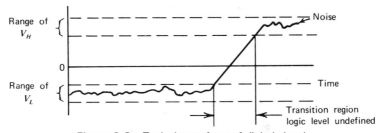

Figure 3-8   Typical waveform of digital signal.

Every signal has some fluctuations in value that we call *noise*. The ranges assigned to V_H and V_L should be large enough so that a signal that belongs in one range is not driven outside that range by this unwanted noise. Similarly, the two bands should be sufficiently separated so that there is no problem in distinguishing a V_H level from a V_L level even if unwanted noise is present.

Fan-in and Fan-out Capabilities

When two or more logic circuits are connected, the output signal of one network is the input signal to one or more following networks. If information is to be propagated through a network, we must have a transfer of energy from the driving logic circuit producing the signal to the receiving logic circuit that is accepting this information. In order to simplify the design of logic networks, input loading (i.e., the amount of energy absorbed by a given input) and output drive capability can be specified in terms of a unit load. When we do this we can describe the ability of a logic network to receive and transmit information in terms of its fan-in and fan-out capabilities.

The maximum number of independent input variables that can be used by a logic circuit is called the maximum *fan-in* of the circuit. For example, a commercial logic circuit might have five input leads available for use by the network designer. This device then has a fan-in of 5.

The number of unit loads that can be driven by a given logic circuit is limited by the way the circuit is constructed. The maximum number of unit loads that can be driven by a particular circuit is called its *fan-out* capability. Usually the input to a logic circuit represents a unit load. Therefore, the fan-out ability of a logic circuit is also a measure of the number of logic circuits that can be driven by the logic circuit under consideration.

Fan-in and fan-out limitations are very important parameters to keep in mind when logic networks are being designed. No logic circuit can be employed in a manner that would require more inputs or outputs than the circuit can accommodate.

Dynamic Behavior

All logic devices contain energy storage elements as an integral part of their construction. Therefore the effect of a change in the input to the device cannot instantly appear at the output. For example, consider the AND circuit shown in Figure 3-9a.

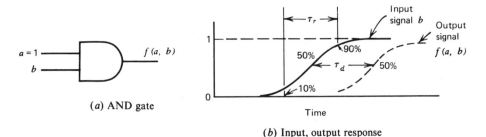

(a) AND gate

(b) Input, output response

Figure 3-9   Dynamic response of logic circuit.

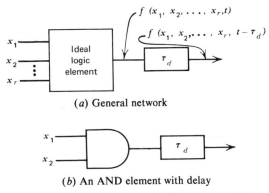

(a) General network

(b) An AND element with delay

Figure 3-10   Logic network with inherent delay.

The a input is initially set to 1 and the input to the b terminal is shown in Figure 3-9b. Examining the input signal we see that it is initially zero producing a steady-state output signal of zero. The b input then changes to a 1 value, but this cannot happen instantaneously. The time τ_r that it takes the signal to go from 10% to 90% of its final value is called the *rise time* of the input signal and is a measure of the speed at which the input can change. The output, which must become a 1, does not respond instantaneously to this input signal. Instead there is a delay of τ_d seconds before the output responds to the input change, measured between 50% points on the input and output waveforms.

The inherent delay found in all logic elements is important in determining the maximum operating speed of a logic network. If we must consider this problem we can approximate the dynamic properties of a given logic element by the circuit diagram shown in Figure 3-10. Figure 3-10b shows a typical model of an AND element.

In this model the logic elements are assumed to be ideal. Thus they introduce no delay. The delay in the circuits is introduced by the ideal delay element, which delays the output signal from the ideal logic element τ_d seconds before it appears at the output terminal. Figure 3-11 illustrates the type of signals we are dealing with if we use this ideal model for an AND element. Note that the delay is important only when the output changes value.

Timing Diagrams

The delay introduced by each logic element in a logic network contributes to the overall delay of the network. In some cases it becomes very important to know the exact effect that each element has on the transient behavior of the complete network. We can study this behavior by using a timing diagram, which provides a time history of each important signal that is found in the network.

The timing diagram for the network shown in Figure 3-12a is shown in Figure 3-12b, where it is assumed that $\tau_2 > \tau_1$.

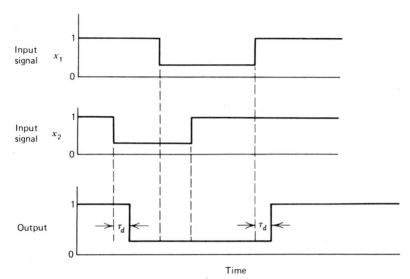

Figure 3-11   An example of the delay in an AND logic element.

The delays in any logic element are determined by the physical structure of the element and can vary quite markedly from element to element of the same type. The delays included in any timing diagram are thus representative values that characterize the average behavior of each element.

The operating speed of any logic network is determined by the total time it takes for the network's output to reach a steady state value after a change in the input signal. In the example illustrated in Figure 3-12, it takes $\tau_1 + \tau_3$ seconds for the network to reach a stable condition after a change in an input to the upper path through the network and $\tau_2 + \tau_3$ seconds after a change in an input to the lower path through the network. Since $\tau_2 > \tau_1$ the overall operating speed of the network is limited by the delay of $\tau_2 + \tau_3$ seconds. Thus the input to this network should be limited to fewer than $1/(\tau_2 + \tau_3)$ changes per second.

EXERCISES

1. The voltage levels associated with a given logic circuit are given in the following table. What logic operation does this device perform if we use (a) negative logic? (b) positive logic?

a	b	$f(a, b)$
− 5v	− 5v	3v
− 5v	3v	− 5v
3v	− 5v	− 5v
3v	3v	− 5v

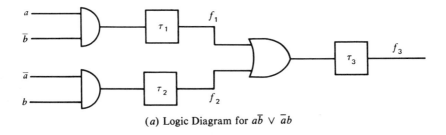

(a) Logic Diagram for $a\bar{b} \vee \bar{a}b$

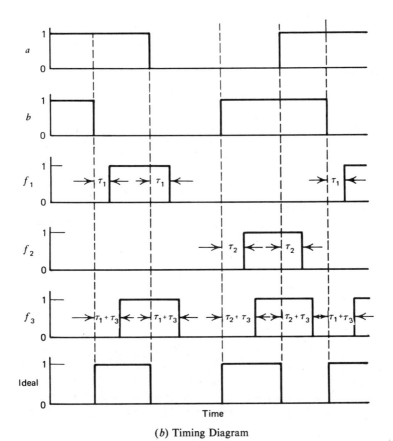

Time

(b) Timing Diagram

Figure 3-12   Logic network timing diagram.

2.   AND and OR logic elements that have a fan-in and fan-out of 5 cost $0.25 each and those with a fan-in and fan-out of 3 cost $0.15 each. What is the minimum cost that we can have for a 5-input, 3-output logic network that will realize the following function?

$$f_1(x_1, x_2, x_3, x_4, x_5) = x_1x_2x_3x_4 \lor x_2x_5 \lor x_1x_3x_4x_5$$
$$f_2(x_1, x_2, x_3, x_4, x_5) = x_2x_3x_5 \lor x_1x_3x_4x_5$$
$$f_3(x_1, x_2, x_3, x_4, x_5) = x_1x_3x_4x_5 \lor x_2x_5$$

3. Sketch a timing diagram for the following logic network. Assume $\tau_2 < \tau_1$.

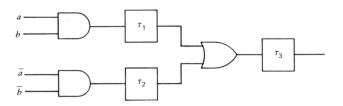

6.   SUMMARY

Modern integrated circuit technology has introduced many changes in the way that we design combinational logic networks. The first types of integrated circuits to be developed consisted of logic packages that contained from one to 12 individual logic elements. Integrated circuits of this form are classed as *small-scale integrated* circuits or SSI circuits. The most common way to package these circuits is to place the microelectronic chip in a *dual inline package* (DIP), which has the general form shown in Figure 3-13 a. The leads to each of the individual logic elements are brought out to the pins on the side of the package. Normally a package will have from 14 to 28 leads depending upon the units included in the package. The internal organization of one typical package is shown in Figure 3-13 b.

A very large family of SSI circuits is available to the designer. All of the logic networks discussed in this book can be realized in a number of different ways using logic units of this type. The references at the end of this chapter give further details about the types of circuits available and how they are constructed. It should be emphasized that very little electronic background is needed to construct a wide range of digital systems using these integrated circuits once the system has been designed using the techniques to be presented in the following chapters.

In this chapter we have considered the different fundamental logic operations that can be used to process information in digital form. Our emphasis has been on the general principles involved in using these operations rather than on specific applications. In the following chapters we extend these ideas to show how a variety of digital systems can be designed using these techniques. However, no matter how complex the networks we are designing become, we will find that the final design will involve applying the basic logic operations developed in this chapter.

Reference Notation

An extensive discussion concerning the construction and design of digital circuits and logic networks can be found in Reference 4, while References 2 and 3 provide an

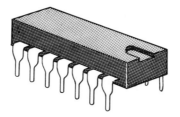

(*a*) Typical DIP package

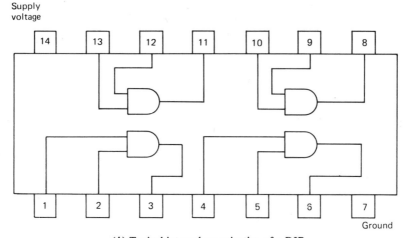

(*b*) Typical internal organization of a DIP

Figure 3-13 A typical SSI package.

overview of many of the LSI and MSI logic circuit elements currently available for the design of digital systems. The graphic symbols used in this text are defined in Reference 1. A new set of logic circuit symbols has been defined to allow a greater range of symbolic representation of logic elements. This notation, which is discussed in detail in Reference 3, has not been used in this book since it often obscures the basic concepts being discussed when someone is encountering logic design for the first time.

REFERENCES

1. American National Standards Institute (1973), *Graphic Symbols for Logic Diagrams*. Institute for Electrical and Electronic Engineers, New York.
2. Blakeslee, T. R. (1975), *Digital Design with Standard MSI and LSI*. Wiley, New York.

3. Fletcher, W. I. (1980), *An Engineering Approach to Digital Design*. Prentice-Hall, Englewood Cliffs, N.J.
4. Taub, H. (1982), *Digital Circuits and Microprocessors*. McGraw-Hill, New York.

HOME PROBLEMS

1. Prove that the two logic networks shown in Figures P3-1a and P3-1b realize the same logical expression.

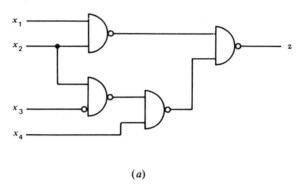

(*a*)

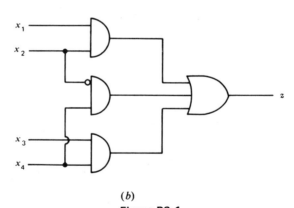

(*b*)

Figure P3-1

2. Binary addition is defined by the following rules

$$
\begin{array}{cccc}
0 & 0 & 1 & 1 \\
+\ 0 & +\ 1 & +\ 0 & +\ 1 \\
\hline
0 & 1 & 1 & 1\,0 \quad \leftarrow \text{sum} \\
& & & \uparrow\!\underline{\qquad}\ \text{carry}
\end{array}
$$

A network of the form shown in Figure P3-2 can be used to realize this simple addition operation. This network, which is called a *half-adder*, is described by the following truth table.

Table PR3-1   The Truth Table for a Half-Adder

a_i	b_i	s_i	c_i
0	0	0	0
0	1	1	0
1	0	1	0
1	1	0	1

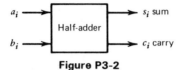

Figure P3-2

(a) Develop logic expressions that describe both s_i and c_i.

(b) Give two possible logic realizations for the half-adder.

3. A *full-adder* is an extension of a half-adder in which provisions are made to process a carry from a lower stage. The general form of a full-adder is shown in Figure P3-3.

Figure P3-3   General form of a full-adder.

The full-adder carries out the operation

$$
\begin{array}{r}
a_i \\
b_i \\
\underline{c_{I-1}} \\
c_i \quad s_i \quad \leftarrow \text{sum} \\
\end{array}
$$
└── carry

(a) Give the addition table for the full-adder.

(b) Develop the truth table that describes the full-adder.

(c) Develop an AND/OR logic network that will realize the full-adder.

4. Error-checking codes are used extensively in digital systems to detect when an error occurs in an information transfer operation. One of the simplest ways to introduce this feature is to introduce an extra bit called a parity bit in the digital representation of the information for the sole purpose of checking for an error. In one code the parity bit is chosen so that the number of 1's (including the parity bit) in the digital representation of the information is even. A way for generating the parity bit is shown in Figure P3-4. Define the logical expression for the parity bit generator network.

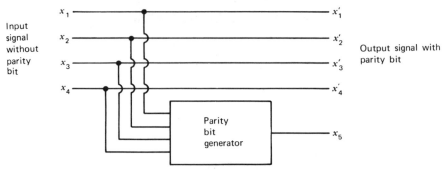

Figure P3-4   Generation of parity bit

5. Let $g(x_1, x_2, x_3, x_4)$ be any logical expression. Give a general method that may be used to find either the canonical sum-of-product or product-of-sums expression for this expression.

6. Let A be a digital signal corresponding to a decimal number between 0 and 9 encoded by a 4-bit gray code. This signal is applied to a logic network that has 10 output lines. Line y_i is connected to a lamp that lights whenever $y_i = 1$. Develop the logic expression for y_i such that the ith lamp will light if and only if the input corresponds to the decimal number i.

7. A combinational logic network has 10 input lines and 4 output lines. At any time, one and only one of the inputs must be set to 1. If input x_i, $i = 0, 1, \ldots,$ 9, is 1, then the output must be the BCD encoded representation for the decimal number i. Develop the logic expressions that describe this network.

8. Smaller logic networks are often interconnected to form larger logic networks. A typical arrangement of this type is shown in Figure P3-5. Assume that the outputs c_i and d_i of the ith sublogic network do not reach a stable steady state value until τ_1 seconds after the inputs to the network reach a steady value.
   (a) How long will it be necessary to wait after an input has been applied before

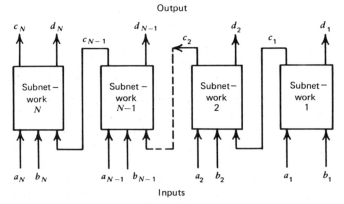

Figure P3-5

we can be sure that the output of the complete network has reached a steady state value?

(b) How many input changes per second can be processed by this network without encountering errors due to this time delay?

9. Assume that the subnetworks shown in Figure P3-5 are full-adders and that $N = 3$. Let

$$A = [0\ 1\ 1]$$
$$B = [0\ 0\ 1]$$

and assume that the inputs are applied at $t = 0$. Draw a set of timing diagrams that shows the values of the variables c_i and d_i as a function of time. Assume that the delay τ associated with each network is 10^{-6} seconds.

10. In the logic circuit shown in Figure P3-6, $z = 1$ will be the steady state value of the output for both $[x_1, x_2, x_3]$ equal to $[0, 1, 0]$ and $[1, 1, 0]$. However,

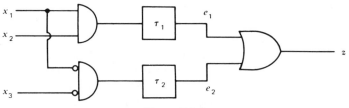

Figure P3-6

when the input is $[0, 1, 0]$, $e_1 = 0$ and $e_2 = 1$, while for the input $[1, 1, 0]$, $e_1 = 1$ and $e_2 = 0$. Thus when the input changes from $[0, 1, 0]$ to $[1, 1, 0]$ or from $[1, 1, 0]$ to $[0, 1, 0]$, there exists a possibility that z_1 will momentarily go to zero. This spurious output produced during such a change in the input is called a *static hazard*. Use a timing diagram to show that a static hazard will exist whenever $\tau_1 \neq \tau_2$.

4

SWITCHING ALGEBRA AND LOGIC NETWORK DESIGN

1. INTRODUCTION

The previous chapters have provided us with an insight into how digital information is represented in a digital system and how we can operate on this information at a basic level. However, if we are to make extensive use of these new ideas, we must develop the algebraic properties associated with these operations and explore how they can be used to carry out a number of important tasks. That is the purpose of this chapter.

In the first part of this chapter we investigate the properties of switching algebra. This is a system of mathematical logic that can be used to manipulate the logical expressions that describe the behavior of logic networks. After we have developed this background we will consider how these ideas can be used by a designer to reduce a set of design specifications to an actual combinational logic network.

2. SWITCHING ALGEBRA

In the mid-1800s George Boole introduced a system of mathematics that provided an algebraic treatment of logic. This algebra, which has become known as Boolean algebra, has a great many interesting applications in mathematics, engineering, and the sciences. Our interest, however, is not in the general theory of Boolean algebra but in the special class of problems associated with investigating the algebra of scalar functions of the type we encountered in Chapter 3. A complete treatment of Boolean algebra as it applies to general problems can be found in several of the references listed at the end of this chapter.

Boolean algebra, like any other algebra, is composed of a set of symbols and a set of rules for manipulating these symbols. In our case, the set of symbols is taken to be the set of binary valued variables and the operations are taken to be the operations of AND, OR, and NOT developed in Chapter 3. This introductory discussion can be formalized by stating the above ideas in terms of the following basic postulates for our particular form of Boolean algebra, which is called *switching algebra*.

Basic Postulates of Switching Algebra

Postulate 1 A Boolean variable, x, has two possible values, 0 and 1. These values are exclusive, that is

$$\text{if } x = 0 \quad \text{then } x \neq 1$$
$$\text{if } x = 1 \quad \text{then } x \neq 0$$

Postulate 2 The NOT operation "⁻" is defined as

$$\bar{0} = 1 \qquad \bar{1} = 0$$

Postulate 3 The logical operations $\wedge$ AND, and $\vee$ OR are defined as

$$
\begin{array}{ll}
0 \wedge 0 = 0 & 0 \vee 0 = 0 \\
1 \wedge 0 = 0 & 0 \vee 1 = 1 \\
0 \wedge 1 = 0 & 1 \vee 0 = 1 \\
1 \wedge 1 = 1 & 1 \vee 1 = 1
\end{array}
$$

Note: When there will be no confusion we use the notation $x_1 x_2$ to indicate the AND operation $x_1 \wedge x_2$.

Using this set of postulates we can build a set of useful theorems that will allow us to manipulate and simplify the logical expressions that we use to represent binary functions. For switching algebra there are two general methods of proof that we can use to prove theorems.

Proof by Perfect Induction

The first method, called *proof by perfect induction,* is a brute force technique. Let us suppose that we wish to prove a theorem that states that the logical expression $f(x_1, \ldots, x_r) = g(x_1, \ldots, x_r)$ is true for all $(x_1, \ldots, x_r)$. Since the variables used in this expression can take on only one of two values at a given time, all that we have to do to test if $f(x_1, \ldots, x_r) = g(x_1, \ldots, x_r)$ is to form the truth table for each function. If the two functions are equal for each entry in the truth table, then the theorem is true. Otherwise, it is false. This method of proof, which we have already used in Chapter 3, is best used when the number of variables is small.

Proof by Deduction

The second method of proof, called *proof by deduction,* is to show that a given expression is true by showing that the expression can be derived by starting with the basic set of postulates and known theorems and then applying mathematical deduction to obtain the desired expression. This method of proof is effective if the expression under investigation is indeed true. However, if the expression is false, the best method of showing this is to find a counter example that shows that the expression is false.

One of the problems that arises when someone first encounters switching algebra is the great similarity between switching algebra and ordinary algebra. This leads to a tendency to automatically apply concepts from ordinary algebra to similar situations in switching algebra. Unfortunately there are several differences between the two algebraic systems and this approach can lead to erroneous results. The following discussion will establish the rules that we can use to manipulate and simplify logical expressions. Examples of both proof techniques are also given.

Basic Properties of Switching Algebra

The amount of work necessary to evaluate a logical expression can often be reduced by applying one or more of the following algebraic relations that hold true for switching algebra. In the following, x can represent a single variable or a general logical function.

1.   Special properties of 0 and 1

$$0 \vee x = x \qquad 0 \wedge x = 0$$
$$1 \vee x = 1 \qquad 1 \wedge x = x$$

2.   The idempotence laws

$$x \vee x = x \qquad x \wedge x = x$$

3.   Complementation laws

$$x \vee \bar{x} = 1 \qquad x \wedge \bar{x} = 0$$

4.   Involution

$$\overline{(\bar{x})} = x$$

5.   Commutative laws

$$x \vee y = y \vee x \qquad x \wedge y = y \wedge x$$

6.   Associative laws

$$x \vee (y \vee z) = (x \vee y) \vee z \qquad x \wedge (y \wedge z) = (x \wedge y) \wedge z$$

7.   Distributive laws

$$x \wedge (y \vee z) = (x \wedge y) \vee (x \wedge z)$$
$$x \vee (y \wedge z) = (x \vee y) \wedge (x \vee z)$$

8.   Absorption laws

$$x \vee (x \wedge y) = x \qquad x \wedge (x \vee y) = x$$
$$x \vee (\bar{x} \wedge y) = x \vee y \qquad x \wedge (\bar{x} \vee y) = x \wedge y$$

If we examine the above relationships we see that there are many identities that are not found in regular algebra. The proof of these relationships is straightforward for our particular form of Boolean algebra. In fact all of these laws are easily proved by the method of perfect induction. For example, let us prove that

$$x \vee \bar{x} = 1$$

The truth table for this expression is

x	$x \lor \bar{x}$	1
0	1	1
1	1	1

Similarly the absorption law

$$x \lor (x \land y) = x$$

is proved by using the following truth table

x	y	$(x \land y)$	$x \lor (x \land y)$	x
0	0	0	0	0
0	1	0	0	0
1	0	0	1	1
1	1	1	1	1

These basic relations can also be proved by deduction. In this case we start off with the expression we wish to prove and then, using only previously proven results, try to show that one side of the equation can be reduced to the other side of the equation. For example, let us prove the absorption law

$$x \lor (\bar{x} \land y) = x \lor y$$

under the assumption that the relationships 1 to 7 have been established. The following steps illustrate the method of proof:

Initial statement	$x \lor (\bar{x} \land y)$
Distributive law	$x \lor (\bar{x} \land y) = (x \lor \bar{x}) \land (x \lor y)$
Complementation law	$(x \lor \bar{x}) \land (x \lor y) = 1 \land (x \lor y)$
Special property of 1	$1 \land (x \lor y) = x \lor y$

Simplification of Logic Expressions

One of our greatest applications of the above relationships is to the problem of simplifying logical expressions. For example, assume that we wish to find a logical expression to represent the following truth table.

x_1	x_2	x_3	$f(x_1, x_2, x_3)$
0	0	0	1
0	0	1	1
0	1	0	0
0	1	1	0
1	0	0	0
1	0	1	1
1	1	0	0
1	1	1	0

From our discussion of Chapter 3 we know that we can represent this function in the following canonical form.

$$f(x_1, x_2, x_3) = \bar{x}_1\bar{x}_2x_3 \vee \bar{x}_1x_2x_3 \vee x_1\bar{x}_2x_3$$

However, this function can be simplified by using the above relationships. This simplification process proceeds as follows:

1. Use the idempotence law to add $\bar{x}_1\bar{x}_2x_3$.

$$f(x_1, x_2, x_3) = \bar{x}_1\bar{x}_2x_3 \vee \bar{x}_1x_2x_3 \vee \bar{x}_1\bar{x}_2x_3 \vee x_1\bar{x}_2x_3$$

2. Combine the first two and last two terms using the distributive law.

$$f(x_1, x_2, x_3) = \bar{x}_1\bar{x}_2(\bar{x}_3 \vee x_3) \vee (\bar{x}_1 \vee x_1)\bar{x}_2x_3$$

3. Use the complementation law.

$$f(x_1, x_2, x_3) = \bar{x}_1\bar{x}_2 \vee \bar{x}_2x_3$$

4. Use the distributive law again.

$$f(x_1, x_2, x_3) = (\bar{x}_1 \vee x_3) \wedge \bar{x}_2$$

This is as far as we can reduce this expression.

Obtaining the Canonical Forms of an Expression

A second problem that we often encounter is that of obtaining a canonical representation of a given logical expression. We could, of course, derive the truth table for the expression and then obtain the canonical representation from the truth table. However, it is also possible, and in most cases easier, to obtain the canonical form of a given expression in a purely algebraic manner.

Assume that we wish to obtain the canonical representation of a given logical expression in the canonical sum-of-product form. To do this we first reduce the expression to a sum-of-product form and then we use the complementation law and the distributive law to transform each product term into its corresponding minterm representation. The following example will illustrate this technique.

Let

$$f(x_1, x_2, x_3) = (\bar{x}_1 \vee x_2)(x_1 \vee \bar{x}_3)$$

be the given function. The canonical sum-of-products representation is obtained by the following steps.

1. Use the distributive law to obtain a sum-of-product representation of the expression.

$$f(x_1, x_2, x_3) = \bar{x}_1x_1 \vee \bar{x}_1\bar{x}_3 \vee x_1x_2 \vee x_2\bar{x}_3 = \bar{x}_1\bar{x}_3 \vee x_1x_2 \vee x_2\bar{x}_3$$

2. Use the complementation law to transform each product term into a corresponding minterm representation.

(a) $\overline{x_1}\overline{x_3} = \overline{x_1}(x_2 \vee \overline{x_2})\overline{x_3} = \overline{x_1}x_2\overline{x_3} \vee \overline{x_1}\overline{x_2}\overline{x_3}$

b) $x_1 x_2 = x_1 x_2 (x_3 \vee \overline{x_3}) = x_1 x_2 x_3 \vee x_1 x_2 \overline{x_3}$

(c) $x_2\overline{x_3} = (x_1 \vee \overline{x_1})x_2\overline{x_3} = x_1 x_2\overline{x_3} \vee \overline{x_1}x_2\overline{x_3}$

Thus

$$f(x_1, x_2, x_3) = \overline{x_1}x_2\overline{x_3} \vee \overline{x_1}\overline{x_2}\overline{x_3} \vee x_1 x_2 x_3 \vee x_1 x_2\overline{x_3} \vee x_1 x_2\overline{x_3} \vee \overline{x_1}x_2\overline{x_3}$$
$$= \overline{x_1}x_2\overline{x_3} \vee \overline{x_1}\overline{x_2}\overline{x_3} \vee x_1 x_2 x_3 \vee x_1 x_2\overline{x_3}$$

A similar technique can be used to obtain the canonical product-of-sum representation of a function.

Principle of Duality

If we examine the above postulates and algebraic relationships, we see that there are two forms for each law. This would seem to imply that we would have to prove both forms. However, the *principle of duality* simplifies our effort. This principle states that each theorem has a dual that can be obtained by:

1. Interchanging the OR and AND operations of the expression.
2. Interchanging the 0 and 1 elements of the expression.
3. Not changing the form of the variables.

To illustrate the use of this property, we note that applying the principle of duality to

	$0 \vee x = x$	replace 0 with 1
gives the dual relationship	$\updownarrow \updownarrow$	and
	$1 \wedge x = x$	replace $\vee$ with $\wedge$

while

$$x \wedge (x \vee y) = x$$

gives the dual relationship

$$x \vee (x \wedge y) = x$$

As a final example consider

$$\overline{x_1}\overline{x_3} \vee \overline{x_1}x_2 \vee x_2 x_3 = \overline{x_1}\overline{x_3} \vee x_2 x_3$$

Then the dual of this expression is

$$(\overline{x_1} \vee \overline{x_3})(\overline{x_1} \vee x_2)(x_2 \vee x_3) = (\overline{x_1} \vee \overline{x_3})(x_2 \vee x_3)$$

WARNING: If the expression $g(x_1, x_2, \ldots, x_r)$ is the dual of the expression $f(x_1, x_2, \ldots, x_r)$ this *does not* imply that these two expressions are equal. The truth of this warning is easily verified.

In particular if

$$g(x_1, x_2, x_3) = \overline{x_1}\overline{x_3} \vee x_2 x_3$$

then its dual is

$$f(x_1, x_2, x_3) = (\bar{x}_1 \vee \bar{x}_3) \wedge (x_2 \vee x_3)$$

However,

$$g(0, 0, 0) = 1$$

while

$$f(0, 0, 0) = 0$$

Thus, $g(x_1, x_2, x_3) \neq f(x_1, x_2, x_3)$.

The principle of duality lets us establish two theorems for the effort of one proof. If we can prove, through a series of logical steps, that a given theorem is true, then we immediately know that the dual of the theorem is also true, since the dual of the logical steps that proved the original theorem proves the dual theorem.

DeMorgan's Theorem

DeMorgan's theorem is a very important and interesting theorem that has many useful applications. In particular, we will find it helpful when dealing with the design of logic networks constructed from NAND and NOR logic elements. This theorem states:

$$\overline{(x \vee y)} = \bar{x} \wedge \bar{y}$$
$$\overline{(x \wedge y)} = \bar{x} \vee \bar{y}$$

The proof of this theorem for our switching algebra is easily accomplished by using the following truth table.

x	y	$\overline{(x \vee y)}$	$\bar{x} \wedge \bar{y}$
0	0	1	1
0	1	0	0
1	0	0	0
1	1	0	0

Thus we see that

$$\overline{(x \vee y)} = \bar{x} \wedge \bar{y}$$

By the principle of duality we then have the dual theorem

$$\overline{(x \wedge y)} = \bar{x} \vee \bar{y}$$

DeMorgan's theorem can easily be extended to give

$$\overline{(x_1 \vee x_2 \vee \cdots \vee x_n)} = \bar{x}_1 \wedge \bar{x}_2 \wedge \cdots \wedge \bar{x}_n$$

and

$$\overline{(x_1 \wedge x_2 \wedge \cdots \wedge x_n)} = \bar{x}_1 \vee \bar{x}_2 \vee \cdots \vee \bar{x}_n$$

Or for a general function we have

$$\overline{f(x_1, \ldots, x_n, \vee, \wedge)} = f(\overline{x_1}, \ldots, \overline{x_n}, \wedge, \vee)$$

The following example illustrates the application of this theorem. If

$$f(x_1, x_2, x_3) = \overline{(x_1 \wedge x_2)} \vee \overline{x_1} \vee (x_2 \wedge \overline{x_3})$$

then the complement of this function is

$$\overline{f(x_1, x_2, x_3)} = (\overline{x_1} \vee \overline{x_2}) \wedge x_1 \wedge (\overline{x_2} \vee x_3)$$

Another interesting result that can be proved by using DeMorgan's theorem is that the NAND operation is a universal operation. By this we mean that any logic expression can be represented only using the NAND operator. To prove this statement, we start with the fact that any logic expression $f(x_1, x_2, \ldots, x_n)$ of n variables can be represented in canonical form using the operations of NOT, AND, and OR. All that we have to do is show that each one of these operations can be represented in terms of the NAND operation.

1. The NOT operation

$$\overline{(x \wedge x)} = \overline{x} \vee \overline{x} = \overline{x}$$

2. The AND operation

$$\overline{\overline{(x \wedge y)} \wedge \overline{(x \wedge y)}} = (x \wedge y) \vee (x \wedge y) = x \wedge y$$

3. The OR operation

$$\overline{\overline{(x \wedge x)} \wedge \overline{(y \wedge y)}} = (x \wedge x) \vee (y \wedge y) = x \vee y$$

This proof is in the form of an existence proof. It shows that we can always express a canonical sum-of-product expression by using only the NAND operation. The direct application of this result is very cumbersome. In the following sections several design techniques that make use of the universality of the NAND operation are illustrated. For these cases, DeMorgan's law proves to be a very useful tool. By the principle of duality it is also possible to show that the NOR operation is a second universal operation.

The best way to become proficient in using switching algebra is to work a number of problems and see how each of the laws and theorems can be used. In the rest of this chapter we illustrate a number of useful applications of switching algebra and show how these results have influenced the design of medium-scale integrated circuits.

EXERCISES

1. Prove the commutative and associative laws using perfect induction.

2. Prove by deduction that the following logical expressions are true.

   (a) $x_1\overline{x_2} \vee \overline{x_1}x_2 = \overline{(x_1 x_2 \vee \overline{x_1}\overline{x_2})}$

(b) $x_1x_2 \lor \overline{x}_1\overline{x}_3 = (\overline{x}_1 \lor x_2)(x_1 \lor \overline{x}_3)$

(c) $x_2\overline{x}_3 \lor x_1\overline{x}_3 \lor x_2x_3 \lor x_1x_3 \lor \overline{x}_1x_2 \lor \overline{(\overline{x}_1 \lor \overline{x}_2)} = \overline{(\overline{x}_1\overline{x}_2)}$

3.   Find the canonical sum-of-product and product-of-sum representations for the following logical functions.

(a) $f(x_1, x_2, x_3) = \overline{(x_1x_2 \lor \overline{x}_1x_3)}$

(b) $f(x_1, x_2, x_3) = \overline{(\overline{x_1x_2} \lor x_1x_3)}$

(c) $f(x_1, x_2, x_3) = (x_1x_2 \lor x_3)(x_1\overline{x}_2 \lor \overline{x}_3)$

3.   LOGIC NETWORK REDUCTION USING BOOLEAN ALGEBRA

As we have seen in Chapter 3, scalar functions describing combinational logic networks can always be represented by logic equations expressed in a canonical form. These equations can, in turn, be realized by simple two-level logic networks. A canonical equation is often much more complex than necessary to realize a given function, and it is possible to reduce the complexity of the expression by algebraic techniques. The goal of the reduction is to remove as many terms and variables as possible from the canonical expression while still realizing the same function. This process of shortening an equation describing a specific function is called *simplifying* or *minimizing* the equation. The minimization process is complicated by the different forms in which a given equation may be written, by the cost of the different types of elements required to construct the networks, and by the operational characteristics of the logic circuit elements that are to be used in the network. In this section we consider some of the general characteristics of these reduction processes.

Simplification of Canonic Networks

In order to see how we can apply Boolean algebra to the simplification of a logic network let us assume that we are dealing with a function described by the following truth table.

x_1	x_2	x_3	$f(x_1, x_2, x_3)$
0	0	0	1
0	0	1	1
0	1	0	0
0	1	1	0
1	0	0	1
1	0	1	1
1	1	0	0
1	1	1	1

This function can be represented in either the sum-of-product or product-of-sum canonical form as

$$f(x_1, x_2, x_3) = \overline{x}_1\overline{x}_2\overline{x}_3 \lor \overline{x}_1\overline{x}_2x_3 \lor x_1\overline{x}_2\overline{x}_3 \lor x_1\overline{x}_2x_3 \lor x_1x_2x_3$$
$$= m_0 \lor m_1 \lor m_4 \lor m_5 \lor m_7$$
$$= (x_1 \lor x_2 \lor x_3)(x_1 \lor \overline{x}_2 \lor \overline{x}_3)(\overline{x}_1 \lor \overline{x}_2 \lor x_3)$$
$$= M_2 \land M_3 \land M_6$$

These two representations of the function $f(x_1, x_2, x_3)$ give rise to the two possible two-level logic networks shown in Figure 4-1. Examining these two networks we see that the product-of-sum representation appears to require fewer logic elements. However, let us see what happens when we apply our algebraic relationships to both canonical forms.

First, we consider the sum-of-product representation. We can reduce this function using the distributive, complementation, and absorption laws as follows.

$$f(x_1, x_2, x_3) = \overline{x}_1\overline{x}_2\overline{x}_3 \lor \overline{x}_1\overline{x}_2x_3 \lor x_1\overline{x}_2\overline{x}_3 \lor x_1\overline{x}_2x_3 \lor x_1x_2x_3$$
$$= \overline{x}_1\overline{x}_2 \lor x_1\overline{x}_2 \lor x_1x_2x_3$$
$$= \overline{x}_2 \lor x_1x_3$$

Thus we have reduced the network of Figure 4-1a to that of Figure 4-2a.

It is also possible to reduce the product-of-sum expression using the idempotence, complementation, and distributive laws as follows.

$$f(x_1, x_2, x_3) = (x_1 \lor \overline{x}_2 \lor x_3)(x_1 \lor \overline{x}_2 \lor \overline{x}_3)(\overline{x}_1 \lor \overline{x}_2 \lor x_3)$$
$$= (x_1 \lor \overline{x}_2 \lor x_3)(x_1 \lor \overline{x}_2 \lor \overline{x}_3)(x_1 \lor \overline{x}_2 \lor x_3)(\overline{x}_2 \lor \overline{x}_2 \lor x_3)$$

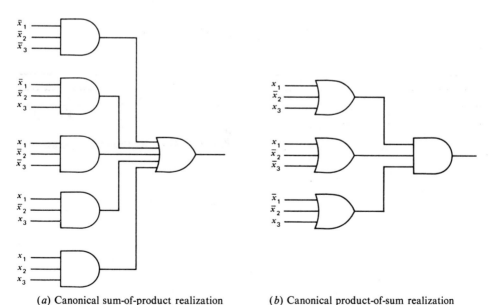

(a) Canonical sum-of-product realization   (b) Canonical product-of-sum realization

Figure 4-1   Canonical representation of $f(x_1, x_2, x_3)$.

$$= (x_1 \lor \bar{x}_2 \lor x_3\bar{x}_3)(x_1\bar{x}_1 \lor \bar{x}_2 \lor x_3)$$
$$= (x_1 \lor \bar{x}_2)(\bar{x}_2 \lor x_3)$$

Thus we have reduced the network of Figure 4-1b to that of Figure 4-2b. These two networks realize the same logic function since, because of the distributive law, we have

$$\bar{x}_2 \lor x_1x_3 \equiv (\bar{x}_2 \lor x_1)(\bar{x}_2 \lor x_3)$$

However, we also note that the product-of-sum now requires one more logic element than the sum-of-product realization.

If the variables x_i and their negation $\bar{x}_i$ are available, we can always construct a two-level logic network to realize any given binary function. These networks have the fastest operating speed since there is a maximum of two delays between any input variable and the output. However, when we work with integrated circuit logic modules we often have other considerations that must be included in the design process.

For example, assume that we are working with a family of integrated circuit logic elements that have only 2-input OR or 2-input AND elements available. Suppose that we wish to realize a logic network with the following sum-of-product form.

$$f(x_1, x_2, x_3, x_4) = x_1x_2\bar{x}_3 \lor x_1x_2x_4 \lor x_2\bar{x}_3x_4$$

This function cannot be constructed from our logic elements as long as it remains in this form. However, we can factor this function into a more desirable form by applying the commutative, distributive, and idempotence laws in the following manner

$$f(x_1, x_2, x_3, x_4) = x_1x_2\bar{x}_3 \lor x_1x_2x_4 \lor x_1x_2x_4 \lor x_2\bar{x}_3x_4$$
$$= x_1x_2(\bar{x}_3 \lor x_4) \lor x_2x_4(x_1 \lor \bar{x}_3)$$

which can be realized by a network of 2-input logic elements as shown in Figure 4-3.

Factoring a logic expression usually reduces the fan-in requirements while increasing the number of logic levels and the number of logic elements in the circuit. The larger the number of levels in the resulting circuit, the greater the total delay time of the complete network. However, in some design problems it is much more important to use standard elements rather than to minimize network delay.

The design of logic networks is an art that depends on many things beside switch-

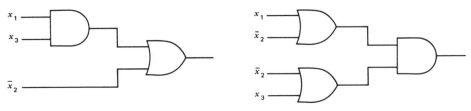

(*a*) Reduced Sum-Of-Product Network   (*b*) Reduced Product-Of-Sum Network

Figure 4-2   Representation of $f(x_1, x_2, x_3)$ in Reducted Form.

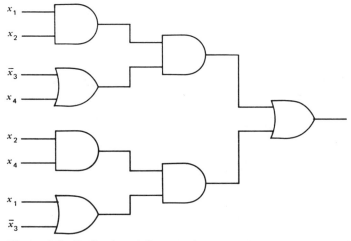

Figure 4-3 Realization of $f(x_1, x_2, x_3)$ using two-input logic elements.

ing algebra. If only a few copies of the network are to be constructed, it is not economical for a designer to spend a large amount of time trying to obtain an optimum minimum network. This is true since the cost of logic elements usually represents a small fraction of the total design cost while the logic designer's time may often be a major part of the design cost. On the other hand, the optimization of the network is very important if the network is to be mass produced. In either case, the availability of algorithmic procedures that can be used to eliminate unnecessary terms and variables can make any minimization process easier to handle. Procedures of this type are presented in Chapter 6.

Logic Network Design Using NAND and NOR Circuit Elements

All of our discussion of switching algebra and logic network design has, so far, assumed that we are working with circuits that can perform the basic logical operations of AND, OR, or NOT. Anyone familiar with the integrated circuit logic elements that are currently available might wonder why we take this approach, since the basic integrated circuit logic elements are NAND and NOR circuits, which have the general form shown in Figure 4-4.

As we previously proved, any binary function $h(x_1, x_2, \ldots, x_r)$ can be realized using only NAND elements or NOR elements. In particular, we now show how any sum-of-product expressions can be realized by a two-level network involving only NAND elements and how any product-of-sum expressions can be realized by a two-level network involving only NOR elements. The following discussion deals only with the sum-of-product realization using NAND elements. The arguments for a NOR element realization of a product-of-sum expression follow from the principle of duality.

From our previous discussion we know that any function $h(x_1, x_2, \ldots, x_r)$ can be

(a) General form of NAND logic elements

$$f(x_1, x_2, \cdots x_r) = \overline{x_1 \wedge x_2 \wedge \cdots \wedge x_r} = \overline{x}_1 \vee \overline{x}_2 \vee \cdots \vee \overline{x}_r$$

(b) General form of NOR logic elements

$$g(x_1, x_2, \cdots x_r) = \overline{(x_1 \vee x_2 \vee \cdots \vee x_r)} = \overline{x}_1 \overline{x}_2 \cdots \overline{x}_r$$

Figure 4-4 NAND and NOR logic elements.

represented in a canonical sum-of-product form. We can then apply, if desired, the basic properties of switching algebra to obtain a minimal sum-of-product realization of the function. The following example will show how any sum-of-product function can be realized using only NAND elements.

Assume that we are given a fucntion $h(x_1, x_2, x_3)$ in canonical sum-of-product form:

$$h(x_1, x_2, x_3) = \overline{x}_1\overline{x}_2\overline{x}_3 \vee \overline{x}_1\overline{x}_2 x_3 \vee x_1\overline{x}_2\overline{x}_3 \vee x_1 x_2\overline{x}_3 \vee x_1 x_2 x_3$$

This canonical expression can be reduced to

$$h(x_1, x_2, x_3) = \overline{x}_1\overline{x}_2 \vee \overline{x}_2\overline{x}_3 \vee x_1 x_2$$

The two-level AND-OR realization is given in Figure 4-5.

Now let us consider how we can realize $h(x_1, x_2, x_3)$ as a two-level NAND network. Using involution we note that

$$h(x_1, x_2, x_3) = \overline{\overline{h(x_1, x_2, x_3)}}$$

$$= \overline{(\overline{\overline{x}_1\overline{x}_2 \vee \overline{x}_2\overline{x}_3 \vee x_1 x_2})}$$

Applying DeMorgan's theorem then gives

$$h(x_1, x_2, x_3) = \overline{(\overline{\overline{x}_1\overline{x}_2} \wedge \overline{\overline{x}_2\overline{x}_3} \wedge \overline{x_1 x_2})}$$

Figure 4-5 AND-OR realization of $h(x_1, x_2, x_3)$.

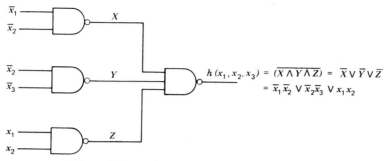

Figure 4-6   NAND representation of $h(x_1, x_2, x_3)$.

However, if we examine this expression we can write

$$h(x_1, x_2, x_3) = (\overline{X \wedge Y \wedge Z})$$

where

$$X = (\overline{x_1 \overline{x_2}}) \qquad Y = (\overline{\overline{x_2} \overline{x_3}}) \qquad Z = (\overline{x_1 x_2})$$

Thus we see that we can realize $h(x_1, x_2, x_3)$ using NAND elements as shown in Figure 4-6.

A graphical proof that the NAND network of Figure 4-6 is equivalent to the AND-OR network of Figure 4-5 is presented in Figure 4-7. The key to the conversion process is shown in Figure 4-7a where the NAND element is converted to an OR element with all of its inputs negated.

From this example we see that the NAND network realization follows directly from the sum-of-product representation. There is one special situation that we must be careful to handle properly. Assume that we have a function such as

$$f(x_1, x_2, x_3) = \overline{x}_1 \vee x_2 x_3$$

to realize. The product term $\overline{x}_1$ involving a single variable must be handled very carefully if a mistake is to be avoided. The NAND network corresponding to $f(x_1, x_2, x_3)$ is given in Figure 4-8.

Initially we need a NAND element to realize the term $\overline{x}_1$ as shown in Figure 4-8a. However, a single input NAND element is an inverter that performs the NOT operation. Thus we can eliminate this NAND element as shown in Figure 4-8b if x_1 is available as an input.

Using the principle of duality, we can realize a product-of-sum expression using NOR elements in a similar manner. For example, the network shown in Figure 4-9 will realize the function

$$g(x_1, x_2, x_3) = (x_1 \vee x_2)(x_1 \vee \overline{x}_3)(\overline{x}_2 \vee \overline{x}_3)$$

We can prove that this realization gives the desired logic function in exactly the same way that we did for the previous example. These calculations are left as an exercise.

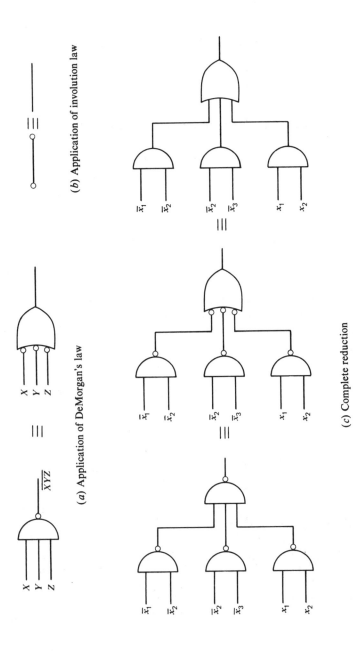

(a) Application of DeMorgan's law

(b) Application of involution law

(c) Complete reduction

Figure 4-7 Graphical interpretation of conversion of NAND-NOR network to an AND-OR network.

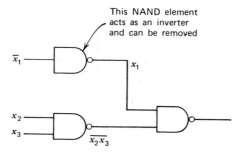

(a) Formal NAND network realization

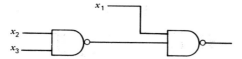

(b) Network after removing unnecessary inverter

Figure 4-8 Treatment of single variable product terms.

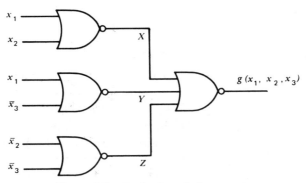

Figure 4-9 Realization of $g(x_1, x_2, x_3)$.

<u>**WARNING:**</u> <u>The above relationships are true only if we are dealing with two-level</u> <u>sum-of-product or product-of-sum expressions.</u> If logic networks with more than two levels are used, the situation is considerably more complicated. An expanded discussion of the logic design problem using NAND or NOR circuits can be found in Reference 2 listed at the end of this chapter.

EXERCISES

1. Find the minimal AND-OR, OR-AND, NAND, and NOR realization for the following truth table

x_1	x_2	x_3	$f(x_1, x_2, x_3)$
0	0	0	1
0	0	1	0
0	1	0	1
0	1	1	1
1	0	0	0
1	0	1	0
1	1	0	1
1	1	1	0

2. Find a NAND logic circuit realization for the following logic expression.

$$f(a, b, c) = a\bar{b} \vee b\bar{c} \vee \bar{a}\bar{b}\bar{c}$$

3. Find the dual of the function $f(a, b, c)$ given in exercise 2. Realize this function using NOR logic elements. Show that the two networks do not realize the same logic expression.

4. Show, using graphical techniques similar to those illustrated in Figure 4-7, that the NOR circuit realized in exercise 3 can also be realized as an OR-AND network.

4.   SPECIFICATION AND DESIGN OF COMBINATIONAL LOGIC NETWORKS

Up until this point we have been concentrating on developing the analytical techniques that can be used to represent and evaluate the behavior of a combinational logic network. The basic assumption in most of our discussions was that we had been given the truth table representation of a given combinational logic network and all we were asked to do was to find a logic expression that could be used to represent this truth table. This is a rather special situation. At the beginning of most design tasks we are given a (rather vague) word description of what we would like a logic network to do and we are then required to translate this word description into a design for this network. To carry out such a design process, a designer must decide which of the analytical techniques we have developed are useful for the problem being solved and then translate the problem into a form that makes it possible to apply these techniques.

Each design problem is different. As we gain experience and confidence we will find that even the most complex design problem can be handled if we undertake the design process in a systematic manner. However, before we can undertake the design of complete systems, we must first be able to design basic combinational logic networks of the form shown in Figure 4-10.

The input to the network is assumed to be a set of signals represented by the vectors, $A, \ldots, E$. These vectors contain the encoded information that is to be processed. The output of the network is represented by the vector Z. The symbol $:=$ is

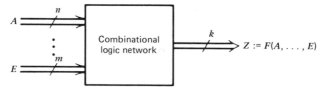

Figure 4-10 General representation of a combinational logic network.

used to indicate that Z is defined or specified by the function $F(A, \ldots, E)$. The number of elements in each vector is indicated by the value associated with the slash ($\neq$) in the line corresponding to the vector. For this figure we see that the vector A is represented as an n-tuple, the vector E is an m-tuple, and the vector Z is defined to be a k-tuple.

The Design Process

The design process starts when a set of requirements are formulated that define a need for a combinational logic network to carry out a specific task. It is the designer's responsibility to first translate these requirements into a set of specifications that describe the network in a formal manner and then realize the network using suitable logic circuit components. Although each design problem will have its own unique set of characteristics, the following systematic approach ensures that the design process will be carried out successfully.

Let us assume that you have been asked to design a combinational logic network that is to be used in a system being developed by your company. This design task can be accomplished by proceeding in the following manner.

Design Step 1

Using the set of requirements provided by the customer, identify and name all of the input signals to be supplied to the network and the output signals that the network must generate. The use of a figure, such as the one shown in Figure 4-10, to summarize this information is often a useful design aid that allows you to visualize the general form that the network will take.

Design Step 2

Establish the exact relationships that exist between the input and output information identified in Step 1. These relationships should be expressed in an analytical form, such as a truth table or a mathematical equation, and should be checked to see whether they conform to the stated requirements of the customer.

Design Step 3

Code (if necessary) each input and output signal into digital form. In some cases the code will be fixed by the system requirements, while in other cases the designer will be free to select the code that will produce the best design.

Design Step 4

Using the information from Steps 2 and 3, develop a set of logic expressions to represent the input/output relationships that must be realized by the combinational logic network. In some cases the logic expressions can be written down directly from the relationships developed in Steps 2 and 3.

Otherwise truth table or analytical techniques can be used to develop the necessary logic expressions.

Design Step 5

Decide upon the type of logic circuit elements that will be used to realize the network. Use appropriate analytical techniques to reduce the complexity of the logic expressions developed in Step 4 and to place the expressions into a form that can be used to realize the network using the selected logic circuit elements.

Design Step 6

Use the logic expressions developed in Step 5 to realize the network. Test the resulting realization to prove that the resulting network performs the tasks called for by the initial system requirements.

The following case studies will illustrate how these steps are applied to a number of typical problems.

An Absolute Value Network

As our first example assume that we have been given the following design task.

Design Requirement

Two 2-bit registers A and B are used to store two positive binary numbers. It is desired to design a logic network that will compute the absolute value of the difference between the two positive numbers.

From the statement of the problem we know that the numbers stored in A and B must have a decimal value in the range 0 to 3. To carry out the desired task we can use a network of the form shown in Figure 4-11a. The output of the network is

$$Z := |A - B|$$

This means that Z will also fall in the range of 0 to 3.

Next we must decide how this information is to be encoded. Examining the problem specification we see that all numbers are to be represented as standard binary numbers. Thus A and B can be represented as

$$[A] := [a_1, a_2] \qquad [B] := [b_1, b_2]$$

This means that the output Z can be represented as

$$[Z] := [z_1, z_2] = [f_1(a_1, a_2, b_1, b_2), f_2(a_1, a_2, b_1, b_2)]$$

Using this information we decide that we can use a network of the form shown in Figure 4-11b to carry out the desired task. Since this network has 4 inputs and 2 outputs, we can use the truth table given in Table 4-1 to describe this network.

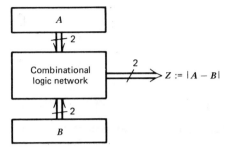

(*a*) General structure of network

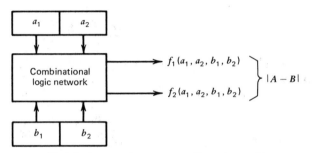

(*b*) A logic network to compute $Z := |A - B|$

Figure 4-11   Development of Logic Network to Compute $Z := |A - B|$.

Table 4-1   Truth Table for $Z := |A - B|$

A		B		$Z := [f_1, f_2]$	
a_1	a_2	b_1	b_2	$f_1(a_1, a_2, b_1, b_2)$	$f_2(a_1, a_2, b_1, b_2)$
0	0	0	0	0	0
0	0	0	1	0	1
0	0	1	0	1	0
0	0	1	1	1	1
0	1	0	0	0	1
0	1	0	1	0	0
0	1	1	0	0	1
0	1	1	1	1	0
1	0	0	0	1	0
1	0	0	1	0	1
1	0	1	0	0	0
1	0	1	1	0	1
1	1	0	0	1	1
1	1	0	1	1	0
1	1	1	0	0	1
1	1	1	1	0	0

The entries in the truth table are obtained by direct calculation. For example, if A has a decimal value of 2 and B has a value of 3, then $|A - B|$ has a decimal value of 1. Thus

$$[A] := [1, 0] \qquad [B] := [1, 1] \qquad [Z] := [0, 1]$$

This means that

$$f_1(1, 0, 1, 1) = 0 \qquad f_2(1, 0, 1, 1) = 1$$

Examining Table 4-1 we can develop the following minterm representation for the two output scalar functions.

$$\begin{aligned}
f_1(a_1, a_2, b_1, b_2) :=\ & \bar{a}_1\bar{a}_2 b_1 \bar{b}_2 \lor \bar{a}_1\bar{a}_2 b_1 b_2 \lor \bar{a}_1 a_2 b_1 b_2 \lor a_1\bar{a}_2\bar{b}_1\bar{b}_2 \lor \\
& a_1 a_2\bar{b}_1\bar{b}_2 \lor a_1 a_2\bar{b}_1 b_2 \\
:=\ & m_2 \lor m_3 \lor m_7 \lor m_8 \lor m_{12} \lor m_{13}
\end{aligned}$$

$$\begin{aligned}
f_2(a_1, a_2, b_1, b_2) :=\ & \bar{a}_1\bar{a}_2\bar{b}_1 b_2 \lor \bar{a}_1\bar{a}_2 b_1 b_2 \lor \\
& \bar{a}_1 a_2\bar{b}_1\bar{b}_2 \lor \bar{a}_1 a_2 b_1\bar{b}_2 \lor a_1\bar{a}_2 b_1 b_2 \lor \\
& a_1\bar{a}_2 b_1 b_2 \lor a_1 a_2\bar{b}_1\bar{b}_2 \lor a_1 a_2 b_1\bar{b}_2 \\
:=\ & m_1 \lor m_3 \lor m_4 \lor m_6 \lor m_9 \lor m_{11} \lor m_{12} \lor m_{14}
\end{aligned}$$

Next we apply our switching algebra to reduce these logic expressions to minimal form. Doing this gives us the following expressions

$$\begin{aligned}
f_1(a_1, a_2, b_1, b_2) :=\ & \bar{a}_1\bar{a}_2 b_1 \lor \bar{a}_1 b_1 b_2 \lor a_1\bar{b}_1\bar{b}_2 \lor a_1 a_2\bar{b}_1 \\
f_2(a_1, a_2, b_1, b_2) :=\ & \bar{a}_1\bar{a}_2 b_2 \lor \bar{a}_1 a_2\bar{b}_2 \lor a_1 a_2\bar{b}_2 \lor a_1\bar{a}_2 b_2 \\
:=\ & \bar{a}_2 b_2 \lor a_2\bar{b}_2
\end{aligned}$$

Using these expressions we obtain the logic network shown in Figure 4-12 as the final network to carry out our desired task. This can be verified by checking that the network corresponds to the truth table in Table 4-1.

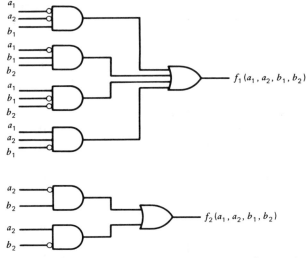

Figure 4-12   Logic network realization for $Z := |A - B|$.

In this example all the input and output variables were specified in a manner such that they could easily be identified and represented in digital form. This is not always the case, as illustrated by the next example.

A Parking Lot Gate Control Unit

Assume that you are working for a company that has three parking lots. Originally each employee was assigned to a specific lot and issued a specially coded card that indicated where he or she could park. However, it was found that many employees were disregarding these assignments, thus causing a very serious parking problem.

The management has decided to erect a gate at the entrance to each lot. To enter the lot an employee will be required to insert a card in a special slot at the gate. If the card entitles the employee to use the lot, the gate will open. Otherwise the gate is to remain closed.

The following parking assignments have been made.

Employee Class	Parking	Area	Allowed
Company officers	1	2	3
Managers	1	2	
Engineers	1	3	
Secretaries	2	3	
Machinists	1	2	
Electricians	1	3	
Accountants	2		

Design Requirement

Develop a logic network that can be used in each gate control system. The input to the network will be a signal produced by a card sensor. Based on the information received from the card sensor, the logic network must generate a signal that indicates whether the gate should or should not be opened.

Examining this problem we see that we must design three combinational logic networks. The input to each network will be a coded digital signal that either indicates no one has inserted a card or indicates which class of employee is seeking admittance. The output will be a 1 if the gate is to open or a 0 if it is to remain closed.

The first task is to assign a coding to the seven different employee groups and the "no input" condition. This coding, which requires at least three bits, can be assigned in an arbitrary manner. Once this coding is completed, the final task is to derive the logic expressions describing the outputs of each network. Table 4-2 indicates one possible solution to this problem.

The next task is to obtain a logical expression describing each output. Using maxterms, these expressions become

Gate 1

$$f_1(x_1, x_2, x_3) := M_0 \wedge M_4 \wedge M_7$$
$$:= (x_1 \vee x_2 \vee x_3) \wedge (\bar{x}_1 \vee x_2 \vee x_3) \wedge (\bar{x}_1 \vee \bar{x}_2 \vee \bar{x}_3)$$

Table 4-2 Encoding of Gate Control Signal

Employee Class	Digital Coding			Output		
	x_1	x_2	x_3	Gate 1	Gate 2	Gate 3
No input	0	0	0	0	0	0
Company officers	0	0	1	1	1	1
Managers	0	1	0	1	1	0
Engineers	0	1	1	1	0	1
Secretaries	1	0	0	0	1	1
Machinists	1	0	1	1	1	0
Electricians	1	1	0	1	0	1
Accountants	1	1	1	0	1	0

Gate 2

$$f_2(x_1, x_2, x_3) := M_0 \wedge M_3 \wedge M_6$$
$$:= (x_1 \vee x_2 \vee x_3) \wedge (x_1 \vee \bar{x}_2 \vee \bar{x}_3) \wedge (\bar{x}_1 \vee \bar{x}_2 \vee x_3)$$

Gate 3

$$f_3(x_1, x_2, x_3) := M_0 \wedge M_2 \wedge M_5 \wedge M_7$$
$$:= (x_1 \vee x_2 \vee x_3) \wedge (x_1 \vee \bar{x}_2 \vee x_3) \wedge (\bar{x}_1 \vee x_2 \vee \bar{x}_3)$$
$$\wedge (\bar{x}_1 \vee \bar{x}_2 \vee \bar{x}_3)$$

These expressions can be simplified using our switching algebra to give

Gate 1

$$f_1(x_1, x_2, x_3) = (x_2 \vee x_3) \wedge (\bar{x}_1 \vee \bar{x}_2 \vee \bar{x}_3)$$

Gate 2

(NOTE: No reduction is possible for this expression)

$$f_2(x_1, x_2, x_3) = (x_1 \vee x_2 \vee x_3) \wedge (x_1 \vee \bar{x}_2 \vee \bar{x}_3) \wedge (\bar{x}_1 \vee \bar{x}_2 \vee x_3)$$

Gate 3

$$f_3(x_1, x_2, x_3) = (x_1 \vee x_3) \wedge (\bar{x}_1 \vee \bar{x}_3)$$

From these expressions we can develop the logic networks shown in Figure 4-13 for the control units for each gate.

Problem Decomposition

The examples given thus far deal with truth tables that have a reasonable number of rows. However, consider the problem of developing a truth table for a function

$$Z := F(A, B)$$

when the information associated with A and B is represented by the r-tuples

$$[a_1, a_2, \ldots, a_r] \quad \text{and} \quad [b_1, b_2, \ldots, b_r]$$

respectively.

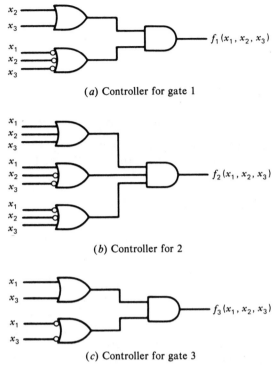

(a) Controller for gate 1

(b) Controller for 2

(c) Controller for gate 3

Figure 4-13   Logic network to control access gates.

The truth table representation of $F(A, B)$ will require 2^{2r} rows. If $r = 2$ we need 16 rows, if $r = 3$ we need 64 rows, and if $r = 5$ we need 1024 rows. Obviously if we are dealing with $r > 2$, it is not practical to try to write down a truth table which represents $F(A, B)$.

To solve this problem we must be able to break the task represented by $F(A, B)$ into component parts. Let us assume that Z is an n-tuple $[z_1, z_2, \ldots, z_n]$. Then the statement

$$Z := F(A, B)$$

really means that there exist n scalar functions

$$f_i(a_1, a_2, \ldots, a_r, b_1, b_2, \ldots, b_r) \qquad i = 1, 2, \ldots, n$$

such that

$$z_1 := f_1(a_1, \ldots, a_r, b_1, \ldots, b_r)$$
$$z_2 := f_2(a_1, \ldots, a_r, b_1, \ldots, b_r)$$
$$\vdots$$
$$z_n := f_r(a_1, \ldots, a_r, b_1, \ldots, b_r)$$

This does not appear to be an improvement. However, when we examine the definition of $F(A, B)$, we may find that the binary function f_i is dependent on only a small number of the variables in the set $a_1, a_2, \ldots, a_r, b_1, b_2, \ldots, b_r$. The following examples illustrate this idea.

A Simple Vector Operation

The next example illustrates how we can design logic networks to carry out operations on vectors.

Design Requirements

Design a logic network to compute

$$Z := A \wedge B$$

where A and B correspond to the information contained in two r-bit registers and the resulting value Z is defined to be formed as the bit by bit ANDing of the contents of each register.

To understand this design problem we can construct a simple example. For example if

$$A := [1, 0, 1, 1] \qquad B := [0, 1, 1, 0]$$

then

$$Z := [1, 0, 1, 1] \wedge [0, 1, 1, 0] = [1 \wedge 0, 0 \wedge 1, 1 \wedge 1, 1 \wedge 0] = [0, 0, 1, 0]$$

In this situation we note that since A and B are represented by r-tuples, Z is represented by the r-tuple $[z_1, \ldots, z_r]$. To realize this operation using a single combinational logic network would require a network of the form shown in Figure 4-14.

Constructing a truth table for this network, even for $r > 3$, would be an impossible task. However, consider the binary function that describes each z_i. Since $A \wedge B$ represents the bit by bit ANDing of the two r-tuples, this means that

$$z_1 := a_1 \wedge b_1 = f_1(a_1, \ldots, a_r, b_1, \ldots, b_r) = f_1(a_1, b_1)$$
$$z_2 := a_2 \wedge b_2 = f_2(a_1, \ldots, a_r, b_1, \ldots, b_r) = f_2(a_2, b_2)$$
$$\vdots$$
$$z_r := a_r \wedge b_r = f_r(a_1, \ldots, a_r, b_1, \ldots, b_r) = f_r(a_r, b_r)$$

Thus the complex combinational network of Figure 4-14 can be decomposed into r subnetworks as shown in Figure 4-15a. To complete the design we must develop the

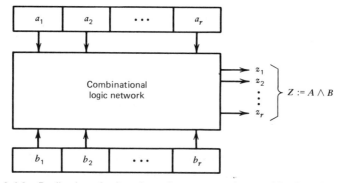

Figure 4-14   Realization of a function using one complex combinational logic network.

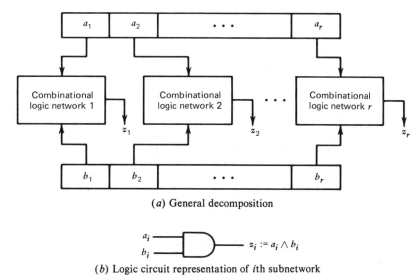

(*a*) General decomposition

$$a_i \quad\quad\quad\quad z_i := a_i \wedge b_i$$
$$b_i$$

(*b*) Logic circuit representation of *i*th subnetwork

Figure 4-15 Decomposition of a complex combinational logic network into subnetwords.

logic circuit for each of the subnetworks. From our analysis we find that the *i*th subnetwork is described by the relationship

$$f_i(a_i, b_i) := a_i \wedge b_i$$

From this we can complete our design by using the circuit shown in Figure 4-15*b* to represent each of the subnetworks in Figure 4-15*a*.

This simple example has illustrated the decomposition process. Our goal in such a design problem is to use the structural features of the problem to decompose the complex combinational logic network that we wish to design into an interconnection of simpler subnetworks. Hopefully the resulting decomposition will produce a set of subnetworks that we can specify using our truth table representation techniques. For this problem we were able to decompose a network that initially required a truth table with 2^{2r} rows into a network made up of *r* subnetworks. Each of the subnetworks could then be described by a truth table with 2^2 rows. The next example expands upon this idea.

A Controlled Combinational Logic Network

There are many applications in which we want to control the operation performed by a combinational logic network. This can be accomplished by using a combinational logic network organized as shown in Figure 4-16. The system consists of two *r*-bit registers *A* and *B* and a third register *I* called an *instruction register*. We wish to build a logic network that carries out the operations described by the following design requirements where [0] indicates that the output should be identically zero.

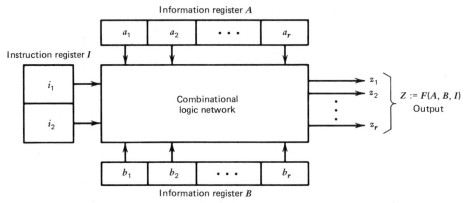

Figure 4-16   Controlled combinational logic network.

Design Requirements

Design a controlled combinational logic network that will carry out the following operations.

Contents of Instruction Register	Operation to be Performed	Meaning
0	$Z := A \wedge B$	Bit by bit AND
1	$Z := A \vee B$	Bit by bit OR
2	$Z := \overline{A}$	Bit by bit NOT
3	$Z := [0]$	Each output bit 0

From the above we see that the register I must have a minimum of 2 bits, since there are four different instructions. Using the same reasoning as in the previous example, we know that the network, which has the form shown in Figure 4-16, can be broken up into r subnetworks, which operate upon the individual bits of A and B. The general form of the network that operates on the jth bits of the A and B registers to form z_i can be represented as shown in Figure 4-17. The truth table representing the function $f_j(i_1, i_2, a_j, b_j)$ is given in Table 4-3.

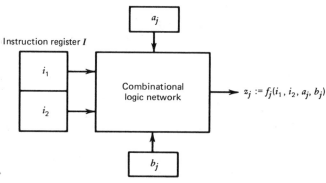

Figure 4-17   Component part of a register logic network.

Table 4-3   Truth Table for Component Network

i_1	i_2	a_j	b_j	$f_j(i_1, i_2, a_j, b_j)$	Operation Performed
0	0	0	0	0	
0	0	0	1	0	$A \wedge B$
0	0	1	0	0	
0	0	1	1	1	
0	1	0	0	0	
0	1	0	1	1	$A \vee B$
0	1	1	0	1	
0	1	1	1	1	
1	0	0	0	1	
1	0	0	1	1	$\overline{A}$
1	0	1	0	0	
1	0	1	1	0	
1	1	0	0	0	
1	1	0	1	0	
1	1	1	0	0	[0]
1	1	1	1	0	

Using Table 4-3, we can develop the minterm representation of $f_j(i_1, i_2, a_j, b_j)$ as

$$f_j(i_1, i_2, a_j, b_j) := \bar{i}_1\bar{i}_2 a_j b_j \vee \bar{i}_1 i_2 \bar{a}_j b_j \vee \bar{i}_1 i_2 a_j \bar{b}_j \vee \bar{i}_1 i_2 a_j b_j \vee i_1 \bar{i}_2 \bar{a}_j \bar{b}_j \vee i_1 \bar{i}_2 \bar{a}_j b_j$$
$$:= m_3 \vee m_5 \vee m_6 \vee m_7 \vee m_8 \vee m_9$$

Using our switching algebra we can reduce these equations to

$$f_j(i_1, i_2, a_j, b_j) := \bar{i}_1 a_j b_j \vee \bar{i}_1 i_2 b_j \vee \bar{i}_1 i_2 a_j \vee i_1 \bar{i}_2 \bar{a}_j$$

From this expression we obtain the logic network shown in Figure 4-18 as the final representation for the subnetwork of Figure 4-17. If we construct r copies of this network, we will have a complete network that carries out the desired set of logic operations on the information contained in the registers A and B.

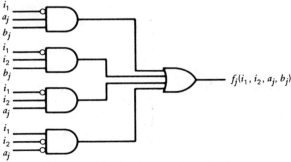

Figure 4-18   Logic network realization.

EXERCISES

1. It is desired to build a combinational logic network that will convert numerical information encoded in a 3-bit gray code into conventional binary number form. Find the logical expressions that will describe this network (*Hint:* See Table 2-10 of Chapter 2).

2. Let A and B be two r-bit registers and I an instruction register. Find the logical expression that describes the logic network that will carry out the following operations

Contents of Instruction Register	Operation to be Performed
0	$\overline{A \wedge B}$
1	$\overline{A \vee B}$
2	$A \vee B$
3	$A\overline{B} \vee \overline{A}B$

5. SUMMARY

In this chapter we have established the analytical tools that we need to specify the behavior of the different logic networks used to process information in digital form. Using these techniques we were then able to investigate the methods that can be used to design medium-size combinational logic networks. However, as the complexity of the task that we wished to perform increased, we found that we could not solve the problem directly. Instead we were required to decompose the design problem into a set of subproblems that could be solved individually. Once each subproblem was solved we then had the solution to the original problem.

Switching algebra is a very useful analytical tool when we are trying to design a combinational logic network that is described by a truth table or a logic expression. However, as we try to design more complex networks, we find that we need a richer set of modeling techniques to specify these networks. This will be our goal in the next chapter, where we first investigate some of the techniques that can be used to describe higher level operations on information described in vector form and then show how these operations can be realized using the techniques just discussed in this chapter.

Reference Notation

A comprehensive discussion of Boolean algebra and its mathematical properties can be found in Reference 4. Applications of Boolean algebra to switching circuits is treated in References 1, 2, 3, and 5. These discussions also provide additional examples of how a combinational logic network can be decomposed into smaller subnetworks to simplify the design process.

REFERENCES

1. Brzuzowski, J. A., and Yoeli, M. (1976), *Digital Networks*. Prentice-Hall, Englewood Cliffs, N.J.
2. Dietmeyer, D. L. (1978), *Logic Design of Digital Systems* (second edition). Allyn and Bacon, Boston.
3. Hill, F. J., and Peterson, G. R. (1981), *Introduction to Switching Theory and Logical Design* (third edition). Wiley, New York.
4. Hone, F. E. (1966), *Applied Boolean Algebra—An Elementary Introduction*. Macmillan, New York.
5. Winkel, D., and Prosser, F. (1980), *The Art of Digital Design—An Introduction to Top-Down Design*. Prentice-Hall, Englewood Cliffs, N.J.

HOME PROBLEMS

1. From our discussion in Chapter 3 we know that any logical function $f(x_1, x_2, \ldots, x_n)$ of n variables can be represented in canonical form using the Boolean operations of AND, OR, and NOT applied to the variables.

   (a) Show, using DeMorgan's theorem, that any logical function of n variables can be represented by a Boolean expression involving only the operations of AND and NOT.

   (b) State the dual of this result.

2. Show that any logic expression can be realized using only NOR elements.

3. Is the NAND operation
   (a) commutative?
   (b) associative?
   (c) distributive with respect to AND?

   Prove each result. State the dual of these results.

4. The cancellation law of regular algebra says that if

$$a + b = a + c$$

   then

$$b = c$$

   Prove, by giving a counter example, that if

$$a \lor b = a \lor c$$

   then

$$b = c$$

   is a false assumption. Thus the cancellation law does not hold true in Boolean algebra.

5. A complex logic network of the form shown in Figure P4-1 can be used to detect whether the contents of the A register and the contents of the B register are equal. Define the logic expression g_i, which describes the r-identical combinational logic networks used to realize the whole network.

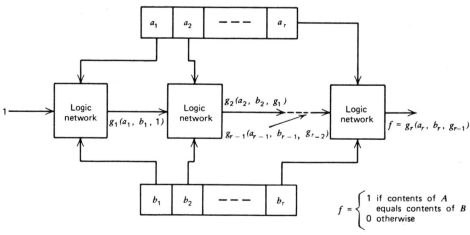

Figure P4-1   Network to test equality of two quantities.

6. Networks of the general form shown in Figure P4-2 are quite common in digital systems. Design a logic network to realize the following values for c_1, c_2, and c_3.

$c_1 = 1$ when the contents of A is an even binary number

$c_2 = 1$ when the contents of A is a binary number corresponding to the decimal numbers 3 or 6

$c_3 = 1$ when the contents of A is a binary number corresponding to the decimal numbers 1, 3, 5, or 7.

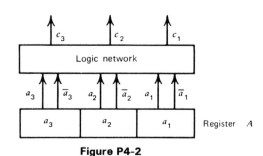

Figure P4-2

7. A multiplexer network of the form shown in Figure P4-3 is to be realized. Give the logical expressions that describe this network, where

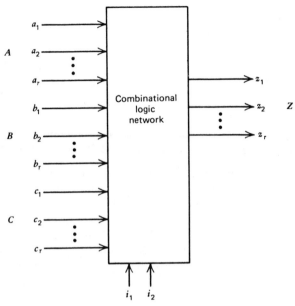

Figure P4-3   A multiplexer network.

$$Z := [0] \text{ if } [i_1, i_2] := [0, 0]$$
$$Z := A \text{ if } [i_1, i_2] = [1, 0]$$
$$Z := B \text{ if } [i_1, i_2] := [0, 1]$$
$$Z := C \text{ if } [i_1, i_2] = [1, 1]$$

8. Numeric displays of the type found on hand calculators are realized using 7-segment displays of the form shown in Figure P4-4*a*.

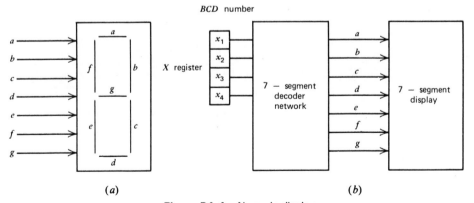

Figure P4-4   Numeric display.

When a 1 is placed on one of the input leads, the corresponding bar in the display lights up. The numbers 0 through 9 are then formed as

Give the logic expressions for the combinational logic functions that describe the 7-segment decoder of Figure P4-4*b*. The input is a BCD encoded number.

9. Assume that a 12-bit register A is designed to hold a 3-digit BCD encoded decimal number. In some situations it might be possible to deposit a digital signal into A that is not an acceptable representation of such a 3-digit number. It is desired to develop an error detection network that will monitor the contents of A. As long as the information in A is an acceptable value, the output of the error detection network must be 0. Otherwise it is to have a value of 1 indicating an error. Design this error detection network. *Reminder:* Each BCD encoded digit requires 4 bits.

5

OPERATIONS ON DIGITAL INFORMATION

1. INTRODUCTION

The preceding chapters have presented the analytical techniques used to describe the behavior of combinational logic networks. From this discussion it might appear that each such network must be custom-designed for a particular application. Fortunately this is not true. We can use the analytical techniques that we have developed to define a collection of standard operations that can be performed upon digital information. When designing a large digital system, we use these operations to describe the tasks performed by the system without having to worry about how each operation is realized. When the system level design is finished, we can use the techniques discussed in the last chapter to define the logic modules that realize the operations included in the design.

When designing combinational logic networks, we deal with networks of the type shown in Figure 5-1a and b. At this level we must consider such details as

1. What coding is used to represent the information being processed.
2. What logic expressions

$$f_i(x_1, \ldots, x_r)$$

or

$$g_i(x_1, \ldots, x_r, y_1, \ldots, y_s)$$

are required to represent the individual scalar functions that describe the network.

When we move to the system level, we suppress these details and concentrate on the system level characteristics of the network. At this level we represent the tasks performed by combinational logic networks as shown in Figure 5-1c and d. In this representation the input and output consist of appropriately encoded digital signals X, Y, and Z. The relationship between the output signal Z and the input information represented by the signals X and Y depends on the operations performed by the networks. These operations are represented by functions of the form $F(X)$ and $G(X, Y)$, which indicate how the information in the input signals is to be acted upon rather than the logical relations that must be realized to carry out the operation.

When designing at this level, we must consider problems such as

1. What information are we dealing with and what is its allowed range of values?
2. What mathematical expression must we evaluate to produce the desired output signal?

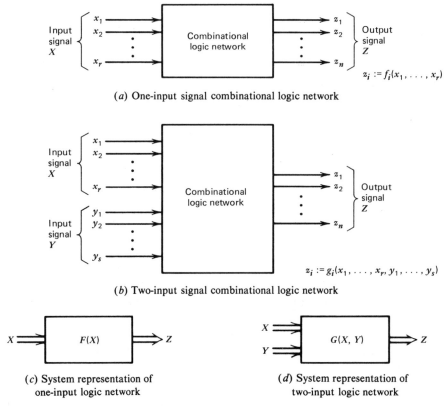

(a) One-input signal combinational logic network

(b) Two-input signal combinational logic network

(c) System representation of
one-input logic network

(d) System representation of
two-input logic network

Figure 5-1   General system representation of high-level processing tasks.

This chapter introduces the notational conventions and operations that are used in later chapters to design complex digital networks. As part of this discussion we show how many of these operations can be realized in terms of standard combinational logic networks. Finally we introduce some of the standard medium-scale integrated (MSI) circuits that are commercially available to realize these operations.

2.   NOTATIONAL CONVENTIONS

One goal of this chapter is to divorce ourselves as much as possible from the logic circuit level details involved in realizing a given information processing operation. Thus we first develop a set of notational conventions that allow us to describe the information content of digital signals and the operations performed on these signals independent of the ultimate way in which these signals are encoded or the operations performed. A number of such conventions are in current use. The conventions used in this book are introduced in this section. Other notational conventions are described in the references listed at the end of this chapter.

Identifiers

Identifiers are used to represent constants, variables, and functions. An *identifier* consists of a letter followed by an indefinite number of letters, digits, or the underscore character (_). In any identifier the letters are either all uppercase or all lowercase. Numerical subscripts can be used with any identifier. The meaning of the subscripts will depend upon the context in which they are used. Some typical identifiers are:

X1   START   J1_GO $ACC_{1,6}$
x1   finish   f3_t6 acc_5

The following character sequences are not valid identifiers;

5FG2   Does not start with a letter
I*F   Invalid character
x3 y2   Contains a space

We also use the conventions that

1. Identifiers formed using lowercase letters represent scalar quantities.
2. Identifiers formed using uppercase letters represent vector quantities.

When discussing a vector we are often interested only in the information represented by the vector and not in the method selected to encode the information. If we need to discuss the structure of a vector, we assume that the vector is represented as an r-tuple. For example, if X represents a vector, then it is assumed that X can be represented by an r-tuple of the form

$$[x_1, x_2, \ldots, x_r]$$

where each of the x_i's is a scalar. When we wish to indicate that we are interested in the exact encoding of X, we use the notation $[X]$ to represent

$$[x_1, x_2, \ldots, x_r]$$

The individual scalars that make up the r-tuple are normally numbered from left to right. In some cases the numbering will be 1 through r while in other cases it is convenient to use 0 through $r - 1$. There is one major exception to this rule. When we use a vector to represent numerical information, the individual scalars that make up the r-tuple are numbered from right to left and are numbered 0 through $r - 1$. Thus, if A represents a 6-bit binary number, $[A]$ would be represented as

$$[a_5, a_4, \ldots, a_1, a_0]$$

Domain of Definition

Identifiers are used to name the signals that are present in a given system. To complete the description of an identifier we must define the values that can be associated with the signal represented by the identifier. As we know from earlier discussions, signals may be classified as either vectors or scalars. When we use an identifier to represent a scalar or a vector, this identifier is assumed to be a variable that may take on a value from a set of allowed values. A scalar is always assumed to have only two values. However, we may give particular meaning, such as 0 or 1 or TRUE or FALSE, to these values. Vectors are used to represent a much wider range of values. When designing at the system level, we are often interested in the information represented by a vector but we do not need to know how this information is actually encoded. Thus when we discuss a vector identifier, one of the first things we must do is to define the domain of definition of the vector.

The *domain of an identifier* is an ordered, finite set of values that may be associated with that identifier. This set is defined by listing the allowed values in the assumed order. The listing has the form

$$\{ \langle 1\text{st value}\rangle, \langle 2\text{nd value}\rangle, \ldots, \langle k\text{th value}\rangle \}$$

where the ith value comes before the jth value if $i < j$. The ordering defined for a domain may be a "natural ordering" or an arbitrary ordering defined by the designer. Some typical domains are listed below.

Identifier	Domain	Description
T	{0, 1, 2, 3, 4, 5, 6, 7, 8, 9}	Vector representing the decimal digits
f	{NOT_READY, READY}	Scalar representing two logical conditions
V	{A, B, . . . , Z, a, b, . . . , z}	Vector representing the upper and lower case letters
INST	{ADD,SUB,MUL,DIV,NOP}	Vector representing five "concepts"
SIGVAL	{−255, . . . , 0, . . . , +255}	Vector representing decimal integers in interval [−255, 255]

In the examples given above, the number of elements in the domain are fixed as well as the ordering. According to these definitions we have $A < a$ when we are dealing with the information represented by the vector V and SUB < MUL when we deal with the vector INST.

Composite Domains

In some designs it is desirable to represent a given signal as being formed from two or more subsignals. For example, assume that $T1$ and $T2$ are two signals that represent identifiable information in a design but that they are combined into a single signal T. The signal T is said to be a *composite signal* and it is represented as

$$T := [T1, T2]$$

where we say that $T1$ and $T2$ are subsignals (or subvectors) of the signal (vector) T.

The domain of T is defined in terms of the domains of $T1$ and $T2$. For example, if $T1$ has the domain $\{A, B, C\}$ and $T2$ has the domain $\{0, 1, 2\}$, then the domain of T consists of all the pairs of values that can be formed by taking a value from the domain of $T1$ and one from the domain of $T2$. The resulting domain of T may have the form

$$\{[A, 0]\ [A, 1]\ [A, 2]\ [B, 0]\ [B, 1]\ [B, 2]\ [C, 0]\ [C, 1]\ [C, 2]\}$$

where we have selected to represent T in the natural "dictionary ordering" suggested by the domains of $T1$ and $T2$. However, the domain of T could also be represented as

$$\{[A, 0]\ [B, 0]\ [C, 0]\ [A, 1]\ [B, 1]\ [C, 1]\ [A, 2]\ [B, 2]\ [C, 2]\}$$

When defining the domain of a composite signal, it is the responsibility of the designer to define the ordering selected for the domain if this ordering is of importance.

The domain associated with a composite signal is called a *composite domain*. If we wish to indicate the relationship between this domain and the domains associated with the domains of the subsignals, we use a notation of the form

$$T = T1 \times T2$$

which indicates that the composite domain consists of pairs of values where the first value is selected from the domain of $T1$ and the second value is selected from the domain of $T2$. Nothing is implied about the ordering of T in this definition.

Operands

Identifiers that appear as arguments in a function or are acted on by specific operations are called *operands*. Operands represent the information being processed. When we use a figure to describe the system being considered, we use the convention shown in Figure 5-2 to represent operands.

Scalar operands are indicated by a single line, as shown in Figure 5-2a. The name of the operand is written near to the line. Vector operands can take two forms. If we are not interested in the number of bits used to represent the vector, we indicate a vector operand as a double line, as indicated in Figure 5-2b. When the operand is known to be an r-bit operand, we use the double line but place a labeled slash through the line to indicate that the operand has r bits. This is illustrated in Figure 5-2c.

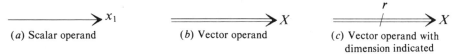

(a) Scalar operand   (b) Vector operand   (c) Vector operand with dimension indicated

Figure 5-2   Graphical representation of operands.

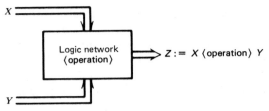

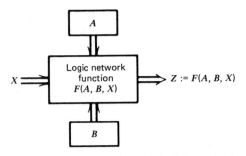

(*a*) Binary operation performed on two signals to produce an output signal

(*b*) Function operating on a signal X and the information in two registers

Figure 5-3   Schematic representation of basic information processing operations.

Specification or Definition

Figure 5-3 illustrates two typical situations where one or more input operands are processed to produce an output signal Z. In this situation we say that Z is *defined* or *specified* to have a particular relationship to the operands. This relationship is indicated by the notation

$$\langle \text{identifier} \rangle := \langle \text{value} \rangle$$

where the operation $:=$ is used to indicate that the quantity on the left-hand side of $:=$ is specified or defined to have the value given by the quantity on the right-hand side. We use this special symbol instead of the equal sign $=$ since, as discussed shortly, the equal sign has another meaning.

The term represented by $\langle \text{value} \rangle$ either is a constant or is obtained by processing the input operands according to a prespecified information processing operation. The following examples show typical applications of the define operation

$$A := B + C$$
$$A := [20]$$
$$z := A \leq B$$

The meaning of these statements will be discussed in the following sections.

The value of the quantity on the left-hand side of the definition operation is assumed to remain unchanged as long as all of the operands used to form the value on the right-hand side remain unchanged.

Constants and Values

A signal can be used to represent a wide variety of information. If a signal is given a fixed value, we say that the signal represents a *constant*. The form that a constant will take depends on its use.

The simplest situation occurs when we wish to specify that a signal has a particular value. For example, if X is known to be a 4-tuple, then

$$X := [1, 1, 0, 1]$$

means that a particular value has been specified for X.

One goal of this chapter is to develop design techniques that can be used to describe the task performed by a complex combinational logic network without having to deal with the details of realizing the network at the logic level. Thus to discuss the value of a signal without having to specify the particular coding used in its representation, we use the following notation.

If we wish to indicate that a given signal X has a numerical value of n, we use the notation

$$X := [n]$$

and assume that an appropriate binary code has been used to encode n. If the base b of the number system is important, we can indicate this as

$$X := [n_b]$$

if the base is not obvious from the context of the discussion.

In particular the notation

$$X := [0]$$

is used to indicate that all of the binary variables that form the signal are identically 0. Thus

$$X := [0] \quad \text{is equivalent to} \quad X := [0, 0, \ldots, 0]$$

In some applications we will be dealing with character information. A character constant is indicated as

$$X := [\text{'}AB\text{'}]$$

The single quotes around the character string AB indicate that the constant is an appropriately encoded version of these characters. For example, if we are told that X is a 16-bit signal and that each character is stored in one byte, then

$$X := [\text{'}AB\text{'}]$$

would be equivalent to

$$X := [0, 1, 0, 0, 0, 0, 0, 1, 0, 1, 0, 0, 0, 0, 1, 0]$$

if we decide to represent character information using the ASCII code.

When a signal, say T, is defined to have a given domain, then it is possible to indicate that T takes on a constant value from that domain. For example, if the domain is

$$\{ADD, SUB, MUL, DIV, NOP\}$$

then the specification that

$$T := [DIV]$$

indicates that T is specified to have the value of the 4th element of the domain.

Functional Representation

The techniques used to represent the behavior of a logic network at the system level are similar to the logic functions used to represent the same network at the logic level. The main difference is that we concentrate upon the information contained in the signals being processed by the network rather than upon how the network operates upon the individual bits that make up the signals. We can identify two classes of functions.

The simplest functions are *scalar functions* that have the form

$$z := f(A, B, \ldots, G)$$

where the scalar output z is defined as a function of the values associated with the input arguments $A, B, \ldots, G$. When such a function is realized by a logic network, the output of the network will be a scalar value while the input operands may be either scalars or vectors.

The second class of functions are *vector functions* that have the form

$$Z := F(W, X, \ldots, Y)$$

where the vector output Z is defined as a function of the values associated with the input arguments $W, X, \ldots, Y$. When a vector function is realized by a logic network, we must know the encoding of both the output information and the information contained in the arguments. The function is realized using the standard logic realization techniques discussed in Chapter 4.

A number of techniques are used to specify functions at the system level. The simplest method is to present the functional relationship between the input and the output in tabular form. For those functions that are in general use, we can give each a name and call it an *operator*.

Some functions can be represented in terms of a mathematical expression made up of basic operations applied to the input signals. The following example illustrates the tabular method of representing a function. The rest of this chapter discusses some of the basic operations we will find useful and shows how they can be used to represent several complex information processing tasks.

Tabular Representation of Functions

The tabular representation of a function is similar to the truth table representation technique used for describing combinational logic networks. The main difference is that we suppress the detailed information about how the arguments associated with

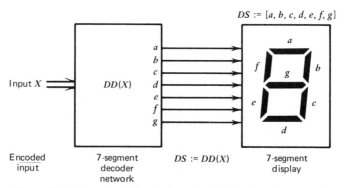

Figure 5-4 Functional description of a display decoder network.

the function are encoded. To illustrate this method of specification consider the system shown in Figure 5-4.

The input signal, X, is assumed to be an encoded decimal digit with domain {[0], ..., [9]}. The task of the network is to generate the signal DS that will drive the 7-segment display. We see that each element of the display is indicated by a letter. If the scalar value applied to an input lead labeled by that letter is 1, the segment indicated by the letter will light. In this way we can form all of the digits from 0 to 9. Thus we wish to define a function $DD(X)$ to describe the operation of this network. The relationship that we must describe is indicated as

$$DS := DD(X)$$

At this point we do not know the encoding that has been used to represent the input values associated with X. However, we do know that DS has the general form

$$DS := [a, b, c, d, e, f, g]$$

The domain of DS corresponds to all of the 7-tuples that correspond to the display of one of the decimal digits. The system level definition of $DD(X)$ can be represented by a table of the form shown in Table 5-1. As shown the rows are labeled with the distinct values that can be assigned to X independent of the encoding used to represent these values. The output signal has a predefined encoding, which we must indicate. For example, using this table we see that

$$DD([4]) := [0, 1, 1, 0, 0, 1, 1]$$

will cause a 4 to be lit on the display when the input argument has the value of 4.

As long as we are only interested in the system level operation of the decoder network, the representation of Table 5-1 is sufficient. If we must design the combinational logic circuit necessary to realize this network, we must supply additional information concerning the encoding of X.

For example, let us assume that X is encoded using the 2, 4, 2, 1 weighted code discussed in Chapter 2. Then if

$$X := [x_1, x_2, x_3, x_4]$$

Table 5-1   Tabular Description of 7-Segment Decoder

X	$DS := [a, b, c, d, e, f, g]$
[0]	[1, 1, 1, 1, 1, 1, 0]
[1]	[0, 1, 1, 0, 0, 0, 0]
[2]	[1, 1, 0, 1, 1, 0, 1]
[3]	[1, 1, 1, 1, 0, 0, 1]
[4]	[0, 1, 1, 0, 0, 1, 1]
[5]	[1, 0, 1, 1, 0, 1, 1]
[6]	[0, 0, 1, 1, 1, 1, 1]
[7]	[1, 1, 1, 0, 0, 0, 0]
[8]	[1, 1, 1, 1, 1, 1, 1]
[9]	[1, 1, 1, 0, 0, 1, 1]
All inputs outside domain	[0, 0, 0, 0, 0, 0, 0]

The value of n represented by X is given by

$$n = 2*x_1 + 4*x_2 + 2*x_3 + x_4$$

The truth table representing the combinational logic network that will realize this decoding network is given by Table 5-2. Since at this level we are dealing with a

Table 5-2   Truth Table Description of 7-Segment Decoder Input Encoded Using the 2, 4, 2, 1 Weighted Code

\multicolumn{4}{c}{2, 4, 2, 1 Encoded Input}		$DD(X)$
x_1	x_2	x_3	x_4	X	$[a, b, c, d, e, f, g]$
0	0	0	0	[0]	[1, 1, 1, 1, 1, 1, 0]
0	0	0	1	[1]	[0, 1, 1, 0, 0, 0, 0]
0	0	1	0	[2]	[1, 1, 0, 1, 1, 0, 1]
0	0	1	1	[3]	[1, 1, 1, 1, 0, 0, 1]
0	1	0	0	[4]	[0, 1, 1, 0, 0, 1, 1]
0	1	0	1	—	[0, 0, 0, 0, 0, 0, 0]
0	1	1	0	—	[0, 0, 0, 0, 0, 0, 0]
0	1	1	1	—	[0, 0, 0, 0, 0, 0, 0]
1	0	0	0	—	[0, 0, 0, 0, 0, 0, 0]
1	0	0	1	—	[0, 0, 0, 0, 0, 0, 0]
1	0	1	0	—	[0, 0, 0, 0, 0, 0, 0]
1	0	1	1	[5]	[1, 0, 1, 1, 0, 1, 1]
1	1	0	0	[6]	[0, 0, 1, 1, 1, 1, 1]
1	1	0	1	[7]	[1, 1, 1, 0, 0, 0, 0]
1	1	1	0	[8]	[1, 1, 1, 1, 1, 1, 1]
1	1	1	1	[9]	[1, 1, 1, 0, 0, 1, 1]

logic design problem, we have arranged the rows in the normal manner for a truth table. Thus the values associated with X do not appear in the same order as they do in Table 5-1.

Once we have the truth table, we can complete the design by forming the minterm logic expression for each of the outputs. For example, the logic expression for the output e is given by the expression

$$e := m_0 \lor m_2 \lor m_{12} \lor m_{14}$$

Expressions for the other outputs can be obtained in a similar manner.

Operations

The concept of a logic operation discussed in Chapter 3 can easily be extended to situations where one or more of the operands are vectors. For our needs, we can identify two classes of operators. They are *unary operators,* which involve a single operand and have the form

$$\langle result \rangle := \langle operator \rangle \langle operand \rangle$$

and *binary operators,* which involve two operands and have the form

$$\langle result \rangle := \langle operand \rangle \langle operator \rangle \langle operand \rangle$$

The operators that we investigated in Chapter 3 operated on scalar operands and produced scalar results. The operators considered in the next sections have a much richer structure.

All of the unary operators that we consider have a vector operand and produce a vector as the result. When we deal with the possible binary operators, we have a number of different possible forms. These forms are summarized in Table 5-3.

In the next sections we introduce a number of useful vector, relational, and mixed mode operations that can be used to describe the tasks performed by complex combinational logic networks. The usefulness of this approach is that we can concentrate upon the information processing task being carried out rather than becoming involved with the fine details of developing the lower level logic equations that describe the network.

Table 5-3 Possible Forms of Binary Operations

Class	⟨operand-1⟩	⟨operand-2⟩	⟨result⟩	Comment
A.	scalar	scalar	scalar	Standard scalar operation
B.	scalar	vector	scalar	No operators of this form
	vector	scalar	scalar	
C.	scalar	vector	vector	Mixed mode operation
	vector	scalar	vector	
D.	vector	vector	scalar	Relational operation
E.	vector	vector	vector	Vector operation

EXERCISES

1.   Assume that X is an 8-bit vector. Show the encoding implied by the following expressions.

(a) $X := [15]$		BCD encoding
(b) $X := [15]$		Binary encoding
(c) $X := ['A']$		ASCII encoding

2.   Find the logic expressions that complete the definition of the mapping $DD(X)$ defined by Table 5-2.

3.   Using the classification given by Table 5-3, classify each of the following binary operations.

(a) $x \wedge y$ (c) $X + Y$
(b) $X \wedge Y$ (d) $X = [5]$

4.   Assume that $D1$ is a vector with a domain corresponding to the octal digits. Form the composite domain for the vector NUM $:= [D1, D1, D1]$ and show some typical values for NUM.

3.   LOGIC AND RELATIONAL OPERATIONS

A number of basic logic operations defined on scalar operands were presented in Chapter 3. These operations, which can easily be extended to vectors, are also of importance at the system level. There are, however, a number of different ways in which these extensions can be introduced. In this section we consider three such extensions. They are:

1.   Vector logic operations
2.   Relational operations
3.   Mixed mode operations

For this discussion we assume that we are dealing with the vector operands X and Y that are represented by the r-tuples

$$[x_1, x_2, \ldots, x_r] \quad \text{and} \quad [y_1, y_2, \ldots, y_r]$$

respectively. We first provide a formal definition of the different operations and then illustrate a number of ways in which they can be used.

Logic Operations on Vectors

The simplest way to extend the basic logic operations to vectors is to apply the operation on a bit-by-bit basis to the components of the vectors involved in the operation. For example, the unary NOT operation is defined on the vector X as

$$\text{NOT operation}$$
$$Z := \overline{X}$$
$$:= [\overline{x_1}, \overline{x_2}, \ldots, \overline{x_r}]$$

Table 5-4 Logic Operations Defined on r-tuples

Operation	Representation	Meaning $i = 1, 2, \ldots r$
NOT	$Z := \overline{X}$	$z_i = \overline{x_i}$
AND	$Z := X \wedge Y$	$z_i = x_i \wedge y_i$
OR	$Z := X \vee Y$	$z_i = x_i \vee y_i$
EXCLUSIVE OR	$Z := X \oplus Y$	$z_i = x_i \oplus y_i$
COINCIDENCE	$Z := X \odot Y$	$z_i = x_i \odot y_i$
NAND	$Z := X \uparrow Y$	$z_i = x_i \uparrow y_i$
NOR	$Z := X \downarrow Y$	$z_i = x_i \downarrow y_i$

Similarly the OR operation is defined as

OR operation
$$Z := X \vee Y$$
$$:= [x_1 \vee y_1, x_2 \vee y_2, \ldots, x_r \vee y_r]$$

Continuing in this manner we can extend the definition of all of the logic operations to vectors. Table 5-4 provides a summary definition of these operations, which operate on vector operands and produce a vector result.

Logic Expressions

These basic operations can be expanded to provide more complex expressions. For example,

$$Z := (A \vee B) \oplus ((C \vee D) \odot (A \wedge D))$$

is such a complex expression in which parentheses have been used to indicate the order of evaluation. If A, B, C, and D were the 3-tuples $[1, 0, 1]$, $[1, 1, 0]$, $[0, 1, 0]$, $[1, 1, 1]$, respectively, then the expression would become

$$Z := ([1, 0, 1] \vee [1, 1, 0]) \oplus (([0, 1, 0] \vee [1, 1, 1]) \odot ([1, 0, 1] \wedge [1, 1, 1]))$$
$$:= ([1, 1, 1]) \oplus ([1, 1, 1] \odot [1, 0, 1])$$
$$:= ([1, 1, 1]) \oplus ([1, 0, 1])$$
$$:= [0, 1, 0]$$

Algebraic Relationships

Because of the way in which we have defined the logical operations on vectors, all of the basic properties of the operations initially developed for switching algebra in Chapter 3 can be extended to an algebra of vectors. To do this we must define the set of elements that we are dealing with and then show that the switching algebra relationships hold for all elements from that set.

For this discussion let $\mathcal{V}$ be the set of all r-tuples, X, defined formally as

$$\mathcal{V} = \{ X \mid X := [x_1, x_2, \ldots, x_r] \}$$

where the x_i's are scalars.

The set $\mathcal{V}$ has 2^r elements. In particular we identify two of these elements for special attention. The "zero" element of the set is

$$[0] := [0, 0, \ldots, 0]$$

and corresponds to the 0 value in our switching algebra. The other special element of $\mathcal{V}$ is the "unit" or "one" element, U, which is defined as

$$[U] := [1, 1, \ldots, 1]$$

This element corresponds to the 1 value in our switching algebra.

With these introductory remarks we can now define the basic postulates of our extended algebra, which, in mathematical terminology, forms a Boolean algebra defined on the set $\mathcal{V}$

Postulate 1 The set $\mathcal{V}$ has two distinct elements $[0]$ and $[U]$

Postulate 2 The unary operation NOT is defined on every element of $\mathcal{V}$. The result of applying NOT to an element in $\mathcal{V}$ is a unique element of $\mathcal{V}$.

Postulate 3 The binary operations AND ($\wedge$) and OR ($\vee$) are defined for every pair of elements of $\mathcal{V}$. The result of these operations is a unique element of $\mathcal{V}$.

Using these postulates and our earlier results from switching algebra, it is a very easy task to prove the following properties about this particular Boolean algebra.

Basic Algebraic Relationships

The following relationships are defined for elements of the set $\mathcal{V}$, and the result of any operation is an element of $\mathcal{V}$. These relations hold independent of the specific meaning assigned to the vectors being operated upon.

1. Special Properties of $[0]$ and $[U]$.

$$[0] \vee X = X \qquad [0] \wedge X = [0]$$
$$[U] \vee X = [U] \qquad [U] \wedge X = X$$

2. The idempotence laws

$$X \vee X = X \qquad X \wedge X = X$$

3. Complementation laws

$$X \vee \overline{X} = [U] \qquad X \wedge \overline{X} = [0]$$

4. Involution

$$\overline{(\overline{X})} = X$$

5. Commutative laws

$$X \vee Y = Y \vee X \qquad X \wedge Y = Y \wedge X$$

6. Associative laws

$$X \vee (Y \vee Z) = (X \vee Y) \vee Z \qquad X \wedge (Y \wedge Z) = (X \wedge Y) \wedge Z$$

7. Distributive laws

$$Z \wedge (Y \vee Z) = (X \wedge Y) \vee (X \wedge Z)$$
$$X \vee (Y \wedge Z) = (X \vee Y) \wedge (X \vee Z)$$

8. Absorption laws

$$X \vee (X \wedge Y) = X \qquad X \wedge (X \vee Y) = X$$
$$X \vee (\overline{X} \wedge Y) = X \vee Y \qquad X \wedge (\overline{X} \vee Y) = X \wedge Y$$

The proofs of these relationships are not difficult. For example, to prove the idempotence law

$$X \vee X = X$$

we note that

$$X \vee X := [x_1 \vee x_1, x_2 \vee x_2, \ldots, x_r \vee x_r]$$
$$:= [x_1, x_2, \ldots, x_r]$$

Thus

$$X \vee X = X$$

By the principle of duality we also have proved

$$X \wedge X = X$$

The proof of the other relationships are left as an exercise.

Relational Operators

In many information processing tasks we find it necessary to compare two items of information and make the logical decision that either

"It is TRUE that the two items compare in the required manner."

or

"It is FALSE that the two items compare in the required manner."

Mathematically such a task is performed using a *relational operator*. Relational operators, which operate on vector operands and produce a scalar result, have the general form

$$z := X \, \mathcal{R} \, Y$$

Table 5-5 The Basic Relational Operations

$<$ Less than	$>$ Greater than
$\leq$ Less than or equal	$\geq$ Greater than or equal
$=$ Equal	$\neq$ Not equal

where z is a scalar that has the value 1 (TRUE) if the comparison indicated by the relational operator $\mathcal{R}$ is satisfied. Otherwise z has the value 0 (FALSE).

The relational operations commonly encountered in the design of digital systems are given in Table 5-5. These relational operators can be used to describe a wide range of decision processes that occur as part of a system design. In particular we note that equality ($=$) is one of the relational operations that has a special and limited meaning. This is why we introduced the notation $:=$ to indicate that an identifier was defined or specified by a given mathematical expression. These two operations are very different, and we must be very explicit in their definition and application.

Inherent in the use of the relational operators defined in Table 5-5 is the idea that they are applied to operands that can be ordered in some manner. For example, X and Y might be vectors that are assumed to have a domain that corresponds to the integers in the range $\{0, 1, \ldots, 4095\}$. Thus both X and Y would have to be represented by r-tuples where r is ≥ 12. The ordering would be the normal numerical ordering of the integers. Similarly X and Y could be from the domain of ASCII encoded characters $\{A, B, \ldots, X\}$. In this case the ordering would be the normal alphabetic ordering.

Whenever we use the relational operators given in Table 5-5 we make the following assumptions:

1. The values of the operands X and Y are from the same ordered domain.
2. The ordering is determined by the domain and not by the digital encoding selected to represent the elements of the set.
3. The result, z, of applying the operation $\mathcal{R}$ to the operands X and Y depends only upon the operation and the ordering of the domain and not upon the coding used to represent X and Y.

To illustrate these assumptions assume that the vectors X and Y are 8-tuples and that

$$X := [11000001]$$
$$Y := [11000101]$$

Then in the relation operation

$$z := X < Y$$

the output z has the following value depending upon the meaning assigned to X and Y.

1. X and Y are selected from the domain $\{0, 1, \ldots, 255\}$ of positive integers. X and Y are encoded as 8-bit unsigned binary numbers

$$X := [193] \qquad Y := [197]$$
$$z := 1$$

2. X and Y are selected from the domain $\{-127, \ldots, 0, \ldots, 127\}$ of positive and negative integers.

   X and Y are encoded as 8-bit sign-magnitude binary numbers.

$$X := [-65] \qquad Y := [-69]$$
$$z := 0$$

3. X and Y are selected from the domain $\{A, B, \ldots, Z\}$ of capital letters.
   X and Y are encoded using the 8-bit EBCDIC code.

$$X := [\text{‘}A\text{’}] \qquad Y := [\text{‘}E\text{’}]$$
$$z := 1$$

These examples illustrate that as long as we consider only the information represented by the operands and not how the information is encoded, we can determine the value produced by applying any of the relational operations to those operands. However, if we must design a combinational logic network to carry out the operation, then we must consider the encoding used to represent the information as well as the ordering of the set from which the operands may be selected. We consider this problem in the next section.

Relations Involving Comparisons to Constants

There are a number of situations where one of the operands in a relation is replaced by a constant. In these cases the constant is given in its symbolic form and it is assumed that the proper encoding is obvious from the context. For example

$$z := X < [108_{10}]$$
$$z := T = [10_2]$$
$$z := Y \leq [\text{‘}F\text{’}]$$

are typical relations of this form. The logic networks used to realize comparisons of this type are usually simpler than the networks used to realize general relational operations.

Collating Sequence

When we apply the relational operations to a given domain, we must first specify the ordering associated with the elements of that domain so that we know how the operators such as $\langle$ and $\rangle$ are to be interpreted. In some cases, such as the a domain $\{0, 1, 2, 3, 4, 5, 6, 7, 8, 9\}$ of decimal digits, the ordering is a characteristic of the elements of the domain. There are many domains, however, where the ordering is not fixed and may be defined by a number of different factors. One common way to establish an ordering is by the way that the code used to represent the elements of the domain is defined. An example of this approach is the ordering associated with the set of alphanumeric characters.

There are two common codes, the ASCII code and the EBCDIC code, used to represent alphanumeric information. The ordering defined for the domain of alphanumeric characters is referred to as the *collating sequence* of the domain. For both of these codes the collating sequence is defined by the coding used to represent the characters. This ordering is generated by assuming that the code used for each character is a positive binary number. The ordering of the characters then corresponds to the numerical ordering of the binary number representing each character. This numerical ordering, for both the ASCII and EBCDIC codes, is given in Appendix A.

This has an interesting result. For example, assume that we are dealing with the domain made up of the following set of characters

$$\{\sqcup, 0, 1, 2, \ldots, 9, A, B, \ldots, Z\}$$

The collating sequence for this set will depend upon the code selected to represent the characters. (Note that $\sqcup$ is used to indicate the blank or space character.) Using the ASCII and EBCDIC codes give the following collating sequences.

1. Collating sequence, ASCII code

$$\sqcup < 0 < 1 < \ldots < 8 < 9 < A < B < \ldots < X < Y < Z$$

2. Collating sequence, EBCDIC code

$$\sqcup < A < B < \ldots < X < Y < Z < 0 < 1 < 2 < \ldots < 8 < 9$$

Examining these two collating sequences we see that the ordering relationship is different. This can have some very dangerous consequences if one is not careful during a design.

Sequence Ordering

Once the collating sequence is established for a given system, the ordering of any two character sequences can be decided very easily. Starting on the left of both sequences a character-by-character comparison is carried out until two dissimilar characters are found. The two character sequences are then ordered according to these two characters. For example

['ABC'] < ['DEF']
['ABC'] < ['ABF']

both have a value of 1 while

['AC'] > ['BC']

has a value of 0. However, consider the relational operation

$z := $ ['2A'] < ['A2']

Until we specify the collating sequence being used, we cannot determine a value for z. If the characters are coded using the ASCII, then z has a value of 1. However, if the EBCDIC code is used, z will have a value of 0.

Relational Expressions

When we apply a relational operator, the resulting value is a scalar. But scalars can be combined by using the standard logic operations of AND, OR, NOT, etc. Thus we can form a relational expression by chaining together a number of relational operations using these logic operations.

There are many situations in which we might like to test a given vector to see whether it is in a given range. The following expression is *not correct*

$$z := [20] < X < [50]$$

since this expression cannot be evaluated. The correct representation for z would be.

$$z := ([20] < X) \wedge (X < [50])$$

In this case z will have a value of 1 only if the first operation produces a value of 1 *and* the second operation produces a value of 1.

As another example let us assume that X and Y correspond to the x and y position of a cursor on a display as shown in Figure 5-5. We might ask the question "Is the cursor in the box in the center of the screen?" This question is answered by evaluating the following expression

$$z := ([45] < X) \wedge (X < [55]) \wedge ([10] < Y) \wedge (Y < [15])$$

This ability to form relational expressions is a very useful analytical tool when we are dealing with the decision process in digital systems.

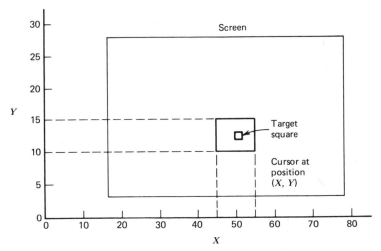

Figure 5-5   Detection if cursor is inside target squarer.

Mixed Mode Operations

There are many situations where we will wish to combine a scalar x (i.e., a 1-tuple) with a vector Y (i.e., an r-tuple) to form a result that is a vector Z (also an r-tuple). To do this we define a set of *mixed mode* operations according to the following conventions:

Let x be a scalar and let Y and Z be the vectors

$$[y_1, y_2, \ldots, y_r] \quad \text{and} \quad [z_1, z_2, \ldots, z_r]$$

respectively. Then let $\langle op \rangle$ be a mixed mode operation if

1. $\langle op \rangle$ is one of the basic logic operations and
2. $Z := x \langle op \rangle Y$ implies $z_i := x \langle op \rangle y_i$ for $i = 1, 2, \ldots, r$.

From this definition we see that the scalar x is combined with each bit of Y according to the rules associated with the operation $\langle op \rangle$. Some typical mixed mode operations are shown in Table 5-6. In particular, note some of the interesting relationships that exist for specific values of x.

As an example, let $\langle op \rangle$ correspond to the AND operation and let

Then

$$
\begin{aligned}
Z :&= x \wedge Y \\
:&= x \wedge [1, 1, 0, 1] \\
:&= [x \wedge 1, x \wedge 1, x \wedge 0, x \wedge 1] \\
:&= [x, x, 0, x]
\end{aligned}
$$

Table 5-6   Some Basic Mixed Mode Operations

Operation	Representation	Meaning	Observations
AND	$Z := x \wedge Y$	$z_i = x \wedge y_i$	
	or	$i = 1, 2, \ldots, r$ $\quad Z := \begin{cases} [0] & \text{if} \quad x = 0 \\ Y & \text{if} \quad x = 1 \end{cases}$	
	$Z := xY$	$z_i = xy_i$	
OR	$Z := x \vee Y$	$z_i = x \vee y_i$	
		$i = 1, 2, \ldots, r$ $\quad Z := \begin{cases} Y & \text{if} \quad x = 0 \\ [1, 1, \ldots, 1] & \\ & \text{if} \quad x = 1 \end{cases}$	
EXCLUSIVE OR	$Z := x \oplus Y$	$z_i = x \oplus y_i$	
		$i = 1, 2, \ldots, r$ $\quad Z := \begin{cases} Y & \text{if} \quad x = 0 \\ \overline{Y} & \text{if} \quad x = 1 \end{cases}$	
		Note: $\quad Z := \overline{x} \wedge Y \vee x \wedge \overline{Y}$	

Applications of Mixed Mode Operations

Mixed mode operations are particularly useful if we wish to select one vector value from a group of values. For example, assume that we have three vectors W, X, and Y and we wish to control which vector value we use in a computation. To do this we may define a vector Z as

$$Z := (a_1 \wedge W) \vee (a_2 \wedge X) \vee (a_3 \wedge Y)$$

Since each term in this expression is a vector, they can be ORed together to form the vector Z. Next we note that we can select a value for Z by specifying particular values for the scalars. To select W we set

$$a_1 = 1 \qquad a_2 = 0 \qquad a_3 = 0$$

This gives the result

$$Z := (1 \wedge W) \vee (0 \wedge X) \vee (0 \wedge Y)$$
$$:= W$$

Similarly if

$$a_1 = 0 \qquad a_2 = 1 \qquad a_3 = 0$$

then

$$Z := X$$

These ideas can be expanded by using relational expressions or logic expressions to compute the values assigned to the a's in the above expression. These scalars are called *control variables* or *selectors*. The next example illustrates how control signals can be used to define which operation is to be performed in a combinational logic network.

Control of Operations

Mixed mode operations are particularly useful if we wish to use a control signal to define which operation is to be performed by a combinational logic network. Networks of this type are quite common in digital systems, and they have the form illustrated in Figure 5-6.

In this network the value of the control signal T is used to generate a set of selector variables that are in turn used to select the operation performed by the network to produce the output signal Z. Assume that T is a 2-tuple, that A and B are r-tuples, and that the network is to be designed to carry out the tasks indicated by Table 5-7.

The following mixed mode expression can be used to define Z:

$$Z := ((T = [1]) \wedge (A \vee B)) \vee ((T = [2]) \wedge (\overline{A}))$$
$$\vee ((T = [3]) \wedge (A \wedge B))$$

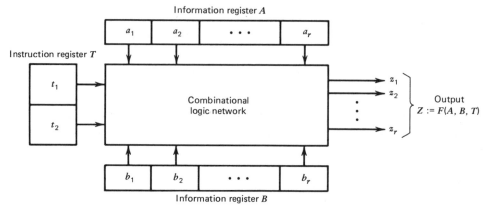

Figure 5-6   Controlled combinational logic network.

In this expression we are using the fact that the relational operations such as $(T = [2])$ produce a scalar result. The selector variables in this expression thus become

$$a_1 := (T = [1])$$
$$a_2 := (T = [2])$$
$$a_3 := (T = [3])$$

It should also be noted that we have not included the term

$$(T = [0]) \wedge [0]$$

since this term is, by definition, $[0]$ for all input conditions.

The three classes of operators that we have defined in this section are useful during a design effort because we can describe a number of different information processing operations in a very compact manner. Once we have reduced a design to a set of such expressions, our next job is to use the expressions to define the combinational logic networks needed to realize the expressions. A design of this type was presented in Section 4 of Chapter 4. Additional examples of this type are considered in the next section.

Table 5-7   Operations to Be Performed by Controlled Network

Value of Control Signal $T := [t_1, t_2]$	Value of Output Signal Z
$[0] := [0,0]$	$[0]$
$[1] := [0,1]$	$A \vee B$
$[2] := [1,0]$	$\overline{A}$
$[3] := [1,1]$	$A \wedge B$

EXERCISES

1. Define the set $\mathcal{V}$ as the set of all 2-tuples $[x_1, x_2]$ where the x_i's have a value of 0 or 1.
    (a)   List the elements of $\mathcal{V}$.
    (b)   Which of the elements correspond to $[0]$ and $[U]$?
    (c)   Define the operations of NOT, AND, and OR for the elements of this set.

2. Prove the commutative, associative, distributive, and absorption laws for a Boolean algebra defined upon sets of r-tuples.

3. Let $X := [0\ 1\ 0\ 1\ 1\ 0\ 1\ 0]$. Evaluate the following relational expressions.
    (a) $z := X < [200_{10}]$ (c) $z := X = [`G`]$ ASCII code
    (b) $z := X > [-25_{10}]$ (d) $z := X = [`G`]$ EBCDIC code

4. Assume that the following set of characters is encoded using the ASCII character code.

    $\{A, B, \ldots, Z, a, b, \ldots, z, 0, 1, \ldots, 9, +, =, -, (,), *, `, ", \langle, \rangle, ?\}$

    Define the collating sequence for this set.

5. Let $T := [t_1, t_2]$, $A := [a_1, \ldots, a_n]$, and $B := [b_1, \ldots, b_n]$. Design a logic network to realize the following expression

    $$Z := ((T = [1]) \land A) \lor ((T = [2]) \land B)$$

4.   REALIZATION OF NETWORKS DESCRIBED BY RELATIONAL AND LOGICAL OPERATIONS

In Section 3 we have introduced a number of operations that involve vector and scalar signals. As long as we are only interested in processing the information contained in these signals, the modeling techniques described in that section are completely general. However, once we have created an analytic expression describing the operations to be performed, our next task is to realize the expression as a logic network. This section discusses how each of the basic logic and relational operations can be realized. Many of these operations are used extensively in the design of digital systems. As a result there are many standard MSI (medium-scale integrated) circuits available that can be used directly to implement these standard operations in a given design.

Realization of Logic Operations

The logic operations applied to vectors are simply an extension of the logic operations as they are applied to scalars. Thus the realization of the operations AND, OR, or NOT can be carried out as shown in Figure 5-7. At the signal level we use the sym-

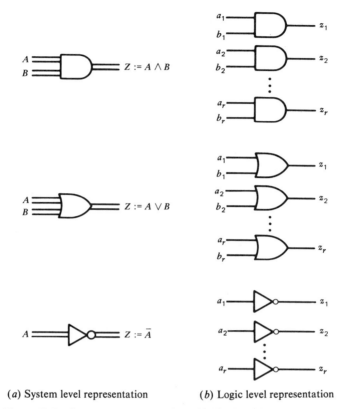

(a) System level representation   (b) Logic level representation

Figure 5-7   Symbolic representation of logic operations on vectors.

bology shown in Figure 5-7a to represent the combination of two signals. The double line indicates that we are dealing with a vector rather than a scalar. This symbol is just a shorthand notation for the combinational logic circuits shown in Figure 5-7b.

Realization of Relational Operations

Realization of the relational operations is complicated by the fact that we must consider how the information represented by the signals involved in the operation is encoded. The following examples will illustrate how various relational operations can be realized.

The simplest relational operation to realize is the equality operation

$$z := A = B$$

In this relation the encoding of the information is assumed to be the same for each signal. Thus the determination of equality is independent of the encoding used. To develop a logic circuit that will test two signals, A and B, for equality we assume that A and B are represented as

$$A := [a_{r-1}, \ldots, a_1, a_0] \qquad B := [b_{r-1}, \ldots, b_1, b_0]$$

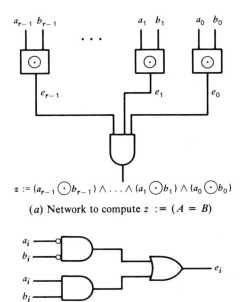

$$z := (a_{r-1} \odot b_{r-1}) \wedge \dots \wedge (a_1 \odot b_1) \wedge (a_0 \odot b_0)$$

(a) Network to compute $z := (A = B)$

(b) AND/OR network to realize COINCIDENCE operation

Figure 5-8   First realization of equality comparator network.

In this case we know that

$$A = B \quad \text{if and only if} \quad a_i = b_i \quad \text{for} \quad i = 0, 1, \dots, r - 1$$

Using the COINCIDENCE binary operation we can express this relation as

$$z := (a_{r-1} \odot b_{r-1}) \wedge (a_{r-2} \odot b_{r-2}) \wedge \dots \wedge (a_1 \odot b_1) \wedge (a_0 \odot b_0)$$

where the COINCIDENCE binary operation is applied on a bit-by-bit basis.

The equality relational operation can be carried out by a combinational logic network of the form shown in Figure 5-8. In this realization it has been assumed that the COINCIDENCE operation is available as a standard logic element. If it is not then the COINCIDENCE operation can be described by the following expression

$$a_i \odot b_i = \overline{a_i} \overline{b_i} \vee a_i b_i$$

and realized using standard AND, OR, and NOT logic elements.

This realization shown in Figure 5-8 requires an r-input AND gate to form z from the individual tests realized by the COINCIDENCE operation. Another possible realization is shown in Figure 5-9a. In this case the logic network that carries out the comparison has been factored into r subnetworks, E, which have three inputs and a single output. These subnetworks are arranged to compute z according to the following factorization of the expression for z.

$$z := e_{r-1} := (a_{r-1} \odot b_{r-1}) \wedge e_{r-2}$$
$$e_{r-2} := (a_{r-2} \odot b_{r-2}) \wedge e_{r-3}$$
$$\vdots$$

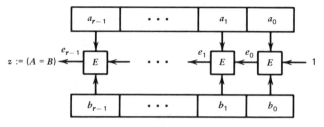

(a) Network to compute $z := (A = B)$

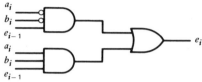

(b) Logic network to realize network E

Figure 5-9   Second realization of equality comparator network.

$$e_1 := (a_1 \odot b_1) \wedge e_0$$
$$e_0 := (a_0 \odot b_0) \wedge 1$$

In this realization e_i is used to indicate whether the subvectors

$$[a_i, \ldots, a_1, a_0] \quad \text{and} \quad [b_i, \ldots, b_1, b_0]$$

are equal. This information is passed to the $(i + 1)$st stage and used to check for equality of the next larger subvector. This continues until equality is checked for the full r-bits. The final answer is e_{r-1}.

From this we see that the subnetwork E that carries out these tests is described by the truth table given in Table 5-8. The realization of E is shown in Figure 5-9b.

Realization of the Less Than (<) Relation

As a somewhat more complex example consider the relational operation

$$z := A < B$$

Table 5-8   Truth Table for Network E

a_i	b_i	e_{i-1}	e_i
0	0	0	0
0	0	1	1
0	1	0	0
0	1	1	0
1	0	0	0
1	0	1	0
1	1	0	0
1	1	1	1

$$e_i = \overline{a_i}\overline{b_i}e_{i-1} \vee a_i b_i e_{i-1}$$

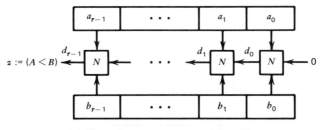

(a) Network to compute $z := (A < B)$

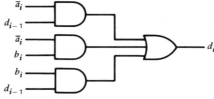

(b) Logic network to realize network N

Figure 5-10   Realization of less than comparator network.

To realize this operation we must first decide upon the coding used to represent the information corresponding to the vectors A and B. In most cases the r-tuples representing A and B are assumed to correspond to positive binary numbers. In that case the operation can be realized by a combinational logic network of the form shown in Figure 5-10a, where the comparison needed to evaluate the $<$ relation is carried out on a bit-by-bit basis. The subnetworks N, which carry out the required comparisons, are defined according to the following rules:

$d_i = 1$ if

    (a) $a_i = 0, b_i = 1$
    (b) $d_{i-1} = 1, a_i = 0, b_i = 0$
    (c) $d_{i-1} = 1, a_i = 1, b_i = 1$

$d_i = 0$ all other cases

These rules are based on the fact that we scan A and B from left to right until we find 2 bits that are not equal. At that point we can make a decision. If $a_i = 0$ and $b_i = 1$, then we know that $A < B$ and we set $d_i = 1$. Otherwise $d_i = 0$. Once we make a decision we must propagate this value to the output. Note that since we are testing for $<$, the input to the rightmost subnetwork must be 0. For example, consider the following cases:

A	B	z	d_2	d_1	d_0
[0, 1, 1]	[0, 1, 1]	0	0	0	0
[0, 1, 0]	[0, 1, 1]	1	1	1	1
[0, 1, 0]	[1, 1, 0]	1	1	0	0

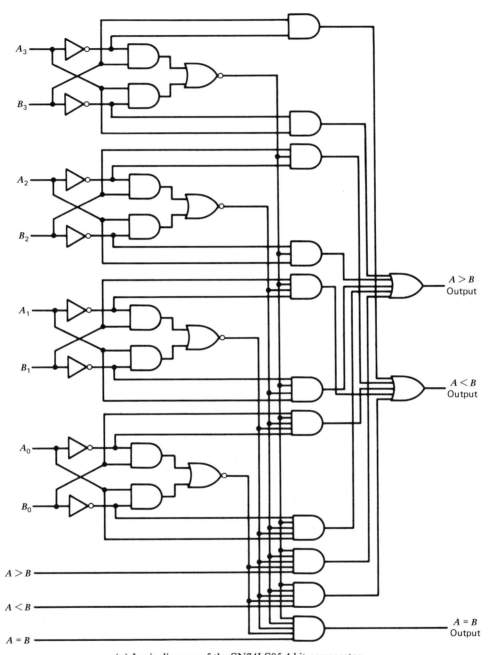

(a) Logic diagram of the SN74LS85 4-bit comparator

Figure 5-11   Use of MSI comparator network.

Table 5-9   Truth Table for Network N

a_i	b_i	d_{i-1}	d_i
0	0	0	0
0	0	1	1
0	1	0	1
0	1	1	1
1	0	0	0
1	0	1	0
1	1	0	0
1	1	1	1

The Truth Table for the subnetwork N is represented by Table 5-9. This means that

$$d_i = \bar{a}_i\bar{b}_id_{i-1} \lor \bar{a}_ib_i\bar{d}_{i-1} \lor \bar{a}_ib_id_{i-1} \lor a_ib_id_{i-1}$$

Using our switching algebra we can reduce this equation to

$$d_i = \bar{a}_id_{i-1} \lor \bar{a}_ib_i \lor b_id_{i-1}$$

The logic circuit for the subnetwork is shown in Figure 5-10b.

A similar network for the other relational operations can be designed using the same techniques. This is left as an exercise.

MSI Realization of the Comparison Operations

The comparison operations occur in many digital system designs. Because of this, several semiconductor manufacturers have developed standard MSI circuits to implement these relational operations. Figure 5-11a is the logic diagram of the SN74L85 4-bit magnitude comparator.

This comparator has two 4-bit input signals, A and B, three comparison propa-

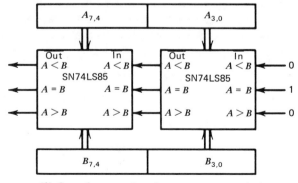

(b) Cascade connection of comparator network

Figure 5-11   (cont.)

gation input lines corresponding to $A < B$, $A = B$, and $A > B$ from a previous stage, and three output lines corresponding to $A < B$, $A = B$, and $A > B$ from the present stage. If there are no previous stages, the input to the $A = B$ input must be 1 and the inputs to the $A < B$ and $A > B$ inputs must be 0.

When the two signals being compared have more than 4 bits, we can carry out the comparison by connecting the basic comparator network in cascade as shown in Figure 5-11b. As shown, the $A < B$, $A = B$, and $A > B$ output of the stage handling the less-significant bits are connected to the corresponding $A < B$, $A = B$, and $A > B$ inputs of the next stage.

Influence of Signal Encoding

The whole discussion leading up to the realization of the less than comparison network shown in Figure 5-10 was based upon the assumption that the information represented by A and B was encoded as standard positive binary numbers. Consider the case where we know that A and B represent numerical information that has been encoded using the gray code discussed in Chapter 2. In this case the encoding is such that we cannot use the network of Figure 5-10 to carry out the comparison operation. For example consider the case where

$$A := [10_{10}] \qquad B := [15_{10}]$$

If a gray code is used to represent A and B, this will mean that

$$A := [1, 1, 1, 1] \qquad B := [1, 0, 0, 0]$$

If A and B were compared using the network of Figure 5-10, the result would be $z := 0$ indicating that A was not less than B. To realize a network that will carry out the $<$ operation when A and B are represented by a gray code requires a much more complex organization. The development of such a network is left as a home problem.

Realization of Mixed Mode Expressions

In the previous section we considered a simple example of a logic network in which a 2-bit control signal T was used to select which operation was to be performed by the network. The output of the network was described by the expression

$$Z := ((T = [1]) \wedge (A \vee B)) \vee ((T = [2]) \wedge (\overline{A}))$$
$$\vee ((T = [3]) \wedge (A \wedge B))$$

To realize this expression we must first evaluate the relational operations of the form

$$f_i := (T = [i]) \qquad \text{for} \quad i = 1, 2, 3$$

If we assume that the control signal is encoded as a binary number, the equality relational operation will have a value of 1 only when the signal T has the binary value of i. This means that

$$f_i = m_i$$

Table 5-10 Truth Table for $(T = [3])$

t_1	t_2	f_3
0	0	0
0	1	0
1	0	0
1	1	1

where m_i is the ith minterm. To see this consider the case where $i = 3$. The truth table for this case is given by Table 5-10. Using this result we see that our mixed mode expression reduces to

$$Z := (m_1 \wedge (A \vee B)) \vee (m_2 \wedge (\overline{A})) \vee (m_3 \wedge (A \wedge B))$$

Completing the expansion shows that the individual components of Z are given by

$$z_i := \overline{t}_1 t_2 (a_i \vee b_i) \vee t_1 \overline{t}_2 \overline{a}_i \vee t_1 t_2 a_i b_i$$

This can be reduced using switching algebra to

$$z_i := \overline{t}_1 t_2 a_i \vee \overline{t}_1 t_2 b_i \vee t_1 \overline{t}_2 \overline{a}_i \vee t_2 a_i b_i$$

The logic circuit to realize the expression for Z can easily be realized from this expression.

Now that we have a general idea of how we can reduce the information flow level expressions to logic circuits, our next task is to investigate how we can carry out the basic arithmetic operations of addition and subtraction.

EXERCISES

1. Let A and B be two positive binary numbers. Show how
    (a) $z := A > B$
    (b) $z := A \geq B$

    can be realized using standard logic elements.

2. Prove that the logic diagram for the SN74LS85 MSI logic network shown in Figure 5-11a computes the indicated output values.

5.   ADDITION AND SUBTRACTION

We are all familiar with the basic arithmetic operations of addition and subtraction as they are carried out using decimal numbers. From an abstract viewpoint we can represent addition and subtraction as

Addition

$$Z := X + Y$$

Subtraction

$$Z := X - Y$$

However, when these operations appear in a digital system, there are several limitations imposed by the fact that all of the numerical information must be stored in fixed size registers or represented by signals with a fixed number of bits. This means that we must consider the following questions.

1. How does the method of encoding used to represent the numerical information influence the realization of these operations?
2. How are negative numbers represented?
3. How many bits are needed to represent the desired numerical information?

In this section we first consider the addition and subtraction of binary numbers. This discussion is then extended to other number systems and methods of encoding. Finally we consider the different classes of logic circuits that can be used to realize these operations.

Binary Addition

Binary addition is carried out in the same way as decimal addition except that we use the following relationships.

0	0	1	1
+0	+1	+0	+1
0	1	1	10

↑————— carry digit

The carry digit becomes important when adding two multiple digit binary numbers. The following example illustrates this point.

	1	1			Carry
1	0	1	1	0	Augend number
0	0	1	1	1	Addend number
1	1	1	0	1	Sum

The arrows indicate that a carry was generated and brought over to be added to the next column. We have also used the relationship that

$$1 + 1 + 1 = 10 + 1 = 11$$

If we add two r-bit binary numbers, the result will be a binary number of no more than $r + 1$ bits. For example

1	1	1	1			Carry
	1	0	1	1	0	Augend number
	0	1	1	1	0	Addend number
1	0	0	1	0	0	

Thus we see that the sum of two 5-bit numbers produces a 6-bit result.

As long as we place no restriction on the number of bits that we can have in a binary number, we have no problem in carrying out the addition of two or more numbers. However, now let us consider the problem that arises if each of the binary numbers involved in the addition process must fit into an r-cell register. Without loss of generality we consider, initially, only integer valued numbers.

From our previous discussion we know that any number that we encounter must fall between 0 and $2^r - 1$. If we add two numbers that give a sum that does not exceed $2^r - 1$ there is no problem. However, if the sum does exceed $2^r - 1$, then we lose the higher order bit. In particular, assume that we form the sum $A + B$ and this gives us a number larger than $2^r - 1$. The number that we will actually form, since we do not retain the $(r + 1)$th bit will be $A + B - 2^r$. The following example illustrates this. Assume that $r = 3$, $A_{10} = 6$, and $B_{10} = 4$. Then in binary notation we have

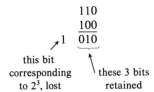

The highest order bit is lost since we can retain only 3 bits. Thus we find that the answer is $(6 + 4)_{10} - (2^3)_{10} = 2_{10} = 010_2$. If we have a means for detecting the fact that we have an extra bit, we can detect that the sum is too large to store in our register. Such a situation is referred to as an *overflow* of our register.

Modular Number System

The above is an example of modular arithmetic that we encounter when we have to work with finite length registers. Normally we can represent numbers as a set of ordered points on a line as illustrated in Figure 5-12. Addition then simply consists of connecting line segments together as shown.

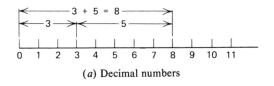

(a) Decimal numbers

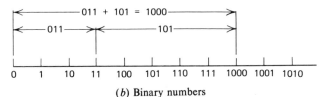

(b) Binary numbers

Figure 5-12 Graphical method of representing the addition of numbers on a linear scale.

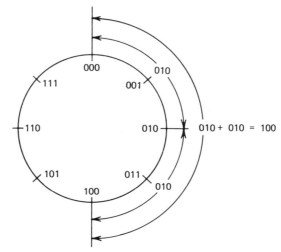

Figure 5-13 Circular representation of numbers stored in a 3-bit register.

When we deal with numbers stored in an r-bit register we must use a different graphical representation. In this case we are dealing with the finite set of numbers between 0 and $2^r - 1$. Graphically we can represent the distinct numbers of this set as points on the circumference of a circle.

For example if $r = 3$ this representation has the form shown in Figure 5-13.

Addition can be represented as before by connecting line segments. The only difference, in this case, is that the line segments lie along the circumference of the circle. If A and B are two r-bit numbers such that their sum is less than 2^r, then addition in this system is the same as before. However, if the sum is equal to or greater than 2^r, we have the situation illustrated in Figure 5-14. The resulting number is the remainder we obtain by subtracting 2^r from the sum. This phenomenon can be formalized in the following manner.

The numbers A and B are said to be *equivalent modulo N* if the remainder obtained when A is divided by N is the same as the remainder that is obtained when B is divided by N. This is indicated by writing

$$A \equiv_N B$$

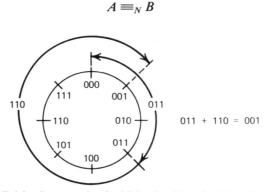

Figure 5-14 An example of addition involving fixed-length registers.

Table 5-11 Addition Table for Addition Modulo 4

+	0	1	2	3
0	0	1	2	3
1	1	2	3	$4 \equiv_4 0$
2	2	3	$4 \equiv_4 0$	$5 \equiv_4 1$
3	3	$4 \equiv_4 0$	$5 \equiv_4 1$	$6 \equiv_4 2$

For example if

$$A = 10 \quad \text{and} \quad B = 18$$

then we say that

$$A \equiv_8 B$$

since

$$10 = 1 \cdot 8 + 2 \overset{\text{remainder}}{\nearrow} \quad \text{and} \quad 18 = 2 \cdot 8 + 2 \overset{\text{remainder}}{\nearrow}$$

In a modular number system we have

$$0 \equiv_N N$$
$$1 \equiv_N N + 1$$
$$\vdots$$
$$N - 1 \equiv_N N + N - 1 = 2N - 1$$

Addition in a modular number system is thus the same as the addition process illustrated in Figures 5-13 and 5-14.

When we deal with numerical information represented by r-bit binary numbers, all of our arithmetic operations are carried out modulo 2^r. With a little practice it is as easy to carry out the arithmetic operations modulo 2^r as it is to carry out the same operations in the standard manner.

For example, the addition table for numbers modulo 4 is given by Table 5-11. Thus, if we wish to add 2 and 3 we go to the table and find that $2 + 3 = 5 \equiv_4 1$.

Binary Subtraction

Binary subtraction is carried out in essentially the same way that we carry out decimal subtraction. There is no problem in carrying out the following subtractions.

$$\begin{array}{r} 0 \\ -0 \\ \hline 0 \end{array} \qquad \begin{array}{r} 1 \\ -0 \\ \hline 1 \end{array} \qquad \begin{array}{r} 1 \\ -1 \\ \hline 0 \end{array}$$

However, when we try to form $0 - 1$ we find that we cannot carry out this operation unless we introduce a borrowing process. For this case we assume that we have

$$\begin{array}{r} 10 \\ -1 \\ \hline 01 \end{array}$$

The extra 1 that we used is borrowed from the next higher order column by subtracting 1 from that column. For example to form $11011 - 01101$ we proceed in the following manner.

-1⋯	-1⋯				Borrow
1	⇢ 11	⇢10	1	1	Minuend
-0	1	1	0	1	Subtrahend
0	1	1	1	0	Difference

In this example the answer is positive because the subtrahend is smaller than the minuend. However, if the reverse condition were true, we would have to account for this by subtracting the minuend from the subtrahend and then assign a negative sign to the answer.

This form of arithmetic is easily handled when we are making hand calculations. However, if we wish to build a computer to carry out both addition and subtraction using this form of arithmetic, we need separate logic networks for each operation. If we wish to minimize the number of logic networks, we can use a special property of modular number systems to replace the subtraction operation by an addition operation.

2's Complement Representation of Negative Numbers

A number B is said to be the negative of a number A if

$$A + B = 0$$

If we are dealing with a regular number system we have the unique relationship

$$B = -A$$

However, let us consider what happens if we are dealing with the set of numbers modulo N. In this case

$$A + B \equiv_N 0$$

implies that B is the negative of A. But B is not unique. In fact any B such that

$$B = kN - A \qquad k = 0, 1, \ldots$$

satisfies the condition that B is the negative modulo N of A. For $k = 0$ we have the standard relationship. However, we have a very interesting situation for the case $k = 1$.

If A is less than N, then $B = N - A$ is seen to be a positive number less than N. Thus, as far as all our calculations are concerned, we can use $B = N - A$ in any calculation calling for $-A$ as long as all the operations are performed modulo N. Thus the calculation

$$C = D - A$$

is equivalent (modulo N) to

$$C = D + (N - A)$$

Therefore if we can find an easy way to find $(N - A)$, not involving subtraction, we see that the subtraction operation can be replaced by addition. We now show how this can be accomplished.

If we are carrying out our operations using r-bit binary integers, then

$$N = 2^r$$

We can represent this N in binary form as

$$
\begin{array}{ccc}
r + 1 \text{ terms} & r \text{ terms} & r - 1 \text{ terms}
\end{array}
$$

$$N = \overbrace{1000 \cdots 0} = \overbrace{111 \cdots 1} + \overbrace{00 \cdots 0\,1}$$

Now let $A = a_{r-1}, a_{r-2}, a_{r-3}, \ldots, a_0$ be any r-bit number. Forming $(N - A)$ we have

$$N - A = (1 - a_{r-1}), (1 - a_{r-2}), (1 - a_{r-3}), \ldots, (1 - a_0) + 000 \cdots 01$$

But a_j is either 1 or 0. Thus $(1 - a_j)$ is 0 if a_j is 1 and 1 if a_j is 0. For example, let $r = 3$ and $A = 010$. Then

$$N = 1000 = 111 + 001$$

and

$$
\begin{aligned}
N - A &= 1000 - 010 = 111 - 010 + 001 = (1 - 0), (1 - 1), (1 - 0) \\
&\quad + 001 \\
&= 101 + 001 = 110
\end{aligned}
$$

The quantity $(N - A)$ is called the *2's complement* of A. The 2's complement of any r-bit binary number is found by using the following expression.

2's Complement of A: $(N - A) := \overline{A} + [1]$

For example, let us assume that we are dealing with 5-bit vectors and let

$$A := [01000]$$

Then the 2's complement of A is computed as

$$
\begin{array}{ll}
\overline{A} & [10111] \\
\underline{+\ [1]} & \underline{+\ [00001]} \\
\text{2's complement of A} & [11000]
\end{array}
$$

The Sign Bit

Table 5-12 gives the binary representation of the decimal numbers between $+7$ and -7. The negative numbers are represented in 2's complement form.

Examining this table we see that we have used 4 bits to represent the numbers.

Table 5-12   Binary Representation of Numbers Between $+7$ and -7 with 2's Complement Representation of Negative Numbers

Binary Number	Decimal Number
0111	7
0110	6
0101	5
0100	4
0011	3
0010	2
0001	1
0000	0
1111	-1
1110	-2
1101	-3
1100	-4
1011	-5
1010	-6
1001	-7

Any number in the table can be represented as

$$A = a_3 a_2 a_1 a_0$$

If a_3 is 0, then A is a positive integer, while if a_3 is 1, then A is a negative integer. Generalizing this observation we see that the leftmost bit always represents the sign of the number no matter what value of r is used.

We also note that if we take the 2's complement of $(N - A)$ we have

$$N - (N - A) = A$$

Thus the relation $-(-A) = A$ also holds true for the 2's complement representation of negative numbers.

2's Complement Subtraction

The 2's complement representation for negative numbers allows us to carry out subtraction by using addition. To see this assume that A and B are two r-bit binary numbers that may represent a decimal value between $\pm (2^{r-1} - 1)$. It is also assumed that negative numbers are represented in 2's complement form.

Assume that we wish to compute $A - B$ where A and B may themselves be positive or negative. To perform this calculation we use the result that

$$A + (N - B) \equiv_N A - B$$

where $N = 2^r$. Thus to form $A - B$ we first form the 2's complement of B and then add the result to A. The following examples illustrate this type of calculation for several different cases.

1. $A = 0111_2 = 7_{10}$ $\qquad B = 0110_2 = 6_{10}$
   $A - B = 0111 + 1010 = 10001 \equiv_{24} 0001$

2. $A = 0011_2 = 3_{10}$ $\qquad B = 1101_2 = -3_{10}$
   $A - B = 0011 + 0011 = 0110$

3. $A = 1101_2 = -3_{10}$ $\qquad B = 0100_2 = 4_{10}$
   $A - B = 1101 + 1100 = 11001 \equiv_{24} 1001$

In the above examples we note that for some values of A and B a carry from the most significant bit (i.e., bit 3 in the example) is produced. The result, if we were doing normal arithmetic, would then be a 5-bit number. However, for 2's complement arithmetic operations we follow the following rule:

Whenever, in performing 2's complement arithmetic, a carry is generated from the most significant bit, this carry is ignored.

This generalization assumes that the true result of the calculation falls within the range

$$\pm (2^{r-1} - 1).$$

Overflow

One of the problems we must continually consider in doing 2's complement arithmetic is the possibility that the result generated will fall outside of the range

$$\pm (2^{r-1} - 1).$$

When this occurs we say that we have an *arithmetic overflow* condition. An arithmetic overflow will occur when

1. The two operands have the same sign.
2. The 2's complement addition produces a result with an opposite sign.

For example if

$$A = 0110_2 = 6_{10} \qquad B = 0011_2 = 3_{10}$$

Then $A + B$, using 2's complement arithmetic, would give

$$A + B = 0110_2 + 0011_2 = 1001_2$$

This would be equivalent to -7 in 2's complement notation instead of the correct answer of 9. The key fact to remember here is that the addition was assumed to be carried out on numbers represented in 2's complement form. Even though the resulting answer appears to be correct (i.e., the binary number corresponding to $6 + 3$), it is incorrect since the most significant bit is used as a sign bit. In this case the sign bit is 1 while the sign bits of the two operands are both 0.

Fractional Parts

Up to this point we have considered that all of the operands being discussed represent integer values. If we wish to allow the operands to have a fractional part, we usually do this by "remembering" where the binary point occurs and then treat the two operands as integer values. After we have completed the operations involving the numbers, we "replace" the binary point in the proper location. For example, let us find $A - B$, where

$$A = 1101.10 \quad \text{and} \quad B = 10.111$$

are two positive binary numbers. If we decide to use 2's complement arithmetic to carry out this calculation, we must first decide on the proper value to use for r. Once we select r we can then find the 2's complement for B. Writing out $A - B$ gives

$$
\begin{array}{l}
\text{add extra 0 to provide for sign bit} \\
\qquad\text{note that we must line up} \\
A = \quad 01101.100 \quad \text{binary point} \\
\qquad\qquad\qquad\text{add a 0} \\
-B = -00010.111 \\
\qquad\qquad\text{add extra 0's}
\end{array}
$$

In forming the expression for $A - B$ we note that before we can determine r we must first line up the binary points and then add 0's to make sure each number has the same number of positions. Finally, we add an extra 0 on the left to allow for the sign digit. After finishing this preliminary organization we can then find r by counting the number of digits in either number. Carrying out this process we find that $r = 8$. Thus the 2's complement of B is

$$N - B = 11101.000 + 00000.001 = 11101.001$$

Thus

$$
\begin{array}{r}
01101.100 \\
11101.001 \\
\hline
1\,01010.101
\end{array}
$$

disregard this carry

Therefore

$$A - B = 1010.101$$

which is a positive number, since the sign bit has a value of zero. In performing this type of arithmetic operation, one should be very careful to account for all of the bit positions *including the sign-bit position.*

1's Complement Representation of Negative Numbers

In forming the 2's complement of a number we had to perform two steps. First we negated each digit of the number and then we added 1 to the result. If we omit the last step, we form what is known as the *1's complement* of a number. For example

Table 5-13 Binary Representation of
Numbers Between +7 and −7
with 1's Complement
Representation of Negative
Numbers

Binary Number	Decimal Number
0111	+7
0110	+6
0101	+5
0100	+4
0011	+3
0010	+2
0001	+1
0000	+0
1111	−0
1110	−1
1101	−2
1100	−3
1011	−4
1010	−5
1001	−6
1000	−7

the 1's complement of

$$0101 \quad \text{is} \quad 1010.$$

Table 5-13 presents the binary representation of the positive and negative integers between +7 and −7 where a 1's complement representation is used for the negative numbers. Examining this table we see that we have both a positive and a negative zero and that this table differs from Table 5-12 only by the fact that an extra 1 must be added to the negative numbers to form the 2's complement.

1's Complement Subtraction

To carry out the subtraction process using 1's complement subtraction we proceed in the same way as for 2's complement subtraction except that we do not neglect the carry at the left end if 1 is generated. This is illustrated in the following example.

Suppose we wish to calculate $A - B$ where $A = 1101.10$ and $B = 10.111$. This is carried out in the following manner with $r = 8$.

$$
\begin{array}{lll}
& 01101.100 & A \\
& \underline{11101.000} & \text{1's complement of } B \\
\text{carry} & 1\ 01010.100 & \\
& \downarrow & \\
& \text{!-----------►1} & \text{add in carry} \\
& \overline{01010.101} &
\end{array}
$$

This example has illustrated the fact that whenever a carry is generated, it is added to the least significant digit of the sum generated by the addition operation. This is known as an *end-around carry*.

To show why we need to include the end-around carry assume that X and Y are both positive r-bit numbers. The 1's complement of Y is represented (in decimal notation) as

$$-Y \equiv_{2'} 2^r - Y - 1$$

To perform the addition $X + (-Y)$ we have

$$X + (\text{1's complement of } Y) = X + 2^r - Y - 1$$
$$= 2^r + (X - Y) - 1$$

We must now consider two possibilities

1. If $X \geq Y$ then $X - Y \geq 0$ and the sum will be a positive number with a carry. If this carry is added to the result this gives

    $$[(X - Y) - 1 + \overset{\overbrace{\hspace{1.5cm}}^{\text{carry added in}}}{1}]$$

    which is $(X - Y)$, the desired result.
2. If $X < Y$ then the sum will be $2^r - (Y - X) - 1$ with no carry, which is the 1's complement of the positive number $(Y - X)$.

Finally we must consider the addition of $(-X)$ to $(-Y)$. This is represented as

$$(2^r - X - 1) + (2^r - Y - 1) = 2^r + [2^r - (X + Y) - 1] - 1$$

Thus the carry represented by the first 2^r can be added in to eliminate the last -1 leaving the result

$$[2^r - (X + Y) - 1]$$

which is the 1's complement representation of $-(X + Y)$. Note that we have assumed that $2^r - 1 \geq X + Y \geq 0$.

Realization of an Adder Logic Network

The basic task performed in the previous discussion is that of addition. Thus let us consider how we can describe the behavior of a combinational logic network that will carry out the operation

$$Z := A + B$$

where A and B correspond to two r-bit registers that hold two binary numbers. This network can be assumed to have the form shown in Figure 5-15. Note that the output Z is assumed to be represented by $r + 1$ bits.

The direct method of using a truth table to represent the behavior of the whole network cannot be easily used except for $r \leq 2$. Instead we must look at the addition process in greater detail. As a first step let us write out the general additon operation in symbolic form. Doing this we have

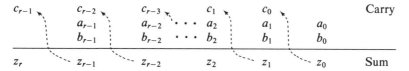

c_{r-1}		c_{r-2}		c_{r-3}		c_1		c_0			Carry
		a_{r-1}		a_{r-2}	$\cdots$	a_2		a_1		a_0	
		b_{r-1}		b_{r-2}	$\cdots$	b_2		b_1		b_0	
z_r		z_{r-1}		z_{r-2}		z_2		z_1		z_0	Sum

In this form the z_i's are the sums and the c_i's are the carries produced at the ith stage. Examining this example we see that we can decompose the general addition network into a collection of r identical subnetworks as shown in Figure 5-16.

These subnetworks are called *full-adders,* since they must not only form the sum of a_i and b_i but also must include the carry information from the previous stage in forming the sum. The first subnetwork could have a different form from the others since there is no need to add in a carry term. However, for uniformity it is easier to use a full-adder and set the carry input to 0. We will also see that this approach is useful when we wish to carry out complement arithmetic.

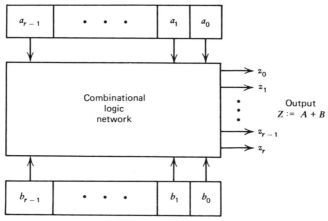

Figure 5-15 General form of adder network.

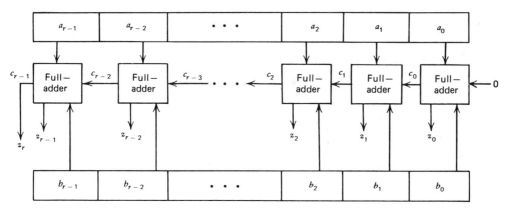

Figure 5-16 Adder network realization using subnetworks to carry out the intermediate summation process.

Table 5-14 Truth Table for a Full-Adder

a_i	b_i	c_{i-1}	z_i	c_i
0	0	0	0	0
0	0	1	1	0
0	1	0	1	0
0	1	1	0	1
1	0	0	1	0
1	0	1	0	1
1	1	0	0	1
1	1	1	1	1

The truth table for a full-adder has the form given by Table 5-14. Examining this table we see that the values of z_i and c_i are given by

$$z_i := \overline{a_i}\overline{b_i}c_{i-1} \vee \overline{a_i}b_i\overline{c_{i-1}} \vee a_i\overline{b_i}\overline{c_{i-1}} \vee a_ib_ic_{i-1}$$
$$= m_1 \vee m_2 \vee m_4 \vee m_7$$
$$c_i := \overline{a_i}b_ic_{i-1} \vee a_i\overline{b_i}c_{i-1} \vee a_ib_i\overline{c_{i-1}} \vee a_ib_ic_{i-1}$$
$$= m_3 \vee m_5 \vee m_6 \vee m_7$$

where the m_i's represent the minterms necessary to represent each expression. To complete the design we note that

$$z_r := c_{r-1}$$

The logical expression for the sum terms, the z_i's, cannot be reduced. However, the carry terms can be reduced using switching algebra to give

$$c_i := a_ib_i \vee a_ic_{i-1} \vee b_ic_{i-1}$$

A logic circuit realization of a full adder can be constructed directly from these equations.

Full-Carry Look-Ahead Adders

One of the problems of using the addition network shown in Figure 5-16 is that we must allow time for the carry signal to propagate through each stage before we use the output value. One way to speed up the operation of an addition network is to calculate the carry information directly for each stage. Such an adder is called a *full-carry look-ahead* adder. Adders of this type are very useful and are available as an MSI integrated circuit from a number of manufacturers. Figure 5-17 shows the logic diagram for the type SN74LS83 4-bit binary full-adder with fast carry. The analysis of this network will show that each sum term is formed at the same time and that there is no need to propagate a carry signal from stage to stage. This analysis is left as a home problem.

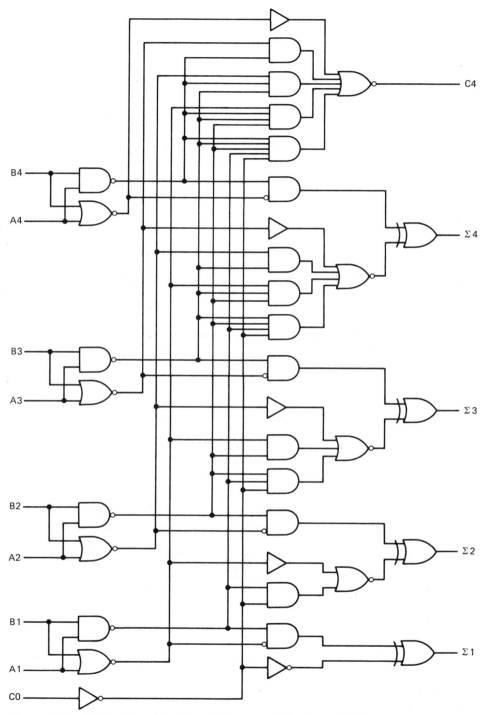

Figure 5-17 A 4-bit binary full-adder with fast carry (type SN74LS83).

Table 5-15 A Combined Addition/
Subtraction Network

Control Signal t	Operation
0	$Z := A + B$
1	$Z := A - B$

$$Z := [z_{r-1}, z_{r-2}, \ldots, z_1, z_0]$$

Realization of a Subtractor Network

Suppose that we wish to compute

$$Z := X - Y$$

One way to do this would be to place the number X in the A register of the adder network and the 2's complement of the number Y in the B register of the adder network. The output would then be the desired value of Z represented in 2's complement notation. However, there are many situations in which we would like to use the same network to do both addition and subtraction. One way to do this is to introduce a control signal as shown in Table 5-15. In this realization we assume that all operations are to be carried out using 2's complement arithmetic. The output Z is described by the relation

$$Z := \bar{t} \wedge (A + B) \vee t \wedge (A - B)$$

But since 2's complement arithmetic is used, this expression can be reduced to

$$\begin{aligned} Z := {} & \bar{t} \wedge (A + B) \vee t \wedge (A + (\bar{B} + [1])) \\ := {} & A + (\bar{t} \wedge B \vee t \wedge \bar{B}) + t \wedge [1] \\ := {} & A + (t \oplus B) + t \wedge [1] \end{aligned}$$

Thus the combined addition/subtraction network can be realized by the network shown in Figure 5-18. The control signal t is used to select which operation is performed. If t is 0 then A and B are applied to the network and the rightmost carry input is set to 0. If t is 1, indicating subtraction, the A input is not changed but $\bar{B}$ is

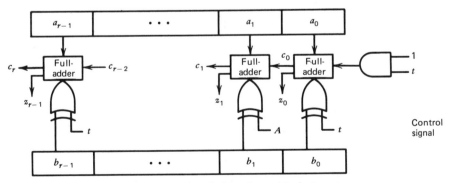

Figure 5-18 The design of an adder/subtractor.

formed and the rightmost carry input signal is set to 1. This small change is accomplished by processing B before it is applied to the full-adders. The only thing that must be remembered about using this network is that all operations are carried out using 2's complement arithmetic. Thus if the $(r\text{-}1)$st bit of the result is 0, then the answer is a positive number, while if the bit is 1, the result is a negative number represented in 2's complement form.

Complement Arithmetic in the Decimal Number System

Although binary arithmetic is very important in digital system design, we often find that some type of decimal encoding of the decimal numbers is used in systems that perform numerical calculations. We could use standard decimal addition and subtraction. However, just as for the binary system, it is easier to use complement arithmetic to perform subtraction. The following discussion describes complement arithmetic in the decimal number system.

Let

$$D = d_{n-1}d_{n-2} \ldots d_0$$

be an n-digit decimal integer. Then the largest value of D is $\overbrace{999 \ldots 9}^{n \text{ terms}}$.

In particular we note that

$$10^n = \overbrace{999 \ldots 9}^{n \text{ terms}} + \overbrace{00 \ldots 01}^{n - 1 \text{ terms}} = \overbrace{1000 \ldots 0}^{n \text{ terms}}$$

The *10's complement* of an n-digit decimal number is thus

$$10^n - D = c_{n-1}c_{n-2} \ldots c_0 + 000 \ldots 01$$

where $c_i = (10 - 1) - d_i = 9 - d_i$.

To form the 10's complement of a decimal number $A = d_{n-1}d_{n-2} \ldots d_0$

1. Subtract each d_i from 9 to give

$$(9 - d_{n-1}), (9 - d_{n-2}), \ldots, (9 - d_0)$$

2. Add 1 to the resulting number.

For example if $n = 6$ and $D = 273245$, then the 10's complement of D is

$$10^6 - D = (9 - 2), (9 - 7), (9 - 3), (9 - 2), (9 - 4), (9 - 5) + 000001$$
$$= 726754 + 000001 = 726755$$

If we use 10's complement arithmetic, then the positive numbers correspond to the numbers between $\overbrace{00 \ldots 0}^{n \text{ terms}}$ and $\overbrace{499 \ldots 9}^{n - 1 \text{ terms}}$ while the negative numbers correspond to the numbers between $\overbrace{99 \ldots 9}^{n \text{ terms}}$ (corresponds to -1) and $50 \ldots 01$ (corresponds to $-499 \ldots 9$). The number $50 \ldots 0$ serves as a dividing line between the positive and negative numbers.

To illustrate how we can perform arithmetic operations using 10's complement addition let

$$A = 22763.425$$
$$B = 13621.2$$

and compute $C = A - B$. This is carried out as follows

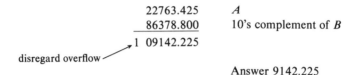

22763.425	A
86378.800	10's complement of B
1 09142.225	

disregard overflow

Answer 9142.225

Note that whenever there is a carry in 10's complement addition, the carry is disregarded.

We can also form the *9's complement* of a decimal number. In this case we form the 10's complement of the number but do not add the 1 to the lowest order digit. When we perform a subtraction, any carry must be added into the lower order digit as we did for 1's complement arithmetic.

For example, let A and B be defined as above. Then

	22763.425	A
	86378.799	9's complement of B
	109142.224	
End around ⟶	⌐---------→1	
carry	09142.225	Answer 9142.255

Hardware Realization of a Decimal Adder

The hardware realization of a decimal adder is much more complex than a binary adder. Assume that a register D contains an encoded decimal number. Each decimal digit is represented by 4 binary bits. Thus the decimal number $d_{n-1}d_{n-2} \cdots d_0$ would require a representation of the form in Figure 5-19.

Thus if we wish to add two numbers, say D and E, represented in this form, we could use a logic network of the form shown in Figure 5-20.

The only difference in this network from the binary adder is the design of the subnetworks that carry out the digit-by-digit addition. In this case the network has the form shown in Figure 5-21.

By examining this figure we see that the network will have $4 + 4 + 1 = 9$ inputs and $4 + 1 = 5$ outputs. Thus a truth table with $2^9 = 512$ rows would be required

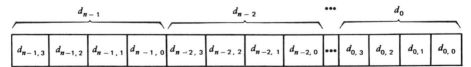

Figure 5-19   Encoded decimal number.

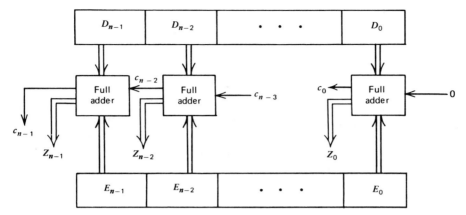

Figure 5-20 General form of a decimal adder.

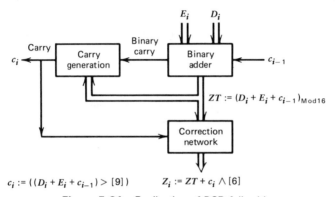

$$c_i := ((D_i + E_i + c_{i-1}) > [9]) \qquad Z_i := ZT + c_i \wedge [6]$$

Figure 5-21 Realization of BCD full-adder.

to formally design this network. In addition, we must specify the coding used to represent the decimal numbers.

To complete the design we will assume that the decimal numbers are encoded using the standard BCD code. The ith decimal digit in D is assumed to be represented as

$$D_i := [d_{i,3}, d_{i,2}, d_{i,1}, d_{i,0}]$$

And similarly the ith digit of E is assumed to be represented as

$$E_i := [e_{i,3}, e_{i,2}, e_{i,1}, e_{i,0}]$$

The BCD code corresponds to the binary equivalent of the given decimal number.

As long as the two decimal digits being added together have a sum that is not greater than 9, a standard binary adder can be used to form the sum. However, when the sum is greater than 9, a correction must be added to the output of the binary adder to give the correct decimal result. The following example illustrates this problem.

	Case I			Case II	
	Sum Less Than 10			**Sum Greater Than 9**	
D_i	4	[0,1,0,0]	D_i	5	[0,1,0,1]
E_i	3	[0,0,1,1]	E_i	6	[0,1,1,0]
	7	[0,1,1,1]		11	[1,0,1,1]

In Case II it appears that the answer is correct. However, remember that the BCD code for the decimal number 11 is the 8-bit number [0,0,0,1,0,0,0,1], which is not the result that was obtained. If we examine this example we see that the problem can be corrected by adding the decimal value of 6 to the binary sum whenever the binary sum has a result in the decimal range of 10 to 15. By adding 6 we skip over these unallowed values of the BCD encoding. To see this consider the following example, which is an extension of Case II.

Decimal Number	BCD Encoded	
05	[0,0,0,0,0,1,0,1]	
+06	+ [0,0,0,0,0,1,1,0]	
11	[0,0,0,0,1,0,1,1]	Uncorrected result
	0,1,1,0	Correction BCD 6
	[0,0,0,1,0,0,0,1]	Corrected result

Carry

The BCD adder shown in Figure 5-21 is thus described by the following equations

Sum Term

$$Z_i := (D_i + E_i + c_{i-1} + ([6]) \wedge ((D_i + E_i + c_{i-1}) > 9))_{\text{Modulo 16}}$$

Carry Term

$$c_i := ((D_i + E_i + c_{i-1}) > 9)$$

Normally the carry should be considered as a BCD encoded number. However, nothing is lost if we specify only the rightmost bit of the carry since the only value a carry will have is [0] or [1].

The general form of the BCD adder realized by the above equations is shown in Figure 5-21. It is left as a Home Problem to reduce this block diagram to a logic circuit realization.

Complements in Number Systems with Radix r

The two systems of complements that we have just considered are special cases of general complement arithmetic. If the base of the number system is r, the r's complement or the true complement of the n-digit number

$$D = d_{n-1}d_{n-2} \cdots d_0$$

is

$$r^n - D = c_{n-1}c_{n-2} \ldots c_0 + 000 \ldots 01$$

where $c_i = (r - 1) - d_i$.

For example, if

$$r = 8 \quad \text{and} \quad D = 157513 \quad \text{then the 8's complement is}$$
$$620264 + 000001$$
$$= 620265$$

If we do not add the 1 to the lowest order digit when we form the r's complement, we form the (radix $-$ 1) complement. Thus the 7's $= (8 - 1)$'s complement of 157513 is 620264. The arithmetic operations using true complements or (radix $-$ 1) complements is carried out in the same manner as that used for the decimal and binary cases. For example, assume that $A = 3763$ and $B = 104$ are two octal numbers. Then $A - B$ can be obtained by forming the 8's complement of B and adding A. This calculation gives the following results

$$
\begin{array}{rr}
A & 3763 \\
-B & 7674 \\
\hline
& 1\ 3657 \\
\end{array}
$$

carry ignored $\nearrow$

$$A - B = 3657$$

Similarly the same computation performed using 7's complement arithmetic is

$$
\begin{array}{rr}
A & 3763 \\
-B & 7673 \\
\hline
& 13656 \\
\end{array}
$$

End around carry $\longrightarrow$ $\dashrightarrow 1$

$$\overline{3657}$$

The result of the 8's complement calculations is positive, since it falls in the range 0000 to 3777. If it had fallen in the range 4000 to 7777, the result would be a negative number represented in 8's complement form.

Similarly the result of the 7's complement calculation is positive, since it falls in the range 0000 to 3777. If it had fallen in the range 4000 to 7777, the result would have been a negative number represented in 7's complement form.

Addition and subtraction are the keys to many of the more complex computational tasks performed in a digital system. For example, multiplication involves a sequence of addition operations, and division requires a sequence of subtractions. Complex operations of this type are considered in later chapters.

EXERCISES

1. Find the r's complement and the (radix $-$ 1) complement of the following numbers, which are all assumed to be positive.
   (a) $r = 2$ 10101.11
   (b) $r = 3$ 121.11
   (c) $r = 8$ 2721.63
   (d) $r = 16$ A6315

2. Compute $A - B$. A and B are assumed to both be positive. Use both r's complement and (radix $- 1$) arithmetic.
   (a) $r = 2$ $A = 101.110$ $B = 11.01011$
   (b) $r = 3$ $A = 212.21$ $B = 22.22$
   (c) $r = 8$ $A = 7644.24$ $B = 77654.21$

3. Show how a BCD adder would carry out the following addition

$$Z := 2983 + 1974$$

6. SUMMARY

In this chapter we have investigated how some of the basic information processing operations can be represented independent of the combinational logic networks necessary to realize the operations. These operations will form, in later chapters, the basic building blocks from which we construct complex systems.

Once we design a system using the operators discussed in this chapter, it is an easy task to realize each of the operations in terms of basic logic elements. As was demonstrated, these realizations may come in a variety of forms. Standard integrated circuit elements have been developed by many manufacturers to perform these operations. Because of the availabliity of these devices, it is possible to design complete digital systems, using operations of the type discussed in this chapter, without considering the details of the electronic techniques that are necessary to realize the particular operation. This is the approach that we follow in the rest of this book.

Reference Notation

Several different methods have been developed to represent the basic information processing operations. References 1, 2, and 6 provide a general insight into the way that the different operations are integrated into complete systems. Additional insight into the problem of designing logic networks to carry out specific operations are given by discussion found in References 3, 4, and 5. Some of the current LSI and MSI networks available to carry out the basic operations are described in the manufacturer handbooks such as Reference 7.

REFERENCES

1. Bell, C. G., and Newell, A. (1971), *Computer Structures: Reading and Examples.* McGraw-Hill, New York.
2. Bell, C. G., Mudge, J. C., and McNamara, J. E. (1978), *Computer Engineering—A DEC View of Hardware Statems Design,* Digital Press, Bedford, Mass.
3. Chu, Y. (1972), *Computer Organization and Microprogramming.* Prentice-Hall, Englewood Cliffs, N.J.
4. Hill, F. J. and Peterson, G. R. (1978), *Digital Systems: Hardware Organization and Design.* (second edition). Wiley, New York.

5. Sloan, M. E. (1976), *Computer Hardware and Organization.* SRA, Chicago.
6. Winkel, D, and Prosser, F. (1980), *The Art of Digital Design—An Introduction to Top-Down Design.* Prentice-Hall, Englewood Cliffs, N.J.
7. *The TTL Data Book for Design Engineers* (current edition). Texas Instruments Inc. Dallas, Tex.

HOME PROBLEMS

1. Define the operation of binary subtraction. Use this definition to design a full-subtractor. Compare the full-subtractor to the full-adder network defined by Table 5-14.

2. Assume that A and B are two gray code encoded n-bit positive numbers. Design a logic network that can compute

$$z := A < B$$

3. Develop a network that will realize the following mixed mode expression

$$z := ((I = [0]) \wedge (A = [0])) \vee ((I = [1]) \wedge (A < [0]))$$
$$\vee ((I = [2]) \wedge (A > [0])) \vee ((I = [3]) \wedge (A \geq [0]))$$

4. Assume that A and B are two n-bit 2's complement numbers. Design a logic network to realize

$$z := A < B$$

5. Complete the design of the BCD full-adder given in Figure 5-21.

6. Prove that the logic network shown in Figure 5-17 is a 4-bit binary full-adder with a fast carry.

7. Assume that A and B are two n-bit 2's complement binary numbers. An *arithmetic overflow* is said to occur when the two numbers are added together if
   (a) The two numbers have the same sign.
   (b) The result of the addition is a number of the opposite sign.
   Design a network to compute

   $$z := OVERFLOW(A, B)$$

8. Let X and Y be two n-bit positive binary numbers. Give the design of a logic network that will realize the following operation

   $$Z := MAX(X, Y)$$

   where Z is defined to be the maximum value of the two.

9. Design a BCD full-subtractor. The inputs will be the two BCD encoded digits D and E and the borrow bit b_{i-1} from the previous stage. The output is to be Z, the BCD encoded difference, and b_i, the borrow bit to the next stage.

6

MINIMIZATION OF COMBINATIONAL LOGIC NETWORKS

1. INTRODUCTION

The final step in the design of a combinational logic network involves the realization of the network from standard logic elements. This step can be carried out in a variety of ways depending on the type of logic elements that are to be used and other constraints that are placed on the network. One approach is to develop a canonical logic expression to represent the function to be realized and then realize the function directly using a standard two-level logic circuit representation. With current integrated circuit technology this approach is often the best one to take. However, there are still many situations in which it is desirable to minimize any logic expression before one attempts to realize it as a logic circuit.

We can use the switching algebra relationships discussed in Chapter 4 to carry out the minimization of any logic expression. Since many of the logic expressions of interest contain a large number of terms, we must develop an organized approach to the reduction process so that all possible reduction steps are considered. Several such methods have been developed. In this chapter we consider two of the most popular reduction techniques.

The problem of interest can be formulated in the following manner. Assume that we are given the task of realizing a combinational logic network of the form shown in Figure 6-1. The inputs to the network are the variables

$$x_1, x_2, \ldots, x_r$$

and the outputs are the variables

$$y_1, y_2, \ldots, y_k$$

which are defined by the set of scalar functions

$$f_1(x_1, \ldots, x_r), \ldots, f_k(x_1, \ldots, x_r)$$

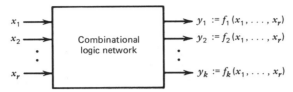

Figure 6-1 General form of combinational logic network.

These functions are assumed to be defined by either a truth table or a logic expression. Our task is to specify a two-level logic circuit, using a minimum number of logic elements, to realize the given network.

Completely Specified and Incompletely Specified Functions

The functions $f_j(x_1, \ldots, x_r)$, which define the relationship between the input variables and the output variables, may be defined in a number of ways. A function is said to be *completely specified* if $f_j(x_1, x_2, \ldots, x_r)$ is assigned a value for all possible values of the r-tuple $[x_1, x_2, \ldots, x_r]$. If, on the other hand, there are values of $[x_1, x_2, \ldots, x_r]$ that never occur because of the way in which the variables are generated, then the function of $f_j(x_1, x_2, \ldots, x_r)$ need not be defined for these values. Such a situation is called a *"don't care"* condition and the function is said to be *incompletely specified*.

Incompletely specified functions are quite common in digital system design. For example, assume that the input to the logic network represents a decimal number encoded in BCD form. Then only 10 of the 4-tuples $[x_1, x_2, x_3, x_4]$ would be specified and the other 6 would correspond to don't care conditions. The following truth table (Table 6-1) also illustrates another incompletely specified function. The don't care entries in this table are indicated by d.

Table 6-1 Typical Incompletely Specified Function

x_1	x_2	x_3	$g(x_1, x_2, x_3)$
0	0	0	1
0	0	1	1
0	1	0	d
0	1	1	1
1	0	0	0
1	0	1	0
1	1	0	d
1	1	1	0

A Preview of the Minimization Problem

There are several methods of finding a minimal representation of the function. In the next few sections we present two of the standard minimization techniques; the map method and the tabular method. However, before proceeding, let us try to obtain an understanding of the minimization problem by finding a minimal representation for two functions.

First consider the completely specified function given by

$$f(x_1, x_2, x_3) = \overline{x}_1 x_2 \overline{x}_3 \vee x_1 \overline{x}_2 \overline{x}_3 \vee x_1 \overline{x}_2 x_3 \vee x_1 x_2 \overline{x}_3 \vee x_1 x_2 x_3$$

If we were to realize this function directly, we would need a logic network with five AND elements and one OR element. However, we can continually apply the laws

$$\overline{x}y \vee xy = y \qquad \text{and} \qquad x \vee \overline{x}y = x \vee y$$

to produce the reduced function

$$f(x_1, x_2, x_3) = x_1 \vee x_2 \overline{x}_3$$

This function can be realized with one AND element and one OR element.

Next let us consider the case where the truth table description of the function contains a don't care condition. The function represented by Table 6-1 is an example of such a situation. Since the 3-tuples [0, 1, 0] and [1, 1, 0] never occur as input combinations, we can assign any value that we want to $g(0, 1, 0)$ and $g(1, 1, 0)$. There are four possible ways in which values could be assigned. If we do this we obtain the following four possible representations of $g(x_1, x_2, x_3)$ that differ only for the don't care values of $[x_1, x_2, x_3]$.

Case 1

$$g(0, 1, 0) = g(1, 1, 0) = 0$$

$$g_1(x_1, x_2, x_3) = \overline{x}_1 \overline{x}_2 \overline{x}_3 \vee \overline{x}_1 \overline{x}_2 x_3 \vee \overline{x}_1 x_2 x_3$$

Case 2

$$g(0, 1, 0) = 1 \qquad g(1, 1, 0) = 0$$

$$g_2(x_1, x_2, x_3) = \overline{x}_1 \overline{x}_2 \overline{x}_3 \vee \overline{x}_1 \overline{x}_2 x_3 \vee \overline{x}_1 x_2 x_3 \vee \overline{x}_1 x_2 \overline{x}_3$$

Case 3

$$g(0, 1, 0) = 0 \qquad g(1, 1, 0) = 1$$

$$g_3(x_1, x_2, x_3) = \overline{x}_1 \overline{x}_2 \overline{x}_3 \vee \overline{x}_1 \overline{x}_2 x_3 \vee \overline{x}_1 x_2 x_3 \vee x_1 x_2 \overline{x}_3$$

Case 4

$$g(0, 1, 0) = 1 \qquad g(1, 1, 0) = 1$$

$$g_4(x_1, x_2, x_3) = \overline{x}_1 \overline{x}_2 \overline{x}_3 \vee \overline{x}_1 \overline{x}_2 x_3 \vee \overline{x}_1 x_2 x_3 \vee \overline{x}_1 x_2 \overline{x}_3 \vee x_1 x_2 \overline{x}_3$$

If we apply the reduction laws to these four functions we find that

$$g_1(x_1, x_2, x_3) = \bar{x}_1\bar{x}_2 \vee \bar{x}_1 x_3$$
$$g_2(x_1, x_2, x_3) = \bar{x}_1$$
$$g_3(x_1, x_2, x_3) = \bar{x}_1\bar{x}_2 \vee \bar{x}_1 x_3 \vee x_1 x_2 \bar{x}_3$$
$$g_4(x_1, x_2, x_3) = \bar{x}_1 \vee x_2 \bar{x}_3$$

Examining the minimal form of these four possible representations of $g(x_1, x_2, x_3)$, we see that $g_2(x_1, x_2, x_3) = \bar{x}_1$ is the simplest expression. Therefore, if we arbitrarily assign the values

$$g(0, 1, 0) = 1 \qquad g(1, 1, 0) = 0$$

to the don't care condition of Table 6-1, we obtain a very simple function to represent $g(x_1, x_2, x_3)$ for all those values of $[x_1, x_2, x_3]$ where $g(x_1, x_2, x_3)$ is defined. This example has illustrated that it is often possible to obtain a simpler minimal expression if we make use of the flexibility provided by the freedom of assigning any value we wish to the don't care entries.

In these two examples we have used algebraic techniques to obtain the minimal expressions. This was easy to do because it was fairly obvious which reduction should be applied to each expression. When there are more variables or when the expressions take on a more complex form, this is not as easy to do. Several minimization algorithms have been developed which, in theory, allow us to handle any minimization problem in a mechanical manner.

2. MINIMIZATION BY THE MAP METHOD

Sometimes the most difficult problem one encounters in trying to reduce logical expressions to minimal form by algebraic means is to identify the terms in the expression that can be combined to form a new term with fewer variables. The map method of minimization uses a visual representation of the expression under investigation to aid us in selecting the terms that can be combined to obtain a simpler expression. This map is called a *Karnaugh map.*

Forming the Map

Basically the Karnaugh map of a function is a visual way of presenting the same information contained in the truth table representation of the function. A map for a function $f(x_1, x_2, \ldots, x_r)$ of r variables contains 2^r squares, there being a square on the map for every possible value of the r-tuple $[x_1, x_2, \ldots, x_r]$. Assume that $[e_1, e_2, \ldots, e_r]$ is a particular value of $[x_1, x_2, \ldots, x_r]$. Then the square corresponding to this particular input assignment is labeled $f(e_1, e_2, \ldots, e_r)$. Under this convention a 1 is placed in each square representing a combination for which an output of 1 is desired; a 0 is placed in each square representing a combination for which an output of 0 is desired; and a d is entered in those squares corresponding to don't care input conditions.

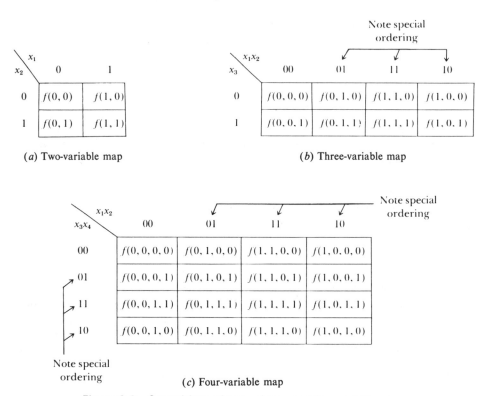

(a) Two-variable map

(b) Three-variable map

(c) Four-variable map

Figure 6-2   General form of two-, three-, and four-variable maps.

The two basic algebraic laws that we make use of in the map method of reduction are

$$xy \vee \bar{x}y = y \qquad \text{and} \qquad x \vee \bar{x}y = x \vee y$$

Therefore when we construct a map of a given function we must arrange the map in such a way that we can apply these laws by inspection. This condition is satisfied, for functions of two, three, or four variables, if we arrange the maps as shown in Figure 6-2. Note that any two adjacent squares in the map correspond to r-tuples which differ in only one variable. Also note that the r-tuple corresponding to the leftmost square of any row differs in only one variable from the r-tuple corresponding to the rightmost square of that row. Similarly the top square of any column differs in only one variable from the bottom square of the column. The significance of this ordering will become evident shortly.

Figure 6-3 gives specific examples of maps corresponding to two, three, and four variables. There are two possible interpretations that we can give to a map. If we concentrate on the 1 and d entries, then the resulting minimal function that we obtain will be in the sum-of-product form. This is true because the 1 entries of a map correspond to the minterms of the function.

However, because of the duality of switching algebra, we can also concentrate on 0 and d entries of a map. In this case the 0 entries correspond to the maxterms of a

x_1	x_2	$f(x_1, x_2)$
0	0	0
0	1	1
1	0	0
1	1	1

x_1	x_2	x_3	$f(x_1, x_2, x_3)$
0	0	0	1
0	0	1	1
0	1	0	d
0	1	1	1
1	0	0	0
1	0	1	0
1	1	0	d
1	1	1	0

x_1

x_2	0	1
0	0	0
1	1	1

(*a*) Two-variable function

x_1x_2

x_3	00	01	11	10
0	1	d	d	0
1	1	1	0	0

(*b*) Three-variable function

x_1	x_2	x_3	x_4	$f(x_1, x_2, x_3, x_4)$
0	0	0	0	1
0	0	0	1	1
0	0	1	0	0
0	0	1	1	1
0	1	0	0	0
0	1	0	1	0
0	1	1	0	0
0	1	1	1	1
1	0	0	0	0
1	0	0	1	1
1	0	1	0	1
1	0	1	1	0
1	1	0	0	0
1	1	0	1	0
1	1	1	0	1
1	1	1	1	0

x_1x_2

x_3x_4	00	01	11	10
00	1	0	0	0
01	1	0	0	1
11	1	1	0	0
10	0	0	1	1

(*c*) Four-variable function

Figure 6-3 Example of two-, three-, and four-variable maps.

given function and the resulting minimal function that we obtain will be in the product-of-sum form.

Minimal Sum-of-Product Functions

To find a minimal sum-of-product function we visualize the map as a representation of the function in its canonical sum-of-product form. Each 1 or *d* entry corresponds to possible minterms that can be combined to simplify our expression. Since we are not interested in the 0 entries in the map, we will adopt the convention that these

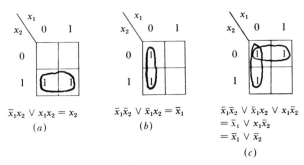

$$\bar{x}_1x_2 \lor x_1x_2 = x_2$$

(a)

$$\bar{x}_1\bar{x}_2 \lor \bar{x}_1x_2 = \bar{x}_1$$

(b)

$$\bar{x}_1\bar{x}_2 \lor \bar{x}_1x_2 \lor x_1\bar{x}_2$$
$$= \bar{x}_1 \lor x_1\bar{x}_2$$
$$= \bar{x}_1 \lor \bar{x}_2$$

(c)

Figure 6-4   Three typical reductions.

entries are left blank in order to reduce the clutter in a map. The maps of Figure 6-4 illustrate this convention.

Our reduction process is based on the use of the following identities,

$$xy \lor \bar{x}y = y \qquad \text{and} \qquad x \lor \bar{x}y = x \lor y$$

to combine and simplify the product terms. The application of these identities is facilitated by the convention that we have used to set up our map. Any two adjacent squares correspond to minterms that differ in only one variable. In one square this variable appears in the negated form and in the other square it appears in its unnegated form.

For example, the map of Figure 6-4a has two adjacent minterm entries $m_1 = \bar{x}_1x_2$ and $m_3 = x_1x_2$. The two terms m_1 and m_3 differ in that the variable x_1 appears in its negated form in m_1 and its unnegated form in m_3. From this we see that we can combine these two terms to obtain

$$\bar{x}_1x_2 \lor x_1x_2 = x_2$$

This simplification is noted on the map by drawing a circle around the two squares that we combined to form the simpler expression.

Two other examples are shown in Figure 6-4b and c. In particular the reduction shown in Figure 6-4c should be considered in detail. This reduction has made use of the fact that the minterm $m_0 = \bar{x}_1\bar{x}_2$ can be combined with both the minterm $m_2 = x_1\bar{x}_2$ and the minterm $m_1 = \bar{x}_1x_2$. It should also be noted that it is not possible to combine minterms such as m_1 and m_2 that fall along the diagonal of the map.

Next consider the case of functions of three or four variables. Maps of these functions will have two or four rows respectively and we can combine either two, four, or eight squares at a time to obtain a reduced function. Figure 6-5 shows some of the possible forms that the four-square at a time combinations can take. The two-square at a time combinations take the same form as in Figure 6-4. Note the use of the top-bottom and left-right combinations on the columns and rows, respectively.

Figure 6-6 shows some of the ways that eight adjacent squares can be combined.

So far we have shown the methods of combining blocks of either two, four, or eight adjacent squares to identify the terms that can be combined to minimize a given

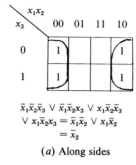

$$\bar{x}_1\bar{x}_2\bar{x}_3 \lor \bar{x}_1\bar{x}_2x_3 \lor x_1\bar{x}_2\bar{x}_3$$
$$\lor x_1\bar{x}_2x_3 = \bar{x}_1\bar{x}_2 \lor x_1\bar{x}_2$$
$$= \bar{x}_2$$

(a) Along sides

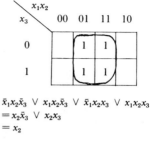

$$\bar{x}_1x_2\bar{x}_3 \lor x_1x_2\bar{x}_3 \lor \bar{x}_1x_2x_3 \lor x_1x_2x_3$$
$$= x_2\bar{x}_3 \lor x_2x_3$$
$$= x_2$$

(b) At the center

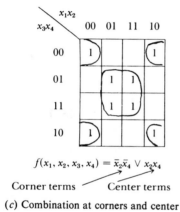

$$f(x_1, x_2, x_3, x_4) = \bar{x}_2\bar{x}_4 \lor x_2x_4$$

Corner terms   Center terms

(c) Combination at corners and center

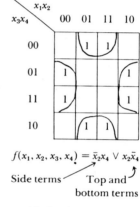

$$f(x_1, x_2, x_3, x_4) = \bar{x}_2x_4 \lor x_2\bar{x}_4$$

Side terms   Top and bottom terms

(d) Combination at sides

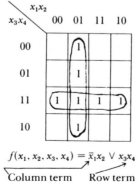

$$f(x_1, x_2, x_3, x_4) = \bar{x}_1x_2 \lor x_3x_4$$

Column term   Row term

(e) Combination along row or column

Figure 6-5 Some typical four adjacent square groupings.

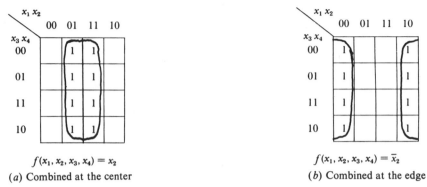

$f(x_1, x_2, x_3, x_4) = x_2$

(a) Combined at the center

$f(x_1, x_2, x_3, x_4) = \bar{x}_2$

(b) Combined at the edge

Figure 6-6 Some possible eight adjacent square combinations.

function. Often we find patterns in which we can combine adjacent squares in a number of different ways. To decide which combinations should be made we can formulate the following general rules.

1. Every one-square must be accounted for at least once.
2. Any combination should be as large as possible. Thus a one-square should not be taken by itself if it can be taken as part of two adjacent squares; a group of two adjacent squares should not be combined if they can be combined in a group of four adjacent squares; etc.
3. All one-squares should be accounted for in the minimum number of groups of adjacent squares.

Figure 6-7 illustrates these general rules. The map of Figure 6-7a is formed in a straightforward manner. Although the two-square term corresponding to $x_2\bar{x}_3x_4$ overlaps the four-square term corresponding to x_1x_4, both terms are required to cover the map. However, consider the map given in Figure 6-7b. It appears that we should include the four-square indicated by the dotted line. But if we examine the map carefully we see that every square in that particular four-square is already contained

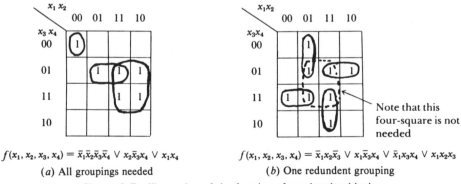

$f(x_1, x_2, x_3, x_4) = \bar{x}_1\bar{x}_2\bar{x}_3\bar{x}_4 \vee x_2\bar{x}_3x_4 \vee x_1x_4$

(a) All groupings needed

$f(x_1, x_2, x_3, x_4) = \bar{x}_1x_2\bar{x}_3 \vee x_1\bar{x}_3x_4 \vee \bar{x}_1x_3x_4 \vee x_1x_2x_3$

(b) One redundant grouping

Figure 6-7 Illustration of the forming of overlapping blocks.

in a two-square that cannot be eliminated; thus the term x_2x_4, corresponding to the four-square is redundant and does not have to be included in the expression for $f(x_1, x_2, x_3, x_4)$.

Reading a Map

Each set of minterms that are combined on a map correspond to a product term that can be formed by algebraically combining these minterms. Each time two minterms are combined we eliminate one of the variables in the product term. The variable that is eliminated is the one that appears in its negated form in one minterm and in its unnegated form in the other minterm. Similarly when four minterms are combined we eliminate two variables and when we combine eight minterms we eliminate three variables.

To find the product term corresponding to any combined set of minterms is easily accomplished if we use the above observation. The rows and columns of a map are labeled so that only one variable changes value as we go from row-to-row or column-to-column. Thus if we combine minterms in adjacent rows or adjacent columns, we see that we are actually eliminating the variable that changes value from one row to the other or one column to the other.

For example, in Figure 6-7*a* consider the two minterms in row 01 and columns 01 and 11. These two terms are combined. We note that the x_1 variable is the variable that changes when we go from column 01 to column 11. Thus x_1 is the variable eliminated from the product term. The three other variables remain 1, 0, and 1, respectively. Thus we see that the resulting product term is $x_2\overline{x}_3x_4$. Similarly we see that the four minterms in rows 11 and 01 and columns 11 and 10 can be combined into a single product term. In this case the variables x_2 and x_3 are the ones that change value and can thus be eliminated. The two variables x_1 and x_4 remain 1 and 1, respectively. Thus the product term corresponding to this grouping is x_1x_4.

The Reduction Process

Now that we have developed an understanding of how we can use a map to locate the minterms that can be combined into single product terms, our next task is to see how these techniques can be used to find a minimal map of a given function. The reduction process that we use involves the systematic grouping of minterms into the largest group possible. Sometimes this grouping will be unique. At other times we will find that more than one grouping can be found. Whenever this occurs we know that there will be several possible minimal representations of a function.

The following algorithm can be used to find a minimal map of a given function.

Algorithm for Finding Minimal Map

1. Identify and circle all one-squares that cannot be combined with any other squares.
2. Identify all one-squares that can be combined with only one other square. Use

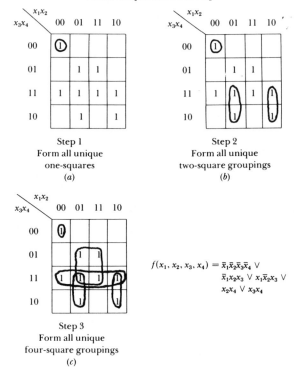

Case I. Unique Minimum Map

Step 1
Form all unique
one-squares
(a)

Step 2
Form all unique
two-square groupings
(b)

Step 3
Form all unique
four-square groupings
(c)

$$f(x_1, x_2, x_3, x_4) = \bar{x}_1\bar{x}_2\bar{x}_3\bar{x}_4 \lor$$
$$\bar{x}_1 x_2 x_3 \lor x_1 \bar{x}_2 x_3 \lor$$
$$x_2 x_4 \lor x_3 x_4$$

Case II. Nonunique map

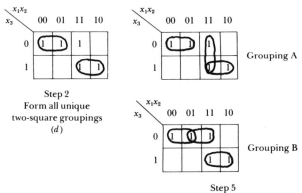

Step 2
Form all unique
two-square groupings
(d)

Grouping A

Grouping B

Step 5
Two possible ways that last one-square can
be assigned to a two-square group
(e)

Resulting Minimal Function
Grouping A $f(x_1, x_2, x_3) = \bar{x}_1\bar{x}_3 \lor x_1 x_3 \lor x_1 x_2$
Grouping B $f(x_1, x_2, x_3) = \bar{x}_1\bar{x}_3 \lor x_1 x_3 \lor x_2 \bar{x}_3$

Figure 6-8 Illustration of minimal map algorithm.

these pairs to form two-square groupings. Leave any square that can be combined in more than one way until later.

3. Identify all squares that can be combined in groups of four in only one way provided all of the squares are not already covered by the groupings of step 2. Use these squares to form four-square groups. Leave any squares that can be combined in more than one way until later.

4. Repeat the combination process for groups of eight squares provided all the squares in the group are not already covered.

5. Next investigate any squares not assigned to a grouping. Arbitrarily form the largest group that can be formed that includes most uncovered squares. Add just enough terms until all the one-squares are covered.

The steps of this algorithm are illustrated in Figure 6-8. Two examples are shown. The first example given by Figure 6-8*a* to *c* illustrates the case where there is no problem in deciding how to assign the blocks. The second example given by Figure 6-8*d* and *e* shows the situation where there is no unique assignment of blocks to cover the one-square corresponding to $f(1, 1, 0)$. Either of the two assignments are equally valid.

Don't Care Condition

The extension of the above minimization process to the case where the function has one or more don't care conditions associated with it is straightforward. As indicated before, don't care conditions are shown by a *d* entry in the map. In combining squares we use a *d* entry whenever possible to form larger blocks of squares. However, any *d*-square not needed to create a larger block is neglected. To illustrate the case, consider the map given in Figure 6-9. The *d*-square corresponding to $f(0, 1, 0)$ is used to form a four-block while the *d*-square corresponding to $f(1, 1, 0)$ is not used.

A Design Example

To illustrate how the map method can be used in the design of a combinational logic network let us assume that we work for a company that makes automatic toll collectors and that we are given the job of designing a logic network that is part of a new model collector.

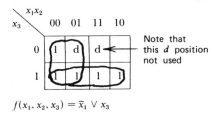

$$f(x_1, x_2, x_3) = \bar{x}_1 \vee x_3$$

Figure 6-9   Use of don't care conditions in the map minimization process.

Design Requirements

The logic network is to count the amount of change placed into the collector. If 15 cents is deposited (nickels and dimes only), then the go light is to be flashed on and a change collect signal is sent out to collect the coins. Otherwise, the stop light is to remain on.

Examining the design requirements we see that two input signals and one output signal are required. These signals and their domain of definition are given by

Input Signals

N number of nickels deposited—$\{0,1,2,3\}$
D number of dimes deposited—$\{0,1\}$

Output Signal

C command to the signal light and collection control

$$(\text{TRUE, FALSE})$$

where

TRUE if 15 cents in change holder
FALSE if 15 cents is not in change holder

It is assumed that the information concerning the number of coins deposited shows up at the same time so that the network does not have to have a "memory."

The first task is to encode the input and output information. One such encoding is

Input Information			**Output Information**		
$N := [n_1, n_2]$	[0,0]	0 nickels	$C := [c_1]$	[0]	FALSE
	[0,1]	1 nickel		[1]	TRUE
	[1,0]	2 nickels			
	[1,1]	3 nickels			
$D := [d_1]$	[0]	0 dimes			
	[1]	1 dime			

The output of the network will be TRUE if we receive 3 nickels or 1 dime and 1 nickel. We also decide that if the driver puts in more than the minimum amount we will give a go signal but no change. (After all, we can give the driver fair warning by putting up a sign saying "Exact Change Only.")

Using this information we next develop the truth table given by Table 6-2, which describes the logical relationship that exists between the inputs and the output. Examining this table we can write the following logical expression for c_1.

$$c_1 := \bar{n}_1 n_2 d_1 \lor n_1 \bar{n}_2 d_1 \lor n_1 n_2 \bar{d}_1 \lor n_1 n_2 d_1$$

To minimize this expression we can use the map shown in Figure 6-10.

Using this map allows us to reduce the logical expression for c_1 to

$$c_1 := n_2 d_1 \lor n_1 n_2 \lor n_1 d_1$$

Table 6-2   Truth Table for Coin Collectors

n_1	n_2	d_1	c_1
0	0	0	0
0	0	1	0
0	1	0	0
0	1	1	1
1	0	0	0
1	0	1	1
1	1	0	1
1	1	1	1

Two possible realizations of the desired logic network are shown in Figure 6-11. In the first network standard AND-OR elements are used while the second network uses NAND elements to realize the same expression.

Minimal Product-of-Sum Functions

As was indicated previously, we can find a minimal product-of-sum function representation for a given map by visualizing the map as a representation of the function in the canonical product-of-sum form. In this case we concentrate on the 0 entries in the map rather than the 1 entries. Each 0 entry corresponds to one of the maxterms of the function. For example, the map shown in Figure 6-12, where the 0 rather than the 1 entries have been retained, corresponds to the logical expression

$$f(x_1, x_2, x_3) = (x_1 \lor x_2 \lor x_3)(x_1 \lor \bar{x}_2 \lor x_3)(x_1 \lor \bar{x}_2 \lor \bar{x}_3)$$

where each sum term corresponds to one of the maxterms associated with a 0 entry. The reduction process makes use of the laws of the form

$$(x \lor y)(x \lor \bar{y}) = x \quad \text{and} \quad (x \lor y)(x \lor z \lor \bar{y}) = (x \lor y)(x \lor z)$$

to simplify the map.

We proceed in exactly the same manner as in the discussion for sum-of-product functions except that we try to enclose the largest number of 0's into groups. The map shown in Figure 6-12 admits two enclosures corresponding to the following applications of the above laws

$$f(x_1, x_2, x_3) = (x_1 \lor x_2 \lor x_3)(x_1 \lor \bar{x}_2 \lor x_3)(x_1 \lor \bar{x}_2 \lor \bar{x}_3)$$
$$= (x_1 \lor x_3)(x_1 \lor \bar{x}_2 \lor \bar{x}_3) = (x_1 \lor x_3)(x_1 \lor \bar{x}_2)$$

Figure 6-10   Map to reduce logical expression for c_1.

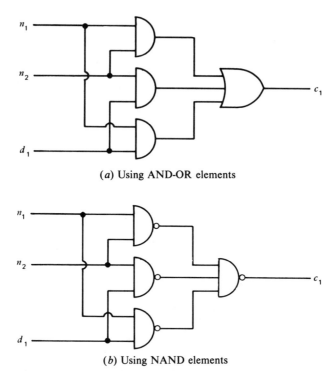

(*a*) Using AND-OR elements

(*b*) Using NAND elements

Figure 6-11 Two realizations of logic network for toll collector.

As another example, consider the map shown in Figure 6-13. This map has three sum terms in the product. The resulting minimal function for this map is

$$f(x_1, x_2, x_3, x_4) = (x_2 \lor x_4)(\overline{x}_2 \lor x_3 \lor \overline{x}_4)(\overline{x}_1 \lor x_2)$$

The minimal product-of-sum expression can be realized by a two-level OR-AND logic network. For the function given by the map in Figure 6-13 the resulting network would require three OR elements and one AND element.

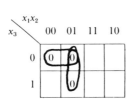

Figure 6-12 A map set up for product-of-sum evaluation.

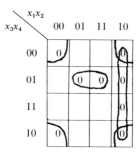

Figure 6-13 A maxterm map.

Prime Implicants

The map method of minimization can be extended to five and even six variables. However, the added complexity involved is usually not worth the bother and the tabular method to be presented in the next section is easier to use for more complex problems. In particular, the tabular technique can be used to develop computer programs that carry out the more tedious aspects of the reduction process.

Besides giving us a quick way to reduce logic expressions of up to four variables, the map of a function has another useful feature. It gives us a visual understanding of an important relationship that exists between logic terms that we use in the next section.

When we use the map method to find a minimal sum-of-product representation of a logic function, we try to combine all adjacent one-squares into groups of $2^n (n = 0, 1, \ldots)$ one-squares. Each such group of squares that we can form *that is not properly contained* in a larger group of squares is a graphical example of what we call a *prime implicant*. To illustrate this idea consider the map shown in Figure 6-14. There are four prime implicants as indicated in this figure.

They have been formed by continually applying the reduction rule $xy \lor x\bar{y} = x$ to the product terms found in the sum-of-product expression until no new reductions can be made. For example

$$\bar{x}_1 x_2 = \bar{x}_1 x_2 \bar{x}_3 \bar{x}_4 \lor \bar{x}_1 x_2 \bar{x}_3 x_4 \lor \bar{x}_1 x_2 x_3 x_4 \lor \bar{x}_1 x_2 x_3 \bar{x}_4$$

is such a prime implicant.

If we examine Figure 6-14 we see that although the function represented by the map can be represented as

$$f(x_1, x_2, x_3, x_4) = \bar{x}_1 x_2 \lor x_2 x_4 \lor x_1 x_3 x_4 \lor x_1 \bar{x}_2 x_3$$

in reality we do not need the prime implicant $x_1 x_3 x_4$ since the block represented by this term contains only one-squares that are already contained in other blocks that must be used in the representation of the function.

In the next section we show how these prime implicants can be found using a tabular method and how we can go about selecting the smallest set of these prime implicants that we need to represent a function.

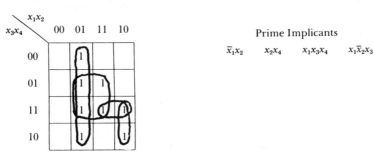

Figure 6-14 Illustration of prime implicants.

EXERCISES

1. Find all minimal sum-of-product and product-of-sum expressions for the following truth tables

x_1	x_2	x_3	$f(x_1, x_2, x_3)$	$g(x_1, x_2, x_3)$
0	0	0	1	1
0	0	1	1	d
0	1	0	0	d
0	1	1	1	0
1	0	0	0	1
1	0	1	0	d
1	1	0	1	0
1	1	1	1	0

x_1	x_2	x_3	x_4	$h(x_1, x_2, x_3, x_4)$
0	0	0	0	1
0	0	0	1	0
0	0	1	0	1
0	0	1	1	0
0	1	0	0	1
0	1	0	1	0
0	1	1	0	0
0	1	1	1	d
1	0	0	0	1
1	0	0	1	1
1	0	1	0	d
1	0	1	1	1
1	1	0	0	1
1	1	0	1	d
1	1	1	0	0
1	1	1	1	0

2. Find the prime implicants of the functions defined in Figure 6-8 and by Table 6-3.

3. MINIMIZATION BY THE TABULAR METHOD

The tabular method of simplification, also called the Quine-McCluskey method, consists of a systematic enumerative technique for reducing functions initially in the sum-of-product form to minimal form. It is based on the relationship $xy \vee x\bar{y} = x$ where x is any product expression representing one or more variables and y is a single variable.

Table 6-3 Truth Table Representation of $f(x_1, x_2, x_3, x_4)$

x_1	x_2	x_3	x_4	$f(x_1, x_2, x_3, x_4)$
0	0	0	0	1
0	0	0	1	0
0	0	1	0	0
0	0	1	1	0
0	1	0	0	1
0	1	0	1	1
0	1	1	0	1
0	1	1	1	0
1	0	0	0	0
1	0	0	1	0
1	0	1	0	0
1	0	1	1	1
1	1	0	0	1
1	1	0	1	1
1	1	1	0	1
1	1	1	1	1

The minimization process is carried out according to the following algorithm.

1. Form the canonical sum-of-product representation of the function to be minimized.
2. Examine all product terms and apply the reduction $xy \vee x\bar{y} = x$ as many times as possible. All of the new product terms so formed will have one less variable than the original terms.
3. Take the new set of product terms and repeat step 2 on this new set of terms. When no further reductions are possible, all of the product terms that were generated by steps 1 and 2 and that cannot be further reduced are the prime implicants associated with the function to be minimized.
4. The set of prime implicants are then inspected to choose a minimal set that can be ORed together to represent the function.

The advantage of the Quine-McCluskey method is that it provides an algorithmic technique that can be used to generate all of the prime implicants associated with a given function. Once all of the prime implicants are found, the second stage of the process allows us to generate all of the possible minimal expressions that represent the function. The following example explains the steps of this simplification technique.

Assume that we are given the function described by the truth table given by Table 6-3. The sum-of-product representation of this function is

$$f(x_1, x_2, x_3, x_4) = \bar{x}_1\bar{x}_2\bar{x}_3\bar{x}_4 \vee \bar{x}_1x_2\bar{x}_3\bar{x}_4 \vee \bar{x}_1x_2\bar{x}_3x_4 \vee \bar{x}_1x_2x_3\bar{x}_4$$
$$\vee x_1\bar{x}_2x_3x_4 \vee x_1x_2\bar{x}_3\bar{x}_4 \vee x_1x_2\bar{x}_3x_4$$
$$\vee x_1x_2x_3\bar{x}_4 \vee x_1x_2x_3x_4$$

Table 6-4 First Step in Tabular Reduction Process

Product Terms	0,1 Representation	
$\bar{x}_1\bar{x}_2\bar{x}_3\bar{x}_4$	0000	Terms in no 1 per row
$\bar{x}_1 x_2\bar{x}_3\bar{x}_4$	0100	Terms with one 1 per row
$\bar{x}_1 x_2\bar{x}_3 x_4$	0101	
$\bar{x}_1 x_2 x_3\bar{x}_4$	0110	Terms with two 1's per row
$x_1 x_2\bar{x}_3\bar{x}_4$	1100	
$x_1\bar{x}_2 x_3 x_4$	1011	
$x_1 x_2\bar{x}_3 x_4$	1101	Terms with three 1's per row
$x_1 x_2 x_3\bar{x}_4$	1110	
$x_1 x_2 x_3 x_4$	1111	Terms with four 1's per row

Note that the product terms are included in this example only for illustrative purposes. They are usually not included in forming the table.

To apply the reduction process we must identify all product terms that differ in only one variable. That variable is negated in one expression and not in the other. All other variables have the same form. The two terms $\bar{x}_1 x_2\bar{x}_3\bar{x}_4$ and $\bar{x}_1 x_2 x_3\bar{x}_4$ are two such product terms, which we can combine to form $\bar{x}_1 \_ x_3\bar{x}_4$. The blank indicates that one variable has been eliminated from the product.

We now form a special table that allows us to identify the product terms that can be combined in this manner. The 0, 1 representation of each product term, where 0 indicates a negated and 1 an unnegated variable, is used in this table.

First we list all terms that do not contain any 1's, then all terms that contain only one 1, then all terms that have two 1's, and so on until the last part of the list contains the term with all 1's if it is present. Table 6-4 shows this listing and the corresponding product term.

Instead of examining all possible pairs of product terms to apply the relationship $xy \lor x\bar{y} = x$, all that we have to do is examine the adjacent groups of the table that were formed by counting the number of 1's in a row. If two rows are to be combined, they can differ in only one column. In that column one row contains a 1 and the corresponding column in the other row must contain a 0. When we locate two rows that can be combined we make the following reduction

$$0000 \qquad 0\_00$$
$$0100$$

The "_" indicates that the variable has been eliminated by application of the relation $xy \lor x\bar{y} = x$.

Table 6-5 shows how we use this technique to carry out the first step of the reduction process for the function described in Table 6-4. The first reduction is obtained by combining 0000 with 0100 to give 0_00, which is entered in the column labeled

Table 6-5 Illustration of Reduction Process

				First Reduction				Second Reduction			
x_1	x_2	x_3	x_4	x_1	x_2	x_3	x_4	x_1	x_2	x_3	x_4
0	0	0	0✓	0	–	0	0*	–	1	0	–*
0	1	0	0✓	0	1	0	–✓	–	1	–	0*
0	1	0	1✓	–	1	0	0✓	1	1	–	–*
0	1	1	0✓	0	1	–	0✓				
1	1	0	0✓	–	1	0	1✓				
1	0	1	1✓	–	1	1	0✓				
1	1	0	1✓	1	1	0	–✓				
1	1	1	0✓	1	1	–	0✓				
1	1	1	1✓	1	–	1	1*				
				1	1	–	1✓				
				1	1	1	–✓				

first reduction. This says that $\overline{x}_1 x_2 \overline{x}_3 \overline{x}_4 \vee x_1 x_2 \overline{x}_3 \overline{x}_4 = x_2 \overline{x}_3 \overline{x}_4$ is a possible simplification. A "✓" mark is placed alongside the rows 0000 and 0100 to indicate that they are not prime implicants. Next we take the row 0100 and try to combine it with the rows containing two 1's. Combining 0100 with 0101 gives 010_, which is the second entry in our second column. Similarly 0100 combines with 1100 to give _100. The terms 0101 and 1100 are checked to indicate that these two rows are not prime implicants. It should be noted that even when a row is checked it is still used to try to find reduced terms. This is because of the law $x \vee x = x$. Continuing in this manner we obtain the table labeled "First Reduction" in Table 6-5. We also see that all of the terms in the original table have been checked so that none of them are prime implicants. If any row had not been checked, that row would have corresponded to one of the prime implicants that we are looking for.

The next step is to compare the rows in the new table, labeled "First Reduction," to find new reductions. Again, for two rows to combine, they must differ in only one column. All other columns must be identical. Thus 0_00 and _101 cannot combine because they differ in the first, second, and fourth column. However, _100 and _101 can be combined to give _10_.

The _'s speed up the reduction process since, in particular, it can be seen that two terms cannot be combined if the _'s do not appear in the same place in both rows. For example 0_00 in the first group of the second table cannot combine with any of the terms in the second group because all three of these terms have a 1 in the x_2 column.

Applying the reduction rules to the table we obtained in the first reduction we obtain the new table labeled "Second Reduction." Here again we observe some interesting properties. We note that _10_ can be obtained by combining either 010_ and 110_, or _100 and _101. Thus all four of these terms are checked as not being prime implicants. We also note that the terms 0_00 and 1_11 cannot be combined. These terms, which are prime implicants, are starred (*).

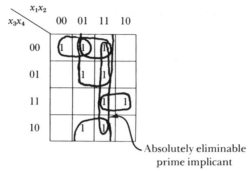

Figure 6-15   A map representation of the prime implicants.

Finally we examine the last table and see that the terms $\_10\_$, $\_1\_0$, and $11\_\_$ are also prime implicants since they cannot be combined. Thus we have completed the first stage of the reduction process and we have identified the five product terms $\overline{x}_1\overline{x}_3\overline{x}_4$, $x_1x_3x_4$, $x_2\overline{x}_3$, $x_2\overline{x}_4$, and x_1x_2 as prime implicants. Figure 6-15 is a map of the function under investigation with the prime implicants indicated.

Now that we have identified all the prime implicants, our final step is to select enough prime implicants to account for all of the original product terms. This is accomplished by constructing a table of choice. Each column of the table corresponds to one of the minterms in the original sum-of-product expression we started with and each of the rows corresponds to one of the prime implicants that we have found in the previous step. For each prime implicant, a check mark is placed in the columns of those minterms accounted for by that prime implicant. For example, consider the column headed by 1100 corresponding to the minterm $x_1x_2\overline{x}_3\overline{x}_4$. This minterm was used to form the prime implicants $\_1\_0$ corresponding to $x_2\overline{x}_4$, $\_10\_$ corresponding to $x_2\overline{x}_3$, and $11\_\_$ corresponding to x_1x_2. Thus we place a check in this column whenever one of the three rows corresponding to these prime implicants intersect the column. Table 6-6 gives the complete table of choice for our example.

Examining this table we can make the following observations:

1.   A prime implicant with no $\_$'s accounts for only 1 minterm, a prime implicant with one $\_$ accounts for 2 minterms, and in general a prime implicant with u $\_$'s accounts for 2^u minterms.

2.   It is possible to have one or more minterms that are accounted for by one and only one prime implicant. Prime implicants of this type are called *essential* or *core* prime implicants. These prime implicants are starred in the table.

In the above example 0_00, $\_1\_0$, 1_11, and $\_10\_$ are essential prime implicants.

3.   A prime implicant is an *absolutely eliminable prime implicant* if all of the columns that are checked in the row corresponding to that prime implicant are also checked in one or more of the rows corresponding to the core prime implicants.

In the above example $11\_\_$ is an absolutely eliminable prime implicant. The reason for this is also graphically illustrated in Figure 6-15.

Table 6-6 Table of Choice

Prime Implicants	Minterms								
	0000	0100	0101	0110	1011	1100	1101	1110	1111
*0_00	✓	✓							
*_1_0		✓		✓		✓		✓	
*1_11					✓				✓
*_10_		✓	✓			✓	✓		
11__						✓	✓	✓	✓

4. The set of prime implicants that are not essential prime implicants or absolutely eliminable prime implicants is called the *set of eligible prime implicants*. A subset of this set must be used together with the core prime implicants to form the minimal logic expression representation of the given function.

In the above example we see that all the prime implicants are either core prime implicants or absolutely eliminable. Therefore there is only one minimal logic expression to represent the function. That expression is

$$f(x_1, x_2, x_3, x_4) = \overline{x}_1\overline{x}_3\overline{x}_4 \vee x_2\overline{x}_4 \vee x_1x_3x_4 \vee x_2\overline{x}_3$$

The next example illustrates the case where we have a set of eligible prime implicants.

Don't Care Conditions

When we have don't care conditions present in the truth table representation of the logic function we wish to synthesize, we proceed in the same way as before except for one small modification. In forming our table for the reduction process we include all the product terms that correspond to the don't care conditions and then proceed with our reduction process. After we have found the prime implicants, we then form our table of choice. However, we do not include any columns in the table for the product terms corresponding to the don't care conditions.

In this case the don't care conditions are used only for the generation of prime implicants with the fewest number of variables. The following example illustrates this process. Assume that we wish to realize the function described in Table 6-7. The reduction process is carried out in Table 6-8. The two-product terms 0000 and 0010 corresponding to the don't care conditions are included when we find the prime implicants but not when we form the table of choice.

Examining the table of choice we see that there is only one essential prime implicant, _1_1. The other five prime implicants form an eligible set and our final problem is to decide which prime implicants actually need to be selected from this set in order to complete our expression. There are a number of possible selections. The only

Table 6-7 A Function with Don't Care Conditions

x_1	x_2	x_3	x_4	$f(x_1, x_2, x_3, x_4)$
0	0	0	0	d
0	0	0	1	0
0	0	1	0	d
0	0	1	1	1
0	1	0	0	0
0	1	0	1	1
0	1	1	0	0
0	1	1	1	1
1	0	0	0	1
1	0	0	1	0
1	0	1	0	1
1	0	1	1	1
1	1	0	0	1
1	1	0	1	1
1	1	1	0	0
1	1	1	1	1

requirement is that the prime implicants must provide checks in those columns that are not accounted for by any of the essential prime implicants. To aid in making this choice we can use a reduced table of choice such as illustrated in Table 6-8c. This table is obtained by eliminating the rows corresponding to the essential prime implicants and the columns containing checks associated with the essential prime implicants.

Table 6-8 (a) Prime Implicant Calculations

	x_1	x_2	x_3	x_4	x_1	x_2	x_3	x_4		x_1	x_2	x_3	x_4
Don't care	0	0	0	0✓	0	0	–	0✓		–	0	–	0*
conditions	0	0	1	0✓	–	0	0	0✓		–	0	1	–*
included	1	0	0	0✓	0	0	1	–✓		–	–	1	1*
only for	0	0	1	1✓	–	0	1	0✓		–	1	–	1*
selection	0	1	0	1✓	1	0	–	0✓					
of Prime	1	0	1	0✓	1	–	0	0*					
Implicants	1	1	0	0✓	0	–	1	1✓					
	0	1	1	1✓	–	0	1	1✓					
	1	0	1	1✓	0	1	–	1✓					
	1	1	0	1✓	–	1	0	1✓					
	1	1	1	1✓	1	0	1	–✓					
					1	1	0	–*					
					–	1	1	1✓					
					1	–	1	1✓					
					1	1	–	1✓					

Table 6-8 (continued) (b) **Table of Choice** (Note that 0000 and 0010 corresponding to don't care conditions are not included as minterms.)

Prime Implicants	Minterms								
	0011	0101	0111	1000	1010	1011	1100	1101	1111
1_00				✓			✓		
110_							✓	✓	
_0_0				✓	✓				
_01_	✓				✓	✓			
__11	✓		✓			✓			✓
*_1_1		✓	✓					✓	✓

(c) **Reduced Table of Choice Associated with the Eligible Set**

Eligible Set		Minterms				
		0011	1000	1010	1011	1100
A	1_00		✓			✓
B	110_					✓
C	_0_0		✓	✓		
D	_01_	✓		✓	✓	
E	__11	✓			✓	

By examining this table we see that any one of the following four possible sets of prime implicants from the eligible set can be used, together with the essential prime implicant to represent the logic function of the example.

Set 1	Set 2	Set 3	Set 4
1_00	1_00	110_	110_
_01_	_0_0	_0_0	_0_0
	__11	_01_	__11

Examining this set we see that set 1 has the fewest terms so we can select this set of terms to complete our expression. The resulting minimum logic expression is

$$f(x_1, x_2, x_3, x_4) = x_2 x_4 \lor x_1 \bar{x}_3 \bar{x}_4 \lor \bar{x}_2 x_3$$

In many cases the selection of the subset of the eligible set necessary to complete the minimal expression representation of a function is obvious. However, in some situations it is desirable to have an algorithm that can be used to find the desired expressions. We now consider this problem.

Algebraic Solution of Reduced Choice Table

To find all of the combinations of prime implicants that can be formed from the eligible set to complete our expression we assign a variable to each element of the eligible set. This is illustrated in Table 6-8c.

For each column in the reduced table of choice we write a logical expression indicating which prime implicants contribute a check to that column. For example, consider the column corresponding to the product term 0011. Both rows D and E contribute a check to that column. Thus we can say that in the final expression we must have the prime implicant D OR the prime implicant E. This condition is indicated by writing $(D \lor E)$. For each column we can form the following logical sums describing the conditions that give a check in that column.

Column	Logical Sums
0011	$(D \lor E)$
1000	$(A \lor C)$
1010	$(C \lor D)$
1011	$(D \lor E)$
1100	$(A \lor B)$

Next we note that we must select our prime implicants so that we have at least one check in each column. For an n column table this can be stated logically as (there must be one check in column 1) *AND* (one check in column 2) *AND* ... *AND* (one check in column n). To satisfy this logical condition all we have to do is to form the logical product of the logical sum terms describing each column.

For our example the resulting logical expression associated with Table 6-8c is found to be

$$(D \lor E)(A \lor C)(C \lor D)(D \lor E)(A \lor B) = F(A, B, C, D, E)$$

But this is a logical expression. Thus we can use our laws of switching algebra to reduce and expand this expression to a sum-of-product form. The steps of this process are given below for our example.

In this reduction we make use of the logical relationship

$$(x \lor w)(x \lor v) = (x \lor xv \lor xw \lor wv) = (x \lor wv)$$

Applying this relationship to our function gives

$$
\begin{aligned}
F(A, B, C, D, E) &= (D \lor E)(A \lor C)(C \lor D)(D \lor E)(A \lor B) \\
&= (A \lor C)(A \lor B)(D \lor E)(D \lor C) \\
&= (A \lor CB)(D \lor EC) \\
&= AD \lor AEC \lor CBD \lor CBE
\end{aligned}
$$

When we obtain the sum-of-product form, as in the above example, we look at each of the product terms. The prime implicants corresponding to the variables in each of the product terms are the ones that form the subsets of the eligible set that we are looking for. Thus we see that $F(A, B, C, D, E)$ tells us that there are four sets, which are

Set 1	Set 2	Set 3	Set 4
A 1_00	A 1_00	C _0_0	C _0_0
D _01_	E __11	B 110_	B 110_
	C _0_0	D _01_	E __11

These sets are the same sets that we have found previously.

A Design Example

The tabular method is commonly used when a computer program is available to carry out the tedious steps of the reduction process. In this case the designer enters a description of the logic function to be designed and the program generates all of the possible solutions. The designer can then select, based upon other criteria, the solution that appears to be best for the given network being designed. The following example illustrates how a preliminary analysis by the designer may make even this design process simpler.

Design Requirements

A company that manufactures temperature control devices uses an electronic thermometer, which measures temperatures between 0 and 99°C in one-degree increments, to monitor the temperature of a chemical process. A warning device is needed that will sound an alarm whenever the temperature goes above 75°C. The temperature measured by the thermometer is encoded as an 8-bit BCD digital signal and the Over Temperature Detector must use this signal to generate a signal, which will be 1 when the alarm is to be sounded and 0 otherwise.

The general organization of this system is shown in Figure 6-16.
The output of the thermometer is represented by the signal

$$T := [T_1, T_0] := [t_{1,3}, t_{1,2}, t_{1,1}, t_{1,0}, t_{0,3}, t_{0,2}, t_{0,1}, t_{0,0}]$$

where T_1 is the encoded ten's digit and T_0 is the encoded unit's digit.
The output of the Over Temperature Detector is given by

$$e := (T > [75])$$

The direct approach to the design of the Over Temperature Detector would be to realize e using an 8 input and 1 output combinational logic network derived directly from a truth table representation for e. To do this we note that there would be 24 values of T that would correspond to over temperature conditions. In addition, since the information represented by T is encoded in BCD form, there are

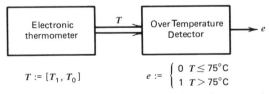

Figure 6-16   An over temperature detection network.

$$2^8 - 100 = 256 - 100 = 156$$

don't care bit patterns associated with T. (For example, $T := [1111, 0000]$ could never occur.) At this point we would probably reach the conclusion that the direct approach would be very difficult to carry out even with the aid of a computer.

As with many other design problems, we should not give up until we consider other ways to formulate the problem. In particular we should consider whether there are any ways in which we can decompose the problem into smaller parts. One way to do this is to consider the conditions that define the output signal e. Figure 6-17 is a graphical representation of the relationship between the ten's digit and the unit's digit of T and the output e. This figure indicates the 256 distinct bit patterns that can be associated with T. Examining this figure we can identify the following regions.

Region 1. Values of T for which $e := 1$

Region 2. Values of T corresponding to don't care conditions

Region 3. Values of T for which $e := 0$

If we combine some of the area from Region 2 that represents a don't care area with the area from Region 1 that represents the $E := 1$ area, we can write the following relational expression to represent e.

$$e := (T_1 > [7]) \lor ((T_1 > [6]) \land (T_0 > [5]))$$

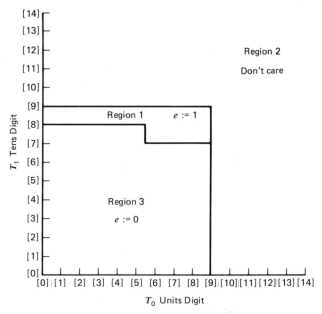

Figure 6-17   Visual representation of allowed temperature regions.

Table 6-9 Truth Table Description of Subexpressions f, g, and h

				$i = 1$		$i = 0$
$t_{i,3}$	$t_{i,2}$	$t_{i,1}$	$t_{i,0}$	f	g	h
0	0	0	0	0	0	0
0	0	0	1	0	0	0
0	0	1	0	0	0	0
0	0	1	1	0	0	0
0	1	0	0	0	0	0
0	1	0	1	0	0	0
0	1	1	0	0	0	1
0	1	1	1	0	1	1
1	0	0	0	1	1	1
1	0	0	1	1	1	1
1	0	1	0	d	d	d
1	0	1	1	d	d	d
1	1	0	0	d	d	d
1	1	0	1	d	d	d
1	1	1	0	d	d	d
1	1	1	1	d	d	d

A combinational logic network to realize this equation can be developed by observing that e can be expressed as the logical combination of three simpler scalars. That is

$$e := f \vee g \wedge h$$

where the three new scalars are defined by

$$f := (T_1 > [7]) \qquad g := (T_1 > [6]) \qquad h := (T_0 > [5])$$

From this we see that f and g depend only upon the value of the ten's digit of T, while h depends only on the unit's digit. It is now possible to realize each of these scalars.

Table 6-9 is a truth table description of each of these scalars. Note that the points that fall in Region 2 of Figure 6-17 generate don't care entries in this table. The next step is to find a minimal expression for the three scalars. From Table 6-9 we have

$$f := m_8 \vee m_9 \vee m_{10} \vee m_{11} \vee m_{12} \vee m_{13} \vee m_{14} \vee m_{15}$$
$$g := m_7 \vee m_8 \vee m_9 \vee m_{10} \vee m_{11} \vee m_{12} \vee m_{13} \vee m_{14} \vee m_{15}$$
$$h := m_6 \vee m_7 \vee m_8 \vee m_9 \vee m_{10} \vee m_{11} \vee m_{12} \vee m_{13} \vee m_{14} \vee m_{15}$$

Using the tabular method we can now find a minimal expression for each of these expressions. The following calculations indicate the steps to compute a minimal expression for g. Similar techniques can be used for f and h.

Finding the Prime Implicants of g

	First Reduction	Second Reduction	Third Reduction
1 0 0 0 ✓	1 0 0 _ ✓	1 0_ _ ✓	1_ _ _ *
‾‾‾‾‾‾	1 0 _ 0 ✓	1 _0 _ ✓	
1 0 0 1 ✓	1 _ 0 0 ✓	1_ _0 ✓	
1 0 1 0 ✓	‾‾‾‾‾‾		
1 1 0 0 ✓	1 0 _ 1 ✓	1 _1 _ ✓	
‾‾‾‾‾‾	1 0 0 1 ✓	1 _ _1 ✓	
0 1 1 1 ✓	1 _ 1 ✓	1 1_ _ ✓	
1 0 1 1 ✓	1 _ _ 0 ✓		
1 1 0 1 ✓	1 1 0 _ ✓		
1 1 1 0 ✓	1 1 _ 0 ✓		
‾‾‾‾‾‾	‾‾‾‾‾‾		
1 1 1 1 ✓	_ 1 1 1 *		
	1 _ 1 1 ✓		
	1 1 _ 1 ✓		
	1 1 1 _ ✓		

This gives the following prime implicants

$$t_{1,2}t_{1,1}t_{1,0} \qquad t_{1,3}$$

Using these prime implicants give the following table of choice

Prime Implicants	Table of Choice for g		
	m_7	m_8	m_9
$t_{1,2}t_{1,1}t_{1,0}$	✓		
$t_{1,3}$		✓	✓

From this we see that the expression for g becomes

$$g := t_{1,2}t_{1,1}t_{1,0} \lor t_{1,3}$$

Using a similar approach we find that

$$f := t_{1,3}$$
$$h := t_{0,2}t_{0,1} \lor t_{0,3}$$

Combining these results we find that

$$e := f \lor g \land h$$
$$:= t_{1,3} \lor t_{1,2}t_{1,1}t_{1,0}t_{0,2}t_{0,1} \lor t_{1,2}t_{1,1}t_{1,0}t_{0,3}$$
$$\lor t_{1,3}t_{0,2}t_{0,1} \lor t_{1,3}t_{0,3}$$

This expression can be further reduced by using the relationship

$$x = x \lor x \land y$$

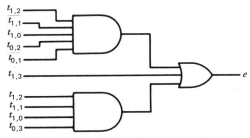

Figure 6-18   Realization of Over Temperature Detector network.

to eliminate the last two product terms since they can be combined with the first product term. Thus the final expression for e is given by

$$e := t_{1,3} \lor t_{1,2}t_{1,1}t_{1,0}t_{0,2}t_{0,1} \lor t_{1,2}t_{1,1}t_{1,0}t_{0,3}$$

The combinational logic network to realize this expression is shown in Figure 6-18.

EXERCISES

1. Use the tabular method to minimize the following logical expressions.
    (a) $f(x_1, x_2, x_3) = m_0 \lor m_2 \lor m_3 \lor m_4 \lor m_7$
    (b) $f(x_1, x_2, x_3, x_4, x_5)$ $m_0 \lor m_2 \lor m_4 \lor m_8 \lor m_{12} \lor m_{19} \lor m_{30}$
          don't care minterms m_6, m_{16}, m_{29}

2. Use the tabular method to find the functions f and h defined by Table 6-9.

4.   SUMMARY

In some ways the problem of finding a minimal logic circuit realization of a given function is not as critical as it once was. Before the development of integrated circuit elements, each logic element involved a relatively high cost, in terms of both money and equipment considerations. The availability of integrated circuits has considerably altered this picture. Integrated circuit logic elements are very cheap, and one logic package may contain several identical logic elements.

Reduction of logic circuits now becomes important in order to simplify the organization of the circuits and the number of interconnections necessary to construct a given network. However, this is not the only reason that we study the minimization process.

Our ability to apply and use logic networks in an efficient manner and to understand their behavior requires us to fully understand how the various components of a logic network interact to realize a given logical expression. This insight is one of the major side products of the ideas discussed in this chapter. From this point it is assumed that any logic network that is needed as part of a system can be designed by the techniques that have been developed to this point. Thus our investigations in the later chapters are concerned with designing higher level networks and complete systems, and we minimize the amount of attention we pay to how particular networks are realized at the logic level.

Reference Notation

With the advent of LSI and MSI technology the importance of logic circuit minimization has decreased in importance. Thus many of the detailed minimization techniques that have been developed are no longer considered in detail in the newer publications dealing with logic design. References 1 and 4 present a very detailed discussion of the minimization process. The newer treatments, such as found in References 2 and 3, provide a general overview of the process and indicate a number of applications.

REFERENCES

1. Bartee, T. C., Lebow, I. L., and Reed, I. S. (1962), *Theory and Design of Digital Machines*. McGraw-Hill, New York.
2. Dietmeyer, D. L. (1978), *Logic Design of Digital Systems* (second edition). Allyn and Bacon, Boston.
3. Hill, F. J., and Peterson, G. R. (1981), *Introduction to Switching Theory and Logic Design* (third edition). Wiley, New York.
4. Miller, R. E. (1965), *Switching Theory,* Vol. 1. Wiley, New York.

HOME PROBLEMS

1. Information is transferred in a digital system using a 4-bit code. Bits 1 through 3 are information bits and bit 4 is a parity bit. The value of the parity bit is chosen so that the number of 1's (including the parity bit) in the 4-bit representation of the information is odd. Design a minimum two-level AND-OR logic network that will indicate (with a 1 output) whenever an error is present in the received information.

2. A minimal logic network is needed to realize the function

$$z := \text{majority } (a, b, c, d, e)$$

where z has a value of 1 if and only if the majority of the variables a, b, c, d, e have a value of 1. For example

$$\text{majority } (0, 1, 0, 0, 1) = 0 \qquad \text{majority } (1, 1, 0, 0, 1) = 1$$

Minimize this function and realize it using NAND gates.

3. Let A and B be two 3-bit binary numbers and let T be a 2-bit control signal. Design a logic network that computes

$$z := ((T = [0]) \wedge (A < B)) \wedge ((T = [1]) \wedge (A = B))$$
$$\wedge ((T = [2]) \wedge (A > B))$$

4. Let A be a BCD encoded decimal digit. Design a logic network that will give a 1 output if the decimal value of A is a nonzero multiple of 3 and 0 otherwise.

5. A digital counter contains a 3-bit register. The counter counts from 0 = [0,0,0] to 7 = [1,1,1] and then resets and starts all over again. This counter is used, as indicated in Figure P6-1, to generate 3 control signals c_1, c_2, c_3. These signals take a value of 1 as indicated by the following conditions.

$$c_1 = 1 \text{ for a count of } 0, 1, 3, 5, 7$$
$$c_2 = 1 \text{ for a count of } 0, 3, 5, 6$$
$$c_3 = 1 \text{ for a count of } 0, 3, 4, 7$$

They are 0 for all other conditions. Design a minimal logic network that will generate c_1, c_2, and c_3.

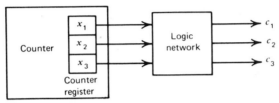

Figure P6-1

6. The minimal logic network shown in Figure P6-2 has a static hazard. (See Home Problem 10, Chapter 3). Use a three-variable map to explain why this hazard exists. How can the addition of an extra AND gate to this network eliminate this hazard?

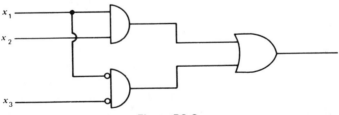

Figure P6-2

7

STANDARD MEDIUM-SCALE LOGIC NETWORKS

1. INTRODUCTION

At one time all logic networks were designed using logic circuits constructed from discrete components such as transistors, resistors, and capacitors. By today's standards these networks were bulky and very costly. Integrated circuit technology has now made it possible to place thousands of these components on a single semiconductor chip. Thus the price and size of complete digital networks are now of the same order of magnitude as the price and size of an individual transistor. The problem faced by the semiconductor manufacturer is to decide which standard logic networks should be developed and marketed. This decision is usually made by evaluating the needs of the logic system designer and trying to identify those networks that provide the greatest flexibility in design or that carry out a commonly required operation. To use this flexibility the logic designer must be able to relate the functional tasks that must be carried out by a network to the way that these tasks can be realized using the standard modules produced by the semiconductor manufacturers.

In this chapter we briefly investigate the characteristics of some typical medium-scale logic networks that, for our purposes, will be considered to be a network that requires from 10 to 100 logic elements to realize. Modules of this type are typically used to carry out many of the standard operations discussed in Chapter 5. Our initial discussion will show how a general multiple-input multiple-output network can be designed using a special class of logic networks called Programmed Logic Arrays (PLAs). We will then consider some of the standard building blocks such as decoders, multiplexers, demultiplexers, and arithmetic logic units, which are available as standard medium-scale integration (MSI) integrated circuits.

2. MULTIPLE-OUTPUT LOGIC NETWORKS

Up to this point we have concentrated most of our effort on developing the techniques that can be used to realize logic networks that have a single output. Most of the networks found in digital systems have multiple outputs. In this section we consider

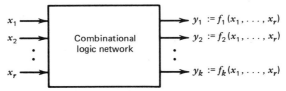

Figure 7-1   General form of multiple-input multiple-output logic network.

the problem of designing networks of the form shown in Figure 7-1 with r inputs and k outputs.

Formally such a network can be described by k canonical sum-of-product functions of the form

$$y_1 := f_1(x_1, \ldots, x_r) = m_{1,1} \lor m_{1,2} \lor \ldots \lor m_{1,n_1}$$
$$y_2 := f_2(x_1, \ldots, x_r) = m_{2,1} \lor m_{2,2} \lor \ldots \lor m_{2,n_2}$$
$$\vdots$$
$$y_k := f_k(x_1, \ldots, x_r) = m_{k,1} \lor m_{k,2} \lor m_{k,n_k}$$

where the terms $m_{i,j}$ are the minterms associated with the function $f_i(x_1, \ldots, x_r)$.

We have already seen that one way to design complex logic networks of this type is to try to decompose the network into smaller subnetworks, hopefully of the same general form, which can be interconnected to form the main network. Although there is a wide range of design problems for which this approach is useful, we may encounter design problems where it is not clear how such a decomposition can take place. In that case the network must be designed as a whole. However, if we can share some of the logic elements among many of the functions, we can reduce the overall complexity of the network. There are a number of different ways that this can be done.

In the following discussion we investigate a few of the design techniques that can be used to design two-level AND-OR multiple-output logic networks that share as many logic circuit elements as possible. In particular the larger the number of minterms common to two or more functions, the greater our chance to share logic circuit elements.

Independent Subnetworks

When the functions describing a given network do not have many common minterms, the most suitable design technique is to design a separate logic network for each function

$$y_i := f_i(x_1, \ldots, x_r)$$

This approach produces a design of the form shown in Figure 7-2. Each network is designed using one of the standard techniques discussed in the previous chapters. For many of the simpler networks this approach is a realistic solution to the problem.

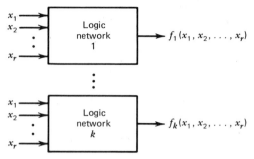

Figure 7-2   A simple realization of a multiple-output network.

Switching Matrix

The most direct method of realizing a multiple output network is to realize the canonical expressions that represent each function. The resulting network is called a switching matrix and is very easily constructed. To illustrate this method, assume that we wish to realize the network described by Table 7-1.

The functions associated with this table are:

$$f_1(x_1, x_2, x_3) = m_1 \lor m_2 \lor m_5 \lor m_7$$
$$f_2(x_1, x_2, x_3) = m_0 \lor m_1 \lor m_4 \lor m_5$$
$$f_3(x_1, x_2, x_3) = m_2 \lor m_4 \lor m_5$$

The realization of these functions using a switching matrix is shown in Figure 7-3.

The complete circuit diagram for a switching matrix can become rather cluttered. To simplify the representation, we can use the alternative representation for the network shown in Figure 7-4. In this representation the minterm generator generates only those minterms necessary to realize the functions. The output is then formed by selecting the minterms for each output function. When a minterm is needed it is ORed to the output, and this is indicated by the fact that the minterm line and output line are connected by the special symbol

shown in Figure 7-4.

Table 7-1   Truth Table for a Multiple-output Network

x_1	x_2	x_3	$f_1(x_1, x_2, x_3)$	$f_2(x_1, x_2, x_3)$	$f_3(x_1, x_2, x_3)$
0	0	0	0	1	0
0	0	1	1	1	0
0	1	0	1	0	1
0	1	1	0	0	0
1	0	0	0	1	1
1	0	1	1	1	1
1	1	0	0	0	0
1	1	1	1	0	0

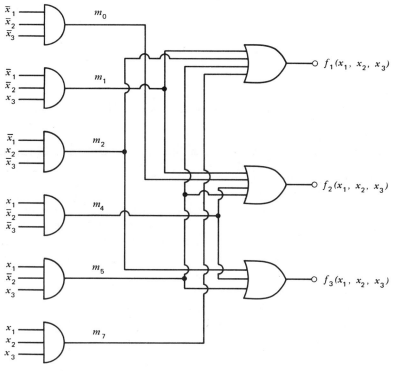

Figure 7-3 Switching matrix representation of Table 7-1.

When a switching matrix had to be constructed using discrete components, they were very costly to use in the design of a digital system. Integrated circuit technology has changed this constraint. When an integrated circuit is designed, one of the goals is to make the circuit as regular as possible. This is one of the major features of a switching matrix. Thus switching matrix techniques are now used extensively in the design of medium- and large-scale integrated circuit logic networks.

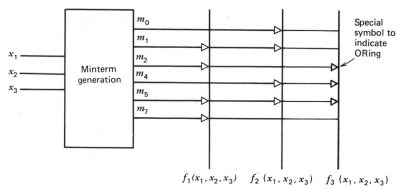

Figure 7-4 Simplified representation of a switching matrix.

Programmable Logic Arrays

Special integrated circuits, called *programmable logic arrays* (PLA), have been developed, making it very easy to realize a switching matrix. A PLA has the general form shown in Figure 7-5a when purchased. This array has not been programmed, so it does not realize any function. In this array only three input lines and three output lines are indicated to simplify our discussion. A typical commercial PLA circuit, such as the 74S330 produced by Texas Instruments, has 12 input lines, 50 internal AND gates, and 6 output lines.

To implement a given network, the designer first uses appropriate analytical techniques to develop a set of sum-of-product logic expressions to describe the network. Each of the distinct product terms found in these expressions is realized using one of the AND gates. These product terms are then ORed together to realize each expression. The programming of the array is accomplished using special equipment to make the necessary interconnections. Usually this is done by applying special voltages or currents that "burn out" unwanted connections or "burn in" desired connections. These operations are quite easy to do and can be carried out either under computer control or manually by a very careful technician.

To illustrate how a PLA may be used we will realize the multiple output network described by Table 7-1. From the previous analysis we know that the three output functions are defined by the following equations:

$$f_1(x_1, x_2, x_3) = m_1 \lor m_2 \lor m_5 \lor m_7$$
$$f_2(x_1, x_2, x_3) = m_0 \lor m_1 \lor m_4 \lor m_5$$
$$f_3(x_1, x_2, x_3) = m_2 \lor m_4 \lor m_5$$

Using the PLA shown in Figure 7-5a, we can program the connections shown in Figure 7-5b to realize the three functions using the canonical representation of each expression.

If the functions to be realized involve a large number of minterms, and if there is considerable commonality among the functions, it may be possible to simplify the network by using simplification techiques of the form discussed in the previous chapter. A number of computer programs have been developed to carry out the simplification process for large networks. The following discussion illustrates a possible simplification for the three equations given above. For this example, simplification will be carried out by using the map method to simplify each function separately. A somewhat more general method of simplification is discussed in Section 5.

The three variable maps associated with each function are shown in Figure 7-6. Using these maps it is seen that the functions reduce to

$$f_1(x_1, x_2, x_3) = \bar{x}_2 x_3 \lor x_1 x_3 \lor \bar{x}_1 x_2 \bar{x}_3$$
$$f_2(x_1, x_2, x_3) = \bar{x}_2$$
$$f_3(x_1, x_2, x_3) = x_1 \bar{x}_2 \lor \bar{x}_1 x_2 \bar{x}_3$$

The PLA realization of these expressions is shown in Figure 7-7. Note that almost as many product terms are needed in this reduced realization as in the minterm realization. The main contribution of the reduction process is to reduce the number of product terms and the number of variables used to form the products.

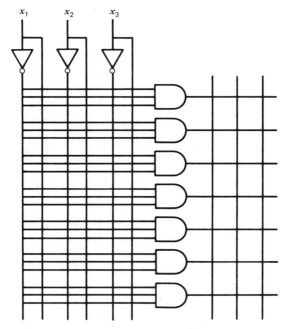

(a) Unprogrammed PLA

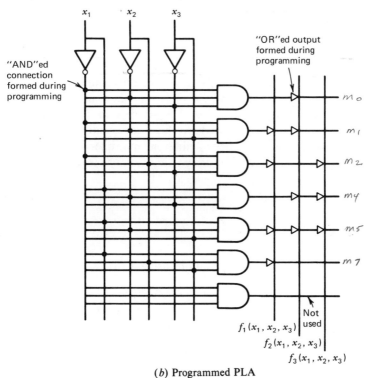

(b) Programmed PLA

Figure 7-5 Illustration of use of a PLA.

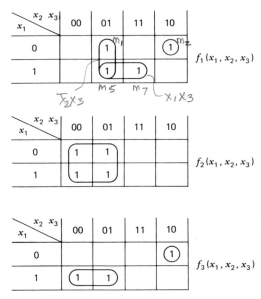

Figure 7-6   Reduction of logic expressions.

A factor that places a limit on the use of a given PLA is the number of internal AND gates that are available to form product terms. PLAs can be used to realize a multiple-output network as long as the number of required product terms for that realization does not exceed the number of AND gates provided by the PLA. For example, assume that we have an n-input network and that the PLA has K AND gates. There are 2^n possible minterms. For $n > 5$ we normally find that $K \ll 2^n$. Thus a PLA cannot be used to realize a given network unless the canonical expressions describing the network involve K or fewer minterms or unless we can reduce the logic expression to the point where they are described by fewer than K product terms. There are many situations where this limit is satisfied. The ability to "program" PLAs to realize a number of different multiple-input multiple-output networks is therefore a very powerful design aid when one is designing complex digital systems.

EXERCISES

1. Realize the following set of equations using a PLA.

$$f_1(x_1, x_2, x_3, x_4) := m_0 \lor m_2 \lor m_5 \lor m_6 \lor m_{13} \lor m_{14}$$
$$f_2(x_1, x_2, x_3, x_4) := m_0 \lor m_5 \lor m_8 \lor m_{13} \lor m_{15}$$
$$f_3(x_1, x_2, x_3, x_4) := m_0 \lor m_3 \lor m_8 \lor m_{12}$$

(a) Realize these equations directly.
(b) Reduce the equations individually before realizing them.

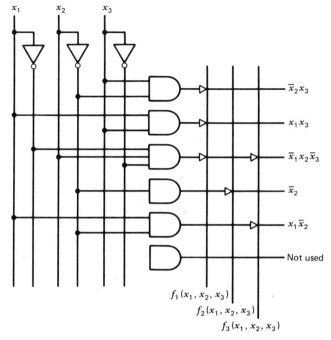

Figure 7-7   PLA realization of reduced logic expression.

2. How many product terms were required for realization 1a and 1b in the above problem? Did the minimization process help?

3.   DECODERS, DEMULTIPLEXERS, AND MULTIPLEXERS

Integrated circuit technology has generated a number of standard logic modules that can be used as the basic components in the design of complex digital systems. In this and the next section we introduce a number of these modules and indicate some typical applications. No attempt is made to discuss specific modules produced by a given manufacturer or to give detailed designs for their internal structure. Instead we talk about a generic class of modules and the specific task they perform. It is assumed that suitable manufacturer's catalogs can be consulted to obtain a detailed description of specific commercial realizations of modules from that class.

Decoders

A basic module encountered in a number of designs is the _decoder,_ which has the form shown in Figure 7-8a. An n-bit signal, S, is applied to the input of the decoder which has $k \leq 2^n$ output lines. The output of the ith line is formally defined as the scalar

$$f_i := (s = [i])$$

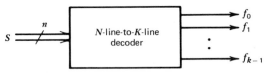

(a) General *N*-line-to-*K*-line decoder

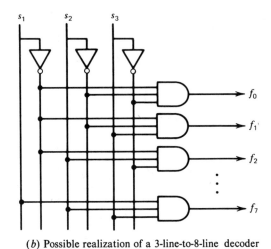

(b) Possible realization of a 3-line-to-8-line decoder

Figure 7-8   Decoder network.

When the input signal is encoded as a standard binary number, then

$$f_i := m_i$$

the ith minterm associated with the input n-tuple. If a different encoding is used for S, then the appropriate minterm associated with the encoded representation of $[i]$ must be used.

Decoders are referred to as *N-line-to-K-line* decoders where $K \leq 2^N$. This designation indicates that the input signal is an N-bit signal and that there are K distinct output lines. For example, the decoder shown in Figure 7-8b is a 3-line-to-8-line decoder. Examining this figure we see that the decoder is nothing more than an array of AND gates such as we have already seen in a PLA.

By itself, a decoder network does not appear to be particularly useful. However, if we add a few more logic elements, we can carry out a very large number of interesting tasks.

Demultiplexers

A *demultiplexer* is equivalent to a multiposition switch with a single input and a multiple number of outputs. Conceptually a demultiplexer carries out the task shown in Figure 7-9a. As shown, there are two inputs to a demultiplexer. Besides the input

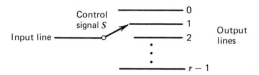

(*a*) Conceptual representation of a demultiplexer as a multiposition switch

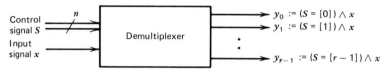

(*b*) Network representation of a demultiplexer

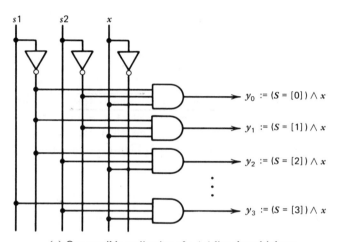

(*c*) One possible realization of a 1-4 line demultiplexer

Figure 7-9   Demultiplexer representation.

signal there is an *n*-bit control signal *S*, which is used to position the switch. If the control signal has a value of [*i*], then the input signal is connected to the *i*th output line.

If we replace the switch of Figure 7-9*a* with the logic network of Figure 7-9*b*, the *i*th output of the network is defined as

$$y_i := (X = [i]) \wedge x$$

If *S* is encoded as a standard binary number, this means that

$$y_i := m_i \wedge x$$

One way in which to realize a demultiplexer using a network similar to a PLA is shown in Figure 7-9*c*.

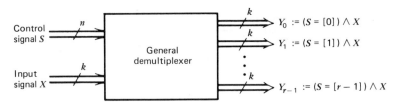

Figure 7-10   General demultiplexer operation on k-bit signal.

Extending this idea we can design a demultiplexer that operates on complete r-bit signals. Suppose that we wish to realize the system shown in Figure 7-10. To do this all that we have to do is make r copies of the circuit shown in Figure 7-9. In this case the output will be given by the vector equation

$$Y_i := m_i \wedge X$$

Multiplexers

The inverse of a demultiplexer is a multiplexer. A *multiplexer* is the equivalent of a multiposition switch with multiple inputs and a single output. This switch functions as shown in Figure 7-11a. The multiplexer receives a set of n input signals and a control signal T. The control signal indicates which one of the input signals is to appear at the output. For the network shown in Figure 7-11a, the output is given by the following relationship

$$Z := ((T = [0]) \wedge X_0) \vee ((T = [1]) \wedge X_1) \vee \ldots \vee ((T = [n]) \wedge X_n)$$

If T is encoded as a binary number, the relationship becomes

$$Z := (m_0 \wedge X_0) \vee (m_1 \wedge X_1) \vee \ldots \vee (m_n \wedge X_n)$$

where the m_i's are the minterms associated with the control signal T. The multiplexer operation may be implemented in a variety of ways.

For some applications, the minterms needed to select the desired input are generated by a separate decoder network as shown in Figure 7-11b. In this case the outputs of the decoder are used to control a set of input gates in a different part of the network. This approach is useful if the signals being multiplexed are physically separated.

A second approach is to build the complete multiplexer as a single integrated circuit. The decoding operation and the ANDing operation are combined in a single package as shown in Figure 7-11c.

These ideas can easily be extended to the case where the inputs are r-bit signals. In the first case r copies of the AND gates are needed, but only one decoder is needed to generate the selection signal. The second realization does not use a separate decoder. Thus r copies of the complete multiplexer network shown in Figure 7-11c are used.

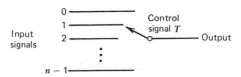

(a) Conceptual representation of a multiplexer as a multiposition switch

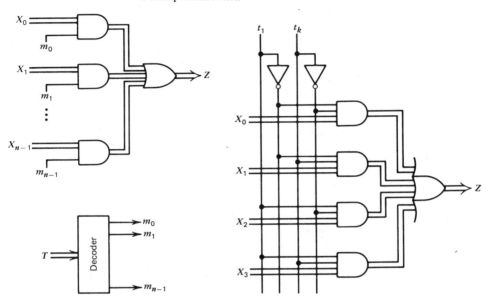

(b) Multiplexer realization with separate decoder

(c) Multiplexer realization with internal decoding

Figure 7-11   Multiplexer realization.

Three-state Logic Element

In the multiplexer circuits shown in Figure 7-11, the AND gates were used to control which signal was transmitted to the output. The output of each AND gate, however, had to be passed through an OR gate to form the output signal. The reason this arrangement is necessary is that each AND gate must be electronically isolated from its neighbors. This circuit could be simplified if we could replace the AND and OR gates with the electronic equivalent of a mechanical switch shown as in Figure 7-12a. The main feature of a switch is that when it is open there is no connection between the input and the output. The "open switch" condition is logically equivalent to having a 0 value applied as one input to a two-input AND gate, while the "closed switch" condition is logically equivalent to having a 1 value applied to the input.

The desirability of having the equivalent of a mechanical switch has led to the development of a special logic element, called a *three-state gate*, which is represented

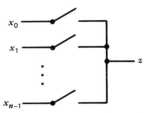

(*a*) Conceptual model of a mechanical switch replacement for AND gates in a multiplexer

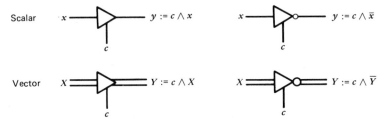

Scalar $\qquad$ $y := c \wedge x$ $\qquad$ $y := c \wedge \bar{x}$

Vector $\qquad$ $Y := c \wedge X$ $\qquad$ $Y := c \wedge \bar{Y}$

(*b*) Logic circuit representation of three-state gates

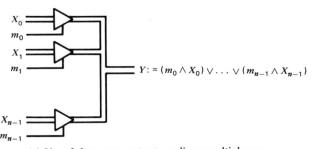

$Y : = (m_0 \wedge X_0) \vee \ldots \vee (m_{n-1} \wedge X_{n-1})$

(*c*) Use of three-state gates to realize a multiplexer

Figure 7-12 Three-state gates.

by the one or the other of the logic symbols shown in Figure 7-12*b*. The behavior of these elements is described by the scalar or vector equations given below.

Scalar Equations	Vector Equations
$y := c \wedge x$	$Y := c \wedge X$
$y := c \wedge \bar{x}$	$Y := c \wedge \bar{X}$

The control signal c is a scalar, while the inputs may be either a scalar or a vector. If the input is an n-bit vector, then n copies of the scalar gate must be used to realize the vector gate. The difference between a three-state gate and an AND gate is that the output signal is electronically disconnected when the control signal is 0. This means that a multiplexer of the form shown in Figure 7-12*c* can be constructed from these gates without using an OR gate to provide electronic isolation.

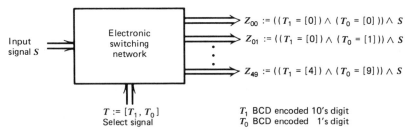

$$Z_{00} := ((T_1 = [0]) \wedge (T_0 = [0])) \wedge S$$
$$Z_{01} := ((T_1 = [0]) \wedge (T_0 = [1])) \wedge S$$
$$Z_{49} := ((T_1 = [4]) \wedge (T_0 = [9])) \wedge S$$

$T := [T_1, T_0]$
Select signal

T_1 BCD encoded 10's digit
T_0 BCD encoded 1's digit

(*a*) General organization of electronic switching system

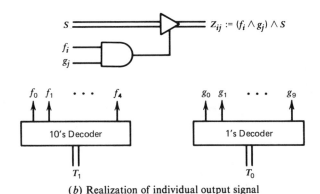

(*b*) Realization of individual output signal

Figure 7-13   Design of an electronic switch using three-state logic.

Three-state gates have many applications other than in multiplexers. The following example illustrates one such application.

An Electronic Switching System

It is becoming quite common to connect a number of computer systems together into what is called a computer network. In such a network it is necessary to be able to send the output produced by one computer to different points within the network. The destination selected will depend upon the information contained in the signal to be transferred. One way to do this is to use an electronic switching system of the form shown in Figure 7-13*a*. There are two input signals to this network; the signal S from the local computer and the line select signal T, which selects which line is to be used to transmit the signal S from the local computer to another computer in the network. Let us assume that the select signal is encoded as a BCD number and that there are 50 different transmission lines that may be selected by the select signal. If these lines are numbered from 00 to 49, then the output found on line i, j is described by the expression

$$Z_{ij} := ((T_1 = [i]) \wedge (T_0 = [j])) \wedge S$$

where

$$T := [T_1, T_0] = [t_{1,3}, t_{1,2}, t_{1,1}, t_{1,0}, t_{0,3}, t_{0,2}, t_{0,1}, t_{0,0}]$$

In this representation T_1 is the BCD encoded ten's digit and T_0 is the BCD encoded unit's digit. The kth element of Z_{ij} is formed as shown in Figure 7-13b. Two decoders are used, one to form the control signal corresponding to the ten's digit

$$f_i := (T_i = [i])$$

and one to form the control signal corresponding to the unit's digit

$$g_j := (T_i = [j])$$

These two signals are then used to control the three-state gate as shown in Figure 7-13b.

Note that if the control signal T has a value that fall outside of the range [00] to [49], then the output of the computer system is not transmitted to any part of the computer network.

Multiplexer Realization of Combinational Logic Networks

Initially multiplexers were designed to solve the problem of producing a particular output signal selected from among n input signals. However, logic designers soon realized that integrated circuit multiplexers provided a compact way to realize general purpose combinational logic networks. A number of design techniques have been developed to do this. Some are quite general while others make special use of the particular properties of the logic expression that is being realized. The following discussion illustrates one way that any truth table can be realized by a multiplexer provided enough input and control lines are available.

Assume that we wish to realize the function

$$z := f(a, b, c)$$

defined by the three-variable truth table of Table 7-2, and that the 4-1 multiplexer shown in Figure 7-14a is to be used for this realization. To carry out this task we must decide how to relate the select signal input

Table 7-2   A Typical Logic Function

a	b	c	$f(a, b, c)$
0	0	0	0
0	0	1	0
0	1	0	1
0	1	1	1
1	0	0	1
1	0	1	0
1	1	0	0
1	1	1	1

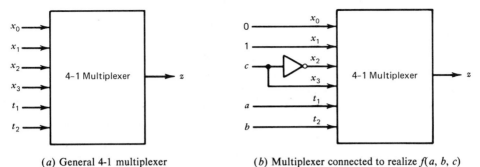

(a) General 4-1 multiplexer   (b) Multiplexer connected to realize $f(a, b, c)$

Figure 7-14   Use of a multiplexer to realize a logic expression.

$$T := [t_1, t_2]$$

and the signals on the input lines

$$x_0, \ldots x_3$$

to the input variables a, b, and c.

The first step of our design process is to partition the truth table of Table 7-2 into subsets. If T is an r-bit control signal, we generate 2^r subsets. Each subset corresponds to one of the distinct values of T. Since T is a 2-bit signal in our example, we will generate four subsets as shown in Table 7-3. To define the partition we use the first two of the three input variables. Rows of the truth table are placed in the same subset if the variables a and b have the same values. The reason for this grouping is that each of these groups will define one of the x inputs to the multiplexer.

For this truth table we interpret the subsets in the following manner. The first subset corresponds to the condition that the output of the multiplexer is identically 0, the second subset corresponds to the condition that the output of the multiplexer is identically 1, the third subset corresponds to the output being equal to $\bar{c}$, and the fourth subset corresponds to the output being equal to c. With these observations we see that the variables a and b are used as the control input to the multiplexer to specify which subset we are dealing with and the appropriate function of c can be

Table 7-3   A Typical Logic Function Grouped by Common First Two Elements

a	b	c	$f(a, b, c)$	
0	0	0	0	Subset [0, 0]
0	0	1	0	$f(0, 0, c) := 0$
0	1	0	1	Subset [0, 1]
0	1	1	1	$f(0, 1, c) := 1$
1	0	0	1	Subset [1, 0]
1	0	1	0	$f(1, 0, c) := \bar{c}$
1	1	0	0	Subset [1, 1]
1	1	1	1	$f(1, 1, c) := c$

applied to the line selected by the control signal. The output of the multiplexer is the function of c associated with that subset.

The realization of the function $f(a, b, c)$ is completed by connecting the multiplexer as shown in Figure 7-14b. The variables a and b are used to form the control signal and an appropriate function of c is used to form the multiplexer inputs.

Any three-variable function can be realized using a 4-1 multiplexer by this technique. Generalizing upon this approach, we see that any function of n variables

$$z := f(y_1, \ldots, y_n)$$

can be realized using a 2^{n-1} to 1 multiplexer. The first $n - 1$ variables are used to generate the control signals applied to the multiplexer, while the subsets associated with the control signals define which input

$$0, 1, y_n, \text{ or } \overline{y}_n$$

is applied to the input line selected by the control signals.

This approach is very useful since we can realize any three-variable function with a 4-1 multiplexer, a four-variable function with an 8-1 multiplexer, and a five-variable function with a 16-1 multiplexer.

EXERCISES

1. What is the difference between a decoder network and a demultiplexer?

2. Use a 4-1 multiplexer to realize the following logic function:

$$f(a, b, c) := m_0 \lor m_3 \lor m_4 \lor m_5$$

4.   OPERATIONAL MODULES

In Chapter 5 we saw that a number of mathematical operations, such as addition and the relational operations, could be defined in terms of the information contained in the operands associated with the operation rather than on how the information was encoded. At that point we demonstrated that standard design techniques could be used to define the logic circuits necessary to realize these operations.

Before the development of integrated circuit technology, all logic networks had to be realized using discrete logic elements. At that time individual logic elements were expensive and a logic designer had to be very careful in the design so that a minimal number of logic elements were used in a given network. Integrated circuit technology has removed this constraint. In fact the greatest problem often faced by a designer is minimizing the number of connections that must be made between circuits rather than the complexity of the circuit inside of the integrated circuit package.

As our discussion of digital system design develops in the following chapters, we will find it useful to assume that a wide variety of integrated circuit modules are available to carry out standard operations. This assumption is consistent with current practice. In this section we introduce a number of modules that perform the standard arithmetic, logical, and relational operations that are used in our later design efforts. These modules are somewhat idealized since they do not have the full range of capabilities found in many of the commercially available units. This approach is taken so that we can concentrate on the general use of functional modules without having to go into detail about some of the more advanced features of specific modules produced by a given manufacturer. Detailed descriptions of specific MSI and LSI modules produced by a given manufacturer can be found in the data books, such as those listed in the References at the end of this chapter, published by the manufacturers.

General Module Representation

Our goal in this section is to describe the functional characteristics of a number of complex modules without considering the module's actual logic circuit realization. This discussion will be aided, however, if we have a general conceptual model to describe how the internal information is being processed by the module. Figure 7-15 shows the general form of the model used.

The external view of a module is illustrated in Figure 7-15a. The module receives

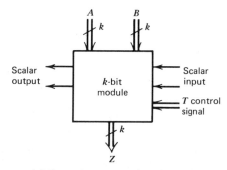

(a) General representation of a module

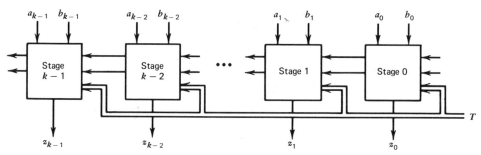

(b) Conceptual functional representation of the internal structure of a k-bit module

Figure 7-15   Symbolic representation of a k-bit module.

both vector and scalar information as input information and generates both vector and scalar information as output. Most modules are designed to operate upon k-bit vectors where k is typically 2, 4, or 8. The scalar inputs and outputs are used to represent status information that is needed by the module or produced as a result of the processing being carried out by the module. Some modules can carry out a variety of operations. In this case a control signal T is used to select the desired task or operation.

The actual logic circuit used to realize a given module can be quite complex and designed in such a way both to aid in its manufacture and to provide desirable timing characteristics. However, when we wish to discuss the functional behavior of a module, it is desirable to use a conceptual model of the internal structure, which has a form such as that shown in Figure 7-15b. Here we assume that the operations performed on the bits are isolated into stages that are connected in cascade to realize the module's overall operation. This conceptual model allows us to indicate when information must be passed from stage to stage and also whether specific items of information are needed to generate specific output signals.

For each of the modules to be described we first present a conceptual model of the module and then an analytical description of the module's functional behavior. The description may be in tabular and/or equation form as appropriate. The following discussion presents several examples of modules that are of use in designing complex digital systems.

The Relational Operations

The six relational operations

$$ < \quad \leq \quad = \quad \geq \quad > \quad \neq $$

play a very important roll in many designs. One way to implement these operations is to use an n-bit comparator network of the form discussed in Section 4 of Chapter 5. A typical 4-bit comparator network is shown in Figure 7-16. In the design of this network it was assumed that the two input vectors, A and B, represented positive binary numbers. The relationship that exists between A and B is reported by the three scalar outputs

$$ l_{n+4} \qquad e_{n+4} \qquad g_{n+4} $$

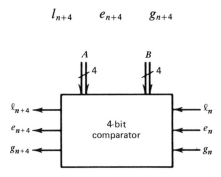

Figure 7-16   Symbolic representation of a 4-bit comparator.

Table 7-4   Relational Operation Realization

Operation	Output Location	Input Conditioning	Functional Expression
$<$	l_{n+4}	$l_n := 0$	$l_{n+4} := (A < B)$
$\leq$	l_{n+4}	$l_n := 1$	$l_{n+4} := (A < B) \lor (A = B)$
$=$	e_{n+4}	$e_n := 1$	$e_{n+4} := (A = B)$
$>$	g_{n+4}	$g_n := 0$	$g_{n+4} := (A > B)$
$\geq$	g_{n+4}	$g_n := 1$	$g_{n+4} := (A > B) \lor (A = B)$
	Special Case		
$\neq$	$\overline{e}_{n+4}$	$e_n := 1$	$\overline{e}_{n+4} := \overline{(A = B)}$
			logic circuit needed to form NOT of e_{n+4}

as defined below. The three scalar inputs

$$l_n \qquad e_n \qquad g_n$$

can be used either to condition the operation to be performed or to propagate information from a preceding stage in a multiple-stage comparison.

The functional description of the 4-bit comparator is given by the following equations

$$l_{n+4} := (A < B) \lor l_n \land (A = B)$$
$$e_{n+4} := e_n \land (A = B)$$
$$g_{n+4} := (A > B) \lor g_n \land (A = B)$$

The six relational operations that can be realized by the 4-bit comparator are summarized in Table 7-4. These relationships form the starting point for constructing a general comparator.

Cascade Connection of Comparators

If we wish to compare more than 4 bits, a cascade connection of comparators as shown in Figure 7-17 is needed. In this design a control signal and an output selector network has been added so that we can define the exact relational operation that is being performed. The relationship between the relational operation performed by the network and the value of the control signal T is defined by Table 7-5.

Assume that we wish to compare two u-bit vectors A and B. To do this we need to use k 4-bit comparators where k is selected to be the smallest integer such that $4*k \geq u$. The output h of this system is defined by the equation

$$h := ((T = [0]) \land (A < B)) \lor ((T = [1]) \land (A \leq B)) \lor ((T = [2]) \land (A = B))$$
$$\lor ((T = [3]) \land (A \neq B)) \lor ((T = [4]) \land (A > B)) \lor ((T = [5]) \land (A \geq B))$$

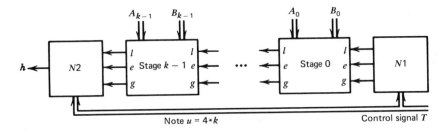

Note $u = 4*k$

$$\text{Input signals} \quad \begin{aligned} A &:= [A_{k-1}, \ldots, A_0] \\ B &:= [B_{k-1}, \ldots, B_0] \end{aligned}$$

Figure 7-17   Multiple-stage comparison network.

This equation represents the functional behavior of the complete network under the assumption that both A and B are positive binary numbers. The network $N2$ is used to form h from the output signals generated from the last comparator. In addition to the network $N2$, we also need the network $N1$ to provide the initial condition signals that must be applied to the first comparator. Using the information contained in Table 7-4, both $N1$ and $N2$ can be designed in a straightforward manner.

First we design $N1$. The initial conditions that must be applied to the first stage are defined by the following set of equations.

$$l_0 := (T = [1])$$
$$e_0 := (T = [2]) \vee (T = [3])$$
$$g_0 := (T = [5])$$

If we assume that T is encoded as a 3-bit binary number, then $N1$ is described by the following logical expressions:

$$l_0 := m_1$$
$$e_0 := m_2 \vee m_3$$
$$g_0 := m_5$$

which are easily realized in using any of the standard methods discussed in previous chapters.

Table 7-5   Relational Operations Performed as a Function of Control Signal Value

Control Signal T	Operation	Control Signal T	Operation
[0]	$<$	[3]	$\neq$
[1]	$\leq$	[4]	$>$
[2]	$=$	[5]	$\geq$

The output network $N2$, which uses the outputs of the last stage to form h, is defined by the equation

$$h := ((T = [0]) \lor (T = [1])) \land l_{4k} \lor (T = [2]) \land e_{4k} \lor (T = [3]) \land \overline{e}_{4k}$$
$$\lor ((T = [4]) \lor (T = [5])) \land g_{4k}$$

This network can also be easily realized using standard techniques.

If the comparison operations must be carried out on numbers represented in 2's complement form, we must use a slightly different organization than that shown in Figure 7-17. The alterations necessary to handle this situation are left as a home problem.

Arithmetic Logic Unit

During the design of many digital systems it is necessary to implement a number of arithmetic and/or logic operations on r-bit vectors. This need has led to the development of a number of integrated circuits that combine a variety of the standard logic and arithmetic operations in a single package. These circuits are called *arithmetic logic units* or *ALUs*. Figure 7-18a illustrates one possible organization for a 4-bit ALU. The input to this unit consists of

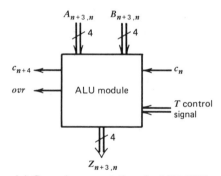

(a) General representation of a 4-bit ALU

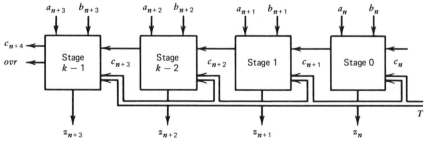

(b) Conceptual functional representation of internal organization of a 4-bit ALU

Figure 7-18 Symbolic representation of a 4-bit ALU.

$$A := [a_{n+3}, a_{n+2}, a_{n+1}, a_n] \qquad \text{first operand}$$
$$B := [b_{n+3}, b_{n+2}, b_{n+1}, b_n] \qquad \text{second operand}$$
$$T := [t_1, t_2, t_3] \qquad \text{control signal}$$
$$c_n \qquad \text{carry bit}$$

The output produced by the unit consists of

$$Z := [z_{n+3}, z_{n+2}, z_{n+1}, z_n] \qquad \text{result}$$
$$c_{n+4} \qquad \text{carry}$$
$$ovr \qquad \text{arithmetic overflow}$$

The conceptual organization of this ALU is indicated in Figure 7-18b. Two basic types of operations are performed—arithmetic and logical. When one of the allowed arithmetic operations is selected by the control signal T, carry information is propagated from stage to stage as indicated. However, when a logic operation is performed, each stage is isolated from the other stages since no carry is generated. Table 7-6 defines the Z output for the ALU shown in Figure 7-18.

If we examine this table we see that the t_1 bit of T acts as a selector bit according to the following rules

$$t_1 := 0 \qquad \text{arithmetic operations}$$
$$t_1 := 1 \qquad \text{logical operations}$$

The Carry Output c_{n+4}

Using the information contained in Table 7-6, we see that the carry output is defined as

$$c_{n+4} := (((T = [1]) \wedge (\overline{A} + B) \vee (T = [2]) \wedge (A + \overline{B})$$
$$\vee (T = [3]) \wedge (A + B) + \overline{t}_1 \wedge c_n \wedge [1]) > [15])$$

The carry bit indicates whether there is a binary carry out of the fourth stage of the ALU.

Table 7-6 Operational Description of Z Output of ALU

Control Signal $[t_1, t_2, t_3]$	Operation	Z
[0, 0, 0]	Clear	$Z := [0]$
[0, 0, 1]	B minus A	$Z := (\overline{A} + B + c_n \wedge [1])_{\text{MOD}16}$
[0, 1, 0]	A minus B	$Z := (A + \overline{B} + c_n \wedge [1])_{\text{MOD}16}$
[0, 1, 1]	$A + B$	$Z := (A + B + c_n \wedge [1])_{\text{MOD}16}$
[1, 0, 0]	A Exclusive Or B	$Z := A \oplus B$
[1, 0, 1]	A OR B	$Z := A \vee B$
[1, 1, 0]	A AND B	$A := A \wedge B$
[1, 1, 1]	Set	$Z := [1, 1, 1, 1]$

Note: $(\ldots)_{\text{MOD}16}$ indicates taking the result modulo 16.

The Arithmetic Overflow Signal *ovr*

When we are carrying out complement arithmetic using r-bit vectors, the leftmost bit of a vector is used to indicate the sign of the number representer by the vector. When two 2's complement numbers are added or subtracted, the result must lie within the range of numbers that can be stored in the vector. If the resulting value lies outside this range, we say that we have an *arithmetic overflow*, which is different from a carry.

An overflow occurs whenever both operands in an arithmetic operation are of the same sign and the result generated is of an opposite sign. This differs from a carry, which is defined simply as a carry out of the most significant bit position when an arithmetic operation is performed on two operands that are assumed not to contain a sign bit. To understand the difference between these two quantities consider the following examples

A	*B*	*Z*	c_{n+4}	*ovr*		**Description**	
[0, 1, 0, 0]	[0, 0, 1, 1]	[0, 1, 1, 1]	0	0	No carry	$4 + 3 = 7$	
					No overflow	$4 + 3 = 7$	
[0, 1, 0, 0]	[0, 1, 0, 1]	[1, 0, 0, 1]	0	1	No carry	$4 + 5 = 9$	
					Overflow	$4 + 5 = -7$	
[1, 1, 1, 0]	[1, 1, 1, 1]	[1, 1, 0, 1]	1	0	Carry	$14 + 15 = 13$	
					No overflow	$-2 + (-1) = -3$	
[1, 1, 0, 0]	[1, 0, 1, 1]	[0, 1, 1, 1]	1	1	Carry	$12 + 11 = 7$	
					Overflow	$-4 + -(5) = 7$	

As illustrated in the above examples, an overflow can occur at both ends of the number range represented by the r-bit vector. If we refer to Figure 7-18b, we see that an overflow will occur when the two operands have the same value for the sign bit and the operation generates a carry into the sign bit location (the leftmost bit). This means that

$$ovr := t_1 \wedge (c_{n+3} \oplus c_{n+4})$$

where the overflow signal is meaningful only when an arithmetic operation is being performed.

Cascade Connections of ALUs

If we must process operands that are larger than the ones that can be handled by a single ALU, we can use a cascade connection such as is shown in Figure 7-19. In this case the operands are 8-bit vectors. Thus two 4-bit ALUs are needed. Note that the carry signal from the rightmost ALU must be connected as an input to the leftmost ALU. However, the overflow signal is ignored since the arithmetic overflow applies only to the sign bits that are processed by the leftmost ALU. If we assume that all of the operations are carried out using 2's complement arithmetic, then the carry c_0 must be set to 0 or 1 depending upon which operation is being performed. If we are carrying out one of the *minus* operations, then c_0 is set to 1, while if the

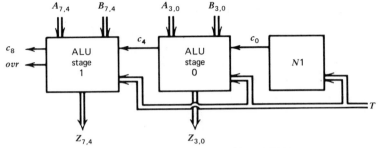

Figure 7-19 Cascade connection of ALUs.

operation is *plus,* c_0 is set to 0. This task is accomplished by use of the network $N1$ shown in the figure. The logic expression for c_0 is

$$c_0 := ((T = [1]) \lor (T = [2])) \land [1]$$

EXERCISES

1. Let A be an 8-bit vector representing a signed integer. Design a network that will compute

$$z := ((T = [0] \land (A = [0])) \lor ((T = [1]) \land (A < [0]))$$
$$\lor ((T = [2]) \land (A \geq [0]))$$

2. Let A and B be two positive binary numbers represented by 8-bit vectors. Design a network that will compute

$$Z := 1A - B1$$

3. Compute all of the output signals generated by the network shown in Figure 7-19 for the following input signals.

T	A	B
[2]	[5]	[25]
[3]	[200]	[80]
[6]	[220]	[64]
[1]	[-50]	[225]

5. TABULAR REDUCTION OF MULTIPLE OUTPUT NETWORKS*

In Section 2 we saw that a multiple output network could be described by a set of canonical logic expressions of the following general form.

$$y_1 := f_1(x_1, \ldots, x_r) := m_{1,1} \lor m_{1,2} \lor \ldots \lor m_{1,n_1}$$
$$y_2 := f_2(x_1, \ldots, x_r) := m_{2,1} \lor m_{2,2} \lor \ldots \lor m_{2,n_2}$$
$$y_3 := f_3(x_1, \ldots, x_r) := m_{3,1} \lor m_{3,2} \lor \ldots \lor m_{3,n_3}$$

*This material is optional.

A switching matrix or PLA can be used to realize such a network by directly implementing the minterms making up the logic functions. The number of AND gates needed in this realization is equal to the number of distinct minterms contained in the set of logic expressions. When the same minterm appears in two or more expressions, we say that commonality exists between the functions. The greater the degree of commonality we find in the logic expressions describing a given network, the fewer the number of AND gates needed to implement the network.

One of the problems with using PLAs is that the number of AND gates available in a given PLA is fixed. If the number of minterms that must be realized is less than the number of AND gates available, then the network can be directly realized using the minterm representation. However, should the number of minterms exceed the number of available AND gates or the logic expressions appear to be overly complex, we may find it desirable to minimize the logic expressions before they are realized. As indicated in Section 2, one method of minimization is to use standard minimization techniques to individually reduce each function. For many design problems this produces satisfactory results. However, this approach does not try to retain any of the commonality that might exist between functions.

The following discussion outlines an algorithm that can be used to simplify the logic expressions that describe a multiple-output network while retaining as much commonality as possible. This process can be very tedious if it is carried out by hand. Computer programs have been developed to carry out this reduction process and are usually available for use where a large amount of logic network design is carried out.

The main difference between the reduction process to be presented and the tabular reduction process presented in Chapter 6 is that we must include a number of steps that allow us to determine which product terms can be used in the realization of more than one logic expression. The reduction process could be presented in a very general manner. However, to aid in understanding the main ideas involved in the algorithm, we restrict this discussion to the case where there are r input variables x_1, ..., x_r and three outputs y_1, y_2, and y_3. The extension to the case with four or more outputs is quite straightforward.

When dealing with a single logic function, our first step was to obtain the set of prime implicants associated with the function. We then eliminated all absolutely eliminable prime implicants from the set. From the remaining set of prime implicants we selected the minimal number that we needed to represent the function. Each prime implicant so chosen covered one or more of the minterms in the canonical description of the function. For the multiple output case the same general procedure is applied except that we are now looking for product terms that can be used as part of the representation of more than one function. To find these terms we make the following observation.

Product Term Selection

A product term can be used in the minimal representation of the functions $f_i(x_1, \ldots, x_r)$ and $f_j(x_1, \ldots, x_r)$ only if the term is a prime implicant of the function.

$$f_{i,j}(x_1, \ldots, x_r) = f_i(x_1, \ldots, x_r) \wedge f_j(x_1, \ldots, x_r)$$

Table 7-7   General Form of a Multiple-output Table of Choice

	Minterms	Function $f_1(x_1, \ldots, x_r)$			Function $f_2(x_1, \ldots, x_r)$			Function $f_3(x_1, \ldots, x_r)$		
Prime Implicants		$m_{1,1}$ $m_{1,2}$ $\cdots$ $m_{1,n1}$			$m_{2,1}$ $m_{2,2}$ $\cdots$ $m_{2,n2}$			$m_{3,1}$ $m_{3,2}$ $\cdots$ $m_{2,n3}$		
f_1	$p_{1,1}$ $\vdots$ $p_{1,u1}$									
f_2	$p_{2,1}$ $\vdots$ $p_{2,u2}$									
f_3	$\vdots$									
$f_{1,2}$	$\vdots$									
$f_{1,3}$	$\vdots$									
$f_{2,3}$	$\vdots$									
$f_{1,2,3}$	$\vdots$									

Similarly, a product term can be used in the minimal representation of the functions $f_1(x_1, \ldots, x_r)$ and $f_2(x_1, \ldots, x_r)$ and $f_3(x_1, \ldots, x_r)$ only if the term is a prime implicant of the function

$$f_{1,2,3}(x_1, \ldots, x_r) = f_1(x_1, \ldots, x_r) \wedge f_2(x_1, \ldots, x_r) \wedge f_3(x_1, \ldots, x_r)$$

From this observation we see that we must evaluate the prime implicants for the functions $f_{1,2}(x_1, \ldots, x_r)$, $f_{1,3}(x_1, \ldots, x_r)$, $f_{2,3}(x_1, \ldots, x_r)$, and $f_{1,2,3}(x_1, \ldots, x_r)$ as well as for the functions $f_1(x_1, \ldots, x_r)$, $f_2(x_1, \ldots, x_r)$, and $f_3(x_1, \ldots, x_r)$. Once we have obtained these prime implicants, using the methods described in Chapter 6, we form a multiple-output table of choice that has the general organization illustrated in Table 7-7.

The columns of this table are partitioned into three groups corresponding to the three functions. Within each group there is a column headed by each of the minterms associated with the given function. The rows of the table correspond to the prime implicants of the seven functions f_1 through $f_{1,2,3}$. The rows are also grouped so that all the prime implicants associated with a given function are in the same group.

A large X is placed in the areas of the table where the prime implicants of a given group cannot be associated with the minterms of a given function. For each prime implicant in the remainder of the table, a check mark is placed in the columns of the minterms accounted for by that prime implicant. Once we complete the table of choice, we proceed in the same manner as for the single output case, except that we disregard that portion of the table that has been X-ed out.

The multiple table of choice can often be simplified if we make the following observation.

1. If p_a is a prime implicant of $f_{i,j}$, then p_a *may* also be a prime implicant of f_i and

f_j. Should this be true then p_a need not be included in the f_i and f_j rows of the multiple table of choice.

2. If p_a is a prime implicant of $f_{i,j,k}$, then p_a *may* also be a prime implicant of f_i, f_j, f_k, $f_{i,j}$, $f_{i,k}$, and $f_{j,k}$. Should this be the case p_a need be included only in the $f_{i,j,k}$ rows of the multiple table of choice.

The reasoning behind these two observations should be clear if the definition of $f_{i,j}$ and $f_{i,j,k}$ is examined. For example, assume that two minterms, m_a and m_b, in $f_{i,j}$ can be combined to form a prime implicant p_a of $f_{i,j}$. These two minterms are also included in f_i and f_j and can also be combined. The resulting product term p_a will be a prime implicant of f_i if there is no other pair of minterms of f_i that are not in $f_{i,j}$ and that can be combined with p_a to form a product term $\hat{p}_a$, which is a reduction of p_a. To illustrate this case assume that

$$f_1 = x_1 x_2 \bar{x}_3 \lor x_1 \bar{x}_2 x_3 \lor x_1 \bar{x}_2 x_3 \lor x_1 x_2 x_3$$
$$f_2 = x_1 x_2 \bar{x}_3 \lor x_1 \bar{x}_2 \bar{x}_3 \lor \bar{x}_1 x_2 x_3$$

then

$$f_{1,2} = x_1 x_2 \bar{x}_3 \lor x_1 \bar{x}_2 \bar{x}_3$$

Thus we see that

$$p_a = x_1 \bar{x}_3$$

is a prime implicant of $f_{1,2}$. Examining f_1 we see that p_a is not a prime implicant of f_1 since

$$\hat{p}_a = x_1 = p_a \lor x_1 x_3$$

However, the prime implicants of f_2 are

$$p_a = x_1 \bar{x}_3 \qquad p_b = \bar{x}_1 x_2 x_3$$

Thus in our multiple table of choice we would have $\hat{p}_a$ as the only prime implicant entry for f_1, p_b as the only prime implicant entry for f_2, and p_a as the only prime implicant entry for $f_{1,2}$.

The following example illustrates our method of approach. Assume that we wish to realize a three-output logic network that is represented by the truth table given by Table 7-8.

The corresponding functions are

$$y_1 = f_1(x_1, x_2, x_3, x_4) = m_{1,3} \lor m_{1,5} \lor m_{1,7} \lor m_{1,13} \lor m_{1,14} \lor m_{1,15}$$
$$y_2 = f_2(x_1, x_2, x_3, x_4) = m_{2,5} \lor m_{2,7} \lor m_{2,10} \lor m_{2,13} \lor m_{2,14} \lor m_{2,15}$$
$$y_3 = f_3(x_1, x_2, x_3, x_4) = m_{3,0} \lor m_{3,4} \lor m_{3,10} \lor m_{3,14} \lor m_{3,15}$$

Using these functions we find that

$$f_{1,2}(x_1, x_2, x_3, x_4) = f_1(x_1, x_2, x_3, x_4) \land f_2(x_1, x_2, x_3, x_4)$$
$$= m_5 \lor m_7 \lor m_{13} \lor m_{14} \lor m_{15}$$

Table 7-8 Truth Table for Three-output Logic Network

Minterm	x_1	x_2	x_3	x_4	y_1	y_2	y_3
m_0	0	0	0	0	0	0	1
m_1	0	0	0	1	0	0	0
m_2	0	0	1	0	0	0	0
m_3	0	0	1	1	1	0	0
m_4	0	1	0	0	0	0	1
m_5	0	1	0	1	1	1	0
m_6	0	1	1	0	0	0	0
m_7	0	1	1	1	1	1	0
m_8	1	0	0	0	0	0	0
m_9	1	0	0	1	0	0	0
m_{10}	1	0	1	0	0	1	1
m_{11}	1	0	1	1	0	0	0
m_{12}	1	1	0	0	0	0	0
m_{13}	1	1	0	1	1	1	0
m_{14}	1	1	1	0	1	1	1
m_{15}	1	1	1	1	1	1	1

$$f_{1,3}(x_1, x_2, x_3, x_4) = m_{14} \vee m_{15}$$
$$f_{2,3}(x_1, x_2, x_3, x_4) = m_{10} \vee m_{14} \vee m_{15}$$
$$f_{1,2,3}(x_1, x_2, x_3, x_4) = m_{14} \vee m_{15}$$

If we go through the standard reduction process we find that the prime implicants for these functions are

Function	Prime Implicant
f_1	0_11, 111_, _1_1
f_2	1_10, 111_, _1_1
f_3	0_00, 1_10, 111_
$f_{1,2}$	111_, _1_1
$f_{1,3}$	111_
$f_{2,3}$	111_, 1_10
$f_{1,2,3}$	111_

Examining this set of prime implicants we see that several of them can be eliminated. For example, 111_ is a prime implicant of $f_{1,2,3}$. Thus it is not necessary to include this term as a prime implicant of the other six functions. Similarly, since 1_10 is a prime implicant of $f_{2,3}$, we do not need to retain 1_10 as a prime implicant of f_2 or f_3. Continuing in this manner we obtain the following reduced set of prime implicants.

Function	Prime Implicant
f_1	0_11
f_2	none
f_3	0_00
$f_{1,2}$	$\_1\_1$
$f_{1,3}$	none
$f_{2,3}$	1_10
$f_{1,2,3}$	$111\_$

Using these results we obtain the multiple output table of choice given by Table 7-9. The rows corresponding to f_2 and $f_{1,3}$ are omitted.

Now that we have the table of choice we must select the prime implicants that can be used in forming a minimal representation for our functions. To do this we start off in the standard manner. First we locate all columns that have only one $\checkmark$ in them. The row that contains the $\checkmark$ thus corresponds to an essential prime implicant. If all of the columns cannot be covered by essential prime implicants, we are then free to choose, from the remaining prime implicants, enough additional prime implicants to complete our covering of the multiple table of choice. This is done in the manner described previously except that we try to select those prime implicants that can be used in forming the maximum number of functions.

Up to this point our selection process has concentrated on the whole multiple table of choice. Our final task is to select the prime implicants that are actually needed to realize each function. The final step then is to examine the columns associated with each function and select the minimal number of prime implicants needed to cover each function.

If we examine Table 7-9 we see that all the prime implicants are essential prime implicants. The logical expressions for f_1 and f_3 can be read directly from the table. However, if we examine the columns of the table associated with f_2, we see that the prime implicant $111\_$ is not needed to cover this function. Thus only the prime implicants $\_1\_1$ and 1_10 are needed to realize f_2. From this we find that the three functions can be represented by the following logical expressions.

Table 7-9 Multiple-output Table of Choice for Network

Prime Implicants	Minterms	$f_1(x_1, x_2, x_3, x_4)$ $m_3\ m_5\ m_7\ m_{13}\ m_{14}\ m_{15}$						$f_2(x_1, x_2, x_3, x_4)$ $m_5\ m_7\ m_{10}\ m_{13}\ m_{14}\ m_{15}$						$f_3(x_1, x_2, x_3, x_4)$ $m_0\ m_4\ m_{10}\ m_{14}\ m_{15}$			
f_1	0_11	$\checkmark$		$\checkmark$													
f_3	0_00													$\checkmark$	$\checkmark$		
$f_{1,2}$	$\_1\_1$	$\checkmark$	$\checkmark$	$\checkmark$		$\checkmark$		$\checkmark$	$\checkmark$		$\checkmark$		$\checkmark$				
$f_{2,3}$	$\_1\_10$									$\checkmark$		$\checkmark$		$\checkmark$	$\checkmark$		
$f_{1,2,3}$	$111\_$				$\checkmark$	$\checkmark$				$\checkmark$		$\checkmark$				$\checkmark$	$\checkmark$

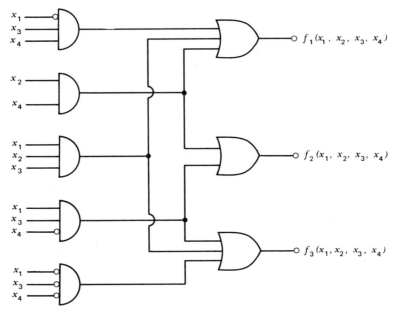

Figure 7-20 Reduced multiple output logic network.

$$f_1(x_1, x_2, x_3, x_4) = x_1 x_2 x_3 \lor x_2 x_4 \lor \overline{x}_1 x_3 x_4$$
$$f_2(x_1, x_2, x_3, x_4) = x_2 x_4 \lor x_1 x_3 \overline{x}_4$$
$$f_3(x_1, x_2, x_3, x_4) = x_1 x_2 x_3 \lor x_1 x_3 \overline{x}_4 \lor \overline{x}_1 \overline{x}_3 \overline{x}_4$$

The logic network corresponding to these expressions is given by Figure 7-20.

A PLA can also be used to realize a network of this type. Figure 7-21 shows the PLA realization. Observe that instead of realizing the minterms of the function, we realize the product terms corresponding to the prime implicants needed to represent the output functions.

This discussion has been of an introductory nature. There are several very detailed algorithms that can be used to design a minimum logic representation of multiple-output networks. References 1 and 2 give a much more extensive discussion of this problem.

EXERCISE

1. Find a minimal two-level logic network that will realize the following functions.

$$f_1(x_1, x_2, x_3, x_4) = m_0 \lor m_2 \lor m_5 \lor m_6 \lor m_{13} \lor m_{14}$$
$$f_2(x_1, x_2, x_3, x_4) = m_0 \lor m_5 \lor m_8 \lor m_{13} \lor m_{15}$$
$$f_3(x_1, x_2, x_3, x_4) = m_0 \lor m_3 \lor m_8 \lor m_{12}$$

Show how these functions are realized using a PLA.

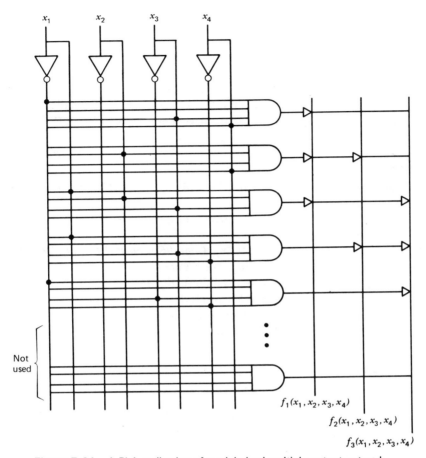

Figure 7-21   A PLA realization of a minimized multiple-output network.

6.   SUMMARY

One of the greatest changes that has occurred in logic design is the availability of MSI networks that can be used as a set of basic building blocks to design a complete digital system. The basic networks discussed in this chapter are only representative of the wide range of integrated circuits that are currently available. By using MSI circuits it is possible to concentrate upon the computational task that must be performed by the system being designed rather than upon the much more detailed problems of realizing the logic networks to do the computation.

The use of MSI circuits allows us to concentrate on the information flow taking place in a system rather than on the gate level structure of the logic circuits or the coding used to represent each signal. As we begin to design larger and larger digital systems, this ability to concentrate on the information flow associated with the signals being processed by the system will be a powerful design tool. After we complete a system level design we can then consider the design of any special logic circuits that may be needed to complete the realization of the system.

Reference Notation

An idea of the range of MSI logic circuitry that is currently available for use in the design of digital systems can be obtained by consulting the data books produced by the semiconductor manufacturers. References 4 and 5 are typical of these books. Additional insight into the methods used to decompose complex digital systems into smaller operational units can be found in References 2 and 3. A detailed discussion of using MSI logic packages as part of the design process is found in Reference 1.

REFERENCES

1. Fletcher, W. I. (1980), *An Engineering Approach to Digital Design.* McGraw-Hill, New York.
2. Hellerman, H. (1973), *Digital System Principles,* (second edition). Mc-Graw-Hill, New York.
3. Hill, F. J., and Peterson, G. R. (1978), *Digital Systems: Hardware Organization and Design* (second edition). Wiley, New York.
4. Advanced Micro Devices (current edition), *Bipolar Microprocessor Logic and Interface Data Book.* Advanced Micro Devices, Inc., Sunnyvale, Calif.
5. Texas Instruments (current edition), *The TTL Data Book for Design Engineers.* Texas Instruments, Inc., Dallas, Tex.

HOME PROBLEMS

1. Assume that *A, B,* and *C* are 8-bit signals. Design a system that will compute

$$Z := \text{MAX}(A, B, C)$$

   Use as many MSI networks as you need.

2. A logic network of the form shown in Figure P7-1 is to be designed, which allows the bidirectional flow of a signal.

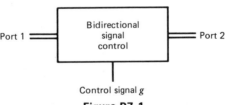

Figure P7-1

$g = 1$ Information flows from Port 1 to Port 2
$g = 0$ Information flows from Port 2 to Port 1

Show how three-state logic elements can be used to realize such a network.

3. The discussion of multiple output logic networks in Section 5 assumed that all output logic expressions were completely specified. Extend the analysis techniques presented in that section to treat the situation where one or more of the logic expressions are incompletely specified.

4. The control logic network shown in Figure P7-2 is described by the following set of requirements.

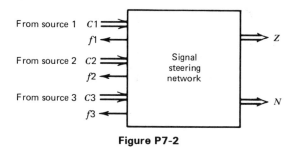

Figure P7-2

(a) The signals Ci are n-bit signals. $Ci := [0]$ indicates that no signal is being transmitted from source i.

(b) $fi := 1$ indicates that a signal is being received from one or both of the other two sources. $fi := 0$ otherwise.

(c) $Z := Ci$ if fi is zero and a signal is being received from source i.
$Z := [0]$ if no signals are being received from any of the sources or if two or more sources are trying to transmit at the same time.

(d) $N := [i]$ if $Z := Ci$. Otherwise $N := [0]$
Design this network.

5. Show how an ALU can be used to compute
(a) $Z := 2*A$
(b) $Z := |A|$
(c) $Z := -A$

6. Let A be a 7-bit ASCII encoded signal. It is desired to design a logic network that will give an output

$Z := [1]$ if A represents a decimal digit between '0' and '9'.
$Z := [2]$ if A represents an uppercase letter 'A' through 'Z'.
$Z := [3]$ if A represents a lowercase letter 'a' through 'z'.
$Z := [4]$ if A is a mathematical symbol '+', '$-$', '*', '/'.

(a) Design this network using MSI logic elements.
(b) Design this network using a PLA. How much can you minimize this network?

7. Let A and B be two u-bit vectors that represent 2's complement encoded numerical information. Show how a general comparator network can be designed that will be able to compare both positive and negative numbers.

8

FLIP-FLOPS, REGISTERS, AND BASIC INFORMATION TRANSFERS

1. INTRODUCTION

Up to this point we have been concentrating on the operation and design of combinational logic networks. These networks are important, since they are used to carry out many of the basic information-processing tasks in a digital system. They are, however, memoryless elements, since their current output depends only on their current input.

There are many situations where we must be able to store information and then use this stored information to influence the future behavior of a given information-processing task. If a system is to possess memory we must have a system element to supply this capability. In digital systems, registers serve this purpose.

The idea of a register was introduced in Chapter 2. In that discussion we indicated that a register was made up of r cells, and that each cell stored one bit of information. We are now ready to start investigating the characteristics of these cells and how they are used to form registers. First, we introduce the basic concept of a flip-flop and show how it can store a single bit of information. Next we consider the common types of flip-flops found in digital systems and how they are used to form different types of registers. The final portion of this chapter is devoted to a discussion of some of the basic information transfers that can be implemented by using registers.

No attempt is made to present a detailed description of the electronic realization of the various flip-flops. Our main concern is with the external properties of these components and how they are used in the design of digital networks and systems.

2. FLIP-FLOPS

A wide variety of devices can be used as cells to store digital information. The only requirement such a device must satisfy is that it have two easily distinguished internal conditions. Each such condition is called a *state of the cell*.

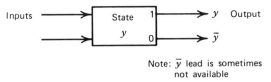

Note: $\bar{y}$ lead is sometimes
not available

Figure 8-1 Basic model of a cell.

The state of a cell is indicated by a *state variable y*, which can take on the value of either 0 or 1. When $y = 0$ we say that the cell is in the zero-state, and when $y = 1$ we say the cell is in the one-state.

To change the state of the cell, we must have some type of input signal. The form of the input signal and the way that it causes the state of the cell to change serves to characterize the cell.

A cell has the general representation shown in Figure 8-1. Two output leads are usually available, one corresponding to the value of the state variable y and the other corresponding to $\bar{y}$. Having both y and $\bar{y}$ available is a very useful feature, particularly when the information is used as the input to a combinational logic network that may require both y and $\bar{y}$ as variables. The cell remains in a fixed state until an activation condition appears on the input that causes the cell to change state. After the change the output remains at a constant value until the next change occurs.

Cells can be realized in a number of different ways. One important group of devices that can be used are called flip-flops. In this section we examine the basic structure of flip-flops and some of the forms that they can take.

Set-Reset (*S-R*) Flip-Flops

All the logic networks that we have considered so far had the property that the signals were propagated from the input terminals to the output terminals without any feedback paths. For this class of networks the inherent delays in the logic elements were not of particular importance in considering the logical behavior of the network. However, let us consider the simple logic network shown in Figure 8-2a where the inherent delay, Δt, of each NOR logic element is indicated. Examining this circuit we see that there exists a feedback path from the output of each NOR element to the input to the other element. Because of these feedback paths the current state of the network depends on its past history.

Let us assume that the network is in an initial steady state condition of $R = 0, S = 0, y = 0$, and $\bar{y} = 1$. At time t_1 assume that a 1 is applied to the S input and the R input remains 0. When this input occurs the output of NOR element 2 goes to 0 and after Δt seconds $\bar{y}$ goes to 0. This in turn drives the output of NOR element 1 to 1 and after another Δt seconds y goes to 1. Now if S goes to 0 and if R remains 0, the complete network will hold the condition $y = 1, \bar{y} = 0$. When this happens we say that the network is in the 1 state.

Next consider what happens when an input condition of $S = 0, R = 1$ occurs while this flip-flop is in the 1 state. When this happens the output of logic element 1 becomes 0 and the output of logic element 2 becomes 1. Thus the state variable has a value of $y = 0$ and we say that the flip-flop is in the 0 state.

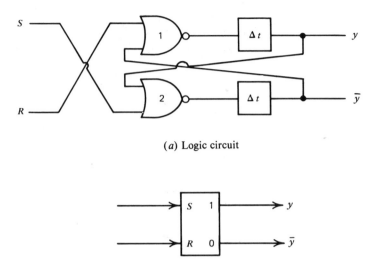

(a) Logic circuit

(b) Symbolic representation

Figure 8-2   Basic S-R flip-flop.

A complete timing diagram illustrating the dynamic behavior of this circuit is shown in Figure 8-3. Note that after the change of state occurs the inputs can both be set to 0 and the outputs hold at a constant value. The only requirement is that the inputs remain applied for a time greater than $2\Delta t$ seconds.

This simple circuit is called a *set-reset flip-flop*, or *S-R* flip-flop for short,* since a 1 on the S input *sets* the circuit to the 1 state while a 1 applied to the R input *resets* the circuit to the 0 state. It should be noted that the input condition $S = 1$, $R = 1$ is an indeterminate condition and should never be allowed to occur. The reason for this restriction can be understood if we examine Figure 8-2. If $S = R = 1$, we see that

$$y = \bar{y} = 0$$

which is inconsistent with our convention that y represents the state of the flip-flop.

The behavior of an S-R flip-flop can be described by a transition table of the form given by Table 8-1 or by the logical expression

$$y(t + \tau) = S(t) \lor y(t)\bar{R}(t)$$

where $y(t + \tau)$ is the state of the flip-flop τ seconds after the input is applied at time t and $y(t)$ is the initial state of the flip-flop. It is also assumed that $\tau > 2\Delta t$.

---

*Flip-flops of this type are also referred to as R-S flip-flops and sometimes as C-S (clear-set) flip-flops.

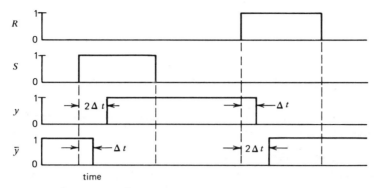

Figure 8-3 Timing diagram for simple *S-R* flip-flop.

The *S-R* Flip-Flop as a Hardware Flag

There are many design situations where we must monitor a given operation and detect whether a given condition has occurred. When that condition is first detected we announce its occurrence by *"setting a flag."* The flag remains set until some action is taken to reset the flag.

The easiest way to create a flag is to use a flip-flop called a *flag flip-flop.* If the flip-flop is in the 1-state, we say that the *flag is set,* while if it is in the 0-state we say that the *flag is cleared.* It is up to the designer to create the necessary signals to set and reset the flag as needed by a given application. The following example illustrates one possible application of a flag.

Assume that you are working for a company that has a laboratory that is processing a dangerous chemical. This is a two-stage process in which containers of the chemical must be passed from the first stage to the second stage through a protective series of doors. The general organization of this protective arrangement is shown in

Table 8-1 Transition Table for *S-R* Flip-Flop

	Input at Time t		Current State	Next State
	$S(t)$	$R(t)$	$y(t)$	$y(t + \tau)$
	0	0	0	0
	0	0	1	1
	0	1	0	0
	0	1	1	0
	1	0	0	1
	1	0	1	1
This input condition must never be allowed to occur	1	1	0	indeterminate
	1	1	1	indeterminate

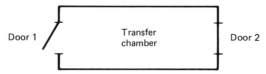

Figure 8-4   Organization of chemical transfer chamber.

Figure 8-4. To insure that the two stages are completely isolated, the following set of rules govern the transfer process.

1. Both doors cannot be open at the same time.
2. If an attempt is made to open both doors, the transfer process must stop. When this occurs the process is said to be locked.
3. If the transfer process is stopped, it can be restarted only by giving a special restart command that unlocks the process. This command will restart operations only if both doors are closed.

To make sure that this set of conditions is satisfied, a special interlock system is being designed to control when a transfer can take place. As part of the design a need for an interlock flag has been identified. This flag must meet the following requirements.

Design Requirements

An interlock flag is to be designed that is to have a value of 1 when a transfer can take place and a value of 0 when no transfer can occur.

A digital network of the form shown in Figure 8-5a is used to realize the flag. Two signals, d_1 and d_2, indicate whether a request has been made to open door 1 or door 2. A third signal u is the unlock signal, which unlocks the process by setting the state of the flag flip-flop to 1. The design of the digital network is completed if we can define the combinational logic network that controls the flag flip-flop. To proceed with this design we encode the input information as

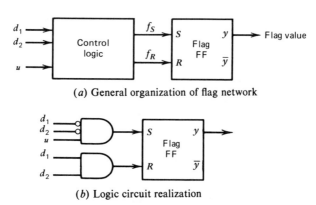

(a) General organization of flag network

(b) Logic circuit realization

Figure 8-5   Realization of interlock flag.

Table 8-2 Truth Table for Flag Flip-Flop Control

d_1	d_2	u	f_S	f_R	
0	0	0	0	0	
0	0	1	1	0	} Unlock condition.
0	1	0	0	0	
0	1	1	0	0	
1	0	0	0	0	
1	0	1	0	0	
1	1	0	0	1	} Danger condition.
1	1	1	0	1	Clear flag to lock system.

$$d_i \begin{cases} := 1 & \text{door } i \text{ is open} \\ := 0 & \text{door } i \text{ is closed} \end{cases} \qquad u \begin{cases} := 1 & \text{request to set flag to 1} \\ := 0 & \text{no request to set flag to 1} \end{cases}$$

Using this encoding we create the truth table of Table 8-2 to describe the operation of the input logic network. As long as the flag is set, operations will continue in the normal manner. If, for any reason, both doors are open at the same time the flag is cleared to indicate that all operations must stop. The flag can be set only if both doors are closed and an unlock command is issued.

From this table we derive the following logic expressions for the S and R inputs to the flip-flop.

$$f_S := \bar{d}_1 \bar{d}_2 u \qquad f_R := d_1 d_2$$

The logic diagram for the complete network is given in Figure 8-5b.

If we examine this network closely, we see that a change in the input that causes a change in f_S and/or f_R will immediately be acted on by the flip-flop. In this type of application the input signals d_i or u are often generated by mechanical switches. One problem with mechanical switches is that the signal produced will fluctuate before the final desired value is reached. These fluctuations may be large enough to cause the flip-flop to make an unwanted transition. We now investigate how these unwanted changes can be eliminated.

Switch Debouncing Using an *S-R* Flip-Flop

Digital data can be entered into a system by a mechanical switch as shown in Figure 8-6a. When the switch is open the output voltage is 0. When the switch is closed the output voltage becomes V_H. However, when the switch is first closed the contacts of the mechanical switch vibrate or *bounce* for a short time before staying closed. As shown in Figure 8-6b, this bounce causes undesirable transients in the output voltage. In a logic circuit this bounce may lead to unwanted circuit behavior.

A mechanical switch can be *debounced* using the circuit shown in Figure 8-6c. The *S-R* flip-flop responds almost instantly to the first positive swing of an input signal on the S line or the R line. Thus when the switch is pushed to the 1 or "ON"

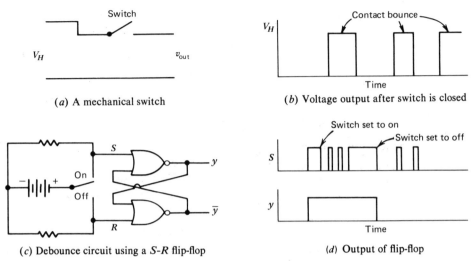

(a) A mechanical switch

(b) Voltage output after switch is closed

(c) Debounce circuit using a S-R flip-flop

(d) Output of flip-flop

Figure 8-6 The use of a flip-flop to debounce a switch.

position, the output of the flip-flop is driven to the 1 state on the first part of the bounce. It stays in the 1 state until the switch is pushed to the "OFF" position. At that point a signal is placed on the R lead and the flip-flop is driven to its 0 state. The relationship between the input and output of the flip-flop is shown in Figure 8-6d.

Switch debouncing is useful when we must condition the signals applied to the system from external devices. However, there are many situations where the time delay in the different logic networks that make up a system means that the control signals that are applied to the flip-flop do not instantaneously reach their required values. To prevent the flip-flop from making a premature transition we introduce the idea of a system clock signal.

Clocked S-R Flip-Flops

To make sure that the flip-flop is not activated at the wrong point, an AND gate can be introduced in the S and R lines as shown in Figure 8-7a. After sufficient time has been allowed for f_S and f_R to reach a steady-state value, a pulse, called a *clock pulse* or *transfer pulse*, can be applied to the other input of the AND gate and the S-R flip-flop is activated. Such a circuit is called a clocked S-R flip-flop. The pulse must last for a sufficient time to allow the flip-flop to assume its new state.

Many integrated circuit flip-flops contain a clock pulse input as part of their basic design. Therefore, we will assume, when necessary, that all flip-flops are internally connected for clocked operation and have an input terminal for a clock pulse. Figure 8-7b shows the symbol we use to indicate a clocked S-R flip-flop.

When a flip-flop is initially placed into service, it is often necessary to make certain that it is in a known initial state. Two inputs are provided to do this as shown in

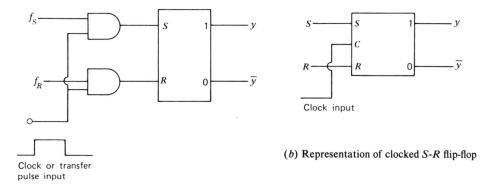

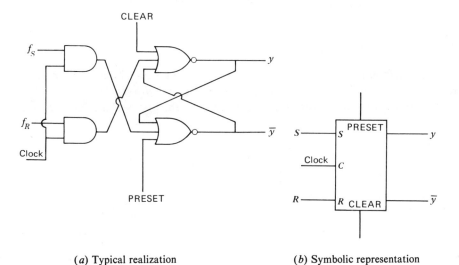

(b) Representation of clocked S-R flip-flop

(a) Clocked input S-R flip-flop

Figure 8-7 S-R Flip-flop.

Figure 8-8a. A 1 on the PRESET input places the flip-flop in the 1-state while a 1 on the CLEAR input places it in the 0-state. The symbolic representation of this flip-flop is shown in Figure 8-8b. These particular inputs are not usually included in a logic diagram unless needed.

S-R flip-flops can be realized in a number of different forms. The actual construction of flip-flops is not of importance to our discussion. However, it is important for us to know the relationship between the inputs and outputs of the flip-flop and the shape of the clock pulse.

For the very simple S-R flip-flop presented in Figure 8-7 the output starts to change Δt seconds after the clock pulse is applied and a new steady state output

(a) Typical realization   (b) Symbolic representation

Figure 8-8   An S-R clocked flip-flop with PRESET and CLEAR.

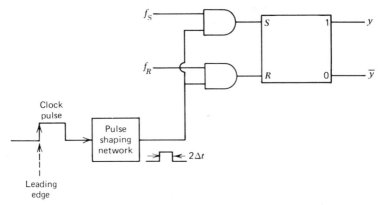

Figure 8-9   A clocked *S-R* flip-flop with a pulse shaping network.

appears in $2\Delta t$ seconds. If the inputs change while the clock pulse is on, the final state of the flip-flop may not be the one that is expected. Several methods have been developed to overcome this problem.

Edge Triggered Flip-Flops

One way to avoid this problem is to make sure that the clock pulse has a width of $2\Delta t$ seconds and that the input remains constant for this period. Since the width of the actual clock pulses in a network may be greater than $2\Delta t$, a pulse shaping circuit can be used in the clock line as shown in Figure 8-9.

The pulse shaping network detects the $0 \rightarrow 1$ transition of the leading edge of the clock pulse. This transition causes the pulse shaping network to generate an output pulse of width $2\Delta t$. Since it is assumed that the signals f_S and f_R remain constant in this interval, the output goes to the desired state no matter how long the clock pulse remains on.

Master-Slave Flip-Flop

A second method to overcome the problem of unwanted transitions is shown in Figure 8-10. This circuit, which is called a *master-slave SR flip-flop*, is basically two S-R flip-flops in series. When the clock pulse goes to 1, the first *S-R* flip-flop is activated

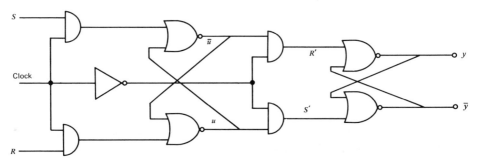

Figure 8-10   Master-slave *S-R* flip-flop.

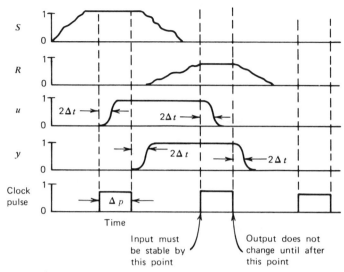

Figure 8-11 Timing diagram for master-slave flip-flop.

by the input, but the inverter in the clock lead cuts the second S-R flip-flop off from the first. Thus the output y is not affected by the input. The clock pulse then goes to 0 and cuts off the input to the first flip-flop. However, the second stage is now connected to the output of the first stage and the intermediate information stored in the first flip-flop causes the second flip-flop to change to the proper state. Thus the output y does not change until after the clock pulse has returned to zero. The timing diagram shown in Figure 8-11 illustrates the operation of this circuit.

We do not use any special symbol to indicate that a given S-R flip-flop is a master-slave flip-flop. However, when we actually try to design a circuit using commercially available flip-flops, we must check the manufacturer's specifications to determine the switching characteristics of the flip-flop before we start the overall circuit design. All of the flip-flops that we use in the following chapters are assumed to be of the master-slave type unless we specifically state otherwise.

We now investigate some of the other types of flip-flops that can be found in digital networks. In each case we could develop a complete logic diagram to illustrate how they operate. However, this would add little to our discussion so we present only the general switching characteristics of each of the following flip-flops and show how they can be constructed from S-R flip-flops. Here again, each of these flip-flops is available in integrated circuit form and the actual circuit that is used to construct the flip-flop will be considerably different from the one we present for discussion purposes.

The D Flip-Flop

One way of making sure that the indeterminate inputs to an S-R flip-flop never occur is to provide only one input to the flip-flop. The D flip-flop, illustrated in Figure 8-12, is a flip-flop of this type. The input at the time that the clock pulse occurs completely determines the output until the next clock pulse. Thus if $D = 1$, the next

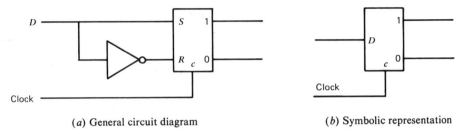

(*a*) General circuit diagram   (*b*) Symbolic representation

Figure 8-12   The *D* flip-flop.

state of the flip-flop will become $y = 1$ when the clock pulse appears regardless of
the value of y before the clock pulse. The transition table for this flip-flop is given in
Table 8-3. Examining this table we see that the following logical expression can be
used to describe the input-output relationships of this flip-flop

$$y(t + \tau) = D(t)$$

where τ is greater than the delay needed for the flip-flop to change its state. This
type of flip-flop is useful when transferring data from one source to another. It is
referred to as a delay flip-flop since it has the property of delaying the input information one clock period.

The *J-K* Flip-Flop

The *J-K* flip-flop has become an extremely popular flip-flop circuit in recent years
because integrated circuit technology has brought their price into the same range as
any of the other types of flip-flop. The operation of the *J-K* flip-flop is exactly the
same as the *S-R* flip-flop except when both inputs are 1. When this occurs the state
of the flip-flop changes when the clock pulse occurs. This type of operation can be
achieved by modifying the *S-R* flip-flop as shown in Figure 8-13. Examining this
circuit we see that the *J* input is equivalent to the *S* input and the *K* input is equivalent to the *R* input of an *S-R* flip-flop. The feedback paths give us the extra flexibility because they ensure that the inputs to the *S-R* flip-flop will never both be 1 at
the same time.

The transition table for this flip-flop is given in Table 8-4. Examining this table

Table 8-3   Transition Table for *D* Flip-Flop

Input $D(t)$	Current State $y(t)$	Next State $y(t + \tau)$
0	0	0
0	1	0
1	0	1
1	1	1

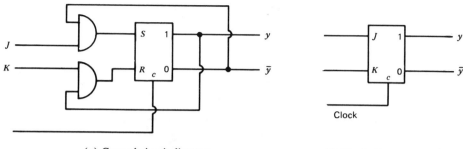

(a) General circuit diagram   (b) Symbolic representation

Figure 8-13 The *J-K* flip-flop.

Table 8-4 Transition Table for *J-K* Flip-Flop

Input		Current State	Next State
J	**K**	**y(t)**	**y(t + τ)**
0	0	0	0
0	0	1	1
0	1	0	0
0	1	1	0
1	0	0	1
1	0	1	1
1	1	0	1
1	1	1	0

we see that the following logical expression describes the input-output relationship of this flip-flop

$$y(t + \tau) = \bar{y}(t)J(t) \lor y(t)\bar{K}(t)$$

where τ is greater than the delay needed for the flip-flop to change its state.

Toggle or *T* Flip-Flop

The *toggle* or *T flip-flop* is another type of flip-flop that is in common use particularly for counting circuits. One way to form a *T* flip-flop is to use a *J-K* flip-flop that is connected as shown in Figure 8-14. As long as the *T* input has a 0 value the state of

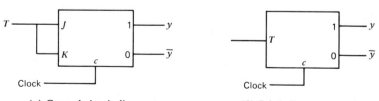

(a) General circuit diagram   (b) Symbolic representation

Figure 8-14 The *T* flip-flop.

Table 8-5   Truth Table for T Flip-Flop

Input T	Current State $y(t)$	Next State $y(t + \tau)$
0	0	0
0	1	1
1	0	1
1	1	0

the flip-flop does not change. However, when T becomes 1 the state of the flip-flop is negated each time a clock pulse appears. The transition table for this flip-flop, which is included in Table 8-5, shows that the input-output relationship for a T flip-flop is

$$y(t + \tau) = \overline{T}(t)y(t) \vee T(t)\overline{y}(t)$$

The Clock Signal

The clock pulse applied to the clock input of a flip-flop can be derived in a number of different ways. In the simplest case we have a special source of clock pulses called a *clock*. The clock generates a sequence of clock pulses that are normally equally spaced and of equal duration as indicated in Figure 8-15.

The pulse width T_p is selected as small as possible to be consistent with the operating characteristics of the flip-flop and the *period* T is selected according to the speed at which the network must operate. The only restriction is that $T - T_p$ must be large enough to allow the flip-flop to shift to its new state before the next clock pulse occurs. For modern digital systems, T can vary anywhere from seconds down to the nanosecond range (1 nanosecond $= 10^{-9}$ seconds).

The operation of any logic network constructed from flip-flops can be controlled by proper use of the clock pulse line. Whenever we wish to activate an information transfer, we allow the clock pulse to pass through to the network. Otherwise we prevent it from reaching the network. A simple way to accomplish this is shown in Figure 8-16. When the control signal is on (has a value of 1), the clock pulses pass through the AND gate and are available to activate the operation of the network. When the control signal is off (has a value of 0), the clock pulses are blocked and thus the network does not receive any activation signal.

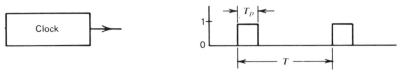

Figure 8-15   A clock pulse sequence.

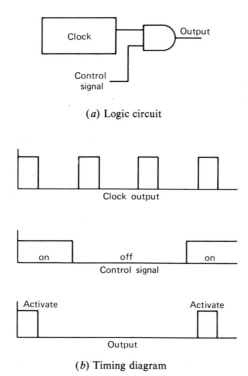

(a) Logic circuit

(b) Timing diagram

Figure 8-16   Control of clock pulses.

Transfer Pulse

In many design situations the pulse applied to the clock line is generated by another portion of the system under design. Since these pulses may not have a regular period, we usually refer to them as *transfer pulses* rather than clock pulses. When we use this convention it is assumed that a transfer pulse will be generated when it is needed to carry out the task of transferring information into the flip-flop. The terminology "clock pulse" and "transfer pulse" is often used interchangeably in the digital system design area.

Special Use of Clock Input

Signal levels, as well as pulses, can be applied to the clock input of some but not all flip-flops. In the simple flip-flops a signal level of 1 allows any input control signals to activate the flip-flop while a signal level of 0 deactivates the flip-flop. A much more interesting situation occurs when we are dealing with a master-slave flip-flop.

In this situation the output of the flip-flop will not change state until the signal at the clock input undergoes a transition from 1 to 0. This situation is indicated in Figure 8-17 for a *J-K* flip-flop in which the *J* and *K* inputs are both 1.

Inputs are both 1

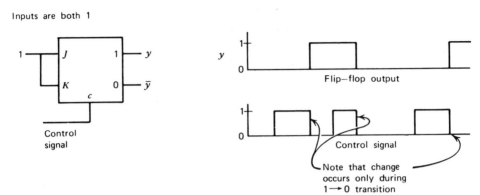

Figure 8-17   Illustration of level control of a master-slave flip-flop.

There are a number of situations where this type of operation is useful. However, for the purpose of this book we restrict our discussions to digital networks, which are constructed from clocked flip-flops. Some of the other classes of networks are discussed in the references listed at the end of this chapter.

Modes of Operation

Originally flip-flops were constructed from discrete components and were made as simple as possible to minimize their cost. With the development of integrated circuits, it is now possible for a manufacturer to produce very complex logic circuits that are not any more expensive than single transistors. Consequently, there are a large number of variations possible in the type of flip-flop integrated circuits that one can use in the design of a system.

In the following discussion we present some of the general applications of flip-flops to various information processing tasks. Most of the circuits that we discuss are *clocked* or *synchronous sequential networks*. In this class of networks the contents of the flip-flops that make up the network do not change until a transfer or clock pulse occurs. Thus we find it easier to analyze and understand the behavior of these networks.

There are many applications where the input information to a network appears in the form of pulses rather than as voltage levels. In this situation the flip-flops in the network must be activated only when the pulses carrying the input information are present. Digital networks of this type are referred to as *pulse-mode circuits*. It is also possible to design circuits where the flip-flops do not have any clock inputs. Transitions take place as soon as the inputs to the flip-flop change to a value that requires the flip-flop to change states. Such circuits are called *level-mode sequential circuits*.

Both pulse-mode and level-mode circuits are somewhat harder to design because care must be exercised to ensure that the sequence of operations that control these circuits occur in the proper order required for correct operation. The operation of level-mode and pulse-mode sequential circuits will not be considered in this book since their design is more complex than synchronous networks.

EXERCISES

1. Let X be a 3-bit binary number. Design the input logic needed to set a clocked S-R flip-flop to the 1 state if X has an odd number of 1's and to the 0 state otherwise. Repeat this problem for clocked D and J-K flip-flops.

2. Describe the operation of the following logic circuits.

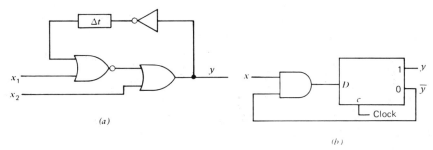

(a)

(b)

Figure 8-E 2.2

3. REGISTERS AND THE INFORMATION TRANSFER OPERATION

Flip-flops provide us with a way to store information during a portion of an information processing task. If we group a number of flip-flops together, we form a register. In this section we first discuss the basic operation of registers and the conventions used to describe their operation. We then consider how registers are constructed from different types of flip-flops.

Register Representation

At the register level of representation we assume that all registers are made up of n cells and that each cell is a clocked flip-flop of an appropriate form. Figure 8-18 shows the basic form of a register. When a signal is to be loaded directly into a register, it is assumed that the signal is also an n-bit vector. There is a one-to-one correspondence between the bits that form the signal vector and the flip-flops that make up the register. The information contained in the signal does not influence the contents of the register until a transfer pulse, τ, is applied. Upon application of the

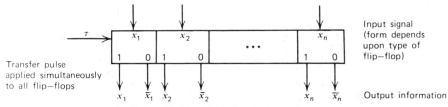

Figure 8-18 Basic form of a register.

transfer pulse, the information contained in the signal is loaded into the register. The following conventions formalize the register level transfer operation.

Transfers can be of two types as shown in Figure 8-19. In Figure 8-19a the information to be transferred into the register is contained in a signal A and it is transferred when the transfer pulse τ is applied. In Figure 8-19b, the information to be transferred is already stored in a register A and this information is transferred to the register X when the transfer pulse τ is applied. The contents of the register A is not changed when this transfer takes place unless a transfer pulse is also applied to that register at the same time. We assume that the registers are constructed from master-slave flip-flops. Thus the output of the register does not take on its new value until the transfer pulse has returned to zero.

Let the contents of the register X correspond to the n-tuple $[x_1, \ldots, x_n]$. We use X to represent both the contents of the register and the register itself. If we refer to "the register X," we mean the register that we have named X; if we say "the contents of X," we mean the particular value assigned to the x_is of the n-tuple $[x_1, \ldots, x_n]$; while if we speak of the "value of X," we are talking about the information stored in the register without considering how it is encoded.

State of a Register

Registers are used to store a wide variety of information. An n-bit register can store 2^n different values. Each of the distinct n-tuples that can be stored in a register corresponds to a distinct *state of the register*. For example, if $n = 3$ then the eight distinct states of the register X are

States of Register X
$$X := [x_1, x_2, x_3]$$

$[0, 0, 0]$	$[0, 1, 1]$	$[1, 1, 0]$
$[0, 0, 1]$	$[1, 0, 0]$	$[1, 1, 1]$
$[0, 1, 0]$	$[1, 0, 1]$	

In this example we have used the 3-tuple representation for each of the possible states of X. Each register state can be associated with a unique item of information. It is up to the system designer to define the meaning of each state. A designer may choose, for example, to state that the register is storing positive binary numbers. In that case the standard correspondence between each number and its binary representation is used. In this case we can set up the following correspondence between the states of X and the 3-tuple encoding the states.

Encoding of Positive Binary Numbers as States of Register X

State	Encoding	State	Encoding	State	Encoding
0	$[0, 0, 0]$	3	$[0, 1, 1]$	6	$[1, 1, 0]$
1	$[0, 0, 1]$	4	$[1, 0, 0]$	7	$[1, 1, 1]$
2	$[0, 1, 0]$	5	$[1, 0, 1]$		

Other information may be stored in X. For example, X may store numerical information in 2's complement form. In this case the distinct states can be indicated as

Encoding of 2's Complement Binary Numbers as States of Register X

State	Encoding	State	Encoding	State	Encoding
0	[0, 0, 0]	3	[0, 1, 1]	−2	[1, 1, 0]
1	[0, 0, 1]	n.d.	[1, 0, 0]	−1	[1, 1, 1]
2	[0, 1, 0]	−3	[1, 0, 1]	n.d.	not defined

There is no need to limit ourselves to numeric information. We can use an arbitrary symbolic representation for the distinct states. One typical representation might be

Symbolic Encoding of the States of Register X

State	Encoding	State	Encoding	State	Encoding
s_0	[0, 0, 0]	s_3	[0, 1, 1]	s_6	[1, 1, 0]
s_1	[0, 0, 1]	s_4	[1, 0, 0]	s_7	[1, 1, 1]
s_2	[0, 1, 0]	s_5	[1, 0, 1]		

During a given design the designer is free to select any encoding of register states that is appropriate for the problem being solved. In some cases the encoding is defined by the form of the information being represented. At other times the designer may select the encoding so that other parts of the design are easier to carry out.

The Assignment Operation

To indicate the transfer of information at transfer time τ we use the *assignment operation* notation:

$$\tau : X \leftarrow A$$

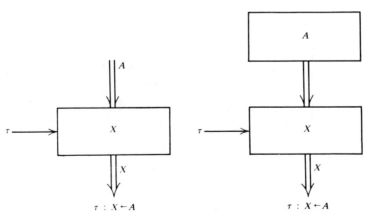

(*a*) Parallel information transfer from an external source

(*b*) Transfer between two registers

Figure 8-19 Register level representation of parallel information transfer.

This notation means that when the transfer pulse τ occurs, the value of the information contained in A is transferred into register X. It is assumed that the value of A is constant while the transfer is taking place.

While we are working at the register transfer level, there is no need to be concerned with the details of how the transfer is actually accomplished. At that level the representation shown in Figure 8-19 is sufficient to indicate the desired flow of information. However, if we are to fully understand the behavior of these transfers, we must examine the different ways that they are implemented using different types of flip-flops.

Realization of a Parallel Transfer

Suppose that we are given a signal A

$$[a_1, \ldots, a_n]$$

and we wish to transfer this information into a register X. The way in which this transfer is accomplished depends upon the type of flip-flop used to form the register. Figure 8-20a shows how the transfer is accomplished for S-R flip-flops. When the transfer pulse τ is applied, the contents of the register X is set to the value represented by the input signal A.

Information can be transferred between registers in a similar manner. Figure 8-20b illustrates how information can be transferred from a register A to a register X. When the transfer pulse τ appears, the information stored in A is transferred to register X. The contents of A is not changed unless a transfer pulse is also applied

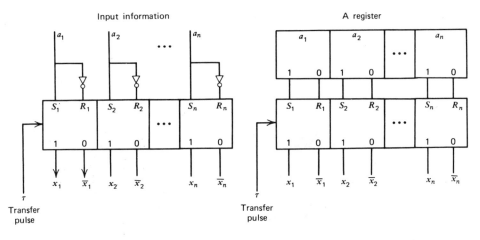

(a) Parallel information transfer from an external source

(b) Transfer between registers

Figure 8-20   Two methods of parallel information transfer.

to A. Similar transfer operations can be defined for registers constructed from D and J-K flip-flops.

Serial Transfer

The parallel transfer of information into an n-bit register requires that the n inputs to the flip-flops that make up the register be available to receive the information. If the information is to be transmitted over a long distance, such as from one office to another, it is not practical to transfer the n bits simultaneously. For situations such as this, information can be transmitted serially one bit at a time instead of using a parallel transfer.

The serial transfer of information can be accomplished by using a register constructed from S-R flip-flops and organized as shown in Figure 8-21. Assume that register X is to receive an n-bit signal A, which is transmitted one bit at a time. Whenever a 1 input is applied to the input lead of the register, the first flip-flop is set to the 1 state when the transfer signal τ is applied. If the input is 0, the first flip-flop is set to 0.

Next we note that the output of flip-flop i is connected to the input of flip-flop $i + 1$ for $i = 1, 2, \ldots, n - 1$. Thus, when the transfer signal occurs, the contents of flip-flop i is transferred to flip-flop $i + 1$. The contents of flip-flop n just before the transfer pulse is lost. If we let

$$X_i := [x_i]$$

represent the ith flip-flop in the register X, then the serial transfer operation is represented as

$$\tau : \quad X_1 \leftarrow a, \quad X_2 \leftarrow X_1, \cdots, X_n \leftarrow X_{n-1}$$

If we are to transfer an n-bit signal A into the register X, this transfer operation must be repeated n times. Each time the new value that is to be transferred must appear at the input to the register.

Figure 8-22 is a timing diagram that illustrates the serial transfer of the signal $A := [1, 1, 0]$ into the register X. Since we are using master-slave flip-flops, the state of each flip-flop does not change until the transfer pulse returns to zero. Also note that the input value must reach a steady value before the transfer pulse is applied.

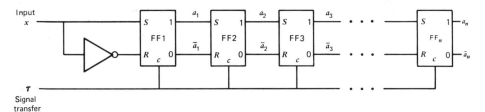

Figure 8-21   Serial transfer to a register A using S-R flip-flops.

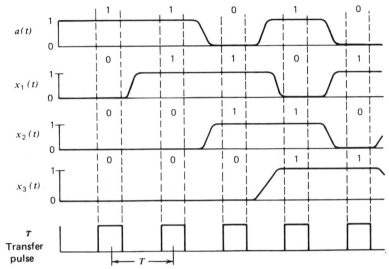

Figure 8-22 Typical time sequence for 3-bit shift register.

If the input is not correct when the transfer signal is given, an erroneous value will be loaded into the register.

Another way to look at the operation of a serial transfer is to consider the sequence of transfers necessary to accomplish the transfer. This form of representation is illustrated in Figure 8-23. In this case we do not consider the time characteristics of the signals involved and only concentrate upon the sequence of transfers necessary to accomplish the desired task.

The serial transfer illustrated in this discussion is accomplished by shifting infor-

Transfer Pulse τ_i	Input When Transfer Pulse Occurs	Contents of Register After It Has Responded To Transfer Pulse. Register Initially Contains All Zeros		
τ_1	1	1	0	0
τ_2	0	0	1	0
τ_3	0	0	0	1
τ_4	1	1	0	0
τ_5	1	1	1	0
τ_6	0	0	1	1

$\rightarrow$
Direction
of Shift

Figure 8-23 Illustration of a shift right serial transfer.

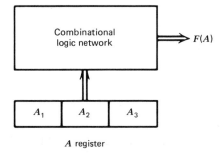

A register

Figure 8-24 Operating on the information in a register *A*.

mation into the register X from left to right. It is just as easy to construct a serial transfer operation that would shift information into the register from right to left. Both forms of serial transfer are found in digital systems.

Register Outputs

The output of a register is constant except during the period where an information transfer is taking place. Since we have assumed that registers are constructed from master-slave flip-flops, the output of each flip-flop remains constant during the time the transfer pulse occurs and changes values only during the time when the transfer pulse is zero. This behavior is demonstrated in Figure 8-22 where one typical timing relationship of a serial information transfer is shown.

Registers are used to store information. This information would be of little value if we could not use it in other parts of the system. We have already seen that we can transfer information from one register to another by using either a serial or parallel transfer. Another major use of the information contained in a register is to provide inputs to combinational logic networks as shown in Figure 8-24.

To illustrate this use of register information, assume that a combinational logic network is used to compute $F(A)$ from the information stored in register A. Table 8-6 is a truth table representation of this function. Using this information we can

Table 8-6 Description of Output Network

| Input Information | | | | Output Generated | | | |
Mnemonic	a_1	a_2	a_3	f_1	f_2	f_3	f_4
CLA	0	0	0	1	1	0	0
CLL	0	0	1	1	0	1	1
CMA	0	1	0	1	1	0	1
RAR	0	1	1	0	0	1	1
RAL	1	0	0	0	0	0	1
IAC	1	0	1	1	0	0	1
RR	1	1	0	0	0	1	0
DEC	1	1	1	0	1	1	1

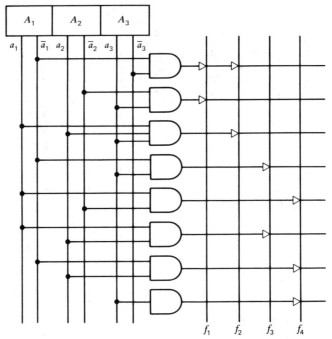

Figure 8-25 Realization of output network.

develop the combinational logic network shown in Figure 8-25 to realize this function.

The output equations describing the combinational logic network become

$$f_1 := \bar{a}_1 \bar{a}_3 \lor \bar{a}_2 a_3$$
$$f_2 := \bar{a}_1 \bar{a}_3 \lor a_1 a_2 a_3$$
$$f_3 := \bar{a}_1 a_3 \lor a_1 a_2$$
$$f_4 := a_1 \bar{a}_2 \lor \bar{a}_1 a_2 \lor a_3$$

Examining the network shown in Figure 8-25, we see that we do not need any inverters in the combinational logic network, since both a_i and $\bar{a}_i$ are available as outputs from the ith flip-flop. We also note that as long as the values of the state variables, a_i, remain constant, the output values are constant. Thus the output value in this case changes only when the state of the register is changing.

At the system level we often are not interested in the way that information is encoded. Thus symbolic names or *mnemonics* may be associated with the different states of the register. When we do this we can then think of the output function in terms of a mapping of the register's states. A possible set of mnemonics associated with the information in the A register is shown in Table 8-6. Using these mnemonics we can define the mapping as

$$F(\text{CMA}) := [1, 1, 0]$$

As we progress to more involved system designs, we will find that this approach allows us to concentrate upon the flow of information in a system without having to think about the encoding used to represent the information.

EXERCISES

1. Give the series of information transfer operations if the 1's complement of the contents of register X is to be serial transferred into the register A.

2. Assume that A and B are 4-bit registers designed from D flip-flops. Design a network that will carry out the following information transfer:

$$\tau: B \leftarrow ((T = [0]) \wedge \overline{A}) \vee ((T = [1]) \wedge (A))$$

4. BASIC REGISTER OPERATIONS AND EVENTS

In the last section we introduced the assignment operation as the basic operation used to store information in a register. This operation was represented as

$$\tau: X \leftarrow A$$

where both the signal A and the register X are n-tuples. There is, however, no reason to limit ourselves to simple transfers of this type. As discussed in Chapter 5, a signal can be generated in a large number of ways. Thus a much more general representation of the assignment operation has the form

$$\tau: X \leftarrow \langle \text{expression} \rangle$$

where $\langle$expression$\rangle$ represents any logical, arithmetic, or functional expression that produces a signal with the same number of bits as used to represent X.

For example, assume that we have the general digital network shown in Figure 8-26a, where we combine the information contained in register A with the information contained in the input signal B to generate a signal that is to be loaded into the X register when the transfer pulse τ occurs. Some typical assignment operations that can be realized using a network of this type are:

τ:	$X \leftarrow A + B$	Arithmetic expression
τ:	$X \leftarrow A \wedge B$	Logical expression
τ:	$X \leftarrow (A < B) \wedge A \vee (A > B) \wedge B$	Mixed-mode expression

More than one information transfer may occur when a transfer pulse is applied. The network shown in Figure 8-26b illustrates a situation in which three transfer operations are performed at the same time. These transfers are represented by the general *transfer expression*

$$\tau: \quad X \leftarrow F(A, B) \quad A \leftarrow G(A, B) \quad B \leftarrow \langle \text{input} \rangle$$

where $F(A, B)$ and $G(A, B)$ are functions defined by the combinational logic networks and $\langle$input$\rangle$ is an input signal generated outside the system. This type of trans-

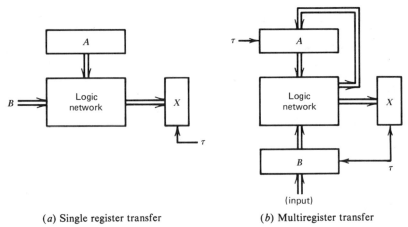

(*a*) Single register transfer   (*b*) Multiregister transfer

Figure 8-26   Representation of information transfers.

fer operation is possible since we assume that the output of the A and B registers do not change value until after the transfer operation has been completed and the transfer pulse removed. A typical transfer expression for the network of Figure 8-26*b* might be

$$\tau: \quad X \leftarrow A + B \qquad A \leftarrow (A > B) \wedge A \vee (A \leq B) \wedge B \qquad B \leftarrow Y$$

where it is assumed that Y is an external signal.

The following examples illustrate a number of typical transfer expressions. Throughout this discussion remember that the value of the expression found on the right-hand side of an assignment operator must have reached a steady state value before the transfer pulse τ is applied to transfer this value into the register. The actual networks used to realize a transfer expression depends upon the type of flip-flops used to form each register. In most of the examples discussed the detailed design of the logic circuits used to realize a transfer expression are not considered. However, when it is necessary to go to this level, we assume, for simplicity, that all registers are constructed from D flip-flops.

Events

As we will shortly see, specific information processing tasks may require a sequence of information transfer operations to complete a task. The transfer action that describes each transfer expression represents an *event,* and the time that the transfer is initiated is called the *event time* of the event. Our normal practice is to use the notation

$$\tau_i: \langle \text{transfer expression} \rangle$$

to denote the fact that the event described by the transfer expression $\langle$transfer expression$\rangle$ occurred at the event time τ_i.

When a sequence of events occur, we order the events according to their associated event times. For example, assume that we wish to add three numbers together and leave the result in a register X. If the numbers are produced external to the system, the following sequence of transfer operations will carry out the desired task.

Addition of Three Values

Event Time 1. Clear X and read first value into Y

$$\tau_1: \quad X \leftarrow [0] \qquad Y \leftarrow \langle \text{input} \rangle$$

Event Time 2. Form first partial sum and read second value into Y

$$\tau_2: \quad X \leftarrow X + Y \qquad Y \leftarrow \langle \text{input} \rangle$$

Event Time 3. Form second partial sum and read third value into Y

$$\tau_3: \quad X \leftarrow X + Y \qquad Y \leftarrow \langle \text{input} \rangle$$

Event Time 4. Form final sum. No change in Y

$$\tau_4: \quad X \leftarrow X + Y$$

Our ability to define complex information processing sequences is enhanced if we have a basic set of transfer operations that can be used as building blocks to form transfer expressions. The following discussion introduces several common transfer operations that are used later.

Multiplexed Inputs

The concept of a multiplexer was introduced in Chapter 7 as a device that would allow us to use a control signal to select as an output one of n possible inputs. If we combine a multiplexer with a register as shown in Figure 8-27, we can use the control signal T to select which signal we wish to load into the register X. The transfer expression describing this operation is

$$\tau: \quad X \leftarrow A \wedge (T = [1]) \vee B \wedge (T = [2]) \vee C \wedge (T = [3])$$

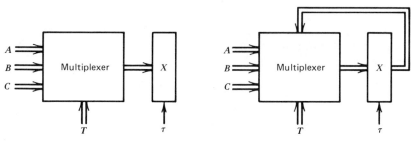

(a) Multiplexer without feedback   (b) Multiplexer with feedback

Figure 8-27 Representation of multiplexed information transfers.

In this expression we see that if the control signal takes on a value of [1], [2], or [3] then A, B, or C, respectively, will be transferred into X. However, if T takes on any other value, such as [0], then the expression on the right-hand side will have the value [0] and [0] will be transferred into the X register. In all cases the value stored in X before the transfer pulse is applied is lost.

There may be situations where we do not wish to lose the current contents of the X register if there is no information to be transferred to X from the outside world. For this case the transfer expression can be modified to

$$\tau: \quad X \leftarrow X \wedge (T = [0]) \vee A \wedge (T = [1]) \vee$$
$$B \wedge (T = [2]) \vee C \wedge (T = [3])$$

where we have introduced the additional term that ensures that X retains its current value when the control signal T has the value [0]. One method to realize this type of transfer is to use a multiplexer with an additional feedback path to include X as one of the inputs. This organization is illustrated in Figure 8-27b.

The Shift Operations

In the last section we saw that information could be shifted into or out of a register one bit at a time using a serial transfer. Since such a shift operation causes the state of the register to be modified, we would like to be able to express the shift operation as an assignment operation.

Registers designed to handle the serial transfer of information are called *shift registers* and come in a variety of forms. Information can be entered at the left end of the register and shifted right or it can be entered at the right end and shifted left. To accommodate either situation we introduce two special operations, the *shift right* operation and the *shift left* operation.

Figure 8-21 illustrated the general internal construction of a shift register. At the register level we are concerned only with the external characteristics of such a register. Thus for this discussion we assume that X is a register formed from the individual cells $X_1, \ldots, X_n$. The contents of X is $[x_1, \ldots, x_n]$ and the contents of cell X_i is $[x_i]$. Also assume that the input signal A is the 1-tuple $[a_1]$. Using these conventions, we define the following basic shift operations.

1. *Shift Right Operation* SR

$$\tau: \quad X \leftarrow SR(A, X)$$

The contents of X are shifted one cell to the right. The value of A is shifted into the leftmost cell of X. The initial content of X_n is lost.

$$\tau: \quad X \leftarrow SR(A, X) \begin{cases} X_{i+1} \leftarrow X_i & i = 1, 2, \ldots, n - 1 \\ X_1 \leftarrow A \end{cases}$$

Example: Initial values $X := [1, 0, 1, 0]$ $A := [1]$

$$\tau: \quad X \leftarrow SR([1], [1, 0, 1, 0])$$

Final value $X := [1, 1, 0, 1]$

2. *Shift Left Operation* SL

$$\tau: \quad X \leftarrow SL(X, A)$$

The contents of X are shifted one cell to the left. The value of A is shifted into the rightmost cell of X. The initial content of X_1 is lost.

$$\tau: \quad X \leftarrow SL(X, A) \quad \begin{cases} X_{i-1} \leftarrow X_i & i = 2, 3, \ldots, n \\ X_n \leftarrow A \end{cases}$$

Example: Initial values $X := [0, 1, 0, 1] \qquad A := [1]$

$$\tau: \quad X \leftarrow SL([0, 1, 0, 1,], [1])$$
Final value $X := [1, 0, 1, 1]$

3. *Special Case*—no input.

If there is no input to a register, then the shift operations can be represented as

$$\tau: \quad X \leftarrow SR(X) \qquad \text{Right shift}$$
$$\tau: \quad X \leftarrow SL(X) \qquad \text{Left shift}$$

where the input signal has been omitted as an argument (i.e., it is assumed to be zero).

Example: Initial value of $X := [1, 1, 0, 1, 1]$

$$\tau: \quad X \leftarrow SR([1, 1, 0, 1, 1,])$$
Final value $X := [0, 1, 1, 0, 1]$
$$\tau: \quad X \leftarrow SL([1, 1, 0, 1, 1])$$
Final value $X := [1, 0, 1, 1, 0]$

The use of these shift operations is illustrated in the following example.

Serial Information Transfer

If we wish to transmit an n-bit digital signal between two points, we have two choices. We can use a parallel information transfer if we have n lines connecting the two points, or we can use a serial information transfer if we have only one line connecting the two points. A parallel transfer is faster since it involves one event time, while the serial transfer takes n event times. If the cost of having n lines connecting the two points is not justified by this speed advantage, then it is quite common to use serial information transfer techniques.

Suppose that we wish to transfer a 3-bit signal A to a 3-bit register X using the serial information transfer system illustrated in Figure 8-28. At the start of trans-

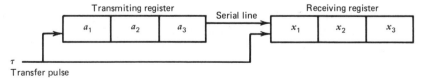

Figure 8-28   Representation of a serial information transfer.

mission the signal A is in the A register and we do not care what is contained in the receiving X register. After three transfers the signal A will have been transfered to X and A will contain $[0]$.

The transfer sequence necessary to carry out this transfer is described by the following sequence of transfer expressions.

$$\tau_1: \quad A \leftarrow SR(A) \qquad X \leftarrow SR(A_3, X)$$
$$\tau_2: \quad A \leftarrow SR(A) \qquad X \leftarrow SR(A_3, X)$$
$$\tau_3: \quad A \leftarrow SR(A) \qquad X \leftarrow SR(A_3, X)$$

To illustrate a serial information transfer assume that before the transfer is started A and X are initialized to

$$A := [1, 0, 1] \qquad X := [0, 0, 0]$$

The transfers take place at event times 1, 2, and 3 as described by the following sequence of events.

			Contents of A and X After Transfer	
Event Time	Transfers		A	X
$\tau_0:$	$A \leftarrow [1, 0, 1]$	$X \leftarrow [0, 0, 0]$	$[1, 0, 1]$	$[0, 0, 0]$
$\tau_1:$	$A \leftarrow SR([1, 0, 1])$	$X \leftarrow SR([1], [0, 0, 0])$	$[0, 1, 0]$	$[1, 0, 0]$
$\tau_2:$	$A \leftarrow SR([0, 1, 0])$	$X \leftarrow SR([0], [1, 0, 0])$	$[0, 0, 1]$	$[0, 1, 0]$
$\tau_3:$	$A \leftarrow SR([0, 0, 1])$	$X \leftarrow SR([1], [0, 1, 0])$	$[0, 0, 0]$	$[1, 0, 1]$

After the transfer has been completed, the final values in the registers are

$$A := [0, 0, 0] \qquad X := [1, 0, 1]$$

This example can easily be extended to any number of bits.

General Information Transfers

A wide variety of techniques can be used to form the expression on the right-hand side of a transfer expression. At the system level, a general information transfer operation performs a specific operation on one or more signals and then stores the result in a given register. Some typical network configurations that may be used to carry out such a transfer are shown in Figure 8-29. The design of such networks, using the techniques discussed in earlier chapters, is easily carried out once we define how the information is encoded and the type of flip-flops used to form the registers in the network.

For example, the network shown in Figure 8-29a has three registers, A, B, and C. The combinational logic network receives the information from registers A and B and produces a result $F(A, B)$. When the transfer pulse τ occurs, this result is loaded into the C register. Symbolically this transfer is indicated as

$$\tau: \quad C \leftarrow F(A, B)$$

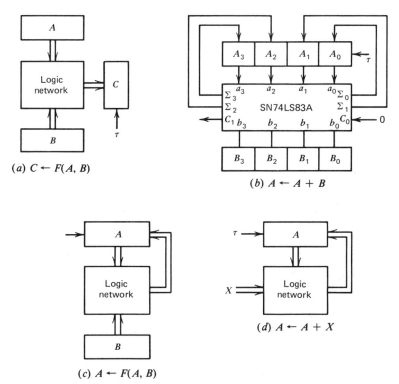

(a) $C \leftarrow F(A, B)$

(b) $A \leftarrow A + B$

(c) $A \leftarrow F(A, B)$

(d) $A \leftarrow A + X$

Figure 8-29   General information transfer.

Sometimes the register C, which receives the information, is actually one of the registers that supplies one of the initial arguments to the function. A typical example of this situation is shown in Figure 8-29c, where the network realizes the transfer operation

$$\tau: \quad A \leftarrow A + B$$

If A and B are 4-bit registers and if A is constructed from D flip-flops, then this transfer operation can be realized using the network shown in Figure 8-29b. In this example we have used a type SN74LS83A 4-bit binary full-adder MSI logic network to implement the addition operation.

Digital networks with inputs can also be handled in a similar manner. For example, consider the system shown in Figure 8-29d, where the B register is replaced with an input signal X. This network performs the transfer operation

$$\tau: \quad A \leftarrow A + X$$

This network can be realized in the same manner as the network shown in Figure 8-29b except that the input signal X serves as input to the 4-bit binary full-adder in place of the B input from the other register.

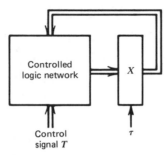

Figure 8-30   General form of a controlled transfer operation.

Controlled Networks

Our previous discussion of combinational logic networks showed that it is very easy to design a network that will realize a number of different operations depending upon the value of a control signal. If we use such a logic network to form the expression on the right-hand side of a transfer expression, then we can realize a number of different transfer operations. A typical network of this type might have the form shown in Figure 8-30. Let us assume that the behavior of this network is defined by Table 8-7. The transfers described by this table can be summarized by the transfer expression

$$\tau: \quad A \leftarrow (T = [0]) \land A \lor (T = [1]) \land SR(X, A) \lor (T = [2]) \land SL(A, X)$$

Using our knowledge of the shift operation, we see that this controlled information transfer can be realized by a network of the form shown in Figure 8-31. The logic networks $M1$ used as the input to each flip-flop are simple multiplexers with a control signal T. This network selects the proper input to each flip-flop depending upon the value of T.

Simple Multiregister Transfers

There is no reason to limit our information transfers to a single register. In the simplest case we might wish to transfer the contents of the register X to three output registers A, B, and C as shown in Figure 8-32. This transfer is represented by the

Table 8-7   A Controlled Information Transfer

Control Signal T	Transfer Operation	Description of Operation
[0]	$A \leftarrow A$	Contents of A remains constant
[1]	$A \leftarrow SR(X, A)$	Shift information right
[2]	$A \leftarrow SL(A, X)$	Shift information left
[3]	$A \leftarrow [0]$	Clear A (i.e., set A to 0)

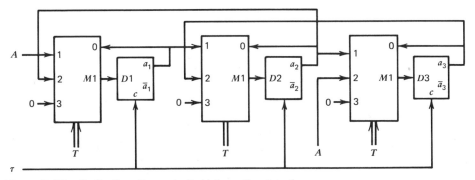

Figure 8-31 Realization of a controlled information transfer.

transfer expression

$$\tau: \quad A \leftarrow X \qquad B \leftarrow X \qquad C \leftarrow X$$

As shown in Figure 8-32, an individual transfer pulse is associated with each register. In this example these pulses are simply connected to the master pulse input τ. We can increase the flexibility of a transfer expression if we introduce a logic network to control the generation of the individual transfer pulses.

Figure 8-33 shows the same system as presented in Figure 8-32 except that a *steering network* has been added to the line carrying the transfer pulse. This steering network is a simple combinational logic network with a control signal. This control signal defines which transfers are to take place when the transfer pulse τ is applied to the system. The following example illustrates how this is accomplished.

Suppose that we wish to use a control signal T to specify which one of the four possible transfer operations shown in Table 8-8 is to be carried out. Examining this

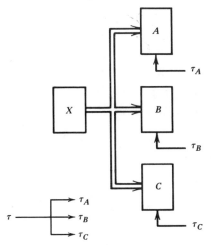

Figure 8-32 A simple multiregister transfer.

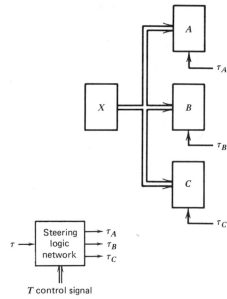

Figure 8-33   Controlled multiple-register transfer.

Table 8-8   Controlled Multiregister Transfers

Control Signal T	Transfer Operation		Transfer Pulses Required
[0]	$A \leftarrow X$	$B \leftarrow X$	τ_A, τ_B
[1]	$A \leftarrow X$	$C \leftarrow X$	τ_A, τ_C
[2]	$B \leftarrow X$		τ_B
[3]	$B \leftarrow X,$	$C \leftarrow X$	τ_B, τ_C

table we can write the following logic expression to define the transfer pulses that must be generated to accomplish the desired transfers.

$$\tau_A := ((T = [0]) \lor (T = [1])) \land \tau$$
$$\tau_B := ((T = [0]) \lor (T = [2]) \lor (T = [3])) \land \tau$$
$$\tau_C := ((T = [1]) \lor (T = [3])) \land \tau$$

If we encode the control signal T as

$$T := [t_0, t_1]$$

then standard logic design techniques allow us to generate the steering network shown in Figure 8-34.

Multiple-Step Transfer Operations

Most of the information processing operations that we are interested in involve a number of steps. For example assume that we wish to compute

$$Z := 4*Y_1 + 2*Y_2 + Y_3$$

where the values for Y_1, Y_2, and Y_3 are read in from an external signal source. One way to compute Z is to use a network of the form shown in Figure 8-35.

In this network we have three registers, a controlled combinational logic network that forms the signals applied to the A register, and a steering network that controls the transfer pulses that are applied to the registers at the proper event times. The following sequence of events can be used to compute the desired value for Z.

Event Time	Transfer Operation Describing Event	Control Signal	Comment
τ_0:	$A \leftarrow [0]$, $\quad X \leftarrow Y$	[0]	CLEAR A, READ Y_1
τ_1:	$A \leftarrow A + X$	[1]	PARTIAL SUM
τ_2:	$A \leftarrow SL(A), X \leftarrow Y$	[2]	MULTIPLY A BY 2 READ Y_2
τ_3:	$A \leftarrow A + X$	[1]	PARTIAL SUM
τ_4:	$A \leftarrow SL(A), X \leftarrow Y$	[2]	MULTIPLY A BY 2 READ Y_3
τ_5:	$A \leftarrow A + X$	[1]	PARTIAL SUM
τ_6:	$Z \leftarrow A$	[3]	FINAL RESULT

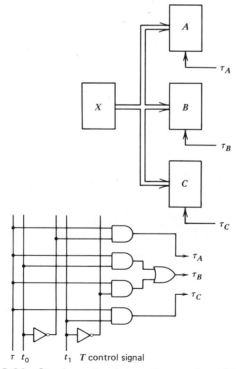

Figure 8-34 Steering network to realize transfers of Table 8-8.

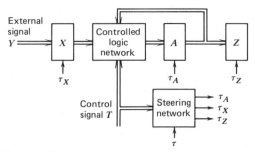

Figure 8-35 A multiple-step computation of $Z := 4*Y_1 + 2*Y_2 + Y_3$

If we examine this sequence of transfer operations, we see that Z is computed using the following expression:

$$Z := ((Y_1*2) + Y_2)*2 + Y_3$$

where we have used the operation of shifting left one bit to carry out the operation of multiplying by 2.

To complete our design we must define the properties of the controlled combinational logic network and the steering network. These networks are defined in Tables 8-9 and 8-10. The logic circuits necessary to realize these two networks can be carried out using our standard techniques. Their design is left as an exercise.

To actually carry out the computation represented by this network we must generate the control signal T and the transfer pulse τ. The only constraint is that the control signal T must have reached a steady state value early enough for the signal $F(A, X, T)$ to have reached its desired value before the transfer pulse τ is applied. The way that these signals are generated is discussed in detail in the next chapter.

Table 8-9 Description of Controlled Combinational Logic Network

Control Signal T	Function $F(A, X, T)$ Formed for Each T
[0]	$F(A, X, [0]) := [0]$
[1]	$F(A, X, [1]) := A + X$
[2]	$F(A, X, [2]) := SL(A)$
[3]	Not defined

Table 8-10 Description of Steering Network

Control Signal T	Transfer Pulses Produced
[0]	τ_A
[1]	τ_A
[2]	τ_A, τ_X
[3]	τ_Z

EXERCISES

1. Design the logic networks necessary to realize the event

τ: $X \leftarrow (T = [1]) \wedge (X + 1) \vee (T = [2]) \wedge (X - 1)$
$$\vee (T = [3]) \wedge (SR(X))$$

2. Design the steering network and the controlled logic network shown in Figure 8-35.

5. SUMMARY

The ability of a digital network to store information about its past behavior or the ability of a digital system to store information concerning the sequence of tasks it is to perform makes it possible to use these networks and systems to carry out time-dependent information processing tasks. In this chapter we first concentrated on the basic operation and characteristics of flip-flops and the registers constructed from these flip-flops. These registers then became one of the building blocks used to realize a number of different information transfer operations.

The main new idea introduced in this chapter is that of an event. In the next chapter we show how any complex information processing task can be represented as a series of events. Since we already know that any event can be represented using a few simple combinational logic networks and one or more registers, we will then be able to design general digital systems and computers.

Reference Notation

The flip-flops currently used in digital circuits are purchased as integrated circuits. Manufacture data sheets and handbooks, such as Reference 5, are the best place to find a detailed description of these circuits. The methods used to design with integrated circuit flip-flops are discussed in Reference 1 while Reference 4 presents a good overview of the internal operation of these elements. Both References 2 and 3 give other views of how flip-flops can be used in the design of digital systems.

REFERENCES

1. Blakeslee, T. R. (1975), *Digital Design with Standard MSI and LSI*. Wiley, New York.
2. Peatman, J. B. (1980), *Digital Hardware Design*. McGraw-Hill, New York.
3. Sloan, M. E. (1976), *Computer Hardware Organization*. SRA, Chicago.
4. Taub, H. (1982), *Digital Circuits and Microprocessors,* McGraw-Hill, New York.
5. Texas Instruments (current edition), *The TTL Data Book for Design Engineers*. Texas Instruments, Inc., Dallas, Tex.

HOME PROBLEMS

1. An input of $S = 1$, $R = 1$ is inadvertently applied to an S-R flip-flop of the type shown in Figure 8-2. If at $t = 0$, S and R both go from 1 to 0. To what

state will the flip-flop go if the upper delay is greater than the lower delay? Draw a timing diagram to show the behavior of the flip-flop.

2. Let A, B be 3-bit registers constructed from J-K flip-flops, and let X be a 3-bit signal. Design a digital network that will realize the following event.

$$\tau: \quad A \leftarrow (A < B) \wedge X \vee (A \geq B) \wedge A$$
$$B \leftarrow (A \leq B) \wedge B \vee (A > B) \wedge X$$

3. Consider the network shown in Figure P8-1 to add two numbers. Assume that the flip-flop delay Δt equals τ_a seconds and that the full-adder attains a constant output value τ_b seconds after all of the inputs assume a constant value. Derive, as a function of τ_a and τ_b, the smallest period T the transfer pulse can have. If $\tau_a = \tau_b = 10^{-6}$ seconds, how many additions can be performed in a second?

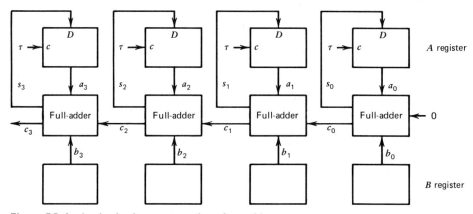

Figure P8-1   Logic circuit representation of an adder.

4. Design a multiple-step digital network that will carry out the following counting sequence

$$[0] \rightarrow [1] \rightarrow [2] \rightarrow [3] \rightarrow [4] \rightarrow [5] \rightarrow [0] \rightarrow [1] \rightarrow \cdots$$

(a) Give the block diagram of the network needed to carry out this task.
(b) Give the sequence of transfer operations needed to carry out this task.
(c) Assume that D flip-flops are used to build this network. Complete the logic design necessary to realize this system.

5. An automatic change counting machine is to be designed. A major component of this machine is a counter which will count the total amount of money deposited in the machine. Assume that the machine can process nickles, dimes and quarters. Design a simple network that will compute the total amount of change received. The output of the network is to be the BCD total of all of the money received by the machine. Assume that the machine always shows a total of $000.00 when processing starts.

9

DIGITAL SYSTEM DESIGN

1. INTRODUCTION

In the earlier chapters we have been slowly building a set of design tools that allow us to describe and analyze the operation of digital systems. Our discussion of combinational logic networks has reached the point where we can describe a wide range of information processing operations that can be used to operate on the information contained in signals or found in registers. In Chapter 8 we saw that we could combine these operations with the concept of an assignment operation to perform multiple-step tasks that required the intermediate storage of information. Those investigations concentrated on the internal or register and logic-level behavior of a digital system.

Starting with this chapter we turn our attention to the macroscopic behavior of digital systems. In particular, we concentrate on the problem of how registers and combinational logic networks can be integrated into a complex information processing system. Our main interest is directed toward the flow of information, the control of information, and the transfer of information rather than on the details of how the circuits that perform these tasks are constructed. When necessary we can use the techniques of the previous chapters to design these circuits.

Our first task is to develop a model that represents the major parts of a digital system and the specific task each part plays in carrying out a multiple step computation. The next step is to show how a "hardware language" can be created to represent the different classes of basic tasks that can be used to carry out a computation. Using this language we then show how a "hardware program" made up of statements from this language can be used to describe the sequence of steps needed to carry out a given computation. In fact, we find that the hardware program that describes a given digital system has many of the same features that would be found in a software program designed to carry out the same task.

Using these concepts we then investigate how a set of design requirements for a given system can be reduced to a complete digital system design. To complete the discussion we use these methods to realize two typical digital systems.

2. THE BASIC MODEL OF A DIGITAL SYSTEM

Digital systems may take on a variety of forms. In most cases, however, we can model a system using the general structure shown in Figure 9-1. This model indicates the two major components of any digital system: the information processing unit and the control unit.

The *information processing unit* defines the basic information transfers and operations that can be performed on information as it flows through the system. By itself, the information processing unit cannot perform a multiple-step computation. Each unit must implement all of the hardware operations required to carry out a desired computation. However, the sequence in which the operations are performed in a multistep computation is determined by the *control unit*.

As each step in a computation is reached, the control unit sends the appropriate control signals and transfer pulses to the information processing unit indicating that a given set of assignment operations are to be performed. When the events associated with these operations have been completed, the control unit goes to the next processing step. In some cases the next step will depend on the current status of the information being processed. To decide which step to perform, the control unit must receive *status information* from the information processing unit. The control unit then uses this information to select the next step in the computational sequence being performed.

Besides the status information received from the information processing unit, the control unit may receive external information that will also influence the computational sequence being performed. Similarly it may also produce output information that can be sent to other control units to influence their operation.

In this section we develop the formal representation techniques used to describe complete system operation and introduce a number of assumptions concerning how the various signals indicated in Figure 9-1 are formed and used. This discussion is based upon the information transfer concepts first introduced in Chapter 8.

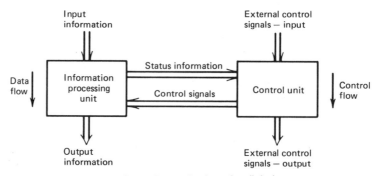

Figure 9-1 General organization of a digital system.

Information Processing Unit Representation

An information processing unit is simply a digital network of the form introduced in Chapter 8. Figure 9-2 presents a conceptual model of the organization of a typical information processing unit. The three major components of such a unit are:

1. A controlled combinational logic network
2. A set of m internal registers
3. A steering network to form specific register transfer pulses

The input signals $X_1, \ldots, X_k$ and the output signals $Z_1, \ldots, Z_n$ represent the information flow through the information processing unit, while the control signal T is produced by the control unit to define which operations are to be performed when the transfer pulse τ is applied. Finally the signal S represents the status information generated inside the unit by using one or more relational operations to test for specific relations that may exist between the input signals and the information stored in the internal registers.

We have already discussed the detailed techniques that can be used to design the logic circuits necessary to realize this unit once the specific tasks it must perform are identified. Our attention in this chapter is directed to the problem of deciding upon the capabilities that must be included in the unit if we are to carry out a specific multiple-step computation.

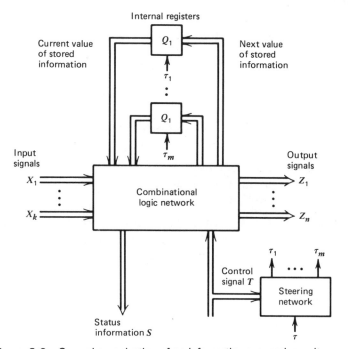

Figure 9-2 General organization of an information processing unit.

A variety of techniques can be used to represent the information processing unit. We have already used the idea of an assignment operation to specify the new values to be loaded into a register when a transfer pulse is applied to a register and the idea of a specification statement to indicate the value of the output signals produced by a combinational logic network. For simple networks this approach provides a compact way to model the behavior of the network. As the number of tasks that must be performed increases, this method of representation can become difficult to understand. We will shortly introduce the idea of a *specification table* as a general technique for defining the exact tasks carried out by an information processing unit. Before doing this we introduce several conventions concerning the relationships that exist among the signals found in the unit.

The Next-state Expression

For the purpose of this model it is assumed that all of the registers in the information processing unit are constructed from master-slave flip-flops. The value stored in a register at the time a transfer pulse is applied is called the *current value* or *current state* of the register. When the transfer pulse is applied, the flip-flop control signal is applied to the input of the register. This will start the process necessary to change the information stored in the register. However, as long as the transfer pulse is on, the output of the register retains its current value. When the transfer pulse is removed, the register now contains the new value defined by the control signal and the output of the register takes on this value. The information stored in the register at the completion of the transfer operation is called the *next-state value* or *next-state* of the register.

The transfer that creates the next-state value of the ith register can be represented by a general transfer expression of the form

$$Q_i \leftarrow F_i(X_1, \ldots, X_k, Q_1, \ldots, Q_m, T)$$

This expression, called the *next-state expression,* emphasizes the fact that the next-state of the register Q_i is a function of

1. The values of the current input signals
2. The values of the current states of the registers
3. The value of the control signal T

and is not influenced in any way by the status signal S or the output signals Z_j. Once the register reaches its new state, the output of the register remains constant until the completion of the next transfer pulse.

The Output Expression

One or more output signals may be produced by the information processing unit. The jth output is defined by the specification statement

$$Z_j := G_j(X_1, \ldots, X_k, Q_1, \ldots, Q_m, T)$$

which is called an *output expression*. This expression is a function of

1. The values associated with the current input signals
2. The values of the current states of the registers
3. The value associated with the control signal T

and is not influenced in any way by the status signal S. Since Z_j is the output of a combinational logic network, the value associated with this signal is defined only when all of the arguments of G_j have reached a steady value. It is assumed that this condition has been reached before the transfer pulse that causes a change of state of one or more of the registers is applied.

For many of the systems discussed in later sections the output signals may depend only on the current values contained in the registers. When this is true the output expression has the form

$$Z_j := G(Q_1, \ldots, Q_m)$$

The output signal is then available for use whenever the arguments of G are constant.

The Status Signal

In all but the simplest computations, we must have the ability to alter the computation sequence being performed based on the status of the information being processed. To do this we must be able to carry out tests on this information to determine its current status. The status information produced by this testing process is reported to the control unit by the status signal S. The control unit must evaluate this information before deciding on the next step in the calculation. The status signal is defined by a general expression of the form

$$S := R(X_1, \ldots, X_k, Q_1, \ldots, Q_m)$$

This expression is governed by the following rules.

1. The status signal S is not a function of the control signal T.
2. The status signal S reaches a steady state value only after the input signals X_i reach a steady state value.
3. The control unit may use the current value of the status signal S in determining the current value of the control signal T.
4. The transfer pulse τ is applied only when the control unit has had enough time to generate the proper control signal T after receiving the current value of the status signal S.

As long as we are dealing only with the information processing unit we do not have to know how the control unit is going to make use of the current value of the status signal. However, when we discuss the control unit, we will see that the information contained in the status signal is very important.

Associated with the status signal will be a set

$$\{S_A, S_B, \ldots, S_L\}$$

of possible values that the signal may assume. It is assumed that each element of this set represents a different condition and that the conditions are mutually exclusive. The values in this set are often represented symbolically by a set of *mnemonics* that suggest the test being conducted. The actual coding used to represent these elements is unimportant at this level of design. However, we will find that there are several situations in which a natural encoding can be defined if the signal S is represented by the u-tuple

$$S := [s_1, s_2, \ldots, s_u]$$

where each of the bits in the u-tuple is defined by a specific relational operation.

For example assume that the status signal is selected from the set

{XGT, XEQ, XNEQ, XGEQ, XLT}

where the mnemonics corresponding to these elements are defined as

XGT—X greater than [0]

XEQ—X equal to [0]

XNEQ—X not equal to [0]

XGEQ—X greater than or equal to [0]

XLT—X less than [0]

In this case we could also define S as a 3-tuple

$$S := [s_1, s_2, s_3]$$

where the s_i are defined by

$$s_1 := (X > [0])$$
$$s_2 := (X = [0])$$
$$s_3 := (X < [0])$$

With this encoding we can define the following relationship between the mnemonic representation of S and its vector representation

XGT	:= [1, 0, 0]	XEQ	:= [0, 1, 0]
XLT	:= [0, 0, 1]	XNEQ	:= [1, 0, 1]
XGEQ	:= [1, 1, 0]		

We use both methods of representing S as appropriate to the design being investigated.

The Control Signal

The control signal T is used to define

1. The information transfers performed by the information processing unit
2. The value of the output signals

when the transfer pulse τ is applied. To carry out a calculation the control unit will generate a sequence of control signals that must assume a steady value before the application of the transfer pulse τ.

As shown in Figure 9-2, the control signal appears as an input to both the combinational logic network at the heart of the processing unit and the combinational logic network used as the steering network to generate the transfer pulses applied to the individual registers. It is the responsibility of the control unit to generate the value of T needed at any given point in a computation. In generating T the control unit may use the information contained in the status signal S, information contained in the external control input signal, or internal information stored within the control unit. The detailed discussion of how the control signal is generated is discussed in Section 3.

Associated with each control signal T is a set

$$\{T_A, T_B, \ldots, T_R\}$$

of possible values that the control signal may assume. Each element of this set is assumed to represent a different information processing task. The actual digital coding used to represent these elements is unimportant at this level of design.

The values that may be assigned to T are represented symbolically by a mnemonic that suggests the operations to be performed. For example, the values associated with a control signal might be taken from the set

$$\{CLR, ADD, SUB, INC, DEC\}$$

where the mnemonics have been selected to suggest the following operations:

CLR—Set registers A and B to [0].

ADD—Add contents of registers A and B and place result in A.

SUB—Subtract contents of register B from A and place result in A.

INC—Add [1] to the contents of register A.

DEC—Subtract [1] from the contents of register A.

We will find mnemonics very useful in both understanding the different operations that the processing unit can perform and in developing "hardware programs" for the control unit.

Specification Tables

A set of mixed mode expressions could be used to describe the transfer operations found in a given information processing unit. This form of representation is, however, better suited to the problem of designing the combinational logic elements needed to realize the different transfer operations. When carrying out a design at the system level, it will be less confusing if we use a *specification table* to describe the specific information processing operations performed by the unit for each value of the control signal.

A specification table for any information processing unit consists of two subtables. The first subtable is the *operation table*. This table describes the transfer actions taken when the transfer pulse τ is applied and the output signals generated by the unit corresponding to this event time. The second subtable is the *status table,* which defines the status information contained in the status signal. The following example illustrates the form that the specification table takes.

Assume that we are given a simple network with the general form shown in Figure 9-3. This network has a single input X, a control signal T, and two registers A and B. It produces two output signals: S, the status signal, and a signal ERR, which is the difference between the value of X and the value contained in A. Table 9-1 provides a formal definition of the behavior of this network.

This example illustrates the major features of a specification table. First we note that we used a set of mnemonics to represent the distinct values of the control signal. We could also have used a simple ordering such as [0], [1], [2], and [3] to represent these values of T. However, the mnemonics make it easier to understand the general operation that will be performed in response to this signal.

When $T := $ NOP we see that there are no internal transfers, but the current value of the output signal is set equal to the current value of the input signal. When $T := $ CLAB we see that both of the registers are set to [0] but that we don't care what value is associated with the current value of the output signal Z. The next state signals applied to the registers to implement the indicated transfers will, of course, depend upon the types of flip-flops used to construct the registers. The steering network used to generate the transfer pulses for each of the registers is defined by the column labeled Transfer Pulses. This column of the operation table may be omitted

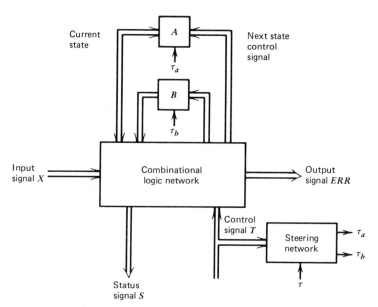

Figure 9-3   A simple information processing network.

Table 9-1 Specification Table for Network of Figure 9-3

Operation Table

Control Signal T	Transfer Expression	Transfer Pulses	Output Signal ERR
NOP	No transfers	No transfer	$ERR := X$
ADDA	$A \leftarrow A + X$	τ_a	$ERR := A - X$
ADDB	$A \leftarrow A + B$	τ_b	$ERR := A - X$
CLAB	$A \leftarrow [0]$ $B \leftarrow [0]$	$\tau_a \quad \tau_b$	Don't care

Status Table
$$S := [s_1, s_2, s_3]$$

Component of S	Relational Expression Defining Component
s_1	$s_1 := (A = X) \vee (B = X)$
s_2	$s_2 := (X > 0)$
s_3	$s_3 := (X < 0)$

since the same information can be derived from the information contained in the Transfer Expression column.

In this example the status information is seen to be encoded as a 3-bit signal. Each bit is defined by a particular relational expression that depends only on the input and the current contents of the A and B registers. With this encoding S can take on eight distinct values. In some design situations it would be desirable to use mnemonics to represent the values of S. In this example the use of mnemonics for S would obscure the relationship that exists between the different tests being conducted and the results of the test that is inherent in the indicated 3-bit encoding used for S.

Timing Considerations

The proper operation of an information processing unit requires that all signal levels be present and at a steady value when they are needed. In all "clocked" systems there is a master clock that generates a standard master transfer pulse sequence or *clock pulse* sequence. This sequence is made up of pulses of a standard width, t_w, and has a fixed period of t_p seconds. The typical form that this master transfer pulse sequence may take is illustrated in Figure 9-4.

The application of a transfer pulse to the transfer pulse input of an information processing unit initiates the event called for by the current value of the control signal T. When the transfer pulse is applied, it is assumed that all signals involved in the transfer operations associated with that event time have reached a steady state value. The values of all input and output signals and the outputs of all registers are assumed to remain constant during the t_w seconds that the transfer pulse is present. When the transfer pulse is completed, the output of the registers involved in the transfer go to

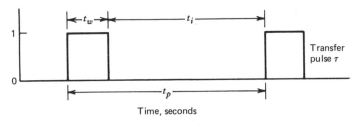

Figure 9-4   The master clock sequence.

their new value, and the other signals in the unit can change in preparation for the application of the next transfer pulse. These changes must be completed in less than t_i seconds when the next transfer pulse occurs. The period of the transfer pulse sequence is thus

$$t_p = t_w + t_i \text{ seconds}$$

Because of the relationships that exist between different signals, there are several restrictions on when a signal must reach a steady value. Figure 9-5 illustrates the timing considerations imposed on the signals found in the information processing unit. In this figure we use the notation

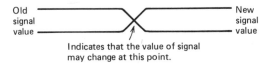

to indicate that the values of the signal being discussed may be *either* 0 or 1 and that a change in the value of the signal *may* occur at the indicated point.

As shown in Figure 9-5, the first signals that must reach steady state values are the signals at the outputs of all registers that have been involved in the last transfer and the input signals that change values. These two groups of signals are used to form the status signal S. This signal must reach a steady state value before the control unit can use the information in the signal to form the control signal T. Once the control signal has reached a steady value, the register control signal and the output signals assume their steady state values. (Note that if the output signals are not dependent upon the control signal T or the input signals, then they will reach a steady state value as soon as the output of the registers reaches a steady state value.) The next transfer pulse can then be applied at this point.

When carrying out a design at the system level, we assume that all of the signal levels are produced in the proper manner to satisfy the indicated timing relationships. However, when the system design is implemented at the logic circuit level, the logic circuit designer must be very careful to make sure that the assumed timing relationships actually exist. In the next section we develop the design techniques necessary to describe how the information processing unit is used to carry out a multiple-step calculation. During that discussion it is assumed that the proper timing relationships are satisfied by all signals involved in the processing.

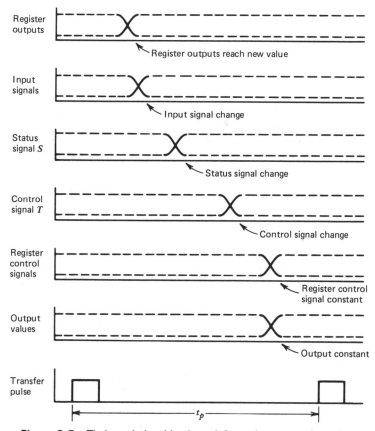

Register outputs — Register outputs reach new value

Input signals — Input signal change

Status signal S — Status signal change

Control signal T — Control signal change

Register control signals — Register control signal constant

Output values — Output constant

Transfer pulse

t_p

Figure 9-5 Timing relationships in an information processing unit.

EXERCISE

1. Assume that the signal X and the two registers A and B in the information processing unit shown in Figure 9-3 are 8-bits. Using MSI circuit elements, realize this information processing unit.

3. THE CONTROL UNIT

To carry out a complex computational task using a digital system we need a formal description of how that task is performed. In Chapter 1 we said that an algorithm for the computation $F(x) = y$ existed if we could define an ordered sequence of operations and tests that could be performed mechanically by a device such that, when given x, the device either:

1. formed $F(x)$ by executing these operations and tests in the prescribed order, or
2. indicated that no y existed that satisfied the conditions of the computation.

The device was required to reach one or the other of these decisions after executing a finite number of steps.

The first requirement that must be satisfied in implementing an algorithm is that we have a device that is capable of performing a number of predefined operations and tests on the information being processed. The information processing unit discussed in Section 2 satisfies this requirement. The second requirement is that we must be able to describe the desired computation as a sequence of these operations. For a digital network this sequence of operations is called the *hardware program* that describes the computation. Finally we need a "mechanical device" that will carry out the steps defined by the hardware program. The mechanical device in this case is the control unit.

It is the responsibility of the system designer to define the basic operations and tests implemented by the information processing unit and to develop the hardware program describing the computation. Once the program is defined, the last task is to realize the control unit needed to implement the program. This section models the operation of the control unit at the system level and introduces a simple hardware language that can be used to define a hardware program to realize a given algorithm. The technique used to define a hardware program using this language is discussed in the next section. This program is then used to define the system level operation of the control unit. The logic level design of the control unit is discussed in the next chapter.

The Basic Assumptions

Although digital systems vary in complexity, conceptually we have represented the major parts of the system as shown in Figure 9-6. To develop a hardware program to carry out a given task we assume:

1. The information processing unit has been defined and the operations and tests that can be performed by the unit are completely described by a specification table. The set of operations that can be performed is defined by the control signal set associated with the control signal T, and the tests that can be performed are defined by the status signal set associated with the status signal S.

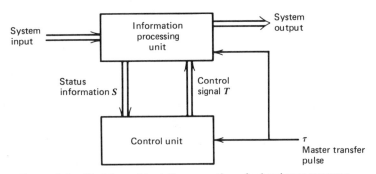

Figure 9-6 Model used to define execution of a hardware program.

2. The operation of the system is *synchronous*. The occurrence of the master transfer pulse τ causes the operations called for by the control signal to be executed and the control unit to move on to the next "instruction".

3. All of the signals associated with the information processing unit have reached their desired steady state value before the transfer pulse τ is applied.

To carry out the computation defined by a given algorithm the control unit must generate a sequence of control signals that indicate the sequence of operations that must be performed. Each control signal in the sequence carries out the operations associated with one step of the algorithm. It is the responsibility of the control unit to make sure that each step of the algorithm is carried out in the proper order.

Our approach in this section is first to consider how to describe the operation of the control unit and then to define a simple "hardware language" that we can use to describe the algorithm that we wish the control unit to implement. A number of simple computational tasks are used to demonstrate how this is accomplished.

The Control Unit Model

An algorithm requires a finite number of steps for its completion. Therefore the control unit must contain an internal representation of the algorithm so that it can determine which event is to occur when the next transfer pulse is applied. The control unit must have some type of "memory" to retain this information. To provide this capability the system model shown in Figure 9-7 is used to represent the general properties of a control unit.

The control unit's internal memory is represented by the *state register Q*. The purpose of this register is to record, in an appropriately encoded manner, where we are in the execution of our algorithm. Using this information, along with the current value of the status signal S, the control unit is able to generate the control signal T. This value defines the event that is to occur when the transfer pulse τ is applied to the information processing unit.

As soon as the transfer pulse is applied, the control unit must progress to the next

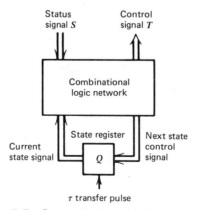

Figure 9-7 System level model of a control unit.

step in the algorithm. The *next state* control signal is responsible for updating the contents of the state register to the value corresponding to the next step in the computation. As shown, this next state signal is a function of the current state Q of the control unit and the value of the status signal S.

Based upon this model, the control unit's behavior can be represented by two equations. They are:

The Control Signal Equation

$$T := F(S, Q)$$

The Next State Equations

$$Q \leftarrow G(S, Q)$$

These equations emphasize that both the current value of the control signal T and the next state of the control unit are dependent upon the current value of the status signal S and the current state Q of the control unit.

To specify a control unit we must define the two equations given above and the following signals.

1. The Status Signal Set

$$\{[s_1, \ldots, s_r]\} \quad \text{or} \quad \{S_A, \ldots, S_U\}$$

2. The Control Signal Set

$$\{[t_1, \ldots, t_m]\} \quad \text{or} \quad \{T_A, \ldots, T_V\}$$

3. The State Set

$$\{[q_1, \ldots, q_n]\} \quad \text{or} \quad \{Q_A, \ldots, Q_W\}$$

As shown, the status signal, the control signal, and the state of the control unit may be represented in either vector or symbolic form. At this point in our discussion we find that the symbolic form is the most useful. However, when we reach the point of realizing the control unit, each signal must be encoded in vector form.

The Control Unit State Transition Table

Several techniques can be used to represent the equations that describe the operation of a control unit. At this point in our discussion these equations are represented by a *state transition table,* which has the general form shown in Figure 9-8.

The rows of the table correspond to the unique states that the control unit can enter, and the columns correspond to the distinct values that the status signal can take on. The entry in the *j*th row and the *i*th column corresponds to

$$G(S_i, Q_j) / F(S_i, Q_j)$$

Status S / State Q	S_A	$\cdots$	S_i	$\cdots$	S_U
Q_A					
Q_j			$G(S_i, Q_j)/F(S_i, Q_j)$		
Q_W		$\cdots$		$\cdots$	

Figure 9-8   General form of a control unit state transition table.

where the *next state* of the control unit is given by

$$G(S_i, Q_j)$$

and the current output of the control unit, corresponding to the *current value* of the control signal *T*, is given by

$$F(S_i, Q_j)$$

Unless otherwise specified, the control unit is assumed to be in state Q_A at the start of a computation.

Not all entries in the transition table must be filled. There may be situations where it is known that a given value for the status signal will never occur when the control unit is in a given state. Situations of this type can be indicated by a "don't care" entry of the form

$$-/-$$

A variety of techniques are used to define a transition table.

The Command Sequence

During a computation the control unit generates the sequence of control signals that instruct the information processing unit how to carry out the steps of an algorithm. In general this sequence is not fixed but is dependent upon the sequence of status signals received by the control unit. Thus one of the first things that we must understand is how to compute the control signal sequence generated by a control unit when we know the state transition table for the control unit and the sequence of status signals that drive the unit.

Assume that we are given the state transition table for a given control unit and that the control unit is initially placed in state Q_A. If we apply the status signal sequence

$$S(1), \ S(2), \ S(3), \ \ldots, \ S(k)$$

then the state sequence and the control signal sequence generated by the control unit in response to this sequence is defined as

Event Time	Status Signal	Current State	Current Control Signal	Next State
1	$S(1)$	$Q(1) = Q_A$	$T(1) := G(S(1), Q_A)$	$Q(2) \leftarrow F(S(1), Q_A)$
2	$S(2)$	$Q(2)$	$T(2) := G(S(2), Q(2))$	$Q(3) \leftarrow F(S(2), Q(2))$
3	$S(3)$	$Q(3)$	$T(3) := G(S(3), Q(3))$	$Q(4) \leftarrow F(S(3), Q(3))$
$\vdots$				
k	$S(k)$	$Q(k)$	$T(k) := G(S(k), Q(k))$	$Q(k + 1) \leftarrow F(S(k), Q(k))$

The following example illustrates how this calculation is performed.

Assume that we are given a simple digital network made up of an information processing unit with a single input signal X and two internal registers A and N. The specification table for this unit is given by Table 9-2a. We wish to use this system to compute the number of times that we must add the value of the input signal to the contents of A before the contents of A is larger than 10. When the contents of A exceeds 10, we wish to output the count corresponding to the number of additions performed to reach this value. The state transition table for the control unit that will implement this calculation is shown in Table 9-2b.

To start the computation process the control unit is placed in state Q_A and the master clock pulse generator is started. After each transfer pulse the control unit goes to the next state and generates the control signal defined by the status signal and the new current state. A typical control sequence produced by the control unit described by Table 9-2 might have the following form. It is assumed that both A and N are cleared and that the control unit is placed in state Q_A before the computation is started.

Step Number	1	2	3	4	5
Input X	[5]	[4]	[3]	[D.C]	[D.C]
Status Signal	LOW	LOW	HIGH	HIGH	HIGH
State Sequence	Q_A	Q_A	Q_A	Q_B	Q_C
Control Signal	ADD	ADD	ADD	OUT	CLR
Output Z	[D.C.]	[D.C.]	[D.C.]	[3]	[0]

[D.C.] = Don't care.

Table 9-2 A Typical Digital Network

(*a*) Specification Table

Operation Table			Status Table	
Control Signal	**Transfer**	**Output**	**Status Signal**	**Definition**
CLR	$N \leftarrow [0]$ $A \leftarrow [0]$	$Z := [0]$	HIGH	$A + X \geq [10]$
ADD	$A \leftarrow A + X$ $N \leftarrow N + [1]$	Don't care	LOW	$A + X < [10]$
OUT	No operation	$Z := N$		

(*b*) State Transition Table of Control Unit

State Set—Q $\{Q_A, Q_B, Q_C\}$	Status Signal Set—S $\{$LOW, HIGH$\}$	Control Signal Set—T $\{$CLR, ADD, OUT$\}$

State Q \ Status S	LOW	HIGH
Q_A	Q_A/ADD	Q_B/ADD
Q_B	–/–	Q_C/OUT
Q_C	–/–	Q_A/CLR

The computation illustrated by this sequence has five steps. At the 5th step the control unit has completed one cycle of the computation and the system has been reset to repeat the computation a second time. The number of steps necessary to reach this reset condition depends upon the values associated with the input X.

This example shows that once we have the specification table and state transition table for a given digital network we can easily describe its operation. To define these tables we must develop a process that allows us to reduce an algorithm for a computation to a specification table that describes the operations and tests that must be performed and a state transition table for the control unit that describes how the algorithm is to be implemented. We now consider this process.

The Programming Process   *skip*

Every algorithm, no matter how complex it becomes, involves five basic tasks that are repeated a number of times. These tasks can be identified as

1. Input information.
2. Perform a sequence of one or more assignment operations.

3. Make a test and decide on the basis of the test the next step to perform.
4. Repeat a sequence of steps a number of times until a particular computational task is completed.
5. Output information.

All high level programming languages have specific statements or groups of statements that a programmer may use to implement these tasks. At the hardware design level the state transition table of the control unit is responsible for carrying out the same tasks. The only difference is that in designing the control unit we must use a much more primitive "language" to represent the algorithm being implemented.

When developing a hardware program for a given information processing unit, the "language" that we use is defined by the specification table associated with the unit. The operations that can be performed are represented by the distinct values assigned to the control signal T, while the decisions that can be made are represented by the tests associated with the status signal S.

At the end of the design process we must have defined the specification table for the information processing unit and we must have reduced the hardware program developed to represent the algorithm to a state transition table for the control unit. To reach this point we proceed in the following manner.

Step 1. Define the Computational Task to Be Performed

A detailed specification of the computation to be performed is developed. This specification defines the inputs to be applied to the system and the outputs desired without trying to indicate how the computation is to be done.

Step 2. Define the Information Processing Unit

The specification table for the information processing unit on which the computation is to be performed must be defined. If the unit already exists, the designer must use the tests and operations built into the unit as the basic building blocks to implement the computation defined in Step 1. If the unit has not been specified, the designer may be able to define the operations and tests that the unit must have in order to implement the desired computation in the most desirable manner. (For the following discussion it is assumed that the unit is already defined.)

Step 3. Define the Algorithm Required to Implement the Computation

Using the operations and tests identified in Step 2, develop an algorithm to represent the computation. This algorithm may be represented in flow-chart form or as a series of statements in the "hardware language" associated with the information processing unit.

Step 4. Create the State Transition Table for the Control Unit

Using the algorithm defined in Step 3, identify the distinct states that the control unit must "remember" and the relationship between the states. Using these states, the values of the status signal, and the values of the control signal, define the state transition table for the control unit.

Step 5. Test the Resulting System to See Whether It Meets Requirements

Define a series of test conditions that exercise all of the possible conditions that might be encountered by the system. Apply these test conditions and verify that the system produces the proper response. If errors are detected modify the design to correct the errors.

As with all programming activities, the creation of a hardware program is a creative process that depends to a considerable extent upon the program designer's past experience and knowledge of the problem being solved. The following discussion presents a number of examples of the design process and illustrates some of the methods that can be used to solve different classes of problems. The only way to build experience, however, is to become involved in the design process. The exercises and home problems in this chapter have been selected so that you may experiment with these design methods and possibly invent a few of your own.

Input and Output Considerations

For the types of digital systems we are discussing, the methods for receiving input information or producing output information are quite straightforward. As explained in Section 2, input information is applied to the digital system in the form of signals. It is assumed that the process generating these signals is synchronized in some manner with the network so that the signals are applied at the proper time. As shown in Figure 9-5, any input signal needed by the information processing unit to carry out a given operation must be present early enough so that they have reached a steady state value before the transfer pulse is applied.

The information processing unit's output is defined by the output expressions. The value of the output signal is a function of the current contents of the registers in the unit, the current value of the input signal, and possibly the current value of the control signal. Here again the output signal is assumed to have reached a steady state value before the current transfer pulse is applied and to hold this value until the transfer has been completed. Formally we consider the current value of the output signal to be defined as the value present when the transfer pulse occurs. In many systems this signal will have reached a steady state value long before this transfer pulse is applied. The output signal, in this case, may be used as soon as the designer is sure that sufficient time has passed to ensure that the signal has reached its steady state value.

When digital networks are interconnected to form large systems, a detailed understanding of the timing relationships that exist between the information exchanged between the networks is of critical importance. We delay these considerations to later chapters. In this chapter it is assumed that all input signals and output signals are present as needed and that any timing problems associated with their generation or use have already been solved. The rest of this section develops techniques that can be used to represent the other three basic programming tasks.

Hardware Programming Language

In theory we could translate an algorithm describing a given computation directly into a state transition table for the control unit that will implement the computation. Such an approach is usually unsatisfactory since the number of tasks involved in such a translation make it quite easy for the designer to make errors. As an intermediate step we can use a hardware language to describe the algorithm and then translate the resulting hardware program into the desired state transition table description.

A large number of hardware description languages have been developed to assist in the various phases of the hardware design process. The symbolic notation presented in the earlier chapters is an example of one such language. This notation was useful when dealing with the information transfers and logical operations that take place inside of a digital network. However, we need a somewhat different notation to describe multistep computations. To provide this notation we now formally define a hardware programming language designed to aid us in representing the tasks that must be carried out by the control unit in a digital system.

Our approach is to first present a formal description of the language and show how the statements in the language are related to the tasks performed by a control unit. We then illustrate how it is used by writing a number of hardware programs using this language. In the following discussion it is assumed that the basic constructs of the language are fixed but that the detailed values of the elements that make up the language are defined by the properties of the information processing unit that must execute the operations described by the language.

Lexical Conventions

A hardware program, as with any program, consists of a sequence of statements defined according to a set of rules that define the language. To write a statement we must formally establish the lexical rules and conventions that are used to form a legal statement. These rules and conventions should be as simple and understandable as possible as well as being closely related to the process they describe. The following discussion provides a description of the language and describes how the statements in the language are related to the operations of a state transition table. The next section shows how this language is used to develop complete hardware programs.

The language is to be used to describe the operation of a control unit. Thus it must represent the same type of information represented by the state transition table.

The states of a transition table represent the internal information we must remember about the computation being performed. The statements that make up a language serve a similar purpose. Thus there is a very close correspondence between the states of the control unit and the statements in the program.

For a given calculation there may be a large number of statements in the program describing the calculation being performed. It is often necessary to reference a particular statement in the program. To do this we introduce the idea of a label.

A *label* is a sequence of from one to seven alphanumeric characters, the first of which must be a letter, which is used to name a statement in a program. For example, some typical labels might be

A1 START LAST A5B2 FINISH

If we wish to talk about the general class of elements we call labels, we use the angle bracket notation ⟨label⟩ to indicate any element from that class.

The input to the control unit is the *status signal S*. The distinct values associated with S are assumed identified by an appropriate set of mnemonics or status vectors. Thus ⟨status value⟩ indicates any possible value that may be assigned to S. For example, typical ⟨status value⟩s might be

Mnemonic form: GT LT NOTEQU EQU XPOS
Vector form: [1, 0, 1] [1, 1, 0]

The form selected depends upon the particular application being programmed.

The output of the control unit is the value of the *control signal T*. This signal causes the information processing unit to take a specific action. The distinct values of T are assumed identified by an appropriate set of mnemonics. Thus ⟨control value⟩ is used to indicate any mnemonic that represents one of the values contained in the control signal set of the information processing unit associated with the system being described by the language. For example, some typical ⟨control value⟩s might be

NOP CLR ADD SUB

An important feature of any programming language is the ability to add comments at appropriate points in the program to describe the task being performed or to indicate the assumptions being made at that point. A *comment*, represented in general as ⟨comment⟩, consists of any sequence of characters preceded by /* and terminated by the end of the line. Comments are used to document the program but do not involve any program action. Comments have the following general form

/*THIS IS A COMMENT
/*COMPUTE THE MAGNITUDE OF X

Statements

Every computation consists of a series of steps. The basic elements defined above are used to build statements that describe these steps. A statement is designed to provide the following information.

1. The operation to be performed when the control unit executes the statement.
2. How to determine the next statement to be executed.

Thus we see that the role of a statement in a hardware program is similar to the role of the ⟨next state⟩/⟨output⟩ entry in a state transition table.

There are two classes of statements, *simple statements* and *compound statements*.

Simple Statements

A simple statement has the following general organization.

⟨label part⟩ ⟨operation part⟩ ⟨next⟩ ⟨comment part⟩

The first component of the statement is the label part indicated by ⟨label part⟩. This component provides a means of attaching a symbolic name or label to the statement, if desired, and corresponds to associating a specific external name to the current state of the control unit that is associated with the labeled statement. The ⟨label part⟩ of a statement is formally defined as

⟨label part⟩ ::= ⟨label⟩: | *null*

where we have used the symbol ::= to indicate that the quantity on the left of ::= is defined in terms of the quantities on the right. In this case ⟨label part⟩ is either a ⟨label⟩ followed by : or ⟨label part⟩ is omitted as indicated by the term *null*. The symbol | is used to indicate that either of the quantities on the right may be used to represent the quantity on the left.

The ⟨operation part⟩ of a statement, which indicates the operation performed when the statement is executed, is defined by

⟨operation part⟩ ::= ⟨control value⟩

This indicates that the ⟨operation part⟩ must always be present and that it must be one of the mnemonics used to represent one of the possible values that can be assigned to the control signal.

The third part of a statement, indicated by the term ⟨next⟩, indicates the next statement to be executed. This provides us with the information that corresponds to the "next state" information of a control unit. The term ⟨next⟩ is defined by

⟨next⟩ ::= ⟨label⟩ | null

This is the "address part" of the statement since it tells us where to find the next statement to evaluate. If ⟨next⟩ is represented by ⟨label⟩, this means that the next statement to be executed is the one that is named by ⟨label⟩. If ⟨next⟩ is null, then the next statement in the sequence is to be executed.

The final part of a simple statement is the ⟨comment part⟩, which is defined by

⟨comment part⟩ ::= ⟨comment⟩ | null

This indicates that a statement may have an attached comment if desired to document the purpose of the statement in the program or to explain what task the designer is trying to carry out with a given segment of code.

Simple statements appear to be quite restricted since they do not use any status information to influence the task that is being performed. However, as we will soon see, large segments of a hardware program are formed from simple statements. The following example illustrates both the form that simple statements can take and how they can be used to describe a complete computational task.

This program illustrates how simple statements can be used to carry out a given task that does not require any decisions during the computation.

```
/* PROGRAM TO REPEATLY ADD A SEQUENCE OF THREE INPUT SIGNALS
/* AND DISPLAY THE RESULTS
SIGAD: CLR                          /* CLEAR ACCUMULATOR
       ADD                          /* ADD FIRST INPUT VALUE
       ADD                          /* ADD SECOND INPUT VALUE
       ADD                          /* ADD THIRD INPUT VALUE
       DISP    SIGAD                /* DISPLAY AND THEN REPEAT
                                    /* CALCULATION
```

In this example the first statement is labeled to provide both a name for the segment of code and an "address" that can be used in a later statement. The next three statements carry out the addition operation. Since they are executed in sequence, there is no need for a ⟨next⟩ value in any of the statements. The final statement displays the value produced by the computation and then transfers control back to the first statement by placing the lable SIGAD in the ⟨next⟩ location. This indicates that the statement labeled SIGAD is to be the next statement executed.

If we wish to build a control unit to implement this hardware program, we must introduce a state for each statement in the program. The first state, Q_A, corresponds to the first statements labeled by SIGAD. The other statements are not labeled. Thus we can assume that they correspond to the states Q_B, Q_C, Q_D, and Q_E. The state transition table corresponding to this program becomes

	State	Next State/Output
This state	Q_A	Q_B/CLR
corresponds to the	Q_B	Q_C/ADD
statement labeled	Q_C	Q_D/ADD
SIGAD	Q_D	Q_E/ADD
	Q_E	Q_A/DISP

In this transition table we see that each step is carried out in sequence until we reach the state Q_E corresponding to the statement

```
DISP    SIGAD
```

At this point we must go back to the beginning of the instruction sequence and repeat the calculation. The entry corresponding to this state accomplishes this by transferring control to state Q_A.

Compound Statements

When writing a hardware program, it is often necessary to group a sequence of statements together and treat them as if they corresponded to a single statement. We can define a *compound statement* as a statement that has the following form

$$\langle\text{compound statement}\rangle ::= \{\langle\text{statement}\rangle$$
$$\vdots$$
$$\langle\text{statement}\rangle\}$$

This definition indicates that a ⟨compound statement⟩ consists of a number of statements grouped together and taken as a unit. The { indicates the beginning and the } indicates the end of the compound statement. If only one statement is included in the compound statement, the {} may be omitted and the compound statement becomes a simple statement.

Compound statements are also statements. Thus it is possible that a ⟨statement⟩ inside of a compound statement is also a ⟨compound statement⟩ or a ⟨case statement⟩, which will be defined next.

In a simple statement the ⟨next⟩ term of the statement indicates the next statement to be executed in the program. The ⟨next⟩ value for a compound statement is defined to be the ⟨next⟩ value of the last statement executed in the compound statement.

The following program segments illustrate the form of a compound statement.

First Example

```
NEW: {ADD          /* ADD TWO NUMBERS AND
      ADD          /* REDUCE BY 1
      DEC    OUT}
```

Note: ⟨next⟩ value is OUT

Second Example

```
OUT: {DISP         /* DISPLAY RESULTS
       {INCA       /* UPDATE POINTERS   Note the included
        INCB       /* A, B, C              compound statement
        INCC}
       DEC         /* COMPLETE PROCESSING
       CLR NEW}
```

Note: ⟨next⟩ value is NEW

The statements presented so far do not provide any way to use the status information generated by the information processing unit. To use this information we must introduce one additional type of statement.

Case Statements

The most complex type of statement in our hardware language is the ⟨case statement⟩. This statement allows us to make decisions based on the value associated with the status signal. A case statement is defined as

⟨case statement⟩ ::= ⟨label part⟩ CASE ⟨status signal⟩

$$\{$$
$$[S1] \ \langle\text{statement}\rangle$$
$$[S2] \ \langle\text{statement}\rangle$$
$$\vdots$$
$$[Sk] \ \langle\text{statement}\rangle$$
$$\text{DEFAULT} \ \langle\text{statement}\rangle$$
$$\}$$

In this statement ⟨status signal⟩ represents the status signal applied to the input of the control unit. The operation to be performed next is defined by the current value of this signal at the time that the case statement is to be executed. The value of the status signal at this point is called the ⟨status value⟩ of the ⟨status signal⟩. When a CASE statement is encountered in a program, the operation to be performed is defined by the current status value of the status signal.

The body of the CASE statement consists of all of the statements between the initial { and the final }. Within the body are a series of statements that are indexed by a term of the form

[⟨status value⟩]

This notation indicates that the specific computational task associated with that statement is to be performed when the status signal has the indicated status value. The following rules govern how the CASE statement is executed.

Execution of a CASE Statement

If ⟨status signal⟩ has a ⟨status value⟩ of Si in the set $\{S1, S2, \ldots, Sk\}$,
then
    the simple or compound statement following [Si] is executed.
If ⟨status value⟩ is not in the set $\{S1, S2, \ldots, Sk\}$,
then
    the simple or compound statement following DEFAULT is
    executed if there is a DEFAULT value.
If there is no DEFAULT value,
then
    the CASE statement is treated as a no operation statement and the next state-
    ment to be executed is the statement immediately after the body of the CASE
    statement.

The ⟨next⟩ value of a CASE statement is selected according to the following rules.

1. When a statement in the body of the CASE statement is selected for execution, the ⟨next⟩ part of the statement defines the current ⟨next⟩ value of the CASE statement and indicates the next statement to be processed when leaving the body of the CASE statement.
2. If ⟨next⟩ is null, control goes to the statement immediately after the body of the CASE statement.

3. If ⟨next⟩ has a value, corresponding to the label of the next statement to be executed, then this statement cannot be located inside the body of the CASE statement containing the statement currently being executed.
4. If no statement is selected for execution within the body of the CASE statement, the ⟨next⟩ value is assumed to be null.

Some typical CASE statements that might be found in a hardware program are:

Example 1

```
CHECK: CASE S
         {
            [XPOS] ADD     B4
            [XNEG] { CMA              /* FORM 2'S
                      INC  B2  }      /* COMPLEMENT OF A
            [XZRO] NOP
         }
```

Example 2

```
TESTA: CASE S1
         {
            [XGT] INCA                    /* INCREASE COUNT

            [XEQ] { ADDA
                    ADDB
                    CASE S2               /* CHECK RESULT
                    {
                       [YPOS]        NOP   OUT1  /* FINISHED
                       [YNEG]        INCB TESTA  /* REPEAT
                    }
                  }

            DEFAULT DECA
         }
```

The above examples indicate a number of interesting properties of the CASE statement. In the first example the CASE statement has a ⟨next⟩ value of B4 if ⟨status value⟩ is XPOS, B2 if ⟨status value⟩ is XNEG, and null if ⟨status value⟩ is XZRO. Example 2 illustrates that the statements in the body of a CASE statement may also include CASE statements. Thus when the ⟨status value⟩ of S1 is XEQ, we go to the compound statement indicated by this value. This compound statement has an embedded CASE statement, which is conditioned on a second ⟨status signal⟩ S2. The way in which CASE statements are used will become clearer as their applications are discussed in the next section.

Implementation of CASE Statements

The state transition table associated with programs that contain one or more CASE statements is somewhat more complex than the table associated with a program without CASE statements. The following examples illustrate how the CASE statements in a given program can be reduced to entries in a transition table. In this discussion it is assumed that the information processing unit has been defined and that the status signal S and the control signal T have been defined as belonging to the following sets.

Status Signal Set S	Control Signal Set T
{XLT, XEQ, XGT}	{ADD, SUB, CLR, DEC, INC, NOP}

The first example involves a program in which all the statements in the CASE statement are simple statements. This is the easiest form of the CASE statement to implement.

```
START:  CLR                  /* START CALCULATION
        ADD
A1:     CASE S               /* CASE STATEMENT
        {                    /* BODY OF STATEMENT
          [XLT]  SUB  OUT
          [XEQ]  INC  A1     /* REPEAT CASE OPERATION
          [XGT]  ADD
        }
        ADD
OUT:    DEC   A1             /* REPEAT CASE OPERATION
```

In this example each statement in the program corresponds to a single state of the control unit. The CASE statement has three parts corresponding to the status values associated with the status signal. Using this observation we can derive the state transition table shown below to implement this program. The initial state is Q_A corresponding to the statement labeled by START.

(Label of corresponding statement)	Input S State	XLT	XEQ	XGT
START	Q_A	Q_B/CLR	Q_B/CLR	Q_B/CLR
	Q_B	Q_C/ADD	Q_C/ADD	Q_C/ADD
A1	Q_C	Q_E/SUB	Q_C/INC	Q_D/ADD
	Q_D	Q_E/ADD	Q_E/ADD	Q_E/ADD
OUT	Q_E	Q_C/DEC	Q_C/DEC	Q_C/DEC

If we examine this table we see that all of the rows, except for the row associated with state Q_C, have identical entries that implement the simple statements associated with the non-CASE statements in the program. The CASE statement is implemented by the row associated with state Q_C. In this row we see that there is a different transition and operation associated with each entry in this row. These entries correspond to the distinct status values found in the CASE statement.

When the CASE statements in a program contain compound statements, the transition table realizing the program is a little more complex. To see how compound statements are implemented consider the following program.

```
START: CLR
NEW:   CASE S                      /*FIRST CASE STATEMENT
       {
          [XLT]    {ADD            /*COMPOUND STATEMENT
                   INC START}      /* NUMBER 1
          DEFAULT {SUB             /*COMPOUND STATEMENT
                   INC             /* NUMBER 2
                   SUB      }
       }
       CASE S                      /*SECOND CASE STATEMENT
       {
          [XGT] ADD NEW            /*BODY OF STATEMENT
       }
       ADD START                   /* REPEAT CALCULATION
```

This program has two CASE statements, which demonstrate a number of different forms that the CASE statement may take. In the first CASE statement we have a number of compound statements associated with the status values. In the transition table given below the realization of this statement is associated with the states with the B subscripts. The second CASE statement uses only one status value. The other status values do not enter into the definition of the statement. This statement is implemented by row Q_C in the transition table. Note that the NOP operation is associated with the status values not included in the body of the CASE statement.

(Label of corresponding statement)	State	Input S — XLT	XEQ	XGT
START	Q_A	Q_B/CLR	Q_B/CLR	Q_B/CLR
NEW	Q_B	Q_{B1}/ADD	Q_{B2}/SUB	Q_{B2}/SUB
	Q_{B1}	Q_A/INC	Q_A/INC	Q_A/INC
	Q_{B2}	Q_{B3}/INC	Q_{B3}/INC	Q_{B3}/INC
	Q_{B3}	Q_C/SUB	Q_C/SUB	Q_C/SUB
	Q_C	Q_D/NOP	Q_D/NOP	Q_B/SUB
	Q_D	Q_A/ADD	Q_A/ADD	Q_A/ADD

These examples illustrate the fact that the hardware program is much easier to understand than the transition table. However, when we must realize the control unit using a logic network, we must use the information in the transition table. This discussion has presented the techniques that can be used to go from a program to a transition table. If necessary, a similar technique can be used to go from a transition table to an equivalent hardware program. A much more interesting problem is that of creating a hardware program to carry out a given computation. This problem is considered in the next section.

EXERCISE

1. Find the transition table for the following hardware programs using the values for S and T given in the example of this section.
   (a)   Program 1   (b)   Program 2

```
        START: ADD                 START: CLR
        A1      CASE S                     ADD
                {                  BGN:     CASE S
                  [XLT]   INC OUT            {
                  [XGT]   DEC OUT               [XLT] {INC
                }                                       ADD
                SUB                                     SUB OUT}
                                            [XEQ]  SUB
        OUT:    CLR   START                 [XGT] {DEC
                                                   CASE S
                                                   {
                                                     [XEQ] {ADD
                                                             INC  BGN}
                                                     DEFAULT { SUB
                                                               DEC
                                                               DEC}
                                                   }|
                                                 }
                                             }
                                             INC
                                    OUT:     CLR BGN
```

4.   THE PROGRAMMING PROCESS

The job of creating a hardware program to describe the operation of a given digital system is quite similar to the process of creating a program in a higher level programming language such as PL/I or Pascal. This section briefly reviews the programming process as it applies to developing programs using the hardware language presented in the last section. Throughout this discussion it is assumed that you are already a competent programmer in a structured high level language such as Pascal or PL/I. Thus the emphasis is on the problem of relating the basic tasks that must be carried out in any program to the structure of the hardware language being used to describe a given digital system.

Autonomous Computations

The simplest type of information processing unit is one that does not generate any status signal. Such a unit is shown in Figure 9-9. This unit receives an input signal X, carries out some form of processing on the input using the internal register A, and then produces an output signal Z. Although there is no status information involved, the control unit must still control the sequence of steps necessary to compute the output Z. The following example illustrates how a hardware language program can be developed to describe a typical computation that might be carried out by a network of this type.

The following design requirement describes a simple calculation that might be carried out using the network shown in Figure 9-9.

Digital Design 1—DD1

Design Requirement—Function Evaluation

Task: Continuously Compute

$$Z := 4*X1 + 2*X2 + X3$$

Input: The input X will provide the sequence of values $X1$, $X2$, $X3$ as needed in the proper order.

Output: The value of Z each time the computation is completed.

The first step in carrying out this design is to develop an algorithm to describe the calculation. This algorithm must use the operations implemented by the information processing unit. Figure 9-10 provides such an algorithm. The next step in developing a transition table for the control unit is to convert the algorithm to the hardware language program given in Figure 9-10b. In forming this program we use the set of mnemonics defined in Table 9-3 as the ⟨control value⟩ set of our language.

The hardware language program is particularly simple since it is constructed entirely of simple statements. Except for the last statement, all statements in the program are executed sequentially. When we execute the last statement, we have completed the calculation of Z and that value can be used as an output. After the execution of that statement is completed, the control unit then prepares to repeat the

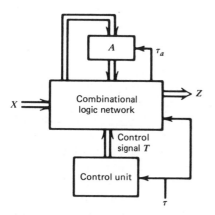

Figure 9-9 A Digital network without a status signal.

Table 9-3 Specification Table for Network of Figure 9-9

Output Expression $Z := A$	
Control Signal *T*	**Transfer Expression**
CLR	$A \leftarrow [0]$
ADD	$A \leftarrow A + X$
MUL2	$A \leftarrow SL(A)$

Note: $SL(A)$—Shift A left 1 bit; also, $\tau = \tau_a$.

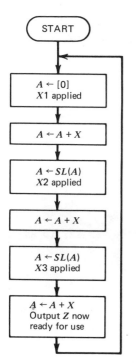

(*a*) General structure of algorithm

```
START:  CLR           /*  START
                      /*  X1 INPUT
        ADD           /*  A := X1
        MUL2          /*  A := 2*X1
                      /*  X2 INPUT
        ADD           /*  A := 2*X1 + X2
        MUL2          /*  A := 4*X1 + 2*X2
                      /*  X3 INPUT
        ADD   START   /*  Z := A
                      /*  REPEAT
```

(*b*) Hardware language program

Note The computed value for *Z* occurs after the ADD START instruction is executed. It is available until the execution of the CLR instruction has been completed.

Figure 9-10 Representation of algorithm for Design 1.

calculation by returning to the statement labeled START. The value of Z during this interval is the value called for in the design specification.

In this example there is no status information so the control unit does not receive any external input. Such a control unit is referred to as an *autonomous control unit* since its behavior is not influenced by any outside information. Autonomous control units are typically found in digital networks that carry out a repetitive computation that does not have to be modified. As shown, an autonomous control unit steps through a sequence of statements until it reaches the last statement. It either stops at that point or reinitializes itself, as in this example, and repeats the computation.

The final step in the design process is to define the state transition table for the control unit. This is an autonomous control unit and the state transition table has a very simple form since the control unit does not need to make any decisions. Each statement in the program corresponds to a state in the control unit and the output associated with that state is given by the ⟨control value⟩ of the statement. The next state is defined by the ⟨next⟩ part of the expression. The complete state transition table for the control unit is given in Table 9-4.

The Basic Decision Process

The last example did not require any status information to perform the desired computation. When a status signal is available to report on the condition of the information being processed, the range of the computations that can be performed is expanded. The next design example illustrates a simple computation where a decision must be made at a number of different points in the calculation.

Digital Design 2—DD2

Design Requirements—Absolute Value Calculation

Task: Compute continually

$$Z := |X1| + |X2| + |X3|$$

Input: The input X will take on the sequence of values $X1$, $X2$, $X3$ as needed.

Output: Two signals Z and C.
         The C flag indicates when an output is ready.

$$C := [0] \quad \text{Output not ready}$$
$$C := [1] \quad \text{Output } Z \text{ is as specified above.}$$

To perform this computation we are to use the information processing unit illustrated in Figure 9-11 and described by the specification table given by Table 9-5.

Table 9-4 State Transition Table for Control
Unit of Design 1

Current State	Next State/Control Signal
Q_A	Q_B/CLA
Q_B	Q_C/ADD
Q_C	$Q_D/\text{MUL2}$
Q_D	Q_E/ADD
Q_E	$Q_F/\text{MUL2}$
Q_F	Q_A/ADD

An algorithm to carry out this computation is illustrated in Figure 9-12. The flow-chart describing the algorithm is shown in Figure 9-12a, while the corresponding hardware program is shown in Figure 9-12b. The ⟨control value⟩ set and the ⟨status value⟩ set for this language is defined by the specification table given in Table 9-5. The new concept introduced is that of making a decision. This occurs at three points in the computation. At each point we use the status information to decide whether the current input is positive, that is, $X \geq 0$, or negative, that is, $X < 0$. On the basis of the results of the test we either ADD X to the partial result or we SUBtract X from the partial result. After doing one or the other of these operations, we go on to the next step in the algorithm. After the third test we carry out the addition/sub-traction called for and also set the C flag to indicate that the calculation of Z has been completed.

The three decisions called for in this flowchart are implemented by three CASE statements in the hardware program. The CASE statement uses the value of S to select the statements that will be executed. The ⟨next⟩ values of all the statements

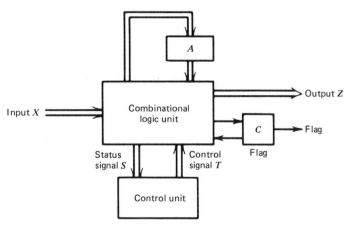

Figure 9-11 An information processing unit with a flag.

Table 9-5 Specification Table for Network of Figure 9-11

| | Output Expression | $Z := A$ |
| | Operation Table | Flag $:= C$ |

Control Signal T	Transfer Expression
CLR	$A \leftarrow [0], C \leftarrow [0]$
ADD	$A \leftarrow A + X$
SUB	$A \leftarrow A - X$
ADDF	$A \leftarrow A + X, C \leftarrow [1]$
SUBF	$A \leftarrow A - X, C \leftarrow [1]$

Status Signal

Value of Status Signal S	Interpretation
XGTE	$X \geq 0$
XLT	$X < 0$

in the body of the first two CASE statements are null, indicating that the next statement to be executed after the CASE statement is the statement following the CASE statement. However, the statements in the body of the last CASE statement have the common ⟨next⟩ value START. This indicates that the next statement to be executed after this CASE statement is the statement labeled START.

The transition table for the control unit described by this program is given by Table 9-6. In this table we see that the case statement provides the information that we need to choose the proper next-state after observing the value of the status signal.

Looping

There are many applications where a given set of statements must be repeated two or more times. In higher level languages a program loop is used to carry out a repetitive calculation. At the hardware level we require the same ability. The general form of a typical loop is shown in Figure 9-13. Before beginning the loop we initialize any parameters needed by the loop. Upon entering the loop we may perform a sequence of operations before testing the status of the information in the information processing unit to see whether the computation is finished. If the test indicates that we are done, we leave the loop. Otherwise we go on and carry out the second sequence of operations. When we reach the end of this sequence, we must go back and start through the loop an additional time.

Loops can take a number of different forms depending upon the tasks performed

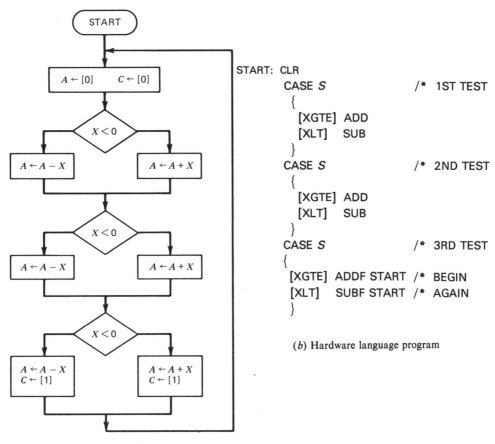

START: CLR
      CASE *S*   /* 1ST TEST
      {
        [XGTE] ADD
        [XLT]   SUB
      }
      CASE *S*   /* 2ND TEST
      {
        [XGTE] ADD
        [XLT]   SUB
      }
      CASE *S*   /* 3RD TEST
      {
        [XGTE] ADDF START /* BEGIN
        [XLT]   SUBF START /* AGAIN
      }

(*b*) Hardware language program

(*a*) General structure of algorithm

Figure 9-12 Representation of algorithm for Design 2.

Table 9-6 Transition Table for Control Unit

Status S State	[XGTE]	[XLT]
Q_A	Q_B/CLR	Q_B/CLR
Q_B	Q_C/ADD	Q_C/SUB
Q_C	Q_D/ADD	Q_D/SUB
Q_D	Q_A/ADDF	Q_A/SUBF

by the computational sequences I and II. There are several ways to implement a loop. However each loop can be represented by the following general form.

```
    {⟨statement⟩                    /*  Statements to
         .                          /*  initialize the
         .                          /*  loop.
      ⟨statement⟩}
LOOP: {⟨statement⟩                  /*  Computation Sequence
         .                          /*  Number I
         .                          /*  and
      ⟨statement⟩}                  /*  Set conditions of test
      CASE S                        /*  Use status information
                                    /*  to make test
        {                           /*  Body of CASE statement
          [S1] {⟨statement⟩         /*  Exit condition satisfied
             .                      /*  execution transferred
             .                      /*  outside loop by last
            ⟨statement⟩}            /*  statement associated with S1.
          [S2] {⟨statement⟩         /*  Exit condition not
              ⟨statement⟩           /*  satisfied. Computation
                .                   /*  Sequence II continues
                                    /*  to carry out loop computations
              ⟨statement⟩           /*  Last statement associated
              ⟨statement⟩}          /*  with S2 transfers execution
                                    /*  to statement LOOP.
        }                           /*  End of CASE statement and
                                    /*  end of body of loop.
```

As before, groups of statements enclosed in { } represent a compound statement. The last statement found in a compound statement has the responsibility of defining where the next statement to be executed is located. We assume that $S1$ is the value of the status signal that indicates that the loop computation is completed. The compound statement associated with $S1$ must complete any calculations necessary to terminate the loop and then transfer control to the next part of the program. If S has a value of $S2$, then the loop calculation continues. The compound statement associated with $S2$ carries out the computation sequence II. The last expression in this compound statement must transfer control back to the statement labeled with LOOP.

To illustrate how a loop may be used consider the system shown in Figure 9-14. This system is designed to act as a timer. The timing cycle starts when the register CNT is set to [0] and the flag register C is set to [1]. When the unit under test detects that C is [1], it starts its operation and at the same time sets its flag D to [0]. As long as D is [0] the value stored in CNT is incremented by 1 each time a

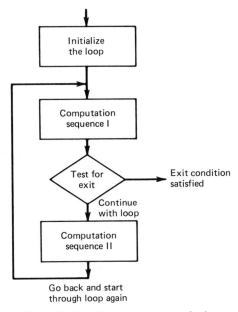

Figure 9-13 General structure of a loop.

transfer pulse occurs. This keeps up until the value of D is set to [1], indicating that the timing interval is over. At this point the timing measurement has been completed and the end of the timing cycle is indicated by resetting C to [0]. The value stored in CNT at this point is a measure of the amount of time required by the device under test to perform its duties. This network can be described by the following design requirements.

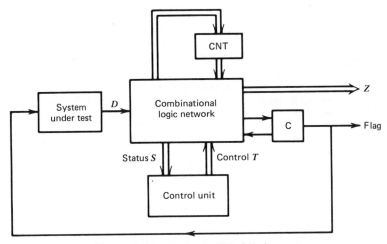

Figure 9-14 A simple digital timing system.

Digital Design 3—DD3

Design Requirements—Digital Timer Network

Task: Compute the number of clock pulses that occur while the input signal to the timing network is [0]. The count is to start when the timer flag C is set to [1] and end when the input signal goes to [1].

Input: The signal D, which will have a value of [0] or [1].

Output: Two signals Z and C

$C := [0]$ Test not running. Output Z indicates value of last count CNT.

$C := [1]$ Test is running. Output Z is not defined.

Table 9-7 is the specification table for the timer network. Using this table we define the program given in Figure 9-15 to carry out the desired task. Note that in this program we use a loop to carry out the timing computation. As long as we are in the loop we ignore the output Z since it is not meaningful at this point. When we leave the loop the output Z corresponds to the number of transfer pulses received while the system being measured was operational. The fact that the value of Z is meaningful is indicated by the fact that C has a value of [0].

In particular note how the hardware program in Figure 9-15b uses labels to control the transfer of control from one statement to the next. Using this program we can define the state transition table for the control unit as shown in Table 9-8.

This section has briefly reviewed the techniques needed to develop hardware programs for a wide variety of digital networks. They are very similar to those we are

Table 9-7   Specification Table for Timer Unit

	Output Expression $Z := $ **CNT**		
Control Expressions		**Status Signal**	
Control Signal T	**Transfer Expression**	**Value of S**	**Meaning**
STCNT	CNT ← [0] , C ← [1]	$D0$	$D = [0]$
INC	CNT ← CNT + [1]	$D1$	$D = [1]$
STOPC	C ← [0]		
NOP	No operation		

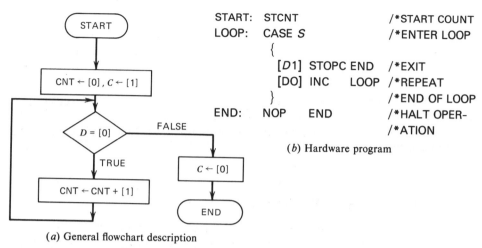

START: STCNT /*START COUNT
LOOP: CASE S /*ENTER LOOP
{
    [D1] STOPC END /*EXIT
    [DO] INC LOOP /*REPEAT
}   /*END OF LOOP
END: NOP END /*HALT OPER-
                 /*ATION

(b) Hardware program

(a) General flowchart description

Figure 9-15 Hardware program for timing unit.

already familiar with from designing programs in a high level language such as Pascal or PL/I. In the next section we consider how these results can be used to design somewhat more complex systems.

EXERCISES

1. Using the information processing unit described in Figure 9-11, develop a hardware program to compute

$$Z := 2*(X1 - X2)$$

Set the flag C to [1] when the output is available for use. The system should compute Z continuously. You may expand the operation table of Table 9-5 if needed.

Table 9-8 State Transition Table for Timer Control Unit

State	Status S [D0]	[D1]
Q_A	Q_B / STCNT	Q_B /STCNT
Q_B	Q_C / STOPC	Q_B/INC
Q_C	Q_C / NOP	Q_C / NOP

2. The testing system shown in Figure 9-14 is to be modified so that it can be used to measure the interval between the occurrence of two pulses. Pulses occur at random. When the first pulse occurs it appears at the D input of the timing system. At that point the system must start counting until the second pulse occurs. When the second pulse is detected the counting stops and the C flag is set to [0] to indicate that the current count is the number of transfer pulses that have occurred between the first and the second pulse. This process is to be repeated continuously. Design the hardware program for the control unit of the timer network.

5. DESIGN OF DIGITAL SYSTEMS

Designing digital systems is a much more complex activity than designing combinational logic networks. One of the main reasons for this is that there are usually a large number of systems that can be defined to carry out a given task and the designer must be able to identify these possible systems and select the "best" one to do the job. Unfortunately there are no algorithms that tell the designer how to find all of the possible systems or how to evaluate them to see which one is the most desirable.

Digital system design is a heuristic process that relies heavily on the experience and know-how of the designer. This section presents a discussion of the various stages of the design process and indicates some of the techniques that can be used to handle the problems encountered at each step. The examples presented in this section and in later chapters indicate some of the different approaches that can be used to carry out a design. Although these examples will provide some understanding of the design process, you will find that the only way to develop your own design ability is to actually carry out a number of designs.

Problem Specification

The first stage of any design process consists of developing a detailed description of the information processing task and selecting an algorithm that provides a detailed description of the steps that must be performed to carry out that task. For all but the simplest task, there will be more than one possible algorithm.

Sometimes the algorithm is suggested by the task to be performed, while at other times the designer must develop special data handling methods so that the task can be carried out within certain operational or equipment constraints imposed on the designer by other system requirements. For example, the designer must take into consideration such factors as the types of logic units that might be used in constructing the system, the operations that these units can perform, their operating speed, and the way that the information is encoded.

After one or more possible algorithms are developed, the designer must decide which algorithm best meets the set of design conditions imposed by the problem specifications. This decision will probably involve minimizing some "cost" criterion that balances the need for special hardware features against the cost of implementing these features and the time required to perform the information processing task. Sometimes it is not possible, at this stage, to select a single algorithm that is obviously better than all other algorithms. In that situation more than one algorithm is retained for additional evaluation.

Initial System Organization

Each algorithm implies a general sequence of information processing steps. The next stage in the design process consists of actually specifying the digital system that will carry out these steps. The system will be made up of one or more digital networks of the form we have been investigating. For each network we must decide upon the specific tasks that must be performed by that network. This information can then be used to develop a formal specification describing the operations that that unit must perform and the "hardware program" that describes its behavior.

Each algorithm carried over from the first stage of the design process will suggest one or more system organizations. All such designs are evaluated and one is selected for further development. The goal of this selection is to obtain the system that comes nearest to the given design goals within the constraints imposed by costs and other performance requirements. A single candidate system organization is usually selected at this point since the following stages of the design process involve a considerable amount of detailed design effort. However, as the detailed design progresses we may find that our initial selection is not suitable. When this happens we must return to this stage of the design process and consider some of the alternate designs that were initially rejected.

Digital Network Specification

The formal specification of a digital network involves two tasks. First we must specify the information processing unit and then, using the operations provided by this unit, define the control unit. At the system level of design we have identified the signals that are received by the network, the signals that the network must produce, and the relationship that must exist between these signals. These specifications form the starting point of the network design process.

At this point it is necessary to make the following decisions

1. How is the information to be stored while it is being processed?
2. What basic information transfer and processing operations are needed to realize the desired computations?
3. What tests must be made upon the information as it is being processed?

A number of possible organizations may be identified at this stage. The designer is responsible for selecting the organization that appears to best satisfy the design requirements. When this point has been reached, the designer can define an initial specification table for the information processing unit.

The next step in the design process is to use the information contained in the specification table to create the hardware program necessary to carry out the required computations. In performing this step it may be found that the initial design selected for the information processing unit may have overlooked one or more needed operations or may have some feature that makes it difficult to define an acceptable program. This information can be used to redefine or modify the specification of this information processing unit. Finally an acceptable hardware program will be developed. This program is used to complete the design by defining the transition table for the control unit.

Final System Realization

When we reach this point in the design process all of the operational characteristics of the networks of the system have been defined. Our final task is to reduce this information to a logic level design that shows how the system will be realized using combinational logic circuits and registers. Since this phase of the design process uses techniques of the type presented in previous chapters, we will not consider this step here.

A Serial Line Receiver

One common task encountered in digital system design is that of transmitting information from one part of a system to another. As long as the source and the destination of the information are close together this can be done by a simple parallel transfer operation. However, when they are widely separated the transmission process must be considered in greater detail.

If the source and the destination locations are separated by large distances, from a few feet to hundreds of miles, it becomes very expensive to transmit data in parallel. For example, if 8-wire cable cost 25¢ a foot and we had to transmit an 8-bit signal 500 feet, it would cost $125 just for the cable to connect the source to the destination. Except for very special cases, such a cost would be unacceptable. The solution to this problem is to use serial rather than parallel transmission techniques, which use less costly 2-wire cable. To do this we require a standard way to encode the signal for transmission.

Figure 9-16 illustrates a simple serial transmission system. The source and the receiver are connected together by a transmission channel that transmits a single bit at a time. Since these two devices are physically separated, all information that is exchanged between them must be encoded in a standard manner. The source must be able to notify the receiver when data are to be transmitted and the receiver must be able to detect when the transmitted data have been received. International standards have been established to accomplish this requirement.

A commonly used standard is the Electronics Industry Association (EIA) RS232C standard, which defines both the electrical and the logical specifications for the bit-serial transmission of digital information. This is a very detailed document. For this discussion we will assume that the information to be transmitted has the form shown

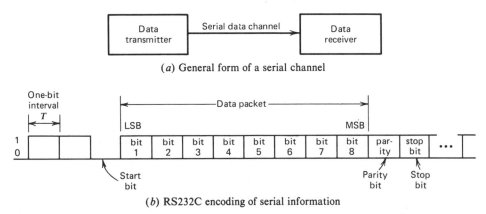

(*a*) General form of a serial channel

(*b*) RS232C encoding of serial information

Figure 9-16 Serial transmission of digital information.

in Figure 9-16*b*. Although this is a simplification of the RS232C standard, it retains all of the logical features that are important in using this standard for information transmission in a digital system.

It is assumed that the transmitted signal is divided into a series of one-bit intervals of length T. During each interval the transmitter will send a 1 or a 0. It is the responsibility of the receiver to detect the value of the signal transmitted in each interval. To transmit information the transmitter uses the following conventions, which are illustrated in Figure 9-16*b*.

1. If no information is being transmitted, the transmitter sends a continuous sequence of 1's. This is a protective feature. If the receiver does not see this sequence, it knows that something is wrong with the transmission channel and that corrective action should be taken.
2. The start of transmission of a data item is indicated by a transition from the sequence of 1 bits to a 0 bit. The first 0 bit in the transmission is called the *start bit*, and it tells the receiver to be ready for the data bits.
3. The number of data bits is prespecified when the system is designed. For this system it is assumed that eight data bits are transmitted. The first data bit is considered to be the least significant bit (LSB) and the eighth bit is considered to be the most significant bit (MSB).
4. To provide some error detection capability a *parity bit* is transmitted after the eight data bits. This system uses the convention that the parity bit is set to 1 to make the total number of 1 bits transmitted, including the parity bit, be an even number. This is called *even parity*.
5. One 1 bit is then transmitted to indicate that the transmission of the eight bits has been completed. This bit is called a *stop bit*.
6. At this point the transmitter may start to transmit the next eight bits of information or it may continually transmit 1's, indicating that nothing more is ready for transmission.

Our design goal is to develop a digital system that will be able to receive digital information encoded as described above. The system must satisfy the following requirements.

Design Requirements—Serial Receiver

Task: Receive serial information encoded using an RS232C type encoding. Output the received information or an indication that no information is ready. If a parity error is detected, the received information is available as an output, but a parity error signal indicates that an error has been detected.

Input: The serial input signal X from the transmission channel. $X := [x_1]$

Output: Three signals Z, C, and P

$P := [0]$ No parity error detected
$:= [1]$ Parity error detected

$C := [0]$ Data not ready. Z not defined.
$:= [1]$ Data received. Z has the value of the received data.

C and P are set to [0] upon reception of the start bit indicating the start of transmission of next data item.

Figure 9-17 shows the general organization selected for the receiver. The information processing unit contains the four registers:

R—The Received Data Register: eight bits

C—The Received Data Flag Register: one bit

P—The Parity Error Flag Register: one bit

CNT—Bit Counter Register: four bits

The input to the receiver is a single one-bit input signal X corresponding to the information received from the transmission channel. The receiver generates three output signals.

$Z := R$ The output of the Received Data Register
C The output of the Received Data Flag Register
P The output of the Parity Error Flag Register

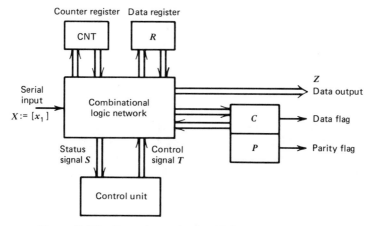

Figure 9-17 General organization of the serial line receiver.

The control unit must synchronize the operation of the receiver to the pattern of the information being received. The status signal S must serve two purposes. It must indicate the value of the received signal from the transmission line, and it must indicate when eight bits have been received by the data register. The operation of the information processing unit is defined by the specification table defined in Table 9-9.

Table 9-9 Specification Table for Serial Receiver

	Operation Table

Control Signal T	**Transfer Operations**
CLR	$CNT \leftarrow [0] \quad C \leftarrow [0] \quad P \leftarrow [0]$
STC	$C \leftarrow [1]$
STCP	$C \leftarrow [1] \quad P \leftarrow [1]$
READ	$R \leftarrow SR(X, R) \quad CNT \leftarrow CNT + [1]$
NOP	No operation

Note: $SR(X, R)$—Shift Right

	Status Table

Component of S	$S := [s_1, s_2]$ **Relational Expression Defining Component**
s_1	$s_1 := x_1$
s_2	$s_2 := (CNT = [8])$

Using the information in this table and the stated requirements for the tasks that the receiver must perform, we can develop the general algorithm shown in Figure 9-18 to describe the operation of the receiver. From this algorithm we then write the hardware program given in Figure 9-19 to implement this algorithm.

The receiver observes the input from the channel until the occurrence of the start bit is detected. This indicates the start of data transmission. The counter is cleared and the system is ready to load the received data into the data register and to keep track of the information needed to compute the parity value at the end of the data packet. After the eight data bits are received, the receiver checks the received parity bit against the expected value generated while the packet was being received. If the two values are the same, there is no parity error and P remains [0] while C is set to

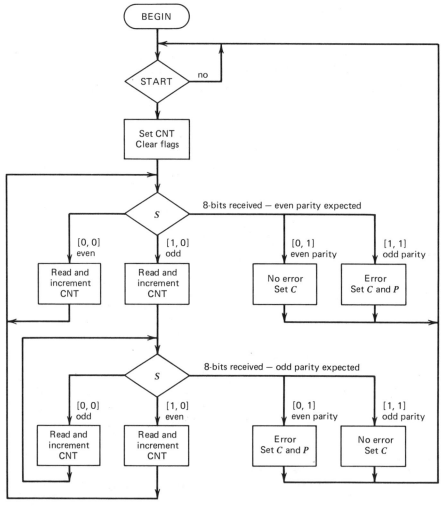

Figure 9-18 Algorithm for serial receiver operation.

```
BEGIN: CASE S                          /* LOOK FOR START BIT
       {
          [0, 0] CLR    EVEN           /* START BIT FOUND
          [0, 1] CLR    EVEN           /* START BIT FOUND
          [1, 0] NOP    BEGIN          /* STILL LOOKING
          [1, 1] NOP    BEGIN          /* STILL LOOKING
       }
EVEN:  CASE S                          /* READING INPUT EVEN
       {                               /* NUMBER 1 BITS RECEIVED
          [0, 0] READ   EVEN           /* 0 DATA BIT RECEIVED
          [1, 0] READ   ODD            /* 1 DATA BIT RECEIVED
          [0, 1] STC    BEGIN          /* 0 PARITY BIT. EVEN PARITY
                                       /* NO PARITY ERROR.
          [1, 1] STCP   BEGIN          /* 1 PARITY BIT. ODD PARITY
       }                               /* PARITY ERROR.
ODD:   CASE S                          /* READING INPUT ODD
       {                               /* NUMBER 1 BITS RECEIVED
          [0, 0] READ   ODD            /* 0 DATA BIT RECEIVED
          [1, 0] READ   EVEN           /* 1 DATA BIT RECEIVED
          [0, 1] STCP   BEGIN          /* 0 PARITY BIT. ODD PARITY
                                       /* PARITY ERROR.
          [1, 1] STC    BEGIN          /* 1 PARITY BIT. EVEN PARITY
       }                               /* NO PARITY ERROR.
```

Figure 9-19   Hardware language program for serial receiver.

[1]. The output Z in this case is assumed to be correct. If there is a parity error, both C and P are set to [1]. The output Z corresponds to the received data, but the fact that the P flag is set indicates that it is probably in error. The outputs remain constant until the next start bit is detected and the overall process is repeated.

In this design we have decided to use a special counter in the receiver to count the number of data bits received. This could also have been done in the control unit, but it would have made the control unit's task somewhat more complex. We did decide, however, to make the control unit responsible for computing parity since all that it has to do is remember whether an even or odd number of 1 data bits have been received at any given point in the transmission of the data bits. This task is easily accomplished without increasing the general complexity of the control unit. Using the information contained in the hardware program, our final task is to define the transition table for the control unit. This is done in Table 9-10.

At this point in the design we have completely defined the functional behavior of both the information processing and the control units. The last step in the design process is to realize these units using appropriate logic networks. The techniques that we use to realize the information processing unit have already been discussed in detail, so we leave that task as an exercise. The techniques that may be used to realize the control unit are discussed in the next chapter. Thus we leave the final design of this unit until later.

Table 9-10 Transition Table for Serial Receiver Controller

State \ Status S	[0, 0]	[0, 1]	[1, 0]	[1, 1]
Q_A	Q_B/CLR	Q_B/CLR	Q_A/NOP	Q_A/NOP
Q_B	Q_B/READ	Q_A/STC	Q_C/READ	Q_A/STCP
Q_C	Q_C/READ	Q_A/STCP	Q_B/READ	Q_A/STC

Design of a Digital Multiplier

It is quite easy to design a logic network to add two binary numbers in a single step. However, if we were to try to use standard logic design techniques to build a combinational logic network to multiply two binary numbers in a single step, we would find that, in general, the resulting network would be much too complex for normal applications. Therefore, multiplication is almost always carried out using a multistep algorithm. We now consider how one such algorithm can be implemented. This example presents a simple way to multiply two r-bit positive binary numbers. The references at the end of this chapter present a number of other algorithms and networks that can be used to carry out the multiplication process.

A digital multiplier performs multiplication by carrying out a series of shifting and addition operations. However, before we develop the design requirements for the hardware multiplier, let us investigate how we would carry out a manual multiplication using paper and pencil. The steps of this process are shown in Table 9-11.

This example illustrates the basic features that we must account for in designing a multiplier. First we note that if we are multiplying two r-bit numbers the result has at most $2r$ digits. Second we note that there must be a relative shift of one bit between each partial product. Finally, we note that the ith partial product is set to zero if the ith bit of the multiplier is zero.

In the above example we first formed all the partial products and then added them together as the last step in the formation of the product. However, it is easier to construct a digital network if we do not wait until we form all of the partial products before we carry out the addition operations. One way to modify the multiplication

Table 9-11 An Example of Manual Multiplication of Two Binary Numbers

1 1 0 1 0	multiplicand	
1 0 1 1 0	multiplier	Multiplier digit
0 0 0 0 0	1st partial product	0
1 1 0 1 0	2nd partial product	1
1 1 0 1 0	3rd partial product	1
0 0 0 0 0	4th partial product	0
1 1 0 1 0	5th partial product	1
1 0 0 0 1 1 1 1 0 0	product = sum of partial products	

process is shown in Table 9-12. In this multiplication process we assume that there is a register, which we will call an *accumulator register,* that can be used to hold the partial sums that are formed during the computation.

Examining Table 9-12 we see that as each new partial product is formed, it is added to the partial sum already in the accumulator. We also note that the $(i + 1)$th partial product is either zero if $y_i = 0$ or equal to the multiplicand shifted i bits to the left if $y_i = 1$.

There are a number of ways that the multiplication operation can be implemented. Before we make a final design decision we must explore some of the advantages and limitations of the different methods. The simplest realization of a multiplier is sketched in Figure 9-20. In this arrangement the multiplier is placed in the Q register, the multiplicand is placed in the r rightmost bits of the M register, and the accumulator register A is set to [0]. The multiplication then takes place according to the algorithm given by the flow chart of Figure 9-20b. This method of multiplication, which is a direct implementation of the operations shown in Table 9-12, is simple and easy to control. However, it makes very inefficient use of the registers. For example, the multiplicand register is a double-length register even though it only holds a single-length operand.

A second method of realizing a multiplier is shown in Figure 9-21. In this realization the accumulator register A has $r + 1$ bits, A_0 through A_r, and the multiplier register has r bits. The leftmost bit, A_0, of the accumulator is needed to handle overflow information during the addition sequence.

The accumulator and multiplier registers do double duty. Instead of shifting the contents of the multiplicand register to the left after we have formed the partial sum, we shift the contents of the accumulator and multiplier registers, treated as a single $2r + 1$ bit register, to the right. In particular the contents of the bit at the right end of the accumulator register A is transferred to the bit at the left end of the multiplier register Q. Thus, we use the multiplier register for the double purpose of holding the

Table 9-12 Multiplication Using Partial Product Accumulation

1 1 0 1 0	multiplicand $= x_4x_3x_2x_1x_0$
1 0 1 1 0	multiplier $\quad = y_4y_3y_2y_1y_0$
0 0 0 0 0 0 0 0 0 0	initial contents of accumulator
0 0 0 0 0	bit y_0 is 0, 1st partial product zero
0 0 0 0 0 0 0 0 0 0	first partial sum
1 1 0 1 0	bit y_1 is 1, 2nd partial product
0 0 0 0 1 1 0 1 0 0	second partial sum
1 1 0 1 0	bit y_2 is 1, 3rd partial product
0 0 1 0 0 1 1 1 0 0	third partial sum
0 0 0 0 0	bit y_3 is 0, 4th partial product
0 0 1 0 0 1 1 1 0 0	fourth partial sum
1 1 0 1 0	bit y_4 is 1, 5th partial product
1 0 0 0 1 1 1 1 0 0	final product = fifth partial sum

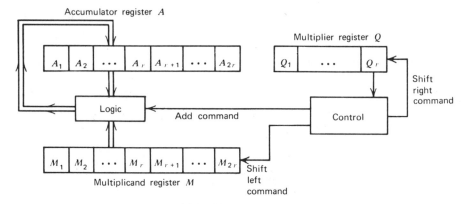

(a) Multiplier organization

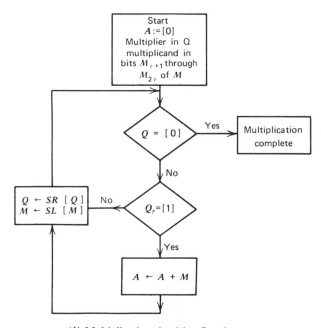

(b) Multiplication algorithm flowchart

Figure 9-20 Organization and operation of simple multiplier.

multiplier at the beginning of the operation and for holding the r least significant bits of the product at the end of the multiplication process. Except for this change in the direction of information transfer, the operation of the multiplier shown in Figure 9-21 is the same as the operation of the one shown in Figure 9-20. The r highest order bits of the final answer are found in the r rightmost bits of A and the r lowest order bits are contained in Q. The price that we must pay for this saving in register space is that every multiplication requires r shift-right operations, whereas in the

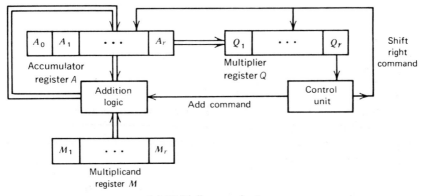

(a) Multiplier organization

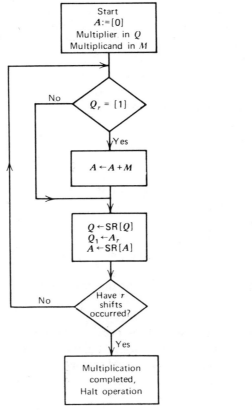

(b) Multiplication algorithm flowchart

Figure 9-21   Multiplier making more efficient use of registers.

algorithm in Figure 9-20 we can stop the multiplication operation any time that we detect that the multiplier register contains [0]. In that case the multiplication process shown in Figure 9-20 may require anywhere from 0 to r shift-right operations.

At this point in the design process we have identified two possible multiplication techniques and we must select one to implement. The two factors that influence this decision are:

1. The multiplication process shown in Figure 9-20 will, on the average, be the faster algorithm since it terminates as soon as $Q = [0]$. The control unit will be simpler since it does not have to count the number of shifts. This method, however, requires larger registers.
2. The multiplication process shown in Figure 9-21 will be the slower algorithm since we must always have r shifts. This means that the system must be able to count the number of shifts that occur. Its advantage is that it requires smaller registers.

At this point the decision between the two multiplication techniques is not clear. Thus we must consider how the multiplication unit is to be used. Normally a multiplier is part of a larger system where the sizes of the registers are fixed. This usually means that the algorithm shown in Figure 9-21 would be selected since it can be implemented more easily using standard register sizes. Thus at this point we decide to use the second algorithm to complete our multiplier design. The following design requirements describe our design goal.

Design Requirements — Digital Multiplier

Task: Multiply two r-bit numbers to obtain a $2r$-bit result.

Input: The multiplier is placed in the Q register and the multiplicand is placed in the M register.

Output: The output Z is to be the $2r$-bit result.

Using this requirement, and the previous discussion, our first attempt at designing this network has the form shown in Figure 9-22. This figure gives both the organization of the proposed network and the specification table for the information processing unit. Figure 9-23 indicates the hardware program that describes the multiplication process.

To implement the multiplier using the system shown in Figure 9-22 we must use the control unit to count the number of shifts that have been made. As shown in Figure 9-23, we do this by using a straight line program that has r decision points. The resulting transition table for the control unit is shown next to the program.

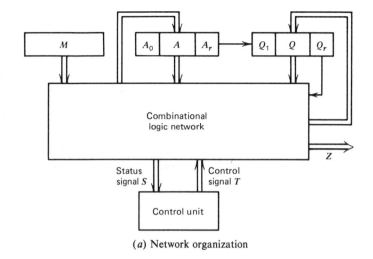

(*a*) Network organization

Operation Table

Control Signal *T*	Transfer Expression	Status Signal
NOP	No operation	$S := [s_1]$
CLR	$A \leftarrow [0]$	$s_1 := [Q_r]$
		Result
ADD	$A \leftarrow A + M$	MSB := A
		LSB := Q
SHIFT	$A \leftarrow SR(A)$ $Q \leftarrow SR(A_r, Q)$	$Z := [MSB, LSB]$

(*b*) Specification table for multiplier

Figure 9-22   Digital network to realize a multiplier.

Although the program and the transition table both look very complex, the actual design of the control unit is quite easy. Basically the repetition of the same test a fixed number of times implies that the control unit must have some type of counter that counts the number of times a given operation, or sequence of operations, has been executed. If we wish to explicitly show that a counting process is an inherent part of the computation, we can use the modified system shown in Figure 9-24. In this case we have included an identifiable counter as part of the system. The resulting specification table for the system must then be modified to provide for the servicing of the counter. The new specification table is also shown in Figure 9-24.

By including a counter external to the control unit we can create a simpler hardware program as shown in Figure 9-25. In this case we have transformed the straight line program into one with a simple loop. Normally we would think that the best way to use the counter would be to initialize it to zero and then count up until the counter reached the final value. This approach requires that we compare the value of the counter to the desired final value. If that value changes we must have a way

START: CLR   /*CLEAR A
     CASE S   /*PROCESS 1ST
     {   /*BIT OF MULTIPLIER
       [0] SHIFT
       [1] {ADD
            SHIFT}
     }
     CASE S   /*PROCESS 2ND
     {   /*BIT OF MULTIPLIER
       [0] SHIFT
       [1] {ADD
            SHIFT}
     }
       ⋮
     CASE S   /*PROCESS RTH
     {   /*BIT OF MULTIPLIER
       [0] SHIFT
       [1] {ADD
            SHIFT}

END: NOP   END
/*MULTIPLICATION COMPLETE

(a) Hardware program

Transition Table

State $\backslash$ S	[0]	[1]
QA	QB/CLR	QB/CLR
QB1	QB2/SHIFT	QB1A/ADD
QB1A	−/−	QB2/SHIFT
QB2	QB3/SHIFT	QB2A/ADD
QB2A	−/−	QB3/SHIFT
⋮		
QBR	QC/SHIFT	QBRA/ADD
QBRA	−/−	QC/SHIFT
QC	QC/NOP	QC/NOP

(b) Transition table

Figure 9-23 Realization of multiplication operation.

to change the test. Another approach is to initially set the counter to the number of times that we wish to go through the loop and count down by one each time we go through the loop. When we reach zero we know that we have executed the loop the desired number of times. In this case the test is always to see whether the count is zero no matter what initial value was placed in the counter. This is the approach used in Figure 9-25. With this hardware program the transition table for the control unit takes on the very simple form shown in Figure 9-25b.

At this point we have completed our design of the multiplier at the system level and all that is left to do is to design the logic circuitry necessary to realize the system. This is left as a home problem.

EXERCISES

1. Design the information processing unit needed to realize the serial receiver shown in Figure 9-17.

2. Design the hardware program for a multiplier based on the algorithm shown in Figure 9-20. Do it both with and without the use of a separate counter.

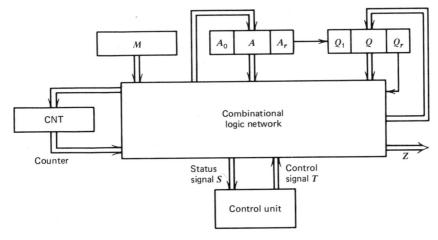

(*a*) Revised system organization

Operation Table

Control Signal T	Transfer Expression
NOP	No operation
CLRSC	$A \leftarrow [0]$ $CNT \leftarrow [r]$
ADD	$A \leftarrow A + M$
SHIFT	$A \leftarrow SR(A)$ $Q \leftarrow SR(A_r, Q)$ $CNT \leftarrow CNT - [1]$

Status Signal
$$S := [s_1, s_2]$$
$$s_1 := [Q_r]$$
$$s_2 := (CNT = [0])$$
Result
$$MSB := A$$
$$LSB := Q$$
$$Z := [MSB, LSB]$$

(*b*) Specification table for multiplier

Figure 9-24   Digital network to realize a multiplier using a counter.

6.   SUMMARY

In this chapter we have investigated, in an introductory manner, the methods that can be used to design a digital system that will carry out a multiple-step computational task. We have seen that the design process consists of defining the basic operations needed to perform a given computation and then designing an information processing unit to carry out these operations. Once we have the information processing unit, we can complete the design process by defining a hardware program that indicates the sequence in which the operations are to be applied to perform the desired computation. The design is then completed by using the program to define the transition table for the control unit that will mechanically generate the commands necessary to have the information processing unit perform the desired operations in the desired sequence.

The methods for designing the information processing unit have been discussed in detail in the previous chapters. These same techniquess can be used to design the

```
START: CLRSC
LOOP:   CASE S
        {
            [0, 0]  SHIFT LOOP   /*STILL
            [1, 0]  {ADD          /*MULTIPLYING
                     SHIFT LOOP}  /*END
            [0, 1]  NOP
            [1, 1]  NOP

        }
END:    NOP  END                 /*FINISHED
```

(*a*) Hardware program

Transition Table

State \ S	[0, 0]	[0, 1]	[1, 0]	[1, 1]
QA	QB/CLRSC	QB/CLRSC	QB/SLRSC	QB/SLRSC
QB	QB/SHIFT	QC/NOP	QB2/ADD	QC/NOP
QB2	–/–	–/–	QB/SHIFT	–/–
QC	–/–	QC/NOP	–/–	QC/NOP

(*b*) Transition table for multipliter control unit

Figure 9-25 Realization of multiplication program with a counter.

control unit. However, a control unit is a special case of a more general type of digital network called a sequential network. The next chapter will develop the properties of these networks and illustrate a number of standard ways in which they can be realized.

Reference Notation

The references listed include a wide range of topics related to the material presented in this chapter. Some of the techniques that can be used to represent the higher level operation of digital systems are presented in References 1, 3, and 4. References 3 and 4 present a general discussion of how various arithmetic operations can be performed using logic networks. Reference 2 discusses some of the trade-offs made during a digital system design, while Reference 5 discusses the general design process from the system module viewpoint.

REFERENCES

1. Bell, G. C., and Newell, A. (1971), *Computer Structures: Readings and Examples*. McGraw-Hill, New York.

2. Bell, G. C., Mudge, J. C., and McNamara, J. E. (1978), *Computer Engineering—A DEC View of Hardware Systems Design.* Digital Press, Bedford, Mass.
3. Hellerman, H. (1973), *Digital Computer System Principles* (second edition). McGraw-Hill, New York.
4. Hill, F. J., and G. R. Peterson (1978), *Digital Systems: Hardware Organization and Design* (second edition). Wiley, New York.
5. Winkel, D., and Prosser, F. (1980), *The Art of Digital Design: An Introduction to Top-Down Design.* Prentice-Hall, Englewood Cliffs, N.J.

HOME PROBLEMS

1. Design a serial line transmitter that will transmit an 8-bit data signal to the serial line receiver shown in Figure 9-17. Indicate how the parity bit is computed and included in the information transmitted.

2. Design the logic circuits necessary to realize the digital multiplier shown in Figure 9-24.

3. Design a hardware multiplier that can multiply two numbers if the numbers are represented in 2's complement form.

4. Design a hardware multiplier that can multiply two numbers if the numbers are represented in sign-magnitude form.

5. Design a hardware divider that will divide two r-bit positive numbers.

10

ANALYSIS AND DESIGN OF SYNCHRONOUS SEQUENTIAL NETWORKS

1. INTRODUCTION

In Chapter 9 we saw that the control unit in a digital system played a very important part in the overall operation of the system. A control unit is a special case of a more general class of digital networks that have the ability to store information temporarily during their operation and then use that information to influence their future behavior. Networks in this class are called *sequential networks*.

The behavior of the control units discussed previously was easily related to the basic information processing tasks that were to be performed. We saw that the control unit received input information, by way of the status signals, and then produced an output control signal T, which was a function of both the current value of S and the past behavior of the unit. Behavior of this type is common to a number of design problems beside the design of control units already considered.

When a sequential network is designed from clocked flip-flops, the state of the network can change only when a transfer pulse or clock pulse is applied. Such a network is called a *synchronous sequential network*. Between pulses logical operations can be performed on the input and stored information, but there is no change in the information stored in the information storage elements.

In Chapter 8 we concentrated on the basic operating characteristics of the different types of flip-flops and the registers that could be constructed from these elements. We now generalize this discussion. First, we show how the operation of a given sequential network can be analyzed. Using this insight we then consider how to design a sequential network to carry out a specific information processing task such as implementing the transition table of a control unit. Finally we show how a synchronous sequential network can be designed to carry out a general information processing operation independent of the need to have a separate information processing unit.

Sequential networks come in a wide variety of forms and are implemented using a number of different techniques. Although the design and analysis processes presented in this chapter are of an introductory nature, they are sufficient to design control units or implement simple digital systems. The references listed at the end of this chapter show how these ideas can be extended to more sophisticated design problems.

2. ANALYSIS OF SYNCHRONOUS SEQUENTIAL NETWORKS

Any synchronous sequential network, such as a control unit, can be represented by the general model shown in Figure 10-1. The heart of this model is the register, which acts as an internal information storage device or memory. It keeps track of important past events that influence the future behavior of the network. This register can be constructed from any of the master-slave flip-flops discussed in Chapter 8.

The other major component of a sequential network is the combinational logic network, which performs two important tasks. First, it forms the register control signals $i_1, \ldots, i_r$ applied to the register. These signals cause the contents of the register to change when the next clock or transfer pulse occurs. Second, it forms the output, $z_1, \ldots, z_v$, of the network. In both cases the signals generated are a function of the input variables $x_1, \ldots, x_u$ and the variables $y_1, \ldots, y_r$ associated with the cells of the register.

The relative timing that must exist between the values of different signals in the network and the transfer pulse is shown in Figure 10-2. All signal values must be constant at the time the transfer pulse appears. While the pulse is present the internal

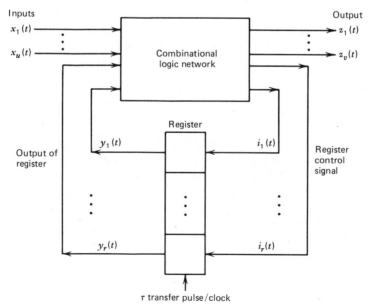

Figure 10-1   General structure of a synchronous sequential network.

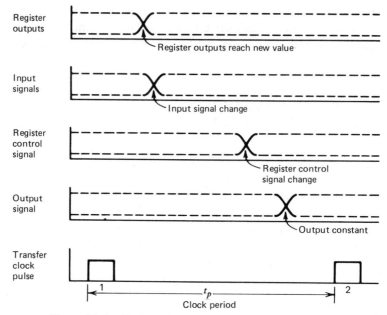

Figure 10-2 Timing relationships in a sequential network.

states of the register flip-flops are updated. When the pulse is removed the output of the register goes to its new value as defined by the register's input at the beginning of the transfer action. The input to the network can change at any time in the inter-pulse interval as long as the value of the output signal and the value of the register inputs have a constant value when needed. In some applications, such as when the network serves as a control unit in a digital system, the output signal must reach a constant value for some prespecified interval before the transfer pulse appears.

The Model

The behavior of the model can be indexed to the sequence of transfer pulses applied to the network. Since the transfer pulses normally occur at a fixed rate, we refer to each pulse as a clock pulse and the sequence of pulses as the clock sequence. As shown in Figure 10-2, the pulses can be numbered to show the order in which they occur.

If we let t, $t = 1, 2, 3, \ldots$, indicate the order in which the pulses appear, then the input, output, and state of the network at the time the tth pulse was applied can be indicated as

$$\begin{aligned}
\text{current input} \quad & X(t) := [x_1(t), \ldots, x_u(t)] \\
\text{current output} \quad & Z(t) := [z_1(t), \ldots, z_v(t)] \\
\text{current state} \quad & Y(t) := [y_1(t), \ldots, y_r(t)]
\end{aligned}$$

In the above expression the variables $y_1, \ldots, y_r$ are the *state variables* of the sequential network and the distinct values that the r-tuple

$$Y := [y_1, \ldots, y_r]$$

can take on are the *states* of the network.

The *current-state* of a synchronous sequential network corresponds to the state (i.e., contents) of the register at the time the clock pulse appears. The state of the register after the transfer pulse has been removed is called the *next-state* of the network since it is the state the network will be in when the next transfer pulse is applied. The relationship between the current-state and the next-state, as defined by the flip-flop control signal

$$I(t) := [i_1(t), \ldots, i_r(t)],$$

is indicated symbolically as

$$Y(t + 1) \leftarrow F_Y'[I(t)]$$

or

$$Y(t + 1) \leftarrow F_Y[X(t), Y(t)]$$

where F_Y' is the next-state function expressed in terms of the flip-flop control signal and F_Y is the same function defined in terms of the current-input and current-state information.

To illustrate these relationships, consider the simple sequential network shown in Figure 10-3. At $t = 0$ (i.e., before any pulse has been applied), assume that

$$\text{current input} \quad X(0) := [x_1(0)] := [1]$$
$$\text{current state} \quad Y(0) := [y_1(0), y_2(0)] := [0, 0]$$

If we examine the network we see that the following logical expressions

$$z(t) := x(t) \vee y_2(t)$$
$$D_1 := y_1(t) \vee \bar{y}_2(t)$$
$$D_2 := x(t)y_1(t)$$

represent the current output and current control signals, respectively. From Chapter 8 we know that the next state of a D flip-flop is given by

$$y(t + 1) = D(t)$$

Thus the next state of this network is given by

$$y_1(t + 1) = D_1(t)$$
$$y_2(t + 1) = D_2(t)$$

Using these expressions we see that for $t = 0$ we have

$$\text{current input} \quad x(0) = 1$$
$$\text{current state} \quad [y_1(0), y_2(0)] := [0, 0]$$
$$\text{current output} \quad z(0) = 1$$

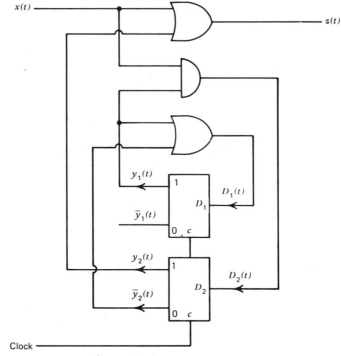

Figure 10-3   A simple synchronous sequential network.

current control $\qquad$ $D_1(0) = 1$ $D_2(0) = 0$

next state $\qquad$ $[y_1(1), y_2(1)] := [1, 0]$

These definitions concerning the behavior of synchronous sequential networks can now be generalized.

Fundamental Equations of Operation

The operation of any sequential network is defined by three sets of equations. They are;

1.   The output equations
2.   The next-state equations
3.   The flip-flop control equations

If we use the convention that the clock pulses occur at $t = 0, 1, 2, \ldots$, then these equations have the following form.

Output Equations

Under the most general conditions, the current output is a function of the current input and the current state of the network. This relationship is given by the following scalar equations.

$$z_1(t) := fz_1[x_1(t), \ldots, x_u(t), y_1(t), \ldots, y_r(t)]$$

$$\vdots$$

$$z_v(t) := fz_v[x_1(t), \ldots, x_u(t), y_1(t), \ldots, y_r(t)]$$

Next-State Equations

The next state of each flip-flop in the register is dependent on the particular class of flip-flops used to form the register. The control and next-state equations for S-R, D, and J-K flip-flops are defined as follows.

S-R Flip-Flops

$$y_1(t + 1) := S_1(t) \vee y_1(t)\overline{R}_1(t)$$

Note: $R(t)S(t) = 1$ not allowed

$$y_r(t + 1) := S_r(t) \vee y_r(t)\overline{R}_r(t)$$

D Flip-Flops

$$y_1(t + 1) := D_1(t)$$

$$\vdots$$

$$y_r(t + 1) := D_r(t)$$

J-K Flip-Flops

$$y_1(t + 1) := \overline{y}_1(t)J_1(t) \vee y_1(t)\overline{K}_1(t)$$

$$\vdots$$

$$y_r(t + 1) := \overline{y}(t)J_r(t) \vee y_r(t)\overline{K}_r(t)$$

Control Equations*

The control equations define the inputs to the control lines of the flip-flops that make up the state register. These equations are defined as follows.

S-R Flip-Flops

$$i_1(t) := \begin{cases} S_1 := f_{S_1}[x_1(t), \ldots, x_u(t), y_1(t), \ldots, y_r(t)] \\ R_1 := f_{R_1}[x_1(t), \ldots, x_u(t), y_1(t), \ldots, y_r(t)] \end{cases}$$

$$\vdots$$

$$i_r(t) := \begin{cases} S_r := f_{S_r}[x_1(t), \ldots, x_u(t), y_1(t), \ldots, y_r(t)] \\ R_r := f_{R_r}[x_1(t), \ldots, x_u(t), y_1(t), \ldots, y_r(t)] \end{cases}$$

D Flip-Flops

$$i_1(t) := D_1(t) := f_{D_1}[x_1(t), \ldots, x_u(t), y_1(t), \ldots, y_r(t)]$$

$$\vdots$$

$$i_r(t) := D_r(t) := f_{D_r}[x_1(t), \ldots, x_u(t), y_1(t), \ldots, y_r(t)]$$

*Note: Two equations are used to represent $i(t)$ for S-R, J-K flip-flops.

J-K Flip-Flops

$$i_1(t) := \begin{cases} J_1 := f_{J_1}[x_1(t), \ldots, x_u(t), y_1(t), \ldots, y_r(t)] \\ K_1 := f_{K_1}[x_1(t), \ldots, x_u(t), y_1(t), \ldots, y_r(t)] \end{cases}$$

$$\vdots$$

$$i_r(t) := \begin{cases} J_r := f_{J_r}[x_1(t), \ldots, x_u(t), y_1(t), \ldots, y_r(t)] \\ K_r := f_{K_r}[x_1(t), \ldots, x_u(t), y_1(t), \ldots, y_r(t)] \end{cases}$$

These scalar equations can be summarized in vector form by the following vector equations

Output Function

$$Z(t) := F_Z[X(t), Y(t)]$$

Flip-Flop Control Function

$$I(t) := F_I[X(t), Y(t)]$$

Next-State Function

$$Y(t + 1) := F_Y'[I(t)] := F_Y[X(t), Y(t)]$$

where $X(t)$, $Y(t)$, and $I(t)$ are the vectors that represent the input, the state, and the control signal in the sequential network.

The next-state function shows that the $(t + 1)$st state of the system is a function of the tth state of the network and the tth input. The following example shows that these equations are useful if we wish to represent the behavior of a given network in terms of its state behavior.

When working with a digital system we may encounter a sequential network, such as that shown in Figure 10-4, and wish to describe its general behavior. The first step would be to develop the output, control, and next-state equations associated with the network. Examining Figure 10-4 we find that these equations become

$$
\begin{aligned}
z(t) &:= x(t)y_1(t)\bar{y}_2(t) \\
J_1(t) &:= \bar{x}(t) \vee \bar{y}_1(t)y_2(t) & K_1(t) &:= \bar{x}(t) \\
J_2(t) &:= x(t) & K_2(t) &:= y_2(t) \\
y_1(t + 1) &:= \bar{y}_1(t)\bar{x}(t) \vee \bar{y}_1(t)y_2(t) \vee y_1(t)x(t) \\
y_2(t + 1) &:= \bar{y}_2(t)x(t) \vee y_2(t)\bar{y}_2(t) := \bar{y}_2(t)x(t)
\end{aligned}
$$

These equations can be evaluated as shown in Table 10-1. Although the information presented in this table completely describes the network, it is hard to understand its behavior as a function of the input. This information can be used to construct a transition table that provides an easier to understand representation of a network's operation.

State Diagrams and Transition Tables

When we described the operation of a control unit in Chapter 9, we used the idea of a transition table. This same method can be used to represent any sequential network. The next-state function $F_Y[X(t), Y(t)]$ and the output function $F_Z[X(t), Y(t)]$

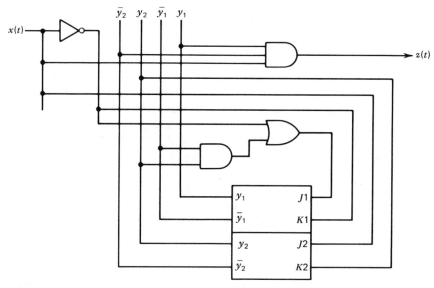

Figure 10-4 A typical sequential network.

of a sequential network can be represented by a *transition table* or we can introduce a graphical representation, called a *state transition diagram,* to represent the same information.

As in our previous discussion, the transition table representation of a sequential network displays the properties of the next-state and output functions in tabular form. The columns of the table correspond to the possible input symbols and the rows correspond to the possible states of the network. The entry found at the intersection of the *k*th row and the *j*th column is

Next State/Current Output

Table 10-1 Tabular Representation of Sequential Network Shown in Figure 10-4

			$F_J[X(t), Y(t)]$				$F_Y[X(t), Y(t)]$		$F_Z[Z(t), Y(t)]$
Current Input $x(t)$	Current State $y_1(t)$	$y_2(t)$	Current Control $J_1(t)$	$K_1(t)$	$J_2(t)$	$K_2(t)$	Next State $y_1(t+1)$	$y_2(t+1)$	Current Output $z(t)$
0	0	0	1	1	0	0	1	0	0
0	0	1	1	1	0	1	1	0	0
0	1	0	1	1	0	0	0	0	0
0	1	1	1	1	0	1	0	0	0
1	0	0	0	0	1	0	0	1	0
1	0	1	1	0	1	1	1	0	0
1	1	0	0	0	1	0	1	1	1
1	1	1	0	0	1	1	1	0	0

For example, the information presented in Table 10-1 concerning the next-state and current output of the network shown in Figure 10-4 can be represented by the transition table given by Table 10-2.

When discussing sequential networks we may wish to indicate the states in symbolic form as we did when we discussed the operation of a control unit. For example, the four distinct states in the above example could be denoted symbolically as q_0, q_1, q_2, and q_3, respectively. This symbolic representation is easier to use when dealing with networks that have a large number of state variables. This representation is also useful during the design process, wherein we must describe the behavior of the network before we consider the problem of realizing it using particular logic elements and flip-flops.

Using the above coding, we can represent Table 10-2 in symbolic form as shown in Table 10-3. The symbolic form of a transition table is called the network's *state transition table* or *state table*. One difficulty with transition tables and state tables is that it is sometimes hard to visualize the response of the network when a given input sequence is applied.

State transition diagrams provide a graphical representation of the operation of a sequential network. Each diagram consists of a set of vertices labeled to correspond to the states of the network. For each ordered pair of (not necessarily distinct) states q_i and q_j, a directed edge connects vertex q_i to q_j if and only if there exists a value, a_k, of the input signal such that

$$q_j = F_Y(a_k, q_i)$$

If a directed edge connects q_i to q_j when the input is a_k, then the edge is labeled as

$$a_k/F_Z(a_k, q_i)$$

Thus the vertices of the transition diagram correspond to the current state of the network; the label on each edge indicates the current input and the current output; and an arrowhead on each edge indicates the next state of the network. Figure 10-5 is the state transition diagram corresponding to the state table given by Table 10-3.

Table 10-2   Transition Table for Network of Figure 10-4

Current State \ Current Input	0	1
[0, 0]	[1, 0]/0	[0, 1]/0
[0, 1]	[1, 0]/0	[1, 0]/0
[1, 0]	[0, 0]/0	[1, 1]/1
[1, 1]	[0, 0]/0	[1, 0]/0

Next State

Current Output

Table 10-3 State Table Representation of a Transition Table

Current State	Current Input	
	0	1
		— Next State
q_1	$q_2/0$	$q_1/0$
q_2	$q_2/0$	$q_2/0$
q_3	$q_0/0$	$q_3/1$ ← Current Output
q_4	$q_0/0$	$q_2/0$

Input, Output, and State Sequences

When we are dealing with a sequential network that forms part of a complex system, we are usually interested in the network's external behavior. In particular, if we apply an input sequence

$$x(0), x(1), x(2), \ldots, x(k)$$

we would like to know what the resulting output sequence

$$z(0), z(1), z(2), \ldots, z(k)$$

will be. The answer to this question is not unique but depends on the initial state of the network at $t = 0$.

For example, consider the network represented by the transition diagram of Figure 10-5. Assume that the input sequence

$$x(0) = 1 \qquad x(1) = 0 \qquad x(2) = 1 \qquad x(3) = 0 \qquad x(4) = 0$$

is applied to this network. If the initial state is q_0, then we see from the transition diagram that the network will go from q_0 to q_1 at $t = 0$, from q_1 to q_2 at $t = 1$, from q_2 to q_3 at $t = 2$, from q_3 to q_0 at $t = 3$, and finally from q_0 to q_2 at $t = 4$. The output sequence corresponding to this input sequence and state sequence, which

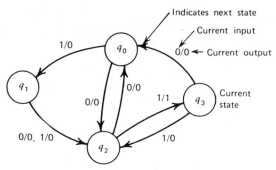

Figure 10-5 State transition diagram corresponding to Table 10-3.

can also be read from the transition diagram, is seen to be

$$z(0) = 0 \qquad z(1) = 0 \qquad z(2) = 1 \qquad z(3) = 0 \qquad z(4) = 0$$

Next consider what happens when the initial state is q_1 instead of q_0. In this case the state sequence is

$$q_1 \rightarrow q_2 \rightarrow q_0 \rightarrow q_1 \rightarrow q_2 \rightarrow q_0$$

and the output sequence is

$$z(0) = 0 \qquad z(1) = 0 \qquad z(2) = 0 \qquad z(3) = 0 \qquad z(4) = 0$$

Thus we obtain a different output sequence and state sequence if we start in a different initial state.

From this discussion we see that the problem of analyzing the behavior of a given sequential network can be handled in a straightforward manner. Although the analytical techniques that we have developed are of importance in themselves, this discussion has also served another important purpose: that of providing the background material that we need to consider the problem of designing a synchronous sequential network to carry out a specific task. The rest of this chapter considers this problem.

EXERCISES

1.   Find the transition table and state diagram for the sequential network below.

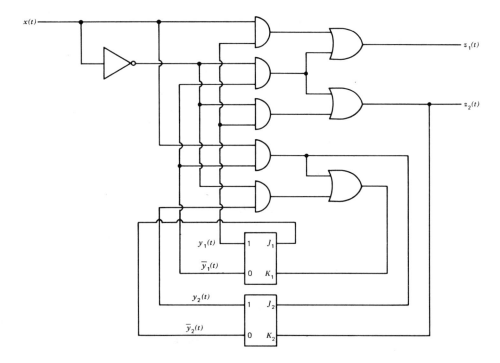

2. Find the state sequence and output sequence for the network of Exercise 1 for the following initial state q_I and input sequence $X(t)$.

(a) $q_I := [0, 0]$ $\quad X(t)$ $\quad$ 1, 0, 1, 1, 0, 1, 0
(b) $q_I := [1, 0]$ $\quad X(t)$ $\quad$ 1, 0, 0, 1, 0, 1, 0, 1

3. REALIZATION OF SYNCHRONOUS SEQUENTIAL NETWORKS

The problem of analyzing the behavior of a given synchronous sequential network is easily overcome provided we have a circuit diagram of the network. The reverse problem, that of realizing a sequential network if we are given the network's state transition table or state transition diagram, is somewhat more difficult. In this situation we must consider two problems.

If we are given the state transition table in symbolic form, the first task that we must consider is how to encode the input, state, and output information into binary form. For example, the transition tables that we developed in the last chapter for different control units used mnemonics to represent both the input and output signals as well as the states of the control unit. To encode this information we may find it useful to consider both how the input signals are generated and how the output signals are used. The encoding of the state information may be influenced by the particular class of flip-flops used in the realization as well as the information "remembered" by the state.

The second problem to be resolved is the selection of the types of flip-flops and logic elements that will be used to implement the network. Once the choice of the flip-flops has been made, the next-state control equations can be defined. The method selected to realize the combinational logic network will similarly influence the form used to represent the logic expressions describing the output and the control signals.

Once these two decisions are made, the final step of the design process, that of actually developing the equations describing the operation of the network, is straightforward. The encoding problem cannot be solved in a completely algorithmic manner. There are a number of decisions that must be made by the designer based on past experience or on special known characteristics about the information being encoded. The selection of the circuit elements to be used for a given realization depends upon factors that are usually independent of the tasks that the network is to perform. In this section we assume that the encoding process has been completed and that the circuit elements to be used in the realization have been specified. Our attention is focused on the techniques that are used to describe the combinational logic network that defines the operation of the sequential network.

Excitation Tables for Flip-Flops

Our initial discussion of flip-flops in Chapter 8 emphasized the response of the different types of flip-flops to various combinations of input signals. This information is very important in analyzing the behavior of a sequential network or in working with flip-flops when there is no feedback information present in the network. However, when we are designing a sequential network, we know the current state and the desired next state for each flip-flop under each input condition. This information is used to determine the control signals that must be supplied to each flip-flop in order to achieve the desired operation.

The transition table description of flip-flops used in Chapter 8 can be rearranged to form an *excitation table* that relates the known state transitions to the control signals necessary to produce the transitions. Table 10-4 gives the excitation tables associated with S-R, D, and J-K flip-flops. These tables are interpreted in the following manner.

Consider the S-R flip-flop and assume that we want to go from the initial state $y(t) = 0$ to the final state $y(t + 1) = 0$. Looking in the first row of Table 10-4a we see that $S(t)$ must be 0 but $R(t)$ can be either 0 or 1 (i.e., a don't care condition) since both values for $R(t)$ will result in $y(t + 1) = 0$. Thus $R(t)$ is indicated as d in this situation. Now consider the case where we want to go from the initial state $y(t) = 0$ to the final state $y(t + 1) = 1$. Looking at the second row of Table 10-4a we see that $S(t)$ must be 1 in order to set the flip-flop to the 1 state and $R(t)$ must be 0 since $S(t) = 1$, $R(t) = 1$ is a prohibited input combination for an S-R flip-flop.

Similar considerations also hold for the J-K flip-flop, as can be seen by inspecting Table 10-4c. These don't care conditions in the excitation tables of both the S-R and

Table 10-4 Excitation Tables for S-R, D, and J-K Flip-Flops

Current State $y(t)$	Next State $y(t + 1)$	Input Required $S(t)$	$R(t)$	Current State $y(t)$	Next State $y(t + 1)$	Input Required $D(t)$
0	0	0	d	0	0	0
0	1	1	0	0	1	1
1	0	0	1	1	0	0
1	1	d	0	1	1	1

S-R Flip-Flop	D Flip-Flop
(a)	(b)

Current State $y(t)$	Next State $y(t + 1)$	Input Required $J(t)$	$K(t)$
0	0	0	d
0	1	1	d
1	0	d	1
1	1	d	0

J-K Flip-Flop

(c)

J-K flip-flops allow us greater flexibility in the design of the combinational logic networks that control these flip-flops.

Network Realization

The realization of a sequential network requires us to design a combinational logic network that generates the proper output signals and control signals to the flip-flops. The following example illustrates how we can carry out this design process.

Assume that we wish to construct a sequential network that is described by the transition table given by Table 10-5. This network has three states that are important to its operation and one state [1, 1] that never occurs. The presence of this state means that there will be several don't care entries in the transition table.

To realize this network we need two flip-flops. Thus the first problem we must consider is what type of flip-flops should we use. Here again the proper choice of flip-flops determines the complexity of the logic circuit that we need. At this point we arbitrarily choose to use two *J-K* flip-flops. Later on we investigate the type of results we can obtain by using other types of flip-flops. Under this assumption our sequential network has the form shown in Figure 10-6, and we must find the logical expressions that describe the combinational logic network.

The five logical expressions that we must find are easily obtained if we use a modified truth table of the form shown in Table 10-6. Beside the standard input signals, we also include the next state of the network that is associated with these signals. We can now use the information in the *J-K* flip-flop excitation table to derive the desired logical expression.

For example, consider the second row of Table 10-6. The first flip-flop remains in the 0 state, and the second flip-flop goes from the 1 to the 0 state when the input is 0. Looking at the *J-K* flip-flop excitation table of Table 10-4c we see that this means that $J_1 = 0$, $K_1 = d$, $J_2 = d$, and $K_2 = 1$. The output $z = 0$ is found by examining Table 10-5.

The final task in our design process is to obtain the logical expressions describing

Table 10-5 Transition Table for a Sequential Network

Current State y_1, y_2	Current Input x_1 0	1	
0, 0	0, 0/0	0, 1/0	
0, 1	0, 0/0	1, 0/0	
1, 0	0, 0/0	1, 0/1	
1, 1	d, d/d	d, d/d	don't care state

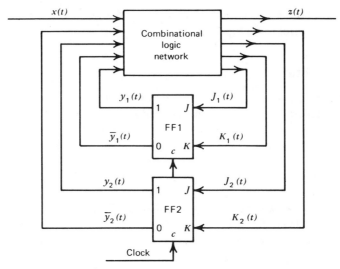

Figure 10-6   General form of sequential network.

the combinational logic network. The simplest approach, and the one that we will use, is to treat each expression separately. If we go through the standard minimization process, we obtain the following logical representation for z, J_1, K_1, J_2, and K_2.

$$z = xy_1$$
$$J_1 = xy_2 \qquad J_2 = x\bar{y}_1$$
$$K_1 = \bar{x} \qquad K_2 = 1$$

Using these equations we obtain the network shown in Figure 10-7. This network could be drawn in a much more compact form but it was drawn in this manner to correspond to the general form of sequential networks presented in Figure 10-6.

Table 10-6   Truth Table for Combinational Network

Input	Current State		Next State		FF1		FF2		Output
x	y_1	y_2			J_1	K_1	J_2	K_2	Z
0	0	0	0	0	0	d	0	d	0
0	0	1	0	0	0	d	d	1	0
0	1	0	0	0	d	1	0	d	0
0	1	1	d	d	d	d	d	d	d
1	0	0	0	1	0	d	1	d	0
1	0	1	1	0	1	d	d	1	0
1	1	0	1	0	d	0	0	d	1
1	1	1	d	d	d	d	d	d	d

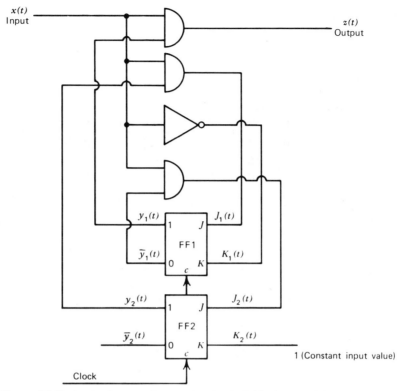

Figure 10-7 Logic diagram of network using individual term minimization.

Flip-Flop Selection

Unfortunately there is no general algorithm that can be used to determine which class of flip-flops will yield the minimum complexity realization for a given design problem.

The selection of which class of flip-flops to use to realize a given network depends on many factors. In some cases the flip-flops are specified by the fact that only one particular type of flip-flop is available to the designer. At other times the designer is free to choose the flip-flop that produces the simplest circuit according to some minimization criterion, such as the minimum number of total circuit elements or the minimum number of connections needed between circuit elements.

To illustrate these considerations let us design a circuit to realize the network described by Table 10-5 using D flip-flops and then one using S-R flip-flops. The truth table for the D flip-flop realization is given by Table 10-7a and the truth table for the S-R flip-flop realization is given by Table 10-7b.

Table 10-7 Truth Table for Realization of Sequential Network Using D and S-R

Input	Current State		Next State		(a) D Flip-Flop Realization FF1	FF2	(b) S-R Flip-Flop Realization				Output
x	y_1	y_2	y_1	y_2	D_1	D_2	S_1	R_1	S_2	R_2	
0	0	0	0	0	0	0	0	d	0	d	0
0	0	1	0	0	0	0	0	d	0	1	0
0	1	0	0	0	0	0	0	1	0	d	0
0	1	1	d	d	d	d	d	d	d	d	d
1	0	0	0	1	0	1	0	d	1	0	0
1	0	1	1	0	1	0	1	0	0	1	0
1	1	0	1	0	1	0	d	0	0	d	1
1	1	1	d	d	d	d	d	d	d	d	d

Going through our standard minimization process we obtain the following logical expressions:

Case I *Using* D *Flip-Flops*

$$D_1 = xy_2 \lor xy_1$$
$$D_2 = x\bar{y_1}\bar{y_2}$$
$$z = xy_1$$

Case II *Using* S-R *Flip-Flops*

$$S_1 = xy_2 \qquad S_2 = x\bar{y_1}\bar{y_2} \qquad z = xy_1$$
$$R_1 = \bar{x} \qquad R_2 = y_2$$

If we examine these expressions and compare them to the expressions we obtained for the previous example where we used J-K flip-flops, we see that the network using the J-K flip-flops is minimal both in terms of the number of logic elements used and the number of connections required to construct the circuit. Again it is important to note that there is no general algorithm that can be used to determine which class of flip-flops gives us a minimal realization. It is simply a combination of trial and error plus design experience.

The Encoding Problem

As just demonstrated, the realization of a transition table is easily accomplished if it is already encoded into digital form. In many designs we generate a transition table in mnemonic form and must encode it to finish the design. For example, in Chapter 9 we carried out the initial design of a serial receiver used for the serial transmission

Table 10-8 Transition Table for Serial Receiver Controller

State \ Status S	[0, 0]	[0, 1]	[1, 0]	[1, 1]
Q_A	Q_B/CLR	Q_B/CLR	Q_A/NOP	Q_A/NOP
Q_B	Q_B/READ	Q_A/STC	Q_C/READ	Q_A/STCP
Q_C	Q_C/READ	Q_A/STCP	Q_B/READ	Q_A/STC

of information between two points in a digital system. As part of that design effort we developed the transition table for the serial receiver controller given by Table 10-8. Looking at this table we see that the input status information has already been encoded, but the output information and the state information is represented by mnemonics. To complete the design of this control unit we must decide upon the encoding to be used for these two items.

The decision on how to encode the output information depends upon the meaning we associate with the mnemonics that represent this information. Table 10-9 summarizes the mnemonics used and their meaning in terms of the operations they invoke when applied to the information processing unit in the receiver. Since there are five mnemonics, we need to use at least 3 bits to encode the signal T. For this example we have arbitrarily selected the encoding shown in the second column of Table 10-9.

To complete the encoding process we must encode the states of the control unit. There are three states. Thus we must use at least 2 bits to encode the state information. One way to do this is to use the "natural" encoding

$$Q_A := [0, 0] \qquad Q_B := [0, 1] \qquad Q_C := [1, 0]$$

for the states.

Table 10-9 Encoded Operation Table for Serial Receiver

Control Signal T		Transfer Operations
Mnemonic	**Code**	
CLR	[1, 0, 0]	CNT ← [0] C ← [0] P ← [0]
STC	[0, 0, 1]	C ← [1]
STCP	[0, 1, 0]	C ← [1] P ← [1]
READ	[1, 1, 0]	R ← $SR(X, R)$ CNT ← CNT + [1]
NOP	[0, 0, 0]	No operation

Note: SR(X, R)—shift right.

Using this encoding we redefine the transition table for the receiver controller as shown in Table 10-10. To complete our realization we assume that the register in the control unit is constructed from D flip-flops. This assumption allows us to generate the truth table shown in Table 10-11 to describe the combinational logic network needed to complete our design.

Using this table and our standard minimization process, we obtain the following logical expressions:

The Control Equations

$$D_1 := \bar{s}_1\bar{s}_2 y_1 \vee s_1\bar{s}_2 y_2$$
$$D_2 := \bar{s}_1\bar{y}_1\bar{y}_2 \vee \bar{s}_1\bar{s}_2\bar{y}_1 \vee s_1\bar{s}_2 y_1$$

The Output Equations $T := [t_1, t_2, t_3]$

$$t_1 := \bar{s}_1\bar{y}_1\bar{y}_2 \vee \bar{s}_2 y_2 \vee \bar{s}_2 y_1$$
$$t_2 := \bar{s}_2 y_2 \vee \bar{s}_2 y_1 \vee \bar{s}_1 y_1 \vee s_1 y_2$$
$$t_3 := \bar{s}_1\bar{s}_2 y_2 \vee s_1\bar{s}_2 y_1$$

These equations are not unique. If we decided to use another encoding of the states and/or the output signals, we would generate a different set of equations. Similarly, if we decided to use $J\text{-}K$ or $S\text{-}R$ flip-flops we would have a different set of control equations.

PLA Realization

In Chapter 7 we introduced the idea of using a Programmable Logic Array (PLA) to realize multiple-input multiple-output logic networks. The availability of PLAs has made the design of sequential networks much easier since, in many cases, we do not need to try to minimize the logic expressions describing the network if we use a PLA realization. For example, the truth table given in Table 10-11 can be realized

Table 10-10   Encoded Transition Table for Serial Receiver Controller

State \ Status S	[0, 0]	[0, 1]	[1, 0]	[1, 1]
[0, 0]	[0, 1]/[1, 0, 0]	[0, 1]/[1, 0, 0]	[0, 0]/[0, 0, 0]	[0, 0]/[0, 0, 0]
[0, 1]	[0, 1]/[1, 1, 0]	[0, 0]/[0, 0, 1]	[1, 0]/[1, 1, 0]	[0, 0]/[0, 1, 0]
[1, 0]	[1, 0]/[1, 1, 0]	[0, 0]/[0, 1, 0]	[0, 1]/[1, 1, 0]	[0, 0]/[0, 0, 1]
[1, 1]	-/-	-/-	-/-	-/-

Table 10-11 Truth Table for Controller Network

Input		Flip-Flop Current State		Flip-Flop Next State		Control Equations D_1	D_2	Output $T := [t_1, t_2, t_3]$ t_1	t_2	t_3
0	0	0	0	0	1	0	1	1	0	0
0	0	0	1	0	1	0	1	1	1	0
0	0	1	0	1	0	1	0	1	1	0
0	0	1	1	d	d	d	d	d	d	d
0	1	0	0	0	1	0	1	1	0	0
0	1	0	1	0	0	0	0	0	0	1
0	1	1	0	0	0	0	0	0	1	0
0	1	1	1	d	d	d	d	d	d	d
1	0	0	0	0	0	0	0	0	0	0
1	0	0	1	1	0	1	0	1	1	0
1	0	1	0	0	1	0	1	1	1	0
1	0	1	1	d	d	d	d	d	d	d
1	1	0	0	0	0	0	0	0	0	0
1	1	0	1	0	0	0	0	0	1	0
1	1	1	0	0	0	0	0	0	0	1
1	1	1	1	d	d	d	d	d	d	d

d represents don't care conditions.

using the PLA implementation shown in Figure 10-8. The control and output equations are represented by the following canonical sum-of-product expressions:

The Control Equations

$$D_1 := m_2 \lor m_9$$
$$D_2 := m_0 \lor m_1 \lor m_4 \lor m_{10}$$

The Output Equations $T := [t_1, t_2, t_3]$

$$t_1 := m_0 \lor m_1 \lor m_2 \lor m_4 \lor m_9 \lor m_{10}$$
$$t_2 := m_1 \lor m_2 \lor m_6 \lor m_9 \lor m_{10} \lor m_{13}$$
$$t_3 := m_5 \lor m_{14}$$

If we examine the way that we have organized the flow of information in Figure 10-8, we see that the identity of each group of signals is easily recognized. Thus our conceptual model for the operation of a sequential network is very closely related to the actual PLA realization.

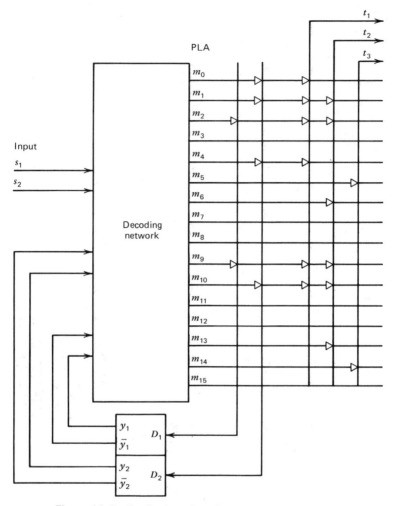

Figure 10-8   Realization of receiver controller using a PLA.

EXERCISES

1. Show how the transition table given by Table 10-10 can be realized using *J-K* flip-flops. Do the realization using minimized logic expressions and using a PLA.

2. Develop a realization of a sequential network that will realize the multiplier control unit given in Figure 9-25. Use a PLA in the final design.

4. THE DESIGN OF GENERAL SYNCHRONOUS SEQUENTIAL NETWORKS

Control units correspond to one important class of synchronous sequential networks. They are designed to work in conjunction with an information processing unit to carry out a complete computational task. There are a number of situations in which it is possible to design a single sequential network to perform the desired computation without separating the network into two subunits.

For example, we might wish to design a sequential network that will compute the correct change to return to a customer of a coin operated vending machine. In that case the input consists of the sequence of coins deposited into the machine and the output is a command to return the specific change that the customer expects. The design of a sequential network to carry out such a task is both an art and a science.

At several stages of the process the designer must call on heuristic procedures and past experience to make decisions about the best way to proceed. At other stages straightforward algorithmic procedures of the type we have just discussed can be employed to carry out the design steps associated with that stage. The design process can be broken down into the following stages.

Stage 1. Description of Desired Network Operation

Prepare a complete set of specifications describing the operation of the network. All inputs and outputs are identified and the relationships between the quantities are defined in a consistent manner.

Stage 2. Determination of State Table

Using the specification established at Stage 1, an initial state table, or state transition diagram, is defined for the network. The resulting description is checked to make sure that it satisfies all design criteria.

Stage 3. State Table Minimization

In the process of developing a state table to satisfy a given set of operational requirements an unnecessarily large number of states may be introduced. Since the complexity of the network increases as the number of states increases, it is often desirable to remove redundant or unnecessary states from the state table.

Stage 4. State Assignments

The information contained in the state table must be encoded into binary form. This is not a unique process and the encoding used can considerably influence the complexity of the resulting circuit. The result of this stage is to transform the state table into a transition table.

Stage 5. Network Realization

Once a transition table has been defined, and a decision made concerning the type of storage and logic elements to be used, the logic expressions relating the input and present state to the output and control signals are developed.

In the above design process, only Stages 3 and 5 can be carried out in a completely algorithmic manner. The state assignment problem of Stage 4 could, in theory, also be carried out in an algorithmic manner by simply trying all the possible state assignments and then selecting the "best" one according to some criteria. Unfortunately the number of possible state assignments is so large that this is an unrealistic approach. Heuristic and advanced analytical techniques have been developed to assist in the solution of this problem.

We have already discussed the problem of realizing a network once we have developed a state transition table. At one time the problem of state table minimization was of great importance when the cost of circuit elements had a major impact upon final system cost. However, this problem is now of interest only at more advanced levels. Therefore, we will not consider it any further.

The problems that must be solved during the first two stages of the design process are not as easily eliminated. The general problem of obtaining a state transition table description of a network is not solved by an algorithmic process. The main reason for this is that the word description of what we would like the network to do, developed during Stage 1, is usually not a formal description of the network's action. Consequently, the designer must use personal insight and past experience to translate the initial word description into a state transition table description of the network to be developed.

The hardware design language introduced in Chapter 9 is a powerful design tool when dealing with complex systems. There are, however, a number of tasks carried out by sequential networks that can be directly described in terms of a state transition diagram or a state table. This section provides a brief discussion of how both transition tables and state tables can be developed to meet specific design requirements. Of necessity, this discussion is heuristic instead of algorithmic since the actual design process must rely extensively on the designer's previous experience and understanding of the operations that the desired network must perform.

Autonomous Networks

A small but important class of sequential networks operate without any input signals. Such networks are called *autonomous networks*. Figure 10-9 illustrates the general form that autonomous networks take. Examining this figure we see that both the network's next state and the output depend only on the current state of the network. Therefore, the transition table or state table representing this network will have only one column.

Autonomous networks are used extensively to generate standard periodic control signal sequences for use in various information processing tasks. In fact, an autonomous network is, in reality, a generalized counter.

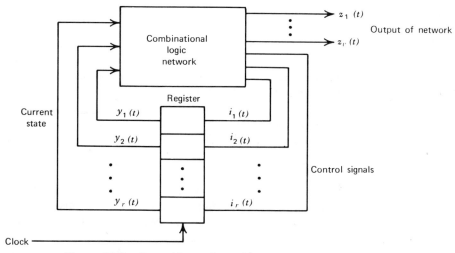

Figure 10-9 General form of an autonomous sequential network.

Counters

Counters are important building blocks in digital systems and can take on a variety of forms depending on the application for which they are used.

A counter will count through a sequence of numbers, then reset itself to an initial value, and then repeat the counting process. The simplest types of counters are binary counters built from r flip-flops. These counters start at 0 and count to $2^r - 1$ and then reset to 0. For example, if $r = 3$, a counter will count through the successive binary numbers 0 through 7. Figure 10-10 gives a transition diagram representation of this counting process. The corresponding transition table representation for this network is also shown. Counters of this type are called *binary up counters* or *modulo 2^r counters*.

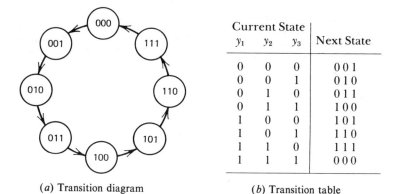

Current State			
y_1	y_2	y_3	Next State
0	0	0	0 0 1
0	0	1	0 1 0
0	1	0	0 1 1
0	1	1	1 0 0
1	0	0	1 0 1
1	0	1	1 1 0
1	1	0	1 1 1
1	1	1	0 0 0

(*a*) Transition diagram   (*b*) Transition table
Figure 10-10 Representation of binary modulo 8 counter.

Several standard circuits are available to realize counters and many manufacturers are currently manufacturing integrated circuits that are complete counters. The design of the necessary logic circuits to realize a counter can be accomplished using the techniques of the last section. For example, let us design the counter of Figure 10-10 using D flip-flops. The control equations for this case are described by Table 10-12. Using the information in this table we find that

$$D_1 = \bar{y}_1 y_2 y_3 \lor y_1 \bar{y}_3 \lor y_1 \bar{y}_2$$
$$D_2 = \bar{y}_2 y_3 \lor y_2 \bar{y}_3$$
$$D_3 = \bar{y}_3$$

The resulting logic diagram is given in Figure 10-11. It is left as an exercise to show that a simpler network is required if J-K flip-flops are used to build this counter.

There is, of course, no reason why we must limit ourselves to a modulo 2^r counter or that we even count in the standard binary order. For example, assume that we have a machining process that requires five steps and that there are three possible operations that can be performed at each step. These operations, which are all performed during the interclock interval of the control network, are

c_1 drill

c_2 move drill right 1 unit

c_3 move drill up 1 unit

When no operation is indicated (i.e., all $c_i = 0$) the machine performing the machining operation returns to its starting position.

The machining process to be carried out is to drill a plate as indicated in Figure 10-12. The operating sequence necessary to accomplish this task is described by the following steps.

Table 10-12   Control Signals Necessary to Realize a Modulo 8 Counter

Current State			Next State			Control Signals		
y_1	y_2	y_3	y_1	y_2	y_3	D_1	D_2	D_3
0	0	0	0	0	1	0	0	1
0	0	1	0	1	0	0	1	0
0	1	0	0	1	1	0	1	1
0	1	1	1	0	0	1	0	0
1	0	0	1	0	1	1	0	1
1	0	1	1	1	0	1	1	0
1	1	0	1	1	1	1	1	1
1	1	1	0	0	0	0	0	0

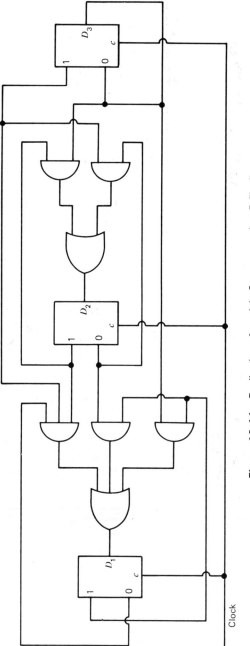

Figure 10-11 Realization of modulo 8 counter using *D* flip-flops.

Clock

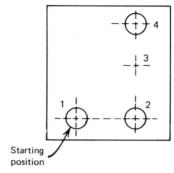

Starting
position

Figure 10-12 Diagram of plate after drilling operation.

Step 1. Initialization of machining operation—position drill in lower left-hand corner.

Step 2. Drill hole 1.

Step 3. Move drill to position 2 and drill hole.

Step 4. Move drill to position 3 and do not drill.

Step 5. Move drill to position 4 and drill hole.

This sequence of operations can be controlled by a counter that will generate the successive values of the 3-tuple $[c_1, c_2, c_3]$ where $c_i = 1$ indicates that an operation is performed and $c_i = 0$ indicates that no operation is performed. In this case the state variables of the counter are identical to the outputs of the counter. The actual sequence that the counter must go through is illustrated by the transition diagram and transition table of Figure 10-13.

Since the output of the network is assumed to be identical to the value of the current state of the control network, the final step in the design of the control unit is to realize an autonomous sequential network that has the behavior described by the transition table of Figure 10-13. Assume that this network is to be realized using S-R flip-flops. Then the flip-flop control signals necessary to realize this network are

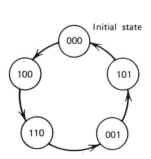

Current State			**Next State**		
0	0	0	1	0	0
0	0	1	1	0	1
0	1	0	d	d	d
0	1	1	d	d	d
1	0	0	1	1	0
1	0	1	0	0	0
1	1	0	0	0	1
1	1	1	d	d	d

Figure 10-13 Transition diagram representation of control sequence.

Table 10-13 Flip-Flop Control Signals Necessary to Realize Control Sequences

Current State			Next State			Flip-Flop Control Signals					
y_1	y_2	y_3	y_1	y_2	y_3	S_1	R_1	S_2	R_2	S_3	R_3
0	0	0	1	0	0	1	0	0	d	0	d
0	0	1	1	0	1	1	0	0	d	d	0
0	1	0	d	d	d	d	d	d	d	d	d
0	1	1	d	d	d	d	d	d	d	d	d
1	0	0	1	1	0	d	0	1	0	0	d
1	0	1	0	0	0	0	1	0	d	0	1
1	1	0	0	0	1	0	1	0	1	1	0
1	1	1	d	d	d	d	d	d	d	d	d

given in Table 10-13. Using this information and our standard logic network realization techniques, we obtain the following expressions for the flip-flop control signals:

$$S_1 = \bar{y}_1 \qquad\qquad S_2 = y_1\bar{y}_2\bar{y}_3 \qquad S_3 = y_2$$
$$R_1 = y_1y_3 \lor y_2 \qquad R_2 = y_2 \qquad\qquad R_3 = y_1y_3$$

The actual circuit of this sequential network is easily obtained from these expressions
and is omitted.

Up to this point the problems have had a form that allowed us to go directly to a
transition table description of the network. This, of course, is not always possible
since there are many situations that occur where the desired operation of the network
is described in terms of a word statement. The design process then involves first
obtaining a state table description of the network. Next the state table is turned into
a transition table by assigning a digital coding to the state, input, and output symbols
associated with the state table. The resulting transition table is then used to complete
the design of the network. Thus our next task is to consider how a state table or a
state transition diagram can be obtained.

State Tables from Word Statements

The process of defining a state table can be divided into two stages.

1. Determine how many different pieces of information about the past history of
   the network must be "remembered" by the network. Each such piece of information is represented by a state of the network.
2. Define, for each input and state condition, the next state and output that occur.

The first stage of this process is probably the hardest since it requires the designer
to have the ability to identify the past events that must be remembered and to classify
these events into the smallest number of classes possible. This is basically a heuristic
process that becomes easier as the designer gains experience.

The problem of forming a state table is not as difficult as it might initially seem.
The reason for this is that there are a number of state tables that correspond to the
same network performance. Thus all we must do is find one of these tables. In some

of the complex problems we often inadvertently include more states than necessary. We will not investigate this problem, however, since it is usually possible to uniquely identify the states we need to represent the stored information in the types of networks that we will be discussing. Although we will not explore this problem, algorithmic procedures do exist that can be used to remove redundant states from a state table or that can transform one state table into another state table without changing the corresponding network performance. The following examples will illustrate how we can define simple state tables.

A Subsequence Detector

Assume that we wish to observe a sequence of 0's and 1's and take the following action based on the patterns observed.

Whenever three consecutive 1's are observed, an output $z = 1$ must be produced when the third 1 is applied. Otherwise the output will be $z = 0$.

In examining this problem statement we observe that we are checking the sequence $x(t - 2)$, $x(t - 1)$, $x(t)$ to see whether the three values are all 1. Since $x(t)$ is the current input we only need to remember information about $x(t - 2)$ and $x(t - 1)$. In particular we note that all we need to know about the past inputs is "how many consecutive 1's have we had prior to $x(t)$."

One of the easiest ways to investigate the interrelationship between the input information and the information that must be stored by the network is to use a state transition diagram. We start out with an "initial node" corresponding to the assumed initial condition of the network when it starts operating. We then consider each possible input and add new states as needed when the input changes the amount of information we have about the input process. This process of constructing a state transition diagram continues until we reach the point where we have a complete diagram or when we cannot add any additional states. This method is illustrated by Figure 10-14.

Initially we assume that the network starts with no stored information. This condition coincides with the initial state "no consecutive 1's" indicated in Figure 10-14a. Next we consider what happens if we receive an input. If the input is 0 we still have the condition "no consecutive 1's." However, a 1 input requires an additional state that will store the information that we have received "1 consecutive 1." This additional state allows us to expand our state transition diagram as shown in Figure 10-14b. We next consider what happens if we are in this new state and we receive an input. If the input is 0 we go back to our initial state, while an input of 1 requires us to introduce an additional state to store the information that we have received "2 consecutive 1's." The expanded state transition diagram is shown in Figure 10-14c.

Continuing with this reasoning, we complete our state transition diagram as shown in Figure 10-14d. Our final task is to indicate what outputs occur during each transition. We do this in Figure 10-14e where we have labeled the states as

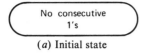

(a) Initial state

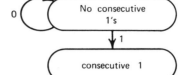

(b) Information added by receiving information while in initial state

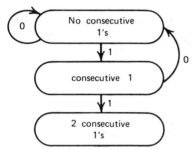

(c) Information added by receiving information while in state "1 consecutive 1"

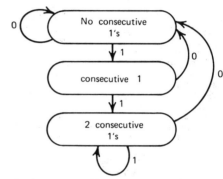

(d) Information added by receiving information in state "2 consecutive 1's"

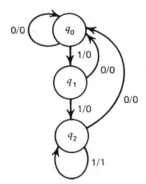

(e) Final state transition diagram

Figure 10-14 Steps in forming a state transition diagram.

q_0—no consecutive 1's (initial state)

q_1—1 consecutive 1

q_2—2 consecutive 1's

Using this information, we form the state table given by Table 10-14 for this network.

Table 10-14 Transition Table for 111
Sequence Detector

State \ Input	0	1
q_0	$q_0/0$	$q_1/0$
q_1	$q_0/0$	$q_2/0$
q_2	$q_0/0$	$q_2/1$

A Controlled Counter

As a second example, assume that we wish to design a special counter that is controlled by three input control signals c_1, c_2, and c_3 in the following manner.

Control Signal	State Behavior Action
c_1	Counter is incremented by 1 each time a clock pulse occurs unless the current count is 4 or 7. If the current count is 4 or 7 when the clock pulse occurs, the counter is reset to 0.
c_2	Counter is incremented by 2 each time a clock pulse occurs if the current count is not 5, 6, or 7. If the current count is 5, 6, or 7 when the clock pulse occurs, the counter is set to 0, 1, and 2 respectively.
c_3	Counter is decremented by 1 each time a clock pulse occurs. If the count is 0 when the clock pulse occurs, the counter is set to 7.

Output Behavior

The output is 0 whenever the current state indicates an even count and 1 whenever the current state indicates an odd count.

Examining these requirements we see that we must remember counts between 0 and 7. Thus we need 8 states that we can label q_i corresponding to "the current count is i." With this convention we can describe the operation of the counter by the state transition diagram shown in Figure 10-15. We have made one slight change in the form of our diagram. Instead of indicating the output as a label on a branch, we have included this information as part of the node label. We do this to emphasize the fact that the output is to depend only on the current state of the network and not the current input. Using the information contained in this diagram, we obtain the state table given by Table 10-15. Since the output does not depend on the input but only on the current state of the network, we include a separate column in the transition table indicating the output.

The Assignment Problem

As we have seen, the state table that we obtain from a word description of the desired behavior of a network is often in a symbolic form that must be encoded into binary notation before we can carry out the rest of the design process. This is known as the

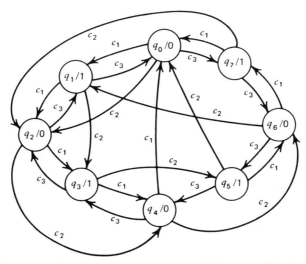

Figure 10-15 State transition diagram representing special counter. *Note:* Label of each node is q_i/z_i where q_i is the current state and z_i is the current output.

assignment problem. For a sequential network any encoding that labels each distinct state, input, and output with a unique binary code can be used to solve the assignment problem. However, the choice of a particular coding assignment can have a very profound effect on the number of logic elements needed to realize the network. Thus it would be desirable to have an algorithm that would tell us which coding assignment would result in the most economical circuit.

One algorithm would simply consist of forming all the possible coding assignments and then selecting the most economical circuit from all those that were formed. Unfortunately, this is not a practical approach even though in theory this algorithm always gives us a minimum circuit. In order to see why this algorithm breaks down, all we have to do is investigate the number of distinct codings that are possible for a transition table with m states.

Table 10-15 State Table for Special Counter

Current State	Input c_1	c_2	c_3	Current Output
q_0	q_1	q_2	q_7	0
q_1	q_2	q_3	q_0	1
q_2	q_3	q_4	q_1	0
q_3	q_4	q_5	q_2	1
q_4	q_0	q_6	q_3	0
q_5	q_6	q_0	q_4	1
q_6	q_7	q_1	q_5	0
q_7	q_0	q_2	q_6	1

When we make up a state table we concentrate on relating the states of the network to the events that we wish to remember. To construct a sequential network corresponding to this table we must relate the states of the table to the state variables of the flip-flops that make up the network. If we have a network with r flip-flops, we know that the 2^r-values of the r-tuple $[y_1, \ldots, y_r]$ represent the possible states of the circuit. Assume that the state table has m states; then the only restriction is that r must be selected such that

$$m \leq 2^r$$

so that it is possible to have a unique assignment between the states of the state table and the r-tuple $[y_1, y_2, \ldots, y_r]$.

For every value of m and r there are many different state assignments that can be used. If we disregard the symmetries that are present between different codings, there are

$$\frac{2^r!}{(2^r - m)!}$$

different ways that we can assign the 2^r combinations of state variables to the m states. McCluskey and Unger have shown that this number can be reduced by taking into account certain symmetries and other special properties of logic circuits. With these restrictions included there are

$$\frac{(2^r - 1)!}{(2^r - m)!r!}$$

distinct assignments of r state variable to m states.

Table 10-16 lists the number of distinct assignments for values of r from 1 to 4 and m from 2 to 9. Examination of this table shows that the brute force method of enumerating all of the possible state assignments would be feasible only for values of m up to 4. For values of m of 9 or greater it becomes a completely unreasonable approach, even if a digital computer were available, to carry out the enumeration. A

Table 10-16   Table of the Number of Distinct State Assignments

Number of States, m	Number of State Variables, r	Number of Distinct Assignments
2	1	1
3	2	3
4	2	3
5	3	140
6	3	420
7	3	840
8	3	840
9	4	10, 810, 800

similar problem also occurs when it is necessary to encode the input and/or the output signal of a network.

Several analytical and rule-of-thumb procedures have been developed to find acceptable if not optimal solutions to the assignment problem. Computer programs have also been developed to help the designer with this problem. Many of these techniques are discussed in detail in References 1, 3, and 5. Fortunately, for the type of networks that we are interested in, the selection of a satisfactory solution to the assignment problem can usually be obtained by making use of the behavioral description of the network.

For example, consider the special counter described by Table 10-15. In this case the states represent the counts 0 through 7. Thus a natural assignment would be

$$
\begin{array}{ll}
q_0 = [0, 0, 0] & q_4 = [1, 0, 0] \\
q_1 = [0, 0, 1] & q_5 = [1, 0, 1] \\
q_2 = [0, 1, 0] & q_6 = [1, 1, 0] \\
q_3 = [0, 1, 1] & q_7 = [1, 1, 1]
\end{array}
$$

Similarly an assignment for the input could be

$$
c_1 = [0, 0] \qquad c_2 = [0, 1] \qquad c_3 = [1, 0]
$$

The state table of Table 10-15 can now be rewritten in terms of this new coding, and the resulting information can be used to find a logic circuit realization for this counter.

A Change Calculator

As a final example of how one might design a sequential network that will carry out a specific time-dependent task, consider the following problem.

Assume that you work for a vending machine manufacturer. The item sold by the machines produced by the company may cost either 10 cents or 15 cents depending on where the machine is installed. The machine will accept nickles, dimes, and quarters one at a time and give the correct change. A sequential network is to be designed that can be used to compute the amount of change to be returned to each customer. There must be a way to control the operation of the network so that the same network can be used if the price of the item is 10 cents or 15 cents.

Examining this problem statement, we must first identify the input information that may be applied to the sequential network and the output information we can expect from the network. To do this, it is helpful to draw a diagram of the form shown in Figure 10-16, indicating the information we know about the problem.

Now that we have identified the input and output, our next task is to formulate the state transition diagram for this network.

The states of the network serve to remember the amount of money that has been deposited before it is necessary to make change. Thus the initial state, q_0, corresponds to the condition "no money received." Starting with this state and going through all

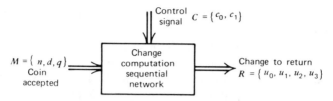

Figure 10-16   General form of network.

The meanings of the symbols shown in Figure 10-16 are as follows:

M	Value of coin deposited	C	Control signal	R	Change returned
n	Nickle	c_0	Item costs 10 cents	u_0 0 cents u_2 10 cents	
d	Dime	c_1	Item costs 15 cents	u_1 5 cents u_3 15 cents	
q	Quarter				

of the possible input combinations provide the state transition diagram shown in Figure 10-17.

Examining this diagram, we see that there are a number of don't care conditions. For example, if we reach state q_1, we assume that the input (c_0, d) would not occur, since the item costs only a dime and thus the person would not have deposited a nickle first. We similarly note that the only time that we will be in state q_2 is when the item costs 15 cents. Thus the inputs $\{(c_0, n), (c_1, d)\}$ never occur in that state.

The state table associated with this network is given by Table 10-17.

The next step in the design process consists of the binary encoding of the input, output, and state information. At this point the designer's experience and insight into

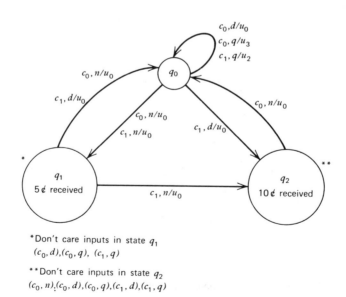

*Don't care inputs in state q_1
$(c_0, d), (c_0, q), (c_1, q)$

**Don't care inputs in state q_2
$(c_0, n), (c_0, d), (c_0, q), (c_1, d), (c_1, q)$

Figure 10-17   State transition diagram for coin change calculator.

Table 10-17 State Transition Table for Coin Change Calculator

Input State	c_0			c_1		
	n	d	q	n	d	q
q_0	q_1/u_0	q_0/u_0	q_0/u_3	q_1/u_0	q_2/u_0	q_0/u_2
q_1	q_0/u_0	-/-	-/-	q_2/u_0	q_0/u_0	-/-
q_2	-/-	-/-	-/-	q_0/u_0	-/-	-/-

the problem will be very important. As we discussed previously, many distinct encodings are possible. The one chosen should be as straightforward as possible to minimize the complexity of the signal.

If we look at the input information, we see that we have six input conditions. ([2 control values] $\times$ [3 coin values]) Thus we need 3 bits to encode the input signal. The input consists of two subparts; one corresponding to the coin received, and one corresponding to the price of the item being sold. This suggests the following encoding.

$$X := [x_1, x_2, x_3]$$

$x_1 = 0$ item costs 10 cents $\qquad$ $x_2, x_3 = [0, 1]$—input a nickle
$x_1 = 1$ item costs 15 cents $\qquad$ $x_2, x_3 = [1, 0]$—input a dime
$\qquad\qquad\qquad\qquad\qquad\qquad$ $x_2, x_3 = [1, 1]$—input a quarter

The output signal may take on four possible values. Two bits are sufficient to encode this information. The following encoding is suggested

$$Z := [z_1, z_2]$$

$u_0 = [0, 0]$ no change $\qquad$ $u_2 = [1, 0]$ 10 cents change
$u_1 = [0, 1]$ 5 cents change $\qquad$ $u_3 = [1, 1]$ 15 cents change

In this encoding, z_1 can be thought of as an indication that 10 cents should be returned and z_2 can be thought of as an indication that 5 cents should be returned. The three states can be encoded as

$$Y := [y_1, y_2]$$

$q_0 = [0, 0]$ no money received $\qquad$ $q_2 = [1, 0]$ 10 cents received
$q_1 = [0, 1]$ 5 cents received

Using this information we can now generate the transition table of Table 10-18 corresponding to the state table of Table 10-17.

At this point we see that a very large number of don't care conditions exist. Our final task is to reduce this transition table to a sequential network. The final logic

Table 10-18   Transition Table for Coin Change Calculations

X Y	000	001	010	011	100	101	110	111
00	-/-	0, 1/0, 0	0, 0/0, 0	0, 0/1, 1	-/-	0, 1/0, 0	1, 0/0, 0	0, 0/1, 0
01	-/-	0, 0/0, 0	-/-	-/-	-/-	1, 0/0, 0	0, 0/0, 0	-/-
10	-/-	-/-	-/-	-/-	-/-	0, 0/0, 0	-/-	-/-
11	-/-	-/-	-/-	-/-	-/-	-/-	-/-	-/-

network necessary to realize this sequential machine can be obtained in the standard manner once we decide on the type of flip-flops we will use. The details of this computation are left as an exercise.

EXERCISES

1.   Design a modulo 8 counter using J-K flip-flops.

2.   Find the state table of a network that counts ⌐→0→1→2→3→⌐ at each clock pulse if the input is 0 and ⌐→0→3→2→1→⌐ if the input is 1. This is an example of an up-down counter.

3.   Find a state assignment for the state table of Exercise 2 and design a sequential network, using J-K flip-flops, that will realize the table.

4.   Realize the sequential network described by Table 10-18 using D flip-flops.

5.   SUMMARY

In this chapter we have investigated, in an introductory manner, the problems that must be solved when designing a sequential network to handle a specific information processing task. There is an extensive body of knowledge concerning techniques that can be used to design sequential networks. Many of these techniques have been reduced to a set of computer programs, thereby reducing the amount of tedious calculations required of the designer. Unfortunately, the hardest part of many design processes, the problem of actually describing the operations that must be performed by the particular network under investigation, cannot be automated to any great extent.

However, many of the networks required to carry out standard information processing operations have reached the point where they are so common that several standardized designs are already available as standard integrated circuits. The system designer will find that this trend makes it much easier to concentrate on the design of a complete system and not have to worry about the details of designing the sequential networks that make up the subunits of the system.

Reference Notation

All the references listed have extensive discussions concerning the analysis of sequential networks. The more theoretical aspects of sequential networks are presented in Reference 3. References 1, 2, 4, and 5 provide an intermediate treatment of the design and applications of various types of sequential networks. They also treat many of the advanced topics of sequential network design such as state assignment and state reduction techniques. These topics are not as central to digital system design as they once were since most designs now use standard LSI or MSI logic networks to carry out the standard operations that once had to be realized using sequential networks.

REFERENCES

1. Dietmeyer, D. L. (1978), *Logic Design of Digital Systems* (second edition). Allyn and Bacon, Boston.
2. Hill, F. J., and Peterson, G. R. (1981), *Introduction to Switching Theory and Logical Design* (third edition). Wiley, New York.
3. Kohavi, Z. (1978), *Switching and Finite Automata Theory* (second edition). McGraw-Hill, New York.
4. Mano, M. M. (1979), *Digital Logic and Computer Design*. Prentice-Hall, Englewood Cliffs, N.J.
5. Mowle, F. J. (1976), *A Systematic Approach to Digital Logic Design*. Addison Wesley, Reading, Mass.

HOME PROBLEMS

1. A widget production line has two conveyer belts. To maintain a balanced production schedule a checkpoint is introduced to monitor the flow of widgets on each conveyer belt. If the number of widgets that passed the checkpoint on belt i exceeds the number of widgets that passed the checkpoint on belt j by three, then belt i must stop. Belt i remains stopped until three additional widgets are detected on belt j. At that point belt i is started. A sequential network is to be used to control this operation. Find a transition table for this network.

2. In a number of digital systems it is necessary to have a controllable counter. Design a synchronous sequential network using *J-K* flip-flops that will have the following characteristics.

Input Signals		
X_1	X_2	Operation
0	0	No change of state
0	1	Modulo 3 counter
1	0	Modulo 5 counter
1	1	Modulo 7 counter

3. Design a digital combination lock that can be opened only if the proper sequence of 5 buttons on a 10-button keyboard has been pushed. Realize this system using a PLA. Explain how the combination can be changed.

4. Design a BCD decade counter. Every time the input clock pulse occurs, the count will increase by 1 until 9 is reached. The counter then resets to 0 and a carry output of 1 is generated. Show how four of these counters can be used to form a 4-digit BCD counter.

5. A vending machine is set to sell six items whose price may range from 10 cents to 50 cents in 5-cent increments. To use the machine a person pushes a button to indicate the item to be purchased and then deposits the money necessary to purchase the item. Assume that the machine will accept only nickles, dimes, and quarters and that it will give the correct change if too much money is deposited. Design a sequential network, similar to the one shown in Figure 10-16, that will indicate when enough money has been deposited and the amount of change that must be returned.

11

INTRODUCTION TO DIGITAL SYSTEM ARCHITECTURE

1. INTRODUCTION

The digital devices discussed in the previous chapters were designed to carry out individual information processing tasks or to perform specific operations on digital information. We have now reached the point where we can combine these individual units to form complex digital systems. This level of design is referred to as developing a *system architecture*. In this chapter we consider the following problems:

1. The interface problem: How do we interconnect a digital device to other digital devices or to the outside world?
2. The memory problem: How do we store the large quantities of information needed by a system to perform a computation?
3. The system design problem: How do we create a system that can perform one or more complex computations using an interconnection of digital devices designed to perform specific tasks?

This discussion emphasizes the information flow that takes place in a digital system rather than the details of how individual devices operate. Several examples are presented, however, to illustrate the relationship that exists between the information flow in the system and the way that the tasks that influence this flow are implemented. The references listed at the end of this chapter provide further insight into many of the problem areas that are introduced in the following sections.

2. THE INTERFACE PROBLEM

Modern digital systems can process information at a very high rate. Unfortunately the outside world cannot always keep pace with this capability. For example, one common input device for a digital system is a video terminal with a keyboard. A typical user will use the keyboard to enter information at a rate considerably below

10 characters per second. However, even the slowest digital system can process hundreds of characters per second. If a digital system is to communicate effectively with the terminal, special techniques must be used to match the operating speed of the input/output device (the terminal) to the operating speed of the system.

The necessity of communicating with the outside world is not the only problem that must be considered. A digital system may be constructed as an interconnection of a number of subsystems, some of which may be physically or logically separated. Special techniques must be used to interchange information between these subsystems in such a way that the overall performance of the system will not be degraded.

The problem of matching the flow of information between portions of a digital system to the rate at which this information is being generated or used is referred to as an *interface problem*. Figure 11-1 illustrates two typical interface problems involving the transfer of information between a digital system and two peripheral devices.

The first problem involves receiving information from the outside world by way of an input device. This device first encodes the information into digital form and then announces to the digital system that the information is ready for use. The system then assumes responsibility for reading the information and informing the input unit that the information has been received.

The second problem involves an output device that receives information from the digital system and processes this information for use by the outside world. Before the system can send information to the output device, it must check to see whether the device is free to receive information. If it is the digital system sends the data. Otherwise it must wait until the output device indicates that it is free.

In each of these devices we have indicated that a separate control unit is available to control the operation of the peripherals. For some devices the control unit will be extremely simple since the tasks that must be controlled are not particularly complex. In other cases the peripheral may be required to carry out extensive pre- or post-processing before the information is ready for use. For those cases the control unit may be quite complex. The following discussion illustrates several of the interfacing techniques found in digital systems.

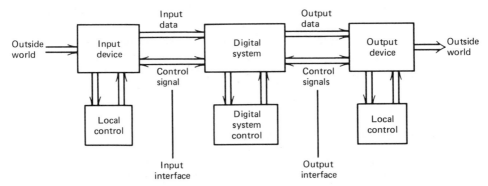

Figure 11-1   General model of interface problem.

Input Interface

Figure 11-2 illustrates the organization of a typical input interface. As shown, the input device receives information from the outside world and, if necessary, encodes it into digital form. The encoded information is placed into the *input-device buffer-register,* or *input buffer,* to await transmission to the digital system. When the input device is operating independently of the digital system, it is necessary to announce that information is in the input buffer and ready for use. This is accomplished by using a *flag.* The flag is a 1-bit register that is set to 1 when information is ready for transmission and set to 0 when no information is available. It is the responsibility of the input device control unit to see that the input buffer is loaded and that the device flag is set.

As soon as the digital system is ready to receive information, it looks at the value of the flag. When it finds that the flag has a value of 1, it issues the control signals necessary to transfer the information from the device-input buffer to the system-input buffer-register. For this example it is assumed that the transmission is carried out as a single-step parallel transfer. A serial transfer could also be used, but this would require a slightly more complex interface unit. When the transfer has been completed, the input flag is set to 0 and the input device can start generating the next input signal. From this model we see that the control unit in the digital system can control when an input transfer is to take place, but the rate of transfer is limited by the speed of the input device.

Output Interface

The output interface shown in Figure 11-3 operates in a manner similar to the input interface. Initially, before any output information has been transferred, the flag in the output device is set to 1 to indicate that it is free to receive information. The information to be transferred to the output device is placed in the *system-output buffer-register.* As soon as the control unit in the digital system detects that the out-

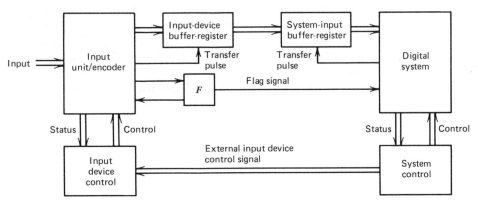

Figure 11-2   General organization of input interface.

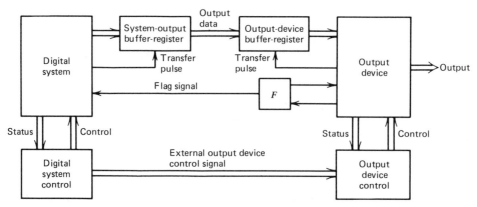

Figure 11-3   General organization of output interface.

put flag is a 1, the control unit issues the command to transfer the information from the system-output buffer to the *output-device buffer-register*. When this transfer is made the control unit in the output device sets the flag to 0, indicating that the output device is busy processing the information that was just transferred to the output buffer. Upon completing the processing, the control unit sets the flag to 1, indicating that the output device is ready to process the next item of information.

Here again we see that the digital system controls when information is sent to the output device, but the rate of transfer is governed by capabilities of the output device.

The use of a flag to control the interchange of information between two devices is called *handshaking*. The design of an interface depends upon the complexity of the task that must be performed by the peripheral device and the rate at which the digital system processes information. The following examples illustrate some of the different forms that an interface may take.

A Keyboard Input

The simplest type of input device is a switch. If we assume that we are dealing with a "debounced" switch of the type discussed in Chapter 8, then the arrangement shown in Figure 11-4 can be interpreted as generating a 1-bit signal. When the switch is in position (i), it has an output value of 1. Similarly, it has an output of 0 when it is in position (ii).

The idea of a switch can be easily extended to a keyboard, such as the one illus-

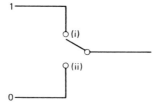

Figure 11-4   Generation of a digital signal using a switch.

trated in Figure 11-5. Each character on the keyboard is assigned a unique digital code, such as the EBCDIC code given in Appendix A. When a key is pushed, a signal is applied to the decoding network that produces the 8-bit code associated with that key. We also assume that a transfer pulse is generated that can be used to control the transfer of information into a buffer-register. If we assume that the letter A is pressed, then a timing diagram showing the output of the decoder network might have the form shown in Figure 11-6.

Using this information, an input interface unit of the form shown in Figure 11-7 can be used with this input device. The input-device buffer is constructed from D flip-flops.

Initially, assume that the flag is in the 0 state. When a key is pressed on the keyboard, an input transfer pulse is generated that is applied, through the AND gate, to the clock input on the input-device buffer. The code corresponding to the pressed key is loaded into the register and the flag, which is a simple unclocked $S\text{-}R$ flip-flop, is set to 1. This prevents any other information from being loaded into the input-device buffer.

The digital system then observes that the flag has a value of 1 and knows that input information is ready for transmission to the system-input buffer. An information transfer signal is sent out by the digital system. The contents of the input-device buffer is then transferred into the system-input buffer, and the flag is reset to 0. This completes the information transfer sequence, and the next key on the keyboard can be pressed.

This whole transfer sequence usually occurs within, at most, a few milliseconds after the keyboard key is pushed. The person using the keyboard will probably take a tenth of a second or more to push the next key. Thus the user assumes that the system is accepting the keyboard information as fast as the keys can be pushed.

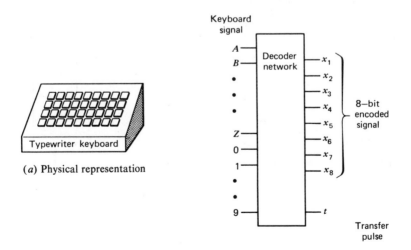

(a) Physical representation

(b) Logic representation

Figure 11-5 A keyboard input device.

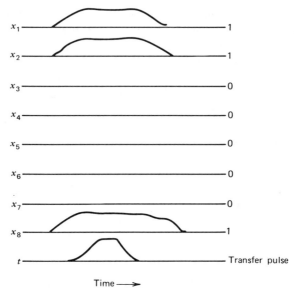

Figure 11-6 Timing diagram of a typical output of keyboard decoder network.

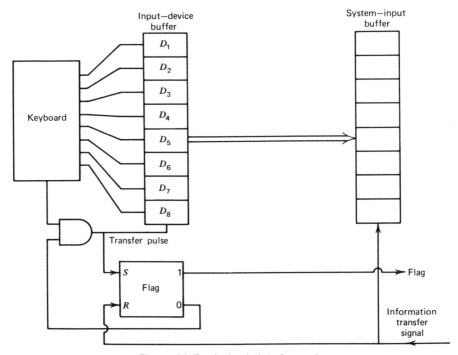

Figure 11-7 A simple interface unit.

A Printer as an Output Device

A common type of output produced by a digital system is a printed record. This type of output is essentially the reverse of the input process just discussed. Figure 11-8 shows the form that a printing output device might take.

The code for the character to be printed is placed in the buffer-register. The printing operation is then started by applying a 1 to the start-print input of the printing unit. After the unit has completed the printing of the character, it emits a printing-complete pulse, which indicates that it is ready to print the next character.

A typical interface for this type of output device is shown in Figure 11-9. Initially the flag is set to 1, indicating that the printer is ready to receive data. The system-output information is placed in the system-output buffer-register. When the system detects that the flag is 1, it transmits a transfer command that transfers the information in the system-output buffer-register into the output-device buffer-register and sets the flag, again a simple unclocked S-R flip-flop, to 0. As soon as the flag goes to 0, the printer is commanded to print the character corresponding to the coded information contained in the output-device buffer-register. On completion of the printing operation the printer issues a printing-complete pulse that sets the flag to 1. This completes the printing cycle and the next character can be transmitted for printing.

Analog Information

Many of the signals processed by digital systems are initially in analog or continuous form. Before the system can operate on the information in the signal, it must be converted into digital form. An input device that performs this task is called an *analog-to-digital converter* or *A/D converter*. Similarly there are many occasions in which the output information generated by a digital system must be converted into analog form before it can be used. An output device that performs this task is called a *digital-to-analog converter* or *D/A converter*.

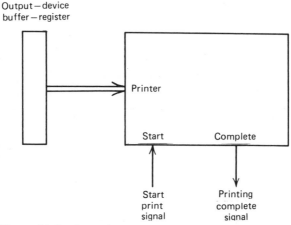

Output — device
buffer — register

Printer

Start   Complete

Start
print
signal

Printing
complete
signal

Figure 11-8   General organization of printing output device.

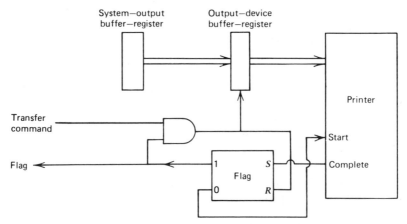

Figure 11-9 An output interface for printer.

The general problems involved with both types of conversion were treated briefly in Chapter 2. In the following discussion we investigate some of the techniques that can be used to construct both D/A and A/D converters.

D/A Converters

The digital-to-analog conversion process is the easiest to realize. Figure 11-10 illustrates the general form that a D/A converter might take if it is used as an output device for a digital system. In this example only one buffer is used to hold the information generated by the digital system and no flag is included in the converter. The reason for this is that it is assumed that we wish to update the analog output signal as fast as possible. Thus, when a new value is ready for conversion, the system loads it directly into the buffer. As long as the time taken to convert the digital signal is

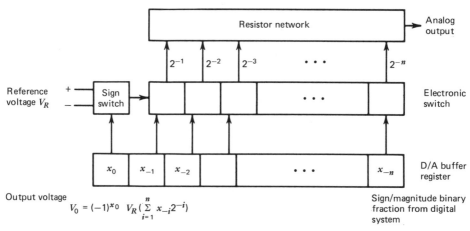

Output voltage
$$V_0 = (-1)^{x_0} V_R \left(\sum_{i=1}^{n} x_{-i} 2^{-i} \right)$$

Figure 11-10 General form of D/A converter.

less than the time it takes the system to generate a new value for the signal, the system will operate correctly. If we should reach the situation where the D/A converter cannot keep up with the rate at which the system generates new values, then we would need to introduce a flag to control the conversion rate.

For this system it is assumed that the digital information is represented as a sign-magnitude binary fraction. This number is placed in the D/A buffer register and has the form

$$[x_0, x_{-1}, x_{-2}, \ldots, x_{-n}]$$

where x_0 represents the sign bit (0 corresponds to plus and 1 to minus) and $[x_{-1}, x_{-2}, \ldots, x_{-n}]$ represents the magnitude of the binary fraction ($.x_{-1} x_{-2} \ldots x_{-n}$). The output of each bit of the buffer register drives an electronic switch that connects an appropriate voltage to the resistor decoding network. The organization of the switches and the decoding network is shown in Figure 11-11 for $n = 4$ and an input of [01010].

The resistor network shown in Figure 11-11 can be generalized for the case where the magnitude is represented by n bits. In this case the expression for the output voltage becomes*

$$V_0 = (-1)^{x_0} V_R \left(\sum_{i=1}^{n} x_{-i} 2^{-i} \right)$$

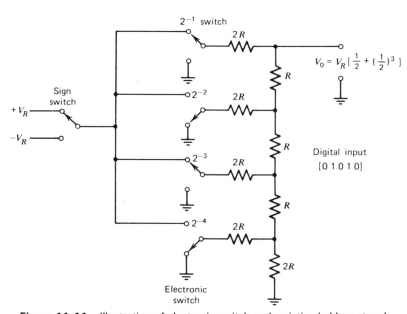

Figure 11-11   Illustration of electronic switch and resistive ladder network.

*This formula can be derived by using standard circuit theory analysis techniques. See the reference at the end of this chapter.

Conversion Rate

The settling time of a D/A converter is the time it takes for the output voltage to reach a steady value after the command is given to load the digital signal into the buffer-register. Current D/A converters have settling times in the range of a few microseconds.

If we let t_s represent the settling time for a D/A converter, then the maximum conversion rate is

$$C_{max} = 1/t_s \text{ samples per second}$$

In many cases this conversion rate will be much faster than needed, and the operating conversion rate will depend on how fast the digital system delivers information to the D/A converter.

A/D Converters

Analog-to-digital converters can take on a number of forms. The most popular types, and the ones that we will discuss, are classified as feedback converters. They have the general form shown in Figure 11-12. This unit operates by generating a sequence of digital values in the register. The content of the register then drives the D/A converter network to produce an output analog voltage V_0. The voltage V_0 is compared to the input voltage V_I in the comparator, which produces an output signal

$$d = \begin{cases} 1 & V_0 \geq V_I \\ 0 & V_0 < V_I \end{cases}$$

Using this value of d, the gating and control network decides on the next value to be placed in the register. This sequence of operations continues until the gating and control network decides that the signal in the register is a satisfactory approximation of V_I.

Counter A/D Converters

The simplest way to realize a feedback A/D converter is to use the register as a counter and count up until a value is reached where $V_0 \geq V_I$. When this condition occurs, the number in the register is the digital approximation of V_I. Figure 11-13

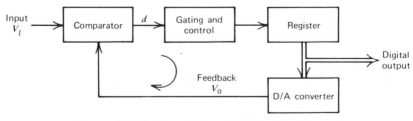

Figure 11-12 General form of A/D feedback converter.

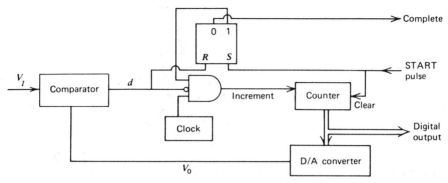

Figure 11-13 A simple counter A/D converter.

shows the general form of this type of A/D converter. For illustrative purposes it is assumed that the input analog signal is always positive.

The counter is a standard binary counter with a clear input and an increment input. When a pulse is applied to the clear input, the counter is set to 0, and when a pulse appears on the increment input, the count increases by 1. Operation starts when a start pulse is applied to the start line. This clears the counter and sets the control flip-flop to the 1 state. As long as $V_0 < V_I$ the gate will allow the clock pulses to be applied to the increment input. Thus the counter will start to count up, which in turn increases the value of V_0. This operation continues until $V_0 \geq V_I$ at which time $d = 1$, the AND gate opens, and the control flip-flop is reset to 0 indicating that the conversion is complete. The digital value in the counter is the digital approximation to V_I.

The conversion operation is illustrated in Figure 11-14. The time frame of operation has been exaggerated somewhat to show the details of operation. However, the figure does show the important characteristics of a counter A/D converter.

First we note that the value of the digital output will always equal or exceed the value of the input at the time the conversion is ended. Second we see that the con-

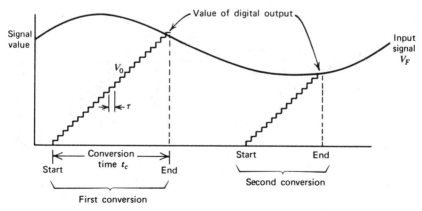

Figure 11-14 Illustration of the operation of a counter A/D converter.

version time is variable. The larger the magnitude of the signal, the larger the conversion time.

The speed of a counter A/D converter depends on the settling time τ of the D/A converter that generates V_0. If the magnitude of the signal is to be represented by n bits, then the conversion time t_c will fall in the range of

$$\tau \leq t_c < 2^n \tau$$

For example, if τ = 2 microseconds and n = 10, then t_c would fall in the range of

$$2 \text{ microseconds} \leq t_c < 2048 \text{ microseconds}$$

For many applications the simplicity of operation of a counter A/D converter outweighs this wide variation in conversion time. However, for high-speed applications a different conversion method must be used to reduce conversion time.

Successive Approximation A/D Converters

In the successive approximation A/D converter we try to match the input signal by successively dividing the possible interval in which the input may fall into smaller and smaller size. To understand the operation of this converter, consider the 4-bit converter shown in Figure 11-15. The register together with the control logic makes up a sequential network. When the start signal is received, the register is driven to [1000]. The output of the D/A converter becomes $V_0 = (V_R/2)$. If

$$\frac{V_R}{2} \leq V_I$$

then d = 0 and the next state of the register is [1100]; otherwise

$$\frac{V_R}{2} > V_I$$

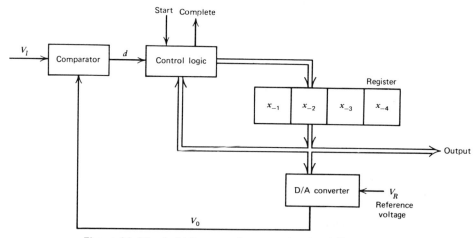

Figure 11-15 A 4-bit successive approximation A/D converter.

which means $d = 1$ and the next state of the register becomes [0100]. Again V_0 is compared to V_I and if $V_0 \leq V_I$, bit x_{-2} is not changed and x_{-3} is set to 1. Otherwise x_{-2} is set to 0 and x_{-3} is set to 1. The comparison then continues to the point where the values for x_{-3} and x_{-4} are fixed. A complete enumeration of all the possible testing sequences is illustrated by the transition diagram shown in Figure 11-16. Examining this diagram we see that if the converter register has n-bits, then exactly n-steps are needed to complete the conversion after the start signal is given.

The way in which a 4-bit successive approximation A/D converter would process an input signal is illustrated in Figure 11-17. Here we see that if the settling time for the D/A converter is τ seconds and if the register has n-bits, then the total conversion time is always $(n + 1)\tau$ seconds independent of the magnitude of the input.

This brief discussion of A/D and D/A converters has introduced the common techniques employed by digital systems to interface digital and analog or continuous systems. The references listed at the end of this chapter give a much more extensive discussion of the organization, construction, and use of A/D and D/A converters.

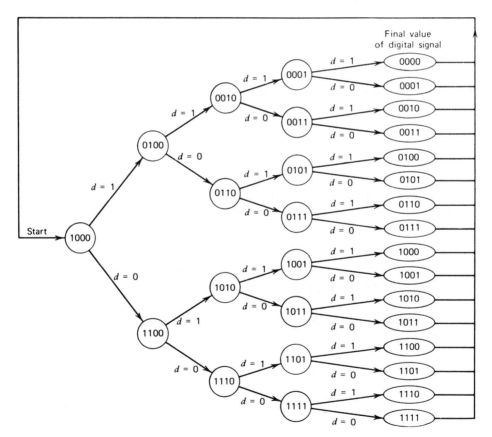

Figure 11-16 Transition diagram illustrating operation of successive approximation D/A converter.

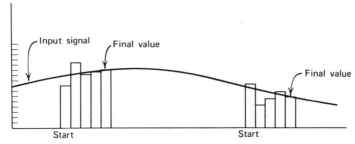

Figure 11-17 Illustration of conversion process for successive approximation A/D converter.

EXERCISES

1. Suppose that the digital device processing the information received from the keyboard interface takes 10^{-4} seconds to process the information. If the keyboard can generate only 10 characters per second, how much time does the digital system spend waiting between inputs?

2. Redesign the interface system of Figure 11-9 if a serial information transfer must take place between the system-output buffer-register and the buffer-register of the printer. Assume that the buffer is an 8-bit register.

3. For an n-bit converter, what is the size of the maximum conversion error that may be introduced in an A/D conversion
(a) If a sign bit is present?
(b) If a sign bit is not present?

4. A 12-bit successive approximation D/A converter with a settling time τ of 1.5 microseconds ($1.5 \ 10^{-6}$ seconds) is used as an output of a digital network. What is the maximum number of distinct output values that this converter may produce in a second? What is the maximum frequency sine wave that can be produced if we assume that we must produce 10 values per period (or cycle) of the sine wave?

3. MEMORY DEVICES

In computers and other digital systems there are many situations in which it is necessary to store large amounts of information in a small space and at low cost. We have already seen that registers constructed from flip-flops can be used to store information. In this section we introduce two classes of memory devices, read-only memory and random access memory, which have been designed to store information in an efficient manner. This discussion concentrates upon the external characteristics of these devices and the way that they may be used in a digital system. The references at the end of this chapter give additional details about the internal structure of these memory units.

Read-Only Memory (ROM)

The simplest type of memory unit is the *read-only memory* or, as they are usually referred to, *ROMs*. These memories store a fixed collection of information that is required by a digital system to perform a given task.

From a functional view, ROMs are used to carry out a mapping from a set X to a set Y. This mapping is represented by

$$Y := F(X)$$

where X is an r-bit input signal and Y is an n-bit output signal. When discussing a ROM, the signal X is referred to as the *address signal* and the signal Y is the *data signal*.

Basically a ROM is a special purpose switching matrix. The structure of a ROM can be represented as shown in Figure 11-18. Two registers, the *Memory Address Register* (MAR) and the *Memory Buffer Register* (MBR) are often used to interface the ROM to the rest of the system. These registers are normally external to the ROM but in special cases may be an integral part of the unit.

To read information out of the ROM it is necessary to apply the address signal X to the input of the ROM. This address information is decoded and used to select one of the 2^r rows of the output matrix. The bit pattern associated with that row then appears as the output data signal from the ROM. If we assume that the read operation begins when an address value is loaded into the MAR, the complete read operation can be described by the transfer sequence:

$$\tau_1: \quad \text{MAR} \leftarrow X$$
$$\tau_2: \quad \text{MBR} \leftarrow F(X)$$

The second transfer pulse τ_2 cannot occur until the data output has reached a steady value after the application of τ_1.

If X is an r-bit vector, there will be 2^r different n-bit data items that can be stored

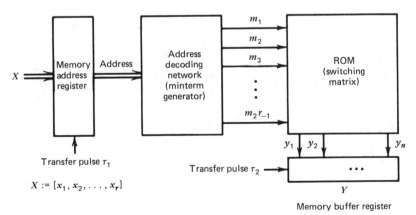

Figure 11-18 General form of a Read-Only memory.

in the ROM. Each such item is called a *word*. The minterm associated with a given row is called the *address* of the row, or the address of the memory word associated with that row.

ROMs have become very important devices in digital system design because of their relative low cost and the ease with which they can be used to carry out specialized tasks. To generate a ROM all that we need to do is to specify the mapping $F(X)$ that defines the output associated with each address X. As shown in the following example, we can use a truth table to represent this mapping.

Output Display Driver

In many digital systems we wish to display the output as a multiple digit decimal number. A common way to display a decimal digit is to use a seven-segment display that has the form shown in Figure 11-19a. When an activate signal (logical 1) is applied to one of the segments of the display, that segment glows. By using this result it is possible to form the digits 0 through 9, the letter E (to indicate an error), and the minus sign as shown in Figure 11-19b.

Each display has seven input leads. If we wish to display the digital value of a BCD encoded number, we can use a ROM as the decoding network. In this case, X is the 4-bit BCD encoded information and Y is the signal needed to activate the corresponding display pattern.

To design the ROM, we must first develop the truth table that describes the relationship F between the input X and the output Y. This is given by Table 11-1. Since there are 16 possible addresses associated with the 4-bit input and only 13 output characters (the 12 characters shown in 11-19b and a blank) to be displayed, we have

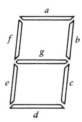

(a) Segment organization of seven-segment display

(b) Character representation

Figure 11-19 Seven-segment display.

Table 11-1 Programming of Seven-Segment Display Decoder

BCD Input X				Decoded Output Y							Display Output
d_3	d_2	d_1	d_0	a	b	c	d	e	f	g	
0	0	0	0	1	1	1	1	1	1	0	0
0	0	0	1	0	1	1	0	0	0	0	1
0	0	1	0	1	1	0	1	1	0	1	2
0	0	1	1	1	1	1	1	0	0	1	3
0	1	0	0	0	1	1	0	0	1	1	4
0	1	0	1	1	0	1	1	0	1	1	5
0	1	1	0	0	0	1	1	1	1	1	6
0	1	1	1	1	1	1	0	0	0	0	7
1	0	0	0	1	1	1	1	1	1	1	8
1	0	0	1	1	1	1	0	0	1	1	9
1	0	1	0	0	0	0	0	0	0	1	—
1	0	1	1	0	0	0	0	0	0	.	Blank
1	1	0	0	1	0	0	1	1	1	1	E
1	1	0	1	1	0	0	1	1	1	1	E
1	1	1	0	1	0	0	1	1	1	1	E
1	1	1	1	1	0	0	1	1	1	1	E

arbitrarily decided to assign an output of E to all unused input values. This will indicate that an error has occurred if one of these inputs is ever generated by the system.

This table can be used to realize a ROM as shown in Figure 11-20. In this realization the memory buffer register is realized from D flip-flops. The switching matrix is the actual "memory." It has sixteen 7-bit words. Each word is accessed by activating (placing a 1) on the appropriate line. The output then appears on the output or *sense* lines.

To illustrate the operation of this system, assume that the input X is [0101]. When τ_1 is applied, X is loaded into the MAR. The decimal value of X is 5. Thus the value we are interested in is in memory word 5. As soon as X is loaded, the address decoding network activates line m_5 and the output [1011011] appears on the output sense lines of the switching matrix. The transfer pulse τ_2 transfers this output into the MBR. Finally the display uses the output of the MBR to form the digit 5 on the display.

Read-only memories come in a number of different forms. The simplest consists of semiconductor arrays in which the 0-bits in a word are realized by actually "burning out" the connection associated with that element during the manufacturing process. ROMs of this type cannot be changed after they are programmed. If a change in the contents of such a ROM must be made, a completely new ROM must be produced.

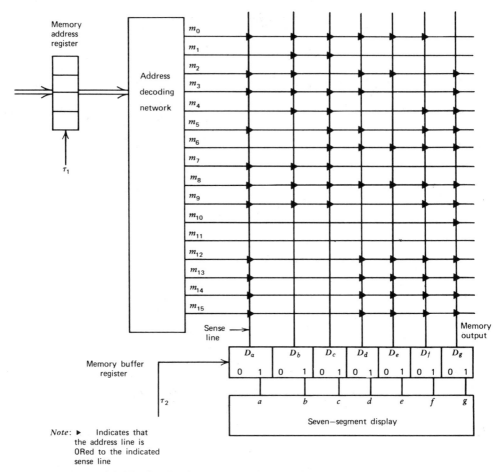

Note: ▶ Indicates that the address line is ORed to the indicated sense line

Figure 11-20 Read-only memory realization of seven-segment decoder.

To overcome this problem a special class of ROMs has been developed called *Programmable Read-Only Memories* or PROMs. Instead of "burning" out a connection in a PROM, we electronically alter the connections in the switching matrix by applying special conditioning signals that are much different from the normal operating signals. Once the PROM is programmed, it acts just like a ROM.

ROMs and PROMs have one disadvantage. Once they are programmed to realize a given truth table, they cannot be changed. A newer type of device has been developed that can erase the stored information by shining an ultraviolet light onto the semiconductor material that makes up the device. Once the information is erased, the device can be reprogrammed. Such a device is called an *erasable programmable read-only memory* (EPROM). These devices are still read-only memories since the technique used to reprogram the device requires that the device be removed from the system in which it is being used and placed in a special ROM programming unit. Thus to change the contents of an EPROM memory unit can take several hours.

Read/Write Memories

If we wish to dynamically change the information stored in a given memory location, we must use some type of register. Figure 11-21 illustrates a simple arrangement for introducing registers as the information storage element.

In this example each memory location is an n-bit register constructed from D flip-flops. If we wish to place information into the ith memory register, we must go through the following steps.

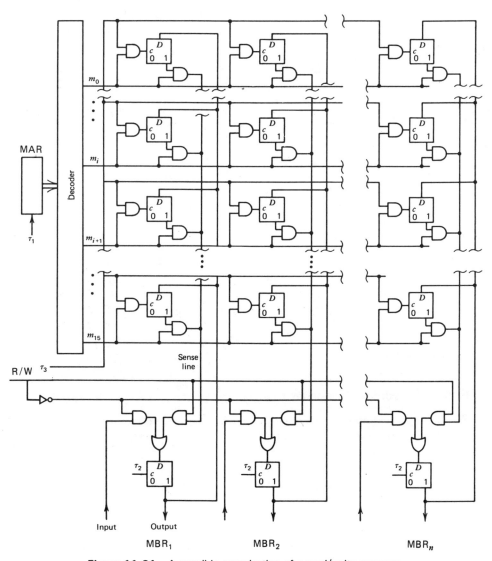

Figure 11-21 A possible organization of a read/write memory.

Writing Information into Memory

1. Place the address of the desired register into the Memory Address Register (MAR). This transfer is accomplished by transfer pulse τ_1.
2. The read/write signal (R/W) must be set to 0, indicating that information is to be written into memory.
3. The information to be placed into memory is loaded into the Memory Buffer Register (MBR) by transfer pulse τ_2.
4. The address information in the MAR corresponds to the binary number i. The ith minterm m_i at the output of the addess decoder goes to 1, selecting the ith memory register as the one to receive the information in the MBR. The pulse τ_3 transfers the information from the MBR into the ith memory word.

If we wish to read the information contained in the ith memory word, we use the following sequence of steps.

Reading Information from Memory

1. The address of the ith word is read into the MAR using transfer pulse τ_1.
2. The R/W signal is set to 1, indicating that infomation is to be read from memory.
3. The ith output of the address decoder network is 1, indicating that the ith word is to be involved in the information transfer.
4. The contents of the ith word appears on the output data line. The transfer pulse τ_2 is used to read the information into the MBR.

In the read operation the contents of the ith word is not changed. This is called a *nondestructive read*. One disadvantage of semiconductor memories is that they lose all of the information stored in the memory when power is removed. Such a memory is called a *volatile* memory. In some applications a special power supply is included in the system that keeps the power on to the memory devices even when the power to the rest of the system is turned off. A number of the programmable hand calculators currently on the market have this feature and are referred to as continuous memory calculators.

Random Access Memories (RAM)

Read/write memories are called *random access memories* or RAMs, since each memory register is directly accessible by placing its address in the MAR. Several different technologies can be used to construct RAMs. Most of the memory units now in use are constructed from integrated circuits. Each circuit is realized on a semiconductor wafer or chip. Thus it is common to refer to such a memory element as a "memory chip." For the discussions in the rest of this book we use the somewhat simplified representation shown in Figure 11-22 to model the external properties of a RAM.

The address signal is used to select the word to be accessed. If the address is represented by an n-bit signal, then the memory normally contains 2^n words. Some typ-

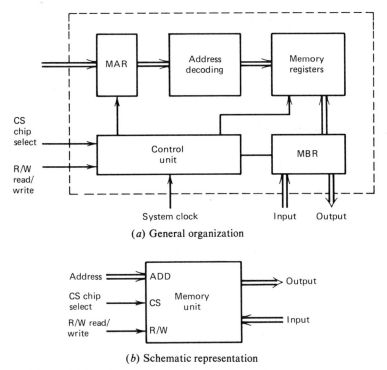

(*a*) General organization

(*b*) Schematic representation

Figure 11-22   General representation of a random access memory.

ical memory sizes currently found in a single semiconductor package are $16K$ ($K =$ 1024), $64K$, $128K$, and $256K$. However, developments in the semiconducter memory area are moving at a rapid pace, and larger memory sizes in a single package can be expected.

When the chip select signal CS is set to 1, it indicates that the particular memory unit is to be used in a memory transfer. This signal allows us to use multiple memory chips to create larger memory sizes. For example, if we wish to construct a $32K$ memory from two 16K memory units, we can use the circuit shown in Figure 11-23. To address $32K$ words of memory we need to use an address signal with 15 bits. If we wish to address 16K, we need 14 bits. Thus to form a 32K memory from two 16K units we use the memory address signal

$$[a_0, a_1, a_2, \ldots, a_{13}, a_{14}]$$

The first bit in this address, a_0, is used as the chip select bit. If this bit is 0 the low order memory unit is selected and a word with an address between 0 and $2^{14} - 1$ is selected. If a_0 is 1 the high order memory unit is selected. The address of the words in this unit fall in the range 2^{14} to $2^{15} - 1$.

The R/W signal is used to indicate whether the information is to be read from memory, R/W := 1, or to be written into memory, R/W := 0. The information

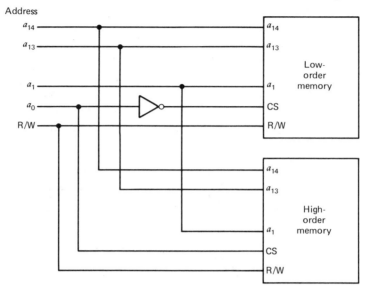

Figure 11-23 Illustration of use of *CS* to select a given memory chip.

transfers needed to carry out either of the operations are controlled by the control unit, which is driven by the system clock signal. The number of clock pulses needed to complete one of the memory transfers will vary depending upon the type of memory unit in use. For this discussion we assume that two clock pulses are required to carry out a memory transfer. The sequence of operations is characterized by the following sequence of information transfer operations.

Write Operations R/W := 0

Transfer Pulse	Transfer Operation
τ_1:	MAR ← ⟨address⟩ MBR ← ⟨input information⟩
τ_2:	$M_{[MAR]}$ ← MBR

Read Operations R/W := 1

τ_1:	MAR ← ⟨address⟩
τ_2:	MBR ← $M_{[MAR]}$

Core Memories

Before the development of semiconductor memories, the central memory of a computer system was normally constructed from small magnetic devices that looked like little doughnuts called *magnetic cores*. These devices can assume two different magnetized states. Thus each core can store 1 bit of information. Information transfers into and out of a core are much slower than the corresponding transfers in a semiconductor memory and require much more power. Thus cores have gone out of general use. Their main advantage is that once information is stored in a core, no additional power is needed to hold the information. Thus power can be turned off and the memory will retain all of the information that was stored in it when the power to the system was on. Memories with this property are called *nonvolatile* memories.

EXERCISES

1. Modify the switching array of Figure 11-20 so that the following input/output pairs are realized

Input	Output Character	Segments
1101	$\lfloor\overline{}\rfloor$	a, b, g, f
1110	$\lfloor\overline{}$	a, f
1111	$-$	d

2. Show how a 64K memory can be constructed from four 16K memory units.

4. BUS DATA TRANSFERS

As the number of registers increases in a digital system, the problem of moving information from one register to another becomes of increasing importance. For example, assume that we have two source registers that contain data that may be transferred to any one of three destination registers. One way to do this is to set up individual connections between each source register and each destination register as shown in Figure 11-24.

If the registers are close together, this type of interconnection may not be much of a problem. However, as the number of registers involved increases, we soon find that the complexity of the data paths that must be provided becomes unacceptable.

In this organization the transfer of information is described by the following set of transfer expressions.

$$\tau_A: \quad A \leftarrow f_1 \wedge X \vee g_1 \wedge Y$$
$$\tau_B: \quad A \leftarrow f_2 \wedge X \vee g_2 \wedge Y$$
$$\tau_C: \quad A \leftarrow f_3 \wedge X \vee g_3 \wedge Y$$

One way to overcome this problem is to use the arrangement shown in Figure 11-25. In this approach a single data path, called a *data bus,* is used to carry the information from the source registers to the destination registers. As shown, information is placed *on the bus* by way of the OR gate. The AND gates at the output of each source register are used to select which signal is to be placed on the bus. Each source register has an associated *output select signal* f_i. When f_i is 1 the information contained in source register i is selected and appears at the input to the OR gate. In this organization it is necessary to ensure that no more than one of the control signals is

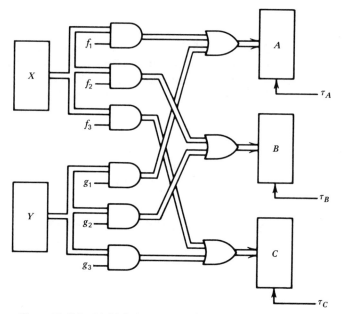

Fiure 11-24 Multiple interconnection between registers.

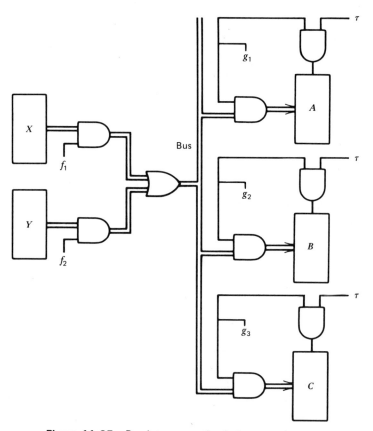

Figure 11-25 Bus interconnection between registers.

1 at a given time. If this restriction is enforced, we know that the information placed on the bus is uniquely defined.

At the other end of the bus it is possible to make use of the information in a number of ways. In the example shown in Figure 11-25 we have assumed that the bus delivers information to the input lines of three registers constructed from D flip-flops. The information found on the bus can be transferred into register j if the input select signal g_j is 1 when the transfer pulse occurs. At the receiving end it may be desirable to load the same information into more than one register. Thus it is not necessary to introduce the requirement that the g_j signals be unique.

When the select signal g_j is 0, we do not want the contents of register j to change. Since it is assumed that the registers are constructed from D flip-flops, it is possible to ensure that the content of a register is not changed by blocking the application of the transfer pulse to that register. An AND gate in the transfer pulse line, as shown in Figure 11-25, is used to accomplish this task.

The information transfers that take place on the bus system shown in Figure 11-25 are described by the following expressions:

$$\tau : \begin{cases} A \leftarrow f_1 g_1 X \lor f_2 g_1 Y \lor \bar{g}_1 A \\ B \leftarrow f_1 g_2 X \lor f_2 g_2 Y \lor \bar{g}_2 B \\ C \leftarrow f_1 g_3 X \lor f_2 g_3 Y \lor \bar{g}_3 C \end{cases}$$

Since we have insisted that at most one f_i can equal 1 at any given time, there is no conflict in these equations. The last terms

$$\bar{g}_1 A \qquad \bar{g}_2 B \qquad \bar{g}_3 C$$

in each equation are included to indicate that the content of a register does not change if the control signal g_j associated with the register is 0. If this term was not included, the transfer expression would indicate that the register would be cleared when the transfer pulse occurred.

Bus Interfacing Using Three-state Gates

In Figure 11-25 we interfaced the input registers to the bus using an AND gate to select the register and an OR gate to place the signal on the bus. This rather cumbersome arrangement can be simplified if we replace the AND gate and the OR gate connection with a single three-state gate of the form discussed in Chapter 7. The three-state gate acts as a simple switch. When the select signal is 1, the output of the source register is connected to the bus. When the signal is 0, the register is disconnected from the bus. Using this approach, the bus system takes the form shown in Figure 11-26.

Bidirectional Bus Operation

The bus organization shown in Figure 11-26 allows information to be transferred in only one direction. Such a bus is a *unidirectional bus*. There are many situations in which we would like to transfer information in both directions. It is not difficult to structure a bus to satisfy this need. Such a bus is said to be a *bidirectional bus*.

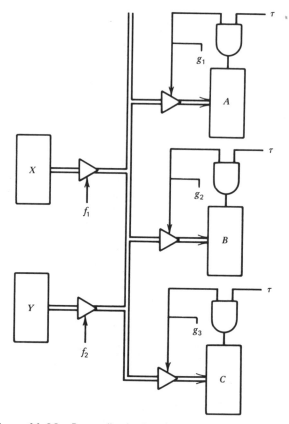

Figure 11-26 Bus realized using three-state logic gates.

An example of the use of a bidirectional bus is shown in Figure 11-27. In this system we have a microprocessor and we wish to transfer data between the microprocessor and one of the four memory units associated with the microprocessor. Two buses are used to accomplish this task. The address bus is a unidirectional bus that is used to indicate the address of the information that the microprocessor wishes to use in the transfer operation. This address information is encoded so that the two leftmost bits of the address indicate the memory unit that holds the data item of interest and the other bits in the address indicate the address of the word in the selected memory unit.

A single control line is used to send the read/write signal (R/W) to each memory unit. This signal is 1 if we wish to read information from the memory unit to the microprocessor and 0 if we wish to write information into memory from the microprocessor. Although this signal is connected to all of the memory units, only the memory unit that has been enabled by having its chip select signal set to 1 will carry out the indicated transfer operation.

Information is transferred between the microprocessor and the memory units by the data bus. The input and the output lines on the memory unit are connected to

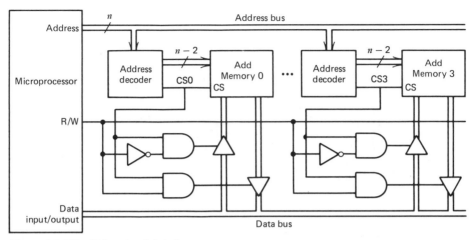

Figure 11-27 Bidirectional data bus.

the data bus through three-state gates as shown. When the control signal indicates that a read operation is to be performed, the output of the selected memory chip is connected to the bus and information is transferred from the chip to the microprocessor on the data bus. If the control signal indicates that a write operation is to be performed, the input to the selected memory chip is connected to the bus and information is transferred from the microprocessor to the chip on the data bus.

In this example we assume that the clock pulses that drive the memory unit are synchronized with the clock pulses in the microprocessor so that all of the steps needed to carry out the desired information transfer are coordinated. In larger systems the bus may be used to interconnect two systems that do not operate using a common system clock. When this situation occurs we must use additional control lines and control signals to synchronize the transfer of information between the units.

Another problem involves the number of lines we need to form the bus. If the address and data require n bits, then the bus must have at least $2n$ lines if separate data and address lines are used. It is possible to reduce the number of lines used if we use one set of lines to carry both address and data information. To do this requires a much more complex transfer operation. The next example illustrates one method used to solve this problem.

Shared Bus Operation

The bus system shown in Figure 11-27 is commonly used in applications where a processor and the memory unit are very close to together, and it is important that the data transfer be carried out in the shortest possible time. Another common design shares a single bus to transmit both address and data information. To do this additional control lines are introduced that carry information that controls the data transfer operations. Figure 11-28 illustrates one form that such a shared bus system might take.

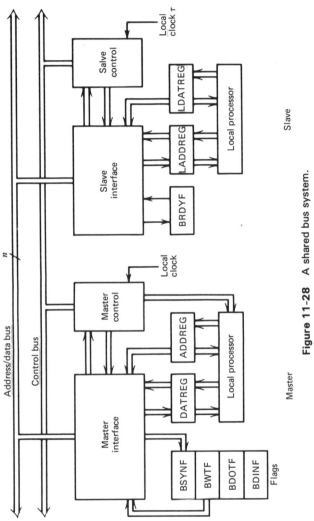

Figure 11-28 A shared bus system.

Figure 11-28 indicates that a number of features have been added to the bus system. Two sub-buses are used to form the bus. The first bus is the *address/data bus* and is used to transmit both address information and data information. The second bus, the *control bus,* is used to carry the control signals that activate the steps necessary to carry out the different data transfers performed by the system. A number of devices can be connected to the bus. During a transfer one of the devices must take control of the transfer operation. This device is called the *bus master*. The other devices are called *slave units*.

The address/data bus is an *n*-bit bidirectional bus. The control bus can take a number of forms depending upon the protocol used to implement the transfer. For this discussion it is assumed that the control bus is a 5 line bus having the form shown in Figure 11-29. The control signals are used to provide the following information.

BSYNC—Bus Synchronization: Signal used to indicate that an information transfer is underway.

BDOUT—Data Out: Indicates that the bus master is ready to send output information to the bus.

BDIN—Data In: Indicates that the bus master is ready to read information from the bus.

BRPLY—Slave Reply: Signal generated by the slave unit to indicate that it is ready to participate in a data transfer.

BWT—Read/Write Signal: Indicate if the bus master will send or receive data.

One of the major features of this system is that the bus master and the slave units are independent. It is assumed that each unit has its own local clock source and that any synchronization that occurs is implemented by the way in which the control signals are used. There are two basic transfer operations. They are:

1. Data Read: Data is read from the local data register, LDATREG, in one of the slave units into the data register, DATREG, in the bus master.
2. Data Write: Data is transmitted from the data register, DATREG, in the bus master to the local data register, LDATREG, in one of the slave units.

We now consider how each of these transfers is implemented.

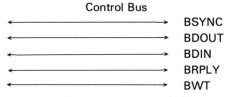

Figure 11-29 General organization of control bus.

The Bus Addresses Cycle

A bus data transfer on a shared bus involves two stages. The first stage, which is called the *address cycle,* establishes communication between the bus master and the slave unit that is to be involved in the transfer. At the completion of the address cycle the bus master initiates the second stage, called the *data transfer cycle,* which carries out the actual data transfer.

The address cycle is the same for both a read and a write transfer. Associated with each slave unit is a unique *address space* consisting of one or more unique address values. For example, we could have three slave units. Unit 1 might have address values in the range 1000_8 to 5000_8, unit 2 might have a single address value of 500_8, and the third unit might have address values in the range of 6000_8 to 6010_8.

To start an information transfer the bus master initiates the address cycle by placing an address on the address/data bus and announcing that a transfer is to be started by setting BSYNC to 1. It also indicates whether the operation will be a read operation by setting BWT to 0 or a write operation by setting BWT to 1. Each slave unit, upon detecting that BSYNC is 1, looks at the address information. If the slave unit sees that the address falls in its address space, it knows that it has been selected by the bus master to participate in a data transfer. For example, if the bus master places an address value of 6005_8 onto the address/data line, this would indicate that the bus master wished to communicate with the third slave unit in the above example.

As soon as a slave unit detects that it has been selected, it must respond with the following actions. First the address information is loaded into the slave unit's local address register, LADDREG, and the slave selected flag BRDYF is set to 1. When the slave's control unit detects that the unit is selected, it acknowledges this selection by setting the BRPLY signal to 1. As soon as the bus master detects that BRPLY has gone to 1, it knows that the address cycle has been completed and that it can start the data transmission cycle. At the start of the data transmission cycle, the bus master starts a data read or a data write operation depending upon the value of BWT. We now consider the details of both types of data transfer operations.

The Data Read Cycle

The data read cycle, which the bus master has indicated by setting BWT to 0 during the address cycle, involves the transfer of information from the slave unit to the master. It is assumed that during the address cycle the data to be read from the slave unit has been placed in the slave data register, LDATREG. When the bus master is ready to read this information, it sets BDINF, and thus BDIN, to 1. Upon detecting that BDIN is 1, the slave control units places the information in LDATREG on the address/data bus and sets BRPLYF, and thus BRPLY, to 0. This indicates that the desired information is on the bus and that it can be read by the bus master. When the master detects that BPLY has gone to 0, it reads the data from the address/data bus into the register DATREG and sets BSYNF, and thus BSYN, to 0, indicating that the data read transfer cycle has been completed. All of the system flags are then cleared and the bus master control waits until the next transfer is needed.

To understand the operation of the read transfer operation on this bus it is necessary to understand the relative timing relationship that exists between the bus master and the slave unit. Figure 11-30 illustrates this relationship in a general manner.

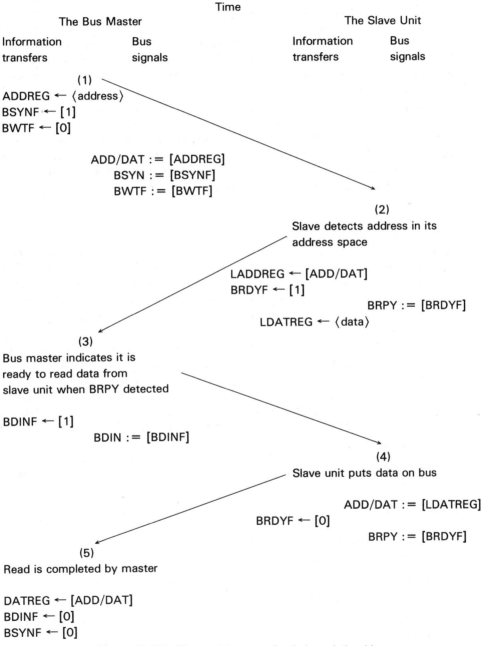

Figure 11-30   The read data transfer timing relationship.

Data Write Cycle

The data write cycle, indicated by BWT being set to 1, is similar to the read cycle except that information is transferred from the bus master to the slave unit. During the address cycle the bus master has loaded this information into the data register, DATREG. As soon as the master detects that BRPLY has gone to 1, it places this information onto the address/data bus and sets the BDOUTF flag, and thus BDOUT, to 1. When the slave unit detects that BDOUT has gone to 1, it knows that the data from the bus master is on the address/data bus and that it can be loaded into the slave data register, LDATREG. As soon as this has been accomplished, the slave control unit sets BRPLYF, and thus BRPLY, to 0, indicating that the data has been received from the bus master and that it can be used by the slave unit. When the bus master detects that BRPLY has gone to 0, it knows that the write operation has been completed and it sets BSYNF, and thus BSYN, to 0, indicating the end of the transfer cycle. The master control unit then clears all flags and waits for the next transfer cycle to begin. The relative timing between the signals that make up a write data transfer is illustrated in Figure 11-31.

Bus Standards

There are a large number of bus structures in use to transfer data between modules. Most manufacturers have selected one or more standard bus designs for use in their systems. In many cases the bus configuration selected by one manufacturer may be quite different from that used by another. This means that it is often difficult to interface a module developed by one manufacturer to a system designed by another company.

A number of attempts have been made to develop standard definitions for particular classes of bus systems. The IEEE-488 standard is one such standard that has been accepted to interconnect digital systems and digital instrumentation. Another standard is the IEEE-696/S100 bus standard, which has been developed to handle intercommunication between modules in a computer system. These standards are now in general use, but there are still many manufacturers who stay with their own bus standards.

EXERCISES

1. Show the steps involved in transferring the ASCII encoded letter A from the bus master to a slave unit with address 6005_8.

2. Design a hardware program that describes the operation of the bus master control unit of the bus system shown in Figure 11-28.

3. Design a hardware program to describe the operation of the slave control unit of the bus system shown in Figure 11-28.

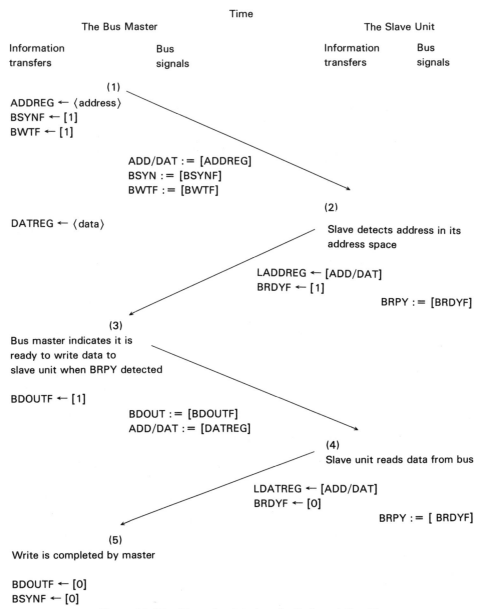

Time

The Bus Master · The Slave Unit

| Information transfers | Bus signals | Information transfers | Bus signals |

(1)
ADDREG ← ⟨address⟩
BSYNF ← [1]
BWTF ← [1]

    ADD/DAT := [ADDREG]
    BSYN := [BSYNF]
    BWTF := [BWTF]

(2)
DATREG ← ⟨data⟩

    Slave detects address in its address space

    LADDREG ← [ADD/DAT]
    BRDYF ← [1]

        BRPY := [BRDYF]

(3)
Bus master indicates it is
ready to write data to
slave unit when BRPY detected

BDOUTF ← [1]

    BDOUT := [BDOUTF]
    ADD/DAT := [DATREG]

(4)
    Slave unit reads data from bus

    LDATREG ← [ADD/DAT]
    BRDYF ← [0]

        BRPY := [BRDYF]

(5)
Write is completed by master

BDOUTF ← [0]
BSYNF ← [0]

Figure 11-31 The write data transfer timing relationship.

5. SYSTEM ARCHITECTURE

The modules discussed in the last sections provide the building blocks we need to construct complex digital systems. We now investigate how these modules, together with the information processing and control units introduced in Chapter 9, can be

used to design complex digital systems that carry out a variety of information processing tasks. Although this discussion is mainly concerned with the system level of
operation, we also illustrate how a system level design provides the information we
need to complete the implementation using standard digital logic design techniques.

Instruction-controlled Controller

The control units developed in Chapter 9 were designed to carry out a single task.
One method of increasing the flexibility of an information processing system is to
use a control unit with a separate instruction register as shown in Figure 11-32. This
instruction register provides an extra input to the control unit since the information
in the register can be used to indicate which computational task, from a set of tasks,
is to be performed by the system. The control unit uses this information to generate
the sequence of control signals necessary to carry out the selected task.

The addition of an instruction register means that we must add another argument
to the control signal and the next-state equations that describe the operation of the
control unit. The expanded equations then have the form

The Control Signal Equation

$$T := F(I, S, Q)$$

The Next-state Equations

$$Q \leftarrow G(I, S, Q)$$

Other than this change, the operation of the control unit is identical to that discussed
in Chapter 9. The following example illustrates how an instruction register is used
to expand the computational capabilities of a system.

A Multiple-task Computation System

To illustrate the use of an instruction register, assume that we wish to design a digital
network of the form shown in Figure 11-33. In this system it is assumed that the n-
bit input signal X delivers numerical information, encoded in 2's complement form,

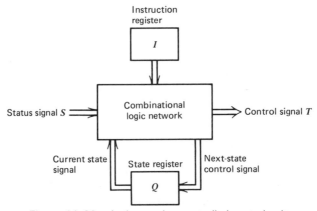

Figure 11-32 An instruction-controlled control unit.

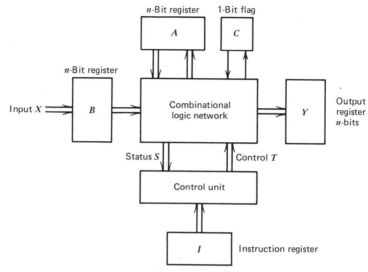

Figure 11-33 A multiple-instruction control unit.

to the network as needed. The information contained in X is processed by the network, and the result of the processing is placed in the register Y. The one-bit flag-register C is used to indicate whether a numerical overflow condition occurred during the processing. Thus when C is set to 1 this indicates that the contents of Y is incorrect.

The four tasks carried out by this network are described by the design requirement given on the following page. The specification table describing the information transfers used to perform these tasks are given by Table 11-2.

To complete the design of this network it is necessary to define the hardware program, using the transfers given in Table 11-2, required to carry out each of the

Table 11-2 Specification Table for Multiple-instruction Network: Operation Table for T

T	Transfer Operation	T	Transfer Operation
NOP	No operation	SLA	$A \leftarrow A + A$†
LDB	$B \leftarrow X$		$C \leftarrow \text{OVF}[A,A]$
LDA	$A \leftarrow B$	OUT	$Y \leftarrow A$
	$C \leftarrow [0]$		
LDNA	$A \leftarrow \bar{B} + [1]$		
	$C \leftarrow [0]$		
ADD	$A \leftarrow A + B$		
	$C \leftarrow \text{OVF}[A,B]$		

†$A \leftarrow A + A$ is equivalent to shifting the contents of A left one bit. $(A + A = 2*A)$
Note: All addition operations MOD 2^{n-1}. OVF$[A,B]$ is the arithmetic overflow function.

Status Signal—S

$$S := [s_1] \quad \text{where } s_1 := [C]$$

Design Requirements—Multiple-task Computation

Task: The output Y is computed using the values of X as input. The instruction register holds a 2-bit code indicating the task to be performed. The signals X and Y are both n-bits. The flag register C is a 1-bit register that indicates whether an arithmetic overflow has occurred.

1. Addition (2's complement) $I := [0, 0]$

$$Y \leftarrow (X1 + X2) \text{ MOD } 2^{n-1}$$
$$C \leftarrow \text{OVF}[X1, X2] \quad \text{Arithmetic overflow}$$

2. Subtraction (2's complement) $I := [0, 1]$

$$Y \leftarrow (X2 - X1) \text{ MOD } 2^{n-1}$$
$$C \leftarrow \text{OVF}[X2, -X1] \quad \text{Arithmetic overflow}$$

3. Multiplication by 2 $I := [1, 0]$

$$Y \leftarrow \begin{cases} 2*X1 & \text{No overflow} \\ \text{undefined} & \text{Overflow} \end{cases}$$
$$C \leftarrow \text{OVF}[2*X1]$$

4. Multiplication by 10 $I := [1, 1]$

$$Y \leftarrow \begin{cases} 10*X1 & \text{No overflow} \\ \text{undefined} & \text{Overflow} \end{cases}$$
$$C \leftarrow \text{OVF}[10*X1]$$

Input: The signal $X := [x_{n-1}, x_{n-2}, \ldots, x_0]$

$X1$ is the first value of X read
$X2$ if needed is the second value of X read

Output: Y the n-bit result of the calculation
C the arithmetic overflow bit

Note: OVF(A, B) = arithmetic overflow

desired tasks. The following observations about the network and the way different steps of the computations can be performed are useful.

All values are read into the network by way of the B register. The A register is isolated from the input and is used to hold the intermediate values generated when an arithmetic operation is performed.

Upon completion of the calculation the result must be transferred to the Y register. The flag register C is used during the computation. Whenever the flag is set to 1, this indicates that an arithmetic overflow has occurred and that any values generated are incorrect.

The arithmetic operations of addition and subtraction are carried out using 2's complement arithmetic. Multiplication by 2 could be done by introducing a shift left operation that would shift the contents of A one bit to the left. This operation is, however, equivalent to

$$A \leftarrow A + A$$

Using this method we can also detect an overflow with the same logic used to detect an arithmetic overflow when this multiplication by 2 is performed.

Multiplication by 10 can be represented as

$$A \leftarrow 2*(2*2*X1 + X1)$$

since

$$10*X1 = 2^3*X1 + 2*X1$$

An overflow can occur during any of the multiplication by 2 operations or when the addition takes place. It is assumed that the multiplication operation is stopped and the overflow flag set when the first such overflow is detected.

Using these observations we can now complete the design of the hardware program that will control the operation of this system.

The Hardware Program

In carrying out the design of this system it is assumed that the value of the control signal has been placed in the instruction register I before the computation is started. Under this assumption the flowchart shown in Figure 11-34 indicates how the

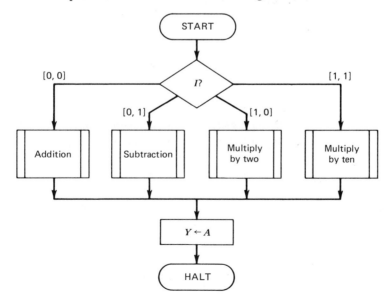

Figure 11-34 Flowchart illustrating instruction execution.

instruction information is used by the system to select one of the four possible tasks. A detailed flowchart describing each task is shown in Figure 11-35.

The hardware program that describes the operation of this digital network, assuming that I holds a fixed value when the processing starts, has the following form:

```
/* HARDWARE PROGRAM TO IMPLEMENT FLOWCHART OF FIGURES 11-34 AND 11-35
START:  CASE I                          /* I assumed preloaded
          {
            [0,0] { LDB                 /* TASK #1
                    LDA                 /* the addition operation
                    LDB
                    ADD   END           /* End of task 1
                  }
            [0,1] { LDB                 /* TASK #2
                    LDNA                /* subtraction operation
                    LDB
                    ADD   END           /* End of task 2
                  }
            [1,0] { LDB                 /* TASK #3
                    LDA                 /* multiplication by 2
                    SLA   END           /* operation
                  }                     /* End of task 3
            [1,1] { LDB                 /* TASK #4
                    LDA                 /* multiplication by 10
                    SLA                 /* Form 2*X1
                    CASE S
                        {[0] SLA A1     /* No overflow. Form 2*X1
                         [1] NOP END    /* Overflow. Halt task.
                        }
                    A1: CASE S
                        {[0] ADD A2     /* No overflow. Form 2*2*X1 + X1
                         [1] NOP END    /* Overflow. Halt task.
                        }
                    A2: CASE S
                        {[0] SLA END    /* No overflow. Form 2*(4*X1 + X1)
                         [1] NOP END    /* Overflow. Halt task.
                        }
                  }                     /* End of task 4
          }                             /* End of instruction execution
                                        /* associated with tasks
END:    OUT                             /* Output result. C set if error
HALT:   NOP HALT                        /* End of program
```

This example has illustrated how an instruction register can be used to control the tasks performed by a given digital system. The next example illustrates how a com-

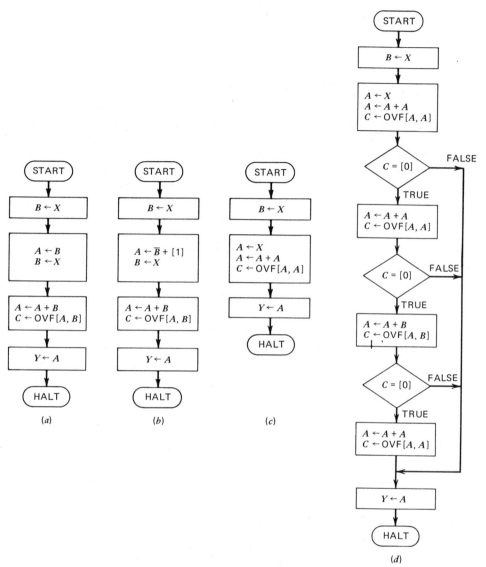

Figure 11-35 Flow diagrams describing the four information processing tasks shown in Figure 11-34.

plex digital system can be designed as a collection of subnetworks each able to carry out a specific set of tasks. The overall operation of the system is under the control of a master control unit, which has the responsibility to define the task performed by each subnetwork. To accomplish this level of operation we use a memory unit to hold the sequence of instructions that we wish to execute. The control unit reads each instruction from memory and uses the information in the instruction to send the proper instruction code to each subnetwork involved in the execution of the instruction. When an instruction is received, the subnetwork carries out its assigned task and notifies the control unit when the task is completed. At that point the control unit goes on to the next instruction.

A Drilling Machine Controller

Many of our examples have illustrated the common types of logic networks used in computer systems. However, it is quite common to use digital techniques to control nondigital devices. The example that we now consider is designed to illustrate how a digital controller can be used to guide the operation of a drilling machine.

For this example assume that we are given the job of designing a digital control system for the drilling machine illustrated in Figure 11-36. The unit to be drilled is placed on the work table in a prespecified position, and the control system must generate the sequence of drilling and positioning operations that must be performed on the unit. It is desired that these operations be carried out automatically.

To automate the drilling operation the manufacturer of the machine has incorporated three position control motors on the machine to adjust the x and y position of the work table and the height of the drill. A stepping motor has also been included to allow the selection of any one of four drill sizes. Initially the manufacturer provided levers that an operator could use to operate these motors and indicators to show the current status of each variable. It is now desired to design an automatic control unit that will be able to carry out a preprogrammed sequence of operations. The programmed sequence of operations is to be placed in random access memory, and the control unit must interpret this information and send appropriate commands to the drilling machine. Our task is to design this control unit and specify how the instructions needed to carry out a given sequence of drilling operations are to be encoded.

The initial step in the design process is to determine the characteristics of each of the devices that we must work with. For this problem there are two devices that are prespecified; the drilling machine and the memory unit. The drilling machine is assumed to have the following characteristics.

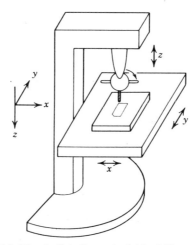

Figure 11-36 A digitally controllable drilling machine.

Work Table Position Characteristics of Drilling Machine

The position of the work table can be adjusted in the x and y directions in increments of 0.1 inch. The x and y positions are adjustable between 0.0 and 9.9 inches. The actual value of x or y is indicated by an 8-bit BCD encoded number of the form

$$\overbrace{XXXX}^{\substack{\text{inch} \\ \text{digit}}} \,.\; \overbrace{XXXX}^{\substack{\text{0.1 inch} \\ \text{digit}}}$$

Two 2-bit control signals CX and CY are used to change the x and y position of the table, respectively. The allowed commands are encoded in the following manner.

Control Signal	CX		CY	
	0 0	no motion	0 0	no motion
	0 1	increase x	0 1	increase y
	1 0	decrease x	1 0	decrease y
	1 1	no motion	1 1	no motion

Drill Selection and Drill Depth Characteristics

The drilling machine has four different size drills mounted as shown in Figure 11-36. The drill mount is rotated in a clockwise direction by a stepping motor. The four drill positions on the mount are numbered 0 through 3 in a clockwise direction. A 2-bit signal M is available to indicate which drill is currently positioned over the work surface.

The rotation of the drill mount is controlled by a 1-bit control signal CM defined as follows:

Control Signal CM	
0	Do not rotate drill mount
1	Rotate drill mount clockwise to the next drill position

Each drill is mounted in the drill mount so that its tip is 0.5 inches above the work table. It can be lowered, under the control of a control signal CD, in increments of 0.01 inches until it touches the work table. The actual displacement, z, of the drill from its at-rest position is indicated by an 8-bit BCD encoded number, Z, of the form:

$$\overbrace{.DDDD}^{\substack{\text{0.1 inch} \\ \text{digit}}} \;\; \overbrace{DDDD}^{\substack{\text{0.01 inch} \\ \text{digit}}}$$

The actual displacement is controlled by the 2-bit control signal *CD* according to the following encoding:

Control Signal	
CD	
0 0	no motion
0 1	increase z
1 0	return drill to zero displacement
1 1	no motion

Block Diagram Representation of Drilling Machine

From the above specifications we develop the block diagram shown in Figure 11-37 to represent the important information and control signals associated with the drilling machine.

Next we investigate the properties of the memory unit before we start designing the system.

The Random Access Memory Unit

The information used to define the operation to be carried out by the machine is stored in a random access memory unit as a series of encoded instructions. The unit has 256 8-bit words and is organized as shown in Figure 11-38. For the purpose of this example it is assumed that the memory unit has been specially designed for use by the drilling controller.

Each instruction requires either 1 or 2 bytes. The system controller reads successive bytes from the memory unit and uses the information contained in these bytes to carry out the desired drilling task. For this example we do not consider how the information is placed in memory. Our interest centers on how the control unit reads and uses the information from the memory.

The control unit may fetch information from memory by issuing one of two commands. The commands and the action taken by the memory unit when they are received are summarized in Table 11-3.

The START command is used when the drilling operation is to be started. When this command is received, the memory unit places [0] in the memory address register, MAR, since it is assumed that the first byte of the command sequence is stored

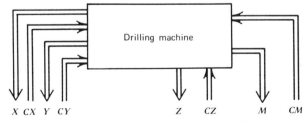

Figure 11-37   Block diagram representation of drilling machine.

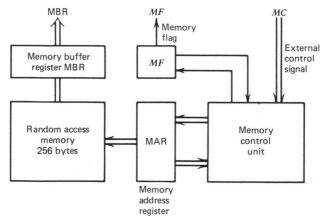

Figure 11-38   Block diagram representation of random access memory.

in memory location 0. It also clears the memory flag, *MF*. Upon receiving this command the memory unit reads the information in memory location 0 and places this information in the memory buffer register, MBR. Next the memory flag, *MF*, is set to [1], indicating that information is ready for use by the control unit. Finally the contents of the MAR is incremented by 1 so that this register now contains the address of the next byte to be read.

When the drilling control unit wishes to fetch the next byte in the command sequence, it issues a READ command to the memory unit. When this command is issued, the contents of the MAR is the address of the next byte to be read from memory. Upon receipt of the READ command the memory flag, *MF*, is cleared and the memory control unit starts a read operation that reads the contents of the memory location indicated by the MAR and places this value in the MBR. The memory flag, *MF*, is then set to [1], indicating that the read operation has been completed and that the MBR contains the next byte needed by the control unit. Finally the contens of the MAR is incremented by 1 to indicate the location of the byte to be read when the next READ command is received.

As long as we are designing at the system level we do not have to consider the

Table 11-3   Memory Unit Commands

Command	Event Time	Transfer Operations	
START	τ_a :	$MF \leftarrow [0]$	$MAR \leftarrow [0]$
	τ_b :	$MBR \leftarrow M_{[MAR]}$	
	τ_c :	$MF \leftarrow [1]$	$MAR \leftarrow MAR + [1]$
READ	τ_a :	$MF \leftarrow [0]$	
	τ_b :	$MBR \leftarrow M_{[MAR]}$	
	τ_c :	$MF \leftarrow [1]$	$MAR \leftarrow MAR + [1]$
WAIT		No operation	

detailed design of the memory unit. Thus for the rest of this example we deal only with the external behavior of the memory unit.

Finally the WAIT command is used when the drilling operation has been completed and the drilling control unit is in a wait state while the next item to be drilled is placed on the work table.

A Typical Control Problem

To obtain an idea of the operations that the controller must perform let us consider the sequence of steps necessary to drill the pattern of holes shown in Figure 11-39 in a 0.25 inch thick piece of steel plate. To carry out this drilling operation would require the following steps. It is assumed that the drilling machine can execute only one step at a time.

DRILL HOLE 1.   (a) Set x to 1.5 in.
                           (b) Set y to 1.5 in.
                           (c) Select drill 2
                           (d) Lower drill .5 in.
                           (e) Raise drill

DRILL HOLE 2   (a) Set x to 3.7 in.
                           (b) Set y to 2.6 in.
                           (c) Select drill 1
                           (d) Lower drill .35 in.
                           (e) Raise drill

DRILL HOLE 3   (a) Set y to 4.2 in.
                           (b) Lower drill .5 in.
                           (c) Raise drill
                         End of drilling operation

In examining the above list, we see that we must be able to vary the sequence of operations. In particular we note that in the drilling of hole 3 we did not have to repeat the x position operation or the drill selection operation, since they were the same as those used for the drilling of hole 2.

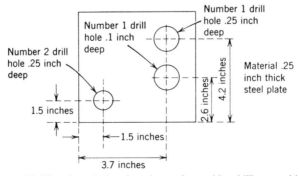

Figure 11-39 A typical task to be performed by drilling machine.

From this observation we can conclude that the controller must have a control unit with an instruction register. We also note that each step of the drilling operation requires the controller to perform two distinct types of operations.

1. Determine which drilling operation is the next one to be performed.
2. Generate the commands necessary to cause the drilling machine to execute the indicated drilling operation.

The next stage of the design process thus consists of determining how these two tasks can be performed.

Generation of Drilling Machine Commands

If we examine the specifications for the drilling machine, we note that we must control the following variables:

1. x position of table
2. y position of table
3. z depth of drill
4. drill selection

Since we have sensors on the drilling machine that provide us with the current value of each of these variables, we can use an arrangement of the form shown in Figure 11-40 to generate the necessary control signals to change the value of each variable.

When the flag signal, OCi, is a 1, this indicates that the machine is ready to receive a new position signal. The load output information control signal, NSi, transmits the desired value of the machine variable into the buffer register and sets the flag to 0. As long as the value of the current variable is not equal to the desired value of the variable, there is an error. An appropriate drilling machine command is generated

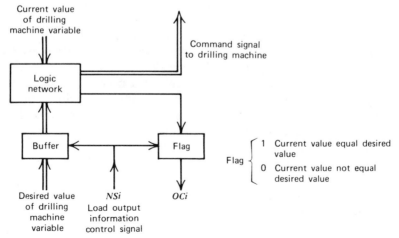

Figure 11-40 General form of output unit used to interface digital drilling control unit to drilling machine.

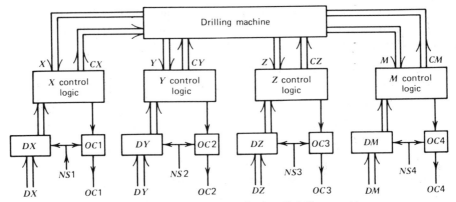

Figure 11-41 Interface organization of drilling machine.

to change the value of the current variable in such a way as to reduce this error to zero. When the two values match, the flag is set to 1 and no further changes are called for in the value of the variable being controlled.

Using this type of approach, we obtain the partial organization of the controller shown in Figure 11-41. The signals X, Y, Z, and M are the actual values of the drilling machine variables, while the signals DX, DY, DZ, and DM are the respective desired values of the same variable and CX, CY, CZ, and CM are the generated control signals. The signals $OC1$ through $OC4$ are the values of the flags and the signals $NS1$ through $NS4$ are the transfer control signals.

The next problem we must consider is that of determining how the signals DX, DY, DZ, and DM are generated. There are two ways in which this problem can be solved.

The value of each signal will be read from memory into the memory buffer register. One approach would be to use this signal directly as an input for the appropriate control logic network. The second approach would be to introduce a separate signal buffer register for the intermediate storage of each signal. In this case the information in the memory buffer would be transferred into the appropriate signal buffer register. The output of each such buffer register would then provide the necessary signal input for each control logic network.

Of the two approaches the second would be more expensive, since four additional buffer registers would be required. However, the added flexibility in the design of the system will justify this added cost. Thus individual registers are added to hold the signals DX, DY, DZ, and DM. The values that are placed in the registers will be found in the memory-buffer register when they are needed. It is the responsibility of the master control unit to see that the proper transfers take place when needed.

The necessary switching between different input lines can be accomplished by using a switching network between the reader buffer and the inputs to the control logic networks. This unit is illustrated in Figure 11-42. This master control unit must include an instruction register, since the order in which the different drilling tasks are performed can vary from job to job.

The transfer pulses MC and $NS1$ through $NS4$ needed to control the interfaces will also be generated by switching the transfer pulse produced by the control unit

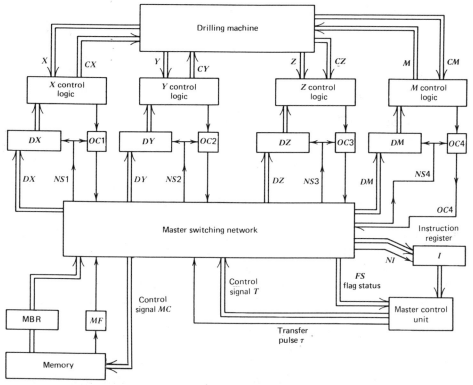

Figure 11-42 Block diagram of complete drilling machine controller.

in the master control unit. Similarly the value of the different flags will be available to the master controller from the signal *FS*, which is the vector

$$FS = [MF, OC1, OC2, OC3, OC4]$$

Now that we have generated a block diagram showing the general operation of the controller, we must next specify the exact operation of each unit in the block diagram.

The Drill Instruction Set

Before we can discuss the operation of the individual units of the controller, we must define the type of instructions that can be interpreted by the master control unit and the method of encoding these instructions. If we examine the types of operations that must be performed, we note that there are two general types of instructions that must be implemented. The first type involves a change of a particular drilling machine variable to a new value that must be specified by an instruction. The second type involves taking some action that does not require the specification of a new value of a drilling machine variable. The particular instructions that must be implemented are summarized in Table 11-4.

Examining this list we see that there are seven different instructions. In instruc-

Table 11-4 Instructions Needed by Controller

Instruction	Variable to Be Specified	I	Assigned Code
(a) No operation	None	i_0	000
(b) Move X	New value of X	i_1	001
(c) Move Y	New value of Y	i_2	010
(d) Drill hole	New value of Z	i_3	011
(e) Select drill	Drill number	i_4	100
(f) Raise drill	None	i_5	101
(g) Halt	None	i_6	110

tions i_1, i_2, and i_3 we need 8 bits to represent X, Y, and Z information, and we need 2 bits to represent drill number information in i_4. Instructions i_0, i_5, and i_6 do not require any such information.

All of these instructions must be encoded in such a way that they can be placed in memory. Since each byte holds 8 bits, this means that instructions i_1, i_2, and i_3 will require more than one byte to encode.

To encode each instruction we must provide 3 bits to indicate which instruction we are dealing with and either 0, 2, or 8 bits to encode the information needed to execute the instruction. The encoding process used to represent an instruction is determined by the fact that every instruction must fit into the memory unit.

Each instruction is encoded using either 1 or 2 bytes. The leftmost 3 bits of the first byte form an *instruction field* that holds the code that indicates the instruction. The rightmost 5 bits are not used except for the select drill instruction. In that case the rightmost 2 bits are used to represent the drill number given in binary notation. When the code in the instruction field indicates that the instruction is a Move x, a Move y, or a Drill instruction, the control unit then knows that a second byte is present that holds the BCD encoded value of the argument associated with the instruction.

Table 11-5 indicates how the instructions are encoded in memory. It is the responsibility of the person who develops the "application" program that will drive the drilling machine to select the values for the arguments associated with the 2-byte instructions. For example, suppose that the drilling operation to be performed was described by the five instructions given below. These instructions would then be encoded as shown in order to place them in memory.

Instruction Number	Instruction Task	Argument Value	Instruction Encoding	Comment
1	Move X	$X = 2.9$ in.	00100000	
			00101001	BCD 29
2	Select drill	$M = 2$	10000010	
3	Drill hole	$Z = .25$ in.	01100000	
			00100101	BCD 25
4	Raise drill		10100000	
5	Stop operation		11000000	

Table 11-5 Encoding of Instructions in Memory

Instruction	Number of Bytes Used	Byte	Byte Encoding 7 6 5 4 3 2 1 0	Comments
(a) No operation	1	1	0 0 0 0 0 0 0 0	
(b) Move X	2	1	0 0 1 0 0 0 0 0	
		2	$X X X X X X X X$	BCD representation of DX
(c) Move Y	2	1	0 1 0 0 0 0 0 0	
		2	$Y Y Y Y Y Y Y Y$	BCD representation of DY
(d) Drill hole	2	1	0 1 1 0 0 0 0 0	
		2	$D D D D D D D D$	BCD representation of DZ
(e) Select drill	1	1	1 0 0 0 0 0 $M M$	MM binary value of drill number
(f) Raise drill	1	1	1 0 1 0 0 0 0 0	
(g) Halt	1	1	1 1 0 0 0 0 0 0	

Specification Table for Master Switching Network

The master switching network shown in Figure 11-42 serves to interconnect the different signals that appear in the system. The following tasks must be accomplished by this network:

1. The information contained in the memory buffer register, MBR, must be sent to the proper control registers or to the instruction register.
2. The flag status information must be delivered to the master control unit.
3. The control signals and transfer pulses generated by the master control unit must be transferred to the proper points in the system.

These tasks are performed under the control of the master control unit. However, before we can design the algorithm that defines the operation of the control unit, we must develop a specification table to describe the transfer operations controlled by the master switching network.

The major function of the switching network is to control the flow of information from one point in the system to another based on the value of the control signals applied to the network. Using the information presented in the previous discussion, we can generate the specification table of Table 11-6 to summarize the tasks accomplished by this network. In this table we have used a distinct mnemonic to represent each of the distinct values of the control signal T.

The master switching network receives a number of input signals and must produce a number of output signals. If we consider that this network has the general form shown in Figure 11-43a, then we can use the information contained in Table 11-6 to decompose this network into a number of subnetworks. These subnetworks

Table 11-6 Specification Table for Master Switching Network
Operation Table

$T := [TM, TD]$ Control Signal

Control Signal T	Transfer Expression	Comments
NOP	No operation	No transfers take place.
STP	$MF \leftarrow [0]$	START command issued to memory unit. Read first instruction in program.
RFM	$MF \leftarrow [0]$	READ command issued to memory unit. Read next instruction in program.
LDX	$DX \leftarrow MBR$ $OC1 \leftarrow [0]$	Command desired X position.
LDY	$DY \leftarrow MBR$ $OC2 \leftarrow [0]$	Command desired Y position.
LDZ	$DZ \leftarrow MBR$ $OC3 \leftarrow [0]$	Command desired Z position.
LDM	$DM \leftarrow MBR[0,1]$ $OC4 \leftarrow [0]$	Read M field of byte. Command desired drill bit.
LRZ	$DZ \leftarrow [0]$ $OC3 \leftarrow [0]$	Reset drill position to 0.
LDI	$I \leftarrow MBR[5,7]$	Read instruction field to instruction register.

Status Signal

$FS := [MF, OC1, OC2, OC3, OC4]$

MF = Value of memory flag

OCi = Value of ith operation complete flag

Mnemonics for Controller Instructions

Instruction	Mnemonic
[000]	NOOP
[001]	MOVX
[010]	MOVY
[011]	DRIL
[100]	CHDR
[101]	RAISD
[110]	HALT

and the tasks they carry out are summarized in Figure 11-43*b* through Figure 11-43*e*.

The control signal *T* produced by the control unit is divided into two subsignals as shown. The signal *TD* is used to transfer information from the memory buffer register to the point in the system where it will be used. The multiplexer *MX*1 indicated in Figure 11-43*b* is used to make this connection, while the multiplexer *MX*2 shown in Figure 11-43*c* is a steering network that sends a transfer pulse to the proper register so that the indicated transfer can take place.

The second subsignal, *TM*, is used to control the operation of the memory unit. Multiplexer *MX*3 shown in Figure 11-43*d* sends a START command or a READ command to the memory unit to carry out the desired memory operation. In this case we note that the memory control signal *MC* is defined as a pulse rather than as a signal level. This form of command signal is used since it is assumed that the memory unit has a source of internal transfer pulses that are used by the memory control unit

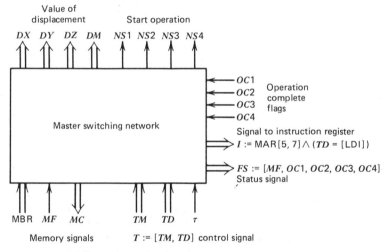

(*a*) General organization of master switching network

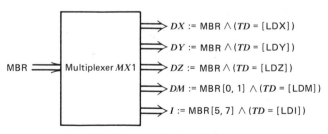

(*b*) Displacement signal multiplexer

Figure 11-43 The Master control switching network.

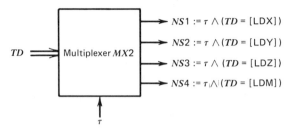

$$NS1 := \tau \wedge (TD = [\text{LDX}])$$
$$NS2 := \tau \wedge (TD = [\text{LDY}])$$
$$NS3 := \tau \wedge (TD = [\text{LDZ}])$$
$$NS4 := \tau \wedge (TD = [\text{LDM}])$$

(*c*) Initiation signal multiplexer

$$MC := ([\text{START}] \wedge (TM = [\text{STP}]) \vee [\text{READ}] \wedge (TM = [\text{REF}])) \wedge \tau$$

(*d*) Memory control signal multiplexer

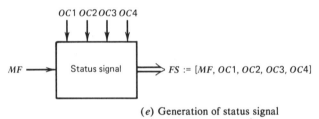

$$FS := [MF, OC1, OC2, OC3, OC4]$$

(*e*) Generation of status signal

Figure 11-43 (Continued).

to carry out the internal information transfers necessary to realize the START or READ operations called for by the control signal.

The final unit is a network that generates the status signal *FS* from the information contained in all of the flag registers connected to the master switching network. As shown in Figure 11-43*e*, *FS* is assumed to be a 5-bit vector. This representation was selected since it allows us to uniquely identify the status of each of the flags in the system.

Now that the major parts of the system have been defined, the final design task at the system level is a definition of the hardware program that describes the operation of the master control unit.

Master Control Unit

The master control unit is a sequential network with two inputs, *FS* and *I*, and two outputs, *T* and *τ*. The control signal *T* is a level signal, but *τ* will be a transfer pulse that causes the appropriate transfers to take place. The hardware program describing the operation of the control unit is given in Figure 11-44.

```
                    /*Initialization of Memory—Fetch First Instruction
BEGIN:   STP                                    /*Start program. Read first
WAITI:   CASE      FS                           /*instruction from memory
         {                                      /*All drill flags assumed 1 when
         [1,1,1,1,1] LDI  EXECU                 /*First instruction ready
         DEFAULT   NOP WAITI                    /*Waiting for memory read
                                                /*to finish
         }

                    /*Execution of Program

EXECU:   CASE      I                            /* Process instruction Code In
         {                                      /* I Register

                    /* No Operation Instruction

         [NOOP]       NOP   FETCH               /* Get next instruction

                    /* Move X Instruction

         [MOVX]   {  RFM                        /* Read next byte of instruction
                     WAITX: CASE FS             /* Wait for value
                        {
                        [1,1,1,1,1] LDX FETCH /* Value ready. Move in X direction
                        DEFAULT   NOP WAITX/* Wait for value
                        }
                  }
                  /* Move Y Instruction

         [MOVY]   {  RFM                        /* Read next byte of instruction
                     WAITY: CASE FS             /* Wait for value
                        {
                        [1,1,1,1,1] LDY FETCH /* Value ready. Move in Y direction
                        DEFAULT   NOP WAITY/* Wait for value
                        }
                  }
                  /* Drill in Z Direction Instruction

         [DRIL]   {  RFM                        /* Read next byte of instruction
         WAI         WAITZ: CASE FS             /* Wait for value
                        {
                        [1,1,1,1,1] LDZ FETCH /* Value ready. Move in Z direction
                        DEFAULT   NOP WAITZ/* Wait for value
                        }
                  }
```

Figure 11-44 Hardware program for master control unit.

```
                    /* Select Drill Bit

        [CHDR]      LDM   FETCH      /* Request the desired drill bit

                    /* Reset Drill to Zero Position

        [RAISD]     LRZ   FETCH      /* Return Z position to zero

                    /* Halt operation

        [HALT]      NOP   FINISH     /* Exit program

        }           /* End of Execution CASE Statement

                    /* Instruction Fetch Cycle

FETCH:  RFM                               /* Read next byte in memory
WAITF:  CASE FS                           /* Wait for value and completion
        {                                 /* of any drill operation
        [1, 1, 1, 1, 1] LDI   EXECU       /* Read instruction code to I register
        DEFAULT         NOP WAITF         /* Wait for value
        }                                 /* End of Fetch cycle

                    /* End of Program

FINISH:  NOP         FINISH               /* Loop until restart of program
```

Figure 11-44   (Continued).

As shown, the program has two distinct phases of operation. The first phase is the fetch phase, in which the command is read from memory and transferred to the instruction register. The fetch phase may be carried out while the drilling machine is in motion. The end of the fetch phase occurs when the next instruction value has been transferred to the instruction register I and all motion of the drilling machine has stopped. At that point the system enters the execution phase of operation.

During the execution phase the control unit uses the value in the instruction register I to decide which task is to be performed. If no additional information is needed (instructions i_0, i_4, i_5, i_6), the control unit sends out the necessary commands to carry out the indicated instruction. However, if the instruction requires additional information (instructions i_1, i_2, i_3), a second read operation must be implemented to read the next byte of the instruction from memory. The operation of the control unit will continue until the halt instruction is encountered. The control system stops operation at this point.

Once we have defined the hardware program for the control unit, we have completed the system level design of the complete system. The next task would be to reduce the system-level design to a logic-level design. This is a straightfoward process and is left as a home problem.

Using a memory unit to store a program that can be executed by a master control unit greatly increases the flexibility of such systems. If we wish to change the task performed, all that we have to do is to change the program in the memory unit. These ideas will be expanded in the next chapter, where we describe how to construct a complete computer system.

EXERCISES

1. Find the state transition table for the control unit that will realize the hardware program shown in Figure 11-35.

2. Write out the binary code representation of the instructions needed to drill the holes in the steel plate shown in Figure 11-39.

6. SUMMARY

In this chapter we have concentrated on the subsystems that form the building blocks of larger computer systems. We have seen that it is not necessary, in many cases, to worry about the actual logic circuit level design of a particular device if we can represent the information processing tasks performed by the device.

The concept of a control unit that can be used to control the operation of a large number of other information processing devices is of particular importance. In simple systems this control unit is completely responsible for determining the sequence of information processing tasks performed by the system. As the complexity and number of information processing tasks that must be handled by a system increase, we find that it is no longer practical to have a system in which the control unit is constrained to one fixed sequence of operations. By introducing the idea of a control unit with an instruction register we saw that we could greatly increase the flexibility of the control unit. Thus we are able to increase the overall computational capability of a system with a small increase in the complexity of the control unit.

Now that we have an understanding of how a control unit with an instruction register operates, our next task is to investigate how this concept can be used to represent a complete computer system. This is done in the next chapter.

Reference Notation

The references listed include a wide range of topics related to the material presented in this chapter. References 2 and 6 develop the idea of information transfers as a design tool. References 2, 3, and 4 discuss various arithmetic operations and their implementation using digital logic networks. A general overview of the interfacing problem can be found in References 1, 3, and 7. The idea of a stored program information processing device is presented in References 3, 5, and 6.

REFERENCES

1. Artwick, B. (1980), *Microcomputer Interfacing.* Prentice-Hall, Englewood Cliffs, N.J.
2. Hellerman, H. (1973), *Digital Computer System Principles* (second edition). McGraw-Hill, New York.
3. Langdon, G. G. Jr. (1982), *Computer Design.* Computeach Press, San Jose, Calif.
4. Mano, M. M., (1979), *Digital Logic and Computer Design.* Prentice-Hall, Englewood Cliffs, N.J.
5. Stone, H. S. (ed.) (1975), *Introduction to Computer Architecture.* SRA, Chicago.
6. Winkel, D., and F. Prosser (1980), *The Art of Digital Design: An Introduction to Top-Down Design.* Prentice-Hall, Englewood Cliffs, N.J.
7. Zaks, R., and L. Austin (1979), *Microprocessor Interfacing Techniques* (third edition). Sybex, Berkeley, Calif.

HOME PROBLEMS

✓**1.** As shown in Figure P11-1, three keyboards are available for people to send information to a computer system. Design, at the register level, a bus system and a control unit that will allow information to be transmitted to the computer as soon as a flag is raised by any keyboard. The control unit should select the keyboard signal that is to be transmitted. How will the control unit operate if more than one flag is up at any given time? How will the computer know which keyboard generated the input information?

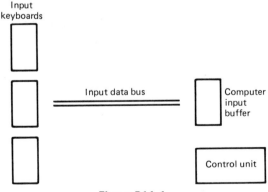

Figure P11-1

2. Because of the large operating speed difference between I/O devices and digital systems, local buffer memories are often built into the I/O device. One such arrangement is shown in Figure P11-2 for a line printer. The digital system deposits one line of characters (80 characters including blanks) into the buffer memory at a very high speed. The system then gives a command to the controller to send these 80 characters to the printer. When the printing is completed, the controller informs the system that it is ready to print the next 80 characters. Complete the register level design of this system.

Figure P11-2

3. Design a digital system that will automatically test the operation of the combinational logic network shown in Figure P11-3. The output should indicate whether the system is acceptable or has failed the test.

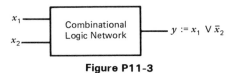

Figure P11-3

4. Complete the design of the drilling machine controller presented in Section 5 by implementing a sequential network that will carry out the hardware program given in Figure 11-44.

12

COMPUTER ARCHITECTURE AND
ORGANIZATION

1. INTRODUCTION

Our previous discussions have shown that any information processing task can be
represented by an algorithm involving a sequence of elementary information processing operations. Up to this point we have considered simple programmed information processors designed to automatically execute a sequence of operations determined by a fixed program. To change the algorithm a redesign of the control unit
was required. This is a reasonable approach when the system is designed to carry out
a single task. However, if we add a few minor changes to the control unit, we can
turn a fixed-program information processor into a full-scale computer.

A large number of computer systems are available. They range in size from simple
microprocessor-based systems, which cost a few thousand dollars, to supercomputers
such as the CRAY-1, which cost millions of dollars. Although the computational
power of a supercomputer is certainly orders of magnitude greater than that of a
microprocessor, the basic architectural concepts that underlie the design of either
system are remarkably similar. In this chapter we investigate the basic structure of
a simple stored program computer system and indicate the major components of such
a system. This computer is used in Chapter 13 to show how programs can be developed to carry out complex information processing tasks.

2. SYSTEM ORGANIZATION

The architecture selected for a given computer system involves many compromises.
The need for special computational capabilities must be balanced against the implementation cost and usefulness of each capability. Thus one of the first tasks undertaken when developing a new computer system is to establish a set of design goals
that the system is expected to satisfy. These goals are influenced by both the class of
problems the system is being designed to handle and the price that the potential users

are expected to be willing to pay for the proposed system. To develop these goals the designer must decide on:

1. The basic operations that the system must be able to perform.
2. The techniques that will be used to control the steps of a calculation.
3. How information will be stored and encoded in the system.
4. The structure of the information flow in the system.
5. The way in which the system will interact with the outside world.

Each designer solves these design problems in a different manner. However, the overall organization of the system will have the general form shown in Figure 12-1.

General System Organization

It is easier to understand the operation of a computer system if we partition the system into the major subunits shown in Figure 12-1. The heart of the system is the *central processing unit* (CPU). The CPU consists of a collection of registers and logic networks that carry out the fundamental logical, arithmetic, and information transfer operations necessary to realize a given computational task. Any program executed by the computer system must be constructed from these operations.

The control unit has two levels of responsibility. At the lowest level it controls the operation of the CPU. Each operation performed by the CPU is made up of a number of steps and the control unit is responsible for making sure that the steps are carried out in the proper order. Each program executed by the system is made up of an encoded sequence of these operations. The second responsibility of the control unit is to read this encoded sequence from memory and to make sure that the operation is performed by the CPU. Thus early in the design process it is necessary to select the set of instructions that can be executed by the control unit as well as the encoding used to represent these instructions.

The memory unit stores the sequence of encoded instructions executed by the control unit and the data needed by the CPU and the system to perform a given computational task. As discussed in Chapter 11, the memory may be of two types—random access memory (RAM) or read-only memory (ROM). Read-only memory is used to store fixed program sequences that do not need to be changed during nor-

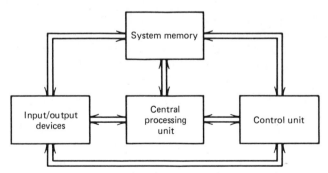

Figure 12-1 Major units of a computer system.

mal system use. The random access memory is used to store both program sequences and data. Both types of memory are commonly found in modern computer systems.

A number of input/output (I/O) devices are used to communicate with the outside world. These devices include such units as keyboards, printers, or video terminals to provide an interface with the human users of the system; mass storage devices such as disk or tape systems to provide for the storage of large amounts of data; or specialized devices such as A/D converters to handle special input/output problems. All of the input/output devices will be under the control of the control unit. Sometimes the I/O information will flow through the CPU and at other times the information transfer may take place directly between memory and a particular I/O device.

One way to understand the problems involved in the design of a computer system is to study the architecture of a given machine in detail. This is the approach we will take. In the following discussion a hypothetical computer system, called SEDCOM II, is used to illustrate the organization of a typical "small" computer system. The architecture of SEDCOM II is very similar to the PDP-11 family of computers manufactured by Digital Equipment Corporation. No attempt was made to reproduce the actual architecture of this family of machines. However, the organization of SEDCOM II, its instruction set, and the way that information is stored in memory are compatible with the PDP-11 family. In fact, any program developed for SEDCOM II can be executed directly on a PDP-11.

Although a specific computer architecture is used in the following discussion, similar capabilities and organizational features are present in the architecture of other computer families. Once you have developed an understanding of the operation and structure of one system, there is little difficulty in understanding the characteristics and internal operation of any other computer family.

SEDCOM II Data Organization

In a computer system most of the registers used for information storage and processing are the same size. If the register size is r-bits then the resulting computer system is referred to as an r-bit machine and we say that the computer system deals with r-bit *words*.

The value of r is usually a power of two. Microprocessors such as the Intel 8080, the Zilog Z80, or the Motorola 6800 are 8-bit machines. Newer microprocessors, such as the Intel 8086, the Zilog Z8000, or the Motorola 68000, are 16-bit machines. There are even some 32-bit microprocessors such as the Intel 432. Minicomputers such as the DEC PDP-11 or the Data General Micronova family of computers are 16-bit machines, while the larger computer systems such as the DEC VAX 11/780 or the Data General MV8000 are 32-bit machines. Larger computers, such as the IBM 3030 series, are 32-bit systems, while super computers such as the CRAY-1 are 64-bit systems.

One of the first design decisions made when a new computer system is developed is to select a value for the system's word size. This decision represents a compromise between cost, complexity, and capability. As the size of r increases, the complexity of the hardware needed to realize the system increases and thus the cost. However, this is compensated for by greater processing speed and flexibility in the range of data types and operations that can be realized without resorting to special programming techniques or increasing the complexity of the control unit.

The way that information is encoded in a system has a major impact upon the selection of word size. In particular, all encoded information should fit into the registers of the system. From our previous discussions we know that there are three basic classes of information. They are:

1. Logical information
2. Character information
3. Numerical information

Logical information can be represented by a single bit, thus logical information does not provide any major constraints on the selection of word size. Character information is usually encoded as 8-bit bytes. Thus, if the system is to be able to easily carry out processing tasks involving character information, the word size should be a multiple of 8-bits.

The selection of the conventions used to represent numerical information provides the greatest opportunity for compromise when selecting a word size for a given computer system. Typically numerical information either is represented directly as a binary number or is encoded using a binary coded decimal (BCD) encoding. In making the selection we must consider a number of factors.

A BCD encoding is useful if we are going to do a large amount of computing with which we must retain the decimal nature of the information. This requirement is typically associated with computers that are designed for use in business data processing. If BCD encoding is used, each encoded decimal digit will require 4 bits. Thus the word size selected must be a multiple of 4.

The second factor that must be considered is the range and the resolution associated with the encoding used to represent numerical information. If the word size is too small, we will need to use special programming techniques to carry out some numerical calculations, while if the size is too large we will waste storage space in memory.

When dealing with signed integers, an r-bit word can store any integer in the range

$$\pm(2^{n-1} - 1)$$

as a binary number. Thus if $n = 8$ the range would be ± 127, while if $n = 16$ the range is $\pm 32,767$.

If we wish to store a k-digit signed BCD integer, we would need a word size of at least

$$r = 1 + 4*k$$

bits. This means that a 3-digit decimal number would require 13 bits and a 5-digit decimal number would need 21 bits.

Finally if we wished to store a binary floating point number of the form

$$\pm . m_{-1}m_{-2} \ldots m_{-r} 2^{\pm e_1 \ldots e_u}$$

we would need $(r + 1)$ bits to encode the mantissa and $(u + 1)$ bits to encode the exponent. Depending upon the range that we wish to represent and the word size of the system, it may require from 2 to 8 words to represent a single floating point number.

For SEDCOM II we assume that the designers have decided to use a word size of 16 bits and that the primary data types will be

1. Characters encoded using the ASCII code (stored in 8 bits)
2. Signed integers represented in 2's complement form (16 bits)
3. Unsigned integers (16 bits)

With this selection we see that each word can store

1. Two characters
2. A signed integer in the range $\pm 32,767$
3. An unsigned integer in the range 0 to 65,535

It has also been decided that BCD encoded numbers and floating point numbers will not be included as basic data types. If we wish to use either of these data types, or if we must represent information that does not fit into the ranges given above, then we will have to develop special programs to extend the capabilities of the system. A number of these programs are presented in the next chapter.

SEDCOM II Machine Organization

The general organization selected for SEDCOM II is illustrated in Figure 12-2. Since this is a hypothetical computer system, we have chosen to make it as simple as possible while still maintaining reasonable capability. The system has four major subunits: the CPU, the control unit, random access memory (RAM), and an input/output unit. These units can interchange information by a bus system called INFOBUS. (INFOBUS is similar to but simpler in operation than the UNIBUS system of the PDP-11 computer.) A separate set of control and status lines allows the CPU and the control unit to interact independent of the operations going on on the INFOBUS.

Most modern computer systems use some type of bus structure to allow the CPU and other system subunits to interact. This approach simplifies the communication process in the machine since all of the subunits can be assigned unique address areas that can hold information that may be used by the other units in the system. This information is then available for use just as if it were in a standard memory unit. For our system, the transfer of information between units will be controlled by the control unit. In more advanced systems it is usually possible for more than one unit to be able to control the transfer of information between units on the bus. Although the complexity of such systems is greater, the transfer process is similar to that presented for the INFOBUS.

In the next section we first look at the operation of the bus and the individual subunits. After we see how each part of the system operates, we then define the set of basic instructions that the control unit can execute. Throughout this discussion we

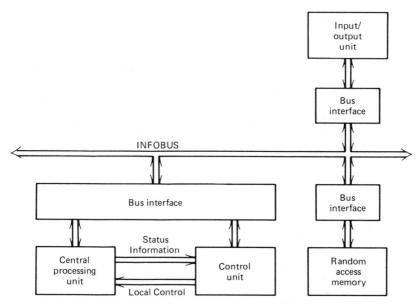

Figure 12-2   General organization of SEDCOM II.

emphasize only the concepts that deal with the general operation of SEDCOM II. It is assumed that the detailed design of the system could be carried out using the techniques discussed in the previous chapters.

EXERCISES

1. Assume that we wish to encode a floating point number in one 16-bit word using $r = 7$ and $u = 7$. What is the range of values that could be represented?

2. What is the smallest unsigned binary fraction that can be represented in one 16-bit word? What is the resolution interval? Is it necessary to encode the "binary point" associated with a fraction?

3.   THE INFOBUS

The general use of a bus to transfer information between different digital devices was discussed in Chapter 11. Our discussion of INFOBUS therefore concentrates on the different information transfers that can take place rather than upon the design of the hardware used to carry out these transfers.

Figure 12-2 shows that the CPU and control unit use the bus to communicate with the memory unit and the I/O unit. The control unit serves as the bus master and the memory and I/O units are the slave units. All information transfer operations are carried out in an asynchronous manner.

The bus is made up of 21 lines, as shown in Figure 12-3. There are 16 address/

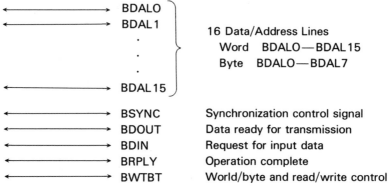

Figure 12-3 The structure of INFOBUS.

data lines and 5 control lines. A transfer is started when the bus master places the address associated with the data to be transferred on the address/data lines and announces that a transfer is to take place by setting the value of BSYNC to 1. Once the slave unit involved with the transfer acknowledges that it is ready to participate in the transfer, the control unit uses the address/data lines to carry out the desired data transfer.

In SEDCOM II information is transferred as either 16-bit words or 8-bit bytes. There are three general classes of transfers. They are:

Data Read—DATI

Information is transferred or read from one of the slave units into a register in the CPU. This is called a Data Input Transfer and given the mnemonic DATI.

Data Write—DATO

Information is transferred or written from a register in the CPU to one of the slave units. This is called a Data Output Transfer and given the mnemonic DATO.

Data Read/Process/Write—DATIO

This transfer operation is a combination of the two previous transfer operations. Data is read from a slave unit to a register in the CPU, processed in the CPU, and then returned to the slave unit. This is called a Data Input/Output Transfer and given the mnemonic DATIO.

Bus Organization

INFOBUS is a bidirectional bus. The function assigned to each line is summarized in Table 12-1.

A simple data read DATI or data write DATO information transfer involves two major steps. The read/process/write DATIO transfer is a combined read/write transfer and requires three steps. The steps can be briefly summarized as follows.

Table 12-1 Description of INFOBUS Signal Lines

Line Number	Mnemonic	Description	Function
0–15	BDAL0–BDAL15	Address/data lines	Transmit address/data information
16	BSYNC	Synchronization signal	Master sets BSYNC to 1 to indicate that information transfer is underway
17	BDOUT	Data ready	Master sets BDOUT to 1 to indicate that data are on the address/data lines and ready for transfer to slave
18	BDIN	Ready to receive	Master sets BDIN to 1 to indicate that it is ready to receive data from slave
19	BRPLY	Slave device ready	Slave sets BRPLY to 1 to acknowledge that it has been selected and is ready to carry out a transfer
20	BWTBT	Control signal	During address transfer the master sets $$BWTBT = \begin{cases} 0 & \text{read data} \\ 1 & \text{write data} \end{cases}$$ During data transfer the master sets $$BWTBT = \begin{cases} 0 & \text{word transfer} \\ 1 & \text{byte transfer} \end{cases}$$

Step 1. Address Transfer

The master places the address information on the address/data lines and announces that a bus transfer is to take place by setting BSYNC to 1. BWTBT is used to indicate whether it is a read or a write transfer.

Step 2. Data Transfer

The data to be transferred is placed on the address/data lines. BWTBT is set to 0 to indicate a word transfer or to 1 to indicate a byte transfer. If it is a read transfer, the master reads the data placed on the data/address lines by the slave.

If it is a write transfer, the slave reads the data that was placed on the data/ address lines by the master. This completes the transfer unless it is a DATIO transfer. In that case the master initiates the third transfer step.

Step 3. Second Data Transfer

In a DATIO transfer the second step reads data from a slave unit and this information is processed in the CPU. At the completion of the processing the result is returned to the same slave unit, which is still connected to the bus. This saves the need for an additional address step.

When a word is transferred, data appears on all 16 of the data/address lines. When byte information is transferred, only lines 0–7 carry the data. The lines not involved in the transfer of the byte information are ignored by the system during the transfer. In SEDCOM II the address of a word must always be even (i.e., BDAL0 is always 0 when the address is a word address).

The following discussion presents a detailed description of each type of transfer independent of the specific slave devices involved. The next sections treat the operation of each subunit in the system and how they make use of the information transferred on the bus.

Bus Addressing—Transfer Step 1

The first step in any bus transfer operation is started when the bus master places the address of the slave device to be accessed on the data/address lines and announces the type of transfer on the control lines. If BWTBT is set to 0, the transfer is to be a read operation, while a 1 indicates a write operation. As soon as these values are set, the bus master sets the control signal BSYNC to 1 to indicate that the information transfer cycle can start.

Each slave unit is assigned a set of distinct addresses. All slave units continually monitor the bus. When they detect that BSYNC is 1, they check the address on the data/address lines. If a slave unit finds that the address on the bus falls in its assigned address space, it enters the activated state and checks BWTBT to see whether the transfer is to be a read or a write. At that point the slave and master initiate the steps necessary to complete the transfer.

The Read Sequence—A DATI Transfer

The DATI transfer is restricted to the reading of full data words from the slave device. This means that the address must always be an even value. Once a read sequence is started a full word is always read by the master. If the CPU needs only the information in one of the bytes in a word, it accesses this information and ignores the other information. However, the slave unit places a full word on the address data lines for transmission to the master.

The sequence of steps necessary to complete a full DATI transfer is shown in Figure 12-4. The first three steps in the bus cycle are associated with setting up the

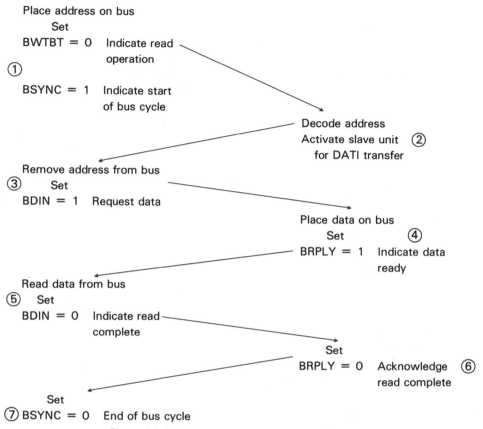

Figure 12-4   The main steps of the DATI bus cycle.

address information as described above. As soon as the slave detects the fact that BDIN is set to 1, it places the data to be transferred on the bus and sets BRPLY to 1 to indicate that data is available to be read by the master. The master then reads this information and sets BDIN to 0 to indicate that it has read the desired information. When the slave detects that BDIN has returned to 0, it resets BRPLY to 0 to acknowledge completion of the transfer and deactivates itself. Finally the master detects that BRPLY is 0 and sets BSYNC to 0 to indicate that the transfer cycle has been completed.

The Write Sequence—A DATO Transfer

During a write sequence either a word or a byte can be transferred from the master to the slave unit. The write cycle is started by setting the address on the bus and setting BWTBT to 1 to indicate the start of a write cycle. After the slave unit has been activated, the data transfer is started.

The steps necessary to carry out the DATO transfer are shown in Figure 12-5. The first two steps activate the slave unit that is to receive the data. The master then places the data on the bus at step 3 and indicates whether a byte (BWTBT = 1) or a word (BWTBT = 0) is to be transferred. When the data is ready, the master sets BDOUT to 1. The slave unit then reads the data and acknowledges that it has been received by sending BRPLY = 1. The final three steps complete the transfer.

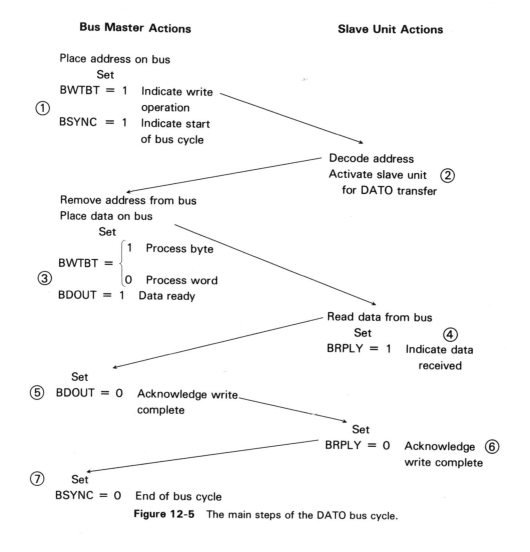

Figure 12-5 The main steps of the DATO bus cycle.

The Read/Process/Write Sequence—A DATIO Transfer

Many of the operations performed by the CPU involve reading data from a memory location, processing this information in some manner, and then returning the result to the same location. This could be done by using a DATI transfer followed by a DATO transfer. Using a two-transfer sequence to accomplish this task means that we must carry out two identical address sequences. This task can be speeded up if the DATI and DATO transfers are combined into a single bus cycle. During the read portion of the cycle, the data to be processed is read from the slave unit to the CPU. The information is then processed at the end of the read operation and the master immediately enters a write cycle. The information is then returned to the slave unit using a standard write sequence.

Figure 12-6 indicates the steps of the DATIO transfer operation. Note that the BWTBT signal is used to indicate whether a byte or a word is to be processed during this transfer operation.

Now that we have an overview of how the bus operates in SEDCOM II, we must define the structure and organization of each of the major units connected to the bus. In the following discussion we consider both the tasks that the unit can perform and the methods used to interface it to the bus.

The Memory Unit

Typical computer applications involve the processing of both character and numerical information. Thus one major design goal is to make it easy for the system to store either numerical or character information in memory. To do this, SEDCOM II uses 16-bit words divided into a high byte and a low byte as shown in Figure 12-7. This flexibility allows us to manipulate both types of information as needed. However, this flexibility also requires a memory organization that allows us to address either whole words or individual bytes.

SEDCOM II is assumed to have a 4096-word memory organized as shown in Figure 12-8*a*. Each memory word is divided into a high-order and a low-order byte. Since we have decided that we want to be able to access both character and word information, we assign a unique address to each byte. Thus our 4096-word memory has 8192 addressable byte locations. Under this convention we see that consecutive words are located at even-number addresses with the address of the low-order byte corresponding to that address and the address of the high-order byte corresponding to the next higher odd address. *Words must always be addressed with an even address!!*

Since memory is one of the slave units connected to INFOBUS, its address space must be uniquely specified. For SEDCOM II the memory address space is arbitrarily assigned to be the 8192 octal addresses between 01000_8 and 20777_8. This means that we can directly address each byte in memory. When we are dealing with words in memory, we can think of memory as being organized as shown in Figure 12-8*a* where

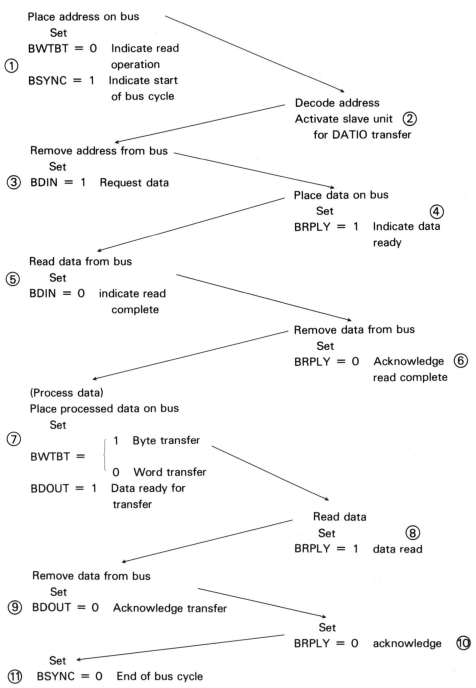

Place address on bus
    Set
BWTBT = 0   Indicate read
①   operation
BSYNC = 1   Indicate start
                of bus cycle

Decode address
Activate slave unit ②
    for DATIO transfer

Remove address from bus
    Set
③ BDIN = 1 Request data

Place data on bus
    Set   ④
BRPLY = 1   Indicate data
                ready

Read data from bus
⑤   Set
BDIN = 0   indicate read
                complete

Remove data from bus
    Set
BRPLY = 0   Acknowledge ⑥
                read complete

(Process data)
Place processed data on bus
    Set
⑦   ⌠ 1   Byte transfer
BWTBT = ⎨
           ⌡ 0   Word transfer
BDOUT = 1   Data ready for
                transfer

Read data
    Set   ⑧
BRPLY = 1   data read

Remove data from bus
    Set
⑨ BDOUT = 0   Acknowledge transfer

Set
BRPLY = 0   acknowledge ⑩

    Set
⑪   BSYNC = 0   End of bus cycle

Figure 12-6   The main steps of the DATIO bus cycle.

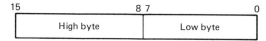

Figure 12-7   Basic word organization.

every word address must be an even octal number. If we wish to work with bytes, then we can think of the memory as being organized as shown in Figure 12-8*b* even though physically it is organized as shown in Figure 12-8*a*. In this case the low-order bytes correspond to even addresses and the high-order bytes correspond to odd addresses.

Memory Unit Organization

From the viewpoint of the outside world, the memory unit is a self-contained device that communicates with the rest of the system by the INFOBUS. The general internal organization of the memory unit is illustrated in Figure 12-9. As shown, the memory unit is subdivided into a device selector, a local control unit, and the actual memory elements. It is also assumed that the master system clock drives the controller so that there is no need to provide a local source of clock pulses.

The memory itself is assumed to be semiconductor memory that is designed so that either byte or word information can be written into or read from memory. As

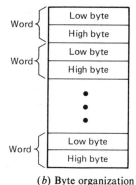

(*a*) Word organization

(*b*) Byte organization

Figure 12-8   Memory organization.

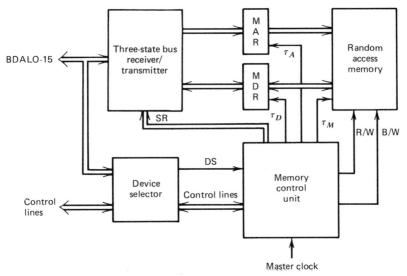

Figure 12-9 General block diagram of memory unit.

shown, the Memory Address Register (MAR) and the Memory Data Register (MDR) are both 16-bit registers. There are two control signals, which are used to indicate the particular task to be performed. The read/write signal (R/W) indicates whether information is to be read (R/W = 1) from memory or written (R/W = 0) into memory. The byte/word signal (B/W) indicates whether a byte (B/W = 1) or a word (B/W = 0) is being processed. Because of the way in which we defined the DATI read operation, we always read a word from memory. However, a write operation may be either a word write or a byte write depending upon the value of B/W. The address in the MAR indicates the location of the information being processed.

Information transfers are controlled by the transfer pulses:

τ_M—Transfer information into the memory location indicated by MAR

τ_A—Transfer address information into MAR

τ_D—Transfer information into the MDR

The MAR and MDR are interfaced to INFOBUS by way of a three-state Bus Receiver/Driver, which is controlled by the 2-bit control signal SR:

SR Operation

[0, 0]—INFOBUS disconnected
[0, 1]—Connection from INFOBUS to MAR input information to memory unit
[1, 0]—Connection from INFOBUS to MDR input information to memory unit
[1, 1]—Connection from MDR to INFOBUS deliver information from memory unit

The device selector monitors both the data/address lines and the control lines. As long as BSYNC is 0 the device selector is in the "NOT SELECTED" state. This is indicated to the control unit by setting the data select signal DS = 0, which informs the control unit that the device is not involved in any memory reference activity. The device selector continually monitors the data/address line. If the address on the data/address line is in the address space of the memory unit when BSYNC goes to 1, this indicates that the bus master wishes to carry out a memory reference operation. The device selector then goes to the "SELECTED" state and DS = 1 is sent to the control unit to indicate that a memory reference operation is to be initiated. The device selector stays in the selected state until BSYNC returns to 0, which causes the device selector to immediately return to the "NOT SELECTED" state.

While the device selector is in the selected state, all of the control signals except BSYNC are transmitted directly to the control unit. The control unit uses these signals, together with the master clock, to generate the control signals and transfer pulses required to perform the memory reference operation requested by the controller. The transfer sequences necessary to carry out the three basic transfer operations, DATI, DATO, DATIO, were given earlier. The details concerning the actual design of the control unit are left as a home problem and can be easily accomplished using the techniques discussed earlier.

The Input/Output Unit

For SEDCOM II we assume that all input information is by way of a keyboard and that the output is printed on a printer. All information is encoded using the ASCII code given in Appendix A. This means that all I/O transfers will involve byte information. The general organization of the I/O slave unit is shown in Figure 12-10.

Basically we can think of the I/O unit as a "special" type of memory device with four words. The organization of the "memory" is shown in Figure 12-10b. The first two words are associated with the keyboard input and the second two words are used for the printer output. These words have been arbitrarily assigned the indicated addresses.

The first word, at the address 177560_8, contains the keyboard ready flag in bit location 7. If we wish to know whether a key has been struck on the keyboard, we must read this word and check whether bit 7 is a 1. If it is we know that the information in the low-order byte of the second word (address 177562_8) is the ASCII code for the key that was struck. If we find that the flag is not 1, then we know that no information is ready. Both of these words are read-only locations that can be accessed using a standard DATI bus cycle. Whenever the keyboard buffer is read, the keyboard flag goes to 0 until the next key is struck. The information in the keyboard buffer can be read only once. The control signal that transfers this information to the bus also clears the keyboard flag and clears the keyboard buffer. This indicates that the unit is ready to process the next input character struck on the keyboard.

The third and fourth words are associated with the printer. The third word at memory location 177564_8 contains the printer flag in bit location 7. When this bit is set, we know that the printer is ready to receive data. To use the printer the control unit uses a DATI bus cycle to read this word and check the value of the flag bit. If the control unit sees that the flag is 1, then it transmits the ASCII code for the

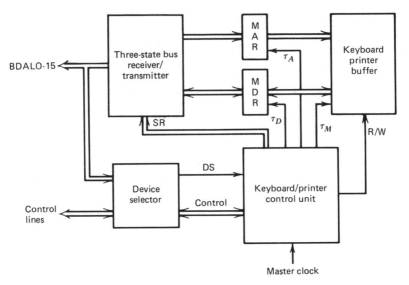

(a) General interface organization

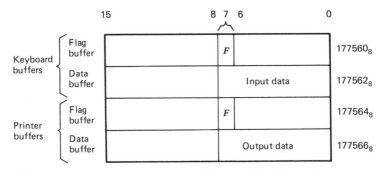

(b) Organization of keyboard/printer buffer addresses

Figure 12-10 General block diagram reader/writer interface.

character to be printed to the low-order bit of the second word (address 177566_8) using a DATO cycle. When this word is received by the I/O unit, the flag bit is set to 0 and the printing operation starts. The printer will not accept any new data until the flag bit is set to 1, indicating that the printing process has been completed.

Since the general operation of the I/O unit is very similar to the operation of the memory unit, we leave it as a home problem to show how the interface can be realized.

4. CENTRAL PROCESSOR AND CONTROL UNIT

The information processing tasks performed on data are carried out in the central processing unit. This unit consists of a collection of registers and the associated logic networks necessary to accomplish the basic logic, arithmetic, and information transfer operations required to carry out a specific information processing task. When a computer is designed, one of the major design decisions involves selecting the basic computational and information transfer operations that will be provided by the CPU.

Each operation that may be executed by the CPU is called an *instruction* and involves a number of steps. It is the responsibility of the control unit to provide the sequence of control signals and transfer pulses required to perform the operation. Each control unit has an *Instruction Register,* which holds a coded representation of the instruction that is used by the control unit to identify the sequence of tasks that must be executed to perform the operations called for by the instruction.

The set of basic instructions associated with a given control unit and CPU form the *machine language instruction set* or *machine language* for that computer. All programs executed by the computer must be expressed as a sequence of these machine language instructions. Such a program is called a *machine language program.*

There are two general classes of instructions: those that involve the operation of the CPU and the other parts of the system, and those that influence the sequence in which the instructions that make up the program are executed. Each instruction is stored in memory. To execute the program the control unit must read the instruction from memory, determine the operation called for by the instruction, and then generate the control signals necessary to carry out the instruction.

Any data needed to execute a given instruction may be stored in memory, in one of the registers of the CPU, or may come from an input device connected to the system. When a point is reached in the execution of an instruction where data is needed, the control unit must know where to find it, how it is to be used, and where to put the results produced by using it in the computation. In some cases this knowledge is designed into the control sequence generated by the control unit, while in other cases the instruction being processed by the control unit must supply this information.

Most computer users do not come into contact with the machine language program that actually carries out the computational tasks that they have described in some higher level language such as Pascal or FORTRAN. As long as we are interested in this level of programming only, we do not have to understand the operation of the computer at the machine language level. However, when we reach a point where we wish to understand how a computer actually operates and the factors that limit its computational capabilities, we must understand how the machine language instructions are implemented and the tasks they perform.

SEDCOM II has been designed to illustrate how one hypothetical computer might be organized to realize a given machine language that is very similar to the machine language of the PDP-11 family of computers. The system being discussed is not meant to duplicate the hardware design of a PDP-11. Instead the hypothetical realization has been designed so that the reader can easily understand how the different types of machine language instructions are executed and the role that the control unit plays in both the execution of a machine language program and the execution of a machine language instruction. Any program that will run on SEDCOM II will also run on machines in the PDP-11 family.

The User's View

From the user's view, the CPU and control unit of SEDCOM II have the organization shown in Figure 12-11. At this level we are not interested in the detailed data paths inside of these units. Both of the units are connected to the INFOBUS. The control unit controls all information transfers that take place on the bus as well as the internal operations of both the CPU and the control unit. All of the data processing activities take place in the CPU.

The CPU contains eight 16-bit registers numbered R0 through R7, an 8-bit processor status (PS) register, an instruction register (IR), an interface to the INFOBUS, and an arithmetic logic unit that can be used to operate on the data in any of the registers or data received from memory by way of the bus. Registers $R0$ through $R5$ are general purpose registers and are used for a number of different purposes as we will shortly discuss. Registers $R6$ and $R7$ are reserved for special use, although the information they contain can be processed by the CPU.

Register R6 is used to implement a stack in memory. A stack is an area of memory set aside by the programmer to temporarily store data during a computation. The stack uses a *last-in first-out* organization where the last item added to the stack is

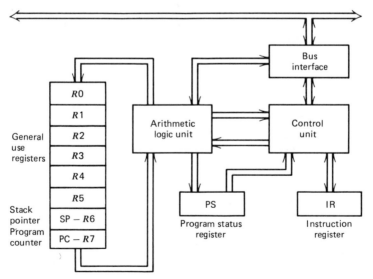

Figure 12-11 The CPU and control unit.

the first one used when an item is removed from the stack. The content of the stack pointer register $R6$ is the memory address of the last item added to the stack. As we will see later, the value of the stack pointer is automatically updated every time an item is added to or removed from the stack. (The registers $R0$ through $R5$ can also be used for stack pointers, but we will single out register $R6$ for this special use.) Register $R6$ is given the special name SP to indicate that it is the *stack pointer register*.

The instructions that make up a machine language program are stored sequentially in memory as illustrated in Figure 12-12. The control unit starts with the first instruction and processes each instruction in order until it reaches an instruction that tells it to go to another instruction sequence someplace else in memory. The control unit must have some way to remember where to find the next instruction when it completes the processing of the current instruction. This is the function served by register $R7$, which is called the system's *program counter* and given the special name PC. The function of the program counter is to store the address of the next instruction to be executed by the control unit.

The Processor Status Vector (PS)

During any computation we will usually have to make a decision by carrying out one or more tests on the data being processed. The 8-bit processor status vector (PS), stored in the processor status register, provides a set of one-bit flags that records the results of these tests or indicates special conditions that result when a given instruction is executed. Although PS contains eight bits, only four of them are used as flag

Address

n	Instruction
$n + 1$	Instruction
$n + 2$	Instruction
$n + 3$	Instruction
$n + 4$	Instruction
$n + 5$	Instruction
$n + k$	Data
$n + k + 1$	Data
$n + k + 2$	Data
$n + k + 3$	Data
$n + k + 4$	
$n + k + r$	Data

Figure 12-12 Representation of the contents of memory.

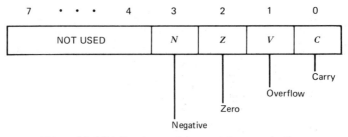

Figure 12-13 Processor status register organization.

bits. Figure 12-13 indicates the organization of the PS register and the symbolic representation of each of the flags.

The flags in the PS register are set following the execution of a given instruction and reflect the status of the result produced by the operation performed. The N, Z, and V flags have a fixed meaning. The C flag is used in two different but related ways depending upon the particular operation being performed. The flags are controlled by the rules given in Table 12-2.

Before we consider the inner workings of the CPU, we must investigate the structure of typical machine language instructions and some of the tasks they perform.

Machine Language Instructions

As a practical matter, all machine language instructions must be encoded so that they occupy one or more words. Thus, for SEDCOM II, we must organize our instructions so that all of the information can be encoded to fit into one or more 16-bit words. Before we consider the detailed specifications of an instruction, it is helpful to consider the general structure that an instruction must take and some of the classes of tasks that must be represented.

Table 12-2 Meaning of the Processor Flags at the Completion of Instruction Execution

$N = 1$	If the result, considered as a 2's complement number, is negative
$N = 0$	If the result, considered as a 2's complement number, is nonnegative
$Z = 1$	If the result of the operation is zero
$Z = 0$	If the result of the operation is not zero
$V = 1$	If there is an *arithmetic overflow* when the operation involves 2's complement arithmetic
$V = 0$	If there is no arithmetic overflow
$C = 1$	If the operation resulted in a carry from the MSB (most significant bit) *or* if during a rotate or shift operation a 1 was shifted from the MSB or LSB (least significant bit).
$C = 0$	If the operation resulted in no carry from the MSB *or* if during a rotate or shift operation a 0 was shifted from the MSB or LSB

Note: Some instructions do not influence the values of particular flag bits.

Each instruction informs the control unit that it should perform a given task. This task may involve using one or more data items to compute a new value for a data item or it may involve controlling how the program is to be executed. Instructions therefore are classified as either

1. Data reference instructions or
2. Program control instructions.

Symbolically we can think of an instruction that performs a data reference operation as having the form

$$\langle result \rangle \leftarrow OP[\langle operand\text{-}1 \rangle, \dots, \langle operand\text{-}k \rangle]$$

where the operation OP has k operands that are used to produce the value assigned to $\langle result \rangle$.

The control unit always finds the address of the next instruction to be executed in a machine language program by going to the program counter (PC). Thus, if we wish to control the sequence in which instructions are executed in a machine language program, we must change the value of the address information stored in the program counter. Program control instructions accomplish this task. They have the same form as data reference operations except that they modify the value of the program counter. Symbolically program control instructions have the form

$$PC \leftarrow OP[\langle operand\text{-}1 \rangle, \dots, \langle operand\text{-}k \rangle]$$

where the first operand is often a logical value that determines whether the control action will take place and the other operands indicate how the new value of the program counter is to be computed.

Structure of Instructions

Since an instruction is encoded into one or more words, a k-word instruction will be $16*k$ bits in length. Theoretically we could arbitrarily define 2^{16*k} distinct k-word instructions. This approach is undesirable since we would find it difficult to keep track of all of the possible instructions. To simplify the interpretation of an instruction we use a more structured approach.

Every instruction is partitioned into sections that contain specific types of information. This is accomplished by assigning special meaning to particular groups of nonoverlapping bits of an instruction. Each such subsection of an instruction is called a *field*. A field is not allowed to cross a word boundary even if the instruction is a multiple-word instruction.

The first field included in an instruction is an *operation code field*, which identifies the instruction to the control unit. The control unit uses this information to determine the number and size of the other fields in the instruction and to select the control sequence necessary to execute the instruction. The remaining fields of an instruction are used to indicate:

1. The location or value of the other operands needed by the instruction.
2. The destination of the results produced by the instruction.

3. Where to find the next instruction.
4. That some basic operation is or is not to be performed.

For practical reasons, machine language instructions usually involve only zero, one, or two operands. If we think of a general instruction as implementing the following task sequence:

Compute   ⟨operand 1⟩⟨operation⟩⟨operand 2⟩
Then place result in   ⟨destination location⟩

Then the instruction representing this task might have the form shown in Figure 12-14. This instruction provides the following information:

1. The ⟨operation⟩ to be carried out.
2. The addresses of the operands or quantities to be operated on.
3. The location to which the result is to be sent.
4. The location of the next instruction.

Instruction Classes

The general form of an instruction indicated in Figure 12-14 implies that all of the information needed to execute a given instruction is contained in the instruction. This form of encoding is very inefficient. For example, if the memory has $2^{16} = 65,536$ memory locations that must be addressed, then each address field would require 16 bits. The instruction would need 64 bits for address information alone. In a machine such as SEDCOM II with 16-bit words, each instruction would require 4 words just for address information. Since memories with this number of locations are not unusual in current computer systems, more efficient instruction encoding methods are required.

The instructions associated with a given calculation are, for the most part, stored in sequential memory locations. The *next-instruction address* field is not needed since we can use a special hardware register, the program counter (PC) register, to keep track of the address of the next instruction to be executed. Register $R7$ serves this purpose in SEDCOM II. The disadvantage of this approach is that additional instructions are needed to alter the sequence in which a set of program instructions is executed.

Next we note that two fields are used to indicate operand addresses and one field is used to indicate where the result of performing the operation is to be placed. There are a number of ways that we can economize at this point. First the need for a result address field is eliminated by introducing the convention that the result produced by an operation is stored in a location that is determined from either the operation code or information contained in one of the operand address fields. This causes few diffi-

Operation code	First operand address	Second operand address	Result address	Next instruction address

Figure 12-14   Four-address instruction format.

culties and saves a considerable amount of memory space by not requiring a result address field in each instruction.

Not all instructions require two operands. We can identify three classes of instructions:

1. Zero-operand instructions
2. One-operand instructions
3. Two-operand instructions

Each time we eliminate the need for an operand we reduce the number of fields we need. Typical examples of each type of instruction will be given shortly.

Sometimes, in order to eliminate the need for an operand, the information needed by a given instruction is assumed to be in a predefined location before the instruction is executed. For example, in SEDCOM II we have a set of flags that form the processor status (PS) vector. To access this information we do not need a complete address field. Instead we can introduce a *tag* field that will have a single bit associated with each location of interest. If the bit is set, we know that we will need to use the information contained in the location associated with that bit. Otherwise the information can be neglected.

There are a variety of ways in which instructions can be encoded for use by a control unit. Figure 12-15 illustrates the general organization used for the instructions in SEDCOM II. Depending upon the type of instruction and the way in which the address of an operand is formed, an instruction may take up from one to three words. The first word always contains the operation code field and

1. A set of tag fields if the instruction is a zero operand instruction.
2. A single operand reference field if the instruction is a single-operand instruction.
3. Two operand reference fields if the instruction is a two-operand instruction.

When an instruction has an operand reference field, the information in that field may be enough to directly locate the referenced operand. However, there are a number of situations in which additional information is needed to determine the value of the operand. In that case additional words are included in the instruction to hold this additional information. Single-operand instructions require at most one additional word for this information. Double-operand instructions may require one or two additional words. Thus a single-operand instruction may be either one or two words while a double-operand instruction may have from one to three words. Before we fully define the machine language of SEDCOM II, we must understand how the control unit executes an instruction and the different techniques that it can use to compute the location of the data needed by a given instruction.

Instruction Execution

Before we can complete the definition of the instruction set that makes up the machine language of SEDCOM II, we must understand how instructions are executed and how we can access specific data contained in memory or in one of the CPU

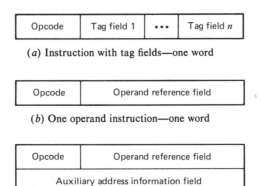

(*a*) Instruction with tag fields—one word

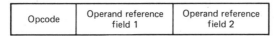

(*b*) One operand instruction—one word

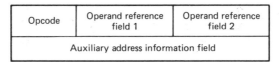

(*c*) One operand instruction—two words

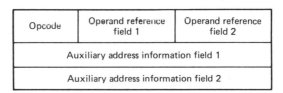

(*d*) Two operand instruction—one word

(*e*) Two operand instruction—two words

(*f*) Two operand instruction—three words

Figure 12-15   Some typical instruction formats.

registers. To do this we must look inside of the CPU to see how it is organized and how various tasks are performed.

Figure 12-16 indicates the assumed data flow within the CPU and the control unit. This diagram shows the registers $R0$ through $R7$ and the processor status (PS) register, which are accessible to the programmer, and the internal ALU registers that are used by the Arithmetic Logic Unit when an instruction is executed but that are not available for use by the programmer. All these registers except the PS register are 16-bit registers. For simplicity, only the major control signal paths are indicated.

Communication between the CPU, the control unit, memory, and the input/output units takes place by way of the INFOBUS as discussed previously. A second bus, linking the registers within the CPU and the control unit, is used for internal infor-

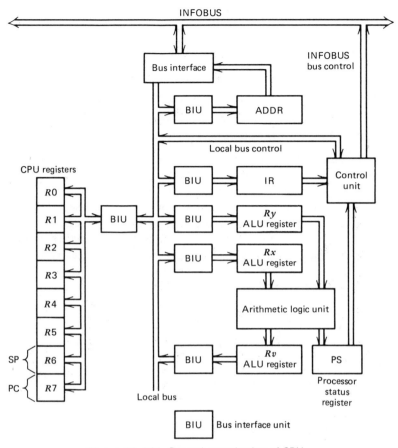

Figure 12-16 General organization of CPU.

mation transfer during the execution of an instruction. We assume that all of the
control signals needed to carry out a transfer on this local bus are produced by the
control unit as needed and we will not be concerned with these details. To further
simplify the discussion we also ignore the details involved in the transfer of data on
the INFOBUS.

The heart of the CPU is the arithmetic logic unit (ALU) and the internal ALU
registers Rx, Ry, and Rv. All of the logic necessary to carry out any of the basic
operations is found in the ALU. The specific operation selected is indicated by a
signal from the control unit. If the operation to be performed is a single-operand
operation, then the value of the operand is placed in internal register Rx, and if a
double-operand operation is being performed, the second operand is placed in internal register Ry. When all of the operands are in place, the operation is carried out
and the result is held in internal register Rv until it is needed to complete the instruction being executed.

When an information transfer is to take place on the INFOBUS, the bus finds the needed address information in the register ADDR. One of the major tasks that must be carried out in the execution of any instruction is that of generating this information. As we will shortly see, there are a number of different ways in which the address information is computed. A complete understanding of the different addressing techniques is mandatory if one is to understand how the different machine language instructions can be used to carry out a given computational task.

Instruction Fetch and Execution

A machine language program is stored in memory in sequential memory locations as shown in Figure 12-17. Each instruction in the program involves from one to three words. It is the responsibility of the control unit to interpret the instructions in the proper order and to see to it that the desired information processing task is executed.

Within the CPU, register $R7$ is the program counter (PC) register. This register is used by the control unit to keep track of which instruction and which word in the instruction is currently being processed. A general flowchart indicating the major steps in executing an instruction is shown in Figure 12-18.

Examining this figure we see that the execution of an instruction is divided into two phases:

1. The fetch phase
2. The execute phase

At the start of the fetch phase the PC contains the address of the first word of the instruction. The control unit uses the address information in this register to initiate a bus input data transfer DATI, which reads the first word of the instruction into the instruction register. Table 12-3 indicates the relative timing of the information transfers involved in this task. The event times indicated in this table are as viewed by the CPU and the control unit. Each memory access is associated with an

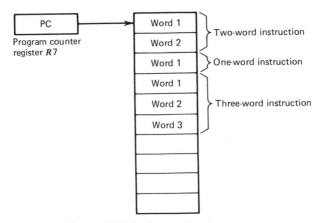

Figure 12-17   Instructions in memory.

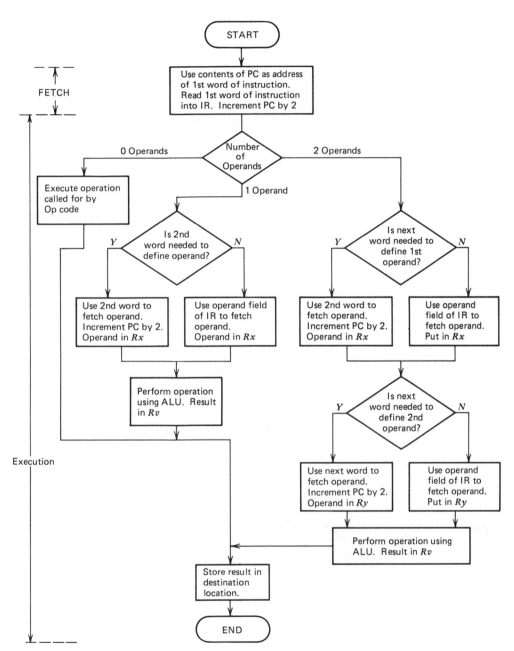

Figure 12-18   General execution sequence.

Table 12-3 The Information Transfer Sequence Involved in the Instruction Fetch Phase of Instruction Execution

Event Time	Transfers	Comment
F1	ADDR ← R7 Rx ← R7	SET ADDRESS TO PC VALUE. START DATI TRANSFER.
F2	MAR ← ADDR	SET MEMORY ADDRESS OF INSTRUCTION.
	Rv ← Rx + [2]	COMPUTE NEW VALUE OF PROGRAM COUNTER.
F3	MDR ← M[MAR] R7 ← Rv	GET INSTRUCTION FROM MEMORY. SAVE NEW VALUE FOR PC.
F4	IR ← MDR	TRANSFER INSTRUCTION TO INSTRUCTION REGISTER. END OF DATI.

INFOBUS information transfer sequence. Only the details of this transfer that are directly related to the fetch cycle are indicated in this discussion.

After the fetch phase has been completed, the PC contains the address of the word following the first word of the instruction. When the instruction is a multiword instruction, this information is used during the execute phase. If the instruction is a single-word instruction, the PC will contain the address of what is anticipated to be the next instruction to be executed by the control unit.

The execute phase is much more complex than the fetch phase. If the operation code of the instruction in the instruction register indicates that the instruction does not require an operand, the control unit will immediately carry out the required task and go on to the next instruction. When the operation code indicates that the instruction involves one or two operands, the control unit must determine the location of these operands and load their values into the proper register in the CPU. SEDCOM II provides a number of methods for locating operands.

Operand Address Calculation

The first word in every SEDCOM II instruction contains the operation code field and either one or two operand reference fields that indicate *how* the values of the operands are to be located. In some instructions all of the information needed is contained in these fields, while in others additional words are needed to augment the information in the operand reference fields.

An operand may be located in either

1. One of the registers, $R0, \ldots, R7$, of the CPU or
2. In memory

When the operand is in one of the registers in the CPU, it is available for immediate use and we do not need an INFOBUS bus transfer to move its value into the CPU. If the operand is in memory, we must first compute the address of the operand and place this value in the address register ADDR. A standard INFOBUS bus transfer operation is then used to transfer the value of the operand found at that address to either the *Rx* or the *Ry* register as determined by the control unit. A number of techniques are used to compute the operand addresses.

For simplicity, we assume that we are dealing with an instruction that has a single operand and that the control unit has completed the fetch phase of instruction execution. Our task is to transfer the value associated with the operand to the *Rx* register. The processing of a two-operand instruction is carried out in a similar manner.

A single-operand instruction has two possible forms. They are:

1. The instruction is a single-word instruction. The address of the operand is indicated by the information contained in the instruction's operand reference field.

2. The instruction is a two-word instruction. The address of the operand is computed using information contained in the second word of the instruction as well as information contained in the instruction's operand reference field.

Single-word Instructions

Single-word instructions are used when all of the information needed to compute the address of the operand is already available in the CPU. The simplest situation occurs when the operand is stored in one of the CPU registers $R0$ through $R7$. In this case the operand reference field indicates the register in which the operand is stored. The control unit then transfers the value of the operand directly to the ALU register *Rx*. This mode of addressing is called *register addressing*.

Register Deferred Addressing

The next form of addressing occurs when the memory address of the operand is stored in one of the CPU registers. The operand reference field of the instruction indicates the register used to hold this address. In this case we can think of the contents of the register as "pointing" to the desired operand value. Figure 12-19a illustrates this interpretation. If we assume that the address is stored in register *Rn*, then the following single information transfer sets ADDR to the needed value.

$$ADDR \leftarrow Rn$$

A DATI or a DATIO bus transfer completes the task of transferring the operand value into the ALU register *Rx*. If the operation does not produce a result that must be saved, the operand is transferred using a DATI transfer. Otherwise a DATIO transfer is used. This mode of addressing is called *register deferred addressing*.

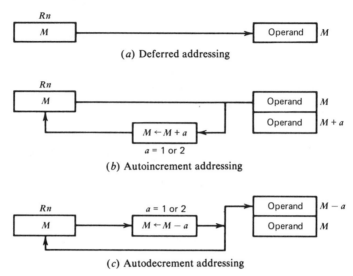

(a) Deferred addressing

(b) Autoincrement addressing

(c) Autodecrement addressing

Figure 12-19   Addressing techniques using only CPU registers.

Autoincrement and Autodecrement Addressing

One common class of information processing activities consists of performing an operation on a sequence of data items stored in contiguous memory locations. Assume that we had a task where we must access each item in order. One way to do this is to set up a pointer that will sequence through the list one item at a time. Either the operation may be performed on the item before the pointer is moved to the next item or the pointer can be moved and the operation then performed on the new item pointed to by the pointer.

Figure 12-19b and c illustrates two different ways that a pointer can be created using one of the CPU registers. In the first case the address of the current data item is stored in register Rn. The address is transferred to the address register ADDR and, at the same time, it is incremented by

(a)   1 if we are accessing bytes or
(b)   2 if we are accessing words.

The updated value is then returned to register Rn. This mode of operation is called the *autoincrement mode* of addressing. Note that the value of the pointer is incremented to its new value *after* the address has been placed into ADDR.

When we use the autoincrement mode of addressing, we process data items that are stored in increasing memory locations. An alternate approach is shown in Figure 12-19c, where we access data in decreasing memory locations. We also introduce the convention that we decrease the address value stored in Rn by

(**a**)   1 if we are accessing bytes or
(**b**)   2 if we are accessing words.

before we load the address into the address register ADDR. This method of address-ing is called the *autodecrement mode* of addressing. The reason that we decrement the address before we use it will become clearer when we start to discuss the use of both modes.

After we have set the ADDR value, the operand is read from memory using either a DATI or a DATIO bus transfer as determined by the operation to be performed. Finally we carry out the operation called for by the instruction's operation code.

Double-word Instructions

The second class of addressing techniques must be used when the operand reference field in the first word of the instruction indicates that additional information is needed to obtain the value of the operand. This information is placed in the word (or words if it is a two-operand instruction) following the first word of the instruction. Single-operand instructions require a maximum of one additional word. If we are dealing with an instruction requiring two operands, we may need up to two additional words, one for each operand.

The information contained in the second word may be the immediate value of the operand or it may supply the additional information needed to compute the memory location of the desired operand value. For both cases, the control unit must transfer the information in the second word to a register in the ALU before it can be used. At the point in the execution of the instruction where this information is needed the program counter, PC, contains the address of the second word. The control unit uses this address to read the contents of this word. After the read operation is completed, the value in PC is incremented by 2 to point to the next word in memory.

When we deal with addresses stored in one of the registers $R0$ through $R7$, we know that they are absolute addresses. That is, they directly indicate the location in memory where we expect to find the desired operand. By using a second word in the instruction we can increase the number of ways that we can access information stored in memory.

Immediate Addressing

The simplest situation for accessing information in memory is shown in Figure 12-20*a*. The value of the operand which we wish to use is stored in the second word of the instruction. This case is of particular use when the operand has a constant value that we wish to use in performing the operation. For example, we often want to carry out a computation such as

$$A \leftarrow 10 + A$$

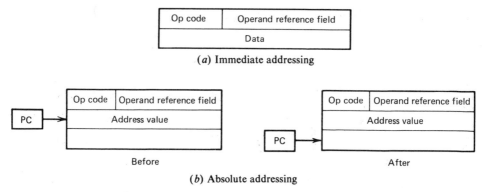

(a) Immediate addressing

(b) Absolute addressing

Figure 12-20 Simple double-word addressing.

where the constant value of 10 is added to the variable A. In some computer systems a specific area in memory is set aside for data storage. The values of all operands, including constants, are stored in that area. When this method is used to store constants, it puts an extra burden on the programmer since it is then necessary for the programmer to remember where this constant is stored. The immediate storage of the operand as part of the instruction (as illustrated in Figure 12-20a) eliminates the need for this special storage location. In addition the constant value, which is uniquely associated with the instruction, is easily read because the program counter already contains the address of this memory location. To read this information we carry out the following information transfer sequence.

Transfer Sequence—Immediate Addressing

CPU—Transfers	INFOBUS—Transfers
ADDR ← PC Rx ← PC	
Rv ← Rx + [2]	MAR ← ADDR
PC ← Rv	MBR ← $M_{[MAR]}$
	Rx ← MBR

When this transfer has been completed, the control unit can then use the constant to carry out the action called for by the instruction's operation code. The program counter has also been set to point to the next word in memory. This form of addressing is called *immediate mode* addressing.

Absolute Addressing

One problem with using a CPU register to hold the address of an operand is that this address must be loaded into the register before it can be used. There are many cases in which we wish to make a calculation that uses an operand that is located in an arbitrary memory location. If we had to use a single-word instruction to access this information, we would have to first transfer the operand's address to a CPU register and then read the operand using this address. This approach adds unnecessary complexity to a program. A simple alternative is to include the absolute address of the operand as part of the instruction. This is illustrated in Figure 12-20*b*. The address of the operand is placed in the second word of the instruction. This address information is transferred to ADDR by the following transfer sequence, which involves one additional bus transfer but is independent of any of the CPU registers other than the program counter register $R7$.

Transfer Sequence to Read Operand Absolute Address

CPU—Transfers		INFOBUS—Transfers
ADDR ← PC	Rx ← PC	
Rv ← Rx + [2]		MAR ← ADDR
PC ← Rv		MBR ← $M_{[MAR]}$
		ADDR ← MBR

At the end of the transfer the program counter is pointing to the next word and the address register ADDR contains the address of the operand to be used in the execution of the instruction. The control unit then uses this address to complete the execution of the instruction. This form of addressing is called *absolute mode* addressing.

Indexed Addressing

All addressing techniques considered so far involve addresses that are stored either in a CPU register or in the second word of the instruction. The final type of addressing to consider is somewhat more complex since the desired address is computed by using two values, one of which is found in a CPU register and one of which is found in the second word of the instruction. The power of this form of addressing can be appreciated if we consider how we might store a complex data structure, such as an array of records, in memory.

Suppose that we wish to store an array of records and that each record has the four data fields shown in Figure 12-21. As shown, each record requires eight words to store the four fields. To access a specific field in a given record we must first determine the location of the record and then the location of the field within the record. This task is simplified if we adopt the convention that the address of a record is the address of the first word of the record and that the locations of the different fields that make up the record are given relative to that address. For example, in Figure 12-21 assume that the first word of Employee Record 1 starts at memory location 5000_8 and that the record takes up the next 16 bytes (8 words) of memory.

Since we use byte addressing in SEDCOM II, the first field, the Name Field, starts in location 0 of the record, the second field, the Salary Field, starts in location 6_8, the third field, the Employee Code Field, starts in location 10_8, and the fourth field, the Department Field, starts in location 12_8.

Indexed addressing allows us to access information stored in this manner in a nat-

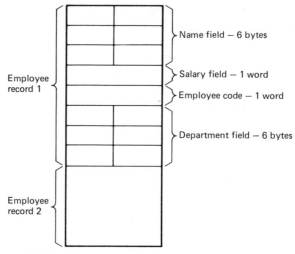

Figure 12-21 Memory organization of a complex data structure.

ural way. As shown in Figure 12-22, we store the record address in one of the CPU registers and we store the field location information in the second word of the instruction. The address of the desired item in the record is formed using the following set of information transfers. It is assumed that the address of the first word in the record is stored in CPU register $R1$.

Information Transfers to Compute Address Using Indexed Addressing

CPU—Transfers		INFOBUS—Transfers
ADDR ← PC	Rx ← PC	
Rv ← Rx + [2],	Ry ← $R1$	MAR ← ADDR
PC ← Rv		MBR ← $M_{[MAR]}$
		Rx ← MBR
Rv ← Rx + Ry		
ADDR ← Rv		

Note: Record address assumed in $R1$.

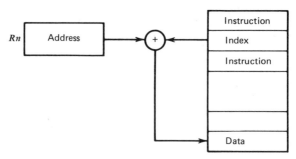

Figure 12-22 Indexed addressing.

This sequence of information transfers indicates that a number of different data transfers are required. First we use a bus data input transfer to transfer the index value, found in the second word of the instruction, to register *Rx*. While this transfer is being carried out, the value of the program counter is also incremented so that it points to the next word in memory and we transfer the record address contained in *R*1 into the temporary register *Ry*. Finally the absolute address of the item in the record being referenced is computed and this value is placed in ADDR.

In the above example the register *R*1 is referred to as an *index register* and the value supplied by the instruction is called the *displacement* value of the address. Note that the displacement value may be either positive or negative if we assume that we use 2's complement addition for the addition operation.

This mode of addressing is called *indexed addressing*. There are several variations of indexed addressing that can be found in different computer systems. One important variation found in SEDCOM II is called *relative addressing*.

Relative Addressing

Suppose that we wish to perform an operation on the data stored in location *A*. We could use direct addressing to access this location. This requires that we know the exact location in memory where both the program and the data are stored. A common software engineering design practice, however, is to develop a complex program by breaking it into a series of subprograms and then to develop each of the subprograms independently before they are combined into the complete program. This means that we may not know the absolute address of the program or the data at the time the program was developed. The only information that we would know about the address of *A* would be its location relative to the instruction that referenced that location. The information contained in location *A* can be accessed by using relative addressing.

To understand relative addressing, assume that we are dealing with a two-word instruction that has its first word stored in memory location *X* and that we wish to use an operand that is stored in memory location *Y*. The *displacement* between the instruction and the data is

$$D = Y - X$$

which may be a positive or negative number. For a given program segment and operand location, all such displacement values are constant and independent of the absolute location in memory used to store this program segment.

If we wish to make use of this fact, we need a method that can be used to compute the location of the value of the operand relative to the location of the instruction. One way to do this for a single operand instruction is to store an offset value as the second word in the instruction. This offset value is then used to compute the absolute location of the operand. Figure 12-23 illustrates the relationship that exists between the different data items necessary to compute the address of memory location *Y*.

After we fetch the first word of the instruction located in memory location *X*, the

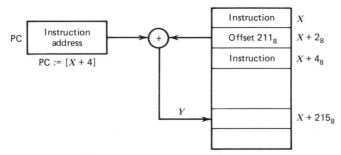

Figure 12-23   Relative addressing.

program counter contains the value $X + 2$, which points to the second word of the instruction. This word holds the offset value needed to compute the value of Y. To make this calculation we must read the value of the offset. After reading this value the program counter contains the memory address $X + 4$. Thus if we define the *offset* value as

$$\langle \text{offset} \rangle = Y - X - 4$$

we can compute the absolute address of the data as

$$
\begin{aligned}
\langle \text{data address} \rangle &= \text{PC} + \langle \text{offset} \rangle \\
&= \text{PC} + (Y - X - 4) \\
&= (X + 4) + (Y - X - 4) \\
&= Y
\end{aligned}
$$

After we complete the computation of $\langle \text{data address} \rangle$ using $\langle \text{offset} \rangle$, we can read the value of the operand stored at that address.

If we are dealing with a two-operand instruction, there are a number of ways in which we may use relative addressing. If relative addressing is used, both operands may be referenced in a relative manner or only one of them might be referenced. In each case the technique used to calculate $\langle \text{data address} \rangle$ will depend upon the location of the offset information. The problem of computing the $\langle \text{data address} \rangle$ for the various forms of relative addressing found in a two-operand instruction is left as a home problem.

Note that the offset may be positive or negative. If it is negative it is represented as a 2's complement number. For example, in Figure 12-23 the displacement is 215_8 since the first word of the instruction is assumed to be at location X and the data element A is assumed to be in location $X + 215_8$. The offset, which is stored in the second word of the instruction, is 211_8.

Relative addressing can easily be implemented since the register $R7$ in the CPU is the program counter register. From this discussion we also see that relative addressing is just a special case of indexed addressing. The information transfers necessary to implement this addressing technique are identical with those used to illustrate indexed addressing. The only modification is that the PC register rather than register $R1$ is used for the index register.

EXERCISES

1. Assume that PC := [10500] and R2 := [10700]. What is the memory location of the operand if
   (a) deferred addressing is used together with *R2*?
   (b) autoincrement addressing is used together with *R2*?
   (c) autodecrement addressing is used together with *R2*?

2. Give the information transfers necessary to calculate the operand address when relative addressing is used.

5. BASIC INSTRUCTION SET FOR SEDCOM II

A key design decision in the development of a new computer system is the selection of the basic instruction set for the computer. The instruction set selected for SED-COM II is representative of the types of instructions found in any computer system. In selecting an instruction set it is necessary to provide instructions that will:

1. Move information between the CPU, memory, and I/O devices.
2. Perform basic arithmetic and logical operations on data.
3. Perform basic tests on data and report the results.
4. Control the sequence in which instructions are executed.
5. Control the operation of the computer system.

The first four classes of instructions provide the capabilities to carry out a normal computation. The fifth class of instructions, which may not be available on all machines, provides the computer system with the capability to respond to situations that are external to a program. For example, if the system tries to execute a nonexistent instruction, the computer may have a built-in response that will aid the user in identifying where and why the error occurred. Instructions of this type are not included in SEDCOM II.

A discussion of the machine language instructions associated with any computer can be presented from two different views—the user's view and the designer's view. The user is mainly interested in the basic set of machine language instructions that can be used to create a program, the way in which these instructions are encoded, and the net result of executing an instruction on the data in the computer. The system designer, on the other hand, must be concerned with how each instruction is implemented by the control unit. Thus the way in which the fields in each instruction are defined and how they are related to the basic operations that must be performed to carry out each instruction is of key importance to the system designer.

This section presents the user's view of SEDCOM II's machine language. We first consider the way an instruction is organized and the different types of information it must supply to the control unit. Using this information we then define the instructions that make up the machine language instruction set of SEDCOM II.

Notation Conventions and Background

SEDCOM II has a word size of 16 bits but uses a memory addressing technique that allows us to address either individual 8-bit bytes or 16-bit words. An instruction is made up of from one to three words. The first word always contains the operation code field and the operand reference fields. If an instruction is a multiple-word instruction, the additional words are used to provide the information needed to compute the address of an operand. A single-operand instruction requires either one or two words, while a double-operand instruction may have a maximum of three words. A single word is all that is needed if the instruction does not involve an operand.

To define the machine language of SEDCOM II we must first decide upon the instructions that are to be included in the language and then define the binary coding used to represent each instruction. If we were to write down the binary pattern used to encode each instruction, we would find this representation much too confusing to be of any use. Two notational aids are used to avoid this problem. If we wish to retain the ability to deal with the actual bit patterns in the words that make up an instruction, we can use octal or hexadecimal numbers to represent the contents of each word. Although this makes it easier to represent the contents of a word, it is still not easy to relate the numerical values to the task that the instruction is designed to carry out. When this becomes important a set of mnemonics is introduced to represent the task of each instruction and the location where the operands needed by the instruction can be found.

Octal and Hexadecimal Coding

It is quite common to use octal or hexadecimal numbers to represent the instructions found in a computer system. Since most computers use word sizes that are multiples of 8 bits, the hexadecimal number system would seem to be the most likely candidate for this task since only two hexadecimal numbers would be required to represent a byte. There are, however, some computer systems in which the pattern of encoding used to represent the instruction set is built around 3-bit groupings of information. For these systems the octal number system provides a better representation of the contents of each instruction. SEDCOM II, like the PDP-11, has this property. Thus we will use octal numbers to describe the content of either a byte or a word.

Figure 12-24 illustrates a typical 16-bit word and shows how a 6-digit octal number can be used to represent the information contained in the word. Note that the

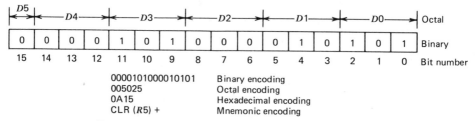

Figure 12-24 Different representations of an instruction.

leftmost digit corresponds to a single bit. Thus the octal number associated with any word must fall in the range of 000000_8 to 177777_8. In the following discussion all numbers are assumed to be given in octal form unless another base is indicated. When we must reference an individual bit, it is assumed that the bits are numbered from right to left as shown. Thus bit 0 is the rightmost bit and bit 15 is the leftmost bit.

Mnemonics

Even though the octal representation of the contents of the word indicated in Figure 12-24 is easier to remember than the equivalent binary encoding, it is not very informative as to what the instruction is designed to do. The *mnemonic representation* of the instruction shown is

$$\text{CLR} \qquad (R5)+$$

This representation suggests that the instruction is to clear a register that is represented by the address $(R5)+$. (The meaning of this address notation is discussed in the next section.) A mnemonic representation is easier for the programmer to remember, but it destroys some of the information about the way that the instruction is actually encoded.

The set of mnemonics used to describe the instruction set of a given machine forms the basis of a language called the *assembly language* of the system. We can write complete programs in this language and use a special program, called an *assembler,* to translate the assembler language program into its corresponding machine language. The next chapter presents the programming techniques that can be used to write assembly language programs, and Chapter 14 investigates the structure of an assembler program that can be used to carry out the translation of these programs to SEDCOM II machine code.

The Basic Instruction Set of SEDCOM II

The machine language instructions selected for a computer system represent a compromise between the number of distinct instructions that can be realized and the computational capabilities a programmer would like to have to develop a program. What is surprising to many people is the small number of instructions that are actually needed to be able to carry out any calculation.

The basic instruction set has four classes of instructions. They are:

1. Zero-operand instructions
2. Single-operand instructions
3. Double-operand instructions
4. Program control instructions

The following discussion presents the formal definition of the instructions that make up SEDCOM II's machine language. The next chapter provides a better insight into how they are used in a program.

Zero-Operand Instructions

Zero-operand instructions are single-word instructions that are executed without reference to any data items in memory or in the CPU data registers. There are four such instructions. Two of them deal with the execution of a program and two deal with the status of the C flag in the processor status (PS) register. Table 12-4 provides a description of the task performed by each one.

The *HALT instruction* provides some protection against the system running away as well as providing for a way of stopping the execution of a program. In normal operation a HALT instruction is the last instruction executed in a program so that you can stop the computer. However, in writing machine level programs it is often very easy to make an error, which causes the control unit to try to execute an instruction from a section of memory that does not contain instructions. When that happens the action of the computer is completely unpredictable and we say that the computer has "run away." This unpredictable operation will continue until the user stops the computer manually or the control unit encounters a word in memory that it interprets as the HALT instruction. If one makes sure that all unused memory locations have a zero value before a program is initiated, then there is a good chance that a runaway situation will be stopped by the control unit encountering a HALT instruction.

The *NOP instruction* is a null instruction in that it does not do anything. There are two uses for this instruction. In developing a program you will often find that you

Table 12-4   The Zero-operand Instructions

---

1. Halt   Mnemonic HALT
   Definition: Causes the processor to stop operation.
   Instruction: 000000

2. No Operation   Mnemonic NOP
   Definition: The control unit carries out one fetch execute
                 sequence without doing anything.
   Instruction: 000240
   Condition: C, V, Z, N unaffected
   Codes

3. Clear C Flag   Mnemonic CLC
   Definition: Set the value of the C flag to 0.
   Instruction: 000241
   Condition: C set to 0, V, Z, N unaffected
   Codes

4. Set C Flag   Mnemonic SEC
   Definition: Set the value of the C flag to 1.
   Instruction: 000261
   Condition: C set to 1, V, Z, N unaffected
   Code

---

must delete one or more instructions from the code that you have generated. If you physically remove the instructions, you will have to recompute a considerable amount of information associated with the address information of the remaining instructions. If you replace the words associated with the instructions that you wish to delete with NOP instructions, these instructions are disregarded during execution. However, in taking this approach, you have not changed the number of words in memory that the program has used. A second use of the NOP instruction is in timing loops where you wish to wait a fixed amount of time before you go on to the next task. If it takes $T1$ seconds to go once around the loop, then a delay of approximately $T2$ seconds can be obtained by going around the loop consisting of the NOP instruction

$$N = T2/T1$$

times.

The C flag in the processor status register PS is used for two purposes. It indicates that a carry from the most significant bit was generated during an arithmetic operation, and it is used as a temporary storage location during shift and rotate operations. In the second case we must often make sure that the value of C has a predefined value before the shift or rotate operation is performed. The clear C flag operation indicated by the mnemonic CLC sets the C flag to 0 and the set C flag indicated by the mnemonic SEC sets the C flag to 1.

Single-operand Instructions

Most single-operand instructions carry out an operation of the following form:

$$A \leftarrow \text{OP}(A)$$

The information represented by the operand A is operated on by the operator OP to produce a new value, which replaces the original value of A. The operand A is referred to as the *destination operand*. As we have seen in Section 4, there are a number of different ways in which the operand A may be addressed.

Single-operand instructions take up either one or two words depending upon the addressing technique used. The format for both types of instructions is illustrated in Figure 12-25. The first word in the instruction contains the *operation code field* and the *operation reference field* which, in a single-operand instruction, is called the *destination address field*. If the destination address field indicates that all of the address information is available in the CPU, a second word is not needed. However, if additional address information is required to locate the value of the operand needed to execute the instruction, a second word is used. This word contains the supplemental information needed to locate the operand value in main memory.

The destination address field is divided into two 3-bit subfields called the *mode field* and the *register field*. The value found in the mode field indicates the addressing mode to be used in locating the value of the operand. The register field, which holds a value between 0 and 7, indicates the CPU register involved in locating the operand. If the register field contains the value n, this means that CPU register Rn is to be

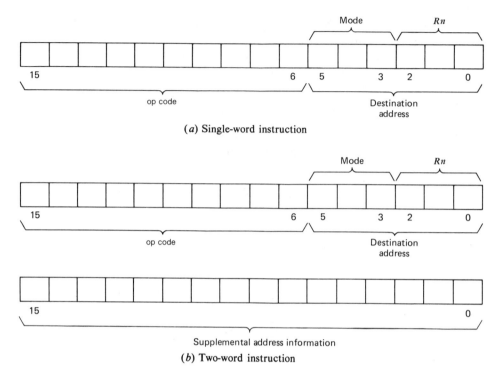

Figure 12-25 Format of single operand instructions.

used. Table 12-5 provides a summary of the different modes of addressing available in SEDCOM II and the numerical value used to represent each of the allowed modes.

There are 13 basic single-operand instructions. Of these 13, 12 can operate on either words or bytes while the other 1 can operate only on words. The following summary briefly describes each of the instructions, the mnemonic used to represent the instruction, and its operation code and illustrates the task it performs. In interpreting the instruction the following conventions are used in encoding the instructions:

1. Bit 15 of the instruction is set to 1 to indicate that the operation is a byte operation.
2. Bits 14–6 indicate the operation code. Note that bits 14, 13, 12 have an octal value of 0 for single-operand instructions.
3. Bits 5–0 form the *destination address field* ⟨DEST⟩. The destination address field has two 3-bit subfields. The address mode subfield indicates the address mode (see Table 12-5) and the register subfield indicates the CPU register used in calculating the address of the operand according to the mode of addressing used. The destination address is represented by the two-digit octal number *DD*, where the first *D* indicates the mode of the operand and the second *D* indicates the CPU register associated with the addressing mode.

Table 12-5 Addressing Modes for SEDCOM II

Addressing Modes for Use When Registers Field Has a Value 0 through 6

Mode	Name	Register Mnemonic	Location of Operand
0	Register	Rn	Operand is in register Rn in the CPU.
1	Indirect	(Rn)	Address of operand is found in CPU register Rn.
2	Autoincrement	$(Rn)+$	Address in CPU register Rn is used to locate operand. The value stored in Rn is then incremented by 1 if the instruction is a byte instruction or by 2 if it is a word instruction. If $n = 6$ then $R6$ is always incremented by 2.
3			This mode is not defined in SEDCOM II
4	Autodecrement	$-(Rn)$	Address in CPU register is first decremented by 1 for a byte operation and by 2 for a word operation or if $n = 6$. The decremented value is then taken as the address of the operand.
5			This mode is not defined in SEDCOM II
6	Index	$X(Rn)$	The number stored in the address supplement field is added to the value in CPU register Rn to form the address of the operand.
7			This mode is not defined in SEDCOM II

Table 12-5 (Continued)

Program Counter Register Address Modes—Register Field Has Value 7

Mode	Name	Register Mnemonic	Location of Operand
2	Immediate	#n	Operand n is contained in the address supplement field of the instruction.
3	Absolute	@#A	The absolute address A of the operand is contained in the address supplement field of the instruction.
6	Relative	A	The address of A relative to the instruction is contained in the address supplement field of the instruction.

4. If the address mode requires an address supplement field, then this field is contained in the second word of the instruction.

The single-operand instructions are summarized in Table 12-6. This table indicates the mnemonic used to represent the instruction, its octal representation, the information transfers performed when the instruction is executed, and a brief discussion of the task performed by the operation.

Table 12-6 Single-Operand Instructions

1. Add Carry

Mnemonic	Word ADC ⟨DST⟩	Byte ADCB ⟨DST⟩
Octal Code	Word 0055DD	Byte 1055DD
Operation:	⟨DST⟩ ← ⟨DST⟩ + C	

Condition
Codes:
N: set if result < 0 cleared otherwise
Z: set if result = 0 cleared otherwise
V: set if ⟨DST⟩ is initially 077777 and C is initially 1 else cleared
C: set if ⟨DST⟩ is initially 177777 and C is initially 1 else cleared

Description: Adds the contents of the C bit into the destination. This permits the carry from the addition of the low order words/ bytes to be carried into the high order result, such as in performing double precision arithmetic.

Table 12-6 Single-operand Instructions (Continued)

2. Arithmetic Shift Left

Mnemonic	Word ASL ⟨DST⟩	Byte ASLB ⟨DST⟩
Octal Code	Word 0063DD	Byte 1063DD

Operation: ⟨DST⟩ ← ⟨DST⟩ shifted one place to the left

Condition
Codes:

N: set if high order bit of the result = 0
Z: set if the result = 0
V: loaded with the exclusive OR of the N bit and C bit (as set by the completion of the shift operation)
C: loaded with the original high order bit of the destination

Description: Shifts all bits of the destination left one place. The low order bit is loaded with a 0. The C bit of the status word is loaded from the high order bit of the destination. ASL performs a signed multiplication of the destination by 2 with *arithmetic* overflow indication.

3. Arithmetic Shift Right

Mnemonic	Word ASR ⟨DST⟩	Byte ASRB ⟨DST⟩
Octal Code	Word 0062DD	Byte 1062DD

Operation: ⟨DST⟩ ← ⟨DST⟩ shifted one place to the right

Condition
Codes:

N: set if the high order bit of the result is set (result < 0)
Z: set if the result = 0
V: loaded from the exclusive OR of the N bit and C bit (as set by the completion of the shift operation)
C: loaded from low order bit of the destination

Description: Shifts all bits of the destination right one place. The high order bit is replicated. The C bit is loaded from the low order bit of the destination. ASR performs signed division by 2.

4. Clear

Mnemonic	Word CLR ⟨DST⟩	Byte CLRB ⟨DST⟩
Octal Code	Word 0050DD	Byte 1050DD

Operation: ⟨DST⟩ ← [0]

Condition
Codes:

N: cleared
Z: set
V: cleared
C: cleared

Description: Contents of specified destination are replaced with 0's.

Table 12-6 Single-operand Instructions (Continued)

5. Complement

   Mnemonic   Word COM ⟨DST⟩   Byte COMB ⟨DST⟩

   Octal Code   Word 0051DD   Byte 1051DD

   Operation: ⟨DST⟩ ← ⟨$\overline{DST}$⟩

   Condition   N: set if most significant bit of result = 1
   Codes: Z: set if result = 0
                   V: cleared
                   C: set

   Description: Replaces the contents of the destination address with its
                   logical complements (each bit equal to 0 is set and each bit
                   equal to 1 is cleared).

6. Decrement

   Mnemonic   Word DEC ⟨DST⟩   Byte DECB ⟨DST⟩

   Octal Code   Word 0053DD   Byte 1053DD

   Operation: ⟨DST⟩ ← ⟨DST⟩−[1]

   Condition   N: set if result < 0
   Codes: Z: set if result = 0
                   V: set if ⟨DST⟩ was 100000
                   C: not affected

   Description: Subtract 1 from the contents of the destination.

7. Increment

   Mnemonic   Word INC ⟨DST⟩   Byte INCB ⟨DST⟩

   Octal Code   Word 0052DD   Byte 1052DD

   Operation: ⟨DST⟩ ← ⟨DST⟩+[1]

   Condition   N: set if result < 0
   Codes: Z: set if result = 0
                   V: set if DST was 077777
                   C: not affected

   Description: Adds 1 to the contents of the destination.

8. Negate

   Mnemonic   Word NEG ⟨DST⟩   Byte NEGB ⟨DST⟩

   Octal Code   Word 0054DD   Byte 1054DD

   Operation: ⟨DST⟩ ← ⟨$\overline{DST}$⟩ + [1]

   Condition   N: set if result < 0
   Codes: Z: set if result = 0
                   V: set if result = 100000
                   C: cleared if result = 0

Description: Replaces the contents of the destination address by its 2's complement. Note that 100000 is replaced by itself.

9. Rotate Left

Mnemonic	Word ROL ⟨DST⟩	Byte ROLB ⟨DST⟩
Octal Code	Word 0061DD	Byte 1061DD

Operation: ⟨DST⟩ ← ⟨DST⟩ rotate left one place

Condition Codes:
- N: set if the high order bit of the result word is set (result > 0)
- Z: set if all bits of the result word = 0
- V: loaded with the exclusive OR of the N bit and C bit (as set by the completion of the rotate operation)
- C: loaded with the high order bit of the destination

Description: Rotates all bits of the destination left one place. The high order bit is loaded into the C bit of the status word and the previous contents of the C bit are loaded into the low order bit of the destination.

10. Rotate Right

Mnemonic	Word ROR ⟨DST⟩	Byte RORB ⟨DST⟩
Octal Code	Word 0060DD	Byte 1060DD

Operation: ⟨DST⟩ ← ⟨DST⟩ rotate right one place

Condition Codes:
- N: set if high order bit of the result is set
- Z: set if all bits of result are 0
- V: loaded with the exclusive OR of the N bit and the C bit as set by the completion of the rotate operation
- C: loaded with the low order bit of the destination

Description: Rotates all bits of the destination right one place. The low order bit is loaded into the C bit and the previous contents of the C bit are loaded into the high order bit of the destination.

11. Subtract Carry

Mnemonic	Word SBC ⟨DST⟩	Byte SBCB ⟨DST⟩
Octal Code	Word 0056DD	Byte 1056DD

Operation: ⟨DST⟩ ← ⟨DST⟩ − C

Condition Codes:
- N: set if result < 0
- Z: set if result = 0
- V: set if ⟨DST⟩ was 100000 and C = 1
- C: cleared if ⟨DST⟩ was 0 and C = 1

Description: Subtracts the contents of the C bit from the destination. This permits the carry from the subtraction of the low order words/bytes to be subtracted from the high order part of the result in order to perform double precision subtraction.

Table 12-6 Single-operand Instructions (Continued)

12. Swap Byte

Mnemonic	Word SWAB ⟨DST⟩
Octal Code	Word 0003DD
Operation	⟨Byte 1⟩ ← ⟨Byte 0⟩ ⟨Byte 0⟩ ← ⟨Byte 1⟩
Condition Codes:	*N*: set if high order bit of low order byte (bit 7) of result is set. *Z*: set if low order byte of result = 0 *V*: cleared *C*: cleared
Description:	Exchanges high order byte and low order byte of the destination (which must be a word address).

13. Test

Mnemonic	Word TST ⟨DST⟩	Byte TSTB ⟨DST⟩
Octal Code	Word 0047DD	Byte 1047DD
Operation:	⟨DST⟩ ⟨ ← ⟨DST⟩	
Condition Codes:	*N*: set if result < 0 *Z*: set if result = 0 *V*: cleared *C*: cleared	
Description:	Sets the condition codes *N* and *Z* according to the contents of the destination address. Contents of ⟨DST⟩ not changed.	

Double-operand Instructions

Most double-operand instructions carry out an operation of the general form

$$B \leftarrow OP(A, B)$$

As indicated, the value of operand A is not changed while, the value of operand B is updated to a new value by performing the operation. The operand A is called the *source operand* and the operand B is called the *destination operand.*

Double-operand instructions occupy from one to three words depending upon the mode of addressing used to reference each operand. The different ways in which a double-operand instruction can be formed are illustrated in Figure 12-26. The first word always contains an *operation code field* and two operand reference fields. The first one is called the *source operand field,* and the second is called the *destination operand field.* Just as in a single-operand instruction, both of these fields have a mode subfield and a register subfield. If either operand field has an address mode that indicates that additional information is needed to calculate the address of the operand, then this information is contained in the second or third word. These words form

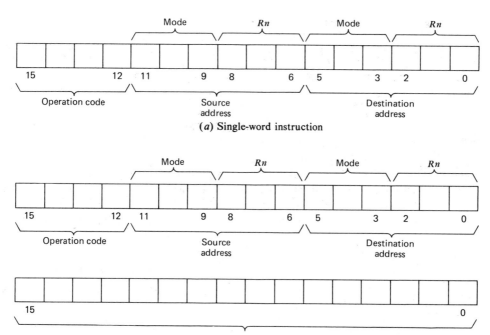

(a) Single-word instruction

(b) Two-word instruction

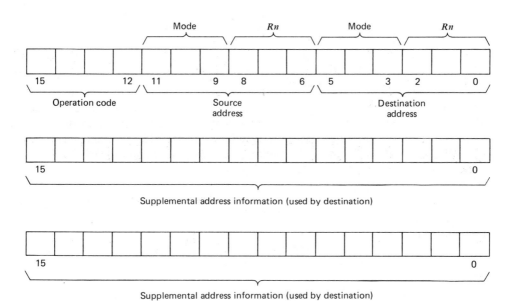

(c) Three-word instruction

Figure 12-26 Format of double operand instructions.

the *supplemental address fields* of the instruction. Since the source operand field is always processed before the destination operand field, the control unit always expects to find the source supplement field, if needed, before the destination supplement field. The different combinations that can occur are shown in Figure 12-26. The addressing modes are the same as those discussed in Table 12-5.

There are seven basic double-operand instructions. Of these seven, five can operate on either words or bytes while the other two can operate only on words. Table 12-7 describes each of the instructions, the mnemonic used to represent the instruction, the operation code, and illustrates the task it performs.

The addition instruction ADD and the subtraction instruction SUB are restricted to word operations. The bit test instructions BIT or BITB are used to compare two words or bytes but do not modify the contents of the location indicated by the destination address information. In interpreting the instruction it is useful to remember that

1. Bit 15 of the instruction is set to 1 to indicate a byte operation and 0 to indicate a word operation except for the ADD and SUB operations.
2. Bits 14–12 indicate the operation code, which indicates the operation to be done. If the operation code is 6, this indicates that the instruction is either ADD, bit 15 set to 0, or SUB, bit 15 set to 1.
3. Bits 11–6 form the source address field.
4. Bits 5–0 form the destination address field.
5. One or two address supplement fields may be included in the instruction depending upon the mode values of the source and destination address field.

Program Control Instructions

Up to this point all of the instructions, except the halt and no-operation instructions, have involved the manipulation of data. However, if we wish to carry out any reasonable computational task, we must be able to make a test and then alter the sequence of instructions to be executed based upon the result of the test. Since the address of the next instruction to be executed is stored in the program counter PC, we can do this if we introduce a set of instructions that can alter the contents of the program counter. Two classes of instructions, *branch instructions* and *jump instructions,* are provided in SEDCOM II for this purpose.

Branch Instructions

Branch instructions, which have the general format shown in Figure 12-27, first test the status of one or more of the flags in the processor status (PS) register. If the test is passed, an offset value, found in the offset field of the branch instruction, is combined with the contents of the program counter to compute the address of the next

Table 12-7   Double-operand Instructions

---

1.   Move Source to Destination

Mnemonic:	Word MOV ⟨SRC⟩, ⟨DST⟩	Byte MOVB ⟨SRC⟩, ⟨DST⟩
Octal Code:	Word 01SS*DD*	Byte 11SS*DD*
Operation:	⟨DST⟩ ← ⟨SRC⟩	
Condition	*N:* set if ⟨SRC⟩ < 0	
Code:	*Z:* set if ⟨SRC⟩ = 0	
	V: cleared	
	C: not affected	

Description: Moves the source operand to the destination location. The previous contents of the destination are lost. The source operand is not affected.

Byte: Same as MOV. The MOVB to a register (mode 0) always moves the byte to the low-order byte of the register and then extends the most significant bit of the low-order byte (sign extension) into the high byte of the selected register. Otherwise MOVB operates on bytes exactly as MOV operates on words. *This is unique among byte instructions.*

2.   Compare the Source and Destination

Mnemonic:	Word CMP ⟨SRC⟩, ⟨DST⟩	Byte CMPB ⟨SRC⟩, ⟨DST⟩
Octal Code:	Word 02SS*DD*	Byte 12SS*DD*
Operation:	⟨SRC⟩ − ⟨DST⟩	
Condition	*N:* set if result < 0	
Code:	*Z:* set if result = 0	

V: Set if there is arithmetic overflow; i.e., operands of opposite signs and the sign of the destination is the same as the sign of the result.

C: cleared if there is a carry from the most significant bit of the result

Description: Compares the source and destination operands and sets the condition codes, which may then be used for arithmetic and logical conditional branches. Both operands are unaffected. The only action is to set the condition codes in PS. The compare is customarily followed by a conditional branch instruction.

3.   Bit by Bit Test

Mnemonic:	Word BIT ⟨SRC⟩, ⟨DST⟩	Byte BITB ⟨SRC⟩, ⟨DST⟩
Octal Code:	Word 03SS*DD*	Byte 13SS*DD* ⟨SRC⟩ ∧ ⟨DST⟩
Operation:	⟨SRC⟩ ∧ ⟨DST⟩	
Condition	*N:* set if high-order bit of result set	
Code:	*Z:* set if result = 0	
	V: cleared	
	C: not affected	

Table 12-7   Double-operand Instructions (Continued)

Description:	Performs logical AND comparison of the source and destination operands and modifies PS accordingly. Neither the source nor destination operands are affected. The BIT instruction may be used to test whether any of the corresponding bits that are set in the destination are clear in the source.

4.   Bit by Bit Clear of Indicated Bits

Mnemonic:	Word BIC $\langle$SRC$\rangle$, $\langle$DST$\rangle$	Byte BICB $\langle$SRC$\rangle$, $\langle$DST$\rangle$
Octal Code:	Word 04SSDD	Byte 14SSDD
Operation:	$\langle$DST$\rangle \leftarrow \overline{\langle\text{SRC}\rangle} \wedge \langle$DST$\rangle$	
Condition	N: set if high-order bit of result set	
Code:	Z: set if result = 0	
	V: cleared	
	C: not cleared	
Description:	Clears each bit in the destination that corresponds to a set bit in the source. The original contents of the destination are lost. The contents of the source are unaffected.	

5.   Bit by Bit OR of Source and Destination

Mnemonic:	Word BIS $\langle$SRC$\rangle$, $\langle$DST$\rangle$	Byte BISB $\langle$SRC$\rangle$, $\langle$DST$\rangle$
Octal Code:	Word 05SSDD	Byte 15SSDD
Operation:	$\langle$DST$\rangle \leftarrow \langle$SRC$\rangle \vee \langle$DST$\rangle$	
Condition	N: set if high order bit of result set	
Code:	Z: set if result = 0	
	V: cleared	
	C: not affected	
Description	Performs the OR operation between the source and destination operands and leaves the result at the destination address. The original contents of the destination are lost.	

6.   Two's Complement Addition

Mnemonic:	ADD $\langle$SRC$\rangle$, $\langle$DST$\rangle$
Octal Code:	06SSDD
Operation:	$\langle$DST$\rangle \leftarrow \langle$SRC$\rangle + \langle$DST$\rangle$
Condition	N: set if result < 0
Code:	Z: set if result = 0
	V: set if there is arithmetic overflow as a result of the operation. This occurs if both operands are of the same sign and the result is of the opposite sign
	C: set if there is a carry from the most significant bit of the result.
Description:	Adds the source operand to the destination operand and stores the result at the destination address. The original contents of the destination are lost. The contents of the source are not affected. Two's complement addition is performed.

7.   Subtraction

Mnemonic:	SUB $\langle$SRC$\rangle$, $\langle$DST$\rangle$

Table 12-7 Double-operand Instructions (Continued)

Octal Code:	16SS*DD*
Operation:	$\langle DST \rangle \leftarrow \langle DST \rangle - \langle SRC \rangle$
	Note: This is regular binary subtraction
Condition	*N:* set if result < 0
Code:	*Z:* set if result $= 0$
	V: set if there is arithmetic overflow as a result of the operation. That is, if the operands were of opposite signs and the sign of the source is the same as the sign of the result.
	C: cleared if there is a carry from the most significant bit of the result. Otherwise *C* is set.
Description:	Normal binary subtraction of the source operand from the destination operand and leave the result at the destination address. The original contents of the destination are lost. The contents of the source are not affected. For double precision arithmetic, the *C* bit, when set, indicates a borrow.

instruction to be executed. This value is then placed in the program counter. When the test is not passed the program counter is not modified and the instruction immediately following the branch instruction is executed by the control unit.

As shown, branch instructions have two fields. The operation code field indicates both that the instruction is a branch instruction and also which test is to be performed on the information contained in the PS register. The offset field indicates the offset, *in words,* that must be added to the contents of the program counter to determine the address of the next instruction. (Remember that after fetching the branch instruction the program counter contains the address of the word following the branch instruction.)

To illustrate the properties and operation of branch instructions consider the unconditional branch instruction represented in mnemonic form as

$$BR \quad A$$

where A is the address of the next instruction we wish to execute. If this instruction is to be executed by SEDCOM II, the first task we must consider is how that symbolic instruction can be converted to the appropriate instruction code.

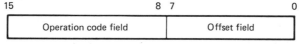

Figure 12-27 General format of a branch instruction.

Examining Figure 12-27 we see that each field corresponds to one byte. Thus the octal code for the branch instructions must be computed in a slightly different manner than for the instructions we have already discussed. The formula that we use to compute the octal representation of the instruction code is given by

$$\text{INSTCODE} := \text{OPCODE} + XXX$$

where

INSTCODE   octal representation of branch instruction code

OPCODE   octal representation of contents of instruction word when it is assumed that the offset field is zero

XXX   octal value of offset in words

The value for the offset is computed by the formula

$$XXX := (DA - BIA - 2)/2$$

where

DA   the octal address of the word that holds the instruction to which the program is to branch

BIA   the octal address of the word holding the branch instruction

This formula is arrived at by remembering that we have introduced the convention that all addresses are given as byte addresses. However, the offset is defined as the *number of words* that separate the address pointed to by the program counter and the address to which we wish to branch. This number is computed after the branch instruction has been fetched from memory. To compute this offset we note that $DA - BIA - 2$ is the offset in bytes of the new address with respect to the address found in the PC after the branch instruction has been fetched from memory. To obtain the word offset we must divide the byte offset by 2.

The offset must fit into one byte and must allow us to transfer control to an instruction that is either higher or lower in memory. Thus the value of *XXX* is limited to an octal range of

$$000_8 \leq XXX \leq 377_8$$

In addition we use the convention that the offset is represented as a 2's complement number. This means that the offset falls in the range of

$$-128_{10} \quad \text{to} \quad 127_{10}$$

If we must transfer control to an instruction that has a greater offset, we must use a jump instruction, which we will discuss shortly.

Table 12-8 The Branch Instructions

Branch Mnemonic	OPCODE	Instruction	Branch Condition
		Single Flag Branch Conditions	
BR	000400	Branch (unconditional)	always
BNE	001000	Branch if *not* equal (to 0)	$Z = 0$
BEQ	001400	Branch if equal (to 0)	$Z = 1$
BPL	100000	Branch if plus (+)	$N = 0$
BMI	100400	Branch if minus (−)	$N = 1$
BVC	102000	Branch if no arithmetic overflow	$V = 0$
BVS	102400	Branch if arithmetic overflow	$V = 1$
BCC	103000	Branch if no carry	$C = 0$
BCS	103400	Branch if carry	$C = 1$
		Signed Conditional Branches	
BGE	002000	Branch if greater or equal (to 0)	$N \oplus V = 0$
BLT	002400	Branch if less than (0)	$N \oplus V = 1$
BGT	003000	Branch if greater than (0)	$Z \vee (N \oplus V) = 0$
BLE	003400	Branch if less than or equal (to 0)	$Z \vee (N \oplus V) = 1$

The SEDCOM II branch instructions are listed in Table 12-8. The octal code for an instruction must be computed by adding the address code to the value given for OPCODE. When a branch instruction is executed, the flags in PS are not altered.

The Jump Instruction

When we use modular programming techniques to develop machine language programs, we find that most transfer of control can be accomplished using branch instructions. This is the most efficient method of control transfer since a branch instruction involves a single word and the execution of the instruction is carried out easily by the control unit. There are situations, however, in which it is necessary to transfer control to a portion of the program that is outside the range of a branch instruction. The jump instruction JMP provides the needed increase in flexibility. Control may be transferred to any memory location addressable by the standard addressing methods. Only addressing mode 0 is prevented since this mode deals with addressing a register in the CPU rather than in memory.

The jump instruction is a one- or two-word instruction depending upon the addressing mode used. Figure 12-28 shows the two formats for a jump instruction. The information associated with the address field is used to compute the location in

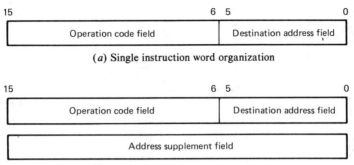

(a) Single instruction word organization

(b) Double instruction word organization

Figure 12-28 Organization of jump instruction.

memory that contains the next instruction to be executed. At the end of the instruction execution cycle, this address is left in the program counter and the original contents of the program counter are lost. Thus once a transfer has been made using a jump instruction, we have no way of knowing from where the transfer was made. Table 12-9 summarizes the major properties of the jump instruction. Note that the flags in PS are not influenced by this instruction.

Subroutine Transfers

When creating large programs a common approach is to divide the program into modules that are designed to do specific, well-defined tasks. In higher level languages this is accomplished by using subroutines or subprocedures. Subroutines are also a major programming tool at the machine level. To include the ability to use subroutines in our machine language programs we must have an instruction that transfers control to a subroutine and an instruction that allows us to return to the main routine.

When we introduce a subroutine we transfer control to a location in memory that contains the first instructions of the subroutine. After executing the instructions that make up the subroutine, we then return to the point in the calling program where the subroutine was called. This means that we must transfer control to a different memory location and, at the same time, remember the location in memory to which we are to return after completing the subroutine. The *jump subroutine* instruction JSR and the *return from subroutine* instruction RTS provide this capability.

The JSR instruction behaves in a manner similar to the jump instruction JMP except that it must save a return address. To do this it makes use of the idea of a stack. An area of memory is set aside as a stack area and is organized as shown in Figure 12-29. Note that the stack grows down in memory. Thus, as each new data item is added, it is added at the next lower word in memory. CPU register $R6$ is defined to be the stack pointer (SP) register. This register contains the address of the last item entered on the stack. To add new data to the stack, the address in SP is first decremented by 2 (i.e., one word) and then this address is used to enter the new data item. When a word is to be read from the stack, the address in SP is used

Table 12-9 Jump and Subroutine Transfers

1. Unconditional Jump
   Mnemonic: JMP ⟨DST⟩
   Octal Code: 0001*DD*
   Operation: PC ← ⟨DST⟩
   Operation Codes: N, Z, V, C, unaffected
   Description: Transfer operation to the memory location indicated by
                          destination address

2. Jump to Subroutine
   Mnemonic: JSR PC, ⟨DST⟩
   Octal Code: 0047*DD*
   Operation: TEMP ← ⟨DST⟩
                          SP ← SP − [2]
                          $M_{[SP]}$ ← PC
                          PC ← TEMP
   Operation Codes: N, Z, V, C, unaffected
   Description: Transfer operation to the memory location indicated by
                          destination address. Save return address on stack.

3. Return from Subroutine
   Mnemonic: RTS
   Octal Code: 000207
   Operation: PC ← $M_{[SP]}$
                          SP ← SP + [2]
   Operation Codes: N, Z, V, C, unaffected
   Description: Pop return address from the stack. Return control to
                          this address.

to locate and read the data contained in the word. The address in SP is then incremented by 2 (i.e., one word) so that SP is now pointing to the word that now appears
at the top of the stack.

The jump subroutine instruction can use any addressing mode except mode 0 to
transfer control to the address corresponding to the subroutine code. Thus a JSR

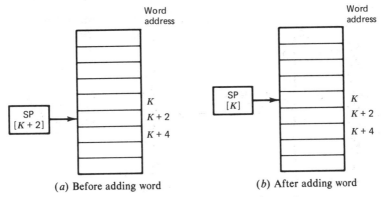

(*a*) Before adding word   (*b*) After adding word

Figure 12-29 Adding a word to the stack.

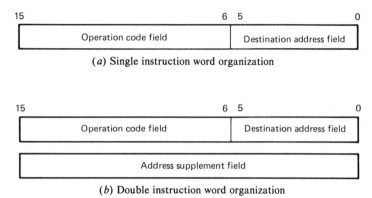

(a) Single instruction word organization

(b) Double instruction word organization

Figure 12-30 Organization of jump subroutine instruction JSR.

instruction may be one or two words, as shown in Figure 12-30. The expected return address is defined to be the address that immediately follows this instruction. Thus if the instruction takes up one word the expected return address will be PC + [2], and if the instruction requires two words the return address will be PC + [4]. The assumption is that the next instruction following the jump subroutine instruction will be the instruction executed upon return from the subroutine. As we will see in the next chapter when we consider the use of subroutines in a program, this is only one of a number of ways that this expected return address information is used. To complete the JSR instruction we must save the expected return address on the stack and then transfer control to the subroutine. The following sequence of information transfers indicates the steps carried out to realize the JSR instruction.

TEMP ← ⟨DST ADDRESS⟩	TEMP is a special internal register
SP← SP − [2]	Stack pointer moved to make room for new value to be placed on stack
$M_{[SP]}$ ← PC	Save return address
PC ← TEMP	Transfer control to first instruction of subroutine

The general characteristics of the JSR instruction are summarized in Table 12-9.

The Return Instruction

To return from the subroutine we must take the return address stored on the stack and place this value in the program counter. This task is accomplished by use of the return from subroutine instruction RTS. As shown in Table 12-9, this is a fixed single-word instruction. It causes the following sequence of information transfers to take place.

PC ← $M_{[SP]}$	Read return address from stack
SP ← SP + [2]	Point to new top of stack

Upon completion of this instruction the PC contains the address of the next instruction to be executed.

EXERCISES

1. Write instructions that will do the following tasks.
   (a)   Add the contents of register $R1$ to the contents of register $R2$.
   (b)   Clear the location in memory pointed to by register $R3$.
   (c)   Decrement the contents of location 1000_8 in memory.
   (d)   Add [5] to the contents of memory location 1000_8.

2. A jump to subroutine instruction
$$\text{JSR} \quad \text{PC,SUBPROG}$$
is located in memory location 2000_8. The subroutine SUBPROG starts in memory location 4000_8. The stack pointer contains 1500_8. Show how this instruction is executed. Also show how the RTS instruction is executed when we return from this subroutine.

6.   SUMMARY

The main purpose of this chapter has been to show how a stored program information processor can be constructed as an interconnection of a number of standard logic networks such as we have studied in earlier chapters. Now that we have an idea of how a simple computer operates, our next task is to investigate how programs can be developed for the computer in order that it can carry out a complete information processing task. This is done in the next chapter.

Reference Notation

The PDP-11 is one of the most popular minicomputers currently manufactured. Reference 8 presents a detailed description of the internal and external specifications of this system. SEDCOM II is based on the instruction set of the PDP-11 family of computers, but no attempt has been made to match the architecture of the two machines. All programs written for SEDCOM II should execute properly on a PDP-11 if one is available for use. The general problems involved in the design of a computer system are discussed in References 1, 6, and 7. Reference 1 gives a particularly good insight into the background of how the PDP-11 was designed. A number of books are available that discuss assembly language programming for the PDP-11. Reference 3 concentrates on the programming process, while References 2, 4, and 5 discuss both programming and the organization of the PDP-11.

REFERENCES

1.   Bell, G. C., Mudge, J. C., and McNamara, J. E. (1978), *Computer Engineering: A DEC View of Hardware Systems Design.* Digital Press, Bedford, Mass.
2.   Frank, T. S. (1983), *Introduction to the PDP-11 and Its Assembly Language.* Prentice-Hall, Englewood Cliffs, N.J.
3.   Gill, A. (1983), *Machine and Assembly Language Programming of the PDP-11* (second edition). Prentice-Hall, Englewood Cliffs, N.J.
4.   Eckhouse, R. E. Jr., and Morris, L. R. (1979), *Minicomputer Systems Organization, Programming, and Applications (PDP-11)* (second edition). Prentice-Hall, Englewood Cliffs, N.J.

5. Kapps, C. A., and Stafford, R. L. (1981), *Assembly Language for the PDP-11*. Prindle, Weber & Schmidt, CBI Publishing Co., Boston.
6. Langdon, G. G. Jr. (1982), *Computer Design*. Computeach Press, San Jose, Calif.
7. Osborne, A. (1980), *An Introduction to Microcomputers: Volume 1 Basic Concepts* (second edition). OSBORNE/McGraw-Hill, Berkeley, Calif.
8. *Microcomputer Processor Handbook* (latest edition). Digital Equipment Corp., Maynard, Mass.

HOME PROBLEMS

1. Design the device selector and the control unit for the memory unit shown in Figure 12-9.
2. Design the device selector and the control unit for the input/output unit shown in Figure 12-10.
3. You will be required to develop a number of machine level programs in the next chapter. Create an Instruction Summary Card for SEDCOM II that lists all of the instructions and their mnemonics in a compact manner.
4. Define the equations necessary to compute the ⟨data address⟩ information for a double-operand instruction in which either or both operands involve relative addressing.
5. It is desired to connect five individual keyboard/printer units to SEDCOM II using a single slave unit. Each keyboard/printer unit is connected to the slave unit, and the slave unit is interfaced to the INFOBUS. Assume that each keyboard/printer unit operates in a manner similar to the input/output unit discussed in this chapter. Design the slave unit necessary to support this interface task. Assign the address space of this unit in the same region as that used for the input/output devices discussed in this chapter.
6. The INFOBUS system allows the CPU to send to or receive information from a slave unit. All such transfers must be initiated by the CPU, but the CPU does not have any way of knowing when the slave unit has information to send or is ready to receive information. Many bus systems have an interrupt capability that allows a slave unit to signal the master control unit that an information transfer should take place.

    Assume that the control line, INTR, is added to the INFOBUS. The signal on this line is to serve as an interrupt. When the bus controller detects that INTR is set to 1, it knows that one of the slave units wishes to perform an information transfer. This is called an interrupt request. The controller must decide which unit wishes to be serviced and then carry out the desired transfer.

    a. Describe how the CPU can determine which slave unit made an interrupt request. What will happen if more than one unit makes an interrupt request at the same time?
    b. Explain how the control unit would process a case where there are multiple interrupt requests.

13

ASSEMBLY LANGUAGE PROGRAMMING

1. INTRODUCTION

The first introduction most persons have to programming a computer is through the use of some higher level language such as Pascal, FORTRAN, BASIC, or PL/I. At that point the novice programmer is told that there is a compiler or, in the case of BASIC, an interpreter that converts the statements written in the higher level "source" language into an "object" program that can be understood by the computer. Little attempt is made to discuss the form of this object language or the structure of the resulting object language program.

Every computer program must ultimately be reduced to a set of machine language instructions for the computer on which it is to be executed. In this chapter we investigate how to write programs in a computer's machine language. This discussion serves a number of purposes. First it provides us with an insight into some of the problems that must be considered in carrying out computations at the machine level. It also illustrates some of the tasks that can be assigned to a compiler when we use a higher level language and identifies some of the properties we must include in a higher level language to make it possible for the compiler to generate the object language program.

A machine language program must ultimately be represented in machine readable form. However, since it is difficult to work with the individual bit patterns that make up each machine language instruction, we have introduced a set of mnemonics to represent the basic machine language instructions used by SEDCOM II. These mnemonics form the basic components of the *assembly language* for this machine. After writing a program in assembly language, we translate it to machine language using a special program called an *assembler* as shown in Figure 13-1.

In this chapter a simple assembly language for SEDCOM II is used to illustrate a number of programming techniques. Throughout this discussion our concern is on identifying the techniques and concepts common to all information processing tasks

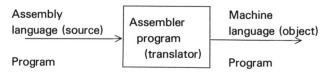

Figure 13-1   The relationship between assembly and machine language programs.

at the machine level rather than on developing advanced programming skills. In the next chapter we investigate the organization and structure of a typical assembler program that might be used to translate our assembly language program into executable machine code.

A large number of minicomputers and microprocessors are in use. SEDCOM II was selected as the instructional computer since it has a relatively simple structure that is representative of most small computers. In particular it has all of the important features one must understand in developing machine-language level programs. Once you have mastered the programming concepts presented in this chapter, it is a straightforward process to apply these concepts to other computer systems.

This discussion assumes that you have previous programming experience in a higher level language such as Pascal, PL/I, or FORTRAN. It is also assumed that the algorithm necessary to represent a given computational task has been developed and that our task is to create the SEDCOM II program necessary to realize the algorithm. Our goal is to develop an insight into the problems associated with programming at the machine level that are hidden from the user when a higher level programming language is used.

2.   ASSEMBLY LANGUAGE PROGRAMMING

Programming a computer to perform a given algorithm would be a tedious, time-consuming, and error-prone process if we were forced to do all the programming using the computer's machine language. These difficulties are mainly a result of the following problems.

1.   All instructions must be expressed in a coded binary form that is difficult for a person to work with.

2.   Every address reference must be absolutely defined. Thus, as a program is written, the programmer must be able to define the locations of all data and program instructions that are referred to in the program. This is often necessary even though locations for these items have not been defined at the time this information is needed.

3.   Changes in instructions, changes in data, or the insertion or deletion of instructions often require reassigning the locations of instructions and data. This usually requires modifying other instructions in the program to account for changes in references to the altered data and instruction locations.

4. The programmer must transform the coding into a machine-readable form, such as punched cards, magnetic disk, or magnetic tape, and check that this transformation is correct.

5. Parts of previously developed programs that are applicable to a new programming effort may not be usable without being completely recoded to conform with the address assignments of the new program.

In presenting the various machine language instructions and addressing techniques associated with SEDCOM II, we used a set of mnemonic terms to indicate each basic operation and addressing technique as well as giving the octal representation of each instruction. We now extend this basic set of mnemonics into a complete language.

The advantage of using mnemonic symbols to represent the basic instructions was clearly evident to early programmers. Initially, programs were written in mnemonic form and then the programmer hand translated the mnemonics into the computer's machine language. It was quickly realized that this translation task was a mechanical process that could be carried out by the computer. Assembly languages and assembler programs were quickly developed to aid the programming process.

Although higher level languages have evolved from the need to go beyond the capabilities of an assembly language, a considerable amount of programming activity still takes place at the assembly language level. For some microcomputers carrying out real-time tasks this is the only way that satisfactory programs can be developed. In other cases special features can be included in a program only by writing critical portions of the code at the machine level. Our reason for studying assembly language programming is much more basic. It gives us an opportunity to understand the way in which a computer actually implements a computation and the limits placed upon such a computation by the architecture of the computer and the operations available in the computer's instruction set.

In this section we present a simple assembly language for SEDCOM II. It is assumed that an assembler program is available to translate the resulting programs into machine language. We will thus be able to see both the assembly language program and the resulting machine language program.

A Simple Assembly Language

Assembly languages take a number of forms. Many include special features that simplify the programming process for an experienced programmer. For our needs it is more instructive to use as simple a language as possible so that we concentrate on the way that each program is organized and not worry about special language features that we do not need. Before giving a formal description of the language, let us look at some of the characteristics that a language should have to make it useful.

Consider the sample program shown in Figure 13-2. Figure 13-2a is an assembly language program before it is translated into machine language. In this program we use the SEDCOM II mnemonics to represent the operations that we wish to perform

```
                TITLE   ZERO_TABLE

; *******************************************************************
;           PROGRAM TO PLACE ZERO VALUE IN ALL LOCATIONS OF A 100  WORD
;           TABLE STARTING AT LOCATION 2000.
; *******************************************************************


            . = 1000                    ;INITIALIZE LOCATION COUNTER TO 1000

START:  MOV         #TAB,R1     ;SET UP POINTER TO POINT TO TABLE
        MOV         #100,R2     ;SET COUNTER TO 100
LOOP:   MOV         #0,(R1)+    ;DEPOSIT ZERO. INCREMENT POINTER
        DEC         R2          ;DECREMENT COUNTER
        BNZ         LOOP        ;REPEAT LOOP IF COUNT NOT ZERO
        HALT                    ;TASK COMPLETED


        . = 2000                ;RESET LOCATION COUNTER
TAB:    .BLKW       100         ;RESERVE TABLE AREA
        .END        START
```

(*a*) A sample assembly language program

```
Line        machine
Number      code (Octal)
 1                              .TITLE ZERO TABLE

 2                      ;*****************************************************************
 3                      ;           PROGRAM TO PLACE ZERO VALUE IN ALL LOCATIONS OF A 100  WORD
 4                      ;           TABLE STARTING AT LOCATION 2000.
 5                      ;*****************************************************************

 6      001000              . = 1000                    ;INITIALIZE LOCATION COUNTER TO 1000

 7 1000 012701  START:  MOV     #TAB,R1     ;SET UP POINTER TO POINT TO TABLE
        002000
 8 1004 012702          MOV     #100,R2     ;SET COUNTER TO 100
        000100
 9 1010 012721  LOOP:   MOV     #0,(R1)+    ;DEPOSIT ZERO. INCREMENT POINTER
        000000
10 1014 005302          DEC     R2          ;DECREMENT COUNTER
11 1016 001174          BNZ     LOOP        ;REPEAT LOOP IF COUNT NOT ZERO
12 1020 000000          HALT                ;TASK COMPLETED

13      002000          . = 2000            ;RESET LOCATION COUNTER
14 2000         TAB:    .BLKW   100         ;RESERVE TABLE AREA
15      001000          .END    START
    memory                              ⎡ indicates the address where program execution is
    address (Octal)                     ⎣ to start
```

(*b*) Assembler listing of program

Figure 13-2   An example of an assembly language program and its listing.

and symbols to represent the operands needed by each operation. When an assembler translates this program, it must substitute the proper machine code for each mnemonic in an instruction and associate a memory or register location with each operand.

When the assembler completes the translation of an assembler language program, it creates two outputs. First it must generate a machine readable version of the machine language program, called the *object code program,* which can be loaded into the computer for execution. Since a program in that form would be unintelligible to a human programmer, the assembler also produces a *program listing* of the form shown in Figure 13-2*b.* This listing shows both the original assembly language program and the resulting machine language program expressed in octal notation.

The listing is a snapshot of the form that the program will take when it is initially loaded into memory. Each line in the listing is numbered with a *line number.* The first column after the line number corresponds to the memory addresses where the instruction or data item defined by that line is stored. The address information is presented in terms of the byte address of the information being located. To make this listing easier to understand we see that the first word of each machine language instruction is listed on the same line as the corresponding assembly language mnemonic representation.

The value of a machine language instruction is obtained by translating the mnemonic representation of the instruction according to the conventions presented in the last chapter. How this is accomplished will be considered in the following sections. Each instruction may generate a machine language instruction that takes from one to three memory words.

Statement Types

Each assembly language statement occupies a single line. Examining the program in Figure 13-2, we identify three classes of statements. They are

1. Instruction statements
2. Data statements
3. Assembly language directives

Instruction statements and data statements are translated directly into machine language code, while assembly language directives are used to control the actions of the assembler program. We now consider the form that these statements can take. The program in Figure 13-2 illustrates typical statements of each type and how they are used in a program.

Statement Structure

Every statement in a program appears on a single line and has the following general organization

$$\langle \text{field-1} \rangle: \quad \langle \text{field-2} \rangle \quad \langle \text{field-3} \rangle \quad ;\langle \text{field-4} \rangle$$

Although four fields are shown, not all of the fields must be present in all statements.

The Label Field—⟨field-1⟩

The first field, ⟨field-1⟩, is the *label field;* it is the *symbolic address* of the statement. Not all statements need to have symbolic addresses, thus the label field may be omitted. If a label is present it must have the following properties:

1. The first character of the label must be in column 1 (i.e., the first character of the statement).
2. It may be made up of from one to eight symbols from the set

$$\{\$, A, \ldots, Z, 0, \ldots, 9\}$$

3. The first character must not be numeric.

Only the first six characters are significant to the assembler. Thus if two labels do not differ in the first six characters, they are taken to be the same. This feature is included so that the programmer can use long labels that have special meaning relative to the problem being solved while at the same time not putting an undue burden upon the assembler program.

The end of the label is indicated by a colon ":" followed by one or more spaces. The colon is not part of the label. If no label field is included in a statement, the colon is omitted and there must be at least one space between the beginning of the line and the next field unless the field is a comment field preceded by a ; .

In Figure 13-2 we can identify three labels: START, LOOP, and TAB. Other allowable labels would be

$$\text{T1} \qquad \text{UP2} \qquad \text{NEXT1} \qquad \text{W1SQS}$$

since they all start with a letter, which is followed with five or fewer uppercase letters or digits. Note that since the colon is not part of the label it is not included when a label is being discussed.

The two labels

$$\text{START11} \qquad \text{and} \qquad \text{START12}$$

are taken to be the same since the first six characters of both labels are the same.

Some unacceptable labels are;

4TTY	Starts with a digit
*HERE	* is not an allowable character
NOT H	A space is not allowed in a label
YES/NO	/ is not an allowable character

The Comment Field—⟨field-4⟩

The fourth field, if present, is always indicated by preceding it with a semicolon ";". This field is called the *comment field.* Anything following the semicolon and up to the end of the statement is ignored by the assembler program during the translation process. You can use this field, as shown in Figure 13-2, to include the comments necessary to document your program. The comment field can appear anywhere except that it must be separated from any other fields by at least one space before the semicolon. In Figure 13-2 we see that comments are used to create a header that describes the task that the program is to carry out. Additional comments are used throughout the program to describe the purpose of each major statement or group of statements. As with programs in a higher level language, a well commented program is much easier to understand.

The Operator and Operand Fields— ⟨field-2⟩ and ⟨field-3⟩

The second and third fields correspond to the *operator* and *operand* fields. The second field is the operator field and indicates which machine level operation is to be performed if the statement is an executable instruction, or which command to the assembler program is to be carried out if it is an assembly language directive.

If the first character in the operand field is a period ".", then it is assumed that the operator is an assembly language directive. Otherwise the operator field is assumed to represent a machine language operation.

In most situations the operator will require one or more operands. These operands are placed in the third field. If the operand field contains more than a single operand, each operand is separated by a comma "," but no spaces. Some typical operator operand combinations from Figure 13-2 are

MOV	#TAB,$R1$	⎫
DEC	$R2$	⎬ Executable statements
MOV	#0,($R1$)+	⎭
.BLKW	100	Assembly language directive

The first three statements are executable statements that will cause the assembler program to generate an appropriate machine level code as shown in Figure 13-2*b*. The last statement is an assembly language directive as indicated by the leading period ".". This statement tells the assembler to save 100 words in memory for use of the program. The operand in this case is an octal number giving the number of words that must be reserved.

The operands in an executable statement refer to registers in the CPU or to a specific memory location. Thus the mnemonics used to represent the operands correspond to the mnemonics that we introduced in the last chapter to discuss the various forms of memory and register reference. The formal rules for representing operands will be presented shortly.

One of the largest sources of error in developing assembly language programs is in expressing operand information in an incorrect manner. Two typical errors are

1. Including spaces in the operand field. For example,

$$R1 ,R2 \qquad (R3)+ ,\#A$$

2. Including the wrong number of operands for the indicated operator. For example,

MOV	C1	Requires two operands
BNZ	A1,(R3)	Requires a single operand

Data Statements

In higher level languages a number of techniques are used to set aside memory space to store data items needed in the computation or to hold values generated as the computation progresses. The necessary memory space may be reserved by using some type of declare statement such as

DECLARE A(10) FIXED, DECIMAL   (PL/1)
A: array[0..9] of integers;   (Pascal)

Each of these statements informs the compiler processing the program that 10 words of memory must be set aside to store the array A. Similarly the assignment statement from Pascal

STRING := "Now is the time";

tells the compiler that 16 bytes must be reserved in memory to store the 15 bytes of the character string "Now is the time" plus one additional byte to store an *end of string* marker (For example the byte of all zeros is often used).

To accomplish the same task at the assembly language level we need to have a special set of statements, called *data statements,* which tell the assembler to reserve an area in memory for the storage of a given collection of data and, in some cases, to place initial values into the reserved space. For our language, data statements have the following form

⟨label⟩:   ⟨data-type⟩   ⟨data-descriptor⟩   ;⟨comment⟩

In a data statement the first field is the label field and, if present, it is used to name the memory area being reserved. The fourth field is the comment field and is used to describe, if desired, the features of the information to be stored in the reserved area.

The second field ⟨data-type⟩ is an operator field that describes to the assembler the type of data to be stored in the reserved area. Since this field contains an assembly directive, the first character in this field is a period ".".

The third field ⟨data-descriptor⟩ describes the amount of memory space that must be set aside in memory to store the information described by ⟨data-type⟩. This field may also contain information indicating the values to be loaded into the reserved memory area.

There are five data-type commands. These are listed in Table 13-1 together with a brief description of their use. The data-descriptor field either tells the assembler the number of words or bytes of memory to reserve or indicates the actual data values to be placed in consecutive memory locations.

Table 13-1 Data Reservation Statements

Data-type Operator	Data-type Descriptor	Description
.BLKW	n	Reserve n consecutive words in memory. No specific value stored in this area.
.BLKB	n	Reserve n consecutive bytes in memory. No specific value stored in this area.
.WORD	$d_1, d_2, \ldots, d_k$	Place the k values d_1 through d_k in the next k memory words.[a]
.BYTE	$b_1, b_2, \ldots, b_k$	Place the k values b_1 through b_k in the next k bytes.[b]
.ASCII	/str/	Place the ASCII code for str in the consecutive bytes. (/ represents any character not in str except ⟨ and ⟩). A nonprinting character can be specified as ⟨n⟩ where n is the numeric value of the code for the nonprinting character.[c]
.ASCIZ	/str/	Same as .ASCII except that a null byte (octal 0) is placed after the last byte in the string str.[c]

[a] Word data values d_i can be any octal number from 000000 to 177777.
[b] Byte data values b_i can be any octal number from 000 to 377.
[c] The delimiter character used for / is not part of str.

Assembly Language Control Statements

All of the statements discussed so far lead to the generation of machine language instructions or the reservation of memory space to store information. The final class of statements is *assembly language control statements*, which are sometimes called *pseudo operations*. These statements do not lead to the generation of any object code or the reservation of memory space. Their purpose is to provide information to the assembler program concerning how the assembly process is to be carried out or to provide information about one or more of the variables that appear in the program being translated by the assembler.

The Assignment Control Statement

There are many occasions when it is useful to use a mnemonic as a symbolic variable to represent a data item in a program. For example, we might have a general program that will go through a loop I times before it exits. While writing the program it is desirable to use the symbolic representation for I rather than giving it a value.

Later on we can add an assignment statement at the beginning of the program to assign a fixed value to *I*. Such an assignment statement may have the form

$$I = 25 \quad ;\text{THERE ARE 25 STUDENTS IN THE CLASS}$$

Later on, if the class size changes, the same program could be reassembled with a new value for *I*. The only change that would be required would be to change the above statement to reflect the new class size.

Assignment statements have the general form

$$\langle\text{symbol}\rangle = \langle\text{expression}\rangle \quad ;\langle\text{comment}\rangle$$

where ⟨symbol⟩ may be any sequence of 1 to 8 alphanumeric characters, the first one of which must be a letter, and ⟨expression⟩ may take any one of the following forms;

⟨number⟩   ⟨symbol⟩ − ⟨number⟩

⟨symbol⟩   ⟨symbol⟩ + ⟨symbol⟩

⟨symbol⟩ + ⟨number⟩   ⟨symbol⟩ − ⟨symbol⟩

If a ⟨symbol⟩ is used in an expression, it must have already been assigned a value in a previous assignment statement. Note that no spaces can appear in the expression. Only the first six characters of a symbol are significant to the assembler. Thus two symbols must differ in the first six characters if they are to represent different quantities.

Some typical assignment statements are;

```
INFLAG = 177560          ;ADDRESS OF INPUT FLAG
INPORT = 177562          ;ADDRESS OF INPUT PORT
TEMPBF = 2000            ;ADDRESS BEGINNING OF TEMPORARY BUFFER
ENDTBF = TEMPBF + 200    ;END OF TEMPORARY BUFFER. BUFFER 200
                         ;BYTES IN SIZE
```

The Location Counter

As we know from our discussion of the architecture of SEDCOM II, we use CPU register *R7* as a program counter to keep track of the next machine language instruction that is to be executed by the computer. When we assemble a program the assembler must keep track of where each translated instruction and each data element is placed in memory. To do this the assembler has a special pointer, called the *location counter* (LC), which indicates the address of the next byte in memory in which information is to be stored. When we must refer to the location counter in a program, we use an isolated period "." to serve this purpose. For example, in Figure 13-2 we have the statement

$$. = 1000$$

This is an assignment statement that tells the assembler to set the location counter LC to a value of 1000_8. The next statement processed by the assembler will be placed in memory starting at this memory location.

Location Counter Control

When laying out a number of data areas in memory, we often will use the .BLKB, .BYTE, or .ASCII pseudo operators to create storage areas for different types of information. In SEDCOM II we know that all word addresses must start at even memory addresses. To make sure that the location counter is pointing to a word address we can use the directive

.EVEN

This will force "dot" to become the next even address if its current value is odd or will not change the value of "dot" if its current value is even.

Terminating a Program

The last statement of every program must be

.END ⟨starting location⟩

where ⟨starting location⟩ is a label assigned to the first instruction to be executed when the program is loaded into memory and started. For example, in Figure 13-2 we note that the last instruction is

.END   START

and we see that START is the label associated with the first instruction, which is found in location 1000.

A special program, called a *loader,* loads the machine readable form of the program into memory and then detects that the starting address is 1000. At this point the loader places 1000 into the program counter, which causes the computer to start execution of the program just loaded by the loader.

The .END directive is also a signal to the assembler program that the end of the assembly language program has been reached and the assembly processing can be completed. If the .END directive is left off of a program, the assembler will sit and wait for additional statements to process.

Documentation

In any programming effort well-thought-out program organization and documentation are essential. Figure 13-3 outlines the program organization that we will use for SEDCOM II assembler language programs.

Each program should be assigned a short descriptive name so that it can be easily referenced. This name can be printed at the head of the program listing if you

```
            .TITLE    ⟨program name⟩


;  *************************************************************
;
;       Description of the task performed by the program.
;
;       Description of the way input information is supplied to the program.
;
;       Description of the way output information is produced by the program.
;
;  *************************************************************
```

Header information in the form of assignment statements defining specific values for symbolic variables used in program.

Statement to initialize value of location counter if necessary.

```
                -
                -
```

BODY OF PROGRAM   ; Comments as needed

```
                -
                -
```

Data Reservation   ; Comments describing data
statements

```
    .END    ⟨starting address⟩
```

Figure 13-3   General program organization.

include the directive

.TITLE ⟨program name⟩

as the first statement in your program. The program name should be a single word. For example, the program of Figure 13-2 is titled ZERO_TABLE by including the statement

.TITLE   ZERO_TABLE

Following the title should be a short description of the program, the computations performed, the inputs expected, the output produced, and any special properties of the computations. This information is supplemented by appropriate comments inserted throughout the program. In all cases the comments should be designed to inform a possible user of the important techniques and concepts used in formulating the program.

   Programming at the assembly language level is similar to programming in a higher
level language. As shown in the next sections, we use the same general techniques to
realize a program. The main difference is that we must be concerned with a greater
amount of detail at the assembly language level. In Section 3 we show how to program simple tasks using the assembly language defined in this section. In the later
sections we design a number of complex programs to carry out both numeric and
non-numeric information processing tasks.

EXERCISE

1. Classify each statement in the following simple program and indicate how it is
   used.


```
        .TITLE DEMO1

; ****************************************************************
;
;
;       TASK:    PROGRAM TO ADD TWO NUMBERS AND STORE THE RESULT
;
;       INPUT:   DATA IN MEMORY LOCATIONS A AND B
;
;       OUTPUT:  RESULT IN MEMORY LOCATION Y
;
; ****************************************************************
;

        . = 1000

START:  CLR      R1          ; CLEAR REGISTER
        ADD      A,R1        ; ADD FIRST NUMBER
        ADD      B,R1        ; ADD SECOND NUMBER
        MOV      R1,Y        ; SAVE RESULT
        HALT                 ; STOP

        . = 2000             ; DATA AREA

A:      .WORD    100         ; VALUE OF FIRST NUMBER
B:      .WORD    50          ; VALUE OF SECOND NUMBER
Y:      .WORD    0           ; RESULT PLACED HERE

        .END     START
```

3. BASIC PROGRAMMING CONCEPTS

Software development is a five-stage iterative process requiring a considerable amount of experience. These stages are identified as:

1. Define program requirements.
2. Translate requirements into program specifications.
3. Develop an algorithm to satisfy the specifications.
4. Use an appropriate programming language to realize the algorithm.
5. Test and verify that the resulting program satisfies the design goals.

The first three stages of program development are essentially independent of the language selected to represent the solution algorithm. When you reach the point where your algorithm satisfies your design goals, an appropriate programming language must be selected to implement the algorithm. Normally, for very large software design efforts, you would select one of the major higher level languages to complete the development process. There are, however, some situations in which you may decide to implement the program using the assembly language of the computer that will run the program.

The following discussion assumes that you are an experienced programmer in some higher level language and that you are familiar with the general software design process. Thus, in this section, we explore how the basic programming constructs necessary to implement specific algorithms are realized using the assembly language for SEDCOM II.

The Programming Process

In developing any algorithm we must consider two basic problems: information flow and control flow. One of the first steps in defining an algorithm consists of identifying the different data structures that will be manipulated by the algorithm, the operations that can be performed upon these structures, and the data that they contain. As the algorithm evolves, the designer must control the sequence in which these basic operations are performed. Chapter 9 demonstrated this relationship between information flow and control flow in the development of hardware systems. Similar relationships exist in the development of assembler language programs.

The placement of data in memory can have a major impact upon program organization. When selecting the data structures to be used in a program, we must consider a number of factors, such as

1. The amount of information associated with each data type.
2. The range of values that will be stored.
3. How the different items in the data structure will be accessed.
4. The amount of memory space available for storage of data.
5. The operations that must be performed upon the data.

Throughout the following discussions an attempt will be made to indicate the considerations used to select specific data organizations in the examples presented.

A complete program often appears to be a complex structure. However, if a program is broken down into a sequence of simpler subtasks, this apparent complexity quickly disappears. In fact, we soon find that most programs are developed by repeatedly applying a few simple programming techniques. In particular, we must be able to carry out the following five basic tasks.

1. Input information.
2. Perform sequential computations.
3. Make decisions.
4. Repeat a fixed procedure a number of times (looping).
5. Output information.

If we can understand how to perform these tasks by using the instructions available in the computer's instruction set, then it is relatively easy to develop a program to realize a given algorithm.

Basic Data Types

In SEDCOM II the basic data elements are 8-bit bytes and 16-bit words. A variety of different data types can be stored in these elements. It is the responsibility of the program designer to select the proper representation for all data used in a program and to decide how it is to be stored and manipulated. For our initial discussions we make use of the following possible data representations.

A Byte May Represent

1. Eight individual binary variables.
2. One ASCII encoded character (See Appendix A for codes).
3. A positive binary number with a decimal value between 0 and 255.
4. A signed binary number (represented in 2's complement form) with a decimal value between -128 and $+127$.

A Word May Represent

1. Sixteen individual binary variables.
2. Two ASCII encoded characters.
3. A positive binary number with a decimal value between 0 and 65535.
4. A signed binary number (represented in 2's complement form) with a decimal value between -32768 and $+32767$.

These basic data types are used to construct more complex data types such as floating point numbers, arrays, and structures.

Addressing Modes

Two important problems in all program development efforts are where to store data and how to access the data. A program may have to process data found in memory, in one of the CPU registers, or in one of the input/output registers. There are a number of techniques used to access this data. They are all based upon the addressing methods discussed in Chapter 12. Eight addressing methods were introduced in Section 5 of Chapter 12. Before progressing to the following programming examples, you should briefly review this material. The main features of each addressing technique, and its corresponding symbolic representation, are summarized in Table 13-2. The uses, advantages, and limitations of each method of addressing will become clearer as we progress with our discussion.

Straight-line Computation

A straight-line computation is a program sequence that does not involve any decisions or looping. Such a sequence is formed using the nonbranching instructions such as CLR, INC, MOV, ASR, and so on.

Table 13-2 Summary of Addressing Methods

Address Method	Assembly Language Representation	Comment
Register mode	Rn	Register Rn contains operand.
Indirect addressing	(Rn)	Register Rn contains address of operand.
Autoincrement	$(Rn)+$	Register Rn contains pointer to operand. Value is incremented after operation.
Autodecrement	$-(Rn)$	Register Rn contains pointer to operand. Value is decremented before operation.
Indexed addressing	$\pm X(Rn)$	X is added to or subtracted from (Rn) to produce the address of the operand. Neither X nor Rn is modified.
Immediate addressing	$\#n$	Operand is contained in instruction.
Relative addressing	A	Address of A, relative to the instruction, is contained in the instruction.
Absolute addressing	$@\#A$	Absolute address of operand is contained in the instruction.

As a simple example let us assume that we wish to carry out the computation described by the following program specification. This task can be carried out as a straight-line computation.

Program Specification

PROGRAM 1

Task: Sum three positive 16 bit numbers (modulo 2^{16}).

$$Y := X1 + X2 + X3$$

Input: $X1$, $X2$, $X3$ in the three memory words following the program.

Output: Y in the word following the input values.

An assembly language program that performs this task is given in Figure 13-4. It is assumed that the values of the input quantities have been prespecified and that all that is required is the result. This simple program is placed in memory starting at memory location 1000.

The computation is carried out by using register $R0$ as a temporary location to store the partial result as each number is added to the partial sum. This register is initialized to zero by the CLR operation that uses register mode addressing to indicate that register $R0$ is to be cleared. The next three addition operations are double-operand operations. The source operand is referenced using relative addressing and the destination is indicated by register mode addressing. We use relative addressing to address the data in memory since we do not have to worry about specifying the actual address. We simply refer to the data by their label values, and the assembler takes care of generating the proper machine language code to realize the desired operation. The task is completed by using the MOV instruction to copy the value contained in $R0$ into the memory location indicated by the label Y.

The assembler directive .WORD is used to load specific numerical values into the memory words set aside to store the data. Note that we use the directive .EVEN to make sure that this data area starts on a word boundary. It is a good practice to insert this directive, or to redefine the value of the location counter, in situations of this type since there is no guarantee that the first free location in memory is at a word boundary. Finally we indicate the end of our program with the directive .END followed by the label indicating the starting point of the program.

Decisions

The ability to select the next instruction to be executed in a calculation based on the current status of the calculation is a very important feature in any computer lan-

```
          .TITLE PROGRAM_1

; ******************************************************************
;
;         SUM THE THREE POSITIVE NUMBERS X1, X2, X3
;         INPUT VALUES IN MEMORY LOCATIONS X1, X2, X3
;         OUTPUT IN MEMORY LOCATION Y
; ******************************************************************
;


          . = 1000                ;SET LOCATION COUNTER
START:    CLR      R0             ;SET R0 TO ZERO.
          ADD      X1, R0         ;FORM PARTIAL SUM
          ADD      X2, R0
          ADD      X3, R0
          MOV      R0, Y          ;SAVE RESULTS
          HALT

          .EVEN                   ;MAKE SURE DATA STARTS
                                  ;ON WORD BOUNDARY
X1:       .WORD    267            ;SOME TYPICAL VALUES
X2:       .WORD    4431
X3:       .WORD    57
Y:        .WORD    0              ;LOCATION OF FINAL ANSWER
          .END     START
```

Figure 13-4   Assembly language program to sum three numbers.

guage. At the machine level this status information is indicated by the flags in the processor status (PS) register. As discussed in Chapter 12, PS has four flags, which indicate the following information:

1. Zero Flag Z. Z is set to 1 at the completion of an instruction if the result is 0.
2. Negative Flag N. N is set to 1 if the result is negative (i.e., the sign bit of the result is 1).
3. Carry Flag C. C is set to 1 if a carry is generated from the MSB (most significant bit) or a 1 was shifted into the C bit by a shift operation.
4. Arithmetic Overflow V. V is set to one if the operation resulted in an arithmetic overflow (2's complement arithmetic assumed).

The branch instructions described in Table 12-8 are used to test the condition of these flags. On the basis of the results of this test, the control unit decides where to obtain the next instruction to be executed in the program.

The general way that these instructions are used is shown in Figure 13-5a. The

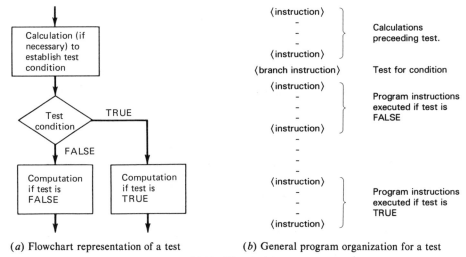

(*a*) Flowchart representation of a test   (*b*) General program organization for a test

Figure 13-5   The decision process.

box preceding the decision point corresponds to the sequence of code used to make the necessary computations on which the test is to be based. One of the appropriate branch instructions is then used to carry out the test. If the test is TRUE, the control unit transfers control to the address indicated by the branch instruction. Otherwise the control unit executes the next instruction.

The general program organization necessary to accomplish this testing process is shown in Figure 13-5b. In SEDCOM II a branch instruction is limited to transferring control to an instruction within a range of -128_{10} to $+127_{10}$ words from the end of the branch instruction. This is usually sufficient for most programming needs. If you must transfer control outside of this range, it is necessary to branch to a location that contains a jump instruction JMP and then use that instruction to make the final transfer. The following examples illustrate some typical decision processes.

Register Overflow Detection

One of the problems with the program developed to add three numbers together is that the result may be larger than $65,535_{10}$. When this happens we say that the result has overflowed the capacity of the 16-bit register $R0$. The program specification for Program 2 accounts for this possibility.

When two numbers are added together using the ADD instruction, a register overflow will be generated if the result exceeds $65,535_{10}$. This overflow condition sets the C flag in PS to 1. Thus if we find that C is 1 after any ADD operation, we know that a register overflow condition has occurred and we can take an appropriate action.

Program Specification

PROGRAM 2

Task: Sum three positive numbers and detect if the result exceeds the numerical size limit $2^{16} - 1$.

$$Y := X1 + X2 + X3$$

Input: $X1$, $X2$, $X3$ in the three memory words following the program.

Output: No overflow $Y \leq 65,535_{10}$.
Y in the word following the input values.
Register $R0$ set to 0.
Overflow $Y > 65,535_{10}$.
Y is set to zero.
Register $R0$ set to 177777.

To illustrate how the C flag is controlled consider the two examples shown below. In the first case there is no overflow and in the second case an overflow occurs. Note that the initial value of C is unimportant.

Operation   ADD   R0,R1

	Case I		Case II	
	Before	**After**	**Before**	**After**
$R0$	002357	002357	073446	073446
$R1$	017554	022133	120303	013751
C	1	0	0	1

Figure 13-6a gives the flowchart of the algorithm needed to solve this problem. Register $R0$ is used to accumulate the partial sum. Thus it is first initialized to zero. The C flag does not have to be initialized since its value is determined by the result of an operation and the value contained in C before the operation is lost. Finally we note that we must check for overflow every time a partial sum is formed. When an overflow occurs we stop the processing and enter the error routine before completing the program. Upon completion of this program we need to know whether the program terminated normally or was terminated because of an error condition. We have chosen to do this by setting $R0$ to 0 if the calculation was completed successfully and to 177777 if it was terminated because of an error.

The assembly language program to carry out this addition is shown in Figure 13-6b. The BCS (Branch if Carry is Set) instruction is used to test C for an overflow

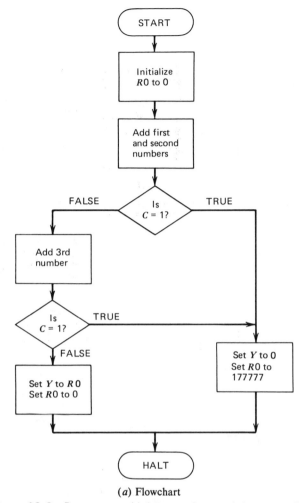

(*a*) Flowchart

Figure 13-6 Program to add three numbers and detect overflow.

after each addition operation. If C is found to be 1, the branch instruction takes us to the error exit point OFLERR, where we set the error condition. Otherwise we continue on with the computation.

Arithmetic Overflow

As long as we know that we are dealing with positive numbers the C flag is used as the overflow indicator. However, when doing 2's complement arithmetic the most significant bits of the operands correspond to the sign bit. In this case we are dealing with numbers with a decimal value in the range $-32,768$ to $+32,767$. Whenever the addition or subtraction operation produces a result that falls outside this range,

```
                .TITLE PROGRAM__2

;   ***************************************************************
;           SUM THE THREE POSITIVE NUMBERS X1, X2, X3
;           AND DETECT ANY REGISTER OVERFLOW
;
;           INPUT VALUES IN MEMORY LOCATIONS X1, X2, X3
;
;           OUTPUT IN MEMORY LOCATION Y
;                   IF NO OVERFLOW R0 SET TO 0 AND RESULT IN Y
;                   IF OVERFLOW R0 SET TO 177777 Y SET TO 0
;   ***************************************************************
;

                . = 1000

START:  CLR     R0              ;SET R0 TO ZERO
        ADD     X1,R0           ;FORM PARTIAL SUM
        BCS     OFLERR          ;BRANCH IF OVERFLOW
        ADD     X2,R0
        BCS     OFLERR          ;BRANCH IF OVERFLOW
        ADD     X3,R0
        BCS     OFLERR          ;BRANCH IF OVERFLOW
        MOV     R0,Y            ;SAVE RESULTS
        CLR     R0              ;SET R0 TO 0
        HALT


OFLERR: CLR     Y               ;PROCESS ERROR CONDITION
        MOV     #177777,R0      ;SET ERROR FLAG
        HALT


        .EVEN                   ;SET  DATA  AREA  TO  START  ON  WORD
                                ;BOUNDARY
X1:     .WORD   267             ;SOME TYPICAL VALUES
X2:     .WORD   4431
X3:     .WORD   57
Y:      .WORD   0               ;LOCATION OF FINAL ANSWER
        .END    START
```

(b) Assembly language program

Figure 13-6   (Continued)

we have an *arithmetic overflow*. The V flag is used to indicate arithmetic overflow. If V is set by an arithmetic operation, then we know that an arithmetic overflow occurred and corrective actions may have to be taken. The following examples illustrate the behavior of the V flag. Note that the initial value of V is of no interest.

	Case 1		Case 2	
	Before	After	Before	After
$R0$	002357	002357	073446	073446
$R1$	017554	022133	020303	113751
V	1	0	0	1

Operation ADD R0, R1

In the second example we are adding two positive numbers that produce a result greater than 077777 (the largest allowable positive number that can be stored in a 16-bit word in 2's complement form). This results in the V flag being set to 1 to indicate an arithmetic overflow condition.

Program Specification

PROGRAM 3

Task: Sum three 2's complement numbers and detect if the result falls outside the range $\pm(2^{15} - 1)$.

$$Y := X1 + X2 + X3$$

Input: $X1$, $X2$, $X3$ in the three memory words following the program.

Output: No overflow $-32{,}768_{10} \leq Y \leq 32{,}767_{10}$
Y in the word following the input values.
Register $R0$ set to 0.
Overflow $Y < -32{,}768_{10}$ or $Y > 32{,}767_{10}$.
Y is set to zero.
Register $R0$ set to 177777.

To illustrate the use of the V flag consider the program specification for Program 3, a slightly revised version of Program 2. In this program we are to add both positive and negative numbers and detect whether there is an arithmetic overflow. The algorithm used for this computation is almost the same as that for Program 2. The only difference is that we now test the V flag and ignore the C flag. The assembly language program necessary to carry out this computation is shown in Figure 13-7. Note

```
        .TITLE PROGRAM-3

; ****************************************************************
;
;          SUM THE THREE 2'S COMPLEMENT NUMBERS X1, X2, X3
;          AND DETECT ANY ARITHMETIC OVERFLOW
;
;          INPUT VALUES IN MEMORY LOCATIONS X1, X2, X3
;
;          OUTPUT IN MEMORY LOCATION Y
;                 IF NO OVERFLOW R0 SET TO 0 AND RESULT IN Y
;                 IF OVERFLOW R0 SET TO 177777 Y SET TO 0
; ****************************************************************

            .= 1000                     ;SET LOCATION COUNTER

START:   CLR      R0                     ;SET R0 TO ZERO
         ADD      X1,R0                  ;FORM PARTIAL SUM
         BVS      OFLERR                 ;BRANCH IF OVERFLOW
         ADD      X2,R0
         BVS      OFLERR                 ;BRANCH IF OVERFLOW
         ADD      X3,R0
         BVS      OFLERR                 ;BRANCH IF OVERFLOW
         MOV      R0,Y                   ;SAVE RESULTS
         CLR      R0                     ;SET R0 TO 0
         HALT

OFLERR:  CLR      Y                      ;PROCESS ERROR CONDITION
         MOV      #177777,R0             ;SET ERROR FLAG
         HALT

         .EVEN                           ;SET DATA AREA
X1:      .WORD    267                    ;SOME TYPICAL VALUES
X2:      .WORD    4431
X3:      .WORD    57
Y:       .WORD    0                      ;LOCATION OF FINAL ANSWER
         .END     START
```

Figure 13-7 Program to add three 2's complement numbers with overflow detection.

that the only change is that every BCS instruction is replaced with a BVS instruction.

Program Loops and Repetitive Calculations

An important property of a computer is that it can carry out the steps in a repetitive task as many times as are necessary to complete the task. For example, suppose in Program 3 we had to sum 100 numbers instead of 3. It would be very wasteful of memory space to write a program that contained 100 copies of the instruction sequence

$$\text{ADD} \qquad Xi, R0$$
$$\text{BVS} \qquad \text{OFLERR}$$

where the only change that has to be made is the value for i. To overcome this problem we can introduce the idea of a loop.

A *program loop* is a set of instructions that are repeatedly executed until a condition is detected that terminates the loop. A loop may be a complete program or it may be part of a more general program. Loops are common in programs written in higher level languages. Depending upon the language, a number of different conventions are used to describe loops. If we disregard some minor variations, it is possible to identify two basic loop organizations. They are illustrated by the flowcharts shown in Figure 13-8.

The loop shown in Figure 13-8a is the DO-WHILE type loop and is the typical way a DO statement is implemented in PL/I or a WHILE statement is implemented in Pascal. In this arrangement the exit condition is always tested before the body of

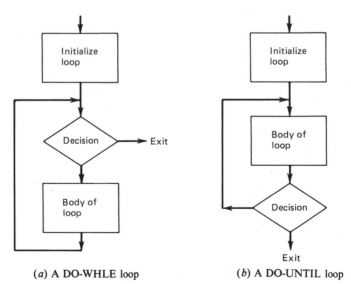

(*a*) A DO-WHLE loop   (*b*) A DO-UNTIL loop

Figure 13-8   Flowchart illustrating basic loop structure.

the loop is executed. Thus, it is possible that the exit condition will be satisfied before the body of the loop is executed for the first time.

The loop shown in Figure 13-8*b* is the DO-UNTIL type of loop and is typical of the way a DO statement is implemented in FORTRAN or a REPEAT-UNTIL statement is implemented in Pascal. In this arrangement the body of the loop is always executed at least once before an exit from the loop is possible.

When programming at the assembly language level, we are free to select either form of loop structure or to introduce variations that are suggested by the problem being solved. The following two examples illustrate some of the general techniques used in realizing a loop. These techniques are expanded and generalized in later examples.

Counters

The simplest type of loop is one in which the body is executed a fixed number of times. In this case we must have some way to count the number of times that the body has been executed. A *counter* is used to do this task. When the loop is entered, the counter is set to the number of times the body is to be executed. Each time the program executes the instructions that make up the body, the counter is decremented. When the body has been executed the proper number of times, the counter goes to zero and the program exits from the loop. The DO-UNTIL loop organization is nicely matched to this type of task.

Since SEDCOM II does not contain a special counter in its CPU, we must use one of the general purpose registers or a memory location for this purpose. The decrementing and testing of the counter is then carried out using standard machine language instructions. The general way in which a counter is represented in a DO-UNTIL loop is outlined in Figure 13-9.

Assume that we wish to execute the body of the program N times and that we have decided to use CPU register $R0$ as a counter. Before entering the loop, we initialize the counter $R0$ to N. Each time the body of the loop is executed we decrement the counter $R0$. If we have gone through the body of the loop N times, the count will go to zero and the Z flag in the program status register will be set to one. Thus by testing Z we can decide whether we should exit the loop or execute the body another time.

The way that we test and branch will depend upon the number of memory words needed to hold the instructions that make up the body of the program. If the body requires less than 127_{10} words, we can use the BNE (Branch Not Equal to zero) instruction to transfer control to the first instruction in the body whenever we must repeat the loop (alternative a in Figure 13-9). If we must branch back more than this distance, then we need a slightly more complex sequence of instructions. In this case we use a BEQ (Branch EQual to zero) instruction to test whether we should leave the loop (alternative b in Figure 13-9). If the loop has not been executed N times, the BEQ instruction finds that Z is 0. Thus the JMP instruction immediately following the BEQ instruction is executed. This takes us to the beginning of the loop.

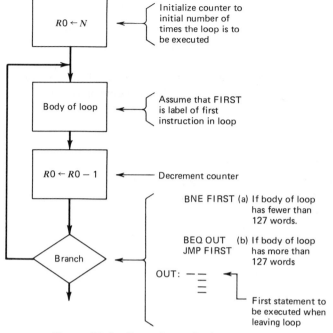

Figure 13-9 General organization of a loop.

When the branch test BEQ finds that Z is 1, indicating that the loop has been executed the correct number of times, we exit the loop by transferring control to the statement labeled OUT.

Program Specification

PROGRAM 4

Task: Sum the numbers 1 through N modulo 2^{16}.

$$Y := 1 + 2 + 3 + \ldots + N$$

Input: The value of N represented by NVAL.

Output: The resulting sum placed in memory location Y.

An Example

As a simple example of how a counter is used in a loop, consider the program specification for Program 4. Two possible solutions to this problem are shown in Figure 13-10.

The first solution uses CPU register $R0$ for the partial sum, $R1$ to hold the current value of I, and $R2$ for the counter. We could have used one or more memory locations

```
                .TITLE PROGRAM_4I

;   ***************************************************************
;
;           SUM THE POSITIVE NUMBERS 1 THROUGH N
;
;           INPUT VALUE OF N IN MEMORY LOCATION NVAL
;
;           OUTPUT IN MEMORY LOCATION Y
;
;   ***************************************************************
;

                . = 1000                    ;SET LOCATION COUNTER

                                ;INITIALIZE LOOP

START:  CLR     R0                          ;SET R0 TO ZERO TO HOLD PARTIAL SUM
        MOV     #1,R1                       ;SET INITIAL NUMBER IN SEQUENCE
        MOV     NVAL,R2                     ;SET COUNTER

                                ;BODY OF LOOP

LOOP:   ADD     R1,R0                       ;FORM PARTIAL SUM
        INC     R1                          ;FORM NEXT NUMBER IN SEQUENCE
        DEC     R2                          ;DECREMENT COUNT
        BNE     LOOP                        ;REPEAT IF COUNT NOT 0

                                ;EXIT FROM LOOP

        MOV     R0,Y                        ;SAVE RESULT
        HALT

        .EVEN                               ;PROVIDE DATA STORAGE AREA
NVAL:   .WORD   67                          ;A TYPICAL VALUE FOR N
Y:      .WORD   0                           ;LOCATION FOR RESULT
        .END    START
```

(*a*) First program using separate counter: DO-UNTIL program structure

Figure 13-10 Two ways to sum the integers 1 through N.

```
        .TITLE PROGRAM_4II
```

```
; *****************************************************************
;
;       SUM THE POSITIVE NUMBERS 1 THROUGH N
;
;       INPUT VALUE OF N SPECIFIED BY ASSIGNMENT STATEMENT
;
;       OUTPUT IN MEMORY LOCATION Y
;
; *****************************************************************
```

```
        NVAL = ⟨value of N⟩      ;DEFINE VALUE FOR NVAL

        . = 1000                 ;SET LOCATION COUNTER

                                 ;INITIALIZE LOOP

START:  CLR     R0               ;SET R0 TO ZERO TO HOLD PARTIAL SUM
        MOV     #1,R1            ;SET INITIAL NUMBER IN SEQUENCE

                                 ;TEST AT HEAD OF LOOP

LOOP:   CMP     #NVAL,R1         ;COMPARE I TO NVAL
        BMI     FINISH           ;I > NVAL EXIT

                                 ;BODY OF LOOP

        ADD     R1,R0            ;FORM PARTIAL SUM
        INC     R1               ;FORM NEXT NUMBER IN SEQUENCE
        BR      LOOP             ;REPEAT

                                 ;EXIT FROM LOOP

FINISH: MOV     R0,Y             ;SAVE RESULT
        HALT

        .EVEN                    ;DATA AREA
Y:      .WORD   0                ;LOCATION FOR RESULT
        .END    START
```

(*b*) Second program without separate counter: DO-WHILE loop structure

Figure 13-10   (Continued)

to substitute for these registers. However, this would slow the calculation since a larger number of memory accesses would be needed. To perform the calculation we start with $I = 1$ and increment I each time we go through the loop and, at the same time, we decrement the counter. This processing is continued until the counter reaches a value of 0.

If this program were written in a higher level language, the variable I would be considered as both a counter variable and the variable used to form the partial sum. However, in the first assembly language program we used two variables. The variable corresponding to I is found in register $R1$ and it is incremented from 1 to N. A second variable is used as a counter and is found in register $R2$. This variable is initially set to N and decremented until it reaches zero. This is not the only way that this calculation can be carried out.

In the second program we use a DO-WHILE loop structure to solve the same problem. For this case we use $R0$ to hold the partial sum and $R1$ to hold the value of I. I starts at 1 and is incremented each time the body of the loop is executed. However, instead of using a separate counter, we use the instruction

$$\text{CMP} \quad \text{\#NUMV}, R1$$

to see whether I is greater than N before the body of the loop is executed. When we find that this condition is true, we exit the loop. Note that the assignment statement

$$\text{NUMV} = \langle \text{value of } N \rangle$$

is used to allow the value of N to be changed as desired by the programmer.

Pointers

There are many situations in which we wish to perform some type of computation that involves a block of data. For example, suppose that we wished to sum N numbers. As long as N is a relatively small value we could use a straight-line program such as Program 1 or Program 2 to do the job. However, consider what would happen if $N = 50$. A straight-line program would become so large that it would be unwieldy. To overcome this problem we can make use of the indirect, autodecrement or autoincrement addressing modes to create *pointers* that point to the data in which we are interested.

When we deal with a block of data, the individual data items in the block are normally stored in sequential memory locations. To process this information we must access this data item by item. One way to keep track of the item currently being processed is to use a "pointer" that points to that item. A pointer can be created by using one of the CPU registers to store the address of the data item to be processed. Then, whenever the data item is needed, the instruction can use the indirect, autodecrement or autoincrement addressing modes to address the item. Figure 13-11 provides a graphical interpretation of the pointer concept.

The use of a pointer can greatly simplify a program, but to obtain the full value of this concept you must understand the way that the indirect, autodecrement and

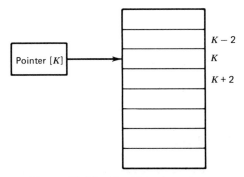

Figure 13-11 The idea of a pointer.

autoincrement modes of addressing operate. The following examples will illustrate some of the simpler applications. Later examples will make greater use of the capabilities of pointers as information processing tools.

Autoincrement Address Mode

In many programs an area in memory is set aside to hold a block of data. For example, a block of N memory locations might be used to hold an array of N numbers generated as part of an experiment. Before starting the experiment all of the elements of the array must be set to zero. The specification for this task is given by the Program Specification for ZROTAB. The assembly language program to accomplish this task is given in Figure 13-12.

Program Specification

ZROTAB

Task: Enter a 0 value in the N words that make up the table TABLE.

Input: The value of N and the location of TABLE are defined in the program.

Output: The zero values inserted into TABLE.

Although this is a very simple program, it illustrates the use of a number of features of the SEDCOM II assembly language.

A major task in the design of any program involves defining the data structures that will be used to hold the data being processed by the program. The central data structure of this program is a table of N words that is to be cleared. There are a

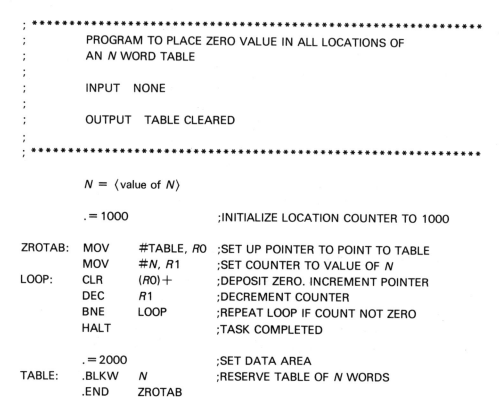

```
          .TITLE ZROTAB

;  **********************************************************
;          PROGRAM TO PLACE ZERO VALUE IN ALL LOCATIONS OF
;          AN N WORD TABLE
;
;          INPUT   NONE
;
;          OUTPUT   TABLE CLEARED
;
;  **********************************************************

          N = ⟨value of N⟩

          . = 1000                    ;INITIALIZE LOCATION COUNTER TO 1000

ZROTAB:   MOV    #TABLE, R0   ;SET UP POINTER TO POINT TO TABLE
          MOV    #N, R1       ;SET COUNTER TO VALUE OF N
LOOP:     CLR    (R0)+        ;DEPOSIT ZERO. INCREMENT POINTER
          DEC    R1           ;DECREMENT COUNTER
          BNE    LOOP         ;REPEAT LOOP IF COUNT NOT ZERO
          HALT                ;TASK COMPLETED

          . = 2000            ;SET DATA AREA
TABLE:    .BLKW  N            ;RESERVE TABLE OF N WORDS
          .END   ZROTAB
```

Figure 13-12   Program to zero an N word table.

number of different ways to introduce this structure into the program. For this example we assume that the table is to be placed directly after the program. However, to add some generality to the program we also assume that the size of the table may vary and that we wish to be able to change the size without a large amount of reprogramming.

Since the size of the table is subject to change, we use the assignment statement

$$N = ⟨\text{number of words in table}⟩$$

to assign a value to N, which is the symbol that we have selected to indicate the number of words in the table. In writing our program we use N whenever we wish to deal with the size of the table. When the program is processed by the assembler, the assembler substitutes the indicated value for N in every place that it is used in the program. If we decide to change the size of the table, all that we must do is to assign a different value to N and reassemble the program with this new value.

The table to be processed involves a block of N words in memory. To set aside the necessary room in memory for this table we use the statement

TABLE: .BLKW   N

The address of the first memory location in this block is indicated by the label TABLE, while the size of the table is given by N. The label TABLE associated with this statement is called the *symbolic address* of this table and its value, indicated as #TABLE, is the address of the first memory word in the block of words set aside to hold the table. For example, the following statement sequence

. = 2000
TABLE: .BLKW   N
—
—

indicates that we wish to reserve N (octal) words in memory starting at memory address 2000. The block is labeled by the symbolic address TABLE, which has a value #TABLE of 2000 (octal). Once we define a symbolic address for a given location in memory, we can use that address whenever we wish to refer to that location in the rest of the program.

To access each word in TABLE we decide to use $R0$ as a pointer and $R1$ as a counter. During the initialization we set $R0$ to the value #TABLE and $R1$ to the value N. A DO-UNTIL loop is then used to clear the N words in the block of memory indicated by TABLE. In this case the instruction

CLR   (R0)+

is used to first clear the memory location pointed to by the value contained in register $R0$. After this memory location is cleared, the value stored in $R0$ is automatically incremented by 2. (Remember that CLR is a word instruction.) As a result, after the instruction has been executed, the pointer is now pointing to the next word in memory that is to be cleared.

Each time we complete the loop we decrement the value of the counter. If the new value of count is not zero, we go back and execute the body of the loop another time. We keep this up until we have cleared the N words in memory that make up the data structure that we have labeled TABLE.

Stacks

Sometimes we must store one or more data items in a temporary memory location while working on other parts of a computation. We could set aside specific memory locations to hold this information, but this would mean that we would have to remember exactly where each data item was stored. One solution to this problem is to use a data structure called a stack.

A *stack* is a data structure that stores a sequence of data elements in consecutive memory locations. Elements can be added or removed from only the top of the stack and an element lower down in the stack cannot be utilized until all elements above this particular element are removed. As soon as the top element is used, it is effectively removed from the stack and it becomes the new top element. When a new element is added to the stack, it becomes the new top element and the old top element is pushed down into the stack. There are a number of different conventions used to realize a stack at the machine level. We adopt the following convention.

It is assumed that the bottom of a stack is located at the highest memory address of the memory area set aside for the stack and that the stack expands linearly *downward* in memory as items are added. As items are removed the stack contracts toward the bottom (higher memory). Figure 13-13 illustrates this organization.

The main advantage of the stack is that you do not have to keep track of the actual locations used to hold a given data item. That is done by a stack pointer. As shown in Figure 13-13, the stack pointer is a CPU register that contains the address of the data item on the top of the stack. In SEDCOM II register *R6* has been specially designed for use as the stack pointer and is given the special symbol SP. The registers *R0* through *R5* can also be used for stack pointers, but special care must be used if a stack is implemented with these registers.

There are three basic operations that we must be able to perform when we include a stack in a program. They are:

1. Initialize the stack.
2. PUSH an item onto the stack.
3. POP an item from the stack.

Each of these tasks can be accomplished by use of a single instruction. If register *R6* is used as the stack pointer, the item pushed onto or popped from the stack is *always a word*. Whenever we use register *R6* as the stack pointer, we use the symbol SP to represent this register. If the other registers are used to act as a stack pointer, either a word or a byte can be processed by these operations.

Stack Initialization

In the initial design of a program we must decide where we are going to place the stack in memory and how much memory we are going to reserve for its use. Normal

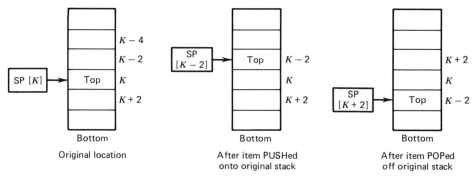

Figure 13-13   Illustration of stack operations.

programming practice is to place the stack area below the area used for the program being developed. For example, in SEDCOM II the memory is located in the address area between 1000 and 20777. If we assume that we wish to reserve 250_8 words for the stack, then the first instruction in the program would start at memory address 1500. (Remember that 250 words corresponds to 500 bytes and that all addresses are given as byte addresses.) To initialize the stack we would use the following assembly code as the first instruction in the program.

```
        . = 1500              ;SET LOCATION COUNTER
                              ;TO START OF PROGRAM AREA
START:  MOV  #START,SP        ;SET STACK POINTER TO WORD
                              ;JUST BELOW STACK
        :                     ;THIS IS THE EMPTY STACK CONDITION
```

The first instruction sets the stack pointer SP to point at the first word of the program. Under the convention that the stack pointer always points at the current word on the stack, this corresponds to the *empty stack* condition (i.e., if the stack is empty the pointer points at the word just below the bottom of the stack). In this example the bottom word in the stack area is the word at memory location 1476_8.

The PUSH Operation

To add a new item to the stack we remember that the stack pointer SP is pointing to the word on the top of the stack. Therefore to add a new word to the stack we must first decrement SP so that it is pointing to the first empty word at the top of the stack. The next step is to transfer the word to be stored to the new location being pointed at by SP. The operation of pushing a word onto the stack is accomplished by the following instruction:

```
MOV  ⟨source⟩,−(SP)           ;PUSH THE WORD AT ADDRESS
                              ;⟨source⟩ ONTO THE STACK
```

The source address, represented by ⟨source⟩, can be any of the standard address modes used to reference an operand. Note that we use the autodecrementing mode of addressing to decrement SP *before* the information is placed onto the stack.

The POP Operation

A word is read from the stack by reversing the PUSH process. In this case SP is pointing to the word that we wish to POP or read from the stack. After reading the word we increment SP so that it points to the word that becomes the new top element. To carry out this operation we use the following instruction:

```
MOV  (SP)+,⟨destination⟩       ;POP A WORD FROM THE STACK AND
                              ;PLACE IT IN ⟨destination⟩
```

The destination address, represented by ⟨destination⟩, can be any of the standard address modes used to reference an operand. Note that we use the autoincrement mode of addressing to increment SP automatically as part of the execution of the MOV instruction after the value of the word on top of the stack has been read.

WARNING1: The size of the stack selected for a given program represents the designer's best estimate of the amount of room that must be reserved in memory to serve as the stack area. If we try to PUSH too many words onto the stack, we will transfer data into a location that has not been reserved for the stack. The instruction sequence used to push information onto a stack makes no attempt to test to see whether the stack is full. Similarly the POP operation always assumes that the stack is not empty and that it can read a word from the stack. If the POP operation is performed on an empty stack, we will have erroneous results. Here again the POP instruction does not have any provision to test for an empty stack. If either of these conditions occurs, the results may be disastrous. It is the program designer's responsibility to ensure that these conditions do not occur.

WARNING2: Register $R6$ is specially designed to be used as a stack pointer for a stack that always PUSHes or POPs one word. Thus any autoincrement or autodecrement reference to SP causes SP to be incremented or decremented by 2. If you wish to form a stack to store bytes instead of words, you must use one of the registers $R0$ through $R5$. In that case the PUSH operation becomes MOVB ⟨source⟩, $-(Ri)$ and the POP operation becomes MOVB $(Ri)+$, ⟨destination⟩.

Input/Output Programming

Information is read into SEDCOM II by use of a keyboard. Output information is printed on a printer. As discussed in Chapter 12, we can receive one character at a time from the keyboard and send one character at a time to the printer. Each character is encoded using the ASCII code given in Appendix A. We now consider the problem of communicating with the outside world using the printer and the keyboard. (In an interactive system the printer would be a display device.)

Both the printer and the keyboard are very slow compared with the operating speed of the CPU. As discussed in Section 3 of Chapter 12, both the printer and the keyboard have device status flags. These flags are used to synchronize the speed of the I/O devices with the need for information by the program. Whenever we wish to transfer information between SEDCOM II and one of the I/O devices, we check the appropriate device status flag to see whether the device is ready for an information transfer. If it is ready the flag will be set to 1 and we know that the transfer can take place. If the flag is 0 this indicates that the device is not ready for a transfer and we must wait until the flag is set before we can continue.

The Keyboard as an Input Device

The checking of the device status flag and the transfer of information is quite simple because of the way the interface to the I/O devices is implemented. Remember from Chapter 12 that both the keyboard and the printer have a status register and a data register that are connected to the INFOBUS. Thus, from the viewpoint of the CPU, each of these registers appears to be a single memory location. Therefore all interactions involving these registers are carried out as if they were memory transfers. The addressing convention used to reference each register is illustrated in Figure 13-14.

The *keyboard status register* is the byte at absolute address 177560 while the *keyboard data register* is the byte at absolute address 177562. Bit 7 of the keyboard status register is the *keyboard status flag*. The status of the keyboard status flag is checked using the test byte instruction TSTB. If the keyboard status flag is 1, the TSTB instruction causes the N bit in the program status register PS to be set (i.e., bit 7 is the sign bit; if it is 1 this indicates a "negative" number). As soon as the program sees that the N bit is set to 1, it knows that a character is ready for transmission to the CPU. A MOVB instruction is used to transfer the information from the keyboard data register to either a CPU register or a register in memory. *When the read instruction is carried out, the keyboard status flag and the keyboard buffer are cleared and the next input character can be entered into the keyboard buffer.* The program sequence necessary to carry out the read operation has the following general form.

```
          ;PROGRAM SEGMENT TO READ A CHARACTER FROM KEYBOARD
     KBSTAT = 177560              ;ADDRESS OF KEYBOARD STATUS REGISTER
     KBDATA = 177562              ;ADDRESS OF KEYBOARD BUFFER

RD:  TSTB  @#KBSTAT               ;IS KEYBOARD STATUS FLAG SET?
     BPL   RD                     ;NO-TRY AGAIN
     MOV   @#KBDATA,⟨dest⟩        ;MOVE DATA TO DESTINATION
     —
     —
```

The Printer as an Output Device

The *printer status register* is the byte at absolute address 177564 while the *printer data register* is the byte at absolute address 177566. Bit 7 of the printer status reg-

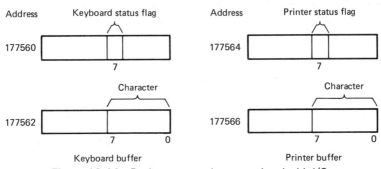

Figure 13-14   Register conventions associated with I/O.

ister is the *printer status flag*. Whenever the printer is able to receive a character, the printer status flag is set to 1. A TSTB instruction can be used to test this flag. When it is found to be 1, a MOVB instruction is used to move the character to be printed to the printer data register. At the completion of the MOVB instruction, the printer status flag is set to 0 and the printer starts to print the character. When the printing is completed, the flag is again set to 1 to indicate that the next character can be sent to the printer data register. The following program segment illustrates the sequence of instructions that can be used to print a character.

```
              ;PROGRAM SEGMENT TO PRINT A CHARACTER ON THE PRINTER
      PRSTAT = 177564              ;ADDRESS OF PRINTER STATUS REGISTER
      PRDATA = 177566              ;ADDRESS OF PRINTER BUFFER

PD:   TSTB  @#PRSTAT               ;IS PRINTER STATUS FLAG SET?
      BPL   PD                     ;NO-TRY AGAIN
      MOV   ⟨sorc⟩,@#PRDATA        ;MOVE DATA FROM SOURCE TO
                                   ;PRINTER
      ──
      ──
```

To illustrate how the I/O operations are used consider the program READ _PRINT given by the following program specification.

Program Specification

READ_PRINT

Task: Read up to 80 characters from the keyboard and store them in a buffer storage area BUFF. The last character read is a Line Feed LF. Reading of characters will stop after reading a LF or reading the 80th character. The characters are to be printed as they are read.

Input: The characters from the reader.

Output: The characters stored in BUFF. The last character is a LF if less than 80 characters are read.
        The printed characters.

We wish to read in a string of up to 80_{10} (120_8) ASCII characters terminated with the Line Feed (LF) character (ASCII code 12_8). As we read in the characters we must store them sequentially in memory in an area labeled BUFF and also print out each character. Figure 13-15 gives a flowchart of the steps that must be carried out to perform this task as well as the necessary program. Note that we have used register $R1$ as a pointer to keep track of where each character is to be deposited.

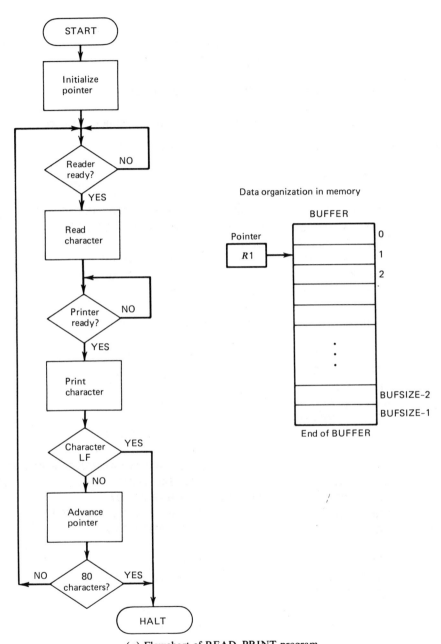

(*a*) Flowchart of READ_PRINT program

Figure 13-15 Program for READ_PRINT.

```
                    .TITLE READ_PRINT

; ****************************************************************
;
;Task:      Read up to 80 characters and store them in BUFFER.
;           Print out characters as they are read.
;
;Input:     A string of characters terminated by a line feed LF.
;
;Output:    The characters stored in BUFFER and the printed output sequence.
;
; ****************************************************************

                    ;SYSTEM CONSTANTS

            KBSTAT = 177560  ;ADDRESS OF KEYBOARD STATUS REGISTER
            KBDATA = 177562  ;ADDRESS OF KEYBOARD BUFFER REGISTER
            PRSTAT = 177564  ;ADDRESS OF PRINTER STATUS REGISTER
            PRDATA = 177566  ;ADDRESS OF PRINTER BUFFER REGISTER
            BUFSIZE = 120    ;MAXIMUM NUMBER OF CHARACTERS (80 DEC)
            LF = 12          ;CODE FOR LINE FEED

            . = 1000         ;INITIAL LOCATION COUNTER

START:  MOV   #BUFFER,R1            ;SET POINTER TO BUFFER
RD:     TSTB  @#KBSTAT             ;CHARACTER READY TO READ?
        BPL   RD                   ;NO-CHECK AGAIN
        MOVB  @#KBDATA,(R1)        ;YES-READ DATA
PR:     TSTB  @#PRSTAT             ;PRINTER READY
        BPL   PR                   ;NO-CHECK AGAIN
        MOVB  (R1),@#PRDATA        ;PRINT CHARACTER
        CMP   (R1)+,#LF            ;IS CHAR A LF? ADVANCE POINTER
        BEQ   DONE                 ;YES-EXIT LOOP
        CMP   #BUFFER+BUFSIZE,R1   ;80 CHAR READ?
        BNE   RD                   ;NO-GET NEXT CHARACTER
DONE:   HALT                       ;YES-INPUT READ

        .EVEN                       ;SET DATA AREA
BUFFER: .BLKB  BUFSIZE              ;RESERVE BUFFER AREA
        .END   START
```

(b) Assembly language program for READ_PRINT

Figure 13-15   (Continued)

The program is to halt after we have read in a LF or if the buffer is full. Thus two checks must be made. First we must check each character to see whether it is a LF and second we must make sure that the buffer is not full before we try to read the next character. There are a number of ways that we can make sure that we do not overflow the buffer. One way would be to use a counter. However, we have decided to use the compare operation CMP to perform this task.

To provide the greatest generality we use an assignment statement to define BUFSIZE to be the number of characters that can be stored in the buffer. In this example

$$BUFSIZE = 120$$

Thus the buffer into which we are loading the characters consists of the 120_8 locations from BUFFER, to BUFFER $+$ BUFSIZE $-$ 1. Initially the pointer in register $R1$ is set to the address represented by BUFFER. As each character is read in, the character is placed in the buffer and $R1$ is incremented by 1 to point to the next free byte in the buffer. If the value in $R1$ reaches a value of BUFFER $+$ BUFSIZE, we know that it is pointing to the first byte outside of the buffer. Thus after depositing each character in the buffer we carry out the following test to see whether the buffer is full.

```
CMP   #BUFFER+BUFSIZE,R1        ;IS THE BUFFER FULL?
BNE   ⟨beginning of loop⟩       ;NO-CONTINUE PROCESSING
—                               ;YES-GO TO NEXT TASK
```

Note that the first operand in the CMP instruction is #BUFFER $+$ BUFSIZE. This value is the address of the first byte following the buffer.

This example illustrates the ease with which we can use the I/O devices. The biggest problem that we have with an I/O device is that it is very slow compared with the speed of the rest of the computer. To get around this problem we can often organize our program so that we carry out a large number of machine operations between each I/O instruction.

ASCII to Binary (Octal) Conversion

The ASCII code used to represent character information must be used when information is read from the keyboard or when we transmit information to the printer to be printed. When we deal with character information inside the computer, we can retain this coding. However, if we wish to work with numerical information, any numerical information represented as a string of ASCII characters must first be converted to an equivalent binary number before the information is processed. Similarly, if we wish to print a binary number, we must first have a program that translates this number into a string of ASCII encoded digits that can be printed by the printer.

In the ASCII code the digits 0 through 9 are represented by the code 060_8, which represents the character 0, through 071_8, which represents the character 9. Thus to convert the ASCII code for a single digit to its corresponding binary value, all that we have to do is subtract 60_8 from the code character. Similarly if we have a binary number with a decimal value between 0 and 9 stored in a given location, we can generate the ASCII code corresponding to that number by adding 60_8 to that location. This relationship is shown in Table 13-3.

To illustrate how this conversion process could be carried out, let us assume that we wish to implement a program to carry out the task described by the program ASCII_NUM. The flowchart representing the conversion process is given by Figure 13-16a and the corresponding assembly language program is given in Figure 13-16b. In developing this program we assume that the input ASCII code string is made up of from 1 to 5 ASCII digits, that the largest number input is the string 77777, and that the input string is terminated with a space.

Program Specification

ASCII_NUM

Task: Read in a character string of from 1 to 5 characters from the set {0, ... , 7} representing an octal number and convert this string to an equivalent binary number. Print ERROR if a nonoctal character is detected or if the input string has more than 5 characters.

Input: A character string of from 1 to 5 ASCII characters from the set {0, ... , 7} and terminated by a space.

Output: If no error the binary number corresponding to the input character sequence stored in memory location BINUM.

If an error is detected ERROR is printed and 177777_8 is placed in BINUM.

The following example illustrates the method used to carry out the conversion. Let us assume that we wish to convert the three-character number string

$$C2 \quad C1 \quad C0$$

to its equivalent binary value. The conversion process we use is based upon the fact that we can express the value assigned to BINUM as

$$\text{BINUM} \leftarrow ((C2-60_8)*8 + (C1-60_8))*8 + (C0 - 60_8)$$

where we assume that we have read the input character string from left to right.

In this program we use $R0$ as a counter, $R1$ as a temporary location to store the

Table 13-3   ASCII to Binary Conversion

Digit (Decimal)	ASCII Code (Octal)	Octal Equivalent After Subtraction of 60_8
0	060	000
1	061	001
2	062	002
3	063	003
4	064	004
5	065	005
6	066	006
7	067	007
8	070	010
9	071	011

intermediate values of the number being read, and $R2$ as a temporary register to hold the current character being processed. The first task is to initialize the counter $R0$ to 5 and register $R1$ to 0. The next step is to read in the character string character by character.

As each character is read it is subjected to a number of tests. First we check to see whether the character is a space (40_8). If it is we know that we have read all characters and we end the processing. Otherwise we check to see if we have already read 5 characters or if the current character is not an octal character. Should we detect any of these conditions, the processing is terminated and an error message is printed. Otherwise the processing of the input character is then completed by multiplying the contents of $R1$ by 8_{10} (this is the same as shifting the contents of $R1$ 3-bits to the left) and then adding the numerical value of the current character to $R1$.

EXERCISES

1. Write a program that will print the character string "HELLO WORLD"

2. Write a program that will multiply the contents of register $R1$ by 10_{10}.

3. Write a program that will read a character string of from 1 to 4 number characters from the set $\{0, 1, 2, \ldots, 9\}$ and convert the string to the equivalent binary value of the string. Print out an appropriate error message if the input string does not represent a decimal number.

4. Generate the machine language program for the assembly language program of Figure 13-4.

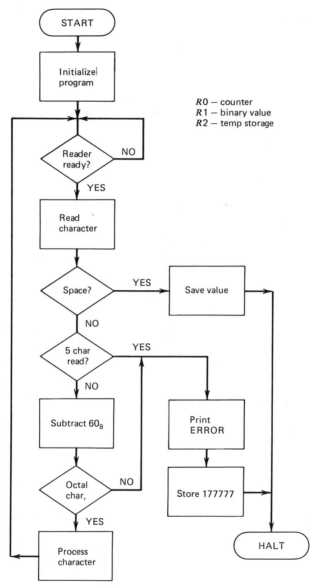

$R0$ — counter
$R1$ — binary value
$R2$ — temp storage

(a) Flowchart of ASCII_NUM

Figure 13-16   Program for ASCII_NUM.

```
        .TITLE ASCII_NUM

; ***********************************************************
;
;Task:    Read in 1 to 5 octal characters and convert them to the equivalent binary
;         number.
;
;Input:   From 1 to 5 characters terminated with a space.
;
;Output:  Binary number stored in BINUM if no error.
;
;         ERROR printed if an error occurs.
;
; ***********************************************************

                ;CONSTANTS USED IN PROGRAM

        KBSTAT = 177560   ;KEYBOARD STATUS BUFFER ADDRESS
        KBDATA = 177562   ;KEYBOARD DATA BUFFER ADDRESS
        PRSTAT = 177564   ;PRINTER STATUS BUFFER ADDRESS
        PRDATA = 177566   ;PRINTER DATA BUFFER ADDRESS

        SPACE = 40        ;SPACE CHARACTER
        . = 1000          ;SET LOCATION COUNTER

START:  MOV   #5,R0       ;SET COUNTER
        CLR   R1          ;SET BINARY VALUE TO 0
RD:     TSTB  @#KBSTAT    ;DATA READY?
        BPL   RD          ;NO-TRY AGAIN
        MOVB  @#KBDATA,R2 ;YES-GET CHAR
        CMPB  #SPACE,R2   ;IS IT A SPACE?
        BEQ   DONE        ;YES-FINISH
        DEC   R0          ;COUNT CHAR READ
        BMI   ERR         ;ERROR IF 6 CHAR READ
        SUB   #60,R2      ;CHAR MINUS 60 OCTAL VALUE
        BMI   ERR         ;ERROR IF CHAR LESS THAN 60
        CMP   #7,R2       ;GREATER THAN 7?
        BMI   ERR         ;YES-ERROR
        ASL   R1          ;SHIFT R1 3-BITS LEFT
        ASL   R1          ;TO MULTIPLY BY 8
        ASL   R1
        ADD   R2,R1       ;UPDATE RECEIVED VALUE
        BR    RD          ;GO AND READ NEXT CHAR

DONE:   MOV   R1,BINUM    ;SAVE BINARY VALUE
        HALT              ;END OF INPUT
```

(b) Assembly language program

Figure 13-16 (Continued)

```
ERR:      MOV  #5,R0              ;SET UP TO PRINT ERROR
          MOV  #MSG,R2            ;MESSAGE.
PR:       TSTB @#PRSTAT           ;CHECK PRINTER
          BPL  PR                 ;NOT READY
          MOVB (R2)+,@#PRDATA     ;SEND CHAR TO PRINTER. INC POINTER
          DEC  R0                 ;COUNT DOWN
          BNE  PR                 ;CONTINUE PRINTING IF NOT 0
          MOV  #177777,BINUM      ;SET ERROR
          HALT                    ;END OF ERROR PROCESSING

          .EVEN                   ;DATA AREA
BINUM:    .WORD  0                ;RESULT
MSG:      .ASCII /ERROR/          ;ERROR MESSAGE

          .END  START
```

Figure 13-16 (Continued)

4. SUBROUTINES

A program, which is often referred to as a routine, usually carries out a computation as a sequence of smaller component computations. The program segment associated with each of these computations is called a *subroutine*.

Some subroutines are so small that they are included in the main body of the program whenever they are needed. Subroutines of this type are called *open subroutines* or *in-line routines*.

Program Specification

DOUBLE_SUM

Task: Compute, modulo 2^{16}

$$Y = \sum_{I=1}^{N_A} A_I + \sum_{J=1}^{N_B} B_J = G(A) + G(B)$$

Input: N_A in memory location 1500
N_B in memory location 1502
A_I an array starting at 2000
B_J an array starting at 3000

Output: Result Y stored in memory location 1504

As a simple example of an open subroutine, consider the computation described by the program specification for the program DOUBLE_SUM. The flowchart for this program is shown in Figure 13-17a and the associated assembly language program is given in Figure 13-17b. This program makes use of two open subroutines, one to compute $G(A)$ and one to compute $G(B)$.

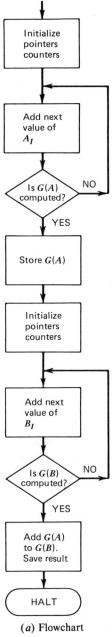

(a) Flowchart

Figure 13-17   Flowchart of program to compute Y of Program DOUBLE_SUM.

```
            .TITLE DOUBLE_SUM

; **************************************************************
;           SUM THE NUMBERS IN THE ARRAYS A AND B MODULO 2^16
;
;INPUT:  BOTH ARRAYS ASSUMED IN MEMORY. NUMBER OF ELEMENTS
;            SPECIFIED BY AN ASSIGNMENT STATEMENT
;
;OUTPUT:RESULT IN MEMORY LOCATION Y
;
; **************************************************************
            NA = ⟨number of elements in A⟩
            NB = ⟨number of elements in B⟩
            . = 1000              ;SET LOCATION COUNTER

                        ;COMPUTE ARRAY SUM OF A

START:   CLR      R0          ;R0 HOLDS PARTIAL SUM
         MOV      NAVAL,R1    ;SET COUNTER
         MOV      #A,R2       ;SET POINTER
LOOP1:   ADD      (R2)+,R0    ;ADD NEXT ELEMENT OF A. INCREMENT POINTER
         DEC      R1          ;SEE IF WE ARE
         BNE      LOOP1       ;FINISHED-NO GET NEXT VALUE
         MOV      R0,R3       ;YES-SAVE SUM IN TEMPORARY STORAGE

                        ;COMPUTE ARRAY SUM OF B

         CLR      R0          ;CLEAR PARTIAL SUM
         MOV      NBVAL,R1    ;SET COUNTER
         MOV      #B,R2       ;SET POINTER
LOOP2:   ADD      (R2)+,R0    ;ADD NEXT ELEMENT OF B. INCREMENT POINTER
         DEC      R1          ;SEE IF WE ARE
         BNE      LOOP2       ;FINISHED-NO GET NEXT VALUE

                        ;COMPUTE TOTAL

         ADD      R3,R0       ;ADD SUM OF A TO SUM OF B
         MOV      R0,Y        ;SAVE RESULT
         HALT                 ;FINISHED

         . = 1500             ;SET DATA AREA
NAVAL:   .WORD    NA          ;NUMBER OF ELEMENTS IN A
NBVAL:   .WORD    NB          ;NUMBER OF ELEMENTS IN B
Y:       .WORD    0           ;LOCATION FOR RESULT
         . = 2000             ;STORAGE LOCATION FOR ARRAY A
A:       .BLKW    NA          ;NA WORDS USED FOR A
         . = 3000             ;STORAGE LOCATION FOR ARRAY B
B:       .BLKW    NB          ;NB WORDS USED FOR B
         .END     START
```

(b) Assembly language program

Both subroutines compute the sum of a sequence of numbers. The only difference between them is the number of elements in the array and the location in memory where the data are stored. Thus before carrying out the summation, we must initialize a counter to count the number of times we traverse the loop and set a pointer to point to the first data element. After completing the initialization, the rest of the instructions carry out the summation. The code that makes up the body of each subroutine is identical except for the way that the initialization takes place.

Closed Subroutines

As the number of lines of code needed to realize a given subroutine increases, it becomes desirable not to repeat that code each time the subroutine is needed. Instead, a special area in memory is set aside and the instructions associated with the subroutine are placed in that area. Whenever it is necessary during the execution of the main program to carry out the computation represented by the subroutine, the main program must transfer control to the subroutine. The calculation is then performed by the subroutine and, when the computation is completed, control is passed back to the main program. Subroutines of this type are called *closed subroutines*.

Figure 13-18 illustrates the major difference between the use of open subroutines and closed subroutines. The in-line subroutine is easily implemented, since it is an integral part of the overall program. Closed subroutines, however, pose a number of special problems.

A closed subroutine consists of a self-contained sequence of instructions that carry out a specific task. Thus the methods used to write the body of a subroutine are the same as those used to write any other program. The only difference is that a closed

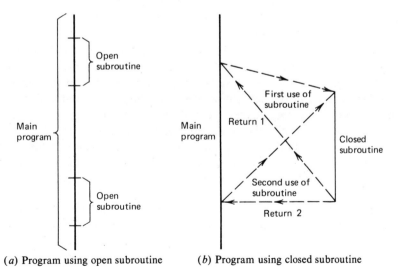

(*a*) Program using open subroutine   (*b*) Program using closed subroutine

Figure 13-18   Illustration of different subroutine structures.

subroutine can be called from any part of the main program. Thus we must consider how we link the main program to a closed subroutine.

There are four questions that must be answered if we are to use closed subroutines in a program. They are:

1. How do we call a subroutine?
2. How does the subroutine locate the data it needs to perform the given task?
3. How does the subroutine determine where it is to store the results of the computation?
4. How do we return to the main program after the subroutine has completed its computation?

Different computers have different ways in which to solve the linkage problem. In SEDCOM II, and many other computer systems, the linkage mechanism involves using a push-down stack and one or more special instructions.

As we discussed in Section 3, a special push-down stack is maintained in memory using the stack pointer (SP) register (CPU register $R6$). One of the purposes of this stack is to assist in the solution of the linkage problem. When a subroutine is called, this stack is used for two purposes:

1. It keeps track of where in the main program the subroutine was called.
2. It is used to pass information between the main program and the subroutine.

To implement a call to a subroutine we use the Jump SubRoutine instruction JSR. This instruction has the form

JSR   PC,⟨destination address⟩

where ⟨destination address⟩ is the address in memory of the first instruction of the subroutine and PC refers to the program counter register $R7$. Figure 13-19 illustrates how this instruction is used.

Just before the JSR instruction is executed, we have the condition shown in Figure 13-19a. The program counter, PC (CPU register $R7$), is pointing at the first word of the JSR instruction. The JSR instruction is a double-operand instruction. The effective address AAA of the subroutine, corresponding to the destination operand, is stored in the supplementary address word of the instruction. Any of the addressing modes may be used to specify the actual address of the subroutine. The easiest one to use, and the one used in this discussion, is the relative addressing mode where the second word of the instruction contains the address of the subroutine relative to the current JSR instruction. In this case the JSR PC,AAA instruction operates in the following manner.

After fetching the instruction the program counter is pointing to the word immediately following the address word. See Figure 13-19b. Unless a change is made by the subroutine, we assume that this is the location to which we wish to return when we have completed the subroutine. At this point the control unit carries out the following steps necessary to execute the JSR instruction.

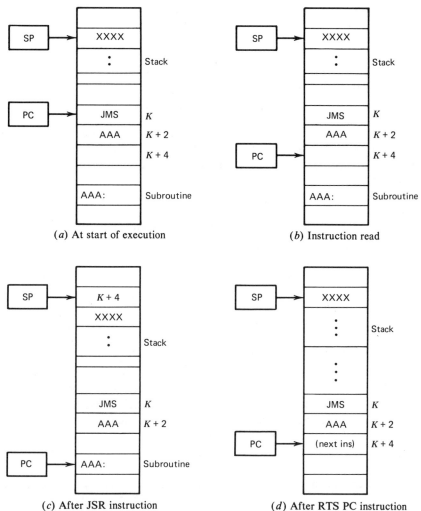

(a) At start of execution

(b) Instruction read

(c) After JSR instruction

(d) After RTS PC instruction

Figure 13-19 Illustration of the execution of the execution JSR   PC, AAA.

1. The content of the program counter is pushed onto the system stack (i.e., the stack pointed to by the stack pointer SP). This is equivalent to the execution of the instruction:

$$\text{MOV} \qquad \text{PC}, -(\text{SP})$$

2. The destination address is computed and placed into the program counter. If AAA is the address of the first word of the subroutine, this is equivalent to the operation:

$$\text{PC} \leftarrow \text{AAA}$$

3. The next instruction is taken from the memory location with address AAA.

The contents of the program counter, the stack pointer, and the stack at the completion of the execution sequence are shown in Figure 13-19c.

To return to the main program from the subroutine, we make use of the ReTurn Subroutine instruction that has the form:

$$\text{RTS} \qquad \text{PC}$$

This instruction *assumes* that the address of the next instruction to be executed in the calling program is stored on the top of the system stack. This address is POPed off the stack and placed into the program counter (PC). Thus the RTS instruction is equivalent to the instruction:

$$\text{MOV} \qquad \text{(SP)+,PC}$$

The behavior of the RTS instruction is illustrated in Figure 13-19d.

The following examples will illustrate the various forms that a subroutine can take and the different ways that information can be passed between the main program and the subroutine. The program holding the JSR instruction is referred to as the *calling routine,* and we say that the subroutine referenced by the JSR instruction has been *called* by the calling routine.

Autonomous Subroutines

The simplest types of subroutines are those that require no information transfer between the main program and the subroutine. This class of subroutine is rather limited, but the following example illustrates how the JSR instruction is used.

Consider the subroutine described by the subroutine specification PRTLINE. This subroutine is used to print a line of the form

_____

on the printer. This line is formed by printing the underline (_) symbol 70_{10} times.

Program Specification

PRTLINE

Task: Print a line of 70_{10} underline symbols on the printer

Input: None

Output: The line of underline symbols printed on the printer. The print head is left positioned at the end of the line.

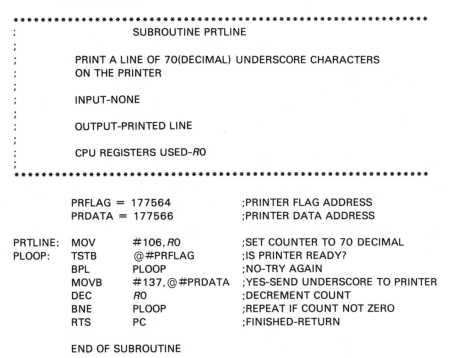

```
          .TITLE PRTLINE

**************************************************************
;                    SUBROUTINE PRTLINE
;
;          PRINT A LINE OF 70(DECIMAL) UNDERSCORE CHARACTERS
;          ON THE PRINTER
;
;          INPUT-NONE
;
;          OUTPUT-PRINTED LINE
;
;          CPU REGISTERS USED-R0
;
**************************************************************

          PRFLAG = 177564          ;PRINTER FLAG ADDRESS
          PRDATA = 177566          ;PRINTER DATA ADDRESS

PRTLINE:  MOV      #106,R0          ;SET COUNTER TO 70 DECIMAL
PLOOP:    TSTB     @#PRFLAG         ;IS PRINTER READY?
          BPL      PLOOP            ;NO-TRY AGAIN
          MOVB     #137,@#PRDATA    ;YES-SEND UNDERSCORE TO PRINTER
          DEC      R0               ;DECREMENT COUNT
          BNE      PLOOP            ;REPEAT IF COUNT NOT ZERO
          RTS      PC               ;FINISHED-RETURN

          END OF SUBROUTINE
```

Figure 13-20   Subroutine to print a line.

Figure 13-20 gives the assembly language program for this task. We have used the rather standard convention of using the name of the subroutine as the label for the first statement in the program. The address of the first instruction of a subroutine must always be a word address. If there is any doubt you should use the .EVEN assembler directive or reset the assembler location counter to an even value before entering the code for the subroutine.

Autonomous subroutines are easy to use. For example, let us assume that we are writing a program to print information on the printer and that we need to print a line. The following segment of code will accomplish this task.

```
          ⟨instruction⟩
                    .
                    .
                    .
          JSR      PC,PRTLINE
          ⟨instruction⟩
                    .
                    .
```

When writing a subroutine we normally assume that we can use any of the CPU registers to hold information while the subroutine is being executed. For example, register $R0$ was used as a counter in the subroutine PRTLINE. This may cause a problem if we are not careful in how this subroutine is used.

Saving Register Values

When we use a subroutine it is prudent to assume that the subroutine may use all of the CPU registers $R0$ through $R5$ in performing the required computation. If these registers are not being used to hold needed information when the subroutine is called, then any changes introduced by the subroutine are of no interest. However, we often call a subroutine while in the middle of a higher level computation and the values stored in one or more of the registers may be needed to continue the computation after returning from the subroutine. When this situation arises we must be very careful about how the needed information is saved. A number of techniques can be used.

One way to save information is to use a sequence of MOV instructions to save the needed information in predefined memory locations. These instructions might have the form

```
        —
        —
MOV   R0,TEMP0
MOV   R1,TEMP1
        —
        —
MOV   R5,TEMP5
        —
```

When we return from the subroutine, we then use the instructions

```
        —
MOV   TEMP0,R0
MOV   TEMP1,R1
        —
        —
MOV   TEMP5,R5
```

to restore the saved values. This approach is somewhat inflexible since special memory locations must be identified and reserved for a special use. A much more flexible approach is to use the system stack as a temporary storage location.

There are two basic methods in common use. They are:

1. Save all important information before the JSR instruction calling the subroutine is executed. The information must be restored after control is returned to the calling routine by the subroutine.

2. Have the subroutine save the information in all of the CPU registers it uses to carry out the required task. The information must be restored before control is returned to the calling routine.

The method selected will often depend upon the particular programming style we favor for implementing programs.

If we adopt a style in which we wish to control which information is saved when we call a subroutine, then we will use method 1 above to save information. This places a greater burden on the programmer but does not waste time storing unneeded information. To illustrate this approach assume that we wish to use the subroutine PRTLINE but that register $R0$ contains important information that we must save before we call the subroutine and restore it after we return. In this situation we can use the following segment of code to call the subroutine.

```
⟨instruction⟩
MOV    R0,−(SP)       ;SAVE CONTENTS OF R0
JSR    PC,PRTLINE     ;CALL SUBROUTINE
MOV    (SP)+,R0       ;RESTORE CONTENTS OF R0
⟨instruction⟩         ;AFTER RETURN FROM SUBROUTINE
```

In this example we first use the stack to temporarily store the contents of $R0$ and then it is used to store the return address when we called the subroutine PRTLINE. After completing the task of printing the line, we return to the calling routine and then restore the value of $R0$ by POPing it off of the stack.

The limitation of this method is that we must know which CPU registers are used by the subroutine or we must save all of the important information. The second approach, method 2, places this burden on the designer of the subroutine. In this case the designer knows exactly which registers the subroutine will use. Upon entry into the subroutine the first task is to save the contents of these registers on the stack. The computation is then performed. When the computation is completed the final task performed by the subroutine is to restore the values of the registers by POPing the saved values from the stack. If we decide to use this approach with the subroutine PRTLINE, the code for the subroutine must be modified as shown on the next page.

In this approach we see that the person writing the portion of the program that calls the subroutine does not have to worry about which register values to save. However, if there is no need to save these values, the subroutine executes several unnecessary steps.

As you gain experience in developing assembly language programs, you will find that both methods of saving register information are useful.

Calling Sequence

A major use of subroutines is to compute the value of a function $F(x_1, x_2, \ldots, x_n)$ for specific values of the arguments $x_1, x_2, \ldots, x_n$. Thus we must provide a way for

```
                —
                —
        JSR   PC,PRTLINE      ;CALL THE SUBROUTINE
                —             ;RETURN FROM SUBROUTINE

            ;REVISED PRTLINE SUBROUTINE

PRTLINE:  MOV  R0,—(SP)       ;SAVE VALUE OF R0 ON STACK
          MOV  #106,R0        ;SET COUNTER TO 70 DECIMAL
PLOOP:    TSTB PRFLAG         ;IS PRINTER READY?
          BPL  PLOOP          ;NO-TRY AGAIN

            ;BODY OF LOOP

          MOVB #137,PRDATA    ;YES-SEND UNDERSCORE TO PRINTER
          DEC  R0             ;DECREMENT COUNT

            ;END OF BODY OF LOOP

          BNE  PLOOP          ;REPEAT IF COUNT NOT ZERO
          MOV  (SP)+,R0       ;RESTORE VALUE OF R0 BEFORE RETURNING
          RTS  PC             ;RETURN TO CALLING PROGRAM
```

the subroutine to have access to these argument values at the time the subroutine is called. After the subroutine has completed its task, it is usually necessary to return one or more values computed by the subroutine back to the calling routine. The technique used to pass information to a subroutine from a calling routine is referred to as the *calling sequence* for the subroutine.

Information to be returned by the subroutine may be transmitted to a known location or it may be transmitted to a location indicated by the calling sequence. There are a variety of methods used to transfer information between the calling routine and the subroutine. The following examples will illustrate some of these techniques.

Local and Global Information

In most subroutines, there are a number of memory locations that store information that is needed only by that subroutine. The contents of these storage areas are of no interest outside of the subroutine. Information of this type is called *local information*, and the memory locations used to store this information are called *local storage*.

One way to pass information between the main program and subroutines or between subroutines is to set aside a set of predefined memory locations that are identified as containing particular items of information. Each subroutine that needs to use that information can then reference it directly. Information of this type is called *global information,* and the locations used to store this information are called *global memory locations.*

Another way to pass information to a subroutine is to use one or more of the registers in the CPU. In this case, the calling sequence brings the information into the proper registers just before the subroutine is called. When the computation performed by the subroutine is complete, the subroutine can also pass information back to the calling program by placing the information into one or more registers before executing the RTS instruction. In this case the registers act as special global memory locations. The following example illustrates these ideas.

Multiplication by Ten

A common task that is used in a number of programs is to multiply a positive integer by 10_{10}. If it is assumed that the number to be multiplied is stored in CPU register $R1$, we can develop a simple subroutine to carry out this task. However, since the largest positive number that can be stored in a 16-bit register is $65,535_{10}$, the largest value that can be placed in $R1$ is $6,553_{10}$. Otherwise the result will be larger than can be held in register $R1$. To realize the subroutine TIME10 defined by the Subroutine Specification given below we must investigate how this multiplication process can be performed.

Subroutine Specification

TIME10

Task: Compute

$$R1 \leftarrow 10_{10} * R1$$

Input: Value placed in $R1$. The value must be $< 6,554_{10}$.

Output: Result is in $R1$.

Registers
Used: None except $R1$.

To understand how this task is performed we consider the following example. Assume that we wish to multiply the following 16-bit binary number

$$0\ 0\ 0\ 1\ 0\ 1\ 1\ 0\ 1\ 0\ 0\ 1\ 1\ 1\ 1\ 1$$

by

$$10_{10} = 1010_2.$$

Carrying out this task by hand gives

```
      0  0  0  1  0  1  1  0  1  0  0  1  1  1  1  1
                                    1  0  1  0
```

```
      0  0  0  0  0  0  0  0  0  0  0  0  0  0  0  0    Shift R1
      0  0  0  1  0  1  1  0  1  0  0  1  1  1  1  1   ← left 1 bit
   0  0  0  0  0  0  0  0  0  0  0  0  0  0  0  0       Shift R1
0  0  0  1  0  1  1  0  1  0  0  1  1  1  1  1          ← left 3 bits
```

```
0  0  0  1  1  1  0  0  0  1  0  0  0  1  1  0  1  1  0
|←  ↘ →|←——————————— 16 bits ———————————————→|
   Disregard these bits
```

Using this example we see that the operation of multiplying the contents of $R1$ by 10_{10} can be represented as

$$R1 \leftarrow SL(R1) + SL(SL(SL(R1)))$$

where $SL(R1)$ is the operation of shifting the contents of $R1$ one bit to the left. The flowchart of this operation is shown in Figure 13-21 a and the corresponding assembly language program is given in Figure 13-21 b.

In this program we use the system stack for the temporary storage of the quantity $SL(R1)$. Note that when we push the value stored in $R1$ onto the stack, the value also remains in the register $R1$. We then shift the contents of $R1$ left two more times.

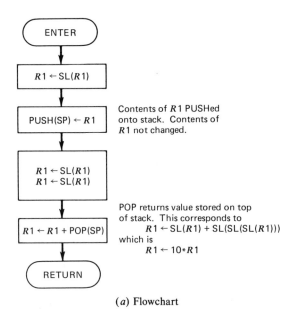

(a) Flowchart

Figure 13-21   Subroutine for TIME 10.

```
                .TITLE TIME10

;  ************************************************************
;
;                SUBROUTINE TIME10
;
;        MULTIPLY THE CONTENTS OF CPU REGISTER R1 BY 10₁₀
;
;        INPUT-THE INITIAL VALUE IN R1. VALUE ( 6,554
;
;        OUTPUT-THE INITIAL VALUE MULTIPLIED BY 10₁₀ IN R1
;
;        CPU REGISTERS USED-R1
;
;  ************************************************************

                           ;ENTER WITH VALUE IN R1
TIME10:   ASL  R1           ;CARRY OUT FIRST SHIFT
          MOV  R1,-(SP)     ;AND PUSH ONTO STACK
          ASL  R1
          ASL  R1           ;SHIFT THREE TIMES
          ADD  (SP)+,R1     ;POP SAVED VALUE AND ADD
          RTS  PC           ;RETURN-ANSWER IN R1
```

(*b*) Assembly language program

Figure 13-21 (Continued)

Finally we complete the operation by adding the value stored on the stack to the current contents of $R1$. This is the desired result and we return to the calling program with this view in $R1$ as required. It should be observed that the operation

$$\text{ADD} \qquad (\text{SP})+, R1$$

serves the dual purpose of POPing the temporarily stored value of $SL(R1)$ from the stack and then adding this value to the current contents of $R1$. At the completion of this operation $SL(R1)$ has been removed from the stack and the quantity on top of the stack is the address to which we want to return when the RTS instruction is executed.

This example shows one simple way to pass information to a subroutine. The next example illustrates the use of pointers and global memory locations to accomplish a somewhat more general information transfer.

Double-precision Addition

In SEDCOM II each 16-bit word can hold a positive decimal integer value between 0 and 65,535. There are some cases in which we may wish to work with integers that exceed this range. One way to do this is to use two words to represent the integer. The resulting integer value is said to be a *double-precision integer*. When we wish to add two double-precision integers we cannot do this by simply using the ADD instruction. Instead we must use a subroutine to carry out this task. The double-precision integer add subroutine DPIADD, defined by the following subroutine specification, illustrates one form that this subroutine might take.

Subroutine Specification

DPIADD

Task: Compute
$$A \leftarrow A + B$$
$C = 1$ if there is an overflow.

Input: A is a double-precision positive integer located in memory locations 1000 and 1002. B is a double-precision positive integer. The address of B is placed in register $R0$ as part of the calling sequence.

Output: The result is left in the memory locations 1000 and 1002. This is called the DOUBLE-PRECISION INTEGER ACCUMULATOR.

Registers   Register $R0$ is used to hold the address of B.
Used: Upon return from the subroutine C is 1 if there is an overflow.

To implement this addition operation we use the two words at memory locations 1000 and 1002 as global memory locations that form the *DOUBLE-PRECISION INTEGER ACCUMULATOR*. This area is denoted by the address DPIAC associated with the word that holds the least significant bits of the argument. The first argument for the addition operation is found in these two words. The first word contains the least significant bits and the second word contains the most significant bits. To locate the second argument we place the address of the first word of the second argument in register $R0$ just before the subroutine DPIADD is called. After the subroutine is completed the result is left in the global memory location we have indicated as DPIAC.

The assembly language program needed to realize DPIADD is given in Figure 13-22. Examining this program we see that we do not use any local storage. Next we note that we add the first words of the double precision operands using the standard ADD instruction. If the result is greater than 65,535, the carry flag C will be set, indicating that a carry was generated. Otherwise C is 0. The carry must be propagated to the second word. Thus the next instruction ADC adds the carry bit to the second word of DPIAC. Finally the second add instruction is used to complete the addition of the second word of the two operands. The double-precision integer accumulator now contains the sum of the two double-precision integers and the C flag will be set if there is an overflow. We return from the subroutine at this point.

.TITLE DPIADD

```
;***************************************************************
;
;                      SUBROUTINE DPIADD
;
;              DOUBLE PRECISION ADD THE NUMBER IN DPIAC.
;              TO THE NUMBER B AND LEAVE RESULT IN DPIAC.
;              OVERFLOW INDICATED BY C = 1
;
;              INPUT-FIRST OPERAND IN DPIAC
;                      SECOND OPERAND ADDRESS IN R0
;
;              OUTPUT-RESULT IN DPIAC
;              C = 1 IF OVERLOW
;
;              CPU REGISTERS USED-R0
;
;***************************************************************
;
```

```
            . = 1000              ;DEFINE DPIAC
DPIAC:      .WORD 0               ;LEAST SIGNIFICANT BITS
DPIACH:     .WORD 0               ;MOST SIGNIFICANT BITS
            . = 2000              ;START OF SUBROUTINE
DPIADD:     ADD  (R0)+,DPIAC      ;ADD LEAST SIGNIFICANT BITS
            ADC  DPIACH           ;ADD CARRY FROM LSB IF GENERATED
            ADD  (R0),DPIACH      ;ADD MOST SIGNIFICANT BITS
            RTS  PC               ;RETURN C = 1 IF OVERFLOW

            ;END OF SUBROUTINE
```

Figure 13-22   Subroutine to do double precision integer add.

A typical calling sequence for DPIADD is shown below. It is assumed that the first operand is already stored in DPIAC. Thus before calling the addition subroutine we must load the address of the second operand into $R0$. As soon as this is accomplished we call the subroutine.

```
            .
            .
            MOV #B,R0             ;PLACE ADDRESS OF OPERAND B IN R0
            JSR PC,DPIADD         ;CALL ADDITION SUBROUTINE
            ⟨next instruction⟩    ;ANSWER IN DPIAC
            .
            .
```

The use of the CPU registers and global memory locations to pass information to or from a subroutine is quite common. It does place a limitation on the programmer, since particular memory locations must be reserved for this global data and only six registers are available for use in the CPU. Some of these difficulties can be removed if we generalize the idea of a pointer so that it can be used to indicate specific collections of data.

Parameter Passing Using Linking Pointers

From the most general viewpoint we can think of a subroutine as a process that evaluates a set of functions that can be represented in the following form:

$$z_1 = F_1(x_1, x_2, \ldots, x_n)$$
$$z_2 = F_2(x_1, x_2, \ldots, x_n)$$

$$.$$
$$.$$
$$.$$

$$x_m = F_m(x_1, x_2, \ldots, z_n)$$

where m or n or both are greater than 1. If we are to use a subroutine to evaluate these functions and to return the results to the calling program, we must provide a systematic means whereby the subroutine can locate the specific values of the arguments

$$x_1, x_2, \ldots, x_n$$

and a way by which the results

$$z_1, z_2, \ldots, z_m$$

can be stored for later use.

One way to do this is to use one or more of the CPU registers as pointer registers. In this case we group data in memory and place the address of the first data word into one of the CPU registers. The data are then accessed using one of the standard deferred modes of addressing. This technique can also be used if we wish to return information to the calling program from a subroutine. The address used to indicate the data areas that will provide or receive information are called *linkage pointers* and the registers that hold these pointers may be called *linkage registers*.

The Subroutine STRSIZE

The way in which linkage pointers are used is illustrated by the subroutine STRSIZE defined by the following subroutine specification. The data being processed consists of a string of ASCII characters that are stored in successive bytes in memory. The end of the string is indicated by an *end marker*. In this case it is assumed that the end marker is the *null byte*, which contains 0_8. The length of the string is the number of characters in the string not counting the end marker. Figure 13-23 illustrates how a character string would appear in memory under this convention.

Byte address   Contents of byte

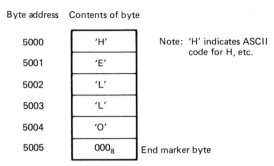

5000	'H'
5001	'E'
5002	'L'
5003	'L'
5004	'O'
5005	000_8

Note: 'H' indicates ASCII code for H, etc.

End marker byte

Figure 13-23   Method used to encode string HELLO in memory.

Subroutine Specification

STRSIZE

Task:
Compute the length (number of characters) in a character string. The end of the string is indicated by an end marker consisting of a byte containing 0_8.

Input:
Address of first byte of the string in $R1$.
Address of memory word to receive value of string length in $R2$.

Output:
Length of the string placed in the memory location whose address is found in $R2$. $R1$ is pointing at the end marker.

Registers Used:
Registers $R1$, $R2$, and $R0$.
Value in $R0$ is saved on stack before subroutine is executed and restored before returning.

When using this subroutine it is the responsibility of the calling sequence to set up the linkage pointers and any data associated with the pointers. The assembly language program used to carry out this computation is shown in Figure 13-24. Examining this program we see that the register $R0$ serves as a counter and registers $R1$ and $R2$ serve as linkage registers. The calling sequence must place the address of the first byte of the character string to be processed in $R1$ and the address of the memory word that will receive the result in $R2$. It is the responsibility of the subroutine to initialize $R0$ to 0 before the counting process begins. However, before we do this initialization, we store the value currently in $R0$ on the system stack since it is assumed that this value may be needed when we return from the subroutine.

After we have scanned the string and counted the number of characters present, we deposit the value of the length of the string in the memory word indicated by $R2$

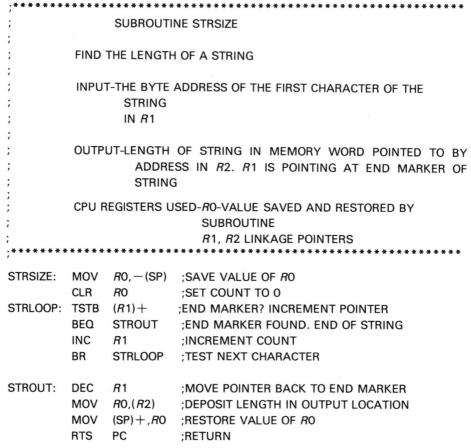

```
                .TITLE STRSIZE

;*************************************************************
;                  SUBROUTINE STRSIZE
;
;          FIND THE LENGTH OF A STRING
;
;          INPUT-THE BYTE ADDRESS OF THE FIRST CHARACTER OF THE
;                  STRING
;                  IN R1
;
;          OUTPUT-LENGTH OF STRING IN MEMORY WORD POINTED TO BY
;                  ADDRESS IN R2. R1 IS POINTING AT END MARKER OF
;                  STRING
;
;          CPU REGISTERS USED-R0-VALUE SAVED AND RESTORED BY
;                  SUBROUTINE
;                  R1, R2 LINKAGE POINTERS
;*************************************************************
STRSIZE:  MOV    R0,-(SP)    ;SAVE VALUE OF R0
          CLR    R0          ;SET COUNT TO 0
STRLOOP:  TSTB   (R1)+       ;END MARKER? INCREMENT POINTER
          BEQ    STROUT      ;END MARKER FOUND. END OF STRING
          INC    R1          ;INCREMENT COUNT
          BR     STRLOOP     ;TEST NEXT CHARACTER

STROUT:   DEC    R1          ;MOVE POINTER BACK TO END MARKER
          MOV    R0,(R2)     ;DEPOSIT LENGTH IN OUTPUT LOCATION
          MOV    (SP)+,R0    ;RESTORE VALUE OF R0
          RTS    PC          ;RETURN
```

Figure 13-24 Subroutine STRSIZE.

and restore the original value of $R0$. Upon returning we find that the linkage pointer in $R1$ is pointing at the end marker associated with the string that has just been processed.

Call-by-Value and Call-by-Reference

When we pass the value of a parameter directly to a subroutine, as we did in the subroutine TIME10, we say that we have used a *call-by-value* to pass the argument to the subroutine. When we pass the address of the information, such as the address of the character string in the subroutine STRSIZE, we say that we have used a *call-by-reference* to pass argument information to the subroutine. Both techniques are used extensively in programming.

When we pass information from a particular memory location to a subroutine using a call-by-value, there is no way for the subroutine to know where that information came from. This value can be modified by the subroutine and will not influence the original value of the information stored in memory. However, when we use a call-by-reference, we actually pass the address of the information that is to be processed to the subroutine. The subroutine may, if desired by the programmer, modify the value of the information stored in memory. Thus we see that a call-by-value isolates the information in memory from the calculations carried out in the subroutine while a call-by-reference allows the subroutine to have access to the original value of the information in memory.

Managing Register Information

As indicated previously, when we use one or more of the CPU registers in a subroutine, it is the responsibility of the subroutine programmer to save the information in the shared registers before starting the subroutine and to restore it after the subroutine has completed its work. This may be done either in the subroutine or as part of the calling sequence. However, when one or more of the CPU registers are needed to pass information to the subroutine as part of the calling sequence, then it is the responsibility of the calling sequence to save any needed information found in the registers used to pass information.

The normal way to store register information is to place it on the system stack. For example, assume that we wish to use a subroutine called EXAMP that uses registers $R2$, $R3$, and $R4$ to carry out a computation and that it is passed information by a calling sequence that uses register $R1$. The following segment of code illustrates how the information currently in these registers is preserved while the subroutine is executed:

```
        MOV  R1,-(SP)        ;SAVE VALUE OF R1
        MOV  (value),R1      ;GET DATA TO BE PASSED
        JSR  PC,EXAMP        ;CALL SUBROUTINE
        MOV  (SP)+,R1        ;RESTORE R1
        .
        .
        .
             ;SUBROUTINE EXAMP

EXAMP:  MOV  R2,-(SP)        ;SAVE R2 ON STACK
        MOV  R3,-(SP)        ;SAVE R3 ON STACK
        MOV  R4,-(SP)        ;SAVE R4 ON STACK
             (CARRY OUT
             (SUBROUTINE
             (UNTIL FINISHED
        MOV  (SP)+,R4        ;RESTORE R4 FROM STACK
        MOV  (SP)+,R3        ;RESTORE R3 FROM STACK
        MOV  (SP)+,R2        ;RESTORE R2 FROM STACK
        RTS  PC              ;RETURN FROM SUBROUTINE
```

Examining this code segment we note that the information is stored on the stack in last-in first-out order. Thus the restoration of the register values is in the reverse order than that in which they were saved.

Whenever we design a subroutine we should be very careful to indicate which registers it uses. It is then the responsibility of the programmer to make sure that any information in those registers that will be needed later in the calculation is stored before the subroutine is called. Failure to do this can lead to program errors that are often very difficult to locate and correct.

Subroutine Usage

Subroutines can be very valuable when developing complex programs. They allow the programmer to divide the program into a collection of manageable modules each of which can be written and tested independently. However, we must be careful not to overuse subroutines in a program since each time we use a subroutine we must introduce the extra code necessary to link the subroutine to the calling program. If the subroutine is small, it might turn out that the code needed to do the linkage exceeds the number of statements in the subroutine. Thus the conceptual advantage of modularizing a program is negated by the inefficiency of the resulting program.

Subroutines can take many forms, and many different types of calling sequences can be used to link a subroutine to the invoking program. The following sections will further illustrate many of the important uses for subroutines. The references at the end of this chapter illustrate a number of other techniques that can be used to link subroutines.

EXERCISES

1. Write a double-precision integer subtraction subroutine SUBINT.

2. Rewrite the program for DOUBLE_SUM. Use a single closed subroutine to compute the array sums $G(A)$ and $\overline{G}(B)$.

3. Write a subroutine SMUL10 that will multiply the signed integer stored in register $R1$ by 10_{10}. What restriction must be placed upon the values stored in $R1$?

4. Write a double-precision addition subroutine that will add two double-precision signed numbers. The V flag should be set if there is an arithmetic overflow.

5. Write a subroutine that will count the number of space characters in a character sequence that is terminated by the null end marker 0_8.

5. NUMERICAL CALCULATIONS

Numerical calculations play a very important role in many information processing tasks. It might therefore seem that we have imposed a considerable limitation on SEDCOM II because we have included only the addition operation ADD and the subtraction operation SUB in the basic instruction set. This limitation can be eliminated by developing special subroutines to provide the mathematical operations not included in the basic instruction set. A time penalty is incurred for this approach since a larger number of machine instructions must be executed to carry out each operation. This section illustrates how different types of subroutines can be developed to perform specific classes of numerical calculations.

Fixed-point Multiplication

In Chapter 9 we saw that we could build a digital network that would multiply two r-bit positive numbers and produce a $2r$-bit result. This task required three r-bit registers, a 1-bit overflow register, and a sequence of shifting and addition operations that were controlled by the network's control unit. To implement the same operation as a subroutine we must perform the same sequence of operations using the available machine language instructions.

The subroutine FIXMUL defined by the following subroutine specification carries out the fixed-point multiplication of two 16-bit positive numbers and produces a 32-bit result. Examining this specification we see that the CPU registers $R0$, $R1$, and $R2$ replace the hardware registers used in the hardware multiplier and the C flag is used as the 1-bit overflow register. The calling sequence for this subroutine must first save the information in registers $R0$, $R1$, $R2$, and $R3$ if any of this information is needed after the multiplication operation is completed. Next the calling sequence places the multiplier in $R1$ and the multiplicand in $R2$. Upon returning from the subroutine we find the result in the 32-bit "register" $[R0, R1]$. The most significant bits of the result are found in $R0$ and the least significant bits are found in $R1$.

Subroutine Specification

FIXMUL

Task: Compute

$$Y \leftarrow A*B$$

Input: A, the multiplier, is a 16-bit positive number stored in CPU register $R1$.
             B, the multiplicand, is a 16-bit positive number stored in CPU reguster $R2$.

Output: Y, the product, is a 32-bit positive number. The higher order 16 bits are stored in $R0$ and the lower order 16 bits are in $R1$. $R2$ is not changed.

Registers Used: $R0$, $R1$, $R2$, $R3$

The flowchart for the algorithm needed to carry out this operation is given in Figure 13-25a and the corresponding assembly language program is given in Figure 13-25b. To understand this subroutine it is necessary to consider the fine details of the tasks performed by the machine language instructions used in this subroutine.

First we note that the C flag does double duty in this program. Each time that we enter the loop the C flag contains the rightmost bit of the multiplier register. If this bit is 1 then the multiplicand is added to $R0$. At this point the C flag is used as an overflow bit. The rotation operation that rotates the combined "register" $[R0, R1]$ one bit right takes the value initially in C and rotates it into the highest order bit of $R0$ and takes the lowest order bit of $R1$ and rotates it into the C register. After this rotation the count in $R3$ is decremented. If the result is 0, we know that we have

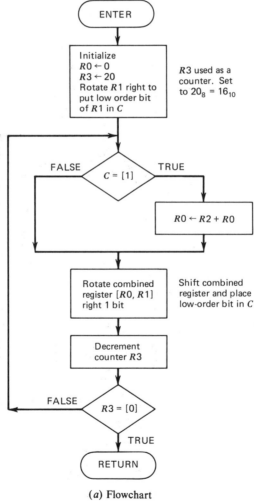

(a) Flowchart

Figure 13-25   The algorithm FIXMUL.

.TITLE FIXMUL

```
;******************************************************************
;
;                SUBROUTINE FIXMUL
;
;        MULTIPLICATION OF TWO 16-BIT POSITIVE NUMBERS TO PRODUCE A
;        32-BIT RESULT.
;
;        INPUT-MULTIPLIER IN REGISTER R1
;                MULTIPLICAND IN REGISTER R2
;
;        OUTPUT-32-BIT RESULT IN [R0, R1]. HIGH ORDER BITS IN R0 AND
;                                LOW ORDER BITS IN R1.
;
;        REGISTERS USED-R0, R1, R2, R3
;
;******************************************************************

FIXMUL:    CLR   R0          ;INITIALIZE REGISTERS
           MOV   #20, R3      ;COUNTER SET TO 16 DECIMAL
           ROR   R1           ;PREPARE TO CHECK 1ST BIT OF R1
FMLOOP:    BCC   FMNEXT       ;IF C IS 0 SKIP NEXT OPERATION
           ADD   R2, R0       ;PARTIAL ADDITION
FMNEXT:    ROR   R0           ;SHIFT RIGHT ONE BIT COMBINED
           ROR   R1           ;REGISTER. SET C TO CHECK 1ST BIT R1
           DEC   R3           ;DECREMENT COUNTER.
           BNE   FMLOOP       ;REPEAT LOOP IF COUNT NOT 0.
           RTS   PC           ;RETURN WITH RESULT IN [R0, R1]

           ;END OF SUBROUTINE FIXMUL
```

(*b*) Subroutine

Figure 13-25 (Continued)

gone around the loop the required number of times and that the result is in [$R0$, $R1$]. If the count is not 0, we know that we must go around the loop another time. Note that when we carry out the DEC operation on $R3$, the value of C is not affected.

The best way in which to completely understand the operation of this subroutine is to carry out each of the steps by hand on typical values. A similar program can be developed to carry out fixed-point division.

Floating-point (Real) Number Representation

In the programming of computations involving noninteger single- or multiple-precision data, the programmer must keep track of the position of the scale point (i.e., binary point in a binary number). Numbers representing such data are called *real numbers* or *floating-point* numbers. Once numbers are entered into the computer, there is no hardware available to keep track of the location of the scale point. This point exists only in the mind of the programmer, who is responsible for keeping track of its imaginary position and correctly interpreting the result of any calculations performed on these numbers.

When discussing real numbers in a computer, we use a binary floating-point notation with the following general form

$$\pm(.m_{-1}m_{-2}\dots m_{-r})2^{\pm e_u e_{u-1}\cdots e_1 e_0}$$

where

$$\pm(e_u e_{u-1}\dots e_1 e_0)$$

is called the *exponent* of the number and

$$\pm(.m_{-1}m_{-2}\dots m_{-r})$$

is the *mantissa*. The exponent is an integer and the mantissa is a binary fraction that is always stored in normalized form where all of the leading 0's are eliminated from the binary representation. Thus the highest order bit, m_{-1}, is always 1 except in the special case where the numerical value of the number is set to zero. In this case the mantissa consists of all 0's and the exponent also has a value of 0. The exponent represents the power of 2 by which the mantissa is multiplied to obtain the number's value when it is used in a computation.

For example, the floating-point representation of
$$101101.101 \text{ is } (.101101101) \times 2^{110}$$
while the representation of
$$.0010101 \text{ is } (.10101) \times 2^{-10}.$$

In the above examples the number in the parentheses represents the mantissa, and the exponent of 2, which is given in binary form, represents the exponent of the number. If a single computer word is large enough, it can store a floating-point number as indicated in Figure 13-26a. The word is divided into two fields. The first field holds the value of the exponent and the second field holds the value of the mantissa.

Sixteen bit words, such as found in SEDCOM II, are much too small to store floating-point values. Thus two words are used to store the value of a floating-point number. The coding used, which has been selected for illustrative purposes only, is shown in Figure 13-26b. (This representation is different from that used in the PDP-11 family of computers.)

The exponent of the number, stored in 2's complement form, is held in the rightmost byte of the first word. The mantissa is represented as a sign-magnitude fraction in which the leftmost bit of the first word is the sign bit and the second word holds the magnitude of the fraction.

With this definition it is seen that the magnitude of a non-zero floating-point number A falls in the range

$$.1 \times 2^{-127_{10}} \leq A \leq .1111111111111111 \times 2^{127_{10}}$$

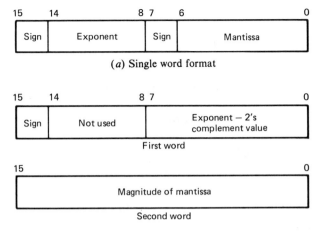

(a) Single word format

(b) Multiple word format

Figure 13-26 Format used to represent floating point numbers.

Any value of A less than the minimum value is taken as 0, while any value larger than the maximum value is considered an *overflow value*. As long as the value of A falls in the allowed range, the magnitude of the mantissia is always adjusted so that the leftmost bit is 1. Whenever A drops below the allowed range (i.e., $A < .1 \times 2^{-127_{10}}$) we have an *underflow condition* and A is set to 0. This is accomplished by setting all of the bits in the mantissa, the sign bit, and the exponent to 0. If there is an overflow, the resulting value is undefined. This is indicated by setting the C flag in the processor status register to 1.

This representation of a floating-point number is wasteful in that it does not use 7 bits of the first word. There are a number of advanced techniques used to represent floating-point numbers in digital systems that make use of these bits. However, the purpose of this discussion is to introduce the problems that must be considered when working with floating-point information. Thus the representation shown in Figure 13-26b was selected to simplify our discussion. It also makes it much easier to write the subroutines needed to carry out the desired floating-point operations.

Some computer systems provide special hardware to carry out all of the basic floating-point operations. SEDCOM II does not have this capability. Calculations involving floating-point arithmetic must use subroutines to carry out the standard arithmetic operations. These subroutines must deal with both the value of the exponent and the value of the mantissa of the numbers involved in the calculation.

Multiplication of Two Floating-point Numbers

To illustrate some of the problems that must be considered when floating-point arithmetic operations are performed we develop a multiplication subroutine that multiplies two positive non-zero floating-point numbers A and B and places the result in the location that held the original value of A. This subroutine is defined by the subroutine specification FLMUL.

Subroutine Specification

FLMUL

Task:	Compute

$$A \leftarrow A * B$$

Input: A is a positive floating point number. The address of the first word of A is in $R0$.
B is a positive floating point number. The address of the first word of B is in $R1$.
Both A and B are assumed to be non-zero

Output: The result replaces the original value of A.
C is set to 1 if there is an overflow. Otherwise C is set to 0.

Subroutines Used: The fixed point multiplication subroutine FIXMUL.

Registers Used: $R0, R1, R2, R3, R4, R5$

Assume that the two numbers have the form

$$A = m_a 2^{e_a} \qquad m_a > 0$$
$$B = m_b 2^{e_b} \qquad m_b > 0$$

Then the product is given by

$$A*B = \begin{cases} \text{overflow} & \text{if } e_a + e_b > 127_{10} \\ m_a m_b 2^{e_a + e_b} & \text{in range} \\ 0 & \text{if } e_a + e_b < -127_{10} \end{cases}$$

Thus to form the product we must add exponents and multiply the mantissas. Since we can treat the mantissa of a number as an integer, provided we keep track of the location of the binary point, we can use the fixed-point multiplication subroutine FIXMUL previously developed to carry out the multiplication of the mantissas. The addition of the exponent is carried out using standard addition. However, we must be careful to see that the result does not exceed the allowed range of our numbers. If there is an underflow the resulting value must be set to 0, and if there is an overflow the C flag must be set.

A flowchart describing the algorithm used to realize FLMUL is given in Figure 13-27a and the corresponding program is given in Figure 13-27b. To start this oper-

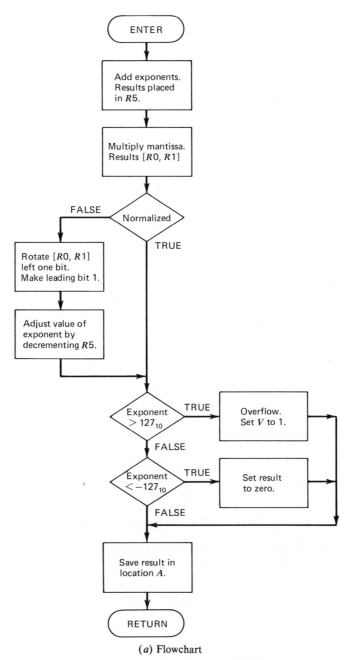

(a) Flowchart

Figure 13-27 The algorithm FLMUL.

```
            .TITLE FLMUL

;*********************************************************************
;                    SUBROUTINE FLMUL
;
;         MULTIPLICATION OF TWO POSITIVE FLOATING-POINT NUMBERS
;
;         INPUT-ADDRESS OF MULTIPLIER A IN REGISTER R0
;         ADDRESS OF MULTIPLICAND IN REGISTER R1
;
;         OUTPUT-RESULT REPLACES THE ORIGINAL VALUE OF A
;                 FLAG C = 1 IF OVERFLOW
;                 FLAG C = 0 IF NO OVERFLOW
;                 RESULT SET TO ZERO IF UNDERFLOW
;
;         REGISTERS USED-R0, R1, R2, R3, R4, R5
;
;         SUBROUTINES USED-FIXMUL
;*********************************************************************

FLMUL:    MOV   R0, -(SP)     ;SAVE ADDRESS OF MULTIPLIER

                  ;ADD THE EXPONENTS OF TWO OPERATORS

          MOVB  (R0),R4       ;GET EXPONENT OF MULTIPLIER
          MOVB  (R1),R5       ;GET EXPONENT OF MULTIPLICAN
          ADD   R4,R5         ;ADD EXPONENTS. SUM IN R5

                  ;MULTIPLY THE MANTISSA

          MOV   2(R1),R2      ;GET MULTIPLICAND MANTISSA
          MOV   2(R0),R1      ;GET MULTIPLIER MANTISSA
          JSR   PC,FIXMUL     ;CALL FIXMUL SUBROUTINE
                              ;RESULT IN [R0,R1]

                  ;CHECK IF RESULT MUST BE NORMALIZED

          TST   R0            ;IS FIRST BIT OF R0 A 1 (R0 NEGATIVE)
          BMI   FNORM         ;YES-NO NORMALIZATION NEEDED
          ROL   R1            ;ROTATE [R0,R1] LEFT 1 BIT TO
          ROL   R0            ;NORMALIZE.
          DEC   R5            ;ADJUST EXPONENT VALUE

                  ;SEE IF THERE IS AN OVERFLOW OR UNDERFLOW

FNORM:    CMP   #177,R5       ;OVEFLOW 127DEC-EXP < 0
          BLT   FOVF          ;OVERFLOW-SET C FLAG
          CMP   #177601,R5    ;UNDERFLOW-127DEC-EXP > 0
          CLC                 ;SET C TO 0 NO OVERFLOW
          BLT   FFIN          ;NO UNDERFLOW FINISH
          CLR   R5            ;SET RESULT TO
          CLR   R0            ;ZERO
          BR    FFIN          ;SAVE RESULT
FOVF:     SEC                 ;SET C TO 1 TO INDICATE OVERFLOW
```

(*b*) Subroutine

Figure 13-27   (Continued)

```
                    ;SAVE RESULT IN MULTIPLIER LOCATION

FFIN:       MOV   (SP)+,R3      ;GET SAVED ADDRESS
            MOVB  #0,1(R3)      ;RESULT A POSITIVE NUMBER. C NOT CHANGED
            MOVB  R5,(R3)       ;SAVE EXPONENT OF RESULT
            MOV   R0,2(R3)      ;SAVE MANTISSA OF RESULT
            RTS   PC            ;RETURN WITH VALUE IN MULTIPLIER LOCATION
                               ;AND C FLAG SET TO 1 IF OVERFLOW

                    ;SUBROUTINE FIXMUL

FIXMUL:     CLR   R0            ;INITIALIZE REGISTERS
            MOV   #20,R3        ;COUNTER SET TO 16 DECIMAL
            ROR   R1            ;PREPARE TO CHECK 1ST BIT OF R1
FMLOOP:     BCC   FMNEXT        ;IF C IS 0 SKIP NEXT OPERATION
            ADD   R2,R0         ;PARTIAL ADDITION
FMNEXT:     ROR   R0            ;SHIFT RIGHT ONE BIT COMBINED
            ROR   R1            ;REGISTER. SET C TO CHECK 1ST BIT R1
            DEC   R3            ;DECREMENT COUNTER.
            BNE   FMLOOP        ;REPEAT LOOP IF COUNT NOT 0.
            RTS   PC            ;RETURN WITH RESULT IN [R0,R1]

            ;END OF SUBROUTINE FIXMUL

                    ;END OF SUBROUTINE FLMUL
```

Figure 13-27   (Continued)

ation it is assumed that $R0$ holds the address of the first word of A and that $R1$ holds the address of the first word of B. Upon returning from the subroutine, A will have the new value and C will be set to 0 if the new value is within the allowed range.

The FLMUL Subroutine

Examining the assembly language program for FLMUL we see that it is much more complex than the previous programs. It is therefore instructive to examine some of the details of this program because a number of new programming techniques are used.

When we enter the program, the first thing that we must do is to save the value of the address of A. This value, which is placed in $R0$ by the calling sequence, is stored on the system stack by the first instruction. The next task is to add the exponents of A and B. To do this we must move the first byte of each floating-point number to a CPU register.

Whenever the MOVB instruction is used to move a byte to a CPU register, the transfer is carried out in a special manner. The byte indicated by the source address is always placed in the low-order byte of the register. The high-order byte of the register is set to zero if bit 7 of the transferred byte is 0 or to 377_8 if bit 7 of the transferred byte is 1. This has the effect of loading the full register with a numerical value, which is the same value as held by the byte involved in the transfer. The following example illustrates this transfer:

Instruction		**MOVB** $A,R4$	
Before		**After**	
A	0000000011101010	A	0000000011101010
$R4$	1011001000101010	$R4$	1111111111101010

Sign
Extended

After the two exponent values are loaded in $R4$ and $R5$, we add them together and leave the result in $R5$. Next we must introduce the calling sequence to set up the call to the subroutine FIXMUL. We use index addressing to read the second word (the mantissa) of each floating-point operand to the registers used by FIXMUL. The fixed point multiplication is then completed and the result is left in combined register $[R0, R1]$.

If the leftmost bit of $R0$ is 0, we must normalize the result by rotating the information in $[R0, R1]$ one bit to the left and decrease the value of the exponent by 1. Otherwise we have completed the operation on the mantissa.

The final task is to check the result to see whether there is an overflow or an underflow. This can be done by testing the value of the exponent. If this value is greater than 127_{10}, we know an overflow condition is present and indicate it by setting C to 1. If the exponent is less than -127_{10}, then an underflow has occurred and the resulting value is set to 0.

The last step in the subroutine consists of POPing the address of A off of the system stack and then using that address to store the result in the memory location indicated by this address. Note that we have again used indexed addressing to transfer the needed information. In particular we use the instruction

MOVB #0,1($R3$)

to make sure that the sign bit of the result is set to 0 to indicate a positive value. This instruction was selected, instead of the instruction

CLRB 1($R3$)

because we wished to preserve the value of C. The MOVB instruction does not affect the current value of C, while the CLRB instruction always sets C to 0.

Having thus completed the floating-point multiplication operation, we then return to the calling program. All of the other basic arithmetic operations can be realized using similar subroutines.

This completes our rather brief discussion of the techniques used for representing the numerical operations that are not included in the basic instruction set of SED-

COM II. However, with many other problems we must be able to deal with symbolic information as well as numeric information. As shown in the next section, we can also develop a number of subroutines to assist with this class of computations.

EXERCISES

1. Modify the multiplication subroutines FLMUL so that any two floating-point numbers (positive or negative) can be multiplied. Assume that neither of the numbers is zero.

2. Write a subroutine DUBCMP that will compare the two double-precision numbers expressed in 2's complement notation. The N, Z, V, and C flags of the processor status register PS are set according to the same conditions that are used when the CMP machine language instruction is executed.

6. SYMBOLIC INFORMATION PROCESSING

Most of the examples considered so far have involved numerical calculations. However, a computer is really a symbol manipulator, and it is just as easy to work with character or symbolic information as it is to work with numeric data. In this section we investigate some of the typical ways that symbolic information may be processed.

Characters and Character Strings

When dealing with symbolic information the basic data types involved are characters and character strings. All modern higher level languages support the character data type and most support the character string data type. If we wish to write a program in one of these languages that involves the manipulation of character or character string information, we find that we have a number of built-in functions and operations that help us in our programming effort. These facilities mean that we can write very complex programs without having to consider either the internal data representation or algorithms used by the programming language to carry out the desired tasks. To provide the same capabilities at the assembly language level we must decide upon a standard method to represent symbolic information and develop a collection of subroutines that can be used to carry out the necessary operations on these data elements. The following conventions are used to represent symbolic information.

Standard Representation of Character Data

In SEDCOM II all characters are represented by the ASCII code given in Appendix A. Each character takes up one byte. A *character string,* or a *string* as it is usually called, is any sequence of zero or more characters. The string without any characters is called the *null string*. A string consisting of a single character is different than the data represented by a character.

The *length of a string* is the number of characters in the string including all space characters, punctuation characters, and special characters. The null string has, by definition, a length of 0. The normal practice in a higher level language is to indicate a string as a sequence of characters enclosed in double quotes such as

"This is a string of length 29"

Under this convention the quotation marks are not considered to be part of the string. At the machine level we must adopt a different convention.

All strings in SEDCOM II are stored as a sequence of bytes in memory. A number of conventions can be used to define how these bytes are used to represent character strings. For this discussion we use the convention that if a string has n characters, then $n + 1$ bytes are used to store the string. The first n bytes hold the ASCII codes for the characters that make up the string. The $(n + 1)$st byte is the null byte (i.e., the byte contains 000_8) and this byte indicates the end of the string. Thus we see that the null string is represented by a single byte, which contains the null byte, and that a character string consisting of a single character is represented by two bytes. The first byte is the encoded character and the second byte is the null byte.

String Declaration

In a higher level language we might declare that an identifier STRING represents a character string with a maximum length of k characters by using a statement of the form

DECLARE STRING[k];

The identifier STRING can then be used to represent a *string variable* that can have up to k characters. This identifier may represent a number of different string values during a given information processing task. The compiler processing the language is responsible for reserving $k + 1$ bytes in memory to hold the information that will be associated with this identifier. At the assembly level we use a statement of the following form to reserve the space in memory that will be associated with the string.

STRING: .BLKB $k + 1$;RESERVE $k + 1$ BYTES FOR STRING

When this statement is processed by the assembler, the identifier STRING is given a value corresponding to the address of the first byte in an array of $k + 1$ bytes. The assembly language directive

.BLKB $k + 1$

tells the assembler program that the array of $k + 1$ bytes must be reserved in memory to hold the data that will be associated with the identifier STRING during the computation. The actual character string found in that area may have any length from 0 (the null string) to k. The end of the string is indicated by the null character 000_8.

String Constants

Just as we have numerical constants we can have *string constants*. For example, we might have a statement such as

PRINT("HELLO");

in a higher level language. The string "HELLO" is a string constant. Constants of this type can be represented at the assembly language level by a statement of the form

$C1:   .ASCIZ   "HELLO"

which was defined in Table 13-1. In this statement the label $C1 is used to indicate the address of the first character in the string. The assembler then allocates 6 bytes to hold the 5 characters that make up the string and places the null character in the 6th byte to indicate the end of the string. The ASCII codes for the characters that make up the string are also generated by the assembler at the time this statement is encountered in the assembly process. The programmer is responsible for the location selected for storing the string constants used in a program. One common practice is to group all such constants in a fixed location in the program so that they are easily accessible by all parts of the program.

The following subroutines illustrate how a number of basic string operations can be performed and show the basic computational techniques we can use to process symbolic information.

String Output

A common task found in many programs involves the printing of a character string stored in memory. The PRTSTR subroutine described by the following subroutine specification carries out this task.

The subroutine to accomplish this task is shown in Figure 13-28. The address information placed in $R0$ by the calling sequence acts as a pointer to the array of

---

Subroutine Specification

PRTSTR

Task: Print a string on the output printing device.

Input: The address of the first byte of the string is placed in CPU register $R0$.

Output: The character string printed on the output device.

Registers Used: $R0$

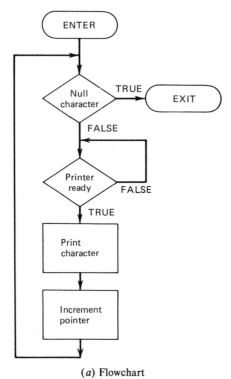

(*a*) Flowchart

Figure 13-28   The subroutine PRTSTR.

bytes that make up the character string. Initially it points to the first byte of the string to be printed. Each time a character is printed, the value of this pointer is incremented by 1 so that it points to the next character in the string. This process continues until we encounter the null byte, which marks the end of the string. At this point the subroutine is completed and control is returned to the calling program.

String Comparison

A fundamental need when dealing with string information is the ability to compare two strings to tell whether they are equal or to determine which is "less than" the other. To carry out this comparison we assume that the collating sequence induced by the ASCII code is used to order string information. The subroutine specification on page 572 defines a typical string comparison subroutine.

The subroutine for STRCMP is given in Figure 13-29. The comparison is carried out byte by byte. Assume that we have just compared the ith bytes in the two strings to see whether they are equal. If they are not, $R0$ is set to the proper value and control is then returned to the calling routine. When the bytes are equal there are two possible conditions. If the bytes being compared are the null bytes, then we are

```
                .TITLE PRTSTR


;********************************************************************
;              SUBROUTINE PRTSTR
;
;       PRINT A STRING ON PRINTER
;
;       INPUT - ADDRESS OF FIRST BYTE IN R0
;
;       OUTPUT - PRINTED STRING
;
;       REGISTERS USED - R0
;********************************************************************


                PRSTAT = 177564              ;PRINTER STATUS
                PRDATA = 177566              ;PRINTER BUFFER

PRTSTR:   TSTB      (R0)                      ;NULL BYTE
          BEQ       PROUT                     ;YES - END
PD:       TSTB      @#PRSTAT                  ;PRINTER READY?
          BPL       PD                        ;NO - TRY AGAIN
          MOVB      (R0)+,@#PRDATA            ;PRINT
          BR        PRTSTR                    ;NEXT CHAR
PROUT     RTS       PC                        ;RETURN


          ;END OF SUBROUTINE
```

(*b*) Assembly language program
Figure 13-28 (Continued)

at the end of the string. When this is true we exit with $R0$ set to 0, indicating that the two strings are equal. Otherwise we continue the process by comparing the next bytes in the string.

String Arrays and Tables

It is quite common to encounter information processing tasks in which it is necessary to deal with an array of character strings. For example, let us assume that we wish to translate the mnemonic symbols associated with a given instruction set into a corresponding machine-language operation code. This task can be accomplished if we form a table that contains all of the mnemonics and their corresponding octal value. Then all that is needed to translate a given mnemonic into its corresponding octal value is a subroutine that can locate the mnemonic in the table and read the octal value associated with that mnemonic. To create such a subroutine we must first define how the table will be stored in memory and then develop an algorithm that can be used to search the table to locate the desired value.

For this example let us assume that we wish to translate the mnemonic symbols shown in Table 13-4 into the indicated octal values. (To simplify the following discussion we have only used eight mnemonics. However, this problem could easily be extended to a table that contained all of the mnemonics used to describe the instruction set of SEDCOM II.) Examining this table we see that a mnemonic may be either 3 or 4 characters in length. Thus 4 or 5 bytes are needed to store the character string associated with each mnemonic since one byte must be provided to store the null byte, which indicates the end of the string. The octal value associated with each mnemonic is represented by 6 octal digits. Thus one word is required to store this information.

Subroutine Specification

STRCMP

Task: Compare ⟨string−1⟩ to ⟨string−2⟩

$$
\begin{array}{ll}
-1 & \langle\text{string}-1\rangle \langle \langle\text{string}-2\rangle \\
\text{Result} \quad 0 & \langle\text{string}-1\rangle = \langle\text{string}-2\rangle \\
1 & \langle\text{string}-1\rangle \rangle \langle\text{string}-2\rangle
\end{array}
$$

Input: Address of ⟨string−1⟩ in CPU register $R1$.
                    Address of ⟨string−2⟩ in CPU register $R2$.

Output: Result in register $R0$.

Registers Used: $R0$, $R1$, $R2$

There are a number of ways that this information can be stored. After considering the programming techniques that can be used, it was decided to store each entry in the table using a data structure of the form shown in Figure 13-30.

Two arrays are used. The first array is an array of string constants that hold the mnemonic values associated with each entry in the table. These strings form the *key values* that we use to look up information in the table. The second array holds the "table." As shown, each entry in the array consists of two words. The first word contains the address of the first character of the string, which acts as the key for that entry. Thus the first word is said to hold a *pointer,* which points to the character string that starts at the address stored in this word. The second word in the entry contains the octal value associated with the key value.

.TITLE STRCMP

```
;**********************************************************************
;               SUBROUTINE STRCMP
;
;       COMPARE TWO STRINGS. RETURN − 1, 0, 1 IF THE FIRST STRING IS
;       LESS THAN, EQUAL TO, GREATER THAN THE SECOND STRING.
;
;       INPUT - R1 CONTAINS THE ADDRESS OF THE FIRST BYTE OF STRING-1.
;               R2 CONTAINS THE ADDRESS OF THE FIRST BYT OF STRING-2.
;
;       OUTPUT
;
;                       − 1  IF STRING-1 < STRING-2
;               RO =     0   IF STRING-1 = STRING-2
;                        1   IF STRING-1 > STRING-2
;
;       REGISTERS USED — RO, R1, R2
;**********************************************************************
;

STRCMP:   CMPB   (R1),(R2)+   ;COMPARE CURRENT BYTE. INC R2 POINTER
          BLT    CMPMIN       ;STRING-1 < STRING-2
          BGT    CMPPOS       ;STRING-1 > STRING-2
          TSTB   (R1)+        ;END OF STRING? INCREMENT R1 POINTER
          BNE    STRCMP       ;NOT NULL BYTE. KEEP TESTING
          CLR    RO           ;STRINGS EQUAL
          RTS    PC

CMPMIN:   MOV    #−1,RO       ;SET RO TO − 1
          RTS    PC

CMPPOS:   MOV    #1,RO        ;SET RO TO 1

          ;END OF SUBROUTINE
```

Figure 13-29 Subroutine STRCMP to compare two strings.

A Linear Table Search Algorithm

To use the table shown in Figure 13-30 we assume that we have a character string stored in an array labeled TOKEN and we wish to test whether this string is in the table. This test is carried out using a simple linear search algorithm to compare the string in TOKEN to each of the key values in the table until we find the key that has the same value or we reach the end of the table. If we find a match, we read out the value of the string. Otherwise we report that the string was not found. To carry out this task we use the subroutine LINSRC defined by the following specification.

Table 13-4 A Table Giving the Relationship between Mnemonic Symbols and Their Corresponding Octal Value

Mnemonic Input	Octal Value of Mnemonic
MOV	010000
MOVB	110000
CMP	020000
CMPB	120000
BIT	030000
BITB	130000
BIC	040000
BICB	140000

Subroutine Specification

LINSRC

Task:
Search a table for the first occurrence of a character string using a linear search algorithm.
Return the value associated with the string if the string is found in the table. Otherwise return a value of −1.

Input:
Address of input character string in CPU register R3.
Address of first table entry in CPU register R4.
Number of entries in the table in CPU register R5.
Assume at least 1 entry in table.

Output:
Result in CPU register R0.

Registers Used:
R0, R1, R2, R3, R4, R5

Subroutines Used: STRCMP

The assembly language program to realize this subroutine is given in Figure 13-31. This subroutine is slightly more complex than the ones discussed up to this point. First we note that the subroutine uses the STRCMP subroutine to compare the two character strings. Thus we have an example of how one subroutine may call a second

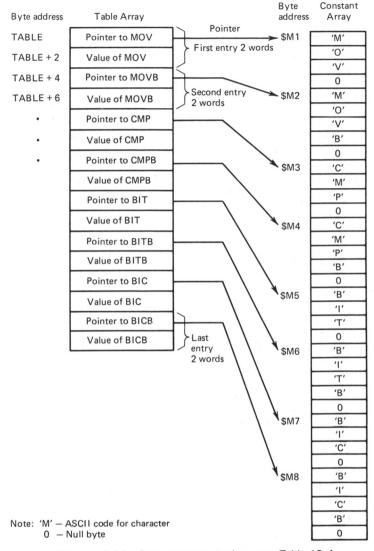

Figure 13-30 Data structure used to store Table 13-4.

subroutine while carrying out a computation. The second thing to be considered is the method used to access the information contained in the table being searched.

When the subroutine LINSRC is entered, register $R4$ contains the address of the first entry in the table. This is the address of the word that contains the pointer to the character string associated with that entry. As part of the calling sequence for STRCMP, we place the value of this pointer in register $R2$. If this is the character string that we are trying to locate, then the next word in the entry contains the value

```
        .TITLE LINSRC

;*************************************************************************
;               SUBROUTINE LINSRC
;
;
;       USE A LINEAR SEARCH TO LOCATE A TOKEN IN A TABLE.
;       THE TOKEN IS A CHARACTER STRING. THE KEYS IN THE TABLE
;       ARE CHARACTER STRINGS. RETURN THE OCTAL VALUE OF THE
;       KEY.
;
;       INPUT - R3 CONTAINS THE ADDRESS OF THE FIRST BYTE OF THE TOKEN.
;               R4 CONTAINS THE ADDRESS OF THE FIRST ENTRY OF THE TABLE.
;               R5 CONTAINS THE NUMBER OF ENTRIES IN THE TABLE > 0.
;
;       OUTPUT        VALUE OF ENTRY IF TOKEN FOUND IN TABLE
;             R0 =
;                     − 1 IF TOKEN IS NOT FOUND IN TABLE
;
;       REGISTERS USED - R0, R1, R2, R3, R4, R5
;
;       SUBROUTINES USED - STRCMP
;*************************************************************************

LINSRC:  MOV R3,R1       ;ADDRESS OF TOKEN
         MOV (R4)+,R2    ;ADDRESS OF MNEMONIC KEY IN TABLE
         JSR PC,STRCMP   ;COMPARE STRINGS - ASSUME SUBROUTINE PRESENT
         TST R0          ;WAS TOKEN = MNEMONIC KEY?
         BEQ FOUND       ;YES - GET VALUE
         ADD #2,R4       ;NO - GO TO NEXT ENTRY
         DEC R5          ;AT END OF TABLE?
         BNE LINSRC      ;NO - CHECK NEXT ENTRY
         MOV #−1,R0      ;YES - KEY NOT FOUND
         RTS PC          ;RETURN NOT FOUND

FOUND:   MOV (R4),R0     ;GET ENTRY VALUE
         RTS PC          ;RETURN WITH VALUE
```

Figure 13-31   Assembly language program for LINSRC.

associated with the string. Thus we also increment $R4$ to point to this value after we have loaded the pointer into $R2$. The

$$\text{MOV} \qquad (R4)+,R2$$

instruction takes care of both of these tasks.

If we locate the string in the table, we know that $R4$ now contains the address of the memory location that holds the value associated with the input string. This information is used to read this value into $R0$ and we return to the calling program. When the comparison fails, we must increment $R4$ by 2 to point to the next entry in the table and then check to see whether we have reached the end of the table. If we have we return with -1 in $R0$. Otherwise we check the next entry.

A Complete Table Read Algorithm

Now that we have formulated all of the tools needed, our last task is to develop a complete program to read a value from the table and report the results. The program to be developed is described by the following specification.

Program Specification

Value Look up in a Table

Task: Read a character string representing a mnemonic that may be in a symbol table. After the string is read it is looked up in the table and its value is printed if it is found. Otherwise the fact that it was not found is indicated.

Input: A character string from the keyboard that represents a possible mnemonic.
The table of mnemonics and their values is built into the program.

Output: If the mnemonic is in the table the printed output is
⟨mnemonic⟩ = ⟨octal value of mnemonic⟩
If the mnemonic is not in the table the printed output is
⟨mnemonic⟩ = -1

The program needed to realize this task is given in Figure 13-32. This program is much more complex than the others presented in this chapter and it serves to review and summarize many of the concepts that have been discussed for individual tasks.

The program is organized in a modular manner where a number of subroutines have been defined to carry out the individual processing tasks that make up the program. The main body of the program is responsible for first setting up the calling sequence for each subroutine and then calling the subroutine. The operation of the program can best be understood by reading the program listing given in Figure 13-32.

From this discussion we see that the manipulation of symbolic information is as easily accomplished as the manipulation of numeric data. In the next chapter we use many of these concepts to show how we can design an assembler program that can be used to translate an assembly language program into a machine language program.

```
        .TITLE FIND_VALUE
```

```
;*************************************************************************
;           PROGRAM FIND__VALUE
;
;   A MNEMONIC IS ENTERED FROM THE KEYBOARD. A TABLE IS SEARCHED FOR
;   THIS MNEMONIC. THE MNEMONIC IS THEN PRINTED FOLLOWED WITH ITS
;   VALUE IF IT IS IN THE TABLE AND WITH A VALUE OF − 1 IF IT IS NOT IN
;   THE TABLE.
;
;   INPUT - CHARACTER STRING FROM KEYBOARD.
;
;   OUTPUT - PRINTED CHARACTER STRING FOLLOWED BY VALUE OF MNEMONIC OR
;            − 1.
;
;   REGISTERS USED - ALL.
;
;   SUBROUTINES USED - RDSTR - READ INPUT CHARACTER STRING
;                      LINSRC - LINEAR SEARCH OF TABLE
;                      PRISTR - PRINT A CHARACTER STRING
;                      PRTOCT - PRINT OCTAL VALUE IN REGISTER
;*************************************************************************
```

```
            ;SYSTEM CONSTANTS

    KBSTAT = 177560  ;ADDRESS OF KEYBOARD STATUS REGISTER
    KBDATA = 177562  ;ADDRESS OF KEYBOARD BUFFER REGISTER
    PRSTAT = 177564  ;ADDRESS OF PRINTER STATUS REGISTER
    PRDATA = 177566  ;ADDRESS OF PRINTER BUFFER REGISTER
    LF = 12          ;CODE FOR LINE FEED
    CR = 15          ;CODE FOR CARRIAGE RETURN
    EQL = 75         ;CODE FOR EQUAL SIGN
    TABSIZ = 10      ;SIZE OF TABLE (8 DECIMAL)

    . = 1500         ;SET LOCATION COUNTER


            ;MAIN PROGRAM

START:  MOV   #START,SP     ;SET SYSTEM STACK POINTER
        MOV   #TOKEN,R0      ;READ INPUT STRING
        JSR   PC,RDSTR       ;INTO TOKEN ARRAY
        MOV   #TOKEN,R3      ;CALLING SEQUENCE FOR LINSRC
        MOV   #TTABLE,R4     ;ADDRESS OF TABLE TO BE SEARCHED
        MOV   #TABSIZ,R5     ;SIZE OF TABLE
        JSR   PC,LINSRC      ;SEARCH TABLE
        MOV   R0, − (SP)     ;SAVE VALUE
        MOV   #TOKENM2,R0    ;PRINT OUT CHARACTER STRING
        JSR   PC,PRTSTR      ;CR LF TOKEN
        MOV   #EQLS,R0       ;PRINT OUT CHARACTER STRING
```

Figure 13-32 An assembly language table read program.

```
        JSR     PC,PRTSTR       ;EQUALS
        MOV     (SP)+,R0        ;GET VALUE OF TOKEN
        CMP     #-1,R0          ;WAS TOKEN IN TABLE
        BEG     NOTFND          ;NO
        JSR     PC,PRTOCT       ;YES - PRINT OCTAL VALUE OF TOKEN
        HALT                    ;TASK COMPLETED

NOTFND  MOV     #MIN1,R0        ;NOT IN TABLE
        JSR     PC,PRTSTR       ;PRINT -1
        HALT                    ;TASK COMPLETED

        ;SUBROUTINES

    .TITLE RDSTR

;********************************************************************
;               SUBROUTINE RDSTR
;
;
;       READ A STRING OF CHARACTERS FROM THE KEYBOARD INTO A BUFFER.
;       END OF INPUT OCCURS WHEN A LINE FEED CHARACTER LF IS DETECTED.
;
;       INPUT - ADDRESS OF BUFFER IN R0.
;               CHARACTER STRING FROM KEYBOARD.
;
;       OUTPUT - CHARACTER STRING IN BUFFER.
;
;       REGISTERS USED - R0
;
;********************************************************************

RDSTR:  TSTB    @#KBSTAT        ;CHARACTER READY?
        BPL     RDSTR           ;NO—TRY AGAIN
        MOVB    @#KBDATA,(R0)   ;YES—READ CHARACTER
        CMPB    (R0)+,#LF       ;END OF INPUT
        BNE     RDSTR           ;NO—GET NEXT CHARACTER
        CLRB    -(R0)           ;SET NULL BIT INDICATING END OF
        RTS     PC              ;INPUT STRING. RETURN

    .TITLE LINSRC

;********************************************************************
;               SUBROUTINE LINSRC
;
;
;       USE A LINEAR SEARCH TO LOCATE A TOKEN IN A TABLE.
;       THE TOKEN IS A CHARACTER STRING. THE KEYS IN THE TABLE
;       ARE CHARACTER STRINGS. RETURN THE OCTAL VALUE OF THE
;       KEY.
;
;       INPUT - R3 CONTAINS THE ADDRESS OF THE FIRST BYTE OF THE TOKEN.
;               R4 CONTAINS THE ADDRESS OF THE FIRST ENTRY OF THE TABLE.
;               R5 CONTAINS THE NUMBER OF ENTRIES IN THE TABLE > 0.
```

Figure 13-32 (Continued)

```
;
;           OUTPUT        VALUE OF ENTRY IF TOKEN FOUND IN TABLE
;                  R0 =
;                         -1 IF TOKEN IS NOT FOUND IN TABLE
;           REGISTERS USED - R0, R1, R2, R3, R4, R5
;
;           SUBROUTINES USED - STRCMP
;
;**********************************************************************
LINSRC:   MOV  R3,R1          ;ADDRESS OF TOKEN
          MOV  (R4)+,R2        ;ADDRESS OF MNEMONIC KEY IN TABLE
          JSR  PC,STRCMP       ;COMPARE STRINGS - ASSUME SUBROUTINE PRESENT
          TST  R0             ;WAS TOKEN = MNEMONIC KEY?
          BEQ  FOUND          ;YES - GET VALUE
          ADD  #2,R4          ;NO - GO TO NEXT ENTRY
          DEC  R5             ;AT END OF TABLE?
          BNE  LINSRC         ;NO - CHECK NEXT ENTRY
          MOV  #-1,R0         ;YES - KEY NOT FOUND
          RTS  PC             ;RETURN NOT FOUND

FOUND:    MOV  (R4),R0        ;GET ENTRY VALUE
          RTS  PC             ;RETURN WITH VALUE


          .TITLE STRCMP


;**********************************************************************
;              SUBROUTINE STRCMP
;
;         COMPARE TWO STRINGS. RETURN -1, 0, 1 IF THE ;FIRST STRING IS
;         LESS THAN, EQUAL TO, GREATER THAN THE SECOND STRING.
;
;         INPUT - R1 CONTAINS THE ADDRESS OF THE FIRST BYTE OF STRING-1
;                 R2 CONTAINS THE ADDRESS OF THE FIRST BYTE OF STRING-2
;
;         OUTPUT           -1    IF STRING-1 < STRING-2
;                  R0 =    0    IF STRING-1 = STRING-2
;                          1    IF STRING-1 > STRING-2
;
;         REGISTERS USED - R0, R1, R2
;
;**********************************************************************
STRCMP:   CMPB (R1),(R2)+    ;COMPARE CURRENT BYTE. INC R2 POINTER
          BLT  CMPMIN        ;STRING-1 < STRING-2
          BGT  CMPPOS        ;STRING-1 > STRING-2
          TSTB (R1)+         ;END OF STRING? INCREMENT R1 POINTER
          BNE  STRCMP        ;NOT NULL BYTE. KEEP TESTING
          CLR  R0            ;STRINGS EQUAL
          RTS  PC
```

Figure 13-32 (Continued)

```
CMPMIN:   MOV    #-1,R0      ;SET R0 to -1
          RTS    PC

CMPPOS:   MOV    #1,R0       ;SET R0 TO 1
          RTS    PC

          .TITLE PRTSTR

;*******************************************************************
;                 SUBROUTINE PRTSTR
;
;         PRINT A STRING OF ASCII CHARACTERS THAT ARE TERMINATED BY THE
;         NULL CHARACTER. ASSUME STRING IS NOT NULL STRING.
;
;         INPUT - ADDRESS OF FIRST CHARACTER IN R0
;
;         OUTPUT - CHARACTER STRING ON PRINTER
;
;         REGISTERS USED - R0.
;
;*******************************************************************

PRTSTR:   TSTB   @#PRSTAT          ;PRINTER READY?
          BPL    PRTSTR            ;NO - TRY AGAIN
          MOVB   (R0)+,@#PRDATA    ;YES - SEND DATA
          TSTB   (R0)              ;AT END OF STRING?
          BNE    PRTSTR            ;NO - GET NEXT CHARACTER
          RTS    PC                ;YES - RETURN

          .TITLE PRTOCT

;*******************************************************************
;
;                 SUBROUTINE PRTOCT
;
;         PRINT THE OCTAL VALUE OF THE POSITIVE NUMBER IN R0.
;
;         INPUT - NUMBER TO BE PRINTED IN R0.
;
;         OUTPUT - 6 DIGIT OCTAL NUMBER CORRESPONDING TO CONTENTS OF R0.
;
;                 REGISTERS USED - R0, R1, R2
;
;*******************************************************************

PRTOCT:   MOV    #60,R1     ;ASCII CODE FOR 0 IN R1
          MOV    #6,R2      ;SET COUNTER TO 6
          TST    R0         ;IS LEFTMOST OCTAL DIGIT 1?
          BGE    PZO        ;NO
          INC    R1         ;ASCII CODE FOR 1 IN R1
PZO:      ASL    R0         ;GET RID OF LEFTMOST BIT OF R0
```

Figure 13-32 (Continued)

```
PZ:         TSTB    @#PRSTAT        ;PRINTER READY?
            BPL     PZ              ;NO - TRY AGAIN
            MOVB    R1,@#PRDATA     ;YES - SEND DATA
            DEC     R2              ;PRINTED 6 CHARACTERS?
            BEG     FIN
            MOV     #6,R1           ;CREATE NEXT CHAR. LOAD LEFTMOST 4 BITS
            ASL     RO              ;MOVE THE NEXT OCTAL VALUE TO R1
            ROL     R1
            ASL     RO
            ROL     R1
            ASL     RO
            ROL     R1              ;ASCII CODE FOR OCTAL NUMBER IN R1
            BR      PZ              ;PRINT VALUE
FIN:        RTS     PC              ;RETURN TO CALLING PROGRAM


                    ;STRING CONSTANTS


            . = 2500

                    ;TABLE OF MNEMONIC STRING VALUES

$M1:        .ASCIZ  /MOV/
$M2:        .ASCIZ  /MOVB/
$M3:        .ASCIZ  /CMP/
$M4:        .ASCIZ  /CMPB/
$M5:        .ASCIZ  /BIT/
$M6:        .ASCIZ  /BITB/
$M7:        .ASCIZ  /BIC/
$M8:        .ASCIZ  /BICB/

EQLS:       .ASCIZ  / = /           ;CHARACTER SEQUENCE ⟨SP⟩ = ⟨SP⟩.   ⟨SP⟩ — SPACE
MIN1:       .ASCIZ  / −1/           ;CHARACTER SEQUENCE −1

                    ;DEFINE TTABLE

            .EVEN                   ;SET TABLE TO START AT WORD

TTABLE:     .WORD $M1,10000,$M2,110000,$M3,20000,$M4,120000
            .WORD $M5,30000,$M6,130000,$M7,40000,$M8,140000

                    ;DEFINE BUFFER

TOKENM2:    .BYTE   CR,LF           ;CODE FOR CR FOLLOWED BY LF
TOKEN:      .BLKW   120             ;RESERVE A BUFFER AREA OF 80 CHARACTERS

            .END    START           ;END OF PROGRAM
```

Figure 13-32   (Continued)

EXERCISES

1. Develop a subroutine PRTDEC that will print the decimal value of the positive number stored in *R*0.

2. Develop a subroutine CONCAT that will concatenate two strings. The operation to be performed is defined by the assignment statement

$$\langle \text{string-1} \rangle := \langle \text{string-1} \rangle | \langle \text{string-2} \rangle$$

where | is used to indicate the concatenation operation. The address of ⟨string-1⟩ is in *R*1 and the address of ⟨string-2⟩ is in *R*2 when the subroutine is called. It is assumed that an area, the first byte of which is labeled ⟨string-1⟩, has been defined that has enough space to hold the new value generated.

7. SUMMARY

The goal of this chapter has been to develop an understanding of how a computer actually carries out the computations associated with a program. To do this we have investigated how the basic operations contained in the instruction set of a typical computer can be used to implement a variety of common computational tasks. Using this background we were then able to write several machine-language level programs to carry out various information processing tasks.

Throughout this discussion we have used a simple assembler language to write all of the programs with the assumption that there was a program available to translate the assembly language program into the machine language program needed to run on the computer. The translation process and the assembler program used to carry out the translation are designed to relieve the programmer of the tedious tasks involved in creating machine language code. The general techniques used to carry out the translation process are introduced in the next chapter.

Reference Notation

As indicated, the SEDCOM II computer is based on the PDP-11. A complete description of the PDP-11 can be found in Reference 6. The fundamentals of program organization are covered in Reference 1. A comprehensive discussion of PDP-11 assembly language programming and many examples of the applications of these techniques can be found in References 2, 3, 4, and 5.

REFERENCES

1. Booth, T. L., and Chien, Y. T. (1974), *Computing: Fundamentals and Applications*. Wiley, New York.
2. Frank, T. S. (1983), *Introduction to the PDP-11 and Its Assembly Language*. Prentice-Hall, Englewood Cliffs, N.J.

3. Gill, A. (1983), *Machine and Assembly Language Programming of the PDP-11* (second edition). Prentice-Hall, Englewood Cliffs, N.J.

4. Eckhouse, R. H. Jr., and Morris, L. R. (1979), *Minicomputer Systems Organization, Programming and Applications (PDP-11)* (second edition). Prentice-Hall, Englewood Cliffs, N.J.

5. Kapps, C. A., and Stafford, R. L. (1981), *Assembly Language for the PDP-11.* Prindle, Weber & Schmidt CBI Publishing Co., Boston, Mass.

6. *PDP-11 Microprocessor Handbook* (latest edition). Digital Equipment Corp., Maynard, Mass.

HOME PROBLEMS

The following problems all involve the writing of a SEDCOM II program to carry out a specific information processing task. The complete solution of the problem should include:

(a) A statement of the algorithm that is used to solve the problem.

(b) A complete flowchart showing how the algorithm is implemented.

(c) The SEDCOM II program that will carry out the algorithm.

(d) (Optional) If a SEDCOM II simulator (or a PDP-11 system) is available, proof should be submitted that the program actually carries out the claimed information processing task. This proof should include a discussion of each test case selected, the reason for the test, the expected results of running the test, and the results observed when the test was executed.

1. Write a program that will read in two octal numbers. The first represents a low memory address and the second a high memory address. The program is then to print out a "memory dump" consisting of the octal information stored in all of the words between the low memory address and the high memory address. This printout should have the form

⟨value of address⟩   ⟨octal value stored in word at that address⟩

2. Write a program that will create a table in memory. The information to be stored in the table is read in using the following format:

⟨key⟩⟨delimitor⟩⟨octal value⟩

where

⟨key⟩ = 3 or 4 uppercase letters
⟨delimitor⟩ = a space or a comma (,)
⟨octal value⟩ = an octal number between 0 and 100000

The end of the input information is indicated when an * is detected. After the table has been completely entered, the program should print out the contents of the table so that it can be verified.

3. Write a program that will read in a series of decimal integers and print out the sum of the numbers. Assume that the largest number that may be found in the series is 999999 and that at most 25 numbers are included in the series.

4. Write a program that will read a series of decimal integers and print out a table that will have the following form:

Table of Numerical Values

Decimal	Octal	Hexadecimal
⟨value read⟩	⟨computed octal value⟩	⟨computed hexadecimal value⟩

5. Write a program that will accept a sequence of character strings. Each character string may have from 1 to 5 characters. The output of the program should be a table giving all of the character strings, listed in alphabetical order and the number of times each character string appears in the input sequence.

6. Write a program that will accept a paragraph of text and count the number of words, lines, and sentences in the text. The output should indicate the word count, the line count, and the sentence count.

7. Write a program that will encrypt an input text string before storing it in memory. A second program should also be written that will decrypt the encrypted string. Encrypt means to encode a string in a secrete code; decrypt means to decode the string. Use any encryption algorithm that you wish as long as every input character is stored as a different value in memory. Show that both programs work properly by reading in a string and then printing out
(a) the original input string,
(b) the encrypted string,
(c) the decrypted string.

8. Write a program that will automatically look up in a directory (table) the telephone number of a person whose name is entered as an input. The output of the program should be the name of the person followed by the telephone number. If the name is not in the directory, the program should ask for the telephone number of that person and create a directory entry for the new name.

14

ASSEMBLER LANGUAGES AND ASSEMBLERS

1. INTRODUCTION

The programming of a computer to carry out a given computational task is tedious, time consuming, and subject to error if it must be done using the computer's machine language. These difficulties are mainly a result of the following problems.

1. All instructions must be expressed in some form of numeric code that is usually difficult for a person to understand.
2. Every address reference must be explicitly defined. Thus, as a program is written the programmer must be able to define the location of all data and program instructions that are referenced in the program. This may occur even though locations for these items have not been defined at the time this information is needed.
3. Changes in instructions, changes in data, or the insertion or deletion of instructions often requires the reassignment of instructions or data locations in memory. This may require modifying other instructions in the program to account for changes in references to the new data and instruction locations.
4. The programmer must create a binary encoded version of the program so that it can be entered directly into the computer. This binary program must be checked to see that it is correct before it is used.
5. Parts of previously developed programs that are applicable to a new programming effort may not be usable without being completely recoded to conform with the address assignments of the new program.

In Chapter 13 we avoided these problems by using mnemonic terms to indicate the basic operations that could be performed by SEDCOM II and the symbolic addresses of the data items that were acted upon by these operations. This method of representing a program made it very easy to define the steps necessary to carry out a computation.

The advantage of using mnemonics to represent the basic instructions was clearly evident to early programmers. Initially, programs were written in mnemonic form and then the programmer translated the mnemonics into the computer's machine language. However, it was quickly realized that this translation task was a mechanical process that could be carried out by the computer. Thus the idea of a simple program that would translate mnemonic terms into their equivalent machine language coding quickly evolved. These translation programs are called *assembler programs* or *assemblers*. The corresponding set of mnemonics and the rules used to form the statements processed by the assembler form the *assembly language* processed by the assembler.

We have already seen how the assembly language for SEDCOM II is used to describe SEDCOM II programs. In this chapter we investigate the operation and structure of a simple assembler designed to translate SEDCOM II assembly language source programs into machine language object programs that can be executed by SEDCOM II. This discussion presents the important concepts used to design assembler programs. Although the code necessary to realize the assembler is not given, enough details are presented so that such a program could be developed if desired.

2. THE SEDCOM II ASSEMBLY LANGUAGE REVISITED

The discussion of the assembly language for SEDCOM II presented in Chapter 13 concentrated on those properties of the language that were directly related to the programming process. In this chapter we have a different problem.

Once we have written an assembly language program we must translate it into machine language if it is to be executed. This is the task of the assembler. However, the information the assembler needs to carry out the translation process is very different from the information needed to write a program in the assembly language. Thus before we can investigate the structure and design of an assembler, we must provide a formal description of the assembly language that is to be processed by the assembler.

The Assembler as an Information Processor

The task performed by an assembler program is illustrated conceptually in Figure 14-1. The assembler reads the statements that make up the assembly language *source program* one statement at a time. As each statement is read the assembler must recognize the various mnemonics and symbols that form the statement. Using this information, the assembler translates the source statements into their corresponding machine language code. The output of the assembler consists of a machine language *object program* and the information needed to indicate where these machine language instructions are to be placed in memory. Figure 14-1 illustrates this translation process.

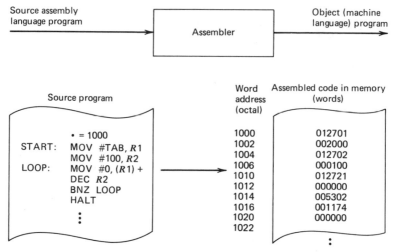

Figure 14-1   The assembly process.

If we examine the translation process implied by Figure 14-1, we see that the assembler program must have the ability to recognize the assembler directives and the mnemonics used to represent the operation codes of each machine-language operation. In addition it must be able to detect and assign values to each of the labels used as symbolic addresses and identifiers found in assignment statements. To provide this capability we can think of the assembler as being organized as shown in Figure 14-2.

The Mnemonic Table

The operation code mnemonics and assembler directives found in an assembly language are defined at the time that the language is designed. Thus the values associated with each mnemonic and directive are known when the assembler program is developed. The *mnemonic table* stores a list of all the mnemonics and directives

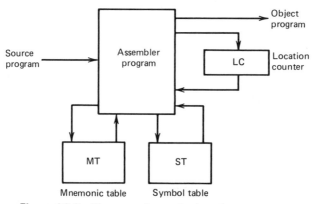

Figure 14-2   The general organization of an assembler.

defined as part of the language. Each entry in the table consists of the character string representing the term and the values associated with the term. When the assembler locates a mnemonic in the table, it reads the value of the mnemonic and then uses this value in forming the machine language instruction corresponding to the statement being processed. When an assembler directive is detected, the assembler uses the value associated with this directive to control the operation of the assembler.

The Location Counter

During the translation process each assembly language statement that corresponds to an operation will produce a binary machine language instruction that must be assigned to a specific location in memory. Thus the assembler is required to keep track of the memory location where the next machine language instruction is to be placed and to update this information as each statement is processed. The *location counter* (LC) serves this purpose. It is the responsibility of the programmer to decide how a program is organized in memory. Assembler directives are used to set the value of LC to ensure that the generated code is placed in the proper memory locations.

The Symbol Table

Labels are used by a programmer to indicate the symbolic location of instructions and data in the assembly language program. Before the translation process can be completed, each symbolic location must be assigned an actual memory location by the assembler. This can be done only during the processing of the assembly language program since the labels used in the program are not known to the assembler until they are actually encountered in the program. Every assembler contains a *symbol table* that records all of the labels found in the assembly language program and the memory address associated with the label. Only after all of the labels have been given values can the assembler complete the translation process.

To understand how the translation of a program is accomplished we must consider how the assembler uses the structural characteristics of the assembly language to carry out the translation process.

Formal Language Definition

From an abstract viewpoint every assembly language program consists of a sequence of characters that have been generated by a programmer to do a given task. In creating this sequence the programmer was required to follow a fixed set of rules, called the *grammar* of the assembly language, which define how a program and the statements that make up the program can be constructed. The assembler has the task of processing this character sequence and translating it into the sequence of machine language instructions that, hopefully, corresponds to the machine language program desired by the programmer.

The assembler assumes that the programmer has formed each statement in the program using the rules of grammar that define the language. If this is the case, the same rules can be used to decompose each statement and generate the machine language code represented by the statement. If a statement is received by the assembler that does not follow these rules, it is assumed that an error has been made and the assembler must produce an error message indicating that an error has been detected. As long as all of the statements in the program are correctly formed, the assembler will produde a machine language program that corresponds to the input assembly language program. There is no guarantee that this program will operate correctly when run by the computer since the assembler cannot check that the algorithm represented by the source program correctly implements the task for which it was designed.

The following discussion presents the formal rules that serve to define the SEDCOM II assembly language. These rules are used in Section 3 to outline the design of an assembler that will process this language.

The SEDCOM II Character Set

The reader and the printer in SEDCOM II are designed to work with the ASCII encoded characters defined in Appendix A. It is possible to use all of these characters in forming an assembler program. However, some of the characters may appear only as data values in data statements and cannot be used to form the assembly language statements that represent other parts of the program.

The basic character set is of importance only in that it defines the building blocks that we use to construct complete statements and programs. The first step in the formal definition of our assembly language is to define a set of primitive program constituents that are recognized by the assembler program as the basic units used to form a statement.

Special Characters and Symbols

In an assembler language we use special characters and symbols to supply special information to the assembler. For example, the character string

$$AB\#\$E69\_+\&**eK78$$

has, in all likelihood, no meaning. However, in the SEDCOM II assembly language we know that

POINT: MOV $(R1)+,-(R2)$;TRANSFER ARRAY 1 TO ARRAY 2

is a valid statement. If an assembler is to process this statement, it must be able to recognize that POINT is a label that represents the symbolic address or name of the statement, that MOV is a mnemonic for a machine language operation, that $(R1)+,-(R2)$ provides the arguments needed by the MOV operation, and that the characters following the ";" make up a comment.

Several characters in the ASCII character set are given special meaning and are used to provide specific information to the assembler. Table 14-1 lists these characters, their octal ASCII representation, and the meaning attached to them by the assembler.

A number of the special characters were identified as *delimiters*. They serve to segment the character string that forms a statement into subunits, which are called *symbols*. There are two basic types of symbols in our assembly language. They are

1. *Permanent symbols* or *system symbols,* and
2. *User-defined symbols—labels* or *identifiers.*

The permanent symbols correspond to the mnemonics used to represent the machine language operation codes, such as MOV, the mnemonics used to represent the assembly language directives, such as .BLKB, or the labels used to indicate the special registers such as $R1$, SP, or PC. These symbols, which are found in all assembly language programs, are predefined and are included as part of the language definition. The system symbols are said to be "reserved" and cannot be used as identifiers or labels.

The user-defined symbols serve as labels to identify memory locations or as iden-

Table 14-1   Table of Special ASCII Characters

Character	ASCII Code (Octal)	Meaning or Use
Space	040	Delimiter—separates substrings
:	072	Delimiter—indicates symbolic address
;	073	Delimiter—start of a comment
↲	015	Delimiter—carriage return end of statement
,	054	Delimiter—separation of argument or operand in argument or operand field
=	075	Delimiter—assignment operator end of identifier and start of identifier value
(	050	Address—beginning of reference to a register pointer
)	051	Address—end of reference to a register pointer
#	043	Address—indicates immediate mode address
+	053	Address—autoincrement
−	055	Address—autodecrement

tifiers to represent constant values that are defined in assignment statements. A value is associated with a user-defined symbol by:

1. Being assigned a value by an assignment statement, or
2. By appearing as the symbolic address of a statement.

When a label acts as the symbolic address of a statement, it is assigned a value corresponding to the address of the instruction or the address of the data defined by the rest of the statement.

In SEDCOM II the characters that can be used to form a symbol are limited to

1. The uppercase alphabetical characters: $\{A-Z\}$
2. The numerical characters: $\{0-9\}$
3. The dollar sign: $
4. The period: .

Using these characters, a symbol is formed according to the following rules:

1. A symbol consists of one or more characters. The first character must not be a numerical character.
2. Although a symbol may be longer than six characters, only the first six characters are significant to the assembler. Thus A1AAAAAA and A1AAAA are considered to be equivalent symbols.
3. If a symbol begins with a period, it must contain at least one additional character.

In general usage we start all assembler directives with a period to distinguish them from operation code mnemonics, labels, and identifiers. This is not required but makes it easier for the assembler to distinguish between assembler directives and other classes of symbols.

Numbers

All the numbers appearing in a SEDCOM II program are assumed to be octal numbers. The number may represent a positive value or a negative number if it is preceded by a negative sign. Depending upon the context in which the number is used, it must be able to fit into one byte or one word.

Tokens

A *token* is any sequence of one or more characters that appears between two delimiters. When a token is detected during the assembly process, it is up to the assembler to attach a meaning to the token. This meaning may be determined by the location of the token in the statement or by the delimiter at the beginning or the end of the token. For example, consider the statement

first character in line
↙

end of line
delimiter

LOOK1:   MOV $(R1)+$,OUT   ; SAVE THE RESULT)

The first token in this statement is LOOK, which starts with the first character in the statement and is delimited by ":". The next token is MOV. The spaces before MOV and the spaces after MOV serve to delimit this symbol. The next token detected is the first operand $(R1)+$, which is delimited by the space before the "(" and the "," following the $+$ character. The meaning associated with this token is obtained by using the structure of the token to recognize that this operand refers to register $R1$, which is used as part of an autoincrement address reference. The next token follows the "," which indicates the separation between two operand values. The symbol OUT is recognized as a second operand token by the fact that it starts immediately after the comma and is delimited on the right by a space. Finally we detect the ";", which indicates that all of the characters between the ";" and the end of line delimiter "⟩" form a comment and can be ignored. The next character after the end of line delimiter is taken to be the first character of the next statement.

In the next section we see that one of the key subprocedures in an assembler program is the subprocedure used to locate and classify the next token in a statement.

Statements

Every statement appears on a single line and has up to four fields. The general structure of a statement has the form

Field 1	Field 2	Field 3	Field 4
⟨label⟩:	⟨operator⟩	⟨operands⟩	;⟨comment⟩
	or	or	
	⟨directive⟩	⟨arguments⟩	

Each field must be separated from the preceding field by at least one space character. As we know from the discussion in Chapter 13, not all fields must be present in a statement. The tokens found in each of the fields determine the class of statement being processed.

There are three general classes of statements. They are

1. Machine command statements
2. Assembler directive statements
3. Data statements

This classification is selected to emphasize the different types of tasks that must be performed by the assembler during the translation process.

Machine Command Statements

Machine command statements are those statements that the assembler translates directly into machine language instructions. These statements are recognized by finding a mnemonic for one of SEDCOM II's operation codes in field 2. When the assembler detects the presence of such an operation code, by finding it in the mnemonic table, it also knows how many operands are associated with that code. It thus expects to find the proper number of operands in field 3. If the contents of field 3 contain too many or too few operand tokens, the assembler reports an error condition and goes on to process the next statement. Otherwise the processing of the character string continues.

Each such instruction generates a machine instruction that requires 1, 2, or 3 words in memory depending upon the instruction and the address modes associated with the instruction's operands. When the statement is read by the assembler, the location counter (LC) contains the address of the first byte of the instruction. After the processing of the statement has been completed, LC will have been incremented by either 2, if it is a one-word instruction, by 4 if it is a two-word instruction, or by 6 if it is a three-word instruction.

Labels are used to provide a symbolic address for machine command statements and data statements although not all machine command statements are labels. Such a symbolic address is normally used only when other instructions reference the labeled machine command or data statement. When a label is found in field 1, it is the responsibility of the assembler to enter this label into the symbol table and to assign it a value equal to the current value stored in LC (i.e., the label takes on a value equal to the address of the first byte of the machine language instruction generated by the statement or the first byte of the area in memory set aside to hold the data indicated by the data statement).

Labels may also be found in field 3. In this case the label is part of one of the operand tokens. For example, in the statement

$$\text{NEW:}\quad\text{MOV}\quad (R1)+,\text{OUT}$$

we note three labels. The first label, NEW, is the symbolic address of the statement and is entered into the symbol table as described above. The second label is the predefined label $R1$ in the first operand, which references register $R1$. The third label found in the statement is OUT and is used to define the second operand of the MOV instruction. In this case OUT refers to the symbolic address of another statement in the program. There are two possible situations that may be present in the program. They are illustrated by the code segments given in Figure 14-3.

Whenever a label is part of one of the instruction's operands, the assembler looks the label up in the symbol table. If the label references one of the CPU registers or if it has been encountered previously, as shown in Figure 14-3*a*, the label will have an assigned value and can be used in the processing of the statement. When this occurs we say that the instruction makes a *backward reference* to the symbolic address represented by the label.

There are many cases where the label in the operand references a symbolic address associated with a statement that has not yet been processed. This case is shown in Figure 14-3*b*. When this occurs the assembler will find that the label has not yet been placed in the symbol table. Such a reference is called a *forward reference*. When

<table>
<tr><td>OUT:</td><td>⟨Statement⟩</td><td></td><td>NEW: MOV</td><td>(R1)+,OUT</td></tr>
</table>

OUT: ⟨Statement⟩   NEW: MOV (R1)+,OUT

NEW: MOV (R1)+,OUT   OUT: ⟨Statement⟩

(*a*) Backward address reference   (*b*) Forward address reference

Figure 14-3 Two forms of references to symbolic address.

a forward reference occurs the assembler enters this new label into the symbol table and marks it as an *undefined label*.

The processing of the statement cannot be completed until a value for this undefined label is defined. Thus the assembler sets the processing of this statement aside and continues the processing of the following statement. Eventually the processing will reach the statement that contains the label as its symbolic address. At that point the assembler assigns a value for the label. It can then go back and complete the processing of all the earlier statements that referenced that label or it can continue the processing of the program. If the second action is taken it is necessary to make a second pass through the program to complete the translation process. During the second pass all unresolved references are procesd.

Assemblers that do not make a second pass through the assembly language program are called *one-pass assemblers*. If a second pass is used the assembler is called a *two-pass assembler*. Two-pass assemblers are simpler to design and are typically used on smaller computer systems. One-pass assemblers are usually found on larger systems since they require more memory space for proper operation. The assembler discussed in the next section is a two-pass assembler.

Assembler Directive Statements

Assembler directive statements provide information to the assembler program. Such a statement may indicate a particular action that the assembler should perform or it may be an assignment statement that assigns a value to an identifier that is to be used in the program. The assembler recognizes an assembler directive statement by finding one of the tokens given in Table 14-2 in field 2 or by detecting the presence of an assignment expression in that field. (The fact that field 2 contains an assign-

Table 14-2 Tokens Representing Direct Assembler Directives

Token	Use
.END	Indicates the last statement of an assembly language program. When this directive is detected by the assembler, it completes the current processing activities. An argument is associated with this directive. It is the address of the first instruction to be executed when the object program is run.
.EVEN	Checks the current value of the location counter LC. If this value is odd, 1 is added to LC to make the value even. After execution of this directive, LC will always contain a word address.
.TITLE	The argument of this directive gives the current title associated with the routine or subroutine being developed. This title is printed at the top of each page of a program listing.

ment expression is detected by finding an = sign as part of the symbol sequence making up the field.)

For the simple assembler that we are using only three assembler directives that influence the operation of the assembler are used. A statement involving the .END directive, such as

.END   START

indicates that the end of the assembly language program has been reached and that the first statement to be executed when the machine language program is run is the one associated with the symbolic address START. When the assembler detects the .END directive, it completes the current phase of the translation process and waits for the user to indicate the next action to be taken.

If the output indicates that the translation has been completed without any detected errors, the user may run the object program produced by the assembler and check that it is operating correctly. A much more common occurrence is to find that the assembler has detected one or more errors during the processing of the source program. In that case the programmer must make corrections in the source program and reassemble the program to see whether all of the errors have been corrected.

The second directive is the .EVEN directive. When this directive is detected, the assembler tests the value of LC. If the location counter holds an even number, indicating that it contains the address of a word in memory, this value is not changed. However, if the location counter holds an odd number, indicating the address of the second byte in a word, the location counter is incremented by 1 so that the address indicated by LC is now a word address.

The third directive is .TITLE. This tells the assembler that the character string found in field 3 is to be taken as the title of the program. The assembler uses this title when printing out any information about the program such as a listing or a list of detected errors. This directive does not have any direct influence on the translation process.

There are two types of assignment statements that can be encountered in a program. Assignment statements of the form

.=1000   ;START PROGRAM AT MEMORY LOCATION 1000

are used to set the location counter (LC) to a specific value. When a period is the only symbol on the left-hand side of the equal sign in an assignment statement, this indicates the location counter. The assembler then uses the expression on the right-hand side of the equal sign to define the new value for LC.

Assignment statements of the form

KBDATA=177562   ;ADDRESS OF KEYBOARD BUFFER

are used to assign a fixed value to the identifier found to the left of the equal sign. Statements of this type are processed by checking to see whether the identifier is in the symbol table. When it is already in the symbol table, the assembler uses the value of the expression on the right-hand side of the equal sign to assign a new value to the identifier. If the identifier is not located in the symbol table, the assembler enters the identifier into the table before assigning it the defined value.

Assignment statements cannot be used to redefine the values associated with labels that have been used as symbolic addresses. The normal use of an assignment statement is to provide a means to define a value for an identifier that may change value if the program is changed or modified for different applications.

Data Statements

Data statements are very closely related to machine command statements. They are used to enter specific values of data into memory or to set aside an area of memory to hold information. Data statements are recognized by finding one of the tokens listed in Table 14-3 in field 2. These tokens are assembler directives that, together with the information contained in the argument field, tell the assembler how much

Table 14-3 Assembler Directives Implementing Data Statements

Token	Associated Arguments	Action
.ASCII	/⟨string⟩/	Load the ASCII code corresponding to ⟨string⟩ into successive bytes. / at start and end are delimiters and not part of ⟨string⟩.
.ASCIZ	/⟨string⟩/	Same as .ASCII except that an additional null byte is added at end of block that holds ⟨string⟩.
.BLKB	n	Set aside a block of n bytes in memory.
.BLKW	n	Set aside a block of n words in memory.
.BYTE	⟨byte-1⟩, . . . , ⟨byte-n⟩	Set the n bytes in memory to the values ⟨byte-1⟩ through ⟨byte-n⟩. ⟨byte-i⟩ must be octal values.
.WORD	⟨word-1⟩, . . . , ⟨word-n⟩	Set the n words in memory to the values ⟨word-1⟩ through ⟨word-n⟩. <word-i> must be octal values.

space must be set aside to store the information and the information that is to be placed in this reserved area.

Labels are typically attached to most data statements since the data represented by the statement is normally referenced by one or more other statements in the program. Thus a typical data statement may have the form

BUFFER: .BLKW   500   ;BUFFER AREA OF 500(OCTAL) WORDS

When the assembler processes this statement, it detects the label BUFFER and places it in the symbol table with a value equal to the current value of the location counter (LC). The directive .BLKW then tells the assembler that we wish to set aside a block of words in memory to hold data. The argument associated with this directive, 500_8 in this example, indicates the actual number of words that are to be set aside. The assembler responds to this request by updating the value of LC according to the relationship

$$LC \leftarrow LC + 2*500_8$$

No attempt is made to initialize the contents of these 500_8 words to any specific value. (In some assemblers the assembler automatically sets all words to 0. This convention is not assumed for SEDCOM II's assembler.)

There are many instances where we will wish to store specific data items in memory. As shown in Table 14-3, there are a number of data statement directives that can be used for this purpose. For example, assume that we wish to store the string of ASCII characters

"What is the next value?"

in memory so that they can be printed out as part of the program. To create this string in memory we might use the following program segment

.=2500   ;SET ADDRESS OF FIRST CHARACTER
NEXTVL: .ASCIZ /What is the next value?/ ;STORE CHAR STRING

When the assembler processes these statements, it first sets LC to 2500 and then it sets aside the next 27_8 bytes to hold the string. One additional byte is then set to 0 to indicate the end of the string. After the 30_8 bytes needed by this statement have been set aside and loaded with the desired character sequence, the value of LC is changed to LC + 30_8. Note that the leading and trailing /'s in the above statement are delimiters that indicate the beginning and end of the string of characters to be stored and are not part of the string. The other data directives are processed in a similar manner.

This completes the definition and discussion of our simple assembler language for SEDCOM II. Our next task is to investigate how an assembler is designed to carry out these tasks.

EXERCISES

1. Assume that the following assembly language program is given.

```
        .TITLE SAMPLE

;****************************************************************
;
;           A SIMPLE PROGRAM TO ILLUSTRATE THE TASKS FACED BY
;           AN ASSEMBLER
;****************************************************************
;

        . = 1000
        NEXTVL = 2                          ;SIZE OF INCREMENT
        COUNT = 10                          ;NUMBER OF ELEMENTS
START:  MOV       #COUNT,R1                 ;SET COUNTER
        MOV       #BUF1,R2                  ;SET POINTER TO FIRST WORD OF BUF1
        MOV       #BUF2,R3                  ;SET POINTER TO FIRST WORD OF BUF2
LOOP:   MOVB      (R2),(R3)+                ;TRANSFER WORD
        ADD       #NEXTVAL,R2               ;INCREMENT BUF1 POINTER
        DEC       R1                        ;BEEN AROUND LOOP 20 TIMES?
        BNE       LOOP                      ;NO - DO AGAIN
        HALT


BUF1:   .ASCIZ    /This is a very long string of characters/
BUF2:   .BLKB     20

        .END      START
```

    (a)   Classify each statement.
    (b)   Construct the symbol table for this program. Show all labels and identifiers contained in the table and their associated values.

2. Assume that you are the assembler. Process each statement of the program given in Exercise 1 and explain the action taken. Show the machine language program generated after this assembly process has been completed. Assume that all errors have been corrected.

3. THE DESIGN OF A SIMPLE ASSEMBLER PROGRAM

In the last section we investigated the formal properties of the SEDCOM II assembly language. This provides the starting point for our investigation of the factors that influence the design of an assembler program. Our investigation starts by exploring some of the tasks that must be performed by the assembler during the translation process.

An assembler is designed to process an assembly language program one statement at a time. After a statement is read, the assembler decomposes it into tokens. These tokens are used to generate the machine language instruction or to carry out the assembler directive represented by the statement. This means that the assembler must be able to process labels, operator mnemonics, operand information, assembler directives, and comments. The processing required for each token type is defined by the role each plays in the assembly language.

Processing Comments

Comments are the easiest token type to process. As soon as the ";" indicating the start of a comment is detected, we know that all of the characters from the ";" to the end of line marker "⏎" can be ignored since comments are not used to produce object code.

Processing Operators and Assembler Directives

Operator mnemonics and assembler directives are also easy to recognize and process. The mnemonics used to represent these tokens are included in the mnemonic table together with the additional information needed to complete the processing of the statement. For example, if the mnemonic being processed represents an operation that requires two operands, this information is included in the table entry for this operand. The assembler then knows that it must look for two operands in the address field. Similarly if the token represents one of the assembler directives that require an argument, this is also indicated by the table entry. The assembler looks for the argument in the third field of the statement.

Processing Labels

Labels require the most effort to process since they are defined by the programmer and are not known at the time the assembler is designed. Labels are detected by the assembler in two ways. When the first token in the statement is found in field 1 and is delimited by a ":" we know that that token is a label that represents the symbolic address of the statement. The assembler uses the current value stored in the location counter to assign a machine address to this token. It then places the token and its assigned address value in the *symbol table* for later use.

Labels also appear in the address field of the statement. The operand tokens found in the address field may take on a number of different forms. If the operand is defined in terms of one of the addressing modes that references one of the CPU registers $R0$, ..., $R5$, the stack pointer (SP), or the program counter (PC), then the assembler recognizes these special symbols and processes the operands in the prescribed manner. If the addressing mode used involves a memory reference, then the memory address will be indicated by a label. During processing the assembler must check to find out whether the label is in the symbol table. If it is, and if it has been assigned a value, then the assembler can use this value to complete the processing of the statement. When the label is not found in the table, the assembler enters it and marks the label to indicate that it must be defined (i.e., given an address value) before the processing can be completed.

Processing Errors

As a statement is scanned, it is quite possible that the assembler will find that the statement is incorrect. The assembler must be designed to detect and report as many of these detectable errors as possible. The assembler will not, however, be able to detect errors in the algorithm represented by the program or errors in logic. Assemblers can be designed to detect errors such as:

1. Undefined labels (i.e., labels that have not been assigned an address value).
2. The use of the same label to indicate more than one symbolic address.
3. Improperly formed statements.
4. Improper operation code mnemonics.
5. Improperly formed labels.
6. Improper number of operands for a given operator.

One must be careful in dealing with the errors detected by an assembler. For example, if the assembler processed the statement

$$\text{START:} \quad \text{MVA} \quad (R1)+, -(R2)$$

it would indicate an error since MVA would be recognized as an improper operator mnemonic. However, if the statement

$$\text{LATE:} \quad \text{BNE} \quad \text{BEFOR}$$

was typed as

$$\text{LATE:} \quad \text{BEQ} \quad \text{BEFOR}$$

the assembler would not be able to detect this error since both BNE and BEQ are valid operator mnemonics.

The Assembly Process

Assemblers can take on many different forms. For this discussion we concentrate upon the basic tasks needed by all assemblers. The more advanced features of assemblers are discussed in the references listed at the end of this chapter.

The simplest type of an assembler, and the one that we discuss, is the *two-pass assembler,* which must read the input source program twice before completing the assembly process. During the first pass over the source program, the assembler performs the following tasks:

1. Locates all identifiers assigned values using an assignment statement; makes sure that all identifiers have been placed in the symbol table and assigned a value before they are used in a statement.
2. Locates all labels used as symbolic addresses and enters these labels into the symbol table.
3. Locates all labels in the operand field and checks that they correspond to one of the labels that have been assigned a value.
4. Checks all statements to see that they are formed according to the rules defining the assembly language being processed.
5. Reports all of the errors at the end of the first pass.

If at the end of the first pass the assembler reports one or more detected errors, the programmer must correct the errors and repeat the first pass to see whether the proper corrections have been made. As soon as an error-free first pass has been completed, the processing can go on to the second pass. The information gathered during the first pass is now used to generate object code. At the end of the second pass the assembler can produce, at the option of the programmer, the following output:

1. The machine language object code corresponding to the input source program.
2. A formatted listing that gives each line of the source program and the corresponding machine language code generated to represent the line.
3. A listing of all the labels and identifiers used and their values.

Upon completing the second pass the programmer has an object code representation of the original assembly language program. This object code program can now be run on the target computer system. Although the program may be assembled without error, there is no guarantee that the object code program correctly carries out the desired computational task for which it was written. The programmer must now test the program. When errors are detected the necessary corrections must be made in the assembly language program. The corrected program must be reassembled before the testing process can be continued on the revised program.

The two passes of a two-pass assembler have the general organization shown in Figure 14-4. Statements are read one at a time and processed. This continues until the .END statement is encountered. At the end of the first pass a check is made to see whether any errors were detected during that pass. If one or more errors are reported, the processing stops and the programmer must make the necessary corrections and repeat the first pass. When no errors are reported, the second pass is started. The statements of the program are scanned for the second time and translated into object code. When the .END statement is detected, the processing is completed by generating a machine-readable object program and a human-readable source listing.

The task of reading each statement is straightforward and was discussed in Chapter 13. Thus for the rest of this section we concentrate on how each statement is processed and how the object code is generated.

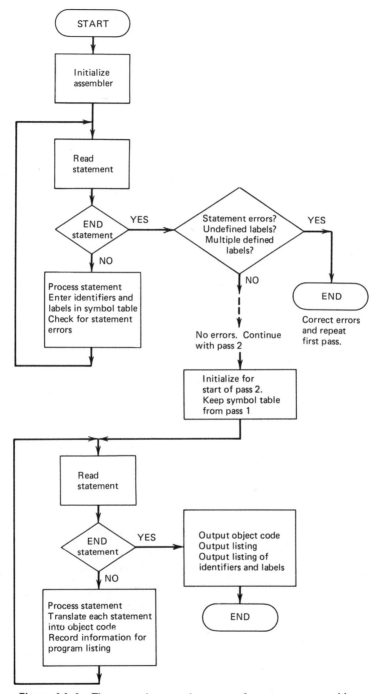

Figure 14-4   The general processing steps of a two-pass assembler.

Assembler Organization

It is easier to understand the operation of an assembler if we develop a conceptual model of the data flow that takes place inside an assembler. To do this we use the block diagram representation of the assembly process shown in Figure 14-5. This diagram is intended to represent the functional relationships that exist within an assembler rather than the actual structure of the assembler program itself.

The assembly operation can be represented in a manner similar to the one we used to investigate the behavior of complex digital systems. At the heart of the system is the *assembler control process,* which is responsible for controlling the flow of information between the various data elements used to hold or store data during the processing. Although the block diagram shown in Figure 14-5 is somewhat simplified and idealized, it serves to indicate the major activities involved in the assembly process.

The processing of a statement begins when it is read into the *statement buffer.*

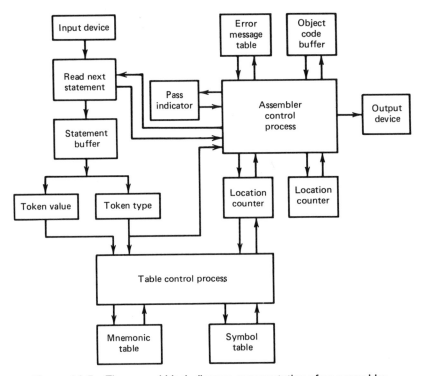

Figure 14-5   The general block diagram representation of an assembler.

Each statement consists of a sequence of tokens that are delimited by the delimiters discussed in the last section. These delimiters serve two purposes. They indicate the beginning and end of a token and may also identify the token type. Processing of the statement is carried out by reading the statement tokens from left to right.

A *statement scanner* is used to read each token from the statement buffer. This scanner outputs a *symbolic token value* and a *token type,* which identifies the type of token found. To do this, the scanner uses the rules defined in the last section to classify each token encountered in the statement buffer as the token is read. If the token cannot be classified, an error is indicated and the control unit places an appropriate error message in the *error message table.* When the scanner reaches the end of the statement, it produces a null output. The assembly control process completes the processing of the current statement and requests the next statement.

The amount of intelligence built into a scanner depends upon the particular method selected to process the statement. For our assembler it is assumed that the scanner can recognize all token types but that additional processing may be needed before deciding whether the recognized token is a valid token. In particular, tokens representing labels, assembler directives, identifiers, or operation codes must be further processed.

The *mnemonic table, symbol table,* and *location counter* (LC) are used to process the tokens. When the scanner indicates that the token is a "possible" operation code token or assembler directive, the assembler control process directs the *table control process* to read a value for this token from the mnemonic table. If the token cannot be found, the table control process reports an error and the assembler control process enters an error message in the error message table. Otherwise the value of the token is placed in the *table buffer.* The value of an operation code token consists of the binary value associated with the operation code mnemonic and an indication of the number of operands needed by the operation. If the assembler directive is a data directive, the value indicates which directive has been detected and the form of the argument associated with that directive.

In some cases the token is a character string representing a numerical value. The table control process translates this string directly to a binary value and places the result in the table buffer.

The token may be an identifier in an assignment statement. When this occurs the table control process tries to find it in the symbol table. If the identifier is found, the scanner is used to read the value of the assignment statement and this value is used to redefine the value of the identifier in the symbol table. When the identifier is not located, the table control process enters the identifier in the table before requesting the value of the identifier. In the one special case where the identifier is a ".", indicating that a new value is to be assigned to the location counter, the assembler control process immediately requests the value of the assignment statement. The table control process generates the binary value of the expression on the right-hand side of the assignment statement and places this value in the table buffer. The assembler control process then transfers this value to the location counter.

Label tokens are the most complex type of tokens to process since the processing depends upon a number of factors. If the processing is being carried out during the first pass, as indicated by the *pass indicator,* then the assembler must build the symbol table. If it is the second pass, the assembler must form the object code for the machine instructions and place this code in the *object code buffer.* This processing is simplified by the use of special token type codes to classify how the label is being used.

All label tokens used as symbolic addresses for statements are defined by the programmer and must be entered into the symbol table during the first pass of the assembler. Label tokens found in the operand portion of a statement may be tokens defined by the programmer or they may be one of the "reserved" tokens that are used to identify the CPU registers $R1$ through $R5$, SP, and PC. When a label is found in an operand, the scanner is responsible for identifying the addressing mode used for the operand. The token value in this case will either be one of the tokens indicating the CPU register associated with the operand or will be a label indicating a symbolic address.

During pass 1 all labels are checked against the contents of the symbol table. As has been described, all symbolic addresses are entered into the symbol table with a value corresponding to the current value of the location counter. Labels in the address portion of a statement are entered into the table, if they have not been previously encountered as symbolic addresses, and marked as undefined. Later, when this symbolic address is found, it is given a value. Whenever we try to use the same label for two different symbolic addresses, we have an error condition. Similarly, if at the end of the first pass we find that a label remains undefined, we also have an error condition.

It is assumed that we do not go on to pass 2 if any errors are detected during pass 1. Thus the processing of labels during pass 2 is much simpler than during pass 1. Whenever a token representing a symbolic address is detected, it is ignored since we know that this address has already been entered into the symbol table. Labels in the address portion of a statement are used to compute the address information associated with the operation code of the operator. The value of the token is read from the symbol table and used by the assembler control process to finish assembling the machine language instruction associated with the statement being processed.

The processing of all the other statement types is the responsibility of the assembler control process. The actual task performed depends upon the contents of the token type register. Data statements are used to reserve an area of memory to hold specific data values while the other assembler directives modify information used by the assembler during the assembly process. In particular the .END statement always indicates the last statement in the program being processed. Upon detection of this statement the current processing pass is completed. For pass 1 this involves printing out any error messages generated during the processing or a message indicating that no errors were detected. Since it is assumed that all errors are corrected before entering pass 2, the output of pass 2 consists of the machine language object code, in a machine-readable form, and, if requested by the programmer, the listing of the assembly language program together with the machine language code generated by each statement.

The First Pass

The sequence of operations carried out during the first pass of the assembly process is outlined by the flowchart given in Figure 14-6. This flowchart indicates the major tasks performed as a statement is being processed. It omits, however, the fine details of how these tasks are accomplished since these details are not of particular importance to the current discussion. Anyone wishing to realize an assembler would, of course, have to develop the operation of these blocks in greater detail.

The structure of the flowchart is determined by the structure that we have defined for our assembler language. The statements of the program are read one at a time and fully processed before going on to the next statement. Each statement consists of a sequence of tokens that are read from left to right. As each token is read it is evaluated and the action implied by the token type is performed.

When the first token in a statement is a label, it corresponds to the symbolic address assigned to that statement by the programmer. The symbol table is searched to find out whether the label has already been entered into the table. If it is not found, the token is entered into the table with a value equal to the value found in the location counter. A somewhat more complex situation occurs when the search finds that the token has been previously entered into the symbol table. There are two possible situations that must be considered. If a value has already been assigned to the label, this means that the same label has been used as the symbolic address for an earlier statement. This is an error and an error message is produced indicating that a label has been doubly defined. When the label is marked as undefined, this means that it has appeared as part of an operand in an earlier statement. A value equal to the value in the location counter is now assigned to the label. This completes the processing of the label token.

When there is no label token or when we complete the processing of the label, the next task is to process the token found in the second field of the statement. This token may be:

1. A comment. The rest of the statement is ignored and a new statement is read into the statement buffer.
2. An assignment statement. If the symbol to the left of the equal sign is a period, this indicates that the location counter is to be given a new value. Otherwise the symbol is an identifier that is to be assigned a value defined by the expression on the right-hand side of the equal sign. This symbol, if not already in the symbol table, is entered in the table and given the defined value. If this task cannot be carried out, an appropriate error message is generated. Upon completing the processing of the assignment operation a new statement is read into the statement buffer.
3. An assembler directive. If it is the .END directive, this terminates pass 1. If it is a data directive, the number of bytes in memory needed to provide the requested storage space is determined and the location counter is incremented by that amount. If it is the .EVEN or .TITLE directive, the assembler carries out the processing corresponding to the directive. Upon completing the appropriate task the assembler reads in the next statement.

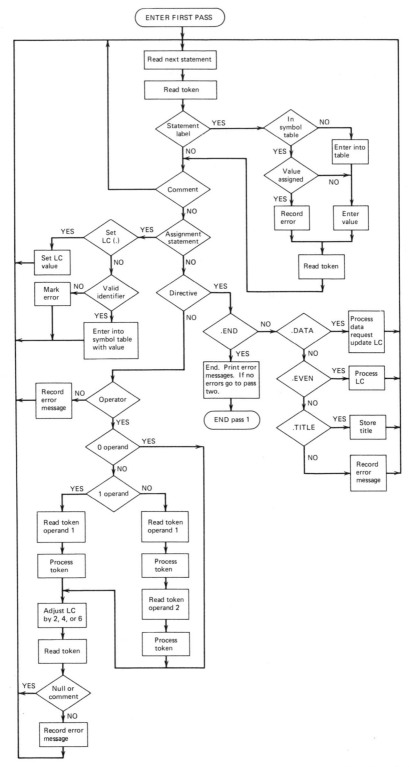

Figure 14-6 A flowchart of first-pass of an assembler showing the creation of symbol table and error detection.

4. An operator. The token is recognized as an operator by finding it in the mnemonic table. The table entry indicates the operation code associated with the token and also the number of operands needed by the operation. The assembler control process uses this information to evaluate the rest of the statement. If the token is a 0 operand operator, the resulting machine language instruction takes up one word and the location counter is incremented by 2. If the token corresponds to a 1 or 2 operand operator, additional processing is needed. Depending upon the information contained in the address field of the statement, 0, 1, or 2 additional words will be needed to complete the instruction. The tokens making up the operands are then read and processed. When the processing of the address information is completed, the location counter is incremented by 2, 4, or 6 depending upon the number of words needed to hold the instruction defined by the statement. The next statement is read after the rest of the current statement is checked for possible errors.
5. An error. The token may not correspond to any of the allowed statement types. An error message is recorded and the next statement is read into the statement buffer.

Upon the completion of pass 1 it is not unusual to find that one or more errors have been detected. The programmer must correct the errors and repeat pass 1. If the corrected source program is now found to be error-free, the programmer can go on to pass 2. As soon as this occurs, pass 2 can be initiated.

An Example

One of the best ways to understand the tasks performed during pass 1 is to consider how an assembler might carry out the processing of a simple program. Let us assume that it is desired to assemble the program given in Figure 14-7. The processing steps necessary to do this are presented in Table 14-4, where the actions taken as each statement is processed are explained.

A number of errors have been inserted in this program to illustrate the action of the assembler. At the end of pass 1 the assembler would print out a set of error messages of the following form

ERRORS DETECTED IN PROGRAM SET_TABLE
LINE 8   TAB UNDEFINED LABEL
LINE 11   DCE UNRECOGNIZED OPERATION CODE

The first error was detected because TAB was entered in the symbol table when line 8 was processed but was never defined as the symbolic address of any statement. Looking at the program the programmer would see that TAB was used as the address of the first word in the table when the correct label should have been TABLE. The second error is detected in line 11 when the assembler tries to find the token DCE in the mnemonic table. Since this is not one of the defined mnemonics, an error is detected.

Note that the error in program logic that occurs because the operation BEQ was

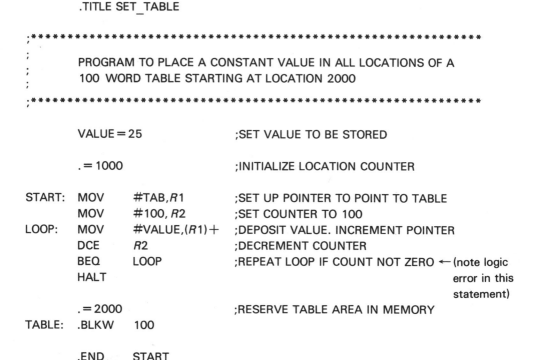

```
              .TITLE SET_TABLE


;***************************************************************

;
;             PROGRAM TO PLACE A CONSTANT VALUE IN ALL LOCATIONS OF A
;             100 WORD TABLE STARTING AT LOCATION 2000
;
;***************************************************************


              VALUE = 25              ;SET VALUE TO BE STORED

              . = 1000                ;INITIALIZE LOCATION COUNTER

START:  MOV       #TAB,R1             ;SET UP POINTER TO POINT TO TABLE
        MOV       #100, R2            ;SET COUNTER TO 100
LOOP:   MOV       #VALUE,(R1)+        ;DEPOSIT VALUE. INCREMENT POINTER
        DCE       R2                  ;DECREMENT COUNTER
        BEQ       LOOP                ;REPEAT LOOP IF COUNT NOT ZERO ← (note logic
        HALT                                                             error in this
                                                                         statement)
        . = 2000                      ;RESERVE TABLE AREA IN MEMORY
TABLE:  .BLKW     100

        .END      START
```

Figure 14-7   A simple assembly language program.

used where the operation BNE should have been used is not detected by the assembler. There is no way that the assembler can detect errors of this type.

At this point in the processing the programmer would correct the detected errors in the source program and repeat the pass 1 processing. If no errors are reported, the next step is to go to pass 2 to generate the final object code program. The object code program would still contain a logic error since the BEQ logic error could not be detected by the assembler.

The Second Pass

The second pass of the assembly process operates in essentially the same way as the first pass except that instead of checking for errors and forming the symbol table the assembler produces the object code equivalent of each source-language statement. At the start of the second pass it is assumed that the symbol table, generated during the first pass, does not contain any undefined values and that the source program does not contain any detectable errors. These assumptions reduce the number of tasks that must be performed during the second pass.

Figure 14-8 presents a flowchart of the major tasks performed during pass 2. Comparing this flowchart with the flowchart for pass 1, we see that since we no longer have to worry about constructing the symbol table or checking for errors, we can

Table 14-4 The Actions Taken during Pass 1 to Process the Program of Figure 14-7

Statement (Comments Not Shown)	Action	Value of LC after Statement Is Processed
.TITLE SET_TABLE	Record string SET_TABLE for later use.	Assume LC is initialized to 0 before reading first statement.
;************	Ignore—comment	LC = 0
; PROG-----	Ignore—comment	LC = 0
; TABLE------	Ignore—comment	LC = 0
;************	Ignore—comment	LC = 0
VALUE = 25	Enter VALUE into symbol table with a value of 25.	LC = 0
. = 1000	Assembler directive. Reset value of LC.	LC = 1000
START: MOV #TAB,R1	START entered in symbol table with a value of 1000. TAB entered in symbol table and marked UNDEFINED.	LC = 1004
MOV #100,R2	Statement checked and found correct. #100 recognized as a number.	LC = 1010
LOOP: MOV #VALUE,(R1)+	LOOP entered in symbol table with a value of 1010. VALUE found in symbol table with a value. No action.	LC = 1014
DCE R2	DCE not recognized. Error message generated. Go to next statement.	LC = 1016 (assume 1 word)
BEQ LOOP	LOOP found in symbol table. BEQ recognized as an operation code mnemonic. Logic error not detected.	LC = 1020
HALT	HALT recognized as a zero operand machine instruction.	LC = 1022
. = 2000	Reset value of LC.	LC = 2000
TABLE: .BLKW 100	Enter TABLE into symbol table with value of 2000. Reserve 100 words (200 bytes) in memory.	LC = 2200
.END START	Detect end of pass 1. Processing is completed by printing out error message	

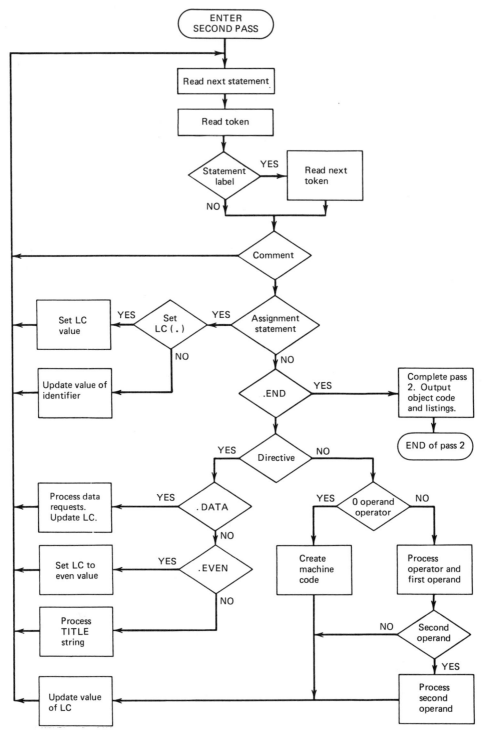

Figure 14-8 A flowchart of the second pass of an assembler showing the generation of object code.

bypass many of the steps. In particular we have to process labels only when they appear as a component of one of the operands, and we can eliminate the various error tests. The following discussion concentrates on those tasks that are related to the generation of object code.

It is tempting to assume that all of the assignment statements, except the one that redefines the value of the location counter (LC), can be neglected. However, one of the properties of an assignment statement is that it can be used to redefine the value of an identifier anywhere in the program. Thus, although we can assume that all assignment statements are error-free, we must process them as we did during pass 1.

The assembler directives play the same role that they did in pass 1 and also must be processed. The new feature that must be introduced arises when we are processing data directives. Data directives that reserve an area of memory, such as .BLKW, are processed by simply generating null values for all of the words or bytes that make up the desired storage area. A somewhat more complicated process is needed to implement the data directives, such as .ASCIZ, which indicate that constant values should be loaded into memory. In this case the assembler must evaluate each of the arguments of the directive and generate the values that are to be stored in the reserved area. For example, the statements

$$. = 2000$$
$$.ASCIZ \quad /TEST \ \#1/$$

would generate the following code:

Word Address	Content of Word (Binary) High-order Byte	Low-order Byte	Content of Word (Symbolic)
2000	01000101	01010100	'E''T'
2002	01010100	01010110	'T''S'
2004	00100110	00100000	'#'' '
2006	00000000	00110001	0 '1'

zero value
end marker

Note that the order of the symbols is determined by the way memory is organized. The seven characters in the character string are stored sequentially in the 7 bytes starting at address 2000. The string is then terminated with the null value in the byte at location 2007. It is the responsibility of the assembly control process to make sure that the proper ASCII codes are placed in the indicated locations and that the sequence is terminated with the null value. The other data directives that have arguments are treated in a similar manner.

The processing of machine command statements is complicated by the fact that these statements may generate machine language instructions that require 1, 2, or 3 memory words. The way in which these statements are processed is best understood by considering a number of examples. Let us assume that the segment of code shown in Figure 14-9a is contained in a program and that during the first pass of the assembler the information shown in Figure 14-9b has been entered into the symbol table.

PACK: MOV (R1)+,(R2)+
        MOV A,R3
        MOV #A,B

(a) The machine command statements

PACK	2000
A	3200
B	2500

(b) The partial symbol table

Token	Octal Value First Word
MOV	010000
(R1)+	002100
(R2)+	000022
Instruction	012122

(c) Translation of the first machine command statement

Token	Octal Value First Word	Second Word
MOV	010000	000000
A	006700	001172
R3	000003	000000
Instruction	016703	001172

(d) Translation of the second machine command statement

Token	First Word	Octal Value Second Word	Third Word
MOV	010000	000000	000000
#A	002700	003200	000000
B	000067	000000	000464
Instruction	012767	003200	000464

(e) Translation of the third machine command statement

Address	Code
2000	012122
2002	016703
2004	001172
2006	012767
2010	003200
2012	000464
2014	⟨next inst⟩

(f) Generated object code

Figure 14-9   The generation of object code for machine command statements.

The calculations used to construct the object code defined by these statements are shown in Figure 14-9*c, d,* and *e*. The resulting object code produced by this processing is given in Figure 14-9*f.*

The translation of machine command statements requires a complete knowledge of the addressing techniques used by SEDCOM II. A review of the different addressing modes used in SEDCOM II, as presented in Chapter 12, is suggested before going on to the following discussion.

The first statement has the symbolic address PACK that, according to the information in the symbol table, corresponds to the memory location 2000. Thus when the translation of this statement is started, the location counter contains the value 2000. When the token MOV is read, the assembler looks this mnemonic up in the mnemonic table and finds that it has a value of 010000_8 and that it requires two operands. The next token read is the source operand $(R1)+$, which indicates that the autoincrement mode of addressing is to be used with register $R1$. Using this information the assembler knows that the mode subfield of the source address field will have a value of 2 since address mode 2 is defined to be the autoincrement mode. The register subfield has a value of 1 since this operand deals with register $R1$. Similarly the second operand, corresponding to the destination address, is defined using the autoincrement mode of addressing in conjunction with register $R2$. The mode and register subfields of the destination address field have the values 2 and 2, respectively. After all of this information is gathered, the instruction is formed by adding the three intermediate values together to produce the single-word instruction indicated in Figure 14-9*c*. The final step in processing this statement consists of incrementing LC by 2 so that it is now pointing at memory location 2002, which is the next word in memory that is to receive an instruction.

The second statement in the program segment requires two words. The source operand indicates that relative addressing is used to locate the value of this operand. The offset value needed to locate A in memory is stored in the second word of the instruction. To assemble this instruction we proceed as shown in Figure 14-9*d*.

First we read MOV and assign it a value of 010000_8. We next find A as the first operand and recognize that this implies the relative addressing mode. Relative addressing uses address mode 6 and the contents of the PC, which is register 7, to form the address of the desired operand. Thus the mode and register subfields of the source field are set to 6 and 7 as shown. To complete the processing of the source operand we must compute the offset value that will be used to compute the address of information represented by this operand. When it is time for the computer to access the information represented by the symbolic address A, it will have read both the first and the second word of the instruction. Thus the program counter (PC) will contain the address of the word following the second word of the instruction. The offset value is added to this value to compute the absolute address of A. Thus the second word of the instruction, which holds this offset value, contains the value

$$\text{OFFSET} = \langle\text{address of } A\rangle - \langle\text{value of PC after fetching the word holding the offset value}\rangle$$
$$= 3200_8 - 2006_8 = 1172_8$$

The evaluation of the first word of the instruction is completed by processing the destination operand. Since this operand indicates that register mode addressing is used, the final value for the first word of the instruction is computed as shown in Figure 14-9*d*. This completes the processing of the second statement, and the location counter is incremented by 4 to indicate that the next instruction will be placed in memory location 2006.

The third instruction is processed as shown in Figure 14-9*e*. It is a three-word instruction. The first word of the instruction is built up in the same manner used in the two previous examples. The source operand #*A* is recognized to be an immediate mode address. Thus the value of *A* is placed in the second word while the mode and register subfields of the source field have the values 2 and 7, respectively. The destination operand is then found to be defined using relative addressing. The third word in the instruction contains the offset value needed to execute the instruction. This value is defined as

$$\text{OFFSET} = \langle\text{address of } B\rangle - \langle\text{value of PC after fetching the offset value}\rangle$$
$$= 2500_8 - 2014_8 = 464_8$$

The three words making up this instruction are stored in memory locations 2006, 2010, and 2012. Thus after this statement is processed, the location counter is incremented by 6 to a value of 2014.

The assembler that we have been discussing is extremely simple because our main interest was in understanding the basic organization of the assembly process. There are, of course, many other routine tasks that can be performed by the assembler. The references at the end of this chapter present additional details about the design and operation of assembler and other translator programs.

EXERCISES

1. What will be contained in the symbol table and what error messages will be produced at the end of the first pass of the assembly process for the following source program?

```
        . = 2000
        NEWLINE = 14
        SPACE = 40


STRT:   MOV   #NEWLINE,R3   ;SET COUNTER
        MOV   #TABL1,R1     ;SET POINTER
LOOP:   CMP   (R1)+,#SPACE  ;FOUND A SPACE
        BRZ   LP3
        ADD   #1,R4                ;INCREMENT COUNT
```

```
LOOP2:     DEC    R3           ;FINISHED?
           BNZ    LOOP         ;NO
           HALT                ;YES

TABEL1:    .ASCII  /HOW MANY LETTERS/
           .END    STRT
```

2. Show how the following statements would be translated by an assembler.

```
           . = 3000
TESTA:     MOV    #500, R1
           CMP    R1,A
           BEQ    TESTB
           JSR    PC,PRINT
TESTB:     MOV    B,A
           HALT

           . = 6000
A:         .BLKW 5
B:         .BLKB  5

           . = 7000
PRINT:     ———
```

4. SUMMARY

This chapter has investigated some of the techniques that can be used to relieve a programmer of many of the routine tasks involved in developing a machine language program. The main concept is that a computer program can be used to translate statements that are meaningful to a programmer into machine language instructions if we are careful in the way that we design these statements. Assembler programs are the simplest of such translator programs.

An assembler language is very closely related to the machine language of the computer that will process the object program. The statements of the language are easy to translate because we have imposed a very rigid limitation on the form that these statements can take. If we wish to have a language that can be used by a general user, we must make the statements of a language have a form that is easily interpreted by the user without requiring the user to know how the computer operates. This requirement means that we need a much more complex program to carry out the translation process from the source program to the object program. Two levels of processing are required. The first level essentially transforms the source language statements into a sequence of assembler-language-like statements. The second level completes the process by translating these statements into an object program. The more advanced topics associated with the first stage of the translation process are discussed in the references.

Reference Notation

A detailed discussion of the advanced features of the PDP-11 assembler language are found in References 2, 3, and 6. The SEDCOM II assembly language is basically a subset of the PDP-11 assembly language. A general overview of other assembler languages and their implementation are found in References 4, 5, and 7. Higher level languages, such as Pascal, PL/1, and FORTRAN, are translated by compiler programs. The design of compilers are discussed in Reference 1.

REFERENCES

1. Aho, A. V., and Ullman, J. D. (1977). *Principles of Compiler Design*. Addison-Wesley, Reading, Mass.
2. Eckhouse, R. H. Jr., and Morris, L. R. (1979), *Minicomputer Systems, Organization, Programming, and Applications (PDP-11)* (second edition). Prentice-Hall, Englewood Cliffs, N.J.
3. Frank, T. S. (1983), *Introduction to the PDP-11 and Its Assembly Language*. Prentice-Hall, Englewood Cliffs, N.J.
4. Freeman, P. (1975), *Software Systems Principles: A Survey*. Science Research Associates, Chicago.
5. Gear, C. W. (1980), *Computer Organization and Programming* (third edition). McGraw-Hill, New York.
6. Stone, H. S., and Sieworek, D. P. (1975), *Introduction to Computer Organization and Data Structures: PDP-11 Edition*. McGraw-Hill, New York.
7. Ullman, J. D. (1976), *Fundamental Concepts of Programming Systems*. Addison-Wesley, Reading, Mass.

HOME PROBLEMS

The following problems deal with developing specific subprocedures to handle different portions of the assembly process. For each program give a flowchart to show the general organization of the algorithm used to carry out the specified task and an assembler language program that implements the given algorithm.

1. Each statement in our assembler language consists of a string of ASCII characters. The end of the statement is indicated by the special delimiter character CR (carriage return), which is encoded as 15_8. To process a statement an assembler reads one statement at a time into the statement buffer according to the following rules.

    The read statement procedure, RDSTAT, ignores all leading blanks and retains only one space between character subsequences that make up the string. The first location of the statement buffer is indicated by the lable STBUF. The number of characters in an input sequence is always less than or equal to 80_{10}.

    Develop the procedure RDSTAT.

2. A token scanner is used to read the next token from the character sequence in

the statement buffer. It must return two values. The first value is the character string that forms the token and the second value is an integer that indicates the type of token detected. The token scanner uses the rules that define the assembler language to make this decision. Design a procedure RDTOKN that carries out this task. The output is a character string corresponding to the token and an integer that indicates the token type. The following values are given to the tokens.

Token Type	Token Value	
Label—symbolic address	1	
Operand	2	
Identifier in assignment	3	
Symbol—possible OP-code	4	
Numerical string	5	
Character string	6	
Assembler directive	7	
Comment	8	(Comment not saved)
Error	9	

3. When the token scanner indicates that the token may be a possible operation code, the token must be checked by searching for the token in the mnemonic table. Design a subprocedure ISTOK that searches for the token in the mnemonic table and returns the value of the operation code associated with the token, if it is found, and a value that indicates the number of operands associated with the token. If the token is not found, an error is indicated by returning a value of 3 for the number of operands.

4. When the token scanner indicates that the token may be a possible symbolic address, the token must be entered into the symbol table. Design a subprocedure SYMTAB that will try to enter the label into the symbol table. An error is indicated if the label is already in the table with a defined value.

5. When the token scanner indicates that the token may be a possible assembler directive, the token must be evaluated to see which task is to be carried out. Design a subprocedure ASDIR that will complete the processing of the statement by deciding which assembly directive has been found and then finish the processing of the statement as specified by the directive.

6. When the token scanner indicates that the token is an operand, the operand must be evaluated. During pass 1 this involves deciding the mode of the operand and the number of words used to hold the information needed to form the operand. If a label is involved, it must be checked in the symbol table to see whether it has been defined. If it is not defined the label must be entered into the table and marked as an undefined label. Design a subprocedure OPPRO that will carry out this processing task.

7. Assume that the subprocedures described in Problems 1 through 6 are available. Write an assembler language program that will implement the first pass of an assembler of the type described in Figure 14-6.

BINARY CODES FOR CHARACTER REPRESENTATION

Standard binary codes have been developed to represent alphanumeric and special characters within a computer. Two such codes are the ASCII (American Standard Code for Information Interchange) and the EBCDIC (Extended Binary Coded Decimal Interchange Code).

The ASCII code is a seven-bit code that is very widely used in almost all microprocessors and minicomputers. It is also used extensively for communication purposes. Some of the code groups included in this code have been defined to represent special tasks found in data communication. Since these tasks are not of importance in most computer applications, the code groups associated with these tasks are often redefined by a given manufacturer to represent some other task. The listing given uses the standard terminology for all of the code groups.

The EBCDIC code, which is an eight-bit binary code, is used mostly by computer systems developed by IBM. It has a larger number of encoded characters and tasks than found in the ASCII code. Only a subset of this code is given.

The ASCII Character Set and Control Codes

	Character	Binary	Octal	Decimal	Hexadecimal
		Numeric Representation			
↑	NUL	00000000	000	0	00
	SOH	00000001	001	1	01
	STX	00000010	002	2	02
S	ETX	00000011	003	3	03
P	EOT	00000100	004	4	04
E	ENQ	00000101	005	5	05
C	ACK	00000110	006	6	06
I	BEL	00000111	007	7	07

The ASCII Character Set and Control Codes (Continued)

	Character	Numeric Representation			
		Binary	Octal	Decimal	Hexadecimal
A	BS	00001000	010	8	08
L	HT	00001001	011	9	09
	LF LINEFEED	00001010	012	10	0A
C	VT	00001011	013	11	0B
O	FF	00001100	014	12	0C
N	CR RETURN	00001101	015	13	0D
T	SO	00001110	016	14	0E
R	SI	00001111	017	15	0F
O	DLE	00010000	020	16	10
L	DC1	00010001	021	17	11
	DC2	00010010	022	18	12
C	DC3	00010011	023	19	13
O	DC4	00010100	024	20	14
D	NAK	00010101	025	21	15
E	SYN	00010110	026	22	16
S	ETB	00010111	027	23	17
	CAN	00011000	030	24	18
	EM	00011001	031	25	19
	SUB	00011010	032	26	1A
	ESC ESCAPE	00011011	033	27	1B
	FS	00011100	034	28	1C
	GS	00011101	035	29	1D
	RS	00011110	036	30	1E
	US	00011111	037	31	1F
	SPACE	00100000	040	32	20
	!	00100001	041	33	21
	"	00100010	042	34	22
	#	00100011	043	35	23
	$	00100100	044	36	24
	%	00100101	045	37	25
	&	00100110	046	38	26
	' APOSTROPHE	00100111	047	39	27
	(	00101000	050	40	28
	)	00101001	051	41	29
	*	00101010	052	42	2A
	+	00101011	053	43	2B
	, COMMA	00101100	054	44	2C
	− MINUS	00101101	055	45	2D
	. PERIOD	00101110	056	46	2E
	/	00101111	057	47	2F

The ASCII Character Set and Control Codes (Continued)

	Numeric Representation			
Character	**Binary**	**Octal**	**Decimal**	**Hexadecimal**
0	00110000	060	48	30
1	00110001	061	49	31
2	00110010	062	50	32
3	00110011	063	51	33
4	00110100	064	52	34
5	00110101	065	53	35
6	00110110	066	54	36
7	00110111	067	55	37
8	00111000	070	56	38
9	00111001	071	57	39
: COLON	00111010	072	58	3A
; SEMICOLON	00111011	073	59	3B
<	00111100	074	60	3C
=	00111101	075	61	3D
>	00111110	076	62	3E
?	00111111	077	63	3F
@	01000000	100	64	40
A	01000001	101	65	41
B	01000010	102	66	42
C	01000011	103	67	43
D	01000100	104	68	44
E	01000101	105	69	45
F	01000110	106	70	46
G	01000111	107	71	47
H	01001000	110	72	48
I	01001001	111	73	49
J	01001010	112	74	4A
K	01001011	113	75	4B
L	01001100	114	76	4C
M	01001101	115	77	4D
N	01001110	116	78	4E
O	01001111	117	79	4F
P	01010000	120	80	50
Q	01010001	121	81	51
R	01010010	122	82	52
S	01010011	123	83	53
T	01010100	124	84	54
U	01010101	125	85	55
V	01010110	126	86	56
W	01010111	127	87	57
X	01011000	130	88	58

The ASCII Character Set and Control Codes (Continued)

| Character | | Numeric Representation | | | |
		Binary	Octal	Decimal	Hexadecimal
Y		01011001	131	89	59
Z		01011010	132	90	5A
[		01011011	133	91	5B
\		01011100	134	92	5C
]		01011101	135	93	5D
^	CARET	01011110	136	94	5E
_	UNDERSCORE	01011111	137	95	5F
`	GRAVE ACCENT	01100000	140	96	60
a		01100001	141	97	61
b		01100010	142	98	62
c		01100011	143	99	63
d		01100100	144	100	64
e		01100101	145	101	65
f		01100110	146	102	66
g		01100111	147	103	67
h		01101000	150	104	68
i		01101001	151	105	69
j		01101010	152	106	6A
k		01101011	153	107	6B
l		01101100	154	108	6C
m		01101101	155	109	6D
n		01101110	156	110	6E
o		01101111	157	111	6F
p		01110000	160	112	70
q		01110001	161	113	71
r		01110010	162	114	72
s		01110011	163	115	73
t		01110100	164	116	74
u		01110101	165	117	75
v		01110110	166	118	76
w		01110111	167	119	77
x		01111000	170	120	78
y		01111001	171	121	79
z		01111010	172	122	7A
{		01111011	173	123	7B
|		01111100	174	124	7C
}		01111101	175	125	7D
~		01111110	176	126	7E
DELET		01111111	177	127	7F

Partial EBCDIC Character Set and Control Codes

Character	Numeric Representation			
	Binary	**Octal**	**Decimal**	**Hexadecimal**
NUL	00000000	000	0	00
CR	00001101	015	13	0D
NL	00010101	025	21	15
LF	00100101	045	37	25
BEL	00101111	057	47	2F
SPACE	01000000	100	64	40
. PERIOD	01001011	113	75	4B
<	01001100	114	76	4C
(	01001101	115	77	4D
+	01001110	116	78	4E
:	01001111	117	79	4F
&	01010000	120	80	50
!	01011010	132	90	5A
$	01011011	133	91	5B
*	01011100	134	92	5C
)	01011101	135	93	5D
;	01011110	136	94	5E
%	01101100	154	108	6C
_ UNDERLINE	01101101	155	109	6D
>	01101110	156	110	6E
?	01101111	157	111	6F
:	01111010	172	122	7A
#	01111011	173	123	7B
'	01111101	175	125	7D
=	01111110	176	126	7E
"	01111111	177	127	7F
a	10000001	201	128	81
b	10000010	202	129	82
c	10000011	203	130	83
d	10000100	204	131	84
e	10000101	205	132	85
f	10000110	206	133	86
g	10000111	207	134	87
h	10001000	210	135	88
i	10001001	211	136	89
j	10010001	221	145	91
k	10010010	222	146	92
l	10010011	223	147	93
m	10010100	224	148	94
n	10010101	225	149	95

Partial EBCDIC Character Set and Control Codes (Continued)

Character	Binary	Octal	Decimal	Hexadecimal
		Numeric Representation		
	Binary	Octal	Decimal	Hexadecimal
o	10010110	226	150	96
p	10010111	227	151	97
q	10011000	231	152	98
r	10011001	232	153	99
s	10100010	242	162	A2
t	10100011	243	163	A3
u	10100100	244	164	A4
v	10100101	245	165	A5
w	10100110	246	166	A6
x	10100111	247	167	A7
y	10101000	250	168	A8
z	10101001	251	169	A9
A	11000001	301	193	C1
B	11000010	302	194	C2
C	11000011	303	195	C3
D	11000100	304	196	C4
E	11000101	305	197	C5
F	11000110	306	198	C6
G	11000111	307	199	C7
H	11001000	310	200	C8
I	11001001	311	201	C9
J	11010001	321	209	D1
K	11010010	322	210	D2
L	11010011	323	211	D3
M	11010100	324	212	D4
N	11010101	325	213	D5
O	11010110	326	214	D6
P	11010111	327	215	D7
Q	11011000	331	216	D8
R	11011001	332	217	D9
S	11100010	342	226	E2
T	11100011	343	227	E3
U	11100100	344	228	E4
V	11100101	345	229	E5
W	11100110	346	230	E6
X	11100111	347	231	E7
Y	11101000	350	232	E8
Z	11101001	351	233	E9
0	11110000	360	240	F0
1	11110001	361	241	F1

Partial EBCDIC Character Set and Control Codes (Continued)

Character	Numeric Representation			
	Binary	**Octal**	**Decimal**	**Hexadecimal**
2	11110010	362	242	F2
3	11110011	363	243	F3
4	11110100	364	244	F4
5	11110101	365	245	F5
6	11110110	366	246	F6
7	11110111	367	247	F7
8	11111000	370	248	F8
9	11111001	371	249	F9

APPENDIX B

ANSWERS TO SELECTED EXERCISES

CHAPTER 2

Section 2

1. [0000] [0001] [0010] [0011] [0100] [0101] [0110] [0111]
   [1000] [1001] [1010] [1011] [1100] [1101] [1110] [1111]

2. Assume 80 characters/line, 50 lines/page, 400 characters/page, 2 characters/ word, 96,000 characters = 240 pages

3. 65,536 bytes

Section 3

1. ADD 001   SUBTRACT 011   CLEAR 111
   MULTIPLY 010   DIVIDE 100

2. 13 characters used. See Appendix A for the code.

Section 4

1. $14.62_8 = 1100.11001_2$
   $123.61_{10} = 1111011.1001110 \ldots_2$
   $A1B.F12_{16} = 101000011011.111100010010_2$

2. $14.65_{10} = 16.5146 \ldots_8$
   $= E.A666 \ldots_{16}$
   $1568.721_{10} = 3040.5611 \ldots_8$
   $= 620.B89 \ldots_{16}$

3. $110101.110_2 = 53.75_{10}$
   $656.46_8 = 426.59375_{10}$
   $777.77_{16} = 1911.46484375_{10}$

4. $10111110101.1101_2 = 2765.64_8$
   $= 5F5.D_{16}$

5. $398.788_{10} = 110001110.1100100 \ldots_2$
   $656.46_8 = 110101110.10011_2$
   $777.77_{16} = 011101110111.01110111_2$

6. $r = 2$ $m = 10$ $r = 5$ $m = 5$ $r = 16$ $m = 3$
   $r = 3$ $m = 7$ $r = 8$ $m = 4$
   $r = 4$ $m = 5$ $r = 10$ $m = 4$

Section 5

1. BCD value of $145.64_{10} = 0001\ \ 0100\ \ 0101\ \ .\ \ 0110\ \ 0100$

2. $10110101_2 = 11101111_{gray}$
   $111111111_2 = 100000000_{gray}$

3.

78934	encoded as a 2 4 2 1 code	1101	1110	1111	0011	0100
	encoded as a 7 4 −2 −1 code	1000	1111	1110	0101	0100

5. Resolution $= (\frac{1}{2})^8 = .00390625$
   Range $= \pm 15.99609375$

6.

	0	1	3	5
100100	−4	−2.0	−.5	−.125
110101	−21	−10.5	−2.625	−.65625
001010	+10	+5.0	+1.25	+.3125

7. 10

8.

n	$.5 \cos(n\omega)$	$X = [b_s b_{-1} b_{-2} b_{-3} b_{-4} b_{-5}]$
0	.5000	010000
1	.49240	010000
2	.46984	001111
3	.43301	001101
4	.38302	001100

CHAPTER 3

Section 2

1. (a)

x_1	x_2	$x_1 \downarrow x_2$	$\overline{(x_1 \vee x_2)}$	$\bar{x}_1 \bar{x}_2$
0	0	1	1	1
0	1	0	0	0
1	0	0	0	0
1	1	0	0	0

(c)

x_1	x_2	$x_1 \wedge x_2$	$\overline{((\bar{x}_1\bar{x}_2)(\bar{x}_1\bar{x}_2))}$
0	0	0	0
0	1	0	0
1	0	0	0
1	1	1	1

2.

x_1	x_2	x_3	x_4	$f(x_1, x_2, x_3, x_4)$	$g(x_1, x_2, x_3, x_4)$
0	0	0	0	1	1
0	0	0	1	0	0
0	0	1	0	1	1
0	0	1	1	1	1
0	1	0	0	0	0
0	1	0	1	0	0
0	1	1	0	1	1
0	1	1	1	1	1
1	0	0	0	1	1
1	0	0	1	1	1
1	0	1	0	1	1
1	0	1	1	1	1
1	1	0	0	1	1
1	1	0	1	1	1
1	1	1	0	1	1
1	1	1	1	1	1

3.

x_1	x_2	x_3	$g(x_1, x_2)$	$f(x_2, x_3)$	$m(x_1, x_2, x_3)$
0	0	0	0	1	0
0	0	1	0	1	0
0	1	0	0	1	0
0	1	1	0	0	1
1	0	0	0	1	0
1	0	1	0	1	0
1	1	0	1	1	1
1	1	1	1	0	0

Section 3

1. $m_0 = \bar{x}_1\bar{x}_2\bar{x}_3\bar{x}_4,$ $m_{13} = x_1x_2\bar{x}_3x_4$
   $M_0 = x_1 \vee x_2 \vee x_3 \vee x_4,$ $M_{13} = \bar{x}_1 \vee \bar{x}_2 \vee x_3 \vee \bar{x}_4$

2. $f(x_1, x_2, x_3, x_4) = m_0 \vee m_1 \vee m_4 \vee m_6 \vee m_7 \vee m_{11} \vee m_{13} \vee m_{14}$
   $= M_2 \wedge M_3 \wedge M_5 \wedge M_8 \wedge M_9 \wedge M_{10} \wedge M_{12} \wedge M_{15}$

3. (a) $x_1 \uparrow x_2 = m_0 \vee m_1 \vee m_2 = M_3$
   (c) $x_1 \oplus x_2 = m_1 \vee m_2 = M_0 \wedge M_3$

Section 4

1.

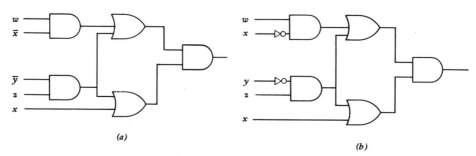

(a)

(b)

2. (a)

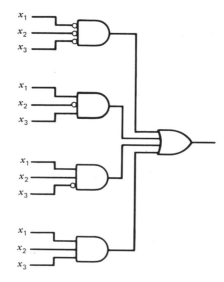

3. $f(x, y, z) = (x\,y\,z) \vee (x\,\bar{y}\,\bar{z}) \vee (\bar{x}\,y\,\bar{z}) = m_7 \vee m_4 \vee m_2$

Section 5

1. (a) NAND   (b) NOR

2. $1.25

CHAPTER 4

Section 2

2. (a) $\overline{(x_1 x_2 \lor \overline{x_1} \overline{x_2})} = (\overline{x_1 x_2})(\overline{\overline{x_1} \overline{x_2}})$
$$= (\overline{x_1} \lor \overline{x_2})(x_1 \lor x_2) = \overline{x_1} x_2 \lor \overline{x_2} x_1$$

(c) $x_2 \overline{x_3} \lor x_2 x_3 \lor x_1 \overline{x_3} \lor x_1 x_3 \lor \overline{x_1} x_2 \lor x_1 x_2 = x_2 \lor x_1 = \overline{(\overline{x_1} \overline{x_2})}$

3. (a) $(\overline{x_1 x_2})(\overline{x_1 x_3}) = (\overline{x_1} \lor \overline{x_2})(x_1 \lor x_3)$
$$= (\overline{x_1} \lor \overline{x_2} \lor x_3 \overline{x_3})(x_1 \lor x_2 \overline{x_2} \lor x_3)$$
$$= (\overline{x_1} \lor \overline{x_2} \lor x_3)(\overline{x_1} \lor \overline{x_2} \lor \overline{x_3})(x_1 \lor x_2 \lor x_3)$$
$$\land (x_1 \lor \overline{x_2} \lor x_3)$$
$$= M_6 M_7 M_0 M_2$$
$$= m_1 \lor m_3 \lor m_4 \lor m_5$$

(b) $\qquad\qquad m_2 \lor m_3 \lor m_4 \lor m_6$

(c) $\qquad\qquad m_5 \lor m_6$

Section 3

1.

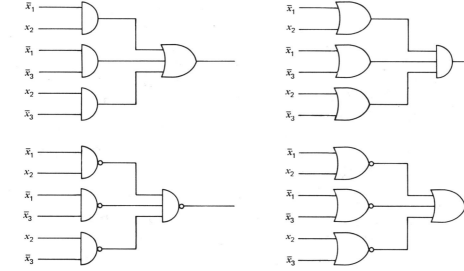

2.

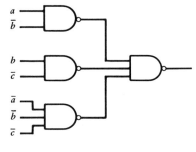

3.

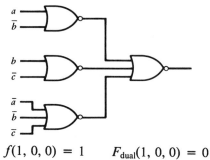

$$f(1, 0, 0) = 1 \qquad F_{\text{dual}}(1, 0, 0) = 0$$

Section 4

1.

Gray Code			Binary Equivalent		
x_1	x_2	x_3	y_1	y_2	y_3
0	0	0	0	0	0
0	0	1	0	0	1
0	1	0	0	1	1
0	1	1	0	1	0
1	0	0	1	1	1
1	0	1	1	1	0
1	1	0	1	0	0
1	1	1	1	0	1

$$y_1 = m_4 \lor m_5 \lor m_6 \lor m_7$$
$$y_2 = m_2 \lor m_3 \lor m_4 \lor m_5$$
$$y_3 = m_1 \lor m_2 \lor m_4 \lor m_7$$

2.

i_1	i_2	Operation
0	0	$\overline{A \land B}$
0	1	$\overline{A \lor B}$
1	0	$A \lor B$
1	1	$A\overline{B} \lor \overline{A}B$

A_k	B_k	i_1	i_2	$f(A_k, B_k, i_1, i_2)$
0	0	0	0	1
0	0	0	1	1
0	0	1	0	0
0	0	1	1	0
0	1	0	0	1
0	1	0	1	0
0	1	1	0	1
0	1	1	1	1
1	0	0	0	1
1	0	0	1	0
1	0	1	0	1
1	0	1	1	1
1	1	0	0	0
1	1	0	1	0
1	1	1	0	1
1	1	1	1	0

$$f(A_k, B_k, i_1, i_2) = M_2 \wedge M_3 \wedge M_5 \wedge M_9 \wedge M_{12} \wedge M_{13} \wedge M_{15}$$

CHAPTER 5

Section 2

1. (a) $X := [0001\ 0101]$
   (b) $X := [1111]$
   (c) $X := [01000001]$

2. $a := m_0 \vee m_2 \vee m_3 \vee m_{11} \vee m_{13} \vee m_{14} \vee m_{15}$

3. (a) A. (b) E. (c) E. (d) D.

4. NUM $:= [6, 5, 2]$ is a typical value

Section 3

1. (a) $[0, 0]$ $[0, 1]$ $[1, 0]$ $[1,1]$
   (b) $[0]$ is $[0, 0]$ U is $[1, 1]$
   (c) NOT $X := [a, b]$ $\overline{X} := [\overline{a}, \overline{b}]$
        OR $X \vee Y$ $[a, b] \vee [c, d] = [a \vee c, b \vee d]$

3. (a) $z := 1$ (b) $z := 1$ (c) $z := 0$ (d) $z := 0$

4. See Appendix A

5. $Z := [z_1, z_2, \ldots, z_n]$
$z_i := \bar{t}_1 t_2 a_i \vee t_1 \bar{t}_2 b_i$

Section 4

1. (a) Use a network of the type shown in Figure 5-10 with d_i defined as

$$d_i := 1 \text{ if}$$

$$
\begin{array}{lll}
\text{(a) } a_i = 1 & b_i = 0 & \\
\text{(b) } d_{i-1} := 1 & a_i = 0 & b_i = 0 \\
\text{(c) } d_{i-1} := 1 & a_i = 1 & b_i = 1
\end{array}
$$

$$d_i := 0 \text{ all other cases}$$

Section 5

1.

Positive Number	r's Complement	(Radix $-$ 1) Complement
(a) 010101.11	101010.01	101010.00
(b) 0121.11	2101.12	2101.11
(c) 2721.63	5056.14	5056.13
(d) 0A6315	F59CEB	F59CEA

2.

	A	r's Complement $-B$	$A - B$	
(a)	0101.11000	1100.10101	10.01101	
(b)	0212.21	2200.01	112.22	
(c)	007644.24	700123.57	707770.03	(-70007.75)

3.

$$
\begin{array}{llllll}
A & 2983 & 0010 & 1001 & 1000 & 0011 \\
B & 1974 & 0001 & 1001 & 0111 & 0100 \\
\end{array}
$$

0011	10010	1111	0111	First sum
0000	0110	0110	0000	correction

0100	1001	0101	0111	Result
4	9	5	7	

CHAPTER 6

Section 2

1. (a) $f(x_1, x_2, x_3)$ $= \bar{x}_1 \bar{x}_2 \vee \bar{x}_1 x_3 \vee x_1 x_2$ or $\bar{x}_1 \bar{x}_2 \vee x_2 x_3 \vee x_1 x_2$
$= (x_1 \vee \bar{x}_2 \vee x_3)(\bar{x}_1 \vee x_2)$

(b) $g(x_1, x_2, x_3)$ $= \bar{x}_2$

(c) $h(x_1, x_2, x_3, x_4) = \bar{x}_3 \bar{x}_4 \vee x_1 \bar{x}_2 \vee \bar{x}_2 \bar{x}_4$
$= (\bar{x}_2 \vee \bar{x}_3)(x_1 \vee \bar{x}_4)$

2. Prime implicants of Figure 6-8

$$(I)\ \overline{x_1}\overline{x_2}x_3\overline{x_4}\quad (II)\ \overline{x_1}\overline{x_3}$$
$$\overline{x_1}x_2x_3\qquad\qquad x_1x_3$$
$$x_1\overline{x_2}x_3\qquad\qquad x_1x_2$$
$$x_2x_4\qquad\qquad x_2\overline{x_3}$$
$$x_3x_4$$

Section 3

1. (a) $\ x_2\,\overline{x_3}\ \vee\ \overline{x_1}\,x_2\ \vee\ x_2 x_3\qquad$ or $\qquad\overline{x_2}\,\overline{x_3}\ \vee\ \overline{x_1}\,\overline{x_3}\ \vee\ x_2 x_3$
(b) $\ \overline{x_1}\,\overline{x_2}\,\overline{x_5}\ \vee\ \overline{x_1}\,\overline{x_4}\,\overline{x_5}\ \vee\ \overline{x_1}\overline{x_2}\,\overline{x_3}x_4x_5\ \vee\ x_1 x_2 x_3 x_4\,\overline{x_5}$

2.
$$f(t_{i,3},\ t_{i,2},\ t_{i,1},\ t_{i,0})\ =\ t_{i,3}$$
$$g(t_{i,3},\ t_{i,2},\ t_{i,1},\ t_{i,0})\ =\ t_{i,3}\ \vee\ t_{i,2}t_{i,1}t_{i,0}$$

CHAPTER 7

Section 2

1. (b)
$$f_1(x_1,\ x_2,\ x_3,\ x_4)\ =\ \overline{x_1}\overline{x_2}\overline{x_3}\ \vee\ x_2\overline{x_3}x_4\ \vee\ x_2 x_3\overline{x_4}$$
$$f_2(x_1,\ x_2,\ x_3,\ x_4)\ =\ \overline{x_2}\overline{x_3}\overline{x_4}\ \vee\ x_2\overline{x_3}x_4\ \vee\ x_1 x_2 x_4$$
$$f_3(x_1,\ x_2,\ x_3,\ x_4)\ =\ \overline{x_2}x_3\overline{x_4}\ \vee\ \overline{x_1}x_3\overline{x_4}\ \vee\ \overline{x_1}x_2 x_3 x_4$$

2. (a) 10   **(b)** 7

Section 3

2. Let the four inputs to the multiplexer be x_0, x_1, x_2, x_3 and the control signals t_0 and t_1. Then

$$t_0 = a\qquad t_1 = b$$
$$x_0 = \overline{c}\qquad x_1 = c\qquad x_3 = 1\qquad x_4 = 0$$

Section 4

1. To solve this problem assume that the desired network can be decomposed into the subnetworks shown.

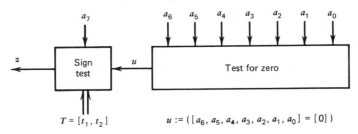

$$T = [t_1, t_2] \qquad u := ([a_6, a_5, a_4, a_3, a_2, a_1, a_0] = [0])$$
$$z := \bar{t_1}\bar{t_2}\bar{a_7}u \lor \bar{t_1}t_2a_7 \lor t_1\bar{t_2}\bar{a_7}$$

2. The network has the form shown below:

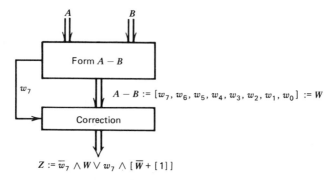

$$Z := \bar{w_7} \land W \lor w_7 \land [\overline{W} + [1]]$$

3. This example shows that the operation of the MSI network is independent of the meaning associated with the data being processed.

	$[A]$	$[B]$	$[Z]$	c_8	ovr
(a)	$[00000101]$	$[00011001]$	$[11101100]$	0	0
(b)	$[11001000]$	$[01010000]$	$[00011000]$	1	1
(c)	$[11011100]$	$[01000000]$	$[01000000]$	0	0
(d)	$[11001110]$	$[11100001]$	$[00010011]$	1	0

Section 5

1. $f_1(x_1, x_2, x_3, x_4) = \bar{x_1}\bar{x_2}\bar{x_4} \lor x_2x_3\bar{x_4} \lor x_2\bar{x_3}x_4$
$\quad f_2(x_1, x_2, x_3, x_4) = x_2\bar{x_3}\bar{x_4} \lor x_1x_2x_4 \lor x_2\bar{x_3}x_4$
$\quad f_3(x_1, x_2, x_3, x_4) = x_1\bar{x_3}x_4 \lor x_1x_2x_3x_4 \lor \bar{x_2}\bar{x_3}\bar{x_4}$

CHAPTER 8

Section 2

1. $X := [x_1, x_2, x_3]$
$\quad S_1 := m_1 \lor m_2 \lor m_4 \lor m_7 := J_1$
$\quad R_1 := m_0 \lor m_3 \lor m_5 \lor m_6 := K_1$
$\quad D := S_1$

2. (a) S–R flip-flop
$\quad$ (b)

$x(t)$	$y(t)$	$y(t + \tau)$
0	0	0
0	1	0
1	0	1
1	1	0

Section 3

1.

$$\tau: \begin{cases} X_2 \leftarrow X_1, \ldots, X_8 \leftarrow X_7 \\ A_1 \leftarrow \overline{X}_8, A_2 \leftarrow A_1, \ldots, A_8 \leftarrow A_7 \end{cases}$$

2. T is a 1-bit signal.

$D_i := \overline{t}\,\overline{a}_i \lor ta_i$

where D_i is the input to the ith bit of the B register.

Section 4

1. Assume that the X register holds

$$X := [x_7, x_6, x_5, x_4, x_3, x_2, x_1, x_0]$$

and that it is constructed from D flip-flops

Flip-Flop Control Equation

$D_i := \overline{t}_1 t_2 \land (x_i \oplus c_{i-1}) \lor t_1 \overline{t}_2 \land (x_i \oplus c_{i-1})$
$\lor t_1 t_2 \land (x_{i+1})$ $Note: x_8 = 0$

Carry Signal

$c_i := \overline{t}_1 t_2 \land (x_i c_{i-1}) \lor t_1 \overline{t}_2 \land (\overline{x}_i c_{i-1})$
$c_{-1} := 1$

2.

$$\tau_A := (m_0 \lor m_1 \lor m_2) \land \tau$$
$$\tau_X := (m_2) \land \tau$$
$$\tau_Z := (m_3) \land \tau$$

CHAPTER 9

Section 2

1. The following equations describe the desired networks:

$\tau_a :$ $A \leftarrow (T = \text{ADDA}) \land (A + X)$
$\tau_b :$ $B \leftarrow (T = \text{ADDB}) \land (B - X)$
      $\text{ERR} := (T = \text{NOP}) \land (X) \lor (T = \text{ADDA}) \land (A - X)$
          $\lor (T = \text{ADDB}) \land (B + X)$
$\tau_a := ((T = \text{ADDA}) \lor (T = \text{CLAB}))\tau$
$\tau_b := ((T = \text{ADDB}) \lor (T = \text{CLAB}))\tau$

Section 3

1. (a)

State \ Input S		XLT	XEQ	XGT
START	Q_A	Q_B/ADD	Q_B/ADD	Q_B/ADD
A1	Q_B	Q_D/INC	Q_C/NOP	Q_D/DEC
	Q_C	Q_D/SUB	Q_D/SUB	Q_D/SUB
OUT	Q_D	Q_A/CLR	Q_A/CLR	Q_A/CLR

(b)

State \ Input S		XLT	XEQ	XGT
START	Q_A	Q_B/CLR	Q_B/CLR	Q_B/CLR
	Q_B	Q_C/ADD	Q_C/ADD	Q_C/ADD
BGN	Q_C	Q_{C1}/INC	Q_E/SUB	Q_D/DEC
	Q_{C1}	Q_{C2}/ADD	Q_{C2}/ADD	Q_{C2}/ADD
	Q_{C2}	Q_G/SUB	Q_G/SUB	Q_G/SUB
	Q_D	Q_E/SUB	Q_{D1}/ADD	Q_E/SUB
	Q_{D1}	Q_C/INC	Q_C/INC	Q_C/INC
	Q_E	Q_{E1}/SUB	Q_{E1}/SUB	Q_{E1}/SUB
	Q_{E1}	Q_{E2}/DEC	Q_{E2}/DEC	Q_{E2}/DEC
	Q_{E2}	Q_F/DEC	Q_F/DEC	Q_F/DEC
	Q_F	Q_G/INC	Q_G/INC	Q_G/INC
OUT	Q_G	Q_C/CLR	Q_C/CLR	Q_C/CLR

Section 4

1. Must add another instruction

$$\text{MUL2F} \quad A \leftarrow A + A, \quad C \leftarrow [1]$$

which multiplies the contents of A by 2 and sets the C flag. The program, with this new instruction, becomes

```
START:  CLR
        ADD
        SUB
        MUL2F START
```

2.
```
START:  CASE S                          /* WAIT FOR FIRST PULSE
        {
            [D0] NOP     START          /* STILL LOOKING
            [D1] STCNT   COUNT          /* STARTING PULSE ARRIVES
        }

COUNT:  CASE S                          /* COUNT TIME BETWEEN PULSES
        {
            [D0] INC     COUNT          /* INCREMENT COUNT
            [D1] STOPC                  /* SECOND PULSE. STOP COUNTING
        }
READ:   NOP     START                   /* VALUE OF THE COUNT AVAILABLE
```

Section 5

1. Assume that all registers are constructed from D flip-flops.

$$\tau_{CNT} : CNT \leftarrow (T = READ) \wedge (CNT + [1])$$
$$\tau_R \quad : R \quad \leftarrow (T = READ) \wedge (SR(X, R))$$
$$\tau_C \quad : C \quad \leftarrow (T = STC) \vee (T = STCP)$$
$$\tau_P \quad : P \quad \leftarrow (T = STCP)$$

$$\tau_{CNT} := ((T = CLR) \vee (T = READ))\tau$$
$$\tau_R \quad := ((T = READ))\tau$$
$$\tau_C \quad := ((T = CLR) \vee (T = STC) \vee (T = STCP))\tau$$
$$\tau_P \quad := ((T = STCP))\tau$$

CHAPTER 10

Section 2

1.

$[y_1 y_2]$ $\diagdown$ x	0	1
$[0, 0]$	$[1, 0]/[1, 1]$	$[1, 1]/[0, 0]$
$[0, 1]$	$[0, 0]/[1, 1]$	$[0, 1]/[0, 0]$
$[1, 0]$	$[1, 0]/[0, 1]$	$[1, 0]/[1, 0]$
$[1, 1]$	$[0, 0]/[0, 1]$	$[1, 1]/[1, 0]$

2. (a)
$$[0, 0] \xrightarrow{1} [1, 1] \xrightarrow{0} [0, 0] \xrightarrow{1} [1, 1] \xrightarrow{1} [1, 1] \xrightarrow{0} [0, 0] \xrightarrow{1} [1, 1] \xrightarrow{0} [0, 0]$$

state sequence

$$[0, 0] \qquad [0, 1] \qquad [0, 0] \qquad [1, 0] \qquad [0, 1] \qquad [0, 0] \qquad [0, 1]$$

output sequence

(b) $[1, 0] \xrightarrow{1} [1, 0] \xrightarrow{0} \cdots$ all transitions state sequence

$\quad\quad [1, 0] \qquad [0, 1] \cdots$ etc. output sequence

Section 3

1.

$$Q := [q_1, q_2] \qquad S := [s_1, s_2] \qquad T := [t_1, t_2, t_3]$$
$$J_1 := q_2 s_1 \bar{s_2} \qquad K_1 := s_1 \lor s_2$$
$$J_2 := \bar{q_1} \bar{s_1} \lor q_1 s_1 \bar{s_2} \qquad K_2 := s_1 \lor s_2$$
$$t_1 := \bar{q_1} \bar{q_2} \bar{s_1} \lor q_2 \bar{s_2} \lor q_1 \bar{s_2}$$
$$t_2 := q_2 \bar{s_2} \lor q_1 \bar{s_2} \lor q_2 s_1 \lor q_1 \bar{s_1}$$
$$t_3 := q_2 \bar{s_1} s_2 \lor q_1 s_1 s_2$$

Section 4

1. Let $[y_1, y_2, y_3]$ be the contents of the counter register.

$$J_1 = y_2 y_3 \qquad J_2 = y_3 \qquad J_3 = 1$$
$$K_1 = y_2 y_3 \qquad K_2 = y_3 \qquad K_3 = 1$$

2.

State	Input	
	0	**1**
q_0	q_1	q_3
q_1	q_2	q_0
q_2	q_3	q_1
q_3	q_0	q_2

3. Let $q_0 = [0, 0]$, $q_1 = [0, 1]$, $q_2 = [1, 0]$, $q_3 = [1, 1]$ in general $q = [y_1, y_2]$, $i = $ input

$$J_1 = y_2 \bar{i} \lor \bar{y_2} i$$
$$K_1 = y_2 \bar{i} \lor \bar{y_2} i$$
$$J_2 = 1$$
$$K_2 = 1$$

CHAPTER 11

Section 2

1. .09999 sec/character. Thus 99.9% of the time is spent waiting for a character.

2. See the discussion of serial transfer in Chapter 8.

3. (a) $5.128 \ 10^4$
    (b) 5.128 kHz

Section 3

1. The changes that must be made involve changing the minterms used to realize the decoded output. This can be done by changing the logic expression for a through g as follows.
    (a) Remove the minterm m_{15} from a.
    (b) Add the minterm m_{13} to b.
    (c) No change.
    (d) Remove the minterms m_{13} and m_{14} from d.
    (e) Remove minterms m_{13}, m_{14}, m_{15} from e.
    (f) Remove minterms m_{15} from f.
    (g) Remove minterms m_{14} and m_{15} from g.

2. Use address lines a_0 and a_1 to generate the chip select signal. The lines $a_2, \ldots ,$ a_{15} are used to address the information on each chip.

Section 4

1.

Step 1	ADDREG ← [6005$_8$]	BSYNF ← [1]	BWTF ← [1]
	DATREG ← ['A']		
Step 2	LADDREG ← ADDREG	BRDYF ← [1]	
Step 3	BDOUT ← [1]		
Step 4	LDATREG ← DATREG	BRDYF ← [0]	
Step 5	BDOUTF ← [0]	BSYNF ← [0]	

2. Define the signals S and T as follows.

S	Meaning
READ	Read operation requested
WRITE	Write operation requested
SR	Slave Ready for read or write BRPY := [1]
SF	Slave Finished read or write BRPY := [0]

T	**Meaning**
READS	ADDREG ← ⟨address⟩, BSYNF ← [1], BWTF ← [0]
MASTRR	BDINF ← [1]
READC	DATREG ← [ADD/DAT], BDINF ← [0], BSYNF ← [0]
WRITES	ADDREG ← ⟨address⟩, BSYNF ← [1], BWTF ← [1]
MASTRW	BDOUTF ← [1]
WRITEC	BDOUTF ← [0], BSYNF < [0]
NOP	No operation

```
            Program
START: CASE S                                    /* START OPERATION
        {
        [READ] {       /* THE READ OPERATION

            RR: CASE S
                {
                [SR] MASTERR              /* SLAVE REPLIES
                DEFAULT NOP RR            /* WAIT FOR REPLY
                }

            RD: CASE S                    /* COMPLETE READ
                {
                [SF] READC                /* FINISH READ
                DEFAULT NOP RD            /* WAIT FOR REPLY
                }
            }

        [WRITE] {      /* THE WRITE OPERATION

            WR: CASE S
                {
                [SR] MASTRW               /* SLAVE REPLIES
                DEFAULT NOP WR            /* WAIT FOR REPLY
                }

            WD: CASE S                    /* COMPLETE WRITE
                {
                [SF] WRITEC               /* FINISH WRITE
                DEFAULT NOP WD            /* WAIT FOR REPLY
                }
            }
        }
    NOP   START                           /* LOOP FOR NEXT TASK
```

Section 5

2.   Drill hole 1

>   (a) 00100000
>   00010101
>   (b) 01000000
>   00010101
>   (c) 10000010
>   (d) 01100000
>   01010000
>   (e) 10100000
>   etc.

CHAPTER 12

Section 2

1.   If it is assumed that m_{-1} is always 1 (i.e., normalized), then the range of the number is

$$.1_2 \times 2^{-128_{10}} \quad \text{to} \quad .1111111_2 \times 2^{128_{10}}$$

2.   The smallest fraction and the resolution interval is 2^{-16}. The binary point does not have to be encoded.

Section 4

1.   (a)   10700
     (b)   10700
     (c)   10677 if a byte address or 10676 if a word address

2.   Transfer sequence to calculate relative address. Assumed that the calculation starts with the PC pointing at the word in memory that contains the address offset

CPU—Transfers	INFOBUS—Transfers
ADDR ← PC, Rx ← PC	
Rv ← Rx + [2]	MAR ← ADDR
PC ← Rv	MBR ← $M_{[MAR]}$
ADDR ← Rv + Rx	Rx ← MDR

Section 5

1. (a) ADD $R1,R2$ 060102
   (b) CLR $R3$ 005003
   (c) DEC @#A 005337 A is data in memory location 1000.
                                    001000   Assume absolute address.
   (d) ADD #5,@#A 062737
                                      000005
                                      001000

2. JSR PC,SUBPROG implies that relative addressing is used to access the subprogram.
   At completion of read cycle the PC has the value 2004. The stack pointer is decremented by 2 to 1476 and 2004 is pushed onto the stack at this location. The address of the subroutine is formed by adding the offset in memory location 2002 to 2004 to produce 4000. Thus the offset value is 1774. The RTS operation reads 2004 from the stack, increments SP to 1500, and then uses 2004 as the new value of the PC.

CHAPTER 13

Section 2

1. The statements with .TITLE, .=, and .END in them are assembler directives. The statements starting with ";" are comment statements. The statements with .WORD in them are data statements. All other statements are instruction statements.

Section 3

1.

```
;**********************************************************
;
;               PROGRAM TO PRINT "HELLO WORLD"
;
;**********************************************************

        PRSTAT= 177564
        PRDATA= 177566

        . = 2000

START:  MOV   #STRING,R1      ;SET POINTER TO DATA
LOOP:   CMPB  #0,(R1)         ;AT END OF STRING?
        BEQ   OUT             ;YES
```

```
PD:        TSTB   @#PRSTAT              ;NO-PRINT CHARACTER
           BPL    PD
           MOVB   (R1)+,@#PRDATA
           JMP    LOOP
OUT:       HALT                         ;END OF PROGRAM

STRING:    .ASCIZ /HELLO WORLD/         ;STRING TO BE PRINTED

           .END   START
```

2. *Hint:* $10_{10} = 2 + 2^3$. Thus $10_{10}*R1$ can be accomplished by adding the original contents of $R1$ shifted one bit left to the original contents of $R1$ shifted 3 bits left.

3. Remember that the characters read are the ASCII characters and that they must be converted to numbers before they are used in the program.

4.

Address	Contents		. = 1000		
1000	005000	START:	CLR	R0	
1002	066700		ADD	X1,R0	
1004	000016				
1006	066700		ADD	X2,R0	
1010	000014				
1012	066700		ADD	X3,R0	
1014	000012				
1016	010067		MOV	R0, Y	
1020	000010				
1022	000000		HALT		
1024	000267	X1:	.WORD	267	
1026	004431	X2:	.WORD	4431	
1030	000057	X3:	.WORD	57	
1032	000000	Y:	.WORD	0	

Section 4

1. Assume that the double precision integers are stored in two words with the first word the low-order bits and the second word the high-order bits. $R1$ points to the first operand and $R2$ points to the second operand. The first operand is the source and the second is the destination.

```
SUBINT:   SUB  (R1)+,(R2)+          ;SUBTRACT LOW-ORDER BITS
          SBC  (R2)                 ;CORRECT HIGH-ORDER DESTINATION BITS
          SUB  (R1),(R2)            ;COMPLETE SUBTRACTION
          RTS                       ;RETURN
```

4. Note that it is assumed that a sign/magnitude representation is used to represent the numbers, not 2's complement. Thus extra care must be taken to process the sign bit of the high-order words.

5. Assume that the address of the first character in the string is in $R1$ and that the count is to be returned in $R0$.

```
CNTSP:   CLR    R0              ;SET COUNT TO ZERO
LOOPC:   CMPB   #0,(R1)         ;AT END OF STRING?
         BEQ    OUT             ;YES-RETURN
         CMPB   #40,(R1)+       ;IS CHARACTER A SPACE?
         BNE    LOOPC           ;NO-CHECK NEXT CHARACTER
         INC    R0              ;YES-INCREMENT COUNT
         JMP    LOOPC           ;PROCESS NEXT CHARACTER
OUT:     RTS    PC              ;RETURN WITH COUNT IN R0
```

Section 5

2. To carry out the CMP operation on two double-precision numbers A and B it is necessary to form $A - B$ where A is assumed to be the source operand and B the destination operand. The CMP operation is a single-precision operation and there is no way to perform the SBC subtract carry destination correction. Thus it is necessary to write DUBCMP using SUB and SBC. Assume that $R1$ points to A and $R2$ points to B. The subroutine uses register $R3$.

```
DUBCMP:   MOV  (R1)+,R3         ;GET LOW BITS OF SOURCE
          SUB  (R2)+,R3         ;SUBTRACT LOW BITS OF DESTINATION
          MOV  (R1),R3          ;GET HIGH BITS OF SOURCE
          SBC  R3               ;MAKE CORRECTION
          SUB  (R2),R3          ;SUBTRACT HIGH BITS OF DESTINATION
          RTS PC                ;RETURN WITH PS BITS SET
```

Section 6

2. Assume that $R1$ points to the first character of string 1 and $R2$ points to the first character of string 2.

```
CONCAT:   CMPB  #0,(R1)+        ;FIND END OF STRING 1
          BNE   CONCAT          ;NOT END
          DEC   R1              ;FOUND END. POSITION POINTER TO FIRST

                                ;LOCATION FOR CHAR FROM STRING 2
MOVCH:    CMPB  #0,(R2)         ;END OF STRING 2?
          BEQ   OUT             ;YES
          MOVB  (R2)+,(R1)+     ;COPY CHARACTER
          JMP   MOVCH           ;PROCESS NEXT CHARACTER
OUT:      MOVB  #0,(R1)         ;SET TERMINATION OF NEW STRING
          RTS   PC              ;RETURN
```

CHAPTER 14

Section 2

1. (b)

Symbol	Value
NEXTVL	2
COUNT	10
START	1000
BUF1	1030
BUF2	1101
LOOP	1014
NEXTVAL	U.A.

2. NEXTVAL is changed to NEXTVL to remove U.A. entry

Address	Contents			
1000	012701	START:	MOV	#COUNT,R1
1002	000010			
1004	012702		MOV	#BUF1,R2
1006	001030			
1010	012703		MOV	#BUF2,R3
1012	001101			
1014	111223	LOOP:	MOVB	(R2),(R3)+
1016	062702		ADD	#NEXTVL,R2
1020	000002			
1022	005301		DEC	R1
1024	001373		BNE	LOOP
1026	000000		HALT	

(The character string is loaded in the next memory words with a terminating null byte. Then 20 bytes are set aside for data.)

Section 3

1.

Symbol	Value
NEWLINE	14
SPACE	40
STRT	2000
TABL1	U.A.
LOOP	2010
LOOP3	2022
TABEL1	2032

ERROR MESSAGES

STATEMENT 7 BRZ LP3 INCORRECT

TABL1 UNDEFINED ADDRESS IN STATEMENT 5

2.

Address	Contents			
3000	012701	TESTA:	MOV	#500, R1
3002	000500			
3004	020167		CMP	R1,A
3006	002770			
3010	001402		BEQ	TESTB
3012	004767		JSR	PC,PRINT
3014	003762			
3016	016767	TESTB:	MOV	B,A
3020	002770			
3022	002754			
3024	000000		HALT	

INDEX